Gowling, Strathy & Henderson
Barristers & Solicitors
Patent & Trade Mark Agents

Suite 2600
160 Elgin Street
Ottawa, Ontario
Canada K1P 1C3

Michael A. Crystal

Telephone (613) 786-0115
Facsimile (613) 563-9869
crystalm@gowlings.com

THE LAW OF EVIDENCE
IN CANADA

THE LAW OF EVIDENCE IN CANADA

John Sopinka
Justice of the Supreme Court of Canada

Sidney N. Lederman, Q.C.
Partner in Stikeman, Elliott

Alan W. Bryant
Professor of law, University of Western Ontario
and member of McCarthy Tétrault

BUTTERWORTHS
Toronto and Vancouver

The Law of Evidence in Canada

© Butterworths Canada Ltd. 1992

The Butterworth Group of Companies
CANADA
Butterworths Canada Ltd.
75 Clegg Road, MARKHAM, Ontario L6G 1A1
and
409 Granville Street, Suite 1455, VANCOUVER, B.C. V6C 1T2
AUSTRALIA
Butterworths Pty Ltd. SYDNEY, MELBOURNE, BRISBANE, ADELAIDE, PERTH, CANBERRA, and HOBART
IRELAND
Butterworth (Ireland) Ltd. DUBLIN
NEW ZEALAND
Butterworths of New Zealand Ltd. WELLINGTON and AUCKLAND
PUERTO RICO
Equity de Puerto Rico, Inc. HATO REY
SINGAPORE
Malayan Law Journal Pte. Ltd. SINGAPORE
UNITED KINGDOM
Butterworth and Co. (Publishers) Ltd. LONDON and EDINBURGH
UNITED STATES
Butterworth Legal Publishers AUSTIN, Texas; BOSTON, Massachusetts; CLEARWATER, Florida (D&S Publishers); ORFORD, New Hampshire (Equity Publishing); ST. PAUL, Minnesota; and SEATTLE, Washington.

Canadian Cataloguing in Publication Data

Sopinka, John, 1933–
    The law of evidence in Canada

Includes bibliographical references and index.
ISBN 0–409–80180–1 (bound) — ISBN 0–409–90639–5 (pbk.)

1. Evidence (Law) - Canada. I. Bryant, Alan W.,
1943-   . II. Lederman, Sidney N., 1943-
III. Title.

KE8440.S66 1992   347.71'06   C92-093403-X
KF8935.ZA2S66 1992

Sponsoring Editor – Fran Cudlipp
Coordinating Editor – Agatha Cinader
Freelance Editor – Janet Sands
Production – Kevin Skinner

Printed and bound in Canada

Reprint #2 1995

T O
Marie, Randy, and Melanie
David and Eli
Sally, Kathryn, and Peter

PREFACE

The predecessor to this book dealt with *The Law of Evidence in Civil Cases*. It was published in 1974 and the authors were extremely gratified by the reception it received not only from judges and advocates working in civil cases but, surprising to us, in the criminal field as well. In considering a second edition we decided that, notwithstanding the success of the earlier work, the reasons which justified a work limited to civil cases were no longer present to justify a revision on this basis.

In contrast with the civil side of the practice where there had been minimal change in the law of evidence, the developments in the criminal law field were quite dramatic. Influenced by the *Canadian Charter of Rights and Freedoms* and the more activist role of the judiciary that it encouraged, the rules of evidence in criminal cases have undergone a spectacular transformation. Illegally obtained evidence is no longer routinely admitted as before but must meet the test of section 24 of the *Charter*, to give but one example. The pervasive influence of the *Charter* on the laws of evidence gives them a peculiar Canadian cast, rendering the English texts less helpful than before. This creates a strong demand for a comprehensive review of the laws of evidence. Proposals for a comprehensive reform of the laws of evidence which might have filled the void, culminating in the ill-fated Bill S-33, died on the order paper. When it was suggested to us that *The Law of Evidence in Civil Cases* should be revised, we decided that, in view of the above circumstances, a new, comprehensive treatment of the subject should replace it. In light of the magnitude of the undertaking, we asked Professor Alan Bryant to join us as a co-author, an assignment which he graciously accepted.

In preparing the new work we endeavoured to preserve the old text as much as possible where no change in the law had occurred. This was frequently impossible when attempting to combine the civil and criminal rules which, while often identical, are not infrequently different, and which are, at times, applied in a stricter fashion. Accordingly, to summarize, the changes are as follows: Chapters 8 and 9 are new, Chapters 10, 11 and 19 are expansions of parts of the former text, and the other chapters are revisions of previous chapters or parts of previous chapters. Because of publishing limitations, the research for this book is up to December 1, 1991.

Authors of a text on a legal subject should strive to identify some trend or unifying theme which can serve as a guide in resolving difficult questions through the application of policy. In the case of the laws of evidence this is a daunting task. One is immediately reminded of the famous observation of C.P. Harvey, Q.C. which, while somewhat harsh, is not far off the mark:

> I suppose there never was a more slapdash, disjointed and inconsequent body of rules than that which we call the Law of Evidence. Founded apparently on the propositions that all jurymen are deaf to reason, that all witnesses are presumptively liars and that all documents are presumptively forgeries, it has been added to, subtracted from and tinkered with for two centuries until it has become less of a structure than a pile of builders' debris. [*The Advocate's Devil*, (London: Stevens & Sons Ltd., 1958), at 79.]

In identifying the direction that the rules should take, the guiding principle which we applied is the one that the Supreme Court of Canada initiated in *Ares v. Venner* in 1970 and has restated more recently in *R. v. Khan*, *Geffen v. Goodman Estate*, *R. v. Gruenke*, and *R. v. Salituro*. Rigid classifications and exceptions must give way to a more flexible approach which recognizes that the rules are there to facilitate proof and not hamper it. Evidence that is relevant and trustworthy should be admitted unless there is a strong policy reason for its exclusion. We do not claim that in following this precept we have succeeded in re-assembling all of the rubble but we do hope that our efforts will enable the glimmer of a structure to be seen.

No work is the product of the authors alone. We are heavily indebted to Margaret Grottenthaler for her invaluable assistance providing research, drafting of some of the material and, perhaps most importantly, co-ordinating the work of the authors, ever urging them to be more prompt. Our thanks as well to the many clerks and students who provided assistance in research and drafting. Special mention should be made of the efforts of Anna Yang, Lionel Smith, Neil Milton and Michael Killeen. We also wish to express our gratitude to the Ontario Law Foundation for providing a research grant to fund salaries for law students.

We also acknowledge the significant contribution of our assistants and secretaries, Mary Brock, Marlene McIvor, Marj Harvey, Kathleen Adair and Fran Meyer who handled the burden of reducing our thoughts to the printed page with only the occasional loss of temper.

Finally, we are grateful to our publishers who encouraged us to undertake this project and were most patient in extending the time to enable us to complete it.

Acknowledgements

The authors and publishers of the following articles and textbooks have been most generous in giving permission for the reproduction in this text of work already in print. References, of course, appear where necessary and possible in the text. It is convenient for us to list below, for the assistance of the reader, the publishers and the authors for whose courtesy we are most grateful. The following list is organized by publisher in alphabetical order.

Canada Law Book
Dawson, D.F., "The Abrogation of Recent Complaint: Where Do We Stand Now?" (1984-85) Vol. 27 *Crim. L.Q.* 57. Reproduced with the permission of the author and Canada Law Book Inc., 240 Edward Street, Aurora, Ontario L4G 3S9.

Canadian Bar Association
Sopinka, J., "Report of the Special Committee on Evidence" (Ottawa, 1968).

Canadian Bar Foundation
Schiff, S., "Evidence — Hearsay & the Hearsay Rule: A Functional View" (1978), 56 *Can. Bar Rev.* 674. With permission from the Canadian Bar Review and the author.

Carswell, a division of Thomson Professional Publishing Canada
Delisle, D.J., "Annotation to *R. v. Potvin*" (1989), 68 C.R. (3d) 193.

Carswell, a division of Thomson Professional Publishing Canada
Report of the Provincial Task Force on the Uniform Rules of Evidence (1982).

Her Majesty's Stationary Office
Eleventh Report, *Evidence (General)*, Cmnd 4991 (1972). Reproduced with permission of the Controller of Her Majesty's Office.

TABLE OF CONTENTS

Preface vii
Acknowledgements xi
Table of Cases xxxvii

SECTION I: GENERAL PRINCIPLES OF ADMISSIBILITY

CHAPTER 1: INTRODUCTION 1

I   WHAT IS EVIDENCE 1
II   GOALS OF THE LAW OF EVIDENCE 1
    A. Search for Truth 1
    B. Efficiency of the Trial Process 2
    C. Fairness of the Trial Process 3
    D. Goals Outside of the Process 4
III DIRECTION OF THE LAW OF EVIDENCE 5

**CHAPTER 2: CONDITIONS FOR THE RECEIPT OF
EVIDENCE** 9

I   TYPES OF EVIDENCE THAT CAN BE RECEIVED
BY THE COURT 9
    A. Sworn Statements 9
        1. General 9
        2. Commission Evidence and Examinations De Bene Esse 10
           (a) In Civil Cases 10

(b) In Criminal Cases 12

3. Discovery Statements 13

4. Affidavits 14

B. Unsworn Statements 14

C. Real Evidence 14

  1. Things 14

    (a) General 14

    (b) Photographs 14

    (c) Videotape 16

    (d) Audiotape 17

  2. Taking a View 18

  3. Appearance or Demeanour of a Person 19

D. Experiments 19

E. Documents 20

II   CONDITIONS FOR THE RECEIPT OF EVIDENCE 21

A. General 21

B. Relevance 22

  1. Definitions 22

  2. Facts in Issue 23

  3. Relevance Distinguished from Exclusionary Rules 24

  4. Relevance Distinguished from Weight 26

  5. Relevance Distinguished from Materiality 27

  6. Conditional Relevance 28

C. Exercise of Judicial Discretion 28

  1. Judicial Discretion in Criminal Cases 28

    (a) In Favour of the Accused 28

    (b) In Favour of the Crown and Third Persons 33

  2. In Civil Cases 33

D. Direct and Circumstantial Evidence 37

  1. Distinction between Direct and Circumstantial Evidence 37

  2. The Treatment of Circumstantial Evidence 40

E. Admissibility Generally 43

  1. Conditional Admissibility 43

  2. Limited Admissibility 43

  3. Curative Admissibility 43

  4. Procedure for Admitting Evidence 45

    (a) Tendering Evidence 45

    (b) Appeals with Respect to Admissibility 47

      (i) Grounds of Appeal 47

      (ii) Significance of Objection at Trial 47

**CHAPTER 3: EVIDENTIAL BURDEN AND
THE BURDEN OF PROOF** 53

I INTRODUCTION 53
II TERMINOLOGY 53
III THE DIFFERENCE BETWEEN THE BURDENS 56
  A. General 56
  B. The Legal Burden of Proof 58
  C. The Evidential Burden 60
IV THE EFFECT OF DISCHARGING THE
EVIDENTIAL BURDEN 65
  A. Two Evidentiary Effects 65
  B. The Terms "Prima Facie Evidence", "Prima Facie Proof" and
    "Prima Facie Case" 69
V TWO MISLEADING CONCEPTS 74
  A. Shifting Burdens 74
  B. Burdens Expressed as Presumptions 80
VI ALLOCATING THE BURDEN 80
  A. Overview 80
  B. Exceptions, Exemptions, Excuses, Qualifications, and
    Provisos 84
  C. Grounds of Policy, Fairness and Probability 91
VII ADMISSIBILITY OF EVIDENCE AND OTHER MATTERS 94

CHAPTER 4: PRESUMPTIONS 97

I INTRODUCTION 97
II PRESUMPTIONS WITHOUT BASIC FACTS 98
III PRESUMPTIONS OF FACT 99
IV CONCLUSIVE PRESUMPTIONS OF LAW 104
V REBUTTABLE PRESUMPTIONS OF LAW 107
  A. What is a Rebuttable Presumption of Law? 107
  B. Evidentiary Effect of a Rebuttable Presumption of Law 109
    1. In Criminal Cases 109
    2. In Civil Cases 112
      (a) General 112
      (b) Presumption of Legitimacy 112
      (c) Presumptions of Life and Death 113
      (d) Presumption of the Order of Death 116

    (e) Presumptions of Advancement and Resulting Trust 117
    (f) Presumption of Regularity 119
VI CONFLICTING PRESUMPTIONS 120
VII THE IMPACT OF THE CHARTER 121

CHAPTER 5: STANDARDS OF PROOF 129

I   INTRODUCTION 129
II   SATISFYING THE EVIDENTIAL BURDEN 130
    A. Motion for a Non-Suit in Civil Proceedings 130
    B. Motion for a Directed Verdict in Criminal Proceedings 135
    C. The Defendant's Evidential Burden 137
III SATISFYING THE LEGAL BURDEN OF PROOF 141
    A. General 141
    B. Civil Cases 141
    C. Criminal Cases 148

SECTION II: EXCLUSIONARY RULES

CHAPTER 6: HEARSAY 155

I   WHAT IS HEARSAY? 155
    A. The Rule 155
        1. Origin of the Rule 156
        2. Hearsay Dangers 157
    B. Conduct Amounting to Hearsay 160
    C. Purpose for Which Evidence is Tendered 160
        1. General 160
        2. Non-Hearsay Use of Words 162
        3. Impliedly Assertive Statements or Conduct 165
II   EXCEPTIONS TO THE HEARSAY RULE 173
    A. General 173
    B. Declarations Against Interest 176
        1. Against Pecuniary or Proprietary Interest 176
        2. Against Penal Interest 177
    C. Declarations Made in the Course of a Business Duty 187

1. The Common Law Exceptions 187
   (a) Nature of Exception 187
   (b) Rationale 188
   (c) Early Preconditions to Admissibility 188
   (d) Judicial Reform of the Common Law Rule:
       Ares v. Venner 192
   (e) Scope of *Ares v. Venner* 192
   (f) Practical Impact of *Ares v. Venner* 195
   (g) The Aftermath of *Ares v. Venner* 195
2. Admissibility by Statute 198
   (a) General 198
   (b) Usual and Ordinary Course of Business 200
   (c) Contemporaneous Record 203
   (d) Personal Knowledge and Duty of Declarant 204
   (e) Record of Facts 208
   (f) Absence of Motive to Misrepresent 210
   (g) Records Made in the Course of Investigation 212
   (h) Business Records Subject to Other Exclusionary Rules 213
   (i) Negative Inferences from Records 213
   (j) Records Kept by Computer Systems 213
   (k) Notice 215
   (l) Reform Proposals 215
D. Declarations as to Reputation 216
   1. General 216
   2. Public or General Rights 217
   3. Marriage 220
   4. Matters of General History 222
E. Declarations as to Pedigree and Family History 222
F. Statements Contained in Ancient Documents as Evidencing
   a Proprietary Interest in Land 228
G. Statements in Public Documents 231
H. Res Gestae 235
   1. General 235
   2. Declarations which by their Assertion Create Legal Rights
      or Liabilities 236
   3. Declarations of Bodily and Mental Feelings and
      Condition 238
      (a) Bodily Feelings and Condition 238
      (b) Declarations Indicating an Existing Mental or Emotional
          Condition, or State of Mind or Intention 242

    4. Declarations Accompanying and Explaining Relevant Act .. 253
    5. Spontaneous Exclamations 257
I. Dying Declarations 267
    1. Scope and Rationale 267
    2. Requirements 268
        (a) Settled Hopeless Expectation of Death 268
        (b) The Trial Must Be One in Which the Accused is
            Charged with Murder or Manslaughter 269
        (c) Injuries Those of Declarant and the Subject of the
            Charge 269
J. Testimony in Former Proceedings 270
    1. Theory of Admissibility 270
    2. Guarantees of Trustworthiness 272
        (a) Issues Substantially the Same 272
        (b) Same Parties 272
        (c) Opportunity by Adversary to Cross-Examine 273
    3. Evidence Taken on Discovery 273
    4. Criminal Proceedings 274
    5. Comparison with Other Rules 277
    6. Previous Testimony Led by the Party Against Whom
       it is Tendered 278
K. Admission of a Party 279
    1. Theory of Admissibility 279
    2. What Constitutes an Admission? 284
    3. Statements by Others who have a Relationship to
       the Party 289
        (a) Vicarious Admissions 289
        (b) Statements by a Representative or by Persons with
            Identity of Interest 293
        (c) Statements by Persons Engaged with Others in a
            Common Purpose or Design 295
    4. Effect of a Party's Admission as Against Others 299
L. Declarations by Children about Sexual Abuse 300
M. Possible New Exceptions 304
N. Non-Applicability of Hearsay Rule in Certain
   Proceedings 305
    1. Administrative Proceedings 305
    2. Sentencing Proceedings 306

CHAPTER 7: SELF-SERVING EVIDENCE 307

I   RULE AND RATIONALE 307
II   EXCEPTIONS 308
    A. General Explanation of Exceptions 308
    B. Evidence to Rebut Allegations of Recent Fabrication by
      the Witness 309
        1. How Must the Allegations Be Raised? 310
        2. Form of Allegation 311
    C. Prior Eye Witness Identification 313
    D. Recent Complaint 315
    E. Res Gestae or to Show Physical, Mental or Emotional State
      of Accused 318
    F. Statements Made on Arrest 319
    G. Explanatory Statements Made by an Accused in Possession
      of Stolen Goods or Illegal Drugs 320

CHAPTER 8: CONFESSIONS 323

I   WHAT CONSTITUTES A CONFESSION? 323
    A. Admissions - Inculpatory Statements 323
    B. Exculpatory Statements as Confessions 324
    C. Spontaneous Statements 326
II   SCOPE OF THE CONFESSION RULE 326
III   HISTORY AND RATIONALE OF THE
    CONFESSION RULE 327
    A. Voluntariness 327
        1. Historical Position 328
        2. Development of the Voluntariness Rule 330
    B. The Operating Mind Requirement 334
IV   THE VOLUNTARINESS TEST 338
    A. Threats or Inducements 338
    B. Oppression 342
    C. Taking Statements and Police Questioning 347
V   PERSONS IN AUTHORITY 350
VI   THE VOIR DIRE 353
    A. The Requirement for a Voir Dire 353
    B. The Procedure on a Voir Dire 354

VII   THE ROLE OF THE TRIAL JUDGE AND OF
     THE TRIER OF FACT 356
VIII THE ONUS AND STANDARD OF PROOF 358
IX   THE EVIDENTIAL VALUE OF A CONFESSION 361
X   USE OF A CONFESSION TO CROSS-EXAMINE THE
     ACCUSED 364
XI   EVIDENCE DISCLOSED AS A RESULT OF AN
     INADMISSIBLE CONFESSION 367
XII CHARTER IMPLICATIONS 369
    A. Right to Counsel — Section 10(b) of the Charter 369
    B. Right Against Self-incrimination — Section 13 of the Charter 373
    C. Right to Remain Silent — Section 7 of the Charter 376
XIII CONCLUSION 377

CHAPTER 9: ILLEGALLY OBTAINED EVIDENCE 379

I   INTRODUCTION 379
II   THE RULE AT COMMON LAW 380
    A. Criminal Cases 380
    B. Civil Cases 384
III THE CANADIAN CHARTER OF RIGHTS AND
    FREEDOMS 387
    A. Historical Background 387
    B. Section 24 388
       1. General 388
       2. Court of Competent Jurisdiction 390
       3. Exclusion Pursuant to Section 24 391
       4. Standing 392
       5. Causation 392
    C. Bringing the Administration of Justice into Disrepute 396
       1. The Burden of Proof 396
       2. "Would" or "Could" 397
       3. Disrepute in Whose Eyes? 398
       4. Discretion or Duty? 399
       5. The Factors 400
    D. The Trial Fairness Rationale 401
       1. Self-Incriminating Statements 401
       2. Other Evidence Affecting Trial Fairness 403
       3. Real Evidence and Trial Fairness 405

4. Admission Notwithstanding Trial Unfairness 407
5. Conclusion 410
E. The Seriousness of the Violation: The Dissociation Rationale 410
1. General 410
2. Good Faith 412
3. Urgency or Necessity 418
4. Availability of Other Investigative Techniques 418
5. Other Factors Affecting the Seriousness of the Violation 422
F. Effect of Exclusion on the Reputation of the Administration
of Justice 423
IV THE CRIMINAL CODE 425
A. Electronic Surveillance 425
1. General 425
2. Illegal Wiretaps 425
3. Establishing Illegality 427
B. Other Statutory Rules 428

CHAPTER 10: CHARACTER EVIDENCE 431

I GENERALLY 431
II CHARACTER AS A FACT IN ISSUE 433
A. In Civil Cases 433
1. Defamation 433
(a) Evidence of Good Character of Plaintiff 433
(b) Evidence of Bad Character of Plaintiff 433
(i) To Support Defences 434
(ii) To Support Mitigation of Damages 435
(iii) Rumour 437
(iv) Summary of Character Evidence in Defamation
Cases 437
2. Breach of Promise to Marry 438
3. Character of Places, Animals or Things 439
B. Criminal Cases 440
III EVIDENCE OF CHARACTER TO PROVE FACTS IN ISSUE 440
A. Civil Cases 440
B. Criminal Cases 443
1. Character of the Accused 443
(a) Evidence of Good Character 443
(i) Reputation 444

        (ii)   Specific Acts of Good Conduct – The Evidence
             of the Accused 447

        (iii) Expert Opinion Evidence 450

        (iv) Use of Evidence of Good Character 453

    (b) Bad Character of the Accused 454

        (i)   The General Rule 454

        (ii)   Bad Character Raised by the Accused 455

        (iii) Bad Character of Co-Accused 456

        (iv) Accused Puts Character in Issue 456

        (v)   Cross-Examination of Accused's Witness 457

        (vi) Cross-Examination of Accused Where Character
             is in Issue 458

        (vii) Cross-Examination of Accused Where Character
             is not in Issue 459

        (viii) Reply Evidence by the Crown Where Character
             is in Issue 460

        (ix) Section 666, Criminal Code 462

        (x)   Section 12, Canada Evidence Act 463

        (xi) Proposal for Reform 465

  2. Character of Persons other than the Accused 467

    (a) Of Non-Victim, Non-Witness, Third Parties 467

    (b) Of Non-Witnesses or Complainants 467

        (i)   In General 467

        (ii)   In Sexual Offences 468

  3. Character of Witnesses in General 474

    (a) In General 474

    (b) Previous Convictions 475

CHAPTER 11: SIMILAR FACT EVIDENCE 477

I   INTRODUCTION 477

   A. The "Similar Facts Rule" 477

   B. Terminology 478

   C. Scope of the Rule 479

II REASONS FOR THE RULE 481

   A. Effect on Trial Process and on the Rights of the Accused Under
      the Charter 482

   B. Effect on System of Law Enforcement 484

III JUDICIAL DEVELOPMENT OF THE RULE 484

A. English Case Law 485
   1. Development of the Rule 485
   2. Formulation of the Rule in *Makin* 485
   3. Application of *Makin* 485
   4. Expansion of the Categories of Admissibility of Similar Fact
      Evidence 486
   5. *Boardman*: Balancing Test of Probative Value versus
      Prejudice to the Accused 490
      (a) Lord Halsham 491
      (b) Lord Morris 493
      (c) Lord Wilberforce 494
      (d) Lord Salmon 495
      (e) Lord Cross 495
B. Canadian Case Law 496
   1. *R. v. C.R.B.* 496
   2. *Sweitzer v. R.* 499
   3. *R. v. Morris* 499
   4. *R. v. Clermont* 501
   5. *R. v. Robertson* 502
   6. *R. v. Morin* 503
   7. *R. v. Green* 504
   8. *R. v. D.(L.E.)* 505
C. Australian Case Law 506
IV PRINCIPLES GOVERNING ADMISSION OF SIMILAR
FACT EVIDENCE IN CRIMINAL CASES 510
  A. Whether Evidence Relevant to Issue in Case 510
  B. Weighing Probative Value Against Prejudicial Effect 512
V ADMISSION OF SIMILAR FACT EVIDENCE
IN CIVIL CASES 512
  A. Evidence of Disposition Alone Not Admissible 514
  B. To Prove a Fact in Issue Where Similar Facts Show "System"
     or "Scheme" 515
  C. To Explain the Animus, Purpose or Object of the Act 518
  D. To Show the State or Condition of Premises, Places or Other
     Objects 519
  E. To Show Ownership or Title 521
  F. To Prove Standard Practice or Market Value 521
  G. To Prove Agency 521
  H. To Rebut Other Evidence 521
VI CONCLUSION 522

CHAPTER 12: OPINION EVIDENCE 523

I   OPINION OF LAY PERSONS 523
    A. Rationale and Development of the Rule 523
        1. Rationale of Exclusion 523
        2. Development of Rule 524
        3. Modern Statement of Rule: Helpfulness 524
    B. Illustrations of Lay Opinion 528
        1. Identity of Persons and Places 528
        2. Identification of Handwriting 530
        3. Mental Capacity and State of Mind 532
II THE OPINION OF EXPERTS 533
    A. General Principles 533
        1. As an Exception to the General Rule 533
        2. Qualifying the Expert Witness 536
        3. Hypothetical Question 537
    B. Opinion on the Ultimate Issue 540
    C. Hearsay Issues and Opinion Evidence 546
        1. As a Component of the Expert's Knowledge 546
        2. As a Component of the Expert's Opinion 547
        3. Surveys and Polls 556
        4. Use of Authoritative Literature 560
        5. Cross-Examination of the Expert 563
    D. The Admissibility of New Scientific Evidence 565
    E. Miscellaneous 571
        1. Limiting Number of Witnesses and Notice Requirement ... 571
        2. Court Appointed Experts 573

SECTION III: RULES RELATING TO THE PRODUCTION OF EVIDENCE

CHAPTER 13: COMPETENCE AND COMPELLABILITY OF WITNESSES 577

I   GENERAL 577
II COMPETENCE 577

A. General 577
B. Witnesses with an Interest in the Proceedings or with a
   Criminal Record 578
C. Mental, Intellectual and Communicative Deficiencies 580
   1. Mental Impairment 580
   2. Children 583
   3. Communicative Deficiencies 585
D. The Oath 586
   1. Necessity at Common Law 586
   2. Form of Oath 586
   3. Affirmation 590
   4. Children 591
      (a) Sworn Evidence 591
      (b) Unsworn Evidence 592
E. Judges, Jurors, Lawyers 597
F. Burden of Proof on Competency Issues 598
III COMPELLABILITY 599
A. The Accused in Criminal Proceedings 600
   1. General 600
   2. Co-Accused 601
   3. Provincial Offences 603
   4. Collateral Administrative Proceedings 604
      (a) Pre-Charter 604
      (b) Post-Charter 607
   5. Parallel Civil Proceedings 611
B. Spouse of Accused in Criminal Proceedings 611
   1. The Common Law Rule 611
   2. Statutory Modifications 615
      (a) General 615
      (b) Exceptions 616
C. Parties in Civil Proceedings 618
D. Spouses in Civil and Criminal Proceedings 619
E. Judges, Lawyers, Jurors 619
F. Foreign Diplomats and the Crown 621
G. Others 621
   1. Illegality of Disclosure Under Foreign Statute 621
   2. Answers to Questions Would be Privileged 622

CHAPTER 14: PRIVILEGE 623

I INTRODUCTION 623
II CONFIDENTIAL COMMUNICATIONS WITHIN SPECIAL
  RELATIONSHIPS 626
  A. A Rule of Evidence as Distinct from Ethical or Equitable
     Principles of Confidence 626
  B. Solicitor and Client 635
     1. Rationale 635
     2. Confidential Nature of the Communication 637
        (a) General 637
        (b) Presence of and Disclosure to Third Parties 637
        (c) Joint Interests 638
        (d) Subject-Matter 639
     3. Scope of the Privilege 640
        (a) Within the Professional Relationship 640
        (b) For Communications Only 641
        (c) Purpose of the Communication 642
            (i) Seeking Legal Advice 642
            (ii) In Furtherance of Unlawful Conduct 644
     4. When the Privilege May be Asserted 645
     5. What Legal Advisers are Included 648
     6. Use of Agents 650
     7. Corporations as Clients 651
        (a) Corporate Counsel 651
        (b) Corporate Client 651
     8. Materials Obtained and Prepared in Anticipation of
        Litigation 653
     9. Duration of Privilege 658
        (a) In Other Proceedings 658
        (b) After Death 660
     10. Loss of Privilege 663
        (a) Who May Waive the Privilege 663
        (b) Voluntary Waiver 664
        (c) Waiver by Implication 666
        (d) By Legislation 672
        (e) Inadvertent Disclosure or Intercepted
            Communications 672
  C. Husband and Wife Communications 677
     1. Origin and Rationale 677

2. Subject-Matter of the Privilege 679
3. Marital Status 681
4. Intercepted Or Overheard Communications Between
   Spouses 684
5. Who May Exercise the Privilege 687
6. Loss of Privilege 688
7. Abolition of the Privilege 690
8. Privilege Respecting Evidence of Sexual Intercourse
   Between Spouses 692
D. Spiritual Advisers 694
E. Journalists 700
   1. Identity of New Sources 700
   2. Newspaper Rule 702
   3. Qualified Privilege 706
      (a) Overriding Judicial Discretion 706
      (b) Application of Wigmore's Four Conditions 708
      (c) Charter, Section 2(b)..
F. Doctor and Patient 712
   1. Psychiatric Consultations 713
   2. Application of Wigmore's Four Criteria 717
   3. Court-Ordered Psychiatric Assessment 718
III COMMUNICATIONS IN FURTHERANCE OF
   SETTLEMENT 719
   A. Policy and General Rule 719
   B. Conditions for Recognition of the Privilege 722
      1. Litigious Disputes in Existence 722
      2. Made with Intention of Non-Disclosure 722
      3. Purpose of Communication 724
   C. Application of the Privilege in Subsequent Proceedings
      Between Different Persons 725
   D. Exceptions to the Privilege 728
      1. Introduction 728
      2. Unlawful Communications 728
      3. Communications Prejudicial to the Recipient 729
      4. Concluded Settlement Agreement in Issue 730
      5. Limitation Periods 731
      6. Costs 731
   E. Involvement of Mediators 732
IV PRIVILEGE AGAINST SELF-INCRIMINATION 734
   A. Introduction 734

B. Recognition of the Privilege at Common Law 735

C. Statutory Modification of the Common-Law Rule 736

D. Charter, Section 13 739

    1. Automatic Protection 739

    2. To What Evidence Does Section 13 Apply 741

    3. "In Any Proceeding" 742

    4. Incriminating Use 743

        (a) Time of Assessment of Nature of Use 743

        (b) Forfeitures and Penalties 744

        (c) Use During Crown's Case in Chief 744

        (d) Crown's Use in Cross-Examination 744

    5. "Any Other Proceedings" 749

    6. Who Can Claim the Protection? 752

E. Charter, Section 7 753

    1. Derivative Use Immunity 753

    2. Right of Silence 757

F. Protecting the Accused's Privilege Against Self-Incrimination

and Right of Silence 760

    1. Commenting on the Accused's Failure to Testify 760

    2. Evidentiary Effect of the Accused's Silence in the Face of an

Accusation from a Person in Authority 765

G. Privilege Against Disclosing Adulterous Conduct 768

    1. General 769

    2. Proceedings in Consequence of Adultery 769

    3. Waiver of the Privilege 771

CHAPTER 15: PUBLIC INTEREST IMMUNITY 773

I   INTRODUCTION 773

II BASIS OF CROWN IMMUNITY 773

III THE DETERMINATION OF IMMUNITY 773

A. General 778

B. Statutory Provisions that give Conclusive Weight to

Government Opinion 779

C. Judge's Determination of Privilege 781

D. Application to Oral Evidence 789

E. The Government's Affidavit 789

IV CRITERIA FOR GRANT OF IMMUNITY 790

A. General 790

B. Contents Claim 791
C. Class Claims 792
   1. The Candour Argument 792
   2. The Interference or Harassment Argument 794
D. Level of Government Involved 795
E. Information Supplied to Government by Outside Sources 796
F. Statements to Police and Police Reports 802
V PROTECTION OF INFORMANTS IDENTITY 805
A. Statement of the General Rule 805
B. Extension of the Rule Beyond the Police Informant
   Relationship 809
C. Exception to the General Rule 809
   1. Criminal Proceedings in General 809
   2. Informant's Evidence as Basis of Search Warrant 813
   3. Informant's Evidence as Basis of Wiretap 815

CHAPTER 16: THE EXAMINATION OF WITNESSES 821

I   GENERALLY 821
II THE EXAMINATION OF WITNESSES BY
     THE TRIAL JUDGE 824
   A. Judge's Right to Examine Witnesses 824
   B. Limits on the Judge's Right 824
   C. Judge's Right to all Witnesses 825
III THE EXCLUSION OF WITNESSES AND PARTIES BY THE
     TRIAL JUDGE 826
   A. Reason for Discretion 826
   B. Discretion to Exclude Parties 827
   C. Effect of Breach of Order 827
IV INTERPRETERS AND THE LANGUAGE OF
     PROCEEDINGS 828
   A. Translation of the Proceedings 828
   B. Translation of a Witness' Evidence 828
   C. Choice of Interpreter 830
   D. Official Languages 831
V EXAMINATION IN CHIEF 832
   A. General 832
   B. Leading Questions 833
     1. Reasons for the Rule 833

2. Form of Leading Questions 833
3. Exceptions to the Rule 834
C. Bolstering, Contradicting and Discrediting One's Own
   Witness 838
   1. Bolstering 838
   2. Contradicting and Discrediting 838
      (a) General Rule at Common Law 838
      (b) Statutory Reform 839
      (c) Provincial Evidence Acts 839
      (d) Canada Evidence Act 842
D. Evidential Value of a Previous Inconsistent Statement 847
E. Refreshing a Witness' Memory 849
   1. General 849
   2. Contemporaneity of Record 850
   3. Absence of Independent Recollection 851
   4. What Records or Devices May be Used to Refresh
      Memory 854
   5. Procedural Matters 856
VI CROSS-EXAMINATION 857
A. Scope 857
B. Cross-Examination Where there are Multiple Parties 862
   1. Civil Cases 862
   2. Criminal Cases 863
C. Cross-Examination on Documents Generally 864
D. Impeachment of a Witness' Credibility 866
   1. Testing Testimonial Capabilities 866
   2. Previous Inconsistent Statements 868
   3. Prior Convictions 873
E. Witness Tendered for Cross-Examination 875
F. The Rule in *Browne v. Dunn* 876
VII RE-EXAMINATION 879
VIII REPLY EVIDENCE 880
A. Limits on Reply Evidence 880
B. The Collateral Fact Rule 883
   1. Bias or Partiality 885
   2. Previous Convictions 885
   3. Previous Inconsistent Statements 885
   4. Physical or Mental Condition for Untruthfulness 886
   5. Evidence of Reputation for Untruthfulness 887

CHAPTER 17: CORROBORATION 891

I   INTRODUCTION 891
II VETROVEC: THE MODERN COMMON LAW 893
II LEGISLATIVE DEVELOPMENTS 896
    A. The Criminal Law 896
       1. Legislative Repeals 896
       2. Statutory Corroboration Requirements 899
    B. The Civil Law 901
       1. General 901
       2. Breach of Promise to Marry 901
       3. Affiliation Proceedings 902
       4. Actions Involving the Estate of Deceased Persons ... 903
       5. Actions Against Mental Incompetents 903
       6. Unsworn Evidence of Children 904
       7. Effect of Repeal on Common Law Rules of Practice ... 904
IV THE NATURE OF CORROBORATION 905
    A. General Requirements 905
    B. Degree and Extent of Corroboration 908
    C. Independence of Corroborative Evidence 909
    D. Corroborative Evidence May be Direct or Circumstantial ... 910
    E. Function of Judge and Jury 911
    F. Difference Between Civil and Criminal Cases 912
V   ILLUSTRATIONS OF THE RULE IN
    CIVIL PROCEEDINGS 917
    A. Actions by or against Heirs, Executors or Assigns of Deceased
       Persons or by or against Mentally Incompetent Persons 917
       1. General 917
       2. The Witness Requiring Corroboration: Opposite and
          Interested Party 919
       3. Action by or against Deceased or Mental Incompetent ... 919
       4. Multiple Claims and Claimants 921
       5. Actions For Negligence 922
    B. Evidence of Children 923

CHAPTER 18: DOCUMENTARY EVIDENCE 927

I   GENERALLY 927
II BEST EVIDENCE RULE 929

A. The History of the Rule 929
B. The Application of the Rule 931
   1. General 931
   2. The Distinction Between Primary and Secondary
      Evidence 932
   3. Circumstances in Which Secondary Evidence is
      Admissible 933
      (a) Loss or Destruction 933
      (b) Documents in Possession of Another Party 935
      (c) Documents in the Possession of a Third Party 936
      (d) Public and Official Documents 936
   4. Proof by Secondary Evidence 938
C. The Modern Rule 938
III DOCUMENTS ADMISSIBLE WITHOUT PROOF 941
A. Public and Judicial Documents 941
B. Documents Admissible Under Statutory Authority 945
C. Other Documents Admitted Without Proof 949
IV DOCUMENTS ADMISSIBLE ON PROOF OF AUTHORSHIP
OR EXECUTION 950
V DOCUMENTS ADMISSIBLE BY REASON OF
CUSTODIAL ORIGIN 955
A. Ancient Documents 955
B. Document in the Possession of a Person 956
   1. Introduction 956
   2. Possession by Individuals 958
   3. Possession by Corporations 960
   4. Possession by Co-conspirators, Agents 962
   5. Evidentiary Value of Possession 963
VI PARTICULAR RULES RELATING TO PROOF OF PRIVATE
DOCUMENTS 965
A. Handwriting 965
B. Attesting Witnesses 966
C. Corporate Seal 967
D. Typewriting 967
E. Photographs and Videotapes 967
F. Plans, Maps and Charts 968

CHAPTER 19: RULES DISPENSING WITH OR FACILITATING PROOF 971

I FORMAL ADMISSIONS 971
   A. In Civil Cases 971
   B. In Criminal Proceedings 974
      1. Guilty Pleas 974
      2. Specific Facts 975
II JUDICIAL NOTICE 976
   A. Notorious Facts 976
   B. Facts Capable of Immediate Accurate Demonstration 979
      1. Official Matters 979
      2. Historical Facts 980
      3. Times, Measures and Weights 981
      4. The Course of Nature and Scientific Facts 981
   C. Judicial Notice by Statute 983
   D. Personal Knowledge 985
   E. The Effect of Judicial Notice 986
   F. Judicial Notice in the Court of Appeal 988
III RES JUDICATA AND RELATED MATTERS 988
   A. Statement of the General Principle 988
   B. In Civil Cases 990
      1. General Rule 990
      2. Final Judicial Decision of a Court of Competent Jurisdiction 991
         (a) Inferior Courts and Tribunals 991
         (b) Foreign Courts 992
         (c) Court or Tribunal With Jurisdiction 992
         (d) Decision Must be Final 993
         (e) Decision on the Merits 994
         (f) Application to Family Law Judgments 996
      3. Identity of Action or Issue 997
         (a) Two Principles at Play 997
         (b) Cause of Action Estoppel 999
            (i) Same Cause of Action 999
            (ii) New Facts or Circumstances 1001
            (iii) Tax Assessments 1002
         (c) Issue Estoppel 1003
         (d) Estoppel as Between Defendants 1005
         (e) Parties and Their Privies 1006

(i) Same Parties 1006
(ii) Same Capacity 1006
(iii) Application to Those in Privity with Parties 1007
(iv) Requirement of Mutuality 1010
(f) Procedural Matters 1012
C. Criminal Law 1013
1. The Special Pleas 1014
(a) Autrefois Acquit 1014
(i) General Principle 1014
(ii) Same Charge 1014
(iii) Final Decision 1015
(iv) Accused Must Have Been in Jeopardy 1020
(b) Autrefois Convict 1020
(i) General Principle 1020
(ii) Same Charge 1021
(iii) Final Order of Court with Jurisdiction 1022
(c) Procedural Matters and Foreign Proceedings 1022
(i) Procedural Matters 1022
(ii) Foreign Proceedings 1023
2. Issue Estoppel 1024
3. *Kienapple v. R.* 1028
(a) General Principle 1028
(b) Sufficient Proximity between Facts and Charges 1029
(c) Procedural Issues 1032
4. Section 11(d) of the Charter 1033
(a) General Principle 1033
(b) "Charged with an Offence" 1034
(c) Same Offence 1035
(d) Final Acquittal or Conviction 1036
(e) Precludes Appeals by Way of Trial de Novo 1038
5. Conclusion 1038
D. Evidentiary Effect of Prior Judicial Determinations 1040
1. General 1040
2. Application of the Rule in Canada 1042
(a) In Civil Cases 1042
(i) Previous Criminal Convictions: Common
Law 1042
(ii) Previous Criminal Convictions: Statutory
Reform 1043
(iii) Previous Acquittal 1045

(iv) Previous Civil Judgment 1045

(b) Criminal Proceedings 1046

Index 1049

TABLE OF CASES

A

A. v. A., ... 771
A., R. v., ... 603
A. & B.C. Chewing Gum Ltd., D.P.P. v., ... 541
A. & D. Logging Co. v. Convair Logging Ltd., ... 639
A. & E. Land Industries Ltd. v. Sask. Crop Insurance, ... 598
Abacus Cities Ltd., Re, ... 990, 998, 1005
Abacus Cities Ltd. v. Bank of Montreal. *See* Abacus Cities Ltd., Re.
Abadom, R. v., ... 548, 570, 571
Abbey, R. v., ... 157, 362, 453, 534, 551, 552, 553, 554
Abel v. Light, ... 271
Abouloff v. Oppenheimer, ... 992, 999
Abrams v. Grant, ... 725
Abrath v. North Easter Railway Co., ... 3-19, 56, 73
Acerro v. Petroni, ... 837
Acosta v. Longsworth, ... 251
Adam v. Campbell, ... 536
Adams v. Public Trustee; Chiasson v. Public Trustee, ... 294
Adams Estate v. Decock Estate, ... 233
Adamson v. Vachon, ... 905
Adderly v. Bremner, ... 205, 206, 208, 209
Adgey v. R., ... 974, 975
Agawa, R. v., ... 183, 184, 601
Agbim, R. v., ... 150
Agnew v. Ont. Assn. of Architects, ... 619
Air Canada v. British Columbia, ... 993
Air Canada v. Secretary of State for Trade, ... 775
Air Canada v. Secretary of State for Trade (No. 2), ... 774
Aladdin Industries Inc. v. Canadian Thermos Products Ltd., ... 535
Alatyppo, R. v., ... 120
Albert v. Tremblay, ... 282, 283
Alberta (A.G.) v. Shepherd, ... 771
Alberta (Public Trustee) v. Walker, ... 182

Alberta Wheat Pool Elevators Ltd. v. S.S. Ensenada, ... 12
Albright, R. v., ... 306
Alcan-Colony Contracting Ltd. v. Minister of National Revenue, ... 650
Alexander v. Vye, ... 525, 530
Alfred Crompton Amusement Machines Ltd. v. Customs and Excise
    Commissioners (No. 2), ... 774, 786, 800
Algoma Central Railway v. Herb Fraser & Associates Ltd., ... 285
Allan v. Bank of Montreal. *See* Duhamel v. R.
Allan and Allan, Re, ... 822
Allcock, Laight & Westwood Ltd. v. Patten, ... 881
Allen v. McDonald, ... 47
Allen, R. v., ... 615
Allen (No. 2), R. v., ... 585
Allen v. St. Louis Public Service Co., ... 208
Allen v. Turk, ... 519
Alston v. Alston, ... 227
Altobelli v. Pilot Insurance Co., ... 1008
Altseimer, R. v., ... 430, 741, 742
Aluminum Goods Ltd. v. Canada (Registrar of Trade Marks), ... 558
Ament, R. v., ... 365
Amway Corp., R. v., ... 600, 615, 618, 630, 735, 736, 744, 749, 752, 753
Amway of Canada Ltd., R. v. *See* Amway Corp., R. v.
Amys v. Barton, ... 239
Anaconda Oil Co. v. Aladdin Oils Ltd., ... 20
Anderson, Re, ... 222
Anderson v. Bank of British Columbia, ... 636, 653
Anderson v. Bradley, ... 920
Anderson, R. v. (1984), ... 369
Anderson, R. v. (1976), ... 749
Anderson, R. v. (1914), ... 547, 560, 561, 562, 982
Anderson v. Walden, ... 224
Anderson v. Woods, ... 972
Andrew, R. v., ... 682
Andrews v. Hopkins, ... 590
Andrews, R. v. (1987), ... 261, 262, 263, 268
Andrews v. R. (1981), ... 354
Andrews v. State, ... 566, 567
Andrews v. Wirral R.D.C., ... 936
Angelantoni, R. v., ... 136
Angle v. M.N.R., ... 989, 999, 1003, 1004, 1011
Ansley v. Ansley, ... 704
Anthes Business Forms Ltd., R. v., ... 962, 964
Anti-Inflation Act, Reference re, ... 979
Antoine, R. v., ... 346
Apostilides, R. v., ... 821, 826
Appleby, R. v., ... 56, 92, 98, 108, 109, 110, 122, 151
Application 15023/89 v. United Kingdom, ... 127

Apsassin v. Canada (Dept. of Indian Affairs & Northern Development),   207, 230, 946

Archer, R. v. (1989), ... 809, 814

Archer, R. v. (1963), ... 29

Archibald v. R., ... 850

Arendale v. Federal Building Corp., ... 134

Ares v. Venner, ... 6, 21, 73, 155, 175, 192, 193, 195, 196, 197, 198, 209, 301, 304, 550

Argyll (Duchess) v. Argyll (Duke), ... 674

Armak Chemicals Ltd. v. Canadian National Railway Co. (1985), ... 853

Armak Chemicals Ltd. v. Canadian National Railway Co. (1984), ... 657

Armstrong v. Canada Atlantic Railway Co., ... 241

Armstrong, R. v. (1970), ... 685, 951, 965

Armstrong, R. v. (1959), ... 591

Army & Navy Department Store (Western) v. R.W.D.S.U. Local No. 535, ... 16

Arnold v. National Westminster Bank, ... 1002

Arrow Transit Lines Ltd. v. Tank Truck Transport, ... 1001

Art, R. v., ... 1013, 1036

Ashburton (Lord) v. Pape, ... 385, 386, 387, 628, 673, 674, 675

Ashby, R. v., ... 19

Ashdown (J.H.) Hardware Co. v. Singh, ... 193

Ashe, R. v., ... 560

Ash-Temple Co., R. v., ... 961

Asiatic Petroleum Co. v. Anglo-Persian Oil Co., ... 791

Askeland, R. v., ... 359

Associated Newspapers Ltd. v. Dingle, ... 435

Atkinson v. Casserley, ... 273

Atkinson v. Morris, ... 252

Atkinson v. Smith, ... 861

Attica Investments Inc. v. Gagnon, ... 10

A.G. v. Bowman, ... 442

A.G. v. Bradlaugh, ... 586, 601

A.G. v. Briant, ... 805

A.G. v. Clough, ... 700

A.G. v. Emerson, ... 228

A.G. v. Foster. *See* A.G. v. Mulholland.

A.G. v. Guardian Newspapers Ltd. (No. 2), ... 627

A.G. v. Hitchcock, ... 884, 885

A.G. v. Horner (No. 2), ... 219

A.G. v. Kelly, ... 736

A.G. v. Mulholland; A.G. v. Foster, ... 624, 700, 701, 703, 706

A.G. v. Radloff, ... 441, 618

A.G. federal or provincial. *See* under Canada or name of province.

Attwood, R. v., ... 965

Atwood, R. v., ... 601

Augustine v. St. John (City), ... 805

Auld v. Auld, ... 997

Aveson v. Lord Kinnaird, ... 238

Aynsley v. Toronto General Hospital, ... 199, 200, 209

Ayscough v. Sheed, Thompson & Co., ... 991
Audy (No. 2), R. v., ... 529

B

B. v. Catholic Children's Aid Society, Metropolitan Toronto. *See* B.(J.) v. Catholic
    Children's Aid Society of Metropolitan Toronto (Municipality).
B. v. R. (1977), ... 646
B., R. v. *See* B.(W.D.), R. v.
B., R. v.; A., R. v., ... 457
B.(A.), R. v., ... 326, 350, 351, 352, 353
B.C. Iron Works Co. v. Buse, ... 294
B.(C.R.), R. v., ... 485, 496, 497, 498, 506, 510, 511
B.F. Goodrich Canada Ltd. v. Mann's Garage Ltd., ... 881, 882
B.(G.), R. v. (1990), ... 300
B.(G.), R. v. (1988), ... 913
B.(G.) (No. 1), R. v. (1990), ... 893, 895, 898, 905, 906, 910, 913-915, 923, 924, 925
B.(J.) v. Catholic Children's Aid Society of Metropolitan Toronto (Municipality), 305
B.(J.E.), R. v., ... 1031
B.(L.M.) v. H.(T.). *See* Bomboir v. Harlow.
B.(W.D.), R. v., ... 745
B.X. Development Ltd. v. R., ... 646
Babcock v. C.P.R., ... 25
Babcock, R. v., ... 162
Bagg v. Budget Rent-A-Car of Washington-Oregon Inc., ... 105, 106
Baig, R. v., ... 369
Bailey, R. v., ... 612
Bailley v. R.C.M.P., ... 803
Baker, R. v. (1984), ... 684
Baker, R. v. (1912), ... 449
Baker v. Spain, ... 1001
Balcombe v. R., ... 95
Baldry, R. v., ... 329
Baldwin v. O'Brien, ... 218
Ball v. Dunsterville, ... 952
Ball, R. v., ... 487, 505, 506, 511, 516, 517
Baltzer, R. v., ... 163
Banbury Peerage Case, ... 221
Bandura, R. v., ... 21
Bank of B.C. v. Singh, ... 1011
Bank of Montreal v. Crosson, ... 1011
Bank of Nova Scotia v. Agronin, ... 996
Bank of Nova Scotia v. MacBrien, ... 742
Bank of Ottawa v. Stamco Ltd., ... 722, 724
Bannerman, R. v., ... 587, 591, 592
Bannister, R. v., ... 968

Banton v. R., ... 12
Barbat v. Allen, ... 579
Barber v. McQuaig, ... 994, 1013
Barbour v. Roberts, ... 47
Barkway v. South Wales Transport Co., ... 82
Barlow v. Kinnear, ... 520
Barnes v. Merritt & Co., ... 515
Barnes, R. v. (1989), ... 13, 32, 529, 577
Barnes, R. v. (1921), ... 618
Barnett v. Brandao, ... 985
Baron, R. v., ... 286, 299
Barrow, R. v., ... 298
Barrs, R. v., ... 572
Barry v. Butlin, ... 65, 146
Bartleman, R. v., ... 980
Bartlett, R. v., ... 612
Barton v. Dundas (Town), ... 189
Barton, R. v., ... 660
Barwell Food Sales Inc. v. Snyder & Fils Inc., ... 992, 993
Bashnick v. Mitchell, ... 1001, 1007
Basken, R. v., ... 468
Baskerville, R. v., ... 892, 894, 900, 906, 912, 913, 914, 915, 916
Basse v. Toronto Star Newspapers Ltd., ... 805
Batary v. Saskatchewan (A.G.), ... 601, 604, 605, 607
Bateman, R. v., ... 975
Bater v. Bater, ... 145, 146
Battersby v. Battersby, ... 771
Baty, Re, ... 972
Baxter v. Canadian Broadcasting Corp., ... 702
Baxter, R. v., ... 41
Bayley v. Trusts & Guarantee Co., ... 909, 920, 921
Beam v. Beatty, ... 519
Beamer v. Darling, ... 639
Beamon v. Ellice, ... 970
Beaton v. Hayman, ... 254
Beaton v. R., ... 354
Beatson v. Skene, ... 791
Bechard, R. v., ... 613
Beckon v. Ontario (Deputy Chief Coroner), ... 144
Beckwith v. Sydebotham, ... 533
Bedere, R. v., ... 877, 973
Bedfordshire Inhabitants, R. v., ... 216, 217, 219
Bedgood, R. v., ... 307
Bedingfield, R. v., ... 258, 261
Beech v. Jones, ... 856
Beeches Working Men's Club and Institute Trustees v. Scott, ... 1003
Begg v. East Hants (Municipality), ... 730

Belair, R. v., ... 1017, 1020
Beland, R. v., ... 307, 308, 319, 453, 534, 567, 568, 569
Belanger v. Gilbert, ... 724, 725, 731
Belanger, R. v. (1978), ... 349, 352
Belanger, R. v. (1975), ... 455, 859
Beliveau, R. v., ... 914
Bell, Re, ... 919
Bell v. Bell, ... 586
Bell v. Holmes, ... 993, 1005
Bell v. Hutchings, ... 988
Bell v. Klein, ... 736, 737, 739, 742, 753
Bell v. Matthewman, ... 253, 954
Bell v. Miller, ... 991
Bell v. Smith, ... 659, 663
Bell and Bruce, R. v., ... 928, 931, 933, 937, 939, 940
Bell Canada v. Olympia & York Developments Ltd., ... 657, 670
Bell Engine etc. Co. v. Gagne, ... 598
Bellerophon, H.M.S., ... 799
Bellman, R. v., ... 969
Belzberg v. B.C.T.V. Broadcasting System Ltd. See Jackson v. Belzberg.
Belzburg, R. v., ... 95
Bencardino, R. v., ... 161, 637, 638, 642, 645, 885
Bengert (No. 5), R. v. (1980), ... 940
Bengert (No. 5), R. v. (1978), ... 852
Bengert (No. 11), R. v. (1980), ... 401
Bennett v. Peattie, ... 116
Bennett, R. v., ... 637
Benning, R. v., ... 108
Benoit v. Higgins, ... 805
Bentley v. Cdn. Bank of Commerce, ... 116
Berger, R. v., ... 140
Bergstrom, R. v., ... 932
Bergwitz v. Fast, ... 633
Berkeley Peerage Case, ... 216
Bernard, R. v., ... 68, 129, 139, 140
Bernardi-Mathews Ltd. v. Malagerio, ... 134
Berndt v. A.H. Rushforth Sec. Ltd., ... 826
Bernier v. Bernier, ... 998
Berry v. Banner, ... 218
Berryman, R. v., ... 1031
Bessela v. Stern, ... 286
Betterest Vinyl Manufacturing Ltd., R. v., ... 929, 933
Beukenkamp v. Canada (Minister of Consumer & Corporate Affairs), ... 189, 933
Beukenkamp and Minister of Consumer and Corporate Affairs, Re. See
    Beukenkamp v. Canada (Minister of Consumer and Corporate Affairs).
Bevan, R. v., ... 894, 898
Biasi, R. v., ... 207

Biasi (No. 2), R. v. *See* Biasi, R. v.
Bickford, R. v., ... 899
Bicknell, R. v., ... 931, 933, 939
Bigaouette v. R., ... 323
Bigras v. C.N.R., ... 285, 286
Bigsby v. Dickinson, ... 20
Binder, R. v., ... 760
Bird v. Keep, ... 945
Bird, R. v., ... 487
Bisaillon v. Keable, ... 778, 805, 806, 807, 808, 817
Biss v. Biss, ... 742
Bissell, R. v., ... 612
Bjarnarson v. Manitoba, ... 1011
Black v. Black, ... 284
Black v. George McKean & Co., ... 909
Black v. Hardwell, ... 280
Black, R. v., ... 393, 395, 406, 407, 409, 424
Blackman v. Davison, ... 118
Blackstone v. Mutual Life Assurance Co. of New York, ... 156, 657
Blackwell, Re, ... 923
Blain, R. v., ... 810
Blais v. Andras, ... 633, 774, 796
Blais, R. v., ... 601
Blake v. Albion Life Assurance Society, ... 515, 516, 517, 518, 521
Blandy-Jenkins v. Earl of Dunraven, ... 179, 228
Blastland, R. v., ... 158, 172, 174, 178, 244
Bleta v. R., ... 532, 538, 539, 540
Blewett v. Tregonning, ... 880
Bliss, R. v. (1936), ... 974
Bliss, R. v. (1837), ... 217, 219
Blonder-Tongue Laboratories Inc. v. University of Illinois Foundation, ... 1010
Blueberry River Indian Band v. Canada (Minister of Indian Affairs & Northern
    Development). *See* Apsassin v. Canada (Dept. of Indian Affairs & Northern
    Development).
Blunt v. Park Lane Hotel Ltd., ... 735, 768
Board v. Board, ... 1007
Boardman, D.P.P. v., ... 483, 490, 491, 492, 493, 494, 495, 496, 497, 512
Bodnarchuk, R. v., ... 479
Bodo v. Bodo, ... 118
Boissonneault, R. v., ... 136
Boland v. The Globe & Mail Ltd., ... 840, 841
Boles, R. v. (1984), ... 207
Boles, R. v. (1978), ... 453
Bomac Construction Ltd. v. Stevenson, ... 1011
Bombardier Ltd. v. Canada (Restrictive Trade Practices Comm.), ... 657, 670
Bomboir v. Harlow, ... 902
Bond v. Loutit (Noonen), ... 105, 107

Bonin, R. v., ... 371
Bonisteel v. Bateman, ... 995
Bonnycastle, R. v., ... 857
Bookman, Re, ... 611
Booth v. Booth, ... 771
Boran v. Wenger, ... 825
Borden & Elliott v. R., ... 645, 646
Borucki v. MacKenzie Bros. Co., ... 208
Boss, R. v., ... 761, 762, 764, 897
Bossman, R. v., ... 326, 342
Boston Belting Co. v. Gabel, ... 47
Bouchard, R. v., ... 826
Bouchard v. Wheeler, ... 1002
Boucher, R. v., ... 468
Boudreau v. R., ... 325, 331, 376
Bouffard v. R. (1979), ... 327
Bouffard, R. v. (1964), ... 966
Boulet v. R., ... 373, 738
Boulianne v. Flynn, ... 658, 660
Bourguignon, R. v., ... 567, 570
Bourne, R. v., ... 1037
Boutilier v. Traders General Ins. Co., ... 134
Bowlen, Re, ... 645
Bowles, R. v., ... 48
Boyce, R. v., ... 316
Boyd v. Simpson, ... 731
Boyer, R. v., ... 41
Boyes, R. v., ... 735
Boyko, R. v., ... 463
Boykowych v. Boykowych, ... 44, 144, 146
Boyle v. R. (1983), ... 64, 68, 97, 107, 125, 126
Boyle, R. v. (1914), ... 479
Boys v. Star Printing & Publishing Co., ... 237
Bracegirdle v. Bailey, ... 875
Bracewell, R. v., ... 457
Bradburn v. Bradburn, ... 770, 771
Bradbury, R. v., ... 463
Bradley v. McIntosh, ... 783
Bradley v. R., ... 103
Bradshaw v. Baptist Foreign Mission, ... 834
Bragg v. Oceanus Mutual Underwriting Association (Bermuda) Ltd., ... 1010
Brain v. Preece, ... 189
Braithwaite v. Haugh, ... 1001
Branzburg v. Hayes, ... 712
Brasier, R. v., ... 586
Bratty v. A.G. for Northern Ireland, ... 54, 61, 139
Breen v. Saunders, ... 1011

Brennan, R. v., ... 842
Breshears v. R. *See* Workman v. R.
Brett v. Brett, ... 598
Briamore Manufacturing Ltd., Re, ... 665
Brick, R. v., ... 404
Briden, R. v., ... 882
Bridlington Relay Ltd. v. Yorkshire Electricity Bd., ... 978
Briginshaw v. Briginshaw, ... 143
Briscoe v. Briscoe, ... 821, 825
Bristow v. Cormican, ... 228
British American Oil Co. v. Born Engineering Co., ... 994
British Columbia (Public Trustee) v. Skoretz, ... 911
British Drug Houses Ltd. v. Battle Pharmaceuticals, ... 540, 541
British Steel Corp. v. Granada Television Ltd., ... 706
Britton, R. v., ... 853
Broad v. Pitt, ... 694
Broken Hill Pty. Co. v. Broken Hill Municipal Council, ... 1002, 1003
Bromley v. Wallace, ... 439
Brooks, R. v., ... 48
Brosseau v. R., ... 974, 975
Brost v. Eastern Irrigation School Division No. 44, ... 292
Brouillard, R. v., ... 824
Brown, Re; Gordon v. Rosenberg, ... 199
Brown v. Argue, ... 692
Brown v. Bonnycastle, ... 996, 1006
Brown v. Brown, ... 920
Brown v. Carter. *See* Woods, Re.
Brown v. Eastern & Midlands Railway Co., ... 513, 519, 520
Brown v. Morrow, ... 933
Brown, R. v. (1978), ... 463, 476
Brown, R. v. (1951), ... 592
Brown v. R. (Aust.), [1913] 148
Brown (No. 2), R. v. (1963), ... 750
Brown v. Sheppard, ... 561
Brown v. Woodman, ... 934
Browne v. Dunn, ... 876, 877
Brownell v. Black, ... 547, 560
Brownell v. Brownell (1890), ... 983
Brownell v. Brownell (1909), ... 28, 442, 860
Browning-Ferris Industries of Winnipeg (1974), R. v., ... 1013
Broyles, R. v., ... 759
Brunsden v. Humphrey, ... 1001
Bryant, R. v., ... 453
Bryce v. Bryce, ... 243
Brydges, R. v., ... 424
Buchanan v. Labrash, ... 912
Buckingham v. Daily News Ltd., ... 20

Buckley, R. v., ... 188, 189, 246
Buckley v. Rice Thomas, ... 573
Buckminster's Estate v. Commr. of Internal Revenue, ... 208
Budin, R. v., ... 584, 592
Building Products Ltd. v. B.P. Canada Ltd., ... 558
Bullen, Re, ... 990, 1002
Bullivant v. A.G. for Victoria, ... 660
Bullock & Co. v. Corry & Co., ... 658
Bullock v. Bullock, ... 115
Bulmer, R. v., ... 62, 136
Bunniss, R. v., ... 537
Burbridge, R. v., ... 977
Burford (Bd. of Education) v. Burford (Township), ... 969
Burgess, R. v., ... 713
Burkart, R. v., ... 886
Burke v. Arab, ... 991
Burke, R. v., ... 829, 830, 889
Burmah Oil Co. v. Bank of England, ... 789
Burnett, R. v., ... 244, 245
Burrows v. R., ... 1017, 1036
Bursil v. Tanner, ... 639
Burton v. Plummer, ... 850
Bury, R. v., ... 1019
Butler v. Board of Trade, ... 386, 645
Butler v. Mountgarret, ... 225
Butterfield, R. v., ... 45
Butterwasser, R. v., ... 450
Buttes Gas and Oil Co. v. Hammer (No. 3), ... 658, 669, 670
Buttrum v. Udell, ... 528, 571, 572, 573
Buxbaum, R. v., ... 752
Byrne v. Frere, ... 995

C

C. v. C., ... 996
C. v. M., ... 543
C.M. Oliver & Co. v. Gilroy, ... 742
C.(D.A.), R. v., ... 1036
C.(M.H.), R. v., ... 498
CNA Assurance Co. v. Altobelli, ... 1009
C.P.R. v. Calgary (City), ... 195
C.P.R. v. Jackson, ... 547
Caccamo, R. v., ... 958, 959, 960
Caffoor (Trustee of Abdul Gaffoor Trust) v. Income Tax
    Commissioner Columbo, ... 992, 1002, 1003
Cahoon v. Franks, ... 1001

Calcraft v. Guest, ... 385, 387, 628, 658, 672, 673, 675
Calder v. British Columbia (A.G.), ... 980
Calder Gravel Ltd. v. Kirkkes Metropolitan Borough Council, ... 119
Calgary Grain Co. v. Nordess, ... 838
California (State) and Meier & Hazelwood (No. 2), Re, ... 937
Callis v. Gunn, ... 29
Cameron v. Moncton (Town), ... 522
Cameron, R. v., ... 87
Cameron v. Rounsefell, ... 1006
Cameron Packaging Ltd. v. Ruddy, ... 724, 730
Camp, R. v., ... 898
Campbell v. Aird, ... 742
Campbell v. Barrie, ... 105
Campbell v. Beamish, ... 47
Campbell v. Cox, ... 116
Campbell v. Lindsey, ... 938
Campbell v. McDonald, ... 935
Campbell v. Paton, ... 805
Campbell, R. v., ... 148, 308, 310, 311, 847, 880, 881
Campbell Flour Mills Co. v. Bowes, ... 1009
Canada v. Schmidt. *See* Schmidt, R. v.
Can. (A.G.) and Restrictive Trade Practices Comm., Re. *See* Bombardier Ltd.
    v. Canada (Restrictive Trade Practices Comm.)
Canada (A.G.) v. Andrychuk, ... 815
Canada Atlantic Railway v. Moxley, ... 193
Canada and Dominion Sugar Co. Ltd. v. Canadian National (West Indies)
    Steamships Ltd., ... 989
Canada Central Railway Co. v. McLaren, ... 520
Canada (Dep. A.G.) v. Brown. *See* Income Tax Act, Re.
Canada (Director of Investigation and Research) v. Canada
    Safeway Ltd., ... 636, 646, 672
Canada (Director of Investigation and Research) v. Shell Canada Ltd., ... 645, 646
Canada Dredge & Dock Co. v. R. *See* R. v. McNamara (No. 1).
Canada Metal Co. v. Heap, ... 620
Canada (Min. of Industry, Trade and Commerce) v. Central Cartage Co.
    (No. 1) (1990), ... 779, 780
Canada (Min. of Trade and Commerce) v. Central Cartage Co. (1978), ... 1008
Canada (Royal Commission in Metropolitan Toronto Police Practices)
    v. Ashton, ... 442
Canada Safeway Ltd. and Manitoba Food & Commercial Workers Union,
    Local 82, Re, ... 558
Canada (Secretary of State) v. Delezos, ... 1038
Canada (Solicitor-General) v. Ontario (Royal Commission of Inquiry
    into Confidentiality of Health Records), ... 631, 805, 808, 810
Canada Safeway Ltd. and Retail Clerks Union, Local 206, ... 558
Canadian Breweries Transport Ltd. v. Johnson, ... 133
Canadian Broadcasting Corp. v. Lessard, ... 708, 711, 712

Canadian Broadcasting Corp. v. New Brunswick (Attorney General), ... 708, 711
Canadian Commercial Bank v. Holman (R.T.) Ltd., ... 105, 107
Canadian Imperial Bank of Commerce v. Val-Del Construction Ltd., ... 720
Canadian Javelin Ltd., Re (*sub nom.* Smallwood v. Sparling), ... 776, 781, 789
Canadian Newspapers Co. v. Canada (A.G.), ... 823
Canadian Newspapers Co. v. Manitoba, ... 233
Canadian Pacific Airlines Ltd. v. British Columbia. *See* Air Canada v. British
    Columbia.
Canadian Pacific Rly. Co. v. Parent, ... 984
Canadian Shredded Wheat Co. v. Kellogg Co., ... 1007
Canary v. Vested Estates Ltd., ... 651
Canpotex Ltd. v. Graham, ... 935, 939, 950
Capital Trust Corp. v. Fowler, ... 282, 283
Carbo v. United States, ... 297
Cardinal, R. v., ... 1036
Carefoot, R. v., ... 828
Carey v. R., ... 773, 774, 775, 781, 782, 783, 784,
                787, 789, 790, 791, 793, 794, 795, 800
Cargil Grain Ltd. v. Davie Ship Building Ltd., ... 196
Cargill, R. v., ... 475
Cariboo Observer Ltd. v. Carson Truck Lines Ltd., ... 839
Carl Zeiss Stiftung v. Rayner and Keeler Ltd. (No. 2), ... 999, 1007, 1010, 1011
Carlson, R. v., ... 1026
Carpenter (No. 2), R. v., ... 843
Carr v. Lyman. *See* Alberta (Public Trustee) v. Walker.
Carr-Briant, R. v., ... 152
Carter, R. v., ... 296, 297, 298, 363, 421, 964
Cartwright v. Toronto (City), ... 273
Caseley, R. v., ... 1035
Cassibo, R. v., ... 843, 845, 846, 847, 878, 870
Cassidy v. Ingoldsby, ... 1007
Castellani v. R., ... 949, 975
Catty v. James, ... 1043
Caughlin, R. v., ... 939, 968
Caulfield, R. v., ... 601
Cavers v. Laycock, ... 1008
Central Trust Co. v. MacDonald, ... 1008
Century 21 Ramos Realty Inc., R. v., ... 545
Cerniuk, R. v., ... 977
Chabot, R. v., ... 41
Challice, R. v., ... 150
Chambers v. Bernasconi, ... 189, 190
Chambers v. Jaffray, ... 742, 749
Chambors, R. v., ... 49, 312, 459, 602, 765, 766, 767, 810
Chandrasekera (alias Alisandiri) v. R., ... 160
Chapin, R. v., ... 389, 398
Chapman v. Amos, ... 945, 946

Chapman v. Seven-Up Sussex Ltd., ... 520
Chard v. Chard (otherwise Northcott), ... 114
Charette v. R. *See* Parsons, R. v.
Charlton, Re, ... 284, 1040
Charlwood v. Greig, ... 520
Chase v. Chase, ... 256
Chase, R. v., ... 62
Chateau Gai Wines Ltd. v. Canada (A.G.), Re, ... 980
Chaulk, R. v., ... 59, 75, 98, 100, 108, 126, 151
Chayko, R. v., ... 913, 914, 915
Cherniak v. Kurchaba, ... 859
Chiasson v. Public Trustee. *See* Adams v. Public Trustee.
Chilcott, Re, ... 978
Ching, R. v., ... 148, 149, 151
Chipchase v. Chipchase, ... 114, 115
Chippendale v. Winnipeg Electric Co., ... 968
Cholmondely (Earl) v. Lord Clinton, ... 658, 659
Choney, R. v., ... 649
Chote v. Rowan, ... 299
Chow, R. v. (1978), ... 344, 354
Chow, R. v. (1930), ... 46
Christenson, R. v., ... 315
Christie, R. v., ... 254, 287
Chromiak, R. v., ... 412
Church of Scientology, R. v., ... 631, 632, 694, 695, 697
Church of Scientology (No. 2), R. v. *See* R. v. Church of Scientology (No. 3).
Church of Scientology (No. 3), R. v., ... 644
Church of Scientology v. R. (No. 6). *See* Church of Scientology, R. v.
Church of Scientology of Toronto, R. v. *See* Church of Scientology, R. v.
Church of Scientology and R., Re. *See* Church of Scientology, R. v.
Churchill Falls (Labrador) Corp. v. R., ... 774
Churchman v. Churchman, ... 143
Circle Film Enterprises Inc. v. Cdn. Broadcasting Corp., ... 54, 67, 70, 71, 108, 112
Cirone, Re, ... 660
City of Philadelphia v. Westinghouse Electric Corp., ... 652
Clark v. Duncan, ... 238
Clark v. Grand Trunk Railway, ... 47, 729
Clark v. Phinney, ... 989, 997
Clark, R. v. (1983), ... 261
Clark, R. v. (U.K.) (1929), ... 974
Clark v. R. (1921), ... 141, 142, 148, 151
Clark, R. v. (1901), ... 760
Clark v. Stevenson, ... 24
Clarke v. British Columbia Electric Railway Co., ... 850
Clarke v. Holdsworth, ... 874
Clarke v. Imperial Gas Light & Coke Co., ... 954
Clarke, R. v. 475

Clarkson, R. v., ... 333, 335, 336, 337, 371, 372, 377, 409, 415, 419
Cleary, R. v., ... 358
Cleaveley, R. v., ... 326
Cleghorn, R. v., ... 826
Cleland v. R., ... 359
Clemens v. Clemens Estate, ... 119
Clemens v. Crown Trust Co., ... 783
Clendenning v. Belleville (Municipality) Commissioners of Police, ... 619, 620
Clergue v. McKay, ... 637
Clergue v. Plummer, ... 176, 177, 183
Clermont, R. v., ... 501
Close, R. v., ... 446, 447, 448, 463
Cloutier, R. v. (1979), ... 22, 25, 26, 940
Cloutier v. R. (1939), ... 46
Clowser v. Samuel, ... 256
Coady, R. v., ... 119
Coates v. Citizen (The), ... 711, 712
Coburn, R. v., ... 949, 975
Cochlin v. Massey-Harris Co., ... 951
Cochran's Trusts, Re; Robinson v. Simpson, ... 227
Coffin, R. v. (1956), ... 612, 836, 837, 844, 856
Coffin, R. v. (1954), ... 682
Cohen v. Cohen, ... 932
Cohen, R. v., ... 399
Cohn, R. v., ... 604
Cokely, R. v., ... 27
Cole & Knowles, Re, ... 45
Collerman, R. v., ... 842
Collier v. Nokes, ... 981
Collins, R. v., ... 95, 372, 373, 389, 390, 392, 397, 398, 399, 400-403, 405
                            407, 408, 410, 411, 412, 414, 418, 420, 423, 424, 559, 560
Colvin, R. v., ... 646
Comba, R. v., ... 41
Cominco Ltd. v. Westinghouse Canada Ltd., ... 732
Commodore Business Machines Ltd. and Ontario (Minister of Labour).
    See Olarte v. Commodore Business Machines Ltd.
Commonwealth v. Webster, ... 37
Commonwealth Shipping Representative v. Peninsular & Oriental
    Branch Service, ... 979, 986
Computer Machinery Co. Ltd. v. Drescher, ... 732
Concha v. Concha, ... 1005
Concord Credits Ltd. v. Frankel, ... 132
Confederation Life Association v. O'Donnell, ... 289
Conkie, R. v., ... 49, 352
Conley v. Conley, ... 189, 190, 211
Conlon v. Conlong Ltd., ... 638
Conlon, R. v., ... 287

1

Connolly v. Murrell, ... 680, 683, 684
Connolly, R. v., ... 936, 962
Connor v. Brant (Township), ... 824, 833
Connors, R. v., ... 601
Conrad, R. v., ... 1017
Consolidated Coal Co. v. Big Chief Woodyard Ltd., ... 295
Construction Association of Thunder Bay Inc., General Contractors' Div. v.
    Lumber & Sawmill Workers' Union, Local 2693 of C.J.A., ... 991
Container Materials Ltd., R. v., ... 295, 956
Continental Ins. Co. v. Dalton Cartage Co., ... 144, 145, 146
Contini v. Canarim Investment Corp., ... 517, 518
Controverted Election for the Electoral District of Shelburne and Queens, ... 47, 518
Conway v. Rimmer, ... 774, 785, 786, 787, 793, 794, 795, 796, 797, 799, 802, 803
Cook v. Grant, ... 922
Cook v. Lewis, ... 93
Cook, R. v. (1980), ... 295
Cook, R. v. (1914), ... 37
Cook v. Tripp, ... 910
Cooke v. Maxwell, ... 775
Coombs, R. v., ... 882
Cooper v. Marsden, ... 188
Cooper v. Molson's Bank, ... 1009, 1012
Cooper v. R. (1980), ... 532, 541, 542
Cooper, R. v. (1978), ... 42, 149
Cooper, R. v. (1833), ... 352
Coopers & Lybrand Ltd. v. Royal Bank of Canada, ... 105
Copp v. Clancy, ... 971, 972
Corbett, R. v., ... 30, 31, 336, 462, 464, 465, 476, 763, 848, 875
Cordell, R. v., ... 928, 931, 933, 943
Cordes, R. v., ... 944
Corke v. Corke, ... 307
Cormier v. LeBlanc, ... 969
Corning Glass Works of Canada Ltd. v. R. *See* General Sessions of the Peace for
    York County, R. v.
Coroner of Langley, R. v. *See* Wilson, Re.
Coroners Act, Re: Re Maddess, ... 605
Corporation professionnelle des médecins (Qué.) v. Thibault, ... 1038
Corran, R. v., ... 613
Cossens, ex parte. *See* Worrall, Re.
Cote, Ex parte, *See* Cote, R. v.
Côté, R. v. (1979), ... 744
Cote, R. v. (1971), ... 612
Côté v. Rooney, ... 729
Cotroni, R. v., Papalia v. R. *See* Swartz, R. v.
Cottrell v. Gallagher, ... 273
Coulson v. Disborough, ... 861
Court v. Holland, ... 271

Court, R. v., ... 29
Covert v. Janzen, ... 994
Cowie v. Fielding. *See* Controverted Election for the Electoral District of
    Shelburne and Queen's, Re.
Cox v. Dublin City Distillery Co. (No. 2), ... 1009
Cox v. Dublin City Distillery Co. (No. 3), ... 1009
Cox v. Robert Simpson Co., ... 1001
Coxon, Henry, The. *See* Henry Coxon, The.
Craig v. Craig, ... 1004
Craig v. Lamoureux, ... 65
Crane v. Ayre, ... 954, 966
Crawford, R. v. (1980), ... 465
Crawford, R. v. (1970), ... 103
Crease v. Barrett, ... 179, 219
Creemer, R. v., ... 967
Crippen, R. v., ... 882, 883
Cripps, R. v., ... 377
Critelli, Re, ... 919
Croft v. Wamboldt, ... 225, 227
Cromarty v. Monteith, ... 284
Crompton (Alfred) Amusement Machines Ltd. v. Customs and Excise
    Commissioners (No. 2), ... 651
Crools, R. v., ... 601
Crothers v. Northern Taxi Ltd., ... 932
Crowley v. Page, ... 886
Crown Trust Co. v. Rosenberg, ... 701, 702, 707, 708
Cruttenden, R. v., ... 612
Cuff v. Frazee Storage & Cartage Co., ... 47, 164, 246, 271
Culpepper, R. v., ... 950
Curr v. R., ... 430
Currie v. Stains, ... 228
Curry, R. v., ... 532, 975
Curry, Re, ... 919
Curry v. R., ... 589
Cusack, R. v., ... 140
Customs and Excise Comrs. v. Harz, ... 340
Customs Comptroller v. Western Lectric Co., ... 363
Cutts v. Head, ... 720, 732
Cyr v. DeRosier, ... 932, 935
Cyr v. O'Flynn, ... 994
Czipps, R. v., ... 612, 613, 617

D

D. v. National Society for Prevention of Cruelty
    to Children, ... 625, 626, 712, 801, 802, 806, 809, 810

D.A.C., R. v. *See* R. v. C.(D.A.).
D.(D.), R. v., ... 584, 594, 597
D.(L.E.), R. v., ... 44, 482, 483, 505
D.(R.R.), R. v., ... 596, 597, 598
D.S.W. v. R.H. *See* W.(D.S.) v. H.(R.).
D.(T.C.), R. v., ... 585
Dacey v. R., ... 1035
Dagle v. Dagle, ... 117, 118
Daigle, R. v., ... 898
Daintrey, Re; ex parte Holt, ... 720, 722, 725, 728, 729
Dalpe v. Edmundston (City), ... 93
Dalrymple v. Sun Life Assurance Co. of Canada, ... 156
Dalton v. Higgins, ... 536
Daly v. Leamy, ... 27
Daniel v. Hess, ... 991, 998
Daniels, R. v., ... 1036
Danson, R. v., ... 464
Danylec v. Kowpak, ... 984
D'Aoust, R. v., ... 600
Darby v. Ouseley, ... 866
Dass, R. v., ... 28
Dauphinee, R. v., ... 120
Davey v. Harrow Corp., ... 978
Davey, R. v., ... 855
Davidson v. R., ... 28
Davidson, R. v., ... 822
Davies v. Harrington, ... 656
Davies, R. v., ... 806, 810, 811
Davis v. Canada Farmers Mutual Insurance Co., ... 598
Davis v. Dinwoody, ... 678
Davis v. McSherry, ... 47
Davis v. Ralls, ... 994
Davis, R. v., ... 479
Davison, R. v., ... 459
Dawson v. Dawson, ... 188
Dawson v. Great Central Rly. Co., ... 973
Daye, R. v., ... 927
Daynes v. British Columbia Electric Rly. Co., ... 854
Deacon, R. v., ... 41, 48, 49, 847, 871
Deacon (No. 2), R. v., ... 847, 871, 872
Debard, R. v., ... 221
Debot, R. v., ... 371, 396, 397, 406, 417
De Champlain v. Maryland Casualty, ... 1004
DeClercq v. R., ... 331, 355
DeCorby v. DeCorby, ... 916, 918
Deep v. Wood, ... 442, 874
Dees, R. v., ... 453

Delafosse, R. v., ... 165
Del Core v. College of Pharmacists (Ontario), ... 1043
Delgamuukw v. British Columbia (1988), ... 670
Delgamuukw v. British Columbia (1987). *See* Uukw v. British Columbia.
Dellow's Will Trusts, Lloyds Bank Ltd. v. Institute of Cancer Research, Re, ... 144
Delong, R. v., ... 660
Delta-Benco-Cascade Ltd. v. Lakes Cablevision Inc., ... 657
Dembie v. Dembie, ... 713, 714, 732
Demenoff v. R., ... 352
Demers, R. v., ... 356, 359
Demeter v. British Pacific Life Insurance Co., ... 1011, 1042, 1043, 1046
Demeter, R. v., ... 179, 180, 181, 183, 184, 185
Demyen, R. v., ... 446
Den Hollander, R. v., ... 815
Denis Shipping Ltd. v. Palmer, ... 211
Denmark, R. v., ... 604
Denn d. Lucas v. Fulford, ... 943
Dennis (W.) & Sons Ltd. v. West Norfolk Farmers' Manure and Chemical
   Co-operative Co., ... 639
Dennison v. Gahans, ... 936
Dennison v. Sanderson, ... 702
Denovan v. Lee, ... 723
Deokinanan v. R., ... 350
Deputy Industrial Injuries Commissioner, R. v.; Ex parte Moore, ... 305
Derby & Co. v. Weldon (No. 8), ... 663, 675
Derco Industries Ltd. v. A.R. Grimwood Ltd., ... 720, 721, 726, 727, 729, 730, 731
Deremore v. Trusts and Guarantee Co., ... 100
Dersch v. Canada (Attorney-General), ... 425, 427, 817
Dersch, R. v. *See* Dersch v. Canada (A.G.).
Desaulniers v. Payette, ... 994, 1027
de Schelking v. Cromie, ... 702
Descôteaux v. Mierzwinski, ... 627, 640, 641, 642, 644, 646,
                                                649, 650, 664, 672, 673, 675, 708
D'Ettore v. R., ... 1035
Devala Provident Gold Mining Co., Re, ... 292
Devasagayum, R. v. *See* Re Praisoody.
Devison, R. v., ... 381
Devlin v. Crocker, ... 882
Dhaliwal, R. v., ... 745
Diamond v. Western Realty Co., ... 994
Dickey v. C.N.R., ... 23
Dickie, R. v., ... 440
Dickson v. McFarlane, ... 938
Dickson v. Pinch, ... 861
Dieleman Planer Co. v. Elizabeth Townhouses Ltd., ... 294
Dietrich, R. v., ... 453, 975, 976
Di Iorio v. Montreal Jail, ... 607

Dilabbio v. R., ... 968
Dillabough, R. v., ... 615, 616
Director of Assessment v. Begg. *See* Begg v. East Hants (Municipality).
Director of Investigation & Research v. Ziegler. *See* Ziegler v. Canada
   (Director of Investigation & Research).
D.P.P. v. *See* under name of accused.
Dixon (No. 2), R. v., ... 953, 965
Djambie Rubber Estates Ltd., Re, ... 190
Dobberthien v. R., ... 826, 827, 828
Dobbs v. Dobbs, ... 771
Dobson, R. v., ... 974
Doe d. Arnold v. Auldjo, ... 227
Doe d. Arundel (Lord) v. Fowler, ... 956
Doe d. Church and Phillips v. Perkins, ... 854
Doe d. Didsbury v. Thomas, ... 218
Doe d. Dunlop v. Servos, ... 225
Doe d. Edgett v. Stiles, ... 955, 956
Doe d. Fleming v. Fleming, ... 220
Doe d. Gilbert v. Ross, ... 934, 936
Doe d. Gilmour v. Witney, ... 936
Doe d. Godsoe v. Jack, ... 934, 938
Doe d. Human v. Pettett, ... 255
Doe d. Jacobs v. Phillips, ... 956
Doe d. King's College v. Kennedy, ... 954, 967
Doe d. Maclem v. Turnbull, ... 955, 956
Doe d. McDonald v. Twigg, ... 954, 966
Doe d. Mariott v. Marquis of Hertford, ... 638
Doe d. Marr v. Marr, ... 222, 735
Doe d. Neale v. Samples, ... 956
Doe d. Patteshall v. Turford, ... 189
Doe d. Shallcross v. Palmer, ... 252
Doe d. Slason v. Hanson, ... 951
Doe d. Spence v. Welling, ... 971
Doe d. Stevens v. Robinson, ... 951
Doe d. Tilman v. Tarver, ... 225
Doe d. Wetherell v. Bird, ... 973
Doe d. Wetmore v. Bell, ... 859, 879
Doe d. Wheeler v. McWilliams, ... 220
Doe d. William IV v. Roberts, ... 937
Doe, Lessee of Banning v. Griffin, ... 226
Doering v. Grandview (Town), ... 998, 999, 1000, 1001, 1002
Doland (George) Ltd. v. Blackburn, Robson, Coates & Co. (a firm) 665
Dombrowski, R. v., ... 389
Dominion Act Co. Ltd. v. Murphy, ... 971, 973
Dominion Bank v. Ewing, ... 286
Dominion Stores and United Steelworkers of America, Re, ... 558
Dominion Telegraph Securities Ltd. v. Minister of National Revenue, ... 189

Dominion Trust Co. v. Inglis, ... 912
Domstad, R. v., ... 463
Domville v. Ferguson, ... 973
Donald v. Law Society (British Columbia), ... 742, 749
Donald, R. v., ... 934
Dooley, R. v., ... 1026
Doré v. Canada (A.G.) (No. 2), ... 1029
Doré v. Canada (A.G.), ... 1029
Doty v. Marks, ... 994
Double-E Inc. v. Positive Action Tool Western Ltd., ... 387, 676
Doull, R. v., ... 736
Dowling v. Bowie, ... 87, 89
Downey, R. v., ... 352
Doyle, R. v., ... 454
Doz, R. v., ... 899
Drabinsky v. Maclean-Hunter Ltd., ... 702, 725
Drake, R. v., ... 364
Drake v. Sykes. See Sykes, Re.
Draper v. Jacklyn, ... 33, 35, 36, 968
Drew (No. 2), R. v., ... 859
Drolex, R. v., ... 594
Drouin, R. v., ... 467
Drummond, R. v., ... 455
Drysdale, R. v. (1969), ... 479
Drysdale, R. v. (1932), ... 974
Dsane v. Hagan, ... 992
Duarte, R. v., ... 409, 410, 415, 416, 417, 423, 426, 684, 685
Dubai Bank Ltd. v. Galadari, ... 657
Dubois, R. v. (1986), ... 135, 137
Dubois, R. v. (1985), ... 124, 374, 376, 735, 740, 743, 744, 750, 751, 752
Dubois, R. v. (1980), ... 41
Dubois, R. v. (1976), ... 467, 533
Dubrule, R. v., ... 977, 978
Duchess of Kingston, R. v., ... 713, 989
Duckworth, R. v., ... 838
Dudas v. Eagle Star Insurance Co., ... 859
Duff Development Co. Ltd. v. Kelanton Government, ... 980
Dufresne Construction Co. v. R., ... 775
Duggan v. Duggan, ... 921
Duguay, R. v. (1985), ... 389, 400
Duguay, R. v. (1966), ... 595
Duhamel v. R., ... 360, 990, 1027
Duke v. Andler, ... 993
Dunbar, R. v., ... 638, 660, 669, 677
Duncan, Re; Garfield v. Fay, ... 648
Duncan v. Cammel, Laird and Co., ... 774, 782, 783, 784, 786, 791
Dunn v. Gibson, ... 905

Dunn, R. v., ... 595
Dunphy v. Phillips, ... 218
Durocher, R. v., ... 348
Duscharm, R. v., ... 28
Dusik v. Newton, ... 641
Duvivier, R. v., ... 612
Dyck, R. v., ... 877
Dyer v. Best, ... 850
Dyer, R. v. (1971), ... 591
Dyer, R. v. (1703), ... 981
Dyment, R. v. (1988), ... 404, 416, 417, 420, 421, 422, 429, 430
Dyment, R. v. (1966), ... 468

E

Eagle Disposal Systems Ltd. v. Ontario (Minister of the Environment), ... 1037
Earnshaw v. Despins, ... 46
Earnshaw v. Dominion of Canada General Insurance Co., ... 144
Eastern Twps. Invt. Co. v. McLellan, ... 20
Eaton, R. v., ... 325
Ebsary, R. v., ... 340
Eccles v. Lowry, ... 1008
Ecker, R. v. (1984), ... 949
Ecker, R. v. (1929), ... 1017
Ed Miller Sales & Rental Ltd. v. Caterpillar Tractor Co., ... 720, 726, 727, 730
Eden, R. v., ... 286
Edmonton Journal (The) v. Alberta (A.G.), ... 823
Edwards, Ex parte, ... 179
Edwards v. Brookes (Milk) Ltd., ... 291
Edwards v. The Ottawa River Navigation Co., ... 25, 442, 520
Edwards, R. v., ... 84, 85, 86, 87, 88
Elder, R. v., ... 854
Elgin v. Stubbs, ... 909
Elliott v. Elliott, ... 771
Ellis v. Allen, ... 972
Ellis v. Home Office, ... 786
Ellis v. Power, ... 735
Ellis-Don Ltd., R. v., ... 151
Elmosri, R. v., ... 453
Elsam v. Faucett, ... 439
Elshaw, R. v., ... 413
Elton v. Larkins, ... 973
Elworthy, R. v., ... 931, 935
Emile, R. v., ... 372
Emsley, R. v., ... 184
Enge v. Trerise, ... 162

Engelke v. Musmann, ... 980
England v. United States, ... 208
English v. Richmond; Laing v. Richmond, ... 284
Enns v. Enns, ... 771
Enoch and Zaretsky, Bock and Co., Re, ... 825
Entrehman, R. v., ... 587
Erco Industries Ltd. v. Allendale Mutual Insurance Co., ... 883
Erickson, R. v., ... 405
Erinco Homes Ltd., Re, ... 728
Ertel, R. v., ... 895
Erven, R. v., ... 326, 375, 376, 752
Ettenfield v. Ettenfield, ... 113
Evans v. Banffshire Apartments Ltd., ... 654
Evans v. Chief Constable of Surrey Constabulary, ... 774, 805
Evans v. Morgan, ... 220
Evans, R. v., ... 370
Evans v. Trusts and Guarantee Co., ... 911
Event Sales Inc. v. Rommco Group Inc., ... 611
"Evgenic Chandris" (The), R. v., ... 983
Excelsior Life Insurance Co. v. Saskatchewan, ... 720, 723

F

F. v. F., ... 997
F. v. A Psychiatrist, ... 633
Faber v. R., ... 606
Fagernes, The, ... 980
Fagnan v. Ure, ... 572
Faid v. R., ... 533
Fairman v. Fairman, ... 143
Falconbridge Ltd. v. Hawker Siddely Diesels & Electronics Ltd., ... 657
Famous Players, R. v., ... 957, 963, 964
Farhat v. Travelers Indemnity Co. of Canada, ... 657
Farley v. Graham, ... 936
Farrant, R. v., ... 102, 103, 448, 459, 460, 461
Farrell v. Collerman, ... 919
Farrell v. Tisdale, ... 725, 731
Farren v. Pejepscot Paper Co., ... 223, 225, 226
Farrer, R. v., ... 810
Fasken, Re, ... 104, 105
Faulkner, R. v., ... 37
Fay v. Prentice, ... 979
Feeley v. R., ... 1025
Feener v. A.G. (N.S.), ... 990
Fehr, R. v., ... 631, 635
Fellichle, R. v., ... 614

Fenerty v. Halifax (City), ... 989
Fequet, R. v., ... 326
Ferber, R. v., ... 162, 164
Ferguson, Ex parte, ... 601
Ferguson v. Veitch, ... 47
Ferraro, R. v., ... 1037
Ferrero and R., Re. *See* Ferrero v. R.
Ferrero v. R., ... 810
Ferrie v. Jones, ... 156
Ferris v. Monahan, ... 27, 284
Feuerheerd v. London General Omnibus Co., ... 649
Fex, R. v., ... 326
Fichter, R. v., ... 940
Fidelitas Shipping Co. Ltd. v. V/O Exportchleb, ... 998, 999
Fields, R. v., ... 45, 46, 860, 861
Fife v. I.C.B.C., ... 1001
Filios v. Morland, ... 828, 829, 830
Finers (a firm) v. Miro, ... 645
Finestone v. R., ... 231, 942
Finlay, R. v., ... 149
Finley v. University Hospital, ... 633
Finnessey, R. v., ... 468, 469
Firkins, R. v., ... 892, 898
First National Bank of Boston v. Christy Crops Ltd., ... 965
Fischer v. Robert Bell Engine & Thresher Co., ... 730
Fisher v. C.H.T. Ltd., ... 12
Fisher, R. v. (1986), ... 612
Fisher v. R. (1961), ... 534, 539, 540, 542
Fisher v. Vaughan (Township), ... 119
Fishman v. R., ... 1045
Fitton, R. v., ... 330, 331
Fitzpatrick, R. v., ... 1028
Flack v. Pacific Press Ltd., ... 636, 653
Flanagan v. Fahy, ... 310
Flavelle, Re, ... 993
Fleet v. Farrel, ... 254
Flegel Construction Ltd. v. Cambac Financial Projects Ltd., ... 723, 725
Fleming v. Canadian Pacific Railway Co., ... 271
Fleming v. Pitirri, ... 978
Fleming, R. v., ... 856
Fleming v. Toronto, Ry. Co., ... 849, 851, 852
Fletcher v. Kondratiuk, ... 982
Fletcher, R. v., ... 587, 588, 591, 592
Foggo v. Foggo, ... 1006
Foley, R. v., ... 913
Folkes v. Chadd, ... 25, 533
Follis v. Albemarle (Township), ... 919

lix

Foncière Cie d'assurance v. Perras, ... 1040
Foothills Pipe Lines (Yukon) Ltd. v. Minister of National Revenue, ... 528
Forbes v. Forbes, ... 221
Forbes, R. v., ... 429
Ford v. Hopkins, ... 929
Forrest v. Davidson, ... 988
Forsythe v. R., ... 469, 471
Fortino v. Randolph, ... 1001
Foster v. Reaume, ... 999
Foster, R. v., ... 220
Fosty, R. v. See Gruenke, R. v.
Foulds v. Bowler, ... 965
Fountain v. Young, ... 649
Fowler v. Fowler, ... 825
Fowler, R. v., ... 349
Fox v. Chief Constable of Gwent. See Fox, R. v.
Fox v. General Medical Council, ... 308, 309, 310, 311, 858
Fox, R. v. (1985), ... 382
Fox, R. v. (1899), ... 742
Fox v. Sleeman, ... 927
Frank, R. v., ... 601
Fraser v. Fraser, ... 849, 850
Fraser, R. v. (1971), ... 974
Fraser, Re (1911), ... 100, 528, 825
Fraser v. Sutherland, ... 638
Frederick, R. v., ... 361, 362
Freel v. Robinson, ... 255
French v. McKendrick, ... 824, 825
French, R. v., ... 543, 544
French's Complex Ore Reduction Co. of Canada v. Electrolytic Zinc
    Process Co., ... 571
Frenette, R. v., ... 215
Frind v. Sheppard, ... 665
Frisbee, R. v., ... 1016, 1023
Frost, R. v., ... 883
Frye v. United States, ... 565, 566, 568, 569
Fuld, Re, Hartley v. Fuld (Fuld intervening), ... 828
Fulling, R. v., ... 343
Fulton v. Creelman, ... 218

G

G., Re, ... 224, 272
G. v. G., ... 714, 715, 732
G.B., R. v. See B.(G.), R. v.
G. & J. Parking Lot Maintenance Ltd. v. Oland Construction Co., ... 18

G.(T.L.) v. L.(D.), ... 902
Gaff, R. v., ... 430
Gagnon v. Quebec Securities Commission, ... 784
Gaich, R. v., ... 957
Gaijic, R. v. See Gaich, R. v.
Gain v. Gain, ... 789
Gaja v. R. See Vetrovec v. R.
Galarce, R. v., ... 931, 934
Galbraith v. Galbraith, ... 1004
Gallant, R. v., ... 36
Gane v. Gane. See Gain v. Gain.
Gardiner v. M.N.R., ... 972
Gardiner, R. v., ... 95, 306, 327, 974
Gardner v. Irvin, ... 637
Garfield v. Fay. See Duncan, Re.
Garlow, R. v., ... 260, 268
Garner v. Garner, ... 713
Garner v. Morin-Heights (Municipalité), ... 984
Garofoli, R. v., ... 213, 425, 427, 811, 812, 813, 817, 818, 819
Garton v. Hunter, ... 930
Gaskill v. Skene, ... 963
Gaskin v. Retail Credit Co., ... 134
Gauthier, R. v., ... 356, 375
Gavin, R. v., ... 329
Gayne, R. v. See Seaboyer, R. v.
Geddie v. Rink, ... 442, 860
Geffen v. Goodman Estate, ... 635, 636, 659, 663, 664
Genaille, R. v., ... 1036
General Films Ltd. v. McElroy, ... 885
General Host Corp. v. Chemalloy Minerals Ltd., ... 949
General Sessions of the Peace for York County, R. v., ... 753
Genest, R. v., ... 402, 405, 406, 407, 416, 417, 418, 419, 420, 424
Gentle v. Gentle, ... 769
George v. Davies, ... 985
George, R. v., ... 317, 318
Georges Contracting Ltd., R. v., ... 1037
Georgia Const. Co. v. Pacific Great Eastern Railway, ... 47
Gerard v. Hudson, ... 922
German v. R., ... 631
Germscheid v. Valois, ... 1012
Gerow v. R., ... 340
Gervais, R. v., ... 896
Gettle Bros. Construction Co. v. Alwinsal Potash of Canada Ltd., ... 997
Giannotti, R. v., ... 102
Gibbs v. Canada Trust Co., ... 919
Gibson, R. v., ... 48
Gibson v. Toth, ... 573

Giffin v. R., ... 979
Giguere, R. v., ... 645
Gilbert v. Campbell, ... 933
Gilbert, R. v. (1988), ... 370, 372
Gilbert v. R. (1907), ... 259
Gilbert v. Ross, ... 932
Gilbert v. Sleeper, ... 935
Gilbey v. Great Western Railway Co., ... 238
Gilham, R. v., ... 341
Gill v. R., ... 1026
Gill, R. v., ... 138
Gill Bros. v. Mission Sawmills Ltd., ... 285
Gillespie, R. v., ... 965
Gilson, R. v, ... 959
Ginesi v. Ginesi, ... 143
Ginsberg, Re, ... 737
Giraldi, R. v., ... 308
Giroux, R. v., ... 613
Girvin, R. v., ... 72, 135
Gladstone, R. v. (1985), ... 412
Gladstone, R. v. (1977), ... 536
Glasgow v. Toronto Paper Mfg. Co., ... 271
Glawe v. Rulon, ... 208
Gleadow v. Atkin, ... 179
Gleeson v. J. Wippell & Co. Ltd., ... 1009, 1010
Gleeson v. Wallace, ... 966, 1008
Glen Bain (Rural Municipality) v. Haley, ... 957
Glidden v. Town of Woodstock, ... 519
Glister, R. v., ... 41
Globe & Rutgers Fire Insurance Co. v. Truedell, ... 237
Gloster, R. v., ... 241
Gloucester Properties Ltd. v. R., ... 789
Goddard v. Nationwide Building Society, ... 385, 386, 675
Godfrey, R. v., ... 108, 126
Goguen v. Bourgeois, ... 911
Goguen v. Gibson, ... 782, 787, 788, 789, 791, 792
Gold v. Canada, ... 789, 790
Goldman, R. v. See Goldman v. R.
Goldman v. R., ... 688
Gollan v. Edmonton Credit Co., ... 978
Goncalves v. Guerra, ... 1000
Gonzague, R. v., ... 464, 888
Goodman v. Geffen. See Geffen v. Goodman Estate.
Goodman & Carr, Re. See Goodman & Carr v. Minister of National Revenue.
Goodman & Carr v. Minister of National Revenue, ... 645, 650, 655
Goodright & Stevens v. Moss, ... 228, 693
Goody v. Odhams Press Ltd., ... 435

Gordon v. Rosenberg. *See* Brown, Re.
Gordon, R. v., ... 974
Gorgichuk v. American Home Assurance Co., ... 543
Gormley v. Canada Permanent Trust Co., ... 182
Gosselin v. R., ... 600, 614, 615, 679
Gottschall, R. v., ... 455
Gough v. Whyte, ... 993, 1001
Gouin v. R., ... 894
Gould, R. v., ... 198, 213
Goulet, R. v., ... 120
Gourand v. Edison Gower Bell Telephone Co. of Europe, ... 639
Government Insurance Office v. Fredrichberg, ... 81
Governor of Brixton Prison, R. v., ... 774, 786, 791
Governor of Pentenville Prison, ex p. Osman, R. v., ... 645, 931, 940
Gowland, R. v., ... 44
Graat, R. v., ... 5, 526, 528, 546
Grady v. Waite, ... 598
Grafstein v. Holme, ... 960
Graham v. Graham, ... 860
Graham v. Law, ... 220
Graham, R. v. (1991), ... 759
Graham, R. v. (1972), ... 266, 267, 320, 362, 483
Grainger v. Hamilton, ... 439
Gran, R. v., ... 471
Grand Trunk Ry. Co. v. McMillan, ... 994
Grandview v. Doering. *See* Doering v. Grandview (Town).
Grant, Re, ... 165
Grant v. Australian Knitting Mills, ... 40
Grant v. Canada (Min. of Indian and Northern Affairs), ... 1000, 1011
Grant, R. v. (1989), ... 280
Grant, R. v. (1924), ... 974
Grant v. Southwestern and County Properties Ltd., ... 928
Gratt, R. v. *See* Graat, R. v.
Gray v. Kerslake, ... 107
Gray v. LaFleche, ... 34, 35
Gray v. New Augarita Porcupine Mines Ltd., ... 164, 243
Gray v. Oshawa (City), ... 119
Graydon v. Graydon, ... 863
Grdic v. R., ... 1026
Great Atlantic Insurance Co. v. Home Insurance Co., ... 663
Great West Uranium Mines Ltd. v. Rock Hill Uranium Mines Ltd., ... 242, 295
Green v. McLeod, ... 911
Green, R. v. (1988), ... 504, 505
Green, R. v. (1983), ... 1037
Green v. R. (1971), ... 149
Green v. Spencer, ... 10
Green v. Tress, ... 237

Greenberg v. Rapaport, ... 99
Greenlaw v. King, ... 643
Greeno, R. v., ... 1026
Greenough v. Eccles, ... 839
Greenough v. Gaskell, ... 636
Greenough v. Woodstream Corp., ... 17
Greenspoon Bros. Ltd., R. v., ... 604
Greenwood v. Fitts, ... 288, 729
Greffe, R. v., ... 405, 406, 416, 417, 419, 420, 422, 423
Greig, R. v., ... 372
Grewal, R. v., ... 352
Grewal v. Small, ... 1008
Griffith, R. v. *See* Bevan v. R.
Griffith, R. v., ... 46
Grimba, R. v., ... 207
Groat v. Kinnaird, ... 892, 921
Gronlund v. Hansen, ... 786, 798
Grosse, R. v., ... 446, 463, 464
Grosvenor Hotel, London (No. 2), Re, ... 786
Gruenke, R. v., ... 623, 624, 626, 632, 634, 635, 636, 694, 695, 696, 697, 698, 699
Guay, R. v., ... 462
Guerin, R. v., ... 761
Guillemette, R. v., ... 1033
Guinness Peat Properties Ltd. v. Fitzroy Robinson Partnership, ... 386
Guiry v. Wheeler, ... 771
Gunn v. Cox, ... 932
Gushue, R. v., ... 1024, 1025, 1030
Guy v. Brady, ... 973

H

Haase, R. v., ... 368
Hacock v. Vallaincourt, ... 633
Hagenlocher v. R., ... 1029, 1039
Haggarty v. Britton, ... 969
Haines v. Guthrie, ... 228
Hair v. Meaford, ... 995, 996
Halam Park Devt. Ltd. v. Hamilton Wentworth Regional Assessment
    Commissioner, Region No. 19, ... 991, 1003
Hales v. Kerr, ... 513, 520
Hall v. Geiger, ... 47
Hall v. Hall, ... 999, 1000
Hall v. R. *See* Simpson, R. v.
Halliday, R. v., ... 41
Hallman v. Bricker, ... 921
Hallmark's Case, ... 959

Halls v. Mitchell, ... 237, 713
Halpin, R. v., ... 234, 235
Hamelyn v. Whyte, ... 637
Hamill, R. v., ... 414, 417, 422
Hamilton v. Laurentian Pacific Ins. Co., ... 1004
Hanes v. Wawanesa Mutual Ins. Co., ... 99, 144
Hanington v. Harshmen, ... 20
Hannam, R. v., ... 957
Hannum v. McRae, ... 618, 736
Hansell v. Spink, ... 934
Hansen v. Saskatchewan Power Corporation, ... 35
Harbuz, R. v., ... 581, 582, 585
Hardy v. Man. Public Insurance Corp., ... 1037
Hardy, R. v., ... 2, 307
Hardy Lumber Co. v. Pickerel River Improvement Co., ... 995
Harich v. Stamp, ... 667
Harlow, Re, ... 115
Harper & Row v. Decker, ... 652
Harriman, R. v., ... 506, 508, 509, 510
Harris v. D.P.P., ... 23, 480, 489, 490, 511
Harris v. Harris, ... 300
Harris, R. v. (1987), ... 1032
Harris, R. v. (1947), ... 108
Harris, R. v. (1946), ... 357
Harris, R. v. (1927), ... 826
Harris v. Tippett, ... 475
Harrison v. King, ... 742
Harrison, R. v. (1977), ... 119
Harrison, R. v. (1946), ... 287
Harrison v. Turner, ... 282
Hart, R. v., ... 877
Hart v. Toronto General Trusts Corp., ... 190
Hartney v. Northern British Fire Insurance Co., ... 723
Hartshorne v. Wilkins, ... 116
Hartz Canada Inc. v. Colgate-Palmolive Co., ... 648
Harvey, R. v., ... 531
Harvie v. Gibbons, ... 909, 910
Harwood v. Wilkinson, ... 821
Hashem, R. v., ... 957
Hatherley, R. v., ... 1016
Hatton, R. v., ... 340, 348
Hawboldt v. Elliott, ... 1009
Hawke, R. v., ... 33, 580, 582, 592, 715, 858, 877, 886
Hawkes, R. v., ... 28, 47
Hawley v. Hand, ... 904
Hay, R. v., ... 694
Hay v. University of Alberta Hospital, ... 627

Hayball v. Shephard, ... 935
Hayes v. Driscoll, ... 955, 956
Hayes, R. v. (1989), ... 895, 896, 916
Hayes, R. v. (1976), ... 591
Hays v. Weiland, ... 702
Haywood Securities Inc. v. Brunnhuber. *See* Haywood Securities Inc.
  v. Inter-Tech Resource Group Inc.
Haywood Securities Inc. v. Inter-Tech Resource Group Inc., ... 608, 611, 759
Heal v. Heal, ... 770
Heany v. Parker, ... 937, 938
Hebert, R. v. (1990), ... 312, 333, 377, 378, 402, 407, 412,
                                                          413, 601, 608, 734, 757, 758, 759
Hébert v. R. (1955), ... 365
Heilman, R. v., ... 213
Hellenius v. Lees, ... 74, 82
Hellyer Farms Ltd. v. Biro, ... 284
Helpard v. R., ... 452
Hemmingway, R. v., ... 1021
Henderson v. Henderson, ... 998
Henderson v. Tudhope, ... 972
Henley v. Henley, ... 733
Hennessy v. Wright, ... 774
Hennessy v. Wright (No. 2), ... 702
Hennig v. Northern Heights (Sault) Ltd., ... 995, 1001
Henry Coxon, The, ... 179, 189, 190
Herodotou (No. 2), R. v., ... 366
Hester, D.P.P. v., ... 893, 915, 922
Hey v. Huss, ... 858
Heywood, R. v., ... 135
Hickey v. Fitzgerald, ... 442, 514, 857, 884
Hickman v. Peacey, ... 116
Hickman v. Taylor, ... 654, 655
Hicks v. Rothermel, ... 638, 643
Higgins, R. v., ... 361
Highland Fisheries Ltd. v. Lynk Electric Ltd., ... 670
Highley v. C.P.R., ... 972
Hill v. Baxter, ... 140
Hill v. East and West India Dock Co., ... 106
Hill v. Hill, ... 996, 998, 1004
Hill, R. v. (1928), ... 49
Hill, R. v. (1851), ... 581, 583
Hillesheim v. Hillesheim, ... 732
Hillier, R. v., ... 981
Himmelman v. Himmelman, ... 113
Hindson v. Ashby, ... 967
Hiuser v. Hiuser, ... 978
H.M.S. Bellerophon, ... 799

Hobart, R. v., ... 297
Hobbins, R. v., ... 347
Hodge's Case, ... 37, 40, 41, 149
Hodgkinson v. Simms, ... 653, 657, 663
Hoffman v. Crerar, ... 637
Hogan v. R., ... 380, 388
Hoilett, R. v., ... 894
Hollington v. F. Hewthorn & Co., ... 436, 1012, 1041, 1042, 1043, 1045, 1046
Hollis v. Burton, ... 972
Holloway v. McFeeters, ... 169
Hollum, Re, ... 770
Holmes v. D.P.P., ... 61
Holmes, R. v., ... 57, 88, 125, 126
Holt, ex parte. *See* Daintrey, Re.
Holt v. Ashfield, ... 1011
Home v. Bentinck, ... 791
Home v. Corbeil, ... 244, 248, 249
Home Juice Co. v. Orange Maison Ltée., ... 536
Homes v. Newman, ... 235
Homestake Mining Co. v. Texasgulf Potash Co. *See* Homestake Mining Co., R. v.
Homestake Mining Co., R. v., ... 801
Honan, R. v., ... 381
Hood v. Cronkite, ... 932, 935
Hope v. Brash, ... 702
Hopper v. Dunsmuir (No. 2), ... 704
Horn v. Sturm, ... 192, 202
Hornal v. Neuberger Products Ltd., ... 99, 144, 145, 146
Horner v. Canadian Northern Ry., ... 877
Horowitz v. Rothstein, ... 638
Horsburgh v. R., ... 583, 588, 591
Horsfall v. Horsfall, ... 997
Horvath v. R., ... 331, 335, 344
Horwood, R. v., ... 488
Hosegood v. Hosegood, ... 103
Hoskyn v. Metropolitan Police Commissioner, ... 613, 614, 615
Howard, R. v. (1989), ... 563, 564, 565
Howard, R. v. (1983), ... 20, 349
Howard Smith Paper Mills, R. v., ... 962
Howe v. Malkin, ... 255
Howith v. McFarlane, ... 252
Hoyle v. Lord Cornwallis, ... 981
Hoystead v. Taxation Commr., ... 999, 1002, 1003
Hrechuk, R. v., ... 519
Hryn, R. v., ... 287
Hubin v. R., ... 915
Hufsky, R. v., ... 342, 429, 430
Hughes, R. v., ... 319

Human Rights Commission v. Canada (A.G.), ... 781
Humphrey v. Archibald, ... 805
Humphries v. Humphries, ... 989
Humphrys, D.P.P. v., ... 1024
Hunnings v. Williamson, ... 736
Hunt v. MacLeod Construction Co., ... 132, 133
Hunt, R. v., ... 65, 87, 89, 90, 91
Hunter v. Chief Constable of West Midlands Police, ... 1010
Hunter v. Hunter, ... 771
Hunter v. Mann, ... 713
Hunter, R. v., ... 806, 810, 814, 815
Hunter v. Rogers, ... 666
Hunter v. Southam Inc., ... 419, 422
Hurd v. Canada (Minister of Employment & Immigration), ... 1037
Hurd v. Minister of Employment & Immigration, see Hurd v. Canada (Minister of
    Employment & Immigration).
Hurd, R. v., ... 28
Huron Steel Fabricators (London) Ltd. v. M.N.R.; Fratschko v. M.N.R., ... 774
Hurst v. Evans, ... 3, 144
Hyde v. Palmer, ... 255, 256

I

IBM Canada Ltd. v. Xerox of Canada Ltd., ... 651
I.C.B.C. v. Sherrell, ... 1005
I.L.W.V. v. Canada, ... 781
Ibrahim v. R., ... 328, 330, 332, 334, 367
Ilich v. Hartford Fire Insurance Co., ... 657
Imperial Bank v. Trusts & Guarantee Co., ... 919
Imperial Oil, R. v., ... 1031
Imrich, R. v., ... 41, 49
Imrie, R. v., ... 585
Income Tax Act, Re; Milner, Re, ... 645
Income Tax Act, Re; Solicitor v. M.N.R., ... 639
Industrial Acceptance Corp. v. Doughan, ... 934
Industrial Acceptance Corp. v. Golisky, ... 994
Industrial Acceptance Corp. v. R., ... 943
Ingram, R. v., ... 942
Inkster, R. v., ... 899
Inquiry re Department of Manpower and Immigration in Montreal, Re, ... 605
Insco Sarnia Ltd. v. Polysar Ltd., ... 273
Interlake Tissue Mills Co. v. Salmond, ... 81
International Corona Resources Ltd. v. LAC Minerals Ltd., ... 628
Ireland v. Taylor, ... 879
Irish Society v. Derry, ... 941
Irvine v. Superintendent of Family and Child Service, ... 302

ITC Film Distributors v. Video Exchange Ltd., ... 676
Iuculano, R. v., ... 1031
I. Waxman & Sons Ltd. v. Texaco Canada Ltd., ... 720, 721, 726, 728, 731
Izzard, R. v., ... 313, 916

J

J.F. Henderson Ltd. v. Athike Enterprises Ltd., ... 994
J.M. Lumber King Ltd. v. Von Transeke-Roseneck Estate, ... 916, 918
Jackman v. Jackman, ... 117
Jackson, Re, ... 892, 920
Jackson v. Belzberg, ... 707
Jackson v. Boyes, ... 683, 685, 687
Jackson v. C.P.R., ... 982
Jackson v. Millar, ... 82
Jackson, R. v., ... 913, 914
Jacobs v. Beaver, ... 992, 1012
Jacobs, R. v. (1988), ... 135, 529
Jacobs, R. v. (1953), ... 761
Jacoy, R. v., ... 390, 403, 405, 414, 415, 423
Jacquard, R. v., ... 765
James Lorimer & Co., R. v., ... 627
Jannette v. The Great Western Ry. Co., ... 972
Janzen, R. v., ... 429
Jarvis v. Connell, ... 877
Jarvis v. Hall, ... 877
Jarvis v. London Street Railway, ... 289
Jarvis, R. v. (1867), ... 341
Jarvis, R. v. (1756), ... 84
Jayasena v. R., ... 55, 56, 65, 139
J-Bailey's Furniture Market Ltd., Re. See Cooper & Lybrand Ltd. v. Royal Bank
  of Canada.
Jean, R. v., ... 690
Jeffrey v. Black, ... 382
Jeffrey v. Johnson, ... 910
Jenion, Re; Jenion v. Wynne, ... 693
Jenion v. Wynne. See Jenion, Re.
Jenkins, Re, ... 752
Jewitt, R. v., ... 1018, 1032
Jobidon, R. v., ... 266
Joe v. Director of Family and Childrens' Services, ... 979, 985, 986
John Morrow Screw & Nut Co. v. Hankin, ... 984
John v. Humphreys, ... 85
John v. R., ... 38, 39
Johnson v. Birkett, ... 273
Johnson v. Lawson, ... 227

Johnson v. Lutz, ... 204, 205, 206
Johnson v. Nova Scotia Trust, ... 909
Johnson, R. v. (1991), ... 602, 603
Johnson, R. v. (1945), ... 974
Johnson, R. v. (1847), ... 238
Johnson and Edwards, R. v., ... 89
Johnston v. Barkley, ... 992
Johnston v. British Columbia (Superintendent of Motor Vehicles), ... 1037
Johnston v. Desaulniers, ... 118
Johnston v. Hazen, ... 190
Johnston v. Occidental Syndicate Ltd., ... 992
Johnston, R. v., ... 759
Johnstone v. Law Society (British Columbia), ... 742, 745
Joly v. R., ... 529
Jones v. Burgess, ... 857, 859, 861, 932
Jones v. Foxall, ... 731
Jones v. James, ... 438
Jones v. Metcalfe, ... 155
Jones v. National Coal Board, ... 825
Jones, R. v. (1988), ... 307, 309
Jones, R. v. (1926), ... 37
Jones v. South Eastern and Chatham Railway Co., ... 307
Jonesco v. Beard, ... 1012
Jordan v. Lewis, ... 384
Jorgensen & News Media (Auckland) Ltd., ... 1040, 1043
Joseph Constantine Steamship Line Ltd. v. Imperial Smelting Corp. Ltd., ... 80, 91
Josiak v. Setler, ... 180
Joy v. Phillips, Mills & Co., ... 515
Jozwiak v. Sadek, ... 243
Junkin v. Davis, ... 943
Jurtyn, R. v., ... 269

K

K.C.F., R. v., ... 150
K.(L.) v. L.(T.W.), ... 902
K.(V.), R. v., ... 894, 897, 898, 923
K & B Ambulance Ltd., R. v., ... 529, 530
Kacherowski, R. v., ... 354
Kadeshevitz, R. v., ... 847
Kaipiainen, R. v., ... 12, 231, 937, 941
Kajala v. Noble, ... 928, 931, 939, 968
Kalashnikoff, R. v., ... 340, 341
Kanester, R. v., ... 683
Kapsales, R. v., ... 472
Kapusta v. Polish Fraternal Aid Society, ... 995

Karpinski, R. v., ... 1017, 1019
Kasteel v. Harris, ... 1006
Kay v. McGay Ltd., ... 611
Kays, R. v., ... 978
Kearns, R. v., ... 853
Keeler, R. v., ... 319
Keizars v. Keizars, ... 732
Kelliher (Village) v. Smith, ... 534
Kelly v. Dow, ... 24
Kelly v. Kelly, ... 670
Kelly, R. v., ... 538, 539, 546
Kemptville Mining Co. v. Village of Kemptville, ... 1013
Ken Ertel Ltd. v. Johnson, ... 909, 918, 919
Ken Ertel Ltd. v. Simonian Estate. See Ken Ertel Ltd. v. Johnson.
Kendall v. Hamilton, ... 1009
Kendall v. Hunt, ... 611
Kendall, R. v. (1987), ... 366, 456
Kendall v. R. (1962), ... 584, 585, 923
Kennealy, R. v., ... 349
Kennedy v. Diversified Mining Interests (Can.) Ltd., ... 665
Kennedy, R. v., ... 349
Kenora (District) Home for the Aged v. Duck Estate, ... 919
Kerenko, R. v., ... 857
Kershaw, R. v., ... 106
Key v. Thomson, ... 46, 521
Keystone Fisheries Ltd., R. v., ... 13
Khan v. R. (1967). See Mawaz Khan v. R.
Khan, R. v. (1990), ... 175, 194, 198, 259, 261, 262, 265, 300-304, 822
Khan, R. v. (U.K.) (1986), ... 599
Khan, R. v. (1982), ... 259, 454
Kibale v. Canada, ... 1011
Kidd v. Henderson, ... 515
Kienapple v. R., ... 1013, 1021, 1028-1035, 1038-1040
Kilbourne, D.P.P. v., ... 455, 492, 493, 893, 915, 922
Kinch v. Walcott, ... 995
Kindylides, R. v., ... 298
King v. King, ... 770
King v. R., ... 382
Kinghorne v. Montreal Telegraph Co., ... 932
Kingsmill v. Kingsmill, ... 255
Kingston, R. v., ... 352
Kingston (City) v. Salvation Army, ... 994
Kinna v. Reilander, ... 996
Kinnon v. Traynor, ... 978
Kirk v. Faugh, ... 991, 1005, 1006
Kirkby, R. v., ... 161
Kirkpatrick v. Lament, ... 20, 917, 921

Kissick v. R., ... 48, 49
Kitchin, Ex parte Young, Re, ... 1009
Kite, The, ... 82
Klein v. Bell. See Bell v. Klein.
Kline, Re, ... 995
Kline, R. v., ... 977
Klippenstein v. R., ... 259
Knapp v. McLeod, ... 238
Knittel, R. v., ... 929
Knowles v. Knowles, ... 112, 113
Knowlton v. Knowlton, ... 220
Knox, R. v., ... 319
Knuff, R. v., ... 457
Knutson v. Sask. Registered Nurses' Assn., ... 750
Ko, R. v., ... 1021
Kobold, R. v., ... 943
Koester, R. v., ... 615
Kok Hoong v. Leong Cheong Kweng Mines Ltd., ... 996
Kokesch, R. v., ... 418, 421
Kolnberger v. R., ... 765
Komarniski v. Komarniski, ... 997, 1005
Kong v. Kong, ... 916, 918
Konkin, R. v., ... 468, 471
Koop v. Smith, ... 904
Kopinsky, R. v., ... 685
Korponay v. Can. (A.G.), ... 353
Kotapski, R. v., ... 670
Koufis, R. v., ... 295, 363, 464, 482
Kowlyk, R. v., ... 100, 101
Kozak, R. v., ... 959, 962
Krack, R. v., ... 597, 598
Krause, R. v., ... 364, 365
Krausz, R. v., ... 468
Kribs v. R., ... 315
Kritz, R. v., ... 149
Krug, R. v., ... 1029, 1030, 1033, 1034, 1035
Kulak, R. v., ... 316
Kulchar v. Marsh, ... 636, 659
Kuldip, R. v., ... 374, 376, 602, 738, 740, 744-747, 749, 751-752
Kurtz & Co. v. Spence & Sons, ... 729
Kuruma, Son of Kaniu v. R., ... 29, 380, 381, 384, 403
K-West Estates Ltd. v. Linemayr, ... 645
Kyling, R. v., ... 899

L

L.E.D., R. v. *See* R. v. D.(L.E.).

L.K. v. T.W.L., *See* K.(L.) v. L.(T.W.).

LAC Minerals Ltd. v. International Corona Resources Ltd. *See* International
Corona Resources Ltd. v. LAC Minerals Ltd.

Lacaille v. Brandl, ... 994

Lachance, R. v., ... 425

Lahay v. Brown, ... 911

Laidlaw Waste Systems Ltd. v. Provincial Sanitation Ltd., ... 1011

Laing v. Richmond. *See* English v. Richmond.

Laird v. Taxicabs Ltd., ... 441

Lake Manitoba Estates Ltd. v. Communities Economic Development
Fund, ... 1002

Lakefield (Village) v. Brown, ... 189

Lal, R. v., ... 959

Laliberté v. R., ... 468

Lamb v. Munster, ... 735, 736

Lamb v. Ward, ... 861

Lambe, R. v., ... 323, 324

Lamberti, Re, ... 1036

Lammens v. Majorcsak. *See* Majorcsak v. Na-Churs Plant Food Co. (Canada) Ltd.

Lamoureux v. Smit, ... 725, 731

Lampert v. Simpson, ... 439

Land v. Kaufman, ... 666

Landreville v. R., ... 781

Landriault, R. v., ... 41

Lanford v. General Medical Council, ... 487

Lang v. Lang, ... 771

Lang, R. v., ... 916

Langille, R. v. (1990), ... 309, 314

Langille, R. v. (1986), ... 745

Language Rights Under Manitoba Act, 1870. *See* Reference re Manitoba
Language Rights.

Langworthy v. McVicar, ... 660, 663

Lapointe, R. v., ... 337, 349

Lapworth, R. v., ... 613

Larson v. Boyd, ... 24, 516, 517, 519

Latham, R. v., ... 1037

Latour v. R., ... 61, 90, 138

Latta v. London Life Insurance Co., ... 1044

Lattoni v. R., ... 1018

Lauder v. Lauder, ... 550

Laughlin v. Harvey, ... 34, 35

Laurie, R. v., ... 978

Laurier, R. v., ... 463

Laurin (No. 4), R. v., ... 269

Laurin, R. v., ... 855
Lavallée, R. v., ... 140, 535, 552-556
Laverty, R. v., ... 188, 197
Law v. Hansen, ... 992, 993, 1006
Lawrence v. Lawrence, ... 118
Lawrence, R. v., ... 184
Lawryshyn v. Aquacraft Products Ltd., ... 638
Laxer, Re, ... 119
Laxton Holdings Ltd. v. Madill, ... 611
Laxton Holdings Ltd. v. Non-Marine Underwriters. See Laxton Holdings Ltd. v.
    Madill.
Laybourn v. R. See Bulmer, R. v.
Layden v. North American Life Assurance Co., ... 683
Leach v. Egar, ... 117
Leach, R. v. (1966), ... 590
Leach v. R. (1912), ... 612
Leadbetter v. Western Shoe Co., ... 572
Leary, R. v., ... 62
Leatham, R. v., ... 379
LeBar v.Canada, ... 1011
LeBlanc v. R., ... 483
LeBrun, R. v. (1954), ... 975
Lebrun, R. v. (1951), ... 315
LeClair, R. v. See Ross, R. v.
Ledingham v. Skinner, ... 921
Lee, R. v., ... 358
Leeds v. Alberta (Minister of the Environment), ... 775, 790
Lee's Poultry Ltd., R. v., ... 87
Leeson v. Darlow, ... 572
Lefebure v. Major, ... 253
Lefebvre v. Worden, ... 188
Lejorte, R. v. 479, 517
Legge, R. v., ... 834
Leggo, R. v., ... 975
Leggott v. Great Northern Rly. Co., ... 1006
Legislative Privilege, Reference re, ... 625, 631
Lego v. Twomey, ... 359, 360
Legrand v. R., ... 978
Leicester (Earl) v. Walter, ... 437
Leier v. Shumiatcher, ... 994
Leland, R. v., ... 41, 258, 261
Lemay v. R., ... 821
Lenoard v. B.C. Hydro & Power Authority, ... 164, 550
Leonard, R. v., ... 591
Lesson v. Darlow, ... 572
Lester, R. v., ... 13
Letnik v. Metropolitan Toronto (Municipality). See Letnik v. Toronto (City).

Letnik v. Toronto (City), ... 93
Leutner v. Garbuz, ... 998, 1006
Lev v. Lev, ... 667, 731
Leveillé, R. v., ... 412
Levesque v. Albert, ... 971
Levin v. Boyce, ... 656
Levy v. Pope, ... 639
Levy, R. v., ... 364, 883
Lew Fun Chaue, Re, ... 783, 785, 797
Lewes JJ., R. v., ... 785, 796, 797
Lewis, R. v., ... 857
L'Hirondelle v. L'Hirondelle, ... 994
Li Kam Kwai (No. 6), R. v., ... 449
Libman v. R., ... 1023
Lichtenberg v. Lichtenberg, ... 771
Lick v. Rivers, ... 977
Lilley v. Pettit, ... 941
Lilwall v. Stockford, ... 933
Lind v. Sweden (Kingdom), ... 590
Lindala v. Canadian Copper Co., ... 539
Lindsay v. Imperial Steel & Wire Co., ... 825
Lines, R. v., ... 775
Linklater, R. v., ... 1037
Linney, R. v., ... 467
Linton v. Wilson, ... 938
Lischka v. Ontario (Criminal Injuries Compensation Board), ... 305
Litke, R. v., ... 978
Little v. Hyslop, ... 909
Littlechild, R. v., ... 631
Livingston v. Gartshore, ... 659
Livingstone v. Livingstone, ... 769, 771
Lizotte v. R., ... 41
Lloyd v. Milton, ... 994
Lloyd v. Mostyn, ... 385
Lloyd v. Powell Duffryn Steam Coal Co. *See* Ward v. H.S. Pitt & Co.
Lloyd, R. v. (1981), ... 677, 686
Lloyd, R. v. (1843), ... 342
Lloyds Bank (sic) Canada v. Canada Life Assurance Co., ... 667, 668
Lobell, R. v., ... 61, 91, 138, 139
Lock v. Lock, ... 771
Lockett v. Solloway, Mills & Co., ... 735
Lockyer v. Ferryman, ... 989
Logan v. Lee, ... 984
Logan, R. v. (1988), ... 327, 365, 366, 676
Logan, R. v. (1981), ... 1020
Logan, R. v. (1947), ... 105
Logiacco, R. v., ... 453, 464

Lomage, R. v., ... 50, 51
Lomas v. DiCecca, ... 531
London (City) v. Grand Trunk Railway, ... 285
London Guarantee & Accident Co. v. Davidson, ... 19-38
London Life Ins. Co. v. Lang Shirt Co. Ltd. (Trustee of), ... 99, 144
Long, R. v., ... 446, 455, 460
Longpré, ex parte. *See* R. v. Quebec (Municipal Commission).
Longaphie, R. v., ... 677
Lonsdale, R. v., ... 613
Lord Audley's Case (The), ... 613
Losier v. Clement, ... 862
Lovis, R. v., ... 958
Low v. Bouverie, ... 989
Lowery v. R., ... 456, 467
Loyer, R. v., ... 1032
Lucas v. Fulford. *See* Denn d. Lucas v. Fulford.
Lucas v. R., ... 319, 459, 460
Lucier, R. v., ... 158, 184, 185
Luffe, R. v., ... 978
Lum, R. v., ... 984
Lumonics Research Ltd. v. Gould, ... 649
Lundy v. Patrick Construction Co., ... 994
Lupien, R. v., ... 450, 451, 541, 549, 550, 886
Luther v. Ryan, ... 909
Lutz, R. v., ... 939, 940
Lyell v. Kennedy, ... 189
Lyles v. United States, ... 208
Lynch v. Attwood, ... 89
Lyone v. Long, ... 861

M

M., R. v. *See* M.(D.), R. v.
M. Brennan & Sons Mfg., Co. v. Thompson, ... 1009
M.(D.), R. v., ... 1036
M.(P.), R. v., ... 150
MacAulay, R. v., ... 979
MacDonald v. Bublitz, ... 680
MacDonald v. Canada Kelp Co., ... 514, 516, 517
MacDonald v. Montreal (City), ... 832
MacDonald, R. v. (1974), ... 456
MacDonald, R. v. (1963), ... 43
MacDonald, R. v. (1952), ... 1019
MacDonald, R. v. (1939), ... 48, 455
MacDonald v. Royal Bank of Canada, ... 933
MacDonald v. Young, ... 117, 118, 911

Macdougall v. Macdougall, ... 24
MacGillivray, Re, ... 251
MacGregor v. Ryan, ... 64, 146, 147
MacIntyre v. Nova Scotia (Attorney General), ... 814
Mack, R. v., ... 94, 95, 388, 440, 1018
MacKay v. Saskatoon (City), ... 285
MacKeigan v. Hickman, ... 619, 620
Mackell v. Ottawa Separate School Trustees, ... 743
MacKenzie, R. v., ... 974
MacKinlay, R. v., ... 895
MacLean, R. v., ... 761
Macleod v. Campbell, ... 991
MacLeod, R. v., ... 760
MacLure, R. v., ... 977
MacMillan Bloedel Ltd. v. West Vancouver Assessment Area Assessors, ... 626, 633
MacPhee, R. v., ... 826
Maddess, Re. See Coroners Act, Re.
Maden v. Catanach, ... 590
Madge v. Thunder Bay (City), ... 642
Madill v. McConnell, ... 954
Magdish, R. v., ... 375, 752
Magel v. Krempler, ... 825
Magnus v. National Bank of Scotland, ... 995
Mahen v. Arkelian, ... 131
Mahoney, R. v., ... 215
Mailloux, R. v., ... 690
Majcenic v. Natale, ... 824
Majorcsak v. Na-Churs Plant Food Co. (Canada) Ltd., ... 133
Makin v. A.G. for New South Wales, ... 480, 485-493, 501
Malcomson v. O'Dea, ... 228
Male, R. v., ... 347
Malik v. Principal Savings & Trust Co., ... 998
Mallios, R. v., ... 977
Maloney v. Winnipeg Free Press Co., ... 703
Maloney (No. 2), R. v., ... 16, 17, 967, 968
Mamarbachi v. Cockshutt Plow Co., ... 11
Manahan, R. v., ... 544
Manchester Brewery Co. v. Coombs, ... 169
Manchev, R. v., ... 763, 764
Mancini v. D.P.P., ... 61, 68, 91
Manderville, R. v., ... 41
Manella v. Manella, ... 993
Mann v. American Automobile Insurance Co., ... 658
Mann v. Balaban, ... 59, 83, 90, 138, 831
Mann v. Mann, ... 997, 1012
Mann, R. v., ... 616
Manninen, R. v., ... 370, 372, 389, 393, 409, 413, 415, 419, 424, 677

Mannion, R. v., ... 365, 374, 376, 747, 748, 750, 847
Manolopoulos v. Paniffe, ... 992
Manos v. R., ... 911
Mapp v. Ohio, ... 384
Maracle v. Travellers Indemnity Co. of Canada, ... 722, 723
Marchand v. Marchand, ... 978
Marchand, R. v., ... 612, 616
Marcil, R. v., ... 50
Marcoux v. R., ... 19, 403, 404, 768
Marcy v. Pierce (No. 2), ... 938
Marek v. Cieslak, ... 776
Marginson v. Blackburn Borough Council, ... 1006
Maritime Electric Co. v. General Dairies Ltd., ... 989
Markadonis, R. v., ... 882
Markin, R. v., ... 984
Markovina, Re, ... 676
Marks v. Beyfus, ... 805, 809
Marks v. Marks, ... 99
Marlborough Hotel Co. v. Parkmaster (Canada) Ltd., ... 655, 665
Marsh v. McKay, ... 702
Marshall, R. v. (1972), ... 842, 855
Marshall v. R. (1961), ... 342
Martel v. Hotel-Dieu St. Vallier, ... 100
Martel, R. v., ... 50
Martin, Re. See MacGregor v. Ryan.
Martin v. Bourque, ... 118
Martin v. Canadian Pacific Railway, ... 133, 134
Martin v. Martin, ... 771
Martin, R. v., ... 357
Marvin v. Hales, ... 935
Mass v. Sheppard, ... 384
Massey v. Allen, ... 179, 189
Massey-Harris Co. v. DeLaval Separator Co., ... 702
Massey-Harris Co. v. Merrithew, ... 514
Matthes, R. v., ... 119
Matheson v. Barnes, ... 203
Matto v. D.P.P., ... 404
Mattouk v. Massad, ... 905
Maves v. Grand Trunk Pacific Ry. Co., ... 833, 834, 835, 836, 859
Maw v. Dickey, ... 189
Mawaz Khan v. R., ... 161, 165, 363
Mawson v. Hartsink, ... 475, 887
May v. Logie, ... 225
Mayflower Bottling Co., R. v., ... 752
Maynard v. Maynard, ... 993, 996, 998, 999
Maynard, R. v., ... 974
Maynes v. Dolan, ... 951

Mayzel v. Storm, ... 995
Mazerall (No. 1), R. v., ... 357
Mazur, R. v., ... 601
McArthur, R. v., ... 395
McBay v. Merritt, ... 687
McCabe Estates, Re. *See* Bentley v. Canadian Bank of Commerce.
McCaig v. Trentowsky, ... 656
McCarroll v. Powell, ... 132
McCarthy v. Morrison-Lamothe Bakery Ltd., ... 770
McClenaghan v. Perkins, ... 921
McClure v. Backstein, ... 744, 752
McClure v. O'Neil. *See* Royal Trust Co. v. McClure.
McColl-Frontenac Oil Co. v. Hamilton, ... 106
McConachy v. Times Publishers Ltd., ... 703, 704
McConnell, R. v., ... 762, 763
McCorriston v. Hayward, ... 1000
McCowan v. Menasco Manufacturing Co., ... 994
McCoy v. O'Donnell, ... 977
McCready v. Grundy, ... 439
McDermott, R. v., ... 327
McDonald v. Murray, ... 973
McDonald, R. v. *See* Re Wilson.
McDougal v. Occidental Syndicate Ltd. *See* Johnston v. Occidental Syndicate Ltd.
McDougall v. Dominion Iron & Steel Co., ... 785, 797
McEwan v. Toronto General Trusts Corp., ... 919
McFadden, R. v., ... 446, 449, 458, 460, 462
McGavin Bakeries Ltd., R. v., ... 961
McGhee v. National Coal Board, ... 93
McGillivray v. Shaw, ... 189, 190
McGinty, R. v., ... 613, 614, 617
McGreevy v. D.P.P., ... 149
McGregor v. Curry, ... 920, 921
McGregor v. Keiller, ... 189
McGregor v. McGregor, ... 1046
McGuigan v. R., ... 1029, 1034
McGuire v. Haugh, ... 1012
McHugh v. Reynolds Extrusion Co., ... 82
McInnis v. University Students' Council of University of Western Ontario, . 702, 705
McInroy v. R., ... 365, 843, 844, 845, 847
McIntosh v. Parent, ... 997, 1002
McIntyre v. Canadian Pacific Ltd., ... 657
McIntyre, R. v., ... 842
McIver, R. v., ... 41, 85
McIvor v. McIvor, ... 772
McKane, R. v., ... 404
McKay v. Chisolm, ... 994
McKay, R. v. (1987), ... 905

McKay, R. v. (1954), ... 43
McKean v. Jones, ... 994
McKenna v. R., ... 337
McKenzie v. Bergin, ... 131, 132, 133
McKenzie, R. v., ... 249
McKergow v. Comstock, ... 435
McKevitt, R. v., ... 578
McKinney, R. v., ... 1013, 1029
McKinnon, R. v., ... 170, 171, 172, 616
McLarty (No. 3), R. v., ... 212, 213
McLaughlin, R. v., ... 601, 863
McLean v. McDonell, ... 937
McLean v. Merchants Bank of Canada, ... 853
McLean, R. v., ... 464
McLeod v. MacLeod, ... 904, 916
McLeod v. Pearson, ... 48, 730
McLeod, R. v., ... 344
McLeod v. Toronto General Trusts Corp., ... 116
McMillan, R. v. (1975), ... 433, 443, 450, 451, 452, 467, 468, 533, 535
McMillan v. Walker, ... 835
McMullen, R. v., ... 214, 928, 931, 937
McNamara, R. v., ... 614
McNamara (No. 1), R. v., ... 295, 447-448, 449, 458, 460, 906, 907, 908, 911
M'Naghten's Case, ... 59, 151
McNeil, Re, ... 113, 114, 115
McPherson v. Institute of Chartered Accountants (British Columbia), ... 675
McPherson, R. v. (1980), ... 614
McPherson, R. v. (1957), ... 139
McPherson, Trusts & Guar. Co. v. Bradford, ... 20
McQuaker v. Goddard, ... 979, 981
McTaggart v. McTaggart, ... 733
McVaught v. McKenzie (Re Claresholm Provincial Election), ... 107
Mead, R. v., ... 269
Meaney v. Busby, ... 660
Meddoni, R. v., ... 308
Medicine Hat Greenhouses Ltd. and R. (No. 3), Re. *See* German v. R.
Medina v. Erickson, ... 208
Medina, R. v., ... 699
Medjedovitch v. R., ... 50
Medvedew, R. v., ... 528, 567, 568
Meek v. Fleming, ... 838
Melcor Developments Ltd. v. Edmonton (City), ... 999
Mellor v. Walmesley, ... 189
Melton v. St. Louis Public Service Co., ... 210
Meltzer v. Meltzer, ... 118
Melville's (Viscount) Case, ... 736
Mercer v. Denne, ... 189, 190, 231, 969

Merchants Bank v. Monteith. *See* Re Monteith.

Mercier, Re, ... 786

Mercure, R. v., ... 832

Merricks v. Knott-Bower, ... 786

Mersey Paper Co. v. Queens (County), ... 882, 883

Meshwa v. Meshwa, ... 1046

Metcalfe, R. v., ... 743

Mete, R. v., ... 877, 878

Metropolitan Asylum District v. Hill, ... 25

Metropolitan Railway Co. v. Jackson, ... 130, 131

Meuckon, R. v., ... 789, 790, 805

Meunier v. Canadian Northern Ry. Co., ... 972

Mexborough (Earl) v. Whitwood Urban District Council, ... 736

Meyer v. Cronkhite, ... 978

Meyer v. Hall, ... 277

Meyers v. Man., ... 18

Mezzo, R. v., ... 72, 130, 135, 149, 529

Michael, R. v., ... 881, 882

Michelson v. U.S., ... 444, 445, 446

Mickey, R. v., ... 41

Mickle v. R., ... 790, 804, 808, 809

Middlemiss v. Middlemiss, ... 114

Middleton v. Bryce, ... 911

Miles v. Miles, ... 783, 785

Milgaard, R. v., ... 843, 845

Milina, R. v., ... 974

Millar, Re, ... 112

Millar v. B.C. Rapid Transit Co., ... 862

Miller, Re (1978), ... 115

Miller, Re (1949), ... 919

Miller v. Miller Estate, ... 905, 916

Miller v. Minister of Pensions, ... 142

Miller, R. v. (1976), ... 295

Miller, R. v. (1959), ... 524

Miller, R. v. (1952), ... 456

Miller v. Shaffran, ... 983

Miller (S.S.) Co. Property Ltd. v. Overseas Tankship (U.K.) Ltd., ... 533

Millett v. Millett, ... 997

Milliken v. British Columbia (A.G.). *See* Thomas v. British Columbia (A.G.).

Mills v. Mercer Co., ... 736

Mills v. Mills (1971), ... 995

Mills v. Mills (1943), ... 113, 114

Mills v. Mills, (1920), ... 188

Mills v. R. (1986), ... 390, 392

Mills, R. v. (1962), ... 854

Milne v. Leisler, ... 266

Milner, Re. *See* Income Tax Act, Re.

Minaker v. Minaker, ... 768, 770
Minister of National Revenue v. Die-Plast Co., ... 783
Minister of National Revenue v. Huron Steel Fabricators (London) Ltd. *See*
    Huron Steel Fabricators (London) Ltd. v. M.N.R.; Fratschko v. M.N.R.
Minors, R. v., ... 933
Minter v. Priest, ... 637, 641
Mirandi v. State, ... 205
Mire v. Northwestern Mutual Ins. Co. (No. 2), ... 998, 1005
Missiaen v. Minister of National Revenue, ... 643, 645
Mitchell v. Hanan, ... 156
Mitchell v. Reiss, ... 989
Mitchell's Claim. *See* River Steamer Co., Re.
Modern Air Spray Ltd. v. Homme, ... 1009
Modern Construction Co. v. Maritime Rock Products Ltd., ... 134
Modeste, R. v., ... 975
Modriski v. Arnold, ... 283
Mohl, R. v., ... 408, 409
Mole v. Mole, ... 733
Monarch Lumber Co. v. Garrison, ... 967
Monarch S.S. Co. Ltd. v. Karlshamns of Oljefabriker, ... 980
Moncini, R. v. *See* R. v. Lovis.
Monckton v. Tarr, ... 120
Monette v. R., ... 364, 365
Monfils, R. v., ... 857
Monkhouse, R. v., ... 208
Monkton v. A.G., ... 228
Monroe v. Toronto Railway, ... 271
Monteith, Re; Merchants Bank v. Monteith, ... 3
Monteleone, R. v., ... 135, 136
Montgomery v. Graham, ... 955, 956
Mood Music Publishing Co. v. De Wolfe Ltd., ... 513, 522
Moore, ex parte. *See* Deputy Industrial Injuries Commissioner, R. v.
Moore, Re, ... 253
Moore v. Lambeth Co. Ct. Registrar, ... 826
Moore v. Moore, ... 220
Moore v. Ransome's Dock Committee, ... 513, 520
Moore, R. v. (1990), ... 304
Moore, R. v. (1988), ... 1016, 1019, 1020
Moore, R. v. (1984), ... 247, 295
Moore, R. v. (1980), ... 870
Moore, R. v. (1956), ... 847
Moore, R. v. (1852), ... 350
Moore v. Whyte (No. 2), ... 687, 688
Moorov v. H.M. Advocate, ... 492
Moosomin School Board and Gordon, Re. *See* Moosomin (School Board)
    v. Gordon.
Moosomin (School Board) v. Gordon, ... 787

Morabito, R. v., ... 130, 135
Moran, R. v., ... 619
Moran v. Richards, ... 910, 911
Moreau, R. v., ... 64
Morgan, D.P.P. v., ... 74
Morgan, R. v., ... 50
Morgan Power Apparatus Ltd. v. Flanders Installations Ltd., ... 1000
Morgentaler, R. v., ... 1038
Moriarty v. London, Chatham & Dover Railway Co., ... 288
Morin, R. v., ... 28, 148, 149, 150, 336, 503, 504, 916
Morris v. New Brunswick (A.G.), ... 922
Morris, R. v. (1983), ... 21, 22, 25, 26, 401, 455, 465, 478, 482, 499-501, 511, 957
Morris v. R. (1979), ... 447, 449, 462, 463, 464
Morris Provincial Election, Re, ... 119
Morris-Jones and R., Re, ... 606
Morrison v. Leyenhorst, ... 133
Morrison Rose & Partners v. Hillman, ... 990, 1012
Morrison-Knudsen Co. v. B.C. Hydro & Power Authority (1973), ... 292, 293
Morrison-Knudsen Co. v. British Columbia Hydro & Power Authority (1972), ... 853
Morrison Knudsen Co. v. British Columbia Hydro & Power Authority (1971), ... 649
Morrow, R. v., ... 631, 660
Mortimer, R. v., ... 479
Mortlock v. Mortlock, ... 732
Moseley v. Davies, ... 217, 220
Mosley, R. v., ... 268
Moss v. Moss, ... 612
Mott v. Trott, ... 909
Moulton, R. v., ... 468
Moysa v. Alberta (Labour Relations Board), ... 632, 710, 712
Mraz v. R. (No. 2), ... 1025
M-T v. M-T, ... 982
Mudie, R. v., ... 215
Mueller Canada Inc. v. State Contractors Inc., ... 727
Mulholland v. Toigo, ... 994
Mulroney v. Coates, ... 622
Murphy, R. v. (1976), ... 913
Murphy, R. v. (1965), ... 382
Murray, Re, ... 905, 918, 923
Murray v. Haylow, ... 860
Murray v. Murray, ... 783
Murray v. Plummer, ... 11
Murray, R. v., ... 358
Muskol v. Benjamin, ... 922
Musqueam Indian Band v. Canada (Min. of Indian and Northern Affairs). *See*
    Grant v. Canada (Min. of Indian and Northern Affairs).
Mustafa, R. v., ... 479
Mutual Life Assur. Co. v. Jeannotte. *See* Mutual Life Assur. Co. v. Lamarche.

Mutual Life Assurance Co. of Canada v. Canada (Deputy Attorney General) 648
Mutual Life Insurance Co. v. Hillmon, ... 246, 247, 248, 249, 250
Mutual Life Assur. Co. v. Lamarche, ... 856
Mutual Life Assurance Co. of New York v. Jonaly, ... 519
Myers v. Director of Public Prosecutions, ... 174, 175, 190, 192, 193, 194, 251, 252
Myers v. Myers, ... 692
Myles v. Elliott, ... 910

N

N.(L.), R. v., ... 308, 317
N.B. Electric Power Commn. v. Barderie, ... 860
N.M. Paterson & Sons Ltd., R. v., ... 630, 753
Nadler v. Chornij, ... 133
Nadeau, R. v., ... 150
Nagel v. Canadian Northern Railway, ... 291
Naglik, R. v., ... 761, 763
Nagotcha v. R., ... 337, 338
Naidanovici, R. v., ... 852
National Fire Insurance Co. v. Rogers, ... 156, 188, 190
National Trust Co. v. Wong Aviation Ltd., ... 74, 75, 76, 91, 93
Naujokat v. Bratushesky, ... 637, 642, 649
Neal v. T. Eaton Co. Ltd., ... 133, 134
Neary v. Fowler, ... 158, 179, 882
Neill v. Duke of Devonshire, ... 218
Nelson v. Murphy, ... 824
Nesbitt Thomson Deacon Inc. v. Everett, ... 1005, 1011
New Hamburg Mfg. Co. v. Webb, ... 876
New West Construction Co. v. R., ... 656
New York Life Insurance Co. v. Taylor, ... 208
New York State v. Phillips' Heirs, ... 144
New York Times Co. v. United States, ... 775
Newall, R. v., ... 872
Newcombe v. Evans, ... 954
Newell v. Barker, ... 933, 936
Newfoundland (A.G.) v. Trahey, ... 806
Newman v. Nemes, ... 667
New's Trustee v. Hunting, ... 293
Nicholls v. Dowding and Kemp, ... 834
Nicholls v. Parker, ... 218
Nichols and Shephard Co. v. Skedanuk, ... 954, 966
Nicholson v. Page, ... 969
Nielsen, R. v., ... 567
Niewiadomski v. Langdon, ... 11
Nigro v. Agnew-Surpass Shoe Stores Ltd., ... 1011
Nimmo v. Alexander Cowan & Sons Ltd., ... 84, 87, 89

Noailles, Re, ... 1037
Noble, R. v., ... 64, 429
Noel, R. v., ... 880
Noor Mohamed v. R., ... 29
Noranda Metal Industries Ltd., Fergus Division v. I.B.E.W., Local 2345, ... 305
North West Water Authority v. Binnie & Partners, ... 1010
Northern Electric Co., R. v., ... 232-233, 942
Northern Regional Health Authority v. Derek Crouch Construction Co., ... 991
Northern Wood Preservers Ltd. v. Hall Corp. (Shipping) 1969 Ltd., ... 211, 212
Norwich Pharmacal Co. v. Customs and Excise Commissioners, ... 797
Nova, an Alberta Corp. v. Guelph Engineering Co., ... 656
Nova Scotia (A.G.) v. Royal Commission (Marshall Inquiry), ... 796
Novalinga, R. v., ... 274
Nowak v. Sanyshyn, ... 667
Nowsco Well Service Ltd. v. Canadian Propane Gas & Oil Ltd., ... 93
Nozaki, R. v., ... 742
Nuttall v. Nuttall, ... 714
Nutting v. Nutting, ... 611

O

Oakes, R. v., ... 56, 91, 97, 98, 99, 111, 122-126, 141, 142, 145
Oakes v. Uzzell, ... 954
Oakley, R. v., ... 50
O'Brien, R. v., ... 161, 177-181, 185, 186
Occidental Petroleum Corp. v. Buttes Gas and Oil Co. (No. 2). See Buttes Gas and
    Oil Co. v. Hammer (No. 3).
Ocean Falls Corp. v. Worthington (Can.) Inc., ... 653
O'Connor v. Dunn, ... 189, 190, 219, 969
O'Connor v. R., ... 380
O'Hara v. Dougherty, ... 929, 937, 1011
Oickle, R. v., ... 276
O'Kelly v. Downie, ... 973
Olarte v. Commodore Business Machines Ltd., ... 305
Oley v. Fredericton (City), ... 1004
Oliphant v. Alexander, ... 835
Oliver v. R. (1981), ... 66
Oliver, R. v. (1943), ... 86
Omand v. Alberta Milling Co., ... 193
Omnia Pelts v. C.P. Airlines Ltd., ... 863
Omnium Securities Co. v. Richardson, ... 730
Omychund v. Barker, ... 586, 930
O'Neil v. Royal Trust Co. See Royal Trust Co. v. McClure.
O'Nory v. Patricia Properties, ... 992
Ontario (Attorney General) v. Bear Island Foundation, ... 217, 222, 932, 940
Ontario (A.G.) v. Brunsden. See Stavely, Re.

Ontario (A.G.) v. Clark. *See* Tilco Plastics Ltd. v. Skurjat.
Ontario (A.G.) v. Gowling & Henderson, ... 627
Ontario Equitable Life and Accident Insurance Co. v. Baker, ... 69, 70, 78, 79, 80
Ontario Gravel Freighting Co. v. Mathews S.S. Co., ... 871
Ontario Salt Co. v. Merchants' Salt Co., ... 967
Ontario (Securities Commission) v. Greymac Credit Corp., ... 641, 642
Ontario Sugar Co., Re, ... 989, 995, 996
Ookpik, R. v., ... 900, 913
Oquataq, R. v., ... 471
O'Quinn, R. v., ... 536
Ord v. Ord, ... 998
Orlias, R. v., ... 979
O'Rourke v. Darbishire, ... 644, 645
Orser v. Vernon, ... 956
Ortt, R. v., ... 103
Osborne, R. v., ... 316
O'Shea v. Wood, ... 637
Ostrom v. Henders, ... 680
Ostrower v. Genereux, ... 688
Ostrowski, R. v., ... 985
Otis, R. v., ... 356, 357
Otney v. United States, ... 202
Ott, Re, ... 662
Ottawa-Carleton (Regional Municipality) v. Consumers' Gas Co., ... 653, 654, 658
Owens, R. v. (1986), ... 317
Owens, R. v. (1969), ... 1025
Owner v. Bee Hive Spinning Co., ... 934

P

P.(D.W.), R. v., ... 1032, 1033
P.M., R. v. *See* R. v. M.(P.).
P.(R.), R. v., ... 245, 247-248, 249, 250
Pacific Press Ltd. v. R., ... 708
Paddock v. Forrester, ... 720, 723
Page v. Faucet, ... 981
Page, R. v., ... 308, 313, 316, 317, 320
Pah-Mah-Guy, R. v., ... 587
Paige v. R., ... 915, 922, 924
Pais v. Pais, ... 734
Palmby v. McCleary, ... 280
Palmer v. Hoffman, ... 200, 202
Palmer v. R., ... 878
Palter Cap Co. v. Great West Life Assurance Co., ... 182, 187, 188
Pamplin v. Express Newspapers Ltd. (No. 2), ... 435
Pangilinan, R. v., ... 311

Pappajohn, R. v., ... 60, 63, 140
Pappin, R. v., ... 310
Paquette v. Chubb, ... 905, 910, 911, 913, 917
Paquette, R. v., ... 832
Paradis v. R., ... 28
Parish, R. v., ... 914
Park v. R., ... 353, 354, 356-357
Parker, R. v. (1985), ... 666
Parker, R. v. (1984), ... 937
Parkin, R. v., ... 882
Parklane Hosiery Co. v. Shore, ... 1010, 1012
Parlee, R. v., ... 1037
Parmas, R. v., ... 814, 815-818
Parna v. G. & S. Properties Ltd., ... 998
Parrot, R. v., ... 295, 962
Parry v. Parry, ... 598
Parry-Jones v. Law Society, ... 626
Parsons, R. v., ... 18
Patel v. Comptroller of Customs, ... 963
Paterson v. Todd, ... 937
Patrick, R. v. (1982), ... 765
Patrick, R. v. (1960), ... 326
Patterson v. Christie, ... 11
Patterson v. Scherloski, ... 972
Paul v. Fadden, ... 18
Paul, R. v., ... 135
Pavel, R. v., ... 405
Pavey v. Furrie, ... 805
Pawliw, R. v., ... 13
Pax Management Ltd. v. A.R. Ristan Trucking Ltd., ... 638
Pax Management Ltd. v. C.I.B.C. *See* Pax Management Ltd. v. A.R. Ristan
   Trucking Ltd.
Payne v. Newberry (No. 2), ... 994
Payne, R. v. (1963), ... 29, 382, 404
Payne, R. v. (1872), ... 601
Peacock v. Cooper, ... 25
Pearce v. Foster, ... 658
Pearlman v. National Life Assurance Co. of Canada, ... 730
Pearson v. A.G. *See* Pearson, Re.
Pearson, R. v., ... 358
Pederson, R. v. (1974), ... 938
Pedersen, R. v. (1956), ... 326
Peel Condominium Corp. No. 199 v. Ontario New Home Warranties Plan, ... 723
Pelletier, R. v. (1986), ... 327, 365, 366
Pelletier, R. v. (1978), ... 181, 183, 184
Pelrine v. Arron, ... 931, 995
Pender v. War Eagle, ... 119

Penn-Texas Corp. v. Murat Anstaldt, ... 1005
Penno, R. v. (1990), ... 978
Penno, R. v. (1977), ... 215
People v. Barker, ... 649
People v. Brown, ... 183
People v. Koklmeyer, ... 208
People v. Spriggs, ... 183
Pepin v. Plamondon, ... 46
Percival v. Nanson, ... 179
Perka v. R., ... 88, 89, 152
Perkins v. Jeffery, ... 23
Perron, R. v., ... 657, 665
Perry v. P.E.I., ... 1037
Perry, R. v. (1977), ... 883
Perry, R. v. (1945), ... 24
Perton, Re; Pearson v. A.G., ... 180
Peters v. Perras, ... 876, 877
Petersen, R. v. (1983), ... 967
Petersen v. R. (1982), ... 1016, 1017, 1020, 1022
Petijevich v. Law, ... 514
Petrie, R. v., ... 48, 598
Petro Can Oil & Gas Corp. Ltd. v. Resource Service Group Ltd., ... 668
Pettit v. Lilley. See Lilley v. Pettit.
Pettitt v. Pettitt, ... 118, 119
Pfeil v. Zinc, ... 387, 675
Phelps v. Prew, ... 385
Phene's Trusts, Re, ... 113, 116
Phillion, R. v., ... 362, 452, 453, 568
Phillips v. Ford Motor Co. of Canada Ltd., ... 81, 573, 825
Phillips v. Rodgers, ... 723, 725
Phosphate Sewage Co. v. Molleson, ... 1001
Piche, R. v., ... 324, 325, 362
Pickett, R. v., ... 358, 359, 360
Pickford v. Daley, ... 989
Piddington v. Bennett and Wood Pty. Ltd., ... 889
Piddington, R. v., ... 41
Pieper v. Zinkann, ... 912
Piercey, R. v., ... 46
Pim v. Curell, ... 218
Ping, R. v., ... 587
Ping Lin, D.P.P. v., ... 329, 334, 338, 339, 359
Pinno, R. v., ... 978, 988
Pinske, R. v., ... 404
Pipe v. Fulcher, ... 218
Pipeline News, R. v., ... 557
Pirie v. Wyld, ... 719, 724, 725
Pitre v. R., ... 530, 531, 965

Pitt, R. v., ... 856
Plainsman Dev. Ltd. v. Builders Contract Mgmt. Ltd., ... 972
Plank, R. v., ... 1015
Plant v. Taylor, ... 225
Plato Films Ltd. v. Speidel, ... 433, 434, 435, 436, 437
Platt v. Buck, ... 639
Playford, R. v., ... 370, 372, 677
Pleet v. Canadian Northern Quebec Railway Co., ... 84
Pleich, R. v., ... 17, 940
Plimpton v. Spiller, ... 533
Plumb v. Royal Trust Co., ... 923
Plumb v. Snow. *See* Plumb v. Royal Trust Co.
Podovinikoff v. Montgomery, ... 723, 724, 731
Pohoretsky, R. v., ... 404, 415, 416, 417, 422, 429, 430
Poirier v. R., ... 905
Poitras v. R., ... 811
Polar Star (The) v. Louis Denker Inc., ... 130, 132, 133, 135
Polini v. Gray. *See* Sturla v. Freccia.
Ponomoroff v. Ponomoroff, ... 829, 830
Poole v. Dicas, ... 188
Poole v. Smith's Car Sales (Balham) Ltd., ... 978
Poole & Thompson Ltd. v. McNally, ... 105, 106
Pople v. Evans, ... 995
Poricanin v. Australian Consolidated Industries, ... 78
Porteous v. Dom. *See* Rosenmeyer, Re.
Porter v. Hale, ... 936
Porter v. Porter, ... 732
Porter, R. v. (1989), ... 1037
Porter, R. v. (1964), ... 233
Porter, R. v. (1961), ... 976
Potapchuk, R. v., ... 984
Potash Corp. of Saskatchewan Mining Ltd. v. Todd. *See* Potash Corp. of
   Saskatchewan Mining, Lanigan Division v. Todd.
Potash Corp. of Saskatchewan Mining, Lanigan Division v. Todd, ... 611
Potts, R. v., ... 976, 977, 985, 988
Potvin, R. v., ... 31, 155, 159, 172, 275-276, 822, 823, 898-899, 913
Powell v. Cockburn, ... 112, 113, 120, 995, 997
Powell v. Guttman, ... 93
Powell v. Powell, ... 255
Power v. MacFarlane, ... 972
Prager v. Prager & Goodison, ... 952
Prager, R. v., ... 342
Prairie Schooner News Ltd., R. v., ... 557
Praisoody v. R., ... 602-603
Pratte v. Maher, ... 760
Pratte, R. v., ... 615, 616
Precourt, R. v., ... 347-348

Preeper v. R., ... 525, 537
Prentice, R. v., ... 638
Prescott v. Jarvis, ... 578
Presswood v. International Chemalloy Corp., ... 646, 651
Preston-Jones v. Preston-Jones, ... 143, 978, 981, 982, 985, 987
Price, Re; Spence v. Price, ... 532
Price v. Manning, ... 837
Price v. Richmond Review (The), ... 703, 704
Price Bros. & Co., R. v., ... 969
Priestley, R. v., ... 342-343, 345
Prince, R. v., ... 1029-1031, 1032, 1035, 1039
Prince v. Samo, ... 879
Procter & Gamble Co. v. Calgon Interamerican Corp., ... 648
Production Equipment Ltd. v. Clayton v. Lambert Manufacturing Co., ... 989
Prosko, R. v., ... 330
Protopappas v. B.C. Electric Railway, ... 132
Proudlock, R. v., ... 64, 71-72, 77, 108, 110-111, 112
Proud, R. v., ... 221
Proulx v. Fraser, ... 994
Prousky v. Law Society (Upper Canada), ... 743
Provo, R. v. See P.(D.W.), R. v.
Prudential Assurance Co. v. Edmonds, ... 115
Pryslak v. Anderson, ... 634
Ptycia v. Swetlishnoff, ... 514
Puczka, Re; Voitko v. Sabados, ... 231
Purdy, R. v., ... 938

Q

Q. v. Minto Management Ltd., ... 1043
Qualifications for Mayor and Aldermen of Calgary of Persons in Receipt of
   Relief, ... 979
Qatar Petroleum Producing Authority v. Shell Internationale Petroleum
   Maatschapij B.V., ... 991
Quebec (A.G.) v. Bégin, ... 380
Quebec (A.G.) v. Canada (A.G.), ... 776
Quebec (Liquor Commission) v. Goulet, ... 810
Quebec (Municipal Commission), R. v., ... 605
Queen Caroline's Case, ... 864, 865-866
Quercia, R. v., ... 313
Quick v. Quick, ... 251, 253
Quinn, R. v. (1976), ... 12-13
Quinn, R. v. (1905), ... 1026
Quintal v. Datta, ... 968

R

R. v. R. *See* Robertson, R. v.

R.L. Crain Inc. v. Couture, ... 759

R.L.R., R. v. *See* R.(R.L.), R. v.

R.(R.L.), R. v., ... 145, 146

R.S., R. v. *See* S.(R.J.), R. v.

R.(T.), R. v., ... 1036

R.(T.) (No. 2), R. v., ... 1036

Rabin v. Mendoza & Co., ... 721

Radford v. Macdonald, ... 891, 908, 909

Rafael, R. v., ... 443, 884

Rahn, R. v., ... 403

Ralston Purina Canada Inc. v. Canada Packers Inc., ... 1011

Ram v. R., ... 589

Randall v. Atkinson, ... 277-278

Rans Construction (1966) Ltd. v. M.N.R., ... 1004

Rarot, Re, ... 45

Rathwell v. Rathwell, ... 117, 118

Ratten v. R., ... 161, 169, 259, 261, 264, 265

Ratti v. R., ... 75

Raviraj v. R., ... 101

Rayner v. Rayner, ... 770

Read v. Bishop of Lincoln, ... 980

Read, R. v., ... 187, 239

Reaney v. Reaney, ... 118

Red Deer Nursing Home Ltd. v. Taylor, ... 702

Redd, R. v., ... 457

Redfern v. Redfern, ... 735, 768

Redgrave, R. v., ... 447

Reed v. Lincoln (Town), ... 145

Reed v. Order of United Commercial Travellers, ... 208

Reese, R. v., ... 783

Reeves, R. v., ... 979

Reference re Alberta Legislation, ... 976

Reference re Anti-Inflation Act, ... 979

Reference re Legislative Privilege, ... 625, 631, 809

Reference re Manitoba Language Rights, ... 1002, 1020

Reference re ss. 222, 224 and 224A of the Criminal Code, ... 547, 850

Regan, Re, ... 601

R. v. *See* under name of accused.

Reichmann v. Toronto Life Publishing Co., ... 704, 706, 928, 931, 933, 935, 938

Reid v. McWhinnie, ... 981

Reid v. Reid, ... 995, 997

Reid v. Telegram Publishing Co., ... 702, 703

Reid v. Watkins, ... 571, 705

Reniger v. Fogossa, ... 105

Rhodes, R. v., ... 44
Riach v. Ferris, ... 65
Rice v. Canada (National Parole Board), ... 809
Rice v. Sockett, ... 537, 572
Richard v. Dunn, ... 963
Richards v. Watch Lake Development Co., ... 704
Richardson v. Nugent, ... 34, 35
Richardson, R. v., ... 994
Rickard, R. v., ... 1033
Riddle, R. v., ... 1015-1017, 1018, 1020, 1022, 1026
Rideout and the Queen, Re. *See* Rideout v. R.
Rideout v. R., ... 813
Re Riffel Estate, ... 905, 918
Rigby v. Nova Scotia Trust Co., ... 911
Riley, R. v., ... 150
Riley v. St. John (City), ... 935
Ringrose v. College of Physicians and Surgeons, ... 991
Risby, R. v., ... 320, 362
River Steamer Co., Re; Mitchell's Claim, ... 721, 730
Rivers v. Hague, ... 836
Robb v. Robb, ... 221, 226
Roberts v. Poitras, ... 589
Roberts, R. v., ... 356
Robertson, R. v. (1987), ... 55, 63, 73, 75, 83, 502, 503, 511
Robertson, R. v. (1975), ... 451, 452, 461, 533, 766, 767
Robichaud, Ex parte, ... 615
Robillard, R. v., ... 974
Robins v. The Empire Printing and Publishing Co., ... 11
Robins v. National Trust Co., ... 60, 64, 528, 532, 571, 573
Robinson v. McQuaid, ... 990
Robinson, R. v., ... 809
Robinson v. Simpson. *See* Cochran's Trusts, Re.
Robinson Bros. (Brewers), Ltd. v. Houghton and Chester-le-Street Assessment
  Committee, ... 930, 931
Robson v. A.G. *See* Monkton v. A.G.
Rocca Construction Ltd. v. Gen. Labourers' & Gen. Workers' Union,
  Local 1079, ... 971
Rock v. Canadian Northern Railway Co., ... 514
Rocking Chair Plaza (Bramalea) Ltd. v. Brampton (City), ... 644
Rodgers, R. v., ... 895, 897
Rodney, R. v., ... 872
Rodych v. Krasey, ... 240
Roe d. Lord Trimlestown v. Kemmis, ... 47, 179
Rogers v. Bank of Montreal, ... 668
Rogers v. Hill, ... 934, 940
Rogers v. Hunter. *See* Hunter v. Rogers.
Rogers v. Porter, ... 992

Rogers v. Secretary of State for the Home Department, . 773, 774, 775, 800, 801, 806
Rogers v. Wood, ... 993
Rolex Watch Co. of Canada Ltd., R. v., ... 964
Romaniuk v. Alberta, ... 1011
Romeo, R. v., ... 75
Roop, R. v. *See* Grant (1924), R. v.
Rosen, R. v., ... 688
Rosenberg v. Rosenberg, ... 771
Rosenblat, Re, ... 253
Rosenmeyer, Re; Porteous v. Dorn, ... 223
Rosik, R. v., ... 44, 452, 453
Ross, Re, ... 922
Ross, R. v. (1989), ... 19, 370, 372, 373, 403, 409, 413, 417, 419, 424
Ross, R. v. (1980), ... 487
Ross, R. v. (1977), ... 1016
Ross, R. v. (1966), ... 984
Ross v. Williamson, ... 938
Rothman, R. v., ... 332, 333, 350, 351, 377, 378, 388, 398
Roud, R. v., ... 479
Rouse, R. v., ... 314
Roviaro v. United States, ... 813
Rowbotham, R. v. (1988), ... 872
Rowbotham, R. v. (1984), ... 392, 528
Rowbotham, R. v. (1977), ... 215
Rowbotham (No. 5), R. v., ... 860
Rowlands v. De Vecchi, ... 189
Rowton, R. v., ... 441, 444, 451, 453, 457, 460, 461, 846, 888
Royal Bank v. Neher, ... 983
Royal Bank v. Sullivan, ... 871
Royal Bank of Canada, R. v., ... 514
Royal Commission into Metropolitan Toronto Police Practices v. Ashton. *See*
  Canada (Royal Commission into Metropolitan Toronto Police Practices)
  v. Ashton.
Royal Insurance Co. v. Duffus, ... 46, 47
Royal Trust Co. v. McClure, ... 532
Royal Victoria Hospital v. Morrow, ... 237
"Ruapehu", The, ... 75
Ruby, Re, ... 902
Rudd v. Frank, ... 643
Rudzinsko v. Warner Theatres, Inc., ... 292
Rumping v. Director of Public Prosecutions, ... 29, 678, 685-687, 691, 692
Rush & Tomkins Ltd. v. Greater London Council, ... 720, 721, 728, 730
Russell v. Fraser, ... 179, 965
Russell, R. v. (1983), ... 126
Russell, R. v. (1920), ... 295, 958, 962
Russell v. Russell, ... 692, 693
Ryan v. Whitton, ... 923

Ryder, Re, ... 644
Ryder v. Wombell, ... 131, 138

S

S. v. Recorder of Manchester, ... 975
S. v. S., ... 442
S.(K.O.), R. v., ... 303
S. & K. Processors Ltd. v. Campbell Avenue Herring Producers Ltd., ... 667
S.(R.J.), R. v., ... 454, 717
Saari v. Nykanen, ... 942
Saccomanno v. Berube. *See* Saccomanno v. Swanson.
Saccomanno v. Swanson, ... 611
St. Ann's Island Shooting and Fishing Club Ltd. v. R., ... 1002
St. Denis and North Himsworth (Township), ... 1000
St. Hilaire v. Kravacek, ... 176, 180
St.-Jean, R. v., ... 33, 689, 690
Saint John (City) v. Irving Oil Co., ... 550, 556, 557
St. Lawrence, R. v., ... 331, 367, 368, 379
St. Leon Village Consolidated School District No. 1425 v. Ronceray, ... 107
St. Pierre, R. v., ... 456
Salekin, R. v., ... 41
Salituro, R. v., ... 612, 615, 682, 683
Salutin v. R., ... 453
Samuel, R. v., ... 449, 461
Samwald v. Mills, ... 604
Sands Estate v. Sonnwald, ... 908, 909, 910, 911, 912
Sanelli, R. v. *See* Duarte, R. v.
Sang, R. v., ... 30, 31, 32, 382, 403, 464, 465
Sanghi, R. v., ... 213, 927, 928
Sangster v. Aikenhead, ... 702
Sankey v. Whitlam, ... 793
Santangelo, R. v., ... 978
Santinon, R. v., ... 335, 337
Sanver, R. v., ... 1020
Sarbit v. Booth Fisheries (Cdn.) Co., ... 288
Saskatchewan Minerals v. Keyes, ... 933, 934
Saskatoon Credit Union Ltd. v. Central Park
    Enterprises Ltd., ... 989, 995, 1008, 1011, 1046
Sat-Bhambra, R. v., ... 324
Sauder Industries Ltd. v. The Molda, ... 656
Sault Ste. Marie (City), R. v., ... 92, 151
Saunders, R. v., ... 48
Saunders v. Saunders, ... 771
Sauvé, R. v., ... 529
Savage v. Futcher, ... 703

Savard v. R., ... 21

Savary, R. v., ... 1036

Savidant, R. v., ... 982, 985

Savion v. R., ... 453

Sawatsky, R. v. *See* Burkart, R. v.

Sawchuk, R. v., ... 943

Saxell, R. v., ... 440

Scamen v. Canadian Northern Railway Co., ... 572

Scappaticci v. A.G., ... 243

Schaffner, R. v., ... 968

Scheel, R. v., ... 940

Schell, R. v., ... 487

Schemerber v. State of California, ... 374, 740

Schetky v. Cochrane, ... 721, 729, 731

Schmidt, R. v. (1987), ... 1034

Schmidt, R. v. (1948), ... 280, 363, 761

Schmuck v. McIntosh, ... 702

Schneider, R. v., ... 578

Schnell v. B.C. Electric Rly. Co., ... 976

Schonberger v. Toronto Transit Commission, ... 657

Schubert, R. v., ... 49

Schwalbe, The, ... 255

Schwartz, R. v., ... 54, 55, 56, 65, 72, 87, 88, 112, 125, 127

Schwartz v. Stinchcombe, ... 742

Schwartzenhauer, R. v., ... 48, 269

Science Research Council v. Nassé, B.L. Cars (formerly Leyland Cars)
    v. Vyas, ... 775

Scopelliti, R. v., ... 450, 467

Scory, R. v., ... 48

Scotia Chevrolet Oldsmobile Ltd. v. Whynot, ... 994

Scotia Construction Co. v. Halifax, ... 994

Scott v. Crerar, ... 966, 967

Scott, R. v. (1990), ... 806, 811, 814

Scott, R. v. (1910), ... 467

Scott v. Sampson, ... 435, 437

Secretary of State for Defence v. Guardian Newspapers Ltd., ... 706

Sederquest v. Ryan, ... 18

Sedlmayr and the Royal Commission into Royal American Shows Inc., ... 607

Seaboyer, R. v., ... 468, 469, 471-474, 660

Seaboyer, R. v.: Gayme, R. v. *See* Seaboyer, R. v.

Sears, R. v., ... 41

Selhi, R. v., ... 1017, 1019

Semayne's Case, ... 422

Sentinel-Review Co. v. Robinson, ... 237

Serack, R. v., ... 345, 346

Seredink v. Kogan, ... 272, 300

Setak Computer Services Corp. v. Burroughs Business
  Machines Ltd., ... 196, 197, 203, 212
Sewers Commrs. of London v. Gellatly, ... 1009
Sewid, R. v., ... 1037
Seymour v. Arrowsmith, ... 877
S. Fremes & Co. v. Neima, ... 643
Shanklin v. Smith, ... 242
Shanks v. J.D. Irving Ltd., ... 993
Shantz v. Hansen, ... 983
Sharpe Estate v. Northwestern General Hospital, ... 632
Sharpe v. Lamb, ... 939
Shaver v. Shaver, ... 515, 521
Shaw v. R., ... 883
Shea v. Halifax & South Western Railway Co., ... 292
Shedd v. Boland, ... 641, 663
Shedden v. A.G., ... 224
Sheehy v. Robinson, ... 114, 115
Shelburne and Queen's Election Case. See Controverted Election for Shelburne
  and Queen's, Re.
Shell Co. of Australia Ltd. v. Federal Taxation Commr., ... 992
Shelley, R. v., ... 92, 122
Shenton v. Tyler, ... 683, 684
Shepard v. United States, ... 250, 251
Shepherd, R. v., ... 352
Shepheard v. Broome, ... 106
Sheppe v. R., ... 1029
Sherrard v. Jacob, ... 524, 528
Shiell v. Coach House Hotel Ltd., ... 904
Short v. Lee, ... 179
Shorten, R. v., ... 924
Shrewsbury v. Blount, ... 959
Shrimpton, R. v., ... 461
Shubley, R. v., ... 1035
Shumardo v. Toronto General Trusts Corp., ... 271
Sidhu v. Grewal, ... 724
Sieben, R. v., ... 414, 423
Sigmund, R. v., ... 922
Sillars, R. v., ... 613
Silverlock, R. v., ... 537
Silverstone, R. v., ... 909, 912
Sim, R. v., ... 977
Simaan General Contracting Co. v. Pilkington Glass Ltd., ... 731
Simmons, R. v., ... 389, 390, 398, 403, 405, 414, 422, 424
Simmons v. R. See Simpson, R. v. (1943).
Simon, R. v., ... 222
Simon v. Simon, ... 188
Simpson v. Lever, ... 205

Simpson v. Monture, ... 933
Simpson, R. v. (1988), ... 310, 319
Simpson, R. v. (1977), ... 75, 440
Simpson, R. v. (1943), ... 736
Simpson Timber Co. (Sask.) Ltd. v. Bonville, ... 17, 968
Sims v. Grand Trunk Railway Co., ... 519
Sims, R. v., ... 492, 493
Siniarski, R. v., ... 339
Sinclair v. Ruddell, ... 441
Sirros v. Moore, ... 619
Skanes, R. v., ... 1026
Skogen v. Dow Chemical Co., ... 208
Skogman v. R., ... 135
Skwarchuk, R. v., ... 850
Slavutych v. Baker, ... 625, 627, 629-632, 634, 635, 675, 698, 708, 717
Slopek, R. v., ... 326
Small v. Belyea, ... 47
Small v. Nemez, ... 140
Smallman v. Moore, ... 908, 909, 910, 911
Smallwood v. Sparling. See Re Canadian Javelin Ltd.
Smart, R. v., ... 959, 960, 962
Smerchanski v. Lewis, Smerchanski v. Asta Securities Corp., ... 774, 803, 804
Smith, Re, ... 905
Smith v. Blakey, ... 179, 183, 189
Smith v. Daniell, ... 643
Smith, D.P.P. v., ... 103
Smith v. Gerow, ... 47
Smith v. Goulet, ... 272
Smith, R. v. (1990), ... 250
Smith, R. v. (1989), ... 372
Smith, R. v. (1986), ... 16
Smith, R. v. (1973), ... 326
Smith, R. v. (1959), ... 341
Smith, R. v. (1915), ... 487, 511
Smith v. Royal Columbian Hospital, ... 632
Smith v. Smith (1958), ... 665
Smith v. Smith (1952), ... 142, 143, 144
Smith v. Smith (1884), ... 972
Smith v. Transcona (Town), ... 838
Smith, Kline and French Laboratories Ltd. v. Canada (A.G.), ... 781
Smith's Field Manor Development Ltd. v. Halifax (No. 2), ... 1002
Smythe v. Campbell, ... 923
Smyth, R. v., ... 68
Snell v. Farrell, ... 79, 94, 100
Snelling, R. v., ... 984
Snider, R. v., ... 775, 784-785, 797-798, 799
Societé des Acadiens v. Association of Parents, ... 832

Sodeman v. R., ... 148, 151, 152
Solicitor v. M.N.R. *See* Income Tax Act, Re.
Solicitor and Income Tax Act, Re. *See* Income Tax Act, Re.
Solomon, R. v., ... 13
Solomon v. Smith, ... 1011
Solosky v. Canada, ... 635, 636, 640, 642, 644, 646, 647, 664
Solosky v. R. *See* Solosky v. Canada.
Solway, The, ... 292
Somerville v. Prudential Insurance Co. of America, ... 240
Sophonow, R. v., ... 750
Sornberger v. Canadian Pacific Railway, ... 34
South American and Mexican Co., Ex parte Bank of England, ... 996
South Staffordshire Water Co. v. Sharman, ... 960
Southam Inc. v. Mulroney. *See* Mulroney v. Coates.
Southam Inc. v. Theriault, ... 776
Southport Corp. v. Esso Petroleum Co., ... 82
Southwark Water Co. v. Quick, ... 653
South-West Oxford (Corp. of the Twp.) v. Ontario (A.G.), ... 792
Speid, R. v., ... 450, 454, 456, 467, 1028
Spence v. Price *See* Price, Re.
Spencer, R. v., ... 915
Spencer, R. v., ... 621, 893
Sperschneider v. Staskiewicz, ... 979
Sproule v. Murray, ... 921
Spurge, R. v., ... 86, 139
Staff Builders International Inc. v. Cohen, ... 995
Staines v. Stewart, ... 252
Stamper v. C.N.R. *See* Stamper v. Finnigan.
Stamper v. Finnigan, ... 993
Standall v. Standall, ... 994
Standard International Corp. v. Morgan, ... 863
Standard Investments Ltd. v. Canadian Imperial Bank of Commerce, ... 626
Staniforth v. R., ... 15
Stanley v. Douglas, ... 598
Stapleton v. R. (1982), ... 327
Stapleton v. R. (1952), ... 102
Starr v. Houlden. *See* Starr v. Ontario (Commissioner of Inquiry).
Starr v. Ontario (Commissioner of Inquiry), ... 609, 610, 760
Stasun, Re; Stasun v. Nesteroff, ... 223
Stasun v. Nesteroff. *See* Stasun, Re.
State v. Davis, ... 537
State v. Russell, ... 649
Stavely, Re, ... 221
Stawycznuj, R. v., ... 24
Steane, R. v., ... 103
Steeves v. Rapanos, ... 653
Steinburg, R. v., ... 582

Steintron International Electronics Ltd. v. Vorberg, ... 627
Stenhouse v. Wright, ... 871
Stephen v. Gwenap, ... 183
Stephens v. Toronto Railway Co., ... 249
Sterling Trusts Corp. v. Postma, ... 869
Stevens, R. v., ... 389, 398, 399
Stevenson v. Dandy, ... 951, 952, 965
Stevenson, R. v., ... 978
Stevenson v. Stevenson, ... 1046
Stewart v. Moore, ... 251-252
Stewart v. Muirhead, ... 720
Stewart, R. v., ... 48
Stewart v. Royal Bank, ... 877
Stewart v. Walker, ... 251, 252, 660-662, 663, 859, 863
Stickney v. Trusz, ... 166
Stills v. R., ... 905
Stinchcombe, R. v., ... 790, 791, 803, 809, 810, 819
Stirland v. D.P.P., ... 49
Stockbridge Mill Co. v. Central Land Board, ... 521
Stockfleth v. De Tastet, ... 384
Stolar, R. v. See Nielsen, R. v.
Storey v. Storey, ... 132
Stotesbury v. Turner, ... 732
Stovel v. Allen, ... 854
Stowe v. Grand Trunk Pacific Railway, ... 280
Stowe v. Querner, ... 951
Strachan, Re, ... 653
Strachan v. McGinn, ... 592, 653
Strachan, R. v., ... 370, 392, 393-395, 396, 405, 420, 424
Straffen, R. v., ... 478, 479, 487, 511
Strand Electric Ltd., R. v., ... 85, 289, 290-91, 293
Strass v. Goldsack, ... 630, 631
Stratton, R. v., ... 464, 465, 476, 1023
Street v. Guelph (City), ... 873, 874
Streu, R. v., ... 280-282, 362, 363
Sturla v. Freccia, ... 179, 180, 189, 190, 228, 231, 937, 941
Subramaniam v. Public Prosecutor, ... 156, 165
Sugden v. Lord St. Leonards, ... 173, 251, 252, 253
Sullivan, R. v., ... 1031, 1033
Sun Alliance Ins. Co. v. Thompson, ... 992
Sunbeam Corp. (Can.) Ltd. v. R., ... 70, 71, 72, 964
Sunila, R. v., ... 212
Sunnyside Nursing Home v. Builders Contract Mgmt. Ltd., ... 18
Sunwell Engineering Co. v. Mogilevsky, ... 649, 650
Susan Hosiery Ltd. v. Minister of National Revenue, ... 650, 653
Sussex Peerage Case, ... 177, 179
Sutherland v. Bell, ... 978

Sutor v. McLean, ... 271
Sutton v. Sadler, ... 64, 100
Sveinsson, R. v., ... 589, 590
Swadron v. North York, ... 18
Swain, R. v., ... 440
Swan v. Miller, Son & Torrance Ltd., ... 292
Swanston, R. v., ... 314
Swartz, R. v., ... 931, 933
Sweeney (No. 2), R. v., ... 44
Sweetman, R. v., ... 1026, 1028
Sweitzer v. R., ... 480, 499, 502
Swietlinski, R. v., ... 538, 549
Switzer v. Boulton, ... 271
Switzer, R. v., ... 1029
Sykes, Re; Drake v. Sykes, ... 253
Symonds, R. v., ... 767
Syms, R. v., ... 135, 136, 151, 359
Szarfer v. Chodos, ... 628
Szlovak, R. v., ... 396

T

T.(F.M.), R. v., ... 1030, 1031
T.L.G. v. D.L. *See* G.(T.L.) v. L.(D.).
Talbot v. Pan Ocean Oil Corp., ... 994
Tally v. Klatt, ... 1044
Tannis Trading Inc. v. Thorne, Ernst & Whinney, ... 993
Tapp v. R., ... 360
Tarafa, R. v., ... 528, 752
Tarrant, R. v., ... 375, 752
Tass, R. v., ... 738
Tateham, R. v., ... 1017
Tatham v. Canada (National Parole Board), ... 790
Tatomir, R. v., ... 937, 938, 943, 944
Taylor, Re; Taylor v. Taylor (1961), ... 220
Taylor, Re (1923), ... 912, 921
Taylor v. Baribeau, ... 1042
Taylor v. Chief Constable of Cheshire (1986), ... 968
Taylor v. Gray, ... 534
Taylor v. Hortop, ... 1009
Taylor v. Massey, ... 850
Taylor v. Regis, ... 921
Taylor, R. v. (1970), ... 591, 922
Taylor, R. v. (1914), ... 1022
Taylor v. Taylor. *See* Taylor, Re; Taylor v. Taylor (1961).
Taylor v. Taylor, ... 120

Teasdale v. Hertel, ... 912
Tecoglas Inc. v. Domglas Inc., ... 188, 928, 931, 933
Teen, Re, ... 944
Telford v. Secord, ... 874
Teper v. R., ... 158, 253, 254, 265
Terlecki v. R., ... 1030, 1033
Terroco Industries Ltd. v. Viking Oldfield Supply Ltd., ... 998
Teskey v. Canadian Newspapers Co., ... 545
Thatcher, R. v., ... 150
Theal v. R., ... 472
Theodoropoulas v. Theodoropoulas, ... 733
Therens, R. v., ... 372, 389, 390, 391, 393, 394, 395, 399, 403,
                                                    404, 408, 409, 412, 415, 418, 419, 423
Thibodeau v. R., ... 975
Thibodeau v. Thibodeau, ... 720, 730
Thiffault v. R., ... 354
Thoday v. Thoday, ... 996
Thomas v. British Columbia (A.G.), ... 235, 300
Thomas v. Connell, ... 242
Thomas v. David, ... 885
Thomas v. Hogan, ... 208
Thomas v. R., ... 148, 149
Thomas v. Watkins Products Inc., ... 200, 954
Thompson v. Bennett, ... 956, 965
Thompson v. Coulter, ... 911, 921
Thompson v. Crawford, ... 995
Thompson v. D.P.P. *See* Thompson v. R.
Thompson, R. v. (1990), ... 425, 426
Thompson, R. v. (1918), ... 480, 488, 957
Thompson, R. v. (1872), ... 612
Thompson, R. v. (1870), ... 612
Thompson v. Thompson (1956), ... 996
Thompson v. Thompson (1902), ... 532, 910, 965
Thompson v. Trevanion, ... 240, 257
Thomson Newspapers Ltd. v. Canada (Director of
  Investigation and Research, Restricted Trade Practices
  Commission), ... 32, 376, 377, 685, 734, 741, 743, 754-757, 758
Thomson, R. v. (1912), ... 246
Thorn v. Worthing Skating Rink Co., ... 533
Thornhill v. Dartmouth Broadcasting Ltd., ... 774, 776, 805
Thornley v. Royal Trust Co., ... 922
Thorson v. Jones, ... 640
Thrasyvoulos Ioannou v. Papa Christoforos Demetrion, ... 231, 941
Ticchiarelli, R. v., ... 666
Tickle v. Tickle, ... 243
Tide Shore Logging Ltd. v. Commonwealth Insurance Co., ... 928
Tierney, R. v., ... 460, 461, 462

Tilco Plastics Ltd. v. Skurjat; Ontario (A.G.) v. Clark, ... 760
Tilton v. McKay, ... 943
Times Square Cinema Ltd., R. v., ... 557
Timm, R. v., ... 314, 315
Timmons, R. v., ... 1036
Tingle Jacobs & Co. v. Kennedy, ... 120
Tipping v. Hornby, ... 284
Tisman v. Rae, ... 703
Tobias v. Nolan, ... 955, 956
Todd, R. v., ... 350
Todish, R. v., ... 465
Toll v. Canadian Pacific Railway, ... 285
Tollemache, Re. See Edwards, Ex parte.
Tolton Mfg. Co. v. Ontario Industrial Standards Advisory Committee, ... 46
Tomaso, R. v., ... 405
Tomlin v. Standard Telephones and Cables Ltd., ... 730
Tompkins, R. v., ... 386
Tompkins v. Ternes, ... 327
Toohey v. Metropolitan Police Commr., ... 886, 887
Topham v. McGregor, ... 854
Topliss Estates, Re, ... 117, 121
Torbiak, R. v., ... 824
Torok v. Torok, ... 713
Toronto General Hospital Trustees v. Matthews. See Aynsley v. Toronto General
  Hospital.
Toronto General Trusts Corp. v. Roman, ... 1001
Toronto Ry. Co. v. Toronto Corp., ... 993
Toulejour, R. v., ... 974
Toussaint v. R., ... 975
Tower, R. v., ... 866
Tracey Peerage Case, ... 533
Trammel v. U.S., ... 616
Trask, R. v., ... 403
Travellers Indemnity Co. of Canada v. Maracle. See Maracle v. Travellers
  Indemnity Co. of Canada.
Tremblay, R. v., ... 372, 373, 407, 408
Trenholme, R. v., ... 352
Tribune Newspaper Co. v. Fort Frances Pulp & Paper Co., ... 577
Tricontinental Investments Co. v. Guarantee Co. of North America, ... 611
Triganzie, R. v., ... 460
Triple A. Invts. Ltd. v. Adams Bros. Ltd., ... 18
Troop, R. v., ... 938
Truscott, Re, ... 584, 591
Tuck, R. v., ... 586, 589
Tucker v. Oldbury Urban District Council, ... 176, 180
Tuckey, R. v., ... 464
Tunke, R. v., ... 48

Tupper v. R., ... 109
Turnbull, R. v., ... 529
Turner, R. v. (1974), ... 475
Turner, R. v., (1816), ... 84-85
Turner v. Turner, ... 997
Tutton, R. v., ... 83
Tylden v. Bullen, ... 966
Tyler v. Minister of National Revenue, ... 608, 760
Tyrell v. Painton, ... 65
Tyson v. Little, ... 27
Tzagarakis v. Stevens, ... 889

U

Udy v. Stewart, ... 584, 585, 830, 831
Uljee, R. v., ... 386, 676
Ulrich, R. v., ... 949, 976
Underwood v. Cox, ... 728, 729
Underwood v. Wing, ... 116
Union Carbide Canada Ltd. v. Trans-Canadian Feeds Ltd., ... 877
Union Carbide Canada Ltd. v. Vanderkop, ... 10
United Cigar Stores Ltd. v. Buller, ... 876
United Motors Service Ltd. v. Hutson, ... 81, 82
United Nurses of Alberta v. Alberta (A.G.), Re, ... 1031
U.S.A. v. Teen. See Teen, Re.
U.S. v. Downing, ... 565, 566, 567, 569
U.S. v. Leon, ... 384
U.S. v. Mammoth Oil Co., ... 639, 648
U.S. v. Nixon, ... 626
U.S. v. Reynolds, ... 774
U.S. v. Shephard, ... 61, 135, 136, 359, 360
U.S. v. Williams, ... 567
University of Guelph v. C.A.U.T., ... 632
Upchurch, R. v., ... 352
Upham v. Yon, ... 627, 713, 717
Upjohn v. United States, ... 652
Upper v. Upper, ... 997
Urquhart v. Butterfield, ... 971
Ussher v. Simpson, ... 729
Uukw v. British Columbia (1987), ... 222
Uukw v. R. See Uukw v. British Columbia.
Uvery, R. v., ... 976

V

V.K., R. v. See K.(V.), R. v.

Valley, R. v., ... 33, 467, 547, 824
Vallières, R. v., ... 401
Vancouver Community College v. Phillips Barratt, ... 670, 671
Vancouver Hockey Club Ltd. v. National Hockey League, ... 676
Van Den Meerssche, R. v., ... 1027
Vanderlinden, R. v., ... 1037
Van Dongen, R. v., ... 359
Van Every v. Drake, ... 969
Van Ginkel v. Van Ginkel, ... 272
Van Koughnet v. Denison, ... 218, 969
Vanlerberghe, R. v., ... 214, 928, 931, 932
Van Rassel, R. v., ... 1013, 1014-1015, 1021, 1023, 1027, 1031, 1035
Van Rooy v. M.N.R., ... 1042
Vardon v. Vardon, ... 730
Vaughan v. Scott, ... 1001
Vautour, R. v., ... 894
Vent, R. v., ... 975
Ventouris v. Mountain, ... 658
Vetrovec v. R.; Gaja v. R. See Vetrovec, R. v.
Vetrovec, R. v., ... 6, 892, 893-896, 905, 913, 923
Vezeau, R. v., ... 761
Vickers v. Vickers, ... 732
Victoria Mutual Fire Insurance Co. v. Davidson, ... 156
Vigeant v. R., ... 761
Vigneault v. Martel. See Martel v. Hotel-Dieu St-Vallier.
Vinette, R. v., ... 1046
Voisin, R. v., ... 965, 966
Voitko v. Sabados. See Puczka, Re.
Vooght v. Winch, ... 1012
Voth Brothers Construction (1974) Ltd. v. North Vancouver School
    District No. 44, ... 656
Voutsis, R. v., ... 1031
Vowles v. Young, ... 228
Voyer v. Lepage, ... 922
Voykin, R. v., ... 215

W

W. v. Egdell, ... 624, 627
W., R. v. (1990), ... 302
W., R. v. (1983), ... 1036
W.(D.S.) v. H.(R.), ... 902
Wahl v. Nugent, ... 998
Wainwright, R. v., ... 246
Waite, R. v., ... 105
Wales v. Wales, ... 521

Walker, Re, ... 115
Walker v. Foster, ... 910
Walker v. McMillan, ... 862
Walker v. Murray, ... 226
Walker v. R. (1939), ... 342
Walker, R. v. (1910), ... 830
Walker v. Wilsher, ... 731, 732
Walkerton (Town) v. Erdman, ... 271
Wallace v. McMaster, ... 979
Wallbridge v. Jones, ... 225, 226
Wallwork, R. v., ... 584
Walmsley v. Humenick, ... 284, 910
Walsh v. R. (1987). *See* Church of Scientology, R. v.
Walsh v. R. (1943). *See* Simpson, R. v.
Walsh, R. v. (1980), ... 932, 940
Walsh, R. v. (1978), ... 583
Walsh v. Walsh, ... 118
Walters v. R., ... 143, 149, 657
Walters v. Toronto Transit Commission, ... 657
Walton v. Bernard, ... 638
Waltson Properties Ltd., Re, ... 215
Wannebo, R. v., ... 310, 879
Ward v. H.S. Pitt & Co.; Lloyd v. Powell Duffryn Steam
 Coal Co., ... 169, 176, 179, 181, 244
Ward v. McIntyre, ... 308, 598
Ward, R. v., ... 326, 332, 334, 335, 337
Warener v. Kingsmill, ... 943
Warickshall, R. v., ... 328, 331, 367
Warkentin, R. v., ... 911, 912, 913, 975
Warren v. Deslippes, ... 937
Warren v. Gray Goose Stage Ltd., ... 722, 725
Warren, R. v., ... 465
Warringham, R. v., ... 352
Warunki v. Warunki, ... 653
Waschuk, R. v., ... 979
Washer, R. v., ... 356
Wasylyshen v. Canadian Broadcasting Corp., ... 702, 703, 704
Watson v. Severn, ... 919
Watt v. Miller, ... 177, 183
Watt, R. v., ... 962
Wattsburg Lumber Co. v. Cooke Lumber Co., ... 970
Waugh v. British Railways Board, ... 656
Wawanesa Mutual Insurance Co. v. Hanes, ... 840-842, 845, 846
Wayte, R. v., ... 931, 934, 939
Weber v. Pawlik, ... 783
Webb, R. v., ... 46
Webster v. Solloway Mills & Co. (No. 2), ... 742

Wednesbury Corp. v. Ministry of Housing, ... 786
Weeks, Re, ... 253
Weeks v. Sparke, ... 216
Weeks v. U.S., ... 384
Weightman, R. v., ... 541
Weil's Food Processing Ltd., R. v., ... 342
Weingarden v. Moss, ... 918
Weis v. Weis, ... 208
Welch, R. v., ... 1017
Wellman v. General Crane Industries Ltd., ... 669, 670
Wells v. Fisher, ... 682
Welstead v. Brown, ... 112, 113, 310, 771
Welton, R. v., ... 602
Wendo, R. v., ... 359
Werner v. Warner Auto-Marine Inc., ... 657
Wert, R. v., ... 354
Westeel-Rosco Ltd. v. Edmonton Tinsmith Supplies Ltd., ... 933, 939
Western Assurance Co. v. Canada Life Assurance Co., ... 665
Western Canada Investment Co. v. McDiarmid, ... 665
Western Grocers Ltd., R. v., ... 961
Westmoreland, R. v., ... 676
Weston v. Middlesex (County), ... 871
Wetherell v. Bird, ... 973
Whalen, R. v., ... 983
Wheeler v. Le Marchant, ... 624, 625, 653
Wheeler v. Wheeler, ... 112
Whelan, R. v., ... 888
Whiffin v. Hartwright, ... 721
Whistnant, R. v., ... 924
White v. Weston, ... 10
White v. White, ... 771
Whitehead, R. v., ... 585
Whitehead v. R.B. Cameron Ltd., ... 190
Whitehead v. Scott, ... 238
Whitelaw, Ex parte. See Re Wilson.
Whitelaw v. McDonald. See Re Wilson.
Whitelocke v. Baker, ... 223
Whitfield v. Fausset, ... 950
Whittaker, R. v., ... 966
Wholesale Travel Group Inc., R. v., ... 90, 93, 151
Whyte v. Armstrong, ... 689
Whyte, R. v., ... 92, 123, 125, 126, 127
Wiedemann v. Walpole, ... 286, 963
Wiggins, R. v., ... 415, 417
Wigglesworth, R. v., ... 1013, 1034, 1035
Wigman v. R., ... 1031
Wilband v. R., ... 548-549

Wildman, R. v., ... 165, 968
William Allan Real Estate Co. v. Robichaud, ... 723, 724
Wilkinson, R. v., ... 46
William Allan Real Estate Co. v. Robichaud, ... 724
Williams v. Davies, ... 882
Williams v. East India Co., ... 99
Williams v. Quebrada Railway Land and Copper Co., ... 644
Williams, R. v. (1987), ... 896
Williams, R. v. (1985), ... 155, 184, 546, 845, 848, 855
Williams, R. v. (1977), ... 16
Williams, R. v. (1893), ... 105
Williams v. Williams, ... 598
Williamson v. Merrill, ... 687
Willoughby-Sumner Ltd. v. Sumner, ... 156
Willshire, R. v., ... 120
Wilmot, R. v., ... 744
Wilsher v. Essex Area Health Authority, ... 93
Wilson, Re (1968), ... 606
Wilson, Re (1963), ... 114
Wilson v. Bell, ... 539
Wilson v. Boltezar, ... 119
Wilson v. Esquimalt and Nanaimo Railway Co., ... 305
Wilson v. McLellan, ... 638
Wilson v. R. (1983), ... 427
Wilson, R. v. (1982), ... 672
Wilson, R. v. (1971), ... 85
Wilson, R. v. (1835), ... 969
Wilson v. Rastall, ... 643
Winfield, R. v., ... 461
Wingold v. W.B. Sullivan Const. Ltd., ... 863
Winnipeg South Child & Family Services v. S.(R.), ... 204
Winnipegosis Boatworks Ltd. v. Holm, ... 994
Winsor v. R., ... 601
Winter v. Henn, ... 439
Wintle v. Nye, ... 147
Wisbey Enterprises Ltd., R. v., ... 934, 935
Wiseman, R. v., ... 471
Wismer v. MacLean-Hunter Publishing Co. (No. 2), ... 703
Wong, R. v., ... 415, 968
Wong Kam-ming v. R., ... 346, 355, 375, 376, 442, 752
Wong On (No. 2), R. v., ... 829
Wong Shue Teen and U.S.A., Re. *See* Teen, Re.
Wood, R. v., ... 612
Woodcock, R. v. (1963), ... 856
Woodcock, R. v. (1789), ... 268
Woodcock v. Woodcock, ... 771
Woodhouse & Co. v. Woodhouse, ... 639

Woods, Re; Brown v. Carter, ... 223
Woods v. Elias, ... 194, 196, 205
Woods v. Mackey, ... 678
Woods, R. v., ... 363
Woodward v. Buchanan, ... 521
Wooey, R. v., ... 587
Woolley, R. v., ... 407
Woolmington v. D.P.P., ... 63, 91, 98, 122, 148, 483
Woolway v. Rowe, ... 294
Workman v. R., ... 1037
Workun v. Nelson, ... 910
Worrall, Re; ex parte Cossens, ... 734
Wray v. R. (1973), ... 164
Wray, R. v. (1970), ... 29-33, 37, 331, 336, 356, 357, 367,
                                              368, 379, 380, 383, 387, 388, 410, 465
Wray (No. 2), R. v. See Wray, R. v.
Wright v. Doe d. Tatham, ... 166-169, 255, 256, 532
Wright v. Kerrigan, ... 239
Wright v. Pepin, ... 972
Wright v. R., ... 760
Wright v. Tatham. See Wright v. Doe d. Tatham.
Wright v. Whiteside, ... 10, 11
Wu v. R., ... 103
Wyer v. Wyer, ... 942
Wyman, R. v., ... 842
Wysochan, R. v., ... 169, 170
Wytinck v. De Grouwe, ... 1012, 1013

X

"X" Ltd. v. Morgan Grampian Publishers Ltd., ... 701, 709

Y

Yachuk v. Oliver Blais Co. Ltd., ... 34, 35
Yacoob, R. v., ... 599
Yakeleya, R. v., ... 750-751
Yanover (No. 1), R. v., ... 894-895
Yerxa, R. v., ... 928, 929
Yes Holdings Ltd., R. v., ... 1037
Yon v. Upham. See Upham v. Yon.
York (County) v. Toronto Gravel Road & Concrete Co., ... 719
Youlden v. London Guarantee & Accident Co., ... 239, 241, 242
Young v. Denton, ... 47, 852, 853, 856, 866
Young v. Rank, ... 134
Young v. Schuler, ... 952

Youngman, R. v., ... 1037
Yuill v. Yuill, ... 132, 133

Z

Zajac v. Zwarycz, ... 591
Zanewich, R. v., ... 41
Zayac v. Coneco Equipment Ltd., ... 978
Zaveckas, R. v., ... 339-340
Zeolkowski, R. v., ... 21
Zeppa v. Coca-Cola Ltd., ... 82
Zevest Dev. Corp. v. K-Mart Canada Ltd., ... 993
Zicari, R. v., ... 761
Ziegler v. Canada (Director of Investigation & Research), ... 736, 741
Ziegler and Hunter, Re. See Ziegler v. Canada (Director of Investigation & Research).
Zielinski v. Gordon, ... 637
Zien v. Canada. See Zien v. R.
Zien v. R., ... 984
Zigelstein v. Kent, ... 520
Zito, R. v., ... 425
Zundel, R. v., ... 203, 228, 231, 980, 986, 987, 988
Zurlo, R. v., ... 602
Zwicker v. Young, ... 871, 886

Section I

GENERAL PRINCIPLES OF ADMISSIBILITY

CHAPTER 1

INTRODUCTION

I   WHAT IS EVIDENCE?

The rules of evidence control the presentation of facts before the court. Their purpose is to facilitate the introduction of all logically relevant facts "without sacrificing any fundamental policy of the law which may be of more importance than the ascertainment of the truth".[1] What are the logically relevant facts in any particular case, whether civil or criminal, is decided by the substantive law governing the cause of action or offence set out in the pleadings or the charge, as the case may be. These matters can tangentially affect the evidentiary principles in any given case, but they do not make up a part of the law of evidence. Rules governing court practice and procedure can govern the conduct of litigation in a manner similar to evidentiary rules, but, again, these are matters ancillary to evidence law and are not considered in any detail in this text. Evidentiary principles, on the other hand, regulate (1) what matters are or are not admissible before the court, and (2) the method by which admissible facts are placed before it.

II   GOALS OF THE LAW OF EVIDENCE

A. *Search for Truth*

The rules of evidence are made up of common law principles, statutory provisions and Constitutional principles. The essential purpose and feature of the trial system in our society is the search for

---

1   C.A. Wright, "The Law of Evidence: Present and Future" (1942), 20 Can. Bar Rev. 714, at 715.

truth. However, because our system is an adversarial one where fact presentation is controlled by the litigants and their counsel, this goal can be elusive in many cases. Apart from this deficiency in the framework in which the evidence is presented, the evidence itself may be inherently weak due, for example, to the imperfect recollection or perception of witnesses. In an attempt to limit these frailties, many of the rules of evidence are concerned with ensuring the reliability or accuracy of the evidence the court receives. For example, the hearsay rule, which seeks to exclude evidence of the out-of-court statements of a person who is not a witness where offered to prove the truth of the contents of the statements, is based in part on a fear of fabrication and on a reluctance to receive evidence where the perception of the actual witness of the events cannot be tested in cross-examination. Many of the exceptions to the hearsay rule[2] have developed in areas where these concerns are not paramount, such as where the out-of-court statements were given under oath in prior proceedings and were subject to cross-examination in that forum. The exception for admissions against interest, for example, recognizes that the fear of fabrication is lessened with this type of evidence, but that it is certainly not lessened with prior consistent statements:[3]

> [T]he presumption . . . is, that no man would declare anything against himself, unless it were true; but that every man, if he was in a difficulty, or in the view to any difficulty would make declarations for himself.

The rules requiring witnesses to take an oath or affirmation and the other rules dealing with the competency of witnesses, such as children or mental incompetents, are also designed to ensure the reliability of the evidence presented to the court.[4]

B. *Efficiency of the Trial Process*

The search for truth is not the only value accommodated in the rules of evidence. The rules are also designed to enhance the efficiency of the trial process itself. The fundamental principle that the evidence

---

2 The hearsay rule and its exceptions are discussed in Chapter 6.
3 *R. v. Hardy* (1794), 24 State Tr. 199, at 1093 per Eyre C.B.
4 See Chapter 13.

presented to the court must be relevant to the facts in issue[5] ensures that the court is not distracted by collateral matters. The collateral fact rule which limits the scope of the evidence that can be presented in testing the credibility of a witness seeks to ensure trial efficiency.[6] Many evidence rules govern the process for examining witnesses and ensure that it is an orderly one. Some of the rules make the proof of matters easier and thereby enhance the process. For example, many statutes permit the introduction of copies of documents as opposed to originals, while others provide that certain types of evidence constitute *prima facie* proof of matters. The principles of issue estoppel and *res judicata* and the rules with respect to judicial notice of facts and formal admissions are concerned with the process itself and not the accuracy or veracity of the evidence.[7] The rules governing the receipt of opinion evidence are also designed in part to define or enhance the role of the trier of fact or law.[8]

C. Fairness of the Trial Process

In criminal cases in particular there is a very great concern with the fairness of the trial process. The rules of evidence can assist in striking an appropriate balance between the power of the state and the individual. Because of the serious consequences which face an accused in a criminal trial, the application of the rules of evidence in criminal cases often differs from their application in civil cases. This affords the accused greater protection against prejudicial evidence.[9] It is not only since the enactment of the *Canadian Charter of Rights and Freedoms*[10] that the evidence rules have been concerned with fairness to an accused. The common law rules governing the admissibility of confessions made to persons in authority is a prime example.[11] Ensuring the voluntariness of such statements is not only an attempt to ensure their accuracy, but also restrains the use of certain interrogation

---

5   Relevance is discussed in Chapter 2. II.B.
6   See Chapter 16. VIII.B.
7   These rules dispensing with or facilitating proof are considered in Chapter 18.
8   Opinion evidence is discussed in Chapter 12.
9   *Hurst v. Evans*, [1917] 1 K.B. 352, at 355; *Re Monteith; Merchants Bank v. Monteith* (1885), 10 O.R. 529, at 545 per Chancellor Boyd (C.A.).
10   R.S.C. 1985, Appendix II, No. 44.
11   Confessions are discussed in Chapter 8.

procedures by the police. Further, at common law a person could not be forced to testify where the answer would incriminate him or her. Although this was later modified by statute, some form of privilege against self-incrimination has long been a part of our law of evidence.[12] Rules restricting the use of evidence of the accused's bad character[13] are also designed to alleviate undue prejudice to an accused that can result from the admission of such evidence. The enactment of the *Charter* has further enhanced the accused's protection. In particular, the effect of s. 24(2) on the reception of evidence obtained in breach of a *Charter* right has had a significant impact on the law of evidence in criminal cases.[14]

D. *Goals Outside of the Process*

The search for truth, the enhancement of the efficiency of the process and the concern for fairness to the parties are all goals which centre on the trial process itself. However, the evidentiary rules also address interests that arise outside of that process. For example, there is a large body of law, both common law and statutory, that governs the production of documents belonging to or in the possession of the government. Exclusion of such materials can sometimes be justified by a need to protect our national security or the process of our government.[15] Rules limiting the evidentiary use of privileged communications are concerned with the maintenance of certain relationships. Although the maintenance of the solicitor–client relationship is ultimately concerned with the trial process, in that communications made within that relationship must be kept confidential to permit lawyers to function within the process, the protection of the confidentiality of other privileged relationships, such as that between spouses, has a more social purpose.

---

12   See Chapter 14. IV.F.
13   See Chapters 10 and 11.
14   See Chapter 9; Chapter 14. IV.
15   See Chapter 15.

III DIRECTION OF THE LAW OF EVIDENCE

Some might say that nothing much has changed in the law of evidence, at least in the law of civil evidence, since the publication of the *Law of Evidence in Civil Cases* in 1974.[16] Estey J. in 1982 in *R. v. Graat* gave his perception of its fossilized nature as follows:[17]

> We start with the reality that the law of evidence is burdened with a large number of cumbersome rules, with exclusions, and exceptions to the exclusions, and exceptions to the exceptions.

Decisions with respect to the admissibility or exclusion of evidence therefore turned on a mastery of these rules and exceptions with little regard as to whether slavish adherence to them made sense in either the circumstances of the particular case or in the context of modern society generally.

Parliament and the provincial legislatures have been slow to effect any kind of statutory reform. Although there was a flurry of activity by law reform bodies in the 1970s resulting in various reports recommending change, none of them reached fruition. A federal/provincial task force on uniform rules of evidence was established in 1977 with six jurisdictions, namely Canada, Ontario, Quebec, Nova Scotia, British Columbia and Alberta, participating in an attempt to bring about uniformity among the provincial and federal rules of evidence. What emerged was a draft Uniform Evidence Act which was introduced into Parliament as a Senate bill. It languished on the order paper, and in the face of opposition from the bar to a comprehensive revision of the rules of evidence there has been virtually no expression of interest in reviving it.

However, the courts have not remained as somnolent as the legislative bodies. They have shown that there still is some vitality in the common law. One can detect a discernible trend emanating from Canadian judicial decisions especially over the last decade. Courts have been prepared to return to basic principles in the examination of whether evidence should be received or not. In certain situations they

---

16   J. Sopinka and S.N. Lederman, *The Law of Evidence in Civil Cases*, Canadian Legal Text Series (Toronto: Butterworths, 1974).
17   [1982] 2 S.C.R. 819, at 835, 2 C.C.C. (3d) 365, at 377, 31 C.R. (3d) 289, 144 D.L.R. (3d) 267, 18 M.V.R. 287, 45 N.R. 451.

have abandoned the application of fixed preconditions as determinative of admissibility and have adopted a principled approach in which the competing policy interests at stake are closely weighed in the context of the circumstances of a particular case. Judges have been assuming a greater discretion in weighing the relevant factors bearing on the question of whether it is safe, or not harmful, to other societal interests to accept certain kinds of evidence. We see this in many areas.

For example: (a) in the area of privilege the courts have made use of the Wigmore principles to determine whether communications made within a particular relationship under particular circumstances should be accorded privilege;[18] (b) courts have carried the Supreme Court of Canada decision in *Ares v. Venner*[19] further, to permit greater elasticity in the admissibility of hearsay evidence of children;[20] (c) the courts have developed pragmatic principles to determine whether certain declarations are against penal interest in such a way as to ensure that they are sufficiently reliable;[21] (d) the courts have introduced more flexibility into the corroboration requirements by eliminating the cumbersome formalism surrounding the law of corroboration and returned it to the basic, common-sense proposition that the evidence of some witnesses should be approached with caution[22] and (e) have emphasized a balancing test for the introduction of evidence of past similar acts evidencing a bad character.[23] The *Charter* has also given the courts the impetus to re-examine previous rulings and develop a more coherent and principled approach to the introduction of evidence which implicates *Charter* rights.

As this introduction has demonstrated, there is something of interest in the law of evidence for every type of lawyer and law student. For those who appreciate the black letter of the law there is a wealth of legal puzzles to solve with the application of specific rules. A working knowledge of the rules of evidence can assist a lawyer in developing sound and creative litigation tactics. For the academic, the

---

18   See Chapter 14. I.
19   [1970] S.C.R. 608, 73 W.W.R. 347, 12 C.R.N.S. 349, 14 D.L.R. (3d) 4; see Chapter 6. II.C.1.(d).
20   See Chapter 6. II.L.
21   See Chapter 6. II.B.2.
22   See Chapter 17. II; *R. v. Vetrovec*, [1982] 1 S.C.R. 811, 27 C.R. (3d) 304, 67 C.C.C. (2d) 1, (*sub nom. Vetrovec v. R.*; *Gaja v. R.*) [1983] 1 W.W.R. 193, 136 D.L.R. (3d) 89.
23   See Chapter 11.

impact of the *Charter* on the law of evidence provides a ripe source for study and commentary. It is our hope that in this text we present the law of evidence in such a way as to accommodate and serve each of these interests.

CHAPTER 2

CONDITIONS FOR THE RECEIPT OF EVIDENCE

I TYPES OF EVIDENCE THAT CAN BE RECEIVED BY THE COURT

While most text writers are agreed that types of admissible evidence may be broken down into three classifications, (1) oral or testimonial evidence, (2) real evidence and (3) documents, there are various ingenious ways of defining the limits of these categories and inventing subclassifications. Although no work on evidence would be complete without an attempt to classify types of admissible evidence, such a classification is of more academic interest than it is of practical value in determining the admissibility of evidence. It appears to the authors that a practical way of classifying types of admissible evidence is to divide the three main categories into the following five: (A) sworn statements, (B) unsworn statements, (C) things, (D) experiments, and (E) documents.

A. *Sworn Statements*

1. General

The most common form in which evidence is produced before the court is the sworn testimony of a witness present in court or who was present at some pre-trial procedure in which the sworn testimony was taken. This, together with the next category of unsworn statements, comprises what is traditionally known as testimonial or oral evidence.

2. Commission Evidence and Examinations *De Bene Esse*

A form of pre-trial sworn statement that deserves some discussion is that taken before trial by a court officer or commissioner.

(a) *In Civil Cases*

The rules of court generally provide for the examination of a witness before an officer of the court or a commissioner appointed by the court prior to a civil trial.[1] The examination which takes place before an officer of the court is known as an examination *de bene esse*. A commissioner is a person named by the court to hear the evidence. Rule 36.01 of the Ontario *Rules of Civil Procedure*[2] sets out the circumstances in which evidence *de bene esse* or before a commissioner can be obtained:

> 36.01 (1) A party who intends to introduce the evidence of a person at trial may, with leave of the court or the consent of the parties, examine the person on oath or affirmation before trial for the purpose of having the person's testimony available to be tendered as evidence at the trial.
>
> (2) In exercising its discretion to order an examination under subrule (1), the court shall take into account,
>
> (a) the convenience of the person whom the party seeks to examine;
>
> (b) the possibility that the person will be unavailable to testify at the trial by reason of death, infirmity or sickness;[3]
>
> (c) the possibility that the person will be beyond the jurisdiction of the court at the time of the trial;[4]

---

1   See, for example, Ontario, *Rules of Civil Procedure*, O. Reg. 560/84, r. 36; Manitoba, *The Queen's Bench Rules,* Man. Reg. 115/86, rr. 241, 245-259; Alberta, *Alberta Rules of Court*, Alta. Reg. 338/83, rr. 270-291, New Brunswick, *Rules of Court*, N.B. Reg. 82-73, r. 53.

2   *Ibid.*

3   *Wright v. Whiteside* (1983), 40 O.R. (2d) 732, 34 C.P.C. 91 (H.C.J.); *Attica Investments Inc. v. Gagnon* (1984), 47 C.P.C. 316 (Ont. Master); *White v. Weston* (1986), 14 C.P.C. (2d) 12 (Ont. H.C.J.).

4   *Union Carbide Canada Ltd. v. Vanderkop* (1974), 6 O.R. (2d) 448 (H.C.J.); *Green v. Spencer*, [1939] O.W.N. 119 (H.C.J.).

(d) the expense of bringing the person to the trial;[5]

(e) whether the witness ought to give evidence in person at the trial;[6] and

(f) any other relevant consideration.

Other jurisdictions simply provide that the court can make the order where justice requires it.[7] The same factors as are expressly set out in Ontario's rule would apply.

Evidence is taken on commission where the witness is outside of the court's jurisdiction and where an examination before an officer of the court is not feasible.[8] If the witness will not attend voluntarily, the court can also issue letters of request.[9]

A transcript of the evidence taken before the court officer or commissioner can be admitted in evidence. A videotape or other form of recording of the examination can also be admitted.[10] The preconditions that must be met for admission of the evidence at the trial depends on the applicable rules of court. The Ontario rules draw a distinction between a party and non-party witness.[11] The evidence of a non-party witness may *prima facie* be used by either party at the trial without proof that the witness is unavailable or not capable of attending the trial. However, the court may require the witness to attend if it finds that the witness ought to give evidence or for any other sufficient reason.[12] On the other hand, leave of the trial judge is required in order to use the *de bene esse* or commission evidence of a witness who is a party.[13] The trial judge's discretion here is wider than

---

5   *Mamarbachi v. Cockshutt Plow Co.*, [1953] O.W.N. 44 (Master); affd. at 52 (H.C.J.); *Robins. v. The Empire Printing and Publishing Co.* (1892), 14 P.R. 488, at 496; *Niewiadomski v. Langdon*, [1956] O.W.N. 762, 6 D.L.R. (2d) 361 (H.C.J.).

6   *Union Carbide Canada Ltd. v. Vandercop et al., supra*, note 4, at 452; *Murray v. Plummer* (1913), 4 W.W.R. 717, at 720, 6 Sask. L.R. 84, 11 D.L.R. 764 (Sask. Q.B.).

7   See, for example, Alberta *Rules of Court, supra*, note 1, r. 270(1).

8   See *Ontario Rules of Civil Procedure, supra*, note 1, r. 36.03.

9   These are a request by one court to the judicial authorities of another court requesting the issuing of such process as is necessary to compel the person to attend and be examined before the commissioner.

10   See, for example, *Wright v. Whiteside, supra*, note 3; *Patterson v. Christie* (1983), 41 O.R. (2d) 145 (H.C.J.).

11   See Ontario *Rules of Civil Procedure, supra*, note 1, r. 36.04.

12   *Ibid.*, r. 36.04(3).

13   *Ibid.*, r. 36.04(4).

his discretion to refuse receipt of the evidence of a non-party. In considering whether to grant such leave the court is to take into account such factors as: (a) whether the party is unavailable to testify by reason of death, infirmity or sickness; (b) whether the person ought to give evidence in person at the trial; and (c) any other relevant consideration.[14] To the trial judge is reserved the right to rule on the admissibility of the witness' answers, notwithstanding that the commissioner has already admitted the evidence.[15] In order to avoid the re-attendance of the witness, it is common practice for the parties to agree that all questions will be answered, subject to the ruling of the trial judge as to their admissibility. The party on whose application the evidence is taken is not required to read the evidence at the trial, but he or she or any other party may do so, in which case the transcript becomes evidence.[16]

(b) In Criminal Cases

Provision for the taking of commission evidence is also made in ss. 709 to 713 of the *Criminal Code*. A party can apply for an order to take evidence on commission where the witness is out of Canada[17] or is not likely to be able to attend the trial by reason of physical disability arising out of illness or some other good and sufficient cause.[18] Section 711 sets out the preconditions for receipt at the trial of the evidence obtained on an examination pursuant to s. 709(a)(i). The party seeking to admit the evidence of a witness must prove, through oral testimony or by affidavit, that the witness is unable to attend by reason of death or physical disability arising out of illness or some other good and sufficient cause. It is also necessary that the evidence be signed by the commissioner. Furthermore, it must be proved to the satisfaction of the court that reasonable notice of the time for taking the evidence was given to the other party and that the accused or the accused's

14 *Ibid.*, r. 36.04(5).
15 *Ibid.*, r. 36.04(6).
16 *Fisher v. C.H.T. Ltd.*, [1965] 2 All E.R. 601, [1965] 1 W.L.R. 1093; on appeal on a different point [1966] 2 Q.B. 475, [1966] 1 All E.R. 88 (C.A.) *Alberta Wheat Pool Elevators Ltd. v. S.S. Ensenada*, [1952] Ex. C.R. 61.
17 *Criminal Code*, R.S.C. 1985, c. C-46, s. 709(b). It would appear that the party also has to show some other valid reason for the witness being unavailable; see *R. v. Kaipiainen* (1953), 107 C.C.C. 377, 17 C.R. 388, [1954] O.R. 43 (Ont. C.A.), and should state in the application that the witness will give material evidence; *Banton v. R.* (1976), 30 C.C.C. (2d) 253 (Ont. H.C.J.).
18 *Ibid.*, *Criminal Code*, s. 709(a).

counsel or the prosecutor, as the case may be, had or might have had the full opportunity to cross-examine the witness. Where the reason for the commission was that the witness was outside of Canada it may be read in (or played in the case of recorded evidence) without meeting these preconditions.[19] The court granting the order can make provisions to enable the accused to be present or represented by counsel. The failure of the accused or accused's counsel to attend will not prevent the reading of the evidence.[20] This provides sufficient protection to the accused so as to make the likelihood of a successful challenge under s. 7 of the *Charter* doubtful.[21] There may be, however, a discretion in the trial judge, exercisable only in rare circumstances, to exclude the deposition when he or she is satisfied that it would be unsafe for a jury to rely upon it. But it must be because of weaknesses arising from factors other than the lack of cross-examination or that it constitutes the only evidence against the accused or that it is in the nature of identification evidence.[22]

Sections 709 to 713 provide a complete code for the taking and receipt of commission evidence in criminal cases.[23] As in civil cases, commission evidence may be videotaped.[24]

3. Discovery Statements

Sworn statements taken on a discovery may be admitted into evidence under the exception to the hearsay rule which allows the receipt of admissions of a party.[25] In certain other circumstances the various rules of court also permit discovery evidence to be read in by either party, even if favourable to the party. For example, the Ontario *Rules of Civil Procedure*[26] grant the trial judge a discretion to allow the evidence to be read in where the person examined has died, is unable

---

19   *Ibid.*, *Criminal Code*, s. 712(2).
20   *Ibid.*, *Criminal Code*, s. 713(1).
21   P.K. McWilliams, *Canadian Criminal Evidence*, 3rd ed. (Toronto: Canada Law Book, 1988). Refer to pp. 8-84 and 8-85.
22   *R. v. Barnes* (1989), 112 N.R. 49 (P.C.), at 55-57.
23   *R. v. Lester* (1971), 6 C.C.C. (2d) 227, [1972] O.R. 330 (Ont. C.A.); *R. v. Solomon* (1958), 28 C.R. 314, 25 W.W.R. 307 (Man. C.A.); *R. v. Keystone Fisheries Ltd.* (1955), 113 C.C.C. 79, 21 C.R. 206, 15 W.W.R. 307, 63 Man. R. 196 (Man. Q.B.); affd. 113 C.C.C. 391, 23 C.R. 180, 17 W.W.R. 255, 63 Man. R. 540 (C.A.).
24   *R. v. Pawliw* (1984), 13 W.C.B. 200 (B.C.S.C.).
25   See a detailed discussion of the admissibility of admissions in Chapter 6. II.K.
26   O. Reg. 560/84, r. 31.11(6)(7).

to testify because of infirmity or illness, or for any other reason cannot be compelled to attend at the trial or refuses to take an oath or affirmation or to answer any proper question.[27]

4. Affidavits

In exceptional circumstances, the trial judge may permit facts to be proved by affidavit evidence. The applicable rules of court may provide for the admission of affidavits. Various legislative provisions may permit evidence in particular proceedings to be in affidavit form.

B. *Unsworn Statements*

At common law, only persons who could swear an oath were permitted to testify. This restriction was altered by statutory enactments, contained in most provincial Evidence Acts and in the *Canada Evidence Act*, which permit young children who do not understand the nature of an oath or affirmation to give unsworn testimony before the court.[28] Unless specifically authorized by statute, unsworn evidence may not be received by the court.

Unsworn statements, either oral or in writing, made out of court are often received in evidence. Such statements will be admitted if they fall within an exception to the hearsay rule.[29] When admissible, the making of the statements must be proved by the ordinary means.

C. *Real Evidence*

1. Things

(a) *General*

Sworn and unsworn statements, lead to proof of facts either directly or indirectly by inference. The court may accept the statements with respect to the facts stated and may draw inferences as to further facts. When things are produced before the court, the court applies its own senses and draws conclusions. The classification commonly used is "real evidence". The classification has been criticized as

---

27 See also New Brunswick, *Rules of Court*, N.B. Reg. 82-73, r. 32.11.
28 R.S.C. 1985, c. C-5. The giving of unsworn testimony by children is discussed in Chapter 13. II.D.4.(b).
29 The admission of hearsay evidence is discussed in Chapter 6.

being both indefinite and ambiguous.[30] The term is used in a number of different ways, but in its widest meaning includes any evidence where the court acts as a witness, using its own senses to make observations and draw conclusions rather than relying on the testimony of a witness. In this sense, it includes not only the production of articles before the court, but the observation by the court of the demeanour of a witness in the witness-box, the viewing of a motion picture and taking a view.

Real evidence (also referred to as demonstrative evidence) cannot be produced before a court without prior testimonial evidence, or at least an admission, in order to establish the identity of the thing. The level of authentication required for admitting real evidence is relatively low.[31] Once the evidence has been admitted, it is for the trier of fact to determine what weight to give it.

For obvious reasons, real evidence will often be more effective than *viva voce* evidence. Although testimony is needed to connect it to the issues at trial, real evidence appeals directly to the trier of fact without passing through the intermediary of a witness. Because of this advantage, it seems the use of real evidence is on the increase. As stated in *McCormick on Evidence*:[32]

> Since 'seeing is believing,' and demonstrative evidence appeals directly to the senses of the trier of fact, it is today universally felt that this kind of evidence possesses an immediacy and reality which endow it with particularly persuasive effect. Largely as a result of this potential, the use of demonstrative evidence of all types has increased dramatically during recent years, and the trend seems certain to continue in the immediate future.

Nonetheless, despite this trend, it should be remembered that real evidence presents several inherent difficulties. Among the most significant are: (i) practical problems associated with bringing objects into a courtroom, (ii) the fact that real evidence cannot be fully recorded in a transcript for appellate purposes, and (iii) the possibility

---

30 J.H. Buzzard et al., *Phipson on Evidence* (11th ed.) (London: Sweet & Maxwell Ltd., 1970), at 3.
31 See *Staniforth v. R.* (1979), 11 C.R. (3d) 84 (Ont. C.A.), at 89.
32 E.W. Cleary (ed.), *McCormick on Evidence*, 3rd ed., (St. Paul: West Publishing, 1984), at 664.

that the evidence has undergone some change since the time of the events at issue.

The case law regarding the introduction of things as evidence presents relatively few complexities. The jurisprudence on other types of real evidence is less straightforward, and is most fruitfully discussed under several headings.

(b) Photographs[33]

The usefulness of photographs as evidence is indisputable. As the Nova Scotia Supreme Court's Appellate Division has put it:[34]

A photograph can often more clearly and accurately portray or describe persons, places or things than a witness can by oral evidence. They are not subject to the difficulty inherent in oral evidence of absorbing and relating the mass of detail and then remembering it.

A widely accepted statement of the requirements for admitting photographs comes from an earlier decision of the same court. In *R. v. Creemer*,[35] the court derived from previous jurisprudence three essential criteria for admissibility: (i) accuracy in representing the facts; (ii) fairness and absence of any intention to mislead; and (iii) verification on oath by a person capable of doing so.

(c) Videotape

These same three criteria have been adopted with regard to videotape evidence.[36] However, there have been cases in which certain videotape passages were found inadmissible because of the manner in

---

33   See B.A. MacFarlane, "Photographic Evidence: Its Probative Value at Trial and the Judicial Discretion to Exclude it from Evidence" (1973-74), 16 C.L.Q. 149.

34   *R. v. Smith* (1986), 71 N.S.R. (2d) 229, 171 A.P.R. 229 (N.S.C.A.), at 237 (N.S.R.).

35   [1968] 1 C.C.C. 14, 1 C.R.N.S. 146, 53 M.P.R. 1 (N.S.C.A.); see *Annotation* (1967), 1 C.R.N.S. 167.

36   *R. v. Maloney (No. 2)* (1976), 29 C.C.C. (2d) 431 (Ont. Co. Ct.); *R. v. Williams* (1977), 35 C.C.C. (2d) 103 (Ont. Co. Ct.) where it was noted that the playing of a tape in slow motion is not a true and accurate reproduction of the event as witnessed. See also *Army & Navy Department Store (Western) Ltd. v. Retail Wholesale & Department Store Union, Loc. No. 535* (1950), 97 C.C.C. 258, [1950] 2 D.L.R. 850, [1950] 2 W.W.R. 999 (B.C.S.C.).

which they were edited, the fact that they were in slow motion, or other similar reasons.[37] It is not necessary that an individual actually have operated the videocamera and have seen the recorded events in order for the tape to be admissible. All that is required is some evidence to support the authenticity of the film.[38]

One British court has gone so far as to admit evidence from witnesses who had observed an offence on a videotape which was accidentally destroyed prior to trial.[39] The court held that the witness' evidence was not inadmissible as hearsay, stating that a video recording is merely an aid to a witness' perception. This suggests that videotape is not in itself evidence from which the trier of fact can draw his or her own inferences, but is only support for a witness' testimony. However, other decisions suggest this issue is open to question.[40]

(d) *Audiotape*

The hearsay issue is more difficult with respect to audio recordings. In *R. v. Pleich*,[41] for example, the Ontario Court of Appeal held that taped conversations between an accused and other persons should be treated much like testimony from a witness who had overheard a conversation and made accurate notes. Thus, unlike *Taylor v. Chief Constable of Cheshire*,[42] the court analogized the recording device to a human witness, and did not treat it merely as a technical aid. Therefore, the court held:[43]

---

37   See, for example, *R. v. Maloney (No. 2), ibid.* For a fuller consideration of cases considering photographic and videotape evidence, see Goldstein, "Photographic and Videotape Evidence in the Criminal Courts of England and Canada", [1987] Crim. L.R. 384.

38   *Greenough v. Woodstream Corp.*, unreported, January 17, 1991, Fleury J. (Ont. Ct. [Gen. Div.]) where the sole proof of an employee's theft of company property was film from a concealed surveillance camera; but see *Simpson Timber Co. (Sask.) Ltd. v. Bonville*, [1986] 5 W.W.R. 180 (Sask. Q.B.).

39   *Taylor v. Chief Constable of Cheshire*, [1987] 1 All E.R. 225, [1986] 1 W.L.R. 1479 (Q.B.).

40   See, for example, *Simpson Timber Co. (Sask.) Ltd. v. Bonville, supra*, note 38, in which the court treated videotape evidence as "illustrated testimony", but raised the possibility that, in other circumstances, it might be considered "a silent witness which 'speaks for itself' or as probative evidence of what it shows."

41   (1980), 16 C.R. (3d) 194, 55 C.C.C. (2d) 13 (Ont. C.A.).

42   *Supra*, note 39.

43   *Supra*, note 41, at 217 (C.R.).

[t]he accused's statements, to the extent that they are against his interest, are admissible against him as admissions. The statements of the other party to the conversation are not, on their own, admissible against him as evidence of the truth of the facts contained in them.

In the criminal context, there are statutory provisions governing the authorization of "intercepted private communications" and their subsequent admissibility as evidence.[44] At trial, the admissibility of such evidence is properly determined in a *voir dire*. However, the *voir dire* is only for purposes of considering the conditions precedent to admissibility, not for the trier of fact to hear and weigh the entire evidence.[45]

2. Taking a View

In both civil and criminal cases, the court has a discretion to take a view, or to order a jury to do so.[46] Here again, the issue arises as to whether a view is evidence which can form the basis of inferences by the trier of fact,[47] or is simply clarification of a witness' testimony.[48] The answer to this question varies according to jurisdiction.[49]

---

44 See, in particular, s. 189 of the *Criminal Code*, R.S.C. 1985, c. C-46. And see Chapter 9. IV.A.1.

45 *R. v. Parsons* (1977), 37 C.C.C. (2d) 497, 40 C.R.N.S. 202, 17 O.R. (2d) 465, 80 D.L.R. (3d) 430, 33 N.R. 161 (Ont. C.A.), affd. (*sub nom. Charette v. R.*), [1980] 1 S.C.R. 785, 51 C.C.C. (2d) 350, 14 C.R. (3d) 191, 33 N.R. 158, 110 D.L.R. (3d) 71 (S.C.C.).

46 In the criminal context, this authority is found in s. 652 of the *Criminal Code*, *supra*, note 44. In civil cases, the authority is granted in provincial rules of civil procedure.

47 In Manitoba and Alberta the trier of fact is entitled to base findings of fact on such observations. See *Meyers v. Man.* (1960), 26 D.L.R. (2d) 550, 33 W.W.R. 461 (Man. C.A.); *G & J Parking Lot Maintenance Ltd. v. Oland Construction Co.* (1978), 16 A.R. 293, at 297 (T.D.).

48 In Ontario, Saskatchewan, New Brunswick and Newfoundland this is the case. See *Swadron v. North York* (1985), 8 O.A.C. 204 (Div. Ct.); *Paul v. Fadden*, [1953] O.W.N. 306 (C.A.); *Triple A Invts. Ltd. v. Adams Bros. Ltd.* (1985), 23 D.L.R. (4th) 587, at 594, 56 Nfld. & P.E.I.R. 272, at 277, 168 A.P.R. 272, at 277 (Nfld. C.A.), *Sederquest v. Ryan* (1939), 14 M.P.R. 64, [1939] 4 D.L.R. 52 (N.B.C.A.); *Sunnyside Nursing Home v. Builders Contract Mgmt. Ltd.*, [1985] 4 W.W.R. 97, 40 Sask. R. 1, 15 C.L.R. 1 (Q.B.).

49 See cases cited at notes 47 and 48. For a discussion of U.S. jurisdictions, see *McCormick on Evidence*, *supra*, note 32, at 680.

3. Appearance or Demeanour of a Person

Particularly in criminal cases, the appearance of a person can constitute important evidence. Physical characteristics such as strength, height, or left-handedness, for example, may be helpful in determining whether an accused committed, or was even capable of committing, a particular crime. It seems that the court has wide discretion to order or deny physical displays.[50]

In civil cases involving personal injuries, it may be instructive for a plaintiff to display injuries (or photographs of them) to the trier of fact. However, this raises a difficult problem of balancing the probative value of the evidence against possible prejudicial effect due to the provocative nature of the evidence.[51]

The Supreme Court of Canada has considered whether forcing an accused to participate in a police line-up for identification is a violation of the right against self-incrimination. The court held that it was not, and went on to state that an accused may equally be obliged to show his features in court.[52]

It is also noteworthy that certain commentators consider the demeanour of a witness during testimony to be a form of "real evidence".[53]

D. *Experiments*

This type of evidence is a combination of sworn statements and the production of things. If the experiment is conducted outside the

---

50   See, for example, *R. v. Ashby*, unreported, October 18, 1988 (B.C.C.A.), in which a crucial issue was the exact manner in which a physical struggle could have taken place. The appellate court upheld the lower court's refusal to order the victim to display the exact location of a stab wound. But, it also upheld the judge's decision to allow a demonstration of the "sleeper hold" which the victim had applied to the accused.

51   The considerable jurisprudence on this point is discussed in II.C.2, under the heading and in more detail in J. Sopinka and S.N. Lederman, *The Law of Evidence in Civil Cases*, Canadian Legal Text Series (Toronto: Butterworths, 1974), at 348 and following.

52   *Marcoux v. R.*, [1976] 1 S.C.R. 763, 24 C.C.C. (2d) 1, 29 C.R.N.S. 211, 60 D.L.R. (3d) 119, 4 N.R. 64; But see more recently *R. v. Ross*, [1989] 1 S.C.R. 3, 46 C.C.C. (3d) 129 (*sub nom. R. v. LeClair*) 67 C.R. (3d) 209, 91 N.R. 81, 37 C.R.R. 369, 31 O.A.C. 321.

53   See, for example, R. Cross and C. Tapper, *Cross on Evidence*, 7th ed. (London: Butterworth & Co., 1990), at 47.

courtroom and merely described, then it falls entirely within the classification of "sworn statements".[54] When conducted in court, it involves the production of things and their manipulation by a witness who is usually an expert. The expert describes to the court what is taking place and the results. The court, however, is free to draw its own conclusions.[55] Generally, in court demonstrations will only be permitted in rare circumstances. The discretion to permit them rests with the trial judge.[56]

E. Documents

A document may be introduced into evidence merely to prove its existence, or to prove that it was in the possession of some person, in which case it is material in itself irrespective of its contents. When so introduced, it falls within the category of "things". When a document is introduced to prove its contents, it merits a separate classification.[57] Although, in many cases, a document does not differ materially from an unsworn statement in that it is introduced as an assertion of fact under an appropriate exception to the rule that prohibits the introduction of hearsay evidence, in other cases it has special characteristics which do not fit within any of the other categories. It may be a photograph. It may be evidence of a transaction, as for instance a written contract, deed or share certificate in which case it is admissible as original evidence quite apart from any exception to the hearsay rule.

Under special statutory provisions documents may be introduced without the aid of other evidence. In the absence, however, of such special provisions for the introduction of a document without

---

54   See, for instance *Kirkpatrick v. Lament*, [1965] S.C.R. 538, [1961] 1 C.C.C. 30, 51 D.L.R. (2d) 699.

55   *Re McPherson, Trusts & Guar. Co. v. Bradford*, [1930] 3 D.L.R. 378, at 383, affd. [1930] 4 D.L.R. 915 (Alta. C.A.); *Hanington v. Harshmen* (1873), Stevens N.D. Dig. 649, N.B. Dig. 1086; *Eastern Twps. Invt. Co. v. McLennan* (1919), 29 B.C.R. 1 (C.A.); *Anaconda Oil Co. v. Aladdin Oils Ltd.*, [1930] 3 D.L.R. 776, [1930] 1 W.W.R. 943 (Alta. T.D.); *Bigsby v. Dickinson* (1867), 4 Ch. D. 24, 46 L.J. Ch. 280 (C.A.); *Buckingham v. Daily News Ltd.*, [1956] 2 Q.B. 534, [1956] 2 All E.R. 904 (C.A.).

56   *R. v. Howard* (1983), 3 C.C.C. (3d) 399 (Ont. C.A.) where the Court of Appeal disagreed with but upheld, the lower court's refusal to allow a witness to take a plasticine impression of a shoe heel in court.

57   The subject of the admissibility of documents to prove the contents is discussed in Chapter 18.

proof of its identity, it, like things, can only be introduced into evidence with the assistance of other evidence.

II CONDITIONS FOR THE RECEIPT OF EVIDENCE

A. *General*

A piece of evidence must satisfy a number of requirements before it can be considered by the trier of fact in the ultimate deliberation on the facts in issue in a civil or criminal proceeding. Once it meets these requirements, the evidence can be received by the court. To be received evidence must meet two basic requirements. First, it must be *admissible*. Second, the trier of law must not have exercised his or her *judicial discretion* to exclude the evidence. Two further concepts make up the principle of admissibility. Evidence is not admissible unless it is: (1) *relevant*; and (2) not subject to exclusion under any other clear rule of law or policy.[58] Therefore, the trier of law in determining whether a particular piece of evidence should be considered by the trier of fact will first consider whether it is relevant. If it is not, then it will be rejected.[59] If it is relevant, then the trier of law will consider whether it is subject to any exclusionary rule of the law of evidence. If it is not, then the trier of law will go on to consider whether he or she has a judicial discretion to reject the evidence and whether that discretion should be exercised in the circumstances. If the evidence is subject to an exclusionary rule or is irrelevant, there is no generally recognized judicial discretion to nevertheless receive the evidence.[60]

---

58 *R. v. Morris*, [1983] 2 S.C.R. 190, 7 C.C.C. (3d) 97, 36 C.R. (3d) 1, 48 N.R. 341, 1 D.L.R. (4th) 385, per Lamer J., at 201, S.C.R. The distinction between the concepts of relevance and the application of evidentiary exclusionary rules is noted in *R. v. Zeolkowski*, [1989] 1 S.C.R. 1378, 50 C.C.C. (3d) 566, 69 C.R. (3d) 281, 61 D.L.R. (4th) 725, [1989] 4 W.W.R. 385, 58 Man. R. (2d) 63, 95 N.R. 149 per Sopinka J., at 1386 (S.C.R.).

59 1 Wigmore, *Evidence* (Tillers rev. 1983), § 9, at 655.

60 *Savard v. R.*, [1946] S.C.R. 20, 85 C.C.C. 254, 1 C.R. 105, [1946] 3 D.L.R. 468. However, inadmissible portions of documents might be admitted along with the admissible portion, but the trier of fact must not act on the inadmissible portion: see *R. v. Bandura* (1933), 61 C.C.C. 15, [1934] 1 D.L.R. 595, [1933] 3 W.W.R. 544 (Alta. C.A.). Although the possibility of the discretionary admission of hearsay evidence was discussed in *Ares v. Venner*, [1970] S.C.R. 608, 12 C.R.N.S. 349, 14 D.L.R. (3d) 4, 73 W.W.R. 347.

The application of the exclusionary rules which make up the second branch of the admissibility test constitute a large part of the law of evidence and are discussed throughout Section II of this text. The concepts of relevance and judicial discretion require some further explanation at this stage.

B. *Relevance*

1. Definitions

A traditionally accepted definition of relevance is that in Sir J.F. Stephen's *A Digest of the Law of Evidence*,[61] where it is defined to mean:

> . . . any two facts to which it is applied are so related to each other that according to the common course of events one either taken by itself or in connection with other facts proves or renders probable the past, present, or future existence or non-existence of the other.

Pratte J. in *R. v. Cloutier*[62] accepted a definition from an early edition of *Cross on Evidence*:[63]

> For one fact to be relevant to another, there must be a connection or nexus between the two which makes it possible to infer the existence of one from the existence of the other. One fact is not relevant to another if it does not have real probative value with respect to the latter.

Although the question of relevance, and admissibility generally, is one for the judge as the trier of law, whether a fact bears the required relationship to another fact is not usually determined by the application of a legal test. It has been said that it is an exercise in the application of experience and common sense.[64] Thayer believed that logic (not the logic of deductive reasoning, but of knowledge and

---

61 (12th ed.), Art. 1 (London: Macmillan & Co. Ltd., 1907).
62 [1979] 2 S.C.R. 709, 48 C.C.C. (2d) 1, 12 C.R. (3d) 10, 99 D.L.R. (3d) 577.
63 *Ibid.*, at 731 (S.C.R.), from *Cross on Evidence*, 4th ed. at 16, see also *R. v. Morris*, *supra*, note 58 and this Chapter, II.B.4.
64 17 *Halsbury's Laws of England*, 4th ed., (London: Butterworths, 1976) at 7, § 5; P.K. McWilliams, *Canadian Criminal Evidence*, 3rd ed. (Toronto: Canada Law Book, 1988), at 3-2.

experience) provided the best guide to the application of this fundamental principle of evidence law.[65]

2. Facts in Issue

The first step in determining what is relevant is to identify the
facts that are in issue in the case. It is the substantive law relating to
the particular charge or cause of action that forms the basis for this
identification exercise. So, in a civil action for negligent misrepresentation, the plaintiff may first have to prove that a representation was
made, that it was false, that it was relied on to the detriment of the
plaintiff, that the defendant was negligent in making the statement and
that damage was suffered. Not every fact may be in issue. For example,
the defendant might admit that the representation was made and that
it was false, dispensing with the need for proof on those issues and
rendering any evidence on those issues irrelevant.[66] The defendant
may still deny that he was negligent in making it or that the plaintiff
relied on it, therefore defining the scope of the facts that are in issue.
In a criminal case the relevance of evidence has to be determined in
reference to all the issues which have to be established by the prosecution for the particular offence charged and any defences raised by
the defence.[67]

Direct or circumstantial evidence of the facts in issue is relevant.[68] Therefore, in the misrepresentation example, evidence given
by the plaintiff's spouse to the effect that the plaintiff admitted
knowledge of the falsity of the statement prior to the purported acts
of reliance would be direct evidence relevant to reliance as a fact in
issue.[69] On the other hand, if the action was based on a false statement
in a prospectus, testimony from the plaintiff's business partner that the
plaintiff admitted that he never reads prospectuses before purchasing
would be circumstantial evidence on the issue of reliance.

---

65   J.B. Thayer, "Presumptions and the Law of Evidence" (1889), 3 Harv. L.R.
141, at 143, and J.B. Thayer, *A Preliminary Treatise on the Law of Evidence at
Common Law*, reprint of 1898 ed. (New York: Augustus M. Kelley Publishers,
1969), at 264-65.
66   See Chapter 19, I.
67   *Perkins v. Jeffery*, [1915] 2 K.B. 702, 84 L.J.K.B. 1554 at 707, K.B.; *Harris
v. D.P.P.*, [1952] A.C. 694, [1952] 2 All E.R. 1044 (H.L.).
68   As to the distinction between direct and circumstantial evidence see this
Chapter, II.D.
69   *Dickey v. C.N.R.*, [1921] 1 W.W.R. 1196, 58 D.L.R. 528 (Alta. C.A.).

A fact will be relevant not only where it relates directly to the fact in issue, but also where it proves or renders probable the past, present or future existence (or non-existence) of any fact in issue.[70] Facts relating to the credibility of the witness giving direct or circumstantial evidence of a fact in issue are relevant.[71] A fact that proves the existence or tends to prove the existence of a pre-condition to the admissibility of a piece of evidence, such as the voluntariness of a confession, the authenticity of a signature on a document or the statutory conditions for a legal wiretap is equally relevant. If no such relationship exists between the evidence offered and any one or more facts in issue the evidence is excluded as irrelevant.

In a civil case the facts in issue are established by the pleadings. Although any detailed discussion of the function of pleadings properly belongs in writings on practice and procedure, a brief mention should be made of the role of pleadings in controlling the admissibility of evidence.

While, in practice, much latitude is allowed, especially in cases tried by judges alone, nevertheless evidence which is completely unrelated to the issues as disclosed in the pleadings will be rejected. An exception is made in divorce cases and in other cases where the interests of the public are concerned. In these cases the courts have, in their discretion, allowed evidence of condonation, connivance or collusion even though not pleaded. This exception does not apply to an alimony action since only the rights of the parties are involved.[72]

Unnecessary or immaterial allegations in the pleadings cannot, however, make evidence relevant that is not.[73]

3. Relevance Distinguished from Exclusionary Rules

The exclusionary rules that make up the bulk of the law of evidence reflect many different policies. Some of the rules are con-

---

70 *Clark v. Stevenson* (1865), 24 U.C.Q.B. 200 (C.A.); *R. v. Perry* (1945), 84 C.C.C. 323, [1945] 4 D.L.R. 762, 18 M.P.R. 144 (P.E.I. C.A.); *R. v. Stawycznuj* (1933), 60 C.C.C. 153, [1933] 4 D.L.R. 725, [1933] 2 W.W.R. 495, 41 Man. R. 281 (Man. C.A.).
71 Although they may still be inadmissible if obnoxious to an exclusionary rule, such as the collateral fact rule (see Chapter 16, VIII.B.).
72 *Macdougall v. Macdougall* (1971), 13 D.L.R. (3d) 696, [1970] 3 O.R. 680, 3 R.F.L. 175 (C.A.).
73 *Larson v. Boyd* (1919), 58 S.C.R. 275, 46 D.L.R. 126, [1919] 1 W.W.R. 808; *Kelly v. Dow* (1860), 9 N.B.R. 435 (C.A.).

cerned with the fear of fabrication (for example, the hearsay rule and its exceptions and the rule that prohibits the receipt of self-serving evidence). Others are concerned with the efficiency of the trial process reflected through the desire to avoid a multiplicity of issues (for example, the collateral fact rule).[74]

Desire to avoid undue prejudice to an accused and so promote the fairness of criminal trials forms at least part of the basis of such rules as exclusion of disposition or bad character evidence and the privilege against self-incrimination. Protection of the broader public interest is the basis of the recognized privilege for solicitor–client communications, communications in furtherance of settlement and Crown claims for immunity from disclosure of information. These policies are all distinct from those that form the basis for the exclusion of evidence which is not relevant. Irrelevant evidence can be of no assistance to the trier of fact. It is, by definition, not "evidence".

Cases applying the exclusionary rules relating to evidence of an accused's bad character illustrate the difficulty that judges occasionally have in distinguishing inadmissibility based on the application of an exclusionary rule and inadmissibility based on irrelevance to any fact in issue. On occasions too numerous to mention the courts have purported to exclude evidence of an accused's bad character because of its irrelevance to the charge.[75] Generally, exclusion of such evidence is based on grounds of policy, not lack of relevance, although it is certainly possible for evidence of this type to be irrelevant. The exclusionary rule for this type of evidence allows its admission if its probative value, or degree of relevance, exceeds its prejudicial effect. Justice Lamer explained the relationship between this exclusionary rule and the concept of relevance in *R. v. Morris*[76] as follows:

---

74 See Chapter 1. Although some courts seem to exclude certain facts which they categorize as "collateral" (although not in the same sense as they are categorized for the purpose of applying the "collateral fact rule") on the basis that they are irrelevant: see *Folkes v. Chadd* (1782), 3 Doug. 157, 99 E.R. 589 (K.B.); *Babcock v. C.P.R.* (1916), 9 W.W.R. 1484, 9 Alta. L.R. 270, 27 D.L.R. 432 (C.A.); *Peacock v. Cooper* (1900), 27 O.A.R. 128 (Ont. C.A.); *Edwards v. The Ottawa River Navigation Co.* (1876), 39 U.C.Q.B. 264 (C.A.); *Metropolitan Asylum District v. Hill* (1882), 47 L.T. 29, 47 J.P. 148 (H.L.).
75 *The Law of Evidence in Civil Cases, supra*, note 51, dealt with the subject of similar fact evidence under the heading of relevance. For one example, see *R. v. Cloutier, supra*, note 62.
76 *Supra*, note 58, at 203 (S.C.R.). Although Lamer J. gave the dissenting

25

Disposition the nature of which is of no relevance to the crime committed has no probative value and as such is as any other fact irrelevant and for that reason excluded. But if relevant to the crime, even though there is nothing else connecting the accused to that crime, it is of some probative value, be it slight, and it should be excluded as inadmissible not as irrelevant. The fact that there is little or even no other evidence connecting the accused to the crime does not diminish the intrinsic probative value proof of disposition would have in the case, but gives "more power" to "its prejudicial effect" were it not to be excluded; it is no less relevant; it is only all the more inadmissible.

Facts which tend to prove a fact which is inadmissible as being within an exclusionary rule, could be legitimately viewed either as being irrelevant (since the logical connection to the facts in issue is broken) or themselves within the exclusionary rule.[77]

4. Relevance Distinguished from Weight

There are no degrees of relevance recognized in Canadian law.[78] Such an idea was put to rest in *R. v. Morris*.[79] A review of the facts of that case is instructive. The accused was charged with trafficking in heroin imported from Hong Kong. A search of the accused's premises disclosed a clipped article on the subject of sources of supply of heroin in Pakistan. At issue was the admissibility of this article.[80] McIntyre J. for the majority held that this was admissible circumstantial evidence. He stated that:[81]

> . . . an inference could be drawn from the unexplained presence of the newspaper clipping among the possessions of the appellant, that he had an interest in and had informed himself on the question of sources of supply of heroin, necessarily a subject

---

judgment in this case, McIntyre J., giving the majority judgment, agreed with Lamer J.'s discussion of relevance.

77   Lamer J. seems to prefer the direct application of the exclusionary rule.

78   As to the English position that the evidence must be "sufficiently relevant", see R. Cross and C. Tapper, *Cross on Evidence*, 7th ed. (London: Butterworths, 1990), at 51.

79   *Supra*, note 58.

80   Distinguish these facts from those in issue in *R. v. Cloutier*, *supra*, note 62.

81   *R. v. Morris*, *supra*, note 58, at 191 (S.C.R.).

of vital interest to one concerned with the importing of the narcotic.

Although McIntyre J. agreed that the probative value of this evidence was low, it was an error for the judge to confuse relevance with weight. His Lordship noted that if the article had been on sources of heroin supply in Hong Kong it would have had greater weight and if it had been a step by step guide to importing heroin its weight would have been greater still. Yet the clipping was nevertheless still relevant evidence and it should have been put before the trier of fact.[82] The trier of law determines if the evidence is relevant. The trier of fact determines what, if any, weight is to be given to it. Obviously, where the judge is the trier of both fact and law the distinction becomes blurred and the weight to be given the evidence becomes the paramount consideration. Without relevance the evidence can have no weight.

5. Relevance Distinguished from Materiality

A distinction has also been drawn between relevance and materiality.[83] Evidence is material in this sense if it is offered to prove or disprove a fact in issue.[84] For example, evidence offered by a plaintiff in a conversion action to prove a loss of profit is not material since loss of profits cannot be recovered in such an action[85] and evidence that an accused charged with forceable entry is the owner of the land is immaterial since the offence can be committed by an owner.[86] This evidence may very well be immaterial, but it is also simply irrelevant. This excluded evidence is no more required to make out the case than is evidence that the accused owns three other properties or owns a black dog for that matter. There is no probative connection between the fact to be proved and the facts in issue as determined by the substantive law. Little is added to the analysis by adding a concept of materiality as different results do not depend on the distinction.[87]

---

82   See also *Ferris v. Monahan* (1956), 4 D.L.R. (2d) 539 (N.B.C.A.).
83   See for example, 11 C.E.D. Ont. (3rd ed.) Title 57, para 11.
84   As defined in this Chapter, II.B.2.
85   *Tyson v. Little* (1852), 8 U.C.Q.B. 434 (C.A.).
86   *R. v. Cokely* (1856), 13 U.C.Q.B. 521 (C.A.). See also *Daly v. Leamy* (1856), 5 U.C.C.P 374 (C.A.).
87   *Cross on Evidence, supra,* note 78, at 61.

6. Conditional Relevance

At the time that evidence is offered by a party its relevance might not yet be established. Relevance hinges on the relationship between facts,[88] yet the order in which those facts are presented to the court does not necessarily reflect the logical order. The practice is for the court to receive the evidence on an undertaking that relevance will be established later. This is a matter within the judge's discretion.[89] If such evidence is not subsequently offered, then the evidence which was received earlier is to be disregarded by the trier of fact. In a criminal trial the judge should direct the jury to this effect[90] or, if appropriate, declare a mistrial.[91]

C. *Exercise of Judicial Discretion*

The trial judge may determine that the evidence offered is relevant and not subject to any exclusionary rule, yet determine through the exercise of judicial discretion that it should not be considered by the trier of fact.

1. Judicial Discretion in Criminal Cases

(a) *In Favour of the Accused*

The scope of the trial judge's discretion to exclude relevant evidence in a criminal prosecution depends upon the effect the reception of the evidence would have on the fairness of the trial and not on the manner in which the evidence was collected.[92] The scope of the

---

88   *R. v. Morin*, [1988] 2 S.C.R. 345, at 370, 44 C.C.C. (3d) 193, 66 C.R. (3d) 1, 88 N.R. 161, 30 O.A.C. 81.

89   *Davidson v. R.* (1876), 16 N.B.R. 396 (C.A.); *R. v. Hawkes* (1915), 25 C.C.C. 29, 25 D.L.R. 631, 9 W.W.R. 445, 32 W.L.R. 720, 9 Alta. L.R. 182 (C.A.); *Brownell v. Brownell* (1909), 42 S.C.R. 368; *Paradis v. R.*, [1934] S.C.R. 165, 61 C.C.C. 184, [1934] 2 D.L.R. 88.

90   *R. v. Dass* (1979), 8 C.R. (3d) 224, at 234 (C.A.); leave to appeal to S.C.C. refd. [1979] 2 S.C.R. vii, 30 N.R. 609*n*.

91   *R. v. Ducsharm* (1955), 113 C.C.C. 1, 22 C.R. 129, 1 D.L.R. (2d) 732, [1955] O.R. 824 (Ont. C.A.). And see generally *Paradis v. R., supra*, note 89; *R. v. Harrison* (1946), 86 C.C.C. 166, [1946] 3 D.L.R. 690, 62 B.C.R. 420 (B.C.C.A.); *R. v. Hurd* (1913), 21 C.C.C. 98, 10 D.L.R. 475, 4 W.W.R. 185, 6 Alta. L.R. 112 (C.A.).

92   However, evidence obtained as a consequence of the violation of a *Charter* right may be excluded as a remedy granted pursuant to s. 24(2) of the *Charter* if its admission would bring the administration of justice into disrepute. This aspect

residual discretion was described by Martland J., speaking for a majority of the Supreme Court of Canada in *R. v. Wray*.[93] The issue considered in *Wray* was whether the trial judge had a discretion to reject evidence even if it was admissible and of significant weight, if he or she considered that the admission would be unjust or unfair to the accused or calculated to bring the administration of justice into disrepute. The Court rejected the notion that there was any discretion to exclude relevant evidence that could bring the administration of justice into disrepute.[94] A discretion to exclude admissible evidence if its admission operates unfairly to the accused was recognized, but the scope of that discretion was in issue. It was argued by counsel for the accused[95] that the trial judge should exclude evidence if its prejudicial effect outweighed its probative value. Martland J. responded to the argument as follows:[96]

> This development of the idea of a general discretion to exclude admissible evidence is not warranted by the authority on which it purports to be based. The dictum of Lord Goddard in the *Kurama* case, appears to be founded on *Noor Mohamed*,[97] and it has, I think, been unduly extended in some of the subsequent cases. It recognized a discretion to disallow evidence if the strict rules of admissibility would operate unfairly against the accused. Even if this statement be accepted in the way in which it is phrased, the exercise of a discretion by the trial judge arises only if the admission of the evidence would operate unfairly. The allowance of admissible evidence relevant to the issue before the court and of substantial probative value may operate unfortunately for the accused, but not unfairly. It is only the allowance of evidence gravely prejudicial to the accused, the admissibility of which is tenuous, and whose probative force in relation to the

of the exclusion of evidence is discussed in Chapter 9. II.

93   [1971] S.C.R. 272, [1970] 4 C.C.C. 1, 11 C.R.N.S. 235, 11 D.L.R. (3d) 673.
94   For an early case holding that such a discretion existed see *R. v. Archer* (1963), 41 C.R. 344, 43 W.W.R. 43 (B.C. Magistrate's Court).
95   Based on *Kuruma, Son of Kaniu v. R.*, [1955] A.C. 197 at 203, [1955] 1 All E.R. 236, at 238 (P.C.); *Callis v. Gunn*, [1964] 1 Q.B. 495, [1963] 3 All E.R. 677; *R. v. Court*, [1962] Crim. L.R. 697 (C.A.); *R. v. Payne*, [1963] 1 W.L.R. 637; and *Rumping v. D.P.P.*, [1962] Cr. App. Rep. 398, at 403, 3 All E.R. 256.
96   *R. v. Wray, supra*, note 93, at 293 (S.C.R.).
97   *Noor Mohamed v. R.*, [1949] A.C. 182.

main issue before the court is trifling, which can be said to operate unfairly.

The scope of the discretion recognized by this *obiter dictum* in *Wray* is very narrow indeed.

Subsequent to the decision in *Wray* the House of Lords considered the issue of the scope of this judicial discretion in *R. v. Sang*.[98] Their Lordships explained that the judicial discretion recognized at common law permitted the trial judge to exclude evidence where its probative effect would be out of all proportion to its prejudicial effect.[99] The application of this principle was not restricted to the case where the probative value of the evidence was minimal or "trifling".

There is a strong indication that the scope of the discretion may widen in Canada. At issue in *R. v. Corbett*[100] was whether s. 12 of the *Canada Evidence Act*,[101] which allows an accused to be cross-examined on a previous criminal record to undermine credibility, offended the accused's right to a fair trial pursuant to s. 11(d) of the *Canadian Charter of Rights and Freedoms*.[102] The accused in this case was charged with murder and his record showed a previous murder conviction. Each judge of the Supreme Court of Canada sitting on this appeal agreed that s. 12 did not offend the accused's right to a fair trial. However, four of the six justices also recognized that the trial judge had a discretion to exclude the record in appropriate circumstances.[103] Dickson J. (with whom Lamer and Beetz JJ. concurred) did not expand on the factors which should guide the exercise of the judge's discretion, but agreed generally with those set out by La Forest J. in his dissenting reasons. (Justice Dickson felt, however, that too little weight was given by La Forest J. to the fact that the accused had vigorously attacked the credibility of the Crown witnesses with reference to their own criminal records.) La Forest J. recognized that the scope of the discretion

---

98 [1980] A.C. 402.
99 *Ibid.*, per Lord Diplock, at 428, 432, 434; Viscount Dilhorne, at 438, 441-42; Lord Salmon, at 445; Lord Fraser, at 446-47; Lord Scarman, at 452.
100 [1988] 1 S.C.R. 678, 41 C.C.C. (3d) 385, 64 C.R. (3d) 1, [1988] 4 W.W.R. 481, 28 B.C.L.R. (2d) 145.
101 R.S.C. 1985, c. C-5.
102 R.S.C. 1985, Appendix II, No. 44.
103 McIntyre and Le Dain JJ. did not feel that a discretion could be exercised with respect to a clear legislative provision such as s. 12 of the *Canada Evidence Act*. To the extent that they recognized the existence of a discretion they relied on *R. v. Wray*.

was described rather restrictively in *Wray* and that it was described in much broader terms in *Sang*. He believed that the precise relationship between the potential prejudice and probative value of the evidence sought to be excluded in order to trigger the exercise of this discretion was not settled.[104] In La Forest J.'s view what was important was not the formulation of the test, but what was required to ensure a fair trial in the circumstances.[105] His approach suggests a loosening of the strict formulation in *Wray*.[106]

> In my view, the recognition of a discretion to exclude evidence when its probative value is overshadowed by prejudicial effect ensures that the legitimate interests of both the public and the accused are taken into account. Justice and fairness demand no less and expect no more. The factors that should be considered in exercising this discretion, which I have earlier set out,[107] ensure that this occurs. Each of them assists in focusing the inquiry on whether the probative value of any previous convictions the Crown seeks to introduce into evidence is sufficient to counterbalance the unjustified prejudice to the accused that would result, thus securing fairness to both. Indeed, as I earlier noted, the touchstone of all these factors is the fairness of the proceedings.

Although this passage indicates that La Forest J. favours a broader test for the exercise of the judicial discretion his comments in this regard are *obiter dicta* only given that he decided that even on the narrow *Wray* formulation the evidence should have been excluded.[108]

The scope of the judicial discretion arose again in *R. v. Potvin*.[109] This time Justice La Forest (with whom Dickson C.J. agreed) expressed his view more clearly:[110]

---

104 *Supra*, note 100, at 738 (S.C.R.).
105 *Ibid.*, at 743-44 (S.C.R.).
106 *Ibid.*, at 745 (S.C.R.).
107 *Ibid.*, at 740-44 (S.C.R.). The most important of which in the context of s. 12 are the nature of the previous conviction and its remoteness or nearness to the present charge.
108 For an interesting comment on *Corbett* and judicial discretion to exclude evidence, see R.J. Delisle, *Comment* (1988), 67 Can. Bar Rev. 706.
109 [1989] 1 S.C.R. 525, 47 C.C.C. (3d) 289, 68 C.R. (3d) 193, 42 C.R.R. 44, 93 N.R. 42.
110 *Ibid.*, at 531-32 (S.C.R.).

... the trial judge may exclude admissible evidence if its prejudicial effect substantially outweighs its probative value; see *R. v. Corbett*, [1988] 1 S.C.R. 670, at pp. 729-36; see also *R. v. Tretter* (1974), 18 C.C.C. (2d) 82. The case most frequently cited for the discretion to exclude is *R. v. Wray*, [1971] S.C.R. 272, where it is referred to in a dictum by Martland J. at pp. 292-93, but it is simply one of the fundamental postulates of the law of evidence.

As my colleague notes, some have interpreted Martland J.'s dictum as limiting the discretion solely to situations where the evidence is highly prejudicial to the accused and is only of modest probative value. I do not accept this restrictive approach to the discretion. As I noted in *Corbett supra*, at pp. 736-740, this narrow view, which can be traced from a statement by Lord du Parcq in *Noor Mohamed v. The King*, [1949] A.C. 182 (P.C.), at p. 192, has now been rejected by the House of Lords: *R. v. Sang*, [1980] A.C. 402. That case, and others he referred to, make it clear that under English law, a judge in a criminal trial always has a discretion to exclude evidence if, in the judge's opinion, its prejudicial effect substantially outweighs its probative value.

The majority preferred not to deal with the scope of the common law discretion and instead determined that s. 643(1) of the *Criminal Code*,[111] which was the provision in issue in the case, recognized a statutory discretion. Given the criticism of the *Wray* formulation, the majority felt it was not appropriate to import a similar restriction into the interpretation of this section. Inherent in the majority judgment is an acceptance that the common law position remains that the evidence may only be excluded if it is highly prejudicial to the accused and of only modest probative value.[112] It would appear, however, that this is an issue that is likely to be reconsidered by the Supreme Court of Canada in the future and there are strong indications that the *Sang* approach will be preferred.[113]

---

111 R.S.C. 1985, c. C-46.

112 *Supra*, note 109, at 552-53, S.C.R.

113 Note also that La Forest J. reaffirmed his position in *Thomson Newspapers Inc. v. Canada (Director of Investigation and Research)*, [1990] 1 S.C.R. 425, at 559-60, 54 C.C.C. (3d) 417, 76 C.R. (3d) 129, 67 D.L.R. (4th) 161, 47 C.R.R. 1, 39 O.A.C. 161, 72 O.R. (2d) 415*n*, 29 C.P.R. (3d) 97, 106 N.R. 161, see also *R. v. Barnes* (1989), 112 N.R. 49 (P.C.).

A discretion to exclude inflammatory photographs or exhibitions of real injury where its prejudicial effect outweighs its probative value may also be recognized in criminal cases.[114]

(b) *In Favour of the Crown and Third Persons*

In *R. v. Valley*[115] the Ontario Court of Appeal held that there was no judicial discretion to exclude evidence on the basis that its admission would operate unfairly to the Crown.[116] There is some indication that evidence might be excluded if prejudicial to third persons.[117]

2. Judicial Discretion in Civil Cases

A judicial discretion to exclude admissible evidence is also recognized in civil cases. It appears that the narrow formulation of the discretion of *R. v. Wray*[118] is not applied. In a civil case evidence can be excluded if, in the judge's view, its prejudicial effect outweighs its probative value. It need not be of minimal probative value.

The discretion normally applies when an attempt is made to introduce real or demonstrative evidence in the court room.[119] In personal injury actions, counsel may attempt to show the trier of fact a graphic photograph of or the actual bodily injury that the plaintiff has incurred. The advantage of exhibiting such injury or photograph is that it constitutes a preferable form of proof to the testimonial evidence of those who have perceived the injury. It may be the very best evidence available. Testimonial evidence, after all, is one step removed from viewing the injury itself and the exposure of it would seem to be the most natural and efficient process of proof. The trier would not have to concern himself or herself with questions of

---

114 See the dicta to this effect of Spence J. in *Draper v. Jacklyn*, [1970] S.C.R. 92, 9 D.L.R. (3d) 264. For a fuller discussion of the development of this particular discretion, see this Chapter, II.C.2.

115 (1986), 26 C.C.C. (3d) 207, at 239, 13 O.A.C. 89 (C.C.C.) (Ont. C.A.); leave to appeal to S.C.C. refd. 26 C.C.C. (3d) 207*n*, 15 O.A.C. 240*n*, 67 N.R. 158*n*.

116 See also *R. v. Hawke* (1975), 22 C.C.C. (2d) 19, at 54-55, 7 O.R. (2d) 145, 29 C.R.N.S. 1 (Ont. C.A.).

117 *R. v. St.-Jean* (1976), 34 C.R.N.S. 378 (Que. C.A.), at 387-88.

118 [1971] S.C.R. 272, [1970] 4 C.C.C. 1, 11 C.R.N.S. 235, 11 D.L.R. (3d) 673. Discussed this Chapter, II.C.1.(a).

119 See B.A. MacFarlane, "Photographic Evidence: Its Protection Value at Trial and the Judicial Discretion to Exclude it from Evidence" (1973-74), 16 C.L.Q. 149.

credibility or possible error in the observation of a witness. Other considerations, however, militate against the use of such evidence:

1. exhibited injuries cannot be recorded so that an appellate court is deprived of such evidence should there be an appeal;

2. the nature and extent of the injury and its treatment could be just as readily explained by medical witnesses giving oral testimony;[120] and

3. its prejudicial effect could far outweigh any probative value that it may have.

Questions then arise as to whether the court will ever refuse to admit real evidence even if it is relevant to an issue in dispute; and, if the court does have such a discretion to exclude this kind of evidence, on what occasions will it do so?

An early statement of the trial judge's discretion, though expressed in inclusionary terms, was made by Chancellor Boyd in *Sornberger v. Canadian Pacific Railway Co.*,[121] after reviewing a number of American authorities, as follows:

... it is within the discretion of the Court to allow the plaintiff to exhibit to the jury his injured limb or body for the purpose of being examined thereon by a physician.

Shortly thereafter, the other division of the same Ontario appellate court, in stronger language, suggested that the possible prejudicial effect of injuries displayed to a jury might be considered by a trial judge in her or his deliberation as to whether the exhibition should be permitted or not.[122] Some later cases seemed to concentrate on whether the part of the body exposed was normally covered,[123]

---

120 See *Gray v. LaFleche*, [1950] 1 W.W.R. 193, [1950] 1 D.L.R. 337, 57 Man. R. 396.

121 (1897) O.A.R. 263, at 270.

122 *Laughlin v. Harvey* (1897), 24 O.A.R. 438, at 440. To the same effect see *Richardson v. Nugent* (1918), 45 N.B.R. 331, 40 D.L.R. 700 (C.A.). For a more detailed discussion of this discretion see J. Sopinka and S.N. Lederman, *The Law of Evidence in Civil Cases*, Canadian Legal Text Series (Toronto: Butterworths, 1974), at 348 and following.

123 *Yachuk v. Oliver Blais Co. Ltd.*, [1944] O.W.N. 412, [1944] 3 D.L.R. 615; revd. on other grounds, [1945] O.R. 18, [1945] 1 D.L.R. 210 (C.A.); revd. on other grounds, [1946] S.C.R. 1; revd. on other grounds and judgment of C.A. restored

although this would appear to be a rather artificial basis for the analysis.

Although an early case[124] suggested that the injuries in question should not be shown to the jury on the ground that it might induce an exaggerated award of damages, other cases that have been cited up to this point considered the prejudicial effect of the injuries as bearing upon liability rather than damages.[125] A later Saskatchewan case, however, indicated that such a display cannot arouse prejudice if liability is not in issue.[126] The court intimated, however, that a trial judge may forbid the exhibition of corporeal injuries even when the issue is only *quantum* if the viewing of the injury might result in an exaggerated impression of the damage to or the suffering of the plaintiff.

In *Draper v. Jacklyn*,[127] a case where quantum of damages but not liability was in issue, Spence J. of the Supreme Court of Canada held that graphic photographs of the plaintiff's face during the course of his surgical treatment should have been put before the jury unless their likely prejudicial effect on the jury was so great as to exceed their probative value. The Supreme Court of Canada felt that the photographs were relevant because they portrayed the nature of the treatment that the plaintiff had to undergo. In this way, they were relevant to the question of damages because the jury could take into account the pain and discomfort and the unattractive nature of the plaintiff's face during the period of convalescence. Moreover, the court agreed with the trial judge's view that the photographs themselves were not overly inflammatory. The Court did, however, lay down the principle that evidence may be excluded, even though it is relevant, if it is prejudicial to the party against whom it is led, in the sense of having slight probative value to a fact in issue in relation to its prejudicial effect. Spence J. put it this way:[128]

> The occasions are frequent upon which a judge trying a case with the assistance of a jury is called upon to determine whether or

---

[1949] A.C. 386; *Gray v. LaFleche, supra*, note 119.
124 *Yachuk* v. *Oliver Blais Co. Ltd., ibid.*
125 *Supra*, note 122.
126 *Hansen v. Saskatchewan Power Corporation* (1962), 31 D.L.R. (2d) 189 (Sask. C.A.), at 192.
127 *Supra*, note 114.
128 *Ibid.*, at 96-97 (S.C.R.).

not a piece of evidence technically admissible may be so prejudicial to the opposite side that any probative value is overcome
by the possible prejudice and that therefore he should exclude
the production of the particular piece of evidence. In the case of
photographs, this occurs more frequently in the trials of criminal
offenses and more usually in murder trials. The matter is always
one which is difficult for the trial judge and in itself essentially a
decision in which the trial judge must exercise his own carefully
considered personal discretion.

Spence J. held that the trial judge is in the best position to determine
whether the photographs would shock the jury and that an appellate
court should not be quick to interfere with the exercise of this
discretion.

It is interesting to note that although the Ontario Court of
Appeal, in enunciating the principle, indicated that the prejudicial
effect of the photographs had to "far outweigh"[129] their potential
probative value for the trial judge to exercise his discretion, Spence J.
did not use equivalent language. He did not suggest that before the
judge may invoke his discretion to exclude the photographs, the
prejudicial effect had to "far outweigh" or be "considerably greater"
than the probative worth of the photographs. He merely placed it on
the basis that if the prejudicial effect "would exceed their probative
value",[130] then the discretion may be exercised. Accordingly, the test
appears to be an even balanced one: if the prejudicial effect of the
photographs, and by analogy, the exposure of bodily injuries, is greater
than the probative or evidentiary value of such evidence, a trial judge
has a discretion to forbid its introduction into evidence. It would also
appear that Spence J. thought that this rule was applicable to both civil
and criminal cases. This is apparent by his reference to the use of
photographs in criminal proceedings, particularly murder trials, and
also by his review of many criminal authorities on this point. One
would expect that the circumstances in which a judge in a civil case
would exclude evidence because of its inflammatory nature would be
rare. People today, because of their exposure to television and motion
pictures, can be expected to be much less sensitive to graphic displays

---

129 *Draper v. Jacklyn*, [1968] 2 O.R. 683 (C.A.), at 685; see also *R. v. Gallant*
(1965), 47 C.R. 309 (P.E.I. S.C.).
130 *Supra*, note 114, at 98 (S.C.R.).

of injuries than the average nineteenth or early twentieth century citizen.

It is unclear whether this particular discretion would apply to other types of potentially prejudicial evidence, but there is no reason why it should not. The test for the exclusion of evidence on the basis of judicial discretion in civil cases would therefore appear to be somewhat wider than the traditional *Wray* formulation applicable in criminal proceedings.

D. *Direct and Circumstantial Evidence*

1. Distinction between Direct and Circumstantial Evidence

Another distinction that is made between types of evidence is the difference between direct and circumstantial evidence. Today, the distinction has very little practical significance. The law used to be that in cases depending solely on circumstantial evidence the jury required a special warning.[131] This is no longer the case and so the distinction has lost much of its significance.

A fact in issue cannot always be proved by direct evidence. A witness cannot always be called to prove the facts from personal observation nor can a document always be introduced which directly establishes the fact. The facts in issue must, in many cases, be established by proof of other facts. As many courts have noted criminals are not likely to commit their crimes within the sight of witnesses and it would be a great blow to the administration of the criminal justice system if such evidence was not admitted.[132] If sufficient other facts are proved, the court may "from the circumstances" infer that the fact in issue exists or does not exist. In such a case proof is said to be circumstantial.

An approved definition is that taken from the judgment of Shaw C.J. in *Commonwealth v. Webster*:[133]

---

131 This was referred to as the rule in *Hodge's case*. Discussed this Chapter, II.D.2, see also Chapter 5. III.C.
132 *R. v. Jones* (1926), 47 C.C.C. 380, [1926] 3 W.W.R. 313, [1927] 3 D.L.R. 679 (Sask. Dist. Ct.); *R. v. Cook* (1914), 23 C.C.C. 50, 18 D.L.R. 706, 48 N.S.R. 150 (C.A.); *R. v. Faulkner* (1911), 19 C.C.C. 47, 16 B.C.R. 229, 18 W.L.R. 634 (B.C.C.A.).
133 (1850) 59 Mass (5 Cush. 295) 52 Am. Dec. 711.

The distinction, then, between direct and circumstantial is this: Direct or positive evidence is when a witness can be called to testify to the precise fact which is the subject of the issue on trial. That is, in a case of homicide, that the party accused did cause the death of the deceased. Whatever may be the kind or the force of the evidence, this is the fact to be proved. But suppose no person was present on the occasion of the death and, of course, there is nobody that can be called to testify to it. Is it wholly unsusceptible of legal proof? Experience has shown that circumstantial evidence may be offered in such a case — that is, that body of facts may be proved, of so conclusive a character as to warrant a firm belief of the fact, quite as strong and certain as that on which discreet men are accustomed to act in relation to their most important concerns.

John v. R.,[134] a manslaughter case, contains a most interesting discussion of the distinction between direct and circumstantial evidence. The learned trial judge charged the jury in part as follows:[135]

All of the evidence that has been given in this trial is what is known as circumstantial evidence. To refresh your memory as to the difference between circumstantial evidence and what is known as direct evidence, I will give you an illustration.

If a witness gives evidence that he saw A stab B with a knife that is direct evidence that A stabbed B. If a witness gives evidence that he found a dagger with an unusually long blade in the possession of A and another witness testified that such a dagger could have caused B's wound, that is circumstantial evidence tending to prove that A did in fact stab B.

The two forms of evidence are equally admissible but the superiority of direct evidence is that it contains only one source of error, namely, the unreliability of human testimony, where circumstantial evidence in addition to the unreliability of human testimony suffers from the difficulty of drawing a correct inference from the circumstantial evidence.

---

134 [1971] S.C.R. 781, 2 C.C.C. (2d) 157, 15 C.R.N.S. 257, 15 D.L.R. (3d) 692, [1971] 3 W.W.R. 401.
135 *Ibid.*, as quoted by Ritchie J., at 788 (S.C.R.).

Mr. Justice Ritchie, speaking for the majority, discussed the adequacy of this charge in the following terms:[136]

> As the trial Judge said, the above illustration was designed exclusively for the purpose of refreshing the memory of the jury as to the difference between direct and circumstantial evidence and although it was so unhappily phrased as to have been potentially misleading if it had stood alone, I think the fact that, as will hereafter appear, it was almost immediately followed by a correct statement of the effect to be given to circumstantial evidence, served to offset any wrong impression of the law which it might have left in the minds of the jurors.

> It seems to me that the only valid criticism of this illustration must relate to the final words "tending to prove that A did in fact stab B". There can be no doubt that it was correct to say "If a witness gives evidence that he saw A stab B with a knife, that is direct evidence that A stabbed B", and I think it was also correct to say that "If a witness gives evidence that he found a dagger with an unusually long blade in the possession of A and another witness testified that such a dagger could have caused B's wound, that is circumstantial evidence", but standing alone it is not evidence "that A did in fact stab B" although, taken in conjunction with evidence of other facts, it might afford a link in a chain of circumstantial evidence so that when the whole was taken together a jury might be justified in reaching the conclusion that the circumstances were consistent only with guilt and inconsistent with any other rational conclusion. Having stated correctly that it was circumstantial evidence, it will be observed that the trial Judge proceeded to point out that while the value of direct evidence is dependent upon the reliability of human testimony, the value of circumstantial evidence suffers also, "from the difficulty of drawing a correct inference" from the testimony as to the existence of the circumstances, and he went on to state correctly the rule which has been established for the evaluation of such evidence, saying:

> > It is therefore my duty to urge you not to find the accused guilty on circumstantial evidence alone, unless you are satis-

---

136 *Supra*, note 134 at 788-90 (S.C.R.).

fied, not only that the circumstantial evidence is consistent with the conclusion that the accused committed the offence with which he is charged, but also that the facts which have been proved are such as to be inconsistent with any other rational conclusion than that the accused is guilty of the offence with which he is charged.

There can be no exception taken to this part of the charge as it is phrased in very much the same language as that employed by Baron Alderson in *Hodge's Case* (1838), 2 Lewin 227, 168 E.R. 1136, which was approved and adopted in this Court in *R. v. Comba*, [1938] 3 D.L.R. 719, 70 C.C.C. 205, [1938] S.C.R. 396.

Justice Ritchie's comments in so far as they relate to the rule in *Hodge's Case* must be read in light of recent jurisprudence which will be discussed below.[137] The discussion of the distinction between direct and circumstantial evidence is nevertheless instructive.

Each piece of evidence need not alone lead to the conclusion sought to be proved. Pieces of evidence, each by itself insufficient, may however when combined, justify the inference that the facts exist.[138] Accordingly, a trial judge must be careful not to exclude individual pieces of evidence if there is an undertaking that the evidence tendered is part of a larger combination.

2. The Treatment of Circumstantial Evidence

In civil cases the treatment of circumstantial evidence is quite straightforward. It is treated as any other kind of evidence. The weight accorded to it depends on the strength of the inference that can be drawn from it and this is a task for the trier of fact.

Circumstantial evidence has given rise to more difficulty in the criminal field. This difficulty arose due to the so-called "rule" in *Hodge's Case*.[139] A court is entitled to convict an accused solely on the basis of circumstantial evidence only, but formerly it was considered necessary to give the special warning in accordance with the rule in *Hodge's Case*. It was there stated that where the Crown's case depended *exclusively* on circumstantial evidence the circumstances must be consistent with the conclusion that the act was committed by the accused

---

137 In this Chapter, II.D.2.
138 *Grant v. Australian Knitting Mills*, [1936] A.C. 85 (P.C.).
139 (1838), 2 Lewin 227, 168 E.R. 1136 (Assize).

and inconsistent with any other rational conclusion. The trial judge's direction to the jury was to reflect this rule.

The Supreme Court of Canada embraced the rule in *R. v. Comba*.[140] Since that time Canadian courts have grappled with such issues as what form the warning had to take,[141] whether the rule applied to the *mens rea* elements of the offence or only the *actus reus*,[142] how to direct the jury where there is other direct evidence that it may or may not accept,[143] whether the warning had to be given where any essential element depended on circumstantial evidence although there was direct evidence on other issues[144] and what constituted "any other rational conclusion" upon which the jury should have been directed.[145] What was most unclear was how the rule related to the Crown's burden to prove its case beyond a reasonable doubt and the judge's direction thereon. The courts appeared to recognize a distinction but the nature of the distinction was never very clear.[146]

---

140 [1938] S.C.R. 396, 70 C.C.C. 205, [1938] 3 D.L.R. 719.

141 *R. v. Mickey* (1988), 46 C.C.C. (3d) 278 (B.C.C.A.).

142 See for example, *R. v. Landriault*, [1968] 2 C.C.C. 379, [1968] 1 O.R. 284 (C.A.); *R. v. Boyer*, [1969] 1 C.C.C. 106, 4 C.R.N.S. 127, 64 W.W.R. 461 (B.C.C.A.); *R. v. Salekin*, [1978] 5 W.W.R. 295 (B.C.C.A.); *R. v. Chabot* (1978), 6 C.R. (3d) 71 (Ont. H.C.J.); revd. on other grounds (1979), 10 C.R. (3d) 324, 49 C.C.C. (2d) 481 (C.A.); affd. [1980] 2 S.C.R. 985, 55 C.C.C. (2d) 385, 18 C.R. (3d) 258, 22 C.R. (3d) 250, 117 D.L.R. (3d) 527, 34 N.R. 361; *R. v. Piddington* (1958), 122 C.C.C. 265 (B.C.C.A.); *R. v. Glister* (1974), 16 C.C.C. (2d) 47 (N.S. C.A.).

143 *R. v. Leland* (1950), 98 C.C.C. 337, 11 C.R. 152, [1951] O.R. 12 (C.A.); *R. v. Deacon*, [1947] 87 C.C.C. 271, 3 C.R. 129, [1947] 1 W.W.R. 545, 55 Man. R. 1 (C.A.); revd. on other grounds [1947] S.C.R. 547, 89 C.C.C. 1, 3 C.R. 265; *R. v. Baxter* (1984), 6 O.A.C. 225 (Ont. C.A.); *R. v. Sears* (1947), 90 C.C.C. 159, 5 C.R. 1, [1948] O.R. 9 (C.A.).

144 *Lizotte v. R.*, [1951] S.C.R. 115, 99 C.C.C. 113, 11 C.R. 357, [1951] 2 D.L.R. 754.

145 *R. v. Zanewich* (1973), 11 C.C.C. (2d) 374 (Man. C.A.); *R. v. Halliday* (1975), 12 N.S.R. (2d) 1, 25 C.C.C. (2d) 131 (C.A.); *R. v. Dubois*, [1980] 2 S.C.R. 21, 52 C.C.C. (2d) 64, 23 A.R. 116, 32 N.R. 176; approving the dissent of McGillivray C.J.A. at (1979), 49 C.C.C. (2d) 501, 17 A.R. 541 (Alta. C.A.); *R. v. Imrich*, [1978] 1 S.C.R. 622, 34 C.C.C. (2d) 143, 39 C.R.N.S. 75, 75 D.L.R. (3d) 243; affg. (1974), 21 C.C.C. (2d) 99, 6 O.R. (2d) 496 (C.A.).

146 *R. v. McIver*, [1965] 1 O.R. 306, [1965] 1 C.C.C. 210; affd. [1965] 2 O.R. 475, 45 C.R. 401, [1965] 4 C.C.C. 182; affd. on other grounds [1966] S.C.R. 254, [1966] 2 C.C.C. 289, 48 C.R. 4; In *R. v. Manderville* (1958), 31 C.R. 154, 124 C.C.C. 268, 44 M.P.R. 42 (N.B.C.A.) McNair C.J.N.B. stated, at 273-74 C.C.C.: "The rule [in *Hodge's case*] is quite distinct from the doctrine of reasonable doubt

In *R. v. Cooper*[147] the Supreme Court of Canada rejected the notion that exclusive reliance on circumstantial evidence requires any special warning to the jury:[148]

There are a few observations I would make on *Hodge's* case specifically. Intent is no less a question of fact than is identity or the *actus reus* of an offence. I would not condone a situation where a trial judge may properly charge a jury under *Hodge's* case in respect of identity, and all other issues except intent, and then in the same case tell them to approach the Crown's burden of proof on a different basis on the question of intent. There must be consistency in a charge where burden of proof is concerned; and to have two different formulae in one case is as unjust to the Crown as it is to an accused.

The judgment of the House of Lords in *McGreevy v. Director of Public Prosecutions* [1973] 1 All E.R. 503 rejects the notion that there ever was any rule arising from *Hodge's* case which judges in England were required to follow where all or most of the evidence in a jury trial was circumstantial. In *Comba v. The King* . . . this Court referred to the formula in *Hodge's* case as "the long settled rule of the common law which is the rule of law in Canada" (at p. 397). Notwithstanding this pronouncement, this Court attenuated the rule in its judgment in *The Queen v. Mitchell, supra,* [[1964] S.C.R. 471] and manifested its discomfort with *Hodge's case* in *Alec John v. The Queen,* [1971] S.C.R. 781. The time has come to reject the forumula [sic] in *Hodge's* case as an inexorable rule of law in Canada. Without being dogmatic against any use of the formula of the charge in *Hodge's* case I would leave the matter to the good sense of the trial judge (as was

---

which applies whether the evidence is direct or circumstantial. Its purpose is to measure the standard of certainty and precision required by the doctrine of reasonable doubt where proof of guilt rests on circumstantial evidence. . . . In order to avoid confusion in the minds of the jury regarding the respective application of the two rules it may be advisable for a trial judge to separate his direction as to circumstantial evidence from his direction on the question of reasonable doubt so that the principles underlying them are kept separate and distinct."

147   [1978] 1 S.C.R. 860, 34 C.C.C. (2d) 18, 37 C.R.N.S. 1, 74 D.L.R. (3d) 731, 14 N.R. 183.
148   Per Laskin C.J.C., *ibid.,* at 865-66 (S.C.R.).

said in *McGreevy*), with the reminder that a charge in terms of the traditional formula of required proof beyond a reasonable doubt is the safest as well as the simplest way to bring a lay jury to the appreciation of the burden of proof resting on the Crown in a criminal case.

This case has removed any relevance of the distinction between direct and circumstantial evidence.

E. *Admissibility Generally*

1. Conditional Admissibility

It has already been mentioned that evidence may only be relevant when viewed together with other evidence.[149] Evidence may not only be conditionally relevant, but, more generally, may be conditionally admissible. Facts which establish the admissibility of evidence may not yet be proved when the evidence is presented to the court. For example, a business record might be referred to in a witness' evidence before the record is admitted into evidence as an exception to the hearsay rule. It is a matter for the court's discretion whether to allow such evidence before the preliminary facts are proved. Clearly, in a criminal trial the judge must be careful in allowing in any evidence which could prejudice the accused if the preliminary facts were not later proved. An instruction to the jury to disregard the evidence may not be sufficient to remove the prejudice and a mistrial might have to be ordered.

2. Limited Admissibility

Evidence might be admissible on one issue, yet not on another. For example, evidence of an accused's criminal record may be used by the Crown to cross-examine the accused. Although admissible on the issue of credibility of the accused, such evidence would not be relevant on the issue of identity, for example, unless it also met the test for introduction of similar fact evidence. Evidence may be admissible against one accused but not a co-accused.[150]

---

149 See this Chapter, II.B.6.
150 *R. v. McKay* (1953), 106 C.C.C. 83, 17 C.R. 88, [1953] O.R. 774 (C.A.), revd. as to *McKay*, [1954] S.C.R. 1, 107 C.C.C. 304, 17 C.R. 412; *R. v. MacDonald*, [1963] 1 C.C.C. 317, 38 C.R. 104, 40 W.W.R. 92 (B.C. Co. Ct.).

Such evidence can nevertheless be received by the court although its admissibility is "limited" to the issues to which it is relevant or upon which it is not excluded. The jury may require a caution against the improper use of the evidence and in certain cases such a caution is mandatory.[151]

3. Curative Admissibility

Where evidence that is technically inadmissible has been received by the court without objection from the opponent, the opponent may present evidence in response, which may also be inadmissible, in order to prevent a distorted picture from being presented to the trier of fact.[152] The exact scope of this discretion is not clear. In *R. v. Rosik*[153] Jessup J.A. suggested that the court's jurisdiction in this regard was very narrow. He stated:[154]

> An exactly contrary view was expressed by Channell, J., delivering the judgment of the Court of Criminal Appeal in *R. v. Cargill*, [1913] 2 K.B. 271 at p. 276. Of the two English and one Canadian cases cited by the learned author to support his proposition, two of them stand only for a rule that inadmissible evidence introduced in cross-examination can be re-examined upon. The third case simply held that a defendant could rebut matters stated in the plaintiff's opening but not afterwards evidenced by him. Unless compelled by authority, I would be reluctant to extend the principle of curative admissibility beyond its application in the cases I have mentioned.

Arguably, a wider jurisdiction was recognized in *R. v. Rhodes*.[155] On a charge of first degree murder committed during the course of a rape the accused's counsel led psychiatric evidence that the accused's per-

---

151 *Boykowych v. Boykowych*, [1955] S.C.R. 151, [1955] 2 D.L.R. 81; affg. [1953] O.R. 827, [1954] 1 D.L.R. 493. *R. v. D. (L.E.)*, [1989] 2 S.C.R. 111.

152 *R. v. Gowland* (1978), 45 C.C.C. (2d) 303, at 310 (Ont. C.A.); *R. v. Sweeney (No. 2)* (1977), 35 C.C.C. (2d) 245, 40 C.R.N.S. 37, 76 D.L.R. (3d) 211, 16 O.R. (2d) 814 (C.A.).

153 (1970), 2 C.C.C. (2d) 351, 13 C.R.N.S. 129 [1971] 2 O.R. 47, 13 Cr. L.Q. 224 (Ont. C.A.); affd. [1971] S.C.R. vi, 2 C.C.C. (2d) 393*n*, 14 C.R.N.S. 400, [1971] 2 O.R. 89*n* (Ont. C.A.).

154 *Ibid.*, at 389 (C.C.C.).

155 (1981), 59 C.C.C. (2d) 426, 21 C.R. (3d) 245 (B.C.C.A.).

sonality was not consistent with the commission of sexual assaults. On cross-examination the psychiatrist admitted that his opinion would change if there was a history of sexual assault. The Crown then led evidence of a previous rape through the victim of that previous rape. The defence wished to adduce other evidence to rebut that evidence. The trial judge would only allow the defence to rebut it through calling the accused as a witness. The British Columbia Court of Appeal held that the evidence of the previous rape was of tenuous relevance and probably should not have been admitted. However, once the evidence was admitted without objection the court saw no basis to limit the witnesses to be called by the defence. If the matter was to be looked into at all, the defence should be entitled to explore it fully.

4. Procedure for Admitting Evidence

(a) *Tendering Evidence*

Normally evidence is presented to the court without objection and without discussion as to its admissibility. However, if an objection is raised counsel should make it clear on the record that he or she is tendering the evidence to the court. This ensures that any improper rejection of the evidence by the judge can be appealed.[156] A vague reference to the evidence is not sufficient formal tender.[157] If the judge in yielding to an objection suggests that the evidence is not admissible, then counsel offering the evidence must make it clear that he or she is not in agreement with the trial judge's suggestion.[158] As stated in *Re Cole and Knowles*:[159]

> The rejection of evidence can be successfully made a ground of appeal only when the evidence is tendered and unequivocally rejected. If counsel yields to a suggestion only of the trial Judge, either from deference to the Judge, as a matter of tactics, or for any other reason, and does not require an express rejection or its equivalent, he cannot on an appeal successfully contend that his evidence is rejected.

---

156 *Re Rarot* (1958), 27 W.W.R. 136 (Man. C.A.); *R. v. Butterfield* (1909), 15 C.C.C. 101, 18 O.L.R. 347 (C.A.).
157 *Ibid.*
158 *Re Cole & Knowles* (1927), 60 O.L.R. 638, [1927] 3 D.L.R. 950 (C.A.).
159 *Ibid.*, at 952, D.L.R.; see also *R. v. Fields* (1986), 28 C.C.C. (3d) 358, 53 C.R. (3d) 260, 56 O.R. (2d) 213, 16 O.A.C. 286 (C.A.).

The trial judge is entitled to inquire as to the purpose of the evidence when it is presented.[160] Opposite counsel may also make such an inquiry.[161] When evidence is formally tendered or an objection is made the trial judge should rule on the evidence right away, indicating why the evidence is or is not relevant.[162] It should not be admitted "subject to objection".[163] Nor should the ruling be made prior to the evidence being offered.[164] Any appeal with respect to incorrect rulings must await judgment in the trial.[165] Counsel must be content with the ruling until that time. Accordingly, Crown counsel cannot remark to the jury that they should disregard the evidence on the basis that it was not admissible.[166]

Occasionally, with respect to documentary or real evidence, the documents or things are marked "for identification only". At this stage they are not evidence. They become evidence when testimony is given which authenticates them.[167] This is often a practical way of dealing with cases involving large numbers of documents. Counsel may prepare bound and tabbed sets of the documents he or she intends to prove and have those books marked for identification at the start of the trial. Reference to the documents is therefore made much easier. One court has remarked however that marking documents for identification only is not a practice that should be encouraged.[168] In large document cases, however, the practicality of the practice cannot be denied.

In a civil case evidence of doubtful admissibility can be admitted with a reservation of the right to reject it in arriving at the decision.[169]

---

160 *Key v. Thomson* (1868), 12 N.B.R. 295 (C.A.); *R. v. Wilkinson* (1878), 42 U.C.Q.B. 492 (C.A.), at 500.
161 *Royal Ins. Co. v. Duffus* (1890), 18 S.C.R. 711.
162 *R. v. Fields, supra*, note 159.
163 *R. v. Griffith* (1959), 127 C.C.C. 209; *Cloutier v. R.*, [1940] S.C.R. 131, 73 C.C.C. 1, [1940] 1 D.L.R. 553.
164 *Tolton Mfg. Co. v. Ontario Industrial Standards Advisory Committee*, [1941] O.R. 79, [1941] 2 D.L.R. 541 (C.A.).
165 *Earnshaw v. Despins*, unreported, September 13, 1989 (B.C.C.A. in Chambers).
166 *R. v. Webb* (1914), 22 C.C.C. 424, 16 D.L.R. 317, 6 W.W.R. 358, 24 Man. R. 437 (C.A.).
167 *R. v. Piercey* (1979), Chitty's L.J. 292 (N.S.Co.Ct.).
168 *R. v. Chow* (1930), 53 C.C.C. 247, [1930] 2 W.W.R. 389, 42 B.C.R. 365 (C.A.).
169 *Pepin v. Plamondon* (1936), 43 R.L.N.S. 1 (C.S.).

(b) *Appeals with Respect to Admissibility*

(i) Grounds of Appeal

Where there is an appeal with respect to the rejection or admission of evidence by the trial judge in a civil case, the appellant cannot advance as a ground of appeal any grounds other than those upon which the evidence was either objected to, or argued to be relevant and admissible at the trial.[170] Where an objection is upheld or overruled, the respondent in whose favour the ruling was made may, on appeal, advance additional grounds for upholding the ruling.[171] In criminal cases an appeal may be successful even though no objection was made at the trial.[172] In such cases any ground of appeal can be heard. Cross-examination on the evidence objected to does not prejudice the objecting party's ability to appeal the admissibility ruling.[173]

(ii) Significance of Objection at Trial

In both civil and criminal cases it is advisable that any objections to the admissibility of evidence be made at the time the evidence is tendered. In a civil case an objection on appeal will not usually succeed unless the objection is made at the trial.[174] A failure to object may constitute the tacit waiver of a privilege that would otherwise apply

---

170 *Royal Ins. Co. v. Duffus, supra,* note 160; *Re Controverted Election for the Electoral District of Shelburne and Queens, Re* (1906), 37 S.C.R. 604, at 611; *Georgia Const. Co. v. Pacific Great Eastern Railway,* [1929] S.C.R. 630, 36 C.R.C. 23, [1929] 4 D.L.R. 161; but see *Cuff v. Frazee Storage & Cartage Co.* (1907), 14 O.L.R. 263 (Div. Ct.) which appears to take a more flexible and preferable approach.
171 *Roe d. Lord Trimlestown v. Kemmis* (1843), 8 E.R. 601 (H.L.); *Clark v. Grand Trunk Railway* (1869), 29 U.C.Q.B. 136 (C.A.).
172 See below this Chapter, II.E.4.(b)(ii) for a discussion of the need to object at the trial.
173 *Ferguson v. Veitch* (1880), 45 U.C.Q.B. 160 (C.A.); but see *Smith v. Gerow* (1874), 155 N.B.R. 425 (C.A.).
174 *Allen v. McDonald* (1881), 20 N.B.R. 533 (C.A.); *Boston Belting Co. v. Gabel* (1880), 20 N.B.R. 347 (C.A.); *R. v. Hawkes* (1915), 22 C.C.C. 29, 25 D.L.R. 631, 9 W.W.R. 445, 32 W.L.R. 720, 9 Alta. L.R. 182 (Alta. C.A.).; *Hall v. Geiger,* [1930] 2 W.W.R. 790, 42 B.C.R. 335, [1930] 3 D.L.R. 644; *Small v. Belyea* (1883), 24 N.B.R. 16 (C.A.); *Barbour v. Roberts* (1884), 24 N.B.R. 211 (C.A.); *Campbell v. Beamish* (1852), 8 U.C.Q.B. 526 (C.A.); *Davis v. McSherry* (1850), 7 U.C.Q.B. 490 (C.A.). But see *Young v. Denton,* [1927] 1 W.W.R. 75, 21 Sask. L.R. 319, [1927] 1 D.L.R. 426 (Sask. C.A.) where an inadmissible document clearly had a material effect on the trial judge's determination.

to make the document inadmissible.[175]

The position in criminal cases is not as clear. As stated by Fauteux J. in *Kissick v. R.*:[176]

> [The] authorities are sufficient to support the proposition that, as to the consequences of the failure to object, there is no steadfast rule, and that, while the failure to object to inadmissible evidence is not always fatal, it cannot be said that it is never so.

Mistakes or oversight of defence counsel with respect to objecting to the admission of evidence cannot prejudice the accused's ability to object to the admissibility on appeal.[177] Nor does it relieve the judge from the duty to ensure that only admissible evidence is put before or considered by the trier of fact, whether that be the judge or a jury.[178] However, if defence counsel fails to object in the hope of a tactical advantage at the close of the trial or in order to create grounds of appeal, a court might treat this as a tacit waiver of the right to object.[179] In *R. v. Deacon*[180] Bergman J.A. of the Manitoba Court of Appeal aptly criticized the placing of an onerous duty on the trial judge to protect that accused against the improper admission of evidence. He noted that the rules imposing such duties arose at a time when the accused was not entitled to be defended by counsel and not allowed to testify. After noting that the U.S. courts treated a failure to object as a waiver,[181] he stated:[182]

---

175 *McLeod v. Pearson*, [1931] 4 D.L.R. 673, [1931] 3 W.W.R. 4 (Alta. S.C.).
176 [1952] 1 S.C.R. 343, 102 C.C.C. 129, at 154, 14 C.R. 1.
177 *R. v. Scory* (1944), 83 C.C.C. 306 (Sask. C.A.) at 323; *R. v. Gibson* (1887), 56 L.J.M.C. 49 per Wills J., at 52; *R. v. Saunders*, [1899] 1 Q.B. 490; *R. v. Stewart*, [1969] 2 C.C.C. 244, 5 C.R.N.S. 75, 66 W.W.R. 144 (B.C.C.A.); *R. v. Petrie* (1890), 20 O.R. 317 (C.A.); *R. v. Brooks* (1906), 11 C.C.C. 188, 11 O.L.R. 525 (C.A.) at 192 C.C.C.; *R. v. MacDonald* (1939), 72 C.C.C. 182, [1939] O.R. 606 (Ont. C.A.).
178 *R. v. Schwartzenhauer*, [1935] S.C.R. 367, 64 C.C.C. 1, [1935] 3 D.L.R. 711 (S.C.C.); *R. v. Scory, ibid.*; *R. v. Gibson, ibid.*; *R. v. Tunke* (1975), 25 C.C.C. (2d) 518 (Alta. S.C.).
179 *R. v. Deacon* (1947), 87 C.C.C. 271, 3 C.R. 129, [1947] 1 W.W.R. 545, 55 Man. R. 1 (Man. C.A.); revd. on other grounds, [1947] S.C.R. 531, 89 C.C.C. 1, 3 C.R. 265, 3 D.L.R. 772 (S.C.C.); *R. v. Bowles* (1974), 16 C.C.C. (2d) 425 (Ont. C.A.).
180 *Ibid.*
181 See E.W. Cleary (ed.), *McCormick on Evidence*, 3rd ed. (St. Paul: West Publishing, 1984), at 54, at para. 140.
182 *R. v. Deacon, supra*, note 179, at 87 C.C.C. 332.

We reverse this and put a premium on the studied silence and the deliberate refraining from making [sic] seasonable objections by the most experienced and most competent counsel by telling them that they need not object, because, if the trial judge makes any slip, they can take full advantage of it in an appellate court.

Such an attitude merited condemnation in this judge's view. The burden of protecting the accused should be shouldered by the defence counsel. Bergman J.A. concluded with the words:[183]

> I reject the implied suggestion that all that it did was to impose on the trial Judge the additional duty of acting as wet nurse to defence counsel.

Furthermore, a failure to object may be taken by the appeal court as evidence that the accused suffered no prejudice by the admission of the evidence, and therefore no miscarriage of justice would have occurred so as to justify a new trial.[184] The words of Viscount Simon L.C. in *Stirland v. D.P.P.* are often cited in this regard:[185]

> It has been said more than once that a judge when trying a case should not wait for objection to be taken to the admissibility of the evidence, but should stop such questions himself . . . If that be the judge's duty, it can hardly be fatal to an appeal founded on the admission of an improper question that counsel failed at the time to raise the matter. No doubt, . . . the court must be careful in allowing an appeal on the ground of reception of inadmissible evidence when no objection has been made at the trial by the prisoner's counsel. The failure of counsel to object may have a bearing on the question whether the accused was really prejudiced. It is not a proper use of counsel's discretion to raise no objection at the time in order to preserve a ground of objection

---

183 *Ibid.*, at 87 C.C.C. 335.
184 *Kissick v. R.*, *supra*, note 176; *R. v. Schubert* (1977), 40 C.R.N.S. 26, [1977] 5 W.W.R. 292 (B.C. Prov. Ct.), at 29 (C.R.N.S.); *R. v. Hill*, [1928] 2 D.L.R. 736, 49 C.C.C. 161, at 164, 61 O.L.R. 645 (C.A.); leave to appeal to S.C.C. refd., [1928] S.C.R. 156, 49 C.C.C. 211, [1928] 2 D.L.R. 779; *R. v. Conkie* (1978), 3 C.R. (3d) 7, 39 C.C.C. (2d) 408, [1978] 3 W.W.R. 493, 9 A.R. 115; *R. v. Imrich*, [1978] 1 S.C.R. 622, at 631, 34 C.C.C. (2d) 143, 39 C.R.N.S. 75, 75 D.L.R. (3d) 243, 15 N.R. 227.
185 [1944] A.C. 315, [1944] 2 All E.R. 13 (H.L.), at 327-28 (A.C.). See also, *R. v. Chambers*, [1990] 2 S.C.R. 1293, 59 C.C.C. (3d) 321, 80 C.R. (3d) 235, 49 B.C.L.R. (2d) 299, 6 W.W.R. 554, 119 N.R. 321, at 1319-320 (S.C.R.).

for a possible appeal, but where, as here, the reception or rejection of a question involves a principle of exceptional public importance, it would be unfortunate if the failure of counsel to object at the trial should lead to a possible miscarriage of justice. . . . The object of British law, whether civil or criminal, is to secure as far as possible, that justice is done according to law, and, if there is substantial reason for allowing a criminal appeal, the objection that the point now taken was not taken by counsel at the trial is not necessarily conclusive.

A number of Canadian cases emphasize the importance of a timely objection to the admission of the evidence as a factor in determining whether a new trial shall be ordered.[186] The extent to which it will be taken into account depends on the circumstances of each case. For example, in *R. v. Lomage*[187] an accused had made exculpatory statements to the police and his trial counsel had agreed to their admission. On appeal, the accused argued that the admission of these statements violated his rights to counsel and silence. The Ontario Court of Appeal held that his rights were not violated because his defence rested on the admission of his statements in full to show his desire to cooperate with the police. In warning against second guessing tactical decisions by competent defence counsel, Finlayson J.A. stated as follows:[188]

I accept that our courts have taken a somewhat paternalistic approach to the trial of an accused person, and certainly the failure to object to a material error has never stood in the way of the court remedying what it perceives to be an injustice. However, we must never forget that ours is an adversarial system and the role of defence counsel is every bit as important as that of any other party to the proceedings, including that of the judge. When we minimize the failure of counsel to object to evidence which he clearly saw as being to his client's advantage, we diminish the role of defence counsel. Defence counsel assumes

---

186 *R. v. Morgan* (1983), 29 Alta. L.R. (2d) 183, 51 A.R. 201, 25 M.V.R. 1 (Q.B.); *Medjedovitch v. R.* (1980), 8 M.V.R. 304, at 312 (Sask. Dist. Ct.); *R. v. Marcil* (1976), 31 C.C.C. (2d) 172 (Sask. C.A.); *R. v. Martel* (1980), 23 A.R. 361, 8 M.V.R. 167 (N.W.T. S.C.); *R. v. Oakley* (1980), 6 M.V.R. 158 (Alta. Q.B.); affd. (1980), 9 M.V.R. 218 (Alta. C.A.).
187 (1991), 44 O.A.C. 131, 2 O.R. (3d) 621 (Ont. C.A.).
188 *Ibid.*, at 138-39 (O.A.C.).

a great deal of responsibility in a criminal case and when he makes a decision both he and his client must live with it. It is no function of this court to play the role of what in football terminology is called a "Monday morning quarterback" when it comes to trial tactics employed by counsel. If we were to do so, it would have the effect of placing an unhelpful burden on the trial judge. Instead of being able to rely on the competence of counsel who must know more about the case than the trial judge, we would effectively be saying that the trial court has an overriding responsibility to vet tactical decisions of counsel and, where necessary, to vary or reverse them. Such overweening paternalism denigrates the adversary system. Had the court taken such an approach in this case it would have amounted to an unjustified interference in the role of both Crown and defence counsel.

Krever J.A. in the same case, although agreeing with Finlayson J.A.'s remarks in the particular circumstances of the case, added a word of admonition:[189]

I do not want to be understood as having the view that in a criminal case, to say nothing of a first degree murder case, in which the liberty of the subject is at stake, the adversary system operates in its pure form. Just as the role of Crown counsel is not that of a pure adversary, so is the role of the judge modified. The judge in a criminal case assumes a greater responsibility to see that justice prevails than that in the pure adversary system controlled by the performance of the opposing parties. Thus, for example, in a criminal case tried by a jury, the judge is obliged to instruct the jury with respect to defences that reasonably arise out of the evidence notwithstanding the defence advanced by counsel and, indeed, even over the objection of defence counsel.

---

189 *Ibid.*, at 140.

CHAPTER 3

EVIDENTIAL BURDEN AND BURDEN OF PROOF

I   INTRODUCTION

The rules relating to the burdens of proof are largely governed by the substantive law.[1] Nonetheless, these rules are commonly dealt with in textbooks on evidence because they are an integral part of the litigation process. Although degrees or standards of proof and presumptions are occasionally referred to in the present analysis, these matters are examined elsewhere.[2]

II   TERMINOLOGY

The term "burden of proof" is used to describe two distinct concepts relating to the obligation of a party to a proceeding in connection with the proof of a case. In its first sense, the term refers to the obligation imposed on a party to prove or disprove a fact or issue. In the second sense, it refers to a party's obligation to adduce evidence satisfactorily to the judge, in order to raise an issue.[3]

---

1   R. Cross and C. Tapper, *Cross on Evidence*, 7th ed. (London: Butterworths, 1990), at 112.
2   See Chapter 5, Standards of Proof and Chapter 4, Presumptions.
3   J.B. Thayer, *A Preliminary Treatise on Evidence at Common Law*, reprint of 1898 ed. (New York: Augustus M. Kelley, 1969), at 353-55; 9 Wigmore, *Evidence* (Chadbourn rev. 1981), §§ 2485, 2490, at 283, 302.

Various labels have been used to describe the burden of proof in its first sense, including the legal,[4] ultimate[5] or fixed[6] burden, the persuasive burden[7] (or the risk of non-persuasion[8]), and the burden on the pleadings.[9] None of these is completely satisfactory. Although each is descriptive of some aspect of the total concept, some of the labels are misleading. It is often preferable simply to describe the effect of the operation of the particular species of burden with which one is dealing rather than to employ a label. Nonetheless, since labels are constantly being used, one should select the most common. In this regard, the term "legal burden", a term apparently initiated by Lord Denning, is most frequently used to describe the first kind of burden of proof.[10]

To differentiate between the two senses in which the term burden of proof is used, the other burden may be called the "evidential burden."[11] Although the evidential burden is sometimes called the "minor" or "secondary burden",[12] these terms neither describe the nature of this burden, nor provide a meaningful way of distinguishing between the legal and the evidential burdens. Where there are multiple issues in a case, for example, negligence, causation, and damages, using the term minor or secondary burden to describe the effect of the evidence in relation to these issues is not helpful and perhaps con-

---

4   *Cross on Evidence, supra*, note 1, at 112.

5   Lord Denning in *Bratty v. A.G. for Northern Ireland*, [1963] A.C. 386, at 413, [1961] 3 All E.R. 523.

6   N. Bridge, "Presumptions and Burdens" (1949), 12 Modern Law Rev. 273, at 277.

7   G. Williams, *Textbook of Criminal Law*, 2nd ed. (London: Stevens & Sons, 1983), at 48; and Dickson C.J.C. in *R. v. Schwartz*, [1988] 2 S.C.R. 443, 66 C.R. (3d) 251, 45 C.C.C. (3d) 97, 55 D.L.R. (4th) 1, [1989] 1 W.W.R. 289, 39 C.R.R. 260, 56 Man. R. (2d) 92, 88 N.R. 90, at S.C.R. 446.

8   9 Wigmore, *supra*, note 3, § 2485, at 283.

9   M.N. Howard, P. Crane and D. Hochberg, *Phipson on Evidence*, 14th ed. (London: Sweet & Maxwell, 1990), at 51.

10   *Cross on Evidence, supra*, note 1, at 112.

11   G. Williams, *supra*, note 7, at 49: ". . . the name 'evidential burden' now has wide acceptance". "The first judicial acceptance of the term appears to have been in *Gill*, [1963] 1 W.L.R. 841" (49, at note 12). See also *R. v. Schwartz, supra*, note 7.

12   These terms are sometimes used by courts to distinguish the evidential burden from the burden of proof which is called the primary burden, see e.g., *Circle Films Enterprises Inc. v. Canadian Broadcasting Corp.*, [1959] S.C.R. 602, at 607. See also *R. v. Schwartz, supra*, note 7.

fusing. The terms "tactical burden"[13] and "provisional burden"[14] are also used to describe the evidential burden. These terms are uninformative and misleading because "evidential burdens are imposed by law not mere matters of tactics."[15]

The terms "burden of adducing evidence"[16] and the "duty of passing the judge"[17] accurately describe the duty of the party that bears the evidential burden and its legal significance. A party, however, may satisfy an evidential burden without doing anything; for example, a witness called by the Crown testifies to facts which raise the issue of self-defence. In these circumstances, the defendant does not adduce evidence but rather, the issue is raised by the evidence. The term "evidential burden", when properly understood, is as informative as the other terms, is less cumbersome, and has gained wide acceptance.[18] Accordingly, for simplicity, conciseness and accuracy, the term "evidential burden" is used in this text. The application and effect of the evidential burden is discussed below.[19]

---

13 R. Cross, *Cross on Evidence*, 4th ed. (London: Butterworths, 1974) speaks of the "tactical shifting" of the evidential burden, at 79. But see the newer edition of *Cross on Evidence, supra*, note 1, at 115-18.

14 Lord Denning, "Presumptions and Burdens" (1945), 61 Law Quarterly Rev. 379.

15 G. Williams, *supra*, note 7. For a criticism of this term, see *R. v. Schwartz, supra*, note 7, at 467.

16 S. Phipson, *Phipson on Evidence, supra*, note 9, at 51.

17 Wigmore, *supra*, note 3, at 293: ". . . each party must first with his evidence pass the gauntlet of the judge".

18 *R. v. Robertson*, [1987] 1 S.C.R. 918, 33 C.C.C. (3d) 481, 58 C.R. (3d) 28, 39 D.L.R. (4th) 321, 75 N.R. 6, 20 O.A.C. 200. G. Williams, *supra*, note 7, states that the term "evidential" has wide acceptance. *Phipson on Evidence, supra*, note 9, at 51, note 15, states: "The phrase 'evidential burden' was described by Professor Cross (5th ed.), p. 87 as accurate and as a phrase which is coming to be increasingly used by the English judges. Lord Devlin however thought it confusing (*Jayasena v. R.*, [1970] A.C. 618, 624). We agree with Professor Cross that it is both accurate and in common use." See also *R. v. Schwartz, supra*, note 7.

19 See this Chapter, III.C. and IV.

III THE DIFFERENCE BETWEEN THE BURDENS

A. *General*

As noted, the term "burden of proof" is ambiguous and it has sometimes been used to mean that there is evidence of a fact, while on other occasions it has been used to mean that a fact has been proved by the evidence.[20] Since the term is applied without discriminating in which sense the term is being used,[21] it is difficult to determine which burden a party has satisfied in a particular case.[22]

The term evidential burden means that a party has the responsibility to insure that there is sufficient evidence of the existence or non-existence of a fact or of an issue on the record to pass the threshold test for that particular fact or issue.[23] As Lord Devlin explained in *Jayasena v. R.*,[24] to satisfy an evidential burden a party is not required to prove anything:[25]

> Their Lordships do not understand what is meant by the phrase *"evidential burden of proof"*. . . . It is doubtless permissible to describe the requirement as a burden, and it may be convenient to call it an evidential burden. But it is confusing to call it a burden of proof. Further, it is misleading to call it a burden of proof, whether described as legal or evidential or by any other

---

20   E.W. Cleary (ed.), *McCormick on Evidence*, 3rd ed. (St. Paul: West Publishing, 1984), at 947.

21   J.B. Thayer, *supra*, note 3, at 355. See, for example, *Abrath v. North Eastern Railway Co.* (1883), 11 Q.B.D. 440 (C.A.); affd. (1886), 11 App. Cas. 247, [1881-5] All E.R. Rep. 614 (H.L.).

22   In *R. v. Appleby*, [1972] S.C.R. 303, at 317, 16 C.R.N.S. 35, 3 C.C.C. (2d) 354, 21 D.L.R. (3d) 325, 4 W.W.R. 601. Laskin J. confuses the evidentiary effect of the incidence of the burden of proof on the accused: see *R. v. Oakes*, [1986] 1 S.C.R. 103, at 123, 50 C.R. (3d) 1, 24 C.C.C. (3d) 321, 26 D.L.R. (4th) 200, 65 N.R. 87, 14 O.A.C. 335, 53 O.R. (2d) 719 (headnote only), where Dickson C.J. points out this confusion.

23   J.B. Thayer, *supra*, note 3, at 355 states: ". . . the duty of going forward in argument or in producing evidence; whether at the beginning of a case or at any moment throughout the trial or the discussion."

24   [1970] A.C. 618, [1970] 1 All E.R. 219 (P.C.).

25   *Ibid.*, at A.C. 624. In *R. v. Schwartz*, Dickson C.J.C. stated: "The party with an evidential burden is not required to convince the trier of fact of anything, only to point out evidence which suggests that certain facts existed", *supra*, note 7, at 467.

adjective, when it can be discharged by the production of evidence that falls short of proof. The essence of the appellant's case is that he has not got to provide any sort of proof that he was acting in private defence. So it is a misnomer to call whatever it is that he has to provide a burden of proof. . . . [emphasis added]

In contrast, the term legal burden of proof means that a party has an obligation to prove or disprove a fact or issue to the criminal or civil standard. The failure to convince the trier of fact to the appropriate standard means that party will lose on that issue.[26] Because the evidential burden and the legal burden will on occasion be distributed between the parties, it is essential that the issues to be tried, and the underlying facts in support of the issues, be clearly identified.[27]

A party who bears an evidential burden is subject to an adverse ruling for failing to meet the threshold test for that particular evidential burden. In a jury trial, the trial judge has the authority to decide that issue without leaving it for the jury's consideration. However, where a party satisfies an evidential burden, the trial judge must leave that issue for the jury's determination. For example, the incidence of the evidential burden in relation to the definitional elements of a crime in a criminal prosecution[28] or the negligence of the defendant in a civil action requires the Crown or plaintiff to call evidence at the commencement of proceedings. To satisfy this evidential burden, these parties must adduce some evidence on these issues to succeed on a motion for a directed verdict of acquittal or a non-suit.[29] The trial judge's determination as to the sufficiency of the evidence to satisfy the evidential burden is a question of law.[30]

---

26   J.B. Thayer, *A Preliminary Treatise on Evidence at the Common Law*, reprint of 1898 ed. (New York: Augustus M. Kelley, 1969), at 355 states: "The peculiar duty of him who has the risk of any given proposition on which the parties are at issue — who will lose the case if he does not make this proposition out, when all has been said and done".

27   R. Cross and C. Tapper, *Cross on Evidence*, 7th ed. (London: Butterworths, 1990), states, at 110: "The key to clarity in this whole area lies in the precise definition and discrimination of the issues to be tried, and of the facts upon the determination of which they depend".

28   It is sometimes difficult to distinguish between definitional elements and defences: see *R. v. Holmes*, [1988] 1 S.C.R. 914, 64 C.R. (3d) 97, 41 C.C.C. (3d) 497, 85 N.R. 21, 27 O.A.C. 321.

29   See Chapter 5, Standards of Proof, for a discussion of these motions.

30   See Chapter 5, Standards of Proof.

The significance of the evidential burden arises when there is a question as to which party has the right or the obligation to begin adducing evidence. It also arises when there is a question as to whether sufficient evidence has been adduced to raise an issue for determination by the trier of fact. The legal burden of proof normally arises after the evidence has been completed and the question is whether the trier of fact has been persuaded with respect to the issue or case to the civil or criminal standard of proof.[31] The legal burden, however, ordinarily arises after a party has first satisfied an evidential burden in relation to that fact or issue.[32] The difference between the two burdens was explained by Professor Williams:[33]

> In short, the rule imposing an evidential burden is applied by the judge, in deciding whether to leave an issue (the general issue or some specific question) to the jury. The rule imposing the persuasive burden is for application by the jury. Putting this in another way, the evidential burden governs what the judge *does*, in leaving the question to the jury or withdrawing it from them; the persuasive burden governs what he *says*, in directing the jury how they are to reach their verdict.

B. *The Legal Burden of Proof*

The incidence of the legal burden of proof means that the party has the obligation to prove or disprove the existence or non-existence of a fact or issue to the civil or criminal standard; otherwise that party loses on that issue. The substantive law, such as the law of torts or the criminal law, and not the adjectival law of evidence, governs which party has the burden of proof in relation to a fact or issue.[34] Consider the resulting uncertainty if the rules governing the legal burden of proof allow the jury to allocate the burden by its perception of fairness

---

31 *McCormick on Evidence, supra*, note 20, at 947, states: "When the time for a decision comes, the jury . . . must be instructed how to decide the issue if their minds are left in doubt."

32 A presumption may obviate the need for a party to satisfy an evidential burden, see Chapter 4, Presumptions. Also, the evidential and legal burdens for an issue may be distributed between the parties, this Chapter, VI.

33 G. Williams, *Textbook of Criminal Law, supra*, note 7, at 55.

34 While this is true as a general proposition, the incidence of the burden of proof is also part of the law of evidence.

or of expediency in a particular case. For instance, in a straightforward motor vehicle negligence action, the jury decides to allocate the onus to disprove negligence to the defendant since he or she was intoxicated. Or, to take an illustration in the context of the criminal law, assume two persons are jointly indicted but separately tried for the same crime.[35] In the trial of one accused, the jury decides that the Crown should negate a common law defence, but at the trial of the other accused, a different jury allocates the legal burden of proof for this defence to the accused. Clearly, the need for predictability in the litigation process demands that the burden of proof be allocated according to rules of law and not *ad hoc* decisions by the trier of fact.

In most cases there are multiple factual and legal issues. Where there are several disputed facts or issues in a case, the legal burden of proof in relation to different issues may be distributed between the parties.[36] For example, the Crown has the legal burden in relation to the external circumstances and the mental element for the crime of murder. However, at common law[37] and under the *Criminal Code*[38] the accused bears the legal burden for the defence of insanity.[39]

In civil proceedings, the legal burden of proof operates in a similar manner. In an action for assault and battery, the plaintiff must prove that there was a non-consensual application of force to the victim, that the blow caused the injury, and the quantum of damages. However, the defendant has the burden of proof in relation to a defence of justification and that he or she used no more force than was necessary.[40]

In civil proceedings, the legal burden does not play a part in the decision-making process if the trier of fact can come to a determinate conclusion on the evidence. If, however, the evidence leaves the trier of fact in a state of uncertainty, the legal burden is applied to determine

---

35   Assume the first accused successfully obtained severance.
36   The criteria used by the courts for allocating the burden of proof is examined in this Chapter, VI.
37   *M'Naghten's Case* (1843), 10 Cl. & Fin. 200, [1843-60] All E.R. Rep. 229, 8 E.R. 718 (H.L.).
38   R.S.C. 1985, c. C-46, s. 16; see this chapter, V.A.
39   *R. v. Chaulk*, [1990] 3 S.C.R. 1303, 62 C.C.C. (3d) 193, 2 C.R. (4th) 1, [1991] 2 W.W.R. 385, 69 Man. R. (2d) 161, 1 C.R.R. (2d) 1, 119 N.R. 161 (S.C.C.); for a criticism of the allocation of the legal burden to the accused, see D. Stuart, *Canadian Criminal Law*, 2nd ed. (Toronto: Carswell, 1987), at 44-45.
40   *Mann v. Balaban*, [1970] S.C.R. 74, 8 D.L.R. (3d) 548.

the outcome. In *Robins v. National Trust Co.*,[41] the Privy Council explained the operation of the legal burden as follows:[42]

> But onus as a determining factor of the whole case can only arise if the tribunal finds the evidence pro and con so evenly balanced that it can come to no sure conclusion. Then the onus will determine the matter. But if the tribunal, after hearing and weighing the evidence, comes to a determinate conclusion, the onus has nothing to do with it, and need not be further considered.

The last sentence of this passage cannot apply in a case in which the standard of proof is higher than on a balance of probabilities. Accordingly, in a criminal case, not only must the trier of fact come to a determinate conclusion as to guilt but he or she must be satisfied beyond a reasonable doubt.[43] In civil cases in which the evidence must be subjected to special scrutiny, the above statement can be applied only after the trier of fact has examined the evidence with the requisite degree of critical appraisal.[44]

C. *The Evidential Burden*

The incidence of an evidential burden means that a party has the obligation to adduce evidence or to ensure that there is sufficient evidence of a fact in the record to raise an issue. Like the legal burden of proof, an evidential burden relates to a particular fact or issue, and where multiple facts or issues are disputed, the evidential burden in relation to different facts or issues may be distributed between the parties. The incidence of the evidential burden,[45] the sufficiency of the evidence required to satisfy it,[46] and the evidentiary effect of its

---

41   [1927] 2 D.L.R. 97, [1927] A.C. 515, [1927] 1 W.W.R. 692 (P.C.).

42   *Ibid.*, at 101 (D.L.R.), 520 (A.C.) E.W. Cleary (ed.), *McCormick on Evidence*, 3rd ed. (St. Paul: West Publishing, 1984), at 947 states: "Clearly, the principal [sic] significance of the burden of persuasion is limited to those cases in which the trier of fact is actually in doubt."

43   There is an exception where the incidence of the legal burden of proof rests with the accused to prove an issue to a balance of probabilities.

44   See Chapter 5, Standards of Proof.

45   *Robins v. National Trust Co.*, *supra*, note 41.

46   *R. v. Pappajohn*, [1980] 2 S.C.R. 120, 52 C.C.C. (2d) 481, 14 C.R. (3d) 243, 111 D.L.R. (3d) 1, [1980] 4 W.W.R. 387, 32 N.R. 104, 19 C.R. (3d) 97 (French).

discharge[47] are all questions of law.

The evidential burden is a product of the jury system[48] and it precludes perverse verdicts as a trial judge will leave a case or an issue for the jury's consideration only if the evidence is capable of such a determination.[49] For example, a trial judge will leave the defence of provocation for the jury's consideration when there is sufficient foundational evidence for this defence.[50] As stated by Lord Morris of Borth-y-Gest:[51]

> . . . it is not every facile mouthing of some easy phrase of excuse that can amount to an explanation. It is for a judge to decide whether there is evidence fit to be left to a jury which could be the basis for some suggested verdict.

Thus, the evidential burden provides a consistency and rough measure of equality to the litigation process. In criminal proceedings, the rule also safeguards an accused's right to silence and protects her or him from self-incrimination unless the Crown has first established a case to meet.[52] In civil actions and criminal prosecutions, once the trial

---

We discuss the measure or sufficiency of the evidence that is required to satisfy or discharge the evidential burden in Chapter 5, Standards of Proof.

47　*United States v. Shephard*, [1977] 2 S.C.R. 1067, 34 C.R.N.S. 207, 30 C.C.C. (2d) 424, 70 D.L.R. (3d) 136, 9 N.R. 215.

48　L.H. Hoffman, *The South African Law of Evidence*, 2nd ed. (Durban: Butterworths, 1970), at 348 as quoted by Australian Law Reform Commission, *Evidence*, Vol. 1 (interim report) (Canberra: Australian Government Publishing Service, 1985), at 16, which states: "By altering the trial procedure it would be possible to dispense with [the evidential burden] altogether. There is no particular reason why one should not have a system under which the court simply listened to all the evidence which the parties had to offer, and then decided the case according to the burden of proof in its ordinary sense."

49　9 Wigmore, *Evidence* (Chadbourn rev. 1981) § 2487, at 292-93. The different procedures in civil and criminal proceedings are discussed in Chapter 5, Standards of Proof. In civil cases, the Canadian procedure renders the non-suit motion more theoretical than real.

50　*Latour v. R.*, [1951] S.C.R. 19, 11 C.R. 1, 98 C.C.C. 258, [1951] 1 D.L.R. 834; see also, *Mancini v. D.P.P.*, [1942] A.C. 1, [1941] 3 All E.R. 272 (H.L.); *R. v. Lobell*, [1957] 1 Q.B. 547, [1957] 1 All E.R. 734 (C.C.A.); *Holmes v. D.P.P.*, [1946] A.C. 588, [1946] 2 All E.R. 124 (H.L.).

51　*Bratty v. A.G. for Northern Ireland*, [1961] 3 All E.R. 523, [1963] A.C. 386, at 417.

52　See G. Williams, *Textbook of Criminal Law*, 2nd ed. (London: Stevens & Sons, 1983), at 44-45, for a discussion of the purpose of the evidential burden in

judge rules that the evidence satisfies the threshold test for that particular issue, her or his ruling is determinative of that issue and the burden is spent. A trial judge does not inform a jury that a party has discharged its evidential burden, as the judge's ruling is not a relevant matter for their consideration.[53] For instance, it would be superfluous to inform the jury that the Crown has survived a motion for a directed verdict or that the accused has adduced sufficient evidence which, if believed, is capable of constituting a defence. Indeed, if the trial judge informed the jury of these rulings it could only confuse them as "once an issue is left to the jury, the only burden left for consideration is the burden of persuasion [legal burden of proof]."[54]

Normally, the incidence of the evidential burden coincides with the legal burden of proof. For example, since the prosecution has the legal burden in relation to all the definitional elements of the crime of sexual assault, the Crown must adduce sufficient evidence on these elements to overcome a motion for a directed verdict of acquittal. If the complainant testifies that the accused applied non-consensual force in circumstances of sexuality[55] and there is an evidential basis to infer that the accused had the requisite mental state for the crime,[56] the prosecution has discharged its evidential burden. Thus, the trial judge must leave the case for the jury's determination where the prosecution's case survives a motion for a directed verdict. In the above circumstances, the criminal law does not allocate an evidential burden to the accused to refute the Crown's case and he or she may decline to adduce any evidence. Nevertheless, if the accused decides not to call any evidence, he or she runs the risk of being convicted and the failure to do so may increase the likelihood of an adverse verdict.[57] In the

---

criminal proceedings.

53　In *R. v. Bulmer*, [1987] 1 S.C.R. 782, 33 C.C.C. (3d) 385, 58 C.R. (3d) 48, 14 B.C.L.R. (2d) 196, 39 D.L.R. (4th) 641, 75 N.R. 271, [1987] 4 W.W.R. 577 (*sub nom. Laybourn v. R.*), at 791 (S.C.C.), McIntyre J. for the court stated: "The first step for the trial judge is to decide if the defence should be put to the jury. It is on this question, as I have said, that the "air of reality" test is applied. It has nothing to do with the jury and is not a factor for its consideration."

54　G. Williams, *Criminal Law: The General Part*, 2nd ed. (London: Stevens & Sons Ltd., 1961), at 880, note 16.

55　*R. v. Chase*, [1987] 2 S.C.R. 293, 59 C.R. (3d) 193, 37 C.C.C. (3d) 97, 45 D.L.R. (4th) 98, 82 N.B.R. (2d) 229, 80 N.R. 247, 208 A.P.R. 229.

56　*R. v. Leary*, [1978] 1 S.C.R. 29, 33 C.C.C. (2d) 473, 37 C.R.N.S. 60, 74 D.L.R. (3d) 103, [1977] 2 W.W.R. 628, 13 N.R. 592.

57　See A. Maloney, Q.C., "Corroboration", *Evidence* (1955), L.S.U.C. Special

absence of any evidence of an excuse or justification, the trier of fact may, not must, convict the accused, since in order to succeed the Crown must also satisfy the legal burden of proof on the definitional elements of the offence beyond a reasonable doubt.[58]

The evidential burden and the legal burden are not always coexistent. Accordingly, in a criminal case, the Crown has the legal burden with respect to all elements of the offence. If, however, the accused wishes to raise a defence which does not simply constitute a denial of an element of the offence, an evidential burden is imposed on the accused. For example, if the accused wishes the jury to consider the "defence" of a mistaken belief in consent for the crime of sexual assault, the criminal law allocates an evidential burden to the accused to adduce a factual basis for this defence.[59] A trial judge will not instruct a jury on this defence unless there is, on the evidence, an "air of reality" for the plea of a mistaken belief in consent.[60] The threshold test and whether the facts proved in evidence meet this test are questions of law.[61] Once the accused has discharged this evidential burden, the Crown has the legal burden to negative the "defence" of mistaken belief in consent, that is, to disprove the existence of this state of mind.[62] The allocation of the two burdens for the crime of sexual assault underlines the need to distinguish between the burdens and to discriminate to which issues they apply.

A statute may expressly or implicitly allocate an evidential burden to the accused. For example, in an impaired driving case, a certificate of analysis, stating the results of the analyses of breath or blood samples is, in the absence of evidence to the contrary, proof that the concentration of alcohol in the blood of the accused at the time of

---

Lectures, at 251-52, for a discussion of a different risk, that is calling the accused person who provides the necessary evidence where the Crown's case is otherwise deficient.

58 *Woolmington v. D.P.P.*, [1935] A.C. 462, at 480, 25 Cr. App. Rep. 72 (H.L.): "[I]f it is proved that the conscious act of the prisoner killed a man and nothing else appears in the case, there is evidence upon which the jury may, not must, find him guilty of murder".

59 *R. v. Robertson*, [1987] 1 S.C.R. 918, 33 C.C.C. (3d) 481, 58 C.R. (3d) 28, 39 D.L.R. (4th) 321, 75 N.R. 6, 20 O.A.C. 200; see A.W. Bryant, "The Issue of Consent in the Crime of Sexual Assault" (1989), 68 Can. Bar Rev. 94, at 143-47 for an analysis of the "defence" of mistake of fact.

60 *R. v. Pappajohn, supra*, note 46.

61 *Ibid.*

62 *R. v. Robertson, supra*, note 59.

driving was in accordance with the analyses.[63] The results stated in the certificate are not conclusive, otherwise the statutory words "in the absence of evidence to the contrary" would be meaningless. If the accused wishes to challenge the accuracy of the results of the analyses (as stated in the certificate) she or he has an evidential burden to overcome.[64] Once the accused adduces sufficient evidence to raise an issue as to the accuracy of the analyses, the Crown then has the legal burden of proof as to the concentration of alcohol in the accused's blood at the time of the offence.

In civil proceedings, the evidential burden normally coincides with the legal burden for a particular fact. In a routine negligence action where the plaintiff pleads that an act or omission by the defendant caused bodily injuries and the defendant pleads that a negligent act or omission by the plaintiff was a cause of, or contributed to, the damages suffered by the plaintiff, each party bears both the evidential and legal burdens for their respective allegations. The plaintiff must adduce sufficient evidence of the defendant's negligence to overcome a motion for a non-suit and the defendant must adduce sufficient evidence of the plaintiff's contributory negligence in order for the trial judge to leave this issue for the jury's consideration.

The evidential burden, however, does not always coincide with the legal burden since the common law or a statutory provision may divide the burdens between the parties. For example, to probate a will, an executrix has the legal burden of proof that the will is that of the testator and that the testator had the capacity to make that will.[65] This burden is frequently discharged by evidence that the testator executed a rational will in accordance with the requisite formalities and that the will was read over to the testator who appeared to understand it.[66] A

---

63   Section 258(1)(c) of the *Criminal Code*, R.S.C. 1985, c. C-46. The conclusion is required to be drawn, *Boyle v. R.* (1983), 5 C.C.C. (3d) 193, 35 C.R. (3d) 34, at 53, 148 D.L.R. (3d) 449, 5 C.R.R. 218, 41 O.R. (2d) 713 (C.A.).

64   *R. v. Proudlock*, [1979] 1 S.C.R. 525, 43 C.C.C. (2d) 321, 5 C.R. (3d) 21, 91 D.L.R. (3d) 449; *Boyle, ibid.*; but see, *R. v. Noble*, [1978] 1 S.C.R. 632, 37 C.C.C. (2d) 193, 40 C.R.N.S. 19, 80 D.L.R. (3d) 69, 17 N.R. 555, 19 N.B.R. (2d) 417, 30 A.P.R. 417; *R. v. Moreau*, [1979] 1 S.C.R. 261, 42 C.C.C. (2d) 525, 89 D.L.R. (3d) 449, 1 M.V.R. 1, 23 N.R. 541.

65   *Robins v. National Trust Co.*, [1927] A.C. 515, at 519, [1927] 2 D.L.R. 97, [1927] 1 W.W.R. 692 (P.C.).

66   *MacGregor v. Ryan*, [1965] S.C.R. 757, 53 D.L.R. (2d) 126; *Robins v. National Trust Co. Ltd., ibid.*; *Sutton v. Sadler* (1857), 3 C.B.N.S. 87, 26 L.J.C.P. 284.

party contesting the will can raise the issue of suspicious circumstances by pointing to circumstances that excite the suspicion of the court that the will was not the product of a free and capable testator or testatrix. The proponent of the will then has the legal burden of dispelling the suspicion and proving that the testator or testatrix knew and approved of the contents of the will.[67] In this respect, the function of the evidential burden in civil cases is the same as it is in criminal cases.

IV THE EFFECT OF DISCHARGING THE EVIDENTIAL BURDEN

A. *Two Evidentiary Effects*

A major source of confusion is the failure to describe the effect of the satisfaction of an evidential burden. A party who has the evidential burden is required by law to adduce evidence of a particular quality or cogency to the satisfaction of the trial judge, but the party is not required to prove a fact or issue either on a balance of probabilities or beyond a reasonable doubt.[68] In this sense, "the discharge of an evidential burden proves nothing — it merely raises an issue."[69]

There are two possible evidentiary effects when a party satisfies an evidential burden.[70] The discharge of some evidential burdens permits the trier of fact to decide that issue. For example, in a prosecution for the crime of theft, when the Crown satisfies the evidential burden as to the definitional elements of the offence, a jury

---

67 *Barry v. Butlin* (1838), 2 Moo P.C.C. 480; *Tyrell v. Painton*, [1894] P. 151, at 157 (C.A.); *Craig v. Lamoureux*, [1920] A.C. 349; *Riach v. Ferris*, [1934] S.C.R. 725, [1935] 1 D.L.R. 118; C.A. Wright, "Wills — Testamentary Capacity — 'Suspicious Circumstances' — Burden of Proof" (1938), 16 Can. Bar Rev. 405, at 414.

68 *Jayasena v. R.*, [1970] A.C. 618, [1970] 1 All E.R. 219 (P.C.). In *R. v. Schwartz*, [1988] 2 S.C.R. 443, 66 C.R. (3d) 251, 45 C.C.C. (3d) 97, 55 D.L.R. (4th) 1, [1989] 1 W.W.R. 289, 39 C.R.R. 260, 56 Man. R. (2d) 92, 88 N.R. 90, at 467 (S.C.R.) Dickson C.J.C. correctly points out that the evidential burden may be satisfied by evidence adduced by the other side.

69 *R. v. Hunt*, [1987] 1 All E.R. 1, [1987] A.C. 352, at 385 (H.L.). However, upon the satisfaction of some evidential burdens, in the absence of evidence to the contrary, there is a compelled fact determination.

70 S. Schiff, *Evidence in the Litigation Process*, 3rd ed. (Toronto: Carswell, 1988), at 1083 labels the effect as "permissible — fact — inference" and "compelled — fact — determination".

direction that demands a conviction would be a reversible error of law. Although the Crown has discharged the evidential burden in relation to the elements of the offence, the jury may, not must, convict in these circumstances. Similarly, if there is sufficient evidence to meet the threshold test for the common law defence of drunkenness, the jury may, not must, determine this issue favourably to the accused.[71] Simply put, the effect of the discharge of this type of evidential burden permits the trier of fact, as a matter of law, to reach a conclusion on the issue.

In civil actions, the satisfaction of some evidential burdens has the same evidentiary effect. Where the plaintiff and defendant adduce sufficient evidence of negligence and contributory negligence to discharge their respective evidential burdens, the trial judge must direct the jury on these issues. Because the jury is not required to decide the case one way or another, the discharge of these burdens allows the jury to determine these issues.

The discharge of other evidential burdens, however, compels a fact determination by the trier of fact that is favourable to the party that satisfies that particular burden. For example, s. 9(1) of the *Narcotic Control Act* states:[72]

> Subject to this section, a certificate purporting to be signed by an analyst stating that the analyst has analyzed or examined a substance and stating the result of the analysis or examination is admissible in evidence in any prosecution for an offence referred to in subsection 7(1) and, in the absence of evidence to the contrary, is proof of the statements contained in the certificate . . . .

Where a certificate of analysis stating that the analyst found the substance to be cannabis (marihuana) is admitted in evidence in a prosecution for possession of a narcotic, absent contradictory evidence, the trial judge must direct the jury to find that the substance is marihuana.[73] In these circumstances, once the Crown discharges its

---

71   The jury must weigh the evidence to determine if they are left with a reasonable doubt on the issue of guilt.

72   R.S.C. 1985, c. N-1. See *Interpretation Act*, R.S.C. 1985, c. I-21, s. 25.

73   *Oliver v. R.*, [1981] 2 S.C.R. 240, 62 C.C.C. (2d) 97, 24 C.R. (3d) 1, 127 D.L.R. (3d) 257, 38 N.R. 314, 32 A.R. 552.

evidential burden the trier of fact is compelled to find the existence of that fact favourable to the Crown.

In civil actions, the discharge of some evidential burdens has a similar effect. In *Circle Film Enterprises Inc. v. Cdn. Broadcasting Corp.*[74] the plaintiff sued for breach of copyright when the defendant corporation broadcast an obscure religious film. In support of its claim, the plaintiff filed a certificate of registration pursuant to s. 36(2) of the *Copyright Act*.[75] The subsection stated:[76]

> A certificate of registration of copyright in a work shall be *prima facie* evidence that copyright subsists in the work and that the person registered is the owner of such copyright.

The Supreme Court of Canada ruled as to the evidentiary value of the certificate:[77]

> A plaintiff who produces this certificate [of registration] has adduced some evidence in support of his case, sufficient to compel the tribunal of fact to act in his favour in the absence of any evidence to contradict it.

Accordingly, a certificate of registration of copyright, in the absence of evidence to the contrary, compels a factual determination that the registrant is the owner of the copyright.

The two possible effects of satisfying an evidential burden must be underlined. When a party satisfies some evidential burdens, the trier of fact *may* make a determination favourable to that party on that issue. Where a party satisfies other evidential burdens, in the absence of evidence to the contrary, the trier of fact *must* make a determination in accordance with the mandated conclusion. The satisfaction of the second type of evidential burden has the effect of casting an evidential burden upon the opponent to adduce some evidence or he or she will lose on that issue.

The consequence of failing to satisfy an evidential burden will

---

74 [1959] S.C.R. 602, 20 D.L.R. (2d) 211, 31 C.P.R. 57, 19 Fox Pat. C. 39.
75 R.S.C. 1927, c. 32 [now R.S.C. 1985, c. C-42, s. 53(2)]. The plaintiff's title was also proven by a series of assignments made in different parts of France, *ibid.* It seems questionable that s. 36(2) applied where the author was not a party to the litigation.
76 *Ibid.*
77 *Supra*, note 74, at 607.

vary depending upon which party the burden rests, upon the nature of the burden, and upon the stage of the proceedings at which the burden arises. For instance, if the Crown fails to discharge the evidential burden for a definitional element of an offence, the trial judge must direct the jury to acquit the accused.[78] If the Crown's case is sufficient to pass the trial judge, then the evidential burden for a common law defence, such as drunkenness, rests on the accused.[79] If the accused fails to adduce sufficient evidence of drunkenness to meet the threshold test for this defence, the trial judge will not leave this issue for the jury's consideration.[80] However, the trial judge's decision on this issue is not fatal to the accused as the Crown must still satisfy the legal burden of proof on the elements of the offence to the criminal standard.

In a civil negligence action, the plaintiff must adduce some evidence of the defendant's negligence to overcome a non-suit. If the trial judge rules adversely to the plaintiff, the plaintiff will lose the case.[81] If the theory of the defence is contributory negligence, the defendant must adduce sufficient evidence of contributory negligence in order for the trial judge to leave this issue for the jury's consideration.[82] If the defendant fails to satisfy this evidential burden, the defendant will lose on this issue but he or she will not necessarily lose the case as the plaintiff must satisfy the legal burden of proof on the issue of the defendant's negligence.

Accordingly, a party who has both the evidential and legal burdens on an issue will lose on that issue as a matter of law if that party fails to satisfy the evidential burden. Conversely, if the party has only an evidentiary burden on an issue, failure to satisfy it will not

---

78 Except where a common law or statutory rule allocates the burden of proof for such element to the defendant. Whether such a burden can be imposed on the accused must overcome a constitutional challenge, see Chapter 4, Presumptions.

79 *Mancini v. D.P.P.*, [1942] A.C. 1, [1941] 3 All E.R. 272 (H.L.); *R. v. Smyth*, [1963] V.R. 737 (Aust. S.C.): see D. Stuart, *Canadian Criminal Law*, 2nd ed. (Toronto: Carswell, 1987), at 392-93; *Boyle v. R.* (1983), 35 C.R. (3d) 34, 5 C.C.C. (3d) 193, 148 D.L.R. (3d) 449, 5 C.R.R. 218, 41 O.R. (2d) 713 (C.A.).

80 *R. v. Bernard*, [1988] 2 S.C.R. 833, 67 C.R. (3d) 113, 45 C.C.C. (3d) 1, 38 C.R.R. 82, 90 N.R. 321, 32 O.A.C. 161.

81 The procedure in civil actions with respect to this motion is discussed in Chapter 5, Standards of Proof.

82 See Chapter 5, Standards of Proof, for a discussion of the degree of proof necessary to raise an issue.

automatically result in a loss on the issue because the trier of fact must still accept the evidence of the party having the legal burden. If that evidence is indeterminate, the legal burden will be applied against the party having the legal burden of proof.

B. *The Terms* "Prima Facie *Evidence,"* "Prima Facie *Proof" and* "Prima Facie *Case"*

The use of imprecise language to describe the effect of satisfying the evidential burden may create confusion.[83] The phrases "*prima facie* proof", "*prima facie* evidence", and "*prima facie* case" are found in the jurisprudence, the texts on evidence, and the statutes. An analysis of five Supreme Court of Canada decisions illustrates how their use has produced uncertainty when courts ascribe different evidential effects to these terms.[84] In *Ontario Equitable Life and Accident Insurance Co. v. Baker*,[85] the trial judge and the Ontario Court of Appeal held that a receipt acknowledging payment was "*prima facie* proof" of payment of a life insurance premium and that the defendant had the legal burden to disprove payment. The Supreme Court of Canada held that a receipt is ordinarily "*prima facie* proof of payment", but in light of all the surrounding circumstances, the receipt was insufficient for the trier of fact to find that the premium had been paid. In this part of their reasons for judgment the Supreme Court used the term "*prima facie* proof" to mean that ordinarily a receipt was sufficient evidence on the issue of payment of the premium to overcome a motion for a non-suit, that is, a permissible fact determination. But in a later passage in their judgment, the Court stated:[86]

> . . . the judgments [of the lower courts] have confounded two different rules connected with proof . . . namely, the rule which requires that the burden of establishing an issue of which the proof is essential to the plaintiff's case shall rest upon the plaintiff, and the rule applicable to the condition which arises in the course

---

83   9 Wigmore, *Evidence* (Chadbourn rev. 1981) §§ 2487, 2494, at 292-300, 378-88.
84   See S. Schiff, *supra*, note 70, at 1082-084.
85   [1926] S.C.R. 297, [1926] 2 D.L.R. 289.
86   *Ibid.*, at 308-09 (S.C.R.).

of a trial, when a stage has been reached at which there is *prima facie* proof or presumption of the truth of an allegation, which ought therefore to be found true in the absence of further evidence. [emphasis added]

Here the Court seems to use the term *"prima facie* proof" to mean, in the absence of evidence to the contrary, there is a compelled fact determination.

In *Circle Film Enterprises v. Canadian Broadcasting Corp.*,[87] the Supreme Court of Canada considered the evidentiary effect of s. 36(2) of the *Copyright Act*.[88] The Supreme Court held that ownership of copyright subsists in the registrant and that the certificate constitutes sufficient evidence "to compel the tribunal of fact to act in [the plaintiff's] favour in the absence of any evidence to contradict it".[89] Because there was no evidence to the contrary, the certificate of registration satisfied the plaintiff's evidential and legal burdens on the issue of ownership.[90] In this decision the Supreme Court of Canada equated the terms *"prima facie* evidence" and *"prima facie* proof" to mean a compelled fact determination absent contradictory evidence.[91]

In *Sunbeam Corp. (Can.) v. R.*,[92] the accused corporation was charged with several offences under the *Combines Investigation Act*.[93] Section 41(2)(c) of the Act provided that documents which were in the possession of the accused "shall be admitted in evidence without further proof thereof and shall be *prima facie* evidence" of the accused's knowledge of the documents and their contents. The Ontario Court of Appeal held that such documents, in the absence of evidence to the contrary, required the trier of fact to find the requisite knowledge. Ritchie J., for the majority of the Supreme Court, disagreed. He stated:[94]

---

87   *Supra*, note 74.
88   R.S.C. 1927, c. 32, as am. [now R.S.C. 1985, c. C-42, s. 53(2)]. Section 36(2) provided: "A certificate of registration of copyright in a work shall be *prima facie* evidence that copyright subsists in the work and that the person registered is the owner of such copyright."
89   *Supra*, note 74, at 607.
90   *Ibid.*
91   See also passage from *Baker, supra*, note 86.
92   [1969] S.C.R. 221, [1969] 2 C.C.C. 189, 56 C.P.R. 242, 1 D.L.R. (3d) 161.
93   Then R.S.C. 1952, c. 314 [now *Competition Act*, R.S.C. 1985, c. C-34].
94   *Supra*, note 92, at 228.

... when the Crown has proved a *prima facie* case and no evidence is given on behalf of the accused, the jury *may* convict, but I know of no authority to the effect that the trier of fact is *required* to convict under such circumstances. [emphasis added]

The majority of the Supreme Court equated the terms "*prima facie* evidence" and "*prima facie* case" to mean a permissible fact inference and expressly rejected the alternative interpretation — a compelled fact determination. In dissent, Spence J., held that a *prima facie* case ". . . by lack of contradiction became conclusive evidence",[95] the construction the Court had earlier adopted in *Circle Film Enterprises Inc. v. Cdn. Broadcasting Corp.*[96]

In *R. v. Proudlock*,[97] the Supreme Court again considered the statutory term "*prima facie* evidence". Section 292(2) of the *Criminal Code* relating to the crime of break and enter with intent to commit an indictable offence stated:[98]

For the purposes of proceedings under this section, evidence that an accused

(a) broke and entered a place is *prima facie* evidence that he broke and entered with intent to commit an indictable offence therein

. . . .

Pigeon J., writing for the majority, held that the term "*prima facie* evidence" meant that a fact shall be established in the absence of evidence to the contrary. Estey J., in a separate judgment, held that the terms "*prima facie* evidence" and "proof, in the absence of evidence to the contrary" differed as to their evidentiary effect. In his view, only the latter phrase compels a factual determination in the absence of contrary evidence.[99]

---

95 *Ibid.*, at 251.
96 [1959] S.C.R. 602, 20 D.L.R. (2d) 211, 31 C.P.R. 57.
97 [1979] 1 S.C.R. 525, 43 C.C.C. (2d) 321, 5 C.R. (3d) 21, 91 D.L.R. (3d) 449.
98 Then S.C. 1953-54, c. 51.
99 *Supra*, note 97, at 535-36 (S.C.R.).

The majority decision in *Proudlock* however was not limited to an interpretation of the statutory provision. Where the Crown adduced sufficient evidence to establish a "*prima facie* case" Pigeon J. held:[100]

> [the accused must] raise a reasonable doubt as to his guilt; if it does not meet this test the *prima facie* case remains and conviction will ensue.

Accordingly, in the absence of evidence to the contrary, there is a compelled fact determination of guilt — an interpretation which was expressly rejected by the Supreme Court in *Sunbeam*.

The better view is that a *prima facie* case does not compel a specific determination unless there is a specific rule of law which demands such a conclusion.[101] The preferable position was stated by the Supreme Court of Canada in its earlier decision in *R. v. Girvin*:[102]

> I have always understood the rule to be that the Crown, in a criminal case, is not required to do more than produce evidence which, if unanswered, and believed, is sufficient to raise a *prima facie* case upon which the jury might be justified in finding a verdict.

Professor Schiff correctly observes that the Supreme Court of Canada interchangeably uses the terms "*prima facie* evidence" and "*prima facie* proof" to mean both a "permissible fact inference" and a "compelled fact determination".[103] To further muddy the water, the

---

100 *Ibid.*, at 551. The Court wrongly analogizes the common law justifiable inference (labelled a presumption of fact) arising out of possession of recently stolen goods to the statutory provision found in s. 306 of the *Criminal Code*, R.S.C. 1970, c. C-34 [now R.S.C. 1985, c. C-46, s. 348]. In *R. v. Schwartz*, [1988] 2 S.C.R. 443, 66 C.R. (3d) 251, 45 C.C.C. (3d) 97, 55 D.L.R. (4th) 1, [1989] 1 W.W.R. 289, 39 C.R.R. 260, 56 Man. R. (2d) 92, 88 N.R. 90 Dickson C.J.C. interprets Pigeon J.'s reasoning to the effect that the accused runs the risk of conviction.
101 See, e.g., section 348(2)(a) of the Criminal Code, R.S.C. 1985, c. C-46; see also Chapter 4, Presumptions.
102 (1911), 45 S.C.R. 167, at 169, 20 W.L.R. 130. This passage was recently adopted in *R. v. Mezzo*, [1986] 1 S.C.R. 802, 52 C.R. (3d) 113, 27 C.C.C. (3d) 97, 30 D.L.R. (4th) 161, [1986] 4 W.W.R. 577, 68 N.R. 1, 43 Man. R. (2d) 161.
103 S. Schiff, *Evidence in the Litigation Process*, 3rd ed. (Toronto: Carswell, 1988), at 1083.

term "*prima facie* case" is sometimes used as a synonym for both terms. Under the former construction, where a party satisfies the evidential burden, the jury may decide the issue in that party's favour ("permissible fact inference"[104]). From the opponent's viewpoint, the failure to adduce any evidence to meet a *prima facie* case renders that party susceptible to an adverse determination on that issue. The second construction mandates that the party will win on that issue unless the opposite party adduces evidence to the contrary ("compelled fact determination"[105]). Put differently, the opposite party now has an evidential burden to adduce sufficient contrary evidence or lose on that issue.

The terms "*prima facie* evidence", "*prima facie* proof", and "*prima facie* case" are meaningless unless the writer explains the sense in which the terms are used. For clarity and conciseness it is preferable, where possible, to explain the evidentiary effect consequent upon the proof of certain facts rather than to indiscriminately use these mixed Latin-English idioms.[106] Under the latter approach, these phrases are superfluous and, as the decisions of the Supreme Court clearly demonstrate, their use is dangerous.[107]

---

104   *Ibid.*
105   *Ibid.*
106   See, for example, *R. v. Robertson*, [1987] 1 S.C.R. 918, at 933, 33 C.C.C. (3d) 481, 58 C.R. (3d) 28, 39 D.L.R. (4th) 321, 75 N.R. 6, 20 O.A.C. 200.
107   See also, in *Ares v. Venner*, [1970] S.C.R. 608, 14 D.L.R. (3d) 4, 12 C.R.N.S. 349, 73 W.W.R. 347, where, at 626 (S.C.R.) Hall J., in reference to business records, stated that the "record should be received in evidence as *prima facie* proof of the facts stated therein. This should, in no way, preclude a party wishing to challenge the accuracy of the records or entries from doing so." But what is the effect of the records in the absence of evidence to the contrary? This problem is not distinctive to Canadian courts: see *Abrath v. North Eastern Railway Co.* (1883), 11 Q.B.D. 440, at 452-53, 456-58 (C.A.); and the comments of R.J. Delisle, *Evidence: Principles and Problems*, 1st ed. (Toronto: Carswell, 1984), at 45.

V TWO MISLEADING CONCEPTS

A. *Shifting Burdens*

The authorities[108] and the jurisprudence[109] often refer to the shifting of the evidential burden or the legal burden of proof. Except for the operation of rebuttable presumptions of law[110] or statutory provisions, these burdens do not shift.[111] In a motor vehicle negligence action the facts supporting the plantiff's and the defendant's allegations of negligence are often intertwined. Nonetheless, each party bears the evidential and legal burdens in relation to their respective versions of the facts. Once the trial judge rules that there is sufficient evidence of the defendant's negligence to leave the case for the jury, the evidential burden in relation to that issue is spent. The defendant must then adduce sufficient evidence of the plaintiff's contributory negligence to pass the trial judge on this issue — a different evidential burden. Assuming both parties adduce sufficient evidence to pass the trial judge, each party also bears a legal burden in relation to her or his respective allegations of negligence. Although the burdens in this case are distributed between the parties, the burdens do not shift.

For the crime of murder, the Crown bears both burdens as to the elements of the *actus reus* and *mens rea*. If the accused is relying on the defence of insanity, the accused has the evidential and legal burdens

---

108 See M.N. Howard, P. Crane and D.A. Hochberg, *Phipson on Evidence*, 14th ed. (London: Sweet & Maxwell, 1990), at 51. R. Cross, *Cross on Evidence*, 5th ed. (London: Butterworths, 1979), at 93-94; R. Cross and C. Tapper, *Cross on Evidence*, 7th ed. (London: Butterworths, 1990), at 115-18.

109 See, for example, *National Trust Co. v. Wong Aviation Ltd.*, [1969] S.C.R. 481, 3 D.L.R. (3d) 55; *Hellenius v. Lees*, [1972] S.C.R. 165, 20 D.L.R. (3d) 369; *D.P.P. v. Morgan*, [1976] A.C. 182, at 217, [1975] 2 All E.R. 347, at 364 (per Lord Simon of Glaisdale).

110 See Chapter 4, Presumptions.

111 Compare the 5th (*supra*, note 108, at 78-82) and 7th editions (*supra*, note 108, at 115-18) of *Cross on Evidence*. In the latter, the text states, at 115: "The definitions of the two principal senses of burden adopted . . . in this book render it difficult to speak meaningfully of the shifting of either of them". "A similar semantic difficulty arises in relation to the phenomenon frequently referred to as *the shifting of the burden*. Although this phrase is used continuously by both academic writers and judges it is, in fact, misleading in that all it means is that, in the same action, both the parties may be required to prove different matters", F. Bates, *Principles of Evidence*, 3rd ed. (The Law Book Co., 1985), at 27-28.

for this defence.[112] In this illustration, burdens allocated to the Crown and the accused are in relation to distinct issues[113] and thus understood, neither burden shifts.

An evidential or a legal burden may be conditional upon the discharge of an evidential burden by the opposite party. For instance, the accused's evidential burden in relation to a defence of a mistaken belief in consent for the crime of sexual assault does not arise until the Crown's case is sufficient to overcome a motion for a directed verdict of acquittal. Because the burdens are in relation to different issues,[114] no shifting of these evidential burdens occurs. Once the accused has met the evidential burden in relation to a mistaken belief in consent, the Crown bears the legal burden to disprove this defence. The legal burden in relation to this defence does not shift, rather it is conditional upon the satisfaction of an evidential burden by the accused.

In bailment cases, the plaintiff bears the evidential and legal burden that there was a bailment relationship and that the goods were not returned. The defendant bears both burdens that the loss or destruction of the goods did not occur by reason of her or his negligent act or omission.[115] Although the incidence of the burdens on the defendant are conditional upon the satisfaction of the burdens allocated to the plaintiff, neither of these burdens shifts.

It may infrequently arise that the incidence of the legal burden depends upon a determination of a fact by the jury. The underlying rationale for allocating the legal burden to the defendant to disprove negligence in bailment actions is concisely stated by Atkin L.J. in *The "Ruapehu"*:[116]

112　*R. v. Simpson* (1977), 35 C.C.C. (2d) 337, 77 D.L.R. (3d) 507, 16 O.R. (2d) 129, 2 L.M.Q. 40 (C.A.); *R. v. Chaulk*, [1990] 3 S.C.R. 1303, 62 C.C.C. (3d) 193, 2 C.R. (4th) 1, [1991] 2 W.W.R. 385, 69 Man. R. (2d) 161, 1 C.R.R. (2d) 1, 119 N.R. 161; *Ratti v. R.*, unreported, March 2, 1987, Callaghan A.C.J.H.C. (Ont. H.C.); affd. November 2, 1988, C.A. Doc. No. 355/87 (Ont. C.A.); leave to appeal to the Supreme Court of Canada granted, June 8, 1989, 1 S.C.R. xiii; *R. v. Romeo* (1991) 62 C.C.C. (3d) 1, 2 C.R. (4th) 307, 110 N.B.R. (2d) 57, 119 N.R. 309 (S.C.C.).

113　D. Stuart, *Canadian Criminal Law*, 2nd ed. (Toronto: Carswell, 1987), at 342-45, argues that the defence of insanity is a denial of *mens rea* and thus the Crown should have the legal burden of proof.

114　*R. v. Robertson, supra*, note 106.

115　*National Trust Co. v. Wong Aviation Ltd., supra*, note 109.

116　(1925), 21 Ll. L. Rep. 310, at 315; this passage was quoted by the Ontario Court of Appeal and referred to by the Supreme Court of Canada in *National*

The bailee knows all about it; he must explain. He and his servants are the persons in charge; the bailor has no opportunity of knowing what happened. These considerations, coupled with the duty to take care, result in the obligation on the bailee to show that that duty has been discharged.

In *National Trust Co. v. Wong Aviation Ltd.*[117] the Supreme Court of Canada held that the defendant's obligation to disprove negligence should occur only where all the considerations stipulated by Lord Atkin are present. Thus, the court held that where the bailee and the chattel disappeared and the defendant had no knowledge or the ability to find out the cause of the disappearance, the legal burden in relation to the defendant's negligence rested on the plaintiff.[118] If both parties discharged their respective evidential burdens, the incidence of the legal burden would be conditional upon the determination of disputed facts by the jury. For example, if the jury found that there was no bailment relationship, the plaintiff would bear the onus to prove that the defendant was negligent. But if the jury found that there was a bailment relationship and rejected the defendant's explanation that he or she had no knowledge of the circumstances surrounding the disappearance of the bailed goods, the defendant must disprove negligence. Although the incidence of the legal burden was conditional upon a determination of these facts by the jury, the burden did not shift.

In criminal law, the incidence of the burden of proof may also be conditional upon the determination of a fact. For the crime of break and enter with intent to commit an indictable offence therein, section 348(2)(a) of the *Criminal Code* provides:[119]

(2) For the purposes of proceedings under this section, evidence that an accused

(a) broke and entered a place or attempted to break and enter a place is, in the absence of evidence to the contrary, proof that he broke and entered the place or attempted to do so, as the case may be, with intent to commit an indictable offence therein . . .

Trust Co. v. Wong Aviation Ltd., ibid., at 489 (S.C.R.).
117 *Ibid.*
118 *Ibid.*, at 489, 491 (S.C.R.).
119 R.S.C. 1985 c. C-46.

Where the Crown establishes that the accused broke and entered a place, the section compels a determination that the accused intended to commit an indictable offence unless there is evidence to the contrary.[120]

Assume the accused testifies that he entered the premises to put out a fire. It is a question of law whether this explanation is capable of a particular determination and it is a question of fact whether it does so. The Supreme Court of Canada has held that an explanation that is disbelieved is not evidence to the contrary.[121] Where an accused offers a plausible explanation of lack of intent to commit an indictable offence, he or she discharges the evidential burden and accordingly the trial judge should direct the jury in the following way. If the accused's explanation is disbelieved by them, there is no evidence to the contrary and the jury must find the requisite intent in compliance with the statutory provision. If the jury does not disbelieve the accused's explanation, the Crown must prove the requisite intent beyond a reasonable doubt. There is no shift in the legal burden of proof, albeit its incidence is conditional upon a finding of fact by the jury.

In many contested actions, a party is obliged to adduce evidence as a matter of tactics and prudence. For instance, if the victim identifies the accused as the assailant who applied non-consensual force, the accused person runs a probable risk of an adverse determination in civil or criminal proceedings for an assault. As the strength of the proponent's case increases and in the absence of an explanation or some exculpatory circumstances arising from the evidence, the risk of an adverse determination also increases. If the theory of the defence is that a battery did not occur, testimony by the defendant to support this theory would be prudent in these circumstances.

Some authorities label the common sense or tactical decision to adduce evidence in such circumstances a "tactical burden" or a "tactical shifting" of the evidential burden. However, the decision by a party to go forward with evidence because the risk of an adverse verdict is too great, is not a question of law but a matter of common sense.[122] Since the defendant is not required by law to do anything,

---

120 *R. v. Proudlock*, [1979] 1 S.C.R. 525, 43 C.C.C. (2d) 321, 5 C.R. (3d) 21, 91 D.L.R. (3d) 449.
121 *Ibid.*, at 546 (S.C.R.).
122 G. Williams, *Textbook of Criminal Law*, 2nd ed. (London: Sweet & Maxwell,

this tactical decision to adduce evidence is not an evidential burden (using the definition in this text) and thus there is no shifting of the evidential burden.

Including the so-called "tactical shifting" of the evidential burden as part of the law of evidence adds nothing to one's understanding of the incidence or satisfaction of the evidential burden. For example, assume that the evidential burden is broadly defined to include situations where counsel adduces evidence as a matter of common sense, such as whenever counsel asks several questions in re-examination to bolster her or his case or calls a witness to refute an opponent's case. Defined as such, the evidentiary burden constantly "shifts" throughout the trial much like the ball at a ping-pong match or a basketball game. However, it would be impossible to determine either the incidence of the evidential burden at any stage of the proceeding or whether a party had satisfied it. Moreover, since there is no requirement for a ruling by the trial judge, its incidence or discharge are not questions of law.[123] Broadly defining the evidential burden to include a tactical or common sense decision to adduce evidence renders the term legally insignificant and of no practical value.[124]

Treating a tactical or provisional burden as forming part of the evidential burden can also lead to confusion as to its legal effect. In *The Ontario Equitable Life and Accident Insurance Co. v. Baker,*[125] the plaintiff executrix filed a receipt of payment as evidence that the insured had paid a premium on a life insurance policy. The defendant insurance company adduced evidence which cast doubt on the validity of the receipt. The central issue at trial and on appeal was the evidentiary value of the receipt. The trial judge held that the receipt

---

1983), at 49, note 16; *Poricanin v. Australian Consolidated Industries*, [1979] 2 N.S.W.L.R. 419, at 425, 429.

123 G. Williams, *Criminal Law: The General Part*, 2nd ed. (London: Stevens & Sons Ltd., 1961), at 877, note 2, states: "Lord Denning in 61 L.Q.R. 379 suggested the term 'provisional burden', apparently contemplating that this could shift backwards and forwards during the trial according to a prediction of how the jury would find if the case stopped at that point. . . . This is not a useful conception, and it is not used in any rule of law. The evidential burden, as that expression is used in the text above, is a legal concept."

124 R. Cross and C. Tapper, *Cross on Evidence*, 7th ed. (London: Butterworths, 1990), at 117, states: ". . . the concept of a provisional burden (sometimes called a 'tactical burden') is devoid of legal significance because there is no means of telling when it has been brought into existence or when it has been discharged".

125 [1926] S.C.R. 297, 2 D.L.R. 289.

was "*prima facie* proof of payment . . . and that the burden was on the defendant to show that the payment acknowledged by the receipt had not been made."[126] The Supreme Court of Canada held that the receipt ought to be found true unless there was evidence to the contrary.

Thus the court treated the receipt as proof of payment which cast upon the defendant an evidential burden which if unsatisfied compelled an inference of payment. In fact, the receipt was only a piece of evidence from which an inference of payment might be drawn. However cogent the evidence might be, it did not demand a finding of payment. In these circumstances, the defendant was in a position of having to adduce evidence as a matter of tactics and not law in order to forestall the likely event of an adverse finding. In *Snell v. Farrell*,[127] the Supreme Court of Canada dealt with the issue of causation in a medical malpractice case. The court referred to cases that spoke of the shifting of the burden, but concluded as follows:[128]

> These references speak of the shifting of the secondary or evidential burden of proof or the burden of adducing evidence. I find it preferable to explain the process without using the term secondary or evidential burden. It is not strictly accurate to speak of the burden shifting to the defendant when what is meant is that evidence adduced by the plaintiff may result in an inference being drawn adverse to the defendant. Whether an inference is or is not drawn is a matter of weighing evidence. The defendant runs the risk of an adverse inference in the absence of evidence to the contrary. This is sometimes referred to as imposing on the defendant a provisional or tactical burden. See Cross [6th ed.] . . . , at p. 129. In my opinion, this is not a true burden of proof, and use of an additional label to describe what is an ordinary step in the fact-finding process is unwarranted.

---

126 *Ibid.*, at 305 (S.C.R.).
127 [1990] 2 S.C.R. 311, 110 N.R. 200, 72 D.L.R. (4th) 289, 107 N.B.R. (2d) 94, 4 C.C.L.T. (2d) 229.
128 *Ibid.*, at 219 (N.R.), 329 (S.C.R.).

B. *Burdens Expressed as Presumptions*

The allocation of the legal burden of proof is sometimes expressed as a presumption. The best known example of this phenomenon is the presumption of innocence, which means that the Crown must prove the guilt of the accused person. Although this particular illustration does not create mischief,[129] the use of the term "presumption" to describe the incidence of a burden or the evidentiary effect of a piece of evidence may cause confusion. In *Baker*,[130] the Supreme Court of Canada used the term "presumption" to describe the evidentiary effect of a receipt:[131]

> . . . the rule applicable to the condition which arises in the course of a trial, where a stage has been reached at which there is *prima facie* proof or *presumption* of the truth of an allegation, which ought therefore to be found true in the absence of further evidence. . . . [emphasis added]

Although a plaintiff may succeed if cogent evidence is uncontroverted, it is misleading to label the effect of such evidence a presumption. The law of presumptions is problematic[132] and the use of the term presumption to describe the evidential effect of an item of evidence or the operation of an evidential burden adds nothing to our understanding of either subject.

VI ALLOCATING THE BURDENS

A. *Overview*

Historically, the incidence of the burdens was developed on a case-by-case basis by trial judges and appeal courts. The famous case of *Joseph Constantine Steamship Line Ltd. v. Imperial Smelting Corp. Ltd.*[133] illustrates this phenomenon. The plaintiff chartered a ship from the defendant and claimed damages for breach of contract when it failed to load a cargo. The defendant pleaded that its ability to

---

129 See Chapter 4, Presumptions.
130 *Supra*, note 125.
131 *Supra*, note 125, at 308-09 (S.C.R.).
132 See Chapter 4, Presumptions.
133 [1942] A.C. 154, [1941] 2 All E.R. 165 (H.L.).

perform the contract was frustrated by an explosion on board the ship. The House of Lords held that the plaintiff had the onus to prove that the defendant's conduct was responsible for the frustration of the contract.[134] Accordingly, this case determined the incidence of the legal burden of proof where frustration of a contract was pleaded.

The tort doctrine of *res ipsa loquitur* illustrates the confusion which results when a legal doctrine is uncertain as to its evidentiary effect or which burden it allocates. *Res ipsa loquitur* applies in situations where the thing which inflicted the damage was under the sole management and control of the defendant, or of someone for whom the defendant is responsible or has a right to control, and the occurrence is such that it would not have happened without negligence.[135] It is stated in *Cross on Evidence* that there are three alternative views as to the doctrine's legal effect.[136]

Res ipsa loquitur, correctly understood, means that circumstantial evidence constitutes reasonable evidence of negligence. Accordingly, the plaintiff is able to overcome a motion for a non-suit and the trial judge is required to instruct the jury on the issue of negligence. The jury may, but need not, find negligence: a permissible fact inference.[137] If, at the conclusion of the case, it would be equally reasonable to infer negligence or no negligence, the plaintiff will lose since he or she bears the legal burden on this issue.[138] Under this construction, the maxim is superfluous. It can be treated simply as a case of circumstantial evidence.

---

134   If neither party is able to prove or disprove fault, in these circumstances the incidence of the burden of proof determines the outcome: see J. Stone, "Burden of Proof and the Judicial Process" (1944), 60 L.Q.R. 262.

135   *Phillips v. Ford Motor Co. of Canada Ltd.*, [1971] 2 O.R. 637, 18 D.L.R. (3d) 641 (C.A.).

136   R. Cross and C. Tapper, *Cross on Evidence*, 6th ed. (London: Butterworths, 1985), at 137-39.

137   *United Motors Service Ltd. v. Hutson*, [1937] S.C.R. 294, [1937] 1 D.L.R. 737, 4 I.L.R. 91; *Interlake Tissue Mills Co. v. Salmon*, [1949] 1 D.L.R. 207, [1948] O.R. 950 (Ont. C.A.). See also *Government Insurance Office v. Fredrichberg* (1968), 118 C.L.R. 403 (H.C. Aust.), at 413.

138   *United Motors Service, Inc.*, *ibid.*, per Duff C.J. In *Hellenius v. Lees*, [1971] 1 O.R. 273, 15 D.L.R. (3d) 147 (C.A.); affd. [1972] S.C.R. 165, 20 D.L.R. (2d) 369, Laskin J.A. stated in a dissenting decision, at (O.R.) 282: "None the less, it appears to me to be the proper principle of law that, whatever be the facts upon which an inference of negligence may be raised (whether or not this be called *res ipsa loquitur*), the injured passenger carries the ultimate burden of proof."

A different construction of the doctrine is that the defendant has an evidential burden to adduce some evidence of a lack of negligence. In the absence of evidence to the contrary, the trier of fact must find for the plaintiff on the negligence issue: a compelled fact determination.[139] If the defendant adduces sufficient evidence of no negligence to satisfy this evidential burden, the plaintiff bears the legal burden on the issue of negligence. The third possible construction is that both the evidential and legal burdens rest on the defendant to disprove negligence to a balance of probabilities.[140]

Since the maxim often leads to confusion, its use might be abandoned and replaced by language that accurately conveys the evidentiary effect of unexplained circumstantial evidence from which negligence may be inferred. For example, in *McHugh v. Reynolds Extrusion Co.*[141] the term *res ipsa loquitur* was referred to by the trial judge both as permitting an inference of negligence and a "shifting" of the onus of proof. Its application, however, is so firmly entrenched that it is likely not possible to do so.

The uncertainty created by the term *res ipsa loquitur* may be contrasted with legislation that clearly allocates the legal burden to the defendant driver/owner to disprove negligence where a pedestrian and a motor vehicle are involved in an accident. Since a pedestrian may be unaware or unable to prove the cause of the collision,[142] s. 167(1) of the Ontario *Highway Traffic Act* states:[143]

> When loss or damage is sustained by any person by reason of a motor vehicle on a highway, the onus of proof that the loss or

---

139   *Hellenius v. Lees*, [1972] S.C.R. 165, 20 D.L.R. (2d) 369, at (S.C.R.) 172, where Ritchie J. quoted from *Clerk and Lindsell on Torts*, 13th ed. (London: Butterworths, 1969), para. 967. See also '*The Kite*', [1933] P. 154, [1933] All E.R. Rep. 234 as cited in *Cross on Evidence, supra*, note 136, at 137.

140   *Zeppa v. Coca-Cola Ltd.*, [1955] O.R. 855, [1955] 5 D.L.R. 187 (C.A.); *United Motors Service Ltd., supra*, note 137. See also *Barkway v. South Wales Transport Co.*, [1948] 2 All E.R. 460; revd. on other grounds [1950] 1 All E.R. 392; *Southport Corp. v. Esso Petroleum Co.*, [1956] A.C. 218, [1955] 3 All E.R. 864. This later rule may be more appropriate in products liability cases because of difficulties of proof where it is more probable than not that the fault was due to negligence by the manufacturer.

141   (1974), 7 O.R. (2d) 336, 55 D.L.R. (3d) 180; affd. 15 O.R. (2d) 325 (C.A.).

142   *Jackson v. Millar* (1972), 31 D.L.R. (3d) 263, [1973] 1 O.R. 399 (Ont. C.A.); revd. on other grounds, [1976] 1 S.C.R. 225, 59 D.L.R. (3d) 246, 4 N.R. 17.

143   R.S.O. 1980, c. 198.

damage did not arise through the negligence or improper conduct of the owner or driver of the motor vehicle is upon the
owner or driver.

Unfortunately, legislation sometimes fails to discriminate between the
burdens or to stipulate the evidentiary effect of a provision and it is
often silent or unclear as to the incidence of a burden. In these
circumstances, the courts must examine the legislation and resolve
these problems on a case-by-case basis.

There have been various attempts to create formulae to determine the allocation of the burdens. Professor Tapper states that "as a
matter of common sense, the legal burden of proving all facts essential
to their claims normally rests upon the plaintiff in a civil suit or the
prosecutor in criminal proceedings", but as the author notes, the
question then arises as to what facts are essential to one's claim. He
concludes, however, that since the incidence of the burden in some
actions is arbitrary, the matter must be determined by precedent[144]
and thus, "it is obviously vain to seek for any set formula . . . ."[145]

After examining various judicial formulae for determining the
incidence of the legal burden, Professor Morgan thought that most of
the suggested formulae had little practical value.[146] For example, one
formula suggests that a party asserting an affirmative of an issue must
prove it. But it is merely a matter of choice whether an issue is stated
positively or negatively. For instance, an allegation of negligence may
be described positively as an act of negligence or negatively as a failure
to exercise due care.[147] Also, the Crown or the plaintiff is often
required to disprove an issue[148] or to prove a negative, for example,
the absence of consent in an assault case.[149] This suggested formula,
like many of its counterparts, should be viewed as a guide for deter-

---

144 R. Cross and C. Tapper, *Cross on Evidence*, 7th ed. (London: Butterworths,
1990), at 120.
145 *Ibid.*, at 124.
146 E.M. Morgan, *Some Problems of Proof under the Anglo-American System of
Litigation* (New York: Columbia University Press, 1956), at 74-76.
147 *R. v. Tutton*, [1989] 1 S.C.R. 1392, 48 C.C.C. (3d) 129, 69 C.R. (3d) 289,
46 C.R.R. 394*n*, 35 O.A.C. 1, 13 M.V.R. (2d) 161, 98 N.R. 19 (S.C.C.).
148 E.g., the accused did not act in self-defence.
149 *R. v. Robertson*, [1987] 1 S.C.R. 918, 33 C.C.C. (3d) 481, 58 C.R. (3d) 28,
39 D.L.R. (4th) 321, 75 N.R. 6, 20 O.A.C. 200; *Mann v. Balaban*, [1970] S.C.R.
74, 8 D.L.R. (3d) 548.

mining the incidence of a burden rather than as a rule of construction.

Two controversial formulae for determining the incidence of the burdens merit special consideration: (1) exceptions, exemptions, excuses, qualifications and provisos; and (2) facts particularly within the knowledge of the party. These doctrines and their underlying rationale are discussed in both criminal and civil cases.[150] For convenience, these intertwined doctrines will be discussed under the following heading.

B. *Exceptions, Exemptions, Excuses, Qualifications, and Provisos*

The origin, rationale and construction of this formula have been thoroughly analyzed by the English Court of Appeal and the House of Lords. In *R. v. Edwards*,[151] the English Court of Appeal traced the origins of the pleading rules governing negative averments in informations and indictments. The court stated that by the end of the seventeenth century a pleading distinction was drawn between a proviso in a statute and an exception: exceptions had to be pleaded and disproved by the Crown whereas there was no need to plead or disprove provisos.[152] In the early nineteenth century case of *R. v. Turner*,[153] the accused was charged with possession of game without a necessary qualification or authorization required under the statute (which set out 10 qualifications). Lord Ellenborough C.J. held that the qualifications were essential to the indictment but that the prosecution did not bear the onus of proof on these issues. He reasoned:[154]

> . . . there would be a moral impossibility of ever convicting on such an information . . . And does not, then, common sense show

---

150 *Nimmo v. Alexander Cowan & Sons Ltd.*, [1968] A.C. 107, [1967] 3 All E.R. 187 (H.L.); *Pleet v. Canadian Northern Quebec Railway Co.* (1921), 50 O.L.R. 223 (C.A.); affd. 26 C.R.C. 238, [1923] 4 D.L.R. 1112 (S.C.R.), at (O.L.R.) 227.
151 [1974] 2 All E.R. 1085, [1975] Q.B. 27 (C.A.).
152 *Ibid.*, at 1089 (All E.R.), citing *R. v. Jarvis* (1756), 1 East., 643, note (e).
153 (1816), 5 M. & S. 206, 105 E.R. 1026.
154 *Ibid.*, at 1028 (E.R.). J.B. Thayer, *A Preliminary Treatise on Evidence at the Common Law*, reprint of 1898 ed. (New York: Augustus M. Kelley, 1969), at 359 wrote: "There is great sense in such a doctrine as indicating a duty of producing evidence, but little or none when it marks a duty of establishing."

that the burden of proof ought to be cast on the person who, by establishing any one of the qualifications, will be well defended?

In the same case, Bayley J. articulated a different justification for the rule:[155]

> I have always understood it to be a general rule that if a negative averment be made by one party, which is peculiarly within the knowledge of the other, the party within whose knowledge it lies, and who asserts the affirmative is to prove it, and not he who avers the negative . . . there is no hardship in casting the burden of affirmative proof on the defendant because he must be presumed to know his own qualification, and to be able to prove it.

Whether Bayley J.'s reasoning gave rise to a distinct formula based on the principle that a party must prove a fact (or a negative averment) particularly within the party's knowledge, or whether this doctrine became intertwined with the exemption and proviso formula is not important for present purposes. What is important is that the reasoning of Bayley J. in *Turner* was extended to many diverse circumstances. For example, in *John v. Humphreys*,[156] a case involving a charge of driving without a licence, Lord Goddard C.J. stated:[157]

> . . . when an Act of Parliament provides that a person shall not do a certain thing unless he has a licence, the onus is always on the defendant to prove that he has a licence because it is a fact peculiarly within his own knowledge . . .

In the modern case of *R. v. Edwards*[158] the accused was charged with selling liquor without a licence, but the prosecution adduced no evidence of a lack of a licence. In upholding the conviction, the

---

155 *Ibid.*
156 [1955] 1 All E.R. 793, [1955] 1 W.L.R. 325 (Q.B.D.).
157 *Ibid.*, at 794. See also *R. v. McIver*, [1965] 4 C.C.C. 182, 45 C.R. 401, [1965] 2 O.R. 475 (C.A.); affd. [1966] 2 S.C.R. 254, [1966] 2 C.C.C. 289, 48 C.R. 4; but see *R. v. Wilson* (1971), 1 C.C.C. (2d) 466, [1971] O.R. 349 (C.A.). For a criticism see Bates, *Principles of Evidence* (The Law Book Co., 1985), at 34-35; R.J. Delisle, *Evidence, Principles and Problems*, 2nd ed. (Toronto: Carswell, 1989), at 98-100. See also *R. v. Strand Electric Ltd.*, [1969] 2 C.C.C. 264, [1969] 1 O.R. 190 (C.A.).
158 *Supra*, note 151.

English Court of Appeal held that the old distinction between provisos and exemptions had been ". . . moribund, if not dead, for well over a century . . .".[159] The "facts particularly within the knowledge of the accused" formula for determining the incidence of the legal burden was rejected. The court stated:[160]

> [t]here is not, and never has been, a general rule of law that the mere fact that a matter lies particularly within the knowledge of the defendant is sufficient to cast the onus on him.

The court also rejected this doctrine as a rationale for the exception and proviso rule:[161]

> [i]n our judgment its application [the exception doctrine] does not depend upon either the fact, or the presumption, that the defendant has peculiar knowledge enabling him to prove the positive of any negative averment. As Wigmore pointed out in his great treatise on evidence this concept of working knowledge furnishes no working rule.

In *Edwards*, the Court of Appeal both reformulated the *Turner* doctrine and limited its scope:[162]

> [i]t is limited to offences arising under enactments which prohibit the doing of an act save in specified circumstances or by persons of specified classes or with specified qualifications or with the licence or permission of specified authorities. Whenever the prosecution seeks to rely on this exception, the court must construe the enactment under which the charge is laid. If

---

159 *Supra*, note 151, at 1093 (All E.R.) citing with approval Viscount Caldecote L.C.J. in *R. v. Oliver*, [1943] 2 All E.R. 800, at 802-03: ". . . it seems to us to be difficult to make the result depend on the question whether the negative is of a proviso or of an exception. We think it makes no difference at all . . . ."

160 *Supra*, note 151, at 1091 (All E.R.). Similarly, in civil proceedings a party "must plead and prove matters as to which his adversary has superior access to the proof" E.W. Cleary (ed.), *McCormick on Evidence*, 3rd ed. (St. Paul: West Publishing, 1984), at 950.

161 *Supra*, note 151, at 1095 (All E.R.). See also *R. v. Spurge*, [1961] 1 All E.R. 577, 45 Cr. App. 213, [1961] 2 Q.B. 205, at 212-13 (C.C.A.).

162 *Ibid.*, at 1095 (All E.R.).

the true construction is that the enactment prohibits the doing of acts, subject to provisos, exemptions and the like, then the prosecution can rely upon the exception.

Because some statutory provisions would fall outside the reformulated rule,[163] the House of Lords subsequently downgraded the status of the suggested formula in *Edwards* to an "excellent guide to construction".[164]

In *R. v. Lee's Poultry Ltd.*,[165] the Ontario Court of Appeal adopted and applied the reformulated *Edwards* rule to the statutory exception proviso governing summary offences under Ontario statutes.[166] As to this, it is important to note that the English Court of Appeal in *Edwards*[167] expressly held that the statutory exceptions and proviso doctrine for summary conviction offences was the same as the common law rule for indictable offences. In *R. v. Hunt*, the House of Lords agreed with this interpretation:[168]

The law would have developed on absurd lines if in respect of the same offence the burden of proof today differed according to whether the case was heard by the magistrates or on indictment.

These words apply to the Canadian scene as it would seem anomalous if the Crown's election of the mode of trial determined the incidence of the legal burden of proof for a hybrid offence.[169]

In *Lee's Poultry Ltd.*, the Ontario Court of Appeal also held that

---

163 *Nimmo v. Alexander Cowan & Sons Ltd., supra*, note 150 (H.L.).

164 *R. v. Hunt*, [1987] A.C. 352, at 375 (H.L.).

165 (1985), 43 C.R. (3d) 289, 17 C.C.C. (3d) 539, 12 C.R.R. 125, 7 O.A.C. 100 (Ont. C.A.).

166 *Ibid.*, at (C.R.) 293-94. In a dissenting judgment in *R. v. Schwartz*, [1988] 2 S.C.R. 443, 66 C.R. (3d) 251, 45 C.C.C. (3d) 97, 55 D.L.R. (4th) 1, [1989] 1 W.W.R. 289, 39 C.R.R. 260, 56 Man. R. (2d) 92, 88 N.R. 90, Dickson C.J.C. reasons at (S.C.R.) 464-69 that the *Edwards* rule violates the presumption of innocence.

167 *Supra*, note 151, at (S.C.R.) 1092. This reasoning was specifically approved by the House of Lords in *Hunt, supra*, note 164, at 375-76. See also *Dowling v. Bowie*, [1952] 86 C.L.R. 136 (Aust. H.C.).

168 *Supra*, note 164, at 373.

169 See *R. v. Cameron*, [1966] 4 C.C.C. 273, 49 C.R. 49, 58 D.L.R. (2d) 486, [1966] 2 O.R. 777 (C.A.); affd. [1967] 2 C.C.C. 195*n*, 1 C.R.N.S. 227, 2 D.L.R. (2d) 326*n*.

the reformulated *Edwards* rule replicates a provision found in s. 794(2) of the *Criminal Code* and similar legislative provisions. Section 794(2) states:[170]

> The burden of proving that an exception, exemption, proviso, excuse or qualification prescribed by law operates in favour of the defendant is on the defendant, and the prosecutor is not required, except by way of rebuttal, to prove that the exception, exemption, proviso, excuse or qualification does not operate in favour of the defendant, whether or not it is set out in the information.

But the statutory language of the English provision is quite different than its Canadian counterparts.[171] The words "burden of proving", like its English forerunner,[172] suggest that the accused has the legal burden of proof. But the unique language in the Canadian statute that "the prosecutor is not required, except by way of rebuttal, to prove that the exception . . . does not operate in favour of the defendant . . ." suggests that the Crown maintains the legal burden once the defendant satisfies an evidential burden. This question may be academic as the Supreme Court has held that an almost identically worded provision in the *Narcotic Control Act*[173] casts the legal burden of proof onto the accused.[174]

The scope of the exception and proviso rule in criminal proceedings will be clarified on a case-by-case basis. For example, in *Perka*

---

170 R.S.C. 1985, c. C-46. See also s. 7 of the *Narcotic Control Act*, R.S.C. 1985, c. N-1 and s. 48(3) of the *Provincial Offences Act*, R.S.O. 1980, c. 400.

171 Section 101 of the *Magistrates' Courts Act 1980* (U.K.), c. 43 provides: "Where the defendant to an information or complaint relies for his defence on any exception, exemption, proviso, excuse or qualification, whether or not it accompanies the description of the offence or matter of complaint in the enactment creating the offence or on which the complaint is founded, the burden of proving the exception, exemption, proviso, excuse or qualification shall be on him; and this notwithstanding that the information or complaint contains an allegation negativing the exception, exemption, proviso, excuse or qualification."

172 *Ibid.*

173 R.S.C. 1985, c. N-1, s. 7(2).

174 *Perka v. R.*, [1984] 2 S.C.R. 233, 14 C.C.C. (3d) 385, 42 C.R. (3d) 113, [1984] 6 W.W.R. 289, 13 D.L.R. (4th) 1, 55 N.R. 1. This case, however, was a pre-*Charter* decision. It will have to be reassessed in light of cases such as *R. v. Holmes*, [1988] 1 S.C.R. 914, 41 C.C.C. (3d) 497, 64 C.R. (3d) 97, 27 O.A.C. 321, 85 N.R. 21 and *R. v. Schwartz, supra*, note 166.

v. R.[175] the Supreme Court of Canada held that common law defences do not fall within the rule. Leaving aside constitutional considerations, the express statutory cases are not troublesome, but as the House of Lords held:[176]

> . . . a statute can, on its true construction, place a burden of proof on the defendant although it does not do so expressly . . . a burden that has to be discharged on the balance of probabilities.

In the absence of linguistic signposts such as "except for",[177] "provided that", and "subject to", it may be a difficult task to determine whether a statutory provision is an essential ingredient, an excuse,[178] or a qualification.[179]

In the cases of *Nimmo v. Alexander Cowan & Sons Ltd.*[180] and *R. v. Hunt*,[181] the House of Lords articulated criteria to determine the incidence of the legal burden where the statute is vague. The criteria include the mischief at which the statute was aimed, the substance and effect of the enactment, and the practical considerations affecting the incidence of the burden such as the ease or difficulty that the respective parties would encounter in discharging the burden.[182] The latter criterion implicitly resurrects the importance of "facts particularly within the knowledge of a party" as being a rationale for the exception and proviso rule. The court stressed, however, that a court should be reluctant to draw the inference that a statute imposes an onerous duty on the defendant to prove his innocence especially if he or she would

---

175 *Ibid.*

176 *Hunt, supra,* note 164, at 374, per Lord Griffiths.

177 See *Lynch v. Attwood,* [1983] 3 N.S.W.L.R. 1 (S.C.).

178 Compare *R. v. Johnson and Edwards,* [1981] Qd. R. 440 (C.A.).

179 See *Hunt, supra,* note 164; *Nimmo v. Alexander Cowan & Sons Ltd.,* [1968] A.C. 107, [1967] 3 All E.R. 187 (H.L.), and *Dowling v. Bowie, supra,* note 167, for examples of statutory language that created difficulties. See also J.C. Smith, *Justification and Excuse in the Criminal Law* (London: Stevens and Sons, 1989).

180 *Ibid.*

181 *Supra,* note 164.

182 *Supra,* note 164, at 374, 380, 383. Also, the arrangement of the clauses in legislation may indicate the incidence of the burdens, *Dowling v. Bowie, supra,* note 167, at 139: ". . . where a statute having defined the grounds of some liability it imposes proceeds to introduce by some distinct provision a matter of exception or excuse, it lies upon the party seeking to avail himself of the exception or excuse to prove the facts which bring his case within it": See also Bates, *Principles of Evidence,* at 33.

encounter practical difficulties discharging it.[183] Obviously, taken to the extreme, a rule of construction based on this rationale would require an accused to prove his or her innocence.[184] On the other hand, to require the Crown to negative every possible qualification or excuse beyond a reasonable doubt for some offences may render the statutory prohibition impotent.[185]

Perhaps there are no hard rules of construction but rather, there are general criteria for determining the incidence of the legal burden. Consider, for example, the tort or crime of assault. In a civil action, the Supreme Court of Canada held that the defendant has the onus of proof that the assault was justified and reasonable force was used.[186] In parallel criminal proceedings, the accused bears only an evidential burden that he or she acted in self-defence.[187] The basis for this distinction does not lie in a mechanical formula or rule of construction but rather our traditional notions of justice. As American writers conclude, the incidence of the burden of proof is dependent upon considerations of policy, fairness and probability, a subject to which we now turn.[188]

---

183 *Supra*, note 164, at 374, 377, per Lord Griffiths.

184 For example, a lack of intent to commit murder. In *R. v. Wholesale Travel Group Inc.* (1991), 67 C.C.C. (3d) 193 (S.C.C.) Cory and Iacobucci JJ. at 257, 266-68 relied on this doctrine to uphold the constitutional validity of a statutory provision allocating the burden of proof for due diligence to an accused charged with a public welfare offence.

185 Section 3(1) of the *Narcotic Control Act*, R.S.C. 1985, c. N-1 states: "Except as authorized by this Act or the regulations, no person shall have a narcotic in his possession". Since numerous pharmacists, hospital staff and doctors are exempted and because a person may lawfully possess a narcotic under a prescription, it would be difficult, if not impossible, to negate every possible lawful possession thereby rendering the law potentially unenforceable.

186 *Mann v. Balaban*, [1970] S.C.R. 74, at 87, 8 D.L.R. (3d) 548.

187 *Latour v. R.*, [1951] S.C.R. 19, 98 C.C.C. 258, 11 C.R. 1, [1951] 1 D.L.R. 834.

188 E.W. Cleary (ed.), *McCormick on Evidence*, 2nd. ed. (St. Paul: West Publishing, 1972), at 789; E.M. Morgan, *Some Problems of Proof Under the Anglo-American System of Litigation* (New York: Columbia University Press, 1956), at 76; 9 Wigmore, *Evidence* (Chadbourn rev. 1981), § 2486, at 291-92 states: "The truth is that there is not and cannot be any one general solvent for all cases. It is merely a question of policy and fairness based on experience in the different situations. . . . There are merely specific rules for specific classes of cases, resting for their ultimate basis upon broad reasons of expedience and fairness". See also R. Cross and C. Tapper, *Cross on Evidence*, 7th ed. (London: Butterworths, 1990), at 123.

C. *Grounds of Policy, Fairness and Probability*

Courts do not examine the underlying reasons for the incidence of a burden unless there is no binding precedent,[189] the common law or a statutory rule is unclear,[190] a party challenges a well-settled rule,[191] or a constitutional consideration arises.[192] The application of the elusive principles of fairness, policy, and probability for the determination of the incidence of the burdens is illustrated in a murder prosecution where the accused relies on self-defence. The Crown must first convince the trial judge that there is sufficient evidence on the definitional elements of the offence for the jury to consider before the accused is put to her or his election to adduce any evidence of a justification or excuse. But as noted, the accused is not obliged to do anything unless he or she wishes the jury to consider additional facts tending to show that the killing was in self-defence. However, the criminal law allocates merely the evidential burden to the accused for this defence.[193] Once the accused discharges this evidential burden, the Crown has the onus to negative this defence.

Let us examine the result if the Crown was required to adduce some evidence negating all possible common law defences as part of its case-in-chief. Because the Crown would not know of the absence of every possible exculpatory circumstances and because it would be unlikely that the Crown could correctly anticipate all possible defences that might be open to the defendant, such a rule would produce unjustified acquittals. Even if the Crown could adduce sufficient evidence negating every possible justification or excuse, it would be an inefficient use of court resources to receive evidence that is unrelated to the merits of the case and its admission could only confuse a jury. The legal *status quo* that distributes the burdens between the parties complies with our historic and present notions of fairness as evidenced by the common law[194] and by the constitutional right of the

---

189   See *Joseph Constantine Steamship Line Ltd. v. Imperial Smelting Corporation Ltd.*, [1972] A.C. 154, [1941] 2 All E.R. 165 (H.L.).

190   *R. v. Hunt*, [1987] A.C. 352 (H.L.).

191   *National Trust v. Wong Aviation Ltd.*, [1969] S.C.R. 481, 3 D.L.R. (3d) 55.

192   *R. v. Oakes*, [1986] 1 S.C.R. 103, 50 C.R. (3d) 1, 24 C.C.C. (3d) 321, 26 D.L.R. (4th) 200, 65 N.R. 87, 14 O.A.C. 335, 53 D.R. (2d) 719 (headnote only).

193   *Supra*, note 188.

194   *Woolmington v. D.P.P.*, [1935] A.C. 462, [1935] All E.R. Rep. 1 (H.L.); *Mancini v. D.P.P.*, [1942] A.C. 1, [1941] 3 All E.R. 272 (H.L.); *R. v. Lobell*, [1957] 1 All E.R. 734, [1957] 1 Q.B. 547 (C.C.A.).

presumption of innocence.[195] Also, because the evidential burden defines the minimum of evidence required to satisfy the burden, the rule prevents a meritless defence from being presented to the jury.[196] Thus, on considerations of policy, fairness and probability the distribution of the burdens for the elements for the crime of murder and the defence of self-defence is reasonably justified in today's society.

The rules governing the incidence of the burdens in true crimes may be contrasted with the rules governing public welfare offences.[197] In *R. v. Sault Ste. Marie (City)*,[198] the Supreme Court of Canada created a new category of responsibility for regulatory offences where there is no express requirement for a mental state. The court held that the Crown had the evidential and legal burdens for the *actus reus* but that the accused had the legal burden to prove that he or she acted without negligence.[199] The creation of strict liability offences was seen by the court as a compromise or "half-way house" between true crimes requiring a subjective mental state and offences of absolute liability where merely doing the act was culpable in law. As the underlying assumptions or factors for allocating a burden for all regulatory offences cannot be empirically tested,[200] it is difficult to argue with certainty which position better reflects the broad considerations of policy, fairness and probabilities. Previously a legislative rule allocating a burden to party was not reviewable by the courts[201] but now the

---

195 Dickson C.J.C. reasoned in *R. v. Whyte*, [1988] 2 S.C.R. 3, 42 C.C.C. (3d) 97, 64 C.R. (3d) 123, 29 B.C.L.R. (2d) 273, [1988] 5 W.W.R. 26, 86 N.R. 328, 6 M.V.R. (2d) 138, that the incidence of any burden to the accused may contravene s. 11(d) of the *Charter* but, presumably, a law might be saved under s. 1; see Chapter 4, Presumptions.

196 G. Williams, *Textbook of Criminal Law*, 2nd ed. (London: Stevens & Sons, 1983), at 58.

197 But see Alan Bruder, "Imprisonment and Strict Liability" (1990), 40 U.T.L.J. 738.

198 [1978] 2 S.C.R. 1299, 40 C.C.C. (2d) 353, 3 C.R. (3d) 30, 85 D.L.R. (3d) 161, 21 N.R. 295, 7 C.E.L.R. 53.

199 This is also known as a due diligence defence. Put differently, the mental state for regulatory offences is an objective one for which the accused has the onus of proof to a balance of probabilities.

200 *Sault Ste. Marie, supra*, note 198, at 1311.

201 See *R. v. Appleby*, [1972] S.C.R. 303, 21 D.L.R. (3d) 325, 3 C.C.C. (2d) 354, 16 C.R.N.S. 35; *R. v. Shelley*, [1981] 2 S.C.R. 196, 59 C.C.C. (2d) 292, 21 C.R. (3d) 354, 26 C.R. (3d) 150 (Fr.), [1981] 5 W.W.R. 481, 9 Sask. R. 338, 3 C.E.R. 217, 37 N.R. 320, 123 D.L.R. (3d) 748.

rule is subject to judicial review under the *Charter*.[202]

In *R. v. Wholesale Travel Group Inc.*,[203] the Supreme Court of Canada examined a statutory reverse onus which allocated the legal burden of proof to an accused to prove due diligence (disprove negligence) for a public welfare offence. Although a substantial majority of the Court found that the provision violated the presumption of innocence guaranteed under the *Charter*, a bare majority upheld its constitutional validity. A significant policy consideration was the effectiveness of the legislative alternatives to induce compliance by prosecutions.

In civil cases, the legal burden is more susceptible to the influence of policy. A party who traditionally has the legal burden has been able to argue, successfully, on policy grounds that the burden should be reversed. The fact that one party is peculiarly situated to prove a fact resulted in the reversal of the traditional burden of a bailee to disprove negligence.[204] This factor plus the rules of fair play saddled two defendants with the legal burden to exculpate themselves of negligence in a shooting accident in which the plaintiff was struck by a bullet fired by one of them.[205]

The difficulty of proving causation in medical malpractice and related cases has resulted in a reversal of the burden of proof in some cases.[206] This trend in England, which was instigated by the *McGhee* case, was halted by a decision of the House of Lords in *Wilsher v. Essex Area Health Authority*.[207] The latter decision followed a report by the Royal Commission on Civil Liability and Compensation for Personal Injury (1978) which recommended against a reversal of the traditional burden of proof because of the likely increase in claims against

---

202 See Chapter 4, Presumptions.

203 *Supra*, note 184.

204 *National Trust Co. v. Wong Aviation Ltd.*, *supra*, note 192.

205 *Cook v. Lewis*, [1951] S.C.R. 830, [1952] 1 D.L.R. 1.

206 *McGhee v. National Coal Board*, [1973] 1 W.L.R. 1, [1972] 3 All E.R. 1008 (H.L.); *Powell v. Guttman* (1978), 89 D.L.R. (3d) 180, [1978] 5 W.W.R. 228, 6 C.C.L.T. 183, 2 L. Med. Q. 279, at 291 (Man. C.A.); *Letnik v. Toronto (City)*, [1988] 2 F.C. 399, 49 D.L.R. (4th) 707 (*sub nom. Letnik v. Metropolitan Toronto (Municipality)*) (C.A.), applied the reversal of proof theory; *Dalpe v. Edmundston (City)* (1979), 25 N.B.R. (2d) 102 (C.A.); *Nowsco Well Service Ltd. v. Canadian Propane Gas & Oil Ltd.* (1981), 122 D.L.R. (3d) 228, 7 Sask. R. 291, 16 C.C.L.T. 23 (Sask. C.A.)

207 [1988] 1 All E.R. 871, [1988] 2 W.L.R. 557 (H.L.).

physicians. In *Snell v. Farrell*,[208] the Supreme Court of Canada reaffirmed that the legal burden respecting causation remains with the defendant. After reviewing policy and fairness considerations, the Court concluded that the difficulties in proving causation could be met without reversing the burden of proof. Rather, what was required was a more pragmatic approach to the weighing of evidence.

VII ADMISSIBILITY OF EVIDENCE AND OTHER MATTERS

In the course of a trial a party may object to the admissibility of evidence. Although the incidence of the burdens in relation to a fact or issue are mainly governed by the substantive law, the burdens in relation to some disputed facts are determined by the adjectival law of evidence.[209] For example, the competency of a witness, the admissibility of a proffered hearsay statement, the voluntariness of a confession and the application of the doctrine of privilege raise questions of fact or mixed fact and law. However, the trial judge, and not the jury, make findings of facts when applying these exclusionary rules.

There are no uniform formulae allocating the evidential and legal burdens in relation to these factual issues.[210] Because the underlying rationales for the various exclusionary rules are often distinct, the incidence of the burdens in relation to the underlying facts are idiosyncratic. For example, the underlying principles governing the hearsay rule[211] and its numerous exceptions are different from those for the solicitor–client privilege.[212] Accordingly, the incidence of the burden and the degree of proof required to satisfy a particular burden are more conveniently examined in the respective chapters on the particular exclusionary rule.[213]

---

208 [1990] 2 S.C.R. 311, 110 N.R. 200.
209 R. Cross and C. Tapper, *Cross on Evidence*, 7th ed. (London: Butterworths, 1990), at 19-20.
210 See *R. v. Mack*, [1988] 2 S.C.R. 903, 67 C.R. (3d) 1, 44 C.C.C. (3d) 513, [1989] 1 W.W.R. 577, 37 C.R.R. 277, 90 N.R. 173 (S.C.C.) for the defence of entrapment.
211 See Chapter 6.
212 See Chapter 14.
213 For example, Chapter 8.

In criminal cases, trial judges make findings of fact in sentencing proceedings. In *R. v. Gardiner*,[214] the Supreme Court decided that the Crown has the evidential and legal burdens to prove aggravating circumstances beyond a reasonable doubt; however, the burden with respect to mitigating circumstances was not raised in the appeal. One approach would allocate the evidential burden to the accused and the burden of proof to the Crown in relation to mitigating factors surrounding the offence. However, in the case of additional facts, such as history of employment, it would not appear too onerous for the accused to prove these factors to a balance of probabilities.

Trial judges must also decide other questions of fact or mixed fact and law, such as procedural[215] or jurisdictional issues,[216] or issues relating to the administration of justice.[217] Although the question of allocating the burdens arises in the determination of these issues, these subjects are more suitably discussed in texts on substantive law or procedure rather than in a text dealing with evidence.

---

214 [1982] 2 S.C.R. 368, 30 C.R. (3d) 289, 68 C.C.C. (2d) 477, 140 D.L.R. (3d) 612, 43 N.R. 361; see also B.C. Bynoe, "The Guilty", in *Defending a Criminal Case*, 1969, L.S.U.C. Special Lectures for a general discussion of evidentiary matters at sentencing.
215 *R. v. Belzberg*, [1951] 2 W.W.R. (N.S.) 568, 101 C.C.C. 210, 12 C.R. 336.
216 *Balcombe v. R.*, [1954] S.C.R. 303, 110 C.C.C. 146; G. Williams, *Criminal Law: The General Part*, 2nd ed. (London: Stevens & Sons Ltd., 1961), at 876.
217 *R. v. Collins*, [1987] 1 S.C.R. 265, 33 C.C.C. (3d) 1, 38 D.L.R. (4th) 508, [1987] 3 W.W.R. 699, 13 B.C.L.R. (2d) 1, 28 C.R.R. 122, 74 N.R. 276, 13 B.C.L.R. (2d) 1; *R. v. Mack, supra*, note 210.

CHAPTER 4

PRESUMPTIONS

I INTRODUCTION

The subject of presumptions is fraught with problems of terminology and classification.[1] In this chapter we discuss the subject according to the general classifications of presumptions without basic facts and presumptions with basic facts.[2] Presumptions with basic facts are subdivided into three categories or types of presumptions: presumptions of fact; conclusive presumptions of law; and rebuttable presumptions of law.[3] We describe the evidentiary effect of these various types of presumptions and briefly discuss the infrequent situation where two presumptions appear to conflict. We conclude the

---

1   McCormick states "one ventures the assertion that 'presumption' is the slipperiest member of the family of legal terms, except its first cousin, 'burden of proof', E.W. Cleary (ed.), *McCormick on Evidence*, 3rd ed. (St. Paul: West Publishing, 1984), at 965. For a discussion of the different purposes served by presumptions, see E.M. Morgan, "Presumptions" (1937), 12 Wash. Law Rev. 255, at 257-59.

2   In *R. v. Oakes*, [1986] 1 S.C.R. 103, at 115, 50 C.R. (3d) 1, 24 C.C.C. (3d) 321, 26 D.L.R. (4th) 200, 65 N.R. 87, 14 O.A.C. 335, 53 O.R. (2d) 719 (headnote only), Dickson C.J.C. adopted Professor Cross's classification of the subject (R. Cross, *Cross on Evidence*, 5th ed. (London: Butterworths, 1979), at 122 ff.). But compare R. Cross and C. Tapper, *Cross on Evidence*, 7th ed. (London: Butterworths, 1990), at 124, 126-27 and 130.

3   *Ibid.* Presumptions of fact and rebuttable presumptions of law are sometimes called permissive presumptions and mandatory presumptions (*Boyle v. R.* (1983), 35 C.R. (3d) 34, 5 C.C.C. (3d) 193, 148 D.L.R. (3d) 449, 5 C.R.R. 218, 41 O.R. (2d) 713 (C.A.)). Rebuttable presumptions of law are sometimes further divided into evidential presumptions and legal presumptions: *Cross on Evidence*, 7th ed., *ibid.*, or evidential and persuasive presumptions (G. Williams, *Criminal Law: The General Part*, 2nd ed. (London: Stevens & Sons Ltd., 1961), ss. 287-88).

97

chapter with an overview of the impact of the *Canadian Charter of Rights and Freedoms*[4] on the law of presumptions.

II PRESUMPTIONS WITHOUT BASIC FACTS

A presumption without a basic fact is a rule of substantive law relating to the incidence of a burden of proof which requires that a conclusion be drawn until the contrary is proved.[5] These presumptions assign an evidential burden or a legal burden of proof to a party as a matter of substantive law. For example, the common law principle that the Crown must prove the guilt of an accused beyond a reasonable doubt has become widely known as the "presumption of innocence".[6] Thus, the presumption of innocence allocates the evidential burden and the legal burden of proof in relation to the essential elements of the crime to the Crown.[7] McCormick writes that the term would be better called an "assumption of innocence" because it describes that, in the absence of contrary facts, a person's conduct upon a given occasion is assumed to be lawful.[8] The term is beneficial because it cautions the trier of fact to ignore the possible suspicions that arise from the arrest and the indictment of an accused and directs the jury to base their decision on the evidence.[9] Under the *Charter*, this rule

---

4   R.S.C. 1985, Appendix 2, No. 44.
5   *R. v. Oakes, supra,* note 2, at 115 (S.C.R.).
6   *Woolmington v. D.P.P.,* [1935] A.C. 462, [1935] All E.R. Rep. 1 (H.L.), at (A.C.) 481-82. For an interesting discussion of this principle see T. Cromwell, W.H. Charles and K. Jobson, *Evidence and the Charter of Rights and Freedoms* (Toronto: Butterworths, 1989), at 125-31. See also *R. v. Chaulk,* [1990] 3 S.C.R. 1303, 62 C.C.C. (3d) 193, 2 C.R. (4th) 1, [1991] 2 W.W.R. 385, 69 Man. R. (2d) 161, 1 C.R.R. (2d) 1, 119 N.R. 161 (S.C.C.) for a discussion of the meaning of the presumption of sanity.
7   G. Williams, *supra,* note 3, at 871. In *R. v. Appleby,* [1972] S.C.R. 303, 3 C.C.C. (2d) 354, 16 C.R.N.S. 35, 21 D.L.R. (3d) 325 Laskin J.A. stated (at S.C.R. 317): "The 'right to be presumed innocent' . . . is, in popular terms, a way of expressing the fact that the Crown has the ultimate burden of establishing guilt . . . . In a more refined sense, the presumption of innocence gives an accused the initial benefit of a right to silence and the ultimate benefit (after the Crown's evidence is in and as well any evidence tendered on behalf of the accused) of any reasonable doubt."
8   *McCormick on Evidence, supra,* note 1, at 967.
9   *McCormick on Evidence, supra,* note 1, at 968; 9 Wigmore, *Evidence*

of substantive law has become enshrined as a constitutional right.[10]

The presumption of innocence has been held to extend to every phase of a person's life.[11] It has, therefore, been applied in civil cases to raise a presumption of law against the imputation of criminal or quasi-criminal conduct.[12] For example, a mortgagee seized mortgaged property and used it. In subsequently selling the goods, the mortgagee took none of the steps required of a mortgagee who sells seized property. It was held that there was a presumption that the mortgagee acted properly and that he had therefore appropriated the goods as owner before he sold them.[13] In civil cases, the opposite party must prove criminal or quasi-criminal conduct to a balance of probabilities in order to discharge this presumption.[14]

III PRESUMPTIONS OF FACT

A presumption of fact is a deduction of fact that may logically and reasonably be drawn from a fact or group of facts found or otherwise established.[15] Put differently, it is a common sense logical inference that is drawn from proven facts.[16] Thus, on proof of Fact A, it is justifiable for the trier of fact to infer the existence or non-existence of designated Fact B. When established facts raise a presumption of fact they give rise to a permissive inference which the trier of fact may,

---

(Chadbourn rev. 1981), § 2511, at 530.

10   *Canadian Charter of Rights and Freedoms*, R.S.C. 1985, Appendix 2, No. 44, s. 11(d); *R. v. Oakes, supra*, note 2.

11   *Marks v. Marks* (1907), 6 W.L.R. 329, 13 B.C.R. 161; affd. (1908), 40 S.C.R. 210.

12   *London Life Ins. Co. Ltd. v. Lang Shirt Co. Ltd. (Trustee of)*, [1929] S.C.R. 117, 51 C.C.C. 31, [1929] 1 D.L.R. 328; *Williams v. East India Co.* (1802), 3 East. 192, 102 E.R. 57 (K.B.).

13   *Greenberg v. Rapaport*, [1970] 2 O.R. 349, 10 D.L.R. (3d) 737 (H.C.J.).

14   *Hanes v. Wawanesa Mutual Insurance Co.*, [1963] S.C.R. 154, [1963] 1 C.C.C. 321, 36 D.L.R. (2d) 718; *Hornal v. Neuberger Products Ltd.*, [1957] 1 Q.B. 247, [1956] 3 All E.R. 970 (C.A.); see also Chapter 5.

15   See sections 600-01 of the *California Evidence Code*, cited in Wigmore, *supra*, note 9, § 2493i, at 343-44 which distinguishes between presumptions and inferences.

16   *Ibid.*

but need not, draw. Thus, a presumption of fact is not a rule of law as it neither compels nor prohibits the drawing of the inference.[17]

Because presumptions of fact vary in force, in some civil cases they *may, not must*, require the party against whom they operate to adduce rebutting evidence or run a substantial risk of losing the case.[18] When used in this sense, it means that the facts are such that a certain inference should, but need not, be logically drawn.[19] But it must be underlined that a presumption of fact does not allocate, as a matter of law, an evidential burden or the legal burden of proof in relation to a factual issue to the other party.

There is a general presumption applicable to civil cases that all persons are of sound mind.[20] In cases to determine the validity of a will in which testamentary capacity is in issue, the presumption is treated as one of fact. Upon production of a properly executed, not irrational will, the court may, in the absence of other evidence, find in its favour.[21] If evidence is led against the validity of the will, the case is decided on all the evidence, and, if the court is not satisfied on a balance of probabilities that the will is valid, the party propounding the will fails.[22]

The so-called doctrine of recent possession is a common sense inference that a person in unexplained possession of recently stolen goods is a thief or is knowingly in possession of stolen goods.[23] In *R. v. Kowlyk*,[24] the Supreme Court of Canada held that upon proof of the unexplained possession of recently stolen property, the trier of fact *may*, but *not must*, draw an inference that the possessor is guilty of theft

---

17   Law Reform Commission of Canada, *Report on Evidence* (Ottawa: Minister of Supply and Services Canada, 1977), at 60.

18   See *Martel v. Hotel-Dieu St-Vallier*, [1969] S.C.R. 745, 14 D.L.R. (3d) 445.

19   *Snell v. Farrell*, [1990] 2 S.C.R. 311, at 329-30, 110 N.R. 200.

20   *Re Fraser* (1910), 24 O.L.R. 222 (Div. Ct.), new trial directed without reference to this point, 26 O.L.R. 508, 28 D.L.R. 955 (C.A.); *Deremore v. Trusts and Guarantee Co.*, [1919] 1 W.W.R. 681, at 687, 14 Alta. L.R. 322 (C.A.). Compare s. 16 of the *Criminal Code*, R.S.C. 1985, c. C-46 as interpreted in *R. v. Chaulk, supra*, note 6.

21   *Sutton v. Sadler* (1857), 3 C.B.N.S. 87, at 98, 140 E.R. 671, at 676 (Common Pleas).

22   *Sutton v. Sadler, ibid., Deremore v. Trusts and Guarantee Co., supra*, note 20.

23   See R. Cross and C. Tapper, *Cross on Evidence*, 7th ed. (London: Butterworths, 1990), at 32-33.

24   [1988] 2 S.C.R. 59, 65 C.R. (3d) 97, 43 C.C.C. (3d) 1, [1988] 6 W.W.R. 607, 55 Man. R. (2d) 1, 86 N.R. 195.

or a related offence.[25] The strength of the inference depends on the recency of the theft and other surrounding circumstances.[26] Where it is unclear if the crime is one of theft or of possession of stolen goods, it is up to the trier of fact to decide which, if either, inference should be drawn.

Inasmuch as it is the usual function of the trier of fact to draw inferences from other facts, one may well wonder why certain facts or a combination of them should be called a presumption. The most plausible explanation is that there are certain circumstances or combinations of fact which recur frequently. It has been found that whenever these circumstances or facts are present, it may safely be inferred that the presumed fact also exists. In order to assist the trier of fact, these recurring circumstances or combination of facts are said to give rise to a presumption of fact.

Some combinations of circumstantial evidence become labelled as a doctrine or a maxim by reason of the frequency of occurrence. Applying logic and common sense, trial judges rule that where a party establishes a particular group of facts or circumstantial evidence, the party has satisfied its evidential burden sufficient to overcome a motion for a non-suit or directed verdict of acquittal. Also, the circumstantial evidence may be sufficiently cogent to support a conviction.[27] Thus, by judicial precedent and familiarity, identifiable recurring circumstantial evidence sometimes becomes labelled as a doctrine or maxim. *Res ipsa loquitur* and the "doctrine of recent possession" illustrate this experience; however, these doctrines do not affect the evidential or legal burden of proof.[28] To hold otherwise would grant circumstantial evidence a greater probative value than direct evidence.[29]

---

25   "The doctrine is only the particular aspect of the general proposition that where suspicious circumstances appear to demand an explanation, and no explanation or an entirely incredible explanation is given, the lack of explanation may warrant an inference of guilty knowledge in the defendant. This again is only part of a wider proposition that guilt may be inferred from unreasonable behaviour of a defendant when confronted with facts which seem to accuse.": *Raviraj v. R.* (1987), 85 Cr. App. R. 93, at 103 (C.A.).

26   *Ibid.*

27   For example, *Kowlyk, supra*, note 24.

28   However, there are authorities which hold that *res ipsa loquitur* has the effect of "shifting" the evidential burden or legal burden of proof, see Chapter 3, V.A.

29   S. Schiff, *Evidence in the Litigation Process*, 3rd ed. (Toronto: Carswell, 1988),

The standardized practice that a group of facts may justify an inference may assist judge and jury alike to perform their respective functions. But the labels themselves or the use of the term presumption to describe these permissible inferences may create difficulties when they are used to imply a greater evidential value.[30] This problem is illustrated when the so-called presumption that a person intends the natural consequences of her or his act is used in the context of criminal proceedings where the issue is the subjective mental state of the accused. Although it may be proper to infer that where a person was engaged in the prohibited conduct that he or she did so with the requisite mental state, it is improper to direct the trier of fact that they *must* draw the inference.[31] Since the term presumption may reasonably be interpreted as an assumption of a fact from the establishment of another fact or group of facts,[32] a jury direction that a person is presumed to intend the natural consequences of her or his act may be misinterpreted by a jury. The jury may erroneously think that they must draw the inference or conclude that the accused has an onus to disprove the "presumed" fact. In *Stapleton v. R.*, Dixon C.J. stated:[33]

> The introduction of the maxim or statement that a man is presumed to intend the reasonable consequences of his act is seldom helpful and always dangerous. For it either does no more than state a self-evident proposition of fact or it produces an illegitimate transfer of the burden of proof of a real issue of intent to the person denying the allegation.

For these reasons, the Ontario Court of Appeal held that a jury direction that a person intends the natural consequences of her or his act was an error in law and that the word presumption should be avoided in this context.[34] Rather, if the circumstances warrant, the

---

at 1146.

30   E.W. Cleary (ed.), *McCormick on Evidence*, 3rd ed. (St. Paul: West Publishing, 1984), at 344, n. 31.

31   See *R. v. Farrant*, [1983] S.C.R. 124 at 144-45, 32 C.R. (3d) 289, 4 C.C.C. (3d) 354, 147 D.L.R. (3d) 511, [1983] 3 W.W.R. 171, 21 Sask. R. 271.

32   The meaning of the word presumption includes ". . . 3. The taking of something for granted; also, that which is presumed; assumption, assumed probability, supposition, expectation, . . .", Shorter Oxford English Dictionary (Oxford: Clarendon Press, 1984), at 1664.

33   (1952), 86 C.L.R. 358, at 365 (Aust. H.C.).

34   *R. v. Giannotti* (1956), 115 C.C.C. 203, 23 C.R. 259, [1956] O.R. 349 (C.A.);

judge should direct the jury that where a person engages in particular conduct it is a reasonable inference which they are entitled to draw that he or she intended to do so.[35] In *R. v. Steane* Lord Goddard C.J. correctly stated the proposition:[36]

> No doubt, if the prosecution prove an act the natural conse-quence of which would be a certain result and no evidence or explanation is given, then a jury may, on a proper direction, find that the prisoner is guilty of doing the act with the intent alleged, but if on the totality of the evidence there is room for more than one view as to the intent of the prisoner, the jury should be directed that it is for the prosecution to prove the intent to the jury's satisfaction, and if, on a review of the whole evidence, they either think that the intent did not exist or they are left in doubt as to the intent, the prisoner is entitled to be acquitted.

There is considerable support amongst writers on evidence that presumptions of fact should not be classified as presumptions.[37] Wigmore states that:[38]

> The distinction between presumptions "of law" and presump-tions "of fact" is in truth the difference between things that are in reality presumptions . . . and things which are not presump-tions at all.
>
> 7. A presumption . . . is in its characteristic feature a rule laid down by the judge and attaching to one evidentiary fact *pro-cedural consequences* as to the duty of production of other evidence

---

R. v. Ortt, [1969] 1 O.R. 461, [1970] 1 C.C.C. 223, 6 C.R.N.S. 233, 10 Cr. L.Q. 456 (C.A.); see also, *Hosegood v. Hosegood* (1950), 66 T.L.R. 735 (C.A.). But see, *R. v. Crawford* (1970), 1 C.C.C. (2d) 515 (B.C.C.A.); *Wu v. R.*, [1934] S.C.R. 609, 62 C.C.C. 90, [1934] 4 D.L.R. 459; *Bradley v. R.*, [1956] S.C.R. 723, 116 C.C.C. 341, 6 D.L.R. (2d) 385.

35 *Farrant, supra*, note 31. See also s. 8, *Criminal Justice Act, 1967*, c. 80 reversing *D.P.P. v. Smith*, [1961] A.C. 290, [1960] 3 All E.R. 161 (H.L.).

36 [1947] 1 K.B. 997, at 1004, 32 Cr. App. Rep. 61 (C.C.A.).

37 J.B. Thayer, *A Preliminary Treatise on Evidence*, reprint of 1898 edition (New York: Augustus M. Kelley Pub., 1969), at 339-42; R.J. Delisle, *Evidence: Principles and Problems*, 2nd ed. (Toronto: Carswell, 1989), at 144-47; Law Reform Com-mission of Canada, *supra*, note 17, at 60.

38 9 Wigmore, *Evidence* (Chadbourn rev. 1981), § 2491, at 304.

by the opponent. It is based, in policy, upon the probative strength, as a matter of reasoning and inference, of the evidentiary fact; but the presumption is not the fact itself, nor the inference itself but the legal consequence attached to it. But the legal consequence being removed, the inference, as a matter of reasoning may still remain; and a "presumption of fact", in the loose sense, is merely an improper term for the rational potency or probative value of the evidentiary fact and is regarded as not having this necessary legal consequence. . . . They have no significance so far as affects the duty of one or the other party to produce evidence because there is no rule of law attached to them and the jury may give to them whatever force or weight it thinks best -just as it may with other evidence.

. . .

So long as the law attaches no legal consequences in the way of a duty upon the opponent to come forward with contrary evidence, there is no propriety in applying the term "presumption" to such facts, however great their probative significance.

Wigmore concluded his analysis by stating that the term presumption of fact "should be discarded as useless and confusing".[39]

IV CONCLUSIVE PRESUMPTIONS OF LAW

Conclusive or irrebuttable presumptions of law are rare and those that exist are mostly statutory. On proof of the basic fact, the presumed fact is conclusively deemed to exist. Because a conclusive presumption is absolute or not rebuttable, evidence is not admissible to rebut the presumed fact. For example at common law, it was conclusively presumed that regardless of age or incapacity, every person was fertile.[40] In *Re Fasken*[41] McRuer C.J.H.C. stated:[42]

In applying the rule against perpetuities the Courts recognize as possible that which is biologically impossible. For 400 years the

---

39 *Ibid.*, § 2491, at 305.
40 R. Gosse, *Ontario's Perpetuities Legislation* (1967), at 35.
41 (1959), 19 D.L.R. (2d) 182 (Ont. H.C.).
42 *Ibid.*, at 188.

English law has maintained that it is possible for a woman 100 years old to bear children.

The Ontario *Perpetuities Act*[43] has altered this conclusive presumption by creating two rebuttable presumptions of fertility and infertility for males and females of certain ages if the person is alive when the question arises.[44] Conclusive presumptions have also been created by federal and provincial legislation. For example, *The Bankruptcy Act*[45] conclusively deems certain transactions made within three months of bankruptcy to be fraudulent and therefore void as against the trustee in bankruptcy.[46] Section 272 of the Prince Edward Island *Highway Traffic Act*[47] makes the owner of a motor vehicle responsible for any loss or damage that occurs while being driven with the owner's consent, expressed or implied, by deeming the driver the agent of the owner.[48]

A conclusive presumption is a rule of substantive law clothed in the language of presumptions. For example, at common law it was conclusively presumed that a child under seven was incapable of committing any criminal offence[49] and proffered evidence that the child was capable of committing the offence was inadmissible.[50] This

---

43   R.S.O. 1980, c. 374, s. 7.
44   Section 7(1)(b), *ibid.*; see R. Gosse, *supra*, note 40, at 35-36; 11 C.E.D. (1988), title 57, at 109-14.
45   R.S.C. 1985, c. B-3, s. 95(1).
46   Section 95(1), *ibid.* In comparison, s. 95(2), *ibid.* creates a rebuttal presumption of law: *Coopers & Lybrand Ltd. v. Royal Bank of Canada* (1977), 25 C.B.R. 118, 25 N.S.R. (2d) 427, 36 A.P.R. 427 (*sub nom. J-Bailey's Furniture Market Ltd., Re*) (N.S.T.D.); *Campbell v. Barrie* (1871), 31 U.C.Q.B. 279 (C.A.).
47   R.S.P.E.I. 1974, c. H-6 [now R.S.P.E.I. 1988, c. H-5, s. 287]; see also *Motor Vehicle Act*, R.S.B.C. 1979, c. 288, s. 79(1); *Highway Traffic Act*, R.S.A. 1980, c. H-7, s. 181; *Highway Traffic Act*, S.M. 1985-86, c. 3-H60, s. 153(3).
48   *Poole & Thompson Ltd. v. McNally*, [1934] S.C.R. 717, at 724, [1935] 1 D.L.R. 161; but see, *Canadian Commercial Bank v. Holman (R.T.) Ltd.* (1986), 57 Nfld. & P.E.I.R. 137, at 141 (P.E.I.S.C.); see also *Bagg v. Budget Rent-A-Car of Washington-Oregon Inc.* (1989), 35 B.C.L.R. (2d) 36, [1989] 4 W.W.R. 586, 14 M.V.R. (2d) 145 (B.C.C.A.); *Bond v. Loutit (Noonen)*, [1979] 2 W.W.R. 154 (Man. Q.B.).
49   Sir Matthew Hale, *The History of the Pleas of the Crown*, (1736) vol. 1, at 27 and 28; *Reniger v. Fogossa* (1816), 1 Plow 1, 75 E.R. 1, at 30 (K.B.).
50   R. Ross and G. McClure, *A Treatise on Crimes and Misdemeanours*, 8th ed. (London: Stevens & Sons Ltd., Sweet & Maxwell Ltd., 1923) vol. 1, at 60; *R. v. Waite*, [1892] 2 Q.B. 600, at 601 (C.C.R.); *R. v. Logan* (1947), 90 C.C.C. 177, at 184-85 (N.B.C.A.); *R. v. Williams*, [1893] 1 Q.B. 320 (C.C.R.); see also *R. v.*

common law presumption became a rule of substantive law in the 1892 *Criminal Code:*[51]

> No person shall be convicted of an offence by reason of any act or omission of such person when under the age of seven years.

Thus, a conclusive presumption is the legal equivalent of a rule of substantive law.

A statutory definition may also be the legal equivalent of a conclusive presumption. For example, s. 198(2) of the *Criminal Code* provides that ". . . a place that is found to be equipped with a slot machine shall be conclusively presumed to be a common gaming house."[52] Parliament could have achieved the same result by a properly worded definition: a common betting house is a place that is found to be equipped with a slot machine.[53]

Writers on evidence have suggested that the term conclusive presumption is not a true presumption. Wigmore writes that "in strictness there cannot be such a thing as a 'conclusive presumption' . . . and [T]hat the term has no place in the principles of evidence . . . and should be discarded."[54] Since the words "conclusively presumed" or similar language in a statute do not improve or clarify the law,[55] it

---

Kershaw (1902), 18 T.L.R. 357 (Assize), where a thirteen year old boy was convicted of manslaughter and sentenced to penal servitude. A male under 14 was incapable of committing the former crime of rape because he was presumed to be impotent and lacking in discretion, but a child between 7 and 14 years of age could be found guilty of committing the lesser crime of indecent assault (Hale, *ibid.*, at 730).

51   55-56 Vict., c. 29, ss. 9 and 266(2); see, s. 13 of the Criminal Code, R.S.C. 1985, c. C-46. Compare s. 50, *Children and Young Persons Act, 1933* (U.K.), 23 Geo. 5, c. 12: "It shall be conclusively presumed that no child under the age of ten years can be guilty of an offence."

52   R.S.C. 1985, c. C-46.

53   R.J. Delisle, *supra*, note 37, at 144.

54   Wigmore, *supra*, note 38, § 2492, at 307-08. Delisle, *ibid.*, states: "It would be best then, in our quest to minimize confusion, to discard the use of the term 'conclusive presumption'."

55   Indeed, they sometimes create confusion. For example the word "deemed" has often been interpreted to mean a conclusive presumption: *Poole and Thompson Ltd. v. McNally, supra*, note 48; *Bagg v. Budget Rent-A-Car, supra*, note 48; *McColl-Frontenac Oil Co. v. Hamilton*, [1953] 1 S.C.R. 127, [1953] 1 D.L.R. 721; *Shepheard v. Broome*, [1904] A.C. 342 (H.L.). However, it has also been interpreted to mean a rebuttable presumption: *Hill v. East and West India Dock Co.* (1884), 9

could be argued that the legislatures could do away with them altogether and replace them with definitions or substantive rules of law.

V   REBUTTABLE PRESUMPTIONS OF LAW

A. *What is a Rebuttable Presumption of Law?*

This type of presumption is the commonest and most significant of the different types of presumptions. A rebuttable presumption of law is a rule of substantive law that has certain consequences directly annexed to proof of particular fact(s).[56] Thus, upon proof of the basic fact and in the absence of rebutting evidence the presumption prescribes a certain legal consequence.[57]

A rebuttable presumption of law differs from a presumption of fact because a presumption of fact does not compel the trier of fact to draw the required inference, albeit the opponent probably runs a risk of an adverse determination in direct proportion to the strength of the inference. Nonetheless, the party against whom it operates is under no obligation, as a matter of law, to adduce rebutting evidence to meet a presumption of fact. In contrast, a rebuttable presumption of law

---

App. Cas. 448 (H.L.); *Gray v. Kerslake*, [1958] S.C.R. 3, [1957] I.L.R. 1-279, 11 D.L.R. (2d) 225; *Canadian Commercial Bank v. Holman (R.T.) Ltd.* (1986), *supra*, note 48. Some courts classify the provision depending upon the context in which it is used and the purpose of the statute: *St. Leon Village Consolidated School District No. 1425 v. Ronceray* (1960), 23 D.L.R. (2d) 32, 31 W.W.R. 385 (Man. C.A.); *Bond v. Loutit, supra*, note 48.

56   James B. Thayer, "Presumptions and The Law of Evidence" (1889), 3 Harvard L. Rev. 141, at 149. *McVaught v. McKenzie (Re Claresholm Provincial Election)* (1912), 8 D.L.R. 58, at 63, 3 W.W.R. 133, 5 Alta. L.R. 286 (Alta. S.C.).

57   Thayer, *ibid.* Presumptions of law are sometimes referred to as mandatory presumptions and reverse onus clauses. The term mandatory presumption emphasizes that upon proof of the basic fact the tribunal of fact must find the presumed fact in the absence of evidence to the contrary. The term reverse onus emphasizes that the accused is required to prove a fact to a balance of probabilities in order to satisfy the presumption: see *Boyle v. R.* (1983), 5 C.C.C. (3d) 193, 35 C.R. (3d) 34, 148 D.L.R. (3d) 449, 41 O.R. (2d) 713, 5 C.R.R. 218 (C.A.). R. Cross and C. Tapper, *Cross on Evidence*, 7th ed., (London: Butterworths, 1990) classify these presumptions as evidential presumptions and legal presumptions, at 126-27, 130.

compels the trier of fact to assume the existence or non-existence of the presumed fact in the absence of contrary evidence.[58]

Both rebuttable presumptions and conclusive presumptions compel the tribunal of fact to draw the required inferences upon proof of the presumed fact. Unlike a conclusive presumption however, a rebuttable presumption of law grants the opponent an opportunity to offer evidence to meet the evidentiary effect of the presumption. This distinguishing feature of rebuttable presumptions has lead some writers on evidence to classify it as a "true presumption", the others being merely permissive inferences or legal definitions. Thayer states that:[59]

> A rule of presumption does not merely say such and such a thing is a permissible and usual inference from other facts, but it goes on to say that this significance shall always, in the absence of other circumstances, be imputed to them . . . .

Thus, a rebuttable presumption is a ". . . rule of law compelling the jury to reach the conclusion *in the absence of evidence to the contrary* from the opponent."[60] No prescribed language or formula is necessary in order to create a statutory rebuttable presumption. Case law has, however, identified certain language as creating such presumptions, for example "in the absence of evidence to the contrary",[61] "*prima facie* proof or evidence",[62] "unless he proves",[63] "until the contrary is proved",[64] and "unless he establishes".[65]

---

58 See this Chapter, V.B.

59 *Supra*, note 56, at 149.

60 Wigmore, *supra*, note 38, at 305.

61 *R. v. Proudlock*, [1979] 1 S.C.R. 525, 43 C.C.C. (2d) 321, 5 C.R. (3d) 21, 91 D.L.R. (3d) 449, [1978] 6 W.W.R. 357, 24 N.R. 199.

62 *Circle Film Enterprises Inc. v. C.B.C.*, [1959] S.C.R. 602, 20 D.L.R. (2d) 211, 31 C.P.R. 57, 19 Fox Pat. C. 39; see also, Chapter 3, IV.

63 *R. v. Benning* (1947), 89 C.C.C. 33, 4 C.R. 39, [1947] 3 D.L.R. 908, [1947] O.R. 362 (C.A.); *R. v. Harris* (1947), 89 C.C.C. 231, 4 C.R. 192, [1947] 4 D.L.R. 796, [1947] O.R. 461 (C.A.).

64 *R. v. Godfrey* (1984), 39 C.R. (3d) 97, 11 C.C.C. (3d) 233, 8 D.L.R. (4th) 122, 26 Man. R. (2d) 61, 9 C.R.R. 176 (Man. C.A.); leave to appeal to S.C.C. refd. (1984), 11 C.C.C. (3d) 233*n*, 40 C.R. (3d) xxvi*n*, 8 D.L.R. (4th) 122*n* (S.C.C.), *R. v. Chaulk*, [1990] 3 S.C.R. 1303, 62 C.C.C. (3d) 123, 42 C.C.C. (3d) 193, 2 C.R. (4th) 1, [1991] 2 W.W.R. 385, 69 Man. R. (2d) 161, 1 C.R.R. (2d) 1, 119 N.R. 161.

65 *R. v. Appleby*, [1972] S.C.R. 303, 16 C.R.N.S. 35, 3 C.C.C. (2d) 354, 21 D.L.R. (3d) 325. For other illustrations see T. Cromwell, W.H. Charles and K.

B. *Evidentiary Effect of a Rebuttable Presumption of Law*

The question arises as to what is the evidentiary effect of a rebuttable presumption. From an opponent's perspective, what quantum of evidence is required to satisfy or discharge the presumption? We address the evidentiary effect in criminal and civil proceedings separately.

1. In Criminal Cases

In several leading pre-*Charter* cases the Supreme Court of Canada held that some statutory provisions created rebuttable presumptions. In *Tupper v. R.*,[66] where the accused was charged with possession of house-breaking instruments the relevant section stated:[67]

> Every one who, without lawful excuse, the proof of which lies upon him, has in his possession any instrument for house-breaking, . . . is guilty of an indictable offence . . . .

The Supreme Court held that once the accused was found in possession of tools that were capable of being used for house-breaking, he or she had the legal burden of proof to prove a lawful excuse for such possession to a balance of probabilities.[68] Thus, once the Crown proved the basic fact of possession of house-breaking instruments, the jury was compelled to find the accused guilty unless he or she proved to a balance of probabilities the existence of a lawful excuse.

In *R. v. Appleby*[69] the Supreme Court of Canada considered a presumption in relation to the offences of care or control of a motor vehicle while impaired and care or control while having more than 80 milligrams of alcohol in the blood. The section stated:[70]

Jobson, *Evidence and the Charter of Rights and Freedoms* (Butterworths: Toronto, 1989), at 126, note 13; R.J. Delisle, *Evidence: Principles and Problems*, 2nd ed. (Toronto: Carswell, 1989), at 156-70.

66 [1967] S.C.R. 589, 2 C.R.N.S. 35, [1968] 1 C.C.C. 253, 63 D.L.R. (2d) 289.

67 *Criminal Code*, S.C. 1953-54, c. 51, s. 295(1) [now R.S.C. 1985, c. C-46, s. 351(1)].

68 *Supra*, note 66, at 593, 595.

69 *Supra*, note 65.

70 *Criminal Code*, S.C. 1953-54, c. 51, s. 224A(1)(a) [am. 1968-69, c. 38, s. 16]; [now R.S.C. 1985, c. C-46, s. 258(1)(a).

(a)   where it is proved that the accused occupied the seat ordinarily occupied by the driver of a motor vehicle, he shall be deemed to have had the care or control of the vehicle unless he establishes that he did not enter or mount the vehicle for the purpose of setting it in motion.

The British Columbia Court of Appeal interpreted the word "establishes" in the provision as equivalent to a requirement that an accused must raise a reasonable doubt.[71] The Supreme Court rejected this construction because it rendered "the statutory presumption ineffective and the section meaningless".[72] The court held that in order to satisfy the presumed fact of care and control the section imposed the legal burden of proof on the accused to prove to a balance of probabilities that he or she did not enter the vehicle to set it in motion.[73] Accordingly, when the Crown proves the basic fact (occupying the driver's seat), the accused must prove a lack of intent to drive in order to satisfy the presumed fact (care and control).

In *R. v. Proudlock*[74] the Supreme Court of Canada considered the rebuttable presumption relating to the offence of break and enter. Section 306(2)(a) provided:[75]

For the purposes of proceedings under this section, evidence that an accused

(a)   broke and entered a place is, in the absence of any evidence to the contrary, proof that he broke and entered with intent to commit an indictable offence therein. . . .

The court unanimously held that evidence which is disbelieved by the trier of fact is not evidence to the contrary and thus such evidence is not capable of satisfying the presumption. Pigeon J., writing for the majority of the court, held that the provision did not cast the legal burden of proof on the accused but rather, upon proof of the basic fact, and in the absence of evidence of lack of intent in the Crown's case, the accused has a burden to adduce evidence.[76] Put differently, this rebuttable presumption cast an evidential burden on the accused to

---

71   *Supra*, note 65, at 307 (S.C.R.).
72   *Ibid.*, at 311.
73   *Ibid.*
74   *Supra*, note 61.
75   R.S.C. 1970, c. C-34.
76   *Supra*, note 61, at 549.

adduce evidence on the issue of intent,[77] but it did not require him or her to prove a lack of intent to a balance of probabilities. The majority also held that this evidential burden required the accused to raise a reasonable doubt. In separate reasons for judgment, Estey J. held that if there was "*any* evidence to the contrary" that was not rejected by the trier of fact the presumption was met and the Crown must prove guilt beyond a reasonable doubt.[78]

All rebuttal presumptions compel a finding of fact in the absence of evidence to the contrary.[79] As noted, Pigeon J. in *Proudlock* held that rebuttable presumptions of law require the accused either to prove a fact or an excuse to a balance of probabilities or to raise a reasonable doubt.[80] More recently, in the leading constitutional case of *R. v. Oakes*,[81] Dickson C.J.C., without reference to *Proudlock*, described the different degrees of proof that may satisfy a presumption resting on an accused in a criminal trial:[82]

> If a presumption is rebuttable, there are three potential ways the presumed fact can be rebutted. First, the accused may be required merely to raise a reasonable doubt as to its existence. Secondly, the accused may have an evidentiary burden to adduce sufficient evidence to bring into question the truth of the presumed fact. Thirdly, the accused may have a legal or persuasive burden to prove on a balance of probabilities the non-existence of the presumed fact.

Accordingly, it is necessary to determine the quantum of evidence which is necessary to satisfy a particular rebuttable presumption. Because some rebuttable presumptions allocate the legal burden of proof for a fact or an issue to the accused, Canadian courts often call them "reverse onus" provisions.

---

77   *Ibid.*, at 550 (S.C.R.).
78   Compare the reasons for judgment at 542, 545 (S.C.R.), *ibid.*, per Estey J. and at 549-51 (S.C.R.), *ibid.*, per Pigeon J.
79   R. Cross and C. Tapper, *Cross on Evidence*, 7th ed. (London: Butterworths, 1990), at 128.
80   *R. v. Proudlock*, *supra*, note 61, at 548, 550 (S.C.R.).
81   [1986] 1 S.C.R. 103, 50 C.R. (3d) 1, 24 C.C.C. (3d) 321, 26 D.L.R. (4th) 200, 65 N.R. 87, 14 O.A.C. 335, 53 O.R. (2d) 719 (headnote only).
82   *Ibid.*, at 116 (S.C.R.).

2. In Civil Cases

(a) *General*

The degree of proof that is necessary to satisfy a rebuttable presumption of law in civil cases may differ from those operating in criminal cases since the two proceedings are fundamentally different.[83] In order to satisfy many statutory presumptions governing a civil action, a party has the onus to prove the existence or non-existence of the presumed fact to a balance of probabilities. However, this is not a universal rule as some civil presumptions merely require the opponent to adduce some contrary evidence. Once a party adduces some contrary evidence, the party satisfies this type of presumption and the evidence giving rise to the presumption has no more than its own weight.[84] There are also a few archaic civil presumptions that require the opponent to prove a fact beyond a reasonable doubt.[85] We will discuss several presumptions to illustrate these different evidentiary effects.

(b) *Presumptions of Legitimacy*

A child born or conceived by a married woman during marriage is presumed to be a legitimate child and this presumption may be overborne only by evidence excluding reasonable doubt.[86] Evidence of non-access by the husband to his spouse during the normal or possible period of gestation,[87] sterility of the husband during the

---

83   *R. v. Schwartz*, [1988] 2 S.C.R. 443, at 462, 66 C.R. (3d) 251, 45 C.C.C. (3d) 97, 55 D.L.R. (4th) 1, [1989] 1 W.W.R. 289, 31 C.R.R. 260, 56 Man. R. (2d) 92, 88 N.R. 90.

84   *Circle Film Enterprises Inc. v. C.B.C.*, [1959] S.C.R. 602, 20 D.L.R. (2d) 211, 31 C.P.R. 57, 19 Fox Pat. C. 39; see also *R. v. Proudlock*, [1979] 1 S.C.R. 525, 43 C.C.C. (2d) 321, 5 C.R. (3d) 21, 91 D.L.R. (3d) 449, [1978] 6 W.W.R. 357, 24 N.R. 199, at 542, 545 (S.C.R.) per Estey J.; *Powell v. Cockburn*, [1977] S.C.R. 218, at 225, 68 D.L.R. (3d) 700, 22 R.F.L. 155, 8 N.R. 215.

85   *Welstead v. Brown*, [1952] 1 S.C.R. 3, 102 C.C.C. 46, [1952] 1 D.L.R. 465; see also, *Cross on Evidence, supra*, note 79, at 132.

86   *Ibid.*

87   *Wheeler v. Wheeler* (1966), 56 D.L.R. (2d) 668, 56 W.W.R. 151 (Sask. Q.B.); *Re Millar*, [1938] O.R. 188, [1938] 2 D.L.R. 164 (Ont. S.C.), *Knowles v. Knowles*, [1962] P. 161, [1962] 1 All E.R. 659 (Prob. & Div.).

period of gestation,[88] and blood tests which negative that the husband is the father rebut the presumption of legitimacy.[89] This presumption does not apply when the parties have separated pursuant to an order of the court, but if the separation is pursuant to a separation agreement or the parties are simply living apart the presumption applies.[90]

Cases in which the legitimacy of a child is in question should be treated in the same way as other civil cases. The gravity of the consequence is no more reason for the imposition of a criminal burden of proof than is a case imputing crime.[91] In the U.K., the presumption of legitimacy may now be rebutted by evidence which shows that it is more probable than not that the person is legitimate.[92] In some jurisdictions the need for the presumption has disappeared because the status of illegitimacy has been abolished.[93]

(c) Presumptions of Life and Death

There is a common sense inference that a person alive and in good health at a certain time was alive a short time after.[94] This inference is sometimes labelled a presumption of continuance of life;[95] however, it is a presumption of fact and not a rebuttable presumption

---

88 *Himmelman v. Himmelman* (1959), 19 D.L.R. (2d) 291 (N.S.S.C.).

89 *Welstead v. Brown, supra,* note 85.

90 *Ettenfield v. Ettenfield,* [1940] P. 96, [1940] 1 All E.R. 293 (C.A.), *Knowles v. Knowles, supra,* note 87. It is questionable whether this distinction or reasoning would prevail today.

91 There was authority that the presumption of validity of marriage could only be overborne by evidence excluding all reasonable doubt, see Sopinka and Lederman, *The Law of Evidence in Civil Cases* (Toronto: Butterworths, 1974), at 381, 387-91 for an analysis of the old authorities. The modern Canadian position is that the effect of this presumption is to cast an evidential burden on the party against whom it operates to adduce some evidence, *Powell v. Cockburn, supra,* note 84.

92 *Family Law Reform Act, 1969,* c. 46, s. 26 cited in A. Keane, *The Modern Law of Evidence,* 2nd ed. (London: Butterworths, 1989), at 469.

93 *Children's Law Reform Act,* R.S.O. 1980, c. 68, ss. 1, 2; *Children and Family Services and Family Relations Act,* S.N.B. 1980, c. C-2.1, Part IV; *Family Maintenance Act,* R.S.M. 1987, c. F20, s. 17; *Children's Act,* R.S.Y.T. 1986, c. 22, s. 5.

94 *Re McNeil* (1906), 12 O.L.R. 208 (Ont. S.C.); *Mills v. Mills,* [1943] O.R. 413, [1943] 4 D.L.R. 113 (Ont. S.C.); *Re Phené's Trusts* (1870), 5 L.R. 139, at 148-49, [1861-73] All E.R. Rep. 514 (Ch. App.).

95 9 Wigmore, *Evidence* (Chadbourn rev. 1981), § 2531, at 602-03; A. Keane, *supra,* note 92, at 462.

of law.[96] In the context of criminal and civil proceedings the question has arisen whether a lapse of time or some other circumstance will satisfy this presumption of fact.[97] The common sense inference that one absent for an extended period of time without explanation may be dead evolved into a rebuttable presumption of law.[98] Thayer states that in the beginning of the nineteenth century "judges as well as text-writers got to expressing what had been put as a cessation of a presumption of life in the form of an affirmative presumption of death; and this was put as a rule of general application wherever life and death were in question."[99]

The basic facts are that a person has been absent for at least seven years and that the person is unheard of by persons who would likely have heard after due inquires have been made.[100] The difficulties in proving death and the high probability that one missing for seven years is in fact dead justify proof of the basic facts as being the legal equivalent of the presumed fact. In *Sheehy v. Robinson*,[101] Mackay J. described the principles of the presumptions of continuance of life and of death:[102]

(1) That there is no presumption of death before the expiration of seven years from the time the missing person was last heard of or seen.

(2) That subject to certain exceptions as to the likelihood of a missing person keeping his identity unrevealed, there is presumption of death after a lapse of seven years.

---

96 *Chard v. Chard (otherwise Northcott)*, [1955] 3 All E.R. 721, at 726, [1953] 1 W.L.R. 954 (P.D.A.).

97 Wigmore, *supra*, note 95, § 2531*b*, at 613-14.

98 J.B. Thayer, "Presumptions and the Law of Evidence" (1889), 3 Harvard Law Rev. 141, at 154.

99 *Ibid.*, at 154.

100 D. Stone, "The Presumption of Death: A Redundant Concept" (1981), 44 Mod. Law Rev. 517, at 518.

101 [1947] O.W.N. 121 (H.C.J.). See also *Mills v. Mills, supra*, note 94; *Re McNeil, supra*, note 94; *Middlemiss v. Middlemiss*, [1955] 4 D.L.R. 801, 15 W.W.R. 641 (C.A.); *Chard v. Chard, supra*, note 94; *Re Wilson*, [1964] 1 W.L.R. 214, [1964] 1 All E.R. 196 (Ch. Div.); *Chipchase v. Chipchase*, [1939] P. 391, 3 All E.R. 895 (P. Div.).

102 *Ibid., Sheehy v. Robinson*, at 122. Wigmore notes that the basic facts for the presumption vary (Wigmore, *supra*, note 95, § 2531*a*, at 603-04.

(3)   That there is no presumption within such seven-year period respecting the time the death took place.

(4)   That if any one claims, or bases a right upon death having taken place within a specific time within the seven years, the onus of proof lies on such person.

However, there is some uncertainty as to the time of death after the seven year period has elapsed.[103] As pointed out by Cross, someone is just as likely to be dead after being missing for six-and-a-half years as seven years.[104] Moreover, courts have found death where a person is absent for a period significantly shorter than seven years.[105] Although the presumption has been criticised,[106] it is widely accepted[107] and is codified in various statutes.[108]

It is uncertain whether the evidentiary effect of the presumption of death is to cast the evidential or the legal burden of proof on the opponent.[109] Part of the confusion may arise because the same evidence may rebut both the basic fact (that the person is alive) and the presumed fact (that the person is dead).[110] Cross states that "this could cause serious problems where the legal burden of proving the basic fact is on the proponent of death, and the legal burden of rebutting

---

103   *Re Miller* (1978), 92 D.L.R. (3d) 255, 22 O.R. (2d) 111 (Ont. H.C.J.); *Re Harlow* (1976), 13 O.R. (2d) 760, 72 D.L.R. (3d) 323 (C.A.); *Re Walker* (1979), 24 Nfld. & P.E.I.R. 80, 65 A.P.R. 80 (P.E.I.S.C.); *Bullock v. Bullock*, [1960] 1 W.L.R. 975, [1960] 2 All E.R. 307 (P.D.); Wigmore, *supra*, note 95, § 2531*a*, at 610.

104   R. Cross and C. Tapper, *Cross on Evidence*, 7th ed. (London: Butterworths, 1990), at 128.

105   D. Stone, *supra*, note 100, at 518.

106   Wigmore, *supra*, note 95, § 2531*b*, at 614; J.C. Shepherd, "Presumption of Death in Ontario" (1979), 4 E. & T. Q. 326; D. Stone, *supra*, note 100.

107   The general presumption is "unquestioned", Wigmore, *ibid.*, § 2531*a*, at 603-04.

108   *Survivorship and Presumption of Death Act*, R.S.B.C. 1979, c. 398, s. 3(1); *Trustee Act*, R.S.O. 1980, c. 512, s. 47(1); *Insurance Act*, R.S.O. 1980, c. 218, s. 186; *Legitimacy Act*, R.S.A. 1980, c. L-11, s. 3; *Family Relief Act*, R.S.A. 1980, c. F-2, s. 2.

109   Compare D. Stone, *supra*, note 100, at 522-23 and A. Shepard, 11 C.E.D., 3rd ed. (1988), title 57, at 341. See also *Chipchase v. Chipchase, supra*, note 101, at [1939] P. 394; *Prudential Assurance Co. v. Edmonds*, [1877] 2 App. Cas. 487; *Re McNeil, supra*, note 94; *Sheehy v. Robinson, supra*, note 101; Wigmore, *supra*, note 95, § 2531, at 603-04; A. Keane, *supra*, note 92, at 469.

110   *Cross on Evidence, supra*, note 104, at 128; see also, *Prudential Assurance Company v. Edmonds, ibid.*

the presumed fact of death upon his opponent."[111]

(d) *Presumption of the Order of Death*

Where two or more persons die in a common disaster, the question often arises as to the order of death. Because the common law did not create a presumption to assist litigants to meet this difficult evidentiary problem,[112] the U.K. Parliament enacted legislation[113] to correct this perceived deficiency.[114] Many Canadian provinces enacted modified versions of the U.K. proviso.[115] The statutory proviso stipulates that upon proof that two or more persons have died in circumstances rendering it uncertain as to who survived whom, the deaths shall be presumed to have occurred in order of seniority.[116]

The evidentiary effect of the presumption is uncertain because evidence which rebuts the presumed fact also rebuts the basic fact. For example, evidence that the younger person predeceased the elder person rebuts both the basic fact that the order of deaths was uncertain

---

111 *Cross on Evidence, supra*, note 104, at 127.
112 *Hartshorne v. Wilkins* (1866), 6 N.S.R. 276 (N.S.S.C.); *Underwood v. Wing* (1854), 19 Beav. 459, 52 E.R. 428 (C.A.); *Re Phene's Trusts* (1870), 5 L.R. 139 (Ch. App.); *McLeod v. Toronto General Trusts Corp.*, [1936] 3 D.L.R. 368, [1936] O.R. 379 (Ont. S.C.); *Campbell v. Cox*, [1930] 1 D.L.R. 649, 42 B.C.R. 120 (B.C.S.C.); *Bentley v. Cdn. Bank of Commerce*, [1922] 69 D.L.R. 730, [1922] 3 W.W.R. 841, 16 Sask. L.R. 109 (Sask. K.B.). See also Wigmore, *supra*, note 95, § 2532, at 618.
113 *Law of Property Act* (1925), c. 20, s. 184(1).
114 In *Bennett v. Peattie* (1925), 57 O.L.R. 233, at 240 (Ont. C.A.), Bennett J.A. stated: "The rules of the Common Law . . . upon the subject of survivorship are alike illogical and unsatisfactory. Where upon the death of two the right depends upon survivorship, and the whole fund must go to one or the other according to the determination as a question of fact that one person killed in a common accident drew his last breath a moment after the other expired, the difficulty of the inquiry and the unsatisfactory nature of the result are obvious. There is no way by which a division of the property can be secured unless the common sense of the contending factions triumphs over the desire to litigate. Where the property is in the hands of a third party, each claimant may in his turn fail to recover because of his inability to satisfy the onus of proof resting upon him."
115 See *Survivorship and Presumption of Death Act*, R.S.B.C. 1979, c. 398; *Survivorship Act*, R.S.A. 1980, c. S-31; R.S.N. 1970, c. 366; R.S.N.B. 1973, c. S-19; R.S.N.S., 1989, c. 454; R.S.S. 1978, c. S-67 [am. 1982, c. 16, s. 65]; *Commorientes Act*, R.S.P.E.I. 1988, c. C-12; and *Survivorship Ordinance*, R.O.N.W.T. 1974, c. S-12 [am. 1976 (1st Sess.), c. 10, s. 1] [now *Survivorship Act*, R.S.N.W.T. 1988, c. S-16]; see also the *Commorientes Act*, S.O. 1940, c. 4. (subsequently renamed the *Survivorship Act*, R.S.O. 1950, c. 382).
116 See *Hickman v. Peacey*, [1945] A.C. 304, [1945] 2 All E.R. 215 (H.L.).

and the presumed fact that the deaths occurred in order of seniority.

These statutory provisions were found lacking in some circumstances and they created fresh interpretation problems.[117] As a result, some jurisdictions repealed the statutory presumptions and enacted new provisions, without creating a presumption, to rectify the perceived shortcomings.[118] For example, s. 55(1) of the Ontario *Succession Law Reform Act* provides:[119]

> Where two or more persons die at the same time or in circumstances rendering it uncertain which of them survived the other or others, the property of each person, or any property of which he is competent to dispose, shall be disposed of as if he had survived the other or others.

(e) *Presumptions of Advancement and Resulting Trust*

Two related common law presumptions, called the presumption of advancement and the presumption of resulting trust, create rebuttable presumptions of law. Where a person makes a voluntary transfer of property to another or where a person supplies the purchase monies but directs that title be taken in the name of another the question arises whether the transfer was a gift or the recipient held the property as trustee.[120] Where there is a conveyance or transfer of property without consideration from a husband to a spouse or from a parent or person standing *in loco parentis* to a child, the law presumes that it was intended as a gift.[121] The same presumption applies where a person buys

---

117 See *Re Topliss Estates*, [1957] O.W.N. 513, [1957] 1 L.R. 1-297, 10 D.L.R. (2d) 654 (Ont. C.A.); *Leach v. Egar* (1990), 46 B.C.L.R. (2d) 158, 70 D.L.R. (4th) 765, 27 R.F.L. (3d) 29, 38 E.T.R. 65 (B.C.C.A.). Wigmore, *supra*, note 95, § 2532, at 618-22.

118 S.O. 1977, c. 40, s. 62(1); *Survivorship Act*, S.M. 1982-83-84, c. 28; *Survivorship Ordinance*, O.Y.T. 1980 (1st Sess.), c. 31.

119 R.S.O. 1980, c. 488.

120 A.H. Oosterhoff and E.E. Gillese, *Text, Commentary and Cases on Trusts*, 3rd ed. (Toronto: Carswell, 1987), at 307-78; *Rathwell v. Rathwell*, [1978] 2 S.C.R. 436, at 450-51, 83 D.L.R. (3d) 289, [1978] 2 W.W.R. 101, 1 E.T.R. 307, 1 R.F.L. (2d) 1.

121 *Jackman v. Jackman*, [1959] S.C.R. 702, 19 D.L.R. (2d) 317; *MacDonald v. Young*, [1934] 4 D.L.R. 172, 7 M.P.R. 602 (N.S.C.A.); *Dagle v. Dagle* (1990), 70 D.L.R. (4th) 201, 38 E.T.R. 164, 81 Nfld. & P.E.I.R. 245, 255 A.P.R. 245 (P.E.I. C.A.).

property and pays the purchase money or part of it but takes title in the name of another who is either the donor's child, spouse, or a person to whom she or he stands in *loco parentis*. The presumption may apply in favour of a woman living with the donor as husband and wife,[122] but it does not apply where there is a marriage breakdown.[123]

The historical basis for the presumption of advancement may not be appropriate in today's society[124] and it has been abolished in some jurisdictions for transfers between spouses.[125] However, the presumption is important for transfers between parent and child[126] and in those jurisdictions where modern matrimonial legislation has not been enacted.[127]

A resulting trust occurs where there is a transfer to, or a purchase in the name of a stranger. In the absence of evidence that the transferor intended to make a gift and in the absence of one of the above relationships, there is a presumption of a resulting trust in favour of the person making the conveyance or transfer.[128]

The presumption of advancement and the presumption of resulting trust are rebuttable.[129] It appears that the presumptions are satisfied if the party adduces evidence of a contrary intention to a balance of probabilities.[130] The evidence required to rebut the pre-

---

122 *Johnston v. Desaulniers* (1910), 46 S.C.R. 620; affg. 20 Man. R. 64 (C.A.).

123 A.H. Oosterhoff and E.E. Gillese, *supra*, note 120, at 322.

124 *Rathwell, supra*, note 120: "In present social conditions the old presumption of advancement has ceased to embody any credible inference of intention", at (S.C.R.) 452, per Dickson J.; see also, *Pettitt v. Pettitt*, [1970] A.C. 777, at 793, at 811, 815, and 824, [1969] 2 All E.R. 385 (H.L.).

125 *Marital Property Act*, S.N.B. 1980, c. M-1.1; *Matrimonial Property Act*, S.N. 1979, c. 32, s. 29; *Family Law Act*, S.O. 1986, c. 4, s. 14; *Family Law Reform Act*, R.S.P.E.I. 1988, c. F-3, s. 11; *Matrimonial Property Ordinance*, R.S.Y.T. 1986, c. 63, s. 7(2); see also A.H. Oosterhoff and E.E. Gillese, *supra*, note 120, at 326; *Meltzer v. Meltzer* (1989), 61 Man. R. (2d) 1, 22 R.F.L. (3d) 38 (Man. Q.B.).

126 *Blackman v. Davison* (1986), 2 B.C.L.R. (2d) 8 (S.C.); affd. (1987), 12 B.C.L.R. 24, 64 C.B.R. (N.S.) 84 (C.A.); *Bodo v. Bodo* (1990), 66 D.L.R. (4th) 700, 25 R.F.L. (3d) 295 (B.C.S.C.).

127 A.H. Oosterhoff and E.E. Gillese, *supra*, note 120, at 324.

128 *MacDonald v. Young, supra*, note 121.

129 *Rathwell, supra*, note 120, at 451 (S.C.R.); *Martin v. Bourque*, unreported, February 8, 1990 (N.S.T.D.).

130 *Dagle v. Dagle, supra*, note 121; *Lawrence v. Lawrence* (1990), 108 N.B.R. (2d) 1, 269 A.P.R. 1 (N.B.Q.B.); *Walsh v. Walsh*, [1948] O.R. 81, [1948] 1 D.L.R. 630 (H.C.J.); affd. [1948] O.W.N. 668, [1948] 4 D.L.R. 876 (C.A.). *Contra: Reaney v. Reaney* (1990), 72 D.L.R. (4th) 532, 28 R.F.L. (3d) 52, 38 E.T.R. 252; *Pettitt v.*

sumption is evidence of the donee's contrary intention at the time of the transfer. Because the courts first examine all the evidence to determine the transferor's or purchaser's intent, the presumption is, practically speaking, operative only in doubtful cases.[131]

(f) *Presumption of Regularity*

The common law presumption of regularity is sometimes referred to by its latin label *omnia praesumuntur rite esse acta*. In its narrower application, the presumption serves to regularize the appointment and acts of persons acting in an official capacity. Where a person is shown to have acted in an official capacity it is supposed that the person would not intrude herself or himself into a public situation without authorization.[132] Furthermore, the person's acts are presumed to be regular.[133] The presumption of regularity also extends to municipal bodies. Accordingly, a by-law need not recite the authority under which it was passed as it will be presumed that council acted with authority.[134] If, however, statutory authority is absent, the by-law is invalid. The absence of a recital is immaterial, however, if the power exists.[135]

It has also been held that by virtue of this maxim a will which appears to be duly executed on its face will be presumed to have been executed in compliance with all statutory requirements.[136] The maxim has been extended in England to raise a presumption that traffic lights erected by public officials were in working order at the relevant

---

Pettitt, supra, note 124: "These presumptions or circumstances may be rebutted by slight evidence . . ." per Lord Upjohn, at 814 (A.C.).

131 A.H. Oosterhoff and E.E. Gillese, *supra*, note 120, at 308. For the nature of circumstantial and direct evidence necessary to rebut the presumptions see *Clemens v. Clemens Estate*, [1956] S.C.R. 286, 1 D.L.R. (2d) 625; *Wilson v. Boltezar*, unreported, April 5, 1989 (B.C.S.C.).

132 *Pender v. War Eagle* (1899), 6 B.C.R. 427 (B.C.S.C.); *R. v. Harrison*, [1977] 1 S.C.R. 238, [1976] 3 W.W.R. 536, 28 C.C.C. (2d) 279, 66 D.L.R. (3d) 660, 8 N.R. 47; *R. v. Coady* (1975), 8 Nfld. & P.E.I.R. 66, 25 C.C.C. (2d) 529 (P.E.I. C.A.); *R. v. Matthes* (1985), 32 M.V.R. 303 (B.C.S.C.).

133 *Re Morris Provincial Election* (1907), 6 W.L.R. 742; affd. 7 W.L.R. 233, 17 Man. R. 132 (C.A.).

134 *Fisher v. Vaughan (Township)* (1853), 10 U.C.Q.B. 492 (C.A.); *Calder Gravel Ltd. v. Kirkkes Metropolitan Borough Council* (1989), Times, October 16 (Ch. D.).

135 *Gray v. Oshawa (City)*, [1972] 2 O.R. 856, 27 D.L.R. (3d) 35 (C.A.).

136 *Re Laxer*, [1963] 1 O.R. 343, at 354-55, 37 D.L.R. (2d) 192 (C.A.).

time.[137] However, the presumption may not be used to establish an ingredient of a crime in criminal proceedings if the regularity and the propriety of the matter in question are disputed at trial.[138]

VI CONFLICTING PRESUMPTIONS

A typical case where courts are required to deal with more than one presumption occurs where there is an issue as to the validity of a marriage and two marriages are proved. In *Powell v. Cockburn*[139] a presumption favoured the validity of both marriages while a different presumption favoured the validity of a foreign divorce decree. Dickson J. held that the presumptions neither conflicted nor cancelled each other out nor artificially added probative value upon proof of the basic fact. Adopting Wigmore's theory of successive presumptions,[140] the court held that the presumptions operated to impose alternating evidential burdens. For example, the petitioner rebutted the presumption of the validity of the present marriage by adducing evidence of his spouse's prior marriage. The presumption of the validity of the spouse's prior marriage was then rebutted by leading evidence of her prior divorce. The court held that these presumptions disappear where the party adduces contrary evidence leaving the trier of fact to determine the case on the evidence and the legal burden of proof. An alternative approach producing the same result is that conflicting presumptions cancel each other out thereby leaving the matter to be decided in accordance with the legal burden of proof.[141]

---

137 *Tingle Jacobs & Co. v. Kennedy*, [1964] 1 W.L.R. 638n, [1964] 1 All E.R. 888 (C.A.).

138 A. Keane, *The Modern Law of Evidence*, 2nd ed. (London: Butterworths, 1989), at 474-75; *R. v. Alatyppo* (1983), 4 C.C.C. (3d) 514, 20 M.V.R. 39 (Ont. C.A.); *R. v. Goulet* (1990), 73 O.R. 492 (Ont. Dist. Ct.); see also *R. v. Harrison*, *supra*, note 132, at 246-47.

139 [1977] 2 S.C.R. 218, 68 D.L.R. (3d) 700, 22 R.F.L. 155, 8 N.R. 215 (S.C.C.).

140 9 Wigmore, *Evidence* (Chadbourn rev. 1981), § 2493, at 308-09.

141 M.N. Howard, P. Crane and D. Hochberg, *Phipson on Evidence*, 14th ed. (London: Sweet & Maxwell, 1990), at 72; *R. v. Willshire* (1881), 6 Q.B.D. 366, 50 L.J.M.C. 57; *Monckton v. Tarr* (1930), 23 B.W.C.C. 504; *R. v. Dauphinee* (1929), 52 C.C.C. 401, [1930] 2 D.L.R. 133, 1 M.P.R. 40 (C.A.); affg., 51 C.C.C. 428, [1929] 3 D.L.R. 622. In *Taylor v. Taylor*, [1965] 1 All E.R. 872 the court held that presumptions cancel each other out only if they relate to the same fact; see also, R. Cross, *Cross on Evidence*, 3rd ed. (London: Butterworths, 1967), at 108.

The Law Reform Commission and the Task Force on Evidence[142] recommended that where presumptions conflict, the judge should apply the one founded on weightier considerations of policy. Since presumptions, like burdens of proof, are founded on principles of fairness, probabilities and policy, this suggested test may be difficult to apply.[143] The revised text of Wigmore, which also recommends this solution, goes on to provide that if there is no such preponderance of policy, then both presumptions are disregarded.[144] Another suggested solution is to apply a purposive approach to the individual presumptions. In *Re Topliss Estates*[145] the court successively applied each presumption in accordance with its underlying purpose thereby avoiding a conflict between them.

VII THE IMPACT OF THE CHARTER

The *Charter*'s influence on the development of the law on presumptions in criminal cases has been significant. Because rebuttable presumptions of law cast either an evidential burden or the legal burden of proof on an accused, the question arises whether a particular presumption that allocates one or the other burden to an accused is contrary to s. 11(d) of the *Charter*. If the answer to this question is affirmative, the next question is whether the particular presumption can be saved under s. 1? As the constitutional validity of specific presumptions is more appropriately discussed in texts on constitutional or criminal law than one on evidence, our discussion is limited to general principles.

A comparative starting point for our discussion is the Supreme Court of Canada's interpretation of section 2(f) of the *Canadian Bill of Rights*[146] which states in part as follows:

---

142 Law Reform Commission of Canada, *Report on Evidence* (Ottawa: Minister of Supply and Services Canada, 1977), at 61; Report of the Federal/Provincial Task Force on Uniform Rules of Evidence (Toronto: Carswell, 1982), at 32-33. See *Family Maintenance Act*, R.S.M. 1987, c. F20, s. 20(5) for a statutory solution.
143 See Chapter 3, VI.C.
144 Wigmore, *supra*, note 140, §2493f, at 332-33.
145 [1957] O.W.N. 513, 10 D.L.R. (2d) 654 (C.A.).
146 *An Act for the Recognition and Protection of Human Rights and Fundamental Freedoms*, R.S.C. 1985, Appendix III.

2. ... no law of Canada shall be construed or applied so as to ...

(f) deprive a person charged with a criminal offence of the right to be presumed innocent until proved guilty according to law . . . .

In *R. v. Appleby*[147] the Supreme Court of Canada held that "s. 2(f) of the *Bill of Rights* must be taken to envisage a law which recognizes the existence of statutory exceptions reversing the onus of proof with respect to one or more ingredients of an offence in cases where certain specific facts have been proved by the Crown in relation to such ingredients."[148] Because a rebuttable presumption that required an accused person to prove a fact to balance of probabilities did not conflict with the presumption of innocence within the meaning of *Woolmington v. D.P.P.*,[149] the presumption was not contrary to s. 2(f) of the *Bill of Rights*. In *R. v. Shelley*,[150] however, the Supreme Court of Canada held that the Crown could not rely upon a reverse onus provision until the prosecution proved that the accused had knowledge or the means of ascertaining the evidence required to rebut the presumption.[151] *In obiter*, the Court held that it would be "clearly incompatible with s. 2(f) for a statute to put upon an accused a reverse onus of proving a fact in issue beyond a reasonable doubt".[152]

In the important *Charter* case of *R. v. Oakes*,[153] the accused was charged with possession of a narcotic for the purpose of trafficking

---

147 [1972] S.C.R. 303, 16 C.R.N.S. 35, 3 C.C.C. (2d) 354, 21 D.L.R. (3d) 325.
148 *Ibid.*, at 316 (S.C.R.).
149 [1935] A.C. 462, 25 Cr. App. Rep. 72 (H.L.).
150 [1981] 2 S.C.R. 196, 21 C.R. (3d) 354, 59 C.C.C. (3d) 292, 123 D.L.R. (3d) 748, [1981] 5 W.W.R. 481, 9 Sask. R. 338, 37 N.R. 320, 3 C.E.R. 217, 26 C.R. (3d) 150 (French).
151 *Ibid.*, at 200 (S.C.R.): "In so far as the onus goes no further than to require an accused to prove as essential fact upon a balance of probabilities, the essential fact must be one which is rationally open to the accused to prove or disprove, as the case may be." "To require less could leave the accused with an impossible burden of proof and would amount to an irrebuttable presumption of guilt against him, depriving him of the right to be presumed innocent under s. 2(f) of the *Canadian Bill of Rights*." (*ibid.*, at 202-03). See also, *R. v. Oakes* [1986] 1 S.C.R. 103, at 124, 50 C.R. (3d) 1, 24 C.C.C. (3d) 321, 26 D.L.R. (4th) 200, 53 O.R. (2d) 719 (headnote only), 14 O.A.C. 335, 19 C.R.R. 308, 65 N.R. 87.
152 *R. v. Shelley, ibid.*, at 200 (S.C.R.).
153 *Supra*, note 151.

contrary to s. 4(2) of the *Narcotic Control Act*.[154] Section 8 of the Act creates a bifurcated trial and a rebuttable presumption by providing that a trial for possession of a narcotic for the purpose of trafficking shall proceed as if it was a trial for simple possession.[155] Where a jury finds that the accused was in possession of a narcotic beyond a reasonable doubt, the accused has the legal burden of proving to a balance of probabilities that she or he was not in possession of the narcotic for the purpose of trafficking. Section 8 was classified as a "reverse onus" provision because it compels, in the absence of rebutting evidence to the civil standard of proof, a finding of guilt.

The Supreme Court held that the jurisprudence under the *Canadian Bill of Rights* was not binding in relation to the interpretation of the *Charter* because the two documents were fundamentally different. Whereas the *Canadian Bill of Rights* was interpreted "... as simply recognizing and declaring existing rights"[156] the *Charter* is a constitutional document under which parliamentary supremacy has been tempered by entrenching important rights and freedoms in the Constitution.[157]

The Supreme Court stated that the presumption of innocence has at least three components:[158]

> First, an individual must be proven guilty beyond a reasonable doubt. Second, it is the State which must bear the burden of proof. Third, criminal prosecutions must be carried out in accordance with lawful procedures and fairness.

Where an accused adduced sufficient evidence to raise a reasonable doubt as to his or her guilt "but did not convince the jury on a balance of probabilities that the presumed fact was true",[159] a conviction for possession for the purpose of trafficking could result. The court held that a "provision which requires an accused to disprove on a balance of probabilities the existence of a presumed fact, which is an important

---

154 R.S.C. 1985, c. N-1.
155 *Ibid.*
156 *Oakes, supra,* note 151, at 124 (S.C.R.).
157 *Ibid.,* at 125 (S.C.R.).
158 *Ibid.,* at 121 (S.C.R.); see also *R. v. Whyte,* [1988] 2 S.C.R. 3, 64 C.R. (3d) 123, 42 C.C.C. (3d) 97, 51 D.L.R. (4th) 481, [1988] 5 W.W.R. 26, 29 B.C.L.R. (2d) 273, 86 N.R. 328, 6 M.V.R. (2d) 138.
159 *Oakes, ibid.,* at 133 (S.C.R.).

element of the offence in question, violates the presumption of innocence in s. 11(d)."[160] Because s. 8 compels the accused to establish that he or she was not in possession of the narcotic for the prohibited purpose, the section was contrary to the right to be presumed innocent.[161]

The second stage of the constitutional inquiry is whether a section that contravenes section 11(d) is nonetheless constitutional because the limit is reasonable and is demonstrably justified in a free and democratic society.[162] The Supreme Court of Canada held that the party seeking to uphold the provision limiting a right or freedom has the onus of proof to a balance of probabilities.[163]

The justification for limiting a right focuses on two central criteria.[164] First, the objective for which the provision is designed to serve must be of sufficient importance to warrant overriding a constitutionally protected right. The court held that the objective must be pressing and substantial in a free and democratic society before it can be characterized as sufficiently important.[165] Second, the means chosen to limit the right are reasonable and demonstrably justified.[166] This latter test, known as the "proportionality test", consists of three components.[167]

> First, the measures adopted must be carefully designed to achieve the objective in question. They must not be arbitrary, unfair or based on irrational considerations. In short, they must be rationally connected to the objective. Second, the means, even if rationally connected to the objective in this first sense, should

---

160 *Oakes, ibid.*, at 132; see also *R. v. Dubois*, [1985] 2 S.C.R. 350, 48 C.R. (3d) 193, 22 C.C.C. (3d) 513, 23 D.L.R. (4th) 503, [1986] 1 W.W.R. 193, 41 Alta. L.R. (2d) 97, 62 N.R. 50, 18 C.R.R. 1, 66 A.R. 202, [1986] 2 D.L.Q. 872 (S.C.C.), where the court held that s. 11(d) includes the obligation on the Crown of the evidential burden of making out a case against an accused before he or she need respond, either by testifying or by calling other evidence.

161 *Oakes, ibid.*, at 134 (S.C.R.).

162 For the courts identification of the contextual elements of a s. 1 analysis and the underlying value and principles for the enshrined rights and freedoms see *Oakes, ibid.*, at 135-36 (S.C.R.).

163 *Ibid.*, at 136-37 (S.C.R.); the evidence must be "clear and cogent" (*ibid.*, at 138).

164 *Oakes, ibid.*, at 138 (S.C.R.).

165 *Ibid.*, at 138-39 (S.C.R.).

166 *Ibid.*, at 139 (S.C.R.).

167 *Ibid.*, at 139 (S.C.R.).

impair "as little as possible" the right or freedom in question. Third, there must be a proportionality between the *effects* of the measures which are responsible for limiting the *Charter* right or freedom, and the objective which has been identified as of "sufficient importance".

The court recognized that limits on rights will vary in degrees of seriousness, thereby incorporating a balancing exercise in relation to the third component of the proportionality test. The court held:[168]

> The more severe the deleterious effects of a measure, the more important the objective must be if the measure is to be reasonable and justified in a free and democratic society.

The *Oakes* test has been applied to various statutory presumptions, albeit there has been some disagreement between members of the Supreme Court of Canada on its application to particular statutory provisions.[169] Since the rights enshrined by the *Charter* are not absolute, some statutory rebuttable presumptions that require an accused to prove a fact to a balance of probability have survived judicial scrutiny. For example, the care and control provision in relation to the drinking and driving sections of the *Criminal Code*[170] and the defence of lawful excuse (innocent purpose) in relation to the offence of possession of instruments suitable for housebreaking[171] have survived constitutional challenge.[172] Nonetheless, there is a noticeable judicial reluctance to uphold a rebuttable presumption that places on the accused the obligation of proving an important fact to a balance of probability. Accordingly, many such provisions may be rendered invalid in the future.

The *Oakes* tests also applies to rebuttable presumptions that place an evidentiary burden on the accused. In *Boyle v. R.*,[173] the Crown

---

168 *Ibid.*, at 140 (S.C.R.).
169 See *R. v. Whyte, supra,* note 158; *R. v. Holmes,* [1988] 1 S.C.R. 914, 64 C.R. (3d) 97, 41 C.C.C. (3d) 497, 27 O.A.C. 321, 85 N.R. 21.
170 *Whyte, ibid.*; see also text *supra,* at note 147 for the pre-*Charter* position.
171 *R. v. Holmes, supra,* note 169.
172 See also, *R. v. Schwartz,* [1988] 2 S.C.R. 443, 66 C.R. (3d) 251, 45 C.C.C. (3d) 97, 55 D.L.R. (4th) 1, [1989] 1 W.W.R. 289, 39 C.R.R. 260, 56 Man. R. (2d) 92, 88 N.R. 90.
173 (1983), 35 C.R. (3d) 34, 5 C.C.C. (3d) 193, 148 D.L.R. (3d) 449, 41 O.R. (2d) 713, 5 C.R.R. 218 (C.A.).

relied on s. 312(2) of the *Criminal Code*.[174] Once the Crown proves the basic fact of possession of a motor vehicle with an obliterated identification number, in the absence of contrary evidence, two distinct facts are presumed by virtue of s. 312(2). First, the motor vehicle was obtained by means of an indictable offence in Canada and secondly, the accused knew that it was so obtained. The Ontario Court of Appeal held that the mandatory nature of all rebuttable presumptions require them to be treated alike for constitutional purposes. The court reasoned that the difference between a reverse onus clause allocating a legal burden of proof to an accused and a rebuttable presumption allocating an evidential burden is merely the amount of evidence that is required to displace the presumption.[175] Martin J.A. held that the presumption that a vehicle with an obliterated identification number had been stolen was reasonable but that the presumption that the accused knew it was stolen was arbitrary and unreasonable.[176] Accordingly, the latter presumption did not survive constitutional review.

The *Oakes* test has also been applied to presumptions of fact.[177] Most presumptions of fact are nothing more than justifiable or common sense inferences. Because these presumptions do not compel a particular conclusion upon proof of the basic fact and they do not require an accused to adduce evidence or prove the existence or non-existence of a fact to a balance of probability, they may not contravene s. 11(d).

Finally, presumptions without basic facts are also subject to constitutional challenge.[178] In *R. v. Chaulk*,[179] the Supreme Court of Canada examined the presumption of sanity found in s. 16 of the *Criminal Code*.[180] The majority of the court held that s. 16(4) contravenes s. 11(d) of the *Charter*. The court reconciles its earlier decisions on 11(d)[181] by holding that the focus of the 11(d) inquiry is the effect

---

174 Now R.S.C. 1985, c. C-46, s. 354.

175 *Supra*, note 173, at 57 (C.R.).

176 *Ibid.*, at 54-62 (C.R.).

177 *R. v. Russell* (1983), 32 C.R. (3d) 307, 4 C.C.C. (3d) 460, 147 D.L.R. (3d) 569, 5 C.R.R. 319, 56 N.S.R. (2d) 701, 5 C.R.R. 319 (N.S.C.A.).

178 *R. v. Godfrey* (1984), 39 C.R. (3d) 97, 11 C.C.C. (3d) 233, 8 D.L.R. (4th) 122, 26 Man. R. (2d) 61, 9 C.R.R. 126 (Man. C.A.), leave to appeal to S.C.C. refd. (1984), 11 C.C.C. (3d) 233n, 40 C.R. (3d) xxvin, 8 D.L.R. (4th) 122*n* (S.C.C.).

179 [1990] 3 S.C.R. 1303, 62 C.C.C. (3d) 193, 2 C.R. (4th) 1, [1991] 2 W.W.R. 385, 69 Man. R. (2d) 161, 1 C.R.R. (2d) 1, 119 N.R. 161.

180 R.S.C., 1985, c. C-46.

181 *Holmes, supra*, note 169; *Whyte*, [1988] 2 S.C.R. 3, 64 C.R. (3d) 123, 42

that the provision has on the issue of guilt or innocence rather than the precise nature or characterization of the provision. The majority of the court adopted the test articulated by Dickson C.J. in *Whyte*:[182]

> It is the final effect of a provision on the verdict that is decisive. If an accused is required to prove some fact on the balance of probabilities to avoid conviction, the provision violates the presumption of innocence because it permits a conviction in spite of a reasonable doubt in the mind of the trier of fact.

Accordingly, it does not matter whether the challenged provision is characterized as an element of the offence, a defence, an excuse or justification, or an exemption since it will violate the presumption of innocence because it permits a conviction in spite of a reasonable doubt as to the guilt of the accused.[183] However, the court found that s. 16(4) was saved under s. 1 as being a reasonable limit on the presumption of innocence.[184]

C.C.C. (3d) 97, 51 D.L.R. (4th) 481, [1988] 5 W.W.R. 26, 29 B.C.L.R. (2d) 273, 86 N.R. 328, 6 M.V.R. (2d) 138; *Schwartz, supra*, note 172.

182 *Ibid.*, at 18 (S.C.R.).

183 *Ibid.*, at 23, 25-26 (S.C.R.).

184 Note that the European Commission on Human Rights has recently held that the presumption of sanity (i.e., the *MacNaghton* rules did not contravene the presumption of innocence enshrined in art. 6(2) of the European Convention on Human Rights, *Application 15023/89 v. United Kingdom* (1990), L.S. Gaz., 22 Aug. 1990.

CHAPTER 5

STANDARDS OF PROOF

I   INTRODUCTION

This chapter concerns the degree of proof necessary to satisfy an evidential burden and the legal burden of proof in relation to a fact or issue in civil and criminal proceedings. We describe the procedure and the test governing a defendant's motion for a non-suit and a directed verdict of acquittal and we discuss the division of responsibilities between the judge and jury on these motions. Although these matters may be classified as substantive law or procedural rules, we discuss them in this text because they are an integral and important aspect of the trial process.[1] Policy considerations are important in determining the sufficiency of evidence that is required to satisfy an evidential burden or the legal burden of proof in both criminal and civil proceedings. If the threshold test to satisfy an evidential burden is too stringent or too low, the substantive law may be altered to meet new considerations.[2]

---

1   See Australian Law Reform Commission, *Evidence*, vol. 1 (interim report) (Canberra: Australian Government Publishing Service, 1985), at 13-16 for a discussion of the scope of the law of evidence.

2   See *R. v. Bernard*, [1988] 2 S.C.R. 833, 67 C.R. (3d) 113, 45 C.C.C. (3d) 1, 38 C.R.R. 82, 90 N.R. 321, 32 O.A.C. 161 where Wilson J. held (at 882-83, S.C.R.) that "[t]he evidence of intoxication withheld from the jury could not possibly have raised a reasonable doubt as to the existence of the minimal intent to apply force" and (at 884, S.C.R.) "[t]here is no evidence that we are dealing with extreme intoxication, verging on insanity or automatism, and as such capable of negating the inference that the minimal intent to apply force was present".

II SATISFYING THE EVIDENTIAL BURDEN

A. *Motion for a Non-Suit in Civil Proceedings*

An important part of the division of responsibilities between judge and jury is the assessment of the sufficiency of the evidence adduced by a party. If a plaintiff fails to lead any material evidence, the plaintiff may be faced with a defendant's non-suit motion[3] at the close of his or her case. If such a motion is launched, it is the trial judge's function to determine whether any facts have been established by the plaintiff from which liability, if it is in issue, may be inferred. In comparison, it is the trier of fact's duty to say at the end of the case whether liability ought to be inferred. In *Metropolitan Railway Co. v. Jackson*[4] Lord Cairns said:

> The Judge has a certain duty to discharge, and the jurors have another and a different duty. The Judge has to say whether any facts have been established by evidence from which negligence *may be* reasonably inferred; the jurors have to say whether, from those facts, when submitted to them, negligence *ought to be* inferred. It is, in my opinion, of the greatest importance in the administration of justice that these separate functions should be maintained, and should be maintained distinct.

The Supreme Court of Canada adopted this passage as a correct statement of the law governing civil and criminal proceedings alike.[5] The trial judge, in performing this function, does not decide whether he or she believes the evidence. Rather, the judge decides whether there is any evidence, if left uncontradicted, to satisfy a reasonable person. The judge must conclude whether a reasonable

---

3   The word "non-suit" originally referred to the practice at common law of a plaintiff, upon discovering some technical defect in his proceeding, terminating his action and retaining the right to commence another for the same cause. Although this practice no longer prevails, the word "non-suit" is still used, but in relation to the motion by a defendant for a final judgment on the ground that the plaintiff has made out no case against him or her: *The "Polar Star" v. Louis Denker Inc.* (1965), 53 D.L.R. (2d) 181 (P.E.I. C.A.), at 183.

4   (1877), 4 L.J.Q.B. 303, 3 App. Cas. 193 (H.L.), at 197.

5   *R. v. Morabito*, [1949] S.C.R. 172, 93 C.C.C. 251, [1949] 1 D.L.R. 609, at 174 (S.C.R.); *R. v. Mezzo*, [1986] 1 S.C.R. 802, 52 C.R. (3d) 113, 27 C.C.C. (3d) 97, 30 D.L.R. (4th) 161, 68 N.R. 1, [1986] 4 W.W.R. 577, 43 Man. R. (2d) 161.

trier of fact could find in the plaintiff's favour if it believed the evidence given in the trial up to that point. The judge does not decide whether the trier of fact should accept the evidence, but whether the inference that the plaintiff seeks in his or her favour could be drawn from the evidence adduced, if the trier of fact chose to accept it.[6]

> It would be a serious inroad on the province of the jury, if, in a case where there are facts from which negligence may reasonably be inferred, the Judge were to withdraw the case from the jury upon the ground that, in his opinion, negligence ought not to be inferred; and it would, on the other hand, place in the hands of the jurors a power which might be exercised in the most arbitrary manner, if they were at liberty to hold that negligence might be inferred from any state of facts whatever.

The ruling by the trial judge on the non-suit motion is a question of law.[7] The judge is not ruling upon whether he or she is satisfied to a balance of probabilities or upon the believability of the evidence since these issues are questions for the trier of fact. If the plaintiff has failed to adduce any evidence in his or her case in chief and the defendant brings a successful non-suit motion, then the plaintiff's action will be dismissed. Because it is a question of law, the judge's assessment of the sufficiency of the plaintiff's evidence, or the defendant's evidence on a counter-claim for that matter, is subject to review by an appellate court.

In keeping with the adversary nature of the trial process, it is clear that a trial judge should not exercise this judicial function until counsel so moves.[8] When the plaintiff's case is completed defence counsel, if so disposed, may move for a non-suit on the ground that there is no evidence to give rise to a reasonable inference in the plaintiff's favour. The trial judge then must put defence counsel to his or her election as to whether the defendant wishes to call evidence.[9] If the defendant

---

6   *Metropolitan Railway Co.*, *supra*, note 4, at 197.
7   *Ryder v. Wombell* (1868), Law Rep. 4 Ex. 32, at 38 per Willes J.: "there is in every case . . . a preliminary question which is one of law, viz, whether there is any evidence on which the jury could properly find the question for the party on whom the onus of proof lies", quoted with approval by Lords Blackburn and Gordon in *Metropolitan Railway*, *supra*, note 4, at 207, 210-11.
8   *McKenzie v. Bergin*, [1937] O.W.N. 200 (C.A.).
9   *Mahen v. Arkelian* (1972), 3 N.S.R. (2d) 405 (C.A.); *McKenzie v. Bergin*,

elects to call no further evidence, the trial judge must then exercise the judicial function to determine if there is any evidence to satisfy a reasonable person of the plaintiff's case.[10] It is rare that a defendant's counsel will elect to call no evidence if he or she has evidence to call, because if the trial judge dismisses the motion for a non-suit, then the defendant is precluded from leading evidence for the purpose of raising a defence to the plaintiff's case.[11] Therefore, defendant's counsel must be sure of his or her success on the motion for a non-suit before making such an election.

In the case where the defendant's counsel elects to call no evidence, the trial judge decides the non-suit motion at that time.[12] If the trial judge concludes that the plaintiff has put forth evidence that may raise a reasonable inference of legal liability, then the judge, if a jury is present, turns the evidence over to the jury to determine the question, to draw the inferences from the evidence and to reach a verdict. But, if the trial judge gives effect to the defendant's motion, the trial judge must dismiss the plaintiff's action, on the basis that the plaintiff has not led sufficient evidence to satisfy the evidential burden.

When the plaintiff is claiming against two defendants alleging fault against both, a non-suit should not be granted at the conclusion of the plaintiff's case against one defendant because a successful non-suit by one defendant would preclude the other defendant from pressing a claim to have the degrees of fault apportioned between them under the provincial *Negligence Acts*.[13] Even though the plaintiff may not have adduced sufficient evidence to go to the jury against both defendants, one defendant, asserting a claim for apportionment, may be able to lead evidence to show that the other defendant is wholly or partly to blame.[14] However, the second defendant may bring a motion

---

[1937] O.W.N. 200 (C.A.); *Yuill v. Yuill*, [1945] P. 15, at 18, [1945] E.R. 183 (C.A.); *Storey v. Storey*, [1960] 3 All E.R. 279 (C.A.).

10 *McKenzie v. Bergin, supra*, note 8.

11 *The "Polar Star" v. Louis Denker Inc., supra*, note 3.

12 Save in exceptional circumstances, the plaintiff should be precluded from adducing any further evidence: *Concord Credits Ltd. v. Frankel*, [1971] 1 W.W.R. 470, 14 D.L.R. (3d) 634 (B.C.S.C.).

13 For example, R.S.O. 1980, c. 315; R.S.B.C. 1979, c. 298. *McCarroll v. Powell*, [1955] O.W.N. 281, [1955] 4 D.L.R. 631, at 635-6, [1955] O.W.N. 281 (Ont. C.A.); *Protopappas v. B.C. Electric Railway*, [1946] 1 D.L.R. 271 (B.C.S.C.); affd. [1946] 1 W.W.R. 232, [1946] 2 D.L.R. 330, 62 B.C.R. 218 (C.A.).

14 *Hunt v. MacLeod Construction Co.*, [1958] S.C.R. 737, at 742, 15 D.L.R. (2d) 529: *McCarroll v. Powell, ibid.*

at the conclusion of the first defendant's case.[15]

Depending on the jurisdiction, the defendant's election to call evidence has different consequences. In Prince Edward Island, British Columbia, Saskatchewan and New Brunswick, if a defendant proceeds to call evidence, the defendant is taken to have abandoned the motion for a non-suit.[16] In Ontario, if defendant's counsel elects to lead evidence, the trial judge will not decide the motion at that time, but he or she will reserve a decision on the motion until all the evidence in the case has been adduced.[17] However, the defendant may renew the non-suit motion at the conclusion of the evidence.[18] The trial judge then decides the motion on the basis of all the evidence led in the trial.[19] Thus, if the defendant's evidence, in part, assists the plaintiff in establishing his or her case, the trial judge considers that evidence along with the plaintiff's evidence in deciding whether or not there is a sufficient quantum of probative evidence before the court.[20] Similarly, the evidence adduced by one defendant may be considered on the question whether the plaintiff has established sufficient evidence against a second defendant who moved for a non-suit and elected to call no evidence.[21]

In either case, whether a defendant elects to call evidence or not, a trial judge should receive the jury's verdict before ruling on the motion.[22] This practice is followed because, should the trial judge grant the non-suit and should the plaintiff appeal that decision and the Court of Appeal holds that the trial judge's ruling was wrong, it is not necessary to remit the case back for a new trial. The appellate court

---

15   *Hunt v. McLeod Construction, ibid.*

16   *The "Polar Star" v. Louis Denker Inc., supra*, note 3; see also *Yuill v. Yuill, supra*, note 9, at 18.

17   *Martin v. Canadian Pacific Railway*, [1932] O.R. 571, at 574, 40 C.R.C. 144, [1932] 4 D.L.R. 191 (C.A.) folld. *Neal v. T. Eaton Co. Ltd.*, [1933] 3 D.L.R. 306, [1933] O.R. 573, at 578 (C.A.).

18   *McKenzie v. Bergin, supra*, note 8.

19   *Martin v. C.P.R., supra*, note 17; *Morrison v. Leyenhorst*, [1968] 2 O.R. 741, 70 D.L.R. (2d) 469 (Ont. Co. Ct.).

20   *Canadian Breweries Transport Ltd. v. Johnson*, [1944] S.C.R. 249, [1944] 3 D.L.R. 140.

21   *Majorcsak v. Na-Churs Plant Food Co. (Canada) Ltd.*, [1964] 2 O.R. 38, 44 D.L.R. (2d) 28 (H.C.); revd. in part on another ground, [1966] 2 O.R. 397, 57 D.L.R. (2d) 39 (C.A.); affd. on other grounds, [1968] S.C.R. 645 (*sub nom. Lammens v. Majorcsak*), 68 D.L.R. (2d) 707.

22   *Nadler v. Chornij* (1973), 32 D.L.R. (3d) 651, [1973] 3 O.R. 1 (Ont. C.A.).

will have before it the jury's verdict and accordingly, it can enter judgment in favour of the plaintiff in accordance with the jury's findings.[23] Because of this practice, the anomalous situation found in *Arendale v. Federal Building Corp.*[24] could conceivably arise where a trial judge allowed a non-suit even though the jury made a finding in favour of the plaintiff. The practice of putting a defendant to an election and taking the verdict of the jury was criticized by Devlin J. in *Young v. Rank.*[25] This problem does not, of course, arise in a non-jury trial. A full discussion of the advantages and disadvantages of this procedure can be found in *The Trial of an Action.*[26]

There is an obvious danger which faces a defendant's counsel who moves for a non-suit and elects to call no evidence. If the defendant is successful on that motion, it may only be a Pyrrhic victory, for, if the plaintiff appeals the trial judge's decision granting the non-suit, the Court of Appeal may well find that the trial judge made an error in law, in which case, the defendant now before the Court of Appeal is bound by the election at trial to call no evidence. Thus, the only evidence before the appellate court will be that of the plaintiff as the defendant is precluded at this time from calling any evidence.[27] The defendant can only argue that it is not possible for the court to draw a rational inference in favour of the plaintiff on the basis of that evidence. Once the defendant has lost the argument in the appellate court, the court will normally decide the case on the merits on the basis of the plaintiff's evidence which is the only evidence before it.[28] Accordingly, the appellate court will probably find in favour of the plaintiff as his or her evidence stands uncontradicted.

---

23 *Boutilier v. Traders General Ins. Co.* (1968), 1 D.L.R. (3d) 379, [1969] I.L.R. 1-262 (N.S.S.C.); affd. 1 N.S.R. 1965-69 810, [1969] I.L.R. 1-299, 7 D.L.R. (3d) 220 (C.A.).
24 [1961] O.W.N. 297 (H.C.); affd., [1962] O.R. 1053, 35 D.L.R. (2d) 202 (C.A.).
25 [1950] 2 K.B. 510, [1950] 2 All E.R. 166.
26 J. Sopinka (Toronto: Butterworths, 1981), at 127-28; see also, R.J. Delisle, *Evidence, Principles and Problems*, 2nd ed. (Toronto: Carswell, 1989), at 142.
27 *Martin v. Canadian Pacific Railway, supra,* note 17.
28 *Modern Construction Co. v. Maritime Rock Products Ltd.*, [1963] S.C.R. 347, 48 M.P.R. 341, 39 D.L.R. (2d) 539, at (S.C.R.) 356; *Gaskin v. Retail Credit Co.*, [1965] S.C.R. 297, 49 D.L.R. (2d) 542, at (S.C.R.) 300-301. See *Neal v. T. Eaton Co. Ltd., supra,* note 17 for conditions imposed on the defendant for a limited re-trial; see also, *Bernardi-Mathews Ltd. v. Malagerio* (1957), 12 D.L.R. (2d) 280 (Ont. C.A.).

This is the practice that is followed in all civil actions except for defamation cases. In actions of libel and slander, on a motion for a non-suit, the defendant is not put to his or her election as to whether he or she intends to call evidence. Rather, the judge decides the question at the moment that the motion is brought.[29] The latter procedure is the same as that applied in criminal prosecutions, which is dealt with in the next section.

B. *Motion for a Directed Verdict in Criminal Proceedings*

There is also a division of responsibilities between judge and trier of fact in criminal proceedings and in prosecutions for other federal and provincial offences. At the conclusion of the Crown's case, the defendant may launch a motion for a directed verdict of acquittal. The trial judge determines whether there is any evidence upon which a reasonable jury, properly instructed, may convict.[30] This test applies whether the evidence presented is circumstantial or direct evidence.[31] Because the trial judge does not determine the guilt or innocence of the accused, the proof beyond a reasonable doubt standard is not applied at this stage of the proceedings.[32]

---

29   *The "Polar Star" v. Louis Denker Inc.* (1965), 53 D.L.R. (2d) 181 (P.E.I. C.A.).
30   *United States v. Shephard*, [1977] 2 S.C.R. 1067, 34 C.R.N.S. 207, 30 C.C.C. (2d) 424, 70 D.L.R. (3d) 136, 9 N.R. 215. For other leading cases see *R. v. Girvin* (1911), 45 S.C.R. 167, 20 W.L.R. 130; *R. v. Mezzo*, [1986] 1 S.C.R. 802, 52 C.R. (3d) 113, 27 C.C.C. (3d) 97, 30 D.L.R. (4th) 161, [1986] 4 W.W.R. 577, 43 Man. R. (2d) 161, 68 N.R. 1; and *R. v. Monteleone*, [1987] 2 S.C.R. 154, 59 C.R. (3d) 97, 35 C.C.C. (3d) 193, 41 D.L.R. (4th) 746, 61 O.R. (2d) 654*n*, 78 N.R. 377. The same test is used to determine whether there is sufficient evidence to commit an accused to stand trial (*Skogman v. R.*, [1984] 2 S.C.R. 93, 41 C.R. (3d) 1, 13 C.C.C. (3d) 161, [1984] 5 W.W.R. 52) or to extradite a person from Canada (*Shephard*, *ibid.*).
31   *Monteleone, ibid.; Mezzo, ibid.; Jacobs v. R.*, [1988] 2 S.C.R. 1047; *R. v. Paul*, [1977] 1 S.C.R. 181, 27 C.C.C. (2d) 1, 64 D.L.R. (3d) 491, 4 N.R. 435.
32   *R. v. Dubois*, [1986] 1 S.C.R. 366, 25 C.C.C. (3d) 221, 51 C.R. (3d) 193, 26 D.L.R. (4th) 481, [1986] 3 W.W.R. 577, 66 N.R. 289, 18 Admin. L.R. 146, 41 Man. R. (2d) 1; *R. v. Morabito*, [1949] S.C.R. 172, 7 C.R. 88, 93 C.C.C. 251, [1949] 1 D.L.R. 609; *R. v. Heywood* (1971), 6 C.C.C. (2d) 141, 17 C.R.N.S. 388, [1972] 2 W.W.R. 209 (B.C.C.A.); *R. v. Syms* (1979), 47 C.C.C. (2d) 114, 28 Chitty's L.J. 66 (Ont. C.A.). For a criticism of failing to incorporate the reasonable doubt standard in the test, see R.J. Delisle, *supra*, note 26, at 120-30.

It is not the function of a trial judge to test the quality or reliability of the evidence, to draw inferences from admissible facts or to weigh the evidence to determine if he or she would be satisfied. These issues are the province of the jury.[33] Thus, the trial judge determines if the Crown has adduced any evidence on every essential definitional element of the crime for which the Crown has the evidential burden.[34] In a murder prosecution, for example, the trial judge determines if there is sufficient evidence on the issues of identity, causation, the death of the victim, and the requisite mental state. If the Crown fails to adduce any evidence to discharge the evidential burden on any of these issues, the trial judge will direct the trier of fact to return a verdict of not guilty. The ruling on this motion is a question of law subject to appellate court review.[35]

There are many similarities between the non-suit motion and a motion for a directed verdict of acquittal, but several important differences exist. Unlike a civil case, the accused is not put to an election whether he or she wishes to call evidence before a ruling is made by the trial judge.[36] Defence counsel would normally make a motion for a directed verdict in the absence of the jury.[37] The trial judge then rules on the motion. If the motion is successful, the trial judge instructs the jury upon their return that there is insufficient evidence for a conviction and directs them to find the accused not guilty. If the Crown satisfies the evidential burden in relation to the requisite elements of the offence, the trial judge will dismiss the motion. After the jury returns, the trial judge will put the accused to his or her election as to whether he or she wishes to call evidence. The trial judge will not inform the jury of his or her decision as it is irrelevant for the purposes of its task of determining the guilt or innocence of the accused.[38] The same procedure applies in a judge

33 *Monteleone, supra,* note 30, at 161.
34 Sometimes the Crown is aided in its task by a presumption, see Chapter 4, V. for a descriptive analysis of rebuttable presumptions of law.
35 *Shephard, supra,* note 30; see also, *R. v. Syms, supra,* note 32 for an example of circumstantial evidence sufficient to justify a conviction.
36 *R. v. Angelantoni* (1975), 31 C.R.N.S. 342, 28 C.C.C. (2d) 179 (Ont. C.A.); see also *R. v. Boissonneault* (1986), 29 C.C.C. (3d) 345, 16 O.A.C. 365 (Ont. C.A.) and cases cited therein.
37 As a matter of tactics, defence counsel would not wish the jury to hear argument and the court's decision in case the motion fails.
38 In *R. v. Bulmer,* [1987] 1 S.C.R. 782, 33 C.C.C. (3d) 385, 58 C.R. (3d) 48,

alone trial where the trial judge instructs himself or herself to dismiss the charge against the accused because the Crown has adduced no evidence in relation to the essential elements of the offence.[39]

Where there are multiple defendants, each defendant may make a motion for a directed verdict of acquittal. In these circumstances the trial judge determines whether there is any evidence against each accused and then rules on the motion in relation to that individual. Accordingly, the Crown could satisfy the evidential burden against one accused, but fail to do so in relation to another accused. In this scenario the jury would be instructed to return a verdict of not guilty against one accused and the trial judge would then put the second accused to his or her election to call evidence. Although evidence called by the remaining accused may implicate the accused who was previously acquitted, this result is justified because it is a principle of fundamental justice that the state must adduce some evidence of culpability on all the essential averments in relation to each accused before that person is required to elect to call evidence.[40]

C. *The Defendant's Evidential Burden*

We now consider those situations where the evidential burden is cast upon the defendant.[41] Since there are various evidential burdens cast on defendants in criminal and civil proceedings, it would be futile to analyze every situation where a defendant must satisfy an evidential burden. Accordingly, we limit our analysis to several illustrative cases to demonstrate the general principles.

---

14 B.C.L.R. (2d) 196, [1987] 4 W.W.R. 57 (*sub nom. Laybourn v. R.*), 39 D.L.R. (4th) 641, 75 N.R. 271, at 791 (S.C.R.), McIntyre J. for the court stated: "The first step for the trial judge is to decide if the defence should be put to the jury. It is on this question as I have said that the 'air of reality' test is applied. It has nothing to do with the jury and is not a factor for its consideration".

39   If the Crown has adduced sufficient evidence to succeed on the motion and the accused intends to testify about a justification or excuse, it is unlikely that defence counsel would bring a motion in a judge alone trial. On the other hand, if the defence does not intend to call evidence and the Crown's case is weak, it is unlikely that counsel will make a motion as it is preferable to argue for an acquittal based upon the reasonable doubt standard rather than on the threshold test for a directed verdict.

40   See *R. v. Dubois, supra*, note 32.

41   In Chapter 4 we discuss the degree of proof necessary to satisfy a presumption that casts an evidential burden on a defendant.

In *Mann v. Balaban*,[42] a civil action for assault, the Supreme Court of Canada held that the defendant bears the evidential and legal burden for the defence of justification and for the issue of the use of reasonable force.[43] The threshold test to discharge an evidential burden allocated to the defendant in a civil action is normally the same as that for the plaintiff.[44] The test is whether a properly instructed trier of fact could draw the desired inference from the evidence adduced up to that stage of the proceedings.[45] The defendant may be able to satisfy the evidential burden by cross-examining witnesses called by the plaintiff or by adducing evidence as part of her or his case. If the defendant fails to satisfy the evidential burden in relation to an issue, the trial judge will withdraw it from the trier of fact's consideration. On the other hand, if the trial judge determines that there is sufficient evidence to pass the threshold test, he or she will leave the issue for the jury's or his or her own consideration with appropriate directions on or considerations of the legal burden of proof. In either event, it is unnecessary for the trial judge to inform the trier of fact of his or her decision.

Where an evidential burden for an issue rests on the defendant in a criminal case, for example self-defence, the accused has the obligation to ensure that there is some evidence on the record to make it a live issue. The evidence necessary to satisfy an evidential burden may arise in the case for the Crown or the defence.[46] In relation to the defence of duress Edmund Davies J. stated:[47]

> The Crown are not called on to anticipate such a defence and destroy it in advance. The accused, either by the cross-examination of the prosecution witnesses or by evidence called on his behalf, or by a combination of the two, must place before the court such material as makes duress a live issue fit and proper to

---

42   [1970] S.C.R. 74, 8 D.L.R. (3d) 548.
43   In *R. v. Lobell*, [1957] 1 All E.R. 734, [1957] 1 Q.B. 547, at 550 Lord Goddard referred to self-defence as a justification: "It is a defence of justification, or, to put it in terms of pleading, a confession and avoidance. In civil cases this plea is always to be proved by the party setting it up; . . .".
44   *Ryder v. Wombell* (1868), L.R. 4 Exch. 32, at 39.
45   *Ibid.*, at 32.
46   *Latour v. R.*, [1951] S.C.R. 19, at 24, 11 C.R. 1, 98 C.C.C. 258, [1951] 1 D.L.R. 834.
47   *R. v. Gill*, [1963] 2 All E.R. 688, 47 Cr. App. Rep. 166 (C.C.A.), at 691 (All E.R.).

be left to the jury. But, once he has succeeded in doing this, it is then for the Crown to destroy that defence in such a manner as to leave in the jury's minds no reasonable doubt that the accused cannot be absolved on the grounds of the alleged compulsion.

An evidential burden cast upon the accused is normally satisfied if there is sufficient evidence as might leave a jury with a reasonable doubt about the guilt of an accused.[48] In *Jayasena v. R.* Lord Devlin stated:[49]

[I]n trial by jury a party may be required to adduce some evidence in support of his case, whether on the general issue or on a particular issue, before that issue is left to a jury. How much evidence has to be adduced depends on the nature of the require- ment. It may be such evidence, as if believed and if left uncon- tradicted and unexplained, could be accepted by the jury as proof.

It is the function of the trial judge to review the evidence supporting a defence to determine if it is fit to be left with the jury.[50] Although judges may be reluctant to withdraw a defence from a jury, not every theory of the defence will be put to the jury. Lord Morris of Borth-y-Gest stated:[51]

. . . it is not every facile mouthing of some easy phrase of excuse that can amount to an explanation. It is for a judge to decide whether there is evidence fit to be left to a jury which could be the basis of some suggested verdict.

---

48 *R. v. Bernard*, [1988] 2 S.C.R. 833, at 884, 67 C.R. (3d) 113, 45 C.C.C. (3d) 1, 38 C.R.R. 82, 90 N.R. 321, 32 O.A.C. 161: "The evidence of intoxication in this case was simply not capable of raising a reasonable doubt as to the existence of the minimal intent required" per Wilson J.; *Lobell, supra*, note 43, at (Q.B.) 551: "If an issue relating to self-defence is to be left to the jury there must be some evidence from which a jury would be entitled to find that issue in favour of the accused, and ordinarily no doubt such evidence would be given by the defence", per Lord Goddard C.J.; *Bratty v. A.G. for Northern Ireland*, [1961] 3 All E.R. 523, [1963] A.C. 386, at 419; *R. v. Spurge*, [1961] 2 Q.B. 205, [1961] 2 All E.R. 688, 45 Cr. App. Rep. 191, at 197-98 (C.C.A.). The matter of presumptions is discussed in Chapter 4.
49 [1970] A.C. 618, at 624, [1970] 1 All E.R. 219 (P.C.).
50 *R. v. McPherson* (1957), 41 Cr. App. Rep. 213, at 215 (C.C.A.).
51 *Bratty v. A.G. for Northern Ireland, supra*, note 48, at (A.C.) 416-17.

Thus, the trial judge may withdraw a fanciful defence from the jury's consideration thereby preventing them from accepting a defence where there is insufficient foundational evidence to support such a plea.[52] For example, in *Lavallée v. R.*[53] the accused's statement to the police introduced as part of the Crown's case, medical records introduced by the defence[54] and some circumstantial evidence was sufficient for the trial judge to leave self-defence for the jury's consideration. Other defences, for example automatism, may require expert medical evidence for their viability[55] and in *Pappajohn v. R.*,[56] the Supreme Court of Canada held that there must be an "air of reality" to the defence of mistaken belief in consent in a sexual assault case before a trial judge will leave it for the jury's consideration.[57] Since the burden of proof for many defences rests on the Crown, the trial judge must direct the jury that the Crown must negate these defences beyond a reasonable doubt in order to find the accused guilty.[58]

---

52   G. Williams, *Textbook of Criminal Law*, 2nd ed. (London: Sweet & Maxwell, 1983), at 52.

53   [1990] 1 S.C.R. 852, 55 C.C.C. (3d) 97, 76 C.R. (3d) 329, [1990] 4 W.W.R. 1, 67 Man. R. (2d) 1 (S.C.C.).

54   *R. v. Lavallée* (1988), 65 C.R. 387, at 388-90, 44 C.C.C. (3d) 113, 52 Man. R. (2d) 274 (Man. C.A.); revd. [1990] 1 S.C.R. 852, 55 C.C.C. (3d) 97, 76 C.R. (3d) 329, [1990] 4 W.W.R. 1, 67 Man. R. (2d) 1, 108 N.R. 321.

55   *R. v. Cusack*, [1971] 3 C.C.C. (2d) 527, 1 Nfld. & P.E.I.R. 496 (P.E.I. S.C.); *R. v. Berger* (1975), 27 C.C.C. (2d) 357 (B.C.C.A.); leave to appeal to S.C.C. refd. 27 C.C.C. (2d) 357n; *Hill v. Baxter*, [1958] 1 Q.B. 277, [1958] 1 All E.R. 193 (C.C.A.); see also, D. Stuart, *Canadian Criminal Law*, 2nd ed. (Toronto: Carswell, 1987), at 99-100.

56   [1980] 2 S.C.R. 120, 52 C.C.C. (2d) 481, 14 C.R. (3d) 243, 111 D.L.R. (3d) 1. In *Pappajohn* Dickson C.J.C. was of the view that the accused had discharged an evidential burden. See also *R. v. Bernard, supra,* note 48.

57   For the views of one of the authors on this issue, see A.W. Bryant, *The Issue of Consent in the Crime of Sexual Assault,* [1989] 68 Can. Bar Rev. 94.

58   A rule of law or a presumption that allocates a burden of proof for a factual issue to an accused is examined in Chapter 4.

III SATISFYING THE LEGAL BURDEN OF PROOF

A. *General*

The legal burden of proof comes into force when the trial judge directs the jury (or himself or herself, as the case may be) at the conclusion of a case as to which party bears the burden to prove a factual issue. The trial judge also directs the jury on the degree of satisfaction that is necessary to find in the proponent's favour. If the proponent has not satisfied the trier of fact to the appropriate degree, the proponent will lose on that issue.

There are two standards of proof. Speaking generally, the degree of satisfaction governing civil actions is the lower standard of a balance of probabilities.[59] This standard is also referred to as proof on a preponderance of probabilities or proof on a preponderance of evidence. Practically speaking, nothing turns on the term used. The higher standard of proof beyond a reasonable doubt is required for a conviction in criminal cases. This standard has become enshrined under the constitutional right to be presumed innocent until proven guilty.[60]

In civil actions the plaintiff normally bears the legal burden of proof because he or she is attempting to change the status quo. But, as discussed, the legal burden in relation to a factual issue may also rest on the defendant. Since society is indifferent to whether the plaintiff or the defendant wins a particular civil suit, it is unnecessary to protect against an erroneous result by requiring a standard of proof higher than a balance of probabilities.[61] In contrast, society values the liberty of the individual very highly and requires a greater degree of certainty to protect against erroneous convictions. Accordingly, the criminal law requires a higher standard of proof.[62] Cross states that "so long as the proportions do not become excessive, it is better that people who

---

59   Some civil presumptions impose a higher standard of proof, *ibid*.

60   *R. v. Oakes*, [1986] S.C.R. 103, 50 C.R. (3d) 1, 24 C.C.C. (3d) 321, 26 D.L.R. (4th) 200, 65 N.R. 87, 14 O.A.C. 335, 53 O.R. (2d) 719 (headnote only).

61   E.W. Cleary (ed.), *McCormick on Evidence*, 3rd ed. (St. Paul: West Publishing, 1984), at 962 states that a "mistaken judgment for the plaintiff is no worse than a mistaken judgment for the defendant".

62   In *Clark v. R.* (1921), 61 S.C.R. 608, 35 C.C.C. 261, 59 D.L.R. 121, [1921] 2 W.W.R. 446, at (S.C.R.) 616, Duff J. stated that the distinction is based on policy; see also, Anthony Hooper, "Discovery in Criminal Cases" (1972), 50 Can. Bar Rev. 445, at 445-52, 485.

are probably guilty should go free than that those whose innocence is reasonably possible should be convicted".[63] Although the standards of proof may be stated simply, judicial attempts to amplify or to apply them has not always been easy.

B. *Civil Cases*

The degree of probability required to discharge the burden of proof in a civil case has been defined by several leading jurists. Lord Denning defined it in these terms:[64]

> It must carry a reasonable degree of probability but not so high as is required in a criminal case. If the evidence is such that the tribunal can say: 'we think it more probable than not', the burden is discharged, but if the probabilities are equal it is not.

Cartwright J. in *Smith v. Smith*[65] put the test as follows:[66]

> . . . that civil cases may be proved by a preponderance of evidence or that a finding in such cases may be made upon the basis of a preponderance of probability and I do not propose to attempt a more precise statement of the rule. I wish, however, to emphasize that in every civil action before the tribunal can safely find the affirmative of an issue of fact required to be proved it must be reasonably satisfied, and that whether or not it will be so satisfied must depend upon the totality of the circumstances on which its judgment is formed including the gravity of the consequences of the finding.

---

63 R. Cross and C. Tapper, *Cross on Evidence*, 7th ed. (London: Butterworths, 1990), at 147.

64 *Miller v. Minister of Pensions*, [1947] 2 All E.R. 372, at 374 (K.B.).

65 [1952] 2 S.C.R. 312, [1952] 3 D.L.R. 449; see also *Clark v. R.* (1921), 61 S.C.R. 608, at 616, where Duff J. concluded that in a civil case a court may act on "such a preponderance of evidence as to shew that the conclusion he seeks to establish is substantially the most probable of the possible views of the facts".

66 *Ibid.*, at (S.C.R.) 331-32; folld. in *Oakes, supra*, note 60, at (S.C.R.) 138.

Simply put, the trier of fact must find that "the existence of the contested fact is more probable than its nonexistence."[67] Conversely, where a party must prove the negative of an issue, the proponent must prove its absence is more probable than its existence.

But how does a trier of fact determine if the standard has been met? It is certainly not the number of witnesses or the volume of evidence adduced.[68] Also, if the nature of the inquiry is serious or the evidence adduced is very unsatisfactory,[69] a jury may not be satisfied as to the existence of a disputed fact even though the proponent of the issue adduced a preponderance of evidence.[70]

There was common law authority that a higher standard of proof applied to divorce proceedings alleging a matrimonial offence such as adultery,[71] or to a civil action alleging criminal-type conduct, for

---

67 *McCormick on Evidence, supra,* note 61, at 957.
68 *Ibid.*
69 See Australian Law Reform Commission, *Evidence* (interim report), vol. 2 (Canberra: Australian Government Publishing Service, 1985), at 321-25.
70 In *Briginshaw v. Briginshaw,* [1938] 60 C.L.R. 336 (Aust. H.C.), at 361-62 Dixon J. held that there must be a subjective belief by the tribunal of fact: "The truth is that, when the law requires the proof of any fact, the tribunal must feel an actual persuasion of its occurrence or existence before it can be found. . . . No doubt an opinion that a state of facts exists may be held according to indefinite gradations of certainty; and this has led to attempts to define exactly the certainty required by the law for various purposes. Fortunately, however, at common law no third standard of persuasion was definitely developed. Except upon criminal issues to be proved by the prosecution, it is enough that the affirmative of an allegation is made out to the reasonable satisfaction of the tribunal. But reasonable satisfaction is not a state of mind that is attained or established independently of the nature and consequence of the fact or facts to be proved. The seriousness of an allegation made, the inherent unlikelihood of an occurrence of a given description, or the gravity of the consequences flowing from a particular finding are considerations which must affect the answer to the question whether the issue has been proved to the reasonable satisfaction of the tribunal", quoted with approval by Cartwright J. in *Smith v. Smith, supra,* note 65, at (S.C.R.) 332. This passage from Dixon J.'s reasons for judgment raised a judicial and academic debate whether the test is subjective or objective, see Australian Law Reform Commission, *ibid.,* for case law and academic articles; see also *Walters v. R.,* [1969] 2 A.C. 26, at 30 (P.C.).
71 *Ginesi v. Ginesi,* [1948] P. 179, [1948] 1 All E.R. 373 (C.A.); *Preston-Jones v. Preston-Jones,* [1951] 1 All E.R. 124 (H.L.); *Fairman v. Fairman,* [1949] 1 All E.R. 938 (D.C.); *Churchman v. Churchman,* [1945] P. 44, [1945] 2 All E.R. 190 (C.A.).

example, fraud.[72] In *Smith v. Smith*[73] and in *Hanes v. Wawanesa Mutual Insurance Co.*[74] the Supreme Court of Canada held that for such causes of action the correct standard of proof was the civil standard of proof on a balance of probability.[75] In *Continental Ins. Co. v. Dalton Cartage Co.*[76] Laskin C.J.C. succinctly stated:[77]

> Where there is an allegation of conduct that is morally blame-worthy or that could have a criminal or penal aspect and the allegation is made in civil litigation, the relevant burden of proof remains proof on a balance of probabilities.

Laskin C.J.C. further stated that the trier of fact could consider the cogency of the evidence and it was entitled to scrutinize the evidence with greater care if there were serious allegations to be established.[78] In support of this position he adopted Lord Denning's oft-cited

---

72   In *Hanes v. Wawanesa Mutual Insurance Co.*, [1963] S.C.R. 154, [1963] 1 C.C.C. 321, 36 D.L.R. (2d) 718, at (S.C.R.) 157 the trial judge applied this standard, see also *London Life Ins. Co. v. Lang Shirt Co. Ltd. (Trustee of)*, [1929] S.C.R. 117, 51 C.C.C. 31, [1929] 1 D.L.R. 328 as interpreted in *Earnshaw v. Dominion of Canada General Insurance Co.* (1943), 80 C.C.C. 35, [1943] 3 D.L.R. 163, 10 I.L.R. 143, [1943] O.R. 385 (C.A.). Compare *New York State v. Phillips' Heirs*, [1939] 3 All E.R. 952 (P.C.) and *Hurst v. Evans*, [1917] 1 K.B. 352, [1916-17] All E.R. Rep. 975.

73   *Supra*, note 65; see also, *Boykowych v. Boykowych*, [1955] S.C.R. 151, [1955] 1 D.L.R. 81.

74   *Supra*, note 72; see also, *Hornal v. Neuberger Products Ltd.*, [1957] 1 Q.B. 247 (C.A.); *Re Dellow's Will Trusts, Lloyds Bank Ltd. v. Institute of Cancer Research*, [1964] 1 All E.R. 771, [1964] 1 W.L.R. 451 (Ch. D.).

75   But see *Beckon v. Ont. (Deputy Chief Coroner)* (1990), 38 O.A.C. 32 (Div. Ct.) where the court held that the criminal standard applied for a coroner's verdict of suicide.

76   [1982] 1 S.C.R. 164, 131 D.L.R. (3d) 559, 40 N.R. 135, 25 C.P.C. 72, [1982] I.L.R. 1-1487.

77   *Ibid.*, at 169.

78   *Ibid.*, at 170.

words[79] in *Bater v. Bater*:[80]

> The case may be proved by a preponderance of probability, but there may be degrees of probability within that standard. The degree depends on the subject matter. A civil court, when considering a charge of fraud, will naturally require a higher standard of probability than that which it would require if considering whether negligence were established. It does not adopt so high a degree as a criminal court, even when it is considering a charge of a criminal nature, but still it does require a degree of probability which is commensurate with the occasion.

Because the civil standard is defined by a degree of satisfaction, Denning L.J.'s view that there are degrees of probabilities could be interpreted to mean that there are varying standards of proof.[81] Laskin C.J.C., however, anticipated and rejected this proposition when he said:[82]

> I do not regard such an approach as a departure from a standard of proof based on a balance of probabilities nor as supporting a shifting standard. The question in all cases is what evidence with what weight that is accorded to it will move the court to conclude that proof on a balance of probabilities has been established.

More recently in *R. v. Oakes*,[83] Dickson C.J.C. held that within the broad category there exist different degrees of probability depending on the nature of the case. Perhaps as Morris L.J. stated in *Hornal v.*

---

79 See, for example *R. v. Oakes, supra,* note 60, at 137-38 and *Hornal v. Neuberger Products Ltd., supra,* note 74, at 263-64.

80 [1950] 2 All E.R. 458, at 459.

81 A. Keane, *The Modern Law of Evidence,* 2nd ed. (London and Edinburgh: Butterworths, 1989), at 68.

82 *Continental Ins. Co. v. Dalton Cartage Ltd., supra,* note 76, at 171.

83 *R. v. Oakes, supra,* note 60, at 137. *Contra:* In *Continental Insurance, ibid.; Reed v. Lincoln (Town)* (1974), 6 O.R. (2d) 391, at 402, 53 D.L.R. (3d) 14; folld. in *R. v. R. (R.L.)* (1988), 65 C.R. (3d) 235, at 243 (Ont. C.A.).

Neuberger Products Ltd.,[84] the apparent conflict is a matter of semantics.[85]

> But in truth no real mischief results from an acceptance of the fact that there is some difference of approach in civil actions. Particularly is this so if the words which are used to define that approach are the servants but not the masters of meaning. Though no court and no jury would give less careful attention to issues lacking gravity than to those marked by it, the very elements of gravity become a part of the whole range of circumstances which have to be weighed in the scale when deciding as to the balance of probabilities.

Thus, the trier of fact will consider the nature of a fact in issue, that is, its physical, religious, moral, ethical, social, or legal character and the consequences of its decision when determining if it is satisfied on a balance of probabilities.[86]

Apart from civil cases alleging a crime, courts have recognized recurring factual situations where the trier of fact should be instructed to carefully scrutinize the evidence. For example, in cases alleging testamentary incapacity where there are suspicious circumstances surrounding the execution of the will, the trier of fact should closely examine the evidence supporting the will.[87] In *MacGregor v. Ryan*,[88] Ritchie J., speaking for the majority, dealt with the standard of proof in circumstances where suspicions were raised in the preparation or execution of a will:[89]

> The extent of the proof required is proportionate to the gravity of the suspicion and the degree of suspicion varies with the

---

84 *Supra*, note 74.
85 *Ibid.*, at 266 (C.A.). "The difference of opinion which has been evoked about the standard of proof in these cases may well turn out to be more a matter of words than anything else" *Bater*, *supra*, note 80, at 459, per Denning L.J. See also A. Keane, *supra*, note 81, at 69; R.J. Delisle, *Annotation, R. v. R. (R.L.)* (1988), *supra*, note 83, at 236 (Ont. C.A.).
86 *Boykowych*, *supra*, note 73, at (S.C.R.) 155.
87 *Barry v. Butlin* (1838), 2 Moo. P.C.C. 480, at 482-83, 12 E.R. 1089, at 1090.
88 [1965] S.C.R. 757, 53 D.L.R. (2d) 126.
89 *Ibid.*, at (S.C.R.) 766-67.

circumstances of each case. It is true that there are expressions in some of the judgments to which I have referred which are capable of being construed as meaning that a particularly heavy burden lies upon the proponents in all such cases, but in my view nothing which has been said should be taken to have established the requirements of a higher degree of proof than that referred to by Sir John Nicholl in *Paske v. Ollat* (1815), 2 Phillim. 323, where he said at p. 324:

> . . . the law of England requires, in all instances of the sort, that the proof should be clear and decisive; — the balance must not be left in equilibrio; the proof must go not merely to the act of signing, but to the knowledge of the contents of the paper. In ordinary cases this is not necessary; *but where the person who prepares the instrument, and conducts the execution of it, is himself an interested person, his conduct must be watched as that of an interested person*; — propriety and delicacy would infer that he should not conduct the transaction; . . . [emphasis added.]

Although such cases require that the evidence be approached with caution, Mr. Justice Ritchie implicitly rejected the criminal standard. In the English case of *Wintle v. Nye*,[90] a solicitor who had prepared a will for an elderly lady with limited intelligence received the bulk of her large estate. Although Lord Reid thought that the jury ought to have been charged that the solicitor was required to satisfy them by evidence "calculated to exclude all doubt"[91] Viscount Simonds, with whom the other judges agreed, did not go that far:[92]

> All these facts and others . . . demanded a vigilant and jealous scrutiny by the judge in his summing-up and by the jury in consideration of their verdict.

This language is consistent with the view of Ritchie J. who cited *Wintle v. Nye* in his reasons for judgment in *MacGregor v. Ryan*.[93] Thus the standard of proof in civil cases is a balance of probabilities.[94] Dixon J.

---

90 [1959] 1 All E.R. 552, [1959] 1 W.L.R. 284 (H.L.).
91 *Ibid.*, at (All E.R.) 561.
92 *Ibid.*, at (All E.R.) 558.
93 *Supra*, note 88.
94 As discussed in Chapter 4, V.B.2., some archaic presumptions may require

summarized it well:[95]

> At common law, as distinguished from ecclesiastical law, no third standard of persuasion appears to have been known. But questions of fact vary greatly in nature and in some cases greater care in scrutinizing the evidence is proper than in others, and a greater clearness of proof may be properly looked for. In the end, however, every issue must be determined by reference to one or the other of these standards.

C. *Criminal Cases*

The classic formulation of the onus and degree of proof applicable in criminal proceedings is Lord Stankey's speech in *Woolmington v. D.P.P.*:[96]

> Throughout the web of the English Criminal Law one golden thread is always to be seen, that it is the duty of the prosecution to prove the prisoner's guilt . . . If, at the end of and on the whole of the case, there is a reasonable doubt, created by the evidence given by either the prosecution or the prisoner . . . the prosecution has not made out the case and the prisoner is entitled to an acquittal.

Judicial attempts to amplify the principle that the prosecution must prove all elements of a charge beyond a reasonable doubt have been criticised by appellate courts.[97] Martin J. A. cautioned:[98]

---

proof beyond a reasonable doubt.

95   *Sodeman v. R.*, [1936] C.L.R. 192, at 216-17 (Aust. H.C.).

96   [1935] A.C. 462, 1 [1935] All E.R. Rep. 1 (H.L.), at 481 (A.C.).

97   *R. v. Morin*, [1988] 2 S.C.R. 345, at 351, 66 C.R. (3d) 1, 44 C.C.C. (3d) 193, 88 N.R. 161, 30 O.A.C. 81; *Thomas v. R.*, [1959-60] 102 C.L.R. 584 (Aust. H.C.).

98   *R. v. Campbell* (1977), 38 C.C.C. (2d) 6, 1 C.R. (3d) 309, 1 C.R. (3d) S-49, 17 O.R. (2d) 673 (Ont. C.A.); see also *Clark v. R.* (1921), 61 S.C.R. 608, 35 C.C.C. 261, 59 D.L.R. 121, [1921] 2 W.W.R. 446, at (S.C.R.) 619, where Duff J. held that the term "reasonable doubt" has passed into common speech. In *R. v. Ching* (1976), 63 Cr. App. Rep. 7, at 11 (C.A.), Lawton L.J. stated: "We point out and emphasize that if judges stopped trying to define that which is almost impossible to define there would be fewer appeals." *Brown v. R.*, [1913] 17 C.L.R. 570 (Aust. H.C.).

The term "reasonable doubt" is, to a great extent, self-defining and its meaning is, I think, generally well understood by the average person. Attempts to further amplify its meaning have often proved unsuccessful and, as a general rule, it is both undesirable and unnecessary to elaborate upon its meaning by departing from the traditional and accepted formulations.

Accordingly, trial judges should avoid using illustrations to explain the kind of doubt that may entitle an accused to an acquittal[99] and they should not incorporate a discussion of possibilities and probabilities in their jury instructions because it may confuse the jury.[100] However, if a jury asks the trial judge for clarification is it satisfactory to simply repeat the traditional and accepted formulations? If a judge does give an illustration should the appellate courts allow the trial judge greater latitude in these circumstances? Perhaps the appellate courts could give the trial judges some guidance for those occasions when a jury requests additional guidance on the meaning of reasonable doubt from the trial judge.[101]

The Supreme Court of Canada has held that it is unnecessary to give a special jury instruction in those cases where part or all of the prosecution's case depends upon circumstantial evidence.[102] The so-called rule in *Hodge's Case* is no more than an alternative explanation

---

99 *R. v. Ching, ibid.*, at 10-11 (C.A.); *Green v. R.*, [1971] 126 C.L.R. 28 (Aust. H.C.).

100 *R. v. Finlay* (1985), 23 C.C.C. (3d) 48, 48 C.R. (3d) 341, 23 D.L.R. (4th) 532, 52 O.R. (2d) 632, 11 O.A.C. 279 (C.A.); leave to appeal to S.C.C. refd. (1986), 65 N.R. 159*n*, 15 O.A.C. 238*n*, 54 O.R. (2d) 504; *Thomas v. R.* (1960), 102 C.L.R. 584, at 587, 593, 595, 604. In *R. v. Morin, supra*, note 97, at 375 (S.C.R.) the court notes that jury studies support the court's concern on the content of a jury instruction.

101 See *Walters v. R.*, [1969] 2 A.C. 26, at 30 (P.C.) where the court cited Lord Goddard C.J. (*R. v. Kritz*, [1950] 1 K.B. 82, at 89, [1949] 2 All E.R. 406 (C.A.)), that it is not the particular formula that matters but the effect of the summing-up. The P.C. held that the summing up is best left to the trial judge to choose the appropriate set of words in making sure that the jury must not return a verdict against an accused unless they are sure of her or his guilt.

102 *R. v. Cooper*, [1978] 1 S.C.R. 860, 37 C.R.N.S. 1, 34 C.C.C. (2d) 18, 14 D.L.R. (3d) 731, 14 N.R. 183; *R. v. Mezzo*, [1986] 1 S.C.R. 802, at 842-43, 52 C.R. (3d) 113, 27 C.C.C. (3d) 97, 30 D.L.R. (4th) 161, [1986] 4 W.W.R. 577, 43 Man. R. (2d) 161, 68 N.R. 1; see also *McGreevy v. D.P.P.*, [1973] 1 All E.R. 503, [1973] 1 W.L.R. 276 (H.L.). See also Chapter 2, II.D.2.

of reasonable doubt. Because it is confusing to have two different jury instructions, the reasonable doubt formula is the simplest and safest way to explain the prosecution's burden of proof.[103]

In *R. v. Morin*,[104] the trial judge invited the jury to apply the criminal standard of proof to individual items of evidence. The Supreme Court rejected a two staged application of the criminal standard (the fact finding stage and the verdict stage), because the function of the standard of proof is not to weigh the individual items of evidence. The court recognized that individual members of the jury may arrive at their verdict by different routes and that each juror did not need to rely on the same facts in order to reach a decision[105] so long as the jury agreed that each essential factual issue was proved beyond a reasonable doubt.[106] The court did not wish trial judges to impose artificial rules on the deliberation process and, subject to two exceptions, the court cautioned against instructing a jury how it should go about its task of weighing evidence. The first exception is that the trial judge should instruct the jury that the facts are not to be examined separately and in isolation with reference to the criminal law standard. Rather, in their deliberations, the jury must consider the evidence as a whole and determine if guilt has been established beyond a reasonable doubt.[107] The second exception applies where the issue of credibility arises between the Crown and the defendant's version of events. It is a misdirection to direct a jury to select one version of the evidence over the other[108] or to determine which version of the evidence was true.[109] Accordingly, to guard against such error, the jury should be instructed that "it is not necessary for them to believe the defence evidence on a vital issue — but that it is sufficient if it, viewed in the context of all the evidence, leaves them in a state of reasonable doubt as to the accused's guilt."[110] These exceptions reinforce for the trier of

---

103 *R. v. Cooper, ibid.*, at 865 (S.C.R.).

104 *Supra*, note 97.

105 *R. v. Thatcher*, [1987] 1 S.C.R. 652, at 697-98, 32 C.C.C. (3d) 481, 57 C.R. (3d) 97, 39 D.L.R. (4th) 275, [1987] 4 W.W.R. 193, 75 N.R. 198, 57 Sask. R. 113; *R. v. Agbim*, [1979] Crim. L.R. 171 (C.A.–Crim. Div.).

106 *R. v. Thatcher, ibid.*, at 698; *R. v. Morin, supra*, note 97, at 361-62.

107 *R. v. Morin, ibid.*

108 *R. v. Nadeau*, [1984] 2 S.C.R. 570, 15 C.C.C. (3d) 499, 42 C.R. (3d) 305, 14 D.L.R. (4th) 1, 56 N.R. 130; *R. v. M.(P.)* (1983), 31 C.R. (3d) 311 (Ont. C.A.).

109 *R. v. Riley* (1978), 42 C.C.C. (2d) 437 (Ont. C.A.); *R. v. K.(F.)* (1990), 73 O.R. (2d) 480 (Ont. C.A.).

110 *R. v. Morin, supra*, note 97, at 357, 362, citing with approval *R. v. Challice*

fact that after reviewing the totality of the evidence presented, the prosecution must prove guilt beyond a reasonable doubt and that if the jury is in a state of doubt after a consideration of all the evidence, they must acquit the accused.[111]

A common law or statutory provision may occasionally allocate the legal burden of proof for an issue to the accused. Where the burden of proof in relation to a factual issue in criminal proceedings rests on the accused, the lower standard of proof on a balance of probabilities applies.[112] This rule applies whether the burden of proof is in relation to a factual issue that is classified as an element of the offence, a defence, or an evidentiary issue, whether the incidence of the burden of proof arises at common law or by statute, or whether the onus is created by means of a presumption.[113] For example, the presumption of sanity requires the accused to prove, on a balance of probabilities, that during the commission of the act he or she was legally insane.[114] For strict liability offences, the accused must prove the common law defence of "due diligence" to a balance of probabilities;[115] however, this is subject to review by the courts under the *Charter*.[116]

The distinction between the degree of satisfaction necessary to meet an evidential burden and the legal burden of proof must be

---

(1979), 45 C.C.C. (2d) 546 (Ont. C.A.). If the jury, however, find that the accused's evidence is a lie and that it constitutes evidence of a consciousness of guilt, this evidence may be used together with the Crown's evidence to infer guilt, *R. v. Syms* (1979), 47 C.C.C. (2d) 114, at 117 (Ont. C.A.).

111 *R. v. Ching, supra*, note 98, at 9.

112 *Clark v. R., supra*, note 98; *R. v. Appleby*, [1972] S.C.R. 303, 21 D.L.R. (3d) 325, 3 C.C.C. (2d) 354, 16 C.R.N.S. 35.

113 *R. v. Chaulk*, [1990] 3 S.C.R. 1303, 62 C.C.C. (3d) 193, 2 C.R. (4th) 1, [1991] 2 W.W.R. 385, 69 Man. R. (2d) 161, 1 C.R.R. (2d) 1, 119 N.R. 161.

114 *Ibid., R. v. Chaulk; McNaghten's Case* (1843), 10 Cl. & Fin. 200, [1843-60] All E.R. Rep. 229, 8 E.R. 718 (H.L.); *Clark, supra*, note 112; *Sodeman v. R., supra*, note 95.

115 *R. v. Sault Ste. Marie*, [1978] 2 S.C.R. 1299, 40 C.C.C. (2d) 353, 3 C.R. (3d) 30, 85 D.L.R. (3d) 161, 21 N.R. 295, 7 C.E.L.R. 53.

116 *R. v. Wholesale Travel Group Inc.* (1989), 73 C.R. (3d) 320, 52 C.C.C. (3d) 9, 63 D.L.R. (4th) 325, 46 C.R.R. 73, 63 D.L.R. (4th) 325, 27 C.P.R. (3d) 129, 35 O.A.C. 331, 70 O.R. (2d) 545 (C.A.); affd. (1991), 67 C.C.C. (3d) 193 (S.C.C.), and *R. v. Ellis-Don Ltd.* (1990), 61 C.C.C. (3d) 423, 2 C.R. (4th) 118, 76 D.L.R. (4th) 347, 1 O.R. (3d) 193, 42 O.A.C. 49 (C.A.); leave to appeal granted June 1991, where a statutory due diligence defence placing the legal burden on the accused was held to be unconstitutional.

underlined. The accused may satisfy an evidential burden by adducing some evidence that may raise a reasonable doubt whereas in order to satisfy the legal burden the accused must persuade the trier of fact to a balance of probabilities in relation to that factual issue or lose on that issue.[117] The English Court of Criminal Appeal succinctly stated the latter principle in the context of presumptions:[118]

> [I]n any case where, either by statute or at common law, some matter is presumed against an accused person "unless the contrary is proved," the jury should be directed that it is for them to decide whether the contrary is proved, that the burden of proof required is less than that required at the hands of the prosecution in proving the case beyond a reasonable doubt, and that the burden may be discharged by evidence satisfying the jury of the probability of that which the accused is called upon to establish.

The allocation of an evidential burden or the legal burden of proof to an accused person raises important policy and constitutional considerations which are discussed in the chapter on presumptions.[119]

---

117 See *Perka v. R.*, [1984] 2 S.C.R. 233, at 258, 14 C.C.C. (3d) 385, 42 C.R. (3d) 113, [1984] 6 W.W.R. 289, 13 D.L.R. (4th) 1, where the Supreme Court distinguished the common law defence of necessity from the statutory exception proviso.

118 *R. v. Carr-Briant*, [1943] 1 K.B. 607, at 612, [1943] 2 All E.R. 156; see also *Sodeman v. R.*, *supra*, note 95, at 216.

119 Chapter 4, see also Chapter 3, VI.

Section II

EXCLUSIONARY RULES

CHAPTER 6

HEARSAY

I   WHAT IS HEARSAY?

A. *The Rule*

Though the exceptions have been increased and broadened, the rule against hearsay has withstood decades of attack[1] and most recently has emerged relatively intact after extensive review by the Ontario and Canada Law Reform Commissions.[2] Nor has the *Charter* weakened its underpinnings, for the Ontario Court of Appeal has held that an accused is not precluded from making full answer and defence because he is prevented by the laws of evidence from introducing hearsay.[3]

---

1   See, e.g., Hall J. in *Ares v. Venner*, [1970] S.C.R. 608, 12 C.R.N.S. 349, 73 W.W.R. 347, 14 D.L.R. (3d) 4, at 672 (S.C.R.) and Diplock L.J. in *Jones v. Metcalfe*, [1967] 1 W.L.R. 1286, [1967] 3 All E.R. 205, at 1290 (W.L.R.); G. Murray, "The Hearsay Maze: A Glimpse at Some Possible Exits" (1972), 50 Can. Bar Rev. 1.

2   Ontario Law Reform Commission, *Report on the Law of Evidence* (Ontario: Ministry of the Attorney General, 1976), at 12-15; Law Reform Commission of Canada, *Report on Evidence* (Ottawa: Information Canada, 1975), at 68-70.

3   *R. v. Williams* (1985), 50 O.R. (2d) 321, 44 C.R. (3d) 351, 18 C.C.C. (3d) 356, 7 O.A.C. 201, 14 C.R.R. 251; leave to appeal to S.C.C. refd. [1985] 1 S.C.R. xiv. Conversely, at least one of the exceptions to the hearsay rule has been held not to be in contravention of the *Charter*. The Supreme Court of Canada in *R. v. Potvin*, [1989] 1 S.C.R. 525, 47 C.C.C. (3d) 289, 68 C.R. (3d) 193, 2 Q.A.C. 258, 93 N.R. 42 found that neither s. 7 nor s. 11(d) of the *Charter* is offended in situations where the Crown is permitted to introduce hearsay evidence (which the accused has not been able to confront or test by cross-examination at trial) pursuant to a recognized exception to the hearsay rule so long as the accused had an earlier opportunity to cross-examine the declarant at the preliminary hearing. See this Chapter, II.J.2.(c).

The rule can be stated as follows:[4]

> Written or oral statements, or communicative conduct made by
> persons otherwise than in testimony at the proceeding in which
> it is offered, are inadmissible, if such statements or conduct are
> tendered either as proof of their truth or as proof of assertions
> implicit therein.

1. Origin of the Rule

The hearsay rule finds its roots in the desire of the eighteenth-century judiciary to control the nature of the evidence that could be presented to the trier of fact. As it first evolved, the jury was allowed, and in fact encouraged, to resolve disputes on the basis of the jurors' personal knowledge of events within their local community. No interdiction prevented the jury from relying on private sources of information, rumour and hearsay, no matter how untrustworthy. Consequently, there was no control on the quality of evidence upon which they based their verdict.

As society became more urban and industrialized, it became increasingly difficult to find jurors who had knowledge, either direct or indirect, of the facts in issue or the ability to find out. As a result, the embryonic jury evolved into a different form, in which witnesses presented evidence to a jury which had no prior knowledge or information on the matters in question.

Since jurors were called upon to scrutinize the evidence of witnesses, the danger of hearsay became readily apparent. To regulate the quality of evidence that could be presented for consideration by the jury, the rule against hearsay was propounded.[5]

---

4   The following sampling of cases has enunciated the rules relating to statements: *Dalrymple v. Sun Life Assurance Co. of Canada*, [1966] 2 O.R. 227, at 231, 56 D.L.R. (2d) 385; affd. [1967] S.C.R., at v, 60 D.L.R. (2d) 192n; *Blackstone v. Mutual Life Insurance Co. of New York*, [1944] O.R. 607, 12 I.L.R. 21, [1945] 1 D.L.R. 165 (C.A.), at 618 (O.R.); *Mitchell v. Hanan*, [1943] 3 W.W.R. 431 (Sask. C.A.); *Willoughby-Sumner Ltd. v. Sumner*, [1924] 3 D.L.R. 381, 21 Sask. L.R. 120 (C.A.); *Victoria Mutual Fire Insurance Co. v. Davidson* (1883), 3 O.R. 378; *Ferrie v. Jones* (1851), 8 U.C.Q.B. 192 (C.A.); *Subramaniam v. Public Prosecutor*, [1956] 1 W.L.R. 965, at 970 (P.C.); *National Fire Insurance Co. v. Rogers*, [1924] 2 W.W.R. 186, 18 Sask. L.R. 585, [1924] 2 D.L.R. 403.

5   For a detailed exposition of the origin of the rule, see R.J. Delisle, "Hearsay Evidence", [1984] *L.S.U.C. Special Lectures*, at 59-64; R.W. Baker, *The Hearsay*

2. Hearsay Dangers

The law assumes that all oral testimony is unreliable, and has accordingly built in such safeguards as the requirement of an oath, the right of cross-examination and the creation of the crime of perjury. Special attention has been given to hearsay as being particularly fraught with untrustworthiness because its evidential value rests on the credibility of an out-of-court asserter who is not subject to the oath, cross-examination or a charge of perjury. As Dickson J. stated in *R. v. Abbey*:[6]

> The main concern of the hearsay rule is the veracity of the statements made. The principal justification for the exclusion of hearsay evidence is the abhorrence of the common law to proof which is unsworn and has not been subjected to the trial by fire of cross-examination. Testimony under oath, and cross-examination, have been considered to be the best assurances of the truth of the statements of facts presented.

Other reasons ascribed for holding hearsay to be a poor form of testimony are the following:

1. The admission of such evidence lends itself to the perpetration of fraud;
2. Hearsay evidence results in a decision based upon secondary and therefore, weaker evidence rather than the best evidence available;
3. There is no opportunity to observe the demeanour of the declarant;

Rule (London: Pitman, 1950), at 7-12. A different opinion was enunciated in "Hearsay Dangers and The Application of the Hearsay Concept" (1948), 62 Harv. L. Rev. 177, at 177-84, by Professor E.M. Morgan, who felt that the rule arose out of the adversarial nature of the proceedings. Counsel would object to the introduction of hearsay evidence because it was not under oath, nor subject to cross-examination. Because counsel could waive both the oath and the right to cross-examine, Morgan suggested that it was the litigants and not the jurors who were to be protected from this evidence. To the same effect, see the Criminal Law Revision Committee, *Evidence (General)*, 11th Report (1972), Cmnd. 4991, § 227, at 133.

6 [1982] 2 S.C.R. 24, 68 C.C.C. (2d) 394, 29 C.R. (3d) 193, [1983] 1 W.W.R. 251, 39 B.C.L.R. 201, 138 D.L.R. (3d) 202, at 41 (S.C.R.), at 216 (D.L.R.).

4.   The introduction of such evidence will lengthen trials.

Thus if the witness states in court that he or she saw the driver's automobile go through a red light and strike a pedestrian, the witness is testifying under oath and is subject to cross-examination by the driver's counsel. The witness' opportunity to observe the event, his or her ability to perceive and recall the incident and to communicate accurately the recollection and other aspects of the witness' credibility may be challenged on cross-examination.

If, on the other hand, the witness testifies that the declarant told him or her that the driver's automobile collided with the pedestrian, then the witness can be cross-examined on only his or her memory and understanding of what the declarant said. There is no guarantee of the veracity of the declarant and the trustworthiness of the declarant's statement. The declarant is not under oath and not subject to cross-examination and, therefore, the declarant's perception, memory and credibility cannot be tested. Thus, this evidence is unreliable and is rejected as hearsay.

These concerns for the most part focus on an expectation that the jury or trier of fact will misjudge the probity of hearsay evidence.[7] The fundamental question, however, is whether there are such inherent frailties in hearsay evidence to warrant its exclusion altogether. As with any relevant direct evidence, it would be more logical that any infirmity or inherent weakness of a piece of evidence would only justify the application of less weight in the decision-making process rather than ignoring it through exclusion. In the same vein, witnesses who are biased in favour of one party or another are not prevented from testifying although their evidence may be discounted by that fact. Other examples in the law of evidence where suspect evidence is received may be multiplied.

Why then does the hearsay rule retain its special prominence of

---

7   *R. v. Lucier*, [1982] 1 S.C.R. 28, 65 C.C.C. (2d) 150, [1982] 2 W.W.R. 289, 14 Man. R. (2d) 380, 132 D.L.R. (3d) 244, 40 N.R. 153, at 31 (S.C.R.); *Teper v. R.*, [1952] A.C. 480, [1952] 2 All E.R. 447 (P.C.), at 486 (A.C.); *R. v. Blastland*, [1986] 1 A.C. 41, [1985] 2 All E.R. 1095, at 1099 (H.L.); *Neary v. Fowler* (1869), 7 N.S.R. 495 (C.A.); R.W. Baker, *The Hearsay Rule, supra*, note 5, at 18; R. Cross and C. Tapper, *Cross on Evidence*, 7th ed. (London: Butterworths, 1990), at 513-15; M.N. Howard, P. Crane and D.A. Hochberg, *Phipson on Evidence*, 14th ed. (London: Sweet & Maxwell, 1990), at 561-62, R.J. Delisle, "Hearsay Evidence", *supra*, note 5.

exclusion? One explanation has to do with social acceptance, in that the hearsay rule assists in maintaining public confidence in the adjudicative system.[8] This is particularly true in criminal law when the liberty of the subject is at stake and there is an underlying need for the perception of fairness.[9] There is something unsavoury about the fact that an accused may be convicted upon secondary and inherently weak evidence, and any abolition of the hearsay rule could be regarded as an inappropriate move towards a stricter law-and-order society. Moreover, the hearsay concept is distinguishable from other evidentiary concepts in that it is well understood by persons outside the legal system.

If the hearsay rule is premised upon an expectation that the jury will erroneously assess the probative value of evidence then it could be said that its retention carries with it a correlated deep suspicion about jury deliberation. Jurors may have before them "good hearsay" which comprise the exceptions to the rule,[10] but they are precluded from even hearing the "bad hearsay". This distinction, if it makes any sense at all,[11] should go to the exercise of weighing evidence, but not to its exclusion. If we trust a jury with some other inherently weak, though direct evidence, there is no reason to keep from it the so-called "bad hearsay". In any event, as with any kind of frailty in the evidence, careful vigilance by the trial judge in his or her cautioning of jurors as to the use of such evidence should afford an adequate safeguard.

Given the generally held view of the deep-seated suspicion of how a jury will handle hearsay evidence, it is not surprising that neither abolition nor extensive liberalization has followed after intensive review and reform proposals in Canada.

---

8   See "The Theoretical Foundation of the Hearsay Rules" (1980), 93 Harv. L.R. 1786.

9   As to the importance of the accused's right to have a full opportunity to cross-examine adverse witnesses, see *R. v. Potvin, supra*, note 3, at 230-31 (C.R.).

10   See this Chapter, II.

11   The classical exceptions do not all necessarily amount to "good hearsay". For example, an admission against pecuniary interest in an amount as low as $5.00 is sufficient to render the statement and collateral matters admissible: see this Chapter, II.B.1.

B. *Conduct Amounting to Hearsay*

Although there is a division of authority on this point, the most prevalent view is that an individual's conduct or non-verbal act which is intended to be assertive falls within the mischief of the hearsay rule and is therefore inadmissible. Assume, for example, that the witness testifies that the declarant, an eye-witness to a motor vehicle accident, nodded his or her head up and down when questioned if the driver went through a red traffic light. In this scenario, the declarant's assertive conduct is equivalent to an oral response assertion, "Yes".[12] Such evidence is tendered for the same purpose as an express statement and the actor is not under oath, cannot be tested by cross-examination, nor can his demeanour be observed by the court. The hearsay dangers are equally implicit in evidence of conduct when the actor is not called as a witness, as when written or oral statements are tendered as evidence of the truth of the contents when the declarant does not testify. There is no way of testing the actor's perception, sincerity and memory and accordingly, evidence of assertive conduct is as frail as evidence of assertive statements. In addition, conduct may convey a message in more equivocal terms than words and therefore is subject to a greater risk of misinterpretation by the trier of fact.[13]

C. *Purpose for Which Evidence is Tendered*

1. General

The hearsay rule is invoked only where extrajudicial statements or conduct are tendered as evidence of proof of the facts asserted therein. If such evidence is presented not for this purpose, but for some other relevant purpose — for example, if it is tendered to show that a person received notice by the fact that a statement was made to her or him — then the statement is admissible as proof, not of its truth, but that the statement was made. When the statement itself, apart from the truth of the assertion therein has relevance to a fact in issue, then the hearsay dangers do not arise and there is no problem about

---

12   See this Chapter, I.C.2. and 3. for a discussion of non-assertive conduct and implied assertions.

13   R.W. Baker, *The Hearsay Rule, supra,* note 5, at 3-6; *Cross on Evidence, supra,* note 7, at 529; *Chandrasekera (alias Alisandiri) v. R.,* [1937] A.C. 220, [1936] 3 All E.R. 865 (P.C.); see this Chapter, I.C.3.

admissibility. In other words, the out-of-court statement is not being offered to prove the truth of the contents of the statement. Thus a distinction must be drawn between statements which evidence a particular conduct or verbal act, and are submitted for this purpose, and those statements which are tendered as evidence of the narration. Only the latter are prohibited by the rule.[14]

The Supreme Court of Canada in *R. v. O'Brien*[15] had occasion to comment on what is and what is not hearsay. O'Brien and Jensen were jointly charged with a narcotic trafficking offence. Jensen left the jurisdiction but O'Brien was convicted. Jensen returned to the jurisdiction and informed O'Brien's lawyer (Simons) in confidence that he alone had committed the offence. Jensen agreed to testify under the protection of subsequent use immunity under the *Canada Evidence Act*. Jensen died prior to trial. On appeal, the question arose as to whether Jensen's statement could be admitted through the testimony of O'Brien's lawyer. On the fundamental question of whether the evidence was hearsay, Dickson J., stated as follows:[16]

> It is settled law that evidence of a statement made to a witness by a person who is not himself called as a witness is hearsay and inadmissible when the object of the evidence is to establish the truth of what is contained in the statement; it is not hearsay and is admissible when it is proposed to establish by the evidence, not the truth of the statement but the fact that it was made. . . .

---

14 "The prohibition of the Hearsay rule, then, *does not apply to all words or utterances merely as such*. If this fundamental principle is clearly realized, its application is a comparatively simple matter. The Hearsay rule excludes extrajudicial utterances only when offered for a special purpose, namely, as *assertions to evidence the truth of the matter asserted*": 6 Wigmore, *Evidence* (3rd ed., 1940), § 1766, at 178; see also *R. v. Kirkby* (1985), 21 C.C.C. (3d) 31, 47 C.R. (3d) 97, 10 O.A.C. 356, at 53 (C.C.C.); leave to appeal to S.C.C. refd. (1986), 72 N.R. 366n; *Mawaz Khan v. R.*, [1967] 1 A.C. 454, [1967] 1 All E.R. 80; *R. v. Bencardino* (1973), 15 C.C.C. (2d) 342, 24 C.R.N.S. 173, 2 O.R. (2d) 351 (C.A.); *Ratten v. R.*, [1972] A.C. 378, [1971] 3 All E.R. 801 (P.C.), at 805 (All E.R.).
15 [1978] 1 S.C.R. 591, 35 C.C.C. (2d) 209, 38 C.R.N.S. 325, [1977] 5 W.W.R. 400, 76 D.L.R. (3d) 512.
16 *Ibid.*, at 593-94 (S.C.R.). Nor was the evidence accepted as an exception to the hearsay rule as it did not meet the constituent elements of a statement against penal interest: see this Chapter, II.B.2.

The evidence of Mr. Simons was offered for the purpose of proving the truth of the matter asserted. It was sought, through that evidence, to prove that Jensen, and not O'Brien, had committed the act with which O'Brien stood charged, or at least to raise a reasonable doubt as to O'Brien's guilt. That is the classic touchstone of inadmissible hearsay.

It should be pointed out that the determination of whether evidence constitutes hearsay or not is a question of law for the trial judge and he or she must not delegate this function to the jury.[17]

2. Non-Hearsay Use of Words

The distinction between hearsay and non-hearsay is illustrated in *Enge v. Trerise*.[18] Following a motor vehicle accident, the plaintiff, a young and attractive girl, became schizophrenic by reason of suffering a large facial scar. Her doctor testified that she told him that people were talking about her and drawing sinister inferences from her scar, for example, that she was sexually promiscuous. The plaintiff did not relate these facts in her testimony. The British Columbia Court of Appeal ruled that the doctor's evidence of this patient's statement could not be admitted to establish the truth of the statements. Sheppard J.A. stated:[19]

> The term "verbal act" applies where the fact to be proved is the making of a statement but not to be used to induce belief in any assertion contained in the statement (6 *Wigmore* [Evidence] (3rd ed.), p. 238). Many of the statements made by the plaintiff to Dr. Leland were used by him as proof of the contents, namely, that she had left a dance because she inferred that people were talking about her, and particularly as to the inferences drawn by her as to what people had thought about the scar. That is in marked

---

17 *R. v. Babcock* (1985), 16 C.C.C. (3d) 26, 57 A.R. 224 (C.A.); leave to appeal to S.C.C. refd. [1985] 1 S.C.R. v.

18 (1960), 33 W.W.R. 577, 26 D.L.R. (2d) 529 (B.C.C.A.).

19 *Ibid.*, at 595-96 (W.W.R.), at 546-47 (D.L.R.); see also *R. v. Ferber* (1987), 36 C.C.C. (3d) 157 (Alta. C.A.); leave to appeal to S.C.C. refd. (1987), 36 C.C.C. (3d) 157n, in which evidence of a telephone call was admitted not to prove the details of the conversation but to prove merely that the caller, who was subsequently murdered, was alone at the time of the call.

contrast to those instances in which a verbal act is admitted, for example, to prove notice by word of mouth, or to prove publication in actions of slander. There the making of the statement is the issue and that may be proven by anyone who has personal knowledge of the statement having been made. The plaintiff's counsel argued that the statement of a patient to a doctor that she was the queen of America would be a verbal act and would be therefore inadmissible. The fact that a person would make such a statement may be evidence of a certain mental condition: in such a case the making of the statement would be the fact to be proved and would be a verbal act. However that may be, it would be quite a different matter for the doctor to testify that the patient had told him that she at some earlier time had stated that she was the queen of America. That she had stated that she was queen of America would be the fact to be proved, but the doctor would be offering hearsay evidence in testifying that she told him that she, at some earlier time, had so stated. That appears to be what has happened in this case.

Again, the purpose for which the statement is tendered is determinative of whether the statement is hearsay. This was emphasized by Macdonald J.A., in *R. v. Baltzer*:[20]

Essentially it is not the form of the statement that gives it its hearsay or non-hearsay characteristics but the use to which it is put. Whenever a witness testifies that someone said something, immediately one should then ask, "what is the relevance of the fact that someone said something". If, therefore, the relevance of the statement lies in the fact that it was made, it is the making of the statement that is the evidence — the truth or falsity of the statement is of no consequence: if the relevance of the statement lies in the fact that it contains an assertion which is, itself, a relevant fact, then it is the truth or falsity of the statement that is in issue. The former is not hearsay, the latter is.

It should be noted that an expert medical witness testifying in a personal injury case may relate hearsay facts (i.e. what a patient has told him or her) as a preliminary to giving opinion evidence, although

---

20 (1974), 27 C.C.C. (2d) 118, 10 N.S.R. (2d) 561 (C.A.), at 143 (C.C.C.).

such narrative would, strictly speaking, otherwise be inadmissible. This evidence, however, is not admissible in proof of the truth of the facts narrated unless given through the testimony of the patient him or herself. It is admissible only because it forms the basis of the expert opinion.[21]

Further illustrations demonstrate how the purpose for which the evidence is tendered is determinative of admissibility. In *Cuff v. Frazee Storage & Cartage Co.*,[22] the Divisional Court of Ontario ruled that answers given by a third party in response to questions asked by the witness as to the whereabouts of a particular person were admissible to prove that an unsuccessful search had been made for the person. It would have been inadmissible if tendered in proof of the whereabouts of that party.

In a murder trial, the Crown was permitted to introduce evidence as to a telephone conversation allegedly held between the deceased and a witness for the limited purpose of proving that the deceased was alive at the time of the call. It was not proof of the details of the conversation.[23]

In order to determine whether a party has been misled by some statement, evidence of the subject of the information received by the party from others is admissible. It is relevant to the issue of the state of mind of the person to whom the information was given. It is, however, not admissible as proof of the facts that comprised the information.[24] For example, a reliable informant advises a police officer that a person possesses narcotics. The information supplied by the informant is admissible for its non-hearsay purpose; that is, to prove that the police officer had reasonable and probable grounds to obtain a warrant, but the statement made by the informant is not admissible to prove that the accused was in possession of the narcotic.

In response to a petition under the British Columbia *Testator's*

---

21   This distinction is fully discussed in *Lenoard v. British Columbia Hydro & Power Authority* (1964), 50 W.W.R. 546, 49 D.L.R. (2d) 422 (B.S.S.C.). Expert opinion is explored more fully in Chapter 12, II and it is mentioned now only to show that evidence which has a hearsay foundation is admissible if it is for a purpose other than proof of the verity of the fact asserted.

22   (1907), 14 O.L.R. 263 (Div. Ct.).

23   *R. v. Ferber, supra*, note 19; see also *Wray v. R.* (1971), 4 C.C.C. (2d) 378 (*sub nom. R. v. Wray (No. 2)*), [1971] 3 O.R. 843; affd. [1974] S.C.R. 565, 10 C.C.C. (2d) 215, 33 D.L.R. (3d) 750.

24   *Gray v. New Augarita Porcupine Mines Ltd.*, [1952] 3 D.L.R. 1 (P.C.).

Family Maintenance Act[25] affidavits were filed indicating the reasons expressed by the deceased in her lifetime to explain the provision in her will for the petitioner (her husband) and her son. On an application to strike out these affidavits it was held that the affidavits were admissible. They were not hearsay because they were admissible as indicating merely that statements had been made, and to shed light on the state of mind of the testatrix, but not for the purpose of establishing the truth of the content of the statements allegedly made by the deceased.[26]

Statements made to the police which prove to be false are admissible if tendered only to show a guilty conscience.[27] Statements by a third party from which the accused could have learned how the deceased was murdered before the details become public are admissible to show that the accused might have acquired such knowledge innocently.[28]

In support of the defence of duress resulting from threats made to the accused, evidence of those threats made by others is admissible not as proof of what they intended, but merely to show what effect they had, and could reasonably have had, upon the accused.[29] In another case, the Crown was permitted to adduce the deceased's statements of her intention to return to live with her husband for the sole purpose of contrasting it with, and to discredit, the accused's evidence that he lacked any motive to kill the deceased since he intended to live with her.[30]

3. Impliedly Assertive Statements or Conduct

Certain statements or forms of conduct are not intended to be assertive. They are not made with the intention of communicating the fact for which they are given in evidence. Such statements or conduct are not strictly tendered as evidence of the truth of the express statement or conduct, but as evidence of an implied assertion. Although the statement or conduct was not intended by the maker to

---

25   Then R.S.B.C. 1960, c. 378.
26   *Re Grant*, [1971] 1 W.W.R. 555 (B.C.S.C.).
27   *Mawaz Khan v. R.*, *supra*, note 14.
28   *R. v. Wildman*, [1984] 2 S.C.R. 311, 14 C.C.C. (3d) 321, 5 O.A.C. 241, 12 D.L.R. (4th) 641, 55 N.R. 27.
29   *Subramaniam v. Public Prosecutor*, [1956] 1 W.L.R. 965 (P.C.).
30   *R. v. Delafosse* (1988), 47 C.C.C. (3d) 165, 28 Q.A.C. 59; affd. [1990] 1 S.C.R. 114, 52 C.C.C. (3d) 576, 107 N.R. 232.

be assertive, it is being proffered as an assertion of some implied fact.

The question of whether the hearsay rule applied to implicitly assertive statements was considered in *Wright v. Doe d. Tatham*.[31] The issue in the case was whether the will of the deceased testator, John Marsden, was valid, and that depended on whether Marsden was mentally competent and of sound mind at the time that he executed the will. Evidence which was adduced in proof of his sanity included three letters addressed and forwarded to Marsden at different times. The first was a friendly note from a cousin, informing Marsden of a recent journey to America. The second letter was from a vicar advising Marsden to instruct his lawyer in connection with some legal controversy. The third was a letter of gratitude from a curate thanking Marsden for all that he had done for him. All of the letters were on subjects and were expressed in language which were suited to the understanding of a person possessing a reasonable intelligence. All of the writers of the letters had died prior to trial.

The letters were tendered as evidence of the writers' opinion that Marsden was of sound mind. This was to be inferred from the nature of the language and topics set out in the letters. If the writers, who were men of intelligence, had thought Marsden was a lunatic, it was inconceivable that they would have sent such letters to him. So the letters were tendered as evidence equal to an express assertion by the writers that Marsden was a sane man. The House of Lords held that the letters were inadmissible for that purpose because they were hearsay. The letters were tendered to show the writers' belief and the truth of that belief, and thus, fell within that class of evidence which the hearsay rule was designed to exclude.

One could come to a different conclusion if an analysis was made of the extent to which the hearsay dangers applied. It is true that the writers of the letters were not under oath and their testimonial factors could not be tested by cross-examination, but how serious was this in the context of the present case? Can it seriously be urged that all three writers may have been insincere? Perhaps it could be imagined that the writers knew Marsden to be mentally defective, but nevertheless, wrote the letters in intelligent language and style merely because they were writing to a man of some influence; or because they knew the letters would be read by others who would translate them into simpler language for Marsden. Although these are possibilities, it is more

---

31   (1837), 7 Ad. & El. 313, 112 E.R. 488 (H.L.).

probable that no thought of Marsden's mental capabilities occurred to the writers at all. The likelihood of insincerity, therefore, was quite small.

Another testimonial factor that could not be tested was the writers' perception. How great a danger was this? We do not know what opportunities the writers had to observe Marsden. Perhaps it could be suggested that the writers might have dealt with Marsden solely on the basis of reputation without any real personal contact with him. This suggestion, however, has little foundation, for the writers appear to have known Marsden fairly well. One writer was a close relative; the other two were clergymen who lived nearby. There is little doubt that they had adequate opportunity to observe those personal qualities in Marsden which were in issue in the case.

Was there any real danger of defective memory on the part of the writers which would not have escaped exposure under cross-examination? It could be hypothesized that passage of time would have resulted in some loss of memory in the writers as to their earlier observations of Marsden. It is difficult to imagine, however, that all three writers suffered from the same lapse of memory, even if it could be established that their last observation of Marsden was at a time well before the letters were written. It would therefore appear that upon analysis of the dangers which the evidence of the letters afforded as hearsay, the risks were minimal, and thus the mischief, which the hearsay rule was intended to avoid, was not present to any great extent. Nevertheless, the House of Lords held that the hearsay rule applied to the implied assertions without any real consideration of the dangers which would ensue if the letters were allowed in as evidence.[32]

The Court in *Wright v. Doe d. Tatham*[33] also referred to other examples of conduct by an actor unavailable at trial, which would be inadmissible as hearsay, if tendered to prove an inference equivalent to an express assertion. Parke B. included the following:[34]

---

32   The result might also be explained on the basis that the letters merely lacked sufficient relevancy. As C. Tapper, the editor of *Cross on Evidence*, 7th ed. (London: Butterworths, 1990), notes, at 518 "[i]t was just not sufficiently relevant to that question that some time before the will had been made, a few laymen had written occasional letters addressed to the testator which on one of several possible explanations were consistent with a belief in his sanity".

33   *Supra*, note 31.

34   *Supra*, note 31, at 516 (E.R.). The House of Lords was inconsistent because it admitted evidence that Marsden was called "Silly Marsden" and children threw

... the conduct of a physician who permitted a will to be executed by a sick testator; the conduct of deceased captain on a question of seaworthiness, who, after examining every part of the vessel, embarked in it with his family; all these, when deliberately considered, are, with reference to the matter in issue in each case, mere instances of hearsay evidence, mere statements, not on oath, but implied in or vouched by the actual conduct of persons by whose acts the litigant parties are not to be bound.

Wigmore, on the other hand, without too much elaboration, feels that evidence of conduct, tendered for the purpose of proving an inference equivalent to an inference from an assertion, is admissible. As examples, he refers to the conduct of persons on a street, observed through a window of a comfortable home, shivering and turning up their collars, as leading to the inference that the temperature outside is low, and to the conduct of drivers who are observed to have turned their vehicles away from a particular spot on the roadway as leading to the inference that something is obstructing the roadway. Wigmore thinks that neither policy nor the spirit of the hearsay rule applies to such conduct:[35]

... that policy is to test the assertions of persons regarded as witnesses, by learning the source of their knowledge and by exposing its elements of weakness and error, if possible; so that where the evidence is not dealing with a person's assertion as deriving force from his personal character, knowledge, or experience, it is not within the scope of the policy of the hearsay rule. No doubt the line is sometimes hard to draw between conduct used as circumstantial evidence and assertion used testimonially. Nevertheless the difference is a real one ...

Other American authorities have also urged that, notwithstanding the decision in *Wright v. Doe d. Tatham*,[36] non-assertive conduct

---

dirt at him. The relevance of such evidence is that it is an implied assertion that Marsden was mentally incompetent to make a will: see J.M. Maguire, "The Hearsay System: Around and Through the Thicket" (1961), 14 Vand. L. Rev. 741.

35   2 Wigmore, *Evidence* (Chadbourn rev. 1970), § 459, at 586.

36   *Supra*, note 31.

should not be included in the hearsay rule.[37] It is said that such conduct has a certain stamp or guarantee of reliability and should not be excluded. This is so because the conduct occurs without any intention to communicate the fact for which it is tendered in proof. There is no question that the actor was sincere in doing what he or she did.

Other courts have considered the admissibility of implicitly assertive conduct. In *Manchester Brewery Co. v. Coombs*,[38] the issue was whether beer supplied to the defendant by the plaintiff was defective. The defendant intended to call as witnesses persons who had heard pub patrons complain about the quality of the beer. The Court had no difficulty in deciding that this was admissible evidence on the basis that it was no different than if the patrons tasted the beer and either left it or threw it away.[39] The reasoning is opposite to that in *Wright v. Doe d. Tatham*.[40] But in *Holloway v. McFeeters*[41] the Supreme Court of Australia took the view that evidence of a driver fleeing the scene of an accident without reporting the accident was a hearsay statement as to his guilt in causing the accident.

Although the fact that conduct is non-assertive does minimize the danger of insincerity, the risk that the actor's perception may have been faulty or distorted continues to exist. This danger is no less reduced in non-assertive conduct than it is when statements or conduct are assertive. A well known example of this may be found in the fact situation of *R. v. Wysochan*,[42] in which the accused was tried for murder. His defence was that the murderer was the victim's husband and not himself. Only he and the husband were present at the time of the shooting of the deceased. To rebut this defence, the Crown called a witness who shortly after the shooting observed and testified to the words of the wife in reference to her husband, which suggested that

---

37 C.T. McCormick, "The Borderland of Hearsay" (1929-30), 39 Yale L.J. 489, at 502-04; J.F. Falknor, "Silence as Hearsay" (1940), 89 U. Pa. L. Rev. 192, at 206.

38 (1900), 82 L.T. 347, [1901] 2 Ch. 608.

39 Of course, the Court's illustration itself is an example of non-assertive conduct amounting to the implied assertion that the beer is no good and is thus hearsay, albeit more reliable than the verbal complaints offered in evidence.

40 So is the reasoning of the House of Lords in *Lloyd v. Powell Duffryn Steam Coal Co.*, [1914] A.C. 733, [1914-15] All E.R. Rep. Ext. 1329, and the Privy Council in *Ratten v. R.*, [1972] A.C. 378, [1971] 3 All E.R. 801, at 805.

41 (1956), 94 C.L.R. 470 (Aust. H.C.).

42 (1930), 54 C.C.C. 172 (Sask. C.A.).

she wanted his comfort, and thereby, in turn, suggested that he had not been the person who had shot her.[43] The Court held the evidence to be admissible.

Professor Stanley Schiff aptly analyzed the dangers that arise by failing to recognize the assertions that are implicit in such words and conduct:[44]

> The purpose for which the Crown offers the testimony, and the only purpose getting it over the basic hurdle of relevancy, is to establish the matter the Crown wants the trier of fact to conclude the wife impliedly asserted by the described conduct — that the husband did not shoot her. But that was the precise purpose for which the hearsay evidence was offered in the original example. Moreover, the testimony here raises the same difficulties as there: the wife was not subject to any of the witness conditions at any time before or while she acted in the way described and, were the evidence admitted, the opponent and the trier of fact would suffer exactly the same disadvantages. To demonstrate in part, I may focus on defense counsel's lack of opportunity to cross-examine her — the rationale for the hearsay rule most often stressed. Quite clearly, he cannot challenge her on any of the elements of credibility I earlier canvassed. Here, two [seem] particularly important. The first is accurate communication of memory to the trier of fact: did she really mean by her conduct what the Crown asks the jury to infer? The second, logically precedent, is perception or opportunity to perceive: did she even see who was actually holding the gun?

The admissibility of all non-assertive conduct is, therefore, not free from difficulties, as it could result in the reception of evidence which, in certain circumstances, would be replete with significant hearsay dangers. Even though such hearsay dangers may be lurking in conduct which was not intended to be an assertive communication, the courts seem to focus only on the issue of assertiveness to determine whether such evidence is admissible. In *R. v. McKinnon*[45] evidence was

---

43   *Ibid.*, at 172.
44   S. Schiff, "Evidence—Hearsay and The Hearsay Rule: A Functional View" (1978), 56 Can. Bar Rev. 674, at 682.
45   (1989), 70 C.R. (3d) 10, 33 O.A.C. 114 (C.A.).

tendered that the police officers who discovered the body in a remote area were accompanied by the accused's wife. The accused objected to this evidence as a jury could only draw the inference that the information which permitted the police officers to find the body must have come from the accused's wife who in turn had received it from the accused. While there was no evidence as to what conversation took place between the wife and the police, the accused's counsel argued that such assertions were implicit in the evidence of her conduct and, therefore, should not be received. Finlayson J.A. rejected this argument and stated:[46]

> In the first place, her presence was a fact, and was part of the police officers' testimony as to the search and discovery, which search and discovery surely was a relevant fact in the light of the Crown's theory of the "plan" to kill and hide the body. In the second place, her presence in the manner described cannot be characterized as hearsay by conduct. It has always been my understanding that such hearsay usually amounted to a description of actions or behaviour which are themselves means of expression, such as shrugs, headshakes, or other gestures that are a substitute for or supplement to oral communication. Evidence of such conduct is tendered as evidence of an assertion by the person who performed the action. As such, it is inadmissible hearsay. On the facts of this appeal I see nothing in the evidence about the wife's accompanying the police officers to the gravesite which amounts to an assertion or a statement that she received information about its location from her husband, from her husband alone, and from no other source. The evidence is not tendered as evidence of an assertion by the wife. It is not hearsay.

Why was this evidence tendered at all? The Crown submitted that the evidence was relevant to help refute the inference that the police obtained the information as to the location of the gravesite from its witness who gave evidence that he had been approached by the accused to assist him in killing the victim but had declined. Thus, the Crown recognized that evidence about knowledge of the whereabouts of the body might be incriminating and adduced it in order to avoid the inference that its witness had such knowledge. Finlayson J.A. held

---

46   *Ibid.*, at 16-17 (C.R.), at 117 (O.A.C.).

that it was admissible for that purpose "even though an incidental result was that the jury might infer that [the accused] was the source of the wife's knowledge."[47] If the Crown was tendering such evidence to ward off the inference that its witness was the source of this information, it naturally follows that the evidence is a telltale that the most likely source of the information was the accused. At the very least, the conduct gives rise to ambiguity of inference, a hearsay danger which poses serious prejudice to the accused.[48]

Moreover, it is not easy to tell whether conduct is assertive or non-assertive, for the actor's intention may be unclear. As *Cross on Evidence* points out:[49]

> Every human action can be presented as an implied assertion of the actor's belief in the satisfaction of the conditions under which he would be prepared to perform it.

Perhaps the best approach would be for courts to analyze all hearsay-by-conduct evidence in terms of the possibility of the dangers of defective perception, insincerity, memory, or communication, and ambiguity of inference raised by such untested evidence. If the dangers are high, then the evidence should be excluded, but not otherwise.[50] *R. v. Potvin*,[51] a decision of the Supreme Court of Canada dealing with out-of-court statements, may point the way in this regard. In that case, the accused and two others, including the declarant, were charged with murder. The Crown proceeded against the accused first. The declarant testified against the accused at the preliminary inquiry but refused to testify at trial. The Crown tendered as evidence the transcript of the declarant's testimony at the preliminary which satisfied the statutory conditions for admissibility under the provisions of the *Criminal Code* permitting such evidence to be received at trial. The

---

47   *Ibid.*, at 15 (C.R.), at 116 (O.A.C.).
48   See also *R. v. Blastland*, [1986] 1 A.C. 41, [1985] 2 All E.R. 1095 (H.L.), at 1099-1100 (All E.R.). It could be argued that this weakness is inherent in any evidence, hearsay or not, which could give rise to competing inferences, and this should be a matter of weight, not admissibility.
49   R. Cross and C. Tapper, *Cross On Evidence*, 7th ed. (London: Butterworths, 1990), at 531.
50   See S. Schiff, *supra*, note 44.
51   [1989] 1 S.C.R. 525, 47 C.C.C. (3d) 289, 68 C.R. (3d) 193, 2 Q.A.C. 258, 93 N.R. 42.

Supreme Court of Canada acknowledged that because the prerequisites to this exception to the hearsay rule had been met, certain safeguards providing some measure of reliability to the evidence had been satisfied. The Court held that a trial judge, nevertheless, has a discretion to exclude evidence, even of high probative quality, if the evidence was obtained unfairly or if its admission would be unfair to the accused in that adverse evidence would be given without the benefit of observing the demeanour of the declarant. Professor R.J. Delisle, in a critical comment, rightly stated that the loss of opportunity to see the demeanour of the declarant at trial is a feature of all hearsay evidence tendered under any recognized exception to the hearsay rule. From that, he infers that:[52]

> The next logical step from *Potvin* might be to recognize a discretion to exclude on the basis of fairness any and all hearsay statements, whether or not they fit within one of our exceptions, which are important to the Crown's case and depend for their worth on the credibility of the out-of-court asserter.

II EXCEPTIONS TO THE HEARSAY RULE

A. *General*

Necessity has given rise to a number of exceptions to the rule against hearsay. The requirement that testimony be subjected to the test of cross-examination has been dispensed with in situations where the declarant of the words in question is unavailable and the oral or written statement was made under circumstances which, it can be presumed, would impress the remarks with a genuinely trustworthy quality. In many situations such declarations are the only cogent evidence available and to exclude them would result in considerable inconvenience.[53]

Exceptions to the hearsay rule therefore developed in situations where, as Sir George Jessel M.R. stated in *Sugden v. Lord St. Leonards,*[54] the following four characteristics existed:

---

52 R.J. Delisle, Annotation, *ibid.*, at 194-95 (C.R.).
53 *Sugden v. Lord St. Leonards* (1876), 1 P.D. 154, [1875-80] All E.R. Rep. 21 (C.A.), at 240 (P.D.).
54 *Ibid.*, at 241.

(1) It was impossible or difficult to secure other evidence.

(2) The author of the statement was not an interested party in the sense that the statement was not in his favour.

(3) The statement was made before the dispute in question arose.

(4) The author of the statement had a peculiar means of knowledge not possessed in ordinary cases.

It remains to be seen whether all of these conditions must be present before a particular exception comes into play.

The courts developed the exceptions in a haphazard fashion to circumvent the rigidity of the hearsay rule in particular instances. Lord Reid in *Myers v. Director of Public Prosecutions*[55] confirmed the manner in which these exceptions arose:

> The rule has never been absolute. By the nineteenth century many exceptions had become well established, but again in most cases we do not know how or when the exception came to be recognized. It does seem, however, that in many cases there was no justification either in principle or logic for carrying the exception just so far and no farther. One might hazard a surmise that when the rule proved highly inconvenient in a particular kind of case it was relaxed just sufficiently far to meet that case, and without regard to any question of principle. This kind of judicial legislation, however, became less and less acceptable and well over a century ago the patchwork which then existed seems to have become stereotyped.

The House of Lords refused to make any further exception and indicated that only legislative reform could do so. The position in *Myers* may be explained on the basis that at the time of the decision the Law Reform Commission was preparing the draft *Civil Evidence Act*, 1968 and the Court may have felt it was inappropriate to make any judicial change in the law. Although the House of Lords reaffirmed this position in *R. v. Blastland*,[56] a number of recent Canadian

---

55 [1965] A.C. 1001, [1964] 2 All E.R. 881 (H.L.), at 884 (All E.R.).
56 *Supra*, note 48, at 52 (A.C.).

cases have made definite inroads into the hearsay rule. The Supreme Court of Canada in *Ares v. Venner*[57] chose not to follow the *Myers* case and initiated judicial reform in creating a new common-law exception in the area of hospital records and nurses' notes.[58] And more recently in *R. v. Khan*, the Supreme Court of Canada chipped away further at the hearsay rule to create an exception for the admission of statements by children to others about sexual abuse. McLachlin J., speaking for the Court, was critical of the rigid nature of the hearsay rule:[59]

> The hearsay rule has traditionally been regarded as an absolute rule, subject to various categories of exceptions, such as admissions, dying declarations, declarations against interest and spontaneous declarations. While this approach has provided a degree of certainty to the law on hearsay, it has frequently proved unduly inflexible in dealing with new situations and new needs in the law. This has resulted in courts in recent years on occasion adopting a more flexible approach, rooted in the principle and the policy underlying the hearsay rule rather than the strictures of traditional exceptions.

Although a wholesale rethinking of the hearsay rule is necessary and is taking place in some quarters,[60] today's litigants continue to be

---

57   [1970] S.C.R. 608, 12 C.R.N.S. 349, 73 W.W.R. 347, 14 D.L.R. (3d) 4.

58   See this Chapter, II.C.1.(d).

59   [1990] 2 S.C.R. 531, 59 C.C.C. (3d) 92, 79 C.R. (3d) 1, 41 O.A.C. 353, 11 W.C.B. (2d) 10, 113 N.R. 53, at 540 (S.C.R.), at 62-63 (N.R.).

60   See R. Graham Murray, "The Hearsay Maze: A Glimpse At Some Possible Exits" (1972), 50 Can. Bar Rev. 1. Statutory reform has taken place in some jurisdictions. In England, The *Civil Evidence Act, 1968*, c. 64, virtually abolished the hearsay rule in civil cases. Scotland eliminated the bar against hearsay evidence in civil proceedings in 1988. In the United States, the *Federal Rules of Evidence for United States Courts and Magistrates* (1975) maintain a broad list of the common-law exceptions to the hearsay rule and, in addition, have a blanket residual clause, permitting any hearsay if the court is satisfied that there is a circumstantial guarantee of trustworthiness to the hearsay statements. In Canada, a Senate bill was introduced in 1982 to enact the *Uniform Evidence Act*, 1980-81-82, Bill S-33, adopted by the Uniform Law Conference of Canada, which contains provisions modifying the hearsay rule and exceptions to some extent but the bill was withdrawn and no further attempt at legislative reform has been made at the federal, or indeed, the provincial levels: see generally, S.A. Schiff, *Evidence in the Litigation Process*, 3rd ed. (Toronto: Carswell, 1988), at 445-46.

plagued, as were their predecessors in the last two centuries, by the vagaries of the rule and its multiple exceptions. It thus becomes important to examine closely each of the customary common-law exceptions.

B. Declarations Against Interest

1. Against Pecuniary or Proprietary Interest

The common law has always recognized an exception to the hearsay rule for declarations against pecuniary or proprietary interest. From a distillation of the relevant cases the classical exception can be stated in the following terms:[61]

> The written or oral declarations of a person, since deceased, which were against his pecuniary or proprietary interest at the time that he made them are admissible as evidence of the facts contained in the declarations, provided that he had competent knowledge of the facts he stated.

The rationale of this exception is the "circumstantial guarantee of truth" that underlies such statements.[62] There exists the belief that when a person asserts a statement against his or her pecuniary or proprietary interest, it is not likely to be false, as a monetary disadvantage can ensue from such a declaration.[63] Mr. Justice Middleton in *Clergue v. Plummer*,[64] in referring to a written receipt of money,

---

61 See *St. Hilaire v. Kravacek* (1979), 26 O.R. (2d) 499, 14 C.P.C. 22, 5 E.T.R. 279, 102 D.L.R. (3d) 577 (C.A.), at 503-04 (O.R.) quoting from J. Sopinka and S. Lederman, *The Law of Evidence in Civil Cases* (Toronto: Butterworths, 1974), at 50.

62 R.W. Baker, *The Hearsay Rule* (London: Pitman, 1950), at 27-28.

63 *Tucker v. Oldbury Urban District Council*, [1912] 2 K.B. 317 (C.A.), at 321. In *Ward v. Pitt (H.S.) & Co.; Lloyd v. Powell Duffryn Steam Coal Co.*, [1913] 2 K.B. 130; revd. on other grounds (*sub nom. Lloyd v. Powell Duffryn Steam Coal Co.*), [1914] A.C. 733 (H.L.), Hamilton L.J. acknowledged this rationale but was critical of its validity, at 138: "As a reason this seems sordid and unconvincing. Men lie for so many reasons and some for no reason at all; and some tell the truth without thinking or even in spite of thinking about their pockets, but it is too late to question this piece of eighteenth century philosophy." One Canadian commentator has described this tenet as the "legal system's primitive view of human nature": see B.P. Elman, Annotation, *Re Myers* (1979-80), 5 E.T.R. 279, at 280.

64 (1916), 37 O.L.R. 432; revd. on other grounds, 38 O.L.R. 54; affd. 12 O.W.N. 367*n* (S.C.C.).

explained it this way:[65]

> In the great majority of cases, the question discussed has been the effect of an entry of a receipt of money made by the recipient. At the time the entry was made, it was, no doubt, against the interest of the recipient; and it was therefore unlikely that he would record the receipt of money which would either discharge an existing debt due to him or create a liability to account on his part, unless the money was actually received. At the time of the entry, its sole effect would therefore be against the interests of the person making the entry. At the time of the trial, the effect of the entry might be favourable to the case of the party making it — e.g., it might have the effect of taking a debt, otherwise statute-barred, out of the statute. Nevertheless, had it been originally against interest, it was admitted.

2. Against Penal Interest

Much judicial activity lately has focused on the broadening of the traditional exception to include declarations against penal interest. The House of Lords decision in the *Sussex Peerage Case*[66] had limited the admissibility to statements against the declarant's monetary or proprietary interest and no other interest. In that case, the statement of a deceased clergyman that he had officiated at a marriage prohibited by statute was ruled inadmissible notwithstanding the fact that the statement was incriminatory in relation to a possible criminal prosecution. So stood the law[67] until 1978 when the Supreme Court of Canada questioned the distinction between declarations against pecuniary or proprietary interest on the one hand and declarations against penal interest on the other. In *R. v. O'Brien*[68] the Court ruled that a declaration against penal interest is admissible for the reason that "a

---

65 *Ibid.*, at 440-41 (37 O.L.R.).
66 (1844), 11 Cl. & Fin. 85, 8 E.R. 1034 (H.L.).
67 Canadian courts, however, had gone so far as to classify a declaration absolving a party of tortious liability as one against pecuniary interest. In *Watt v. Miller*, [1950] 2 W.W.R. 1144, [1950] 3 D.L.R. 709 (B.C.S.C.), a British Columbia court held admissible as a statement against pecuniary interest a declaration by an injured motor vehicle passenger who died prior to trial. The statement tended to exonerate the driver.
68 [1978] 1 S.C.R. 591, 35 C.C.C. (2d) 209, 38 C.R.N.S. 325, [1977] 5 W.W.R. 400, 76 D.L.R. (3d) 513, 16 N.R. 271.

person is as likely to speak the truth in a matter affecting his liberty as in a matter affecting his pocketbook."[69]

The Supreme Court of Canada thus struck out in a direction which English Courts have been hesitant to take. In *R. v. Blastland*[70] Lord Bridge, in refusing leave to appeal to the House of Lords on one of the two issues in that case, simply indicated that the principle was well established in English law that it is for the legislature and not for the judiciary to create any new exception to the hearsay rule. He stated:[71]

> To admit in criminal trials statements confessing to the crime for which the defendant is being tried made by third parties not called as witnesses would be to create a very significant and, many might think, a dangerous new exception.

Although the Supreme Court of Canada acknowledged that statements exposing a declarant to criminal liability now fell outside the exclusionary hearsay rule, judicial suspicion of such statements still requires that there be in each case sufficient circumstantial guarantee of trustworthiness. Such circumstances were not present in *O'Brien*. There, the accused, O'Brien, and a co-accused were jointly charged with possession of a narcotic for the purpose of trafficking. O'Brien was arrested and convicted. His co-accused fled the country. After O'Brien's conviction the co-accused returned and told O'Brien's counsel that it was he and not O'Brien who had committed the crime and that he was prepared to testify to that effect. The co-accused, however, died before the scheduled hearing. After leave to adduce fresh evidence had been obtained from the British Columbia Court of Appeal, O'Brien's counsel gave evidence as to the statement of the co-accused. On the basis of this testimony the British Columbia Court of Appeal allowed the appeal and directed an acquittal. An appeal was taken to the Supreme Court of Canada.

In determining whether the statement in question could properly be admitted as a declaration against penal interest, the Supreme Court of Canada reconfirmed that the traditional pre-conditions necessary for the admissibility of declarations against pecuniary or

---

69   *Ibid.*, at 599 (S.C.R.).
70   [1986] 1 A.C. 41, [1985] 2 All E.R. 1095 (H.L.).
71   *Ibid.*, at 52-53 (A.C.).

proprietary interests as stated in *Ward v. H.S. Pitt & Co.; Lloyd v. Powell Duffryn Steam Coal Co.*[72] had to be established:[73]

1. It is essential that the deceased should have made a statement of some fact, of the truth of which he had peculiar knowledge. The rule applies only to statements as to "acts done by the deceased and not by third parties" . . . It does not extend to cover statements made by a deceased person of what others had told him . . .

2. It is essential that such fact should have been "to the deceased's immediate prejudice," that is against his interest at the time when he stated it. If it may be construed for his interest or against it . . . or may only be against his interest in certain future events . . . it is inadmissible.

3. It is essential that the deceased should have known the fact to be against his interest when he made it, because it is on the guarantee of truth based on a man's conscious statement of a fact "even though it be to his own hindrance," that the whole theory of admissibility depends. It is "a necessary element, that the subject-matter of the declaration . . . must have been within the direct personal knowledge of the person making the declaration . . ."; . . . "to support the admissibility it must be shewn that the statement was, to the knowledge of the deceased, contrary to his interest."[74]

---

72 *Supra*, note 63, at 137-38. These pre-conditions were also adopted by the Supreme Court of Canada in *R. v. Demeter*, [1978] 1 S.C.R. 538, 38 C.R.N.S. 317, 34 C.C.C. 137, 75 D.L.R. 251, 16 N.R. 46, at 545 (S.C.R.).

73 *Ibid., Ward*. See also *R. v. O'Brien*, [1978] 1 S.C.R. 591, 38 C.R.N.S. 325, 35 C.C.C. (2d) 209, [1977] 5 W.W.R. 400, 76 D.L.R. (3d) 513, 16 N.R. 271, at 599 (S.C.R.). See also *Ex parte Edwards*; *Re Tollemache* (1884), 14 Q.B.D. 415 (C.A.), at 416; *Smith v. Blakey* (1867), L.R. 2 Q.B. 326, at 332; *Massey v. Allen* (1879), 13 Ch. D. 558.

74 *R. v. O'Brien, ibid.*, at 599 (S.C.R.). See also *The Henry Coxon* (1878), 3 P.D. 156, at 158; *Roe d. Lord Trimlestown v. Kemmis* (1843), 9 Cl. & F. 749 (H.L.), at 780, 785; *Short v. Lee* (1821), 2 Jac. & W. 464; *Gleadow v. Atkin* (1833), 1 Cr. & M. 410, at 424; *Sussex Peerage Case* (1844), 11 Cl. & Fin. 85 (H.L.), at 112; *Sturla v. Freccia* (1880), 5 App. Cas. 623 (H.L.), at 632-33; *Blandy-Jenkins v. Earl of Dunraven*, [1899] 2 Ch. 121 (C.A.), at 127; but see *contra, Crease v. Barrett* (1835), 1 Cr. M. & R. 919, 4 L.J. Ex. 297; *Neary v. Fowler* (1869), 7 N.S.R. 495 (C.A.); *Russell v. Fraser* (1865), 15 U.C.C.P. 375 (C.A.); *Percival v. Nanson* (1851), 21 L.J.

Given the risk of fabrication, the Supreme Court of Canada additionally recognized as a valuable guide the following safeguards, articulated by the Ontario Court of Appeal and accepted by the Supreme Court of Canada itself in *R. v. Demeter*,[75] a decision that it rendered a few weeks before it delivered the *O'Brien* judgment:[76]

1. The declaration would have to be made to such a person and in such circumstances that the declarant should have apprehended a vulnerability to penal consequences as a result . . .

2. The vulnerability to penal consequences would have to be not remote.

3. ". . . the declaration sought to be given in evidence must be considered *in its totality*. If upon the whole tenor the weight is in favour of the declarant, it is not against his interest . . ."

4. In a doubtful case a Court might properly consider whether or not there are other circumstances connecting the declarant with the crime and whether or not there is any connection between the declarant and the accused.

5. The declarant would have to be unavailable by reason of death, insanity, grave illness which prevents the giving of testi-

---

Ex. 1; *Re Perton; Pearson v. A.G.* (1885), 53 L.T. 707. The Ontario Court of Appeal in *St. Hilaire v. Kravacek, supra*, note 61 affirmed the proposition that a declaration must have been against the interest of the declarant at the time it was made in order to qualify as an exception. That was an action brought by an executor upon a promissory note. By way of defence it was asserted that the requisite limitation period had expired. To rebut this defence the executor attempted to adduce evidence in the form of a written statement by the deceased that partial payment had been made on the note thereby extending the limitation period so that the action would not be statute-barred. The issue became one of determining whether this written statement by the deceased was made prior to the expiry of the limitation period thereby in fact making it a declaration against interest at the time it was made. The Court held that the deceased made the statement prior to the expiry of the limitation period and therefore it constituted a declaration against interest and fell within the exception.

75 *R. v. Demeter, supra*, note 72; see also *R. v. O'Brien, supra*, note 73, at 600. See also *Josiak v. Setler*, [1971] 1 O.R. 724, 16 D.L.R. (3d) 490 (H.C.J.); *Tucker v. Oldbury Urban District Council*, [1912] 2 K.B. 317 (C.A.); *Sturla v. Freccia, ibid.*, at 633.

76 *R. v. Demeter, supra*, note 72, at 544 (S.C.R.).

mony even from a bed, or absence in a jurisdiction to which none of the processes of the Court extends . . .

The Supreme Court of Canada thought that the second and third criteria enumerated in *Ward*,[77] and the first and second criteria set out in *Demeter*,[78] were absent in the circumstances in *O'Brien*[79] and concluded that the statement of the co-accused did not constitute a declaration against penal interest and hence was inadmissible. The statement had been made ten months after O'Brien had been convicted and almost six months after the charges against the co-accused had been stayed. Furthermore, the statement had been made in the privacy of the office of O'Brien's counsel. Moreover, his public confession, had he lived, was to be in circumstances in which his words could not be used nor be receivable in evidence in any criminal proceeding against him since he had indicated that he would seek the protection of the *Canada Evidence Act*[80] when he gave his testimony.

Subsequently, the Ontario Court of Appeal in *R. v. Pelletier*[81] had occasion to consider two other criteria laid down in *Demeter*,[82] namely, the requirement that the declaration be weighed in its totality, and the unavailability of the declarant. In *Pelletier* the charge was manslaughter and the accused attempted to introduce at trial a statement made by the declarant to the police to the effect that it was the declarant who had assaulted the deceased, but that it was in self-defence. The Court determined that the declarant's statement, when considered in its totality, was against his interest. In assessing the tenor of the statement it should be noted that the Court of Appeal had regard to extrinsic evidence beyond the statement itself.

The approach taken by the Ontario Court of Appeal in *Pelletier* with respect to a mixed statement containing both prejudicial and favourable aspects is to examine the statement in its entirety and to decide, having regard to all of the evidence, whether its tenor is such that the statement is against the declarant's interest. If so, then it is to be admitted.

A different view maintains that when a declaration contains not

---

77 *Ward v. Pitt (H.S.) & Co.; Lloyd v. Duffryn Steam Coal Co.*, *supra*, note 63.
78 *Supra*, note 72.
79 *Supra*, note 73.
80 R.S.C. 1970, c. E-10, s. 5(2) [now R.S.C. 1985, c. C-5, s. 5(2)].
81 (1978), 38 C.C.C. (2d) 515 (Ont. C.A.).
82 *Supra*, note 72.

only matters acknowledged to be against the interest of the declarant but also collateral matters which are favourable to his interest, it is proper for the court to admit the whole declaration in evidence and then to ascribe to that declaration including the collateral matter an appropriate weight in the overall context of the evidence. Rather than considering the general tenor of the entire declaration to determine admissibility, this approach prefers to review the statement in terms of weight or probative value. That certainly was the view of the majority of the Alberta Court of Appeal in *Alberta (Public Trustee) v. Walker*,[83] which was an action for the return of certain savings bonds. The bonds with an aggregate face value of $10,500, together with a letter written by the deceased, were found in his safety deposit box. The letter indicated that the bonds had been deposited with the deceased as security for a loan of $12,000 but also that interest and small payments on the loan had been paid. The aspect of the letter that was contrary to the declarant's interest (i.e., the acknowledgment of the partial repayment) was rather insignificant in monetary terms in comparison with the collateral acknowledgment in the letter that was favourable to the declarant's interest (i.e., the assertion that he had made a loan of $12,000). Notwithstanding the relative insignificance of the declaration against interest the Alberta Court of Appeal admitted the letter in its entirety.[84] The probative value of the respective elements of the letter were then to be assessed according to the totality of the evidence presented at trial.

---

83   (1981), 122 D.L.R. (3d) 411, [1981] 3 W.W.R. 199 (*sub nom. Carr v. Lyman*), 26 A.R. 581 (C.A.).

84   There have been many civil cases where the pecuniary or proprietary interest against which the statement is directed was not sizeable. In *Palter Cap Co. v. Great West Life Assurance Co.*, [1936] O.R. 341, [1936] 2 D.L.R. 304 and 327, 3 I.L.R. 285 and 308 (C.A.), a written entry by a deceased physician in his cash book, indicating receipt of $20.00 from a patient, was admitted within the exception to the hearsay rule as evidence that the doctor had examined the individual and that the individual paid for those services. In *Gormley v. Canada Permanent Trust Co.*, [1969] 2 O.R. 414, 5 D.L.R. (3d) 497 (H.C.J.), a statement against interest was admitted even though the pecuniary disadvantage to the declarant was as small as $4.00. When the amount of pecuniary interest is that insignificant, can the declarant's motive for truth-telling be highly reliable? It could be argued that the size of the interest should be considered as a factor in determining whether the declarant believed the statement to be against his interest or whether the interest was so trivial that he probably never considered it when he made the statement.

The Ontario Court of Appeal's approach in *Pelletier*[85] is more consistent with the rationale underlying this exception to the hearsay rule. A declaration against interest is admitted into evidence as an exception on the basis of the circumstantial probability of trustworthiness arising from the purity of motive in an individual making a statement to his or her monetary or penal disadvantage. A self-serving statement which is admitted into evidence as concomitant to a statement which is only marginally against the declarant's interest does not have the same underlying credibility. The fact that less weight may ultimately be attributed to such a self-serving statement may be an inadequate safeguard in the circumstances.

The *Pelletier* decision is notable for another reason. The Ontario Court of Appeal held that the declarant was unavailable to testify within the meaning of the fifth criterion in *Demeter*. Therefore, as that pre-condition and all the others to admissibility had been satisfied, the declaration was received. While this is not entirely clear, it appeared that the declarant's whereabouts were unknown and that he was probably merely absent from the jurisdiction rather than deceased. This represents a dramatic departure from the rigidity of the earlier common-law rule which insisted as a precondition to admissibility that the declarant be deceased before his or her statement against interest would be admissible.[86]

This expansion of the notion of unavailability is contrary to the earlier decision of the Ontario Court of Appeal in *R. v. Agawa*,[87] where the same Court, while differently composed, held that the exception was confined to the declarations of deceased persons. In the circumstances of that case the Court stated that even if the exception extended to persons who were unavailable to give testimony for any other reason it would certainly not apply to a person present in court and competent to testify if that person chooses to invoke the right against self-incrimination and refuses to testify.[88]

---

85 *R. v. Pelletier, supra,* note 81.

86 *Stephen v. Gwenap* (1831), 1 Mood. & R. 120, 174 E.R. 41; *Smith v. Blakey* (1867), L.R. 2 Q.B. 326, 36 L.J.Q.B. 156; *Clergue v. Plummer* (1916), 37 O.L.R. 432; revd. on other grounds, 38 O.L.R. 54, which was affd. by S.C.C. (unreported) but noted at 12 O.W.N. 367; *Watt v. Miller,* [1950] 2 W.W.R. 1144, [1950] 3 D.L.R. 709 (B.C.S.C.).

87 (1975), 31 C.R.N.S. 293, 28 C.C.C. (2d) 379, 11 O.R. (2d) 176 (C.A.).

88 A number of American cases had previously extended the exception to such a situation: *People v. Brown,* 257 N.E. 2d 16 (N.Y.C.A., 1970); *People v. Spriggs,*

Subsequently, the Alberta Court of Appeal in *R. v. Emsley*[89] referred to the *Agawa* decision but, curiously, not *Pelletier*, in concluding that a declaration against interest was admissible only when the declarant was dead and not when he was merely unavailable to testify. This decision was reached despite the fact that the Supreme Court of Canada had endorsed the fifth criterion articulated in the *Demeter* case which spoke of the unavailability rather than the demise of the declarant.

The Supreme Court of Canada once again in *R. v. Lucier*[90] adopted the five criteria of *Demeter* including the one which merely required that the declarant be unavailable in counter-distinction to the requirement that the declarant be deceased. In fact, in *Lucier*, while it was not strictly necessary to state whether mere unavailability of the declarant would suffice, Ritchie J. stated:[91]

> . . . in a proper case, statements tendered on behalf of the accused and made by an *unavailable* person may be admitted at trial if they can be shown to have been made against the penal interest of the person making them. (emphasis added)

The adherence to the requirement that the declarant be deceased rather than just unavailable no longer seems to be the law.[92] Nor should it be. If one justification for the admission of hearsay evidence is necessity, then surely there is no real distinction between a declarant who is dead and a declarant who is unavailable. In either situation, if all of the other requisite conditions have been satisfied, then the evidence should be admissible because, simply put, it is needed.

The decision by the Supreme Court of Canada in *R. v. Lucier*[93] represents a further refinement in the development of this exception to the hearsay rule. It laid down the principle that a declaration against

---

389 P. 2d 377 (Calif. S.C., 1964).

89   (1980), 21 A.R. 145 (C.A.); leave to appeal to S.C.C. refd. 24 A.R. 16.

90   [1982] 1 S.C.R. 28, 65 C.C.C. (2d) 150, [1982] 2 W.W.R. 289, 14 Man. R. (2d) 380, 132 D.L.R. (3d) 244, 40 N.R. 153.

91   *Ibid.*, at 32-33 (S.C.R.). See also *R. v. Lawrence* (1989), 52 C.C.C. (3d) 452, 36 O.A.C. 198 (C.A.).

92   See *R. v. Williams* (1985), 44 C.R. (3d) 351, 18 C.C.C. (3d) 356, 50 O.R. (2d) 321, 7 O.A.C. 201, 14 C.R.R. 251, at 362 (C.R.). Leave to appeal to S.C.C. refd. (1985), 50 O.R. (2d) 321*n*.

93   *Supra*, note 90.

penal interest can only be admitted if its purpose is to exculpate the accused rather than to incriminate him. One wonders why the court should make this distinction once it has concluded that the statement is trustworthy. Logically it should be reliable for all purposes and therefore admitted even if it is to be used against the accused.[94] Nevertheless a notion of fairness seems to prevail in this situation. Ritchie J. put it this way:[95]

> The difference is a very real one because a statement implicating the accused in the crime with which he is charged emanating from the lips of one who is no longer available to give evidence robs the accused of the invaluable weapon of cross-examination which has always been one of the mainstays of fairness in our courts.

Of course, every exception to the hearsay rule robs the party against whom it is being tendered of the opportunity of cross-examination, but it is received nevertheless because the evidence is needed and the circumstances provide it with some assurance of truth. In any event, in criminal cases such declarations can only be used to benefit an accused and therefore cannot be adduced by the Crown to incriminate him.

Where do *O'Brien* and *Demeter* leave the state of the law? Although the Supreme Court of Canada referred to the principles set out in *Demeter* as being "a valuable guide" it did not go so far as to say that they constitute strict conditions which must be fully satisfied before a declaration against penal interest is admissible. If one can read between the lines in the two judgments, one has the impression that although the Court was prepared to accept the fact that it defied logic for the law to recognize declarations against pecuniary or proprietary interest but not those against penal interest, the Court had a residual, nagging concern that the mere recognition of this extended exception to the hearsay rule might increase the risk of fabricated declarations. Thus the added feature arising in these decisions — a realization by the declarant of the peril of having his or her statement used to incriminate him or her subjecting the declarant to penal consequences.

---

94 For a critical analysis of the Supreme Court of Canada's reasoning, see M. Gold, "Case Comment" (1983), 21 Osgoode Hall L.J. 142.
95 *Supra*, note 90, at 33 (S.C.R.).

It is important to distinguish between the use of these criteria as mere guidelines to assist in the court's assessment of the general trustworthiness of the statement, on the one hand, and the laying down of preconditions to admissibility which in all cases must be strictly satisfied, on the other. If the Court was doing the latter, the additional condition in *O'Brien* that the declarant must realize that his statement places him in jeopardy of punishment might be counterproductive to the apparent expansion of the hearsay exception. As pointed out in a commentary on the case:[96]

> The focus on the mind of the declarant and his apprehension of prosecution would render inadmissible an entry in a private diary in which the person could be shown to have recorded all his darkest and deepest secrets. Clearly the diarist did not apprehend prosecution since the entries were for his eyes alone and remained so until his death.

In this interpretation of the criteria, it is possible that the 'apprehension of prosecution' condition would limit admissibility to only that quality of statement which virtually constitutes a confession to the police or to someone who the declarant felt would pass it on to the police. This narrow interpretation would result perhaps in the exclusion of other statements which in the circumstances might generally be reliable but did not satisfy this test.[97]

It is to be hoped that the Supreme Court of Canada judgments can be taken to mean that there must be a careful review of all the circumstances which may vary from case to case, with a view to determining whether on balance the Court is satisfied that there is sufficient degree of reliability in the statement to warrant its admissibility. The criteria that the Supreme Court outlined were appropriate to the facts of the case before it. They may not be in other cases, or

---

96 I. Bushnell, "Declaration Against Penal Interest — *R. v. O'Brien*" (1979-1980), 22 Crim. L.Q. 371, at 374.

97 The Federal Rules of Evidence in the United States provide as a condition precedent to the admissibility of a statement tending to expose the declarant to criminal liability, and offered to exculpate an accused, that there be corroborating circumstances clearly indicating the trustworthiness of the statement: Rule 804(b)(3). Also see P.B. Carter, "Hearsay, Relevance and Admissibility: Declarations as to State of Mind and Declarations against Penal Interest" (1987), 103 L.Q.R. 106, at 113-16.

there may well be other matters peculiar to those cases to be considered in the determination of the trustworthiness of the statement.

In *R. v. Read*,[98] for example, passages of a diary in which the deceased described her possession and purchase of marijuana were held to be admissible as declarations against penal interest notwithstanding the fact that the deceased may not have perceived a vulnerability to penal consequences in the circumstances. McDonald J. of the Alberta Queen's Bench concluded that this was not an essential condition to admissibility of personal diary entries.

C. Declarations Made in the Course of a Business Duty

1. The Common-Law Exception

(a) *Nature of Exception*

At common law, statements made by a deceased person under a duty to another person to do an act and record it in the ordinary practice of the declarant's business or calling are admissible in evidence, provided they were made contemporaneously with the facts stated and without motive or interest to misrepresent the facts.[99]

The importance of this exception has been overshadowed by federal and provincial legislation which allow for the admissibility of written business documents if certain criteria are met.[100] Medical reports are also expressly admissible by statute in some provinces.[101] In addition, statutory provisions permit the admissibility of banking records and microfilm records.[102] Although this legislation has made the common-law exception somewhat redundant, it still remains of considerable value in situations where counsel is faced with the problem of adducing evidence of an oral statement[103] or where counsel

---

98 (1982), 18 Alta. L.R. (2d) 188 (Q.B.).
99 Similar statements appear in *Palter Cap Co. v. Great West Life Assurance Co.*, [1936] O.R. 341, [1936] 2 D.L.R. 304 at 310 and 327, 3 I.L.R. 285 and 308 (C.A.), at 357-58 (O.R.); R. Cross and C. Tapper, *Cross on Evidence*, 7th ed. (London: Butterworths, 1990), at 646-50; R.W. Baker, *The Hearsay Rule* (London: Pitman, 1950), at 78; J.B.C. Tregarthen, *The Law of Hearsay Evidence* (London: Stevens & Sons Ltd., 1915), at 113.
100 See this Chapter, II.C.2.
101 See *ibid*.
102 See this Chapter, II.C.2.(j).
103 See *Palter Cap Co. v. Great West Life Assurance Co.*, *supra*, note 99, at 319-20

wishes to introduce a written business record which fails to meet the requirements of the relevant statutory provisions.[104]

(b) *Rationale*

An exception for this type of hearsay was justified on the basis of necessity, the declarant no longer being available to give evidence.[105] Moreover, the statement was said to possess a circumstantial guarantee of truth based upon the assumption that a declarant would fear censure and dismissal should an employer discover an inaccuracy in the statement. Also, the constant routine and habit in making entries provided some likelihood of accuracy.[106]

(c) *Early Preconditions to Admissibility*

Much of the earlier case law dwelt at length with each of the facts that had to be established as preconditions to admissibility, namely:

(1) The declarant must be deceased;[107]
(2) The duty of the declarant must be one to do a specific act and then to record it when done;[108]

(D.L.R.); *R. v. Buckley* (1873), 13 Cox C.C. 293; *R. v. Laverty* (1979), 9 C.R. (3d) 288, 47 C.C.C. (2d) 60 (Ont. C.A.).

104 See *Tecoglas Inc. v. Domglas Inc.* (1985), 51 O.R. (2d) 196, 19 D.L.R. (4th) 738, 3 C.P.C. (2d) 275 (Ont. H.C.J.), in which it was held that failure to give the notice required by statute did not affect admissibility under common law. It also may be that business records which contain opinions as opposed to setting out facts would be excluded under provincial legislation but admitted under common law. See this Chapter, II.C.2.(e).

105 *Lefebure v. Worden* (1750), 2 Ves. Sen. 54.

106 *Poole v. Dicas* (1835), 1 Bing. N.C. 649, at 652. See J.D. Ewart, "Admissibility at Common Law of Records" (1981), 59 Can. Bar Rev. 52, at 54.

107 In *National Fire Insurance Co. v. Rogers*, [1924] 2 W.W.R. 186, [1924] 2 D.L.R. 403, 18 Sask. L.R. 585 (C.A.) and in *Cooper v. Marsden* (1793), 1 Esp. 1, statements were excluded because there was no evidence that the declarants were deceased, although they were clearly unavailable for attendance at trial.

108 See *Palter Cap Co. v. Great West Life Assurance Co., supra,* note 99, where the records of the deceased heart specialist who had examined the insured, including the written medical history, a cardiograph and screen tracing bearing the insured's name, and a letter by the specialist to the family physician reporting on the examination were made in the ordinary course of the specialist's business and in pursuance of a duty; see C.A. Wright, "Case Note" (1936), 14 Can. Bar Rev. 688; see also *Mills v. Mills* (1920), 36 T.L.R. 772; *Simon v. Simon*, [1936] P. 17; *Dawson v. Dawson* (1905), 22 T.L.R. 52, where medical reports and histories made by

(3)   The act must have been completed;[109]

(4)   The act must have been performed by the declarant him or herself;[110]

(5)   The statement must have been made contemporaneously with the act;[111]

---

deceased physicians were excluded because no duty to another in preparing such documents could be established; *McGillivray v. Shaw* (1963), 39 D.L.R. (2d) 660 (Alta. C.A.), where a solicitor's memorandum to explain a transaction between the plaintiff and defendant was held to have been made in the course of his duty; *Maw v. Dickey* (1974), 6 O.R. (2d) 146, 52 D.L.R. (3d) 178 (Co. Ct.), at 190 (D.L.R.), where a solicitor's notes made during an interview with a client to take instructions for the drafting of a will was held to come within the solicitor's duty to make observations about testamentary capacity and to reduce them to writing; *Conley v. Conley*, [1968] 2 O.R. 677, 70 D.L.R. (2d) 352 (C.A.), where notes of a deceased private investigator regarding his observations of the respondent and co-respondent were admissible; *Mellor v. Walmesley*, [1905] 2 Ch. 164 (C.A.) per Romer L.J., at 167-68, holding admissible an engineer's field book containing survey figures and measurements. That the duty must be owed to some person other than the declarant himself is illustrated by *Massey v. Allen* (1879), 13 Ch. D. 558; *O'Connor v. Dunn* (1877), 2 O.A.R. 247; *McGregor v. Keiller* (1883), 9 O.R. 677 (H.C.J.); *Lakefield (Village) v. Brown* (1910), 15 O.W.R. 656, 1 O.W.N. 589 (C.A.). That the duty must be specific in nature is illustrated by *Smith v. Blakey* (1867), L.R. 2 Q.B. 326, 36 L.J.Q.B. 156; *Dominion Telegraph Securities Ltd. v. Minister of National Revenue*, [1947] S.C.R. 45, [1946] 4 D.L.R. 449, [1946] C.T.C. 239, 60 C.R.T.C. 161; *Mercer v. Denne*, [1905] 2 Ch. 538 (C.A.); *Beukenkamp v. Canada (Minister of Consumer & Corporate Affairs)* (1974), 43 D.L.R. (3d) 118 (*sub nom. Re Beukenkamp and Minister of Consumer & Corporate Affairs*), [1973] F.C. 1401 (T.D.); and *Chambers v. Bernasconi* (1834), 1 Cr. M. & R. 347 (Exch.).

109   E.g., in *Rowlands v. De Vecchi* (1882), 1 Cab. & El. 10, a record kept by a deceased clerk in postage books setting out letters to be posted was excluded when tendered to prove that a certain letter had been mailed; but see *contra, R. v. Buckley* (1873), 13 Cox C.C. 293 (Chester, Spring Assizes), in which a report, made by a police officer to his superior that he was proceeding to a particular location to observe the accused, was admitted as evidence that the murdered policeman and the accused had met each other at that place. This latter case appears to be of doubtful authority and was not considered in *Rowlands*.

110   The declarant must have performed the act or taken an active part in it: *Polini v. Gray* (1879), 12 Ch. D. 411; affd. (*sub nom. Sturla v. Freccia*) (1880), 5 App. Cas. 623 (H.L.); *Lyell v. Kennedy* (1887), 56 L.T. 647 per Bowen L.J., at 657; *Dominion Telegraph Securities Ltd. v. Minister of National Revenue*, [1947] S.C.R. 45, [1946] 4 D.L.R. 449, [1946] C.T.C. 239, 60 C.R.T.C. 161, at 463 (D.L.R.), at 62 (S.C.R.), per Estey J.; *Brain v. Preece* (1843), 11 M.W. 773; *The Henry Coxon* (1878), 3 P.D. 156, at 158, per Sir Robert Phillimore.

111   *Doe d. Patteshall v. Turford* (1832), 3 B. & Ad. 890, at 989; *Barton v. Dundas*

(6)   The declarant must not have had any motive or interest to misrepresent;[112]

(7)   Collateral matters contained in the statement are inadmissible.[113]

The insistence that these prerequisites be strictly met often led to anachronistic results as in the case of *Myers v. Director of Public Prosecutions.*[114] In that case, the accused were charged with conspiracy to receive stolen cars and to defraud the purchasers of the stolen cars. In order to prove its case, the Crown wished to show that the numbers on the cylinder blocks of the cars corresponded with the numbers contained in the car manufacturers' records which were entered by employees as the cars left the assembly line. The House of Lords held that such records were inadmissible as hearsay and failed to come within any of the recognized exceptions. The Court indicated that the tenet of the hearsay rule has been firmly established for the better part of two centuries and although fresh exceptions had been judicially created in the nineteenth century, the creation of any new exceptions in the twentieth century was to be left to the legislators and not to the

---

(Town) (1865), 24 U.C.Q.B. 273 (C.A.); *O'Connor v. Dunn, supra,* note 108, at 259, 261 *et seq.*; *Polini v. Gray, ibid.,* at 425, 430; *Mercer v. Denne, supra,* note 108, at 558; *Re Djambie Rubber Estates Ltd.* (1912), 107 L.T. 631; *Hart v. Toronto General Trusts Corp.* (1920), 47 O.L.R. 387. There appears to be no sound reason for the distinction between declarations against interest (where contemporaneity goes to weight) and declarations in the course of duty (where contemporaneity is a condition precedent to admissibility): see this Chapter, II.B.

112   *Polini v. Gray, supra,* note 110, at 430; *The Henry Coxon, supra,* note 110; *Hart v. Toronto General Trusts Corp., ibid.; McGillivray v. Shaw, supra,* note 108; but see *Conley v. Conley, supra,* note 108. Again there is no logical reason for the distinction between declarations against interest and declarations in the course of duty in this regard.

113   Extraneous matters accompanying that part of the statement made in the course of duty are not admissible: *Chambers v. Bernasconi, supra,* note 108; *Polini v. Gray, supra,* note 110; *Johnston v. Hazen* (1905), 3 N.B. Eq. 147, 26 C.L.T. 317, in particular, at 162.

114   [1965] A.C. 1001, [1964] 3 W.L.R. 145, [1964] 2 All E.R. 881 (H.L.). In Canada, the Saskatchewan Court of Appeal rejected the evidence of the business records of an automobile manufacturer made by unascertained persons in *National Fire Insurance Co. v. Rogers, supra,* note 107. In *Whitehead v. R.B. Cameron Ltd.* (1967), 63 D.L.R. (2d) 180 (N.S.C.A.) a Nova Scotia court rejected a witness' evidence as to certain disbursements because of lack of personal knowledge and because the information came from entries in the books of account of the company, which were not made by him, nor under his observation and control.

courts. If, however, it could have been proven that the original makers of the record were dead, the records would have been admissible under the traditional common-law rule as a declaration made in the course of a business duty.

How important a fact, in the *Myers* case, was the failure to show that the declarant was dead at the time of trial? In deciding that the evidence of the records was inadmissible, the House of Lords made no analysis as to which of the hearsay dangers, if any, were present. No analysis was made of how the evidence might be received and yet afford some measure of protection to the accused.

If the Court had allowed the business records to go in, what hearsay dangers would have resulted? Was there any danger of fabrication on the part of the workmen who entered the numbers in the records? Surely there was no deliberate insincerity on their part as they had had nothing to gain by making false entries. They made these records when the cars were first manufactured, and accordingly, there was no real risk of fabrication. Thus, cross-examination of the workmen would not in all likelihood have disclosed any insincerity.

Could there have been faulty perception on the part of the workmen? Of course it is possible that an employee could have mistaken one number for another; however, cross-examination could never have disclosed this deficiency.

Furthermore, the House of Lords ignored the fact that these business records formed the best evidence available. Had the original workmen been found, their evidence would have been no better than the record itself. Their testimony would have been dependent entirely upon the business record itself, one of hundreds they would have made, and their personal appearance in court as witnesses would have no effect whatsoever on the validity of that record. Thus, having the workmen present for cross-examination would have added nothing to the proceeding. So, in the *Myers* case, there existed a situation where the hearsay evidence posed few, if any, of the customary dangers and the protection for the accused and the guarantee of trustworthiness of the evidence would not have been improved if the original declarants were called to testify. Nothing was to be gained by barring the hearsay evidence.

The House of Lords also ignored the question of necessity. How could the Crown ever locate the workmen who made the original records? In the modern-day world of giant corporations, there is the problem of anonymously-prepared records. Considerations of necessity and convenience dictate the admissibility of such business records.

(d) *Judicial Reform of the Common-Law Rule:* Ares v. Venner

Aware of these criticisms, the Supreme Court of Canada in *Ares v. Venner*,[115] in the absence of any statutory provision, chose not to follow the decision in the *Myers* case and indicated an acceptance of the reasoning of the minority in that case. In *Ares*, a malpractice suit against a physician, the Court held that the nurses' notes were admissible without the necessity of the original makers of the notes being called as witnesses.

This judicial reform of the common-law exception made sense for a number of reasons. First, there is the consideration of mercantile convenience. To call all the persons responsible for keeping a record in a large institution is too inconvenient and may in fact serve to disrupt the business of that institution by taking a multitude of witnesses away from their work. Secondly, one must consider the expense to the litigants in seeking out and subpoenaing all relevant witnesses. Thirdly, the cost to the public and the great length of time that will be consumed at trial by the testimony of witnesses called merely to prove a business record should be considered. Fourthly, with records of a hospital, involving the health of patients, it can be taken for granted that nurses will make every effort to keep accurate notes.[116] The nurses have no interest, apart from their duty, in keeping the notes and therefore, in all likelihood, it is an impartial and trustworthy record of the patients' condition. Furthermore, nothing is to be gained by calling the nurses themselves. In all probability they will have no independent memory apart from the notes that they made, and therefore, the notes as evidence are superior to the testimony of the nurses. All of these factors give rise to a circumstantial guarantee of trustworthiness which justifies the reception of the document without the necessity of calling the declarants.

(e) *Scope of* Ares v. Venner

The innovative decision of the Supreme Court of Canada in *Ares v. Venner* is admirable in opening the road of admissibility to allow in

---

115   [1970] S.C.R. 608, 12 C.R.N.S. 349, 14 D.L.R. (3d) 4, 73 W.W.R. 347.
116   See *Horn v. Sturm* (1965), 408 P. 2d 541 (Okl. S.C.), at 549.

business records which do not fall under the umbrella of the traditional common-law exception. It claimed to have adopted the minority opinion in the *Myers* case. There is, however, a major distinction between the two cases. The records kept in the *Myers* case (and in *Omand v. Alberta Milling Co.*,[117] *Ashdown (J.H.) Hardware Co. v. Singer*,[118] and *Canada Atlantic Railway v. Moxley*,[119] which were referred to by the Supreme Court of Canada) all dealt with situations where the declarant merely recorded data that was presented to him. It amounted to no more than a transcription of numbers and other mathematical or monetary data. In making such a record, the declarant did not have to interpret what he observed. His opinion or interpretation was not material as he merely had to copy the results of a test or other scientific or technical material. In *Ares v. Venner*, however, the nurses were not just recording the objective data of blood pressure or pulse rate; they were observing the condition of the patient and interpreting his condition in a subjective way. The notes stated at times that the patient was "blue", or "blueish pink", or "cool", or "cold". Unlike the *Myers* case, these records give rise to the spectre of hearsay dangers. The nurses' perception, observation and interpretation may have been subject to error. The opponent has lost his opportunity to cross-examine on the nurses' ability to perceive and to interpret accurately what they saw. It may be that records which are based on such subjective factors do not stand on the same footing as the manufacturers' records of numbers in the *Myers* case. It is one thing to allow in objective business records where it is too inconvenient to call the declarant. It is another matter entirely to extend this to business records which turn greatly on the declarant's ability to perceive. Mr. Justice Hall thought that it was a sufficient safeguard to the opponent who wishes to challenge the accuracy of the nurses' notes that he or she can call the nurses to the stand himself. The nurses were present in the courtroom during the trial and thus were available to be called as witnesses by the opponent. But does this afford a sufficient protection against the hearsay dangers? If the opponent calls them to testify, how can he or she cross-examine them? They are his or her witnesses and thus he or she can only examine them in chief.

---

117 [1922] 3 W.W.R. 412, 18 Alta. L.R. 383, 69 D.L.R. 6 (C.A.).
118 (1951), 3 W.W.R. (N.S.) 145 (Alta. S.C.); affd. [1953] 1 S.C.R. 252, [1953] 2 D.L.R. 625.
119 (1888), 15 S.C.R. 145.

That does not allow counsel to properly test the nurses' perception.[120]

What if the nurses were not available in the courtroom for examination? Would the Supreme Court of Canada still have adopted the minority decision in the *Myers* case and applied it to the nurses' records which were dependent upon subjective criteria? Are the hearsay dangers eliminated only because the declarants were in the courtroom and could be examined by opposing counsel?[121] It was McLachlin J.'s view in *R. v. Khan*[122] that admissibility was not dependent on an ability to cross-examine the nurses, since it probably would have been futile given the circumstances. Commenting on this aspect of *Ares*, she stated that the nurses' absence would not have raised any real hearsay dangers:[123]

> The nurses were present in court at the trial, but in the absence of some way of connecting particular nurses with particular entries, meaningful cross-examination on the accuracy of specific observations would have been difficult indeed.

In any event, the Supreme Court of Canada has trodden where no English court has. It ignored the admonition of the majority opinion in the *Myers* case that it is for the legislature, not the courts, to extend the common-law exceptions to the hearsay rule to admit business documents. The minority in the *Myers* case would have allowed in business records because of the anonymity of the makers of the records and the impossibility of tracing them. The Supreme Court of Canada did not even think that unavailability of the declarant was a necessary precondition to the admissibility, as the nurses were not only identifiable but were available in the courtroom.

---

120 But see Ontario Rules of Civil Procedure, O. Reg. 560/84, r. 53.07 where the person is an adverse party. For the view of one of the authors, see A.W. Bryant, "The Common Law Rule Against Impeaching One's Own Witness" (1982), 32 U.T.L.J. 412; "The Statutory Rule Against Impeaching One's Own Witness" (1983), 33 U.T.L.J. 108.

121 See *Woods v. Elias* (1978), 21 O.R. (2d) 840 (Co. Ct.), in which this qualification is emphasized.

122 [1990] 2 S.C.R. 531, 59 C.C.C. (3d) 92, 79 C.R. (3d) 1, 41 O.A.C. 353, 11 W.C.B. (2d) 10, 113 N.R. 53.

123 *Ibid.*, at 548 (S.C.R.).

(f) *Practical Impact of* Ares v. Venner

The decision in *Ares v. Venner*, though important to those provinces which have no statutory provision with respect to the admissibility of business records, has had little practical impact in the provinces which have enacted legislation to circumvent the narrow scope given by the traditional common-law exception. One qualification, however, is necessary here. As will be seen, the provincial legislation does allow in hospital records. But *quaere* whether this provision sanctions the admissibility of hospital records which contain not only the objective data of temperature, pulse rate, etc., but the impressions and diagnostic opinions of doctors and nurses? If it does not, then in this context *Ares v. Venner* may still be of relevant and practical importance in those provinces which do have business record statutes.

(g) *The Aftermath of* Ares v. Venner

The Supreme Court of Canada decision in *Ares v. Venner* significantly expanded the exception and loosened the rigid adherence to the preconditions listed above. First, the requirement that the declarant be deceased has been jettisoned. In fact, in the circumstances of the *Ares* case itself the nurses who made the record were not only very much alive but they were present in the courtroom; however, neither party had any interest in calling them as witnesses.

Furthermore, as to the two-fold duty test (i.e., a duty to do the act and a duty to record it), the nurses were duty bound to observe and record the patients' condition and therefore the test was satisfied. The nurses' observations, however, comprised both the mechanical reading of numbers and subjective interpretation of the patient's condition. Accordingly, the exception now appears to include recorded opinions so long as they fall within the declarant's normal scope of duty.

Most courts which subsequently considered the impact of the decision in *Ares v. Venner* felt that it did represent an expansion of the existing common law; however, the limits of the newly broadened exception have not always been clearly articulated. The first appellate court to consider *Ares* was that of the Alberta Supreme Court in *C.P.R. v. Calgary (City)*.[124] *Ares* was applied to admit business records where the makers thereof were not readily available. In an action by the

---

124 [1971] 4 W.W.R. 241 (Alta. C.A.).

railway against the city for damages resulting from a train derailment, caused by the collapse of a culvert contracted under the track by the city, the Court admitted a summary of facts and figures extracted from the business records of the railway which it tendered on the question of damages to show which cars were destroyed. Unlike that in *Ares*, the data recorded in the document was purely objective.

In *Cargil Grain Ltd. v. Davie Ship Building Ltd.*,[125] the Supreme Court of Canada seemed to be prepared to apply the *Ares* principle to circumstances outside the hospital setting. That case involved a claim for extra structural steel delivered by the plaintiff to the defendant. The issue was whether an accurate, commercially acceptable and verifiable method for the calculation of the weight of the steel shipped by the plaintiff had been used. While the Supreme Court of Canada rejected the application of the *Ares* principle to a document containing conclusions as to the weight of the shipment, it did so because the document merely contained conclusions without any of the supporting calculations and because the draught displacement method of calculating weight was not established to be accurate and commercially acceptable, and not because it was perceived that the *Ares* doctrine was inapplicable to the situation. If the Supreme Court of Canada was of the view that *Ares* established only a hospital records exception it would have so stated and the other reasons given for excluding the records would not have been necessary (this throws into doubt the conclusion in *Woods v. Elias*[126] in which the Court held that the *Ares* principle was restricted in its application to hospital records).

Some express clarification was provided by Griffiths J. in *Setak Computer Services Corp. v. Burroughs Business Machines Ltd.*,[127] who in discussing *Ares*, stated:[128]

> That case [*Ares*] settles the common law in Ontario. Although the statement [in *Ares*] refers only to hospital records, it may be inferred that this decision also settles the law applicable to records of other businesses made in similar circumstances.

---

125 [1977] 1 S.C.R. 569, 10 N.R. 347 (S.C.C.).
126 (1978), 21 O.R. (2d) 840 (Co. Ct.).
127 (1977), 15 O.R. (2d) 750, 76 D.L.R. (3d) 641 (H.C.J.).
128 *Ibid.*, at 755 (O.R.).

But Griffiths J. also pointed out that the exception had certain limits. In *Setak* the plaintiff initiated an action against the defendant for breach of contract and misrepresentation alleging that the defendant had manufactured and leased to the plaintiff two computer systems which were defective and inadequate and that the defendant failed to provide the necessary technical support for the systems when they were installed. The plaintiff attempted to adduce in evidence the minutes of certain meetings between its representatives and the representatives of the defendant, Burroughs, which recorded the discussions that took place in an effort to resolve some of the difficulties with the computer systems. The plaintiff also sought to introduce in evidence a set of minutes which consisted of notes of internal meetings of the plaintiff's personnel and the minutes of meetings involving the technical representatives of the plaintiff and the defendant. In determining whether these minutes were admissible pursuant to the common-law exception to the hearsay rule, Griffiths J. considered *Ares* and stated:[129]

> In my opinion, the common law exception applies only to writings or records made by a person speaking from personal observation or knowledge of the facts recorded. In the *Ares* case, the nurses were recording observations they had made of the plaintiff as a patient and the entries thereof describe matters within their personal knowledge. In my view, the minutes here do not meet this requirement of the common law exception; the authors of the minutes did not have personal knowledge of all the facts recorded. At most, it can be said that [the authors of the minutes] had personal knowledge that the statements attributable to those who attended the meeting, which were duly recorded in the minutes, were in fact made, and it is on this narrow basis only that I would admit the minutes under the common law as modified in *Ares v. Venner*.

The Ontario Court of Appeal in *R. v. Laverty*[130] emphasized another limitation on the exception. That was a case of arson in which certain notes prepared by the deceased fire investigator were held to

---

129 *Ibid.*, at 755 (O.R.). The admissibility of these minutes on a wider basis under provincial business records legislation is discussed in this Chapter, II.C.2.
130 ((1979), 47 C.C.C. (2d) 60, 9 C.R. (3d) 288 (Ont. C.A.).

be inadmissible as hearsay. The notes were merely an *aide-mémoire*, that is, notes taken at random that the investigator kept for himself from which he may or may not have prepared a report and not records that he was under a duty to make. The Ontario Court of Appeal concluded that the *Ares v. Venner* doctrine was only applicable to records kept pursuant to a duty, since otherwise the circumstantial guarantee of trustworthiness was absent.

A broader limitation was expressed by Wood J.A. of the British Columbia Court of Appeal in *R. v. Gould*:[131]

> [In *Ares v. Venner*], on what I consider from reading the judgment to be a very narrow basis, the Supreme Court of Canada adopted the minority position taken in *Myers v. The Director of Public Prosecutions*, which essentially was to the effect that where logistical problems are encountered in applying the laws of evidence to problems of modern life, novel solutions ought to be constructed by the courts.
>
> I do not understand that it has ever been suggested that such an approach could or should be taken to such evidence where it is apparently essential to proof of a criminal charge. I am not aware of any case in which the principle of *Ares v. Venner* has been adopted en route to proof of criminal charge. The application of the principle in the decision has been confined largely to cases in which the facts are similar.

Shortly after this decision, however, the Supreme Court of Canada in *R. v. Khan*[132] took the very approach that Wood J.A. cautioned against.[133]

2. Admissibility by Statute

(a) *General*

In order to obviate the difficulties of adducing evidence of business records under the narrow, traditional common-law exception, legislatures enacted, in a piecemeal fashion, provisions which

---

131 (1990), 57 C.C.C. (3d) 500, 78 C.R. (3d) 151 (B.C.C.A.), at 505 (C.C.C.).
132 [1990] 2 S.C.R. 531, 59 C.C.C. (3d) 92, 79 C.R. (3d) 1, 41 O.A.C. 353, 11 W.C.B. (2d) 10, 113 N.R. 53.
133 See this Chapter, II.L.

facilitated the admission of particular documents and records without the attendant disruption of, or interference with, the commercial, business, or government world. Thus, banking records, letters patent, foreign judgments of certain jurisdictions, copies of statutes, official gazettes, ordinances, regulations, proclamations, journals, orders, appointments to office, notices thereof and other public documents purporting to be printed under the authority of the United Kingdom Parliament, or of the English government, or by or under the authority of the government or any legislative body of any state within the Queen's dominions,[134] were made admissible without any necessity of calling the makers of the documents.

The culmination of this legislative reform has been the provincial and federal business record provisions modelled on comparable American enactments.[135] Under these statutes, business records of a great variety are now admissible;[136] but a close examination of the various provisions reveals serious limitations on the scope of admissibility.

These statutory provisions contain a number of constituent elements which have posed some interpretive difficulties for the courts.

---

134 See, for example, *Canada Evidence Act*, R.S.C. 1985, c. C-5, ss. 19-24, 26-29 and 32, and the Ontario *Evidence Act*, R.S.O. 1980, c. 145, ss. 25-30, 32, 34 and 39-42.

135 The *Canada Evidence Act*, R.S.C. 1985, c. C-5, s. 30, and the Evidence Acts: British Columbia, R.S.B.C. 1979, c. 116, ss. 47-49; Manitoba, R.S.M. 1987, c. E150, ss. 48-49; New Brunswick, R.S.N.B. 1973, c. E-11, ss. 46-49; Northwest Territories, R.S.N.W.T. 1988, c. E-8, s. 47; Nova Scotia, R.S.N.S. 1989, c. 154, s. 23; Ontario, R.S.O. 1980, c. 145, s. 35; Prince Edward Island, R.S.P.E.I. 1988, c. E-11, ss. 32-33; Saskatchewan, R.S.S. 1978, c. S-16, s. 31; Yukon, R.S.Y. 1986, c. 57, s. 37.

136 ". . . this section would cover such diverse things as, perhaps, pages and pages of stockbrokers' dealings with a client, pages and pages of a credit company's business affairs, perhaps pages and pages of records of one of the big stores in the community . . .": per Morand J. in *Aynsley v. Toronto General Hospital*, [1968] 1 O.R. 425, 66 D.L.R. (2d) 575, at 431 (O.R.), at 581 (D.L.R.); varied on other grounds [1969] 2 O.R. 829, 7 D.L.R. (3d) 193; affd. (*sub nom. Toronto General Hospital Trustees v. Matthews*), [1972] S.C.R. 435, 25 D.L.R. (3d) 241. In *Re Brown; Gordon v. Rosenberg* (1967), 11 C.B.R. (N.S.) 17 (O. Reg.), Registrar Cook admitted as business records: (1) documents of the bankrupt, possession of which was taken by the trustee pursuant to his statutory duty, and (2) all records prepared by the trustee in performance of his statutory obligations.

(b) Usual and Ordinary Course of Business

It should be noted that although the wording of the provincial provision is cast in broad terms so as to encompass practically every type of writing utilized in connection with any operation,[137] whether it be profitable or not, two criteria must be met as preconditions to admissibility:

1. The record must have been made in the usual and ordinary course of business; and
2. It was in the usual and ordinary course of the business to make such writing.[138]

It is the latter qualification which severely restricts the type of documents that may be admitted; for, notwithstanding that documents may be made in the usual and ordinary course of business, if it is not the business custom of the activity or operation to maintain such a record, they are inadmissible. An American case is illustrative of this point. In *Palmer v. Hoffman*,[139] the Supreme Court of the United States considered these two criteria in a Federal provision worded similarly to the enactments in most Canadian provinces. That was an action arising out of a railroad crossing accident in which the defendant tried to put in as evidence a statement made by the deceased train engineer to some officials at the defendant's freight office. Although

---

137 In *Thomas v. Watkins Products Inc.* (1965), 54 D.L.R. (2d) 252, 51 M.P.R. 321 (N.B.C.A.), the Appeal Division of the New Brunswick Supreme Court, however, in interpreting the phrase in the New Brunswick provision, *supra*, note 135, s. 49, "a record or entry of an act, condition or event made in the regular course of a business" held that it did not include monthly statements of account or invoices. It said that the entry or record had to be in a book of account or something similar to it or related to it such as an employee's time card. The Ontario statute includes "any writing" and therefore may not be subject to such a restricted interpretation.

138 The Evidence Acts of British Columbia, Nova Scotia, Manitoba, Ontario and Saskatchewan, *supra*, note 135, impose these two criteria. In New Brunswick, *supra*, note 135, s. 49, the record need only be shown to have been made in the "regular course of a business". Another requirement of admissibility is that the record be qualified by a witness who can testify that these two criteria have been fulfilled, or, in New Brunswick, that the document was made in the "regular course of a business": *Aynsley v. Toronto General Hospital*, *supra*, note 136, at 434 (O.R.), at 584 (D.L.R.); *Thomas v. Watkins Products Inc.*, *ibid*.

139 318 U.S. 109, 63 S. Ct. 477 (1943).

the engineer's report of the accident was a record made in relation to his employment, the Court held that that was insufficient for the purposes of admissibility under the statute. Mr. Justice Douglas, speaking for the Court, stated that in order to come within the business records statute, it must be shown to be a record which is necessary for the systematic and mechanical conduct of the business as a commercial enterprise. It must be a record that is routinely kept to run the business as a business. Most businesses are concerned about prospective litigation, and, therefore, have a practice of taking statements from employees when an accident occurs. The primary purpose of such a document, however, is to assist in the lawsuit and not to assist in the running of the railway business. The Court was fearful that there would be abuse should it allow in the report in question. The Court speculated that a business could thereby introduce self-serving evidence, i.e., the statements which reflect its own version of the accident. Such documents have nothing to do with the day-to-day operation and management of the railroad business. The trustworthiness of business documents is based on the reliability placed on such records by the commercial world. In the absence of routineness, there exists the danger that the maker of the record may not be motivated to be accurate. It is the mercantile nature of the record which attracts trustworthiness, not just the fact that the document was prepared in the regular course of business. The implied introduction into business record legislation of the requirement that there be no motive to misrepresent is consistent with the requirements of the traditional common-law exception.[140] Because there is scarcely any business record which could avoid exclusion on this ground, it may be best to give the court power to inquire into the circumstances of the record-making, and to exclude it only if the self-serving nature of the document would indicate a serious lack of trustworthiness.[141]

It could be argued that, even within the Court's strict definition of the business record section, the train engineer's report was admissible on the ground that it was within the railroad's business as such to investigate mishaps and to record observations in order to improve and ensure the efficient running of trains. Moreover, in the United States, the railroad has to deliver monthly reports of accidents to the

---

140 See this Chapter, II.C.1.(c).
141 See *Federal Rules of Evidence for United States Courts and Magistrates* (1975), Rule 803(6), 28 U.S.C.A.

appropriate governmental agency setting forth the nature and causes of the accidents and accordingly, it could be said that the engineer's statement relates in substance to the operation of the railroad as a business enterprise.[142]

In *Otney v. United States*,[143] the issue was whether certain documentary diagnostic evidence of the accused's mental competency could be introduced by the prosecution under the Federal business records statute to establish the accused's sanity. The United States Court of Appeals, while acknowledging that the statute was to be interpreted broadly, held the document inadmissible on the ground that the statute was never intended to apply to written psychiatric opinions made for purely evidentiary purposes. The purpose of the accused's mental examination was not for treatment or cure, which is the normal business of a hospital, but solely to enable psychiatrists to inform the Court whether he was fit to stand trial. It was therefore found to be outside the regular course of the hospital's business. Even in situations where the hospital report has been prepared for both a 'business' and litigation purpose, it will be excluded. In *Horn v. Sturm*[144] there were two reasons for the preparation of an autopsy report: (1) to obtain information which would be helpful in the treatment of future patients; and (2) to obtain information useful in prosecuting or defending a damage action. The Court held the report inadmissible in the malpractice action because one of the reasons for its preparation was for use in litigation. The commercial aspect of the document as it relates to business must be paramount.

The *Canada Evidence Act* has its own business records provision which differs in some material respects from those of the provinces. Under the *Canada Evidence Act* the only major condition of admissibility is that the document be made in the usual and ordinary course of business. It does not contain the second condition as found in the provincial statutes, that it is in the usual and ordinary course of such business to make such a record. Thus, a train engineer's report of an accident as in *Palmer v. Hoffman*,[145] for example, might be admissible under the *Canada Evidence Act* if it were applicable, whereas it would be inadmissible under the provincial statute. Although the train

---

142 Now see (1970), 45 U.S.C., s. 38.
143 340 F. 2d 696 (10th c., O.S.C.A., 1965).
144 408 P. 2d 541 (Okl. S.C., 1965).
145 *Supra*, note 139.

engineer's report would be made in his usual and ordinary course of business, it may not have been the usual and ordinary course of business of the railroad to make such documents. Even though the business necessity test may not be as stringent under the federal statute, there must be some demonstration that the document was made in the usual and ordinary course of business. The mere fact that a document was prepared by a business organization, without more, may not be sufficient to qualify.

In *R. v. Zundel*,[146] a document prepared by the International Red Cross denying the compilation of statistics was tendered as a business record of that organization at a trial of an accused charged with publishing a knowingly false statement. The accused, in a pamphlet that he published, denied the existence of the Holocaust in World War II, relying upon statistics allegedly compiled by the International Red Cross. The Ontario Court of Appeal held that the International Red Cross' document, and therefore any excerpts from it, were not established to have been made in the usual and ordinary course of business of the Red Cross and therefore were inadmissible under s. 30 of the *Canada Evidence Act*.

(c) *Contemporaneous Record*

The provincial statutory provisions expressly require that the record be made "at the time of such act, transaction, occurrence or event or within a reasonable time thereafter". Although the *Canada Evidence Act* does not contain such an express temporal condition, s. 30(6) allows the court to investigate the total "circumstances in which the information contained in the record was written, recorded, stored or reproduced, and draw any reasonable inference from the form or content of the record". In the *Setak*[147] case it was emphasized:[148]

A substantial factor in the reliability of any system of records is the promptness with which transactions are recorded. Unless it

---

146 (1987), 31 C.C.C. (3d) 97, 56 C.R. (3d) 1, 18 O.A.C. 161, 58 O.R. (2d) 129, 35 D.L.R. (4th) 338, 29 C.R.R. 349 (C.A.), at 208-09 (O.A.C.). Leave to appeal to S.C.C. refd. (1987), 61 O.R. (2d) 588*n*.
147 *Setak Computer Services Corp. v. Burroughs Business Machines Ltd.* (1977), 15 O.R. (2d) 750, 76 D.L.R. (3d) 641 (H.C.J.).
148 *Ibid.*, at 760-61 (O.R.). In *Matheson v. Barnes*, [1981] 2 W.W.R. 435, at 438 (B.C.S.C.), a three-week delay was held not to be sufficiently contemporaneous.

appears from the context of the record, or the testimony of the witness introducing the writings or records into evidence, that the act, transaction, occurrence or event described therein occurred within a reasonable time before the making of the writing or record, then such writing or record should not be admitted for the purpose of proving those matters. Where there is evidence of some delay in transcribing, then in each case, it would seem to me, the Court must decide, as a matter of fact, whether the time span between the transaction and the recording thereof was so great as to suggest the danger of inaccuracy by lapse of memory.

(d) *Personal Knowledge and Duty of Declarant*

Another notable feature of the provincial enactments is that they contemplate the admissibility of a record based upon hearsay. It is expressly provided that lack of personal knowledge by the maker of the record will not affect the admissibility of the document, although it may go to the question of weight.[149] Thus, a record based upon information given to the maker is nevertheless admissible. This provision, however, may not necessarily receive a broad interpretation from the courts. The New York Court of Appeal's decision in *Johnson v. Lutz*,[150] which has been referred to by a number of Canadian courts, is of importance in this regard. In the *Johnson* case, which was an action arising out of a motorcycle accident, entries contained in a police officer's report were held to be inadmissible on the ground that they were not based upon the officer's personal knowledge but upon information given to him by a bystander. The Court held that the police report did not fall within the New York equivalent of the provincial business records provisions notwithstanding the explicit provision contained in the New York statute to the effect that:

> All other circumstances of the making of . . . [the] record, including lack of personal knowledge by the entrant or maker . . . shall not affect its admissibility.

---

149 In *Winnipeg South Child & Family Services v. S. (R.)* (1986), 40 Man. R. (2d) 64, at 68 (Q.B.), no weight was given to second-hand hearsay.
150 253 N.Y. 124, 170 N.E. 517 (1930, N.Y.C.A.).

The Court held that the police report of the accident was not a record made in the regular course of business in the sense that the legislature intended.[151] The report was based on statements made voluntarily to the police officer. The party informant was under no duty to make a statement to the police officer. To come within the statutory provision, the Court held that it had to be shown not only that the maker of the record was acting pursuant to a business duty, but that the person from whom he received the information was acting under a business duty as well. It is the business element of the record which gives it credence and efficacy. Without it, the purpose of the legislation is lost. The reliability of the record turns on the maker's duty to make the entry and upon the duty of the informant to give the information to the maker. Neither the New York statute nor the provincial equivalents precludes the maker of the record from relying on hearsay information. He need not have firsthand personal knowledge of the fact that he is recording. It can be based on the information given to him by others; but, in light of *Johnson v. Lutz*, it could be said that the informant must be under a business duty to impart that information to the maker. Both the statement and its basis must be made entirely in the course of business.[152]

Unless there is some guarantee of reliability in the particular circumstances, the general practice of allowing in business records based on hearsay is inherently dangerous. However, the wording of the provincial enactments is explicit and has taken heed of the weakness of multiple hearsay. The legislatures expressly stated that such weakness was to go to the question of weight alone and not to admissibility. In the decisions that have involved these provisions the courts, however, have shown a propensity to follow the rationale in *Johnson v. Lutz* rather than the literalness of the provision.

In *Adderly v. Bremner*,[153] Brooke J. held that only that part of the hospital record which relates to occurrences taking place in the

---

151 See also *Woods v. Elias* (1978), 21 O.R. (2d) 840 (Co. Ct.).
152 But see *Simpson v. Lever*, [1962] 3 All E.R. 870 (Q.B.), where Winn J. admitted a police officer's book containing an unsigned statement of an unavailable witness under a differently worded English provision. Most of the American authorities have confirmed the principle in *Johnson v. Lutz, supra*, note 150; see *Mirandi v. State*, 707 P. 2d 1121 (1985), cert. denied 106 S. Ct. 1239, and E.W. Cleary (ed.), *McCormick on Evidence*, 3rd ed. (St. Paul: West Publishing, 1984), at 879.
153 [1968] 1 O.R. 621, 67 D.L.R. (2d) 274 (H.C.J.).

hospital and routinely recorded is admissible, but not that part of the record which relates to occurrences or events taking place prior to admission to the hospital and recorded as part of the case history. He stated:[154]

> . . . I do not think that the intention of the Legislature was to permit a plaintiff to prove his case by introducing as proof of the truth of its content the history that may be amongst the hospital records — being a history that the plaintiff or some other person had recounted on the plaintiff's admission to or while in hospital. Nor do I think it was the intention of the Legislature to open to a plaintiff a means of escaping the test of truth through cross-examination by resort to the hospital history record.

Thus, notwithstanding the express statutory provision, the court ruled inadmissible self-serving statements made by a patient to his doctor and recorded in a hospital note. The case suggests that such statements by the patient do not fall within the purely business nature of hospital treatment and thus the decision in *Adderly v. Bremner* is consistent with *Johnson v. Lutz*.[155] Griffiths J. put it this way in the *Setak* case:[156]

> In my view . . . the limitations imposed by the *Johnson* case are sound and are in accord with the basic philosophy of the Act. The Act was intended to make admissible records which, because they were made pursuant to a regular business duty, are presumed to be reliable. The mere fact that recording of a third party statement is routine imports no guarantee of the truth of the statement, and to construe [the business record provision] as admitting hearsay evidence of any third party would make the section an almost limitless dragnet for the introduction of random testimony from volunteers outside of the business whose information would be quite beyond the reach of the usual test of accuracy. In my opinion, [the business record provision] of the *Evidence Act* should be interpreted as making hearsay statements admissible when both the maker of the writing or the entrant of

---

154 *Ibid.*, at 623 (O.R.), at 276 (D.L.R.).
155 The effect on admissibility of a motive to misrepresent facts in the record is discussed in this Chapter, II.C.2.(f).
156 *Supra*, note 147, at 762-63 (O.R.).

the record, and the informant or informants, if more than one, are each acting in the usual and ordinary course of business in entering and communicating an account of an act, transaction, occurrence or event.

Unlike the provincial counterparts, there is some ambiguity as to whether s. 30 of the *Canada Evidence Act* will sanction records based on information provided by others even if under a duty to do so. It should be noted that the opening words of s. 30 read:

> Where oral evidence in respect of a matter would be admissible in a legal proceeding . . .

The statute merely provides a method of proof of an admissible fact. It does not make the document admissible when oral testimony of the same fact would be inadmissible. One interpretation that is open is that if the maker of the record took the witness stand he could not testify as to what someone else told him. That would be inadmissible as hearsay and the same limitation applies to business records under s. 30 of the *Canada Evidence Act*. The federal provision does not have a subsection similar to the provincial provisions which state that a lack of personal knowledge does not affect the admissibility of the business record.

Only a few judicial decisions have considered this aspect of the *Canada Evidence Act* provision and they have tended not to be so restrictive in interpretation, and, in fact, have accepted the proposition that double hearsay is admissible under s. 30. In *R. v. Grimba*,[157] the Crown tendered expert fingerprint evidence to demonstrate that the fingerprints taken from the accused on his arrest were the same as those on a fingerprint record over the name of another individual obtained from the FBI identification records. The expert had not made the fingerprint record and had no personal knowledge of its accuracy but had been with the FBI for eleven years and described the FBI as serving as a reservoir for fingerprints. Callaghan J. admitted the evidence and stated:[158]

---

157 (1977), 38 C.C.C. (2d) 469 (Ont. Co. Ct.).
158 *Ibid.*, at 471. See also *R. v. Biasi* (1981), 62 C.C.C. (2d) 304, at 307 (B.C.S.C.); additional reasons at (1981), 66 C.C.C. (2d) 563 (*sub nom. R. v. Biasi (No. 2)*), and *R. v. Boles* (1984), 57 A.R. 232, at 235 (C.A.); *Apsassin v. Canada (Dept. of Indian*

Section 30 was placed into the *Canada Evidence Act* in 1968 . . . It would appear that the rationale behind that section for admitting a form of hearsay evidence is the inherent circumstantial guarantee of accuracy which one would find in a business context from records which are relied upon in the day to day affairs of individual businesses, and which are subsequent to frequent testing and cross-checking. Records thus systematically stored, produced and regularly relied upon should, it would appear under s. 30, not be barred from this Court's consideration simply because they contained hearsay or double hearsay.

(e) *Record of Facts*

The *Adderly v. Bremner*[159] case would also exclude hospital records, which contain subjective data such as a doctor or nurse's diagnosis, opinion or impression, on the ground that these do not constitute "an act, transaction, occurrence or event", within the meaning of the words in the provincial provision.[160] The Court's concern was, presumably, that the subjective opinion of doctors and

---

Affairs & Northern Development) (1987), 37 D.L.R. (4th) 257, [1987] C.N.L.R. 14, 10 F.T.R. 122 (*sub nom. Blueberry River Indian Band v. Canada (Minister of Indian Affairs & Northern Development)*), 17 C.P.C. (2d) 187; *R. v. Monkhouse*, 61 C.R. (3d) 343, [1988] 1 W.W.R. 725, 56 Alta. L.R. (2d) 97, 83 A.R. 62 (C.A.). An analysis of this issue is found in J.D. Ewart, *Documentary Evidence in Canada* (Toronto: Carswell, 1983), at 87-91.

159 *Supra*, note 153.

160 American Federal courts have been ambivalent in interpreting records of an "act, transaction, occurrence or event". Some have preferred a narrow interpretation so as to exclude medical diagnoses and prognoses: *New York Life Insurance Co. v. Taylor*, 147 F. 2d 297 (1945); *England v. United States*, 174 F. 2d 466 (1949); *Lyles v. United States*, 254 F. 2d 725 (1957), cert. denied 356 U.S. 961; *Skogen v. Dow Chemical Co.*, 375 F. 2d 692 (1967). Others have liberally admitted diagnostic records: *Reed v. Order of United Commercial Travellers*, 123 F. 2d 252 (1941); *Buckminster's Estate v. Commr. of Internal Revenue*, 147 F. 2d 331 (1944); *Medina v. Erickson*, 226 F. 2d 475 (1955); *Thomas v. Hogan*, 308 F. 2d 355 (1962); *Glawe v. Rulon*, 284 F. 2d 495 (1960). State courts, for the most part, have admitted such entries: *Borucki v. MacKenzie Bros. Co.*, 125 Conn. 92, 3 A. 2d 224 (1938); *People v. Koklmeyer*, 284 N.Y. 366, 31 N.E. 2d 490 (1940); *Weis v. Weis*, 147 Ohio St. 416, 72 N.E. 2d 245 (1947); *Allen v. St. Louis Public Service Co.*, 365 Mo. 677, 285 S.W. 2d 663 (1956). The *Federal Rules of Evidence for United States Courts and Magistrates* (1975), Rule 803(6), adopts the view of liberal admissibility by expressly including "opinions or diagnoses" in addition to "acts, events, conditions".

nurses, based on their perception and not being subject to cross-examination, is not as trustworthy as the recording of purely objective data. This is particularly true of psychiatric opinions and thus reports of this nature are not admissible under the provincial enactments. As indicated by Morand J., in *Aynsley v. Toronto General Hospital*,[161] the Ontario provision contemplates the admissibility of records containing only objective facts:[162]

> ... that would mean that such routine entries in a hospital record as the date of admittance, the time of admittance, the name of the attending physician, the routine orders as to care of the patient such as the administration of drugs, notation by the nurse of taking temperatures ...

In this context, the result in *Adderly v. Bremner*[163] should be compared with the decision by the Supreme Court of Canada in *Ares v. Venner*.[164] The subjective opinions of doctors and nurses contained in hospital records are inadmissible under the business record legislation, according to the *Bremner* case, but admissible at common law according to the *Ares* case. Thus, notwithstanding the existence of business record statutes in Canada, the decision in *Ares v. Venner* is of considerable practical importance.

It is curious that the exclusion of statements of opinion is recognized in view of the fact that the *Canada Evidence Act* allows for the admissibility of records "in respect of a matter". It could be argued that the use of the general word "matter" contemplates records containing opinions and other subjective data. As noted, the provincial business records provisions permit records of "any act, transaction, occurrence or event". There are no words of limitation so as to restrict the nature of the record; yet the courts have done so. McCormick is of the view that "the opinion rule should be restricted to governing the manner of presenting courtroom testimony and should have little application to the admissibility of out-of-court statements".[165] More-

---

161 [1968] 1 O.R. 425, 66 D.L.R. (2d) 575; varied on other grounds [1969] 2 O.R. 829, 7 D.L.R. (3d) 193; affd. (*sub nom. Toronto General Hospital Trustees v. Matthews*), [1972] S.C.R. 435, 25 D.L.R. (3d) 241.
162 *Ibid.*, at 432 (O.R.), at 582 (D.L.R.).
163 *Supra*, note 153.
164 [1970] S.C.R. 608, 12 C.R.N.S. 349, 14 D.L.R. (3d) 4, 73 W.W.R. 347.
165 *McCormick on Evidence, supra*, note 152, at 875.

over, this narrow interpretation by the courts is not in keeping with the Supreme Court of Canada's expansion of the common-law exception which clearly encompassed statements of opinion. It is illogical to maintain a restrictive interpretation in respect of business records legislation.

(f) *Absence of Motive to Misrepresent*

Is the admissibility of business records which are based on hearsay information affected if the information is essentially self-serving? Does the legislation mandate admissibility in such circumstances or may courts insist upon a requirement that there be the absence of any motive to misrepresent by the declarant? These questions have been raised in the context of hospital records.

First, it has been held that hospital records constitute business records. Although the hospital record relates to matters extraneous to the business of running a hospital (e.g., the cause of a patient's injury), these matters are important to the administration of medical care to the patient. Information provided by the patient as to the cause of injury is required in the diagnosis and treatment of the injury, and that is the very business of a hospital. In *Melton v. St. Louis Public Service Co.*,[166] the Supreme Court of Missouri held admissible under a comparable business records statute a hospital record containing statements describing the cause of the accident in which the patient was injured. In so doing, the Court expressed its conclusion in this way:[167]

The hospital wanted to know how the patient got hurt. This was helpful to the hospital because it aided in determining the nature and extent and proper treatment of the plaintiff's injury. The patient stated how he got hurt. The statement was recorded for the apparent purpose of furthering the hospital's business of determining the nature and extent and proper treatment of the injury; and the record of the statement was apparently made by some one of the hospital staff who presumably, in the circumstances of the recording, had no occasion to falsify the record. The record was surely of something — an act, condition or event — in the regular course of the hospital's business.

---

166 363 Mo. 474, 251 S.W. 2d 663 (1952).
167 *Ibid.*, at 671 (S.W.).

But would this open the door to the admissibility of self-serving statements by a declarant who had a motive to misrepresent the facts? Are such statements so unreliable as to warrant exclusion, even in the face of the clear words of the statute? It has been urged that if the maker of the statement has a motive to falsify he should not be allowed to have such evidence admitted under the guise of business records without any test of cross-examination.[168] In *Northern Wood Preservers Ltd. v. Hall Corp. (Shipping) 1969 Ltd.*,[169] Lacourcière J. excluded an entry in a log book which was tendered as a business record under the Ontario *Evidence Act*, because, notwithstanding it was made contemporaneously with the event and in pursuance of a duty to record, such motive to misrepresent may have been present. Yet the Ontario Court of Appeal has not considered the motive to misrepresent too great a hazard in admitting business records under this provision in other areas. In *Conley v. Conley*,[170] for example, the notes of a private investigator as to observations of the adulterous conduct of the respondents were admitted under the Ontario *Evidence Act*, notwithstanding the fact that they were prepared for and tendered on behalf of the party litigant. Are such records any more reliable than hospital records containing self-serving statements by patients? Or, for that matter, are the latter any the less trustworthy than medical reports prepared on behalf of a party litigant which are admissible specifically under s. 52 of the Ontario *Evidence Act*?[171] With respect to all of these reports, the record was prepared in situations where there existed the possibility of a motive to misrepresent. They are not records merely setting out objective data of a business nature. They were made either for the purpose of litigation or at a time when

---

168 The British Columbia *Evidence Act*, R.S.B.C. 1979, c. 116, s. 48(3) provides that a business statement will be inadmissible if it was made by a person interested at a time when proceedings were pending or anticipated involving a dispute as to a fact which the statement might tend to establish. This provision was interpreted in *Denis Shipping Ltd. v. Palmer* (1973), 33 D.L.R. (3d) 760 (B.C. Co. Ct.), as applying to situations where a controversy has arisen and a statement is made expressly as a result thereof. But the fact that a statement, such as that contained in time books, is made for the express purpose of preventing disputes does not render the record inadmissible.

169 [1972] 3 O.R. 751, 29 D.L.R. (3d) 413 (H.C.J.); affd. 2 O.R. (2d) 335, 42 D.L.R. (3d) 679 (C.A.).

170 [1968] 2 O.R. 677, 70 D.L.R. (2d) 352 (C.A.).

171 R.S.O. 1980, c. 145, s. 52 [re-en. 1989, c. 68, s. 1].

litigation was foreseeable and contemplated.

Or should the legislative provision permitting the admissibility of hearsay-based business records prevail and any evidence of the existence of a motive to misrepresent on the part of the declarant only go to weight and not cause exclusion? In *Setak*,[172] Griffiths J. disagrees with the decision in *Northern Wood*.[173] He stated:[174]

> It is my view that once the writings or records meet the criteria of s. 36, the Court has no discretion as to whether or not they should be admitted, but may in the circumstances attach no weight to them.

Different considerations apply in the prosecution of regulatory offences, specifically if there are substantial penalties or penal consequences. In the context of quasi-criminal statutes the reasoning in *Northern Wood* is applicable. Also, unlike civil proceedings, there is no opportunity to examine the opposite party with respect to the documents.

(g) *Records Made in the Course of Investigation*

In the *Canada Evidence Act*, s. 30(10)(a) expressly denies admissibility to records made "in the course of an investigation or inquiry".[175] In the absence of such words in the provincial legislation the statements should be admitted and any circumstances of motivation should be left to the question of weight.

---

172 *Setak Computer Services Corp. v. Burroughs Business Machines Ltd.* (1977), 15 O.R. (2d) 750, 76 D.L.R. (3d) 641 (Ont. H.C.J.).

173 *Northern Wood Preservers Ltd. v. Hall Corp. (Shipping) 1969 Ltd.*, *supra*, note 169.

174 *Supra*, note 172, at 758 (O.R.).

175 In *R. v. McLarty (No. 3)* (1978), 45 C.C.C. (2d) 184 (Ont. G.S.P.) the Ont. Co. Ct. held that the investigation or inquiry contemplated by this section is of the type envisaged by the *Inquiries Act* and in the form of a coroner's inquest and not one carried on by a police force as part of its normal business. Yet in *R. v. Sunila* (1986), 26 C.C.C. (3d) 331, 73 N.S.R. (2d) 308, 176 A.P.R. 308 (*sub nom. R. v. Sunila (No. 2)*) (N.S.T.P.), it was held that records which set out details of the surveillance of ships suspected of transporting drugs were inadmissible since the surveillance constituted an investigation.

(h) *Business Records Subject to Other Exclusionary Rules*

The *Canada Evidence Act* in s. 30(10)(a) specifically preserves a right to assert privilege in respect of the matters contained in the record.[176] Moreover, if the record was made by or alludes to someone who would not be competent and compellable as a witness to disclose the matters contained in the record, then such record will not be received.[177]

Although provincial legislation contains no such provision, it is logical to believe that there would be exclusion for these reasons as well.

(i) *Negative Inferences from Records*

Section 30(2) of the *Canada Evidence Act* expressly provides for a negative inference which the court can draw from the absence of relevant information in the record and may conclude that the matter which was not recorded did not occur or exist. In *R. v. Garofoli*[178] the Ontario Court of Appeal suggested that resort to this provision is the appropriate way of leading evidence of this fact rather than merely calling a witness to testify that he could not find any relevant entry in the record. In that case, the Court stated that such a witness who testifies that he personally examined customs records to see whether any cars had been imported by the accused, would be stating non-admissible hearsay. The Court said the proper method of adducing such evidence is to utilize s. 30(2) of the *Canada Evidence Act* and produce the custom records thus giving rise to the inference of the non-occurrence of the importation from the fact that there was no entry of it in the records.

No similar provision is contained in provincial legislation, but it appears that there is nothing to prevent a trial judge from drawing such an inference.

---

176 See *R. v. McLarty (No. 3), ibid.*, at 187; *R. v. Sanghi* (1971), 6 C.C.C. (2d) 123, 3 N.S.R. (2d) 70 (C.A.).
177 See *R. v. Heilman* (1983), 22 Man. R. (2d) 173 (Co. Ct.).
178 (1988), 41 C.C.C. (3d) 97, at 149, 64 C.R. (3d) 193, 27 O.A.C. 1, at 39-40 (C.A.); revd. on other grounds (1990), 60 C.C.C. (3d) 161, 80 C.R. (3d) 317 (S.C.C.). See also *R. v. Gould* (1990), 57 C.C.C. (3d) 500, 78 C.R. (3d) 151 (B.C.C.A.).

(j) Records Kept by Computer Systems

Computer printouts are now a part of everyday business life. Such methods of record-keeping were not contemplated when the business records legislation was originated. Accordingly, in the absence of special legislation to deal specifically with computer records, it would appear that the courts will apply principles to this type of record analogous to those they apply to general business documents. Courts have permitted the introduction of computer bank records under s. 29 of the *Canada Evidence Act* but have required as a condition of admissibility that a foundation be established to demonstrate the reliability generally of the input of entries, storage of information and its retrieval and presentation.[179] Some courts have accepted the reliability of computers without stipulating any preconditions to the admissibility of their printouts under s. 30.[180] Although the cases to date have dealt primarily with bank computer records and their admissibility pursuant to s. 29 of the *Canada Evidence Act*,[181] there is no reason to believe that computer-generated records would not be admissible under s. 30 of the *Canada Evidence Act*. To admit them, however, would require acknowledgement that double or multiple hearsay would not be a bar to the application of s. 30.[182] Moreover, there would have to be some relaxation of the strict interpretation of the double duty test.[183]

As stated by Bull J.A., in *R. v. Vanlerberghe*:[184]

[Section 30] clearly covers mechanical as well as manual bookkeeping records and the keeping of records, and the flow-out or printout of that bookkeeping system clearly falls within the meaning of "records" in s. 30 and was therefore admissible.

---

179 See *R. v. McMullen* (1979), 47 C.C.C. (2d) 499, 25 O.R. (2d) 301, 100 D.L.R. (3d) 671, at 506 (C.C.C.).

180 *R. v. Vanlerberghe* (1978), 6 C.R. (3d) 222 (B.C.C.A.); *R. v. Sanghi, supra,* note 176.

181 The admissibility of banking records under this provision is discussed in detail in J.D. Ewart, *Documentary Evidence in Canada* (Toronto: Carswell, 1983), Chapter 4.

182 See this Chapter, II.C.2.(d). See also Chapter 18, I., II.B.3.(c) and III.B.

183 See this Chapter, II.C.2.(b).

184 *Supra,* note 180, at 224.

(k) *Notice*

There is a major distinction between the federal and provincial provision with respect to the requirement of notice. Both s. 30(7) of the *Canada Evidence Act* and the provincial sections provide that the party who intends to introduce the business record must give an opponent seven days' notice of his or her intention to do so and the opposite party has the right of inspection of the record within five days thereafter. Under both federal and provincial legislation, notice is a condition precedent to admissibility.[185] Under s. 30(7) of the *Canada Evidence Act*, such notice, however, may be dispensed with by an order of the court. If the record is simple and not detailed, the court may well exercise its statutory discretion and make an order allowing for the admission of the business record, notwithstanding the absence of notice, if it feels that the opposite party will not be severely prejudiced as a result of such lack of notice. By way of contrast, it is interesting to note that the Ontario *Evidence Act* gives no similar discretion to the trial judge to dispense with notice. Thus, under s. 35 of the Ontario *Evidence Act*, no relief is available to the proponent of a business record if he fails to give the requisite notice, in which case he must resort to calling as witnesses the persons who made the actual entries on the record.[186] Both statutes are silent as to the form of notice to be given, but it is clear that the notice should contain a sufficient description of the record to be tendered so that the opposite party is informed of the precise documents to be submitted.

(l) *Reform Proposals*

The proposed draft *Uniform Evidence Act*[187] prefers the singular standard found in s. 30 of the *Canada Evidence Act* that the record be made in the usual and ordinary course of business over the dual business requirement as found in the provincial legislation. Moreover,

---

185 *R. v. Mudie* (1974), 20 C.C.C. (2d) 262 (Ont. C.A.); *R. v. Frenette* (1977), 23 N.S.R. (2d) 74, 32 A.P.R. 74 (C.A.); *R. v. Rowbotham* (1977), 33 C.C.C. (2d) 411, 2 C.R. (3d) 244 (Ont. G.S.P.); *R. v. Mahoney* (1986), 47 Alta. L.R. (2d) 185, 73 A.R. 226 (C.A.). Notice need not be given if the document had been admitted at a preliminary inquiry: see *R. v. Penno* (1977), 35 C.C.C. (2d) 266, 37 C.R.N.S. 391, [1977] 3 W.W.R. 361, 76 D.L.R. (3d) 529 (B.C.C.A.); *R. v. Voykin* (1986), 29 C.C.C. (3d) 280, 71 A.R. 241 (C.A.).
186 *Re Waltson Properties Ltd.* (1976), 17 O.R. (2d) 328, 80 D.L.R. (3d) 271, 23 C.B.R. (N.S.) 188 (H.C.J.), at 331 (O.R.).
187 See Bill S-33, 1980-81-82 (withdrawn: see *supra*, note 60).

with the removal of the opening words of s. 30 and the express provision, "whether or not any statement contained in it is hearsay" it would be made clear that double hearsay poses no problem for the admissibility of evidence under this provision. The proposed enactment also expressly acknowledges the admissibility of opinions so long as proof is tendered that the opinion was given in the usual and ordinary course of business and, therefore, is not collateral. What is troubling is, however, the maintaining of the right in a court by s. 155(1) of the draft *Uniform Evidence Act* to take into account for the purposes of admissibility all the circumstances surrounding the making of the record. One would have preferred that these factors go to the weight of the evidence alone, as is the case in the provincial legislation. By leaving full discretion to the courts to consider all manner of circumstances it would not be surprising to see the limitations which have traditionally affected the question of admissibility (such as the declarant's motives) creeping back into judicial decisions. On the other hand, in prosecutions for quasi-criminal or regulatory offences, more stringent conditions of admissibility are justified.

D. *Declarations as to Reputation*

1. General

Statements made by persons as to reputations of public or general rights, marital relationships and ancient historical matters are admissible under this common-law exception. The rationale for this head of admissibility, like the other exceptions, turns on the elements of necessity and circumstantial probability of reliability. It is necessary because the subject-matter of the declaration is so ancient in time that no primary evidence to substantiate the fact exists.[188] It also carries with it a certain degree of reliability on the ground that because the reputation affects the community as a whole or a family, it is probably trustworthy for the reputation would not have developed otherwise. Lord Campbell in *R. v. Bedfordshire Inhabitants*[189] summed it up as follows:[190]

---

188 *Weeks v. Sparke* (1813), 1 M. & S. 679, 105 E.R. 253; *Berkeley Peerage Case* (1811), 4 Camp. 401, at 415, 171 E.R. 128, at 134-35.
189 (1855), 4 E. & B. 535, 24 L.J.Q.B. 81, 119 E.R. 196.
190 *Ibid.*, at 542 (E. & B.), at 84 (L.J.Q.B.), at 198 (E.R.).

The admissibility of the declarations of deceased persons in such cases is sanctioned, because these rights and liabilities are generally of ancient and obscure origin, and may be acted upon only at distant intervals of time; because direct proof of their existence therefore ought not to be required; because in local matters, in which the community are interested, all persons living in the neighbourhood are likely to be conversant; because, common rights and liabilities being naturally talked of in public, what is dropped in conversation respecting them may be presumed to be true; because conflicting interests would lead to contradiction from others if the statements were false; and thus a trustworthy reputation may arise from the concurrence of many parties unconnected with each other, who are all interested in investigating the subject.

The evidence must be of a reputation that exists. Since a reputation is a distillation of numerous opinions and individual statements, it follows that a statement by a deceased declarant, respecting a mere rumour or a few isolated comments or an observation of a fact from which reputation is inferred, is insufficient to constitute a true reputation.[191] It is the existence of an unchallenged reputation together with its longevity which assures its reliability.

2. Public or General Rights

Declarations by individuals relating to the reputation of a public or general right have been held admissible if certain conditions are established. As with other common-law exceptions to the hearsay rule, it is a precondition to admissibility that the declarant be dead.[192] Since

---

191 Baron Wood in *Moseley v. Davies* (1822), 11 Price 162, stated at 180: "[I]t must further be proved that the declarations establishing the reputation, and the acts done [by the community] in consequence, were the result of a received reputation . . . the principle use of evidence of this sort is to shew that the act done or declaration made was not a new thought adapted to serve some particular occasion, but the consequence of a received notion of the existence of a custom requiring the performance of the act, and accounting for or explaining it by such declaration. Such evidence should always be general . . ."; see also *R. v. Bliss* (1837), 7 Ad. & El. 550, [1835-42] All E.R. Rep. 372.
192 But see *Ontario (Attorney General) v. Bear Island Foundation* (1984), 15 D.L.R. (4th) 321, 49 O.R. (2d) 353, [1985] 1 C.N.L.R. 1 (H.C.J.), at 338 (D.L.R.), where the evidence was admitted even though the declarants were living or unidentified.

the subject-matter of the declaration usually involves reputation of ancient rights, the statements, in all likelihood, would be those of deceased persons. This precondition, however, is just as applicable where the right in question is contemporary.

The right or interest in question must be of a public or general nature as opposed to private. Rights are public if they affect the interest of the community as a whole, and such matters as right of highway,[193] or ferry,[194] or the right of the public to make use of ports or fishery in tidal waters,[195] have been recognized as such. General rights, on the other hand, are those affecting a segment of the community only, and usually fall within the category of customs and land boundaries of a particular township, county, or a municipal region.[196] Thus, reputation evidence with respect to such matters is admissible. Evidence of private rights, however, is not. Accordingly, if the right in question is one in which the inhabitants of the community as a whole do not have a common interest, then it cannot be said to be public in nature. Evidence on a boundary to show that land was owned by a particular person would not affect the community at large and therefore, it has been held inadmissible.[197] In *VanKoughnet v. Denison*[198] maps of the City of Toronto made by city surveyors in 1857 and 1858, showing a square marked "Bellevue Square", were tendered as evidence of the boundaries of the square. It was held that the maps could not be introduced to establish the demarcation of the boundaries, and were only admissible to show that there existed a public square known as "Bellevue Square".[199]

The reputation of the public or general right contained in the declaration must relate directly to the right itself and not to particular facts from which the existence or non-existence of the right may be

---

193 *Baldwin v. O'Brien* (1917), 40 O.L.R. 24, at 49 (C.A.); *Fulton v. Creelman*, [1931] S.C.R. 221, [1931] 1 D.L.R. 733.

194 *Pim v. Curell* (1840), 6 M. & W. 234, 151 E.R. 395 (Exch. Ct.).

195 *Neill v. Duke of Devonshire* (1882), 8 App. Cas. 135, at 186 (H.L.).

196 *Nicholls v. Parker* (1805), 14 East. 331*n*; *Berry v. Banner* (1792), Peake 156.

197 *Doe d. Didsbury v. Thomas* (1811), 14 East. 323, 104 E.R. 625. See also *Dunphy v. Phillips* (1929), 1 M.P.R. 227 (N.B.C.A.).

198 (1885), 11 O.A.R. 699 (C.A.).

199 Stephen J., in *Pipe v. Fulcher* (1858), 1 E. & E. 111, quoted in *VanKoughnet v. Denison, ibid.*, at 708, stated: "Statements of facts in issue, made in published maps or charts, generally offered for public sale, as to matters of public notoriety, such as the relative positions of towns or countries, are themselves relevant facts, but such statements are irrelevant if they relate to matters of private concern."

inferred. In *R. v. Bliss*,[200] the question in issue was whether a specific road was a public highway and a statement by a deceased resident of the community that he had planted a willow tree to mark the boundary of the roadway was tendered as proof thereof. The Court rejected the statement, for it of itself was not evidence of reputation but merely evidence of a particular fact.[201] Similarly, the Ontario Court of Appeal in *O'Connor v. Dunn*[202] rejected a surveyor's note of the location of a boundary of a township based upon measurements that he had taken, for such a note constituted an act that he performed and was not reputation evidence within the purview of the exception.[203]

Furthermore, the right or interest of the community must be pecuniary in nature. It is insufficient if the community interest is merely one of curiosity. It must affect the legal or proprietary rights of the populace.[204]

With respect to public rights, it is not necessary to establish that the declarant had competent knowledge of the reputation, for the right being a public one, everyone is presumed to have the requisite knowledge. That is not the case, however, with respect to declarations relating to general rights. In the case of the latter, it must be shown that the declarant bore some relationship to the community. The distinction was articulated by Parke B., in *Crease v. Barrett*,[205] as follows:[206]

> . . . in cases of rights or customs, which are . . . of a general nature . . . hearsay evidence is not admissible, unless it is derived from persons conversant with the neighbourhood . . .
>
> . . . Where the right is really public . . . it seems difficult to say that there ought to be any such limitation; and we are not aware that there is any case in which it has been laid down that such exists.

---

200 (1837), 7 Ad. & El. 550, 7 L.J.Q.B. 4.
201 *Ibid.*, at 554 (Ad. & El.): ". . . proof of declarations that the line of road in question had always been used as public would have been admissible": per Patteson J.
202 (1876), 39 U.C.Q.B. 597; revd. on other grounds, 2 O.A.R. 247 (C.A.).
203 See also *A.G. v. Horner (No. 2)*, [1913] 2 Ch. 140 (C.A.).
204 *R. v. Bedfordshire Inhabitants* (1855), 4 E. & B. 535, 24 L.J.Q.B. 81, 119 E.R. 196, at 542 (E. & B.), at 198 (E.R.).
205 (1835), 1 Cr. M. & R. 919, 149 E.R. 1353.
206 *Ibid.*, at 1357 (E.R.).

One other condition that must be met is that the declaration must have been made *ante litem motam*, i.e., before any dispute or controversy over the right has arisen.[207] This requirement would eliminate more than declarations made after the initiation of litigation. If the dispute had advanced to the point where it would be likely to produce bias in the mind of the declarant, the statement would not be allowed even if a formal legal action has not been instituted.

3. Marriage

Reputation evidence is admissible to establish the existence or non-existence of the marriage between two parties.[208] Such evidence was accepted in the case of *Re Taylor; Taylor v. Taylor*[209] to show that a marriage between gypsies had been celebrated. Not only is general reputation evidence admissible under this head but, even if there is no other corroborative evidence, it may be sufficient to prove the existence or non-existence of marriage.[210] Reputation evidence includes the general opinion of persons who may be interested in the marriage. It is not limited to the testimony of relatives or neighbours but also encompasses the opinion of persons who knew the parties and their reputation.[211] Its rationale has been expressed as follows:[212]

> The public had an interest in the question of the existence of a marriage between two persons — the propriety of visiting them,

---

207 *Moseley v. Davies* (1822), 11 Price 162, at 180.

208 The reputation may either support the fact of marriage or negative it. "The evidence of general reputation that the parties were not married was just as strong as, if not stronger than, any evidence of reputation in favour of a marriage": per Orde J.A., in *Knowlton v. Knowlton* (1924), 26 O.W.N. 164, at 165 (C.A.).

209 [1961] 1 W.L.R. 9 (C.A.).

210 *Doe d. Fleming v. Fleming* (1827), 4 Bing. 266; *Graham v. Law* (1857), 6 U.C.C.P. 310, at 313 (C.A.); *Doe d. Wheeler v. McWilliams* (1846), 2 U.C.Q.B. 77, at 79 (C.A.). Although reputation evidence may be sufficient proof of marriage in civil proceedings, it will not suffice in criminal cases involving charges of bigamy or adultery, where proof of marriage is essential, on the ground that it is the right of the accused to have the marriage strictly proven: *R. v. Foster* (1935), 62 C.C.C. 263, [1935] 1 D.L.R. 252, 8 M.P.R. 10 (N.B.C.A.). Nor will it be conclusive in civil actions for criminal conversation in those remaining jurisdictions where this cause of action has not been abolished.

211 *Moore v. Moore*, [1947] O.R. 249, [1947] 3 D.L.R. 531 (C.A.), at 251-52 (O.R.); *Evans v. Morgan* (1832), 2 C. & J. 453, at 456 (Exch.).

212 R.W. Baker, *The Hearsay Rule* (London: Pitman, 1950), at 132.

the liability of the man for the woman's debts (at that time), the competency of either to enter into new relationships — these were matters which necessarily interested the community in which the parties lived. Such being the case, it was reasonable to suppose that due inquiry had been made as to the relationship and therefore the community repute had sufficient trustworthiness to justify it being received in evidence despite its hearsay character.

Unlike reputation evidence of public or general rights, it need not be shown that the declarant is deceased. Thus, living individuals may testify with respect to the existence of the reputation in the community.[213]

The form of reputation evidence is not limited to oral opinion. Evidence of the parties' relationship to one another or their conduct may be sufficient to establish reputation. In *Forbes v. Forbes*,[214] evidence that a party introduced the other party to his friends as his wife was admissible. In *R. v. Proud*,[215] a widow claimed against the Crown under an insurance policy taken out by the deceased under the *Returned Soldiers' Insurance Act*. In defence, the Crown alleged that satisfactory evidence of the marriage had not been adduced. In rejecting this contention, Duff J. held that the evidence that the applicant lived with the deceased openly, had children by him, whom he acknowledged to be legitimate, and was accepted by people of repute as his wife, was quite sufficient. Similarly, documentary evidence between the parties is also admissible to establish reputation of a marriage. In *R. v. Debard*[216] the Court admitted letters between a husband and wife to prove the marital status of the parties.

With respect to family relationships other than marriage, there is some doubt as to whether community reputation will be admissible. In *Re Stavely; Ontario (A.G.) v. Brunsden*[217] it was acknowledged that reputation evidence was admissible to establish the illegitimacy of a person.[218] A different view, however, was taken by a New Brunswick

---

213 *Robb v. Robb* (1891), 20 O.R. 591, at 598; *Evans v. Morgan, supra*, note 211.
214 (1912), 20 O.W.R. 924, 3 O.W.N. 557, 3 D.L.R. 243 (H.C.J.).
215 [1926] S.C.R. 599, [1926] 3 D.L.R. 664.
216 (1918), 44 O.L.R. 427, 31 C.C.C. 122 (C.A.).
217 (1893), 24 O.R. 324 (C.P.).
218 General reputation of legitimacy was also considered proper evidence in favour of the legitimacy of the party in question in *Banbury Peerage Case* (1811),

court in *Re Anderson*[219] where in probate proceedings, community repute was held inadmissible to prove illegitimacy. Similarly, in *Doe d. Marr v. Marr*,[220] in which legitimacy had to be established in order to claim a right of inheritance, reputation evidence as to the mother having had illicit intercourse with another was rejected.

4. Matters of General History

Closely aligned to reputation evidence of public or general rights is reputation evidence of historical facts of general and public notoriety. Such reputation may be proven by written historical works known to be authorities in their field.[221] The event which is sought to be proved by the history or treatise must be an ancient one or at least one which was not observed by any living witness.[222] Furthermore, the event in question must be of general interest which would ensure that the matter was subjected to general public scrutiny so that the reputation thereof had become settled.

Recently, in claims for aboriginal title to lands, courts have received oral history to prove the existence of ancient culture and civilization, its antiquity and its assertion of rights over specific lands and fishing sites.[223]

E. *Declaration as to Pedigree and Family History*

One of the earliest exceptions to the hearsay rule was the admission of declarations by deceased individuals with respect to matters of family history relating to such things as familial relationship and descent, details of births, deaths, and marriages. The importance of

---

1 Sim. & St. 153, as referred to in 5 Wigmore, *Evidence*, § 1605, note 3.
219 [1947] 3 D.L.R. 302, 19 M.P.R. 339 (N.B.C.A.).
220 (1853), 3 U.C.C.P. 36, at 49 (C.A.).
221 5 Wigmore, *Evidence*, §§ 1597-99.
222 See *Ontario (Attorney General) v. Bear Island Foundation* (1984), 49 O.R. (2d) 353, [1985] 1 C.N.L.R. 1, 15 D.L.R. (4th) 321 (H.C.J.), at 339 (D.L.R.); affd. (1989), 68 O.R. (2d) 394, 32 O.A.C. 66, [1989] 2 C.N.L.R. 73, 58 D.L.R. (4th) 117, 4 R.P.R. (2d) 252 (C.A.); affd. (1991), 4 O.R. (3d) 133 (S.C.C.).
223 *R. v. Simon*, [1985] 2 S.C.R. 387, 23 C.C.C. (3d) 238, 71 N.S.R. (2d) 15, 171 A.P.R. 15, 24 D.L.R. (4th) 390, [1986] 1 C.N.L.R. 153, 62 N.R. 366, at 408 (S.C.R.); *Uukw v. British Columbia*, [1987] 6 W.W.R. 155, (*sub nom. Uukw v. R.*) 15 B.C.L.R. (2d) 326, (*sub nom. Delgamuukw v. British Columbia*) 40 D.L.R. (4th) 685 (S.C.).

this exception has been superseded to a great extent by the provincial statutes which require the maintenance of a uniform system of registration of births, marriages, deaths, adoptions, divorces, and changes of name.[224] The statutes also facilitate the proof of issues of pedigree by providing that certified copies of the registration are *prima facie* evidence of the facts so certified.[225] Nevertheless, this exception is still of some importance, particularly where the issue at trial is paternity of illegitimate children or the distribution of estates in which remote relatives have an interest.

As with declarations relating to public or general rights, the rationale for admitting this type of evidence is the general inability to secure other evidence of family relationships, and the inherent reliability or accuracy of statements made by relatives with respect to family matters with which they are intimately concerned. In *Re Stasun; Stasun v. Nesteroff*,[226] statements by the deceased to the effect that he had a brother in the old country and also that he had a brother named Peter Stasun in Lithuania, were admitted as evidence of the latter's status as next-of-kin to the deceased. Such declarations are:[227]

> The natural effusions of a party who must know the truth, and who speaks upon an occasion when his mind stands in an even position without any temptation to exceed or fall short of its truth.

The reliability is ensured only if the statements are made *ante litem motam*. The *lis* may encompass more than actual litigation. Rinfret J. in *Farren v. Pejepscot Paper Co.*[228] stated:[229]

> The phrase *ante litem motam* in itself might be capable of misconstruction. It contemplates a time anterior to the commencement of any actual controversy upon the point at issue.

---

224 For example, see *The Vital Statistics Act*, R.S.O. 1980, c. 524, s. 2 [am. 1990, c. 12, s. 2].

225 *Ibid.*, s. 42 [re-en. 1990, c. 12, s. 15].

226 (1967), 61 W.W.R. 694, 65 D.L.R. (2d) 340; revd. on other grounds (1969), 67 W.W.R. 224, [1969] 3 D.L.R. (3d) 22*n* (S.C.C.).

227 *Whitelocke v. Baker* (1807), 13 Ves. 511, at 514, quoted in *Re Woods; Brown v. Carter* (1912), 23 O.W.R. 353, 4 O.W.N. 388, at 355 (O.W.R.).

228 [1933] S.C.R. 388, [1933] 4 D.L.R. 92 (N.B.).

229 *Ibid.*, at 392 (S.C.R.), at 95 (D.L.R.); see also *Re Rosenmeyer; Porteous v. Dorn*, [1973] 4 W.W.R. 709, 37 D.L.R. (3d) 120, 12 R.F.L. 109; affd. (*sub nom. Porteous v. Dorn*), [1974] 6 W.W.R. 176, 45 D.L.R. (3d) 596, 2 N.R. 501.

Thus, if a dispute has arisen which is likely to create bias in members of the family, then a subsequent declaration as to pedigree will be inadmissible. The fact that the declarant was not aware of the controversy in question at the time that he made the statement is irrelevant.[230] In *Anderson v. Walden*,[231] a declaration of a deceased wife was tendered to the effect that her husband was the father of her child but was rejected because at the time that the declaration was made, proceedings had been launched by the husband for an order to commence a divorce action against her without naming the alleged father of the child in question as co-respondent. The Ontario Court of Appeal was not impressed with the argument that the declarant wife was unaware of that proceeding when she made the statement. Schroeder J.A. stated:[232]

> It does not appear that the deceased wife was aware of the institution or the contemplated institution of such proceedings founded upon the birth of the child Pauline, but upon the authorities cited, that fact would appear to be irrelevant. At the time of the making of the questioned declaration the dispute had already arisen although, for all that appears, the dispute was unknown to the declarant.

Statements, however, will not be rejected if they are made before any real dispute arose but with a view to their use in a prospective controversy over pedigree.[233] But declarations made by deceased relatives have been held inadmissible merely because they are favourable to the interest of the declarant. The statement made by the wife as to the legitimacy of her child was excluded in *Anderson v. Walden*[234] because *inter alia* she had an interest in making it, as divorce proceedings in which it was alleged that the child was born out of an adulterous relationship were pending against her. The Court took the view that "there was that degree of interest on the part of the deceased wife to make the declaration which was sufficient to exclude it as evidence against the defendant."[235]

---

230   *Shedden v. A.-G.* (1860), 2 Sw. & Tr. 170, 164 E.R. 958.
231   [1960] O.R. 50, 21 D.L.R. (2d) 279 (C.A.).
232   *Ibid.*, at 56 (O.R.).
233   *Shedden v. A.-G., supra*, note 230.
234   *Supra*, note 231.
235   *Supra*, note 231, at 56-57 (O.R.), at 284 (D.L.R.). See also *Re G.* (1973), 1

In addition to the requirements that the statement be made before the origin of the controversy giving rise to the action in which the statement is tendered, and that there be absent any motive to misrepresent, other prerequisites must be established. In keeping with the other common-law exceptions, it must be shown that the declarant is deceased.[236] Moreover, it must be established that the declarant bore a family relationship to the person whose pedigree is in issue.[237] By requiring proof of the family relationship of the declarant to the subject whose pedigree is in issue, the court is given some assurance that the declarant had an opportunity to learn the relevant facts by reason of his or her relationship and position. The assumption is that by reason of the declarant's relationship, he or she must have had a fairly accurate knowledge of the family affairs for he or she would be expected to have an interest in such matters. Generally, the proof of the declarant's family relationship must be independent of the declaration itself. In *Farren v. Pejepscot Paper Co.*[238] the Supreme Court of Canada put it this way:[239]

The declarant's relationship must be proved independently and cannot be established by his own statement.

The rule, we think, must be understood in this sense, that the party on whom the onus lies to establish the affirmative of the issue and who, for the purposes of the issues, must show that A was in family relation with B (as, for example, in such cases as the present where the party seeks to establish a right to property through inheritance from B) must adduce some evidence that the

---

O.R. (2d) 318, 50 D.L.R. (3d) 198, 14 R.F.L. 201 (Surr. Ct.), at 322 (O.R.); revd. on other grounds (1974), 5 O.R. (2d) 337, 50 D.L.R. (3d) 321, 19 R.F.L. 45 (C.A.); *Plant v. Taylor* (1861), 7 H. & N. 211; but see *contra, Doe d. Tilman v. Tarver* (1824), Ry. & Mood. 141, 171 E.R. 972 (N.P.); and R.W. Baker, *The Hearsay Rule* (London: Pitman, 1950), at 107.

236 *May v. Logie* (1897), 27 S.C.R. 443; *Doe d. Dunlop v. Servos* (1849), 5 U.C.Q.B. 284, at 288-89 (C.A.); *Butler v. Mountgarret* (1859), 7 H.L.C. 633, at 648.

237 *Farren v. Pejepscot Paper Co.*, [1933] S.C.R. 388, [1933] 4 D.L.R. 92, at 390-91 (S.C.R.); *Croft v. Wamboldt* (1930), 1 M.P.R. 415, [1930] 2 D.L.R. 996 (N.S.C.A.); *Wallbridge v. Jones* (1873), 33 U.C.Q.B. 613, at 618 (C.A.).

238 *Ibid.*

239 *Supra*, note 237, at 390-91 (S.C.R.).

declarant was *"de jure* by blood or marriage" a member of the family of B.

It was said by Lord Brougham, apparently, in *Monkton v. Attorney General* [(1831), 2 Russ. & M. 147, at 156, 157,] that it would be sufficient to show that the declarant was a member of the family of A; and this view of Lord Brougham has been acted upon in other cases and has been very vigorously supported by a well known and very able American writer on the law of evidence, Professor Wigmore.

The weight of authority, however, is decisively in favour of the rule as stated.

Although independent evidence must establish the family relationship of the declarant when he or she is talking about the pedigree of other members of his or her family, no such requirement exists when the declarant is talking about his or her own lineage, i.e., about the declarant's own relationship to the person in question. One must distinguish the circumstances where a declaration is tendered for the purpose of claiming a right to the declarant's estate from the situation in which the declaration is used to establish a right through the declarant to the property of others. The declarations in the first situation are considered statements of the declarant's own pedigree and are admissible as such without any corroborative, independent evidence of the relationship. In the former case, if it were necessary to prove that the declarant was related to the subject by independent evidence, without reference to the declarations, it would then be necessary to prove the very fact for which the declarations were tendered.[240] In the latter situation, although it must be established that the declarant is a blood relation or related by marriage to the subject, the witness who is testifying as to what the declarant said need not be a relative.[241]

Furthermore, it is not a condition of admissibility that the declarant be shown to have personal knowledge of the subject-matter contained in the statement.[242] Hearsay upon hearsay has been admit-

---

240 *Robb v. Robb* (1891), 20 O.R. 591, at 598 (C.P.); *Walker v. Murray* (1884), 5 O.R. 638, at 641 (Q.B.).
241 *Wallbridge v. Jones, supra,* note 237.
242 *Doe, Lessee of Banning v. Griffin* (1812), 15 East. 293.

ted to establish pedigree facts because the matters often relate to events so far in the past that they would be beyond the realm of the declarant's personal knowledge.

The declarant must be related to the person whose pedigree is in issue either by blood or by marriage. Relationship by marriage, however, is limited to spouses of the person in question and does not include the blood relatives of the spouse. In *Croft v. Wamboldt*,[243] a declaration by a brother of the spouse of the person in question was held inadmissible. In *Johnson v. Lawson*,[244] the Court held inadmissible declarations of the housekeeper who had intimate knowledge of the affairs of the family.[245] In a country such as Canada where families tend to be more mobile and tend to separate and live in various parts of the land, the test of intimacy rather than relationship with family would be more sensible.[246] In *Alston v. Alston*[247] an American court admitted statements by foster parents to establish the relationship of the child that they had reared.[248]

Under this exception, not only are oral declarations of pedigree admitted, but assertions by way of conduct, or evidence showing that

---

243 (1930), 1 M.P.R. 415, [1930] 2 D.L.R. 996 (N.S.C.A.).

244 (1824), 2 Bing. 86.

245 See also *Re Cochran's Trusts; Robinson v. Simpson* (1919), 47 D.L.R. 1 (S.C.C.), at 7; *Doe d. Arnold v. Auldjo* (1848), 5 U.C.Q.B. 171 (C.A.).

246 Baker in *The Hearsay Rule, supra*, note 235, at 104, criticized Best C.J.'s admonition in *Johnson v. Lawson* (1824), 2 Bing. 86, as follows: " 'If the admissibility of such evidence (in pedigree cases),' said Best C.J., 'were not restrained we should on every occasion before the testimony could be admitted have to enter upon a long inquiry as to the degree of intimacy or confidence that subsisted between the party and the deceased declarant.' This argument, weak enough in the circumstances then before the Court, can be criticised on *a priori* grounds. Firstly, in many other kinds of case the Courts have to inquire into the qualifications of witnesses and secondly, the proof of family relationship would often be just as difficult and lengthy as proof of the intimacy of servants or friends. It is submitted that there is no sufficient reason for this restriction of the class of declarants and that the law ought to be amended to put declarations by family servants and intimate friends on the same footing as members of the family. This is the course recommended by the American Model Code." Rule 803(19) of the *Federal Rules of Evidence for United States Courts and Magistrates* (1975) extends the category of declarant to the person's associates or to those in the community who are aware of the reputation.

247 (1901), 114 Iowa 29, 86 N.W. 55.

248 For a further analysis of the Court's admitting declarations of non-relatives, see 15 A.L.R. (2d) 1412.

the person "acted upon [the statements], or assented to them, or did anything that amounted to showing that they recognized them"[249] will be accepted. Moreover, entries contained in family bibles, inscriptions on tombstones, engravings on rings are all admissible as proper declarations.[250]

There is one further restriction on admissibility. All other conditions of admissibility having been met, the declaration will be admitted to prove pedigree only when the issue in question is genealogical, i.e., a question of family. Baker described matters of genealogical issue as follows:[251]

> ... primarily they are the ordinary incidents of family life, such things as family succession, descent, relationship, legitimacy or illegitimacy.

In *Haines v. Guthrie*[252] the defence of infancy was pleaded in an action for goods sold and delivered. In order to prove the defendant's age, an affidavit of his deceased father, which had been used in an earlier and different proceeding, was tendered. The Court rejected it because no question of family was raised. The evidence must be given on a question of pedigree to prove pedigree.[253]

F. *Statements Contained in Ancient Documents as Evidencing a Proprietary Interest in Land*

Ancient documents such as deeds or leases which affect an interest in property have been admitted by the courts as evidence of possession of the realty.[254] This exception is usually restricted in its application to property deeds and similar documents.[255] Most authors

---

249   *Sturla v. Freccia* (1880), 5 App. Cas. 623, [1874-80] All E.R. Rep. 657 (H.L.), at 641 (App. Cas.).
250   *Currie v. Stairs* (1885), 25 N.B.R. 4 (C.A.); *Goodright d. Stevens v. Moss* (1777), 2 Cowp. 591, at 454; *Monkton v. A.-G.* (1831), 2 Russ. & M. 147, at 162-63; affd. (*sub nom. Robson v. A.-G.*) (1843), 10 Cl. & Fin. 471 (H.L.); *Vowles v. Young* (1806), 13 Ves. 140.
251   R.W. Baker, *The Hearsay Rule* (London: Pitman, 1950), at 102.
252   (1884), 13 Q.B.D. 818 (C.A.).
253   *Ibid.*, at 828.
254   *Malcomson v. O'Dea* (1863), 10 H.L.C. 593; *Bristow v. Cormican* (1878), 3 App. Cas. 641, at 668 (H.L.); *A.-G. v. Emerson*, [1891] A.C. 649, at 658 (H.L.); *Blandy-Jenkins v. Earl of Dunraven*, [1899] 2 Ch. 121 (C.A.).
255   *R. v. Zundel* (1987), 31 C.C.C. (3d) 97, 56 C.R. (3d) 1, 58 O.R. (2d) 129, 18

do not treat the admissibility of such evidence as an exception to the hearsay rule.[256] They are inclined to treat such evidence as presumptive evidence of possession and thus as original evidence in its own right. Other authors, however, feel that the documents are tendered not only to establish the inference of possession from the mere existence of the document, but are submitted as proof of the truth of the statements contained therein, and can only be accepted as an exception to the hearsay rule.[257] The latter view is persuasive. It is clear that the courts have been prone to receive ancient writings because the fact of their age, their unsuspicious appearance, and the fact that they were produced from a place of natural safekeeping, all suggest that they are authentic. Once admitted as authentic documents, it is illogical to limit their use as evidence to the drawing of inferences of possession and not allow them as evidence of the facts contained therein. An American author who urged that ancient writings be received on this basis argued as follows:[258]

> The recognition of the ancient documents rule as a new exception to the hearsay rule is clearly desirable. To say to litigants that the burden of proving the authenticity of their documentary evidence will be lightened, because of the unavailability of witnesses, where the document is 'ancient', and then to refuse to permit the use of the recitals to prove the facts therein stated is, in most cases, a hollow mockery. The evidence to prove the facts recited in an ancient document is usually as unobtainable as the evidence to prove the document is what it purports to be. In addition, it would seem that none of the safeguards which impart reliability to the other exceptions to the hearsay rule is lacking in this one. The declarations are usually *ante litem motam*; the document must come from such custody as does not generate suspicion of its genuineness; there is usually apparent no motive

---

O.A.C. 161, 35 D.L.R. (4th) 338, 29 C.R.R. 349, at 168 (C.C.C.). Leave to appeal to S.C.C. refd. (1987), 61 O.R. (2d) 588n.

256 2 Wigmore, *Evidence*, § 157; R.W. Baker, *supra*, note 251, at 162-63.

257 E.W. Cleary (ed.), *McCormick on Evidence*, 3rd ed. (St. Paul: West Publishing, 1984), § 323, at 903-04. See also *Best on Evidence*, 11th ed. (London: Sweet & Maxwell, 1911), § 499, at 471, and R.P. Croom-Johnson and G.F.L. Bridgman (eds.), *Taylor on Evidence*, 12th ed. (London: Sweet & Maxwell, 1931), Vol. 1, at 421.

258 A. Winokur, "Notes: The Effect of the Ancient Document Rule on the Hearsay Rule" (1935), 83 U. Pa. L. Rev. 247, at 253-54.

in the declarant to fabricate; and, in addition, the courts have shown a strong tendency to require corroborative evidence. Other protections could supplement those already existing.

Moreover, facts contained in ancient documents are more likely to be reliable than the memory of witnesses testifying as to what happened without referring to such records.[259]

It should be noted that there exists a statutory exception to the hearsay rule for the admissibility of ancient writings in a dispute between a vendor and purchaser with respect to the completion of a contract of sale of land. For example, the Ontario *Vendors and Purchasers Act*[260] provides as follows:

> Recitals, statements and descriptions of facts, matters and parties contained in statutes, deeds, instruments or statutory declarations twenty years old at the date of the contract, unless and except in so far as they are proved to be inaccurate, are sufficient evidence of the truth of such facts, matters and descriptions.

If such documents are of sufficient reliability to be used as evidence in litigation between a vendor and purchaser over an agreement of purchase and sale of land, there is no reason why a statutory exception should not be created with respect to other types of ancient documents, admitting them as evidence of the truth of the facts contained in them in proceedings involving issues other than those arising between a vendor and purchaser in a land sales transaction. The draft *Uniform Evidence Act* would permit statements contained in a formally executed document that is at least 20 years old and is produced from the appropriate custody to be admitted in evidence.[261] There is no limitation as to its subject matter.

---

259 See *Apsassin v. Canada (Dept. of Indian Affairs & Northern Development)* (1987), 17 C.P.C. (2d) 187, at 195, 37 D.L.R. (4th) 257, [1987] 4 C.N.L.R. 14, 10 F.T.R. 122 (*sub nom. Blueberry River Indian Band v. Canada (Minister of Indian Affairs & Northern Development)*).

260 R.S.O. 1980, c. 520, s. 1, para. 1; Ontario *Evidence Act*, R.S.O. 1980, c. 145, s. 59.

261 Draft *Uniform Evidence Act*, Bill S-33, 1980-81-82 (withdrawn: see *supra*, note 60), s. 62(1)(d).

G. *Statements in Public Documents*

Founded upon the belief that public officers will perform their tasks properly, carefully, and honestly, an exception to the hearsay rule was created for written statements prepared by public officials in the exercise of their duty. When it is part of the function of a public officer to make a statement as to a fact coming within his knowledge, it is assumed that, in all likelihood, he will do his duty and make a correct statement.[262] The circumstance of publicity also adds another element of trustworthiness. Where an official record is necessarily subject to public inspection, the facility and certainty with which errors would be exposed and corrected provides an additional guarantee of accuracy.[263] Before this exception to the hearsay rule comes into play, the following preconditions, cumulatively providing a measure of dependability, must be established:

(1) The subject matter of the statement must be of a public nature;
(2) The statement must have been prepared with a view to being retained and kept as a public record;
(3) It must have been made for a public purpose and available to the public for inspection at all times;
(4) It must have been prepared by a public officer in pursuance of his duty.[264]

As with some of the other exceptions to the hearsay rule, necessity is a further justification for admissibility, but it is necessity of a different kind. It has never been a precondition to admissibility that the maker of the public document be dead. The special necessity, therefore, for this type of hearsay evidence is not so much the unavailability of alternative modes of proof; rather, it is based upon

---

262 *Finestone v. R.*, [1953] 2 S.C.R. 107, 17 C.R. 211 (Que.); *Re Puczka; Voitko v. Sabados* (1973), 38 D.L.R. (3d) 234 (Sask. Q.B.).
263 *Sturla v. Freccia, supra*, note 249; *Mercer v. Denne*, [1904] 2 Ch. 534; affd. [1905] 2 Ch. 538 (C.A.).
264 See R.W. Baker, *The Hearsay Rule, supra*, note 251, at 138; *Thrasyvoulos Ioannou v. Papa Christoforos Demetriou*, [1952] A.C. 84 (P.C.); *R. v. Kaipiainen* (1953), 17 C.R. 388, 107 C.C.C. 377, [1954] O.R. 43 (C.A.); *R. v. Zundel* (1987), 31 C.C.C. (3d) 97, 56 C.R. (3d) 1, 58 O.R. (2d) 129, 18 O.A.C. 161, 35 D.L.R. (4th) 338, 29 C.R.R. 349 (C.A.), at 167-68 (C.C.C.). Leave to appeal to S.C.C. refd. (1987), 61 O.R. (2d) 588*n*.

expediency, for, without such an exception, many public officials would have to be taken away from necessary governmental tasks in order to testify in court. Therefore, the work of the government and the needs of the public are given priority, and the law, accordingly, has not insisted upon court attendance of public officials. Moreover, little would be accomplished by demanding the *viva voce* testimony of the public officer since he probably would possess no recollection of the event independent of the document itself.

Where the admissibility of a statement contained in a report prepared by a public official after conducting an investigation is at issue, more than mere accessibility by the public to such report must be demonstrated. This is illustrated in *R. v. Northern Electric Co.*,[265] in which the Crown, in an attempt to prove an illegal combine, sought to tender as evidence the reports of the Dominion Bureau of Statistics which indicated the total production of wire and cable products manufactured in Canada. It was the Crown's purpose to demonstrate that the accused companies manufactured and sold virtually all of the wire and cable that was produced in this country. McRuer C.J.H.C. came to the conclusion that the report was inadmissible as a public document. The *Statistics Act*[266] provided that any individual company's figures were not to be disclosed and, accordingly, the public could not become aware of the components which made up the total production figure set out in the report. Since mere accessibility to the report did not provide the public with a means of verifying the accuracy of the figure, the test of publicity, which is the hallmark of trustworthiness, was lost. McRuer C.J.H.C. put it this way:[267]

> [The reports of the Dominion Bureau of Statistics] . . . stand on a very different footing from a record of the registration of events or facts, whether they be births, marriages, deaths, or climatic conditions. They are a summation of the results of inquiries

---

265 [1955] O.R. 431, 21 C.R. 45, 111 C.C.C. 241, [1955] 3 D.L.R. 449, 24 C.P.R. 1 (H.C.J.).

266 Now see R.S.C. 1985, c. S-19.

267 *Supra*, note 265, at 468. But see the New Brunswick *Evidence Act*, R.S.N.B. 1973, c. E-11, s. 43, which provides for the admissibility of any report, publication, or statement on any matter of science, technology, geography, population, natural resources, engineering or other matter of fact or fact and opinion purporting to have been prepared by or under the authority of any department of the federal or any provincial government.

made pursuant to public duty. Although they are made for the use of the public they can gain little or no authority by reason of the public or any member of the public being in a position to challenge or dispute them, because the constituent material that goes to make up the reports is secret.

Public documents which are admissible under this exception encompass more than governmental reports and surveys prepared by an official whose duty it was to investigate and record his findings in such form. Public registers and records, official certificates, statutes, parliamentary journals and gazettes all fall within the purview of this exception.[268] These documents are accessible to the public; however, that is generally not the major factor asserted in support of the admissibility of such documents. Rather, it is the inconvenience of insisting on alternative modes of proof. As Baker suggests in his work on the hearsay rule:[269]

> . . . the bare possibility of inspection by members of the public cannot have very much influence on the official responsible for the records to ensure that he keeps them accurately, nor is it likely that members of the public would discover any errors or discrepancies in their chance perusal of such a thing as a register of births, deaths, and marriages, for example. Most public documents expand greatly from day to day and the coincidence that a person affected by an entry should see it and notice any inaccuracies is so improbable that it could be ignored.

Accordingly, there is some question that the test of publicity as enunciated by McRuer C.J.H.C. in the *Northern Electric Co.* case[270] would be applicable to the day-to-day records that are kept on file in a government bureaucracy.

Earlier cases had held that it was a condition of admissibility that

---

268 See M.N. Howard, P. Crane and D.A. Hochberg, *Phipson on Evidence*, 14th ed. (London: Sweet & Maxwell, 1990), at 770.
269 *The Hearsay Rule, supra*, note 251, at 137. But see *R. v. Porter* (1964), 48 D.L.R. (2d) 277 (N.S.S.C.); *Adams Estate v. Decock Estate*, [1987] 5 W.W.R. 148, 49 Man. R. (2d) 261 (Q.B.); *Canadian Newspapers Co. v. Manitoba*, [1986] 2 W.W.R. 673, 25 D.L.R. (4th) 321, 39 Man. R. (2d) 161, 34 L.C.R. 307 (C.A.); leave to appeal to S.C.C. refd. [1986] 4 W.W.R. lxix.
270 *Supra*, note 265.

the official making the record should either have had personal knowledge of the matters which he was recording or should have inquired into the accuracy of the facts.[271] This is no longer the case. In *R. v. Halpin*,[272] the accused faced a charge of conspiracy to defraud a municipal authority by submitting false claims for work allegedly done by the accused's company. The Crown sought to adduce the file from the Companies Register containing the annual returns made pursuant to the pertinent *Companies Act* to prove the accused and his wife were the sole shareholders and directors of the company during the relevant period. When faced with the objection that the official who recorded the entries had no duty to inquire and satisfy himself as to the truth of the recorded facts, the English Court of Appeal held that the common law was sufficiently flexible to accommodate modern society and held the records to be admissible. It said:[273]

> The common law, as expressed in the earlier cases which have been cited, was plainly designed to apply to an uncomplicated community when those charged with keeping registers would, more often than not, be personally acquainted with the people whose affairs they were recording and the vicar, as already indicated, would probably himself have officiated at the baptism, marriage or burial which he later recorded in the presence of the churchwardens on the register before putting it back in the coffers. But the common law should move with the times and should recognise the fact that the official charged with recording matters of public import can no longer in this highly complicated world, as like as not, have personal knowledge of their accuracy.

> What has happened now is that the function originally performed by one man has had to be shared between two: the first having the knowledge and the statutory duty to record that knowledge and forward it to the Registrar of Companies, the second having the duty to preserve that document and to show it to members of the public under proper conditions as required.

---

271 These cases are reviewed by Geoffrey Lane L.J. in *R. v. Halpin*, [1975] 1 Q.B. 907, at 913-15 (C.A.).

272 *Ibid.*

273 *Supra*, note 271, at 915.

Where a duty is cast upon a limited company by statute to make accurate returns of company matters to the Registrar of Companies, so that those returns can be filed and inspected by members of the public, the necessary conditions, in the judgment of this court, have been fulfilled for that document to have been admissible. All statements on the return are admissible as prima facie proof of the truth of their contents.

This common-law exception to the hearsay rule is rarely resorted to by counsel. A number of statutes currently provide for the admissibility of diverse governmental and public documents and for the admissibility of certified copies of such records.[274]

H. *Res Gestae*

1. General

Much confusion surrounds the formula *res gestae* which has been used by the courts in diverse situations to avoid the rigours of the hearsay rule. Lord Tomlin in *Homes v. Newman*[275] emphasized the ambiguity of the phrase:[276]

What is meant by saying that a document or act is admissible because it is part of the *res gestae* has never so far as I am aware been explained in a satisfactory manner. I suspect it of being a phrase adopted to provide a respectable legal cloak or a variety of cases to which no formula of precision can be applied.

The courts have unwittingly employed the doctrine of *res gestae* not only to admit declarations as an exception to the hearsay rule, but have also used it to admit non-hearsay statements for which no exception was required.[277] It is only where the statement is tendered

---

274 These statutory provisions are discussed in this Chapter, II.G.
275 [1931] 2 Ch. 112.
276 *Ibid.*, at 120. Similar views have been expressed by commentators: C.A. Wright, "The Law of Evidence: Present and Future" (1942), 20 Can. Bar Rev. 714, at 716; E.M. Morgan, "A Suggested Classification of Utterances Admissible as Res Gestae" (1922), 31 Yale L.J. 229, at 229.
277 See this Chapter, I.C.2. An example can be found in *Thomas v. British Columbia (A.G.)*; *Milliken v. British Columbia (A.G.)* (1973), 34 D.L.R. (3d) 521, at 527 (B.C.C.A.), wherein Bull J.A. said that a statement if forming part of the

as evidence of the truth of the matter asserted in it that an exception is needed. There are two basic situations in which the courts have properly invoked the *res gestae* doctrine to admit utterances offered for their truth. They may be categorized as:

Declarations accompanying and explaining relevant acts; and

Spontaneous Exclamations.

In addition, under the guise of *res gestae*, the courts have admitted declarations for a purpose other than proving the truth of the acts asserted therein in the following circumstances:

Declarations which by their assertion create legal rights or liabilities; and

Declarations of bodily and mental feelings and condition.

Although evidence of such statements is admissible without the assistance of an exception to the hearsay rule, it is convenient to consider them in this chapter because of their confusing similarity with statements for which an exception is necessary. The latter statements shall be examined first.

2. Declarations which by their Assertion Create Legal Rights or Liabilities

Statements which accompany and explain an otherwise ambiguous act in issue will be discussed shortly, and it will be shown that it is preferable to treat the admissibility of such declarations as a true exception to the hearsay rule rather than as original evidence, being a verbal part of a fact in issue, because it is impossible for the trier of fact to receive such evidence as other than proof of the truth of the assertion.[278] A different view, however, is taken with respect to words which, when spoken, effect a legal result. In such cases, the truth of the statement is immaterial, the only issue being whether the statement was made. Unfortunately, some have treated such statements as hearsay and have justified their admissibility as forming a part of the

---

res gestae is admissible not to prove the truth thereof but to prove only that the statement was made. It is submitted that if the statement is tendered for the latter purpose, it is admissible whether it forms part of the *res gestae* or not.
278   See this Chapter, II.H.4.

res gestae.[279] This, however, ignores the purpose for which the out-of-court assertion is tendered. It is only hearsay if it is put forth to prove the truth of the statement, but not otherwise. When the statement itself constitutes a fact in issue, any analysis of the doctrine of *res gestae* is a confusion of terms. This was emphasized by Baker in his work:[280]

> There is obviously not only no necessity for using a shadowy phrase like *res gestae* to cover the admission of this kind of evidence but also every reason for not doing so. For example, in an action for breach of contract, the testimony of a witness as to statements he had heard which constituted the offer of acceptance or revocation is admissible under the issue. Similarly, with the words of an alleged slander in an action for defamation. Therefore it only makes for uncertainty to talk about *res gestae* in such cases.

Thus, conversations which have the legal result of the creation or the termination of contracts are admissible, not as part of the *res gestae*, but as original evidence of the very fact in issue.[281] So, if X says to Y, "I offer to sell my car to you for $300.00", his words are legally operative in their very nature to bind him to a contract if Y accepts. The articulation of those words is an objective act and constitutes original evidence. In the same vein, a statement which is alleged to be defamatory constitutes in itself a material fact in issue and is accordingly admissible.[282] So, also, the giving of a notice may be a fact in issue

---

279 See G.D. Nokes, "Res Gestae as Hearsay" (1954), 70 L.Q. Rev. 370, at 380.

280 R.W. Baker, *The Hearsay Rule* (London: Pitman, 1950), at 158. 6 Wigmore, *Evidence* (Chadbourn rev. 1976), § 1770, at 259, agrees with that proposition: "Where the *utterance of specific words* is itself *a part of the details of the issue under the substantive law and the pleadings*, their utterance may be proved without violation of the hearsay rule, because they are not offered to evidence the truth of the matter that may be asserted therein." See also the remarks by Pigeon J. in *Royal Victoria Hospital v. Morrow*, [1974] S.C.R. 501, 42 D.L.R. (3d) 233, at 509 (S.C.R.), at 239 (D.L.R.).

281 *Green v. Tress* (1927), 60 O.L.R. 151, [1927] 2 D.L.R. 180 (C.A.); *Globe & Rutgers Fire Insurance Co. v. Truedell* (1927), 60 O.L.R. 227, [1927] 2 D.L.R. 659 (C.A.).

282 *Boys v. Star Printing & Publishing Co.* (1927), 60 O.L.R. 592, [1927] 3 D.L.R. 847 (C.A.); *Sentinel-Review Co. v. Robinson* (1927), 60 O.L.R. 93, [1927] 2 D.L.R. 60 (Master); *Halls v. Mitchell* (1926), 59 O.L.R. 355, [1926] 4 D.L.R. 202; revd. 59 O.L.R. 590, [1927] 1 D.L.R. 163; revd. [1928] S.C.R. 125, [1928] 2 D.L.R. 97;

and evidence thereof may be received without the necessity of any exception to the hearsay rule.[283]

3. Declarations of Bodily and Mental Feelings and Condition

(a) *Bodily Feelings and Condition*

A person's declaration about his contemporaneous bodily state is admissible evidence of the existence of that state, although he is not called as a witness.[284] Some courts have interpreted this as an exception to the hearsay rule, while other courts have said that the declaration is not hearsay at all, on the basis that it is being tendered not for the purpose of proving the truth of what is asserted, but merely to indicate a particular bodily feeling. In other words, the statement is received as circumstantial evidence from which the bodily condition may be inferred. In the case of *Gilbey v. Great Western Railway Co.*,[285] in which there was a claim for workmen's compensation, the issue was whether the deceased died as a result of an injury that he sustained in his employment. An autopsy revealed that his death was caused by a tear in his lung. It was alleged that the deceased, while carrying a side of beef, so strained himself as to cause the damage to his lung. In considering the admissibility of statements made by the deceased workman to his wife about his physical condition, Cozens-Hardy M.R. said this:[286]

> I do not doubt that all statements made by a workman to his wife of his sensations at the time, about the pain in the side or head, or what not — whether those statements were made by groans or by actions or were verbal statements — would be admissible to prove the existence of those sensations. But to hold that those statements ought to go further and be admitted as evidence of the acts deposed to is, I think, open to doubt; such a contention is contrary to all authority.

Knapp v. McLeod (1926), 58 O.L.R. 605, [1926] 2 D.L.R. 1083 (C.A.); *Clark v. Duncan* (1923), 53 O.L.R. 287 (C.A.).

283   *Whitehead v. Scott* (1830), 1 M. & Rob. 2, 174 E.R. 1 (N.P.).

284   *Aveson v. Lord Kinnaird* (1805), 6 East 188, 102 E.R. 1258 (K.B.).

285   (1910), 102 L.T. 202 (C.A.).

286   *Ibid.*, at 203. Statements are admissible to prove either poor or good health. In *R. v. Johnson* (1847), 2 Car. & Kir. 354, 175 E.R. 146 (N.P.), the deceased's statements of his health made shortly before his death were admitted to establish his well-being.

Thus, the statements of the workman as to his physical sensations and feelings were held admissible, but the Court of Appeal refused to admit that part of the statement which referred to the cause and occasion of the injury from which the deceased was suffering.[287] A similar issue was considered by an Ontario court in *Youlden v. London Guarantee & Accident Co.*[288] In that case, the deceased had been insured with the defendant against accident and the Court was required to determine the cause of death. The ultimate issue was whether the deceased had died of physical strain. The second issue was whether he had strained himself by lifting a piece of lumber. The insurance company's defence was that the deceased had perished by reason of an infection which could have resulted from a number of causes, the most obvious being from the consumption of impure ice cream on the evening prior to his death. The plaintiff alleged that it was a physical strain, caused by the exertion of lifting the lumber, that brought about the physical condition which enabled bacteria in the digestive tract to develop to such an extent that death resulted. The plaintiff called as a witness the deceased's partner who testified that the deceased, after lifting the lumber, had told him that he was afraid that he had injured himself. Middleton J. admitted the statement, not for the purpose of proving the cause of the deceased's suffering which was the issue in question, but only for the limited purpose of showing the existence of bodily sensation. The statement then became a piece of circumstantial evidence in a chain of reasoning helping the Court to determine what the probable cause of suffering was. The Court accordingly drew the inference from the existence of these physical symptoms that the deceased, at that time, did suffer an injury in lifting the timber, and that the injury was the cause of his death.

Not all Canadian courts, however, have taken the view that statements made by someone who has been injured as to the cause of

---

287 In a subsequent Irish case, *Wright v. Kerrigan*, [1911] 2 I.R. 301, the Irish Court of Appeal in a claim under the Workmen's Compensation Act, admitted a statement made by the deceased to a doctor as to how the injury was received. The English Court of Appeal in *Amys v. Barton*, [1912] 1 K.B. 40 (C.A.), however, rejected this extension to the rule of admissibility and stated that although the statement as to the deceased's physical symptoms would be admissible, the statements as to their cause would not. More recently, see *R. v. Read* (1982), 18 Alta. L.R. (2d) 188 (Q.B.), at 192.

288 (1912), 26 O.L.R. 75, 4 D.L.R. 721 (S.C.); affd. 28 O.L.R. 161, 12 D.L.R. 433 (C.A.).

his or her injury should be excluded. Two courts in Western Canada have expressly admitted such statements, but these decisions are of questionable authority on the question of the admissibility of declarations indicating physical sensation. Rather, the justification of admissibility of the statements in the two cases is better founded on spontaneous declarations accompanying the act.[289] In *Rodych v. Krasey*[290] the deceased had sustained fatal injuries as a result of being crushed between his motor vehicle and the defendant's truck. Matas J. of the Manitoba Queen's Bench admitted statements made by the deceased shortly after the accident, to the effect that the defendant's truck had struck him. It is unclear, however, whether the Court admitted the statements as declarations of bodily feelings or whether they were admitted as spontaneous declarations accompanying relevant acts. The statements were made after the act causing the injury had been completed and the statement was merely a narrative of what had taken place. They were clearly not statements of physical sensation or pain and their admissibility under this head to prove the cause of the injury goes against the grain of well established authority. Much earlier, in *Somerville v. Prudential Insurance Co. of America*,[291] an action on a life insurance policy providing for double indemnity in case of accidental death, MacLean J. of the Saskatchewan King's Bench, in *obiter dicta*, admitted statements made by the deceased as to the cause of his pain or distress, as evidence of the manner in which the deceased received his injury. In support of this principle of admissibility, MacLean J. relied on *Thompson v. Trevanion*[292] which was decided in 1693. In that action, the plaintiff and his spouse sued the defendant for an alleged assault upon the woman. In a report which is only a few lines long, Holt C.J. stated that "What the wife said immediate upon the hurt received, and before she had time to devise or contrive anything for her own advantage . . ." could be admitted as evidence. That is all we know of the case. There is no indication as to the content of the woman's statement or the basis upon which Holt C.J. made his ruling. It is clear that such a ruling does not justify MacLean J.'s holding that the statements were admitted as evidence of the cause of the injury. The Saskatchewan court also relied upon an Ontario decision, *Arm-*

---

289 See this Chapter, II.H.5.
290 [1971] 4 W.W.R. 358 (Man. Q.B.).
291 [1935] 3 W.W.R. 81, 2 I.L.R. 543 (Sask.).
292 (1693), Skin 402, 90 E.R. 179 (K.B.). See this Chapter, II.H.5.

strong v. Canada Atlantic Railway Co.,[293] in which the Divisional Court thought it proper to admit statements made by a deceased immediately after being run over by a railway car, as to how the accident had occurred. On appeal, the Court of Appeal did not rule on this point, but thought that the statement was irrelevant in any event. It is clear, however, that the *Armstrong* case was decided well before the decision in the *Youlden* case[294] and can no longer be considered an authority for the admissibility of statements of the cause of injury under this exception to the hearsay rule, although they may be admitted as excited utterances accompanying an act.

In any case, it is difficult to believe that a court is capable of restricting the use of the statement as proof of the physical symptom only and not extending it to its cause; and thus the court may well be admitting such statements as evidence for one purpose and then using it for another without acknowledging it. Nevertheless, in Canada, rather than recognizing declaration of physical sensation as an exception to the hearsay rule which would encompass declarations as to the cause of that sensation, the courts have preferred to admit such statements on the basis that they constitute original circumstantial evidence of only the bodily feeling in issue.

The only precondition to their admissibility is that the statements be made contemporaneously with the physical sensation.[295] If the declaration amounts to a narrative of the declarant's past symptoms, it will not be admissible under this exception. As to how soon after the incident the declaration must be made, the courts have been flexible and a reasonable passage of time will not destroy the contemporaneous character of the declaration. In the *Youlden* case the statement was made "shortly after [the declarant] had lifted the timber."[296] The circumstances of each case must be examined and if the statement is made at a time too remote from the actual experience of the bodily feeling so as to rob it of any contemporaneity and to amount only to an account of the past state of the declarant's health, it would be inadmissible. Only the recognition of such a statement as an exception to the hearsay rule could justify its reception into evidence. It need

---

293 (1902), 4 O.L.R. 560; 2 C.R.C. 339 (C.A.), reversing 2 O.L.R. 219, 1 C.R.C. 444 (C.A.).

294 *Youlden v. London Guarantee & Accident Co.*, *supra*, note 288.

295 *R. v. Gloster* (1888), 16 Cox C.C. 471.

296 *Supra*, note 288, at 77 (O.L.R.), at 722 (D.L.R.).

not, however, be shown that the declaration arose in such a spontaneous way as to amount to an involuntary exclamation at the time that the physical sensation was incurred.[297] The fact that it was made relatively soon upon the experience of the sensation will suffice, whether the utterance was calculated or not.

Again, as with other exceptions to the hearsay rule, the foundation or trustworthiness of statements of such unavailable declarants is that one who is experiencing the feelings or sensations in question is best able to describe them accurately. Moreover, the fact that the individual's description is uttered at the precise moment that he is experiencing the sensation proves some measure of sincerity.[298]

(b) Declarations Indicating an Existing Mental or Emotional Condition, or State of Mind or Intention

If the mental state of the declarant is directly in issue at trial, then statements of his mental state are generally admissible in proof of the fact. For example, in *Great West Uranium Mines Ltd. v. Rock Hill Uranium Mines Ltd.*[299] the issue before the Court was whether the defendant had participated in a fraudulent conspiracy to deprive the plaintiff of certain mining claims that it had staked. Statements made by one co-conspirator to the plaintiff's employees, instructing them to terminate the staking of the mineral site, was admitted as evidence of the co-conspirator's fraudulent intention. Similarly, in *Thomas v. Connell*,[300] the Court had to determine whether a bankrupt had made a fraudulent preference, and that determination turned upon his knowledge at the material time. The Court admitted the bankrupt's statement that he knew that he was insolvent, not as proof of his insolvency, but as proof of his knowledge of that fact at the time that he made the payment to the defendant. In issue in *Shanklin v. Smith*[301]

---

297 *Supra*, note 288, at 78 (O.L.R.), at 724 (D.L.R.).
298 Section 62(1)(f) of the draft *Uniform Evidence Act*, Bill S-33, 1980-81-82, maintains the common law by providing for admissibility of a "statement as to the physical condition of the declarant at the time the statement was made, including a statement as to the duration but not as to the cause of that condition." The duration of the physical state is a curious extension of the perimeters of the existing common law. It is not entirely clear why this expansion and no other was created.
299 [1955] 4 D.L.R. 307, 15 W.W.R. 404 (Sask. C.A.).
300 (1838), 4 M. & W. 267, 150 E.R. 1429 (Exch. Ct.).
301 (1932), 5 M.P.R. 204; affd. [1933] S.C.R. 340, [1933] 4 D.L.R. 815.

was whether the execution of a conveyance by the deceased had been obtained by fraud. Subsequent to making the conveyance regarding his property, statements of the deceased which were at variance with the conveyance were admitted as evidence of his mental condition, from which the Court inferred that he never considered that he had made such previous conveyance. Moreover, in *Jozwiak v. Sadek*[302] the Court admitted statements made by anonymous telephone callers as evidence that reasonable persons believed that the plaintiff was the person described in a libelous newspaper account.

In *Gray v. New Augarita Porcupine Mines Ltd.*,[303] an action against a director of a company for fraud, the Privy Council held that information the other directors had received from the Ontario Securities Commission was admissible. This evidence was relevant and important to the issue of fraud and deceit, for it would otherwise be impossible to show that the other directors had been misled by statements made by the defendant unless they were able to establish what they knew at the time that these statements were made to them. Other examples in which declarations have been admitted to establish the declarant's state of mind include statements of intention to make a particular country one's home in proof of domicile,[304] and the statements of a physician to a patient about his or her mental health as evidence of the latter's belief that it would be unsafe to resume cohabitation with one's spouse as justification for living separate and apart.[305]

The reception of these statements into evidence has been justified by the fact that in the absence of any evidence of the individual's conduct, these statements may be the only means by which the court can determine the declarant's state of mind. Moreover, by requiring that the statement be made contemporaneously with the existence of the state of mind, there is some guarantee of reliability and sincerity on the part of the declarant.

Although most authors accept the premise that declarations with respect to a declarant's state of mind are hearsay and can be admitted only as an exception, Canadian and English courts have acknowledged

---

302 [1954] 1 All E.R. 3 (Q.B.).
303 [1952] 3 D.L.R. 1 (P.C.).
304 *Scappaticci v. A.G.*, [1955] 2 W.L.R. 409, [1955] 1 All E.R. 193n; *Bryce v. Bryce*, [1932] All E.R. 788.
305 *Tickle v. Tickle*, [1968] 1 W.L.R. 937, [1968] 2 All E.R. 154 (D.C.).

such evidence as verbal acts constituting original evidence.[306] In *R. v. Burnett*[307] such a declaration was held to be original circumstantial evidence since it was not tendered for its truth but rather to establish the extent of the declarant's knowledge. Hartt J. was of the view that so long as the declarant's mental condition is a relevant issue[308] then his words do not constitute hearsay:[309]

> Utterances made outside a particular proceeding have been received to evidence the declarant's state of mind, either testimonially under an exception to the hearsay rule or circumstantially as indicating the speaker's mental condition. In the latter case the statement is not hearsay; it is a verbal utterance employed indirectly, like wordless conduct, to indicate circumstantially a mental condition . . .

> Where the mental condition sought to be proved circumstantially is knowledge or belief, there is an increased risk that the evidence will be used for its hearsay value, particularly in a criminal case where the mental condition of the declarant is not itself an essential ingredient of the crime charged. If the words are used to support an inference of knowledge or belief of certain

---

306 *Great West Uranium Mines Ltd. v. Rock Hill Uranium Mines Ltd.*, *supra*, note 299; *Home v. Corbeil*, [1955] O.W.N. 842, [1955] 4 D.L.R. 750 (S.C.); affd. on other grounds [1956] O.W.N. 391, 2 D.L.R. (2d) 543 (C.A.); *R. v. Blastland*, [1986] A.C. 41, [1985] 3 W.L.R. 345, [1985] 2 All E.R. 1095, at 1098-99 (H.L.); in *Ward v. H.S. Pitt & Co.*; *Lloyd v. Powell Duffryn Steam Coal Co. Ltd.*, [1914] A.C. 733 (H.L.), Lord Moulton stated, at 751-52: "Now, it is well established in English jurisprudence, in accordance with the dictates of common sense, that the words and acts of a person are admissible as evidence of his state of mind. Indeed, they are the only possible evidence on such an issue. It was urged at the Bar that although the acts of the deceased might be put in evidence, his words might not. I fail to understand the distinction. Speaking is as much an act as doing.

"It must be borne in mind that there is nothing in the admission of such evidence which clashes with the rooted objection in our jurisprudence to the admission of hearsay evidence."

307 (1986), 25 C.C.C. (3d) 111, 54 O.R. (2d) 65 (H.C.J.).

308 ". . . the admissibility of a statement tendered in evidence of proof of the maker's knowledge or other state of mind must always depend on the degree of relevance of the state of mind sought to be proved to the issue in relation to which the evidence is tendered.": per Lord Bridge in *R. v. Blastland*, *supra*, note 306, at 1105 (All E.R.).

309 *Supra*, note 307, at 67-68 (O.R.).

events and the belief is in turn used to support an inference that those events occurred, the rule against hearsay is violated. Employed in this manner, the assertion is used to prove the matter asserted. Although an intermediate inference is imposed, the assertion stands alone as evidence of the facts asserted. In my view, assertions tendered to prove the fact known are hearsay — and this is so whether the inference drawn is direct or indirect.

That is not to say, however, that an out-of-court statement is necessarily hearsay when the inference sought to be drawn from the assertion coincides with the actual assertion itself. If knowledge or awareness of a fact is relevant, the fact of the assertion can be evidence of awareness provided that the matter asserted is otherwise independently proved . . . . The statement, "I know the brakes are bad", is hearsay if offered to prove that the brakes were bad, but if offered to show the declarant's knowledge of the bad brakes (the bad brakes being otherwise proved) the statement is not hearsay notwithstanding that the inference of knowledge coincides with the assertion made. In this respect, the heart of the distinction between hearsay and non-hearsay evidence lies in the use to which the out-of-court statement is put.

The distinction, however, seems insignificant, for as Cross suggested, in an early edition of his work,[310]

. . . there does not seem to be a single practical consequence that may or may not ensue according to whether the evidence is received as original or received by way of exception to the hearsay rule.

The state of mind of intention is troublesome. Should the court treat an expression of intention in the same way as a statement indicating bodily or mental feelings of pain or good health? The distinction between the two is that the former is usually a deliberate and calculated statement, whereas the latter is more often than not a reflex verbal action indicating the declarant's present mental attitude. The crucial question in cases where the declarant's mental state is not

---

310 R. Cross, *Evidence*, 3rd ed. (London: Butterworths, 1967), at 475. See also *R. v. P. (R.)* (1990), 58 C.C.C. (3d) 334, at 341 (Ont. H.C.J.).

in issue, is whether declarations of intention should be admissible to prove that the intention was carried out. In other words, can it be inferred that the declarant performed the act on the ground that he had earlier professed such an intention? The obvious danger of admitting such evidence is that there is no guarantee that persons will do what they say they intend to do and thus a person's intention may not be very probative evidence that he or she in fact carried it out. As has been suggested, evidence of a person's state of mind, when such is in issue, is justifiably admissible or there may not be any other evidence going to that question, and there is more of a likelihood that an expressed mental state is actually held by the declarant. When it is not in issue, there is less necessity to admit declarations of intention to prove subsequent conduct. Other circumstantial evidence is usually available to prove the latter. Accordingly, courts were at first resistant to permitting the introduction of such evidence.

A statement of intention in proof of subsequent conduct was held inadmissible in *Cuff v. Frazee Storage & Cartage Co.*[311] The question in that case was whether a person named Brown, who gave testimony in a previous proceeding, was out of the jurisdiction, so that his previous testimony could be read in as evidence in the present action. The Court held that Brown's statement to the witness that "he was going to the other side" and statements made by others that Brown had "gone to the States" were inadmissible as proof of the fact that Brown was absent from the jurisdiction.[312]

American courts have treated such statements quite differently. The Supreme Court of the United States in *Mutual Life Insurance Co. v. Hillmon*[313] considered the issue in the context of an action by a wife to recover on an insurance policy on the life of her husband, John Hillmon. By way of defence, the insurance company alleged that the body that was found at Crooked Creek, Kansas, was not that of the insured, but rather that of a man named Walters who had also disappeared. It was the defendant's contention that Hillmon had murdered Walters in order to enable Mrs. Hillmon to collect the

---

311 (1907), 14 O.L.R. 263 (Div. Ct.).

312 Statements of intention in proof of a subsequent act were also excluded in two early criminal cases: *R. v. Thomson*, [1912] 3 K.B. 19 (C.C.A.) and *R. v. Wainwright* (1875), 13 Cox C.C. 171; but see *contra*, *R. v. Buckley* (1873), 13 Cox C.C. 293 (H.L.).

313 145 U.S. 285, 12 S. Ct. 909 (1892).

proceeds of the insurance policy which had recently been issued on Hillmon's life. As evidence of the fact that the deceased was Walters and not Hillmon, the defendant tendered letters which Walters had written to his sister and fiancée expressing an intention of leaving Wichita, Kansas, with a man by the name of Hillmon, "for Colorado or parts unknown to me". The Court ruled the letter admissible on the following ground:[314]

> The letters in question were competent, not as narratives of facts communicated to the writer by others, nor yet as proof that he actually went away from Wichita, but as evidence that, shortly before the time when other evidence tended to show that he went away, he had the intention of going, and of going with Hillmon, which made it more probable both that he did go and that he went with Hillmon, than if there had been no proof of such intention.

The decision in *Hillmon* has won favour in Canada, at least to the extent of admitting statements of present intention to establish the state of mind of the declarant. In *R. v. Moore*[315] the Ontario Court of Appeal had no difficulty in holding that the statements were admissible as a recognizable exception to the hearsay rule to show the declarant's state of mind of intention as a basis for an inference that the declarant carried out his or her intention. In *R. v. P. (R.)*[316] Doherty J. gave the following illustration of the principle:[317]

> Evidence of the deceased's state of mind may, in turn, be relevant as circumstantial evidence that the deceased subsequently acted in accordance with that avowed state of mind. Where a deceased says, "I will go to Ottawa tomorrow", the statement affords direct evidence of the state of mind — an intention to go to Ottawa tomorrow — and circumstantial evidence that the deceased in fact went to Ottawa on that day. If either the state of mind, or the

---

314 *Ibid.*, at 295-96 (U.S.). An interesting analysis of the implications of this case may be found in J.M. Maguire, "The Hillmon Case — Thirty-three Years After" (1925), 38 Harv. L. Rev. 709.
315 (1984), 15 C.C.C. (3d) 541, 5 O.A.C. 51 (C.A.); leave to appeal to S.C.C. refd. (1985), 7 O.A.C. 320.
316 *Supra*, note 310.
317 *Supra*, note 310, at 343.

fact to be inferred from the existence of the state of mind is relevant, the evidence is receivable subject to objections based on undue prejudice.

The *Hillmon* case, however, can stand for an even broader proposition. One of the criticisms that has been lodged against the decision in the *Hillmon* case is that Walters' statements tended to show that he went away with Hillmon only, if it is assumed that Hillmon consented to go with him. Walters' letters are no evidence of Hillmon's intention or Hillmon's agreeing to go with Walters. McCormick put it this way:[318]

> If completion of a plan or design requires not only the continued inclination and ability of the declarant to complete it but also the inclination and ability of someone else, arguably the likelihood that the design or plan was completed is substantially less. Despite some objection, however, courts have not imposed the limitation. In *Hillmon* itself, in fact, Walters' successful completion of his plan to leave Wichita depended upon the continued willingness of Hillmon to have Walters as a companion and upon Hillmon's willingness and ability to leave at the time planned.

The problem is further compounded by the danger that the trier of fact may use one person's statement of intention as proof of another person's intention and thus infer that it was carried out.

A statement of intention was admitted by an Ontario court in *Home v. Corbeil*.[319] That was an action by a wife under the *Fatal Accidents Act* arising from a motor vehicle accident which caused her husband's death. In defence, it was alleged that at the time of the husband's death, the wife was living apart from him under circumstances which would have disentitled her to alimony from him. Since the wife claimed as a dependant, the question arose as to whether she had lost any monetary advantage by her husband's death since they had been living separate and apart at the time. The ultimate issue before the Court was whether there was a reasonable expectation that

---

318 E.W. Cleary (ed.), *McCormick on Evidence*, 3rd ed. (St. Paul: West Publishing, 1984), § 295, at 848.
319 [1955] O.W.N. 842, [1955] 4 D.L.R. 750; affd. [1956] O.W.N. 391, 2 D.L.R. (2d) 543 (C.A.).

the wife would have received pecuniary benefits from her deceased husband. The plaintiff tendered statements by the deceased indicating a desire to return to cohabitation with his wife and promising to support her financially upon their reconciliation. It was argued that such evidence was relevant in that it could be inferred that there would be a reconciliation, and that, therefore, there would be a likelihood that the wife had a reasonable expectation of pecuniary benefit.[320]

It could be said that in the *Home v. Corbeil* case[321] the decision to admit the statement of intention was without some of the attendant dangers that accompanied the decision in the *Hillmon* case. The statements in *Home v. Corbeil* seem to be more cogent to the ultimate issue to which it was directed than were Walters' letters in the *Hillmon* case. In issue in the *Corbeil* case was the reasonable expectation of the wife to receive benefits from her husband, and the husband's intention was quite closely related and relevant to that issue, whereas in the *Hillmon* case, the letters were not as probative of the ultimate issue, being the identification of the body.[322] The inability to test or gauge the strength of the declarant's intention however, is common to both cases.

The reluctance to fully adopt the *Hillmon* principle in Canada has been expressed in two recent Ontario cases. In *R. v. P. (R.)*[323] the Court drew the line of admissibility to cover only the state of mind of the declarant:[324]

> The rules of evidence as developed to this point do not exclude evidence of utterances by a deceased which reveal her state of mind, but rather appear to provide specifically for their admission where relevant. The evidence is not, however, admissible to show the state of mind of persons other than the deceased (unless

---

320 A similar finding was made in *Stephens v. Toronto Railway Co.* (1905), 11 O.L.R. 19 (C.A.).
321 *Supra*, note 319.
322 The reasonableness of the inference that the declarant acted in accordance with the stated intention, "will depend on a number of variables including the nature of the plan described in the utterance, and the proximity in time between the statement as to the plan and the proposed implementation of the plan": per Doherty in *R. v. P. (R.)* (1990), 58 C.C.C. (3d) 334, at 343-44 (Ont. H.C.J.). See also *R. v. McKenzie* (1986), 32 C.C.C. (3d) 527 (B.C.C.A.), at 534-35.
323 (1990), 58 C.C.C. (3d) 334 (Ont. H.C.J.).
324 *Ibid.*, at 344.

they were aware of the statements), or to show that persons other than the deceased acted in accordance with the deceased's stated intentions, save perhaps cases where the act was a joint one involving the deceased and another person.

The Ontario Court of Appeal made it clear in *R. v. Smith*[325] that the admissibility of statements of intention were to be limited to the declarant's state of mind; they cannot be used to prove the act or intention of any other person:[326]

> In *R. v. Moore, supra,* this court considered the earlier United States decision in *Mutual Life Insurance Co. v. Hillm[o]n, supra.* The issue in *Moore* was confined to the admissibility of the declarant's statements of his intention to show his state of mind and intention. The evidence made no reference to any past act or any intention of any other person. It was not tendered as proof of such facts. We do not consider the reference in the *Moore* case to the *Mutual Life* case as authority for the extension of the doctrine to admit such statements to prove such facts. The *Mutual Life* case has been criticized for suggesting that this is so: *Cross on Evidence*, 6th ed. by Rupert Cross and Colin Tapper (London: Butterworths, 1985) pp. 586-88.

Carried to its logical conclusion, it could be argued that the decision in the *Hillmon* case would render admissible a presently existing state of mind to prove a past act. Such a ruling, however, would virtually emasculate the hearsay rule altogether. The Supreme Court of the United States in *Shepard v. United States*[327] refused to extend the *Hillmon* principle that far. The Court stated:[328]

---

325   (1990), 2 C.R. (4th) 253, 61 C.C.C. (3d) 232, 75 O.R. (2d) 753 (C.A.); leave to appeal to S.C.C. granted (1991), 2 O.R. (3d) xi. See also R.J. Delisle, "*R. v. Smith*: The Relevance of Hearsay", 2 C.R. (4th) 260.

326   *Ibid.,* at 757 (O.R.).

327   290 U.S. 96, 54 S. Ct. 22 (1933).

328   *Ibid.,* at 105-06 (U.S.). The same conclusion was reached by an Ontario Court in *R. v. P. (R.), supra,* note 323, at 344. Section 62(1)(g) of the draft *Uniform Evidence Act*, Bill S-33, 1980-81-82, preserves this common-law exception but expressly excludes statements of a presently existing state of mind to prove a past act. It permits admissibility of "a statement, made prior to the occurrence of a fact in issue, as to the state of mind or emotion of the declarant at the time the

Declarations of intention, casting light upon the future, have been sharply distinguished from declarations of memory, pointing backwards to the past. There would be an end, or nearly that, to the rule against hearsay if the distinction were ignored.

Declarations of intention or state of mind made by testators stand on a special footing. Courts have traditionally taken a more liberal stance in will cases and have admitted a testator's post-testamentary statement of memory or belief to establish antecedent facts. The famous case of *Sugden v. Lord St. Leonards*[329] allowed evidence of declarations made prior to and after the execution of a will to prove the nature of the executing act, i.e., the contents of a will which was allegedly lost.[330] Subsequently, in *Stewart v. Walker*,[331] post-testamentary statements of a testator were tendered in proof of the contents of a will which was not produced upon his death, although its execution was established. The Ontario Court of Appeal accepted the proposition asserted in the *Sugden* case and accordingly admitted the statements:[332]

---

statement was made". This provision is somewhat open-ended in that it does not appear to be limited to situations where the declarant's state of mind is itself a material fact. Moreover, the effect of such a provision would be that declarations would be received to prove a state of mind from which an inference could be made of the performance of an act consistent with that declared state of mind regardless of the inherent hearsay dangers that might otherwise be present.

329 (1876), 1 P.D. 154, 24 W.R. 860 (C.A.).

330 See also *Re MacGillivray*, [1946] 2 All E.R. 301 (C.A.) and *Acosta v. Longsworth*, [1965] 1 W.L.R. 107 (P.C.). The *Sugden* case overruled *Quick v. Quick* (1864), 3 Sw. & Tr. 442, 164 E.R. 1347 (P. & D.), which had established the principle that post-testamentary declarations were inadmissible to prove the contents of a will. The declarations of the testator in the *Sugden* case were admitted only as corroboration of other direct evidence of the contents of the will. The result can be justified only by the court recognizing the admissibility of post-testamentary declarations of a testator as a separate exception to the hearsay rule, for as Lord Morris of Borth-y-Gest stated in *Myers v. D.P.P.*, [1965] A.C. 1001, [1964] 3 W.L.R. 145 (H.L.), at 1027 (A.C.): "With every respect I cannot think that there is any principle that if first there is admissible evidence it may be added to by calling inadmissible evidence. That which is not evidence is not to be made evidence by saying that if it were evidence it would confirm other evidence." Thus, hearsay evidence is no more admissible merely because it is tendered for corroborating purposes.

331 (1903), 6 O.L.R. 495 (C.A.).

332 *Ibid.*, at 503-04.

There is further support from acts and expressions of the deceased subsequent to the making of the will. It has been urged that these should not be received as evidence on this branch of the case. It is argued that, although they may be regarded as throwing light on the question of intention to adhere to the will, and as therefore rebutting the presumption arising from non-production, they should not be looked at as evidence in proof of the contents. But while the decision in *Sugden v. Lord St. Leonards*, 1 P.D. 154, stands, it must be accepted as the law that declarations subsequent to the making of a will are admissible as secondary evidence of its contents . . .

And it is still an authority to be followed in similar cases. The declarations are receivable for what they may be worth, and it is for the Court to judge of the weight to be attached to them.

In addition, the courts have readily admitted pre-testamentary and contemporaneous statements of a testator or testatrix to show his or her state of mind when speaking, from which it may be inferred that he or she made a will consistent with that frame of mind.

It should be noted that neither pre-testamentary nor post-testamentary declarations are admissible to prove the execution of a will[333] since the formalities of execution are governed by statute[334] which cannot be circumvented by the mere introduction of the testator's or testatrix's assertions. This is so even though there is little distinction between a testator's or testatrix's statement referring to the contents of his or her will and a statement as to the execution of the will. From each state of mind may be inferred the existence of the fact, whether it be the contents of the will or the execution of the will, which resulted in that state of mind.

A testator's or testatrix's statement cannot be used to establish revocation of a will,[335] but they are admissible as original evidence in

---

333 *Sugden v. Lord St. Leonards, supra,* note 329; *Doe d. Shallcross v. Palmer* (1851), 16 Q.B. 747, 117 E.R. 1067. In *Howith v. McFarlane*, [1925] 2 D.L.R. 395 (C.A.), post-testamentary statements were admitted as corroboration of other evidence of testamentary execution. The correctness of this decision must be questioned in light of the statement in *Myers v. D.P.P., supra,* note 330.

334 For example, *The Succession Law Reform Act,* R.S.O. 1980, c. 488, ss. 4, 7.

335 *Staines v. Stewart* (1861), 2 Sw. & Tr. 320, 164 E.R. 1019 (P. & D.), at 329; *Atkinson v. Morris,* [1897] P. 40 (C.A.).

proof of his or her mental state at the relevant time. Accordingly, the declarations of a testator are admissible not as evidence of the revocation *per se*, but to establish or to rebut the presumption of *animus revocandi*. The non-production of a will raises a presumption in favour of revocation if the will was shown to have been lost in the testator's or testatrix's possession. In *Lefebvre v. Major*[336] the Supreme Court of Canada admitted declarations of the testator, uttered shortly before his death, indicating that he had left everything to his sister, for the purpose of rebutting the presumption of revocation of a will, the original of which had disappeared and which was in his sister's favour.[337]

In addition to admitting pre- and post-testamentary declarations of state of mind as evidence of the contents of a will and to establish whether the testator possessed an *animus revocandi*, courts have also admitted them to impeach the validity of a will on the ground of fraud, duress, undue influence or lack of testamentary capacity.[338]

4. Declarations Accompanying and Explaining Relevant Acts

There is contradicting judicial opinion as to the basis of admissibility of statements which are part of or accompany and explain the fact or transaction in issue. One view is that such statements constitute hearsay and can only be admitted as an exception to the hearsay rule.[339]

---

336 [1930] S.C.R. 252, [1930] 2 D.L.R. 532 (Ont.).

337 See also *Re Weeks*, [1972] 3 O.R. 422, 28 D.L.R. (3d) 452 (Ont. Surr. Ct.); *Re Moore*, [1941] 2 D.L.R. 112 (N.B.C.A.); *Bell v. Matthewman* (1920), 48 O.L.R. 364 (H.C.J.); *Re Sykes; Drake v. Sykes* (1907), 23 T.L.R. 747 (C.A.).

338 In *Quick v. Quick, supra*, note 330, at 447 (Sw. & Tr.), it was said: "It is familiar practice enough to receive the unsworn declarations of the testator in evidence, for the purpose of arriving at his general intentions where his competency is in dispute, or where there is any imputation of fraud in the making of his will. For in such cases the state of his mind and affections is in itself a material fact, of which such statements are the fair exponents." Although this case was overruled by the House of Lords in *Sugden v. Lord St. Leonards, supra*, note 329, on the issue of admissibility of a testator's post-testamentary statements to prove the contents of a will, no quarrel was taken with this point. In *Re Rosenblat*, [1932] 4 D.L.R. 518, [1932] 2 W.W.R. 433, 40 Man. R. 380 (C.A.), however, a testator's statements relating to mistreatment by his wife were excluded as evidence of undue influence at the time of making the will. Such statements were not expressive of a state of mind and the decision does not necessarily derogate from the principle stated in *Quick v. Quick*.

339 *Teper v. R.*, [1952] A.C. 480, at 487, [1952] 2 All E.R. 447 (H.L.).

The other is that such statements are received as original evidence, being merely a verbal part of the act.[340] The matter is still unsettled and the reason for it seems to arise as Lord Normand suggested in *Teper v. R.*[341] from the "two propositions, that human utterance is both a fact and a means of communication, and that human action may be so interwoven with words that the significance of the action cannot be understood without the correlative words, and the disassociation of the words from the action would impede the discovery of truth."[342] This uncertainty was revealed in a Nova Scotia case in which both theories were apparently adopted. In *Beaton v. Hayman*,[343] the plaintiff, an adopted son of the deceased, conveyed a certain property to her during her lifetime. Upon her death, the property descended to the defendant. The plaintiff maintained that the deed was merely one of convenience to his mother and that neither he nor she intended that the property was to become hers in fact. In support thereof, the plaintiff tendered as evidence, *inter alia*, a statement, made by the deceased to the person who drafted the deed, to the effect that the deed was given to her to facilitate a loan to remodel the house. The statement was made at the time when she instructed that person to draw the deed. Dubinsky J. admitted the statement as original evidence because it accompanied and explained the fact in issue, thus forming part of the *res gestae*. He went on, however, to add that this statement could also be accepted as to the truth of what it contained. The consequences either way are not significant, but the better view would be to treat such statements as hearsay for it would be virtually impossible for the trier of fact to receive such statements as original evidence without referring to the truth of the contents.[344] As Phipson has suggested,[345]

---

340 Lord Atkinson in *R. v. Christie*, [1914] A.C. 545 (H.L.), stated, at 553, that such statements "are not, as against the accused, affirmative evidence of the facts stated, but only of the knowledge of, or the belief in, those facts by the person who makes the statement, or of his intention in respect of them."

341 *Supra*, note 339.

342 *Supra*, note 339, at 486 (A.C.).

343 (1970), 16 D.L.R. (3d) 537, 3 N.S.R. (2d) 325 (N.S.S.C.).

344 In *Fleet v. Farrel* (1985), 71 N.S.R. (2d) 124, 171 A.P.R. 174 (C.A.), statements by a deceased as to her intention in executing a deed were admissible as falling within this exception.

345 D.W. Elliott, *Phipson's Manual of the Law of Evidence*, 10th ed. (London: Sweet & Maxwell, 1972), at 31-32.

A statement of this sort is said to explain the fact in issue, but in most cases it can only do so if it is assumed to be true. What, for instance was the relevance of the pilot's utterance [in *The Schwalbe*]:[346] "The damned helm is still a-starboard"? Of what is this *original* evidence except that pilots occasionally use bad language? It seems impossible to deny that the object of the evidence was to prove that the helm was a-starboard, and to prove it by assertion of one not called as a witness, *i.e.*, by hearsay evidence.

The principle of admissibility is: "Where an act done is evidence per se, a declaration accompanying that act may well be evidence if it reflects light upon or qualifies the act."[347] Necessity has played a strong hand in securing the admissibility of such statements, for where an act which is in issue is ambiguous or equivocal, then words which accompanied it may be the only means affording an explanation of the act. For example, the transfer of money from A to B may have been by way of loan, gift, or the retirement of an indebtedness. Statements which were made either by A or B contemporaneously with the handing over or receipt of the money would explain its purpose. Similarly, statements which accompany the delivery of the deed would tend to show whether it was by way of gift or advancement. So, too, declarations have been admitted to explain the legal nature of such equivocal acts as a transfer of chattels[348] or the taking of possession of land,[349] or the destruction of a will,[350] thus revealing the *animus* of the parties in performing the act. In such circumstances, the legal effect of the act can be understood only when evidence of the accompanying words is given.

All words are not admitted under this exception merely because they accompany an act. The words themselves must be such as to explain or qualify an otherwise ambiguous act.[351] An illustration of this

---

346 (1859), Sw. 521, 166 E.R. 1244 (Adm.).
347 Per Coltman J., in *Wright v. Doe d. Tatham* (1837), 7 Ad. & E. 313, 112 E.R. 488 (K.B.), at 361 (Ad. & E.); affd. 5 Cl. & Fin. 670, 7 E.R. 559 (H.L.). To the same effect see *Howe v. Malkin* (1878), 40 L.T. 196 (C.P.).
348 *Kingsmill v. Kingsmill* (1917), 41 O.L.R. 238, at 240 (S.C.).
349 *Doe d. Human v. Pettett* (1821), 5 B. & Ald. 223, 106 E.R. 1174 (K.B.).
350 *Powell v. Powell* (1866), L.R. 1 P. & D. 209, [1861-73] All E.R. Rep. 362.
351 *Freel v. Robinson* (1909), 18 O.L.R. 651, at 654-55 (Ont. C.A.); *Hyde v. Palmer* (1863), 3 B. & S. 657, 122 E.R. 246 (K.B.).

is found in *Clowser v. Samuel*.[352] A money order was sent together with a letter of instructions as to its application. The letter was lost and evidence of its contents was admitted as explaining the ambiguous act of sending the money order. Ritchie C.J. said:[353]

> In general, what a man says is not evidence for himself. But what he says accompanying an act, if the act cannot be understood without what is said at the time being given in evidence, the statements are admissible as forming part of the act.

In *Chase v. Chase*,[354] objection was taken by the plaintiff to the admissibility of a statement made by a deceased grantor at the time that he executed a deed of his real property to the defendant. After executing the deed, he handed it to the defendant saying, "There's the deed, Ruth, do what you want with it." The Chancery Division of the New Brunswick Supreme Court held that the statement was part of the *res gestae* because it accompanied, qualified and explained the act and gave it legal significance. It showed the grantor's intention when he gave the deed to the defendant.

Moreover, the act which is accompanied by the declaration must be either a fact in issue or relevant to it. Blackburn J., in *Hyde v. Palmer*,[355] indicated that declarations under this head of admissibility could be received only if they relate to "some act, the nature, object or motives of which are the subject of the inquiry".[356]

Furthermore, contemporaneity is an essential factor. The declarations must closely accompany the act or transactions, and be uttered at the time of or shortly before or after the commission of the act. The circumstances of each case must be examined to determine whether there is a sufficient nexus in time between the utterance and the act. There should not be such a hiatus of time as to raise the spectre of fabrication nor to reduce the statement to a mere narrative of facts.

---

352 (1873), 15 N.B.R. 58 (C.A.).
353 *Ibid.*, at 58-59.
354 (1963), 48 M.P.R. 12, 36 D.L.R. (2d) 351 (N.B.); affd. by C.A. without written reasons.
355 *Supra*, note 351.
356 *Supra*, note 351, at 661 (B. & S.). See also *Wright v. Doe d. Tatham* (1837), 7 Ad. & E. 313, 112 E.R. 488 (K.B.), at 361 (Ad. & E.); affd. (*sub nom. Wright v. Tatham*) 5 Cl. & Fin. 670, 7 E.R. 559 (H.L.).

5. Spontaneous Exclamations

The doctrine of *res gestae* has also been invoked to admit statements "made by those present when a thing took place, made about it, and importing what is present at the very time . . ."[357] The origin of the admissibility of such statements can be traced to the year 1693 when Holt C.J. in *Thompson v. Trevanion*,[358] an action for assault upon the plaintiff's wife, said:[359]

> . . . What the wife said immediate upon the hurt received, and before she had time to devise or contrive any thing for her own advantage, might be given in evidence . . .

Thus the statement is received because it was made contemporaneously with the event to which it related so as to be inextricably connected with that event. The mere intimacy of the utterance with the event makes the statement relevant.[360]

The hallmark of admissibility was the contemporaneity of the statement with the act. Because of the coincidence in time of the statement to the event, the hearsay dangers are minimized: (1) there is little time for calculated insincerity on the part of the declarant, as the physical and mental shock of the event stills conscious reflection; (2) there is no problem of faulty memory as the event is still transpiring or has been just completed; (3) the perception of the declarant may well be heightened by the event.

There is another school of thought which holds the opposite viewpoint as to the psychological impression caused by a surprising event: that because the event itself was startling, the perception of the observer may well be impaired. James Marshall in *Law and Psychology in Conflict* showed his concern as follows:[361]

> Danger and stress also affect the estimate of time and distance. This overestimate tends to increase as danger increases. As laymen we are accustomed to the concept that in emergencies

---

357 J.B. Thayer, "Bedingfield's case — Declarations as a part of the *res gesta*" (1881), 15 Am. L. Rev. 1, at 83.
358 (1693), Skin. 402, 90 E.R. 179 (K.B.).
359 *Ibid.*
360 J. Stone, "Res Gesta Reagitata" (1939), 55 L.Q.R. 66, at 80-81.
361 2nd ed. (Indianapolis, Bobbs-Merrill Co. Inc., 1969), at 19-20.

time seems endless, but as lawyers we ignore the reality that with increasing danger 'space and time stretch' and so accept the validity of a party's testimony that the car was a hundred yards away when he stepped off the curb, or the statement of a car driver as to when he sounded his horn. Not only the duration, but the *sequence* of events may be difficult to perceive. This too may be an important issue of fact, as when the question in an assault case is who struck first, or in a matrimonial proceeding, who spoke first. The law of evidence takes a contrary view concerning the impact of stress. The *res gestae* rule governing the admission of spontaneous explanations by a participant in an event is justified on the theory that the impact of intensity, the 'stress of nervous excitement' as Dean Wigmore calls it, will make for 'a spontaneous and sincere response . . .' That is, legal theory maintains that in the 'stress of nervous excitement' the witness does not consciously try to make self-serving declarations as to his perceptions, and therefore his statements are more reliable. It ignores, however, the distorting impact of trauma on the capacity to perceive.

Canadian courts have had difficulty with respect to the degree of proximity in time between the act and the making of the statement so as to meet the requirement of contemporaneity. An extreme position was taken by the Ontario Court of Appeal in *R. v. Leland.*[362] In that case, the victim, shortly after being stabbed, called out to his wife, "Rose, she stabbed me through the heart." The statement was tendered by the Crown as proof of the truth of the assertion, the inference being that it was the accused who killed him. The Ontario Court of Appeal felt that the statement, though it may have been spontaneous, did not form any part of the *res gestae*. When the victim made the statement, the transaction had been completed; the stabbing had ceased and no one was chasing him. Because there was no precise contemporaneity between the statement and event, the Court excluded evidence of the assertion. The words had to be absolutely contemporaneous with the event in time, place and circumstances.[363]

---

362 [1951] O.R. 12, 98 C.C.C. 337, 11 C.R. 152 (C.A.).
363 This requirement emanates from the landmark case of *R. v. Bedingfield* (1879), 14 Cox C.C. 341. There, the accused who was charged with murder was seen going into a house. Moments later, the deceased ran out with her throat cut

The rigidity of the contemporaneity requirement was loosened by the Privy Council in *Ratten v. R.*[364] In that case the accused was charged with murdering his wife by shooting her with a shotgun. His defence was that although he had shot her, it was accidental, explaining that the gun went off while he was cleaning it. Evidence was adduced indicating that his wife had been alive and was behaving normally at 1:12 p.m. and within ten minutes thereafter she had been shot. The prosecution challenged that defence by calling a telephone operator who testified as to a telephone call which she had received at 1:15 p.m. from the deceased's home. She stated that the call was from a female who sounded hysterical and who said "Get me the police please", and gave her address, but before she was able to connect the caller to the police station the phone went dead. Objection was taken to the evidence on the ground that it was hearsay and did not fall within any of the recognized exceptions. The Privy Council held that the operator's testimony constituted original evidence, not hearsay, and was relevant in that it served to rebut the accused's statement that his call for the ambulance after he shot his wife was the only call that emanated from the house between 1:12 p.m. and 1:20 p.m., by which time his wife was dead, and secondly, that the operator's evidence that the caller was a woman speaking in a hysterical voice was capable of relating to the state of mind of the deceased from which it could be inferred that the deceased was suffering from anxiety or fear of some existing or impending emergency.

Lord Wilberforce also dealt with the admissibility of the operator's statements on the assumption that the words *were* hearsay and that they involved an assertion of the truth of the facts stated therein. He then proceeded to set out the modern theory upon which a hearsay statement relatively contemporaneous with some event which produces nervous excitement or stress may be admitted:[365]

---

exclaiming, "See what Harry [the accused] has done." This statement was excluded by Cockburn C.J. because the transaction was over. See also *Gilbert v. R.* (1907), 38 S.C.R. 207, 12 C.C.C. 124.

364 [1972] A.C. 378, [1971] 3 W.L.R. 930, 115 Sol. Jo. 889, [1971] 3 All E.R. 801 (P.C.).

365 *Ibid.*, at 807-08 (All E.R.). These principles have been adopted in Canada: see *R. v. Khan* (1988), 27 O.A.C. 142, 64 C.R. (3d) 281, 42 C.C.C. (3d) 197 (C.A.), at 148-51 (O.A.C.); affd. [1990] 2 S.C.R. 531, 59 C.C.C. (3d) 92, 79 C.R. (3d) 1, 41 O.A.C. 353, 11 W.C.B. (2d) 10, 113 N.R. 53; *R. v. Khan* (1982), 66 C.C.C. (2d) 32, 36 O.R. (2d) 399 (C.A.), at 42-43 (C.C.C.); *Klippenstein v. R.* (1981), 57

The possibility of concoction, or fabrication, where it exists, is on the other hand an entirely valid reason for exclusion, and is probably the real test which judges in fact apply. In their Lordships' opinion this should be recognised and applied directly as the relevant test: the test should be not the uncertain one whether the making of the statement was in some sense part of the event or transaction. This may often be difficult to establish: such external matters as the time which elapses between the events and the speaking of the words (or vice versa), and differences in location being relevant factors but not, taken by themselves, decisive criteria. As regards statements made after the event it must be for the judge, by preliminary ruling, to satisfy himself that the statement was so clearly made in circumstances of spontaneity or involvement in the event that the possibility of concoction can be disregarded. Conversely, if he considers that the statement was made by way of narrative of a detached prior event so that the speaker was so disengaged from it as to be able to construct or adapt his account, he should exclude it. And the same must in principle be true of statements made before the event. The test should be not the uncertain one, whether the making of the statement should be regarded as part of the event or transaction. This may often be difficult to show. But if the drama, leading up to the climax, has commenced and assumed such intensity and pressure that the utterance can safely be regarded as a true reflection of what was unrolling or actually happening, it ought to be received. The expression 'res gestae' may conveniently sum up these criteria, but the reality of them must always be kept in mind: it is this that lies behind the best reasoned of the judges' rulings . . .

These authorities show that there is ample support for the principle that hearsay evidence may be admitted if the statement providing it is made in such conditions (always being those of approximate but not exact contemporaneity) of involvement or pressure as to exclude the possibility of concoction or distortion to the advantage of the maker or the disadvantage of the accused.

C.C.C. (2d) 393, 19 C.R. (3d) 56, [1981] 3 W.W.R. 111, 26 A.R. 568 (C.A.), at 399-400 (C.C.C.), at 65 (C.R.); *R. v. Garlow* (1976), 31 C.C.C. (2d) 163 (Ont. H.C.J.).

Ultimately, *R. v. Leland* was reconsidered by the Ontario Court of Appeal in 1983. In *R. v. Clark*[366] shortly after the deceased was stabbed by the accused she yelled "Help, I've been murdered, I've been stabbed". The Court held that the narrow test of exact contemporaneity should no longer be followed[367] and it acknowledged that the significance of the *Ratten* decision was "to move the test from asking whether the statement was part of the *res gestae* or the transaction to asking whether its spontaneity was such that concoction or distortion could safely be excluded."[368] The Court admitted these statements because they were made spontaneously in circumstances where there was no danger of concoction or distortion and the fact that they were not made exactly contemporaneously with the events to which they related was irrelevant.

The Supreme Court of Canada, however, in *R. v. Khan*[369] has held that contemporaneity is still an important condition for admissibility. The issue was the admissibility of a statement made by a 3-year-old child to the effect that the accused had committed a sexual assault upon her. The child's statement was made to her mother 15 minutes after the assault allegedly occurred. The trial judge did not admit the statement. On his reading of *Ratten* and *Clark*, to be admissible, a spontaneous declaration must occur within the unfolding of the events surrounding it even if not exactly contemporaneous with it. In his reasons the trial judge stated:[370]

> It seems to me that in all the circumstances what the child said to her mother was narrative. She was speaking of a prior event and was so located by time and place sufficiently distant by intervening activities from the event itself as to be disengaged from it. She could have intentionally or subconsciously adapted or fudged her account.

---

366 (1983), 42 O.R. (2d) 609, 35 C.R. (3d) 357, 7 C.C.C. (3d) 46, 1 D.L.R. (4th) 46; leave to appeal to S.C.C. refd. (1983) 39 C.R. (3d) xxvii.

367 The House of Lords in *R. v. Andrews*, [1987] 2 W.L.R. 413, at 422 stated that *R. v. Bedingfield* (*supra*, note 363) could not be decided the same way today: "Indeed, there could . . . hardly be a case where the words uttered carried more clearly the mark of spontaneity and intense involvement".

368 Quoted in M.N. Howard, P. Crane and D.A. Hochberg, *Phipson on Evidence*, 14th Ed. (London: Sweet & Maxwell, 1990), at 717.

369 [1990] 2 S.C.R. 531, 59 C.C.C. (3d) 92, 79 C.R. (3d) 1, 41 O.A.C. 353, 11 W.C.B. (2d) 10, 113 N.R. 53.

370 *Supra*, note 365, *R. v. Khan* (1988), at 291 (C.R.).

I am not satisfied that the shock or pressure created by the event, if indeed that occurred, was present when the child spoke. The chain of occurrence has been broken. Any occurrence that did in fact take place could not be said, on the evidence I heard, to be ongoing. The declaration, for those reasons, will therefore not be admitted.

The Court of Appeal disagreed with the trial judge's approach on the question of contemporaneity and held that the inherent reliability of the child's statement was such that the usual requirements for spontaneous declarations of contemporaneity and intensity or pressure should be relaxed.[371]

McLachlin J. in the Supreme Court of Canada held, however, that these circumstances did not fit within the conceptual framework of the spontaneous declaration exception and that to permit it on this basis would "deform it beyond recognition".[372] She stated:[373]

I am satisfied that applying the traditional tests for spontaneous declarations, the trial judge correctly rejected the mother's statement. The statement was not contemporaneous, being made fifteen minutes after leaving the doctor's office and probably one-half hour after the offence was committed. Nor was it made under pressure or emotional intensity which would give the guarantee of reliability upon which the spontaneous declaration rule has traditionally rested.

The statements, however, were admitted on another basis, a newly created exception for children's hearsay.[374]

The House of Lords has provided a set of guidelines to assist a trial judge in applying the *res gestae* exception to the hearsay rule in a criminal case. In *R. v. Andrews*[375] the House of Lords held that it was quite proper for the trial judge to have admitted the victim's statement to the police in which he named his assailants shortly after being attacked. He had been attacked by two men who had entered his

---

371 *Supra*, note 365, *R. v. Khan* (1988), at 148-51 (O.A.C.).
372 *Supra*, note 369, at 544 (S.C.R.).
373 *Supra*, note 369, at 540 (S.C.R.).
374 See this Chapter, II.L.
375 [1987] A.C. 281, [1987] 2 W.L.R. 413, 84 Cr. App. Rep. 382, [1987] 1 All E.R. 513 (H.L.).

apartment and received knife wounds which ultimately proved to be fatal. After the attack he managed to obtain some assistance and the police arrived within minutes, at which time he informed them of the identity of his attackers. Two months later, the victim died as the result of his injuries. At the trial of the two accused, the Crown sought to have the deceased's statement admitted, not as a dying declaration but as evidence of the truth of the facts that he had asserted, namely, that he had been attacked by the two accused and that the statement was therefore admissible in the circumstances as evidence within the *res gestae* exception. The Court agreed and held that the circumstances here were such as to satisfy the trial judge that the event was so unusual or startling or dramatic as to dominate the thoughts of the victim so as to exclude any possibility on his part of concoction or distortion. The statement was made in conditions of approximate but not exact contemporaneity justifying its admissibility. In coming to this conclusion the House of Lords set out five fundamental guidelines that a trial judge should take into account in determining whether the *res gestae* doctrine is applicable to the circumstances in question:[376]

1. The primary question which the judge must ask himself is — can the possibility of concoction or distortion be disregarded?

2. To answer that question the judge must first consider the circumstances in which the particular statement was made, in order to satisfy himself that the event was so unusual or startling or dramatic as to dominate the thoughts of the victim, so that his utterance was an instinctive reaction to that event, thus giving no real opportunity for reasoned reflection. In such a situation the judge would be entitled to conclude that the involvement or the pressure of the event would exclude the possibility of concoction or distortion, providing that the statement was made in conditions of approximate but not exact contemporaneity.

3. In order for the statement to be sufficiently 'spontaneous' it must be so closely associated with the event which has excited the statement, that it can be fairly stated that the mind of the declarant was still dominated by the event. Thus the judge must be satisfied that the event, which provided the trigger mechanism

---

376 *Ibid.*, at 422-23 (W.L.R.).

for the statement, was still operative. The fact that the statement was made in answer to a question is but one factor to consider under this heading.

4.   Quite apart from the time factor, there may be special features in the case, which relate to the possibility of concoction or distortion. In the instant appeal the defence relied upon evidence to support the contention that the deceased had a motive of his own to fabricate or concoct, namely, a malice which resided in him against O'Neill [an accused] and the appellant [also an accused] because, so he believed, O'Neill had attacked and damaged his house and was accompanied by the appellant, who ran away on a previous occasion. The judge must be satisfied that the circumstances were such that having regard to the special feature of malice, there was no possibility of any concoction or distortion to the advantage of the maker or the disadvantage of the accused.

5.   As to the possibility of error in the facts narrated in the statement, if only the ordinary fallibility of human recollection is relied upon, this goes to the weight to be attached to and not to the admissibility of the statement and is therefore a matter for the jury. However, here again there may be special features that may give rise to the possibility of error. In the instant case there was evidence that the deceased had drunk to excess, well over double the permitted limit for driving a motor car. Another example would be where the identification was made in circumstances of particular difficulty or where the declarant suffered from defective eyesight. In such circumstances the trial judge must consider whether he can exclude the possibility of error.

No court has carried the spontaneous exclamation exception to the hearsay rule to its logical conclusion. Wigmore stresses the occurrence of the startling event and feels that it is of no consequence whether the statement is related to the event or whether that event is or is not a fact in issue.[377] Both English and Canadian cases have insisted that the declaration must be directly in relation to an event or transaction which is in issue. In *Ratten*,[378] the Privy Council stated that

---

377   6 Wigmore, *Evidence* (Chadbourn rev. 1976), § 1750, at 222.
378   *Ratten v. R., supra,* note 364.

what had to be shown was "the involvement of the speaker in the pressure of the drama, or the concatenation of events leading up to the crisis."[379]

Wigmore believes that this is "a cautionary rather than a logically necessary restriction",[380] and Professor Morgan has added that: "If spontaneity of itself is to be accepted as a guaranty of trustworthiness, then the subject matter of the declaration should not be limited to the startling event which operated to still the reflective faculties."[381] That principle, however, has not yet been accepted in Canada.

There is some question as to whether the startling occurrence which gives rise to a spontaneous statement can be proven by the statement alone or whether proof, independent of the statement, is required.[382] McCormick suggests that under generally prevailing practice, the statement alone is considered sufficient but adds that some courts insist on independent evidence of the exciting event as a precondition to the admissibility of the utterance.[383]

Wigmore has also urged that a declaration of a bystander induced by some excitement-producing event should be equally admissible as a declaration made by the principal actor in the event.[384] In *Teper v. R.*,[385] the Privy Council had an opportunity to consider the admissibility of a bystander's exclamation upon seeing an individual fleeing from the scene of a fire, "Your place burning and you going away from the scene of a fire." The Court did not seem to be concerned about the fact that the statement had been made by a bystander rather than a participant in the act. The distinction may be of some importance for there is a greater danger of faulty perception relating to identity when the declaration is made by a non-participant in the transaction. The Privy Council worried about the possibility of error in identification, not because it was a statement made by a bystander, but because the statement had not been made contemporaneously with the com-

---

379   *Ibid.*, at 808 (All E.R.).
380   *Supra*, note 377, § 1750, at 222.
381   E.M. Morgan, "A Suggested Classification of Utterances Admissible as Res Gestae" (1922), 31 Yale L.J. 229, at 239.
382   Per Robins J.A. in *R. v. Khan* (1988), *supra*, note 365, at 148-51 (O.A.C.); affd. *supra*, note 369.
383   E.W. Cleary (ed.), *McCormick on Evidence*, 3rd ed. (St. Paul: West Publishing, 1984), at 855-56, quoted by Robins J.A. in *R. v. Khan, ibid.*
384   *Supra*, note 377, § 1755, at 228-30.
385   [1952] A.C. 480, [1952] 2 All E.R. 447 (P.C.).

mission of the crime. In *R. v. Jobidon*[386] Campbell J. of the Ontario Supreme Court accepted the testimony of bystanders who had witnessed a fist fight. He stated:[387]

> The absolutely spontaneous words "It's a fair fight," spoken during the affray with no possibility of contrivance are evidence of the character of the fight, or at least of its character as it appeared to the onlookers . . .
>
> There is no reason in principle to treat the statements of the onlookers any differently from the statements of the participants.

What if the event to which the statement relates is not startling in any way? Can spontaneous statements nevertheless be admitted? Few cases have dealt with this issue, probably because statements are not usually made in the absence of some excitement-provoking event. However, much can be said in favour of admitting such statements even if some reliability may be lost[388] by reason of the fact that the declarant was not startled into making the exclamations. The fact that the statement is made contemporaneously with the declarant's observations of the event in question removes doubts about sincerity and faulty memory.[389] In *R. v. Graham*,[390] the accused was charged with possession of stolen goods. The Supreme Court of Canada considered the admissibility of two statements, a verbal statement made by the

---

386 (1987), 59 C.R. (N.S.) 203, 36 C.C.C. (3d) 340 (H.C.J.); revd. on other grounds (1988), 45 C.C.C. (3d) 176, 67 C.R. (3d) 183, 30 O.A.C. 172 (C.A.); affd. by S.C.C., but not yet reported, September 26, 1991.

387 *Ibid.*, at 209-10 (C.R.); in *Milne v. Leisler* (1862), 7 H. & N. 786, 158 E.R. 686 (Exch. Ct.), Pollock C.B., at 796 (H. & N.), intimated that statements by bystanders are admissible: ". . . in the case of an exclamation by anyone in a crowd, when an accident occurs, and the conduct of a particular person is in question, it may be asked whether some one did not call out 'shame', for it is part of the res gestae." The draft *Uniform Evidence Act* would clearly allow for spontaneous declarations by anyone including a bystander. Section 62(1)(h) allows for the admissibility of "a spontaneous statement made in direct reaction to a startling event perceived or apprehended by the declarant". It should be noted that there would still have to be a direct relationship between the exclamation and the event.

388 There is some question whether excitement provides any assurance of reliability: see this Chapter, II.H.5.

389 *McCormick on Evidence, supra*, note 383, at 860.

390 [1974] S.C.R. 206, 7 C.C.C. (2d) 93, 19 C.R.N.S. 117, [1972] 4 W.W.R. 488, 26 D.L.R. (3d) 579.

accused contemporaneously with the police discovering the attaché case containing the stolen goods, and a written statement made two hours later. No event of a startling or exciting nature caused the remarks. Ritchie J. stated:[391]

> In the present case the respondent's verbal statement made when the attache case was found, that he had never seen it before in his life, being one which was immediately connected with the initial discovery of the stolen goods, was properly admitted in evidence. Explanatory statements made by an accused upon his first being found "in possession" constitute a part of the *res gestae* and are necessarily admissible in any description of the circumstances under which the crime was committed ... and his written statement was not made contemporaneously with the discovery but rather after ample time had elapsed for reflection. In my view if this statement were to be admitted it would mean that any person accused of receiving stolen goods could, after due consideration, devise an explanation which might easily be true for the goods having been found in his possession and could thus avoid the necessity of presenting himself as a witness and be afforded the full benefit of his explanation without being subjected to cross-examination. Such an explanation is, in my view, inadmissible under the general rule in criminal cases that self-serving statements made by an accused cannot be introduced on the cross-examination of third parties because they cannot themselves be tested by cross-examination of the accused person who made them, and their introduction in such manner deprives the jury of the benefit of appraising his credibility from observing his demeanour.

Determination of whether the statement was admissible turned solely upon its contemporaneous nature.

I. *Dying Declarations*

1. Scope and Rationale

An early common-law exception to the hearsay rule was the admissibility at trial against an accused charged with murder or

---

391   *Ibid.*, at 99 (C.C.C.).

manslaughter of statements by a deceased pertaining to the cause of death, provided that the deceased had been under a settled or hopeless expectation of death when he or she made the statement, and, provided that the individual could have been a competent witness if he or she had been available to testify at the trial. The rationale for the exception had been expressed by Eyre C.B. in the eighteenth-century case of *R. v. Woodcock*[392] as follows:[393]

> . . . the general principle on which this species of evidence is admitted is, that they are declarations made in extremity, when the party is at the point of death, and when every hope of this world is gone: when every motive to falsehood is silenced, and the mind is induced by the most powerful considerations to speak the truth; a situation so solemn, and so awful, is considered by the law as creating an obligation equal to that which is imposed by a positive oath administered in a Court of Justice.

Given that such evidence is most incriminating by its nature and without the traditional safeguards of cross examination, courts have insisted on strict adherence to the prerequisites of the exception before granting admissibility.

2. Requirements

(a) *Settled Hopeless Expectation of Death*

The declarant must have possessed the belief that he or she was mortally injured and was going to die when he or she made the statement and the evidence must establish this fact.[394] It is immaterial whether another person in a similar situation would have harboured the same feeling or that a physician would not have considered the situation hopeless.[395] The feeling to be possessed is not merely fear that the declarant may succumb to death, but that in fact the declarant has a solemn conviction that he or she will soon die and that there is no hope whatsoever of recovery. The fact that death does not take place until sometime thereafter will not affect the admissibility of the

---

392 (1789), 1 Leach 500, 168 E.R. 352.
393 *Ibid.*, at 353.
394 *R. v. Garlow* (1976), 31 C.C.C. (2d) 163 (Ont. H.C.J.); *R. v. Andrews*, [1987] 2 W.L.R. 413, [1987] 1 All E.R. 513 (H.L.), at 417 (W.L.R.).
395 See *R. v. Mosley* (1825), 1 Mood. C.C. 97, 168 E.R. 1200 (C.C.R.).

statement so long as it occurs within a certain proximity of the making of the statement.[396]

(b) *The Trial Must Be One in Which the Accused is Charged with Murder or Manslaughter*

The nature of the cases in which such evidence is admitted is limited to homicide. In *R. v. Mead*,[397] Abbot C.J. stated that "evidence of this description is only admissible where the death of the deceased is the subject of the charge, and the circumstances of the death the subject of the dying declaration."[398]

In addition to murder and manslaughter, criminal negligence causing death has been held to be an appropriate charge since that crime may also fall under the rubric of manslaughter.[399] If the rationale for the admissibility of such statements is the general confidence in the trustworthiness of the statement grounded in the circumstances under which it is given, there is no logical reason to limit the situations in which such evidence is admissible. One would have thought that if the evidence has such a hallmark of reliability as to be receivable in homicide cases, then *a fortiori* it should be received in the trial of any charge.[400]

(c) *Injuries Those of Declarant and the Subject of the Charge*

Dying declarations are also limited to situations where the death or injuries in question are those of the declarant him or herself whose

---

396 *R. v. Laurin (No. 4)* (1902), 6 C.C.C. 104 (Que. K.B.), at 106.
397 (1824), 2 B. & C. 605, 107 E.R. 509 (K.B.), at 510 (E.R.).
398 *Ibid.*, at 510 (E.R.); see also *R. v. Schwartzenhauer*, [1935] S.C.R. 367, 64 C.C.C. 1, [1935] 3 D.L.R. 711 (B.C.).
399 *R. v. Jurtyn*, [1958] O.W.N. 355, 28 C.R. 295, 121 C.C.C. 403 (C.A.).
400 See R.J. Delisle, *Evidence: Principles and Problems*, 2nd ed. (Toronto: Carswell, 1989), at 385, wherein the author points out that the restriction of dying declarations to homicide charges was an accident of history. Such evidence had been readily received in both civil and criminal cases until a statement appeared in a leading text on homicide indicating that such evidence was admissible in that type of prosecution and the matter evolved from there by judicial interpretation to restrict its application to homicide prosecutions. Section 51(1) of the draft *Uniform Evidence Act*, Bill S-33, 1980-81-82, would extend the nature of the charge with respect to which dying declarations would be admissible. It would include an attempt to commit murder or any other charge arising out of the transaction leading to the declarant's death or injuries that is joined with the main charge.

death is the subject of the charge. Again, the limitation is not a logical one.[401] Wigmore gives numerous examples from American cases including:[402]

> M. and L. fought with the deceased W.; W. and L. were killed; M. is charged with the killing of W.; L.'s dying declaration as to the circumstances was excluded when offered by defendant; another example of the crass stupidity of this limitation.

J. Testimony in Former Proceedings

1. Theory of Admissibility

Consistent with the broad, sweeping definition of hearsay set out at the beginning of this chapter,[403] evidence at trial of statements made by a witness in a former adjudicative proceeding falls within this classification if it is tendered as proof of the truth of the facts testified to in the other forum.[404] Wigmore, however, felt that such evidence does not fall under the rubric of hearsay. The hearsay rule was propounded to exclude testimonial statements which were not subjected to cross-examination and which were not given under oath. Thus, a statement which was earlier made under oath, subjected to cross-examination and admitted as testimony at a former proceeding, is received in a subsequent trial because the dangers underlying hearsay evidence are absent.[405] Under either view, the evidence is admissible. If considered hearsay, its trustworthiness is assured by the conditions of admissibility. Certain weaknesses, however, are inherent

---

401 Wigmore described this restriction as an "irrational and pitiful absurdity of this feat of legal cerebration": see 5 Wigmore, *Evidence* (Chadbourn rev. 1974), § 1433, at 282.

402 *Ibid.*, § 1433, at 281.

403 See this Chapter, I.A.

404 E.M. Morgan, *Basic Problems of Evidence* (Joint Committee on Continuing Legal Education of the American Law Institute and the American Bar Association, 1962), at 255.

405 5 Wigmore, *Evidence* (Chadbourn rev. 1974), § 1370, at 55. Rules of Court in a number of Provinces specifically permit the admissibility of such evidence: see Alberta *Rules of Court*, Alta. Reg. 390/68, r. 262; British Columbia *Supreme Court Rules*, B.C. Reg. 221/90, r. 40(4); New Brunswick *Evidence Act*, R.S.N.B. 1973, c. E-11, ss. 33 to 35; Newfoundland *Rules of Supreme Court*, 1986, rr. 30.13(1)(c), 46.13(b); Quebec *Code of Civil Procedure*, R.S.Q. 1977, c. C-25, s. 320; Saskatchewan *Queen's Bench Rules*, r. 304.

in such evidence. For one thing, the cross-examination in the earlier proceeding may have been directed to a specific issue or conducted with a particular and narrow purpose in mind. Secondly, the trier of fact in the second hearing will be deprived of an opportunity of observing the declarant's demeanour under the stress of cross-examination. Demeanour, of course, may be important on the question of credibility. Notwithstanding such drawbacks, the general reliability of such evidence has overridden these considerations. Moreover, the unavailability of the declarant at the time of trial has necessitated its admissibility.[406]

Trustworthiness is guaranteed only if there is insistence on certain requirements in addition to demonstrating that the witness is unavailable. The Supreme Court of Canada considered the extent of such requirements in *Walkerton (Town) v. Erdman*.[407] Erdman had commenced an action against the town with respect to injuries that he had sustained as a result of a fall into a ditch on a public street. Prior to trial, an examination *de bene esse* was held.[408] Such an examination was granted, apparently because Erdman was too ill to travel to the place of trial. In addition to being examined on the *de bene esse* proceeding by his own counsel, he was also cross-examined by the town's solicitor. The transcript of that proceeding was to be used at the subsequent trial, but Erdman died before the action had reached that stage. His widow then commenced a second action under the then Ontario *Fatal Accidents Act*[409] on behalf of herself and her children. She attempted to introduce at the trial of that action the transcript of

---

406 That the declarant is unavailable may be established by proving that he or she is dead: *Walkerton (Town) v. Erdman* (1894), 23 S.C.R. 352; *Court v. Holland* (1880), 8 P.R. 213, at 221; or that he or she is absent from jurisdiction: *Sutor v. McLean* (1859), 18 U.C.Q.B. 490 (C.A.); *Cuff v. Frazee Storage & Cartage Co.* (1907), 14 O.L.R. 263 (C.A.); *Shumardo v. Toronto General Trusts Corp.*, [1940] 2 W.W.R. 564; varied as to quantum of damages, [1941] 1 W.W.R. 448, 49 Man. R. 82 (C.A.); *Monro v. Toronto Railway* (1904), 9 O.L.R. 299, at 312 (C.A.); or that he or she was insane or too infirm: *Abel v. Light* (1866), 11 N.B.R. 423 (C.A.); *Glasgow v. Toronto Paper Mfg. Co.* (1905), 5 O.W.R. 104 (C.A.); or that he or she was incarcerated at the time of trial: *Switzer v. Boulton* (1851), 2 Gr. 693; or that he or she just could not be found after a diligent search had been made: *Fleming v. Canadian Pacific Railway Co.* (1905), 5 O.W.R. 589 (H.C.J.).
407 (1894), 23 S.C.R. 352.
408 See r. 36 of the *Rules of Civil Procedure* of Ontario, O. Reg. 560/84, as am. for present rules for taking evidence before trial.
409 Now see *Family Law Act, 1986*, S.O. 1986, c. 4, Part V.

evidence *de bene esse* but the trial judge refused to admit it. The town then successfully non-suited the plaintiff because she had adduced no evidence of the cause of her husband's injury. An appeal was eventually taken to the Supreme Court of Canada.

The Supreme Court of Canada held that the testimony of Erdman in his examination *de bene esse* was admissible in the subsequent case because the defendant town had the opportunity to, and in fact did, cross-examine Erdman on the same facts and issues that were involved in the second action. Moreover, when Erdman was examined in chief and cross-examined, he was under oath. So there was some assurance of the trustworthiness of his evidence.

2. Guarantees of Trustworthiness

(a) *Issues Substantially the Same*

It is of importance that the issues in the two actions were substantially the same.[410] The main issue in both cases was whether Erdman's injury was caused by the negligence of the town. Since the issues were the same, the defendant town could not say that it would have cross-examined Erdman in a different way and on different issues in the second trial had he been alive and given his testimony at trial.

Insistence upon identity of issues assures that the motive of the party to test the evidence on cross-examination when the witness first gave evidence is the same as that of the present party against whom the evidence is now tendered.[411] "Identity of interest in the sense of motive, rather than technical identity of cause of action or title, is the test."[412]

(b) *Same Parties*

Another requirement that the Court mentioned as a pre-condition to the admissibility of the prior testimony is that the two actions should be between the same parties, or those claiming under them.[413] The rationale, presumably, is that a new party in the second action

---

410   See also *Re G.* (1973), 1 O.R. (2d) 318, 14 R.F.L. 201, 40 D.L.R. (3d) 198, at 323 (O.R.); revd. on other grounds (1974), 5 O.R. 337, 19 R.F.L. 45, 50 D.L.R. (3d) 321 (C.A.); and *Van Ginkel v. Van Ginkel* (1975), 20 R.F.L. 359 (Man. Q.B.).
411   See *Smith v. Goulet* (1975), 19 R.F.L. 45, at 55 (Ont. C.A.).
412   E.W. Cleary (ed.), *McCormick on Evidence*, 3rd ed. (St. Paul: West Publishing, 1984), at 765.
413   See also *Serediuk v. Kogan*, [1976] 5 W.W.R. 571, 28 R.F.L. 237 (Man. C.A.).

should not be bound by the cross-examination conducted by some other party who had a different counsel and a different interest in the first action, and whose cross-examination may have been limited to specific areas relevant to his particular interest. Would not these considerations be satisfied, even if the parties to the two proceedings were different, so long as the cross-examining party in the first action had the same interest and motives as the new party in the second action? If so, would not sufficient elements of trustworthiness be present so as to justify the admissibility of the testimony in the former proceeding against new parties in a subsequent action?[414]

(c) *Opportunity by Adversary to Cross-Examine*

It is imperative that the opponent had an opportunity to cross-examine the declarant at the previous proceeding. Consequently, the previous testimony of a witness in a criminal case is generally not admissible in a subsequent civil action even though it involved the same fact situation. Parties and issues in criminal and civil cases are different, and, consequently, a cross-examination for the purposes of civil action could be totally different from the cross-examination conducted in the criminal proceeding which would focus upon different issues. To permit such evidence to be admitted would effectively deprive the opponent of his or her right to test its accuracy.[415]

3. Evidence Taken on Discovery

Similar considerations apply when an attempt is made to introduce at trial a transcript of a party's own examination for discovery. If a party's representative were allowed to put into evidence at trial that party's examination for discovery, it would have been untested by cross-examination under rules of procedure in some provinces, and, accordingly, the circumstantial guarantee of trustworthiness which is the guiding principle behind this exception to the hearsay rule would be lost.[416]

---

414 Rule 40(4) of the British Columbia *Rules of Court* permits admissibility of evidence given in an earlier proceeding regardless of whether or not it involved the same parties.

415 See *Insco Sarnia Ltd. v. Polysar Ltd.* (1990), 45 C.P.C. (2d) 53 (Ont. Ct. (Gen. Div.)); *Cottrell v. Gallagher* (1919), 16 O.W.N. 76 (C.A.).

416 *Johnson v. Birkett* (1910), 21 O.L.R. 319 (H.C.); *Atkinson v. Casserley* (1910), 22 O.L.R. 527 (C.A.); *Cartwright v. Toronto (City)* (1913), 29 O.L.R. 73, 13 D.L.R.

The new *Rules of Civil Procedure* in Ontario, however, have brought about a significant change, in that cross-examination is now permitted on discovery except for issues of credibility,[417] but more importantly, the transcript of an examination for discovery of a person may, at the discretion of the trial judge, be received in evidence in circumstances where he or she is unavailable.[418] In deciding whether to grant leave to admit such evidence the trial judge is to consider:[419]

(a)   the extent to which the person was cross-examined on the examination for discovery;

(b)   the importance of the evidence in the proceeding;

(c)   the general principle that evidence should be presented orally in court; and

(d)   any other relevant factor.

4. Criminal Proceedings

With respect to criminal proceedings, s. 715 of the *Criminal Code* embodies the exception[420] and expressly allows for the admissibility at trial of evidence given at a previous trial upon the same charge or taken in the investigation of the charge against the accused or upon the preliminary inquiry into the charge if certain conditions are met, namely, where a witness refuses to be sworn or to give evidence, or, if the facts are proved upon oath from which it can be inferred reasonably that the person is dead, has since become and is insane, is so ill[421] that he or she is unable to travel or testify or is absent from Canada.[422]

604; affd. (1914), 50 S.C.R. 215, 20 D.L.R. 189.

417   *Rules of Civil Procedure*, O. Reg. 560/84, as am., r. 31.06(1).

418   *Ibid.*, r. 31.11(6).

419   *Ibid.*, r. 31.11(7).

420   *Quaere* whether the *Criminal Code* provision completely replaces the common-law exception: see S. Schiff, *Evidence in the Litigation Process*, 3rd. ed. (Toronto: Carswell, 1988), at 301-02.

421   Illness is not to be limited to physical illness alone. In *R. v. Novalinga* (1985), 19 C.C.C. (3d) 190 (Ont. H.C.J.), the witness in question who had given evidence at the preliminary inquiry was suffering from a mental illness which was "real and incapacitating". It was held that mental illness is a form of illness sufficient to satisfy the statutory requirement.

422   Section 204 of the draft *Uniform Evidence Act*, Bill S-33, 1980-81-82, would expand the list of reasons for the unavailability of the witness at trial to include the fact that the witness cannot with reasonable diligence be found, or, if the witness testifies to a lack of memory of his evidence despite an attempt, where

Such earlier evidence, if it had been taken in the presence of the accused, may be read in at trial without further proof unless the accused did not have a full opportunity to cross-examine the witness.

It has been held that it is the opportunity by the accused to cross-examine an adverse witness which provides sufficient fairness to the accused. Accordingly, the fact that the witness is unavailable at trial does not constitute an infringement of s. 7 of the *Charter*. In *R. v. Potvin*[423] Wilson J. stated the accused's rights as follows:[424]

What rights then does an accused have under s. 7 of the *Charter* with respect to the admission of previous testimony? It is, in my view, basic to our system of justice that the accused have had a full opportunity to cross-examine the witness when the previous testimony was taken if a transcript of such testimony is to be introduced as evidence in a criminal trial for the purpose of convicting the accused. This is in accord with the traditional view that it is the opportunity to cross-examine and not the fact of cross-examination which is crucial if the accused is to be treated fairly.

Wilson J. did recognize that certain deprivations exist, namely, that the trier of fact loses the ability to assess the credibility of the witness by observing his or her demeanour, that when the evidence is taken at a preliminary inquiry the credibility of that evidence is not an issue, and that the accused at the preliminary inquiry may have strategic reasons for not testing the credibility or even conducting any cross-examination of the witness. Wilson J., however, was of the view that such matters were not of such magnitude and effect as to deprive the accused of the basics of a fair trial. The cornerstone of fairness in this context is the full opportunity of the accused to cross-examine the witness. The failure of the accused to avail himself of that opportunity at the time defeats any suggestion that his or her s. 7 *Charter* rights have been infringed because of an absence of the witness at trial.

Nor did the Court accept the argument that this statutory provision constitutes a contravention of s. 11(d) of the *Charter*. The fact that the accused and not the Crown has the burden of proving that

required by the court, to refresh his memory.
423 [1989] 1 S.C.R. 525, 68 C.R. (3d) 193, 47 C.C.C. (3d) 289, 21 Q.A.C. 258.
424 *Ibid.*, at 543 (S.C.R.).

the accused did not have a full opportunity to cross-examine the witness at the time the evidence was given does not deny the accused the presumption of innocence protected under s. 11(d) of the *Charter*. This burden is quite different from legislation which requires an accused to disprove an essential element of an offence or which specifies that in the absence of proof by the accused of some fact on the balance of probabilities, there is to be a conviction. The Court found that it is perfectly reasonable to expect an accused to be able to prove whether or not he or she was deprived of a full opportunity to cross-examine the witness, for after all only the accused can explain the extent to which there may have been such a denial or restriction.

The Court in *Potvin* also held that the trial judge under the statutory provision has a discretion whether or not to admit the previous testimony even if the conditions as set out in the section are met. The Court held that the discretion should be construed broadly enough to deal with situations where the testimony was obtained in a manner which was unfair to the accused or where its admission at trial would not be fair to the accused. Accordingly, it was held that this *Criminal Code* provision confers upon a trial judge a discretion wider than the traditional evidentiary principle that evidence should only be excluded if its prejudicial effect exceeds its probative value.

It is not all previous testimony which can be introduced under this exception. As stated by Jones J.A. in *R. v. Oickle*:[425]

> The purpose of the section is to introduce admissible evidence which would otherwise be excluded by reason of the absence of the witness. Parliament could hardly have intended that evidence otherwise inadmissible would become admissible simply by the application of s. 643 [now s. 715] of the *Code*.

But can an objection that could originally have been made successfully, but was not, prevail, when an attempt is made to adduce the former testimony at trial? McCormick's view is that it depends on the nature of the objection:[426]

---

425   (1984), 11 C.C.C. (3d) 180, 61 N.S.R. (2d) 239, 133 A.P.R. 239 (C.A.), at 189 (C.C.C.).

426   *Supra*, note 412, § 259, at 770. Phipson, on the other hand, makes no such distinction: see M.N. Howard, P. Crane and D.A. Hochberg, *Phipson on Evidence*, 14th ed. (London: Sweet & Maxwell, 1990), at 676.

The more widely approved view . . . is that objections which go merely to the form of the testimony, as on the ground of leading questions, unresponsiveness, or opinion, must be made at the original hearing, when they can be corrected, but objections which go to the relevancy or the competency of the evidence may be asserted for the first time when the former testimony is offered at the present trial.

5. Comparison with Other Rules

With respect to the requirement that the witness in the previous proceeding be subject to cross-examination, an interesting comparison may be made with the situation in which a witness at trial, having given his or her evidence in examination-in-chief, dies before being cross-examined by the opposing party. Does the deprivation of the opportunity to cross-examine the witness result in the expunging of the evidence given in chief? It appears that it does not, and the fact that the witness' evidence was not tested in cross-examination is a matter which goes to weight only.[427] The reason for permitting such evidence not subject to cross-examination, and yet rejecting evidence taken in a previous proceeding, similarly untested by cross-examination, is unclear. Rose J., in *Randall v. Atkinson*,[428] however, reasoned that more good than harm would follow if the testimony given in examination-in-chef was retained:[429]

I am unable to see any distinction in principle between admitting an affidavit or a deposition where there has been no opportunity of cross-examining, and retaining evidence which has been given in chief without an opportunity to cross-examine. The practice governing the admission of affidavit evidence and depositions may, in a sense, be said to be distinct from that governing the admission of oral testimony, but the difference is in favour of the retention of the oral testimony. It is given in open Court before the Judge and jury, or the Judge alone, under the careful supervision of the Court, and it may be presumed that no improper

---

427 But see *Meyer v. Hall* (1972), 26 D.L.R. (3d) 309, [1972] 2 W.W.R. 481, in which the Alberta Court of Appeal held that the trial judge has a discretion to ignore the witness' evidence completely.
428 (1899), 30 O.R. 242; affd. 30 O.R. 620 (C.A.).
429 *Ibid.*, at 255.

questions will be permitted. It was good evidence when received and must remain upon the record to affect the mind of the Judge or jury, as the case may be, unless expunged. It seems to me that the inconvenience of expunging it or withdrawing it from consideration would be much greater than any possible hardship that might ensue from retaining it.

6. Previous Testimony Led by the Party Against Whom it is Tendered

We have been examining this exception from the standpoint of the offer of previously given testimony against the party *against* whom it was formerly submitted. American statutory provisions also allow, as an exception to the hearsay rule, the admissibility of prior testimony in a subsequent proceeding when the party against whom the testimony is tendered was the party in the previous proceeding who offered the testimony on his or her own behalf.[430] The rationale for admissibility in the latter case turns upon a somewhat different ground. It could be said that the party tendering the witness in the first proceeding did so because the witness' evidence was favourable to that party's cause and he or she put the person forth as a credible witness, and, accordingly, is taken to have adopted the witness' evidence. This theory, however, unfortunately smacks of the concept that a party, by tendering a witness, vouchsafes his or her credibility. The better justification is that because the party in the earlier proceeding did examine the witness in chief and also had the opportunity to re-examine this witness, there is a sufficient check upon its trustworthiness as to warrant its use against that party in subsequent litigation.[431] Only New Brunswick has enacted legislation which, in addition to codifying the common-law exception, specifically provides for the admissibility of previous testimony against the party who adduced it in the former proceeding.[432]

---

430 See Rule 804(b)(1) of *Federal Rules of Evidence for United States Courts and Magistrates* (1975).
431 See J.F. Falknor, "Former Testimony and the Uniform Rules: A Comment" (1963), 38 N.Y.U.L. Rev. 651; *McCormick on Evidence, supra,* note 412, at 762.
432 *Evidence Act,* R.S.N.B. 1973, c. E-11, ss. 33-35.

K. *Admissions of a Party*

1. Theory of Admissibility

Traditionally, out-of-court assertions made by a party to the proceedings have been regarded as admissible at the instance of the opposite party as an exception to the hearsay rule, and although there has been some doubt about the validity of this classification, it has been included in this chapter for the purposes of convenience.[433] Although there is a consensus among the noted writers on the subject of evidence that admissions constitute admissible evidence, they disagree as to its rationale and its use. According to Morgan, admissions properly fall within an exception to the hearsay rule because *prima facie* they fit within the definition of hearsay, being out-of-court statements, not subject to cross-examination, and introduced as evidence of the truth of the facts contained therein. He added that an exception is justified not on the usual ground of trustworthiness but because of the general adversary theory:[434]

> The admissibility of an admission made by the party himself rests not upon any notion that the circumstances in which it was made furnish the trier means of evaluating it fairly, but upon the adversary theory of litigation. A party can hardly object that he had no opportunity to cross-examine himself or that he is unworthy of credence save when speaking under the sanction of an oath.

Wigmore, on the other hand, does not think that any exception is necessary to permit admissibility of admissions because the mischief, which the hearsay rule was designed to prevent, is nonexistent. Wigmore's and Morgan's reasoning, however, follow the same pattern. The main objection to hearsay evidence is that the declarant is not in court under oath and not subject to cross-examination. It is illogical to suggest that it is objectionable for the admission to be received because there is no opportunity to cross-examine the declarant. If the party made the statement, the party cannot argue that he or

---

433 See E.W. Cleary (ed.), *McCormick on Evidence*, 3rd ed. (St. Paul: West Publishing 1984), at 775.
434 E.M. Morgan, *Basic Problems of Evidence* (Joint Committee on Continuing Legal Education of the American Law Institute and the American Bar Association, 1962), at 266.

she has lost the opportunity of cross-examining him or herself, nor complain about the lack of personal oath. Moreover, it is always open to that party to take the witness box and testify either that he or she never made that admission or to qualify it in some other way.[435] Strahorn articulated a different basis of admissibility. To him, all admissions are evidence of conduct and are offered as circumstantial rather than assertive evidence.[436] These theories are not mutually exclusive. Elements of trustworthiness and the adversary theory and original evidence all combine together to justify the reception of this kind of evidence.

Admissions of a party are admissible against him or her in both civil and criminal cases. A complainant in a sexual assault case, while not formally a party, is in the position of a party so far as concerns admissions made by the complainant affecting the vital issue of consent.[437] If, however, the accused in a criminal case made the admission to a person in authority, it will be admissible only if the Crown satisfies the confession rule[438] and establishes that it was made voluntarily.

The restrictions which normally apply to the admissibility of hearsay exceptions have not been totally extended to admissions. For example, while in most instances, statements based upon hearsay or unqualified opinion will not be accepted, that is not the case with respect to admissions. As held in *Stowe v. Grand Trunk Pacific Railway*[439] and more recently in *R. v. Streu*,[440] a statement made by another and accepted as true or adopted by a party as his or her own in an out-of-court admission is receivable as evidence.[441] Thus an admission made by a party who relied upon the information of others and possessed no personal knowledge of his or her own with respect to the fact contained in the admission will nevertheless be accepted as his or her own admission.[442]

---

435   4 Wigmore, *Evidence* (Chadbourn rev. 1972), § 1048, at 4-5.
436   J.S. Strahorn, "A Reconsideration of the Hearsay Rule and Admissions" (1937), 85 U. Pa. L. Rev. 564.
437   *R. v. Grant* (1989), 71 C.R. (3d) 231, 49 C.C.C. (3d) 410, 58 Man. R. (2d) 281 (C.A.).
438   See Chapter 8.
439   [1918] 1 W.W.R. 546, 39 D.L.R. 127; affd. 59 S.C.R. 665, 49 D.L.R. 684.
440   [1989] 1 S.C.R. 1521, 70 C.R. (3d) 1, 48 C.C.C. (3d) 321, [1989] 4 W.W.R. 577, 97 A.R. 356, 96 N.R. 58.
441   See also *Black v. Hardwell*, [1935] 2 W.W.R. 172 (Sask. C.A.).
442   See also *R. v. Schmidt*, [1948] S.C.R. 333, 6 C.R. 317, 92 C.C.C. 53, [1948] 4 D.L.R. 217, at 336 (S.C.R.); *Palmby v. McCleary* (1886), 12 O.R. 192, at 195

The key element is the party's adoption of or belief in the hearsay statement as true. Its reliability comes from the fact that the party was satisfied or at least was in a position to satisfy him or herself as to its truth. Sopinka J. speaking for the Supreme Court of Canada in *R. v. Streu*[443] explained it this way:

> The rationale underlying the exclusion of hearsay evidence is primarily the inherent untrustworthiness of an extra-judicial statement which has been tendered without affording an opportunity to the party against whom it is adduced to cross-examine the declarant. This rationale applies equally in both criminal and civil cases. It loses its force when the party has chosen to rely on the hearsay statement in making an admission. Presumably in so doing, the party making the admission has satisfied himself or herself as to the reliability of the statement or at least had the opportunity to do so. The significance of this factor is evident in the decision of this Court in *Ares v. Venner*, [1970] S.C.R. 608, in which evidence was admitted as an exception to the hearsay rule where the party against whom the evidence was tendered had the opportunity to test the accuracy of the evidence.
>
> . . .
>
> Accordingly, once it is established that the admission was in fact made, there is no reason in principle for treating it any differently than the same statement would be treated had it been made in the witness box. In the latter case, if a party indicates a belief in or acceptance of a hearsay statement, that is some evidence of the truth of its contents. The weight to be given to that evidence is for the trier of fact. On the other hand, if the party simply reports a hearsay statement without either adopting it or indicating a belief in the truth of its contents, the statement is not admissible as proof of the truth of the contents.

But how strong or probative is an admission which is not based upon any firsthand knowledge or experience? Although the party intended to acknowledge the existence of the fact against his interest, and although such an admission is admissible, the court will examine the extent of the party's knowledge when he or she made the state-

---

(C.A.).
443 *Supra*, note 440, at 1529-30 (S.C.R.).

ment.[444] If the admission was made without any knowledge of the facts, the probative value of the admission in the view of the trier of fact may not be regarded as high and its weight discounted.

Admissions made by a party are receivable only as evidence against him or her. Normally, a party who has made a self-serving or favourable admission cannot take advantage of such. The reason for the prohibition against self-serving statements made by a party out of court is considered elsewhere in this book,[445] but suffice it to say that if such statements were admissible, the danger would exist that every person would seek to improve his or her own position in pending or anticipated litigation by making statements in his or her own favour.

One word of qualification, however, is necessary. The whole of a statement which is alleged to be an admission must be put into evidence, and there may be parts thereof which are in fact favourable to the maker of the statement. Thus, if an admission contains statements both adverse and favourable to a party and if an opponent tenders it, he or she may thereby be adducing evidence both helpful and damaging to his or her cause. In *Capital Trust Corp. v. Fowler*,[446] the plaintiff, who was seeking to prove that the defendant agreed to purchase certain shares in a company, tendered a letter in which the defendant stated that he had purchased the shares. Included in the letter, however, was a statement by him that there had been misrepresentations made to him in respect of the sale which supported his defence at trial. The Court held that the letter did constitute some evidence of misrepresentation in favour of the party against whom the letter was adduced. Such evidence, however, was not conclusive against the plaintiff tendering the admission, for he was at liberty to call qualifying evidence to rebut the unfavourable portion of the letter. Another illustration is found in the case of *Albert v. Tremblay*.[447] That was an action for the price of goods sold and delivered to the defendant and installed at the defendant's premises. The defendant claimed that the materials were different from those that he bargained for. The plaintiff, in proving his case at trial, put in the entire examination for

---

444 "Any evidentiary weakness in the information on which the admission was based was a matter of weight and not admissibility": per Sopinka J. in *R. v. Streu*, *ibid.*, at 1530 (S.C.R.).
445 See Chapter 7.
446 (1921), 50 O.L.R. 48, 64 D.L.R. 289 (C.A.); *Harrison v. Turner* (1847), 10 Q.B. 482.
447 (1963), 49 M.P.R. 407 (N.B.C.A.).

discovery of the defendant. Under the provincial rules of court, a party is permitted to read in at trial parts of the other party's examination for discovery.[448] Here, the plaintiff read into evidence the entire transcript of the defendant to put before the Court the admissions against the defendant's interest that he had made on discovery. But the defendant had also stated on his examination for discovery that the materials he received were different from those that he contracted for. An examination for discovery is merely an admission made under oath and is the same as other admissions.[449] The discovery in question contained not only admissions which were unfavourable to the defendant's case but also some statements which were helpful to his case. The Court held that the whole statement, including those parts favourable to the maker, was admissible into evidence. If a party uses an admission, he or she therefore may make it evidence for both his or her case and the opponent's case. The rationale for the principle that the whole of an admission is receivable is based on the fact that a party does not usually make a statement which is both damaging and helpful in the hope that he or she can get the favourable part before the court. The self-serving aspect of the admission is receivable in evidence only after the unfavourable part goes in. It is difficult to believe that an individual will make an incriminating statement in order to ensure that some self-serving evidence goes in as well. Moreover, if the opponent feels that the unfavourable portion does not outweigh the self-serving portion, he or she will not tender it as evidence. In any event the part of the admission which is self-serving will in all likelihood receive less weight because of its nature.

The plaintiff, in the *Tremblay*[450] case, in tendering the admission which contained certain statements not necessary for his cause but in fact helpful to the other side, was permitted, however, to lead other evidence contradicting or qualifying those parts. The Court then weighed the contradictory or qualifying evidence with the statements contained in the admission in determining whether the admitted fact had been established.

---

448 For example, see r. 31.11(1) of the *Rules of Civil Procedure*, O. Reg. 560/84.
449 *Capital Trust Corp. v. Fowler, supra*, note 446; *Modriski v. Arnold*, [1947] O.W.N. 483 (C.A.).
450 *Albert v. Tremblay, supra*, note 447.

2. What Constitutes an Admission?

An admission may consist of an oral or written statement or conduct made directly by or on behalf of a party litigant and tendered as evidence at trial by the opposing party.

An admission may take many forms. A plea of guilty in a criminal proceeding or a proceeding arising out of the commission of a provincial offence is considered an admission which is admissible as such in a subsequent civil proceeding.[451] As in the case of all admissions except those known as "judicial or formal admissions",[452] the party who made it may later lead evidence at trial to reveal the circumstances under which the admission was made in order to reduce its prejudicial effect.[453] It should be noted that before a plea of guilty is admissible in the subsequent civil action, the latter proceeding must have arisen out of the same or similar circumstances which formed the basis of the criminal charge.[454]

Similarly, a statement by a party while under oath or contained in an affidavit may be used as an admission in the course of subsequent civil litigation.[455]

At times, conduct of a party may constitute an admission. Under certain circumstances, payment by one party of the other's medical expenses may be considered an admission of liability but the court will look to the motivating factors. Where the parents of a child who had injured a playmate accepted the responsibility of paying the doctor's fees without first consulting a solicitor, the Court held that they were acting out of compassion and not out of guilt and were not thereby admitting liability.[456] Where the conduct of the parties and their

---

451 *Cromarty v. Monteith* (1957), 8 D.L.R. (2d) 112 (B.C.S.C.); *English v. Richmond; Laing v. Richmond*, [1956] S.C.R. 383, 3 D.L.R. (2d) 385 (Ont.).

452 See Chapter 19, I. In addition to the expressed admissions made by a party himself, judicial admissions made by his legal representative in court documents such as pleadings or in formal admissions to the court may be used adversely to the interests of the party.

453 *Cromarty v. Monteith, supra*, note 451; *Re Charlton*, [1969] 1 O.R. 706, 3 D.L.R. (3d) 623 (C.A.); *Black v. Black* (1960), 32 W.W.R. 477 (B.C.S.C.); *Ferris v. Monahan* (1956), 4 D.L.R. (2d) 539 (N.B.C.A.).

454 *Hellyer Farms Ltd. v. Biro*, [1971] 2 O.R. 583, 18 D.L.R. (3d) 527 (Co. Ct.).

455 *Tipping v. Hornby* (1960), 32 W.W.R. 287 (B.C.).

456 *Walmsley v. Humenick*, [1954] 2 D.L.R. 232 (B.C.S.C.). In any event, with universal medical and hospital coverage in Canada, this situation should rarely arise.

counsel during the course of the trial is such that the court could infer that counsel accepted the existence of a contract, the fact of its existence was treated as being admitted.[457]

If a manufacturer or proprietor improves or repairs equipment or premises after an accident has occurred, then one might surmise that the pre-existing condition must have been faulty. However, if the courts received evidence of such measures as an admission of liability, it might serve as a deterrent to the taking of such remedial steps. Because of public policy, therefore, such conduct has not been admitted in civil cases as proof of negligence.[458] This viewpoint, however, is not universally shared. The majority of the Ontario Divisional Court in *Algoma Central Railway v. Herb Fraser & Associates Ltd.*[459] questioned the rationale excluding such evidence:[460]

> We are of the view that the rationale for the rule must be looked at anew. It is axiomatic that evidence which is relevant is admissible unless some policy reason exists for its exclusion. Here, it has always been admitted that evidence of remedial measures has at least some probative value. However, the evidence is excluded on policy grounds in order that people are not discouraged from taking precautionary measures which may be later used against them. This is a fallacious argument. It cannot be said that, rather than furnishing some evidence which may or may not be prejudicial to one's defence of an action, one will instead take no remedial measures, thus risking further actions being brought by later injured plaintiffs.

In coming to this conclusion, we agree with the comments of Trainor J. in *Bigras v. C.N.R.*:

---

457   See *Gill Bros. v. Mission Sawmills Ltd.*, [1945] 2 W.W.R. 337, [1945] 3 D.L.R. 506; affd. [1945] S.C.R. 766, [1945] 4 D.L.R. 449.
458   *Toll v. Canadian Pacific Railway* (1908), 1 Alta. L.R. 318, 8 C.R.C. 294 (S.C.); *MacKay v. Saskatoon (City)* (1960), 26 D.L.R. (2d) 506 (Sask. C.A.); *London (City) v. Grand Trunk Railway* (1914), 32 O.L.R. 642, 18 C.R.C. 174, 20 D.L.R. 846 (C.A.).
459   (1990), 36 C.P.C. (2d) 8 (Ont. Div. Ct.).
460   *Ibid.*, at 14-15. White J. in a dissenting opinion reviewed and agreed with the policy considerations behind the traditional exclusionary rule and would have held the evidence to be inadmissible on the basis that "[t]he slight probative value of such evidence is outweighed by the desire to promote the policy goal." *Ibid.*, at 17.

"I cannot agree that a responsible citizen would be influenced by considerations of liability in deciding whether or not repairs or alterations should be made to improve a site under his control. Therefore, I cannot agree that the evidence should be excluded for policy reasons."

The Court permitted, at least at the discovery stage, questions concerning subsequent remedial measures. Matters of admissibility and the weight to be given to such evidence at trial were to be for the trial judge's determination.

This type of evidence might be admitted in criminal cases on the basis that concealment may be probative evidence of guilt. For example, an accused's conduct in taking his car to a body shop for a new paint job following a hit and run accident may constitute such evidence.[461]

Mere silence *per se* does not constitute an admission or an adoption of liability but such silence when coupled with material loss or prejudice to the party who should have been informed that liability was not accepted will operate as such.[462] Silence can also be taken as an admission where a denial would be the only reasonable course of action expected if that person were not responsible.[463]

In *R. v. Baron*,[464] Martin J.A. put the principle as follows:[465]

The silence of a party will render statements made in his presence evidence against him of their truth if the circumstances are such that he could reasonably have been expected to have replied to them. Silence in such circumstances permits an inference of assent . . .

---

461 See *Report of the Federal/Provincial Task Force on Uniform Rules of Evidence* (Toronto: Carswell, 1982), at 169.

462 *Dominion Bank v. Ewing* (1904), 35 S.C.R. 133; leave to appeal to P.C. refd., [1904] A.C. 806.

463 Compare *Bessela v. Stern* (1877), 46 L.J.C.P. 467 (C.A.), with *Wiedemann v. Walpole*, [1891] 2 Q.B. 534 (C.A.), as to whether silence by a defendant in the face of accusations that he breached his promise to marry constitutes an admission. In *R. v. Eden*, [1970] 3 C.C.C. 280, [1970] 2 O.R. 161 (C.A.), it was held that it was not unreasonable for an accused to fail to respond to statements made by his co-accused when they were both sitting in a police cruiser.

464 (1976), 31 C.C.C. (2d) 575, 14 O.R. (2d) 173, 73 D.L.R. (3d) 213 (C.A.).

465 *Ibid.*, at 187 (O.R.).

No such assent can be inferred, however, when an accused remains silent in the presence of a police officer conducting an investigation, since to hold otherwise would breach a fundamental right of an accused.[466]

If it would be reasonable to expect a denial in the face of an accusation, then the party's failure to do so could constitute an implied admission against him or her.[467] Much, of course, turns upon the circumstances, whether such an expectation is reasonable. Before such conduct can constitute an admission, the court must be satisfied that there is sufficient evidence from which a jury might reasonably find that the conduct amounted to an acknowledgement of responsibility.[468]

Failure to deny an accusation is not the only conduct that may constitute an implied admission. Any conduct, action or demeanour may amount to an acceptance of the accusation. In fact, an express denial in certain circumstances may help to constitute the exact opposite. Lord Atkinson in *R. v. Christie*[469] stated:[470]

> It by no means follows, I think, that a mere denial by the accused of the facts mentioned in the statement necessarily renders the statement inadmissible, because he may deny the statement in such a manner and under such circumstances as may lead a jury to disbelieve him, and constitute evidence from which an acknowledgement may be inferred by them.

Much care must be taken with this kind of evidence, particularly since it is open to different interpretations. A person may choose to remain silent when accused of a crime or a civil wrong for many reasons other than that he or she is guilty. A knowledgeable person may choose to say nothing in such circumstances for fear that any response might be misinterpreted or used against him or her in

---

466 *R. v. Conlon* (1991), 1 O.R. (3d) 188 (C.A.); see Chapter 14, IV.E.2.
467 *R. v. Christie*, [1914] A.C. 545 (H.L.).
468 *R. v. Harrison*, 86 C.C.C. 166, 62 B.C.R. 420, [1946] 3 D.L.R. 690, at 696; *R. v. Hryn* (1981), 63 C.C.C. (2d) 390 (Ont. G.S.P.). The draft *Uniform Evidence Act*, Bill S-33, 1980-81-82, s. 57, maintains this exception. It provides that "a statement is admissible against a party to prove the truth of the matter asserted . . . if he expressly adopted it or it is reasonable to infer that he adopted it . . .".
469 *Supra*, note 467.
470 *Ibid.*, at 554.

litigation.[471] Because of the possibility of ambiguity in interpreting the lack of a response or the nature of a particular response, a court should examine all of the circumstances in order to conclude whether the individual has behaved in such a way so as to adopt the statement made to him or her as true. Some of the factors that a court may look for are the following:

1. The party must have heard the statement clearly and understood it;
2. The statement must have been about subject-matter of which he or she was aware;
3. The party must not have been suffering from some physical or mental disability or confusion;
4. The individual who made the statement should not be someone to whom one would expect the party to reply, as for example, when the speaker is a young child.

Other factors peculiar to the circumstances in question could also be taken into account.[472] For example, if one party in a business relationship forwards to the other a statement of account, the tendency would be to respond if the account was not correct.

Where one person receives a bill for goods sent to another and that person makes no objection after a reasonable lapse of time, the bill and lack of objection are some evidence to the effect that the goods were delivered for the credit of that person.[473]

A party, while not making an admission of certain facts essential to the opponent's case, can, by his or her conduct, suggest inferentially that he or she realized that he or she did not have a valid defence or action. Such was the case in *Greenwood v. Fitts*,[474] where one party made statements to the effect that he would perjure himself and leave the jurisdiction if the action proceeded to trial. Resort to perjury is evidence of that party's belief that the cause or defence that he or she is putting forth is weak.[475]

---

471 An accused when questioned by the police should be warned that he or she is not obliged to say anything: see Chapter 14, IV.E.2.

472 E.W. Cleary (ed.), *McCormick on Evidence*, 3rd ed. (St. Paul: West Publishing, 1984), at 800-01.

473 *Sarbit v. Booth Fisheries (Cdn.) Co.*, [1951] 2 D.L.R. 108, 1 W.W.R. (N.S.) 115, 58 Man. R. 377 (C.A.).

474 (1961), 29 D.L.R. (2d) 260 (B.C.C.A.).

475 See also *Moriarty v. London, Chatham & Dover Railway Co.* (1870), L.R. 5

An unfavourable inference can be drawn when a party litigant does not testify or fails to call a witness who would have knowledge of the facts, and who might have given important supporting evidence if the case of the litigant had been sound.[476]

3. Statements by Others who have a Relationship to the Party

(a) *Vicarious Admissions*

Statements made by a representative of a party in his or her capacity as such may be binding as admissions against the party. Following a concept of admissions as conduct, it was at one time believed that an agent's statement could be used against his or her principal only when such statement was made contemporaneously with and in relation to the performance of the agent's duty. Early courts preferred to justify admissibility of such statements on the basis of a *res gestae* theory rather than upon a separate and independent admissions exception to the hearsay rule. In *Confederation Life Association v. O'Donnell*,[477] Gwynne J. held that:[478]

> An agent's declaration of a past transaction is not admissible although it may have some relation to an act which the agent may be doing for the principal when he makes the declaration, but if the declaration be made at a time when the agent is not transacting any business for his principal it can not be received, there being in such case no *res gesta* of which the declaration forms a part.

Strong J., however, referring to the declarant's role as an insurance agent, to whom the respondents would turn for settlement of a loss, felt that the agent had the implied authority to recognize the validity of the respondent's claim and anything he said to that effect was an admission and binding on his principals in the absence of evidence showing that the agent's authority was restricted.

Eventually, a theory more in line with the vicarious liability principle in tort law developed. In *R. v. Strand Electric Ltd.*,[479] the

---

Q.B. 314.

476 See Chapter 16, VI.E.

477 (1886), 13 S.C.R. 218.

478 *Ibid.*, at 230; see also *Jarvis v. London Street Railway* (1919), 45 O.L.R. 167, 48 D.L.R. 61 (C.A.).

479 [1969] 2 C.C.C. 264, [1969] 1 O.R. 190 (C.A.).

accused appealed its convictions of offences against the *Construction Safety Act*.[480] The main question for the consideration of the Court was whether or not a supervisor on a job site was an agent and employee of the appellant company, with authority to make the admissions that he did, and whether such statements were admissible as evidence against the company. MacKay J.A. adopted the following passage from *Cross on Evidence*:[481]

> Statements made by an agent within the scope of his authority to third persons during the continuance of the agency may be received as admissions against his principal in litigation to which the latter is a party . . . the admission must have been made by the agent as part of a conversation or other communication which he was authorised to have with a third party.

Since the relevant sections of the *Construction Safety Act* were such as to compel the agent to make the statements to the inspector, it followed as a corollary that the employer was compelled to authorize the agent to supply the information, as was done in this case.

Laskin J.A., dissenting, recognized two guiding principles for the admissibility of an agent's admissions against his or her employer. There had to exist proof of the agency, and the admission of the agent to a third party must have been made within the scope of his or her authority during the subsistence of the agency. As to the first point, a third party cannot testify that the agent him or herself asserted the existence of an agency relationship because that would be hearsay; accordingly, the agency had to be established by means other than by out-of-court statements of the alleged agent him or herself. As to what constitutes the scope of authority so as to warrant admissibility, Laskin J.A. suggested the following test:[482]

> The concept of authority, taken literally, would exclude as against the principal any admission of an agent tending to show liability in tort or penal liability, unless the agent is shown to have been authorized to make admissions to charge his principal. . . . Authority as between agent and principal has in respect of vicarious liability of the principal to third parties, been translated

---

480 Then S.O. 1961-62, c. 18.
481 Now R. Cross and C. Tapper, *Cross on Evidence*, 7th ed. (London: Butterworths, 1990), at 585-86.
482 *R. v. Strand Electric Ltd.*, *supra*, note 479, at 200 (O.R.).

into an issue of the scope of the agent's duties or employment, and I would apply the same test in relation to admissions by an agent which are tendered in evidence against the principal.

As there was no evidence that the agent had the authority to direct a workman onto the defective scaffold, the prosecution, Laskin J.A. said, had not established that the agent was acting for the accused in the course of his duties. This failure was, according to Laskin J.A., fatal to the Crown's case for while it was not necessary to show that the accused *expressly* authorized the agent to make admissions, it had not been demonstrated that the statement accepting fault was reasonably related to the discharge of the agent's duties. Laskin J.A. stated that if it had been shown to his satisfaction that the agent was acting within the scope of his authority in directing the workman to use the scaffold, he would have accepted the admission of the agent as admissible evidence against the accused.

MacKay J.A., quoting from *Cross*, suggests that the agent must have been authorized to engage in the conversation in which the admission was made for such to be admissible as evidence against his or her principal.[483] This test is too narrow and Laskin J.A.'s opinion is preferred. So long as the statements were made by the agent within the scope of his or her authority, it should be irrelevant whether or not he or she had the express authorization to make the statement on behalf of his or her employer. Justification for extending admissibility to such statements can be found in the words of one noted American commentator:[484]

> The agent is well informed about acts in the course of the business, his statements offered against the employer are against the employer's interest, and while the employment continues, the employee is not likely to make the statements unless they are true. Moreover, if the admissibility of admissions is viewed as arising from the adversary system, responsibility for statements

---

483 For an illustration of an agent being clothed with express authority to make statements to bind his employer, see *Edwards v. Brookes (Milk) Ltd.*, [1963] 1 W.L.R. 795, [1963] 3 All E.R. 62 (D.C.); for an example of a court finding an absence of such authority, see *Nagel v. Canadian Northern Railway*, [1930] 2 W.W.R. 431, 24 Sask. L.R. 502, 37 C.R.C. 225, [1930] 4 D.L.R. 366 (C.A.).

484 *McCormick on Evidence*, *supra*, note 472, at 788-89; see also *Federal Rules of Evidence for United States Courts and Magistrates* (1975), Rule 801(d)(2)(C) and (D).

of one's employee is a consistent aspect. Accordingly, the predominant view now favours broader admissibility of admissions by agents if the statement concerned a matter within the scope of the declarant's employment and was made before that relationship was terminated.

This wider test has been accepted by a British Columbia court in *Morrison-Knudsen Co. v. B.C. Hydro & Power Authority*[485] in the context of a statement made by an agent to his principal. There had been a divergence of authority as to whether an agent's statement, made within the scope of his authority, but made only to the principal himself, was admissible against the principal as an admission.[486] Macdonald J. reviewed the authorities, including the Canadian decisions,[487] and came to the conclusion that in this country a statement made by an agent to his principal is admissible against the principal as an admission so long as it was made within the scope of the agent's authority. In determining what the limits of an agent's authority are, Macdonald J. adopted the reasoning of an American court[488] in holding that the question of admissibility in all cases turns on whether the declaration falls within the ambit of the subject-matter of the agent's employment.[489] He quoted from the American decision as follows:[490]

The test of admissibility should not rest on whether the principal gave the agent authority to make declarations. No sensible employer would authorize his employee to make damaging statements. The right to speak on a given topic must arise out of the nature of the employee's duties. The errand boy should not be able to bind the corporation with a statement about the issuance of treasury stock, but a truck driver should be able to bind his employer with an admission regarding his careless

485   (1973), 36 D.L.R. (3d) 95, [1973] 3 W.W.R. 600 (B.C.S.C.).
486   The cases of *Re Devala Provident Gold Mining Co.* (1883), 22 Ch. D. 593, and *Swan v. Miller, Son & Torrance Ltd.*, [1919] 1 I.R. 151, should be contrasted with *The 'Solway'* (1885), 10 P.D. 137.
487   *Shea v. Halifax & South Western Railway Co.* (1906), 47 N.S.R. 366 (C.A.); *Brost v. Eastern Irrigation School Division No. 44*, [1955] 3 D.L.R. 159 (Alta. C.A.).
488   *Rudzinsko v. Warner Theatres, Inc.*, 114 N.W. 2d 466 (1962).
489   This is the test propounded by Rule 801(d)(2)(D) of the *Federal Rules of Evidence for United States Courts and Magistrates* (1975).
490   *Supra*, note 485, at 101 (D.L.R.).

driving. Similarly, an usher should be able to commit his employer with an observation about a slippery spot on the lobby floor.

It is enough to show the existence of the employment and the general nature of the employee's work . . .

In criminal cases and prosecutions for regulatory offences, attribution is more restrictive because the nature of the proceedings is quite distinct and different policy considerations favour a more restrictive approach.[491]

(b) *Statements by a Representative or by Persons with Identity of Interest*

Statements made by a trustee, executor or administrator of an estate in that capacity will constitute an admission against the beneficiaries.[492] Accordingly, if statements are made by a party in a representative capacity and were made in that connection, those statements are admissible against the party he or she represents.[493] The rationale is that there is a sufficient identity of interest to allow for attribution of the statement to the party.

---

491 See *R. v. Strand Electric Ltd., supra*, note 479. *The Federal/Provincial Task Force on the Uniform Rules of Evidence* (Toronto: Carswell, 1982), at 167-68 recommended that in relation to summary conviction proceedings the same rules apply in relation to vicarious admissions that apply in civil cases; however, in relation to proceedings by indictment only statements by those servants or agents exercising a management function and in respect of that function be admissible against the principal. The Task Force settled on this compromise because "it takes into account the interest of both the State and the individual". However, this compromise fails to recognize the substantial penalties which may be imposed for summary conviction proceedings.

492 *New's Trustee v. Hunting*, [1897] 1 Q.B. 607, at 611; affd. [1897] 2 Q.B. 19.

493 The draft *Uniform Evidence Act*, Bill S-33, 1980-81-82, has an express provision for this situation: "In a civil proceeding, a statement made by a trustee, executor or administrator of an estate or any other person in a representative capacity is admissible against the declarant and the party represented to prove the truth of the matter asserted without having to establish that the declarant made the statement as part of the exercise of his representative capacity." This provision does not require any preconditions to admissibility such as the establishment of the fact that the statement was actually made in a representative capacity and that it was made at a time when the declarant was a representative. Apparently these are matters which affect merely the weight and not the admissibility of the statement.

Identity of interest also serves to permit the reception of an admission in various disparate situations: for example, a statement by one partner to a business enterprise made in the course of the business affairs of the partnership is admissible as evidence against all partners;[494] an admission of a deceased tortfeasor is evidence against his executor or administrator;[495] and the admission of an officer of a bankrupt company is evidence against the trustee in bankruptcy in an action by a lien claimant.[496]

Similarly, admissions made by predecessors in title, or other persons in privity with a party, are admissible in evidence against the party. In *Woolway v. Rowe*,[497] it was held that a statement made by the plaintiff's father, the previous owner of the plaintiff's lands, to the effect that he did not possess the right asserted by the plaintiff in the present action, was admissible as against the plaintiff.

It is difficult to delineate all the relationships which would qualify as constituting a sufficient privity or identity of interest as to permit the admissibility of vicarious submissions. Suffice it to say that it would include any relation which permits one persons's rights, obligations or remedies to be affected by the acts of another person and, therefore, includes what has become known as privity of obligation and privity of title.[498]

---

494 *B.C. Iron Works Co. v. Buse* (1894), 4 B.C.R. 419 (C.A.).

495 *Adams v. Public Trustee; Chiasson v. Public Trustee* (1971), 23 D.L.R. (3d) 557 (B.C.C.A.).

496 *Dieleman Planer Co. v. Elizabeth Townhouses Ltd.* (1972), 27 D.L.R. (3d) 692, [1972] 4 W.W.R. 236, 17 C.B.R. (N.S.) 58; affd. [1973] 5 W.W.R. 743, 18 C.B.R. (N.S.) 105, 38 D.L.R. (3d) 595 (B.C.C.A.); affd. [1975] 2 S.C.R. 449, [1975] 2 W.W.R. 752, 20 C.B.R. (N.S.) 81, 48 D.L.R. (3d) 635, 3 N.R. 376.

497 (1834), 1 Ad. & El. 114, 110 E.R. 1151.

498 4 Wigmore, *Evidence* (Chadbourn rev. 1972), § 1076, at 153. The draft *Uniform Evidence Act*, Bill S-33, 1980-81-82, would no longer permit such statements to constitute admissions. Section 60 expressly abrogates the common-law rule whereby a statement is admissible against a party made by a person in privity with the party in estate or interest or by blood relationship. It may be that the mere fact of some identity of interest whether it arises from joint ownership, joint obligation or privity of title of itself does not provide sufficient assurance of reliability as to escape the hearsay dangers. See also E.M. Morgan, "Admissions" (1937), 12 Wash. L. Rev. 181, at 202.

(c) *Statements by Persons Engaged with Others in a Common Purpose or Design*

Conspirators also have an identity of interest, albeit criminal or tortious. Statements made by a person engaged in an unlawful conspiracy are receivable as admissions as against all those acting in concert if the declarations were made while the conspiracy was ongoing and were made towards the accomplishment of the common object.[499] The admissions of a co-conspirator by words or conduct may be used as proof against the others on the basis that there is an implied authority given to all members of the conspiracy to act or speak in furtherance of the common purpose on behalf of the others. This rule applies to both civil[500] and criminal conspiracies.

The rule applies not only to charges for the crime of conspiracy but to any offence committed pursuant to a common design or as a result of pre-concert.[501] Indeed the rule is applicable even if the conspirator whose words or acts are tendered as evidence has not been charged him or herself.[502] If a conspirator is found with the documents in his or her possession which constitute acts or statements in furtherance of the common design, they are admissible under this rule.[503]

In order to be admissible against the others, the statements must be made while the conspiracy is proceeding and not after the common design has been effected.[504] If the conspiracy has been completed or

---

499 *R. v. Moore* (1984), 15 C.C.C. (3d) 541, 5 O.A.C. 51, at 570 (C.C.C.); leave to appeal to S.C.C. refd. (1985), 7 O.A.C. 320*n*.
500 *Consolidated Coal Co. v. Big Chief Woodyard Ltd.*, [1934] 3 D.L.R. 668, [1934] 2 W.W.R. 433, 48 B.C.R. 241 (C.A.); *Great West Uranium Mines Ltd. v. Rock Hill Uranium Mines Ltd.*, [1955] 4 D.L.R. 307, 15 W.W.R. 404 (Sask. C.A.).
501 *R. v. Parrot* (1979), 27 O.R. (2d) 333, 51 C.C.C. (2d) 539, 106 D.L.R. (3d) 296 (C.A.), at 548 (C.C.C.); leave to appeal to S.C.C. refd. (1980), 27 O.R. (2d) 333*n*.
502 *R. v. Parrot, ibid.*; *R. v. Koufis*, [1941] S.C.R. 481, 76 C.C.C. 161, [1941] 3 D.L.R. 657, at 168 (C.C.C.).
503 *R. v. Parrot, supra*, note 501; *R. v. Russell* (1920), 33 C.C.C. 1, [1920] 1 W.W.R. 624, 51 D.L.R. 1 (Man. C.A.), at 6 (C.C.C.); *R. v. Container Materials Ltd.* (1940), 74 C.C.C. 113, [1940] 4 D.L.R. 293 (Ont. H.C.); vard. 76 C.C.C. 18, [1941] 3 D.L.R. 145 (C.A.); affd. [1942] S.C.R. 147, 77 C.C.C. 129, [1942] 1 D.L.R. 529. For a full discussion of documents in possession, see Chapter 18, V.B.
504 *R. v. Miller* (1976), 24 C.C.C. (2d) 401, 33 C.R.N.S. 129, [1975] 6 W.W.R. 1, 63 D.L.R. (3d) 193 (B.C.C.A.), at 221 (D.L.R.); affd. [1977] 2 S.C.R. 680, 38 C.R.N.S. 139, 31 C.C.C. (2d) 177, [1976] 5 W.W.R. 711, 70 D.L.R. (3d) 324; *R. v. Cook* (1980), 53 C.C.C. (2d) 217 (Ont. C.A.); *R. v. McNamara (No. 1)* (1981),

abandoned, the statement is admissible only against the maker and not against his or her former co-conspirators.

Another essential condition to admissibility is proof that the accused was a member of the conspiracy. The difficulty for the courts is that this is also the very issue that must be proven beyond a reasonable doubt at the end of the trial in order to convict the accused. Accordingly, what standard of proof is required to prove membership in the conspiracy relevant to the preliminary question of admissibility and who is to make that finding, judge or jury?

McIntyre J. in *R. v. Carter*[505] posed the issues as follows:[506]

> There are many expositions of the conspirators' exception to the hearsay rule which attempt to resolve the logical problem inherent in its application. The problem may be simply stated. Where an accused is charged with the crime of conspiracy, proof of his agreement in the illegal design alleged, that is, his participation or membership in the conspiracy, is sufficient for a conviction. The conspirators' exception to the hearsay rule may be applied to afford evidence of the accused's membership through acts and declarations of fellow members of the conspiracy performed and made in pursuance of the objects of the conspiracy. The exception, however, depends on the preliminary fact of membership in the same conspiracy. Membership must therefore be proven before the exception is operative. Since membership is the gist of the offence, however, once that is proven the hearsay exception appears to be unnecessary.

> It is only if the preliminary proof of membership is on a standard less than the ordinary standard in criminal cases that this exception can be brought into operation without, at the same time, disposing of the final issue in the matter. Once the membership has been established on a lesser burden, then the hearsay evidence made admissible by the application of the exception may be considered by the trier of fact on the issue of proof of the

---

56 C.C.C. (2d) 193, at 487-91 (Ont. C.A.); affd. [1985] 1 S.C.R. 662, 45 C.R. (3d) 289 (*sub nom. Can. Dredge & Dock Co. v. R.*), 19 C.C.C. (3d) 1, 9 O.A.C. 321, 19 D.L.R. (4th) 314, 59 N.R. 241.

505 [1982] 1 S.C.R. 938, 31 C.R. (3d) 97, 67 C.C.C. (2d) 568, 137 D.L.R. (3d) 387, 46 N.B.R. (2d) 142, 121 A.P.R. 142, 47 N.R. 289.

506 *Ibid.*, at 572-73 (C.C.C.).

offence beyond a reasonable doubt. While the rule in general terms is simple to state, the difficulty arises in its practical application. Who should make the preliminary finding of membership, and what standard of proof is appropriate at that stage?

In attempting to deal with this question, judges are confronted, on the one hand, with the well-settled rule that recognizes the agency principle in connection with conspiracy at criminal law, but must, none the less, be deeply sensible of the grave injustice which could result from the application of the conspirators' exception to the hearsay rule to a person not, in fact, shown to be a member of the conspiracy. The approach generally adopted has been to take the matter in two stages, and to require a determination in the case of each accused of the issue of his membership in the conspiracy, on the basis of evidence directly admissible against him before permitting the application of the exception in order to reach a determination of the larger issue of his guilt, or innocence, on the charge in the indictment.

In order to maintain a clear distinction between the two stages, some courts felt that it should be the trial judge who rules on a *voir dire* on the question and either excludes the operation of the exception or directs the jury to apply it.[507]

The Supreme Court of Canada in *Carter*, however, rejected this approach for fear that it would not necessarily separate the two issues sufficiently in the jury's mind as to avoid confusion, and might even cause the jury to use the hearsay declarations to connect the accused with the conspiracy.[508]

Without a *voir dire*, therefore, *all* the evidence is adduced during the trial, including the statements of co-conspirators, and it is left to the trial judge to separate the two issues carefully for the jury in his or her charge. The Supreme Court of Canada gave the following guid-

---

507 *Carbo v. United States*, 314 F. 2d 718 (1963); see also J. Sopinka, "Commentary on the Proposed Uniform Evidence Act" (1981-82), 24 Crim. L.Q. 331, at 344, who felt that ". . . the reasoning in *Carbo* that it is a question for the judge is difficult to resist".

508 The Court adopted the position taken by Martin J.A. in *R. v. Hobart* (1982), 65 C.C.C. (2d) 518, 25 C.R. (3d) 214, 36 O.R. (2d) 257 (C.A.), at 530-31 (C.C.C.) who rejected the *voir dire* approach enunciated in the *Carbo* case. For a different view, see Sopinka J. in "Commentary on the Proposed Uniform Evidence Act", *ibid.*

ance in how the appropriate instructions are to be given to the jury:[509]

1. The trial judge should instruct the jury to consider whether on all the evidence they are satisfied beyond a reasonable doubt that the conspiracy charged in the indictment existed;
2. If they are not satisfied then the accused charged with participation in the conspiracy must be acquitted;
3. If the jury concludes that a conspiracy did exist they must decide whether there is some evidence of the accused's membership in the conspiracy directly admissible against him which raises the probability that he in fact was a member of the conspiracy;
4. If the jury so finds, they then become entitled to apply the hearsay exception and consider evidence of the acts and declarations performed and made by the co-conspirators in furtherance of the objects of the conspiracy as evidence against the accused on the issue of his or her guilt. This evidence, taken with the other evidence, may be sufficient to satisfy the jury beyond a reasonable doubt that the accused was a member of the conspiracy and that he or she is accordingly guilty.

Certain cautions must be given by the trial judge in order to impress upon the jury the distinction between evidence for the purpose of determining the preliminary issue of membership in the conspiracy, and evidence for the purpose of determining the ultimate issue of guilt. The jury should be told that the ultimate determination is for it alone and that the mere fact that it has found sufficient evidence directly admissible against the accused to enable it to consider the accused's participation in the conspiracy probable and to apply the hearsay exception does not automatically result in a conviction. It is only after the jury has become satisfied beyond a reasonable doubt on the entirety of the evidence on both issues, that is, the existence of the conspiracy and the accused's membership in it, that the jury may convict; and that it is open to the jury to acquit the accused even if it initially determines an accused's probable membership in the conspiracy which enabled the application of the hearsay exception.[510]

---

509 *Supra*, note 505, at 575 (C.C.C.). See also *R. v. Barrow*, [1987] 2 S.C.R. 694, 38 C.C.C. (3d) 193, 61 C.R. (3d) 305, 45 D.L.R. (4th) 487, 81 N.R. 321, at 229-30 (S.C.R.); *R. v. Kindylides* (1990), 57 C.C.C. (3d) 257, at 266, 274 (B.C.C.A.).
510 *Ibid.*, at 575-76 (C.C.C.).

One issue that has not been considered by the courts is the degree of proof necessary to establish that the co-conspirators whose declarations are being tendered were in fact themselves parties to the conspiracy. It appears that once it is established on the basis of evidence directly admissible against an accused that he or she was a party to the conspiracy charged, the acts and declarations of the "alleged co-conspirators" may be used as evidence against him or her.[511] This would mean that the acts and declarations of persons not proven to be agents of the accused are admissible against him or her. There does not appear to be a restriction that the acts and declarations which become admissible must be those of conspirators shown to be a party to the conspiracy. Accordingly, an accused could be shown to be a member of the IRA and then all other alleged members of the IRA could implicate the accused by their acts and declarations.[512] It would, therefore, be reasonable for the courts to import a requirement that it be established by appropriate proof that the declarant was a co-conspirator before his or her statements become admissible against the accused.

4. Effect of a Party's Admission as Against Others

Admissions are binding only as against the party who made them.[513] Accordingly, an admission by one party is not evidence against a co-defendant, and in a jury trial, the jury is to be cautioned

---

511 Per Martin J.A. in *R. v. Baron* (1976), 31 C.C.C. (2d) 525, 14 O.R. (2d) 173, 73 D.L.R. (3d) 213 (C.A.), at 545 (C.C.C.).

512 See J. Sopinka, "Commentary on the Proposed Uniform Evidence Act", *supra*, note 512, at 345. The draft *Uniform Evidence Act*, Bill S-33, 1980-81-82, s. 58, codifies the common-law exception in the following provision: "A statement by a person who was engaged with a party in an unlawful common purpose, or a lawful common purpose to be carried out by unlawful means, made in furtherance of the common purpose, is admissible against the party to prove a truth of the matter asserted if it is established by evidence from a source other than the declarant that the party was engaged in the common purpose." This provision, however, leaves ambiguous the degree of proof to establish the preliminary issue by the accused's membership in the conspiracy. Was the intention to require proof beyond a reasonable doubt or merely *prima facie* evidence? If the former, it obviously would run counter to the degree of proof necessary for admissibility as articulated by the Supreme Court of Canada. Moreover, this proposed legislation does not clear up the problem of the degree of proof required to show that the declarant is a co-conspirator.

513 *Chote v. Rowan*, [1943] O.W.N. 646 (C.A.).

against using the admission in that manner.[514] Thus, in a matrimonial proceeding where a spouse is accused of adultery and B is named as the co-respondent, if the spouse made an out-of-court admission of adultery with B, such admission is admissible as against the spouse only and does not constitute any evidence against B. The reason for this is that as against B, the extra-judicial statement of the spouse is hearsay. While a party who has made an out-of-court admission cannot rationally complain of its admissibility as against him or her,[515] the question of its admissibility as against B stands on a different footing. B has had no opportunity to cross-examine the declarant who may well have lied or wished to falsely implicate B for some personal reason. If B is deprived of an opportunity to test the validity of the statement, then the spectre of the hearsay dangers would haunt the statement's admissibility against B. Thus, an anomaly exists in that the spouse may be found guilty of adultery with B, but B can be exonerated.[516] An admission by one party will be evidence against another as to the truth of the contents only if that other person was present and assented, or is deemed under the circumstances to have assented by silence when he or she might reasonably have been expected to make some observation, explanation or denial. Accordingly, in *Thomas v. British Columbia (Attorney-General); Milliken v. British Columbia (Attorney-General)*,[517] the British Columbia Court of Appeal held that a statement made by one party in the presence of the other party but not heard by him or her was inadmissible to prove the truth of the matter asserted therein as against the latter party.

L. *Declarations by Children about Sexual Abuse*

In *R. v. Khan*[518] the Supreme Court of Canada recognized the need for more flexibility in the reception of hearsay evidence of children who may have been the victims of sexual abuse.[519] Rather

---

514 *Harris v. Harris* (1931), 40 O.W.N. 269, [1931] 4 D.L.R. 933 (S.C.).
515 See this Chapter, II.J.1.
516 See *Serediuk v. Kogan*, [1976] 5 W.W.R. 571, 28 R.F.L. 237 (Man. C.A.).
517 (1973), 34 D.L.R. (3d) 521 (B.C.C.A.).
518 [1990] 2 S.C.R. 531, 59 C.C.C. (3d) 92, 79 C.R. (3d) 1, 41 O.A.C. 353, 11 W.C.B. (2d) 10, 113 N.R. 53.
519 This is in keeping with a general loosening of the strictures that have traditionally circumscribed the evidence of children. Wilson J. in *R. v. B. (G.)*, [1990] 2 S.C.R. 30, 56 C.C.C. (3d) 200, 77 C.R. (3d) 347, (*sub nom. R. v. B. (G.)*

than trying to fit it artificially into the doctrine of spontaneous declarations[520] in order to achieve admissibility, the Court judicially created a new exception to the hearsay rule to accommodate this evidence.[521]

The criteria for admissibility are necessity and reliability of the hearsay statements, together with fairness to the accused. It was in *Ares v. Venner*[522] that the Court first referred to the twin requirements of necessity and reliability as the basis for judicially created exceptions to the hearsay rule and the Court returned to that theme in *Khan*. Necessity, according to the Court, means "reasonably necessary". If the child's evidence were not otherwise admissible, that might make the hearsay necessary. The Court also alluded to the possibility that it might be found to be too traumatic an experience for the child to give testimony in court. If so, that may satisfy the requirement of necessity.[523] In *Khan* the child's hearsay statements to her mother were necessary as evidence because the trial judge refused to admit her *viva voce* unsworn testimony.[524]

In terms of reliability, the trial judge should have regard to the timing of the statement, the demeanour, personality, intelligence and understanding of the child and the absence of any reason to expect fabrication. In *Khan*, reliability came from the fact that the child had no motive to fabricate her story, which came forth naturally and

---

(*No. 2*)) 111 N.R. 31, at 55 (S.C.R.) said: "In recent years we have adopted a much more benign attitude to children's evidence, lessening the strict standards of oath taking and corroboration, and I believe that this is a desirable development."

520 See this Chapter, II.H.5.

521 Several provinces have legislation permitting hearsay evidence of children in child welfare proceedings: see, e.g., *Child Welfare Act*, S.A. 1984, c. C-8.1, s. 74(4). In England, the hearsay rule has been abolished in respect of evidence given in civil proceedings before the High Court, County Courts and in Magistrates Courts in connection with the upbringing, maintenance or welfare of a child: see *The Children (Admissibility of Hearsay Evidence) Order 1991*, SI 1991/1115.

522 [1970] S.C.R. 608, 12 C.R.N.S. 349, 14 D.L.R. (3d) 4, 73 W.W.R. 347 (Alta.).

523 Unavailability of the declarant is not a condition of admissibility; nor is it under the *Ares v. Venner* exception. See this Chapter, II.C.1.(d).

524 The Supreme Court of Canada ruled, however, that the trial judge erred and should have received the trial judge's *viva voce* evidence. If such testimony is admitted, the necessity of the hearsay evidence in this case is gone: *supra*, note 518.

without prompting. Furthermore, it was held that such a young child could not be expected to have knowledge of the sexual acts in question and was, therefore, unlikely to have concocted such a story.

The Court did advise caution in receiving such evidence since it was untested by cross-examination. The court was careful to say that although in some cases a trial judge may insist on cross-examination of the child as condition to admissibility, generally, fairness to the accused can be dealt with by appropriate submissions as to the weight to be given to such evidence and the quality of any corroborating evidence.

The Court also stressed that this decision "does not make out-of-court statements by children generally admissible; in particular the requirement of necessity will probably mean that in most cases children will still be called to give *viva voce* evidence."[525]

In *Irvine v. Superintendent of Family and Child Service*,[526] the principle in *Khan* was extended to allow the hearsay statements of children in an application by government social workers for custody of two other children because of alleged sexual abuse by their father. MacDonald J. of the British Columbia Supreme Court held that as long as the evidence in question involved allegations of sexual abuse, it was irrelevant that the children whose statements were tendered were not the children who were the subject of the custody application. Evidence was therefore permitted from two parents whose children complained that the defendant had sexually abused them while babysitting. MacDonald J. stated that the ages of the children (three and eight) combined with their expressed fear of the defendant provided circumstances that made it reasonably necessary for their hearsay statements to be admitted. As for the requirement of reliability, he accepted the opinion of a psychologist who testified that the children had not been coached by their parents.

---

525 *Per* McLachlin J., *supra*, note 518, at 106 (C.C.C.). In *R. v. W.* (1990), 2 C.R. (4th) 204 (Ont. Ct. Prov. Div.), the Court held that the "necessity" test had not been met in that case since the child abuse specialist had not actually assessed the child for the purpose of determining potential trauma or harm to her in giving evidence. To the extent that considerations related to the court room setting were linked to a general feeling of uneasiness in the child witness and were otherwise not linked directly to issues of trauma and harm to the specific child victim, then it could not be said that such hearsay evidence satisfied the requirement of necessity.

526 [1991] B.C.J. No. 2154, June 10, 1991, not yet reported.

The notion of necessity was considered sufficiently elastic in *R. v. S. (K.O.)*[527] to permit the introduction of the hearsay evidence of the three-year-old victim of an alleged sexual assault on the basis that the calling of the child as a witness would not produce useful testimony. As acknowledged by both counsel, the child either would not or could not recount the events and thus, it was found to be pointless to have her testify. In this sense, the direct evidence of the child was just as "unavailable" as it was in *Khan* and therefore, the hearsay statements passed the test of necessity.

The Ontario Law Reform Commission has recommended that legislation be enacted to make hearsay statements of children admissible in all civil proceedings. While retaining the requirement of reliability, it would discard the need to demonstrate necessity. In its report, the Commission stated:[528]

> The Commission takes the position that providing the judge is satisfied that the hearsay statement of a child is sufficiently reliable, the statement should be admitted into evidence. The trier of fact can then assess the appropriate weight to be given to the out-of-court statement. We do not believe that the new legislation ought to be restricted to cases of physical or sexual abuse, but rather should be applicable to all civil proceedings. Nor should the admissibility of hearsay statements of children be contingent on whether the child testifies. In other words, the "necessity" requirement specified in *Ares v. Venner* should not be a criterion for the admissibility of hearsay statements of children. Rather, reliability should be the sole requirement for the admissibility of out-of-court statements of young witnesses. It is our opinion that the new rule respecting the hearsay evidence of children proposed by the Commission will introduce clarity into the law and will permit what may be extremely probative evidence to reach the courts, without sacrificing the fundamental common law principle for the exclusion of hearsay statements.

---

527 (1991), 63 C.C.C. (3d) 91 (B.C.S.C.).
528 Ontario Law Reform Commission, *Report on Child Witnesses* (Ontario Government, 1991), at 68-69.

M. *Possible New Exceptions*

A further occasion to create a new exception to the hearsay rule arose in *R. v. Moore*.[529] There, an accused was unable to remember acts leading to the death of the deceased. She had so repressed the event that she had no memory of what actually happened in the incident itself. The Court held admissible statements made by the accused in an interview with a psychiatrist while under the influence of sodium amytol in which she did recount what took place. In specifically referring to *R. v. Khan*,[530] Moldaver J. of the Ontario Court (General Division) emphasized that historically, the requisite ingredients to warrant the admissibility of hearsay evidence were necessity and reliability, and concluded that in recent years courts have adopted what appears to be a somewhat less rigid approach to the extension of those categories considered to be exceptions to the hearsay rule. In applying these requirements to the facts of the case, Moldaver J. concluded that the hearsay evidence was reasonably necessary because he was satisfied that the accused from her own memory could not give the critical evidence regarding the incident immediately preceding the deceased's death. Moreover, he was satisfied that the evidence was reliable because of several factors such as the expertise of the psychiatrist who administered the test; the fact that the psychiatrist was of the opinion that the accused was an appropriate candidate for such testing; the indicia of reliability put forward by the psychiatrist and especially the fact that the accused's version went to incriminate her in a very serious criminal offence, though short of what she was being charged for in this case. In applying the principles enunciated in *Ares v. Venner*[531] and *R. v. Khan* to broaden the reach of the hearsay exceptions, Moldaver J. did caution:[532]

I do not wish my ruling to be interpreted that every time a person claims memory loss and undergoes sodium amytol testing, the evidence from such testing will automatically be admissible as an exception to the hearsay rule. Each case will, of necessity, depend upon its own facts.

---

529 (1990), 63 C.C.C. (3d) 85 (Ont. Ct. (Gen. Div.)).
530 *Supra*, note 518.
531 [1970] S.C.R. 608, 12 C.R.N.S. 349, 73 W.W.R. 347, 14 D.L.R. (3d) 4.
532 *Supra*, note 529, at 91.

N. Non-Applicability of Hearsay Rule in Certain Proceedings

1. Administrative Proceedings

In proceedings before administrative tribunals and labour arbitration boards, hearsay evidence is freely admissible and its weight is a matter for the tribunal or board to decide[533] unless its receipt would amount to a clear denial of natural justice.[534] So long as such hearsay evidence is relevant, it can serve as the basis for the decision whether or not it is supported by other evidence which would be admissible in a court of law.[535]

The rationale for shying away from strict adherence to the hearsay rule and the rules of evidence generally is that administrative proceedings are not normally as adversarial as criminal and civil cases. Moreover, policy and social issues are often considered in such proceedings. Evidence with respect to these issues by their nature contain a hearsay component which cannot be separated out. Furthermore, individuals who are not legally trained are often members of the tribunal or act as representatives of the parties and would not be familiar with the rules of evidence.[536]

---

533 *Wilson v. Esquimalt and Nanaimo Railway Co.*, [1922] 1 A.C. 202; *R. v. Deputy Industrial Injuries Commr.; Ex parte Moore*, [1965] 1 All E.R. 81. See also *Statutory Powers Procedure Act*, R.S.O. 1980, c. 484, s. 15(1), which permits a tribunal not only to admit hearsay evidence but to act upon it as well; *Olarte v. Commodore Business Machines Ltd.* (1984), 49 O.R. (2d) 17 (*sub nom. Re Commodore Business Machines Ltd. and Ontario (Minister of Labour)*), 10 Admin. L.R. 130, 84 C.L.L.C. 17,028, 6 O.A.C. 176, 14 D.L.R. (4th) 118, 6 C.H.R.R. D/2833, 13 C.R.R. 338 (Div. Ct.), at 21 (O.R.).

534 *B. (J.) v. Catholic Children's Aid Society of Metropolitan Toronto (Municipality)* (1987), 59 O.R. (2d) 417 (*sub nom. B. v. Catholic Children's Aid Society, Metropolitan Toronto*), 27 Admin. L.R. 295, 7 R.F.L. (3d) 441, 38 D.L.R. (4th) 106 (Div. Ct.), at 420-21 (O.R.); *Lischka v. Ontario (Criminal Injuries Compensation Board)* (1982), 37 O.R. (2d) 134, at 135 (Div. Ct.).

535 *Noranda Metal Industries Ltd., Fergus Division v. I.B.E.W., Local 2345* (1983), 44 O.R. (2d) 529, 1 O.A.C. 187, 84 C.L.L.C. 14,024.

536 See M. Gorsky, "Effective Advocacy and the Continuing Significance of the Rules of Evidence Before Administrative Tribunals" (1987), in *Pitblado Lectures on Evidence: Recent Developments and Directions* 74, at 77-78.

2. Sentencing Proceedings

The Supreme Court of Canada in *R. v. Albright*[537] made it clear that all credible and trustworthy evidence is admissible at a sentencing hearing whether it is technically hearsay or not. The Court reiterated the statement made by Dickson J. in *R. v. Gardiner*[538] as follows:[539]

> It is a commonplace that the strict rules which govern at trial do not apply at a sentencing hearing and it would be undesirable to have the formalities and technicalities characteristic of the normal adversary proceeding prevail. *The hearsay rule does not govern the sentencing hearing. Hearsay evidence may be accepted where found to be credible and trustworthy.* The judge traditionally has had wide latitude as to the sources and types of evidence upon which to base his sentence. He must have the fullest possible information concerning the background of the accused if he is to fit the sentence to the offender rather than to the crime. [emphasis added]

---

537 [1987] 2 S.C.R. 383, 37 C.C.C. (3d) 105, 60 C.R. (3d) 97, [1987] 6 W.W.R. 577, 18 B.C.L.R. (2d) 145, 45 D.L.R. (4th) 11, 4 M.V.R. (2d) 311, 79 N.R. 129.
538 [1982] 2 S.C.R. 368, 68 C.C.C. (2d) 477, 30 C.R. (3d) 289, 140 D.L.R. (3d) 612, 43 N.R. 361.
539 *Ibid.*, at 414 (S.C.R.).

CHAPTER 7

SELF-SERVING EVIDENCE

I   RULE AND RATIONALE

There is a general exclusionary rule against the admission of self-serving evidence to support the credibility of a witness unless his or her credibility has first been made an issue.[1] The rule is generally applied to prior consistent statements of the witness. Although contradictory statements may be used against a witness,[2] "you are not entitled to give evidence of statements on other occasions by the witness in confirmation of her testimony".[3]

The rule is not limited to statements, but is applicable to any out-of-court evidence which is entirely self-serving and would shed no light on the material issues in the case. Polygraph evidence tendered by the accused would be precluded on this basis.[4]

Two different rationales have been given for the exclusion of such evidence. The one most commonly relied on is that, due to the risk of fabrication, no person should be allowed to create evidence for him or herself.[5] The other view emphasizes the valuelessness of such

---

1   *R. v. Beland*, [1987] 2 S.C.R. 398, 36 C.C.C. (3d) 481, 60 C.R. (3d) 1, 9 Q.A.C. 293, 43 D.L.R. (4th) 641, 79 N.R. 263, at 489 (C.C.C.).
2   See Chapter 16, V.C.2. (as to a party's own witness) and VI.D.2. (as to an opposite party's witness).
3   *Jones v. South Eastern and Chatham Railway Co.* (1918), 87 L.J.K.B. 775, at 779 (C.A.). See Chapter 16, V.E. for the use of prior consistent statements to refresh the memory of a witness.
4   *R. v. Beland, supra*, note 1. In *R. v. Bedgood* (1990), 60 C.C.C. (3d) 92, 80 C.R. (3d) 92, 98 N.S.R. (2d) 426 (N.S.C.A.), it was held that evidence that an accused had requested and was refused a polygraph test was inadmissible as an improper attempt to bolster one's own credibility.
5   *R. v. Jones* (1988), 44 C.C.C. (3d) 248, 66 C.R. (3d) 54, 29 O.A.C. 214, at 255 (C.C.C.); *R. v. Hardy* (1794), 24 State Tr. 199, at 1093; *Corke v. Corke*, [1958]

evidence since a witness' story is not made more probable or trustworthy by any number of repetitions of it.[6] Moreover, it would take needless trial time in order to deal with a matter that is not really in issue;[7] for it is assumed that the witness is truthful until there is some particular reason for assailing his or her veracity.[8]

II   EXCEPTIONS

A. *General Explanation of Exceptions*

A number of exceptions to the rule have developed in common law permitting the introduction of a witness' prior consistent statement when credibility has been impeached. The purpose of such evidence is limited to bolstering the witness' credibility by showing consistency with his or her testimony, and is not evidence of the truth of the earlier assertion.[9]

P. 93, [1958] 1 All E.R. 224 (C.A.); *Ward v. McIntyre* (1920), 56 D.L.R. 208, 48 N.B.R. 233 (C.A.). The validity of this rationale is questioned in M.T. MacCrimmon, "Consistent Statements of a Witness" (1979), 17 Osgoode Hall L.J. 285, at 288.

6   *R. v. Beland, supra,* note 1, at 499 (C.C.C.); *R. v. Meddoui* (1990), 61 C.C.C. (2d) 345, 2 C.R. (4th) 316, [1991] 2 W.W.R. 289, 77 Alta. L.R. (2d) 97 (C.A.), at 353 (C.C.C.); 4 Wigmore, *Evidence* (Chadbourn rev. 1972), § 1124, at 255; *Fox v. General Medical Council,* [1960] 3 All E.R. 225, at 230 (P.C.); *R. v. Campbell* (1977), 38 C.C.C. (2d) 6, 1 C.R. (3d) 309 and 1 C.R. (3d) S-49, 17 O.R. (2d) 673 (C.A.), at 18 (C.C.C.).

7   *R. v. Meddoui, ibid.*

8   *R. v. Giraldi* (1975), 28 C.C.C. (2d) 248, [1975] W.W.D. 166 (B.C.C.A.), leave to appeal to S.C.C. refd. 28 C.C.C. (2d) 248n.

9   Except when it compromises part of the *res gestae* (see this Chapter, II.E.) or except when it is prior identification evidence (see *infra,* II.C.) in which case it is admitted for its truth. Also see *R. v. Page* (1984), 12 C.C.C. (3d) 250, 40 C.R. (3d) 85 (Ont. H.C.J.), at 252, 254 (C.C.C.); *R. v. N.(L.)* (1989), 52 C.C.C. (3d) 1, [1990] N.W.T.R. 28 (C.A.), at 6 (C.C.C.). The Ontario Law Reform Commission recommended that all such statements should be admitted for their truth as an exception to the hearsay rule: see Ontario Law Reform Commission, *Report on the Law of Evidence* (Ontario: Ministry of the Attorney General, 1976), Draft *Evidence Act,* s. 28(1); the Federal/Provincial Task Force on Uniform Rules of Evidence would limit admissibility for this purpose to only those prior consistent statements given under oath and subject to cross-examination at the time: see *Report of the Federal/Provincial Task Force on Uniform Rules of Evidence* (Toronto:

Not all situations of impeachment, however, open the door to this exception. The prior consistent statement must be highly relevant to rebut the particular mode of impeachment. When evidence of a general reputation for untruthfulness[10] or evidence of prior convictions[11] has been adduced to attack credibility, the fact that the witness had made an earlier statement consistent with his or her testimony in the stand is not very relevant.[12] The common law has in fact limited prior consistent statement evidence of a witness to situations where its admissibility is sought specifically:

(1) to rebut allegations of recent fabrication;
(2) to establish eye-witness prior identification of the accused;
(3) to prove recent complaint by a sexual assault victim;
(4) to establish that a statement was made that forms part of the *res gestae* or to prove the physical, mental or emotional state of the accused;
(5) to prove that a statement was made on arrest;
(6) to prove that a statement was made on the recovery of incriminating articles.[13]

B. *Evidence To Rebut Allegations of Recent Fabrication by the Witness*

The Privy Council stated the exception for evidence to rebut allegations of recent fabrication by a witness as follows:[14]

> If, in cross-examination, a witness's account of some incident or set of facts is challenged as being a recent invention, thus presenting a clear issue whether, at some previous time, he said or thought what he has been saying at the trial, he may support himself by evidence of earlier statements by him to the same effect. Plainly the rule that sets up the exception cannot be formulated with any great precision, since its application will

---

Carswell, 1982), at 247.
10 See Chapter 16, VI.D.1.
11 See Chapter 16, VI.D.3.
12 4 Wigmore, *Evidence* (Chadbourn rev. 1972), § 1125, at 258.
13 *R. v. Jones, supra,* note 5, at 256 (C.C.C.); *R. v. Langille* (1990), 59 C.C.C. (3d) 544, at 551-52, 75 O.R. (2d) 65, 40 O.A.C. 355 (C.A.).
14 *Fox v. General Medical Council, supra,* note 6, at 230.

depend on the nature of the challenge offered by the course of cross-examination and the relative cogency of the evidence tendered to repel it. Its application must be, within limits, a matter of discretion, and its range can only be measured by the reported instances, not in themselves many, in which it has been successfully invoked.

The lack of clear definition raises certain questions. In what manner must the allegation of recent fabrication be made before confirmatory evidence of credibility may be adduced? What has to be the nature of the challenge to credibility before the exception is triggered?

1. How Must the Allegation Be Raised?

The allegation of recent fabrication is often made in cross-examination of the witness, in which case the previous statement may be adduced on re-examination or through the evidence of another witness.[15] The allegation may be made in a pleading,[16] in the evidence of other witnesses called by the opposite party, or in cross-examination of witnesses other than the witness whose evidence is attacked. If, in such a case, the witness whose credibility is attacked has not already given evidence, the statement may be admitted in the examination-in-chief of the witness.[17] In criminal cases, if the allegation of contrivance is made against the accused (if the accused testifies), the prior consistent statement should be elicited in the examination-in-chief of the accused, and not through other witnesses.[18]

In *R. v. Campbell*,[19] Martin J.A. of the Ontario Court of Appeal indicated that the imputation need not even be express, but may be implied from the circumstances of the case or the way in which it is presented:[20]

---

15 *R. v. Wannebo* (1972), 7 C.C.C. (2d) 266, [1972] 5 W.W.R. 372 (B.C.C.A.); *Fox v. General Medical Council, supra,* note 6; *Flanagan v. Fahy,* [1918] 2 Ir. R. 361 (C.A.).

16 *Welstead v. Brown,* [1952] 1 S.C.R. 3, 102 C.C.C. 46, [1952] 1 D.L.R. 465.

17 *Ibid.*

18 *R. v. Campbell, supra,* note 6, at 19.

19 *Ibid.*

20 *Ibid.,* at 18-19 (C.C.C.); but note that in *R. v. Pappin* (1970), 12 C.R.N.S. 287 (Ont. C.A.), the same court seemed to suggest that the allegation had to be "expressly raised". The Supreme Court of Canada in *R. v. Simpson,* [1988] 1

I accept the proposition that an express allegation of recent fabrication in cross-examination is not necessary before the exception with respect to rebutting an allegation of recent fabrication becomes operative, and that a suggestion that the accused's story has been recently contrived may also arise implicitly from the whole circumstances of the case, the evidence of the witnesses who have been called, and the conduct of the trial. Where the circumstances are such as to raise the suggestion that the accused's evidence is a recent fabrication, counsel may properly anticipate the allegation of recent fabrication in cross-examination, and examine the accused in chief with respect to previous statements to other persons, prior to his being cross-examined.

2. Form of Allegation

The allegation that the witness' testimony is recent fabrication may take a number of different forms. It may be alleged, for example, that the witness is biased or has some other improper motive in giving his or her testimony. In the face of such allegations, counsel may tender a statement of the witness made at a time when it could not be said that such influences existed.[21]

Another kind of allegation to impeach the witness' credit is ". . . that the witness did *not* speak of the matter before, at a time when it would have been natural to speak."[22] The imputation is that a witness who is truthful would have raised the issue at an early opportunity. This allegation, therefore, can be refuted with the admission of a consistent statement made by the witness at the relevant time to demonstrate that in fact he or she did speak out on that earlier occasion.[23]

When the accused is the witness whose testimony is being impeached, the making of the allegation, whether explicitly or implicitly, that he or she did not speak out at an early opportunity

---

S.C.R. 3, 38 C.C.C. (3d) 481, 62 C.R. (3d) 137, [1988] 2 W.W.R. 385, 23 B.C.L.R. (2d) 145, 46 D.L.R. (4th) 466, 81 N.R. 267, at 498 (C.C.C.), approved the *Campbell* view.

21　*Fox v. General Medical Council, supra,* note 6; *R. v. Campbell, supra,* note 6.
22　4 Wigmore, *Evidence* (Chadbourn rev. 1972), § 1129, at 271.
23　*R. v. Campbell, supra,* note 6, at 20 (C.C.C.); *R. v. Pangilinan* (1987), 60 C.R. (3d) 188 (B.C.C.A.).

would conflict with the accused's right to remain silent.[24] At the time of arrest when a caution has been administered to the accused by the police, the accused has a right to remain silent.[25] Cory J. in *R. v. Chambers*[26] made it clear that the Crown cannot allege a failure to speak out by the accused. He gave the following reason:[27]

> It has . . . been recognized that since there is a right to silence, it would be a snare and a delusion to caution the accused that he need not say anything in response to a police officer's question but none the less put in evidence that the accused clearly exercised his right and remained silent in the face of a question which suggested his guilt.

Thus the Crown is precluded from making the allegation and no inference that if the accused was innocent he would have asserted his defence when arrested can be drawn. There is nothing, therefore, that the accused need rebut.

Further, prior consistent statements have been allowed to be tendered when a witness' credibility has been attacked by a prior inconsistent statement. It has been said, however, that if the making of the prior inconsistent statement is not in dispute then the fact that the witness had made a consistent statement earlier in time than the inconsistent statement has little bearing on his credibility since it has already been demonstrated that the witness has been capable of self-contradiction.[28] He or she has already been trapped into an inconsistency. The fact that the witness had on a third occasion made a consistent statement with the testimony in the witness box provides no explanation for the inconsistency. Truly, the prior consistent statement would only be relevant if there was some doubt that the witness had in fact made the inconsistent statement which is alleged.[29]

---

24   See Chapter 14, IV.E.2.
25   *R. v. Hebert*, [1990] 2 S.C.R. 151, 57 C.C.C. (3d) 1, 77 C.R. (3d) 145, 47 B.C.L.R. (2d) 1, [1990] 5 W.W.R. 1, 110 N.R. 1, 49 C.R.R. 114; see Chapter 14, IV.E.2.
26   [1990] 2 S.C.R. 1293, 59 C.C.C. (3d) 321, 80 C.R. (3d) 235, 49 B.C.L.R. (2d) 299, [1990] 6 W.W.R. 554, 119 N.R. 321 (S.C.C.).
27   *Ibid.*, at 341.
28   See M.T. MacCrimmon, "Consistent Statements of a Witness" (1979), 17 Osgoode Hall L.J. 285, at 288.
29   Commentators seem to feel, however, that although there is logic to this

C. *Prior Eye-Witness Identification*

There is an inherent suspicion in testimony given by a witness identifying with certainty, for the first time, the accused in the witness box as the perpetrator of a crime that had occurred months and perhaps years before.[30] It is natural to assume that a witness would identify the accused since he or she was the one arrested by the police and is prominently sitting in the prisoner's dock. Questions may legitimately be asked whether the witness is truly relying on present recollection in making such identification or whether he or she has been strongly influenced by the circumstances. Because such eye-witness identification evidence in the court room is subject to frailty, it is permissible for the witness to testify about previous acts of identification to support his or her testimony; and this evidence can be given without any impeaching allegation having first been made.[31]

What is the purpose of tendering prior identifying statements? Is it merely to establish consistency with the identification testimony given by the witness in the box? Is it also admissible to establish the truth of the earlier identification?

Besides the need to strengthen the credibility of the eye witness, another policy interest is met by permitting the introduction of earlier identification evidence. It is obviously not in the accused's interests to be identified for the first time in the court room. Identification is much more reliable if it takes place closer to the event in question and is conducted under circumstances which ensure accuracy and are fair to the accused.[32] That being the case, the more reliable evidence is in fact the earlier identification evidence rather than the testimony identifying the accused in court. Accordingly, it is difficult to adhere to the proposition that the only purpose for which the prior identification can be tendered should be to establish the fact of consistency and not

---

distinction, practical considerations warrant admissibility of the prior consistent statement in *all* cases where an inconsistent statement has been alleged: see M.T. McCrimmon, "Consistent Statements of a Witness", *ibid.*, at 303-04; *Report of the Federal Provincial Task Force on Uniform Rules of Evidence, supra*, note 9, at 307.

30   *R. v. Izzard* (1990), 54 C.C.C. (3d) 252, 75 C.R. (3d) 342, 38 O.A.C. 6: "The spectre of erroneous convictions based on honest and convincing, but mistaken eye-witness identification haunts the criminal law.": per Doherty J.A. in *R. v. Quercia* (1990), 60 C.C.C. (3d) 380 (Ont. C.A.), at 383.

31   *R. v. Page* (1984), 12 C.C.C. (3d) 250, 40 C.R. (3d) 85 (Ont. H.C.J.), at 252 (C.C.C.).

32   See Chapter 12, I.B.1.

as proof of actual identification. Consider the situation, a not uncommon one, where a witness who has positively identified the accused in a line-up shortly after the occurrence, has some difficulty in court, years later, in identifying the same person, who may have changed his or her appearance. Is there any valid reason why evidence of the prior identification should not be permitted even though it is being tendered for a purpose other than to demonstrate consistency, i.e. to prove actual identification? In *R. v. Swanston*,[33] due to the accused's change in appearance, the victim of a robbery was able to testify at trial only that the accused *resembled* his attacker although he had positively identified the accused as his assailant on previous occasions (at a line-up and at a preliminary hearing). The British Columbia Court of Appeal allowed the victim to give evidence of the earlier identifications and permitted police officers to testify that the person identified by the victim on those occasions was in fact the accused. Accordingly, the law appears to be that evidence of extra-judicial identification is admissible not only to corroborate an identification made at trial but as independent evidence going to identity,[34] at least in situations where the witness who made the earlier identification is in the stand and can be subjected to cross-examination.

Different considerations, of course, apply where the identifier does not take the witness box at all and an attempt is made to adduce evidence of his or her prior identification through someone else. Such evidence would be presented solely for a hearsay purpose, i.e. to prove actual identity without the accused having an opportunity to conduct a cross-examination of the witness and is therefore inadmissible.[35]

---

33   (1982), 65 C.C.C. (2d) 453, 25 C.R. (3d) 385, [1982] 2 W.W.R. 546, 33 B.C.L.R. 391 (C.A.).
34   It would constitute evidence in the nature of "past recollection recorded": *R. v. Rouse* (1977), 36 C.C.C. (2d) 257, 39 C.R.N.S. 135, [1977] 4 W.W.R. 734 (B.C.C.A.), affirmed on other grounds, [1979] 1 S.C.R. 588, 42 C.C.C. (2d) 481, 5 C.R. (3d) 125, [1978] 6 W.W.R. 585, 89 D.L.R. (3d) 609, 23 N.R. 589; *R. v. Langille* (1990), 59 C.C.C. (3d) 544, 75 O.R. (2d) 65, 40 O.A.C. 355 (C.A.); see also Chapter 16, V.E.3.
35   See *R. v. Timm*, [1981] 2 S.C.R. 315, 59 C.C.C. (2d) 396, at 414, 21 C.R. (3d) 209, [1981] 5 W.W.R. 577, 29 A.R. 509, 124 D.L.R. (3d) 582, 37 N.R. 204.

D. Recent Complaint

The common law permitted the credibility of a victim of a sexual offence who testified at trial to be supported by evidence that she made a complaint about the incident within a short time after it occurred. The rule arose in rape cases centuries ago. There was concern that there might be an assumption that if a complainant had not raised a "hue and cry" at an early opportunity then the victim's present testimony was suspect. Fauteux J. in *Kribs v. R.*[36] stated the basis of admissibility of evidence of a recent complaint as follows:[37]

> The principle is one of necessity. It is founded on factual presumptions which, in the normal course of events, naturally attach to the subsequent conduct of the prosecutrix shortly after the occurrence of the alleged acts of violence. One of these presumptions is that she is expected to complain upon the first reasonable opportunity, and the other, consequential thereto, is that if she fails to do so, her silence may naturally be taken as a virtual self-contradiction of her story.

Because such presumption was considered so strong, a complainant was permitted to give this supporting evidence in her examination-in-chief without there first being an attack on her credibility.

In this century the admissibility of recent complaint evidence was expanded to include a victim of any sexual offence, whether male or female.[38] A large body of law developed around the doctrine of recent complaint evidence and a trial judge had to be satisfied as a matter of law that the following conditions had been met:[39]

(1) The words of an extra-judicial statement had to be capable of constituting a "complaint", i.e. any statement made by the victim which, given the circumstances of the case, will, if believed, be of

---

36 [1960] S.C.R. 400, 33 C.R. 57, 127 C.C.C. 22.

37 *Ibid.*, at 405 (S.C.R.).

38 See *R. v. Lebrun* (1951), 100 C.C.C. 16, 12 C.R. 31, [1951] O.R. 387 (C.A.). It has also been suggested that recent complaint evidence can be given in trials of all violent crime whether sexual or not: see *R. v. Christenson* (1923), 39 C.C.C. 203, [1923] 1 W.W.R. 1307, 19 Alta. L.R. 337, [1923] 2 D.L.R. 379 (C.A.).

39 These conditions were set out by the Supreme Court of Canada in *R. v. Timm*, *supra*, note 35, at 413-14 (C.C.C.).

some probative value in negating the adverse conclusions the trier of fact could draw as regards the victim's credibility had she or he been silent;

(2) The complaint must have been recent, i.e. made "at the first opportunity after the offence which reasonably offers itself";[40] and

(3) The complaint must not have been elicited from the complainant by questions of a leading and inducing or intimidating character. "What is sought to be guarded against is the admission as a recent complaint of statements which have been put into the complainant's mouth. Whether a particular question is likely to have brought about that result depends on the nature of the question, the relationship of the parties and the entire circumstances."[41]

The entire rationale of the doctrine of recent complaint has been subjected to justified criticism. An example appears in the *Report of the Federal/Provincial Task Force on Uniform Rules of Evidence*:[42]

The doctrine of recent complaint is an anomalous and arbitrary exception to the rule against narrative. Fauteux J.'s attempt [in *Kribs v. R.*] to formulate a modern basis for the rule cannot be justified in reason. The expectations of medieval England as to the reaction of an innocent victim of a sexual attack are no longer relevant. A victim may have a genuine complaint but delay making it because of such legitimate concerns as the prospect of embarrassment and humiliation, or the destruction of domestic or personal relationships. The delay may also be attributable to the youth or lack of knowledge of the complainant or to threats of reprisal from the accused. In contemporary society, there is no longer a logical connection between the genuineness of a complaint and the promptness with which it is made.

---

40   *R. v. Osborne*, [1905] 1 K.B. 551, at 561; also see *R. v. Kulak* (1979), 46 C.C.C. (2d) 30, 7 C.R. (2d) 304 (Ont. C.A.).

41   *Per* Martin J.A. in *R. v. Kulak, ibid.*, at 38 (C.C.C.).

42   (Toronto: Carswell, 1982), at 301. See also *R. v. Page* (1984), 12 C.C.C. (3d) 250, 40 C.R. (3d) 85 (Ont. H.C.J.), at 252 (C.C.C.); *R. v. Boyce* (1974), 23 C.C.C. (2d) 16, at 33, 28 C.R.N.S. 336, 7 O.R. (2d) 561 (C.A.).

In 1983 an amendment was made to the Criminal Code purport-edly abolishing the use of such evidence.[43] It provided that the rules relating to evidence of recent complaint in sexual assault cases are abrogated.

How is this section to be interpreted? Does it mean that all manner of recent complaint evidence is now inadmissible? Or was it intended merely to prohibit evidence to support a witness' testimony before that witness was even impeached? Does abrogation of the rule mean that the complainant cannot be cross-examined on whether she or he made an earlier complaint nor the jury instructed with respect to the fact that no complaint was made?

The Ontario Court of Appeal in R. v. Owens[44] held that the amendment did not preclude admissibility in all cases. The Court indicated that in certain circumstances the statements may be received as an important part of the narrative[45] or be admissible to show the witness' consistency of position after an allegation of recent fabrica-tion was made.[46]

It appears that the effect of the statutory amendment is that recent complaint evidence may not be led in anticipation of the adverse inference drawn from silence. However, defence counsel are not precluded from cross-examining a complainant about the lack of a prior complaint. If they do, they take the risk that the Crown may adduce a prior complaint to rebut the allegation. This was the view taken by one commentator:[47]

> Excursions by defence counsel in this area are not forestalled by the general law of evidence. Certainly prior to the enactment of s. 246.5 defence counsel had always been free to elicit the absence of a complaint, or emphasize its untimeliness.

---

43   S.C. 1980-81-82-83, c. 125, s. 19 [s. 246.5]; now see R.S.C. 1985, c. C-46, s. 275 [am. R.S.C. 1985, c. 19 (3rd Supp.), s. 11].

44   (1986), 55 C.R. (3d) 386, 18 O.A.C. 125 (C.A.).

45   See this Chapter, II.E. and Chapter 6, H.4; see also R. v. George (1985), 23 C.C.C. (3d) 42 (B.C.C.A.).

46   R. v. Page, supra, note 31, at 253 (C.C.C.); R. v. N.(L.) (1989), 52 C.C.C. (3d) 1, at 4-5, [1990] N.W.T.R. 28 (N.W.T.C.A.).

47   D.F. Dawson, "The Abrogation of Recent Complaint: Where Do We Stand Now?" (1984-85), 27 Crim. L.Q. 57, at 69-70.

To this last point some will argue that questions by the defence designed to elicit the absence or untimeliness of a complaint can only have probative value if the underlying assumptions and rationale for the rule in the first place (that an adverse inference will be drawn from silence) are accepted as valid. If the underlying assumption has been invalidated by statute as suggested above, then questioning in this area should be prohibited as irrelevant. This suggestion however, again fails to recognize the importance of the concept of *anticipatory* rehabilitation in the rationale and assumptions underlying the original rule. The original rule assumes that if mention is *not* made of a complaint by the victim, an adverse inference will be drawn. That is a far cry from saying that if specific mention of absence or untimeliness of complaint *is* made an adverse inference should be drawn, which is logically what the original rationale and assumption would have to have been before its elimination by statute would lead to the conclusion that such questions should not be permitted by the defence. Put differently, it does not logically follow that if we assume no adverse inference should be drawn when no mention is made of the issue one way or another, no adverse inference should be drawn when the issue is specifically raised.

Furthermore, the ability of the defence to question a complainant on the absence or untimeliness of a complaint has had nothing to do in the past with the doctrine of recent complaint. One of the most common means of suggesting that a witness's testimony is fabricated is to allege failure to speak when it would have been expected, and this has always been recognized.

E. Res Gestae *or to Show Physical, Mental or Emotional State of Accused*

An earlier statement made by the witness while the event in question is taking place may be part of the *res gestae* and be admissible evidence as an exception to the hearsay rule.[48] Such statements are admissible in their own right as proof of the contents therein and there need not be consistent testimony given in court on the same point. Accordingly, even if the prior consistent statement would have been

---

48   See Chapter 6, II.H.; see also *R. v. George, supra*, note 45.

inadmissible because no allegation of recent fabrication had been made, it may still be received provided that the statement was made during the carrying out of an act or transaction and so related in time as to be part of it.

By the same token, the Supreme Court of Canada in *R. v. Simpson*[49] stated that whenever the physical, mental or emotional state of an accused is material to be proved, any statements made by him or her at or about the time in question are admissible.

F. *Statements Made on Arrest*

The statements made by an accused upon his or her arrest, which are exculpatory in nature, have been said to be admissible as an exception to the general rule prohibiting self-serving evidence. The problem, however, is that it appears that it is receivable in evidence only if tendered by the Crown but not by the defence.[50] However, it should be noted that in the Supreme Court of Canada decision in *R. v. Hughes*[51] defence counsel elicited upon the cross-examination of a Crown witness the earlier exculpatory remarks made by the accused in a conversation with that witness. The Supreme Court of Canada was more explicit in *Lucas v. R.*[52] wherein it indicated that it was permissible for an accused to testify in his examination-in-chief about an exculpatory statement made to the police upon arrest similar to the testimony that the accused was giving in the court room. In essence, the prior exculpatory statement is tendered to rebut any inference of his guilt arising from any silence on his part at the time of arrest. Although such an inference cannot be drawn as a matter of law by reason of the right to remain silent, it might be drawn in fact. The accused can adduce the exculpatory statement as a matter of good tactics.

---

49 [1988] 1 S.C.R. 3, 38 C.C.C. (3d) 481, 62 C.R. (3d) 137, [1988] 2 W.W.R. 385, 23 B.C.L.R. (2d) 145, 46 D.L.R. (4th) 466, 81 N.R. 267, at 496-97 (C.C.C.); see also *R. v. Beland*, [1987] 2 S.C.R. 398, 36 C.C.C. (3d) 481, 60 C.R. (3d) 1, 9 Q.A.C. 293, 43 D.L.R. (4th) 641, 79 N.R. 263, at 490 (C.C.C.).
50 *R. v. Knox*, [1968] 2 C.C.C. 348, 62 W.W.R. 8 (B.C.C.A.); *R. v. Keeler* (1977), 36 C.C.C. (2d) 9, 4 A.R. 449, [1977] 5 W.W.R. 410 (C.A.).
51 [1942] S.C.R. 517, 78 C.C.C. 257, [1943] 1 D.L.R. 1.
52 [1963] 1 C.C.C. 1, 39 C.R. 101 (S.C.C.), at 10-11 (C.C.C.).

G. *Explanatory Statements Made By an Accused in Possession of Stolen Goods or Illegal Drugs*

An accused who is charged with possession of stolen goods may tender evidence of his or her innocent explanation made at a time when the accused had been found in possession. This evidence is allowed because of the inference that could arise that an accused would have given an explanation at that material time if the possession was in fact innocent. The question arises as to whether the evidence is to be used only for the limited purpose to rebut that inference or whether it can be received as proof of the assertion as well. The Supreme Court of Canada seems to favour the latter view, for in *R. v. Graham*,[53] it stated:[54]

> ... the respondent's verbal statement made when the attache case was found, that he had never seen it before in his life, being one which was immediately connected with the initial discovery of the stolen goods, was properly admitted in evidence. Explanatory statements made by an accused upon his first being found "in possession" constitute a part of the *res gestae* and are necessarily admissible in any description of the circumstances under which the crime was committed ...

If an essential element of *res gestae* is the spontaneity of the exclamation in order to still any reflective instinct, can it be said that the statement to the police officer in *Graham* truly comes within the *res gestae* exception?[55] The Supreme Court of Canada went further in *R. v. Risby*[56] holding that an explanatory statement with respect to possession of illegal drugs was admissible. In these cases, mere possession of the stolen goods or the drugs is the crime. Accordingly, there is an implication that it would have been natural for the accused to speak up when this possession was discovered and thus the accused's state-

---

53   [1974] S.C.R. 206, 7 C.C.C. (2d) 93, 19 C.R.N.S. 117, [1972] 4 W.W.R. 488, 26 D.L.R. (3d) 579.
54   *Ibid.*, at 99 (C.C.C.).
55   See Chapter 6, II.H.5. See *R. v. Page* (1984), 12 C.C.C. (3d) 250, 40 C.R. (3d) 85 (Ont. H.C.J.), where it was held that for the recent complaint to fall within the *res gestae* exception, it must have been a spontaneous exclamation as a result of nervous excitement.
56   [1978] 2 S.C.R. 139, 39 C.C.C. (2d) 567.

ments at the time are received to rebut any implied allegation of recent fabrication. These cases may have to be reconsidered in light of the accused's right to remain silent which is entrenched in s. 7 of the *Charter*. The exculpatory statements are properly admissible even though as a matter of law no inference of guilt can be drawn from the silence of the accused. The accused may not wish to leave it there in order to expressly negate any inference that may be drawn in fact. If admitted, the statement would presumably be admissible to rebut any suggestion of recent fabrication.

CHAPTER 8

CONFESSIONS

I WHAT CONSTITUTES A CONFESSION?

A. *Admissions — Inculpatory Statements*

In its earliest formulation, a confession was simply a guilty plea and was thought to constitute "the best and surest answer that can be in our law for quieting the conscience of the judge and for making it a good and firm conviction".[1] The definition has been gradually expanded and now includes any written or oral communication made by the accused stating or inferring that he or she committed the crime. A confession may be either a complete admission of all the elements of the crime or an admission of one or more material facts tending to prove the guilt of the accused.

Like other admissions, a confession is an exception to the hearsay rule and can be admitted as evidence of the truth of its contents.[2] In *Bigaouette v. R.*,[3] Greenshields J. considered the probative value of a confession:[4]

The general rule . . . is, that a free and voluntary confession made by a person accused of an offence is receivable in evidence against

---

1   Sir William Staunford, *Les Plees del Coron* (1557); reprinted, *Classic English Law Texts* (P.R. Glazebrook, ed.) (London: Professional Books Ltd., 1971), b. 2, c. 51.
2   See E.W. Cleary (ed.), *McCormick on Evidence*, 3rd ed. (St. Paul: West Publishing, 1984), at 363-64 for different theories of admissibility of confessions.
3   (1926), 46 C.C.C. 311 (Que. K.B.); new trial ordered on other grounds, [1927] S.C.R. 112, 47 C.C.C. 271, [1927] 1 D.L.R. 1147 (K.B.).
4   *Ibid.*, at 320 (C.C.C.). The passage was quoted with approval from the judgment of Grose J. in *R. v. Lambe* (1791), 2 Leach 552, at 554-55, 168 E.R. 379 (Assizes).

him, . . . as the highest and most satisfactory proof of guilt, because it is fairly presumed that no man would make such a confession against himself, if the facts confessed were not true.

B. *Exculpatory Statements as Confessions*

In the beginning, only inculpatory statements were considered confessions. The basis for distinguishing between inculpatory and exculpatory statements was that the latter were not offered to prove the truth of the matter asserted in them but to prove circumstantially a state of mind, that is, a consciousness of guilt.[5] An exculpatory statement might also be used for a different non-hearsay purpose, that is, to impeach the accused's credibility by proof of a prior inconsistent statement. As a result, exculpatory statements, such as a statement denying or intending to deny guilt, were not subject to controls governing the admissibility of confessions which had been gradually developing.

This distinction resulted in a great deal of controversy at trial as to whether a statement was inculpatory or exculpatory since a statement which appeared to be exculpatory might be inculpatory in the context of other evidence. Typically, this would occur when an exculpatory statement was collaterally proved false, as when an alibi was found to be untrue.[6] Moreover, the fact that the Crown was tendering an apparently exculpatory statement raised questions as to its real effect.

This controversy was laid to rest by the Supreme Court of Canada in *R. v. Piche*[7] which rejected the distinction between exculpatory and inculpatory statements for the purposes of the confession rule. In *Piche*, the accused was charged with murdering her common-law husband. Immediately after the shooting, Piche told the police that she spent the evening with the victim, that there had been an argument, but that when she left the apartment, the deceased was sleeping. At trial she testified that she shot the victim accidentally.

---

5   McCormick, *supra*, note 2, at 362.
6   This may be contrasted with a statement which was intended to be exculpatory when made but at trial it was proffered by the prosecution to prove one or more elements of the crime.
7   [1971] S.C.R. 23, [1970] 4 C.C.C. 27, 12 C.R.N.S. 222, 11 D.L.R. (3d) 700, 74 W.W.R. 674. But see *R. v. Sat-Bhambra*, [1988] Crim. L.R. 453, where the English C.A. rejected the reasoning in *Piche*.

Because the trial judge held that the statement to the police was inculpatory (it disclosed an opportunity and a motive), he did not consider whether the confession rule should also apply to an exculpatory statement. The Supreme Court, however, held that both exculpatory and inculpatory statements should be subject to the confession rule. Hall J., speaking for the majority, stated:[8]

> In my view the time is opportune for this Court to say that the admission in evidence of all statements made by an accused to persons in authority, whether inculpatory or exculpatory, is governed by the same rule and thus put to an end the continuing controversy and necessary evaluation by trial judges of every such statement which the Crown proposes to use in chief or on cross-examination as either being inculpatory or exculpatory.

Cartwright C.J.C. exposed the inconsistency of the Crown's position in this pithy statement:[9]

> I find it difficult to see how the prosecution can consistently urge that a statement forced from an accused is in reality exculpatory while at the same time asserting that its exclusion has resulted in the acquittal of the accused and that its admission might well have resulted in conviction.

For practical reasons, the rejection of this distinction is sound. As illustrated in *Piche*, a statement may be both inculpatory (opportunity and consciousness of guilt) and exculpatory (lack of intent) and, accordingly, it is not always possible to label a statement as being one or the other.[10] Because an exculpatory false statement may have the same effect on the outcome of the proceedings as an inculpatory statement, and because a false confession which is the product of an inducement may not be a reliable basis for showing a consciousness of guilt or for rejecting the accused's testimony,[11] the underlying justification for the confession rule should also apply to exculpatory statements.

---

8   *Ibid.*, at 36 (S.C.R.).
9   *Ibid.*, at 26 (S.C.R.).
10   Compare the characterization of the accused's statement by Taschereau J. and Kerwin J. in *Boudreau v. R.*, [1949] S.C.R. 262, 94 C.C.C. 1, 7 C.R. 427, 3 D.L.R. 81.
11   *R. v. Eaton* (1978), 39 C.C.C. (2d) 455, at 461 (Man. C.A.).

C. *Spontaneous Statements*

The early common law held that statements made to a person in authority that appear to be volunteered or forming part of the *res gestae* were not subject to the confession rule. In *R. v. Erven*,[12] the Supreme Court of Canada decided that all statements must be proven to be voluntary on a *voir dire*. It may also be argued that because admissions include conduct, conduct meant to be assertive (for example, an accused's affirmative nod to a police officer's question about owner- ship of stolen goods) should also be subject to the confession rule.[13]

II SCOPE OF THE CONFESSION RULE

The rule applies to *all* oral or written statements made by an accused to a person in authority proffered by the Crown in criminal[14] or quasi-criminal proceedings, such as the prosecution of provincial regulatory offences. The rule also applies when a third party offers an inducement in the presence of a person in authority and the former is the agent or is clothed with authority.[15] Even a statement apparently made under statutory compulsion must be dealt with in a *voir dire* to determine whether, apart from such compulsion, it was voluntary.[16]

---

12   [1979] 1 S.C.R. 926, 44 C.C.C. (2d) 76, 6 C.R. (3d) 97, 92 D.L.R. (3d) 507.
13   *R. v. Fequet* (1985), 16 C.R.R. 66 (Que. S.C.).
14   *R. v. Erven, supra*, note 12; *Young Offenders Act*, R.S.C. 1985, c. Y-1, s. 56.
15   *R. v. B.(A.)* (1986), 50 C.R. (3d) 247, at 256, 26 C.C.C. (3d) 17, 13 O.A.C. 68 (Ont. C.A.); leave to appeal to S.C.C. refd. 50 C.R. (3d) xxv, 26 C.C.C. (3d) 17*n*.
16   *R. v. Bossman* (1984), 28 M.V.R. 223, 15 C.C.C. (3d) 251, 56 A.R. 103 (Alta.C.A.); *R. v. Cleaveley* (1966), 49 C.R. 326, 57 W.W.R. 301 (Sask.Q.B.); *R. v. Fex* (1973), 12 C.C.C. (2d) 239, 21 C.R.N.S. 360, [1973] 3 O.R. 242 (H.C.); affd. (1973), 1 O.R. (2d) 280, 14 C.C.C. (2d) 188, 23 C.R.N.S. 368 (C.A.), leave to appeal to S.C.C. refd. (1973), 14 C.C.C. (2d) 188*n*, 1 O.R. (2d) 280*n*; *R. v. Slopek* (1974), 21 C.C.C. (2d) 362 (Ont. C.A.). In *R. v. Ward* (1977), 38 C.C.C. (2d) 353, [1978] 1 W.W.R. 514, 7 A.R. 587; revd. [1979] 2 S.C.R. 30, 7 C.R. (3d) 153, 44 C.C.C. (2d) 498, 94 D.L.R. (3d) 18, [1979] 2 W.W.R. 193, the Alberta Court of Appeal, in *dicta*, indicated that it had doubts about its own decision in *R. v. Smith* (1973), 15 C.C.C. (2d) 113, 25 C.R.N.S. 246, [1974] 2 W.W.R. 4 (Alta. C.A.); but see, *contra*: *R. v. Pedersen* (1956), 114 C.C.C. 366, 23 C.R. 198, [1956] O.W.N. 212 (H.C.); *R. v. Patrick* (1960), 128 C.C.C. 263, 32 C.R. 338, [1960] O.W.N. 206 (C.A.).

However the rule does not apply at bail hearings[17] and, on principle, at the sentencing stage of a trial where guilt or innocence is not an issue.[18] If the accused disputes the accuracy of a statement proffered by the Crown during submissions on sentencing, the normal rules of evidence would adequately safeguard the accused's rights.

The rule does not apply when the utterances themselves constitute an element of the *actus reus* of the offence, for example, the words spoken by an accused on refusing to give a breathalyzer sample.[19] In that situation, the Crown proffers the accused's statement as an element of the offence and not as an admission. There is also authority to support the proposition that, in a joint trial, counsel for one accused may cross-examine a co-accused on a prior inconsistent statement made to the police without first proving the statement was voluntary.[20] Finally, the rule does not apply to civil proceedings.[21]

III HISTORY AND RATIONALE OF THE CONFESSION RULE

A. *Voluntariness*

Statements made against one's interest are normally admitted because of their inherent reliability and trustworthiness. However, where a confession is made by an accused to a person in authority, concerns about reliability or trustworthiness may arise. For that

---

17 *Bouffard v. R.* (1979), 16 C.R. (3d) 373 (Que S.C.).

18 See by analogy *R. v. McDermott* (1981), 31 A.R. 433 (Alta. Q.B.), where the court did not require a *voir dire* in a proceeding to transfer a juvenile to adult court. In *R. v. Gardiner*, [1982] 2 S.C.R. 368, 30 C.R. (3d) 289, 68 C.C.C. (2d) 477, 140 D.L.R. (3d) 612 Dickson J. stated, at 414 (S.C.R.): "It is a commonplace that the strict rules which govern at trial do not apply at a sentencing hearing and it would be undesirable to have the formalities and technicalities characteristic of the normal adversary proceeding prevail."

19 *Stapleton v. R.* (1982), 66 C.C.C. (2d) 231, 26 C.R. (3d) 361, 134 D.L.R. (3d) 239 (Ont. C.A.).

20 *R. v. Pelletier* (1986), 29 C.C.C. (3d) 533 (B.C.C.A.); *R. v. Logan* (1988), 68 C.R. (3d) 1, 46 C.C.C. (3d) 354, 67 O.R. (2d) 87, 30 O.A.C. 321, 57 D.L.R. (4th) 58, 45 C.R.R. 201 (C.A.); affd. [1990] 2 S.C.R. 731, 73 D.L.R. (4th) 40, 58 C.C.C. (3d) 391, 79 C.R. (3d) 169, 74 O.R. (2d) 644*n*, 41 O.A.C. 330, 112 N.R. 144, 50 C.R.R. 152.

21 *Tompkins v. Ternes* (1960), 32 W.W.R. 299 (Sask. Q.B.); affd. (1960) 33 W.W.R. 455, 26 D.L.R. (2d) 563 (Sask. C.A.).

reason, the trial judge has the authority to exclude a confession where there is a reasonable doubt as to its voluntariness. In *Ibrahim v. R.*,[22] Lord Sumner articulated a test for admissibility which still dominates the law today. He stated:[23]

> It has long been established as a positive rule of English criminal law, that no statement by an accused is admissible in evidence against him unless it is shewn by the prosecution to have been a voluntary statement, in the sense that it has not been obtained from him either by fear of prejudice or hope of advantage exercised or held out by a person in authority.

In order to understand the reason for the above rule and the direction of the future development of the law of confessions, it is important to review its historical underpinnings.

1. Historical Position

Confessions were admitted as pleas of guilt until the 1750s when it was first recognized that some confessions were untrustworthy. The first clear and explicit judicial airing of the rationale for the modern rule occurred in *R. v. Warickshall*,[24] when Nares J. held:[25]

> Confessions are received in evidence, or rejected as inadmissible, under a consideration whether they are or are not entitled to credit. A free and voluntary confession is deserving of the highest credit, because it is presumed to flow from the strongest sense of guilt, and therefore it is admitted as proof of the crime to which it refers; but a confession forced from the mind by the flattery of hope, or by the torture of fear, comes in so questionable a shape when it is to be considered as the evidence of guilt, that no credit ought to be given to it; and therefore it is rejected.

The underlying rationale was that a statement which was not obtained voluntarily was not credible. Confessions would be excluded if they had been extracted by methods which would likely result in statements

---

22   [1914] A.C. 599, [1914-15] All E.R. Rep. 874 (P.C.).
23   *Ibid.*, at 609 (A.C.).
24   (1783), 1 Leach 263, 168 E.R. 234 (Cr. Cas. Res.).
25   *Ibid.*, at 234-35 (E.R.).

that were unreliable as affirmations of guilt.

By the 1800s, a general suspicion of all confessions developed and they were frequently excluded upon proof of the most trivial inducements. In *D.P.P. v. Ping Lin*,[26] Lord Hailsham attributed this trend to prevailing social conditions:[27]

> It bears, it is true, all the marks of its origin at a time when the savage code of the eighteenth century was in full force. At that time almost every serious crime was punishable by death or transportation. The law enforcement officers formed no disciplined police force and were not subject to effective control by the central government, watch committees or an inspectorate. There was no legal aid. There was no system of appeal. To crown it all the accused was unable to give evidence on his own behalf and was therefore largely at the mercy of any evidence, either perjured or oppressively obtained, that might be brought against him. The judiciary were therefore compelled to devise artificial rules designed to protect him against dangers now avoided by other and more rational means.

Ultimately, exclusion became the practice, and admission the exception. The nadir of this practice was probably reached in *R. v. Gavin*[28] where Smith J. suggested: "When a prisoner is in custody, the police have no right to ask him questions."[29]

Some judges, however, attempted to relax the strictness of the exclusionary rule. In *R. v. Baldry*,[30] the alleged inducement had been a constable's warning to the accused that what he said could be taken down and used in evidence against him. Because some of the rigours of penal law had been eased by statute, Pollock C.B. attempted to put an end to the judge's habit of seizing upon the slightest pretext in order to exclude a confession. In reacting against the perceived excesses of the judiciary in excluding confessions, he emphasized the need to balance the right of an accused person to a fair trial against the common interest in securing the conviction of the guilty.

---

26 [1976] A.C., at 588, [1975] 3 All E.R. 175 (H.L.).
27 *Ibid.*, at 600 (A.C.)
28 (1885), 15 Cox C.C. 656 (Assizes).
29 *Ibid.*, at 657.
30 (1852), 2 Den. 430, 169 E.R. 568 (C.A.).

2. Development of the Voluntariness Rule

During the next fifty years, the law changed little. It was clear that judges still had strong reservations about the use of confessions. These reservations, however, were now being couched in terms about voluntariness as much as reliability. Then, in 1914, Lord Sumner enunciated a rule, commonly referred to as the *Ibrahim* rule, that set the tone for much of this century: a statement was inadmissible unless it was voluntary "in the sense that it has not been obtained from him either by fear of prejudice or hope of advantage exercised or held out by a person in authority."[31] If it was found that the hopes and fears of the accused had not been preyed upon, the statement was admitted. In 1921, the Supreme Court adopted the *Ibrahim* rule in *R. v. Prosko*.[32] Since then, the test of "voluntariness" has become entrenched in the common law and courts have laboured under the difficulty of adapting this rule of policy to all the different factual circumstances present in each case and to the manifold and changing circumstances and values of modern society.

Initially, the *Ibrahim* rule was an objective test centred around the probable effect of the inducement rather than its actual effect. Gradually, subjective factors became relevant to determine voluntariness. In *R. v. Fitton*,[33] Rand J. stated:[34]

> [t]he cases of torture, actual or threatened, or of unabashed promises are clear; perplexity arises when much more subtle elements must be evaluated. The strength of mind and will of the accused, the influence of custody or its surroundings, the effect of questions or of conversation, all call for delicacy in appreciation of the part they have played behind the admission, and to enable a court to decide whether what was said was freely and voluntarily said, that is, was free from the influence of hope or fear aroused by them.

The underlying rationale for the traditional *Ibrahim* rule is that a confession which is the product of an inducement made by a person in authority may be unreliable or untrustworthy. The position of the

---

31 *Supra*, note 22, at 609 (A.C.).
32 (1922), 63 S.C.R. 226, 37 C.C.C. 199, 66 D.L.R. 340.
33 [1956] S.C.R. 958, 116 C.C.C. 1, 24 C.R. 371, 6 D.L.R. (2d) 529.
34 *Ibid.*, at 962 (S.C.R.).

majority of the Supreme Court in *R. v. Wray*[35] demonstrates a strong commitment to the reliability principle. The court held that Wray's confession was involuntary and therefore inadmissible. However, the confession led police to discover the murder weapon. The majority held that the derivative evidence (the murder weapon) and those parts of the confession that were collaterally proven to be true (the accused's knowledge of the location of the murder weapon) were admissible.[36] When the confession rule is justified on the basis of reliability, the important factors to determine voluntariness are the circumstances surrounding the taking of the statement, including the apprehension created by the presence of police officers[37] and some subjective characteristics of the accused, such as age and gender. Voluntary, in this sense, is determined negatively — "a statement obtained by hope of advantage, (a promise), or fear of prejudice, (a threat), exercised, held out or inspired by a person in authority, is involuntary in the eyes of the law"[38] since such a statement may be unreliable.

The Supreme Court has not always based the rationale of the confession rule on reliability. In *DeClercq v. R.*,[39] the trial judge asked the accused during a *voir dire* whether the statement was true. Although the majority of the Court held that this question was relevant to the accused's credibility, both majority and dissenting judgments held that the issue on the *voir dire* was whether the statement was voluntary and not whether it was true[40] — presumably

---

35 [1971] S.C.R. 272, 11 C.R.N.S. 235, [1970] 4 C.C.C. 1, 11 D.L.R. (3d) 673.
36 *Ibid.*; see also *R. v. St. Lawrence* (1949), 7 C.R. 464, 93 C.C.C. 376, [1949] O.R. 215 (H.C.); and *R. v. Warickshall, supra*, note 24.
37 ". . . the rule is directed against the danger of improperly instigated or induced or coerced admissions", per Rand J. in *Boudreau v. R.*, [1949] S.C.R. 262, 94 C.C.C. 1, 7 C.R. 427, [1949] 3 D.L.R. 81, at 269 (S.C.R.); but, "Questions without intimidating or suggestive overtones are inescapable from police enquiry", per Rand J. in *R. v. Fitton, supra*, note 33, at 963-64: ". . . to render a statement . . . inadmissible there must be the compulsion of apprehension of prejudice or the inducement of hope of advantage whether that apprehension or hope be instigated, induced or coerced", per Martland J. in *Horvath v. R.*, [1979] 2 S.C.R. 376, at 387-88, 44 C.C.C. (2d) 385, 7 C.R. (3d) 97, 93 D.L.R. (3d) 1, [1979] 3 W.W.R. 1, 25 N.R. 537.
38 *Horvath v. R.*, *ibid.*, at 424 (S.C.R.), per Beetz J.
39 [1968] S.C.R. 902, [1969] 1 C.C.C. 197, 4 C.R.N.S. 205, 70 D.L.R. (2d) 530.
40 See the reasons for judgment of Cartwright C.J., Martland, and Spence JJ., *ibid.*

factors other than reliability were relevant to the voluntariness test.

The old rationale that predicates admissibility primarily on reliability lies behind the reasoning in both *Ibrahim* and *R. v. Ward*[41] A different rationale is developing that focuses on the protection of the accused's rights and fairness in the criminal process. In *R. v. Rothman*[42] Lamer J. articulated a rationale for exclusion where the means of extracting a confession bring the administration of justice into disrepute. In that case, after the accused was charged with a narcotic trafficking offence he was cautioned and he refused to make a statement. The police then planted an undercover agent in his cell. Rothman was led to believe that the undercover agent was a truck driver jailed as a result of an unpaid traffic ticket. Rothman eventually made certain incriminating statements to the undercover officer. The case was primarily concerned with whether the officer was a person in authority. In a separate concurring judgment, however, Mr. Justice Lamer held that there should be a discretion to exclude evidence which has been uncovered unfairly. He suggested that the courts have a duty not only to protect the innocent against conviction but also to protect the integrity of the criminal justice system itself. Voluntariness was merely a factor to be considered along with many others and he formulated the following test:[43]

> 1. A statement made by the accused to a person in authority is inadmissible if tendered by the prosecution in a criminal proceeding unless the judge is satisfied beyond a reasonable doubt that nothing said or done by any person in authority could have induced the accused to make a statement which was or might be untrue;

> 2. A statement made by the accused to a person in authority and tendered by the prosecution in a criminal proceeding against him, though elicited under circumstances which would not render it inadmissible, shall nevertheless be excluded if its use in the proceedings would, as a result of what was said or done by

---

41　[1979] 2 S.C.R. 30, 44 C.C.C. (2d) 498, 7 C.R. (3d) 153, 94 D.L.R. (3d) 18, [1979] 2 W.W.R. 193, 10 C.R. (3d) 289, 25 N.R. 514.

42　[1981] 1 S.C.R. 640, 59 C.C.C. (2d) 30, 20 C.R. (3d) 97, 121 D.L.R. (3d) 578, 35 N.R. 485.

43　*Ibid.*, at 696 (S.C.R.).

any person in authority in eliciting the statement, bring the administration of justice into disrepute.

Estey J., delivering a dissenting judgment for himself and Laskin C.J.C., explained the rationale for the confession rule as follows:[44]

> The rules of evidence in criminal law, and indeed in civil law, are all concerned with relevancy, reliability and fairness as well as other considerations such as the reasonable economy and efficiency of trial. The rules with reference to confessions have an additional element, namely the concern of the public for the integrity of the system of the administration of justice. If the reliability of an accused's statements were the only consideration in determining their admissibility the courts would not have adopted distinctive principles applicable only to statements to persons in authority and not to statements against interest generally. Reliability cannot be the ticket for admission because statements may have enough of the appearance of reliability to ensure reference to the trier of fact but still have been excluded by the confession standard.

This emerging rationale for the confession rule will no doubt be strengthened and indeed in some cases it may be pre-empted by the application of the *Charter*.[45] Unfairness to the accused or police misconduct may attract the provision of the *Charter* in which case the reliability of the evidence is of minimal, if any, relevance. The constant concern for fairness and integrity as a result of the *Charter* will likely have an impact on the application of the confession rule in cases in which no *Charter* violation takes place. If the *Rothman* case[46] had occurred in 1990 rather than 1981 it is likely the decision would have been the other way.[47]

---

44 *Ibid.*, at 646-47 (S.C.R.).
45 *Canadian Charter of Rights and Freedoms*, R.S.C. 1985, Appendix II, No. 44: *R. v. Clarkson*, [1986] 1 S.C.R. 383, 50 C.R. (3d) 289, 25 C.C.C. (3d) 207, 26 D.L.R. (4th) 493, 66 N.R. 114, 69 N.B.R. (2d) 40, 19 C.R.R. 209.
46 *Supra*, note 42.
47 See *R. v. Hebert*, [1990] 2 S.C.R. 151, 57 C.C.C. (3d) 1, 77 C.R. (3d) 145, [1990] 5 W.W.R. 1, 47 B.C.L.R. (2d) 1, 110 N.R. 1, 49 C.R.R. 114 (S.C.C.) in which the Supreme Court reversed the result in *Rothman, supra*, note 42 on the basis of an accused's right to remain silent protected under s. 7 of the *Charter*.

In England, the voluntariness test has been replaced by several different tests. For example, s. 76(2)(b) of the *Police and Criminal Evidence Act, 1984*,[48] provides that the prosecution must prove that a confession was not or may not have been obtained in consequence of anything said or done which was likely to render the statement unreliable. Unlike the traditional test, the question is whether the acts or words cause the statement to be unreliable, not whether they cause the statement to be made.[49]

B. *The Operating Mind Requirement*

In *Ward v. R.*,[50] the accused made a confession in a police cruiser shortly after regaining consciousness following a car accident. Unknown to the police, the accused was in a state of shock when he made the statement. The trial judge excluded the statement because the Crown failed to prove the statement was voluntary. Spence J., in dealing with the relevance of the accused's state of mind on the issue of voluntariness, broadly interpreted the *Ibrahim* rule. He stated that the question of voluntariness should be examined in two stages:[51]

firstly, to determine whether a person in his condition would be subject to hope of advancement or fear of prejudice in making the statements, when perhaps a normal person would not; and, secondly, to determine whether, due to the mental and physical condition, the words could really be found to be the utterances of an operating mind.

The first stage of Spence J.'s test is the traditional rule but the second stage fashioned what has become known as the "operating mind" doctrine. It is now part of our law of confessions that a statement which is not the product of an operating mind is involuntary. The causes for a lack of an operating mind include physical

---

48   (U.K.) 1984, c. 60.
49   This was the former common law test in *D.P.P. v. Ping Lin*, [1976] A.C., at 588, [1975] 3 All E.R. 175 (H.L.).
50   *Supra*, note 41.
51   *Ibid.*, at 40 (S.C.R.).

shock,[52] lack of intellectual capacity,[53] hypnosis[54] or self-induced drunkenness.[55]

In some circumstances, the traditional *Ibrahim* rule and the operating mind test overlap. For example, a custodial interrogation of a mentally deficient person may be involuntary under either test. However, in other circumstances, for example, as in *Ward* where the police officer, who was investigating an accident pursuant to a statutory duty, was unaware of the accused's condition and did not obtain the statement by an inducement, such statements would be admissible under the original *Ibrahim* test.

The operating mind test of voluntariness focuses on the accused's state of mind at the time he or she makes the statement. The traditional view is that the rationale for the operating mind test is also reliability.[56] This view has recently been challenged in *R. v. Clarkson*[57] Although the accused's confession during police interrogation was excluded under s. 24(2) of the *Charter*, Wilson J. also considered the admissibility of the confession of an intoxicated person under the common law. Clarkson telephoned her sister and, according to one version of this conversation, the accused admitted to shooting her spouse. Subsequently, the police arrived at the house, charged the accused with murder, cautioned her, and informed her of her right to counsel. While en route to a hospital, the police overheard an incriminating conversation between the accused and her aunt. Approximately four and one half hours after the telephone call, the accused consented to the taking of a blood sample which showed that her blood alcohol level was almost three times the statutory level of impairment for driving a motor vehicle. At the hospital, the police overheard the accused speaking to the medical staff during her medical examination. The accused subsequently made a statement at the

---

52 *Ibid.*, at 41 (S.C.R.).
53 *R. v. Santinon* (1973), 11 C.C.C. (2d) 121, 21 C.R.N.S. 323, [1973] 3 W.W.R. 113 (B.C.C.A.)
54 *Horvath v. R.*, *supra*, note 37, at 425 (S.C.R.), per Beetz J.
55 *R. v. Clarkson, supra*, note 45.
56 "Had the Crown sought to introduce the statements made while the appellant was in a light hypnotic state, it is clear that they would not have been admitted by the trial judge . . . because the appellant, at the time those statements were made, was not in a condition which would make it safe to admit them," per Martland J. in *Horvath, supra*, note 37, at 392 (S.C.R.).
57 *Supra*, note 45.

police station during formal interrogation. The trial judge admitted the first statement in evidence, but he excluded the three subsequent statements by reason of the accused's intoxicated condition.

Wilson J., for the majority, reviewed the judicial precedents and concluded that there were two competing tests to determine the admissibility of the confession of an intoxicated offender: (1) the operating mind test; and (2) the knowledge of consequence test. She held that the focus of the operating mind test was whether the accused was coherent enough to understand her own words to make the statement reliable. She held that the focus of the knowledge of consequence test "reveals a concern not so much for probative value of the statement as for adjudicative fairness in the criminal process and for control of police conduct in interrogating accused persons."[58] Wilson J. concluded that the pre-*Charter* common law position was that a judge had a *discretion* to exclude a confession of an intoxicated offender if its prejudicial effect outweighed its probative value:[59]

> It is perhaps entirely appropriate then that the common law has left the task of balancing these two concerns to the discretion of the trial judge who has the unique advantage of hearing the entire body of evidence and who can consequently best assess both the probative value and the prejudice to the accused in the overall context of the case.

While this statement is at variance with the decision in *R. v. Wray*,[60] the principle in *Wray* has been considerably eroded by more recent Supreme Court of Canada decisions such as *R. v. Corbett*,[61] *R. v. Morris*,[62] and *R. v. Morin*.[63]

There are two additional considerations for the operating mind test: (1) the allocation of the evidential burden and persuasive burden of proof; and (2) the threshold level of the operating mind test. Inasmuch as the accused may be the only person who has knowledge

---

58   *Ibid.*, at 391 (S.C.R.).
59   *Ibid.*, at 393 (S.C.R.).
60   [1971] S.C.R. 272, 11 C.R.N.S. 235, [1970] 4 C.C.C. 1, 11 D.L.R. (3d) 673.
61   [1988] 1 S.C.R. 678, 64 C.R. (3d) 1, 41 C.C.C. (3d) 385, [1988] 4 W.W.R. 481, 28 B.C.L.R. (2d) 145.
62   [1983] 2 S.C.R. 190, 36 C.R. (3d) 1, 7 C.C.C. (3d) 97, 1 D.L.R. (4th) 385, 48 N.R. 341.
63   [1988] 2 S.C.R. 345, 66 C.R. (3d) 1, 44 C.C.C. (3d) 193, 88 N.R. 161, 30 O.A.C. 81.

of these subjective matters,[64] the evidentiary burden to adduce sufficient evidence to raise the issue should be allocated to the accused. The accused may be able to meet this evidential burden through the cross-examination of witnesses called by the Crown or by adducing expert evidence but, in many cases, it will be necessary for the accused to testify in order to adduce sufficient evidence to discharge the evidential burden. Once the accused has adduced sufficient evidence to make it a live issue, the Crown must then satisfy the trial judge beyond a reasonable doubt that the statement was voluntary.[65]

In order to render the statement involuntary, the accused's intellectual ability must be significantly diminished, otherwise every impaired driver's admission of drinking "only two beers" would render a statement involuntary. In *Clarkson*, McIntyre J. held that a high degree of intoxication is required to render a confession involuntary.[66] This threshold requirement is consistent with earlier decisions of the Supreme Court. In *McKenna v. R.*,[67] Kerwin C.J. stated:[68]

> . . . notwithstanding the evidence of drunkenness on the part of the appellant the latter knew what he was saying. It is not a case where a trial judge considered that the words used by an accused did not, because of his condition, amount to his statement.

In the context of mental incapacity, the Supreme Court of Canada also approved a high test of incapacity to render a free and voluntary confession inadmissible. For example, in *Nagotcha v. R.*,[69] the court adopted the test enunciated by the British Columbia Court of Appeal:[70]

---

64 See, for example, the trial judge's reasoning in *Ward v. R.*, [1979] 2 S.C.R. 30, at 41, 44 C.C.C. (2d) 498, 7 C.R. (3d) 153, 94 D.L.R. (3d) 18, [1979] 2 W.W.R. 193, 10 C.R. (3d) 289, 25 N.R. 514.
65 *R. v. Lapointe* (1983), 9 C.C.C. (3d) 366, at 383, 1 O.A.C. 1 (Ont. C.A.); affd., [1987] 1 S.C.R. 1253, 35 C.C.C. (3d) 287, 21 O.A.C. 176, 76 N.R. 228.
66 *R. v. Clarkson*, [1986] 1 S.C.R. 383, 50 C.R. (3d) 289, 25 C.C.C. (3d) 207, 26 D.L.R. (4th) 493, 66 N.R. 114, 69 N.B.R. (2d) 40, 19 C.R.R. 209, at 399 (S.C.R.).
67 [1961] S.C.R. 660.
68 *Ibid.*, at 663.
69 [1980] 1 S.C.R. 714, 51 C.C.C. (2d) 353, 32 N.R. 204, 109 D.L.R. (3d) 1.
70 *Ibid.*, at 717 (S.C.R.) per Laskin C.J., quoting with approval Bull J.A. in *R. v. Santinon* (1973), 11 C.C.C. (2d) 121, at 124, 21 C.R.N.S. 323, [1973] 3 W.W.R. 113 (B.C.C.A.). See also, *R. v. Lapointe* (1983), 9 C.C.C. (3d) 366, 1 O.A.C. 1 (Ont. C.A.); affd., [1987] 1 S.C.R. 1253, 35 C.C.C. (3d) 287, 21 O.A.C. 176, 76 N.R.

THE LAW OF EVIDENCE IN CANADA

. . . having regard to the infinite degrees of insanity, if such incapacity is shown that the accused, for example, is so devoid of rationality and understanding, or so replete with psychotic delusions, that his uttered words could not fairly be said to be his statement at all, then it should not be held admissible.

IV   THE VOLUNTARINESS TEST

The voluntariness test should not be mechanically applied to the facts of a particular case. Rather, the trial judge should evaluate the facts of each case to determine whether an inducement by a person in authority was capable of causing an unreliable confession. The cases should be seen as illustrative of factual situations in which trial judges or appeal courts have decided that a particular statement was involuntary. Moreover, even though some circumstances may be conveniently collected in categories, the existence of a particular circumstance in a case does not automatically render a statement admissible or inadmissible. Accordingly, the following analysis of common factors found in many cases should be viewed as illustrative of the application of the confession rule in particular circumstances and not of the rule itself. Because we dealt with the operating mind and appreciation of consequences test earlier in this chapter,[71] we will not analyze those principles in the present subject.

A. *Threats or Inducements*

The touchstone for voluntariness according to *Ibrahim* is that the statement has not been obtained by hope of advantage or fear of prejudice held out by a person in authority. In the leading case of *D.P.P. v. Ping Lin*[72] Lord Salmon stated:[73]

The judge's decision is, in reality, a decision on the facts. He has to weigh up the evidence and decide whether he is satisfied that no person in authority has obtained the confession or statement,

---

228 (S.C.C.).
71   See III.B.
72   [1976] A.C. 588, at 606, [1975] 3 All E.R. 175 (H.L.).
73   *Ibid.*, at 606 (H.L.).

directly or indirectly, by engendering fear in the accused that he will be worse off if he makes no confession or statement or by exciting hope in the accused that he will be better off if he does make a confession or statement. If the judge is so satisfied, he may admit evidence of the confession or statement. If he is not so satisfied, he must exclude it.

The intention of the person in authority is not determinative. Rather, it is the fact of the inducement that is important. The test, however, is not solely dependent on how the alleged inducement was perceived by the accused but it is a combination of subjective and objective considerations. Schrager analyses it in this way:[74]

> . . . the House of Lords appears in *Ping Lin* to have adopted a view which is partly objective and partly subjective, holding that the test is concerned with the reasonable reaction by the suspect in question to what was said.

Where an inducement is a figment of the accused's imagination, that is, the motivation for the statement comes from within the accused, his declaration is admissible. The court in *R. v. Siniarski*[75] explained:[76]

> This evidence clearly indicates that the motivation for the statement came from within the appellant himself and did not emanate from any one in authority. This being so, the statement could not be considered involuntary.

If, however, the accused initiates an inducement which the person in authority adopts, that statement may be inadmissible. In *R. v. Zaveckas*,[77] for example, the accused asked a police officer: "If I make a statement, will you give me bail now?" The officer replied "Yes", and the accused then admitted his guilt. In the Court of Appeal, it was conceded by the Crown that an unsolicited statement by a police officer about bail would have been regarded as an improper inducement. But, it was argued that here it was the accused himself who

---

74   M. Schrager, "Recent Developments in the Law Relating to Confessions: England, Canada, and Australia" (1981), 26 McGill L.J. 435, at 447.
75   [1969] 3 C.C.C. 228 (Sask. C.A.).
76   *Ibid.*, at 231.
77   [1970] 1 All E.R. 413, [1970] 1 W.L.R. 516 (C.A.).

raised the question. The officer simply answered. Fenton Atkinson L.J. rejected this argument:[78]

> It makes no difference, in our view, that it was the appellant who said, "If I make a statement will you give me bail now?" and the officer said, "Yes". It is exactly the same situation as if it had been the other way round and the officer had said, "You make a statement and I will see that you get bail." In our opinion the statement should have been excluded as it followed on an inducement held out by a person in authority of the advantage of getting bail.

However, not every unsolicited inducement, even if purportedly adopted or fulfilled by the authorities, will render a statement involuntary.[79] It depends on the nature of the inducement and the responses of the authorities.

The threat or promise does not have to relate to the crime confessed. In *Customs and Excise Comrs. v. Harz*,[80] the House of Lords said that the remoteness of a threat so far as it concerns either the accused personally or the offence in respect of which the confession is induced goes only to the weight of the evidence supporting the accused's contention that the confession was involuntary. For example, in *R. v. Kalashnikoff*[81] the accused, after being stopped for a traffic violation, was told that if he provided police with information on a certain robbery, his traffic ticket would not be processed. He did not answer immediately. Several days later, however, he went to the police station, provided the information and then inquired as to the status of the ticket. Lambert J.A. concluded:[82]

> If the passage of time had given rise to a conclusion that the offer of advantage did not induce the statement and that the statement was induced by some other factor, then the statement would have

---

78   *Ibid.*, at 416 (All E.R.).
79   *R. v. Hatton* (1978), 39 C.C.C. (2d) 281, at 294-98 (Ont. C.A.); *Gerow v. R.* (1981), 22 C.R. (3d) 167, at 172-73 (B.C.C.A.); *R. v. Ebsary* (1986), 27 C.C.C. (3d) 488, at 493-97; leave to appeal to S.C.R. refd. (1986), 75 N.S.R. (2d) 270, 73 N.R. 240*n*, 186 A.P.R. 270*n*.
80   [1967] 1 A.C. 760, at 800, [1967] 1 All E.R. 177 (H.L.).
81   (1981), 57 C.C.C. (2d) 481 (B.C.C.A.).
82   *Ibid.*, at 483.

been admissible. That is not the case here. The evidence that I have quoted indicates that the offer of advantage induced the statement.

An inducement may be ineffective through lapse of time or because of some intervening cause. As the Court of Criminal Appeal in *R. v. Smith*[83] explained:[84]

> . . . if the threat or promise under which the first statement was made still persists when the second statement is made, then it is inadmissible. Only if the time limit between the two statements, the circumstances existing at the time and the caution are such that it can be said that the original threat or inducement has been dissipated can the second statement be admitted as a voluntary statement.

When an accused confesses because of a spiritual inducement, the statement is admissible. Apparently, reliability is ensured given that the motivation for confessing is fear of God.[85] This is so even if a confession is induced by a person in authority, provided that it results from a spiritual exhortation.[86] As the author in *Cockle's Cases and Statutes on Evidence*[87] stated:[88]

> If a magistrate were to tell a prisoner that if he did not confess he would get six months' longer sentence, a confession induced thereby would undoubtedly be inadmissible. But, if he told him he would go to Hell, that would not render it inadmissible, apparently. The latter threat might appear the worse, but it would scarcely have the same effect on the mind of the prisoner, who would for the moment be more troubled with his immediate difficulty of getting out of his present trouble, than with his affairs thereafter. Moreover, the magistrate has no jurisdiction with reference to the place mentioned in the latter threat. The prisoner therefore might naturally ignore it.

---

83   [1959] 2 Q.B. 35, [1959] 2 All E.R. 193 (C.A.).
84   *Ibid.*, at 41 (Q.B.).
85   *R. v. Gilham* (1828), 1 Mood. C.C. 186, 168 E.R. 1235 (Cr. Cas. Res.).
86   *R. v. Jarvis* (1867), 10 Cox C.C. 574 (C.C.A.).
87   8th ed., by L.F. Sturge (London: Sweet & Maxwell Ltd., 1952).
88   *Ibid.*, at 191-92.

Courts have also suggested that confessions resulting from an appeal to conscience or morality will be admissible. Accordingly, in *R. v. Lloyd*,[89] an individual said to the accused "I hope you will tell, because Mrs. Gurner can ill afford to lose the money". The confession was admitted because the words were deemed to be appeals to morality.

Finally, a statement made by compulsion of a statute may be admissible even though the accused would not have replied to a policeman's question had there been no statutory duty to do so. In *Walker v. R.*,[90] Duff C.J.C. said:[91]

> . . . there is no rule of law that statements made by an accused under compulsion of statute are, because of such compulsion alone, inadmissible against him in criminal proceedings. Generally speaking, such statements are admissible . . . .

This common law principle is now subject to challenge under the *Charter*. It is premature to speculate whether a particular statutory provision violates s. 7 or 11(c) of the *Charter* and, if so, whether such provision will be saved by s. 1.[92]

B. *Oppression*

In England, evidence of oppression has been used to justify exclusion of confessions since the 1964 revision of the Judges' Rules.[93] In *R. v. Prager*,[94] the Court of Appeal treated the revision, which was originally intended as a guide for police officers, as a valid basis for exercising a discretion to exclude statements. The court quoted at length from *R. v. Priestley*,[95] the only previous case to consider the

---

89   (1834), 6 C. & P. 393, 172 E.R. 1291 (Assize).

90   [1939] S.C.R. 214, 71 C.C.C. 305, 2 D.L.R. 353; see also *Marshall v. R.*, [1961] S.C.R. 123, 129 C.C.C. 232, 34 C.R. 216, 26 D.L.R. (2d) 459.

91   *Ibid.*, at 217 (S.C.R.). See also *Marshall, ibid.*, at 127 (S.C.R.); *R. v. Bossman* (1984), 28 M.V.R. 223, at 228, 15 C.C.C. (3d) 251 (Alta. C.A.).

92   See, for example, *R. v. Hufsky*, [1988] 1 S.C.R. 621, 63 C.R. (3d) 14, 40 C.C.C. (3d) 398, 27 O.A.C. 103, 4 M.V.R. (2d) 170, 84 N.R. 365, 32 C.R.R. 193 where an arbitrary detention under provincial highway legislation was upheld but see *R. v. Weil's Food Processing Ltd.*, unreported, November 19, 1990 (Ont. Ct., Gen. Div.).

93   Practice Note, [1964] 1 All E.R. 237; now, see *Police and Criminal Evidence Act, 1984*, c. 60, s. 76(2)(a) (U.K.).

94   [1972] 1 All E.R. 1114, [1972] 1 W.L.R. 260 (C.A.).

95   (1965), 51 Cr. App. R. 1n (C.C.A.).

meaning of oppression. In that case, Sachs J. stated:[96]

> I mentioned that I had not been referred to any authority on the meaning of the word 'oppression' as used in the preamble to the Judges' Rules, nor would I venture on such a definition, and far less try to compile a list of categories of oppression, but, to my mind, this word in the context of the principles under consideration imports something which tends to sap, and has sapped, that free will which must exist before a confession is voluntary. . . . Whether or not there is oppression in an individual case depends upon many elements. . . . They include such things as the length of time of any individual period of questioning, the length of time intervening between periods of questioning, whether the accused person has been given proper refreshment or not, and the characteristics of the person who makes the statement. What may be oppressive as regards a child, an invalid or an old man or somebody inexperienced in the ways of this world may turn out not to be oppressive when one finds that the accused person is of a tough character and an experienced man of the world.

Under s. 76(2)(a) of the *The Police and Criminal Evidence Act 1984*,[97] oppression renders a confession inadmissible. Section 76(8) of the Act defines oppression: "In this section 'oppression' includes torture, inhuman or degrading treatment, and the use or threat of violence (whether or not amounting to torture)."[98] In *R. v. Fulling*,[99] the English Court of Appeal criticized the common law definition as being artificially wide but then fashioned a working definition of the statutory term which is vague and, perhaps, contradictory.[100]

---

96 *Ibid.*, at 1*n*; with the enactment of the *Police and Criminal Evidence Act, 1984*, *supra*, note 93, oppression is a separate basis for exclusion. Also, a Code of Practice promulgated under the Act sets out guidelines for police in questioning suspects, the breach of which may result in exclusion pursuant to s. 78(1) of the Act recognizing a judge's discretion to exclude evidence that would have an adverse effect on the fairness of the proceedings.

97 *Supra*, note 93; for an interesting analysis of the confession provisions, see D. Birch, "The Pace Hots Up: Confessions and Confusions Under the 1984 Act", [1989] Crim. L.R. 95.

98 *Ibid.*

99 [1987] 2 All E.R. 65, 2 W.L.R. 923 (C.A.).

100 See D. Birch, *supra*, note 97, at 102.

In Canada, there is some judicial authority that oppression may render a confession inadmissible. In *R. v. McLeod*,[101] the police officers created an emotional impact of fear by lying to the accused who was in custody.[102] The trial judge ruled that the statement was involuntary. In his decision, Laskin J.A. apparently recognized oppression as a distinct ground for excluding a confession:[103]

> I do not rule out as a matter of law all stratagems that the police or persons in authority may employ in questioning a person under arrest. The issue in every case, under the governing law, must be whether they operate . . . upon the person to rouse hope of advantage or fear of prejudice, or by their oppressiveness (to borrow a term from the English Judges' Rules) put in doubt at least whether any ensuing inculpatory statement has been properly elicited. In my view, reinforced by a reading of the whole record, the lies and associated incidents in this case had the forbidden effect in inducing the forbidden statement.

The predominant Canadian view, however, is that oppression is not a distinct justification for excluding evidence. Rather, it has been used as a convenient word to describe a variety of circumstances which put the voluntary nature of a confession in doubt. For example, in *Horvath v. R.*,[104] the accused's first statement took place while he was under a light hypnotic state. Two judges[105] held that the first statement was the product of non-consensual but inadvertently-induced hypnosis. Because subsequent statements were tainted by the first statement, they upheld the trial judge's exclusion of all of the statements on the narrow ground of lack of voluntariness. Three judges[106] agreed that the first statement was inadmissible but that the subsequent state-

---

101 (1968), 5 C.R.N.S. 101 (Ont. C.A.); see also *Andrews v. R.* (1981), 21 C.R. (3d) 291 (B.C.C.A.). *Contra: R. v. Chow* (1978), 43 C.C.C. (2d) 215, at 224 (B.C.C.A.).

102 See Jessup J.A. in *R. v. Rothman* (1978), 42 C.C.C. (2d) 377, at 381 (Ont. C.A.) (Estey J. concurring); affd. [1981] 1 S.C.R. 640, 20 C.R. (3d) 97, 59 C.C.C. (2d) 30, 121 D.L.R. (3d) 578, 35 N.R. 485.

103 *McLeod, supra*, note 101, at 104.

104 [1979] 2 S.C.R. 376, 44 C.C.C. (2d) 385, 7 C.R. (3d) 97, 93 D.L.R. 1, [1979] 3 W.W.R. 1, 25 N.R. 537.

105 Beetz and Pratte JJ.

106 Martland, Ritchie, Pigeon JJ. (dissenting).

ments were admissible. In their view, the subsequent statements were not prompted by oppression and that to exclude a statement on this ground, there must be some conduct on the part of the authorities which was improper or unjustified. In a separate judgment, Spence J.[107] subscribed to the trial judge's view that the cross-examination of an unstable 17-year-old accused by two police officers, which was followed by a skillful interviewer whose questioning unwittingly produced a "light hypnotic state", caused the complete emotional disintegration of the accused. Spence J. accepted the dictum in *R. v. Priestley*[108] and concluded that no statement made by the accused in those circumstances would be voluntary. Schrager suggests:[109]

> Nowhere does Spence J. say explicitly that the doctrine of oppression is part of Canadian law, but his judgment strongly implies that circumstances construed as oppressive by an English Court should also give rise to exclusion in Canada under a broad view of the notion of voluntariness set out in *Ibrahim*.

Oppression, like the term voluntariness, is a concept more easily understood by illustration than by definition. While not formally embracing the oppression doctrine, Canadian courts will exclude involuntary statements not induced by fear of prejudice or hope of advantage where the conduct of the police officers or the circumstances of the detention raise doubts as to the motivation of the accused in making the statement. The circumstances which can be considered oppressive are manifold and can arise in unique situations. For example, in *R. v. Serack*,[110] the accused was placed in a cell and his clothing was taken away for examination. He was given only a blanket with which to cover himself. Some hours later, he was taken, wrapped only in the blanket, to an interview room where a statement was obtained from him. While Berger J. found nothing "sinister" in what the police did, he excluded the statement. He said:[111]

> A man's trousers are, in a situation like this, essential to his dignity and his composure. When a man is questioned at a time when

---

107 Estey J. concurring.
108 *Supra*, note 95.
109 M. Schrager, "Recent Developments in the Law Relating to Confessions: England, Canada and Australia" (1981), 26 McGill L.J. 435, at 437.
110 [1974] 2 W.W.R. 377, 24 C.R.N.S. 295 (B.C.S.C.).
111 *Ibid.*, at 378 (W.W.R.).

he is clad only in a blanket, by a police officer who is properly dressed, the police officer has the advantage and it is a palpable advantage, one that may quite disarm an accused of a wholly independent recollection and separate will.

More common, however, are cases where a number of different events occur which, when taken together, suggest oppression. For example, in *R. v. Antoine*,[112] the accused was convicted of manslaughter following a trial at which the Crown was permitted to introduce an inculpatory statement made by the accused to the police. Huband J.A. outlined the circumstances of her detention and confession:[113]

> There were sounds emanating from the room where Winnie Cobela was being interrogated, and those sounds would tend to accentuate the accused's feelings of anxiety. Additionally, there was the persistence on the part of the police officers. The accused had given both verbal and written statements, yet she remained in a locked room without charge. The accused had been offered no nourishment other than coffee.

The court went on to say:[114]

> Exclusive of the confinement without charge, the other factors ought not to render the statement inadmissible. But given the confinement without charge, those other factors take on a more significant dimension which, in concert with the unlawful detention, give rise to an atmosphere of compulsion.

In Canada, an accused's belief which is not based on objective circumstances does not constitute an atmosphere of oppression capable of rendering a statement involuntary. The responses of the accused are significant only insofar as there is evidence that the atmosphere created by the authorities was objectively oppressive.[115] In *R. v.*

---

112   (1982), 70 C.C.C. (2d) 140, 16 Man. R. (2d) 303 (Man. C.A.).
113   *Ibid.*, at 148 (C.C.C.).
114   *Ibid.*
115   This was probably also the position in England prior to the enactment of the *Police and Criminal Evidence Act 1984*, *supra*, note 93, as illustrated by the statement by Lord Hailsham in *Wong Kam-ming v. R.*, [1980] A.C. 247, at 261, [1979] 1 All E.R. 939, at 946, 69 Cr. App. R. 47, at 55 (P.C.): "in a civilised society it is vital that persons in custody or charged with offences should not be subjected to ill treatment or improper pressure in order to extract confessions."

Hobbins,[116] Laskin C.J.C. commented as follows:[117]

> ... an accused's own timidity or subjective fear of the police will not avail to avoid the admissibility of a statement or confession unless there are external circumstances brought about by the conduct of the police that can be said to cast doubt on the voluntariness of a statement or confession by the accused or there are considerations affecting the accused, as in the *Ward* case, ... which would justify doubt as to voluntariness.

C. *Taking Statements and Police Questioning*

Due to the perceived lack of control over the interrogative processes, courts have cautiously reviewed any exchange of comments between an accused and a person in authority after the accused had been charged with an offence. In the nineteenth century, this skepticism was so pervasive that Cave J. suggested in *R. v. Male*[118] that: "... a policeman should keep his mouth shut and his ears open."[119]

The Canadian judiciary, which was not as concerned about abuse of power by the police, quickly acknowledged that police interrogation would not, in itself, result in the exclusion of a confession. Implicit in an acceptance of legitimate police methods of investigation is the understanding that certain standards of propriety must be observed. Leaving aside constitutional concerns which will be examined below, general considerations about the manner in which police obtain a confession when an accused is under interrogation are relevant to the issue of voluntariness. As Martin J.A. pointed out in *R. v. Precourt*,[120] it is a question of balancing the rights of the accused and society's interest through proper police investigative methods:[121]

> Although improper police questioning may in some circumstances infringe the governing [confession] rule, it is essential to

---

116　[1982] 1 S.C.R. 553, 135 D.L.R. (3d) 244, 66 C.C.C. (2d) 289, 27 C.R. (3d) 289, 41 N.R. 433.
117　*Ibid.*, at 557 (S.C.R.).
118　(1893), 17 Cox. C.C. 689 (Assize).
119　*Ibid.*, at 690.
120　(1976), 36 C.R.N.S. 150, 39 C.C.C. (2d) 311, 18 O.R. (2d) 714; leave to appeal to S.C.C. refd., 39 C.C.C. (2d) 311*n*, 18 O.R. (2d) 714*n*.
121　*Ibid.*, at 158-59 (C.R.N.S.).

bear in mind that the police are unable to investigate crime without putting questions to persons, whether or not such persons are suspected of having committed the crime being investigated. Properly conducted police questioning is a legitimate and effective aid to criminal investigation.... On the other hand, statements made as the result of intimidating questions, or questioning which is oppressive and calculated to overcome the freedom of will of the suspect for the purpose of extracting a confession, are inadmissible.

If the police engage in extensive or intrusive cross-examination, it may render a confession involuntary. For example, in *R. v. Durocher*,[122] the accused was cross-examined a number of times after being told on each occasion that his answers were not satisfactory. According to the trial judge:[123]

> He was treated worse than had he received blows, he lost all control of his freedom, all mastery of his intelligence and his free will, he is obliged to speak, he didn't have a choice and he was made to give a declaration which pleased the officers and this he signed, and all that is an absolute nullity because this is a declaration obtained by violence.

But not all forms of questioning will render a statement involuntary. In *R. v. Hatton*,[124] the accused was held in custody for a lengthy period but he was not mistreated, coerced, or subjected to incriminating or oppressive questioning. However, during interrogation, the police officer informed the accused that he did not believe his exculpatory statement. Martin J.A. found that this statement did not constitute a threat or an inducement which would render the statement involuntary.[125]

The accuracy with which a statement was reproduced is also a concern on the *voir dire*. If the police officer is transcribing questions and answers, a complete record should be kept in order to reduce the suggestion that only the incriminating portions of an accused's

---

122   (1966), unreported, No. 15899, Crown Office, Montreal (Que.S.C.).
123   *Ibid.*
124   (1978), 39 C.C.C. (2d) 281 (Ont. C.A.).
125   *Ibid.*, at 298-99.

responses were selected. Even if there is no suggestion of bad faith, an incomplete record of a statement may affect admissibility.[126] However, trial judges must not confuse the issues of authenticity, completeness, or reliability of the recording of a statement, which are matters for the jury's determination, with the different issue of the failure of the Crown to satisfy the court beyond a reasonable doubt that the statement was voluntary. In *R. v. Lapointe*,[127] the trial judge found that the accused's statements were freely and voluntarily given. But since the accused experienced language difficulties, he ruled the statements inadmissible because he was not satisfied beyond a reasonable doubt that the statements were in fact and in law the accused's statement. The Ontario Court of Appeal ordered a new trial:[128]

> ... issues of accurate or inaccurate recording of the respondents' words, of unconscious or deliberate inaccuracy, editing or deliberate fabrication ... are issues of authenticity and are not to be confused with issues of admissibility.

There is an ongoing debate as to whether an interrogation should be electronically recorded or videotaped instead of relying on witnesses to make notes and testify from their memory (refreshed by reviewing their notes) as to what occurred in a private interview room. Although it is recognized that one can erase tapes or otherwise falsify the recording of an interview, the Law Reform Commission of Canada[129] recommended that police questioning should take place in a police station and be electronically recorded. Such a procedure, the paper stated, "... will not only assist the court and expedite the *voir dire*, but in a large measure it should protect the police against unwarranted allegations of misconduct".[130]

---

126   Inadmissible: *R. v. Belanger* (1978), 40 C.C.C. (2d) 335, at 345 (Ont. H.C.J.); *R. v. Fowler* (1981), 27 C.R. (3d) 232, at 242-43, 36 Nfld. & P.E.I.R. (Nfld. C.A.); and *R. v. Kennedy* (1981), 63 C.C.C. (2d) 244, at 249, 10 Man. R. (2d) 104, at 110. Admissible: *R. v. Howard* (1983), 3 C.C.C. (3d) 399 (Ont. C.A.); *R. v. Kennealy* (1972), 6 C.C.C. (2d) 390, at 394-95 (B.C.C.A.).
127   (1983), 9 C.C.C. (3d) 366, at 380-82 (Ont. C.A.); affd., [1987] 1 S.C.R. 1253, 35 C.C.C. (3d) 287, 21 O.A.C. 176, 76 N.R. 228 (S.C.C.).
128   *Ibid.*, at 380 (C.C.C.).
129   Law Reform Commission of Canada, *Questioning Suspects* (Working Paper no. 32) (Minister of Supply and Services Canada, 1984).
130   *Ibid.*, at 59.

V   PERSONS IN AUTHORITY

To exclude a confession, the inducement must emanate from a person in authority.[131] Professor Cross[132] suggests that a person in authority is:

anyone whom the prisoner might reasonably suppose to be capable of influencing the course of the prosecution . . .

In *Deokinanan v. R.*,[133] the Privy Council proposed a broad definition:[134]

A person in authority means, generally speaking, anyone who has authority or control over the accused or over the proceedings or the prosecution against him.

In *R. v. B.(A.)*,[135] the trial judge excluded a 13-year-old accused's confessions to his mother and to two psychiatrists on the basis that they were persons in authority. Cory J.A. carefully reviewed the jurisprudence on who is a person in authority for the purposes of the confession rule. He summarized the common law principles:[136]

(1)   As a general rule, a person in authority is someone engaged in the arrest, detention, examination or prosecution of the accused. When the word "examination" is used, I believe it refers to interrogation by police officers, detention or security guards and members of the Crown attorney's office.

---

131   *R. v. Moore* (1852), 2 Den. 522, at 527, 169 E.R. 608, at 610 (Cr. Cas. Res.): "If not held out by one in authority, they are clearly admissible . . ."; *R. v. Rothman*, [1981] 1 S.C.R. 640, at 664, 20 C.R. (3d) 97, 59 C.C.C. (2d) 30, 121 D.L.R. (3d) 578, 35 N.R. 485: "Once it is accepted that the confession of the appellant was not made to a person in authority, it was properly admissible without any requirement for the Crown to establish that it was voluntary", per Martland J.
132   R. Cross, *Cross on Evidence*, 5th ed. (London: Butterworths, 1979), at 541.
133   [1969] 1 A.C. 20, [1968] 2 All E.R. 346 (P.C.).
134   *Ibid.*, at 33 (A.C.); the P.C. adopted this definition of Bain J. in *R. v. Todd* (1901), 13 Man. R. 364, at 376.
135   (1986), 50 C.R. (3d) 247, at 257-59, 26 C.C.C. (3d) 17, 13 O.A.C. 68 (Ont. C.A.); leave to appeal to S.C.C. refd. 50 C.R. (3d) xxv, 26 C.C.C. (3d) 17*n*.
136   *Ibid.*, at 256-57 (C.R.).

(2) In some circumstances, the complainant in a criminal prosecution may be considered to be a person in authority.

(3) The parent of an infant who is the injured party or complainant in a criminal prosecution may be a person in authority. . . .

(4) An inducement made by one who is not in authority but made in the presence of persons in authority who do not dissent from it may be deemed to have been made by a person in authority. In those circumstances, the person making the inducement can be considered as the agent of the person in authority. . . .

Cory J.A. also held that normally a witness for the prosecution would not qualify as a person in authority, nor would doctors or psychiatrists when examining an accused as a dangerous offender.[137] Although a mother in the ordinary sense of the word is an authority figure, in the circumstances of this case (a dining room confession) she was not a person in authority at law. Accordingly, even if it can be established on objective criteria that the person who obtains the statement could be characterized as an authority figure, that is not determinative of the issue.

In *Admissibility of Confessions*,[138] Kaufman states that the test is subjective: did the accused truly believe, at the time he made the declaration, that the person he dealt with had some degree of power over him? In *R. v. Rothman*,[139] the accused made incriminating statements to an undercover police officer disguised as a truck driver. Martland J., speaking for the majority of the Supreme Court, stated:[140]

> . . . a subjective test should be applied in the circumstances of this case. I also agree . . . that McKnight [the undercover policeman] was not a person in authority because he was not regarded as such by the appellant.

---

137 *Ibid.*, at 257.
138 F. Kaufman, *The Admissibility of Confessions*, 3rd ed. (Toronto: Carswell, 1979), at 81.
139 *Supra*, note 131.
140 *Ibid.*, at 664 (S.C.R.); in a separate concurring judgment Lamer J. also held that the test was a subjective one, *ibid.*, at 680 (S.C.R.).

But what if the accused mistakenly believed that the person was a peace officer, but there was no objective basis for such a belief? It is questionable if the courts would apply a purely subjective test in these circumstances. The Task Force recommended extending the test to include a person not in actual authority but whom the accused reasonably believed had authority over him or her in relation to criminal proceedings.[141] Although an accused can state that he or she believed the receiver of the statement to be a person in authority, it is a question of law whether it would have been reasonable for the person to believe that such person had authority over him or her or the prosecution of the crime.[142] The Ontario Court of Appeal in *B.(A.)*, *supra*, applies this construction of the test.

In short, the trial judge applies a combined subjective/objective test to make the factual determination of a person in authority.[143] Given the variety of potential persons in authority[144] and the test's lack of precision, it is not surprising that there has been some impetus to do away with the requirement completely. The general rule in the United States is that the prosecution must prove all confessions by the accused to be voluntary, whether they were made to a person in authority or

---

141 Uniform Law Conference of Canada, *Report of the Federal/Provincial Task Force on Uniform Rules of Evidence* (Toronto: Carswell, 1982), at 177. 11 C.E.D. Ont. 3rd ed., Title 57 (Toronto: Carswell), at para. 926, at 503 correctly suggests that the accused has an evidential burden in these circumstances.

142 *Demenoff v. R.*, [1964] 1 C.C.C. 118, 43 W.W.R. 610 (B.C.C.A.); appeal dismissed for want of jurisdiction, [1964] S.C.R. 79, 41 C.R. 407, 46 W.W.R. 188, [1964] 2 C.C.C. 305: ". . . a person whom the accused might reasonably believe to be a person in authority", per Wilson J.A., at 133 (C.C.C.). See also Task Force Report, *ibid.*, at 177.

143 *R. v. B.(A.)*, *supra*, note 135, at 259 (C.R.).

144 The following individuals have been held to be persons in authority *in the context of particular cases*: a constable or other officer having an accused in custody (*R. v. Shepherd* (1836), 7 C. & P. 579, 173 E.R. 255); a customs officer investigating a suspected drug offence (*R. v. Grewal*, [1975] Crim. L.R. 159 (Cem. Cr. Ct.)); a prosecutor or his wife (*R. v. Upchurch* (1836), 1 Mood. C.C. 465, 168 E.R. 1346; *R. v. Warringham* (1851), 2 Den. 447*n*, 169 E.R. 575); a magistrate (*R. v. Cooper* (1833), 5 C. & P. 535, 172 E.R. 1087); a parent of the victim (*R. v. Trenholme* (1920), 35 C.C.C. 341, 61 D.L.R. 316, 30 Que. K.B. 232 (Que. K.B.)); the wife of a co-accused (*R. v. Belanger* (1978), 40 C.C.C. (2d) 335 (Ont. H.C.J.)); the crime victim (*R. v. Downey* (1976), 32 C.C.C. (2d) 511, 38 C.R.N.S. 57, 17 N.R.S. (2d) 541 (N.S.C.A.); and physicians called by the police (*R. v. Kingston* (1830), 4 C. & P. 387, 172 E.R. 752; see also, *R. v. Conkie* (1978), 3 C.R. (3d) 7, 39 C.C.C. (2d) 408, [1978] 3 W.W.R. 493, 9 A.R. 115 (C.A.)). This list is illustrative only.

not. The English Criminal Law Revision Committee reasoned that "the risk that an inducement will result in an untrue confession is similar whether or not the inducement comes from a person in authority".[145] The English legislation governing confessions adopted this recommendation and abandoned the person in authority requirement.[146] Since an underlying justification for the rule was that the Crown should not be allowed to benefit from an inducement, the Task Force concluded that the distinction ought to be kept as this reasoning did not apply when a non-Crown agent induced the statement.[147] The person in authority requirement may also be justified on the discipline principle (deterrence of police misconduct which may cause a statement to be unreliable) and a narrow doctrine of self-incrimination (the authorities should not be able to compel a statement).[148]

VI THE VOIR DIRE

A. *The Requirement for a Voir Dire*

A *voir dire* must be held whenever it is sought to introduce a statement made by the accused to a person in authority.[149] The accused or his counsel may expressly waive the necessity for holding a *voir dire*.[150] Mere silence or a lack of objection is not sufficient to constitute a valid waiver since it can be equivocal. As Lamer J. stated in *Korponay v. Can. (A.G.)*:[151]

> the validity of such a waiver . . . is dependent upon it being *clear and unequivocal that the person is waiving the procedural safeguard and is doing so with full knowledge of the rights the procedure was enacted to protect and of the effect the waiver will have on those rights in the process.* [original emphasis]

---

145 Eleventh Report, *Evidence (General)* (London: Her Majesty's Stationery Office, 1972), Cmnd. 4991, at 39.
146 Section 82(1) of the *Police and Criminal Evidence Act, 1984*, c. 60 (U.K.).
147 *Supra*, note 141, at 175.
148 *R. v. B.(A.)*, *supra*, note 135, at 254 (C.R.).
149 See this Chapter, II.
150 *Park v. R.*, [1981] 2 S.C.R. 64, 59 C.C.C. (2d) 385, 21 C.R. (3d) 182, 122 D.L.R. (3d) 1, 37 N.R. 501.
151 [1982] 1 S.C.R. 41, at 49, 132 D.L.R. (3d) 354, 65 C.C.C. (2d) 65, 26 C.R. (3d) 343, 44 N.R. 103.

The trial judge has a discretion whether to accept the waiver and dispense with the holding of a *voir dire*.[152] If the trial judge accepts the waiver, the statement is admissible without a *voir dire*. In these circumstances, the waiver is not an acknowledgment of its evidential value, but is merely an acknowledgment of its voluntariness.

B. *The Procedure on a Voir Dire*

In a *voir dire*, in the absence of the jury, the Crown calls witnesses who testify to the surrounding circumstances of the arrest and subsequent events culminating in the taking of the statement. The focus of the evidence is the absence of threats or promises by persons in authority. Generally, all witnesses involved in the taking of the statement must be called to testify concerning the surrounding circumstances. There must be some evidence, however, that the person was a person in authority and involved in conversations leading to the statement. There is no rule of law that a statement must be rejected because of the mere possibility or conjecture of an earlier conversation in which threats may have been made.[153]

The issue on the *voir dire* is not who was present when the statement was made or who had contact with the accused. Rather, the issue is whether the Crown has discharged the burden of proof in the context of the facts of a particular case that the statement was voluntary.[154] In some circumstances, however, the unexplained absence of a witness who was present or had control over the accused may raise a reasonable doubt on the issue of voluntariness.[155] But if an officer was merely present at the crime scene[156] or he or she had minimal contact with the accused,[157] such officer will not be a necessary witness.[158] For example, a cell sergeant who was present when the accused was

---

152 *Park v. R.*, *supra*, note 150.
153 *R. v. Chow* (1978), 43 C.C.C. (2d) 215, at 224-25 (B.C.C.A.).
154 *R. v. Wert* (1979), 12 C.R. (3d) 254 (B.C.C.A.).
155 *Thiffault v. R.*, [1933] S.C.R. 509, 60 C.C.C. 97, 3 D.L.R. 591. See *R. v. Kacherowski* (1977), 37 C.C.C. (2d) 257, [1978] 1 W.W.R. 209, 7 A.R. 284 (C.A.). For an example of a satisfactory explanation, see *R. v. Chow*, *supra*, note 153, at 224.
156 *Beaton v. R.* (1981), 12 M.V.R. 307, 49 N.S.R. (2d) 78, 96 A.P.R. 78 (N.S.C.A.).
157 *Andrews v. R.* (1981), 21 C.R. (3d) 291 (B.C.C.A.).
158 *Ibid.*

admitted and placed in a holding cell may have had little or no involvement with the accused apart from noting particulars of the accused's physical condition, clothing and articles in his possession, etc. Accordingly, the cell sergeant would not be a necessary witness. If however, the accused alleges that the police assaulted him or her in order to obtain a statement, the cell sergeant's observations may be essential evidence on the issue of voluntariness. In such case, the accused's testimony, together with the unexplained absence of an essential witness, may raise a reasonable doubt on the issue of voluntariness.

A practical evidentiary problem is whether the Crown should produce and file the statement as an exhibit or adduce the content of an oral statement during the *voir dire* proceedings. Since the form and content of the statement may assist the judge in determining voluntariness, the trial judge has a discretion to observe the form and ascertain the contents of a statement.

The defence is entitled to cross-examine the Crown's witness and to call witnesses, including the accused on the *voir dire*. The question then arises whether the trial judge or the Crown may ask the accused if the statement is true. There are three judicial positions. In *DeClercq v. R.*,[159] the majority of the Supreme Court of Canada held that, though the issue on the *voir dire* was voluntariness and not the truth of the statement, the admitted truth or falsity of the statement was relevant to that inquiry.[160] Three judges dissented on the ground that the truth of the statement was irrelevant to the inquiry. Hall J. reasoned that this rule would operate most unfairly in cases tried by the judge alone because it would be difficult to give an accused the benefit of the doubt on the issue of guilt or innocence where an accused had admitted under oath that the statement was true.[161] This reasoning of the dissenting judges was adopted by the Privy Council in *Wong Kam-ming v. R.*[162] In a separate judgment, Cartwright J. held that the trial judge had a discretion to exclude certain questions put to a witness because of their trifling probative value and prejudicial

---

159 [1968] S.C.R. 902, [1969] 1 C.C.C. 197, 4 C.R.N.S. 205, 70 D.L.R. (2d) 530.
160 *Ibid.*, at 911 (S.C.C.).
161 *Ibid.*, at 923 (S.C.C.). This concern for judicial tainting does not appear to apply to judicial decisions under the *Charter*.
162 [1979] 1 All E.R. 939, 2 W.L.R. 81, [1980] A.C. 247 (P.C.). The Task Force agreed, *supra*, note 141, at 186.

effect. Since an accused's answer to such questioning has triflingly probative value on the voluntariness issue[163] and it has the appearance of unfairness, this question should not be allowed.

After witnesses have been examined and cross-examined, counsel make final arguments and the judge rules on the admissibility of the statement. However, even when all the requirements for voluntariness are met, the judge still has a limited discretion to exclude the statement.[164]

VII THE ROLE OF THE TRIAL JUDGE AND OF THE TRIER OF FACT

The admissibility of a confession is within the exclusive jurisdiction of the judge. Simply put, the trial judge decides the issue of voluntariness and the trier of fact decides all other issues. For example, in *Park v. R.*,[165] the issue was whether the trial judge ought to have conducted a *voir dire* in order to determine whether there was some evidence that the statement was made. Dickson J. for the court stated:[166]

> In every case in which the Crown seeks to adduce evidence of a statement made by an accused, there must, by definition, be "some evidence" that the statement was made. This exists by virtue of the fact that a police officer (or other "person in authority") is seeking to tender direct evidence of the making of the statement. Whether or not the officer is to be believed, and

---

163 Task Force Report, *ibid.*, at 186.
164 See *R. v. Washer* (1947), 92 C.C.C. 218, at 218-19, [1948] O.W.N. 393 (Ont. H.C.J.) and *R. v. Demers* (1970), 13 C.R.N.S. 338 (Que. Q.B.). This discretion is limited by the *Wray* doctrine, [1971] S.C.R. 272, [1970] 4 C.C.C. 1, 11 C.R.N.S. 235, 11 D.L.R. (3d) 673, see *R. v. Otis* (1978), 39 C.C.C. (2d) 304, at 308 (Ont. C.A.) for an application of this discretion.
165 *Supra*, note 150; see also, *R. v. Gauthier*, [1977] 1 S.C.R. 441, 27 C.C.C. (2d) 14, 33 C.R.N.S. 46, 64 D.L.R. (3d) 501, 10 N.R. 373. But see *R. v. Roberts*, [1953] 2 All E.R. 340, 37 Cr. App. R. 86, at 94: "I shall inquire into the two questions whether the statements which are alleged to have been made by the accused were in fact his statements and, if so, whether they were made voluntarily . . .": per Devlin J.
166 *Park v. R.*, *ibid.*, at 77 (S.C.R.).

the weight to be given to the statement, is a matter for the trier of fact. The special rules of evidence relating to statements made to persons in authority flow from the concern of the courts to ensure that such statements are made voluntarily. Once the issue of voluntariness is resolved, normal principles of evidence apply. The fact that the testimony of the police officer is contradicted by the accused cannot affect the admissibility of the officer's evidence. Where there are conflicting versions of what was said by the accused, the jury will decide which is to be believed.

In some cases, a trial judge may be required to edit a confession to protect the accused or to prevent confusion of the jury because of the length of the statement.[167] Because parts of an involuntary confession which are confirmed by the discovery of other evidence may be admissible,[168] the trial judge may also be required to edit a statement in these circumstances. The trial judge should be careful that editing does not alter the meaning of the statements.[169] When editing, the judge should request the assistance of both counsel to ensure that the accused and the Crown are not prejudiced by the editing process.[170]

The jury must be given an opportunity to review the circumstances of the confession so that it can assess the probative value of such evidence. Usually, the confession is introduced during the prosecution's case and Crown counsel will call witnesses who will attest to the making of the statement and its content. In practice, those witnesses will include many of the same people who testified during the *voir dire* and they will simply repeat what they said earlier. It is not necessary to call every person who was present when the statement was taken — it may be that only one or two are needed to enlighten the jury as to the reliability of the confession, including the lack of threats. It should be noted that, in a trial by judge alone, with the consent of both parties, the evidence given in the *voir dire* may be used by the judge at trial.

---

167 *R. v. Harris* (1946), 86 C.C.C. 1, 1 C.R. 509, [1946] 3 D.L.R. 520, [1946] O.R. 407 (Ont. C.A.).

168 *R. v. Wray, supra*, note 164.

169 *Otis, supra*, note 164, at 308-09 (C.C.C.). See also, *R. v. Martin* (1905), 9 C.C.C. 371, 9 O.L.R. 218 (Ont. C.A.).

170 *R. v. Mazerall (No. 1)* (1946), 86 C.C.C. 137, 2 C.R. 1, [1946] 4 D.L.R. 336, [1946] O.R. 511 (Ont. H.C.); affd. in effect (1946), 86 C.C.C. 321, 2 C.R. 261, [1946] 4 D.L.R. 791, [1946] O.R. 762 (Ont. C.A.).

The accused may try to create doubt in the minds of the jurors by cross-examining witnesses called by the Crown or by adducing evidence concerning the probative value of the confession. As stated in *R. v. Murray*:[171]

> It has always, as far as this court is aware, been the right of counsel for the defence to cross-examine again the witnesses who have already given evidence in the absence of the jury; for if he can induce the jury to think that the confession was obtained through some threat or promise, its value will be enormously weakened. The weight and value of the evidence are always matters for the jury.

In closing argument before the trier of fact, counsel may address the issue of the voluntariness of the confession as it relates to its reliability.

VIII THE ONUS AND STANDARD OF PROOF

The voluntariness issue requires the trial judge to make factual determinations and to apply a legal rule to those facts. As noted, the jury may also be required to determine the same factual issue, for example if there were any inducements that affected the reliability of the statement.[172] On a preliminary hearing[173] and at trial,[174] the Crown has the burden of proof to establish the voluntariness of a statement beyond a reasonable doubt. However, it is debatable if this standard was always required.[175] The standard of proof has been examined by the Task Force on Evidence,[176] the English Criminal Law Revision Committee,[177] and the Law Reform Commission of Canada,[178] and

---

171 [1951] 1 K.B. 391, at 393, [1950] 2 All E.R. 925 (C.C.A.).

172 *R. v. Cleary* (1963), 48 Cr. App. Rep. 116, 107 Sol. Jo. 77 (C.C.A.).

173 See *R. v. Pearson* (1957), 117 C.C.C. 249, 25 C.R. 342, 21 W.W.R. 337 (Alta. C.A.); see *R. v. Lee* (1952), 104 C.C.C. 400, 15 C.R. 397, [1953] O.R. 34 (Ont. C.A.).

174 *R. v. Pickett* (1975), 28 C.C.C. (2d) 297, 31 C.R.N.S. 239 (Ont. C.A.).

175 *Report of the Federal/Provincial Task Force on Uniform Rules of Evidence* (Toronto: Carswell, 1982), at 190; see also R. Cross and C. Tapper, *Cross on Evidence*, 7th ed. (London: Butterworths, 1990), at 620, note 6.

176 *Ibid.*, the Task Force, at 189-90.

177 Eleventh Report, *Evidence (General)* (London: H.M.S.O., 1972), at 213.

178 Law Reform Commission of Canada, Report of Evidence, Cat.# J31-15/1975, at 62-63, s. 16(1) draft Evidence Code.

also by superior courts in the many English speaking jurisdictions.[179] The present law in Canada[180] and the U.K.[181] is that the prosecution must prove voluntariness beyond a reasonable doubt. This view is based on the reasoning that since a confession is potentially determinative of the issue of guilt or innocence, the criminal standard of proof should be maintained. The Task Force suggested that, in practice, this requirement did not appear to present an insurmountable burden on the Crown and also it had the salutory effect of protecting the rights of accused persons.[182]

The contrary position is that the standard for admissibility of a confession is out of step with the rules governing admissibility for other evidence. Because the test for admissibility of other factual matters is whether there is some evidence to go before the jury, the reasonable doubt standard for confessions is higher than the admissibility standard for other contested evidence. Also, the test to measure the sufficiency of the Crown's case on a motion for a directed verdict is whether there is some evidence upon which a reasonable jury could convict.[183] Since the reasonable doubt standard does not apply at the committal stage of proceedings,[184] the admissibility standard for a confession is higher than the test for committal.

The High Court of Australia[185] and the United States Supreme Court[186] recognize the lower standard of a balance of probabilities. The U.S. Supreme Court held:[187]

---

179 *D.P.P. v. Ping Lin*, [1976] A.C. 588, [1975] 3 All E.R. 175 (H.L.).

180 *R. v. Pickett* (1975), 28 C.C.C. (2d) 297, 31 C.R.N.S. 239 (Ont. C.A.); *R. v. Van Dongen* (1975), 26 C.C.C. (2d) 22, 31 C.R.N.S. 346, [1975] 4 W.W.R. 246 (B.C.C.A.); *R. v. Demers* (1970), 13 C.R.N.S. 338 (Que. K.B.).

181 Section 76(2) of the *Police and Criminal Evidence Act, 1984*, c. 60 (U.K.).

182 *Supra*, note 175, at 191; see also Law Reform Commission of Canada, *supra*, note 178, at 63: ". . . a high standard of proof will place an onus on the police to ensure that they take statements from an accused person under conditions in which there can be no doubt of the statements reliability."

183 *United States v. Shephard*, [1977] 2 S.C.R. 1067, 30 C.C.C. (2d) 424, 34 C.R.N.S. 207, 70 D.L.R. (3d) 136.

184 *R. v. Syms* (1979), 47 C.C.C. (2d) 114 (Ont. C.A.), see Chapter 5.

185 *R. v. Wendo* (1963), 109 C.L.R. 559 (Aust. H.C.); *Cleland v. R.* (1982), 57 A.L.J.R. 15, at 20 (per Murphy J.) and, at 23 (per Deane J.); but see *R. v. Askeland* (1983), 8 A.C.R. 338 (S.C. Tas.).

186 *Lego v. Twomey*, 92 S. Ct. 619 (1972).

187 *Ibid.*, at 626.

. . . no substantial evidence has accumulated that federal rights have suffered from determining admissibility by a preponderance of the evidence. Petitioner offers nothing to suggest that admissibility rulings have been unreliable or otherwise wanting in quality because not based on some higher standard. Without good cause, we are unwilling to expand currently applicable exclusionary rules by erecting additional barriers to placing truthful and probative evidence before state juries and by revising the standards applicable in collateral proceedings. . . . [S]ince the exclusionary rules are very much aimed at deterring lawless conduct by police and prosecution and it is very doubtful that escalating the prosecution's burden of proof . . . would be sufficiently productive . . . to outweigh the public interest in placing probative evidence before juries for the purpose of arriving at truthful decisions about guilt or innocence.

It appears that the U.S. Supreme Court and the Task Force arrive at contradictory positions to maintain the status quo in their respective jurisdictions on the basis of assumptions unsupported by objective data.

Leaving aside the standard of proof for voluntariness at trial, a strong case can be made for a lower standard at the preliminary hearing. The purpose of a preliminary hearing is simply to determine if there is some evidence upon which a reasonable jury properly instructed could convict and not to determine the accused's culpability.[188] Also, the trial judge is not bound by a prior determination on the issue of voluntariness.[189] The Task Force correctly suggests that the standard should be on a preponderance of probabilities at the preliminary hearing stage.[190]

---

188 *United States v. Shephard, supra*, note 183.
189 *Duhamel v. R.*, [1984] 2 S.C.R. 555, 15 C.C.C. (3d) 491, 43 C.R. (3d) 1, 14 D.L.R. (4th) 92, [1985] 2 W.W.R. 251, 35 Alta. L.R. (2d) 1, 57 N.R. 162; see also the unusual case of *Tapp v. R.* (1985), 47 C.R. (3d) 397 (Que. C.A.) where this principle was recognized but not applied.
190 Task Force Report, *supra*, note 175, at 191. *Contra: R. v. Pickett, supra*, note 180, at 303 (C.C.C.).

IX THE EVIDENTIAL VALUE OF A CONFESSION

Some statements have inculpatory and exculpatory parts. Once the Crown tenders the statement, it is obligated to introduce the good with the bad and the whole of the statement is received as evidence of its truth. A jury, however, is not bound to accept the truth of the exculpatory element. Rather, its duty is to consider that part of the confession in light of the other evidence to assess whether it is true. As Parke B. explained in *R. v. Higgins*:[191]

> Now, what a prisoner says is not evidence, unless the prosecutor chooses to make it so, by using it as a part of his case against the prisoner; however, if the prosecutor makes the prisoner's declaration evidence, it then becomes evidence for the prisoner, as well as against him; but still, like all evidence given in any case, it is for you to say whether you believe it.

The fact that the Crown is required to introduce the whole of a declaration when it chooses to offer any part of it as evidence does not mean that the accused can write out a statement to police and require the Crown to tender it. In *R. v. Frederick*,[192] the Court explained the dangers of allowing this practice:[193]

> . . . there is no practice in this Court that would justify such a departure from established procedure which would lead to many dangerous results, the most obvious of which are, the escape from cross-examination; the safe introduction of a concocted defence; the securing of all the benefits of sworn evidence in accused's favour without incurring the consequences of perjury by refraining from going into the witness box; and also depriving the jury of the benefit of appraising his credibility in general from his demeanour therein.

Accordingly, an accused is not able to adduce his explanation through the Crown's witnesses unless the Crown tenders it as part of its case. This ruling is justified on the basis of the hearsay rule and the

---

191 (1829), 3 C. & P. 604, 172 E.R. 565.
192 (1931), 57 C.C.C. 340, [1931] 3 W.W.R. 747, 44 B.C.R. 547 (B.C.C.A.).
193 *Ibid.*, at 342 (C.C.C.).

rule against the admissibility of self-serving statements.[194] Because confessions are a species of admissions, they are admissible as an exception to the hearsay rule on the basis that a person would not admit his guilt unless it was true. A statement exonerating the accused and proffered by defence counsel cannot be characterized as an admission.[195] The reasoning by the court in *Frederick* also applies when an accused attempts to use experts to put his version of events or self-serving statements before the trier of fact without entering the witness box and undergoing cross-examination.[196]

There is an exception to this rule. If the exculpatory statement qualifies as being part of the *res gestae*, the Supreme Court has held that an accused's statement is admissible without the necessity of his testimony in court.[197] Professor Delisle[198] and the Task Force[199] question this ruling. Although an accused's spontaneous utterance, for example, when found in possession of drugs, may be spontaneous in one sense, the possibility for concoction and the practical considerations outlined in *Frederick* are not satisfied.

The question arises as to the evidential value of an admission by an accused concerning an act or event of which she or he has no personal knowledge. In *R. v. Streu*,[200] the Supreme Court stated:[201]

> . . . if a party indicates a belief in or acceptance of a hearsay statement, that is some evidence of the truth of its contents. The weight to be given to that evidence is for the trier of fact. On the

---

194 *R. v. Graham*, [1974] S.C.R. 206, 7 C.C.C. (2d) 93, 19 C.R.N.S. 117, 26 D.L.R. (3d) 579, [1972] 4 W.W.R. 488.

195 For the converse proposition, see *R. v. Piche*, [1971] S.C.R. 23, [1970] 4 C.C.C. 27, 12 C.R.N.S. 222, 11 D.L.R. (3d) 700, 74 W.W.R. 674.

196 *R. v. Phillion*, [1978] 1 S.C.R. 18, 37 C.R.N.S. 361, 10 C.C.C. (2d) 562, 34 D.L.R. (3d) 99, [1973] 2 O.R. 291 and *R. v. Abbey* [1982] 2 S.C.R. 24, 29 C.R. (3d) 193, 68 C.C.C. (2d) 394, 138 D.L.R. (3d) 202, [1983] 1 W.W.R. 251, 39 B.C.L.R. 201.

197 *R. v. Graham, supra*, note 194; *R. v. Risby*, [1978] 2 S.C.R. 139, 39 C.C.C. (2d) 567.

198 R.J. Delisle, *Evidence Principles and Problems*, 2nd ed. (Toronto: Carswell, 1989), at 418.

199 *Report of the Federal/Provincial Task Force on Uniform Rules of Evidence* (Toronto: Carswell, 1983), at 209-10.

200 [1989] 1 S.C.R. 1521, 70 C.R. (3d) 1, 48 C.C.C. (3d) 321, [1989] 4 W.W.R. 577, 96 N.R. 58.

201 *Ibid.*, at 9 (C.R.).

other hand, if the party simply reports a hearsay statement without either adopting it or indicating a belief in the truth of its contents, the statement is not admissible as proof of the truth of the contents.

A party may adopt or accept a hearsay statement as his or her own for the purpose of admitting the facts therein. Its weight will depend on all of the surrounding circumstances. If a person makes an admission that is not based on personal knowledge or information, the admission is admissible but it has little, if any, evidential weight.[202] Depending on the circumstances and the nature of the crime, such as possession of stolen goods[203] or incest,[204] an admission of knowledge of the prohibited circumstance even if based on hearsay, is admissible and may be of sufficient probative value to warrant a conviction.

In a trial of joint accused for a common unlawful purpose or a conspiracy, a confession by one accused after the conspiracy or joint enterprise is concluded is admissible only against him or her and is inadmissible hearsay against the other accused.[205] The trial judge should make it clear to a jury the use that may be made of the accused's confession in these circumstances.[206] However, statements made in furtherance of a joint enterprise, are admissible against persons who are *prima facie* members of the conspiracy.[207] This is commonly referred to as the co-conspirator exception to the hearsay rule.[208] Also, if while testifying, an accused adopts a co-accused's statement as true, then this constitutes an adoptive admission.[209] Finally, a joint fabrication of a defence, such as an alibi, is admissible against both accused for the non-hearsay purpose of indicating a consciousness of guilt of both accused.[210]

---

202 See *Customs Comptroller v. Western Lectric Co.*, [1966] A.C. 367, at 371, [1965] 3 All E.R. 599 (P.C.).
203 *Streu, supra*, note 200.
204 *R. v. Schmidt*, [1948] S.C.R. 333, 6 C.R. 317, 92 C.C.C. 53, [1948] 4 D.L.R. 217.
205 *Ibid*. See Chapter 6, II.K.
206 *Ibid*.
207 *R. v. Carter*, [1982] 1 S.C.R. 938, 31 C.R. (3d) 97, 67 C.C.C. (2d) 568, 137 D.L.R. (3d) 387, 46 N.B.R. (2d) 142, 47 N.R. 289.
208 *R. v. Koufis*, [1941] S.C.R. 481, 76 C.C.C. 161, 3 D.L.R. 657; see Chapter 6, II.K.3.(c).
209 *R. v. Woods* (1980), 19 C.R. (3d) 136, 57 C.C.C. (2d) 220 (Ont. C.A.).
210 *Mawaz Khan v. R.*, [1967] A.C. 454, [1967] 1 All E.R. 80 (P.C.).

X USE OF A CONFESSION TO CROSS-EXAMINE THE ACCUSED

On occasion, the Crown may wish to use the confession only if the accused testifies. This is particularly so if the statement contains matters helpful to the defence which would not be introduced unless the accused testifies.

In *R. v. Krause*,[211] the Crown proved the voluntariness of a statement in a *voir dire*, but the Crown did not adduce the statement at trial before the close of its case. The Crown then used the statement to cross-examine the accused. Although the case turned on a different point, the Supreme Court appeared to accept this trial practice. The only requirement is that the statement pass the voluntariness test.[212]

The question arises whether the Crown can prove voluntariness after the close of its case. In *R. v. Drake*,[213] the Crown sought to cross-examine the accused on his statement without having established its voluntariness as part of its case. The trial Judge, MacPherson J., held a *voir dire*, found the statement voluntary and allowed cross-examination on it. In doing so, he said:[214]

> There is a well-known principle that evidence which is clearly relevant to the issues and within the possession of the Crown should be advanced by the Crown as part of its case, and such evidence cannot properly be admitted after the evidence for the defence by way of rebuttal. In other words, the law regards it as unfair for the Crown to lie in wait and to permit the accused to trap himself. The principle, however, does not apply to evidence which is only marginally, minimally or doubtfully relevant.

This suggested procedure has been adopted elsewhere.[215] Since the Crown is unaware whether the accused will testify, it would be an inefficient use of the court's time to require the Crown to conduct a *voir dire* before the close of its case only to inform the trial judge that

---

211 [1986] 2 S.C.R. 466, 54 C.R. (3d) 294, 29 C.C.C. (3d) 385, [1987] 1 W.W.R. 97, 7 B.C.L.R. (2d) 273, 33 D.L.R. (4th) 267, 14 C.P.C. (2d) 156.
212 *Monette v. R.*, [1956] S.C.R. 400, 23 C.R. 244, 114 C.C.C. 363.
213 (1970), 1 C.C.C. (2d) 396, 12 C.R.N.S. 220, [1971] 1 W.W.R. 454 (Sask. Q.B.).
214 *Ibid.*, at 397 (C.C.C.).
215 *R. v. Levy* (1966), 50 Cr. App. R. 198 (C.A.).

the Crown does not intend to adduce the statement in evidence. Moreover, if the accused testifies in accordance with his or her statement, the Crown will probably not cross-examine the accused on the prior statement, because it is not inconsistent with his or her statement. The Crown should, however, advise the accused of its intention and provide the accused with a copy of the statement before he or she elects to testify; otherwise, it would be unfair to surprise the accused with the alleged statement after he or she has testified in chief.

A voluntary statement first tendered by the Crown in cross-examination which is admitted to have been made is an admission and is admissible as proof of the truth of the contents. It is submitted that *R. v. Ament*,[216] which suggests the contrary, is wrongly decided. Furthermore, if the accused denies making the statement, the Crown may prove the statement subject to the collateral fact rule.[217] It is then admissible with respect to the truth of its content.[218]

The Crown may not cross-examine an accused on an involuntary statement. Once a statement is ruled involuntary, no further use may be made of it by the Crown.[219] Where two accused are jointly tried, however, different considerations arise. Assume one accused testifies and incriminates a co-accused. In this scenario, the accused may wish to cross-examine the other accused *qua* witness on a prior inconsistent statement and prove it pursuant to the *Canada Evidence Act*[220] to impeach the witness' credibility or to implicate him or her.[221] The question that arises is whether the trial judge must first rule that the statement was voluntary. The provincial courts of appeal in British Columbia and Ontario have held that when an accused testifies, his co-accused may cross-examine him on his out-of-court statement without proving the statement was voluntary.[222] The only limitation

---

216 (1972), 7 C.C.C. (2d) 83, 19 C.R.N.S. 15 (Ont. H.C.J.).

217 *R. v. Krause*, [1986] 2 S.C.R. 466, 29 C.C.C. (3d) 385, 54 C.R. (3d) 294, 33 D.L.R. (4th) 267, [1987] 1 W.W.R. 97, 14 C.P.C. (2d) 156, 71 N.R. 61 (S.C.C.). See Chapter 16, VI.D.2.

218 *R. v. Mannion*, [1986] 2 S.C.R. 272, 278; *McInroy v. R.*, [1979] 1 S.C.R. 588, 42 C.C.C. (2d) 481, 5 C.R. (3d) 125, 89 D.L.R. (3d) 609, [1978] 6 W.W.R. 585, 23 N.R. 589 (per Estey J.); and see Chapter 16, VI.D.2.

219 *Monette v. R., supra*, note 212; *Hébert v. R.*, [1955] S.C.R. 120, 113 C.C.C. 97, 20 C.R. 79.

220 R.S.C. 1985, c. C-5, ss. 10 and 11.

221 *R. v. Logan* (1988), 68 C.R. (3d) 1, 46 C.C.C. (3d) 354, 67 O.R. (2d) 87, 30 O.A.C. 321 (Ont. C.A.).

222 *Ibid., R. v. Pelletier* (1986), 29 C.C.C. (3d) 533 (B.C.C.A.); but see *R. v.*

is that the cross-examination must be confined to the matters in issue or to credibility.[223] This position has not been maintained consistently. In *R. v. Herodotou (No.2)*,[224] the trial judge refused to permit such cross-examination because the involuntary confession had no probative value. These conflicting positions are concerned with balancing the competing rights of the two accused: the right of one accused to make full answer and defence against the right of the other accused not to have unreliable and improperly obtained evidence presented in evidence. Perhaps no fixed rule can be made and the matter ought to be left to the trial judge's discretion to be exercised by balancing these competing rights.[225]

It has been suggested that permitting a statement of the accused to be used which has not been proved to be voluntary is open to abuse.[226] First the Crown might be tempted to make a deal with a co-accused to cross-examine on a statement which the Crown could not prove to be voluntary. Moreover, two co-accused might make a deal to have one co-accused cross-examine the other on a statement that exculpates the maker of the statement. Furthermore, a co-accused may seek to cross-examine on a statement that exculpates the cross-examining co-accused. These are all matters which a trial judge must take into account in exercising his or her discretion. In addition, however, in the latter two situations it is doubtful that the statements will be inconsistent with the testimony of the witness which is a pre-condition to the right to cross-examine on and to prove the statements.[227]

Kendall (1987), 35 C.C.C. (3d) 105, 57 C.R. (3d) 249, 20 O.A.C. 134 (Ont. C.A.) where the prejudice to the accused of cross-examination on a previous statement that had not shown in a *voir dire* to be voluntary was held to be an important factor for consideration by the trial judge when exercising his or her discretion to grant a motion for severance.

223   *Pelletier, ibid.*, at 533.

224   (1978), 40 C.C.C. (2d) 542, 6 C.R. (3d) 336 (Ont. Co. Ct.).

225   *Logan, supra*, note 221, at 36-38 (C.R.).

226   *Report of the Federal Provincial Task Force on Uniform Rules of Evidence* (Toronto: Carswell, 1982), at 193. If the maker of the statement goes to the witness box, then one of the badges of hearsay is missing, that is, absence of the cross-examination of the declarant.

227   *Supra*, note 220.

XI EVIDENCE DISCLOSED AS A RESULT OF AN INADMISSIBLE CONFESSION

While the law respecting exclusion of confessions was developing, an issue arose as to whether incriminating evidence discovered in consequence of an involuntary confession should be received. In *R. v. Warickshall*,[228] the accused was charged as an accessory after the fact to theft and as a receiver of stolen goods. As a result of an improper inducement she admitted where the stolen property could be found. The police found the property and sought to adduce it as evidence. The court first noted that the rationale for excluding confessions was doubtfulness as to its reliability. It added:[229]

> This principle respecting confessions has no application whatever as to the admission or rejection of facts, whether the knowledge of them be obtained in consequence of an extorted confession, or whether it arises from any other source; for a fact, if it exists at all, must exist invariably in the same manner, whether the confession from which it is derived be in other respects true or false. Facts thus obtained, however, must be fully and satisfactorily proved, without calling in the aid of any part of the confession which they may have been derived.

At common law Canadian courts adopted this principle and it was affirmed by the Supreme Court in *R. v. Wray*[230]

The more difficult question is whether that part of a declaration which is confirmed by the subsequent discovery of facts may be admitted notwithstanding it was inadmissible under the *Ibrahim* test. In *R. v. St. Lawrence*,[231] McRuer C.J.H.C. was faced with this problem. In that case, the accused made an inadmissible statement in which he told the police where a twitch and the deceased's wallet could be found. He was subsequently taken to that location and the articles were located. The Crown theorized that the accused had used the twitch to murder the deceased and then to rob him. The Chief Justice commented that the question was a difficult one and then concluded:[232]

---

228 (1783) 1 Leach 263, 168 E.R. 234 (Cr. Cas. Res.).
229 *Ibid.*, at 235 (E.R.).
230 [1971] S.C.R. 272, [1970] 4 C.C.C. 1, 11 C.R.N.S. 235, 11 D.L.R. (3d) 673.
231 (1949), 93 C.C.C. 376, 7 C.R. 464, [1949] O.R. 215 (Ont. H.C.).
232 *Ibid.*, at 391 (C.C.C.).

Where the discovery of the fact confirms the confession — that is, where the confession must be taken to be true by reason of the discovery of the fact — then that part of the confession that is confirmed by the discovery of the fact is admissible, but further than that no part of the confession is admissible.

The underlying principle is that the finding of the article simply confirms the fact of the accused's knowledge of where the article was located. The confession is therefore admissible for that purpose only. It is not admissible to show that the accused said he put the articles where they were found as the finding of them does not confirm the statement. In *R. v. Wray*,[233] the Supreme Court of Canada confirmed McRuer C.J.H.C.'s ruling.

The rule has limits however. For example, anything found by the police before the confession cannot, *ex post facto*, confirm the confession.[234] Nor does the finding of "subsequent facts" confirm more than that part of a confession which is directly connected with the discovery.

The common law concerning the admissibility of derivative evidence and those parts of confessions collaterally proven to be true is now subject to challenge under the *Charter*. If a statement is obtained in a manner which violated an accused's rights under the *Charter*, the derivative evidence may be also excluded if its admission would bring the administration of justice into disrepute. If the infringement was pursuant to the law, the derivative evidence may be admissible if the court finds that the statutory or common law rule is a reasonable limit prescribed by law.[235]

It is useful to compare this result with that under the *Police and Criminal Evidence Act 1984*.[236] Under that Act the derivative evidence is admissible.[237] The acused's involuntary confession showing how the derivative evidence was discovered is inadmissible unless evidence of how it was discovered is given by the acused or on his behalf.[238] But the Act also gives the trial judge a residual discretion to exclude

---

233 *Supra*, note 230.
234 *R. v. Haase*, [1965] 2 C.C.C. 56, 45 C.R. 113, 50 W.W.R. 321 (B.C.C.A.); affd. without further reasons [1965] 2 C.C.C. 123*n*, 45 C.R. 321, 50 W.W.R. 386*n* (S.C.C.).
235 See Chapter 14, IV.E.1.
236 (1984), c. 60 (U.K.).
237 *Ibid.*, s. 76(4).
238 *Ibid.*, ss. 76(5) and 76(6).

evidence if its admission would have an adverse effect on the proceedings.[239] It is premature to suggest the way these interrelated sections will be interpreted by the English courts. Similarly, the *Charter's* impact on the Canadian law of evidence may affect the old common law rules of admissibility if the courts are of the view that admission of the evidence would operate unfairly or adversely reflect on the integrity of the judicial process.

XII CHARTER IMPLICATIONS

Several *Charter* provisions have added to or strengthened the common law exclusionary rules relating to admissions by persons charged with or suspected of the commission of a crime. The provisions referred to are:

1. the right to counsel under s. 10(b) of the *Charter*;
2. the right against self-incrimination under s. 13; and,
3. the right to remain silent under s. 7.

A. *Right to Counsel — Section 10(b) of the Charter*

Section 10(b) of the *Charter* provides:

Everyone has the right on arrest or detention

. . . .

(b) to retain and instruct counsel without delay and to be informed of that right.

The Supreme Court of Canada has held that the police must comply with s. 10(b) by informing an accused of her or his right to counsel. Absent proof of circumstances indicating the accused did not understand the right to counsel, the accused has the onus to prove that he or she asked for the right and was denied the right or the opportunity to ask for it.[240]

---

239 *Ibid.*, s. 78.
240 *R. v. Baig*, [1987] 2 S.C.R. 537, 61 C.R. (3d) 97, 37 C.C.C. (3d) 181, 45 D.L.R. (4th) 106, 25 O.A.C. 81, 81 N.R. 87, 32 C.R.R. 355 quoting Tarnopolsky J.A. in *R. v. Anderson* (1984), 10 C.C.C. (3d) 417, 39 C.R. (3d) 193, 7 D.L.R. (4th) 306, 45 O.R. (2d) 225, 2 O.A.C. 258, 9 C.R.R. 161 (Ont. C.A.).

Once an accused asserts his or her right to counsel, the courts have broadly interpreted the detainee's rights under s. 10(b). The Supreme Court has held that the section also imposes correlative duties on a police officer. In *R. v. Manninen*,[241] the police arrested Manninen and informed him of his right to retain and instruct counsel. They also gave him the standard police caution. The accused said, in reply: "Prove it. I ain't saying anything until I see my lawyer. I want to see my lawyer". The police simply continued to question the accused and obtained an incriminating statement. The Supreme Court found that the accused's rights under s. 10(b) of the *Charter* had been seriously infringed. When Manninen claimed his right to remain silent and see his lawyer, the court held that the officer should have allowed the detainee the use of a telephone so that he might exercise that right. The court reasoned that, otherwise, the right would be illusory.

Speaking generally, the Supreme Court has held that s. 10(b) imposes at least three duties on the police: (1) to inform the accused of his or her right to counsel in a manner which ensures that it is understood;[242] (2) to give an accused who wishes to contact counsel a reasonable opportunity to exercise the right without delay;[243] and, (3) to refrain from attempting to elicit evidence until a detainee has had a reasonable opportunity to retain and instruct counsel.[244] However, circumstances of urgency may justify a delay by the authorities in carrying out their duties.[245] An accused, however, may be subjected to other investigative techniques in urgent situations before consultation with counsel, for example, a demand for a breath sample within the statutory period and police action to preserve physical evidence.[246] Also, an accused may be required to perform physical tests if he or she

---

241   [1987] 1 S.C.R. 1233, 58 C.R. (3d) 97, 34 C.C.C. (3d) 385, 41 D.L.R. (4th) 301, 61 O.R. (2d) 736 (note), 21 O.A.C. 192.

242   *R. v. Evans* (1991), 63 C.C.C. (3d) 289, 124 N.R. 278.

243   In *R. v. Playford* (1987), 61 C.R. (3d) 101, 40 C.C.C. (3d) 142, 63 O.R. (2d) 289, 24 O.A.C. 161 the Ont. C.A. held that this right included the ability to retain and instruct counsel in privacy.

244   *Manninen, supra*, note 241; *R. v. Ross*, [1989] 1 S.C.R. 3, 67 C.R. (3d) 209, 46 C.C.C. (3d) 129, 31 O.A.C. 321, 91 N.R. 81, 37 C.R.R. 369 (*sub nom. R. v. LeClair*).

245   *R. v. Strachan*, [1988] 2 S.C.R. 980, 67 C.R. (3d) 87, 46 C.C.C. (3d) 479, 56 D.L.R. (4th) 673, [1989] 1 W.W.R. 385, 90 N.R. 273, 37 C.R.R. 335 (S.C.C.).

246   *R. v. Gilbert* (1988), 61 C.R. (3d) 149, 40 C.C.C. (3d) 423, 24 O.A.C. 150 (Ont. C.A.).

is suspected of impaired driving without being advised of her or his 10(b) right to counsel[247] or be subjected to a search that is otherwise constitutional.[248]

The Supreme Court has considered whether an accused may waive his or her s. 10(b) rights. In *R. v. Clarkson*,[249] the Crown sought to introduce a statement made by the accused to the police shortly after her arrest. At the time of her arrest, she was in a highly intoxicated state and very emotional. After being given the customary police caution and informed of her right to counsel, she nodded when asked if she understood. Her aunt was present with her during the interrogation and on several occasions attempted to persuade her to stop answering questions until a lawyer was present. The accused stated that there was "no point" and that she did not need the assistance of a lawyer. Wilson J. stated:[250]

> Unlike the confession itself, there is no room for an argument that the court in assessing such a waiver should only be concerned with the probative value of the evidence so as to restrict the test to the accused's mere comprehension of his or her own words. Rather, the purpose of the right, as indicated by each of the members of this Court writing in *Therens*, *supra*, is to ensure that the accused is treated fairly in the criminal process. While this constitutional guarantee cannot be forced upon an unwilling accused, any voluntary waiver in order to be valid and effective must be premised on a true appreciation of the consequences of giving up the right.

Accordingly, a waiver of the right to counsel requires a knowledge by the accused of the consequences of the waiver.

---

247 *R. v. Bonin* (1989), 47 C.C.C. (3d) 230, 11 M.V.R. (2d) 31 (B.C.C.A.); leave to appeal refd. October 19, 1989 (S.C.C.).

248 *R. v. Debot*, [1989] 2 S.C.R. 1140, 52 C.C.C. (3d) 193, 73 C.R. (3d) 129, 102 N.R. 161, 37 O.A.C. 1, 45 C.R.R. 49, at 1178 per Sopinka J.; see also the reasons of Lamer J. who found the accused's rights were suspended.

249 [1986] 1 S.C.R. 383, 50 C.R. (3d) 289, 25 C.C.C. (3d) 207, 26 D.L.R. (4th) 493, 69 N.B.R. (2d) 40, 66 N.R. 114.

250 *Ibid.*, at 395-96 (S.C.R.).

Speaking generally, once an accused asserts the right to counsel, there must be a clear indication that he or she changed his or her mind and subsequently waived this right.[251] But when an accused is not reasonably diligent in the exercise of the right to counsel, the correlative duties on the police are suspended.[252] Moreover, once an accused has effectively retained and instructed counsel, police are not precluded from then obtaining an incriminating statement.[253]

Where the court finds that a police officer violated s. 10(b) of the *Charter*, the statement will be excluded if it is established that, having regard to all the circumstances, the admission of the evidence could bring the administration of justice into disrepute.[254] In both *Manninen* and *Clarkson*, the accused's statements were voluntary but their confessions were excluded under s. 24(2). In *Manninen*, the Court found that the accused's rights were seriously violated when the police ignored his expressed desire to remain silent. In *Clarkson*, the Court found that the police interrogated an obviously intoxicated accused because they wanted to extract a confession which they feared they might not be able to obtain when she sobered up and appreciated the need for counsel. In several decisions, the Supreme Court has held that an incriminating statement that was obtained in violation of an accused's s. 10(b) rights will go to the fairness of the trial.[255] Unlike

---

251   *R. v. Ross, supra,* note 244.

252   *R. v. Tremblay,* [1987] 2 S.C.R. 435, 45 D.L.R. (4th) 445, 37 C.C.C. (3d) 565, 60 C.R. (3d) 59, 25 O.A.C. 93, 79 N.R. 153, 2 M.V.R. (2d) 289, 32 C.R.R. 381; *R. v. Smith,* [1989] 2 S.C.R. 368, 50 C.C.C. (3d) 308, 71 C.R. (3d) 129, [1989] 6 W.W.R. 289, 39 B.C.L.R. (2d) 145, 99 N.R. 372.

253   *R. v. Gilbert, supra,* note 246; *R. v. Playford, supra,* note 243; *R. v. Emile* (1988), 65 C.R. (3d) 135, 42 C.C.C. (3d) 408, [1988] 5 W.W.R. 481, [1988] N.W.T.R. 196 (N.W.T.C.A.); *Contra: R. v. Greig* (1987), 56 C.R. (3d) 229, 33 C.C.C. (3d) 40, 26 C.R.R. 136 (Ont. H.C.J.).

254   Section 24(2) of the *Charter* reads: "Where, in proceedings under subsection (1), a court concludes that evidence was obtained in a manner that infringed or denied any rights or freedoms guaranteed by this Charter, the evidence shall be excluded if it is established that, having regard to all the circumstances, the admission of it would bring the administration of justice into disrepute." In *R. v. Collins,* [1987] 1 S.C.R. 265, at 287, 33 C.C.C. (3d) 1, 56 C.R. (3d) 193, 38 D.L.R. (4th) 508, [1987] 3 W.W.R. 699, 13 B.C.L.R. (2d) 1, 28 C.R.R. 122, 74 N.R. 276, the Supreme Court held that the French version of s. 24(2) should prevail: "could bring the administration of justice into disrepute". See Chapter 9, for a full discussion of s. 24(2) and its application.

255   *R. v. Manninen, supra,* note 241; it also applies to bodily fluids (see *R. v. Therens,* [1985] 1 S.C.R. 613, 18 C.C.C. (3d) 481, 45 C.R. (3d) 97, 18 D.L.R. (4th)

real evidence which existed apart from the breach,[256] the admission of a confession so obtained will bring the administration of justice into disrepute. It appears that the courts will automatically exclude a confession unless circumstances of urgency justify delaying the crystallization of a detainee's right to counsel or unless the accused is not reasonably diligent in exercising this right.[257] But, it appears that the Supreme Court distinguishes between evidence emanating from the accused as a result of the *Charter* violation and physical evidence which existed apart from the breach.[258]

B. *Right Against Self-incrimination — Section 13 of the Charter*

Before the *Charter*, a witness could claim the protection of s. 5(1) of the *Canada Evidence Act*[259] and the witness' testimony could not be used as an admission in a subsequent proceeding against that person. This provision required an express claim of the privilege by the witness while testifying. If a witness did not claim the statutory protection, for whatever reason, such testimony would be admissible in a subsequent proceeding without the necessity of a *voir dire*.[260] Because the trial judge was under no obligation to inform a witness of this right, there was a premium on knowledge of this proviso. Section 13 of the *Charter* addresses similar concerns. It states:

> A witness who testifies in any proceedings has the right not to have any incriminating evidence so given used to incriminate that witness in any other proceedings, except in a prosecution for perjury or for the giving of contradictory evidence.

Unlike the *Canada Evidence Act*, s. 13 does not require the witness to claim the protection of subsequent use immunity.[261] This alteration of

---

655, [1983] 4 W.W.R. 286, 40 Sask. R. 122, 38 Alta. L.R. 99, 13 C.P.R. 193, 32 M.V.R. 153, 59 N.R. 122) and an accused's physical appearance, (see *R. v. Ross*, *supra*, note 243).

256 *R. v. Collins*, *supra*, note 254.

257 *R. v. Tremblay*, *supra*, note 252.

258 *R. v. Collins*, *supra*, note 254, at 284 (S.C.R.).

259 R.S.C. 1985, c. C-5.

260 *Boulet v. R.*, [1978] 1 S.C.R. 332, 75 D.L.R. (3d) 223, 34 C.C.C. (2d) 397, 40 C.R.N.S. 158, 15 N.R. 541.

261 For a more detailed discussion of s. 13 see Chapter 14, IV.D.

the law is an improvement because, in some cases, the main suspect or the accused had been subpoenaed to testify in a collateral proceeding, such as a coroner's inquest, where he or she was subject to discovery by the Crown. An unrepresented person who was unaware of his or her rights was put in an unfair position.

In *R. v. Dubois*,[262] the Supreme Court considered the scope of s. 13. Dubois testified at his trial for second degree murder but his conviction was overturned on appeal and a new trial was ordered. At the re-trial, the Crown adduced his prior testimony as part of its case. The Supreme Court ruled that s. 13 precludes the admission of the previous testimony in other proceedings and that for the purposes of s. 13, the original trial was another proceeding. The Court held that it was irrelevant whether the previous testimony was voluntarily given or made under compulsion, or whether a charge was outstanding at the time the previous testimony was given. It also appears that it was irrelevant that Dubois was represented by counsel at both proceedings. By contrast under the broad concept of self-incrimination in the United States, compulsion is a requirement to trigger the right against self-incrimination.[263]

The scope of s. 13 was further extended in *R. v. Mannion*.[264] The Supreme Court ruled that the Crown is not entitled to cross-examine an accused or use his previous testimony as a prior inconsistent statement. Accordingly, if an accused put forth an unsuccessful alibi defence at his first trial, he may take a fresh approach and put forward self-defence at his re-trial. By reason of the court's ruling, the trier of fact would be unaware of the divergent statements.[265] In *R. v. Kuldip*,[266] the majority reversed its previous decision in *Mannion*. Lamer C.J., speaking for the majority, held that s. 13 does not preclude use of

---

262 [1985] 2 S.C.R. 350, 22 C.C.C. (3d) 513, 48 C.R. (3d) 193, 23 D.L.R. (4th) 503, [1986] 1 W.W.R. 193, 41 Alta. L.R. (2d) 97, 62 N.R. 50, 18 C.R.R. 1, 66 A.R. 202.

263 *Schemerber v. State of California* 86 S. Ct. 1826 (1966). See D. Doherty, "Annotation", 48 C.R. (3d) 194, at 196-97. For a different justification for the result in *Dubois* see L. Arbour, *ibid.*, at 194-96.

264 [1986] 2 S.C.R. 272, 31 D.L.R. (4th) 712, 28 C.C.C. (3d) 544, 53 C.R. (3d) 193, [1986] 6 W.W.R. 525, 47 Alta. L.R. (2d) 177, 69 N.R. 189, 25 C.R.R. 182.

265 See R.J. Delisle, "Annotation", 53 C.R. (3d) 194 and D. Doherty, *supra*, note 263 for a criticism of this result.

266 (1990), 61 C.C.C. (3d) 385, 1 C.R. (4th) 285, 43 O.A.C. 340, 114 N.R. 284, 1 C.R.R. (2d) 110.

previous testimony for the purpose of cross-examination if the sole purpose of the cross-examination is to challenge the credibility of the accused who has chosen to testify in a subsequent proceeding.

A related issue is whether an accused's testimony at the *voir dire* is admissible at trial. If the statement is ruled involuntary, an accused's testimony on the *voir dire* cannot be introduced by the Crown as part of its case-in-chief.[267] In the pre-*Charter* case of *R. v. Erven*,[268] the Supreme Court indicated that the accused's testimony on the *voir dire* was not admissible at trial. Dickson J. stated in *obiter*:[269]

> The accused may testify on the *voir dire* while remaining silent during the trial. Evidence on the *voir dire* cannot be used in the trial itself. The fundamental nature of this functional separation was recently reaffirmed by this Court in *The Queen v. Gauthier*.

According to this view, regardless of the ruling on voluntariness, the Crown cannot use the *voir dire* testimony of the accused as part of its case.

The final question is whether the Crown is able to cross-examine an accused on testimony given in the *voir dire* proceedings when the statement is ruled voluntary. In the pre-*Charter* case of *R. v. Tarrant*,[270] the accused testified on a *voir dire* at the preliminary hearing. At trial, he was cross-examined with respect to evidence he gave at the preliminary hearing. Martin J.A. held:[271]

> If an accused chooses to testify on a *voir dire* to determine the admissibility of the statement he takes the calculated risk that if the statement is ruled admissible, *then* or *later*, his evidence may be used to cross-examine him in a later proceeding.

This follows the practice in England and Wales which also permits such cross-examination.[272] Presumably, this is made more palatable by

---

267 *R. v. Magdish* (1978), 41 C.C.C. (2d) 449, 3 C.R. (3d) 377 (Ont. C.A.); *Wong Kam-ming v. R.*, [1979] 2 W.L.R. 81, 1 All E.R. 939, [1980] A.C. 247 (P.C.).

268 [1979] 1 S.C.R. 926, 44 C.C.C. (2d) 76, 6 C.R. (3d) 97, 92 D.L.R. (3d) 507, 30 N.S.R. (2d) 89, 25 N.R. 49.

269 *Ibid.*, at 932 (S.C.R.), citing *R. v. Gauthier*, [1977] 1 S.C.R. 441, 27 C.C.C. (2d) 14, 33 C.R.N.S 46, 64 D.L.R. (3d) 501.

270 (1981), 25 C.R. (3d) 157, 63 C.C.C. (2d) 385, 34 O.R. (2d) 747 (Ont. C.A.).

271 *Ibid.*, at 163 (C.R.).

272 *Report of the Federal/Provincial Task Force on Uniform Rules of Evidence* (Toronto: Carswell, 1982), at 192.

reason of the related practice which does not permit cross-examination of the accused as to the truth of the statement in the *voir dire*.[273] Whether the common law relating to cross-examination on evidence given at a *voir dire* has been altered in Canada depends on the judicial interpretation of the words "in any other proceedings" found in s. 13 of the *Charter*. On the basis of the *obiter* in *Erven* and the above decisions in *Dubois* and *Mannion*, the Supreme Court might find that the *voir dire* is a separate proceeding. Accordingly, s. 13 will provide subsequent use immunity except for cross-examination on previous testimony at the *voir dire* solely for the purpose of challenging credibility.[274]

C. *Right to Remain Silent — Section 7 of the Charter*

The right to remain silent has deep roots in the common law.[275] It was and is a police practice to caution a detainee that there is no obligation to speak. At common law, the failure to give a caution, however, is only one of the circumstances which is taken into consideration in determining whether a statement is voluntary. As Kerwin J. stated in *Boudreau v. R.*:[276]

> The mere fact that a warning was given was not necessarily decisive in favour of admissibility but, on the other hand, the absence of a warning should not bind the hands of the Court so as to compel it to rule out a statement. All the surrounding circumstances must be investigated and, if upon their review the Court is not satisfied of the voluntary nature of the admission, the statement will be rejected. Accordingly, the presence or absence of a warning will be a factor and, in many cases, an important one.

The right can be exercised by a person under arrest, detention or accusation. In such circumstances, silence in the face of an allegation

---

273 *Wong Kam-ming v. R.*, *supra*, note 267.
274 See *Kuldip*, *supra*, note 266. See also Chapter 14, IV.D.3.
275 The common law cases are reviewed by Sopinka J. in *Thomson Newspapers Inc. v. Canada (Director of Investigation and Research, Restrictive Trade Practices Commission)*, [1990] 1 S.C.R. 425, 54 C.C.C. (3d) 417, 76 C.R. (3d) 129, 67 D.L.R. (4th) 161, 39 O.A.C. 161, 29 C.P.R. (3d) 97, 106 N.R. 161, 72 O.R. (2d) 415*n*, at 599-601 (S.C.R.).
276 [1949] S.C.R. 262, at 267, 94 C.C.C. 1, 7 C.R. 427, 3 D.L.R. 81.

of criminal conduct does not constitute a circumstantial admission of guilt.[277]

The *Charter* right was first recognized by the majority in *Thomson Newspapers*.[278] The content and application of the right were more fully explained in *R. v. Hebert*,[279] a case whose facts closely resemble those of *R. v. Rothman*.[280] The accused, who was arrested on a charge of robbery and who, after consulting counsel, chose to remain silent, was placed in a cell with an undercover police officer posing as a cell-mate. The officer engaged the accused in conversation during which the accused made various incriminating statements. The majority held that under s. 7 the state is not entitled to override the exercise of choice by a detainee to remain silent. The right is not absolute, however, and can in some circumstances be overborne by state interest. Thus, the police are entitled to question an accused or a suspect who has not chosen to remain silent. Police persuasion, short of denying the suspect the right to choose, does not violate the right. The exercise of choice does not have to amount to waiver in accordance with the standards in *R. v. Clarkson*[281] This approach appears to be inconsistent with the position taken with respect to other *Charter* rights which can only be forfeited by waiver.[282]

XIII CONCLUSION

The law of confessions is in a state of flux. There is still a lack of agreement as to the basic rationale for the existence of the rule. As illustrated by the *R. v. Rothman*[283] decision, the admissibility of a confession is very much influenced by a determination of the foundation on which the confession rule rests. One of the bases of the rule is the right to remain silent. The application of that right in *R. v.*

---

277 The cases are summarized in *R. v. Hebert*, [1990] 2 S.C.R. 151, 57 C.C.C. (3d) 1, 77 C.R. (3d) 145, at 156 (S.C.R.), and see *R. v. Cripps*, [1968] 3 C.C.C. 323, 3 C.R.N.S. 367, 63 W.W.R. 532 (B.C.C.A.).
278 *Supra*, note 275.
279 *Supra*, note 277.
280 [1981], 1 S.C.R. 640, 59 C.C.C. (2d) 30, 20 C.R. (3d) 97, 121 D.L.R. (3d) 578, 35 N.R. 485.
281 [1986] 1 S.C.R. 383, 50 C.R. (3d) 289, 25 C.C.C. (3d) 207.
282 See Sopinka J. in *R. v. Hebert*, *supra*, note 277, at 204.
283 *Supra*, note 280.

Hebert[284] in a fact situation similar to *Rothman*[285] yielded a different result. It is expected that this branch of the law will continue to develop to bring together what are at present two strains of an essentially common theme. Futhermore, with the development of the emerging operating mind requirement, there is less and less justification for maintaining the person in authority prerequiste. This will continue to be a requirement in cases in which a right to remain silent is asserted under the *Charter*.

Finally, we can expect that there will be strong support for lowering the standard of proof for the admission of confessions at a preliminary hearing. This will be in keeping with the purpose of such proceeding which is to screen out cases not fit to be presented to a trial court.[286] Moreover, there is support for reducing the standard of proof for the admissibility of the confession at trial to require a preponderance of evidence rather than to require proof beyond a reasonable doubt.

---

284 *Supra*, note 277.
285 *Supra*, note 280.
286 See this Chapter, VIII.

CHAPTER 9

ILLEGALLY OBTAINED
EVIDENCE

I   INTRODUCTION

The manner in which evidence is obtained, no matter how
improper or illegal, is not an impediment to its admission at common
law. The point was put starkly in England by Crompton J. in the
nineteenth century: "It matters not how you get it; if you steal it even,
it would be admissible in evidence."[1] This position remains the
common law of both England and Canada. The strict inclusionary
rule is, however, subject to exceptions. At common law, a confession
obtained through improper police conduct may be inadmissible,[2]
though derivative evidence obtained as a consequence of information
contained in the confession is admissible.[3] Under s. 189 of the *Criminal Code*,[4] an illegal interception of private communications is inadmissible, but again, derivative evidence is admissible unless the presiding judge is of the opinion, in the resonant words of s. 189(2), ". . .
that the admission thereof would bring the administration of justice
into disrepute." The most significant derogation from the common
law inclusionary rule in Canada is the express power vested in courts
of competent jurisdiction by s. 24(2) of the *Canadian Charter of Rights*

---

1   *R. v. Leatham* (1861), 8 Cox C.C. 498, at 501, [1861-73] All E.R. Rep. Ext.
1646.
2   See Chapter 8, I.
3   See *R. v. St. Lawrence* (1949), 93 C.C.C. 376, 7 C.R. 464, [1949] O.R. 215
(Ont. H.C.J.), approved in *R. v. Wray*, [1971] S.C.R. 272, at 296, [1970] 4 C.C.C.
1, 11 C.R.N.S. 235, 11 D.L.R. (3d) 673, per Martland J. See Chapter 14, IV.E.1.
as to the effect of s. 7 of the *Charter* in this context.
4   R.S.C. 1985, c. C-46.

and Freedoms[5] to exclude evidence obtained through a violation of constitutional rights, to be discussed in detail in the present Chapter.

II THE RULE AT COMMON LAW

The rationale for the general inclusionary rule is that the trier of fact should have the benefit of all relevant evidence irrespective of how it was obtained. If illegal or improper acts committed in the acquisition of evidence do not affect its probative value, they should not distract the court from its primary task of fact finding. Furthermore, the law of evidence should not be used as a means of disciplining the police or others. The person aggrieved can, at least theoretically, resort to other proceedings, criminal or civil, to obtain recourse against the wrongdoer.

Far from expressing outrage at illegal conduct, our courts have traditionally stressed the lack of logical connection between illegal conduct and the probative value of the evidence in establishing a fact in issue. Lord Goddard C.J. summed up the matter in *Kuruma, Son of Kaniu v. R.*,[6] in the following language:

> In their Lordships' opinion, the test to be applied in considering whether evidence is admissible is whether it is relevant to the matter in issue. If it is, it is admissible and the court is not concerned with how the evidence was obtained.

The strict inclusionary rule has been adopted and applied by the Supreme Court of Canada in several cases.[7]

A. *Criminal Cases*

In criminal matters, some courts went far beyond the tenor of the inclusionary rule, and firmly evinced the belief that an accused

---

5   R.S.C. 1985, Appendix II, No. 44.
6   [1955] A.C. 197, at 203, [1955] 1 All E.R. 236 (P.C.).
7   See e.g., *Quebec (A.G.) v. Bégin*, [1955] S.C.R. 593, 112 C.C.C. 209, [1955] 5 D.L.R. 394 (see 21 C.R. 217 for Eng. trans.); *O'Connor v. R.*, [1966] S.C.R. 619, 48 C.R. 270, [1966] 4 C.C.C. 342, 57 D.L.R. (2d) 123; *R. v. Wray, supra*, note 3, discussed in this Chapter, III.A.; and *Hogan v. R.*, [1975] 2 S.C.R. 574, 18 C.C.C. (2d) 65, 48 D.L.R. (3d) 427, 26 C.R.N.S. 207.

criminal ought not to expect exemplary conduct from the police. The statement of Meredith J.A. in *R. v. Honan*[8] is illustrative. In refusing to reject evidence obtained as a result of the unlawful execution of a search warrant, his Lordship stated:

> Nor can I think that the Magistrate erred in admitting the evidence objected to; the question is not, by what means was the evidence procured; but is, whether the things proved were evidence; and it is not contended that they were not; all that is urged, is, that the evidence ought to have been rejected, because it was obtained by means of a trespass — as it is asserted — upon the property of the accused by the police officers engaged in the prosecution. The criminal who wields the 'jimmy' or the bludgeon, or uses any other criminally unlawful means or methods, has no right to insist upon being met by the law only when in kid gloves or satin slippers; it is still quite permissible to 'set a thief to catch a thief'. . . .

Further, in *R. v. Devison*,[9] the Nova Scotia Court of Appeal approved a statement of the trial judge that ". . . even if he had been knocked down and beaten and the blood sample extracted from him, it would be admissible . . ."

Notwithstanding this well-established rule of admissibility, there remained a question whether a trial judge possessed a discretion to exclude improperly or illegally obtained evidence if its introduction would be unfair to the accused. The existence of such a discretion was adverted to by Lord Goddard C.J. in *Kuruma*,[10] in the following terms:

> No doubt in a criminal case the judge always has a discretion to disallow evidence if the strict rules of admissibility would operate unfairly against an accused. . . . If, for instance, some admission of some piece of evidence, e.g., a document, had been obtained from a defendant by a trick, no doubt the judge might properly rule it out.

The availability of this discretion may be seen as a palliative to the harshness of the inclusionary rule. But in the United Kingdom, the scope of the discretion is very narrow indeed. Cases of entrap-

---

8   (1912), 20 C.C.C. 10, at 16, 6 D.L.R. 276, 26 O.L.R. 484, at 489 (C.A.).
9   (1974), 21 C.C.C. (2d) 225, at 230, 10 N.S.R. (2d) 482 (N.S.C.A.).
10 *Supra*, note 6, at 204.

ment,[11] illegal personal searches,[12] illegal searches of premises,[13] and illegal demands for breath samples,[14] have all failed to attract an exercise of the discretion favourable to the accused. The only significant English case in which improperly obtained evidence was excluded is *R. v. Payne*.[15] In *Payne*, a suspected drunk driver was asked to submit to a police doctor's examination on the understanding that the doctor's opinion of the accused's sobriety would not be sought. A subsequent change in procedure led to an attempt by the Crown to call the doctor as a witness to the accused's drunkenness at the relevant time. Lord Parker C.J. excluded the doctor's evidence ". . . on the basis that if the defendant realised that the doctor was likely to give evidence on the matter, he might refuse to subject himself to examination."[16] On the basis that the evidence was excluded, *Payne* represents an anomaly; but the result in the case may be explicable on the basis that the Crown was estopped from leading the doctor's evidence contrary to an undertaking to the accused not to do so.[17] This may be the only sort of "trick" within the contemplation of Lord Goddard C.J.'s dictum.

Payne was reaffirmed by the House of Lords in *R. v. Sang*, a case concerning evidence obtained by an *agent provocateur*. Lord Diplock's statement of the rule in *Sang* was unanimously concurred in by the Law Lords, and seemed to settle the matter, as follows:[18]

> Save with regard to admissions and confessions and generally with regard to evidence obtained from the accused after commission of the offence, [the trial judge] has no discretion to refuse to admit relevant admissible evidence on the ground that it was obtained by improper or unfair means.

Shortly after *Sang*, however, the Parliament of the United Kingdom enacted the *Police and Criminal Evidence Act, 1984*.[19] Section 78(1) of

---

11   *R. v. Murphy*, [1965] N.I. 138 (C.-M. C.A.).
12   *King v. R.*, [1969] 1 A.C. 304, [1968] 2 All E.R. 610 (J.C.P.C.).
13   *Jeffrey v. Black*, [1978] Q.B. 490 (D.C.).
14   *R. v. Fox*, [1986] A.C. 281, [1985] 1 All E.R. 230 (H.L.); affd. [1985] 3 All E.R. 392, 82 Cr. App. R. 105 (*sub nom. Fox v. Chief Constable of Gwent*).
15   [1963] 1 W.L.R. 637 (C.C.A.); see also *R. v. Court*, [1962] Crim. L.R. 697 (C.C.A.), a case with identical facts.
16   *Payne, ibid.*, at 639.
17   See M. Gelowitz, "Section 78 of the Police and Criminal Evidence Act: Middle Ground or No Man's Land?" (1990), 106 L.Q.R. 327, at 334-41.
18   [1980] A.C. 402 (H.L.), at 437.
19   U.K. 1984, c. 60.

the Act grants to trial judges a limited exclusionary discretion which may be exercised in circumstances in which the admission of impugned evidence ". . . would have such an adverse effect on the fairness of the proceedings that the court ought not to admit it."[20]

The question of a residual discretion to exclude relevant evidence has been academic in Canada since the judgment of the Supreme Court of Canada in *R. v. Wray*,[21] which severely limited the exclusionary discretion that was thought to reside in trial judges. Martland J., speaking for a majority of the Court, articulated the limits of the discretion as follows:[22]

> . . . the exercise of a discretion by the trial judge arises only if the admission of the evidence would operate unfairly. The allowance of admissible evidence relevant to the issue before the court and of substantial probative value may operate unfortunately for the accused, but not unfairly. It is only the allowance of evidence gravely prejudicial to the accused, the admissibility of which is tenuous, and whose probative force in relation to the main issue before the court is trifling, which can be said to operate unfairly.

Thus, in Canada, a trial judge has no power at common law to exclude evidence of considerable probative worth regardless of the manner in which it was obtained, even if its admission would be extremely prejudicial to the accused.[23]

By contrast, the American position is (or at least has been until recently) an almost automatic exclusionary rule for evidence obtained in violation of an accused's constitutional rights. The exclusionary rule

---

20   For general discussion of s. 78, see P. Mirfield, "The Evidence Provisions", [1985] Crim. L.R. 569, at 572-4; R. May, "Fair Play at Trial: An Interim Assessment of s. 78 of the Police and Criminal Evidence Act 1984", [1988] Crim. L.R. 722; D. Birch, "The PACE Hots Up: Confessions and Confusions Under the 1984 Act", [1989] Crim. L.R. 95; I. Dennis, "Reconstructing the Law of Criminal Evidence", [1989] Current Legal Problems 21; Allen, "Discretion and Security: Excluding Evidence Under s. 78(1) of the Police and Criminal Evidence Act 1984", [1990] C.L.J. 80; and M. Gelowitz, "Section 78 of the Police and Criminal Evidence Act: Middle Ground or No Man's Land?" *supra*, note 17.

21   [1971] S.C.R. 272, [1970] 4 C.C.C. 1, 11 C.R.N.S. 235, 11 D.L.R. (3d) 673.

22   *Ibid.*, at 293 (S.C.R.).

23   Although see the discussion in Chapter 2, II.C. on the judicial discretion to exclude evidence, noting the possibility of future expansion of this discretion.

was established for federal prosecutions in *Weeks v. U.S.*,[24] and was extended to state prosecutions half a century later in *Mapp v. Ohio*.[25] The application of the American rule remains highly controversial; but for the most part an accused against whom illegally obtained evidence is adduced can expect exclusion.[26] It should be noted, however, that cracks are beginning to develop in the rule as a conservative majority takes hold in the Supreme Court of the United States. In *U.S. v. Leon*,[27] and *Mass. v. Sheppard*,[28] the Supreme Court recognized a "good faith" exception to the exclusionary rule. It remains to be seen whether further inroads will be made on the American rule.

B. *Civil Cases*

The general inclusionary rule applies equally in civil cases. Lord Goddard C.J. stated in *Kuruma, Son of Kaniu v. R.*:[29] "There can be no difference in principle for this purpose between a civil and a criminal case." As early as the mid-eighteenth century it was held that in civil cases a court would not inquire into the method by which evidence was obtained if it were otherwise admissible.[30] In *Stockfleth v. De Tastet*,[31] a civil proceeding, Lord Ellenborough stated:

> ... I cannot refuse to receive in evidence an examination signed by one of the defendants, however it may have been obtained .... What is proved to have been written or signed by any of the defendants I must admit as evidence against them without considering how it was obtained.

---

24   232 U.S. 383 (1914) (S.C.).
25   367 U.S. 643 (1961) (S.C.).
26   The volume of literature on the American exclusionary rule is breathtakingly large. For an overview, see: Driscoll, "Excluding Illegally Obtained Evidence in the United States", [1987] Crim. L.R. 553; Note, "Sixteenth Annual Review of Criminal Procedure: The Exclusionary Rule" (1987), 75 Georgetown L.J. 845; Kamisar, " 'Comparative Reprehensibility' and the Fourth Amendment Exclusionary Rule" (1987), 86 Mich. L. Rev. 1; and Stutz, "The American Exclusionary Rule and Defendants' Changing Rights", [1989] Crim. L.R. 117.
27   468 U.S. 897 (1984) (S.C.).
28   468 U.S. 981 (1984) (S.C.).
29   [1955] A.C. 197, at 204, [1955] 1 All E.R. 236 (P.C.).
30   *Jordan v. Lewis* (1740), 14 East 305*n*, 104 E.R. 618*n*.
31   (1814), 4 Comp. 10, 171 E.R. 4 (K.B.), at 4 (Comp.).

This principle has stubbornly persisted in English common law.[32] In *Calcraft v. Guest*,[33] the rule was extended to permit the admission of secondary evidence of privileged documents obtained by improper means from the rightful owner and holder of the privilege.[34] In *Calcraft* the principle of "once privileged, always privileged" was subordinated to the general inclusionary rule for improperly obtained evidence. However, if improperly obtained confidential or privileged information is sought to be adduced against the holder of the privilege, the holder may, if he is quick off the mark, obtain an injunction restraining such use under the rule in *Ashburton v. Pape*.[35] In *Ashburton*, the defendant had obtained by a trick confidential letters from Lord Ashburton to his solicitor. Before the defendant had the opportunity to adduce copies of the letters in Bankruptcy Court, Lord Ashburton sought and obtained an order for delivery up of the original documents, and an injunction restraining the defendant and others from making any use, including evidentiary use in court, of the copies. Swinfen Eady L.J. stated:[36]

> The fact . . . that a document, whether original or a copy, is admissible in evidence is no answer to the demand of the lawful owner for the delivery up of the document, and no answer to an application by the lawful owner of confidential information to restrain it from being published or copied.

The *Ashburton* remedy is available to the person to whom the privilege attaches whether or not he is a party to the proceeding in which the evidence is sought to be adduced. A party may seek an *Ashburton* injunction at any time prior to the adduction against him of the improperly obtained confidential or privileged information.[37] However, a party who mistakenly hands over privileged documents

---

32 See, e.g., *Phelps v. Prew* (1854), 3 E. & B. 430, 118 E.R. 1203 (Q.B.); *Lloyd v. Mostyn* (1842), 10 M. & W. 478, 152 E.R. 558 (Exch.); *Calcraft v. Guest*, [1898] 1 Q.B. 759, [1895-9] All E.R. Rep. 346 (C.A.); and *Ashburton (Lord) v. Pape*, [1913] 2 Ch. 469, [1911-13] All E.R. Rep. 708 (C.A.).

33 *Ibid.*

34 For a discussion of *Calcraft v. Guest*, see Chapter 14, II.B.10.(e).

35 *Supra*, note 32.

36 *Ibid.*, at 477 (Ch.).

37 *Goddard v. Nationwide Building Society*, [1986] 3 All E.R. 264, [1987] Q.B. 670 (C.A.).

on discovery must generally apply for an *Ashburton* injunction prior to the opposing party's inspection of the evidence; but where the evidence was obtained by fraud, or viewed by the opposing party in the knowledge that it had been disclosed under an obvious mistake, the party holding the privilege may apply for the injunction subsequent to inspection.[38]

The equitable exception to the general rule represented by *Ashburton* has been held not to apply in criminal cases. In *Butler v. Board of Trade*,[39] Goff J. stated:

> In my judgment it would not be a right or permissible exercise of the equitable jurisdiction in confidence to make a declaration at the suit of the accused in a public prosecution in effect restraining the Crown from adducing admissible evidence relevant to the crime with which he is charged.

Goff J. reached this conclusion on the dual bases that: (1) a third party in possession of a document could not be restrained from introducing it at the trial; and (2) the interest of the state in apprehending and prosecuting criminals takes priority over an accused's private ownership rights.[40]

In civil cases the rationale for enjoining the use of improperly obtained confidential or privileged documents is stated to be a distinction between the law of confidence (which provides an equitable remedy) and the inclusionary rule of evidence (which does not). As Swinfen Eady L.J. stated in *Ashburton*:[41]

> There is here a confusion between the right to restrain a person from divulging confidential information and the right to give

---

38 See *Guinness Peat Properties Ltd. v. Fitzroy Robinson Partnership*, [1987] 2 All E.R. 716 (C.A.). Both *Goddard, ibid.*, and *Guinness Peat Properties* have been harshly criticized: see A. Zuckerman, [1986] All E.R. Rev. 160; and [1987] All E.R. Rev. 109, at 123-25.

39 [1971] 1 Ch. 680, at 690, [1970] 3 All E.R. 593.

40 See also *R. v. Tompkins* (1977), 67 Cr. App. R. 181 (C.A.). The English position on this issue has been rejected in New Zealand: see *R. v. Uljee*, [1982] 1 N.Z.L.R. 561 (C.A.), in which the court excluded the testimony of a police officer who overheard a privileged communication between an accused and his counsel by lurking near a window.

41 *Supra*, note 32, at 476 (Ch.).

secondary evidence of documents where the originals are privileged from production, if the party has such secondary evidence in his possession. The cases are entirely separate and distinct.

But is the law of confidence enough? *Ashburton* and the cases that followed it purport to restrain the use of otherwise admissible documents on the basis of the confidential nature of the document, and the proprietary right of the owner. This is shaky ground upon which to stand against the general inclusionary rule. It could not be suggested, for example, that the owner of a confidential (though not privileged) document could assert his proprietary rights to defeat a subpoena. Thus it would seem that the underlying sentiment that informs the equitable remedy is a revulsion with the prospect that recognized grounds of privilege can be destroyed by a wrongful act. It would be far preferable to overrule *Calcraft v. Guest*,[42] and abolish the rule that privilege can be destroyed by the improper acquisition of a privileged document, as has been done by the Federal Court of Canada in *Double-E Inc. v. Positive Action Tool Western Ltd.*[43]

III THE CANADIAN CHARTER OF RIGHTS AND FREEDOMS

A. *Historical Background*

Prior to the enactment of the *Charter*, there was considerable dissatisfaction with the inflexible inclusionary effect of *R. v. Wray*.[44] Although a court could, according to the terms of *Wray*, exclude evidence the admissibility of which was tenuous if its admission would operate unfairly for the accused, there was no power to exclude evidence that could tarnish the image of the justice system by reason of the manner in which it was obtained.

In its *Report on the Law of Evidence* (1975), the Law Reform Commission of Canada recommended a change in the law that would empower judges to exclude evidence in exceptional cases if its use in the proceedings would tend to "bring the administration of justice

---

42   *Supra*, note 32.
43   [1989] 1 F.C. 163, 21 C.P.R. (3d) 195, 21 F.T.R. 121, 20 C.I.P.R. 109 (T.D.); but *cf. Pfeil v. Zink* (1984), 60 B.C.L.R. 32 (S.C.).
44   [1971] S.C.R. 272, [1970] 4 C.C.C. 1, 11 C.R.N.S. 235, 11 D.L.R. (3d) 673.

into disrepute".[45] The Ontario Law Reform Commission and the Commission of Inquiry Concerning Certain Activities of the RCMP (the MacDonald Commission) made similar recommendations in 1976 and 1981 respectively. Pre-*Charter* proposals for reform suggested leaving the criteria for exclusion of such evidence to the courts and Parliament. This was regarded as unsatisfactory by provincial officials, who feared that the courts would adopt the American rule of absolute exclusion, and by civil libertarians, who feared that the Supreme Court of Canada would not overrule *Wray* and *Hogan*.[46]

Apart from proposals for reform of the law of evidence in this respect, there existed before the enactment of the *Charter* a strong undercurrent in the law of evidence and criminal procedure to protect the reputation of the administration of justice. For example, confessions are excluded if obtained, *inter alia*, by threats, fear of prejudice or hope of advantage. Concern over the conduct of persons in authority and a refusal to condone improper conduct are perhaps the best explanations for the confession rule. If the reliability of a confession were the only factor, an impugned confession would be submitted to the trier of fact, and the misconduct of the person in authority would simply go to the weight of the evidence.[47] This attitude is also evident in the development of the defence of entrapment. The Supreme Court of Canada held in *R. v. Mack*,[48] that ". . . the basis upon which entrapment is recognized lies in the need to preserve the purity of [the] administration of justice."

B. *Section 24*

1. General

Section 24 of the *Charter* reflects its historical background. It is a compromise between the strict Anglo-Canadian inclusionary rule and the strict American exclusionary rule. Section 24 reads as follows:

---

45   This phrase may have been coined by Aylesworth J.A. in *R. v. Wray*, [1970] 3 C.C.C. 122, at 123 (Ont. C.A.); revd., [1970] 4 C.C.C. 1 (S.C.C.).

46   See R. Tassé, "The Exclusion of Evidence in Charter of Rights Cases: Four Years Later" (1986) a paper delivered to The Stanford Lectures, Canadian Institute for Advanced Legal Studies, July 1986, at 10-11.

47   See Estey J. in *R. v. Rothman*, [1981] 1 S.C.R. 640, at 646-47, 59 C.C.C. (2d) 30, 20 C.R. (3d) 97.

48   [1988] 2 S.C.R. 903, at 942 [emphasis omitted], 67 C.R. (3d) 1, 44 C.C.C. (3d) 513, [1989] 1 W.W.R. 577, 37 C.R.R. 277, 90 N.R. 173.

24. (1) Anyone whose rights or freedoms, as guaranteed by this Charter, have been infringed or denied may apply to a court of competent jurisdiction to obtain such remedy as the court considers appropriate and just in the circumstances.

(2) Where, in proceedings under subsection (1), a court concludes that evidence was obtained in a manner that infringed or denied any rights or freedoms guaranteed by this Charter, the evidence shall be excluded if it is established that, having regard to all the circumstances, the admission of it in the proceeding would bring the administration of justice into disrepute.

In the early stages of the application of s. 24(2), a number of interpretational theories competed for prominence in the provincial courts of appeal. These ranged from the view that a failure to exclude evidence obtained by a *Charter* violation would render *Charter* rights hollow,[49] to the view that exclusion was a drastic remedy that would be granted only on rare occasions.[50] Other disagreements centred on the nature of the test to be applied,[51] and the availability of exclusion

---

49 See, e.g., *R. v. Therens* (1983), 5 C.C.C. (3d) 409, at 426-27, 33 C.R. (3d) 204, 148 D.L.R. (3d) 672, [1983] 4 W.W.R. 385 (Sask. C.A.) per Tallis J.A.; affd. [1985] 1 S.C.R. 613, 18 C.C.C. (3d) 481, 18 D.L.R. (4th) 655, 45 C.R. (3d) 97, [1984] 4 W.W.R. 286, 40 Sask. R. 122, 38 Alta. L.R. (2d) 99, 13 C.P.R. 193, 32 M.V.R. 153, 59 N.R. 122; *R. v. Manninen* (1983), 8 C.C.C. (3d) 193, at 203 (Ont. C.A.), per MacKinnon A.C.J.O.; affd., [1987] 1 S.C.R. 1233, 34 C.C.C. (3d) 385, 41 D.L.R. (4th) 301, 58 C.R. (3d) 97, 61 O.R. (2d) 736*n*; and *R. v. Dombrowski* (1985), 18 C.C.C. (3d) 164, at 172, 44 C.R. (3d) 1, 37 Sask. R. 259, 14 C.R.R. 165 (Sask. C.A.), per Tallis J.A.

50 See, e.g., *R. v. Collins* (1983), 5 C.C.C. (3d) 141, at 154, 148 D.L.R. (3d) 40, 33 C.R. (3d) 130, [1983] 5 W.W.R. 43, 5 C.R.R. 1 (B.C.C.A.), per Seaton J.A.; revd. [1987] 1 S.C.R. 265, 33 C.C.C. (3d) 1, 38 D.L.R. (4th) 508, 56 C.R. (3d) 193; *R. v. Duguay* (1985), 18 C.C.C. (3d) 289, at 306, 18 D.L.R. (4th) 32, 50 O.R. (2d) 375, 45 C.R. (3d) 140 (Ont. C.A.), per Zuber J.A. (dissenting); affd. [1989] 1 S.C.R. 93, 46 C.C.C. (3d) 1, 56 D.L.R. (4th) 46, 67 C.R. (3d) 252, 67 O.R. (2d) 160*n*, 91 N.R. 201, 31 O.A.C. 177.

51 The "community shock" test was applied in *R. v. Stevens* (1983), 7 C.C.C. (3d) 260, at 263, 1 D.L.R. (4th) 465, 35 C.R. (3d) 1 (N.S.C.A.); and *R. v. Chapin* (1983), 7 C.C.C. (3d) 538, at 542, 43 O.R. (2d) 458, 2 D.L.R. (4th) 538, 7 C.R.R. 206 (Ont. C.A.); see *contra R. v. Simmons* (1984), 11 C.C.C. (3d) 193, at 218, 7 D.L.R. (4th) 719, 45 O.R. (2d) 609, 39 C.R. (3d) 233, 3 O.A.C. 1, 26 M.V.R. 168, 7 C.E.R. 159 (Ont. C.A.), per Howland C.J.O.; affd. [1988] 2 S.C.R. 495, 66 C.R. (3d) 297, 45 C.C.C. (3d) 296, 67 O.R. (2d) 63, 30 O.A.C. 241, 89 N.R. 1, 38 C.R.R.

of evidence as a s. 24(1) remedy.[52] These and other controversies concerning s. 24(2) have eventually been settled in the Supreme Court of Canada,[53] and there is now a considerable body of Supreme Court authority interpreting the subsection. Indeed, the court has indicated that cases prior to the landmark decision in *R. v. Collins*[54] have been overtaken.[55]

Several issues arise from the text of s. 24. These will be dealt with in the remainder of this chapter.

2. Court of Competent Jurisdiction

By the terms of the section, any application for a s. 24 remedy must be made before a court of competent jurisdiction. Early in the development of the *Charter*, a controversy brewed over whether a magistrate or Provincial Court Judge conducting a preliminary inquiry is a court of competent jurisdiction for the purposes of granting a s. 24 remedy. The Supreme Court of Canada settled the point in *Mills v. R.*,[56] and held, by a majority, that a judge conducting a preliminary inquiry lacks the jurisdiction to entertain any s. 24 application, including an application for the exclusion of evidence.[57] The Court held that in criminal matters trial courts below the level of the provincial superior courts are courts of competent jurisdiction for the purposes of s. 24 if they have statutory jurisdiction over the applicant and the offence, and further, that the provincial superior courts are always courts of competent jurisdiction at first instance.[58]

252.

52   See *R. v. Therens* (Sask. C.A.), *supra*, note 49, at 426-27 (C.C.C.); see *contra R. v. Simmons* (Ont. C.A.), *ibid.*, at 219 (C.C.C.).

53   These issues and cases are discussed in the remaining parts of this Section III.

54   [1987] 1 S.C.R. 265, 38 D.L.R. (4th) 508, 56 C.R. (3d) 193, discussed this Chapter, III.C.

55   *R. v. Jacoy*, [1988] 2 S.C.R. 548, at 588, 45 C.C.C. (3d) 46, 66 C.R. (3d) 336, [1989] 1 W.W.R. 354, per Dickson C.J.C.

56   [1986] 1 S.C.R. 863, 26 C.C.C. (3d) 481, 52 C.R. (3d) 1, 29 D.L.R. (4th) 161, 58 O.R. (2d) 544*n*, 16 O.A.C. 81, 67 N.R. 241.

57   See *ibid.*, per McIntyre J., at 954-55 (S.C.R.), Beetz and Chouinard JJ. concurring; and per La Forest J., at 970-71 (S.C.R.).

58   *Ibid.*, at 955-56 (S.C.R.). A discussion of the broader question whether inferior tribunals can constitute courts of competent jurisdiction in non-criminal matters is beyond the scope of this work.

3. Exclusion Pursuant to Section 24?

The language of s. 24 is, it must be said, ambiguous on the question whether exclusion of evidence is a permissible remedy under both subsections (1) and (2). If s. 24(2) had not been enacted, there is nothing in the wording of s. 24(1) that would have prevented the exclusion of evidence pursuant to s. 24(1). Given both subsections, it is conceivable that a judge who has found a *Charter* violation could determine that the exclusion of particular evidence is the remedy that is "appropriate and just in the circumstances", but at the same time not be satisfied that its admission "would bring the administration of justice into disrepute." The inevitable consequence of restricting the availability of exclusion to s. 24(2), therefore, is that in some cases the court of competent jurisdiction is precluded from granting the remedy that it regards as appropriate and just in the circumstances.

A majority of the Saskatchewan Court of Appeal in *R. v. Therens*[59] held that an applicant could seek exclusion of evidence under either or both of subss. 24(1) and (2). Tallis J.A., speaking for the majority, was concerned that an accused who could not meet the test in s. 24(2) would otherwise be deprived of the exclusion remedy in circumstances in which the trial judge was satisfied that exclusion of evidence was the appropriate and just remedy.[60] Bayda C.J.S. closely considered the wording of s. 24, and concluded that if Parliament had intended to contain the exclusion remedy in s. 24(2), the subs. would read: "the evidence shall be excluded [only] if it is established . . . ."[61] When the case came before the Supreme Court of Canada, a majority of the Court, speaking through Le Dain J. on this point,[62] held that s. 24(2) is the "sole basis for the exclusion of evidence" in the *Charter*.

This interpretation of the relationship between subsections (1) and (2) seems preferable. As Le Dain J. explained, the contrary view would lead to the inevitable redundancy of s. 24(2). Furthermore, the framers of the *Charter* could not have intended that the clear conditions for exclusion set out in s. 24(2) be avoided by resort to s. 24(1). The presence of s. 24(2) is a signal from the framers that the exclusion

---

59 *Supra*, note 49.
60 *Ibid.*, at 426-27 (C.C.C.).
61 *Ibid.*, at 414 (C.C.C.).
62 *R. v. Therens*, *supra*, note 49, at 647-48 (S.C.R.), McIntyre J. concurring; Estey, Beetz, Chouinard and Wilson JJ. concurring, at 621; Dickson C.J. and Lamer J. (as he then was) left the question open.

of evidence is *never* an appropriate and just remedy where the conditions of s. 24(2) are not met.

The unavailability of s. 24(1) in an application for the exclusion of evidence was confirmed by the Supreme Court of Canada in *R. v. Strachan*.[63]

4. Standing

Standing to challenge the admissibility of evidence pursuant to s. 24(2) is limited to the express standing requirements of s. 24(1). An application under s. 24(2) can occur, on its terms, only within the context of "proceedings under subsection (1)".[64]

It follows that an applicant under s. 24(2) must establish that one or more of his or her *Charter* rights, and not merely the rights of a third party, have been infringed or denied.[65] The burden of persuasion that lies upon the applicant to establish a *Charter* violation is the civil standard of the balance of probabilities.[66]

5. Causation

A precondition to the exclusion of evidence pursuant to s. 24(2) is that the impugned evidence be found to have been "*obtained in a manner* that infringed or denied any rights or freedoms guaranteed by this Charter . . ." [emphasis added]. The meaning of the phrase "obtained in a manner" could plausibly lie on a spectrum running from a relationship of strict causation (i.e., obtained as a direct result of a *Charter* violation) to a relationship of mere temporality (i.e., obtained in the course of a larger transaction in which a *Charter* violation occurred). The Supreme Court of Canada touched on the question, but left it undecided, in its first direct encounter with s. 24(2). *R. v. Therens*,[67] was a case concerning the acquisition of an inculpatory breath sample following a violation of the accused's s. 10(b) right to be informed of the right to counsel. As Estey J. pointed out for half of

---

63 [1988] 2 S.C.R. 980, at 1000, 46 C.C.C. (3d) 479, 56 D.L.R. (4th) 673, 67 C.R. (3d) 87, [1989] 1 W.W.R. 385, 90 N.R. 273, 37 C.R.R. 335.

64 *Mills v. R.*, *supra*, note 56, at 954-55 (S.C.R.), per McIntyre J.: "Exclusion of evidence under s. 24(2) is a remedy, its application being limited to proceedings under s. 24(1)."

65 See *R. v. Rowbotham* (1984), 13 W.C.B. 104 (Ont. H.C.J.), per Ewaschuk J. Note that Lamer J. (as he then was) left this question open in *R. v. Collins*, *supra*, note 54, at 276-77.

66 *R. v. Collins*, *ibid*., at 277 (S.C.R.).

67 *Supra*, note 49.

the Court,[68] the impugned evidence was obtained directly as a consequence of the *Charter* violation, and it was not therefore necessary to consider further the required connection between impugned evidence and *Charter* violations. However, Le Dain J. chose to explore the matter further, and expressed his conclusions as follows:[69]

> In my opinion the words 'obtained in a manner that infringed or denied any rights or freedoms guaranteed by this *Charter*', particularly when they are read with the French version, *obtenus dans des conditions qui portent atteinte aux droits et libertés garantis par la présente charte*, do not connote or require a relationship of causation. It is sufficient if the infringement or denial of the right or freedom has preceded, or occurred in the course of, the obtaining of the evidence. It is not necessary to establish that the evidence would not have been obtained out [sic] for the violation of the *Charter*. Such a view gives adequate recognition to the intrinsic harm that is caused by a violation of a *Charter* right or freedom, apart from its bearing on the obtaining of evidence. I recognize, however, that in the case of derivative evidence, which is not what is in issue here, some consideration may have to be given in particular cases to the question of relative remoteness.

Lamer J. expressly disagreed with Le Dain J.'s view that the necessary connection for engaging s. 24(2) could be met by a merely temporal relationship between the *Charter* violation and the impugned evidence.[70]

The issue came before the Court squarely in the case of *R. v. Strachan*,[71] in which an accused challenged the admissibility of evidence of cannabis found in his apartment subsequent to a violation of

---

68   Beetz, Chouinard and Wilson JJ. concurring. (The coram in *Therens* was reduced to eight by the resignation of Ritchie J. prior the release of judgment.) In the subsequent case of *R. v. Manninen*, [1987] 1 S.C.R. 1233, at 1245, 34 C.C.C. (3d) 385, 41 D.L.R. (4th) 301, 58 C.R. (3d) 97, 61 O.R. (2d) 736n, per Lamer J. (as he then was), the Court unanimously reiterated that "a sufficient relationship or connection is obviously made out where . . . the evidence was obtained as a direct consequence of the violation of the *Charter* . . . ." See also *R. v. Black*, [1989] 2 S.C.R. 138, at 163, 50 C.C.C. (3d) 1, 70 C.R. (3d) 97, 98 N.R. 281, 93 N.S.R. (2d) 35, 47 C.R.R. 171.

69   *Supra*, note 49, at 649 (S.C.R.), McIntyre J. concurring.

70   *Ibid.*, at 624 (S.C.R.), Dickson C.J. concurring.

71   *Supra*, note 63.

the accused's s. 10(b) right to retain and instruct counsel. The police were present in the accused's apartment pursuant to a valid search warrant, and thus the evidence was not obtained, as in *Therens*, directly as a consequence of the s. 10(b) violation. Dickson C.J., speaking for the Court,[72] canvassed the views that had been expressed in *Therens*, and concluded that a requirement of strict causation between a *Charter* violation and impugned evidence would have several undesirable effects.

First, a causation requirement would force courts to speculate in a highly artificial manner about whether certain evidence would or would not have been obtained but for the *Charter* violation. Dickson C.J. regarded such an inquiry as inappropriate for the courts.[73] Second, a causation requirement would focus attention on specific details in the transaction between the police and an accused, and divert attention from the whole course of conduct. A microscopic examination of the transaction for the purpose of determining whether a particular *Charter* violation did or did not cause the acquisition of evidence engenders a far too restrictive view of the rights protected by the *Charter*.[74] Third, a causation requirement would result in the automatic admission of virtually all real evidence obtained following a violation of the s. 10(b) right to counsel, save derivative evidence obtained directly as a consequence of an accused's statement.[75] Fourth, and finally, a causation requirement would necessarily result in different treatment for real evidence obtained following a violation of the right to counsel depending upon whether the advice of counsel might have prevented the acquisition of the evidence in the first place.[76]

In view of these considerations, Dickson C.J. adopted the approach suggested by Le Dain J. in *Therens*, according to which a temporal link between the *Charter* violation and the impugned evidence is all that is required to engage s. 24(2). Dickson C.J. stated:[77]

---

72   *Ibid.*; Beetz, McIntyre, La Forest and L'Heureux-Dubé JJ. concurring; Lamer J. concurring, at 1009 (S.C.R.). Wilson J.'s concurrence with Dickson C.J.'s conclusion that the admission of this evidence would not bring the administration of justice into disrepute, at 1013 (S.C.R.), is implicit concurrence with the proposition that s. 24(2) is engaged on these facts.

73   *Ibid.*, at 1002 (S.C.R.).

74   *Ibid.*, at 1002-03 (S.C.R.).

75   *Ibid.*, at 1003-04 (S.C.R.).

76   *Ibid.*, at 1004-05 (S.C.R.).

77   *Ibid.*, at 1005 (S.C.R.).

Ordinarily only a few *Charter* rights, ss. 8, 9 and 10, will be relevant to the gathering of evidence and therefore to the remedy of exclusion under s. 24(2). So long as a violation of one of these rights precedes the discovery of evidence, for the purposes of the first stage of s. 24(2) it makes little sense to draw distinctions based on the circumstances surrounding the violation or the type of evidence recovered. A better approach, in my view, would be to consider all evidence gathered following a violation of a *Charter* right, including the right to counsel, as within the scope of s. 24(2).

Dickson C.J. went on to explain that there could come a point at which evidence, even though obtained following a *Charter* violation, is too remote from the violation to be regarded as "obtained in a manner" that violated the *Charter*;[78] but his Lordship did not elaborate, and left the matter to be decided on a case-by-case basis. Dickson C.J. did, however, indicate that while s. 24(2) comes into play upon a finding of a temporal connection between the *Charter* violation and the evidence, the absence of a causal connection will be a factor in the decision whether the admission of the evidence would bring the administration of justice into disrepute.[79]

Some caselaw on remoteness of evidence not obtained as a direct consequence of a *Charter* violation has begun to develop. In *R. v. Black*,[80] there was a direct causal connection between a violation of the accused's s. 10(b) right to counsel and evidence concerning the recovery of the murder weapon. But Wilson J., speaking for the Supreme Court of Canada, expressed the view that even if this were not so, the whole course of dealings between the accused and the police was a "single transaction" which brought the recovery of the weapon under the scrutiny of s. 24(2).[81] In *R. v. McArthur*,[82] however, the Ontario Court of Appeal held that an accused's voluntary statement to a cellmate, which occurred six days after a violation of the accused's s. 10(b) right to counsel, was too remote from the violation to require consideration under s. 24(2).

---

78 *Ibid.*, at 1005-06 (S.C.R.).
79 *Ibid.*, at 1006 (S.C.R.).
80 *Supra*, note 68.
81 *Ibid.*, at 162 (S.C.R.).
82 (1989), 34 O.A.C. 1, at 12 (C.A.).

An evaluation of the significance of remoteness in s. 24(2) will have to await future developments. But it would seem, from the strong statement of principle in *Strachan*, that impugned evidence will have to be very remote indeed to fall entirely outside the purview of s. 24(2). If it can be shown that particular evidence was obtained in the course of a larger transaction between the accused and the state in which a *Charter* violation preceded the acquisition of the evidence, the evidence is susceptible to consideration under s. 24(2). It can be expected that only evidence that is patently unconnected or unrelated to a *Charter* violation will escape s. 24(2) scrutiny. However, the Supreme Court has subsequently indicated, in *R. v. Debot*,[83] that as the connection between *Charter* violations and impugned evidence becomes more tenuous, the likelihood of exclusion diminishes.

C. *Bringing The Administration of Justice into Disrepute*

An applicant seeking exclusion of evidence who has overcome the hurdles of standing, jurisdiction and temporality is left with the task of satisfying the central test in s. 24(2): Would the admission of the evidence "bring the administration of justice into disrepute"? The seminal authority on the interpretation and application of this phrase in s. 24(2) is the judgment of Lamer J. for the majority of the Supreme Court of Canada in *R. v. Collins*.[84] Lamer J. established a framework for the determination of disrepute that has been adverted to and applied at every opportunity by the Supreme Court of Canada. The elements of the *Collins* test will be discussed in turn.

1. The Burden of Proof

The terms of s. 24(2) suggest clearly that the burden of persuasion lies upon the party seeking exclusion. Lamer J. noted this point summarily in *Collins*, and confirmed that, in common with the standard for establishing a *Charter* violation under s. 24(1), the standard

---

83   [1989] 2 S.C.R. 1140, at 1149, 52 C.C.C. (3d) 193, 73 C.R. (3d) 129, 102 N.R. 161, 37 O.A.C. 1, 45 C.R.R. 49, per Lamer J.; see also *R. v. Szlovak* (1989), 96 A.R. 73, 66 Alta. L.R. (2d) 326 (C.A.); affd. [1989] 2 S.C.R. 1114, 102 N.R. 78, 101 A.R. 353.
84   [1987] 1 S.C.R. 265, 56 C.R. (3d) 193, 38 D.L.R. (4th) 508.

for establishing disrepute is the civil standard of the balance of probabilities: ". . . the applicant must make it more probable than not that the admission of the evidence would bring the administration of justice into disrepute."[85]

The applicant's burden under s. 24(2) is quite unlike an ordinary civil burden to establish facts. Once the *Charter* violation and circumstances surrounding it are proved, the inquiry departs the realm of pure fact and becomes concerned with matters that are not susceptible of proof in the ordinary sense, such as the possible effect of admission on the fairness of the trial, the relative seriousness of the *Charter* violation, and the very concept of the reputation of the administration of justice. Furthermore, the true burden is in practice bound to drift towards the Crown, since many factors in the equation are within the peculiar knowledge of the Crown (e.g., good faith, urgency, availability of other investigative techniques); and, perhaps more important, it is the Crown that is functionally responsible for the maintenance of the administration of justice.[86]

Before exercising the exclusionary power of s. 24(2), the court must be satisfied that the *admission* of the impugned evidence would bring the administration of justice into *further* disrepute than the investigative technique that produced the evidence already has. This refinement is necessary to preserve the view that s. 24(2) cannot be used to discipline the police,[87] and is "not a remedy for police misconduct",[88] but the distinction may be too subtle for application.

2. "Would" or "Could"

The words of the English text of s. 24(2) require that the applicant establish that the administration of justice "would" be brought into disrepute by the admission of the impugned evidence. An important, though infrequently mentioned, modification to this term in s. 24(2) was made in *Collins* as a consequence of the equally authoritative French text of s. 24(2). Lamer J. translated the French phrase *"est susceptible de déconsidérer l'administration de la justice"* as "could

---

85   *Ibid.*, at 280 (S.C.R.).

86   For an illuminating discussion of these matters, see K. Jull, "Exclusion of Evidence and the Beast of Burden" (1987), 30 Crim. L.Q. 178.

87   *R. v. Collins, supra*, note 84, at 275 (S.C.R.).

88   *Ibid.*, at 281 (S.C.R.).

bring the administration of justice into disrepute".[89] Lamer J. held that s. 24(2):[90]

> ... should thus be read as "the evidence shall be excluded if it is established that, having regard to all the circumstances, the admission of it in the proceedings *could* bring the administration of justice into disrepute". [emphasis in the original]

This test was described by Lamer J. as "less onerous",[91] and in logical terms it must be so. Proof that something could occur is a subset of proof that it would occur. Consequently, the burden imposed by s. 24(2) has been reduced from a burden to establish an almost-certain effect, to a burden to establish a potential effect.

3. Disrepute in Whose Eyes?

Disrepute is not an abstract notion. It is an empirical value that implicates the views of the community at all levels. But the disrepute at the centre of s. 24(2) is not to be discovered by empirical investigation. Public opinion polls concerning the effect of admission or exclusion of evidence on the reputation of the administration of justice are inadmissible for the purposes of s. 24(2).[92] Disrepute in s. 24(2) is a legal standard that must be assessed with an eye to community values, but with judicial detachment from the pressures that can render a community's mood unreasonable.

Initially, some appellate courts applied a test for exclusion taken from Lamer J.'s judgment in *R. v. Rothman*,[93] which came to be known as the "community shock" test.[94] Lamer J. rejected the "community

---

89   *Ibid.*, at 287-88 (S.C.R.).
90   *Ibid.*, at 288 (S.C.R.).
91   *Ibid.*, at 287 (S.C.R.).
92   *Ibid.*, at 281-82 (S.C.R.); see, however, A. Bryant, M. Gold, M. Stevenson and D. Northrup, "Public Attitudes Toward the Exclusion of Evidence: Section 24(2) of the *Canadian Charter of Rights and Freedoms*" (1990), 69 Can. Bar Rev. 1.
93   [1981] 1 S.C.R. 640, 59 C.C.C. (2d) 30, 20 C.R. (3d) 97, 121 D.L.R. (3d) 578, 35 N.R. 485.
94   See *R. v. Stevens* (1983), 7 C.C.C. (3d) 260, at 263, 1 D.L.R. (4th) 465, 35 C.R. (3d) 1 (N.S.C.A.); and *R. v. Chapin* (1983), 7 C.C.C. (3d) 538, at 542, 43 O.R. (2d) 458, 2 D.L.R. (4th) 538, 7 C.R.R. 206 (Ont. C.A.); see *contra R. v. Simmons* (1984), 11 C.C.C. (3d) 193, at 218, 7 D.L.R. (4th) 719, 45 O.R. (2d) 609, 39 C.R. (3d) 233, 3 O.A.C. 1, 26 M.V.R. 168, 7 C.E.R. 159 (Ont. C.A.), per Howland

shock" test for the purposes of s. 24(2) in *Collins*, and instead adopted the test proposed by Professor Morissette in his influential article,[95] in the following terms: "Would the admission of the evidence bring the administration of justice into disrepute in the eyes of the reasonable man, dispassionate and fully apprised of the circumstances of the case?"[96]

4. Discretion or Duty?

The presence of the word "shall" in s. 24(2) mandates exclusion when the conditions of the subsection have been met. A judge who has found that the admission of impugned evidence would bring the administration of justice into disrepute does not possess a discretion to admit the evidence on the basis of other factors.[97] Le Dain J. came to this conclusion in *Therens*,[98] and noted the importance of the distinction between discretion and duty for the purposes of appellate review. It was, therefore, established early that a determination under s. 24(2) is, like any question of admissibility, a question of law.[99]

In *Collins*, Lamer J. expressed general agreement with the proposition that s. 24(2) ". . . does not confer a discretion on the judge but a duty to admit or exclude as a result of his finding."[100] It would be an error, however, to conclude that there is no discretionary element to the judge's task. Later in *Collins*, Lamer J. pointed out that the judge's ". . . discretion is grounded in community values"[101] and his Lordship described a successful application of s. 24(2) as one with which a Court of Appeal would not interfere, on the basis of a reasonableness standard akin to that used to review discretionary judicial acts.[102] A

C.J.O.; affd. [1988] 2 S.C.R. 495, 66 C.R. (3d) 297, 45 C.C.C. (3d) 296, 67 O.R. (2d) 63, 30 O.A.C. 241, 89 N.R. 1, 38 C.R.R. 252, 55 D.L.R. (4th) 673.

95   Y.-M. Morissette, "The Exclusion of Evidence under the *Canadian Charter of Rights and Freedoms*: What to Do and What Not to Do" (1984), 29 McGill L.J. 521, at 538.

96   *R. v. Collins, supra*, note 84, at 282 (S.C.R.).

97   See *contra, R. v. Stevens, supra*, note 94, at 264 (C.C.C.).

98   [1985] 1 S.C.R. 613, at 654, 18 C.C.C (3d) 481, 18 D.L.R. (4th) 655, 45 C.R. (3d) 97, [1984] 4 W.W.R. 286, 40 Sask. R. 122, 38 Alta. L.R. (2d) 99, 13 C.P.R. 193, 32 M.V.R. 153, 59 N.R. 122.

99   *Ibid.*, at 653 (S.C.R.); see also *R. v. Cohen* (1983), 5 C.C.C. (3d) 156, at 165, 33 C.R. (3d) 151, 148 D.L.R. (3d) 78 (B.C.C.A.), per Taggart J.A.

100   *Supra*, note 84, at 275 (S.C.R.).

101   *Ibid.*, at 283 (S.C.R.).

102   *Ibid.*

distinction emerges, then, between the judicial adjudication of disrepute (which necessarily involves discretionary decision-making) and the judicial act of exclusion (which does not). The scope of the discretion, such as it is, is constrained by the legal principles that are rapidly developing around the meaning of "disrepute" in s. 24(2). To ignore, overemphasize or misapply one of these principles will attract appellate review. Conversely, the very brief majority judgment of the Supreme Court of Canada in *R. v. Duguay*[103] makes clear that the Court, while it has the jurisdiction to do so, will not substitute its opinion on a s. 24(2) question for that of the courts below, ". . . absent some apparent error as to the applicable principles or rules of law, or absent a finding that is unreasonable . . . ."

5. The Factors

A judge presented with a s. 24(2) application is required, by the terms of the subsection, to consider "all the circumstances". Lamer J. in *Collins* set out a list of factors that had been regarded as relevant to s. 24(2) by lower courts, as follows:[104]

— what kind of evidence was obtained?

— what *Charter* right was violated?

— was the *Charter* violation serious or was it of a merely technical nature?

— was it deliberate, wilful or flagrant, or was it inadvertent or committed in good faith?

— did it occur in circumstances of urgency or necessity?

— were there other investigatory techniques available?

— would the evidence have been obtained in any event?

— is the offence serious?

— is the evidence essential to substantiate the charge?

— are other remedies available?

Lamer J. did not purport to state the above list as exhaustive,[105] and

---

103 [1989] 1 S.C.R. 93, at 98, 46 C.C.C. (3d) 1, 56 D.L.R. (4th) 46, 67 C.R. (3d) 252, 67 O.R. (2d) 160n, 91 N.R. 201, 31 O.A.C. 177, per Dickson C.J., and McIntyre, Lamer, Wilson, La Forest and Sopinka JJ.
104 *Supra*, note 84, at 283-84 (S.C.R.).
105 *Ibid.*, at 284 (S.C.R.).

expressly held that the final factor, the availability of other remedies, is irrelevant to the evaluation of disrepute: "Once it has been decided that the administration of justice would be brought into disrepute by the admission of the evidence, the disrepute will not be lessened by the existence of some ancillary remedy . . . ."[106]

Lamer J. chose to group the relevant factors into three separate categories, according to the nature of their effect on the reputation of the administration of justice. These three categories, which have been applied in all of the significant s. 24(2) cases decided by the Supreme Court of Canada subsequent to *Collins*, are: (1) factors relevant to the effect of admission on the fairness of the trial;[107] (2) factors relevant to the seriousness of the *Charter* violation;[108] and (3) factors relevant to the effect of exclusion on the reputation of the administration of justice.[109] The first two categories provide separate rationales for the exclusion of evidence, and the third provides a rationale for admission.

D. *The Trial Fairness Rationale*

1. Self-Incriminating Statements

It seems uncontroversial that if the admission of certain evidence would adversely affect the fairness of an accused's trial, the evidence ought to be excluded. For example, the general rules of admissibility reflect the precept that the fairness of an accused's trial would be compromised by the admission of evidence the probative value of which is outweighed by its prejudicial effect.[110] But one does not need s. 24(2) to exclude unfairly prejudicial evidence. What concerned Lamer J. in *Collins* was the unfairness at trial that would result from admitting evidence obtained, following a *Charter* violation, by "conscripting" an accused against himself. Lamer J. stated:[111]

---

106 *Ibid.*, at 286 (S.C.R.).
107 *Ibid.*, at 284-85 (S.C.R.).
108 *Ibid.*, at 285 (S.C.R.).
109 *Ibid.*, at 285-86 (S.C.R.).
110 See e.g., *R. v. Vallières* (1969), 9 C.R.N.S. 24, [1970] 4 C.C.C. 69 (Que. C.A.); *R. v. Bengert (No. 11)* (1980), 15 C.R. (3d) 49, 47 C.C.C. (2d) 552 (B.C.S.C.), at 52 (C.R.); and *Morris v. R.*, [1983] 2 S.C.R. 190, at 201, 36 C.R. (3d) 1, 7 C.C.C. (3d) 97, 1 D.L.R. (4th) 385, 48 N.R. 341.
111 *R. v. Collins*, [1987] 1 S.C.R. 265, at 284-85, 56 C.R. (3d) 193, 38 D.L.R. (4th) 508.

Real evidence that was obtained in a manner that violated the *Charter* will rarely operate unfairly for that reason alone. The real evidence existed irrespective of the violation of the *Charter* and its use does not render the trial unfair. However, the situation is very different with respect to cases where, after a violation of the *Charter*, the accused is conscripted against himself through a confession or other evidence emanating from him. The use of such evidence would render the trial unfair, for it did not exist prior to the violation and it strikes at one of the fundamental tenets of a fair trial, the right against self-incrimination. Such evidence will generally arise out of an infringement of the right to counsel. Our decisions in *Therens, supra,* and *Clarkson v. The Queen,* [1986] 1 S.C.R. 383, are illustrative of this. The use of self-incriminating evidence obtained following a denial of the right to counsel will generally go to the very fairness of the trial and should generally be excluded.

Later, in *R. v. Genest,*[112] Dickson C.J. stated the essence of the trial fairness rationale this way: "Would the admission of the evidence change the balance of the trial because of the nature of the particular *Charter* infringement in that case?"

The premise underlying the trial fairness rationale for exclusion is that it is fundamentally unfair to support a criminal prosecution with evidence created by the accused himself in circumstances in which the evidence would not have come into existence but for the state's failure to accord the accused a constitutionally protected right. The powerfully inculpatory effect of this sort of unconstitutionally obtained evidence effectively deprives the accused of the presumption of innocence, and places a high cost (almost certain conviction) on the accused's exercise of the privilege against self-incrimination at trial.[113]

The distinction that activates the trial fairness rationale is that between real evidence, which existed irrespective of a *Charter* violation, and "conscripted" evidence, which was created by an accused as a consequence of a *Charter* violation. This distinction has not escaped

---

112 [1989] 1 S.C.R. 59, at 83, 45 C.C.C. (3d) 385, 67 C.R. (3d) 224, 91 N.R. 161, 19 Q.A.C. 163.
113 See *R. v. Hebert,* [1990] 2 S.C.R. 151, 57 C.C.C. (3d) 1 (S.C.C.), 77 C.R. (3d) 145, 47 B.C.L.R. (2d) 1, [1990] 5 W.W.R. 1, 110 N.R. 1, 49 C.R.R. 114, per Sopinka J. at 20 (C.C.C.), and per McLachlin J. at 45 (C.C.C.).

criticism,[114] but it is sound in principle. The distinction has firm roots in pre-*Charter* jurisprudence,[115] and it reflects a judicial sentiment against improperly caused self-incrimination. Furthermore, it seems intuitively obvious that the exclusion of pre-existing real evidence could have a different effect on the reputation of the administration of justice than the exclusion of evidence created by an accused as a direct result of police misconduct.

2. Other Evidence Affecting Trial Fairness

Apart from self-incriminatory statements, a few other categories of evidence have been authoritatively characterized as falling within the trial fairness rationale for exclusion. Before *Collins*, the Supreme Court of Canada excluded evidence of breath samples in *R. v. Therens*,[116] on the basis of the effect of the admission of the evidence on the fairness of the trial.[117] Later, in *R. v. Ross*,[118] the Court excluded evidence of an identification parade on the same footing.[119] Lamer J.,

---

114 See R. Delisle, "*Collins*: An Unjustified Distinction" (1987), 56 C.R. (3d) 216; R. Delisle, "*Woolley*: Finding Keys in the Distinction between Statements and Real Evidence" (1988), 63 C.R. (3d) 347; R. Delisle, "The Exclusion of Evidence Obtained Contrary to the *Charter*: Where are We Now?" (1989), 67 C.R. (3d) 288; and N. Gold, "Comment on *Simmons, Dyment, Strachan* and *Genest*" (1989), 31 Crim. L.Q. 260.

115 In *Kuruma, Son of Raniu v. R.*, [1955] A.C. 197, at 205, [1955] 1 All E.R. 236 (P.C.), Lord Goddard C.J. made clear that the general inclusionary rule for real evidence has no application to confessions. See also *R. v. Sang*, [1980] A.C. 402 (H.L.), at 437.

116 [1985] 1 S.C.R. 613, 18 C.C.C. (3d) 481, 45 C.R. (3d) 97, 18 D.L.R. (4th) 655, [1984] 4 W.W.R. 286, 50 Sask. R. 122; see also *R. v. Trask*, [1985] 1 S.C.R. 655, 18 C.C.C. (3d) 514, 45 C.R. (3d) 137, 19 D.L.R. (4th) 123, 54 Nfld. & P.E.I.R. 221, 79 N.R.; additional reasons (1987), 59 C.R. (3d) 179, [1987] 2 S.C.R. 304, 37 C.C.C. (3d) 92; and *R. v. Rahn*, [1985] 1 S.C.R. 659, 45 C.R. (3d) 134, 18 C.C.C. (3d) 516, 19 D.L.R. (4th) 126, [1985] 5 W.W.R. 190, 38 Alta. L.R. (2d) 97, 59 N.R. 144.

117 This was later explained in *R. v. Collins, supra*, note 111, at 284 (S.C.R.); *R. v. Simmons*, [1988] 2 S.C.R. 495, at 534, 45 C.C.C. (3d) 296, 55 D.L.R. (4th) 673, 66 C.R. (3d) 297, 67 O.R. (2d) 63; and *R. v. Jacoy*, [1988] 2 S.C.R. 548, at 559, 45 C.C.C. (3d) 46, 66 C.R. (3d) 336, [1989] 1 W.W.R. 354.

118 [1989] 1 S.C.R. 3, 46 C.C.C. (3d) 129, 67 C.R. (3d) 209, 31 O.A.C. 321, 91 N.R. 81, 37 C.R.R. 369 (*sub nom. R. v. LeClair*).

119 *Cf.* the pre-*Charter* case of *Marcoux v. R.*, [1976] 1 S.C.R. 763, 24 C.C.C. (2d) 1, 60 D.L.R. (3d) 119, 29 C.R.N.S. 211, 4 N.R. 64.

speaking for the majority of the Court in *Ross*, stated:[120]

> . . . the use of any evidence that could not have been obtained but for the participation of the accused in the construction of the evidence for the purposes of the trial would tend to render the trial process unfair.

The applicability of this *dictum* from *Ross* to other investigative procedures is difficult to gauge. We know from *Therens* that it applies to breath samples; and it would seem on its terms to fit well also with other participatory tests, such as roadside sobriety tests.[121] The question remains, however, whether the trial fairness rationale will be held to extend to non-participatory investigative techniques involving, for example, the acquisition of bodily samples from an accused. In the two blood sample cases that have reached the Supreme Court of Canada, *R. v. Pohoretsky*[122] and *R. v. Dyment*,[123] the impugned evidence was excluded; but a close reading of the cases discloses that exclusion resulted from the seriousness of the *Charter* violations at issue,[124] and not from the trial fairness rationale. The Court was invited to deal directly with the question in *R. v. Pinske*,[125] but declined to do so on the basis that there was to be a new trial in any event, and the Court of Appeal had not ruled on the matter.

The Alberta Court of Appeal has held in *R. v. Brick*[126] that blood samples are real evidence, and thus do not raise trial fairness concerns. The Ontario Court of Appeal, on the other hand, has held in *R. v.*

---

120   *Supra*, note 118, at 16 (S.C.R.).
121   See *R. v. McKane* (1987), 35 C.C.C. (3d) 481, 58 C.R. (3d) 130, 49 M.V.R. 1, 21 O.A.C. 73, 31 C.R.R. 354 (Ont. C.A.). Recall that in the United Kingdom, the admission of an improperly obtained sobriety test was regarded as unfair to the accused, even in the absence of a statutory or constitutional exclusionary provision: *R. v. Payne*, [1963] 1 W.W.R. 637 (C.C.A.). See also *Matto v. D.P.P.*, [1987] R.T.R. 337, [1987] Crim. L.R. 641 (Q.B.), in which an improperly obtained breath sample was excluded pursuant to s. 78 of the *Police and Criminal Evidence Act, 1984* (U.K.), c. 60.
122   [1987] 1 S.C.R. 945, 33 C.C.C. (3d) 398, 58 C.R. (3d) 113, 39 D.L.R. (4th) 699, [1987] 4 W.W.R. 590, 47 Man. R. (2d) 295, 75 N.R. 1.
123   [1988] 2 S.C.R. 417, 66 C.R. (3d) 348, 45 C.C.C. (3d) 244, 55 D.L.R. (4th) 503, 10 M.V.R. (2d) 1.
124   See this Chapter, III.E.
125   [1989] 2 S.C.R. 979, 40 B.C.L.R. (2d) 151, 100 N.R. 399, 18 M.V.R. (2d) xxxiv.
126   (1989), 19 M.V.R. (2d) 158 (Alta. C.A.).

Pavel[127] that blood samples are ". . . of a self-incriminatory nature emanating from the [accused]." The point is clearly ripe for decision in the Supreme Court of Canada.

In principle, it is suggested that such evidence is more properly regarded as real evidence, since it exists notwithstanding any *Charter* violation, and is not created by the accused against whom it is adduced.[128] There can be no doubt that the acquisition of bodily samples is qualitatively more invasive than a frisk search or even a fingernail scrape. But subsequent cases have shown that invasiveness is not what triggers the trial fairness rationale. In *R. v. Greffe*,[129] the majority of the Supreme Court of Canada excluded evidence of narcotics obtained by a rectal search involving the insertion of a sigmoidoscope eight inches into the accused's anal canal, but specifically noted that the impugned evidence did not raise trial fairness concerns.[130] The acquisition of evidence of bodily samples squarely raises important issues of personal privacy; but these are more appropriately dealt with in the context of the seriousness of the *Charter* violation, rather than further stretching the notion of trial fairness.[131]

3. Real Evidence and Trial Fairness

The application of the trial fairness rationale to real evidence is, as we have seen, apparently precluded by *Collins*.[132] But there have

---

127 (1989), 53 C.C.C. (3d) 296, 74 C.R. (3d) 195, 36 O.A.C. 328, 19 M.V.R. (2d) 294, at 312 (M.V.R.) (Ont. C.A.); see also *R. v. Tomaso* (1989), 70 C.R. (3d) 152, 33 O.A.C. 106, 14 M.V.R. (2d) 10 (Ont. C.A.).

128 See M. Gelowitz, "Two Aspects of Pohoretsky: A Rejoinder" (1989), 9 M.V.R. (2d) 69, at 75; *cf.* D. Paciocco, "The Judicial Repeal of s. 24(2) and the Development of the Canadian Exclusionary Rule" (1990), 32 Crim. L.Q. 326, at 357-58.

129 [1990] 1 S.C.R. 755, 55 C.C.C. (3d) 161, 75 C.R. (3d) 257, 73 Alta. L.R. (2d) 97, 107 N.R. 1, [1990] 3 W.W.R. 577, 46 C.R.R. 1.

130 *Ibid.*, at 788 (S.C.R.). The evidence was excluded on the basis of the second category of factors, i.e., the seriousness of the violation, discussed this Chapter, III.E.

131 See the remarkable decision in *R. v. Erickson* (1989), 49 C.C.C. (3d) 33, 14 M.V.R. (2d) 122 (B.C.C.A.), in which paint scrapings taken from the accused's boat without his consent were held *not* to constitute pre-existing real evidence.

132 [1987] 1 S.C.R. 265, at 284, 56 C.R. (3d) 193, 38 D.L.R. (4th) 508; see also *R. v. Simmons, supra,* note 116, at 534; *R. v. Jacoy, supra,* note 117, at 559; *R. v. Strachan,* [1988] 2 S.C.R. 980, at 1007, 46 C.C.C. (3d) 479, 56 D.L.R. (4th) 673, 67 C.R. (3d) 87, [1989] 1 W.W.R. 385, 90 N.R. 273, 37 C.R.R. 335; *R. v. Genest,*

been *obiter dicta* in recent judgments of the Supreme Court of Canada that suggest the possibility that in certain circumstances the protective shield of the trial fairness rationale will cover real evidence. In *R. v. Genest*,[133] Dickson C.J., speaking for the Court, held that the admission of evidence of weapons found in the course of an illegal (and therefore unconstitutional) search of the accused's house would not adversely affect the fairness of the accused's trial, on the following grounds:[134]

> The evidence was not created by the breach of a *Charter* right, nor was it found by forcing the appellant to participate in the illegal search or to identify the objects seized in the search.

The implication, of course, is that if either of the latter two conditions had been satisfied, the evidence of the weapons, real evidence, might have triggered the trial fairness rationale for exclusion.

In *R. v. Black*[135] it was necessary for the Court to consider the admissibility of a knife, the alleged murder weapon. The accused had handed the knife over to the police at her apartment, where she had been taken following (indeed, during) a violation of her s. 10(b) right to counsel. Wilson J., speaking for the Court, stated:[136]

> [The knife] did not come into existence as a result of the participation of the accused although the police obtained it as a result of such participation. I have little doubt that the police would have conducted a search of the appellant's apartment with or without her assistance and that such a search would have uncovered the knife.

After noting the principles set out in *Collins* for the treatment of real evidence, Wilson J. continued:[137]

---

133 [1989] 1 S.C.R. 59, at 83, 45 C.C.C. (3d) 385, 67 C.R. (3d) 224, 91 N.R. 161, 19 Q.A.C. 163; *R. v. Black*, [1989] 2 S.C.R. 138, at 164, 50 C.C.C. (3d) 1, 70 C.R. (3d) 97, 98 N.R. 281; *R. v. Debot*, [1989] 2 S.C.R. 1140, at 1176, 52 C.C.C. (3d) 193, 73 C.R. (3d) 129, 102 N.R. 161, 37 O.A.C. 1; and *R. v. Greffe, supra*, note 129, at 788.

133 *Ibid.*

134 *Ibid.*, at 83 (S.C.R.). The evidence was, however, excluded on the basis of the seriousness of the violation: see this Chapter, III.E.

135 *Supra*, note 132.

136 *Ibid.*, at 164 (S.C.R.).

137 *Ibid.*, at 165 (S.C.R.).

Given Lamer J.'s comments [in *Collins*] and the fact that the knife would undoubtedly have been uncovered by the police in the absence of the *Charter* breach and the conscription of the appellant against herself, I do not think that the administration of justice would have been brought into disrepute by the admission of the knife.

This disposition leaves open the question whether real evidence obtained as a consequence of a s. 10(b) violation, but which would not have been discovered but for the violation, can be characterized as falling within the trial fairness rationale for exclusion. The above *dicta* from *Genest* and *Black* appear to suggest an affirmative answer; but a resolution of this question will have to await future cases.[138] In light of the strong indications in *Collins* and *Ross*, it is difficult to see how real evidence, no matter how obtained, could be said to affect the fairness of the trial. The better view seems to be that the admission of real evidence (i.e., tangible evidence not created by the accused as a consequence of a *Charter* violation) must stand or fall on the basis of the seriousness of the *Charter* violation by which it was obtained.

4. Admission Notwithstanding Trial Unfairness

Once impugned evidence has been found to come within the trial fairness rationale, exclusion is virtually certain to follow. The Supreme Court of Canada's consideration of the trial fairness rationale suggests a direct relationship between trial fairness and the reputation of the administration of justice.[139] There have, however, been two instances in which the Supreme Court has admitted evidence which plainly fell within the trial fairness rationale. In *R. v. Tremblay*,[140] the Court admitted breathalyzer evidence obtained following a violation of the accused's s. 10(b) right to counsel on the basis that the police officers'

---

138 See *R. v. Woolley* (1988), 40 C.C.C. (3d) 531, 53 C.R. (3d) 333, 25 O.A.C. 390 (Ont. C.A.), in which the keys to a stolen car were treated as real evidence notwithstanding that the police had been directed to them by an involuntary confession obtained in violation of the accused's s. 7 right to remain silent.

139 See *R. v. Collins, supra*, note 131, at 284 (S.C.R.); *R. v. Black, supra*, note 131, at 160; and *R. v. Hebert*, [1990] 2 S.C.R. 151, 77 C.R. (3d) 145, 57 C.C.C. (3d) 1, at 20-21, 47 B.C.L.R. (2d) 1, [1990] 5 W.W.R. 1, 110 N.R. 1, 49 C.R.R. 114, per Sopinka J.

140 [1987] 2 S.C.R. 435, 37 C.C.C. (3d) 565, 45 D.L.R. (4th) 445, 60 C.R. (3d) 59, 25 O.A.C. 93, 79 N.R. 153, 2 M.V.R. (2d) 289, 32 C.R.R. 381.

haste in requesting a breath sample before the accused had contacted his counsel was provoked by the accused's "violent, vulgar, and obnoxious" behaviour.[141] The outcome in *Tremblay* may represent an emerging principle that an accused will be essentially estopped[142] from seeking the exclusion of evidence obtained as a consequence of reasonable (though unconstitutional) police behaviour that occurs in response to unreasonable behaviour on the part of the accused, even if the evidence would, within the *Collins* framework, render the trial unfair.

In *R. v. Mohl*,[143] the Supreme Court of Canada again admitted breathalyzer evidence, this time in circumstances in which the violation of the accused's s. 10(b) rights was constituted by the fact that the accused, a suspected drunk driver, was too drunk to understand his rights at the time they were read to him.[144] The Court gave no reasons for reversing the judgment of the majority of the Saskatchewan Court of Appeal, but expressed agreement with Sirois J. of the Court of Queen's Bench that the admission of this evidence would not bring the administration of justice into disrepute. The relevant portion of Sirois J.'s judgment reads as follows:[145]

> The logic of my Brother Maher's decision in [*R. v. Schmidt* (1984), 36 Sask. R. 298 (Q.B.)] appeals to me. In summary it is this. Where an accused has by his own actions placed himself in a position of being unable to understand his rights under the Charter, it is not appropriate or just to provide a remedy to the accused. To avoid a conviction by an order for the exclusion of evidence in such circumstances would bring the administration of justice into disrepute.

Given the Supreme Court's repudiation in *Therens* of the view that evidence may be excluded pursuant to s. 24(1),[146] it may be

---

141 *Ibid.*, at 438 (S.C.R.).
142 See D. Paciocco, *supra*, note 128, at 359.
143 [1989] 1 S.C.R. 1389, 47 C.C.C. (3d) 575, 69 C.R. (3d) 399, [1989] 5 W.W.R. 66, 95 N.R. 381, 77 Sask. R. 35.
144 The irony of excluding evidence in a drunk-driving prosecution because the accused was *too* drunk was not lost on Wakeling J.A. (dissenting) in the court below: *R. v. Mohl* (1987), 34 C.C.C. (3d) 435, at 450, 56 C.R. (3d) 318, [1987] 4 W.W.R. 31, 55 Sask. R. 22, 50 M.V.R. 237, 30 C.R.R. 28 (Sask. C.A.).
145 *R. v. Mohl*, Sask. Q.B., unreported, January 9, 1985.
146 See discussion of s. 24(1), text this Chapter, III.B.

inferred that the Court's holding in *Mohl* is an application of the principle that where the administration of justice would be brought into greater disrepute by the exclusion of evidence than by its admission, the evidence ought to be admitted.[147] In *Mohl*, therefore, the exclusionary effect of the trial fairness rationale was overcome by the disrepute that would have resulted from acquitting a plainly guilty accused who had voluntarily rendered himself incapable of comprehending his s. 10(b) rights, *where the reason for the incapacity coincided with an element of the offence charged*. *Mohl* must in this sense be distinguished from *R. v. Clarkson*,[148] in which the police proceeded to interrogate an obviously intoxicated murder suspect without giving her the opportunity to become sufficiently sober to knowingly exercise her s. 10(b) right to counsel. *Clarkson's* inability to understand or effectively waive her rights did not, as in *Mohl*, implicate the central element of the offence with which she was charged.

In this connection, it should be observed that while the decision of the Supreme Court of Canada in *R. v. Duarte*[149] might appear at first glance to be a case in which evidence was admitted contrary to the trial fairness rationale,[150] the case is more properly understood as not implicating the trial fairness rationale at all. *Duarte* concerned evidence of interceptions of private communications by way of "participant surveillance", in violation of s. 8 of the *Charter*, but in accordance with the provisions of the *Criminal Code*.[151] The impugned evidence (the accused's statements) existed apart altogether from the s. 8 violation (the taping of the statements). In no sense did the *Charter* violation in *Duarte* cause the "creation" of evidence by the accused against himself, as was the case in, for example, *Therens, Clarkson, Manninen, Ross,* and *Black*.[152] In these circumstances, the evidence in

---

147 See discussion of the third category of factors, concerning the effect of exclusion, this Chapter, III.B. and E.5.

148 [1986] 1 S.C.R. 383, 25 C.C.C (3d) 207, 26 D.L.R. (4th) 493, 50 C.R. (3d) 289, 69 N.B.R. (2d) 40, 66 N.R. 114.

149 [1990] 1 S.C.R. 30, 53 C.C.C. (3d) 1, 74 C.R. (3d) 281, 65 D.L.R. (4th) 240, 103 N.R. 86, 37 O.A.C. 322, 45 C.R.R. 278; see also *R. v. Wiggins*, [1990] 1 S.C.R. 62, 53 C.C.C. (3d) 476, 74 C.R. (3d) 311, 42 B.C.L.R. (2d) 1, 103 N.R. 118.

150 This interpretation is favoured by D. Paciocco, "The Judicial Repeal of s. 24(2) and the Development of the Canadian Exclusionary Rule" (1990), 32 Crim. L.Q. 326, at 360-62.

151 R.S.C. 1970, c. C-34, s. 178.11(2)(a) [now R.S.C. 1985, c. C-46, s. 184(2)(a)].

152 *R. v. Therens*, [1985] 1 S.C.R. 613, 18 C.C.C. (3d) 481, 18 D.L.R. (4th) 655*n*,

Duarte could not be said to raise trial fairness concerns, and the admissibility of the impugned evidence depended upon the other categories of factors set out in *Collins*.[153]

5. Conclusion

In summary, the trial fairness rationale for exclusion under s. 24(2) is engaged in circumstances in which an accused creates evidence for the prosecution as a consequence of a violation of a *Charter*-protected right, most frequently the s. 10(b) right to counsel. Exclusion of such evidence will usually, but not invariably, follow. This ground for exclusion is not available in principle in respect of real evidence that existed independent of the *Charter* violation. Such evidence may be excluded, if at all, if the court concludes that it is unable to condone the police conduct that resulted in the acquisition of the evidence, in view of the seriousness of the *Charter* violation.

E. *The Seriousness of the Violation: The Dissociation Rationale*

1. General

Much of the discontent with the common law inclusionary rule was generated by the powerlessness of the judicial system in the face of egregious police conduct. The *Wray* rule prevented judges from dissociating themselves from unacceptable means of gathering evidence. Admission of evidence obtained through improper means was seen as judicial condonation of the means themselves. In *R. v. Collins*, Lamer J. indicated that such condonation could bring the administration of justice into disrepute.[154] To determine whether this is so in the circumstances requires a consideration of factors relating to the seriousness of the *Charter* violation that preceded the acquisition of the

---

45 C.R. (3d) 97, [1984] 4 W.W.R. 286, 50 Sask. R. 122; *R. v. Clarkson*, *supra*, note 147; *R. v. Manninen*, [1987] 1 S.C.R. 1233, 34 C.C.C. (3d) 385, 41 D.L.R. 301, 58 C.R. (3d) 97, 61 O.R. (2d) 736*n*; *R. v. Ross*, [1989] 1 S.C.R. 3, 46 C.C.C. (3d) 129, 67 C.R. (3d) 209, 31 O.A.C. 321, 91 N.R. 81, 37 C.R.R. 369 (*sub nom. R. v. LeClair*); *R. v. Black*, [1989] 2 S.C.R. 138, 50 C.C.C. (3d) 1, 70 C.R. (3d) 97, 98 N.R. 281.

153 The evidence was admitted on the basis of good faith: see this Chapter, III.E.2.

154 [1987] 1 S.C.R. 265, at 281, 38 D.L.R. (4th) 508, 56 C.R. (3d) 193.

impugned evidence. If the court concludes that the *Charter* violation was sufficiently serious that the court cannot, by admitting the evidence obtained through the violation, condone it, and must therefore dissociate itself from the unacceptable conduct, the evidence will be excluded in accordance with what might be referred to as the dissociation rationale for exclusion under s. 24(2).

The range of possible *Charter* violations that might fall to be considered under the dissociation rationale is broader than that under the trial fairness rationale, and the range of possible factual circumstances is infinite. There are, however, some important principles that have developed in the decided cases. In his general comments in *Collins* concerning the factors relevant to the seriousness of the *Charter* violation, Lamer J. stated:[155]

> There are other factors which are relevant to the seriousness of the *Charter* violation and thus to the disrepute that will result from judicial acceptance of evidence obtained through that violation. As Le Dain J. wrote in *Therens, supra,* at p. 652:
>
>> The relative seriousness of the constitutional violation has been assessed in the light of whether it was committed in good faith, or was inadvertent or of a merely technical nature, or whether it was deliberate, wilful or flagrant. Another relevant consideration is whether the action which constituted the constitutional violation was motivated by urgency or necessity to prevent the loss or destruction of the evidence.
>
> I should add that the availability of other investigatory techniques and the fact that the evidence could have been obtained without the violation of the *Charter* tend to render the *Charter* violation more serious. We are considering the actual conduct of the authorities and the evidence must not be admitted on the basis that they could have proceeded otherwise and obtained the evidence properly. In fact, their failure to proceed properly when that option was open to them tends to indicate a blatant disregard for the *Charter*, which is a factor supporting the exclusion of the evidence.

---

155 *Ibid.,* at 285 (S.C.R.).

A number of discrete issues arise from consideration of this category of factors. The first, and perhaps most important, of these is the effect of the presence or absence of "good faith" on the part of the state agent whose conduct has been found to violate the *Charter*.

2. Good Faith

Given that the stated purpose of examining the seriousness of the *Charter* violation is to determine whether the violation was so serious that the court must dissociate itself from the resulting evidence,[156] it is not surprising that the *bona fides* of police officers who commit a *Charter* violation is a relevant factor in s. 24(2). A *Charter* violation caused by a reasonable misapprehension of the scope of a police officer's authority is more likely to be condoned than is a "flagrant" violation committed in full knowledge of the absence of authority. However, some early appellate decisions suggested that good faith could serve as a complete answer to an application for exclusion pursuant to s. 24(2). In *R. v. Leveillé*,[157] Anderson J.A. stated:

> Where a police officer acts in good faith and does not act carelessly, maliciously or in deliberate defiance of the rights of an accused person there is *no basis for asserting* that the admission of the evidence would bring the administration of justice into disrepute. [emphasis added]

This extreme position did not survive subsequent developments in the s. 24(2) jurisprudence. It is now clear that good faith cannot rehabilitate evidence that is subject to exclusion in accordance with the trial fairness rationale. In *R. v. Therens*,[158] for example, the police officers' good faith reliance upon the definition of "detention" in the previous Supreme Court of Canada decision in *R. v. Chromiak*[159] did not avail to render the breathalyzer evidence admissible. Further, in *R. v. Hebert*,[160] the Supreme Court of Canada rejected the Crown's

---

156 *Ibid.*
157 (1984), 15 C.C.C. (3d) 258, 13 C.R.R. 327 (B.C.C.A.), at 261 (C.C.C.); applied in *R. v. Gladstone* (1985), 22 C.C.C. (3d) 151, at 174, 47 C.R. (3d) 289, [1985] 6 W.W.R. 504, 18 C.R.R. 99 (B.C.C.A.), per Anderson J.A.
158 *Supra*, note 152.
159 [1980] 1 S.C.R. 471, 49 C.C.C. (2d) 257, 102 D.L.R. (3d) 368, 12 C.R. (3d) 300, 11 Alta. L.R. (2d) 295, 29 N.R. 441.
160 [1990] 2 S.C.R. 151, 77 C.R. (3d) 145, 57 C.C.C. (3d) 1, 47 B.C.L.R. (2d)

argument that evidence of statements made by the accused to an undercover officer in the accused's jail cell (in violation of the accused's s. 7 right to remain silent) ought to be admitted on the basis that the police employed the tactic in reliance upon the common law authority of *R. v. Rothman*.[161] McLachlin J., speaking for the majority in *Hebert*, pointed out that police ignorance of the effect of the *Charter* does not "cure an unfair trial".[162] Sopinka J. (Wilson J. concurring), stated:[163]

> This court's cases on s. 24(2) point clearly, in my opinion, to the conclusion that where impugned evidence falls afoul of the first set of factors set out by Lamer J. in *Collins* (trial fairness), the admissibility of such evidence cannot be saved by resort to the second set of factors (the seriousness of the violation). These two sets of factors are alternative grounds for the *exclusion* of evidence, and not alternative grounds for the *admission* of evidence. It seems odd indeed to assert that evidence the admission of which would render a trial unfair ought to be admitted because the police officer thought he was doing his job. From the accused's perspective (whose trial is *ex hypothesi* proceeding unfairly), it makes little difference that the police officer has a clean conscience in the execution of his duty. [emphasis in the original]

Thus good faith, along with the other factors relating to the seriousness of the *Charter* violation, are determinative only in cases in which the impugned evidence does not raise trial fairness concerns. The absence of good faith may provide an alternative basis for the exclusion of evidence,[164] but it cannot provide an alternative basis for the admission of evidence that would render a trial unfair.[165]

Even in cases in which good faith is relevant, there are important objective prerequisites to a successful allegation that a *Charter* viola-

---

1, [1990] 5 W.W.R. 1, 110 N.R. 1, 49 C.R.R. 114 (S.C.C.).

161 [1981] 1 S.C.R. 640, 59 C.C.C. (2d) 30, 20 C.R. (3d) 97, 121 D.L.R. (3d) 578, 35 N.R. 485.

162 *Supra*, note 160, at 45 (C.C.C.).

163 *Ibid.*, at 20 (C.C.C.).

164 See, e.g., *R. v. Manninen*, *supra*, note 152; and *R. v. Ross*, *supra*, note 152, at 17.

165 See *contra*, *R. v. Elshaw* (1989), 70 C.R. (3d) 197, 45 C.R.R. 140 (B.C.C.A.); leave to appeal to S.C.C. granted, March 1, 1990.

tion was committed in good faith. The first Supreme Court of Canada cases concerning real evidence in which good faith turned the tide were *R. v. Sieben*,[166] and *R. v. Hamill*,[167] both of which were decided simultaneously with *Collins*. In *Sieben* and *Hamill*, the police had executed searches under writs of assistance issued pursuant to the then-existing s. 10(3) of the *Narcotic Control Act*.[168] (The legislation was subsequently repealed,[169] and the Crown did not attempt to support its constitutionality on appeal.) In these circumstances, the police officers' reliance on the authority purportedly granted by the legislation was objectively reasonable, as they could not have been expected to anticipate the unconstitutionality of writs of assistance. In *Sieben*, Lamer J., speaking for the majority, stated:[170]

> The only reason that [the police officers] did not obtain a search warrant is that they believed in good faith that a writ of assistance was sufficient. At that time, the statute authorizing a search under a writ of assistance had not been declared to be inconsistent with the *Charter*.

Sieben and *Hamill* demonstrate that a court will not feel compelled to dissociate itself from evidence obtained by police officers who were entitled to believe that their conduct was proper. The Supreme Court confirmed this interpretation of the effect of good faith in *R. v. Simmons*,[171] and admitted evidence of narcotics which had been obtained ". . . in accordance with existing statutory requirements."[172] Similarly, in *R. v. Jacoy*,[173] released simultaneously with *Simmons*, the Court endorsed the good faith of customs officers who had acted ". . . on a policy directive based on a decision of the Ontario

---

166 [1987] 1 S.C.R. 295, 32 C.C.C. (3d) 574, 38 D.L.R. (4th) 427, 56 C.R. (3d) 225, [1987] 3 W.W.R. 722, 13 B.C.L.R. (2d) 30, 74 N.R. 271, 28 C.R.R. 145.
167 [1987] 1 S.C.R. 301, 33 C.C.C. (3d) 110, 56 C.R. (3d) 220, 38 D.L.R. (4th) 611, 13 B.C.L.R. (2d) 24, [1987] 3 W.W.R. 726, 75 N.R. 126.
168 R.S.C. 1970, c. N-1.
169 S.C. 1985, c. 19, s. 200.
170 *R. v. Sieben, supra*, note 165, at 299 (S.C.R.); see also *R. v. Hamill, supra*, note 167, at 308 (S.C.R.).
171 [1988] 2 S.C.R. 495, 45 C.C.C. (3d) 296, 66 C.R. (3d) 297, 67 O.R. (2d) 63, 55 D.L.R. (4th) 673.
172 *Ibid.*, at 535 (S.C.R.).
173 [1988] 2 S.C.R. 548, 45 C.C.C. (3d) 46, 66 C.R. (3d) 336, [1989] 1 W.W.R. 354.

Court of Appeal."[174] More recently, in *R. v. Duarte*,[175] the Court admitted evidence of unconstitutionally obtained interceptions of private communications in circumstances in which the police relied upon the validity of wiretap provisions of the *Criminal Code* which legalize "participant surveillance". La Forest J., speaking for the majority, stated:[176]

> The police officers acted entirely in good faith. They were acting in accordance with what they had good reason to believe was the law — as it had been for many years before the advent of the *Charter*.

Subsequently, in *R. v. Wong*,[177] the Supreme Court of Canada admitted evidence derived from videotape surveillance on the basis that the surveillance, while contrary to s. 8 of the *Charter*, was not illegal and had not been judicially held to constitute a search within the meaning of s. 8 at the time of the surveillance. Again, the Court regarded the police error to be "an entirely reasonable misunderstanding of the law . . . "[178]

At the opposite end of the spectrum from these cases of good faith are cases in which the *Charter* violation was committed in demonstrable bad faith. Where lawful authority is absent or a legal requirement is circumvented, the Court has effectively ruled out good faith. A "wilful", "deliberate" or "flagrant" *Charter* violation would necessarily be regarded as a far more serious violation from the perspective of the reputation of the administration of justice.[179] In *R.*

---

174 *Ibid.*, at 560 (S.C.R.).
175 [1990] 1 S.C.R. 30, 53 C.C.C. (3d) 1, 74 C.R. (3d) 281, 65 D.L.R. (4th) 240, 103 N.R. 86, 37 O.A.C. 322, 45 C.R.R. 278; see also *R. v. Wiggins*, [1990] 1 S.C.R. 62, 53 C.C.C. (3d) 476, 74 C.R. (3d) 311, 42 B.C.L.R. (2d) 1, 103 N.R. 118.
176 *Ibid.*, at 59 (S.C.R.).
177 (1990), 60 C.C.C. (3d) 460, 1 C.R. (4th) 1, 120 N.R. 34, 45 O.A.C. 250, 2 C.R.R. (2d) 277.
178 *Ibid.*, at 468 (C.C.C.).
179 These terms have become terms of art in the s. 24(2) jurisprudence: see, e.g., *R. v. Therens*, [1985] 1 S.C.R. 613, at 621, 18 C.C.C. (3d) 481, 18 D.L.R. (4th) 655n, 45 C.R. (3d) 97, [1984] 4 W.W.R. 286, 50 Sask. R. 122; *R. v. Clarkson*, [1986] 1 S.C.R. 383, at 397, 25 C.C.C. (3d) 207, 26 D.L.R. (4th) 493, 50 C.R. (3d) 289, 69 N.B.R. (2d) 40, 66 N.R. 114; *R. v. Manninen*, [1987] 1 S.C.R. 1233, at 1245, 34 C.C.C. (3d) 385, 41 D.L.R. 301, 58 C.R. (3d) 97, 61 O.R. (2d) 736n; *R. v. Pohoretsky*, [1987] 1 S.C.R. 945, at 949 (quoted *infra*), 33 C.C.C. (3d) 398,

v. Pohoretsky,[180] a police officer obtained a sample of blood from an unconscious accused suspected of having driven while impaired. At the relevant time, s. 237(2) of the *Criminal Code*[181] provided that no person was required to give a blood sample for the purposes of a drunk driving investigation. Lamer J., speaking for the Supreme Court of Canada, stated that the *Charter* violation:[182]

> ... was wilful and deliberate, and there is no suggestion here that the police acted inadvertently or in good faith, as in, to give examples, the cases of [*Hamill* and *Sieben*], two decisions handed down on the same day as the decision in *Collins*. Quite the contrary. They took advantage of the appellant's unconsciousness to obtain evidence which they had no right to obtain from him without his consent had he been conscious.

An equally serious violation occurred in *R. v. Genest*,[183] in which the police deployed a large number of officers to execute an obviously invalid search warrant, in violation of s. 8 of the *Charter*. Dickson C.J., speaking for the Court, stated:[184]

> Well-established common law limitations on the powers of the police to search were ignored. No attempt was made to justify the amount of force used. There is strong reason to believe that this search is part of a continuing abuse of the search powers, since it follows so closely the pattern set the previous month. While the purpose of s. 24(2) is not to deter police misconduct, the courts should be reluctant to admit evidence that shows the signs of being obtained by an abuse of common law and *Charter* rights by police.

---

39 D.L.R. (4th) 699, 58 C.R. (3d) 113, [1987] 4 W.W.R. 590, 47 Man. R. (2d) 295, 75 N.R. 1; *R. v. Dyment*, [1988] 2 S.C.R. 417, at 439, 66 C.R. (3d) 348, 45 C.C.C. (3d) 244, 55 D.L.R. (4th) 503, 10 M.V.R. (2d) 1; *R. v. Duarte, supra*, note 175; and *R. v. Greffe*, [1990] 1 S.C.R. 755, at 796, 55 C.C.C. (3d) 161, 75 C.R. (3d) 257, 73 Alta. L.R. (2d) 97, 107 N.R. 1, [1990] 3 W.W.R. 577, 46 C.R.R. 1.
180 *Ibid*.
181 R.S.C. 1970, c. C-34; blood samples are now permitted under the Code in certain circumstances: see R.S.C. 1985, c. C-46, s. 254(3)(b).
182 *Supra*, note 179, at 949 (S.C.R.).
183 [1989] 1 S.C.R. 59, 45 C.C.C. (3d) 385, 67 C.R. (3d) 224, 91 N.R. 161, 19 Q.A.C. 163.
184 *Ibid*., at 91 (S.C.R.).

Perhaps the most serious, and certainly the most uncomfortable, instance of bad faith recorded in the Supreme Court's s. 24(2) precedents is the execution in *R. v. Greffe*[185] of a rectal search under the pretext of a search incident to arrest for outstanding traffic warrants. The evidence of narcotics obtained in this search was excluded by a majority of the Court. Lamer J., speaking for the majority, characterized the police conduct as "extreme bad faith",[186] and pointed out that their wilful attempt to circumvent the *Charter* militated in favour of excluding the evidence of narcotics obtained. Significantly, there was no reliance by the police in *Greffe* upon a statutory provision or a previously unchallenged procedure. Lamer J. expressly distinguished *Greffe* from *Duarte*, *Wiggins* and *Hamill* on this basis.[187]

The area that falls between good faith and bad faith is less certain, but it is now clear that good faith cannot be claimed if a *Charter* violation is committed on the basis of a police officer's unreasonable error or ignorance as to the scope of his authority. For example, in *R. v. Dyment*,[188] evidence of the alcohol content of the accused's blood was excluded notwithstanding that the police officer did not knowingly breach the accused's s. 8 rights. The Court refused to condone the "lax police procedures" that led to the acquisition of the evidence.[189] The standard to which the police will be held was adverted to in *R. v. Ross*,[190] in which Lamer J. stated: "The police cannot be excused for misconstruing and misinterpreting the scope of their duty to provide a reasonable opportunity to retain and instruct counsel." In *R. v. Genest*,[191] Dickson C.J. expressed the view that:

---

185 *Supra*, note 179.

186 *Ibid.*, at 798 (S.C.R.).

187 *Ibid.*, at 798-99 (S.C.R.).

188 *Supra*, note 179.

189 *Ibid.*, at 440 (S.C.R.). The seriousness of the s. 8 violation in *Dyment*, as in *Pohoretsky*, *supra*, note 179, was enhanced by the fact that it involved the "sanctity of a person's body": see *infra*.

190 [1989] 1 S.C.R. 3, at 17, 46 C.C.C. (3d) 129, 67 C.R. (3d) 209, 31 O.A.C. 321, 91 N.R. 81, 37 C.R.R. 369 (*sub nom. R. v. LeClair*).

191 *Supra*, note 183, at 87 (S.C.R.). *Cf.*, however, *R. v. Debot*, [1989] 2 S.C.R. 1140, at 1177, 52 C.C.C. (3d) 193, 73 C.R. (3d) 129, 102 N.R. 161, 37 O.A.C. 1, in which Wilson J., speaking for herself on this point, suggested that whether or not the police erred in construing their authority "does not affect the issue of their *bona fides*."

While it is not to be expected that police officers be versed in the *minutiae* of the law concerning search warrants, they should be aware of those requirements that the courts have held to be essential for the validity of a warrant.

. . . the defects in the search warrant were serious and the police officers should have noticed them.

In *R. v. Kokesch*,[192] the Supreme Court of Canada confirmed the objective element of good faith. The Court declined to accede to the Crown submission that good faith was present in circumstances in which the police conducted a warrantless perimeter search of a dwelling house in full knowledge that they did not possess the reasonable and probable grounds necessary to obtain a warrant. Sopinka J., speaking for the majority, stated:[193]

. . . The police must be taken to be aware of this Court's judgments in *Eccles* [[1975] 2 S.C.R. 417] and *Colet* [[1981] 1 S.C.R. 2], and the circumscription of police powers that those judgments represent.

Either the police knew they were trespassing, or they ought to have known. Whichever is the case, they cannot be said to have proceeded in 'good faith', as that term is understood in s. 24(2) jurisprudence.

Ultimately, a finding of good faith (or the lack of it) will turn on the subjective question of the honesty of the mistaken belief said to constitute good faith, and on the objective question of the reasonableness of that belief. Police officers will generally be on safe ground in the execution of express statutory powers, even if those powers are subsequently found to infringe *Charter*-protected rights.

3. Urgency or Necessity

The courts are less likely to feel compelled to dissociate themselves from evidence obtained in circumstances in which urgency or the necessity to preserve evidence caused a *Charter* violation.[194] The

---

192 (1990), 61 C.C.C. (3d) 207, 1 C.R. (4th) 62, 51 B.C.L.R. (2d) 157, [1991] 1 W.W.R. 193, 121 N.R. 161, 50 C.R.R. 285.
193 *Ibid.*, at 230 (C.C.C.).
194 *R. v. Collins*, [1987] 1 S.C.R. 265, at 285, 38 D.L.R. (4th) 508, 56 C.R. (3d) 193 quoting *R. v. Therens, supra*, note 179, at 652 (S.C.R.).

effect of this factor has not been fully canvassed in the authorities, but it would seem in principle to be suitable for application to cases of search and seizure in which exigent circumstances preclude the acquisition of a warrant.[195] The primary use of the notions of urgency and necessity, interestingly, has been in cases in which the court has observed that the seriousness of the *Charter* violation at issue was enhanced by the *absence* of urgency or necessity.[196]

An important example of the positive application of this factor was referred to in *R. v. Genest*.[197] In *Genest*, an aspect of the unreasonableness of the search of the accused's dwelling was the use of excessive force. On appeal, the Crown sought to support the degree of force used on the basis that the police had knowledge of facts which led them to believe that the accused was dangerous, and further, that the eventual discovery of weapons in the search itself indicated the reasonableness of this belief. However, no evidence had been led at trial of any such facts within the knowledge of the police prior to the search. Dickson C.J., speaking for the Supreme Court of Canada, considered the view expressed by Le Dain J. in *Therens*,[198] that urgency is a relevant factor, and continued:[199]

> To this I would add another factor that can be considered, whether the circumstances of the case show a real threat of violent behaviour, whether directed at the police or third parties. Obviously, the police will use a different approach when the suspect is known to be armed and dangerous than they will in arresting someone for outstanding traffic tickets. The consideration of the possibility of violence must, however, be carefully

---

195 *Query* whether it is necessary to incorporate this principle in the application of s. 24(2), given that the warrant requirement in s. 8 is operative only where it is feasible to obtain a warrant: *Hunter v. Southam Inc.*, [1984] 2 S.C.R. 145, at 161, 14 C.C.C. (3d) 97, 41 C.R. (3d) 97, 11 D.L.R. (4th) 641, 33 Alta. L.R. (2d) 193, [1984] 6 W.W.R. 577, 55 N.R. 241, 27 B.L.R. 297, 2 C.P.R. (3d) 1, 9 C.R.R. 355, 84 D.T.C. 6467.

196 See, e.g., *R. v. Clarkson, supra*, note 179, at 397 (S.C.R.); *R. v. Manninen, supra*, note 179, at 1245 (S.C.R.); *R. v. Ross, supra*, note 190; and *R. v. Greffe, supra*, note 179, at 796 (S.C.R.).

197 *Supra*, note 191.

198 *Supra*, note 179, at 652 (S.C.R.), adopted by the Court in *R. v. Collins, supra*, note 194, at 285 (S.C.R.).

199 *R. v. Genest, supra*, note 191, at 89 (S.C.R.).

limited. It should not amount to a *carte blanche* for the police to ignore completely all restrictions on police behaviour. The greater the departure from the standards of behaviour required by the common law and the *Charter*, the heavier the onus on the police to show why they thought it necessary to use force in the process of an arrest or a search. The evidence to justify such behaviour must be apparent in the record, and must have been available to the police at the time they chose their course of conduct. The Crown cannot rely on *ex post facto* justifications.

The argument that additional force was justified in *Genest* failed, because the necessary evidence to substantiate the argument had not been led: "The Crown cannot try to rehabilitate its case later on appeal."[200]

Urgency and necessity are probably best understood as elements of good faith. This factor will militate against exclusion of impugned evidence only where there has been a sincere effort to comply with the *Charter* that has been thwarted by circumstances beyond the control of the investigating officers.[201]

4. Availability of Other Investigative Techniques

The terms in which Lamer J. stated in *Collins* that the availability of other investigative techniques is a relevant factor are crucial to an understanding of the direction in which this factor can cut.[202] A *Charter* violation will be *more* serious if it is committed despite the availability of other constitutional investigative techniques. It does not follow, however, that a *Charter* violation will be *less* serious if it is committed in circumstances in which no constitutional investigative technique is available. For example, the s. 8 violation in *R. v. Dyment*[203] was

---

200 *Ibid.*, at 91; see also *R. v. Greffe*, [1990] 1 S.C.R. 755, at 775, 790 and 798, 55 C.C.C. (3d) 161, 75 C.R. (3d) 257, 73 Alta. L.R. (2d) 97, 107 N.R. 1, [1990] 3 W.W.R. 577, 46 C.R.R. 1, in which Lamer J. confirmed that the subsequent discovery of evidence cannot influence the court's evaluation of the existence of reasonable and probable grounds, or of the seriousness of the *Charter* violation.
201 See *R. v. Strachan*, [1988] 2 S.C.R. 980, at 1008, 46 C.C.C. (3d) 479, 56 D.L.R. (4th) 673, 67 C.R. (3d) 87, [1989] 1 W.W.R. 385, 90 N.R. 273, 37 C.R.R. 335.
202 *R. v. Collins, supra*, note 194, at 285 (S.C.R.).
203 [1988] 2 S.C.R. 417, 6 C.R. (3d) 348, 45 C.C.C. (3d) 244, 55 D.L.R. (4th) 503, 10 M.V.R. (2d) 1.

regarded as more serious than it would otherwise have been precisely because the police officer did not have the necessary reasonable and probable grounds that would have permitted him to obtain a search warrant to obtain the blood sample that had previously been collected for medical purposes.[204] La Forest J., speaking for the majority of the Court concerning s. 24(2), regarded the acquisition of this blood sample as a "flagrant breach of personal privacy", in circumstances in which ". . . there are well-known and recognized procedures for obtaining such evidence when the police have reasonable and probable grounds for believing a crime has been committed."[205]

In *R. v. Kokesch*,[206] in which a warrant was not obtained precisely because the requisite grounds were not present, the Court clearly expressed the conclusion that the absence of other investigative techniques cannot serve as a justificatory factor in s. 24(2). To the contrary, Sopinka J. stated for the majority.[207]

> In my respectful view, the unavailability of other, constitutionally permissible, investigative techniques is neither an excuse nor a justification for constitutionally impermissible investigative techniques.
>
> . . .
>
> Where the police have nothing but suspicion and no legal way to obtain other evidence, it follows that they must leave the suspect alone, not charge ahead and obtain evidence illegally and unconstitutionally. Where they take this latter course, the Charter violation is plainly more serious than it would be otherwise, not less. Any other conclusion leads to an indirect but substantial erosion of the *Hunter* standards: the Crown would happily concede s. 8 violations if they could routinely achieve admission under s. 24(2) with the claim that the police did not obtain a warrant *because* they did not have reasonable and probable grounds. The irony of this result is self-evident. [emphasis in the original]

---

204 See *R. v. Carter* (1982), 2 C.C.C. (3d) 412, 2 C.R. (3d) 76, 31 C.R. (3d) 76, 39 O.R. (2d) 439, 18 M.V.R. 9, 2 C.R.R. 280, 144 D.L.R. (3d) 301 (Ont. C.A.), cited in *R. v. Dyment, ibid.*, at 437 (S.C.R.).

205 *Ibid.*, at 439 (S.C.R.).

206 *Supra*, note 192.

207 *Ibid.*, at 227 (C.C.C.).

5. Other Factors Affecting the Seriousness of the Violation

As was pointed out at the outset of this section, the variability of factual circumstances that may fall to be considered under the rubric of the seriousness of the *Charter* violation is infinite. There are, however, a few contextual facts that have been identified as being relevant to the assessment of seriousness, particularly in cases of unreasonable search and seizure, contrary to s. 8 of the *Charter*.

First, the fact that an unreasonable search is conducted in a person's dwelling-house renders the *Charter* violation more serious than it would otherwise have been, as indicated by the Supreme Court of Canada in *R. v. Hamill*.[208] This principle may harken back to the common law's solicitude for an individual's dominion over his or her home: ". . . the house of every one is to him as his (a) castle and fortress . . . ."[209] In any event, it is a recognition that an unjustified intrusion into an individual's living space is a serious encroachment on the individual's reasonable expectation of privacy — the core value protected by s. 8 of the *Charter*.[210]

Second, the judgments of the Supreme Court in *R. v. Pohoretsky*,[211] *R. v. Dyment*[212] and *R. v. Greffe*,[213] represent the common-sense principle that ". . . a violation of the sanctity of a person's body is much more serious than that of his office or even of his home."[214] This heightened scrutiny of evidence obtained by searches involving an individual's bodily integrity is consistent with the heightened scrutiny of the reasonableness of the searches themselves.[215]

And third, it has consistently been held to be a relevant mitigating factor under s. 24(2) that an unreasonable search was conducted

---

208 [1987] 1 S.C.R. 301, at 307, 33 C.C.C. (3d) 110, 56 C.R. (3d) 220, 38 D.L.R. (4th) 611, 13 B.C.L.R. (2d) 24, [1987] 3 W.W.R. 726, 75 N.R. 126.
209 *Semayne's Case* (1604), 5 Co. Rep. 91a, 77 E.R. 194, at 195 [E.R.].
210 *Hunter v. Southam Inc., supra*, note 195, at 159-60 (S.C.R.).
211 [1987] 1 S.C.R. 945, 33 C.C.C. (3d) 398, 39 D.L.R. (4th) 699, 58 C.R. (3d) 113, [1987] 4 W.W.R. 590, 47 Man. R. (2d) 295, 75 N.R. 1.
212 *Supra*, note 203.
213 [1990] 1 S.C.R. 755, 55 C.C.C. (3d) 161, 75 C.R. (3d) 257, 73 Alta. L.R. (2d) 97, 107 N.R. 1, [1990] 3 W.W.R. 577, 46 C.R.R. 1.
214 *R. v. Pohoretsky, supra*, note 211, at 949 (S.C.R.); see also *R. v. Dyment, supra*, note 203, at 439 (S.C.R.), and *R. v. Greffe, ibid.*, at 795 (S.C.R.).
215 See *Hunter v. Southam Inc., supra*, note 195, at 168 (S.C.R.); and *R. v. Simmons*, [1988] 2 S.C.R. 495, at 517, 45 C.C.C. (3d) 296, 55 D.L.R. (4th) 673, 66 C.R. (3d) 297, 67 O.R. (2d) 63.

on the basis of reasonable and probable grounds. In *Collins*, the Crown at trial had been prevented by a wrongly upheld defence objection from proving that the police officer who had applied a choke hold on the accused had reasonable and probable grounds to believe that she was carrying drugs in her mouth. The majority of the Court took the view that if reasonable and probable grounds were established at the new trial, the evidence would not be excluded.[216] Cases in which the existence of reasonable and probable grounds lessened the seriousness of the violation include *R. v. Sieben*,[217] *R. v. Jacoy*[218] and *R. v. Duarte*.[219] Conversely, as we have seen, the absence of reasonable and probable grounds in a s. 8 case can significantly augment the seriousness of the violation, as in *R. v. Greffe*.[220]

F. *Effect of Exclusion on the Reputation of the Administration of Justice*

The final category of factors relevant to the evaluation of disrepute set out by the Supreme Court in *Collins* consists of factors relevant to the effect that exclusion of impugned evidence could have on the reputation of the administration of justice. It was apparent as early as *Therens* that in some circumstances the exclusion, and not the admission, of evidence could bring the administration of justice into disrepute.[221] In *Collins*, Lamer J. held that such disrepute, which would be greater in proportion with the seriousness of the offence charged, could arise from ". . . the exclusion of evidence essential to substantiate the charge, and thus the acquittal of the accused, because of a trivial breach of the *Charter*."[222] This factor has been employed in cases of

---

216 *R. v. Collins*, [1987] 1 S.C.R. 265, at 288-89, 38 D.L.R. (4th) 508, 56 C.R. (3d) 193.
217 [1987] 1 S.C.R. 295, at 299, 32 C.C.C. (3d) 574, 38 D.L.R. (4th) 427, 56 C.R. (3d) 225, [1987] 3 W.W.R. 722, 13 B.C.L.R. (2d) 30, 74 N.R. 271, 28 C.R.R. 145.
218 [1988] 2 S.C.R. 548, at 560, 45 C.C.C. (3d) 46, 66 C.R. (3d) 336, [1989] 1 W.W.R. 354.
219 [1990] 1 S.C.R. 30, at 60, 53 C.C.C. (3d) 1, 74 C.R. (3d) 281, 65 D.L.R. (4th) 240, 103 N.R. 86, 37 O.A.C. 322, 45 C.R.R. 278.
220 *Supra*, note 213, at 793 (S.C.R.).
221 See *R. v. Therens*, [1985] 1 S.C.R. 613, at 622-23, 18 C.C.C. (3d) 481, 18 D.L.R. (4th) 655, 45 C.R. (3d) 97, [1984] 4 W.W.R. 286, 50 Sask. R. 122, per McIntyre J. (dissenting).
222 *R. v. Collins, supra*, note 216, at 286 (S.C.R.).

good faith to support the finding that the *Charter* violation was not serious, and that the evidence ought not to be excluded.[223]

It would seem, however, that the effect of exclusion on disrepute will not salvage the admissibility of evidence that was obtained through a serious *Charter* violation. In *R. v. Genest*,[224] in which a serious s. 8 violation was held to have occurred, Dickson C.J. dealt with this category of factors in a single paragraph and concluded that it could not assist, on the basis that ". . . the breach was not merely technical or minor."[225]

Furthermore, it was made clear in *Collins* that this third category of factors could not operate to admit evidence otherwise excluded in accordance with the trial fairness rationale, regardless of the seriousness of the offence charged:[226]

> If any relevance is to be given to the seriousness of the offence in the context of the fairness of the trial, it operates in the opposite sense: the more serious the offence, the more damaging to the system's disrepute would be an unfair trial.

This point has been reiterated by the Court in *R. v. Manninen*,[227] *R. v. Black*[228] and *R. v. Brydges*.[229] It is significant that in *R. v. Ross*,[230] a case concerning the trial fairness rationale, the effect of exclusion on the reputation of the administration of justice was not even mentioned.

It is evident from the s. 24(2) jurisprudence that has developed to date that the effect of exclusion is primarily a tool for reinforcing a conclusion that a particular *Charter* violation was not sufficiently serious to warrant exclusion. It is doubtful that this category of factors will emerge as an independent ground of admission.

---

223 See *R. v. Simmons, supra*, note 215, at 535 (S.C.R.); and *R. v. Strachan*, [1988] 2 S.C.R. 980, at 1008, 46 C.C.C. (3d) 479, 67 C.R. (3d) 87, 56 D.L.R. (4th) 673, [1989] 1 W.W.R. 385, 90 N.R. 273, 37 C.R.R. 335.

224 [1989] 1 S.C.R. 59, 45 C.C.C. (3d) 385, 67 C.R. (3d) 224, 91 N.R. 161, 19 Q.A.C. 163.

225 *Ibid.*, at 92 (S.C.R.).

226 *Supra*, note 216, at 286 (S.C.R.).

227 [1987] 1 S.C.R. 1233, at 1246, 34 C.C.C. (3d) 385, 58 C.R. (3d) 97, 41 D.L.R. 301, 61 O.R. (2d) 736*n*.

228 [1989] 2 S.C.R. 138, at 160, 50 C.C.C. (3d) 1, 70 C.R. (3d) 97, 98 N.R. 281.

229 [1990] 1 S.C.R. 190, at 211, 53 C.C.C. (3d) 330, 74 C.R. (3d) 129, 71 Alta. L.R. (2d) 145, 103 N.R. 282, [1990] 2 W.W.R. 220, per Lamer J.

230 [1989] 1 S.C.R. 3, 46 C.C.C. (3d) 129, 67 C.R. (3d) 209, 31 O.A.C. 321, 91 N.R. 81, 37 C.R.R. 369 (*sub nom. R. v. LeClair*).

IV   THE CRIMINAL CODE

A. *Electronic Surveillance*

1. General

A significant source of illegally obtained evidence arises from the widespread use of electronic surveillance (hereinafter also referred to as wiretaps) by law enforcement agencies. By virtue of the peremptory provisions of the *Criminal Code*, the interception of private communication is a criminal offence and, absent compliance with these provisions, the evidence obtained is inadmissible. These provisions are contained in Part VI of the *Criminal Code* under the heading "Invasion of Privacy". The terms under which the interception of private communication is authorized are technical and complex. A detailed examination of these provisions is beyond the scope of a work on evidence.[231] Tension is created between these provisions and s. 24(2) of the *Charter* when the interception of private communication is carried out in a manner that violates constitutional rights.

2. Illegal Wiretaps

The prohibition with respect to wiretaps extends to all private communication by means of any "electro-magnetic, acoustic, mechanical or other device". Any oral communication or telecommunication in respect of which there is a reasonable expectation that it will not be intercepted except by the person intended to receive it qualifies as a private communication.[232] The requirement that the communication be "intercepted" appears to exclude from the prohibition the recording of a communication by the person who is

---

231 For a comprehensive treatment of this subject, see D. Watt, "Law of Electronic Surveillance in Canada" (Toronto: Carswell, 1979). Many of these provisions and their application and non-application are discussed in a series of wiretap cases in the Supreme Court of Canada. See *R. v. Thompson*, [1990] 2 S.C.R. 1111, 59 C.C.C. (3d) 225, 80 C.R. (3d) 129, 73 D.L.R. (4th) 596, 49 B.C.L.R. (2d) 321, [1990] 6 W.W.R. 481, 114 N.R. 1, 50 C.R.R. 1; *Dersch v. Canada (A.G.)*, [1990] 2 S.C.R. 1505, 60 C.C.C. (3d) 132, 80 C.R. (3d) 299, 77 D.L.R. (4th) 473, 51 B.C.L.R. (2d) 145, 116 N.R. 340, [1991] 1 W.W.R. 231, 43 O.A.C. 256 (*sub nom. R. v. Dersch*); *R. v. Garofoli*, [1990] 2 S.C.R. 1421; *R. v. Lachance*, [1990] 2 S.C.R. 1490, 60 C.C.C. (3d) 449, 80 C.R. (3d) 374, 116 N.R. 325, 43 O.A.C. 241, 50 C.R.R. 260; *R. v. Zito*, [1990] 1 S.C.R. 1520, 60 C.C.C. (3d) 216, 80 C.R. (3d) 311, 116 N.R. 357, 43 O.A.C. 273.
232 R.S.C. 1985, c. C-46, ss. 183 and 184(2).

expected to receive it. Furthermore, by virtue of s. 184(2), the interception of a communication with the consent of one of the participants is exempted. In *R. v. Duarte*,[233] the Supreme Court of Canada held that, in the absence of an authorization, an interception in the circumstances giving rise to the exemption in s. 184(2) constituted an unreasonable search and seizure. Moreover, while the interception in *Duarte* was illegal in that it violated the *Charter*, it was not unlawful within the terms of s. 184 so as to be rendered automatically inadmissible. Its exclusion turned on the application of s. 24(2) of the *Charter*.

It is still arguable that in circumstances in which the intended recipient records the communication there is no interception and that the *Criminal Code* provisions do not apply. Furthermore, this may constitute a lesser invasion of privacy than the situation in *Duarte* and therefore not run afoul of s. 8 of the *Charter*. Although no point of this was made in *Duarte*, a further significant distinction may be that, in the situation dealt with in that case which involved an interception, an authorization could have been obtained under ss. 185 and 186. Where there is no interception, ss. 185 and 186 do not apply and no authorization can be obtained.[234]

Tension is set up between the provisions of the *Criminal Code* and s. 24(2) of the *Charter* where the evidence is obtained in a manner that is both unlawful and unconstitutional. By virtue of s. 189 of the *Criminal Code*, the evidence is automatically excluded, whereas s. 24(2) requires that the party seeking exclusion discharge the burden of satisfying the court that its admission would bring the administration of justice into disrepute. The matter has been resolved by the Supreme Court of Canada. A party against whom evidence is tendered which is tainted with the dual illegality referred to above, is entitled to the benefit of the rule of absolute exclusion in the *Criminal Code*. Section 24(2) cannot be used to render admissible what Parliament has said is inadmissible.[235]

---

233 [1990] 1 S.C.R. 30, 53 C.C.C. (3d) 1, 74 C.R. (3d) 281, 65 D.L.R. (4th) 240, 103 N.R. 86, 37 O.A.C. 322, 45 C.R.R. 278.
234 *Criminal Code*, R.S.C. 1985, c. C-46, s. 183 defines authorization as "an authorization to *intercept* a private communication . . ." [emphasis added].
235 *R. v. Thompson, supra*, note 231, at 1153. *R. v. Garofoli, supra*, note 231, at 1453.

3. Establishing Illegality

The procedural mosaic to determine admissibility of wiretap evidence was set out in *R. v. Garofoli*[236] as follows:

> First there is a "*Parsons voir dire*," named after *R. v. Parsons* (1977), 37 C.C.C. (2d) 497 (Ont. C.A.), affd [1980] 1 S.C.R. 785, *sub nom. Charette v. The Queen*. The function of this hearing before the trial judge is to determine such issues as whether the authorization is valid on its face, whether the police executed the interception within the terms of the authorization, and whether statutory requirements such as reasonable notice were complied with. The remedy is exclusion under s. 178.16. The second is the "*Wilson* application." This hearing takes place before the issuing court, to determine the substantive or subfacial validity of the affidavit. The remedy is the setting aside of the authorization. The third is a "*Garofoli* hearing." This is a hearing before the trial judge to determine the compliance of the authorization with s. 8 of the *Charter*. The remedy is a determination under s. 24(2) of the *Charter*. The fourth, and last, procedure is a "*Vanweenan* hearing," so-called after one of the appellants in *R. v. Chesson*, [1988] 2 S.C.R. 148. This again is a *voir dire* before the trial judge, but with the object of determining whether the authorization names all "known" persons as required by ss. 178.12(1)(*e*) and 178.13(2)(*c*). The remedy again is exclusion under s. 178.16.

In *Garofoli*, the Court reviewed its decision in *Wilson v. R.*[237] and concluded that where there is an attack on an authorization on the basis of the *Charter*, the so-called "*Wilson* application" can be made before the trial judge even if the authorization was granted by a higher court. The Court also expanded the right to cross-examine on the affidavit filed in support of the authorization. While the application to unseal the "packet" containing the documents relating to the application must still be made to a judge designated by s. 187 of the *Criminal Code*, the granting of an order to open the packet is virtually *pro forma*.[238]

---

236 *Ibid*, at 1445 (S.C.R.).
237 [1983] 2 S.C.R. 594, 9 C.C.C. (3d) 97, 37 C.R. (3d) 97, 4 D.L.R. (4th) 577, 51 N.R. 321, 26 Man. R. (2d) 194, [1984] 1 W.W.R. 481.
238 *Dersch v. Canada (A.G.)*, *supra*, note 231.

B. *Other Statutory Rules*

The *Criminal Code* contains statutory pre-conditions for the reception of certain types of evidence relating to the seizure of breath and blood samples from drivers of motor vehicles for use in prosecutions for several drinking and driving offences.[239] Several interrelated provisions of the *Criminal Code* create investigative, procedural and evidentiary rules which address particular concerns that arise in this area, such as the need to gather reliable evidence, the placing of limits on police powers, and the protection of an individual's right against self-incrimination. Although failure to comply with these conditions does not mean that the sample is obtained "illegally" (in the way that a wiretap is if the statutory conditions are not met[240]), it is useful to consider this type of evidence in this context since the lack of express authorization could ultimately result in the exclusion of the evidence, or at least the certificate of analysis, on the basis of the *Charter* or other general evidentiary rules.

The rules governing police powers to obtain breath and blood samples reflect a balancing of the degree of intrusion and the seriousness of the offence being investigated. For example, if a police officer reasonably suspects that a person operating a motor vehicle has alcohol in his or her body, the police officer may obtain on demand a sample of breath suitable for analysis by a roadside screening device.[241] In contrast, a non-consensual seizure of a sample of blood requires that the officer first obtain a warrant. A warrant may be issued if a justice is satisfied that the police officer has reasonable and probable grounds to believe that the driver has within the preceding two hours committed a drinking and driving offence, that the driver was involved in an accident resulting in death or bodily harm, and that a qualified medical practitioner is of the opinion that the driver is unable to consent and that the taking of the samples of blood would not endanger the life or health of the person.[242]

---

239 See for example, R.S.C. 1985, c. C-46, ss. 254, 256.
240 See this Chapter, IV.A.2.
241 *Supra*, note 239, s. 254(2).
242 *Ibid.*, s. 256.

Where the taking of a bodily sample is without the individual's properly obtained consent, *Charter* issues can arise. The search may be an unreasonable search and seizure under s. 8 of the *Charter* and therefore be subject to exclusion by virute of s. 24(2) of the *Charter*.[243] The same evidence that shows that the statutory conditions were not met, may be proof that the search was obtained in contravention of the *Charter*. But leaving aside such constitutional considerations,[244] the absence of these statutory grounds would mean that the certificate evidence of the blood alcohol analysis was inadmissible hearsay evidence.[245] It may still be open to the Crown to call the analyst to prove the breath or blood sample in a non-hearsay manner and this expert could testify on the basis of the sample as to the state of the accused's intoxication at the time of the offence. Failure to meet the statutory conditions, however, deprives the Crown of the statutory presumptions that would assist in making out the case against the accused. The *Criminal Code* provisions create procedural rules, such as the requirement to take breathalizer samples forthwith or as soon as practicable, to take a first sample no later than two hours after the alleged offence was committed, and to take the second sample after a fifteen minute interval has elapsed.[246] Failure to comply with these statutory requirements deprives the Crown of the benefit of a statutory presumption to prove the blood alcohol concentration of the accused at the time the offence was alleged to have been committed by means of a certificate.[247] Additionally, the Crown must give the accused reasonable notice of its intention to adduce at trial a certificate of analysis of

---

243 See P.K. McWilliams, *Canadian Criminal Evidence*, 3rd ed. (Aurora: Canada Law Book, 1988), at 4-40 to 4-45 for a discussion of these *Charter* concerns. The effect of s. 24(2) on the exclusion of evidence was discussed in this Chapter, III.
244 Cases considering such issues include *R. v. Hufsky*, [1988] 1 S.C.R. 621, 63 C.R. (3d) 14, 40 C.C.C. (3d) 398, 27 O.A.C. 103, 4 M.V.R. (2d) 170, 84 N.R. 365, 32 C.R.R. 193 (S.C.C.); *R. v. Dyment* (1986), 49 C.R. (3d) 338, 25 C.C.C. (3d) 120 (P.E.I. C.A.); affd. [1988] 2 S.C.R. 417, 45 C.C.C. (3d) 244, 66 C.R. (3d) 348, 55 D.L.R. (4th) 503, 73 Nfld. & P.E.I.R. 13, 10 M.V.R. (2d) 1 (S.C.C.); *R. v. Pohoretsky*, [1987] 1 S.C.R. 945, 33 C.C.C. (3d) 398, 58 C.R. (3d) 113, 39 D.L.R. (4th) 699, [1987] 4 W.W.R. 590, 47 Man. R. (2d) 295, 75 N.R. 1.
245 *R. v. Janzen* (1986), 49 Sask. R. 312, 41 M.V.R. 1 (C.A.); *R. v. Forbes* (1986), 40 M.V.R. 224, 72 N.S.R. (2d) 308, 173 A.P.R. 308 (N.S.C.A.).
246 *Supra*, note 239, s. 258.
247 *R. v. Noble*, [1978] 1 S.C.R. 632, 40 C.R.N.S. 19, 37 C.C.C. (2d) 193, 80 D.L.R. (3d) 69, 17 N.R. 555, 19 N.B.R. (2d) 417 (S.C.C.).

the seized sample together with a copy of the certificate.[248] Again, failure to satisfy the statutory pre-conditions renders the certificate of analysis inadmissible. As the case law demonstrates, these provisions have been thoroughly challenged and reviewed by the courts.[249]

---

248 *Supra*, note 244.

249 E.g., *Curr v. R.*, [1972] S.C.R. 889, 7 C.C.C. (2d) 181, 18 C.R.N.S. 281, 26 D.L.R. (3d) 603; *R. v. Altseimer* (1982), 1 C.C.C. (3d) 7, 29 C.R. (3d) 276, 142 D.L.R. (3d) 246, 38 O.R. (2d) 783, 17 M.V.R. 8 (Ont. C.A.); *R. v. Gaff* (1984), 15 C.C.C. (3d) 126, 36 Sask. R. 1 (C.A.); leave to appeal to S.C.C. refd 37 Sask. R. 160*n*, 57 N.R. 75*n*.

CHAPTER 10

CHARACTER EVIDENCE

I GENERALLY

In the decisions that we make about the conduct of others in our daily lives, character is perhaps the most important single factor. People act and react and go about their everyday business on their expectations of what others will do. It is common sense when asked to judge a person's conduct on a particular occasion to enquire how that person behaved on other occasions. The conclusion may be expressed in terms of moral and mental qualities, but these are in turn determined only by what a person says and does. Wigmore defines character as:[1]

> a person's disposition — i.e., a trait, or group of traits, or the sum of his traits . . . .

McCormick defines character:[2]

> Character is a generalized description of one's disposition, or of one's disposition in respect to a general trait, such as honesty, temperance or peacefulness . . .

Character in its wider sense is simply a compendious summary of a person's past actions, good and bad.

In the early history of the law, character was the major determinant of a person's fate at the hands of the law. The following is an

---

1 1A Wigmore, *Evidence* (Tillers rev. 1983), § 52, at 1146.
2 E.W. Cleary (ed.), *McCormick on Evidence*, 3rd ed. (St. Paul: West Publishing, 1984), at 574.

account of the role of character in an eleventh century trial:[3]

> The opinion of neighbours always prevailed, and a trial was a test of character: the question was, 'can the oath of the defendant be relied upon?' Notoriety in England, as in many primitive societies, was for long as good a reason for condemning a man as proof of a particular crime: a man 'regarded with suspicion by all the people', said Canute, was to be put under surety by the king's reeve to answer any charges brought against him, and if he had no surety he was to be slain and to lie in unconsecrated ground.

When the ordeal was the favourite mode of trial, character and reputation became especially important.[4]

> The more notorious a criminal, the greater was his ordeal. He must fast, go to Mass and swear to his innocence; then he holds the hot iron (if the burn festers, he is guilty); or is lowered into water (he is guilty if he floats, for the water rejects him); or, if he is a clerk, swallows the sacred morsel which has been adjured to choke the guilty man.

While it would be difficult to argue from a common sense point of view that evidence of an accused person's bad or criminal character is not logically relevant or is lacking in probative value, the danger that it will be used illogically or given too much weight is considerable.[5] The logical function of character evidence may be shown by the following illustration. If a person is accused of stealing, his or her reputation as a thief logically weighs heavily against him or her. There is strong tendency, however, that evidence of bad character will produce a dislike or hatred for the person against whom the evidence is tendered which may result in an adverse finding to vindicate the trier's feelings. Other drawbacks are that its introduction may create unfair surprise, may detract from the issues, or be too time-consuming having regard for its probative value. It was perhaps because of these

---

3   Harding, A., *A Social History of English Law* (Baltimore: Penguin, 1966), at 22.

4   Harding, *ibid.*, at 24.

5   For a fuller explanation of the danger inherent in the use of evidence of the accused's bad character, see Chapter 11, II.

possible prejudicial effects on juries that for a period of time in English legal history the use of bad character evidence was in disrepute, epitomized by the abolition of its use in criminal cases.[6] There has been a gradual erosion of this ultraprotective attitude. Character evidence is, as a general rule, now excluded, not because it is irrelevant, but on policy grounds.[7] It is the purpose of this chapter to examine the extent to which the erosion of the ultraprotective attitude has taken place with respect to both civil and criminal cases. In each of these areas, evidence of character can be introduced either as tending to prove or negate a fact in issue or because it is a fact in issue.[8]

II   CHARACTER AS A FACT IN ISSUE

A. *In Civil Cases*

Character may be directly in issue, either on the question of liability or the quantum of damages. In such cases, no special rules apply. The cause of action in which this most frequently occurs is a defamation action. In a number of jurisdictions, causes of action can still be maintained for breach of promise to marry, seduction and actions in which damages for adultery are claimed. Character may often be in issue in these proceedings.

1. Defamation

(a) *Evidence of Good Character of Plaintiff*

In an action for libel or slander, although the good character of the plaintiff is presumed at the outset, the plaintiff may adduce evidence through witnesses as to his or her reputation.[9] It is generally accepted that the plaintiff cannot give evidence as to his or her own reputation.[10]   The types of question which the character witnesses

---

6   1A Wigmore, *Evidence* (Tillers rev., 1983), § 57 at 1180-197.
7   *R. v. McMillan* (1975), 23 C.C.C. 160, at 167, 29 C.R.N.S. 191, 7 O.R. (2d) 750 (Ont. C.A.); affd. [1977] 2 S.C.R. 824, 33 C.C.C. (2d) 360, 73 D.L.R. (3d) 759.
8   The exception to the exclusion of bad character evidence for admissible similar fact evidence is considered in Chapter 11.
9   *Plato Films Ltd. v. Speidel*, [1961] 1 All E.R. 876, at 889, [1961] A.C., at 1105 (H.L.).
10   *Ibid.*, at 892 (All E.R.).

may answer are:[11]

> What are you? [i.e. what is your profession or occupation?]
>
> How long have you known him?
>
> Have you known him well? Have you had an opportunity of observing his conduct?
>
> What character has he borne during that time for honesty, morality or loyalty [according to the nature of the case]?
>
> As far as you know, has he deserved that character?

A character witness called by the plaintiff cannot, however, be asked questions in examination-in-chief about particular facts to illustrate the plaintiff's good behaviour. In cross-examination, however, the witness may be asked about particular facts known to him or her in order to test the grounds of his or her belief.[12] In general, the plaintiff cannot be cross-examined about specific acts of misconduct. The exception to this is the case where plaintiff's credit is in issue, in which case he or she may be cross-examined as to credit through reference to specific acts. Questions put to witnesses in cross-examination may refer to specific acts, but the cross-examiner will be bound by the answers.[13] A roving cross-examination as to specific acts of misconduct in the guise of a cross-examination as to credit should be discouraged by the trial judge so that the battle with respect to the plaintiff's reputation is waged on the basis of general evidence of reputation.[14]

(b) *Evidence of Bad Character of Plaintiff*

(i) To Support Defences

The defendant, in support of a defence of justification, can adduce evidence tending to show the bad character of the plaintiff, either by evidence of general reputation or specific acts of misconduct. Furthermore, if the defendant pleads qualified privilege, but not justification, and the plaintiff alleges malice in order to deprive the

---

11   *Ibid.*
12   *Ibid.*
13   See Chapter 16, VI.D. and VIII.B.
14   See Chapter 16, VIII.B.

defendant of the qualified privilege defence, to rebut the imputation of malice the defendant may be permitted to adduce evidence of specific acts, tending to prove the truth of the defamatory statement in order to show *bona fides*.[15]

(ii) To Support Mitigation of Damages

Even where the defendant does not plead justification or lack of malice, a defendant may, in mitigation of damages, adduce evidence of the plaintiff's bad reputation so long as the reputation evidence is directed to the aspect of the plaintiff's character which is relevant.[16] The defendant may not, however, adduce evidence of instances of bad character in the examination-in-chief of his or her witnesses. But, as in the case of evidence of the plaintiff's good character, the defendant's witnesses may be cross-examined by the plaintiff as to specific instances demonstrating good or bad character to test their general evidence.[17] Specific acts of misconduct which have been adduced in support of a defence of justification should not be considered by the trier of fact on the issue of damages. Nevertheless, in *Pamplin v. Express Newspapers Ltd. (No.2)*,[18] the English Court of Appeal refused to direct a new trial when a trial judge instructed the jury that they could take such evidence of specific acts of misconduct into account on this issue of damages. The court concluded that there was no wrong or substantial miscarriage of justice occasioned by this instruction in view of the fact that the evidence was before the jury in any event.

Prior to *Pamplin* there were other indications that English judges were not content with the exclusion of specific acts of conduct in assessing the worth of a plaintiff's reputation. Lord Denning in *Plato Films Ltd. v. Speidel*[19] held that evidence of specific acts of the plaintiff's past misconduct was, as a general rule, not admissible. Lord Radcliffe, however, dissented on the ground that specific conduct was the very material of which reputations are made. The generality of the exclusionary rule was eroded in *Goody v. Odhams Press Ltd.*[20] where Lord

---

15   *McKergow v. Comstock* (1906), 11 O.L.R. 637 (C.A.).
16   *Plato, supra*, note 9, at 890.
17   *Ibid.*; *Scott v. Sampson* (1882), 8 Q.B.D. 491, [1881-5] All E.R. Rep. 628; *Associated Newspapers Ltd. v. Dingle*, [1964] A.C. 371, [1962] 2 All E.R. 737 (H.L.).
18   [1988] 1 All E.R. 282, [1988] 1 W.L.R. 116*n* (C.A.).
19   *Supra*, note 9.
20   [1966] 3 All E.R. 369, [1967] 1 Q.B. 333 (C.A.).

Denning (now Master of the Rolls) was faced with his previous decision in *Plato Films* and the following fact situation.

A newspaper owned by the defendants published a story containing many references to the plaintiff in connection with the great mail bag robbery. The story alleged that the plaintiff had been in prison for three years for his part in the robbery. The defendants at first pleaded justification, but, in order to establish this defence, the defendants would have been required to prove that the plaintiff was in fact one of the robbers. It would not have been sufficient to prove his conviction by reason of the rule in *Hollington v. F. Hewthorn & Co. Ltd.*[21] The defendants then amended their defence to plead partial justification, namely, that the plaintiff was in prison and had been convicted. In mitigation of damages the defendants further pleaded eight previous convictions of the plaintiff. The case came before the Court of Appeal on the question of whether the amended pleading was proper. Notwithstanding the previous decision in *Plato Films* the plea was allowed to stand. Lord Denning distinguished his previous decision as follows:[22]

> I think that previous convictions are admissible. They stand in a class by themselves. They are the raw material on which bad reputation is built up. They have taken place in open court. They are matters of public knowledge. They are accepted by people generally as giving the best guide to his reputation and standing. They must of course be relevant, in this sense, that they must be convictions in the relevant sector of his life and have taken place within a relevant period such as to affect his current reputation; but being relevant, they are admissible. They are very different from previous instances of misconduct, for those have not been tried out or resulted in convictions or come before a court of law. To introduce those might lead to endless disputes. Whereas previous convictions are virtually indisputable.

The Report of the Committee on Defamation[23] criticised the rule and recommended its replacement with the following:

---

21 [1943] 2 All E.R. 35, [1943] K.B. 587. This rule applied in England to prevent a previous conviction from being used as evidence in a subsequent civil proceeding. As to its application in Canada see Chapter 19, III.
22 *Supra*, note 20, at 372-73 (All E.R.).
23 (London: Her Majesty's Stationery Office, 1975), at 103, § 372.

In all the circumstances we *recommend* that there should be admissible in mitigation of damages evidence of any matter, general or particular, relevant at the date of the trial to that aspect of the plaintiff's reputation with which the defamation is concerned. Rules of Court should provide that notice should be given of any matter on which a party intends to reply.

In light of Lord Radcliffe's statement concerning the nature of reputation, it would be logical to extend this recommendation to permit reputation to be proved by reference to specific conduct.

(iii) Rumour

Prior to the decision in *Scott v. Sampson*[24] the defendant was allowed, in mitigation of damages, to adduce evidence that, prior to the defamatory statement complained of, there were rumours to the same effect as the statement complained of.[25] This evidence was admitted on the theory that, if people were saying these things about the plaintiff in any event, he had received little injury.[26] In *Scott v. Sampson*, however, it was finally decided that evidence of such rumours was inadmissible. This decision was affirmed by the House of Lords in *Plato Films Ltd. v. Speidel*.[27] Lord Denning buried rumour once and for all with the following eulogy:[28]

Rumour is a lying jade, begotten by gossip out of hearsay, and is not fit to be admitted to audience in a court of law.

(iv) Summary of Character Evidence in Defamation Cases

To summarize, in a defamation action:

(1) the plaintiff can, through other witnesses, adduce good character reputation evidence;

(2) the defendant can cross-examine such witnesses on specific acts showing the plaintiff's misconduct so as to test the foundation for their belief;

---

24 *Supra*, note 17.
25 *Leicester (Earl) v. Walter* (1809), 2 Camp. 251, 170 E.R. 1146 (C.P.).
26 *Ibid.*
27 *Supra*, note 9.
28 *Supra*, note 9.

(3)   the plaintiff cannot be cross-examined as to specific acts of bad conduct, except insofar as they are to test credibility (in which case the collateral fact rule applies);

(4)   the defendant can adduce evidence of the plaintiff's bad character in the form of general reputation evidence to support a defence of justification, the absence of malice or to mitigate damages;

(5)   with the defences of justification and malice, specific acts showing the plaintiff's bad conduct may be adduced by the defendant;

(6)   with respect to mitigation of damages, the defendant cannot adduce evidence of such specific bad acts in the case in chief, except, perhaps, evidence of previous convictions;

(7)   evidence of rumours against the plaintiff cannot be admitted; and

(8)   the plaintiff can test the evidence of the defendant's witness by reference to specific acts demonstrating good conduct or in such a manner that elicits bad character evidence.

2.   Breach of Promise to Marry

In a few jurisdictions actions may still be maintained for breach of promise to marry,[29] adultery,[30] and enticement or seduction of a wife.[31] In such actions evidence as to the moral character of the spouse or defendant may be in issue.[32]

---

29   The action for breach of promise to marry has been abolished in a number of jurisdictions. See Ont., *Marriage Act*, R.S.O. 1980, c. 256, s. 32; B.C., *Family Relations Act*, R.S.B.C. 1979, c. 121, s. 75(2) [new 1985, c. 72, s. 36]. See also Chapter 17, III.B.2.

30   The action for damages for adultery or criminal conversation has been abolished in a number of jurisdictions. See B.C., *Family Relations Act, ibid.*, s. 76 (rep. 1985, c. 72, s. 37); Man., *The Equality of Status Act*, R.S.M. 1987, c. E130, s. 1(1); Ont., *Dower and Miscellaneous Abolition Act*, R.S.O. 1980, c. 152, s. 69(1); Sask., *The Equality of Status of Married Persons Act*, S.S. 1984-85-86, c. E-10.3, s. 6; N.B., *Compliance Act*, S.N.B. 1985, c. 41, s. 4(6); Nfld., *Family Law Act*, S. Nfld. 1988, c. 60, s. 76.1 [new 1989, c. 11, s. 2]. The statutory cause of action still exists in Alberta, see *Domestic Relations Act*, R.S.A. 1980, c. D-37, s. 13, s. 40.

31   This common law cause of action has been abolished in a number of jurisdictions. See B.C., *Family Relations Act*, R.S.B.C. 1979, c. 121, s. 75(2) [new 1985, c. 72, s. 36]; Ont., *Dower and Miscellaneous Abolition Act, ibid.*, s. 69(2); P.E.I., *Charter of Rights (Consequential Amendments) Act*, c. 6, s. 5; Sask., *The Equality of Married Persons Act, ibid.*, s. 6; N.B., *Charter Compliance Act*, S.N.B. 1985, c. 41, s. 4(7); Nfld., *Family Law Act, ibid.*, s. 76.2 [new 1989, c. 11, s. 2]. But see Alta., *Domestic Relations Act*, R.S.A. 1980, c. D-37, s. 42.

32   See *Jones v. James* (1868), 18 L.T. 243, 16 W.R. 762 [Exch.] for an example

In an action for seduction the defendant may adduce evidence of general reputation for immorality and of specific acts on the part of the person seduced, committed prior, but not subsequent, to the act complained of.[33] The reason is that subsequent acts may have been brought about by the defendant's own misconduct.[34] The character of the plaintiff may also be in issue as it can affect the amount of damages suffered.[35]

In actions for criminal conversation, alienation of affections and enticement, the wife's general moral character and previous acts of adultery (not subsequent acts for the same reason as in seduction cases) may be proved by the defendant.[36] The defendant may also prove that the other plaintiff was a philanderer as this depreciates the loss.[37]

3. Character of Places, Animals or Things

Evidence may be adduced of the character of places, things or animals where this is directly in issue. The dangerous nature of places or things may be in issue in occupiers' liability or negligence cases. For example, in *Lampert v. Simpson*[38] evidence of previous incidents of slipping and falling were admissible to show the dangerous condition of premises where the plaintiff had slipped and fallen. Also, in actions based on the actions of animals, the character of the particular animal or of the species may be in issue.[39]

---

of such evidence in an action for breach of promise of marriage. See also the first edition, this text, Chapter 3, F.3(b), (c), (d) for a more detailed examination of this subject.

33   *McCready v. Grundy* (1876), 39 U.C.Q.B. 316 (C.A.); *Elsam v. Faucett* (1797), 2 Esp. 562, 170 E.R. 455 (K.B.); *Winter v. Henn* (1831), 4 C. & P. 494, 172 E.R. 796.

34   *Phipson on Evidence*, 11th ed. (London: Sweet & Maxwell, 1970), § 541, at 238-39. This subject is not dealt with in any detail in the 14th ed. of Phipson.

35   *Grainger v. Hamilton* (1902), 1 O.W.R. 819 (Div. Ct.); *Bromley v. Wallace* (1803), 4 Esp. 237, 170 E.R. 704 (C.P.).

36   *Bromley v. Wallace, ibid.*

37   *Ibid.*

38   (1985), 34 R.P.R. 39, 57 N.B.R. (2d) 227 (N.B.Q.B.); affd. (1986), 75 N.B.R. (2d) 128 (C.A.); leave to appeal to S.C.C. refd. (1987), 79 N.B.R. (2d) 90*n*, 79 N.R. 348*n*.

39   M.N. Howard, P. Crane and D.A. Hochberg, *Phipson on Evidence*, 14th ed. (London: Sweet & Maxwell, 1990), at 416.

B. *Criminal Cases*

In most cases, the good or bad character of the accused is not a fact in issue with respect to innocence or guilt of the accused. Three minor exceptions to character as a fact in issue deserve mention. In an application under Part XXIV of the *Criminal Code*,[40] s. 757 authorizes the admission of evidence tendered by the Crown to support a finding that the offender is a "dangerous offender". The "defence" of insanity can, in certain circumstances, be raised by the Crown. The evidence tendered by the Crown on an insanity allegation may include character evidence in the form of evidence of past conduct and disposition. Cases which permitted the Crown to introduce insanity as an issue during the trial of the issue of guilt and innocence are no longer applicable due to the decision of the Supreme Court of Canada in *R. v. Swain*.[41] The Crown may still introduce the issue but only after there has been a finding of guilt against the accused. A third exception is where the accused puts forth the defence of entrapment.[42]

III EVIDENCE OF CHARACTER TO PROVE FACTS IN ISSUE

A. *Civil Cases*

Evidence of character may be tendered in proof or disproof of a fact in issue apart from character, for example, to show the doing or failure to do the act in question by the person against whom the evidence is tendered. For example, evidence of specific past acts of negligence may be admitted to prove a person failed to take reasonable steps. It may also be used to bolster or attack credibility.

A strong reaction against the use of evidence of character to circumstantially prove a fact in issue has resulted in its total prohibition in civil cases, subject to some limited exceptions. The modern rationale for its exclusion was enunciated in *Attorney-General v.*

---

40 R.S.C. 1985, c. C-46.
41 (1991), 63 C.C.C. (3d) 481, 125 N.R. 1, 3 C.R.R. (2d) 1 (S.C.C.). See *R. v. Simpson* (1977), 35 C.C.C. (2d) 337, 77 D.L.R. (3d) 507, 16 O.R. (2d) 129, 2 L.M.Q. 40 (C.A.); *R. v. Dickie (No. 2)* (1982), 67 C.C.C. (2d) 218, 38 O.R. (2d) 530 (Ont. C.A.); *R. v. Saxell* (1980), 59 C.C.C. (2d) 176, 123 D.L.R. (3d) 369, 33 O.R. (3d) 78 (Ont. C.A.).
42 *R. v. Mack* (1988), 67 C.R. (3d) 1, 44 C.C.C. (3d) 513 (S.C.C.).

Radloff.[43] In the course of his judgment, Martin B. made the following statement:[44]

> In criminal cases evidence of the good character of the accused is most properly and with good reason admissible in evidence, because there is a fair and just presumption that a person of good character would not commit a crime; but in civil cases such evidence is with equal good reason not admitted, because no presumption would fairly arise, in the very great proportion of such cases, from the good character of the defendant, that he did not commit the breach of contract or of civil duty alleged against him.

While the above statement deals with the introduction of evidence of good character, the same prohibition applies with respect to evidence of bad character,[45] unless the evidence meets the rigid standards relating to the admission of evidence of similar acts.[46]

In criminal cases the exception referred to by Martin B. was introduced at the beginning of the nineteenth century.[47] The rationale for allowing this evidence in criminal cases was clearly based on its relevance. Thus, in *R. v. Rowton*,[48] Willes J. said:

> Such evidence is admissible, because it renders it less probable that what the prosecution has averred is true. It is strictly relevant to the issue . . . .

If the logical relevance of the evidence was the test of admissibility, it would be difficult to rationalize its exclusion in civil cases and its admission in criminal cases. In tort actions such as assault, deceit and negligence, evidence of good character on the part of the defendant would appear to be as relevant as the evidence of good character of the accused in a criminal case.

While the courts appear to exclude character evidence in civil

---

43 (1854), 10 Exch. 84, 23 L.J. Ex. 240, 156 E.R. 366.
44 *Ibid.*, at 371 (E.R.).
45 *Laird v. Taxicabs Ltd.* (1914), 6 O.W.N. 505, 17 D.L.R. 847 (C.A.); *Sinclair v. Ruddell* (1906), 3 W.L.R. 532, 16 Man. R. 53 (C.A.).
46 See Chapter 11.
47 1A Wigmore, *Evidence* (Tillers rev., 1983), § 57 at 1180-147.
48 (1865), L. & C. 520, 10 Cox. C.C. 25, 169 E.R. 1497, at 1506 (C.C.A.).

cases on the basis of irrelevance,[49] the real rationale is the policy to restrain civil proceedings within manageable limits and to prevent unfairness to civil litigants. Without previous notice such litigants cannot be expected to be prepared to protect themselves against imputations which may range over their whole career.[50]

There are very few reported civil cases in which character evidence has been sought to be introduced by the examination of witnesses-in-chief.[51] The vast majority of cases which deal with the use of evidence of character are cases where such evidence is attempted to be introduced by way of cross-examination. Here character evidence is admitted as part of a broader rule. On cross-examination, subject to the discretion of the trial judge to disallow any question which is vexatious or oppressive,[52] a witness can be asked literally anything as a test of his or her credibility.[53] This broader rule is subject to the qualification that if the question is irrelevant to the facts in issue, but is asked purely for the purpose of testing credibility, the cross-examiner is bound by the answer. Evidence cannot be led in reply to contradict the witness.[54]

The foregoing discussion has, perhaps, demonstrated that the law relating to character evidence in civil cases is somewhat of a hodge-podge. There does not seem to be a consistent, logical connection between the various rules. Some evidence is excluded which appears to be logically relevant. This over-zealousness on the part of the courts to protect character is perhaps the hallmark of an advanced civilization. A person must be free to indulge in his or her idiosyn-

---

49 *Deep v. Wood* (1983), 33 C.P.C. 256, 143 D.L.R. (3d) 246 (Ont. C.A.).

50 *Edwards v. Ottawa River Navigation Co.* (1876), 39 U.C.Q.B. 264 (C.A.); 17 *Halsbury's Laws of England,* 4th ed. (London: Butterworths, 1976), § 50.

51 In *A.G. v. Bowman* (1791), 2 Bos. & P. 532*n*, 126 E.R. 1423: "a defendant to an information for keeping false weights was precluded from calling a witness as to good character on the ground that the proceedings although criminal in form were civil".

52 *Brownwell v. Brownwell* (1909), 42 S.C.R. 368; *Wong Kam-ming v. R.*, [1980] A.C. 247, at 260, [1979] 1 All E.R. 939, at 946 (P.C.), per Lord Edmund-Davies. Generally, see Chapter 16, IV.A.

53 *Geddie v. Rink,* [1935] 1 W.W.R. 87 (Sask. C.A.); *Canada (Royal Commission into Metropolitan Toronto Police Practices) v. Ashton* (1975), 27 C.C.C. (2d) 31, 10 O.R. (2d) 113, 64 D.L.R. (3d) 477 (Div. Ct.); *Deep v. Wood, supra,* note 49.

54 *Ibid.; Hickey v. Fitzgerald* (1877), 41 U.C.Q.B. 303 (C.A.); *S. v. S.,* [1954] 2 D.L.R. 765, 12 W.W.R.; revd. on other grounds [1955] S.C.R. 658, [1955] 4 D.L.R. 6. Discussed in Chapter 16, VIII.B.

crasies, oddities and peculiar habits without fear of having them exposed when seeking civil redress.

B. *Criminal Cases*

Unlike civil proceedings, evidence of the accused's good character is admissible on the issue of innocence or guilt, so long as the character trait relates to a relevant issue. It is also admissible to support the accused's credibility. Policy considerations preclude the Crown from adducing evidence of the accused's bad character in the first instance. Accordingly, neither evidence of reputation nor of specific acts designed to show a bad disposition can be adduced by the Crown against the accused unless character is put in issue by the accused. However, evidence of the accused's bad character may sometimes be used to prove a fact in issue, and this is discussed below.[55] Although sometimes allowed in rebuttal, its use is hedged about with significant restrictions. With respect to character evidence introduced by way of cross-examination as to credibility, the wide scope accorded to the cross-examiner in civil cases is tempered in criminal cases by the policy against the introduction of evidence of the bad character of the accused. Moreover, the collateral fact rule applies to the cross-examination of either the accused or an ordinary witness in a criminal proceeding.[56] Because of the different policy reasons applicable to evidence of the accused's character it is convenient to deal separately with the character of the accused.

1. Character of the Accused

(a) *Evidence of Good Character*

The accused can introduce evidence of good character in three ways:
(1)   by adducing evidence as to his or her good reputation;
(2)   by personally testifying as to specific acts of good conduct;
(3)   by calling expert opinion evidence as to disposition.[57]

---

55   See this Chapter, III.B.1.(b). See also Chapter 11, Similar Acts.
56   *R. v. Rafael*, [1972] 3 O.R. 238, 7 C.C.C. (2d) 325 (C.A.). Discussed in Chapter 15, VIII.B.
57   *R. v. McNamara (No.1)* (1981), 56 C.C.C. (2d) 193, at 348; leave to appeal to S.C.C. refd. 56 C.C.C. (2d) 576; *R. v. McMillan* (1975), 23 C.C.C. (2d) 160, 29

(i) Reputation

The early common law permitted third parties to be called as witnesses as to the general reputation of the accused in the community for specific relevant character traits. In the leading case, *R. v. Rowton*,[58] Cockburn C.J. explained the rationale for such evidence:[59]

> In the first instance, it becomes necessary to consider what is the meaning of evidence to character. It is laid down in the books that a prisoner is entitled to give evidence as to his general character. What does that mean? Does it mean evidence as to his reputation amongst those to whom his conduct and position is known, or does it mean evidence of disposition? I think it means evidence of reputation only. I quite agree that what you want to get at, as bearing materially on the probability or improbability of the prisoner's guilt, is the tendency or disposition of his mind to commit the particular offence with which he stands charged; but no one ever heard of a question put deliberately to a witness called on behalf of a prisoner as to the prisoner's disposition of mind. The way, and the only way the law allows of getting at the disposition and tendency of his mind is by evidence as to general character founded upon the knowledge of those who know anything about him and of his general conduct. Now that is the sense in which I find the word character used and applied by all the text writers of authority upon the subject of evidence. Mr. Russell in his book, which now has become a standard work of authority, puts the admissibility or the reception of evidence to character upon this ground, that the fact of a man having had an unblemished reputation up to the time of the particular transaction in question, leads strongly to the presumption that he was incapable of committing, and therefore did not commit the offence with which he stands charged.

Jackson J., delivering the majority judgment of the Supreme Court of the United States in *Michelson v. U.S.*,[60] was less certain of

---

C.R.N.S. 191, 7 O.R. (2d) 750 (C.A.); affd. [1977] 2 S.C.R. 824, 33 C.C.C. (2d) 360, 73 D.L.R. (3d) 759, 15 N.R. 20.

58   *Supra*, note 48.

59   *Ibid.*, at 29 (Cox C.C.).

60   335 U.S. 469, 69 S.Ct. 213 (1948).

the probative value of this compendium of opinion and hearsay but recognized the necessity of imposing this restriction in order to avoid a plethora of collateral issues. The learned justice reasoned as follows:[61]

> When the defendant elects to initiate a character inquiry, another anomalous rule comes into play. Not only is he permitted to call witnesses to testify from hearsay, but indeed such a witness is not allowed to base his testimony on anything but hearsay. What commonly is called "character evidence" is only such when "character" is employed as a synonym for "reputation". The witness may not testify about defendant's specific acts or courses of conduct or his possession of a particular disposition or of benign mental and moral traits; nor can he testify that his own acquaintance, observation, and knowledge of defendant leads to his own independent opinion that defendant possesses a good general or specific character, inconsistent with commission of acts charged. The witness is, however, allowed to summarize what he has heard in the community, although much of it may have been said by persons less qualified to judge than himself. The evidence which the law permits is not as to the personality of defendant but only as to the shadow his daily life has cast in his neighbourhood. This has been well described in a different connection as 'the slow growth of months and years, the resultant picture of forgotten incidents, passing events, habitual and daily conduct, presumably honest because disinterested, and safer to be trusted because less prone to suspect. . . . It is for that reason that such general repute is permitted to be proven. It sums up a multitude of trivial details. It compacts into the brief phrase of a verdict the teaching of many incidents and the conduct of years. It is the average intelligence drawing its conclusion.' Finch, J., in *Badger v. Badger*, 88 N.Y. 546, 552, 42 Am. Rep. 263.

While courts have recognized logical grounds for criticism of this type of opinion-based-on-hearsay testimony, it is said to be justified by 'overwhelming considerations of practical convenience' in avoiding innumerable collateral issues which, if it were attempted to prove character by direct testimony, would

---

61   *Ibid.*, at 477-78 (U.S.) and 219 (S.Ct.).

complicate and confuse the trial, distract the minds of jurymen and befog the chief issues in the litigation. *People v. Van Gaasbeck*, 189 N.Y. 408, 418, 82 N.E. 718, 22 L.R.A., N.S., 650, 12 Ann. Cas. 745.

The evidence cannot be an expression of the witnesses' own opinion of the accused's character or refer to particular acts of conduct tending to show the character trait in issue. The witnesses must therefore have knowledge of the accused's reputation in the community with respect to the character trait in question.[62] Provided that they have relevant knowledge, the accused can adduce evidence of his or her reputation by cross-examining Crown witnesses.[63] The same restrictions apply whether the evidence is adduced in chief or in cross-examination. For example, in *R. v. Close*[64] the accused was charged with breaking and entering with the intent to steal and do damage. The owner of the home and the owner's son knew the accused, and on cross-examination by defence counsel they testified that it was out of character for the accused to steal and that they still trusted him. This evidence was held to be inadmissible character evidence as it was not in the form of general reputation in the community.

The following is the appropriate form for questions concerning reputation:

Q.1 Do you know the accused?

Q.2 How long have you known him or her?

Q.3 In what circumstances have you known him or her? (Witness must identify the community, i.e., work place, church, neighbourhood, etc.)

Q.4 Do you know his or her reputation for (identify relevant character trait)?

---

62   *R. v. Demyen* (1976), 31 C.C.C. (2d) 383, [1976] 5 W.W.R. 324 (Sask. C.A.); *R. v. Long* (1902), 5 C.C.C. 493, at 499, 11 Que. K.B. 328 (C.A.); *R. v. Close* (1982), 68 C.C.C. (2d) 105, 38 O.R. (2d) 453, 137 D.L.R. (3d) 655 (C.A.); *R. v. Grosse* (1983), 9 C.C.C. (3d) 465, 61 N.S.R. (2d) 54 (N.S.C.A.); leave to appeal to S.C.C. refd. 61 N.S.R. (2d) 447*n*, 52 N.R. 397*n*; *R. v. McFadden* (1981), 65 C.C.C. (2d) 9, at 13, 28 C.R. (3d) 33, 33 B.C.L.R. 96 (B.C.C.A.).

63   E.g., *R. v. Long, ibid.*; *R. v. Demyen, ibid.*

64   *Supra*, note 62.

Q.5   Please describe that reputation.

It is generally not objectionable to have the witness relate some specific events involving the accused and the witness in order to illustrate the circumstances in answer to Q.3.

(ii)   Specific Acts of Good Conduct — The Evidence of the Accused

Accused persons can also testify as to their own good character. The restriction to evidence of general reputation does not apply in such situations.[65] Obviously, accused persons are not in a position to speak to their own reputation because what they hear about themselves, if anything, is, in all probability, more favourable than the views people actually hold. This exception to the requirement of general reputation evidence was explained by the Ontario Court of Appeal in *R. v. McNamara (No. 1)*,[66] where the court said:

> Mr. Robinette also argued that character means general reputation and that the accused can only put his character in issue by adducing evidence of general reputation. With respect, we do not agree. The common law rule was that evidence of good character can only be given by evidence of reputation, and could only be rebutted by evidence of reputation and not by specific acts of bad conduct: *R. v. Rowton* (1865), Le. & C.A. 520, 169 E.R. 1497. That rule was, however, established at a time when the accused could not himself give evidence. A long series of cases in England (two of which were cited with approval in *Morris v. The Queen*, [[1979] 1 S.C.R. 405]) have held that an accused may put his character in issue by testifying as to his good character. The word 'character' in the *Criminal Evidence Act, 1898* has uniformly been held to mean not only reputation, but actual moral disposition: *Cross on Evidence*, 4th ed. (1976), p. 426; *Phipson on Evidence*, 12th ed. (1976), p. 218. It is true that when the accused wishes to adduce extrinsic evidence of good character by calling witnesses, such evidence is confined to evidence of gen-

---

65   *R. v. McNamara (No. 1)*, *supra*, note 57; *R. v. Close*, *supra*, note 62; *Morris v. R.*, [1979] 1 S.C.R. 405, 6 C.R. (3d) 36, 43 C.C.C. (2d) 129, 91 D.L.R. (3d) 161, 23 N.R. 109; but see *R. v. Redgrave*, [1981] Crim. L.R. 556 (C.C.A.).
66   *Ibid.*, at 348.

eral reputation, but that has no application where the accused himself gives the evidence.

This passage was cited with approval in *R. v. Close*,[67] in which Brooke J.A. remarked that it seemed more logical that the exception to the general rule requiring general reputation evidence should be limited to the case where the accused gives the evidence. In his view, it was difficult to see how an accused could give evidence of his own reputation.

The accused may testify as to his or her good character by any evidence that projects the image of a law-abiding citizen.[68] This may be in the form of opinion or comment on his or her own disposition with respect to a trait relevant to an issue in the case or by relating specific acts which portray the accused in a good light in relation to such traits. A preliminary issue is whether the accused has put his or her good character in issue so as to permit rebuttal evidence by the Crown of evidence of bad character.[69] Because the issue of what constitutes evidence of good character is integrally tied to the question of whether the accused has made character an issue, it is convenient to deal with both questions here.

An example of opinion evidence is found in *R. v. Farrant*[70] where the accused, who was charged with second degree murder, testified as follows:[71]

> Well, think about it now there's no way I would, you know, it's not my character to be violent, you know, use violence or a rifle, you know, to get my own way. That's not my character.

The Supreme Court of Canada held that the accused's testimony in examination-in-chief had put his character for non-violence in issue.[72]

The accused puts his or her character in issue by evidence of his

---

67   *Supra*, note 62, at 460 (O.R.).

68   *Morris v. R.*, *supra*, note 65, at 156 (C.C.C.).

69   See this Chapter, III.B.1.(b).(iv).

70   [1983] 1 S.C.R. 124, 4 C.C.C. (3d) 354, 32 C.R. (3d) 289, 147 D.L.R. (3d) 511, [1983] 3 W.W.R. 171, 21 Sask. R. 271, 46 N.R. 337 (S.C.C.).

71   *Ibid.*, at 526 (D.L.R.).

72   The fact that the accused puts his or her character in issue is relevant to the question of what character evidence the Crown can adduce in rebuttal. See, this Chapter, III.B.1.(b).(iv).

or her own specific past conduct or acts, such as never having been arrested;[73] earning an honest living for four years;[74] returning lost property to owners on two previous occasions;[75] and that he thought his activities were legal.[76] In each of these instances the accused put character in issue. The accused does not give evidence of good character or, in other words, put character in issue by merely denying guilt and repudiating the allegations.[77] Nor do introductory questions put to the accused as to place of residence, marital status and employment have this effect.[78]

It is sometimes difficult to determine when an accused is giving evidence of good character as opposed to simply meeting the substance of the prosecution's case or giving background information. Evidence adduced to establish innocence normally has the coincidental effect of showing the accused in a morally favourable light. This alone should not put character in issue. Clear cases of putting character in issue are those where the accused states or suggests that he or she has never been arrested for or convicted of an offence or where the accused suggests in some other way that he or she is a law abiding citizen or would never engage in the type of conduct alleged in the charge. In other cases character is not so obviously placed in issue. For example, in *R. v. McFadden*[79] an accused charged with a murder occurring during the course of a sexual assault denied the offence, stating that he had "the most beautiful wife in the world". The court accepted that the effect of this statement was that he had a good character for sexual fidelity and that he had, therefore, put his character in issue. It is doubtful whether the strategy of the defence was to do so. Before removing the protection of the exclusionary rule, courts should be careful to consider whether the accused is offering evidence of innocence rather than deliberately appealing to the trier of fact on his or her moral record. Only in the latter case should the Crown be entitled to elicit evidence of bad character.

By introducing evidence of a victim's character for violence where the defence is self-defence, the accused may impliedly be

---

73   *Morris v. R.*, *supra*, note 65.
74   *R. v. Baker* (1912), 7 Cr. App. R. 252 (C.A.).
75   *R. v. Samuel* (1956), 40 Cr. App. R. 8 (C.C.A.), where the charge was larceny.
76   *R. v. Li Kam Kwai (No. 6)* (1980), 6 W.C.B. 44 (B.C.S.C.).
77   *R. v. McNamara (No. 1)*, *supra*, note 57, at 346.
78   *Ibid.*
79   *Supra*, note 62.

adducing evidence of good character and thereby put his or her own character in issue.[80] However, in *R. v. Butterwasser*[81] the English Criminal Court of Appeal considered a case where the accused was charged with wounding with intent to do grievous bodily harm. The accused's counsel cross-examined the victims called as Crown witnesses on their previous convictions, including convictions for violent offences in order to show that they were more likely to have been the aggressors than the accused. The accused did not testify and the issue was whether the Crown could lead evidence of the accused's bad character and previous convictions. The Court held that merely by attacking the witnesses for the prosecution and suggesting they were unreliable the accused did not put his own character in issue. This decision appears to be eminently sound if the right of an accused to make full answer and defence is to be preserved. On the other hand, a distorted picture of events should not be permitted to go before the jury and evidence that the accused was a peaceful person may result in losing the protection of the exclusionary rule.[82]

(iii) Expert Opinion Evidence

The accused may also adduce psychiatric evidence to prove an abnormal disposition making the carrying out of the crime by the accused less probable. However, this opinion evidence with respect to disposition is limited to certain traits. In *R. v. Lupien*[83] the accused was charged with an act of gross indecency having been found in a compromising position with another man dressed as a woman. The defence was that the accused believed this other man to be a woman and, therefore, the accused did not have the intent to commit the act alleged. To prove that he did not have the requisite intent, the accused called psychiatric evidence to show that he had a particular defence mechanism that made him react violently against homosexual behaviour. Ritchie J.[84] considered the effect of introducing this evidence in

---

80   *R. v. Scopelliti* (1981), 63 C.C.C. (2d) 481, 34 O.R. (2d) 524 (C.A.); *R. v. Speid* (1985), 20 C.C.C. (3d) 534, 46 C.R. (3d) 22, 9 O.A.C. 237; *R. v. McMillan* (1975), 23 C.C.C. (2d) 160, 29 C.R.N.S. 191, 7 O.R. (2d) 750 (C.A.); affd. [1977] 2 S.C.R. 824, 33 C.C.C. (2d) 360, 73 D.L.R. (3d) 759.
81   [1948] 1 K.B. 4, [1947] 2 All E.R. 415 (C.C.A.).
82   *R. v. McMillan, supra*, note 80.
83   [1970] S.C.R. 263, [1970] 2 C.C.C. 193, 9 C.R.N.S. 165, 9 D.L.R. (3d) 1, 71 W.W.R. 110.
84   Although Ritchie J. gave the dissenting judgment, technically, in effect, he

view of the rule in *R. v. Rowton*. He stated:[85]

> This was not a question of adducing character evidence in the sense of reputation, and I think the rule laid down in 1865 by Cockburn, C.J., in *R. v. Rowton*, 10 Cox C.C. 25 at p. 29 to the effect that evidence of character can only be introduced by seeking evidence of the accused's general reputation in the neighbourhood to which he belongs, is, singularly inappropriate to the introduction of evidence from psychiatrists as to the accused's disposition.

> The *Rowton* case was decided many years before the development of psychiatry as an accepted branch of medicine and we were not referred to any case in which the rule there stated was applied so as to exclude such evidence.

Ritchie J. was of the view that as a general rule such psychiatric evidence of a person's disinclination to commit the kind of crime with which he or she is charged should not be admitted, but felt that the particular crime was in a special class making such evidence particularly relevant.[86]

In *R. v. Robertson*[87] the accused was charged with the violent murder of a nine-year-old girl. The defence sought to introduce psychiatric opinion evidence to show that a propensity for violence was not a part of the accused's psychological make-up.[88] Martin J.A., speaking for the court on this issue, held that psychiatric evidence was not admissible to establish a propensity for such normal character traits as violence. He was prepared, however, to admit such evidence if it related to character traits of an abnormal group falling within the range of study of the expert witness. Martin J.A. summed up the proposed rule of admissibility as follows:[89]

> In my view, psychiatric evidence with respect to disposition or its absence is admissible on behalf of the defence, if relevant to

---

gave the decision of the majority on the question of admissibility.

85   *Supra*, note 83, at 202 (C.C.C.), 276 (S.C.R.).
86   *Supra*, note 83, at 203 (C.C.C.), 277 (S.C.R.).
87   (1975), 21 C.C.C. (2d) 385, 29 C.R.N.S. 141 (Ont. C.A.); leave to appeal to S.C.C. refd. 21 C.C.C. (2d) 385*n*.
88   *Ibid.*, at 423 (C.C.C.).
89   *Ibid.*, at 429 (C.C.C.); see also *R. v. McMillan, supra*, note 80.

an issue in the case, where the disposition in question constitutes a characteristic feature of an abnormal group, falling within the range of study of the psychiatrist, and from whom the jury can, therefore, receive appreciable assistance with respect to a matter outside the knowledge of persons who have not made a special study of the subject. A *mere* disposition for violence, however, is not so uncommon as to constitute a feature characteristic of an abnormal group falling within the special field of study of the psychiatrist and permitting psychiatric evidence to be given of the absence of such disposition in the accused.

In *R. v. McMillan*[90] Martin J.A. left open the question whether an accused charged with an offence assumed to be committed by a "normal person e.g., rape" could adduce psychiatric evidence to the effect that he is a member of an abnormal group and hence has an aversion to heterosexual relations. His Lordship was, however, disposed to think that such evidence would be admissible.[91]

The limitations on calling expert psychiatric evidence are sensible, because they prevent criminal trials from becoming a battle of the experts relating to the accused's propensities. The difficulty with the limitations is defining what is an abnormal group and its characteristics falling within the range of study of the expert.

Although it is unclear, it seems that expert psychiatric evidence cannot be adduced by the defence solely for the purpose of bolstering the credit of the accused.[92] In *R. v. Phillion*[93] the trial judge admitted psychiatric evidence that the accused was unstable and had lied to the police when he confessed. The accused did not testify. The accused was convicted, and appealed on the ground that the trial judge improperly excluded the results of a polygraph which, along with the opinion of a psychiatrist, tended to support the credibility of the accused's story to the psychiatrist. The appeal was dismissed by both

---

90   *Supra*, note 80.
91   *Ibid.*, at 175 (C.C.C.).
92   *Helpard v. R.* (1979), 49 C.C.C. (2d) 35, at 50, 10 C.R. (3d) 76, 33 N.S.R. (2d) 1 (N.S.C.A.); *R. v. Rosik* (1970), 2 C.C.C. (2d) 351, at 390-91, [1971] 2 O.R. 47, 13 C.R.N.S. 129, 13 C.R.L.Q. 224 (C.A.), per Jessup J.A.; affd. 42 C.C.C. (2d) 393*n*, [1971] 2 O.R. 89n, 14 C.R.N.S. 400.
93   (1972), 21 C.R.N.S. 169, 10 C.C.C. (2d) 562, [1973] 2 O.R. 209 (Ont. H.C.J.); affd. 20 C.C.C. (2d) 191, 53 D.L.R. (3d) 319, 5 O.R. (2d) 656 (C.A.); affd. [1978] 1 S.C.R. 18, 37 C.R.N.S. 361, 33 C.C.C. (2d) 535.

the Ontario Court of Appeal and the Supreme Court of Canada. The Supreme Court of Canada was careful to express no opinion on the propriety of the admissibility of the psychiatric evidence as to the accused's credibility.[94] In *R. v. Dietrich*,[95] the Ontario Court of Appeal confirmed the admissibility of psychiatric evidence supporting a propensity of the accused to lie, which evidence tended to explain his inculpatory statement to the police. Apparently, a psychiatrist is also permitted to express his or her opinion on the veracity of the accused's statements to the psychiatrist in a case in which the psychiatrist's evidence is otherwise admissible. The evidence is admitted as part of the basis for the expert's opinion.[96] *R. v. Abbey*,[97] has however, cast doubt on the admissibility of the accused's statement to the psychiatrist.[98]

(iv) Use of Evidence of Good Character

Evidence of good character is relevant on the issue of innocence or guilt[99] as well as on the issue of the accused's credibility.[100] Failure to direct the jury that good character evidence can be used in deciding on the issue of innocence or guilt is a misdirection.[101] The character evidence must, however, be relevant to the particular charge. For

---

94 *Ibid.*, at 539 (C.C.C.). See also *R. v. Beland*, [1987] 2 S.C.R. 398, 43 D.L.R. (4th) 641, 36 C.C.C. (3d) 481, 79 N.R. 263.

95 (1970), 1 C.C.C. (2d) 49, [1970] 3 O.R. 725, 11 C.R.N.S. 22 (Ont. C.A.); leave to appeal to S.C.C. refd. 1 C.C.C. (2d) 68n, [1970] 3 O.R. 744n, [1970] S.C.R. xii.

96 *R. v. Rosik, supra*, note 92, at 390-91 (C.C.C.); *R. v. Abbey*, [1982] 2 S.C.R. 24, [1983] 1 W.W.R. 251, 68 C.C.C. (2d) 394, 29 C.R. (3d) 193, 138 D.L.R. (3d) 202, 39 B.C.L.R. 201, 43 N.R. 30.

97 *Ibid.*

98 See Chapter 12 in which the use of an accused's statements as part of an expert's opinion is fully discussed.

99 *R. v. Rowton* (1865), L. & C. 520, 10 Cox C.C. 25, 169 E.R. 1497 (C.C.A.), per Cockburn J., at 60 (Cox C.C.) and Willis J., at 66 (Cox C.C.); *Salutin v. R.* (1979), 11 C.R. (3d) 284 (Ont. C.A.); *R. v. Elmosri* (1985), 12 O.A.C. 161, 23 C.C.C. (3d) 503 (Ont. C.A.); *R. v. Boles* (1978), 43 C.C.C. (2d) 414 (Ont. C.A.); *Savion v. R.* (1980), 52 C.C.C. (2d) 276, 13 C.R. (3d) 259 (Ont. C.A.); *R. v. Logiacco* (1984), 11 C.C.C. (3d) 374, 2 O.A.C. 177 (Ont. C.A.); *R. v. Dees* (1978), 40 C.C.C. (2d) 58 (Ont. C.A.); *R. v. Bryant*, [1979] Q.B. 108, [1978] 2 All E.R. 689 (C.A.).

100 *R. v. Boles, ibid.*; *R. v. Logiacco, ibid.*; *R. v. Dees, ibid.*; *R. v. Elmosri, ibid.*

101 *R. v. Elmosri, ibid.*; *R. v. Boles, ibid*; *Savion v. R., supra*, note 99; *R. v. Logiacco, ibid.*; *R. v. Dees, ibid.* This does not appear to be the case in England: see R. Cross and C. Tapper, *Cross on Evidence*, 7th ed. (London: Butterworths, 1990), at 331.

example, in *R. v. S. (R.J.)*,[102] the accused was charged with five counts relating to three different sexual offences. He adduced evidence of his good reputation for honesty. Failure of the judge to refer to the evidence was held not to amount to a misdirection. The accused's reputation for honesty was not relevant to his innocence or guilt in respect of the offences charged. Although good character evidence is a relevant fact on the issue of guilt, it is not "evidence to the contrary" to discharge an evidentiary burden borne by the accused.[103]

(b) *Bad Character of the Accused*

(i) The General Rule

Once an accused person was made competent to give evidence for the defence, it became necessary for the courts to deal with the correlative issues of the extent to which the accused could claim the privilege against self-incrimination and the extent to which the accused should be treated as an ordinary witness for the purpose of cross-examination as to credibility. An ordinary witness is subject to wide cross-examination on the issue of credibility, including cross-examination as to previous convictions or a bad reputation and disposition. To expose the accused to such cross-examination would be unfair because of the tendency of juries to give such evidence undue weight on the issue of guilt. On the other hand, it would be unfair to the Crown to confer complete immunity from such questioning, particularly where an accused is relying on an unblemished character which he or she does not possess. The principles respecting the admissibility of evidence of the accused's bad character attempt to balance these concerns.

The general rule is that the Crown is not permitted to adduce evidence of the accused's bad character either by evidence of reputation or specific acts unless the accused has put character in issue or the evidence is otherwise relevant to an issue, as for instance as evidence of similar acts.[104] The reason for this prohibition is not that the

---

102 (1985), 19 C.C.C. (3d) 115, 45 C.R. (3d) 161, 8 O.A.C. 241 (Ont. C.A.); leave to appeal to S.C.C. refd. (1985), 61 N.R. 266*n*, 11 O.A.C. 317*n*.

103 See *R. v. Khan* (1982), 36 O.R. (2d) 399, 66 C.C.C. (2d) 32 (C.A.).

104 As to when an accused puts character in issue, see this Chapter, III.B.1.(a).(ii): *R. v. Doyle* (1916), 26 C.C.C. 197, at 199, 28 D.L.R. 649, at 650, 50 N.S.R. 123 (N.S.S.C.); *R. v. Speid* (1985), 46 C.R. (3d) 22, 20 C.C.C. (3d) 534,

evidence is not logically relevant,[105] but that its reception would cause undue prejudice to the accused[106] and would result in investigation into tangential issues resulting in lengthy trials.[107]

The reception of such evidence may be justified under the rules relating to similar acts.[108] Evidence of bad character may, however, also be elicited in cross-examination and adduced in rebuttal in order to discredit the evidence of the accused. This will be discussed in the next section.

The Crown also cannot do indirectly what it is not permitted to do directly. In *R. v. Belanger*,[109] Crown counsel cross-examined the wife of the accused who was called as an alibi witness. She was asked whether she had given alibi evidence in respect of a previous charge against her husband. The Court of Appeal held that this question was not relevant to her credibility and constituted an attack on the character of the accused. Given the wide latitude accorded to the cross-examiner, it is difficult to rationalize this case on the ground that the question was not relevant to the wife's credibility. The preferable explanation is that a trial judge's discretion to control cross-examination can be exercised to exclude questions that, although relevant to credibility, transgress an exclusionary rule which operates in favour of the accused.

(ii) Bad Character Raised by the Accused

No rule of policy prevents the accused from raising evidence of his or her own bad character. It would be difficult, however, to justify this on tactical grounds unless the accused decides to put his character

---

9 O.A.C. 237 (C.A.); *R. v. Long* (1902), 11 Que. K.B. 328, 5 C.C.C. 493 (C.A.); *R. v. Morris*, [1983] 2 S.C.R. 190, [1984] 2 W.W.R. 1, 48 N.R. 341, 36 C.R. (3d) 1, 7 C.C.C. (3d) 97, 1 D.L.R. (4th) 385 (S.C.C.); *R. v. Gottschall* (1983), 10 C.C.C. (3d) 447, 61 N.S.R. (2d) 86 (N.S.C.A.); *R. v. Drummond* (1979), 8 C.R. (3d) 180 (Ont. C.A.); leave to appeal to S.C.C. refd. (1979), 29 N.R. 261*n* (S.C.C.); *R. v. MacDonald*, [1939] O.R. 606, 72 C.C.C. 182, [1939] 4 D.L.R. 60 (C.A.).
105 Some judges do, however, refer to this type of evidence as irrelevant: see, for example, *R. v. Gottschall, ibid.*; *R. v. Long, ibid.*, at 498 (C.C.C.).
106 *R. v. Morris, supra*, note 104; *R. v. Speid, supra*, note 104; *D.P.P. v. Kilbourne*, [1973] A.C. 729, at 757, [1973] 1 All E.R. 440, per Lord Simon (H.L.).
107 K. Chasse, "Exclusion of Certain Circumstantial Evidence: Character and Other Exclusionary Rules" (1978), 16 Osgoode Hall, L.J. 445, at 451.
108 See Chapter 11.
109 (1975), 24 C.C.C. (2d) 10 (Ont. C.A.).

in issue and adduces instances of bad conduct to neutralize its use by the Crown. For instance, the defence may wish to raise the accused's criminal record in examination-in-chief in order to soften the impact of such evidence when it is brought up by the Crown.[110] When the defence does so, the trial judge must make it clear to the jury that this evidence is relevant only to the issue of the accused's credibility as a witness and not for a direct inference that he or she committed the offence.[111] However, where the accused uses the evidence of his or her record in a more probative way, a warning to the jury is not necessary. In *R. v. MacDonald*[112] the accused testified as to his previous convictions for assault in order to show that he had never been convicted of assaulting the woman he was accused of killing. The Ontario Court of Appeal held that no warning to the jury was necessary in these circumstances.

(iii) Bad Character of Co-Accused

The rule which prevents the Crown from leading evidence of bad character does not apply to an accused leading evidence of bad character of a co-accused, so long as such evidence is relevant.[113] In such a case the accused is entitled to cross-examine witnesses and lead evidence without waiting for the co-accused to put his or her character in issue. The trial judge cannot exclude the evidence by reason of the prejudicial effect of the evidence relative to its probative value.[114] The trial judge, however, has the power to order a severance which should be exercised if the introduction of such evidence is likely to prejudice the co-accused.

(iv) Accused Puts Character in Issue

The accused's protective shield cannot be removed unless the accused puts his or her character in issue. Accordingly, the Crown cannot put the accused's character in issue by introducing a statement

---

110 *R. v. St. Pierre*, [1973] 1 O.R. 718, 10 C.C.C. (2d) 164; revd. on other grounds 3 O.R. (2d) 642, 17 C.C.C. (2d) 489, 16 R.F.L. 26 (C.A.).
111 *Ibid.*, at 499 (C.C.C.) (C.A.).
112 (1974), 20 C.C.C. (2d) 144, 27 C.R.N.S. 212 (Ont. C.A.).
113 *R. v. Miller*, [1952] 2 All E.R. 667, 36 Cr. App. Rep. 169 (Assize); *Lowery v. R.*, [1974] A.C. 85 (P.C.); *R. v. Speid, supra*, note 104.
114 *R. v. Kendall* (1987), 57 C.R. (3d) 249, 20 O.A.C. 134 (Ont. C.A.); *Cross on Evidence, supra*, note 101, at 336.

made by the accused which bolsters his or her character.[115] Moreover, the fact that a defence witness volunteers such evidence should not result in a loss of the protection.[116]

Where the accused puts his character in issue, the Crown is entitled to refute the good character evidence.[117] The circumstances in which the accused puts character in issue were considered above.[118] The Crown may refute the evidence by (i) cross-examining the accused, (ii) cross-examining any witness called by the defence to give such evidence, and (iii) by adducing rebuttal evidence. Evidence in any of these forms is admissible to negate or refute the character evidence of the accused. If the purpose succeeds, then the accused's credibility is undermined because the evidence that the accused is of good character is impeached. Impeaching the reliability of evidence of character and of the accused, if he or she testified as to his or her character, is the only use to which the evidence can be put no matter the method by which it is elicited. The trial judge should so instruct the jury.

(v) Cross-Examination of Accused's Witness

The Crown may cross-examine the accused and witnesses called on behalf of the accused who testified as to the accused's good reputation in the community for the relevant trait. The accused's witnesses can be asked about their knowledge of the accused's criminal record[119] and even with respect to previous bad acts of the accused.[120] Such evidence goes to the knowledge of the witness as to the accused's reputation and the collateral fact rule precludes contradicting their testimony by extrinsic evidence.[121]

---

115 *R. v. Knuff* (1980), 52 C.C.C. (2d) 523, 12 Alta. L.R. (2d) 7, 19 A.R. 168 (Alta. C.A.).

116 *R. v. Redd*, [1923] 1 K.B. 104, [1922] All E.R. Rep. 435 (C.C.A.).

117 *R. v. Rowton, supra,* note 99.

118 See this Chapter, III.B.1.(a).(ii).

119 *R. v. B; R. v. A.,* [1979] 3 All E.R. 460, [1979] 1 W.L.R. 1185 (C.A.).

120 *R. v. Bracewell* (1978), 68 Cr. App. Rep. 44 (C.A.).

121 Although, on the basis of s. 666 of the *Criminal Code*, R.S.C. 1985, c. C-46, the Crown could prove the previous convictions in any event. Also in an early edition of *Cross on Evidence* (4th ed.), at 349 the author suggests that the convictions could be proved at common law. As to the collateral fact rule see Chapter 16, VIII.

(vi) Cross-Examination of Accused
Where Character is in Issue

When the accused testifies and gives evidence of his or her good character, the scope of cross-examination allowed the Crown is quite wide. In *R. v. McNamara (No. 1)*[122] a fraud case arising out of bid-rigging in respect of tenders on certain dredging contracts, an accused testified as to his good character for honesty and integrity, including specific acts. The Crown was permitted to cross-examine the accused on the details of a previous transaction where the accused had pleaded guilty to tax evasion. The Court of Appeal agreed that the cross-examination was proper.[123]

> Here the appellant had asserted a good disposition in relation to honesty and integrity. The cross-examination on the . . . transaction related to that particular moral disposition and was highly relevant to rebut the appellant's assertion of good character.

Unless an accused has put his or her character in issue by adducing evidence of specific acts of good conduct, he or she cannot be cross-examined on specific acts of misconduct.[124] It has been held that where the accused puts his or her character in issue by adducing evidence of acts of good conduct, rebuttal evidence by the Crown must be in the form of general reputation.[125] This would appear to place an unwarranted restriction on the Crown, compromising its ability to effectively cross-examine in order to show the falsity of the evidence of the accused. The rule should be the same whether rebuttal is by means of cross-examination or independent witnesses.

If the accused in *McNamara* had asserted the evidence of good *reputation* through third parties and had not personally testified, the Crown would not have been entitled to prove the details of the transaction by reason of the restriction respecting specific acts of misconduct. The Court of Appeal made it clear that this restriction applied but did not apply to cross-examination of a testifying

---

122 (1981), 56 C.C.C. (2d) 193, at 348 (Ont. C.A.); leave to appeal to the S.C.C. refd. 56 C.C.C. (2d) 576 (S.C.C.).
123 *Ibid.*, at 349 (C.C.C.) (C.A.).
124 *R. v. McNamara (No.1)*, *supra*, note 122.
125 *R. v. McFadden* (1981), 65 C.C.C. (2d) 9, 28 C.R. (3d) 33, 33 B.C.L.R. 96 (B.C.C.A.).

accused.[126] It is not clear whether the Crown would have been able to adduce extrinsic evidence of the details of the transaction had knowledge of the details been denied by the accused. If an accused may be cross-examined on a matter relevant to an issue in the case, then presumably this matter may also be the subject of reply evidence by the Crown, unless the court bars the evidence under the collateral fact rule.[127]

(vii) Cross-Examination of Accused Where Character is not in Issue

An accused who takes the stand can also be cross-examined as to credibility in a way which brings the bad character of the accused to light. This can be done in two ways with an accused who has not put character in issue. A cross-examination with respect to evidence in chief may indirectly bring before the trier of fact evidence of, or at least suggestions of, bad character.[128] The accused can also be cross-examined on facts not dealt with in chief to show the falsity of the accused's evidence-in-chief. If the questions are not relevant to a fact in issue, but only to credibility, then reply evidence is subject to the collateral fact rule.

In *R. v. Chambers*,[129] the accused was charged with conspiracy to import cocaine. The defence was that despite his participation in the scheme he had no desire that the conspiracy succeed; his only interest was regaining the affections of a lost lover. As the credibility of the defendant was absolutely crucial for the resolution of this issue, it was permissible for the Crown to cross-examine on matters relating to character to show the falsity of the accused's evidence. Accordingly, cross-examination concerning alleged bribery of a defence witness to procure perjured testimony, and concerning an alleged incident of bribery of Panamanian justice officials in 1982, was permissible,

---

126 See also *R. v. Farrant*, [1983] 1 S.C.R. 124, 4 C.C.C. (3d) 354, 32 C.R. (3d) 289, 147 D.L.R. (3d) 511, [1983] 3 W.W.R. 171, 21 Sask. R. 271, 46 N.R. 337 (S.C.C.), which suggests that even when the accused adduces evidence of general reputation, the Crown can cross-examine on specific acts.

127 The collateral fact rule is discussed in Chapter 16, VIII.

128 *R. v. Davison* (1974), 20 C.C.C. (2d) 424, 6 O.R. (2d) 103 (Ont. C.A.); *Lucas v. R.*, [1963] 1 C.C.C. 1, 39 C.R. 101 (S.C.C.).

129 (1989), 47 C.C.C. (3d) 503 (B.C.C.A.); revd. [1990] 2 S.C.R. 1293, 59 C.C.C. (3d) 321, 80 C.R. (3d) 235, 49 B.C.L.R. (2d) 299, [1990] 6 W.W.R. 554, 119 N.R. 321.

notwithstanding that the evidence adduced might be characterized as evidence of bad character. Furthermore, an accused may be cross-examined on previous convictions pursuant to s. 12 of the *Canada Evidence Act*.[130]

(viii) Reply Evidence by the Crown
Where Character is in Issue

Where the accused adduces evidence of his good reputation in the community, the Crown may call independent evidence of the same type, but to the opposite effect. Although this evidence, like the good character evidence introduced by the accused, goes to the issue of guilt or innocence, it can do no more than rebut the good character evidence. In other words, it neutralizes it. The policy behind allowing this evidence by the Crown is that the court should not be misled by being left with the impression that the accused enjoys a certain reputation, when, in fact, he or she does not possess such a reputation at all.[131] The evidence of bad character to rebut the accused's case cannot be used to show that the person was likely from his character to have committed the offence.[132] The trial judge should instruct the jury with respect to the limited use of such evidence.

The principle laid down in *R. v. Rowton* provides that the evidence adduced by the Crown must, like the evidence led by the accused, be in the form of reputation in the community.[133] There is support in the cases for this as the general rule relating to Crown witnesses even where the accused has testified and given evidence of specific incidents of good character.[134] In *R. v. Farrant*,[135] Dickson J., however, was of the opinion that where the accused had put his character as a non-violent person in issue, he could be cross-examined as to a specific assault. He states:[136]

---

130   R.S.C. 1985, c. C-5. See discussion of s. 12, this Chapter, III.3.1.(b).(viii).

131   *R. v. Rowton* (1865), L. & C. 520, 10 Cox C.C. 25, 169 E.R. 1497 (C.C.A.), per Cockburn J., at 60 (Cox C.C.) and Willis J., at 66 (Cox C.C.).

132   *R. v. McNamara (No. 1), supra*, note 122; *Lucas v. R., supra*, note 128.

133   *R. v. Rowton, supra*, note 131; *R. v. McNamara (No.1), ibid.*; *Lucas v. R., ibid.*; *R. v. Triganzie* (1888), 15 O.R. 294 (C.A.); *R. v. Long* (1902), 11 Que. K.B. 328, 5 C.C.C. 493 (C.A.).

134   See this Chapter, III.B.1.(b).(vi). See also *R. v. Tierney* (1982), 70 C.C.C. 481, at 485, 31 C.R. (3d) 66 (Ont. C.A.); *R. v. McFadden, supra*, note 125.

135   *Supra*, note 126.

136   *Ibid.*, at 526 (D.L.R.), 145 (S.C.R.).

... [it was alleged by the appellant that the trial judge] erred in permitting the prosecutor to cross-examine the accused about alleged incidents of assault which purportedly occurred many months prior to the date of the offence charged. During examination-in-chief Farrant testified:

> 'Well, think about it now there's no way I would, you know, it's not my character to be violent, you know, use violence or a rifle, you know, to get my own way. That's not my character.'

The judge allowed the Crown to cross-examine in respect of alleged incidents of earlier assault. I do not think he erred in so doing, having regard to the fact that Farrant had put his non-violent character in issue in earlier testimony.

If the accused can be cross-examined on specific acts and if psychiatric evidence can be adduced by the Crown to rebut evidence of good character for non-violent behaviour,[137] there is little to be said for maintaining the strict *Rowton* rule in respect of independent rebuttal evidence.

Whatever the other restrictions on independent rebuttal evidence, it is well established that the Crown is not limited to the specific trait on which the accused led evidence. As stated by Goddard L.C.J., in *R. v. Samuel*:[138]

> [I]f a prisoner puts his character in issue, he puts his whole character in issue, not such parts as may be convenient to him, leaving out the inconvenient parts.

This principle has been subject to considerable criticism.[139] For example, an accused who is charged with robbery should not be required to defend against imputations of sexual immorality. What

---

137 *R. v. Tierney, supra,* note 134; *R. v. Robertson* (1975), 21 C.C.C. (2d) 385, at 426, 29 C.R.N.S. 141 (Ont. C.A.); leave to appeal to S.C.C. refd. 21 C.C.C. (2d) 385*n*.

138 (1956), 40 Cr. App. Rep. 8, at 11 (C.C.A.). See also *R. v. Shrimpton* (1851), 2 Den. 319, 3 Car. & Kir. 373: *R. v. Winfield* (1939), 27 Cr. App. Rep. 139, [1939] 4 All E.R. 164 (C.C.A.).

139 *Cross on Evidence,* 5th ed. (London: Butterworths, 1979), at 407-08; and G.D. Nokes, *An Introduction to Evidence,* 4th ed. (London: Sweet & Maxwell, 1967), at 140, quoted in Cross, *ibid.,* both quoted by John Sopinka, Q.C., "A Commentary on the Proposed Uniform Evidence Act" (1982), 24 C.L.Q. 331.

relevance does a reputation for womanizing have to a charge of criminal negligence?[140]

Evidence of specific acts of misconduct on the part of the accused may also be introduced in rebuttal if they meet the test for the admission of similar fact evidence[141] and the evidence is otherwise appropriate for rebuttal.[142]

(ix) Section 666, Criminal Code: Previous Convictions

A further exception to the rule that restricts the Crown to evidence of general reputation is that found in s. 666 of the *Criminal Code*. That section provides as follows:

> Where, at a trial, the accused adduces evidence of his good character the prosecutor may, *in answer thereto*, before a verdict is returned, adduce evidence of the previous conviction of the accused for any offences, including any previous conviction by reason of which a greater punishment may be imposed. [emphasis added]

The purpose of this provision is to ensure that prior convictions will be allowed as evidence of bad character even though they offend the rule that bad character cannot generally be proved by specific acts of misconduct.[143] On the theory that the accused cannot divide his character, all convictions could be proved. However, some convictions would lack sufficient probative value.[144]

The precondition that the accused adduce evidence of good character is the same as that which attracts the common law principle.[145] Accordingly, evidence of good character elicited on cross-examination which is merely the personal opinion of the witness (and

---

140 *R. v. Tierney*, *supra*, note 134. For the circumstance in which the accused can adduce expert evidence of good character, see this Chapter, III.B.1.(a).(iii).

141 *R. v. Guay*, [1979] 1 S.C.R. 18, 42 C.C.C. (2d) 536, 6 C.R. (3d) 130, 89 D.L.R. (3d) 532, 23 N.R. 451, per Pigeon J., at 547 (C.C.C.); *R. v. McNamara (No. 1)*, *supra*, note 122; *R. v. McFadden*, *supra*, note 125.

142 I.e., the Crown is not splitting its case; see Chapter 16, VII and VIII.

143 *Morris v. R.*, [1979] 1 S.C.R. 405, 43 C.C.C. (2d) 129, at 158, 6 C.R. (3d) 36, 91 D.L.R. (3d) 161, 23 N.R. 109.

144 *R. v. Corbett*, [1988] 1 S.C.R. 670, 41 C.C.C. (3d) 385, 64 C.R. (3d) 1, 28 B.C.L.R. (2d) 145, [1988] 4 W.W.R. 481, 85 N.R. 81, 34 C.R.R. 54.

145 As discussed this Chapter, III.B.1.(a).

therefore not properly admissible as evidence of good character) will not attract the application of the section.[146]

Where s. 666 applies, it is not restricted to convictions registered prior to the date of the alleged offence, but can include later registered convictions so long as they were close enough in time as to be relevant to the accused's disposition at the time of the alleged offence.[147]

(x) Section 12, Canada Evidence Act

Section 12(1) of the *Canada Evidence Act* provides as follows:

> A witness may be questioned as to whether he has been convicted of an offence, and on being so questioned, if he either denies the fact or refuses to answer, the opposite party may prove the conviction.

The cross-examination permitted by s. 12 is limited to the identity of the crime, the substance and effect of the indictment, the place of conviction and the penalty.[148] Questions surrounding the details of previous convictions are allowed in cross-examination if defence counsel has brought out many of the details in the examination-in-chief.[149]

As with s. 666 of the Code, proof of young offender convictions is permitted where the offence is one which would have been punishable under the Code had the accused been an adult at the time of its commission.[150] The offences which may be proved under s. 12 do not include only offences which bear on veracity, but includes "any offence".[151] Also, it is not only how the witness answers the questions on a previous record which goes to credibility, but the fact that a

---

146 *R. v. Close* (1982), 68 C.C.C. (2d) 105, 137 D.L.R. (3d) 655, 38 O.R. 453 (C.A.); leave to appeal to S.C.C. refd. 61 N.S.R. (2d) 447*n*, 52 N.R. 397*n*.
147 *Ibid.*
148 *R. v. Laurier* (1983), 11 W.C.B. 165, 1 O.A.C. 128 (Ont. C.A.).
149 *R. v. Grosse* (1983), 9 C.C.C. (3d) 465, 61 N.S.R. (2d) 54 (N.S.C.A.); leave to appeal to S.C.C. refd. 52 N.R. 397*n*, 61 N.S.R. (2d) 447*n*.
150 *Morris v. R.*, *supra*, note 143; *R. v. Boyko* (1975), 28 C.C.C. (2d) 193 (B.C.C.A.); *R. v. Bradbury* (1973), 14 C.C.C. (2d) 139, 23 C.R.N.S. 293 (Ont. C.A.); *R. v. Domstad* (1982), 65 C.C.C. (2d) 355, 27 C.R. (3d) 126, 134 D.L.R. (3d) 66, [1982] 2 W.W.R. 294 (Alta. C.A.); see *Young Offenders Act*, R.S.C. 1985, c. Y-1, s. 36.
151 *R. v. Brown* (1978), 38 C.C.C. (2d) 339 (Ont. C.A.).

criminal record exists.[152] Accused persons cannot be cross-examined with respect to offences they are only suspected of having committed[153] or in such a way as to suggest that they have previously been suspected of other crimes.[154] Nor can they be cross-examined on dispositions other than convictions.[155]

An issue that has arisen in the context of s. 12 is whether the judge has a discretion to disallow questions on prior convictions if the probative value of such questions is outweighed by the prejudice to the accused.[156] The courts in England, considering a differently worded provision, have held that the judge does have such a discretion.[157] Until the decision of the Supreme Court of Canada in *R. v. Corbett*,[158] the prevailing view was that the judge had no such discretion, but could give guidance to the jury if he or she viewed the questions to be of limited value.[159] In *Corbett*, the majority concluded that s. 12 of the *Canada Evidence Act* did not violate s. 11(d) of the *Canadian Charter of Rights and Freedoms* because a trial judge has a discretion to exclude evidence of prior convictions in an appropriate case.

In this regard, La Forest J., with whom the majority agreed in this respect, proposed a non-exhaustive list of factors to be considered by the trial judge in the exercise of this discretion. The factors are: (i) the temporal proximity of the previous conviction to the present charge; (ii) the nature of the previous conviction — if it was credit- or integrity-related then clearly admission is favoured, but if the previous offence was similar to the present charge, that increases the prejudice substantially and favours exclusion; and (iii) the fairness to the prosecution of exclusion following an attack by the accused on the credi-

---

152 *R. v. Gonzague* (1983), 34 C.R. (3d) 169, 4 C.C.C. (3d) 505 (Ont. C.A.); *R. v. Tuckey* (1985), 20 C.C.C. (3d) 502, 46 C.R. (3d) 97, 9 O.A.C. 218 (Ont. C.A.).
153 *R. v. Koufis*, [1941] S.C.R. 481, 76 C.C.C. 161, [1941] 3 D.L.R. 657 (S.C.C.).
154 *R. v. Logiacco* (1984), 11 C.C.C. (3d) 374, 2 O.A.C. 177 (C.A.).
155 *R. v. Danson* (1982), 66 C.C.C. (2d) 369, at 372, 35 O.R. (2d) 777 (Ont. C.A.).
156 *R. v. McLean* (1940), 73 C.C.C. 310, [1940] 2 D.L.R. 733 (N.B.S.C. C.A.); *Morris v. R., supra*, note 143, at 153 (C.C.C.).
157 *R. v. Sang*, [1980] A.C. 402, [1979] 2 All E.R. 1222 (H.L.).
158 *Supra*, note 144; see also *Morris v. R., supra*, note 143, at 431-34.
159 *R. v. Stratton* (1978), 42 C.C.C. (2d) 449, 3 C.R. (3d) 289, 90 D.L.R. (3d) 420, 21 O.R. (2d) 258 (C.A.); *R. v. Grosse* (1983), 9 C.C.C. (3d) 465, 61 N.S.R. (2d) 54 (N.S.C.A.); leave to appeal to S.C.C. refd. 52 N.R. 397*n*, 61 N.S.R. (2d) 447*n*.

bility of Crown witnesses. Inasmuch as the jury should not be given an imbalanced picture of credit, this factor will depend on the circumstances of the evidence tendered, and in particular whether there is other less prejudicial evidence which attacks the credibility of the accused. While these factors are to be considered, it is unclear what the precise relationship between prejudice and probity must be to warrant exclusion.[160] The narrow formulation of the exclusionary standard, that the probative value must be of trifling value and of grave prejudice to the accused,[161] appears to be losing favour to a test more favourable to the accused, namely, whenever the prejudicial effect of the evidence of prior conviction would be out of all proportion to its true evidential value, it should be excluded.[162]

Section 12 also applies to convictions in foreign jurisdictions, as criminal conduct in another country impairs credibility no less than a conviction in Canada.[163] The jury must be properly charged that evidence admitted pursuant to s. 12 goes *only* to credibility and cannot otherwise be used to show that the accused likely committed the offence.[164] It is for the jury to decide what weight is to be given to the conviction. Accordingly, it is misdirection to charge the jury that prior convictions could seriously affect the accused's credibility.[165]

(xi) Proposal for Reform

The present rules relating to character evidence in criminal cases are badly in need of reform. Draft proposals for reform have been studied extensively for years and never implemented.[166]

It is submitted that the *Rowton* rule limiting the evidence of character witnesses to evidence of reputation be revised to permit

---

160 Referred to and left open by Lamer J. in *Morris*, [1983] 2 S.C.R. 190, at 203-04, 7 C.C.C. (3d) 97, 36 C.R. (3d) 1, 1 D.L.R. (4th) 385, [1984] 2 W.W.R. 1 and by La Forest J. again in *Corbett*, *supra*, note 144.

161 *R. v. Wray*, [1971] S.C.R. 272, at 293, [1970] 4 C.C.C. 1, 11 C.R.N.S. 235, 11 D.L.R. (3d) 673, per Martland J.

162 Per La Forest J. in *R. v. Corbett*, *supra*, note 144, at 733, quoting Lord Fraser in *Sang*, *supra*, note 157. See also Chapter 2, II.C.1.

163 *R. v. Stratton*, *supra*, note 159.

164 *R. v. Warren* (1976), 11 C.R.N.S. 217 (Ont. C.A.); *R. v. Crawford* (1980), 54 C.C.C. (2d) 412, 18 C.R. (3d) 171 (Ont. C.A.).

165 *R. v. Todish* (1985), 18 C.C.C. (3d) 159, 7 O.A.C. 336 (Ont. C.A.).

166 For the history of Bill S-33, see *Report of the Special Committee of the Canadian Bar Association on Evidence*.

evidence of personal knowledge of specific acts. While this rule might have been appropriate in an age when persons generally belonged to a well-defined community, this is no longer the case. In this age of ultra-mobility, asking a witness to describe the reputation of the accused in the community usually leads to a wholly artificial answer or a disguised conclusion based on the witness' knowledge of specific conduct. Such evidence is most unreliable and encourages hearsay, gossip and rumour.[167]

Rebuttal evidence by the Crown, whether in the form of cross-examination or extrinsic evidence, should also be permitted by reference to specific acts. By reason of the greater cogency which such evidence would acquire, the rebuttal evidence should be restricted to the relevant character trait.

Finally, by reason of the serious consequences to the accused who drops his protective shield, the law should be altered to prevent this from happening inadvertently. In the absence of a statement by counsel that the accused is putting character in issue, evidence of the accused should not be construed as character evidence unless the Crown has objected to its introduction as being otherwise irrelevant. The accused would then be on notice that, if he or she persists, he or she has placed character in issue.[168]

---

167 R. Cross and C. Tapper, *Cross on Evidence*, 7th ed. (London: Butterworths, 1990), at 333.

168 See J. Sopinka, *Report of the Special Committee of the Canadian Bar Association on Evidence* (Ottawa: Canadian Bar Association, 1986), at 7: "The most difficult problem facing practising defence counsel in relation to character evidence is determining when the accused has put his character in issue, thereby triggering the Crown's right to lead rebuttal evidence. The great concern is that an accused will inadvertently put his character in issue, or that some general comment will later be construed by the judge as character evidence. In order to address this practical problem, the Committee is strongly of the view that the Bill should be amended so as to require the prosecution to state its position that evidence being led is character evidence as a condition precedent to the Crown being able to call rebuttal evidence. By requiring the Crown to state its position at the commencement of the accused's introduction of character evidence, defence counsel can have the issue clarified by the judge in advance and, if the judge feels the evidence about to be led is character evidence, the accused's counsel can make an informed tactical decision as to whether to proceed to adduce that evidence. The Committee considers this to be eminently fair. It is not burdensome to the Crown and would eliminate any surprise at a later stage. This obligation on the Crown is included in the proposed revisions of the Committee below".

2. Character of Persons other than the Accused

(a) *Of Non-Victim, Non-Witness, Third Parties*

Unlike the case of the accused, evidence of the character of a third party is not excluded by any rule of policy. So long as it is relevant and not otherwise excluded by a rule of evidence, evidence of the bad character of a third party can be adduced by the defence.[169] For example, in *R. v. McMillan*[170] the accused, charged with the murder of his child was entitled to adduce psychiatric evidence of his wife's personality in order to prove that she was more likely to have committed the offence than he was.[171] However, by this evidence the accused put his character in issue.

(b) *Of Non-Witnesses or Complainants*

(i) In General

As stated above, no policy rule excludes evidence of the character of a third party led by the accused in support of his defence, and this includes a victim or complainant.[172] The accused generally introduces such evidence in putting forward the defence of self-defence or provocation.[173] For example, in *R. v. Scopelliti*[174] the accused raised the defence of self-defence to a murder charge and was permitted to call evidence of the deceased's reputation and disposition for violence. The accused can prove such disposition by (a) evidence of reputation, (b) proof of specific acts, and (c) expert opinion evidence of dis-

---

169 *R. v. McMillan* (1975), 23 C.C.C. (2d) 160, 29 C.R.N.S. 191, 7 O.R. (2d) 750 (Ont. C.A.); affd. [1977] 2 S.C.R. 824, 33 C.C.C. (2d) 360, 73 D.L.R. (3d) 759; *R. v. Scopelliti* (1981), 63 C.C.C. (2d) 481, 34 O.R. (2d) 524 (Ont. C.A.).
170 *Ibid.*
171 To similar effect are the decisions in *R. v. Speid* (1985), 46 C.R. (3d) 22, 20 C.C.C. (3d) 534, 9 O.A.C. 237 (C.A.) and *Lowery v. R.*, [1974] A.C. 85, [1973] 3 All E.R. 662 (P.C.).
172 *R. v. Scopelliti, supra*, note 169; special rules apply where the complainant is a victim of a sexual assault.
173 *Ibid.*; *R. v. Valley* (1986), 26 C.C.C. (3d) 207, 13 O.A.C. 89 (Ont. C.A.); leave to appeal to S.C.C. refd. 26 C.C.C. (3d) 207n, 67 N.R. 158n, 15 O.A.C. 240n; *R. v. Linney*, [1978] 1 S.C.R. 646, 32 C.C.C. (2d) 294, 73 D.L.R. (3d) 4, [1977] 2 W.W.R. 158, 13 N.R. 217 (S.C.C.); *R. v. Dubois* (1976), 30 C.C.C. (2d) 412 (Ont. C.A.); *R. v. Drouin* (1909), 15 C.C.C. 205 (Que. K.B.); *R. v. Scott* (1910), 15 C.C.C. 442 (Ont. H.C.J.).
174 *Supra*, note 169.

position.[175] With respect to the specific acts evidence, this does not have to meet the test of similar fact evidence. Where the reputation and acts are known to the accused at the time of the incident, such evidence is admissible to show the accused's reasonable apprehension of violence from the deceased when that state of mind is a relevant issue.[176]

The previous reputation or acts of violence need not have been known to the accused at the time of the incident so long as there is some other evidence of aggression on the part of the deceased during the incident. This evidence is relevant to show the probability of the deceased having been the aggressor and to support the accused's evidence. It would be open for the Crown to refute this evidence with evidence of the deceased's peaceable character.[177]

(ii) In Sexual Offences

The old common law position regarding the character of the victim of a sexual assault is that set out in *R. v. Finnessey*,[178] where Osler J.A. stated:[179]

The prosecutrix may be asked the questions to shew that her general character of chastity is bad. She is bound to answer such questions and if she refuses to do so the fact may be shewn. . . . So too she may be asked whether she has previously had connection with prisoner and if she denies it that may be shown. . . . Such evidence is relevant to the issue since in both cases it bears

---

175 *Ibid.*
176 *Ibid.*
177 *Ibid.*
178 (1906), 11 O.L.R. 338, 10 C.C.C. 347 (C.A.).
179 *Ibid.*, at 341 (O.L.R.); *Cross on Evidence, supra*, note 167, at 322-23 and at 295-96. See also *R. v. Boucher*, [1963] 2 C.C.C. 241, 39 C.R. 242, 40 W.W.R. 663 (B.C.C.A.); *R. v. Dyment* (1966), 5 W.W.R. 575 (B.C.C.A.); *R. v. Basken* (1974), 28 C.R.N.S. 359, 21 C.C.C. (2d) 321 (Sask. C.A.); *Laliberté v. R.* (1877), 1 S.C.R. 117; *R. v. Konkin*, [1983] 1 S.C.R. 388, 3 C.C.C. (3d) 289, 34 C.R. (3d) 1, [1983] 6 W.W.R. 292, 27 Alta. L.R. (2d) 193, 145 D.L.R. (3d) 577, 44 A.R. 10, 47 N.R. 124; *R. v. Krausz* (1973), 57 Cr. App. Rep. 466 (C.A.); *R. v. Moulton* (1979), 51 C.C.C. (2d) 154, 13 C.R. (3d) 143, [1980] 1 W.W.R. 711, 19 A.R. 286 (Alta. C.A.); *R. v. Seaboyer; R. v. Gayme* (1987), 58 C.R. (3d) 289, 37 C.C.C. (3d) 53, 35 C.R.R. 300, 20 O.A.C. 345 (C.A.); (1991), 66 C.C.C. (3d) 321, 83 D.L.R. (4th) 193, 4 O.R. (3d) 383n (S.C.C.).

directly upon the question of consent and the improbability of the connection complained of having taken place against the will of the prosecutrix.

And she may be asked, but, inasmuch as the question is one going strictly to her credit, she is not generally compellable to answer whether she has had connection with persons other than the prisoner. This seems to rest to some extent in the discretion of the trial Judge. Whether, however, she answers it or not that is an end of the matter, otherwise as many collateral, and therefore irrelevant issues might be raised as there were specific charges of immorality suggested, and the prosecutrix could not be expected to come prepared to meet them, though she might well be prepared to repel an attack upon her general character for chastity.

The common law rule had been seen as producing, through the cross-examination, a traumatic ordeal for the complainant to the point where for some observers it appeared that the complainant and not the accused was on trial. This process was seen to inhibit complainants from laying complaints and, if accurate, then the course of justice was being adversely affected. Also, it is now the general view that sexual relations outside marriage are more common and not subject to public opprobrium as in earlier times. The reasons for engaging or refusing to engage in those relations had less to do with morality and more to do with other factors such as the choice of partner and the circumstances of the occasion.[180]

In response to the changing social times, Parliament enacted s. 142(1) of the Code which provided some unforeseen and unfortunate effects for complainants.[181] The section has been superseded by more recent *Criminal Code* amendments found in ss. 276 and 277.[182]

These sections provide as follows:

276 (1) In proceedings in respect of an offence under sections

---

180   R. v. Seaboyer, ibid., at 297-98.

181   See Forsythe v. R., [1980] 2 S.C.R. 268, 53 C.C.C. (2d) 225, 15 C.R. (3d) 280, 112 D.L.R. (3d) 385, 32 N.R. 520 (S.C.C.) interpreting R.S.C. 1970, c. C-34, s. 142 [rep. & sub. 1974-75-76, c. 93, s. 8; rep. 1980-81-82-83, c. 125, s. 6].

182   R.S.C. 1985, c. C-46, ss. 276, 277 [rep. & sub. R.S.C. 1985, c. 19 (3rd Supp.), ss. 12, 13].

151, 152, 153, 155 or 159, subsections 160(2) or (3), or sections 170, 171, 172, 173, 271, 272 or 273, no evidence shall be adduced by or on behalf of the accused concerning the sexual activity of the complainant with any person other than the accused unless

(a) it is evidence that rebuts evidence of the complainant's sexual activity or absence thereof that was previously adduced by the prosecution;

(b) it is evidence of specific instances of the complainant's sexual activity tending to establish the identity of the person who had sexual contact with the complainant on the occasion set out in the charge; or

(c) it is evidence of sexual activity that took place on the same occasion as the sexual activity that forms the subject-matter of the charge, where the evidence relates to the consent that the accused alleges he believed was given by the complainant.

(2) No evidence is admissible under paragraph (1)(c) unless

(a) reasonable notice in writing has been given to the prosecutor by or on behalf of the accused of his intention to adduce the evidence together with particulars of the evidence sought to be adduced; and

(b) a copy of the notice has been filed with the clerk of the court.

(3) No evidence is admissible under subsection (1) unless the judge, magistrate or justice, after holding a hearing in which the jury and the members of the public are excluded and in which the complainant is not a compellable witness, is satisfied that the requirements of this section are met.

. . .

277   In proceedings in respect of any offence under section 151, 152, 153, 155 or 159, subsection 160(2) or (3) or section 170, 171, 172, 173, 271, 272 or 273, evidence of sexual reputation, therefore, whether general or specific, is not admissible for the purpose of challenging or supporting the credibility of the complainant.

Evidence of sexual reputation therefore, whether general or specific, is not admissible for attacking or supporting the credibility of the complainant.[183] Where such evidence is relevant to an issue in the trial other than credibility, it can be admitted.[184] The comments of Grange J.A. in *R. v. Seaboyer*[185] reflect the purpose of this provision:

> I think that s. 246.7 [now s. 277] which excludes evidence of sexual reputation for the purpose of challenging or supporting credibility is a true reflection of modern standards. Sexual reputation is no more an indicator of credibility in a woman than it is in a man. It should no longer be recognized as relevant to that issue. It may, of course, be relevant to other issues such as an honest belief in consent but the section does not exclude cross-examination for that purpose or indeed any other purpose than credibility.

Neither of these provisions addresses the question of the complainant's sexual relations with the accused, only third parties. The latter remains a permissible line of inquiry, subject to the trial judge's discretion to forbid degrading questions. Because s. 277 only prohibits evidence going to credibility, it would not deprive an accused of evidence relevant to the defence. Its constitutional validity stands on a different footing than s. 276, which concerns not only evidence going to credibility, but also evidence that may go to a legitimate defence. By virtue of s. 276, evidence of the complainant's sexual relationship with a party other than the accused was admissible only under the following conditions:

> (a) it is evidence that rebuts evidence of the complainant's sexual activity or absence thereof that was previously adduced by the prosecution;[186]

---

183   Section 277; this is narrower than the position under the former s. 142. See, for example, *Forsythe v. R., supra,* note 181; *R. v. Konkin, supra,* note 179.
184   *R. v. Seaboyer, supra,* note 179, at 299 (O.R.).
185   *Ibid.*
186   For cases and commentary considering this section see, D. Watt, *The New Offences Against the Person: The Provisions of Bill C-127* (Toronto: Butterworths, 1984), at 193; *R. v. Gran* (1984), 13 W.C.B. 86, [1984] B.C.D. Crim. Conv. 6105-03 (C.A.); *R. v. Oquataq* (1985), 18 C.C.C. (3d) 440, 13 C.R.R. 370, [1985] N.W.T.R. 240 (S.C.); *R. v. Wiseman* (1985), 22 C.C.C. (3d) 12 (Ont. D.C.).

(b) it is evidence of specific instances of the complainant's sexual activity tending to establish the identity of the person who had sexual contact with the complainant on the occasion set out in the charge;[187] or

(c) it is evidence of sexual activity that took place on the same occasion as the sexual activity that forms the subject-matter of the charge, where that evidence relates to the consent that the accused alleges he believed was given by the complainant.[188]

The list was exhaustive. The trial judge retained no judicial discretion to allow questioning or evidence that is relevant to a defence which does not fit into these categories. The exact scope of these provisions was unclear. They seemed rather vague and one could only foresee a great deal of difficulty in interpretation.

There is no doubt that s. 276 could have the effect of prohibiting the accused from adducing evidence relevant to a legitimate defence. The examples offered by Grange J.A. who delivered the majority decision of the Ontario Court of Appeal in *R. v. Seaboyer*[189] illustrate two possible scenarios in which this might occur because it would be sexual conduct on a different occasion.[190]

If, for example, the defence was that the complainant was a prostitute who sought after the act to obtain a larger fee on threat of exposure or false accusations of assault, evidence of similar acts of that nature in the past would be relevant; if by way of another example, the complainant notoriously attended a certain place and regularly offered herself to anyone there without charge, that might go to an honest belief in consent if that were the defence. It might also be noted that the latter example would not fall within para. (c) of the subsection because it would be sexual conduct on a different occasion.

Grange J.A. was of the view that s. 276 might operate to deprive an accused person of a fair trial in these circumstances. The accused

---

187 For cases and commentary considering this section, see Parker, "The 'New' Sexual Offences" (1982), 31 C.R. (3d) 317, at 327; *R. v. Kapsales* (1985), 15 W.C.B. 433, [1986] Ont. D. Crim. Conv. 5108-02 (Dist. Ct.).
188 Parker, *ibid.*; Watt, *supra*, note 186, at 194.
189 *Supra*, note 179, 61 O.R. (2d) 290 (C.A.); the Court of Appeal in this case commented on the validity of the section but decided the case on other grounds.
190 *Ibid.*, at 300 (O.R.).

might be denied the opportunity for full answer and defence and in that event s. 7 or 11(d) of the *Charter* would be violated.

As to the effect of s. 1 of the *Charter*, Grange J.A. was of the view that s. 276 could not be saved.[191]

> I think it would be a most unusual result that a law which offends s. 7 in that it deprives an accused person of making full answer and defence could ever be found 'to be demonstrably justified in a free and democratic society'.
>
> . . .
>
> In any event it would, at least in theory, have been possible to list the exceptions more fully so as not to offend s. 7 and it certainly would have been feasible to leave a residual discretion in the trial judge so that evidence genuinely relevant to a legitimate defence would not be excluded.

The majority of the Ontario Court of Appeal was not, however, of the opinion that s. 276 was, on its face, contrary to any provision of the *Charter*, because it was only in very limited circumstances that an accused would be deprived of the right to call such relevant evidence. It was open for an accused to argue an infringement of the *Charter* on a case-by-case basis.[192]

The Supreme Court of Canada in *R. v. Seaboyer*[193] and *R. v. Gayme*[194] struck down s. 276 on the ground that it is inconsistent with ss. 7 and 11(d) of the *Charter*. The Court laid down guidelines as to what evidence of past sexual misconduct was admissible. Evidence that the complainant has engaged in consensual sexual conduct on other occasions (including past sexual conduct with the accused) is not admissible solely to support the inference that the complainant is more likely to have consented to the conduct in issue or is less worthy of belief as a witness. Examples of admissible evidence are provided as follows:[195]

---

191 *Ibid.*, at 302-03.

192 *Ibid.*, at 304.

193 (1991), 66 C.C.C. (3d) 321, 83 D.L.R. (4th) 193, 4 O.R. (3d) 383*n*, 128 N.R. 81 (S.C.C.).

194 Hereinafter referred to as *R. v. Seaboyer*, *ibid.*

195 *Supra*, note 193 at 407-08 (C.C.C.).

(A) Evidence of specific instances of sexual conduct tending to prove that a person other than the accused caused the physical consequences of the rape alleged by the prosecution;

(B) Evidence of sexual conduct tending to prove bias or motive to fabricate on the part of the victim;

(C) Evidence of prior sexual conduct, known to the accused at the time of the act charged, tending to prove that the accused believed that the complainant was consenting to the act charged (Without laying down absolute rules, normally one would expect some proximity in time between the conduct that is alleged to have given rise to an honest belief and the conduct charged.);

(D) Evidence of prior sexual conduct which meets the requirements for the reception of similar act evidence, bearing in mind that such evidence cannot be used illegitimately merely to show that the complainant consented or is an unreliable witness;

(E) Evidence tending to rebut proof introduced by the prosecution regarding the complainant's sexual conduct.

These examples are by way of illustration only and are not intended to limit the general rule that [evidence] of consensual sexual conduct on the part of the complainant may be admissible for purpose other than an inference relating to the consent or credibility of the complainant where it possesses probative value on an issue in the trial and where that probative value is not substantially outweighed by the danger of unfair prejudice flowing from the evidence."[196]

The admissibility of this type of evidence is to be determined in an *in camera* hearing by way of *voir dire*. If admitted, the jury must be cautioned as to the use that may be made of the evidence.

3. Character of Witnesses in General

(a) *In General*

The special rules and considerations which apply to the accused or a complainant as witness have previously been dealt with. This section is concerned with introducing evidence of the character of a witness who is neither an accused nor a complainant. Such evidence

---

196   *Ibid.*, at 409 (C.C.C.).

generally goes to the issue of credibility only. Broadly speaking, the same rules apply to witnesses in criminal proceedings as were dealt with above in relation to witnesses in civil proceedings.[197]

As in civil proceedings, bolstering the credibility of one's own witness with evidence of good character is generally not permitted, and such practice is commonly referred to as "oath-helping".[198] The Crown can reclaim with good character evidence the character of a witness whose credibility has been impugned, but such reclamation cannot go beyond reasonable limits.[199]

The credibility of an ordinary witness can be impugned in a number of ways, including ways tending to prove the bad character by evidence of disposition or past acts of the witness. On this basis, evidence of previous convictions, bias and corruption, general lack of veracity or discreditable acts can be raised.[200] Because this type of evidence goes only to credibility, the collateral fact rule applies to any answers given by the witness on cross-examination.[201] There are a number of exceptions to the collateral fact rule in this context which have been reviewed elsewhere in this text.[202]

(b) *Previous Convictions*

Section 12 of the *Canada Evidence Act* applies to all witnesses in a criminal proceeding, and the same considerations apply as were dealt with above in relation to the accused as witness. It is, however, doubtful that the trial judge has a discretion to refuse to permit cross-examination of an ordinary witness. The interpretation of s. 12 arrived at in *Corbett* was largely due to the fact that the section would otherwise have violated the *Charter*. In the case of an ordinary witness,

---

197 See this Chapter, II.A.
198 *R. v. Turner*, [1975] Q.B. 834, at 842, [1975] 1 All E.R. 70, at 75; *R. v. Clarke* (1981), 63 C.C.C. (2d) 224, [1981] 6 W.W.R. 417, 32 A.R. 92 (Alta. C.A.), leave to appeal to S.C.C. refd. (1981), 63 C.C.C. (2d) 224, 34 A.R. 270n, 41 N.R. 445 (S.C.C.), R. Cross and C. Tapper, *Cross on Evidence*, 7th ed. (London: Butterworths, 1990), at 312.
199 *R. v. Clarke, ibid.*; *Mawson v. Hartsink* (1802), 4 Esp. 102; *R. v. Whelan* (1881), 14 Cox C.C. 595 (Q.B.).
200 *Cross on Evidence, supra*, note 198.
201 *Cross on Evidence, ibid.*, at 314; P.K. McWilliams, *Canadian Criminal Evidence*, 2nd ed. (Aurora: Canada Law Book, 1984); *R. v. Cargill* (1913), 8 Cr. App. Rep. 224, [1913] 2 K.B. 271 (C.A.); *Harris v. Tippett* (1911), 2 Camp. 637.
202 See the discussion, Chapter 16, II.

these conditions do not arise. Moreover, in the case of an ordinary witness, cross-examination on the facts surrounding the commission of the crime is permitted where relevant to credibility.[203]

Although the trial judge may have no discretion to disallow questioning or proof coming within s. 12,[204] where the offence is not one strictly relevant to credibility the judge can, in the charge to the jury, advise that they consider the evidence to be of little probative value.[205]

---

203 Not on the basis of s. 12 but because of the wide scope for cross-examination of witnesses about discreditable acts in general.

204 *R. v. Stratton* (1978), 3 C.R. (3d) 289, 42 C.C.C. (2d) 449, 21 O.R. (2d) 258. The decision in *R. v. Corbett*, [1988] 1 S.C.R. 670, 41 C.C.C. (3d) 385, 64 C.R. (3d) 1 (C.A.) is not applicable to an ordinary witness and therefore this is still a good authority.

205 *R. v. Brown* (1978), 38 C.C.C. (2d) 339, per Martin J.A., at 342 (Ont. C.A.).

CHAPTER 11

SIMILAR FACT EVIDENCE

I INTRODUCTION

A. *The "Similar Facts Rule"*

In Chapter 10, the chapter on character evidence, we described a general exclusionary rule of evidence which prohibits a party from adducing evidence of the bad character of an opposite party to prove or disprove a fact in issue when that person's character is not an issue in the proceedings.[1] In criminal cases, it prohibits the prosecution from adducing evidence of the accused's disposition or propensity to commit crimes or evidence of specific instances of misconduct by the accused on other occasions. This exclusionary rule is an exception to one of the basic principles of the law of evidence that all relevant evidence is admissible.

The so-called "similar facts rule" is an exception to the general exclusionary rule barring evidence of the bad character of a party. In exceptional circumstances, a party may adduce evidence of the bad character of the opposite party to prove or disprove a fact in issue. Similar fact evidence is admissible if it is relevant to an issue in the case other than a relevance that derives simply from showing the party is a bad person *and* its probative value outweighs the prejudice to the party that may arise from the admission of such evidence. Under the rule, a party may adduce expert opinion or general reputation evidence to prove the opposite party's disposition, specific incidents of misconduct on other occasions, possession of documents or past associations if such evidence is relevant to an issue in the case *and* the probative value

---

1 As to when character is in issue see Chapter 10, II. Character may be a fact in issue, for example, where the defence to libel is justification or where entrapment is alleged.

of such evidence outweighs its prejudicial effect. Thus, the Crown may adduce evidence of previous misconduct by the accused if the evidence is relevant to prove that the accused was the perpetrator of the crime *and* the admission of the identity evidence outweighs its prejudicial effect: for example, it constitutes a hallmark of the way the accused has previously committed the same or similar crimes. While the rule applies equally to both civil and criminal cases, the dangers which attach to the admission of similar fact evidence are substantially greater in criminal cases, the context in which the rule has primarily developed. As demonstrated by the jurisprudence and academic commentary, the scope and application of the rule remain controversial.

B. *Terminology*

The expression "similar facts rule"[2] or "similar facts evidence rule" is an umbrella term which encompasses a loose category of evidence tending to show a person's discreditable disposition, past conduct, possessions or reputation.[3] The expression is misleading in a number of respects. First, it refers to an exception to the general rule excluding evidence of bad character or disposition rather than to the rule itself, i.e., evidence of similar facts will be admitted in certain circumstances. Second, the exclusionary rule is not limited to evidence of facts or acts similar to those in issue in the proceedings but also includes non-similar evidence. In this respect, the label is neither very accurate nor descriptive. For example, in *R. v. Straffen*,[4] evidence that the accused had recently escaped a psychiatric institution was adduced in part to show that the accused had the opportunity to commit the offence with which he was charged. Similarly, in *R. v. Morris*,[5] evidence of a newspaper clipping on the heroin trade found in the apartment of the accused was adduced to show intention to commit the crime of trafficking in narcotics. One may rightly question whether the term "similar fact evidence" is the appropriate expression with which to capture this often incoherent body of evidence. The only response,

---

2   It is also referred to as "the similar fact" and "the similar acts rule".

3   R. Cross and C. Tapper, *Cross on Evidence*, 7th ed. (London: Butterworths, 1990), at 339.

4   [1952] 2 All E.R. 657, [1952] 2 Q.B. 911 (Q.B.D.).

5   [1983] 2 S.C.R. 190, 7 C.C.C. (3d) 97, 36 C.R. (3d) 1, [1984] 2 W.W.R. 1, 1 D.L.R. (4th) 385, 48 N.R. 341.

admittedly unsatisfactory, is that the terminology is "too deeply engrained to be abandoned".[6]

C. Scope of the Rule

The nature of the evidence admitted under the "similar facts" rule share the general trait of being adduced to show past discreditable conduct tending to prove that the accused is a morally corrupt person or has a propensity or disposition to commit the type of crime of which he or she is accused or to commit crimes in general. In order for such evidence to be admissible, or, in other words, to come within the category of "similar facts" or "similar acts" evidence, it must be relevant to some issue in the case other than merely to show general disposition or moral defect. As will be discussed further, how this exception for evidence of bad character is framed is the subject of some controversy.

There are different types of evidence admitted under the similar facts rule even though they will show the accused to have a *bad* character or disposition. The types of evidence can be usefully described as follows:

True similar acts evidence are proven facts that the accused acted on other occasions in a way which he or she is alleged to have acted on the occasion in dispute. For example, the evidence may be of acts of previous violence by the accused against the victim of an assault or homicide,[7] or even on a third party.[8] A pattern of similarity need not necessarily relate to events or facts that create a negative impression in themselves. For example, in *R. v. Mustafa*,[9] the accused was charged with procuring goods by deception by proffering a stolen credit card in payment for some meat purchased at a frozen food store. The

---

6   *Cross on Evidence, supra*, note 3, at 339.
7   For example, see *Theal v. R.* (1882), 7 S.C.R. 397; *R. v. Roud* (1981), 21 C.R. (3d) 97, 58 C.C.C. (2d) 226 (Ont. C.A.); leave to appeal to S.C.C. refd. 58 C.C.C. (2d) 226n; *R. v. Bodnarchuk* (1949), 94 C.C.C. 279, 8 C.R. 293, [1949] 1 W.W.R. 161, 57 Man. R. 291, [1949] 3 D.L.R. 565 (C.A.); *R. v. Drysdale*, [1969] 2 C.C.C. 141, 66 W.W.R. 664 (Man. C.A.); *R. v. Leforte* (1961), 130 C.C.C. 318, 35 C.R. 227, 29 D.L.R. (2d) 459 (B.C.C.A.); revd. 131 C.C.C. 169, 36 C.R. 181, 31 D.L.R. (2d) 1 (S.C.C.).
8   To list but a few examples, *R. v. Boyle*, [1914] 3 K.B. 339 (C.C.A.); *R. v. Davis*, [1963] Crim. L.R. 40 (C.C.A.); *R. v. Mortimer* (1936), 25 Cr. App. R. 150 (C.C.A.) and *R. v. Straffen, supra*, note 4.
9   (1976), 65 Cr. App. R. 26.

accused's defence was misidentification. The prosecution adduced evidence that the accused had been in the store on previous occasions, had loaded a shopping cart with meat and had left the store, abandoning the cart. These acts, viewed objectively, were innocent on their own, but coupled with the other direct evidence on the charge, gave rise to the possibility of a trial run for a later crime or a botched previous attempt.

Unproven similar acts evidence is evidence of acts on other occasions which the accused is alleged to have committed, but which remain as yet unproven. This occurs when the indictment charges the accused with the commission of several offences, all of a similar nature, but the evidence is inconclusive on all or any one of the charges to prove that they were committed either by the accused or by the same person in each case.[10] Each of the acts is criminal and there is a strong inference that they were committed by the same person.

Evidence of similar events may indicate the repetition of a pattern of similar events which is unlikely to have resulted from coincidence, but may not establish that the accused has behaved in a similar way on any other occasion. The classic example is found in *Makin v. A.G. for New South Wales*.[11] The Makins were a couple who were charged with the death of a baby left in their care whose body was found buried in the back garden of the house in which they lived. The prosecution was permitted to adduce evidence that the bodies of a large number of other children fostered by the couple which had been found beneath the back gardens of various of the Makins' previous homes. The evidence was adduced to show that the accused were baby-killers. None of the events in themselves pointed to criminal conduct but their cumulative effect did, and was sufficiently connected to the accused to implicate them.

Evidence of disposition is evidence of non-similar acts or facts which show the accused to have a disposition likely to be possessed by the perpetrator. For example, in *R. v. Thompson*,[12] two young boys had identified the accused as a person who had made homosexual advances towards them. Through certain articles found in the accused's home the prosecution sought to demonstrate that the accused was a

---

10   For example, *Harris v. D.P.P.*, [1952] 1 All E.R. 1044, [1952] A.C. 694 (H.L.); *Sweitzer v. R.*, [1982] 5 W.W.R. 555, 37 A.R. 292, 42 N.R. 550 (S.C.C.).
11   [1891-1894] All E.R. Rep. 24, [1894] A.C. 57 (P.C.).
12   [1918] A.C. 221, [1918-19] All E.R. Rep. 521 (H.L.).

paedophile, and therefore, of a disposition most likely to be possessed by the perpetrator of the crime.

Therefore, as stated above, the heading of similar fact evidence includes evidence that is neither similar to the facts or events of the alleged crime nor is evidence of a criminal disposition. Evidence in any of these categories may or may not show that the accused has a criminal disposition or is generally morally corrupt. It is only when the evidence is of such a nature that the similar facts rule need be considered. Admissibility will depend on relevance and probative value. In determining relevance, it is submitted that the essential ingredient of the similar facts rule, that is, that the evidence tendered must be relevant to the case in some way other than merely to show a general criminal or immoral disposition, cannot be abandoned in view of the concerns underlying the rule. In other words, evidence of similar facts is relevant in the required sense and thereby admissible when there is some nexus between the similar fact evidence and the facts in issue.[13] As will be discussed further, the categories of evidence or situations in which this nexus may be found to be present are not closed and evidence will be considered to be relevant when the necessary nexus is found in the circumstances of a particular case.[14] In assessing when an exception should be made to the general rule that evidence of past discreditable conduct is inadmissible, it is of paramount importance to keep in mind the logical and policy considerations which have necessitated the similar facts rule.

II   REASONS FOR THE RULE

There are two approaches to evidence of bad character. The first is that general evidence of bad disposition is logically irrelevant and should be excluded. From this perspective, no number of similar offences can connect a particular person with a particular crime. Such evidence simply has no probative value and should be rejected on that ground. The second and clearly more prevalent view is that evidence of disposition or propensity is pertinent to establishing the guilt of the

---

13   17 *Halsbury's Laws of England*, 4th ed., § 48, at 36.
14   J. Stone, "The Rule of Exclusion of Similar Fact Evidence: England" (1932-33), 46 Harv. L. Rev. 954, at 973-76; J.L. Montrose, "Basic Concepts of the Law of Evidence" (1954), 70 L.Q. Rev. 527, at 544-46.

accused and is inherently relevant.[15] For example, if an accused is charged with breaking and entering with intent to commit theft and has raised the defence that he was present in the place for an innocent purpose, the fact that he has a lengthy record for theft would certainly discredit that defence. From this viewpoint, the obvious reason for admitting such evidence is the effective prosecution of criminals.

However, even proceeding from the basis that such general disposition evidence is intrinsically relevant to establishing the guilt of the accused, the objective of effective prosecution is not absolute and the admission of bad character evidence must be tempered not only to ensure the efficient functioning of the criminal justice system but to assure that the rights of the accused under the *Canadian Charter of Rights and Freedoms*[16] are respected. The dangers which attach to the admission of evidence of past criminal behaviour, discreditable conduct, bad reputation or the past record of an accused are substantial, especially in the context of criminal proceedings. The dangers may be identified at two levels: first, the effect on the trial process and the potential infringement of the rights of the accused under the *Charter* and second, its detrimental effect on the system of law enforcement.[17]

A. *Effect on Trial Process and on the Rights of the Accused Under the* Charter

Two fundamental principles of the Canadian criminal justice system are jeopardized when evidence of an accused's past "bad" acts or general criminal disposition is brought to the attention of the trier of fact. The first is the principle that the accused is only to stand trial on those charges set out in the indictment.[18] This principle is enshrined in ss. 7, 9, 11(a) and (h) of the *Charter*. Evidence of past convictions undermines the right not to be tried or punished twice for an offence.

---

15 See the explanation by Lamer J. in *R. v. Morris*, [1983] 2 S.C.R. 190, at 201, 7 C.C.C. (3d) 97, 36 C.R. (3d) 1, [1984] 2 W.W.R. 1, 48 N.R. 341, 1 D.L.R. (4th) 385, cited in Chapter 2, II.B.3.

16 R.S.C. 1985, App. II, No. 44.

17 See *Cross on Evidence, supra*, note 3, at 356-60; *R. v. D.(L.E.)*, [1989] 2 S.C.R. 111, 50 C.C.C. (3d) 142, 71 C.R. (3d) 1, [1989] 6 W.W.R. 501, 39 B.C.L.R. (2d) 273, 97 N.R. 321.

18 *R. v. Koufis*, [1941] S.C.R. 481, 76 C.C.C. 161, [1941] 3 D.L.R. 657 (S.C.C.) per Taschereau J., at 170 (C.C.C.).

The second principle is that the accused is to be presumed innocent until guilt is proven by the Crown beyond a reasonable doubt.[19] This right entrenched in s. 11(d) of the *Charter* is threatened by evidence of past misconduct which tends to show guilt on the part of the accused. In *R. v. D.(L.E.)*,[20] the Supreme Court of Canada noted that the inherent prejudicial effect of such evidence may be felt by a jury in several ways. One is that the jury may assume that the accused is a "bad person" who is likely to be guilty of the offence charged. A second potential prejudicial effect is that the jury might tend to punish the accused for past misconduct by finding the accused guilty of the offence charged. Both of these effects potentially undermine the presumption of innocence. A third potential prejudicial effect is that the jury might become confused as it concentrates on resolving whether the accused actually committed the past acts and the attention of the trier of fact is deflected from the main purpose of the deliberations. Having resolved the question of committing the previous misconduct, there is the danger that the jury will substitute its verdict on that matter for its verdict on the issue which it is in fact trying.

Evidence of bad disposition or discreditable past conduct therefore has the tendency to persuade the trier of fact to enter a conviction for reasons unrelated to the logical force of the remaining evidence. In other words, there is a danger that the trier will be compelled to find the accused guilty, notwithstanding that the Crown may not have proved the case beyond a reasonable doubt, on the basis that the accused should not escape punishment for those past crimes for which he or she was not convicted, or charged, or which were not detected.[21] The trier may also be inclined not to give the accused with such a past the benefit of doubt. Or, as Professor P.B. Carter expressed it, the jury may not give due regard to the possibility that the accused may have mended his or her ways or that criminal propensities only manifest themselves intermittently.[22] In other words, the dangers are that the

---

19   *Woolmington v. D.P.P.*, [1935] A.C. 462 (H.L.); *R. v. Graham*, [1974] S.C.R. 206, 7 C.C.C. (2d) 93, 19 C.R.N.S. 117, [1972] 4 W.W.R. 488, 26 D.L.R. (3d) 579.

20   *Supra*, note 17, at 127-28 (S.C.R.).

21   See comments of Dickson J. in *LeBlanc v. R.*, [1977] 1 S.C.R. 339, 29 C.C.C. (2d) 97, 68 D.L.R. (3d) 243.

22   P.B. Carter, "Forbidden Reasoning Permissible: Similar Fact Evidence a Decade After *Boardman*" (1985), 48 M.L.R. 29, at 29; *cf.* also *D.P.P. v. Boardman*, [1974] 3 All E.R. 887, [1975] A.C. 421, per Lords Hailsham and Cross.

jury may be too quick to infer the guilt of the accused or that the jury will simply infer from the evidence that the accused is the sort of person who ought to be punished, whether or not he or she has been proved guilty of the subject crime. Simply put, the jury may misuse the evidence for a prohibited reason or may give it too much weight.

B. *Effect on System of Law Enforcement*

A different aspect of prejudice concerns the effective functioning of the system of law enforcement which may be threatened by the liberal admission of bad character evidence. The detrimental effects on the system are possible in three significant respects. First, the increased reliance on bad disposition evidence by the prosecution as opposed to other evidence renders the system less fair and thwarts the investigative aspect of the system of administration of justice. If the police know that this type of evidence is relevant to the conviction of accused persons, they are more likely to concentrate their investigative efforts on those criminals and felons known to have committed the type of offence in question in the past, instead of in the search for direct evidence of the crime. The accused's past conduct follows him or her and makes it impossible to overcome a criminal past. This leads to the second important prejudicial effect. As the authors of *Cross on Evidence* note,[23] if having a criminal record becomes a "passport to police scrutiny, harassment and unjustified reconviction", the aim of rehabilitation of offenders would be frustrated. Third, the frequent or routine admission of bad character evidence could very well bring the administration of justice into disrepute by the continual dependence on past misdeeds contrary to the rational and dispassionate analysis upon which the criminal process should rest. These important prejudicial effects attaching to the admission of similar fact evidence should be kept in mind in examining the judicial development of the rule.

III JUDICIAL DEVELOPMENT OF THE RULE

An examination of the origins and development of the rule for the admission of similar fact evidence (i.e., the exception to the general exclusionary rule for evidence of bad character) by the English courts

---

23   *Supra*, note 3, at 360.

will be followed by a study of the Supreme Court of Canada's application of the rule in Canada. A review of the Australian case law then follows.

A. *English Case Law*

1. Development of the Rule

In *R. v. B.(C.R.)*,[24] the Supreme Court's recent decision on the similar fact doctrine, McLachlin J. traced the development of the rule in England. The rule of excluding evidence which was considered "foreign to the point in issue" in criminal prosecutions only developed in the late seventeenth century. Prior to this time, English law had not yet conceived of a rule to prevent the admission of bad character evidence. However, McLachlin J. noted that the legal formalism which characterized the nineteenth century tended to "pigeon-hole" situations in which similar fact evidence would be admitted as exceptions to the general exclusionary rule. For example, similar fact evidence was admitted to show intent, a system, a plan, malice, or identity, as well as to rebut the defences of accident, mistake and innocent association. It was in this context that the Privy Council rendered its decision in the seminal case, *Makin v. A.G. for New South Wales*.[25] The formulation of the rule in *Makin* still provides the springboard for the development of and debate on this area of the law.

2. Formulation of the Rule in *Makin*

Makin was the first case in which an appellate court considered the necessity of excluding evidence tending to show the bad character of the accused. Lord Herschell's famous statement of the rule gave birth to the doctrine of similar fact evidence:[26]

> It is undoubtedly not competent for the prosecution to adduce evidence tending to show that the accused has been guilty of criminal acts other than those covered by the indictment for the purpose of leading to the conclusion that the accused is a person likely from his criminal conduct or character to have committed the offence for which he is being tried. On the other hand, the

---

24 [1990] 1 S.C.R. 717, [1990] 3 W.W.R. 385, 109 A.R. 91.
25 *Supra*, note 11.
26 *Ibid.*, at 25-26 (All E.R. Rep.).

mere fact that the evidence adduced tends to show the commission of other crimes does not render it inadmissible if it be relevant to an issue before the jury, and it may be so relevant if it bears upon the question whether the acts alleged to constitute the crime charged in the indictment were designed or accidental, or to rebut a defence which would otherwise be open to the accused. The statement of these general principles is easy, but it is obvious that it may often be very difficult to draw the line and to decide whether a particular piece of evidence is on the one side or the other.

The first branch of the test must be viewed as carving out from the full range of relevant evidence that evidence which is relevant only for the purposes of displaying the discreditable character of the accused. The rationale for the exclusion of such evidence has been discussed above, and focuses on the possibility that the jury might be influenced in its decision by treating evidence of bad disposition alone as more relevant or weighty than it logically is.

However, the second limb of Lord Herschell's test makes it clear that the mere fact that the evidence may display bad disposition will not disqualify such evidence from being admissible. Such evidence may be relevant to some issue in the case, that is, to rebut the suggestion of accident or to rebut a defence. By identifying some of the specific situations in which the probative value of the evidence may justify its admission, the second limb of Lord Herschell's test was viewed as suggesting a list of exclusionary categories, depending on its relevance to an issue in the case.

3. Application of *Makin*

Makin was immediately followed by the English courts on the basis that similar fact evidence is admissible as long as the forbidden reasoning, i.e., reasoning based solely on general criminal disposition, was not employed. As is evident from the discussion of the cases below, the courts at first tended towards a restrictive approach to the second limb of Lord Herschell's test, viewing *Makin* as a general rule of exclusion subject to certain exceptions, partially enumerated in the second branch.[27]

---

27   See P.K. McWilliams, *Canadian Criminal Evidence*, 3rd ed. (Toronto: Canada Law Book, 1988), at 11-4 for an illustration of the number of times *Makin*

In *R. v. Straffen*,[28] the accused was charged with strangling a young girl. The prosecution was permitted to adduce evidence of two previous killings by the accused of young girls in similar circumstances (i.e., where there was no evidence of sexual interference, no apparent motive, no evidence of struggle, no attempt to conceal the body, and death by manual strangulation). The court admitted it on the basis that it was relevant to the issue of identity and hence fell within the second branch of the *Makin* test.[29]

In the notorious "brides in the bath" case, *R. v. Smith*,[30] the accused was charged with the murder of a woman with whom he had gone through a bigamous form of marriage. She was found dead in her bath and the accused, who was bound to benefit financially from her death through insurance policies taken out on her life, testified that her death was caused by an epileptic fit. The prosecution adduced evidence that two other women had also gone through similar forms of marriage ceremonies with the accused and had died in their baths in similar circumstances. This suggested that the three wives could not all have died of natural causes, but only by design. The evidence was considered relevant to rebut the defence of coincidence raised by the accused.[31]

Makin was also unanimously followed by the House of Lords in *R. v. Ball*.[32] In that case, a brother and sister were charged with incest and the prosecution adduced evidence that the accused had slept in the same bed. In addition, the prosecution adduced evidence that three years previously, prior to incest being made into a criminal offence, they had been lovers. The evidence was adduced because it effectively rebutted the defence of innocent association. The other evidence in the case, i.e., the fact that the accused still shared the same bed, was considered highly relevant because it dispelled any doubt as to whether the Balls slept together for the purpose of having sexual relations.

---

has been applied in Canada.

28   [1952] 2 All E.R. 657, [1952] 2 Q.B. 911.

29   For cases employing similar reasoning, see *R. v. Bird*, [1970] 3 C.C.C. 340, 9 C.R.N.S. 1, 71 W.W.R. 256 (B.C.C.A.); *R. v. Ross*, [1979] 6 W.W.R. 435; affd. [1980] 5 W.W.R. 261 (B.C.C.A.); *R. v. Schell* (1977), 33 C.C.C. (2d) 422 (Ont. C.A.).

30   (1915), 11 Cr. App. R. 229, [1914-15] All E.R. Rep. 262 (C.C.A.).

31   *Cf.* also *Lanford v. General Medical Council*, [1989] 2 All E.R. 921 (P.C.).

32   [1911] A.C. 47 (H.L.).

Similar fact evidence was also admitted where it was seen to constitute a "hallmark". In *Thompson v. R.*,[33] the accused was charged with homosexual offences against two young boys. The prosecution tendered evidence of "powder puffs" found on the person of the accused, as well as pictures of naked boys in various poses found in his apartment. This was not evidence of previous bad acts, but went to show that the accused had a particular propensity that the type of person who committed the crime was likely to have, and was relevant inasmuch as it was an unlikely coincidence that the accused would be wrongly identified as the perpetrator by the young victims. Lord Sumner stated:[34]

> Persons, however, who commit the offences now under consideration, seek the habitual gratification of a particular perverted lust, which not only takes them out of the class of ordinary men gone wrong, but stamps them with the hall-mark of a specialised and extraordinary class . . .

Although it is clear today that evidence of homosexual tendencies would not be considered a special or extraordinary identifying factor, the reasoning in *Thompson* is that where there is such a "hallmark", it may be relevant to the issue of identity.

The degree to which a characteristic must be "special" in order to qualify as a hallmark is evidenced in *R. v. Horwood*[35] in which the accused was charged with attempting to incite a 14-year-old boy to commit an act of gross indecency. The incident was alleged to have occurred when the accused was giving the boy a ride in his car. The accused denied the incident. The court did not permit the prosecution to ask the accused if he was a homosexual as the circumstances were such that having a homosexual disposition would prove very little.[36]

As Lord Herschell had forewarned, it was clear that the rule conceived in *Makin* was difficult to apply. First, as noted above, it resulted in excessive categorization of the evidence offered so as to bring such evidence within the second branch of the test. Evidence

---

33   [1918] A.C. 221, [1918-19] All E.R. Rep. 521 (H.L.).
34   *Ibid.*, at 528 (All E.R.).
35   [1969] 3 All E.R. 1156, [1970] 1 Q.B. 133 (C.A.).
36   The evidence in this case may also have been simply irrelevant. In essence, it is no more relevant than if it was evidence of the accused's heterosexual nature and the victim was female.

could be admitted, even if it was evidence of disposition, so long as it could be considered to rebut a defence of accident or involuntary conduct, to rebut the accused's plea of ignorance or mistake of fact, to rebut the accused's "innocent" explanation, primarily by showing a system, disproving an alibi by identifying the accused, or rebutting a defence of innocent association. Case law developed through attempts to clarify these particular issues, instead of using an approach which would examine the evidence for its particular relevance to the issues in the case. The traditional *Makin* approach was known as the "catchword" approach, so-called because once one of the exempt labels attached to the evidence it was presumed to be admissible.[37] The catchword approach was qualified to some extent by the decision of Viscount Simon in *Harris v. D.P.P.*,[38] in which it was confirmed that the list of exceptions enumerated in the second branch of the *Makin* test was not intended to be exhaustive.

4. Expansion of the Categories of Admissibility of Similar Fact Evidence

In *Harris v. D.P.P.*, the accused, a member of the Bradford police force, was tried on eight counts of office-breaking and larceny for breaking into and entering the premises of a fruit and vegetable merchant and stealing therefrom various sums of money. Each case of theft shared striking similarities, but on the first seven, there was no further evidence to associate the accused specifically with the thefts. It was held that the evidence as to the thefts which occurred on the first seven occasions was not admissible for the purpose of the trial of the accused on the eighth count.[39] However, in reaching this conclusion, Viscount Simon uttered the following important caveat:[40]

> In my opinion, the principle laid down by Lord Herschell, L.C., in *Makin's* case . . . has been constantly relied on ever since. It is, I think, an error to attempt to draw up a closed list of the sort of cases in which the principle operates. Such a list only provides instances of its general application, whereas what really matters

---

37   See Sklar, "Catchwords and Cartwheels" (1977), 23 McGill L.J. 60.
38   *Harris v. D.P.P.*, [1952] 1 All E.R. 1044, [1952] A.C. 694 (H.L.).
39   Query whether the evidence on the eighth would have been admissible on the first seven if the accused had been convicted on the eighth count.
40   *Supra*, note 38, at 1046.

is the principle itself and its proper application to the particular circumstances of the charge that is being tried.

Harris may be seen as an important step towards a more coherent understanding of the similar fact evidence rule. However, with the expansion of the categories in which similar fact evidence will be considered admissible, there was obviously the greater danger of prejudice referred to above. In *D.P.P. v. Boardman*,[41] the House of Lords revisited *Makin* bringing to bear the importance of the balancing test in which the probative value of the evidence is weighed against its prejudice to the accused.

5. *Boardman*: Balancing Test of Probative Value versus Prejudice to the Accused

D.P.P. v. Boardman is considered to have conducted the most important examination of the similar facts rule since *Makin* and the various interpretations of it which have ensued have laid the groundwork for competing theories as to the scope and basis of the rule. In *Boardman*, the issue was whether, on a charge of buggery with one boy, evidence was admissible that the accused had incited another boy to buggery and vice versa. The accused was the principal of a school that catered especially to teaching foreign boys the English language. Boardman was tried on three counts, buggery with a boy, S., and incitement to commit buggery with two other boys, H. and A. There was evidence of several other incidents in respect of each boy outside of the acts that were the subject of the charge.

In his summing up, the judge told the jury that it was not merely a straightforward case of a schoolmaster indecently assaulting a pupil, but that there was an "unusual feature" in that a grown man had attempted to get an adolescent boy to take the "male" part while he himself played the passive part in acts of buggery. On that basis, the judge directed the jury that it was open to them to find in H.'s evidence on count 2 corroboration of S.'s evidence on count 1 and vice versa. The question of law put to the House of Lords was whether, on a charge involving an allegation of homosexual conduct, evidence that the accused was a man whose homosexual proclivities took a particular form was admissible even though it tended to show that the accused had been guilty of criminal acts other than those charged.

---

41   [1974] 3 All E.R. 887, [1975] A.C. 421.

The House of Lords held that in certain cases evidence of past offences was admissible if it showed that those offences shared with the offence with which the accused is charged "features of such an unusual nature" and "striking similarity" that it would be an affront to common sense to assert that the similarity was explicable on the basis of coincidence. In such cases, the judge has a discretion to admit the evidence if he or she is satisfied that its probative force in relation to an issue in the trial outweighs its prejudicial effect and there is no possibility of collaboration between the witnesses. Some commentators and courts have taken this decision to mean that the second branch of Lord Herschell's test, concerning the ways in which the evidence may be relevant to an issue in the case, is to be replaced by the blanket test of "probative value over prejudice". Such an interpretation, however, ignores the rationale underlying the rule. Given the importance of *Boardman* in the development of the similar facts rule in Canada, and the possible confusion flowing from the fact that each of the five Lords expressed separate views, it is necessary to examine the decision closely.

(a) Lord Hailsham

Lord Hailsham wrote the most forceful argument in favour of maintaining the integrity of the principle in *Makin*. Evidence of the accused's bad character is to be excluded under the first rule in *Makin* because of its prejudicial effect; that is, it may endanger a fair trial because it tends to undermine the presumption of innocence. As Lord Hailsham notes, it is a rule of English law which has its root in policy, and by which logicians would not be bound.[42]

His Lordship stressed that the rule contained in the first limb of the *Makin* test cannot be relaxed in any circumstances:[43]

> Contrary to what was suggested in argument for the appellant, this rule [the second branch] is not an exception grafted on to the first. It is an independent proposition introduced by the words: 'On the other hand', and the two propositions together cover the entire field. If one applies, the other does not.

. . .

---

42   *Ibid.*, at 904-05 (All E.R.).
43   *Ibid.*, at 905 (All E.R.).

The fact is that, although the categories are useful classes of example, they are not closed (see per Viscount Simon in *Harris v. Director of Public Prosecutions*) and they cannot in fact be closed by categorisation. . . . What is important is not to open the door so widely that the second proposition merges in the first.

It is clear that Lord Hailsham saw the similar fact test as requiring relevance beyond mere "bad character" or "propensity" in order for it to qualify as evidence which may be admissible. He stated further:[44]

> There must be something more than mere repetition. What there must be is variously described as 'underlying unity' (*Moorov*) 'system' (see per Lord Reid in *Kilbourne*) 'nexus', 'unity of intent, project, campaign or adventure' (*Moorov*) 'part of the same criminal conduct', 'striking resemblance' (*Sims*).

His oft-quoted speech referring to the "forbidden line of reasoning" is:[45]

> It is perhaps helpful to remind oneself that what is *not* to be admitted is a chain of reasoning and not necessarily a state of facts. If the inadmissible chain of reasoning be the *only* purpose for which the evidence is adduced as a matter of law, the evidence itself is not admissible. If there is some other relevant, probative, purpose than the forbidden type of reasoning, the evidence is admitted, but should be made subject to a warning from the judge that the jury must eschew the forbidden reasoning. The judge also has a discretion, not as a matter of law, but of good practice, to exclude evidence whose prejudicial effect, though the evidence be technically admissible on the decided cases, may be so great in the particular circumstances as to outweigh its pro-bative value to the extent that a verdict of guilty might be considered unsafe or unsatisfactory if ensuing . . .

Lord Hailsham concluded that there is no ground for reducing the first branch of Lord Herschell's rule in *Makin*. If this were done the result would be to admit a number of cases in which the forbidden type of inference would be the real reason for adducing the evidence.

---

44   *Ibid.* The cases referred to are *Moorov v. H.M. Advocate* (1930), J.C. 68; *D.P.P. v. Kilbourne*, [1973] 1 All E.R. 440, [1973] A.C. 729 (H.L.); and *R. v. Sims*, [1946] 1 All E.R. 697, [1946] K.B. 531 (C.C.A.).
45   *Ibid.*, at 905-06 (All E.R.).

(b) Lord Morris

Lord Morris also clearly reiterated the requirement that similar fact evidence must be relevant other than to show a general criminal disposition in order to be admissible. Lord Morris noted at the outset that the words of Lord Herschell in *Makin* have always been accepted as expressing "cardinal principles". He then stressed that the judge in each case must determine whether a particular piece of evidence falls on the side of exclusion — that is, adduced for the purpose of leading to the conclusion that the accused committed the crime, since he or she is the sort of person likely to have done so — or on the side of admission — that is, relevant to an issue in the case and admissible even though it tends to show that an accused person has committed other crimes. The judge must decide whether the evidence is on one side or the other and whether "the evidence is sufficiently substantial having regard to the purpose to which it is professedly directed to make it desirable in the interest of justice that it should be admitted".[46] The judge must exercise his discretion having in mind the requirements of both justice and fairness. Lord Morris noted:[47]

> The first limb of what was said by Lord Herschell L.C. in *Makin's* case was said by Viscount Sankey L.C. in *Maxwell v. Director of Public Prosecutions* [[1934] All E.R. Rep. 168, at 172] to express "one of the most deeply rooted and jealously guarded principles of our criminal law". Judges can be trusted not to allow so fundamental a principle to be eroded.

In other words, evidence of bad character should be excluded unless such evidence has a "really material bearing on the issues to be decided".[48] He then confirmed the view expressed by the Court of Criminal Appeal in *R. v. Sims*[49] and followed in *Kilbourne's* case[50] that similar fact evidence is admissible where the features in each accusation bear a striking resemblance to each other so as to show a particular "pattern", "technique" or a proclivity which takes a particular form.

---

46   *Ibid.*, at 892-93 (All E.R.).
47   *Ibid.*, at 893 (All E.R.).
48   *Ibid.*, at 893.
49   [1946] 1 All E.R. 697 (C.C.A.).
50   *Director of Public Prosecutions v. Kilbourne*, [1973] 1 All E.R. 440, [1973] A.C. 729 (H.L.).

(c) Lord Wilberforce

Lord Wilberforce commenced by stating that in each case, it is necessary to estimate (1) whether, and if so how strongly, the evidence as to other facts tends to support, i.e. to make more credible, the evidence given as to the fact in question; (2) whether such evidence, if given, is likely to be prejudicial to the accused. Both these elements involve questions of degree. With respect to the evidence sought to be adduced, he stated:[51]

> If, as I believe, the general rule is that such evidence cannot be allowed, it requires exceptional circumstances to justify the admission. *This House should not, in my opinion, encourage erosion of the general rule.* [emphasis added]

Lord Wilberforce correctly shied away from distinctions between "normal" homosexual acts and "abnormal" homosexual acts which may tend to show some pattern, remarking that distinctions such as this "lend an unattractive unreality to the law".[52] He focused on the importance of "striking similarity" which lends the probative force to the similar fact evidence:[53]

> The basic principle must be that the admission of similar fact evidence (of the kind now in question) is exceptional and requires a strong degree of probative force. This probative force is derived, if at all, from the circumstance that the facts testified to by the several witnesses bear to each other such a striking similarity that they must, when judged by experience and common sense, either all be true, or have arisen from a cause common to the witnesses or from pure coincidence.

Lord Wilberforce was of the view that the case before them was borderline, given that the striking similarity as presented to the jury was only the active character of the sexual performance to which the accused was said to have invited the complainants. However, while he feared that the case might be setting the standard of "striking similarity" too low, he did not consider that the intervention of the House was necessary in this case.

---

51 *Supra*, note 41, at 896 (All E.R.).
52 *Ibid.*, at 897 (All E.R.).
53 *Ibid.*

(d) Lord Salmon

Lord Salmon also adhered to the principles enunciated in *Makin* and affirmed that evidence against an accused which tends only to show bad character or general criminal disposition is inadmissible in English law. His Lordship stressed also that the basis of this fundamental rule is not founded in logic, but on policy, as to admit such evidence would be unjust and would offend our concept of a fair trial to which we hold that everyone is entitled.

He formulated the test to be as follows:[54]

> [W]hether or not evidence is relevant and admissible against an accused is solely a question of law. The test must be — is the evidence capable of tending to persuade a reasonable jury of the accused's guilt on some ground other than his bad character and disposition to commit the sort of crime with which he is charged?
>
> . . .
>
> If a trial judge rightly rules that the evidence is relevant and admissible, he still, of course, has a discretion to exclude it on the ground that its probative value is minimal and altogether outweighed by its likely prejudicial effect.

(e) Lord Cross

Lord Cross was alone in distancing himself from the view that the difference between disposition evidence and evidence which is otherwise relevant is not merely one of degree but of kind. He noted that the reason for the general rule excluding evidence of similar facts is that jurors would attribute a disproportionate degree of relevance to the evidence such that its prejudicial effect would outweigh its probative value. He stated, however, that circumstances might arise in which such evidence is so very relevant that to exclude it would be an "affront to common sense".[55] Lord Cross's view appears to be that the line between admissible and inadmissible evidence is a question of degree of probative value as opposed to relevance.

Therefore, a close reading of the case would not appear to

---

54   *Ibid.*, at 913 (All E.R.).
55   *Ibid.*, at 908 (All E.R.).

support, as some have suggested, the displacing of the two-step approach in favour of the blanket test of probative value versus prejudice. Rather, the preferable view would seem to be the balancing test articulated by the House of Lords as a final safeguard in the application of the rule. *Boardman* has been the subject of competing interpretations by the Canadian Supreme Court in its formulation of the test for admissibility.

B. Canadian Case Law

Since *Boardman*, the Supreme Court of Canada has wrestled with the principles governing the admissibility of similar fact evidence in a series of cases. Prior to its recent decision in *R. v. B.(C.R.)*[56] [hereinafter referred to as *C.R.B.*], the Court appeared explicitly to reject the admission of evidence demonstrating the accused's bad character where its only relevance to the case was to show a general criminal propensity or bad disposition on the part of the accused. In *C.R.B.*, the Supreme Court may have appeared to relax the rigorous application of the rule in certain circumstances. It is submitted that the case should not be seen as a renunciation of the principles developed in the previous jurisprudence of the Court.

1. R. v. C.R.B.

In this case, the accused was charged with sexual offences against his natural daughter who was in his custody subsequent to the death of her mother. To support the testimony of the complainant, the Crown sought to introduce evidence that in 1975 the accused had had sexual relations with a 15-year-old girl, the daughter of his common-law wife, with whom he had also enjoyed a father-daughter relationship. McLachlin J. (for the majority) stated that the trial judge had erred in considering that the similar fact evidence went to the identity of the perpetrator, which was not in issue, rather than to corroborate the testimony of the complainant. McLachlin J. interpreted the test in *Boardman* as suggesting that bad character evidence showing the accused's disposition to the sort of criminal conduct in issue may in exceptional cases be admissible if it meets the test of probative value versus prejudice:[57]

---

56   [1990] 1 S.C.R. 717, [1990] 3 W.W.R. 385, 109 A.R. 91.
57   *Ibid.*, at 731-32.

While the language of some of the assertions of the exclusionary rule admittedly might be taken to suggest that mere disposition evidence can *never* be admissible, the preponderant view prevailing in Canada is the view taken by the majority in *Boardman* — evidence of propensity, while generally inadmissible, may exceptionally be admitted where the probative value of the evidence in relation to an issue in question is so high that it displaces the heavy prejudice which will inevitably inure to the accused where evidence of prior immoral or illegal acts is presented to the jury.

The majority of the Court was of the view that the balancing of the probative value against the prejudice and the rejection of the category approach leaves a residue of discretion entrusted to the trial judge.

Applying these principles to the facts of the case, the majority reached the conclusion that in cases such as this, where the word of the child alleged to have been sexually assaulted is pitted against the word of the accused, similar fact evidence may be central to the issue of credibility. Thus, the fact that in each case the accused established a father-daughter relationship with the girl before the sexual violations began might be argued to show, if not a system or design, a pattern of similar behaviour suggesting that the complainant's story is true.

The minority (per Sopinka and Lamer JJ.) stressed that in order to be admitted, the alleged similar acts "must have relevance other than simply to show a general disposition to commit the crime charged".[58] The case law preceding *C.R.B.* makes it clear that a crucial factor in the application of the similar fact evidence rule is identification of the probative value of the evidence. It must be identified in order to determine whether the evidence has relevance beyond mere propensity to commit crimes of this general type or that it shows the accused to be of poor moral character, and if it does, whether its probative value exceeds its prejudicial effect.

In speaking of "probative value" the dissenting judges stressed that it is not "logically probative" but "legally probative". The minority focused on the reasoning behind the rule and rejected the proposition that *Boardman* effected a radical change in the law:[59]

The principal reason for the exclusionary rule relating to propensity is that there is a natural human tendency to judge a

---

58   *Ibid.*, at 740.
59   *Ibid.*, at 744.

person's action on the basis of character. Particularly with juries there would be a strong inclination to conclude that a thief has stolen, a violent man has assaulted and a pedophile has engaged in pedophilic acts. *Yet the policy of the law is wholly against this process of reasoning.* [emphasis added]

Applying the principles to the facts of the case, the minority was of the opinion that the trial judge erred in admitting the evidence. In their view, to say the evidence supports the credibility of the complainant is to say no more than that the evidence supports guilt, which itself is tantamount to affirming that the accused must be guilty because he engaged in similar conduct on a prior occasion. In order to be admissible, the similarities must be such that, in the absence of collaboration, it would be an "affront to common sense" to suggest that they were due to coincidence. In this case, the minority was of the view that the similarities were not sufficiently remarkable, and the admission of the evidence would be setting the standard of "striking similarity" so low as to be virtually non-existent.

It is submitted that the decision of the majority in *C.R.B.* does not establish a rule that evidence of a general propensity to commit a similar crime may be admissible. Rather, the majority found the evidence to be probative by reason of its role in the case. In other words, in a situation such as that in *C.R.B.*, where the only evidence against the accused is the testimony of the complainant, it may be argued that similar fact evidence should be admitted to support the credibility of the complainant as to reject such evidence may effectively deprive the complainant of the only means of convincing the trier of fact of the validity of the complaint. A certain degree of flexibility has always been inherent in the "striking similarity" test. This case is an example of the low end of the scale in its application. The position of the majority should not, however, be taken to signal a displacement of the general condition of admissibility that bad character evidence must have an otherwise material bearing on the facts in issue.[60] Inherent in the majority's application of the prejudice versus probity test is an understanding that the probative force will never outweigh the prejudicial value if the only relevance of the evidence is that the accused is morally reprehensible or has a general

---

60   This view of the case was confirmed in *R. v. C. (M.H.)*, not yet reported, April, 1991 (S.C.C.); McLauchlin J. wrote the decision of the Court.

criminal disposition for this type of crime. As the following review of the previous decisions of the Supreme Court reveals, there is little support for the view that general criminal disposition is relevant unless the evidence goes beyond such generality and is therefore otherwise relevant.

2. *Sweitzer v. R.*[61]

Sweitzer v. R. concerned the admissibility of unproven similar acts.[62] The accused was charged with fifteen counts of rape and indecent assault. The counts were severed. The issue was whether evidence of other assaults and attempts was properly admissible as evidence of similar facts. The Court held that evidence of episodes not shown to be connected with the accused could not be admitted and the admission of such evidence was to be confined to cases where there was some evidentiary link, direct or circumstantial, with the accused. In reaching its conclusion, the Court (per McIntyre J.) seemed to focus only on probative value and neglected the purpose for which such evidence was adduced. The case turned on whether there was some strong link between the evidence sought to be introduced and the accused. If there was some such link with the accused, the Court appeared to be prepared to admit the evidence without consideration of the purpose for which such evidence was adduced. Decisions of the Court subsequent to *Sweitzer*, however, have adhered to the reasoning underlying the similar fact evidence rule and have emphasized the importance of distinguishing between evidence relevant solely for the purpose of showing general criminal propensity and evidence which is otherwise relevant to an issue in the case.

3. *R. v. Morris*[63]

Morris did not really concern "similar fact" evidence, but rather circumstantial evidence. However, the case is usually examined under this heading, presumably because the evidence sought to be introduced relates to the character or disposition of the accused. The accused was convicted at trial for conspiracy to import heroin from

---

61 [1982] 1 S.C.R. 949, [1982] 5 W.W.R. 555, 42 N.R. 550, 37 A.R. 294.
62 See this Chapter, I.C. for an explanation of the term "unproven similar acts".
63 [1983] 2 S.C.R. 190, 7 C.C.C. (3d) 97, 36 C.R. (3d) 1, [1984] 2 W.W.R. 1, 1 D.L.R. (4th) 385, 48 N.R. 341.

Hong Kong and to traffic in heroin. At issue was the admissibility of newspaper clippings found in the accused's home dealing with the heroin trade in Pakistan. Lamer J., for the minority, was of the view that the sole relevancy of the clipping went to the accused's disposition, whose ultimate purpose was to place the accused in the category of people whose character indicates a propensity to commit the offences of which he was charged. Lamer J. drew a rather fine line by stating that the evidence would have been relevant to prove the accused's participation in the conspiracies through his possession of a document that might have been instrumental in the commission of the crimes had the clipping been of the heroin trade in Hong Kong. However, given that the clipping concerned the trade in Pakistan, in Lamer J.'s view it went only to disposition.[64]

The majority took the view that the difference was one of kind and not of degree.[65] McIntyre J., speaking for the majority, agreed with Lamer J. on the principles concerning relevancy of evidence and with the reason for and the development of the exclusionary rules relating to evidence of bad character. However, he disagreed with the characterization of the newspaper clipping as indicating only a general criminal disposition on the part of the accused:[66]

> In my view, an inference could be drawn from the unexplained presence of the newspaper clipping among the possessions of the appellant, that he had an interest in and had informed himself on the question of sources of supply of heroin, necessarily a subject of vital interest to one concerned with the importing of the narcotic. It is this feature which distinguishes the case at bar from *Cloutier v. The Queen*, [1979] 2 S.C.R. 709, where the purpose of the impugned evidence was to show that the accused was a user of marijuana and had the necessary *mens rea* for the offence of importing.

The majority was consequently of the view that the connection or nexus, clearly absent in the *Cloutier* case, was present, as an inference could be drawn that the preparatory steps in respect of importing narcotics had been taken or were contemplated. The majority con-

---

64   Clearly, the only difference in the evidence was as to weight.
65   *Supra*, note 63, at 192-93, 204 (S.C.R.).
66   *Supra*, note 63, at 191-92 (S.C.R.).

sidered the clipping not merely to be evidence of a propensity to traffic in drugs, but circumstantial evidence of preparatory steps in the commission of the crime of importing, in the same way that evidence of the possession of house-breaking implements would be relevant evidence on a charge of burglary.

4. *R. v. Clermont*[67]

Clermont is a clear-cut case in which evidence of criminal disposition alone was considered inadmissible. In a charge for rape, the question was whether evidence of a rape committed five years previously by the accused was admissible. The only issue was whether the complainant in the case had consented. The Court, per Lamer J., held that such evidence was not admissible:[68]

> Though very relevant, evidence of an earlier rape is not admissible when its only probative value is to establish that the accused is someone capable of disregarding the absence of consent by his victim, and that therefore he should not be believed when he says that she did consent or at least that he honestly and reasonably believed she had ... This would in fact be its sole probative value in the present case.

> It would have been otherwise, having regard to the particular circumstances, if for example the earlier rape had been similar in that the accused had alleged a belief in consent in similar circumstances. That evidence would then be led to counter the credibility of the accused in his defence of an honest mistake as to consent, and as such would be admissible, subject of course to the court balancing its probative value as evidence against the obvious damage caused the accused by evidence of a prior record for rape.

Given that the evidence offered in this case did not meet the conditions necessary to fall into the second branch of the *Makin* test, it was not necessary to apply the balancing test of probative value versus prejudice.

---

67   [1986] 2 S.C.R. 131, 29 C.C.C. (3d) 105, 53 C.R. (3d) 971, 3 Q.A.C. 46, 32 D.L.R. (4th) 306, 69 N.R. 202.
68   *Ibid.*, at 135-36 (S.C.R.).

5. R. v. Robertson[69]

R. v. Robertson makes it clear that the similar facts rule extends beyond acts which are criminal. In a charge for sexual assault, the accused conceded identity and argued that the complainant had consented or, in the alternative, that he believed she consented. One of the issues concerned the admissibility of the evidence of the complainant's roommate that the accused had also made a sexual proposition to her. Wilson J. referred to the decision of the Court in Sweitzer v. R. and stated the test as follows:[70]

> A general statement of the exclusionary rule is that evidence of the accused's discreditable conduct on past occasions [tendered] to show his bad disposition is inadmissible unless it is so probative of an issue or issues in the case as to outweigh the prejudice caused.

Wilson J. first noted that the accused's conduct toward the complainant's roommate was not criminal. However, discreditable conduct extends beyond criminal acts and the similar facts evidence rule extends equally to acts other than criminal acts. In this case, Wilson J. considered the evidence to be relevant for the following reasons:[71]

> In discussing the probative value we must consider the degree of relevance to the facts in issue and the strength of the inference that can be drawn. The bulk of Eileen's testimony is, of course, highly relevant to the case. It provides the background for the circumstances in which the assault occurred. It makes it clear how the respondent came to arrive at the complainant's doorstep on the morning in question, how he knew to use Eileen's name, why he might be interested in the victim, and why he could have anticipated that the complainant would be home alone at the relevant time.

. . .

---

69   [1987] 1 S.C.R. 918, 33 C.C.C. (3d) 481, 58 C.R. (3d) 28, 20 O.A.C. 200, 39 D.L.R. (4th) 321, 75 N.R. 6 (sub nom. R. v. R.).
70   Ibid., at 941 (S.C.R.).
71   Ibid., at 943 (S.C.R.).

The degree of probative value required varies with the prejudicial effect of the admission of the evidence. The probative value of evidence may increase if there is a degree of similarity in the circumstances and proximity in time and place. However, admissibility does not turn on such a striking similarity: see L.H. Hoffmann, "Similar Facts After *Boardman*" (1975), 91 L.Q.R. 193, at p. 201.

Thus, while her statement of the test theorizes that purely disposition evidence may be admitted provided its probative value is significant, it is clear that Wilson J. considered the evidence to have significant non-propensity relevance. Not only did the evidence explain much of the background to the case and make credible the roommate's assertion that she had not sent the accused over to the apartment, it was also relevant to the question of motive and intent. The Crown suggested that the accused, rebuffed by the roommate, had a motive for turning his attention to the complainant. Wilson J. concluded in the circumstances of this case that the prejudicial effect was very slight and that the evidence was properly admitted.

6. *R. v. Morin*[72]

In this case, the Court made clear that the reasoning which excludes evidence of general disposition applies equally to expert evidence. The Court considered the admissibility of psychiatric evidence to the effect that the accused suffered from an illness that put him into a class of persons capable of committing the type of offence with which he was charged. The accused was charged with the murder of a young girl. The Court found that the trial judge was correct in instructing the jury that the evidence elicited on the Crown's examination of the defence psychiatrist was inadmissible as proof of identity on the basis that it is not sufficient to establish that the accused is a member of an abnormal group with the same propensities as the perpetrator. There must be some further distinguishing feature. Sopinka J. stated:[73]

It is illogical to treat evidence tending to show the accused's propensity to commit the crime differently because such propen-

---

72   [1988] 2 S.C.R. 345, 44 C.C.C. (3d) 193, 66 C.R. (3d) 1, 30 O.A.C. 81, 88 N.R. 161.
73   *Ibid.*, at 370 (S.C.R.).

sity is introduced by expert evidence rather than by means of past similar conduct. If in the latter case the evidence is admitted provided its probative value exceeds its prejudicial effect, then the same test of admissibility should apply in the former case.

Accordingly, when the prosecution tenders expert psychiatric evidence, the trial judge must determine whether it is relevant to an issue in the case apart from its tendency to show propensity. If it is relevant to another issue (e.g. identity), it must then be determined whether its probative value on that other issue outweighs its prejudicial effect on the propensity question. In sum, if the evidence's sole relevance or primary relevance is to show disposition, then the evidence must be excluded.

The accused in that case was a schizophrenic. That a small percentage of schizophrenics has the tendency or capability of committing the crime in question in an abnormal fashion is extremely weak evidence that the accused also has these tendencies. It is noteworthy that the Court was unanimous in the formulation of the similar fact evidence rule. The reasons of Wilson J. concurring in the result disagreed with the majority only with respect to the first issue in the case concerning reasonable doubt.

7. R. v. Green[74]

In *R. v. Green*, the evidence was admitted on the basis that there was "striking similarity". The accused was convicted of sexual assault on a young girl. The evidence was that the accused had touched the breasts of the girl and the accused was denying the incident, or, in the alternative, alleging that it was an accidental touching in the course of an innocent hug. The prosecution was permitted to adduce evidence of other children testifying that the accused had touched them in a sexual way. The evidence was admitted on the basis that the accused had a "system", that is, that the incidents shared a striking similarity:[75]

> The only issue argued before us concerned the admission at trial of similar fact evidence, which came from children other than the complainant concerning the respondent's behaviour with

---

74   [1988] 1 S.C.R. 228, 40 C.C.C. (3d) 333, 62 C.R. (3d) 398, 52 Man. R. (2d) 64, 82 N.R. 194.
75   *Ibid.*, at 229 (S.C.R.).

them. This evidence was admissible to show a system adopted by the respondent, and its probative force was sufficient to outweigh any prejudicial effect upon the respondent.

In this case, which is comparable in some respects to *C.R.B.*, it could be argued that the standard of "striking similarity" was set too low, or, alternatively, artificially attributed a "system" to the accused.

8. *R. v. D.(L.E.)*[76]

In this case, evidence of past similar acts which had given rise to charges and subsequently to a stay of proceedings was rejected as having no material bearing to the facts in issue in the case other than the disposition of the accused. The issue concerned the admissibility of evidence of alleged previous acts of sexual misconduct by the appellant against his daughter. The appellant was charged with two counts of sexual assault arising out of separate incidents in July 1985. The Crown wished to adduce evidence of numerous incidents of sexual fondling and intercourse from December 1978 to May 1981, and further incidents of sexual touching in December 1983 and the spring of 1985. The appellant had faced several charges arising from the incidents alleged prior to May 1981, but the Crown had entered a stay of proceedings on all of these charges. The majority, per Sopinka J. (L'Heureux-Dubé J. dissenting), stated:[77]

> The process of reasoning therefore is to determine whether the evidence of similar acts has probative value in relation to a fact in issue, other than its tendency to lead to the conclusion that the accused is guilty because of the disposition to commit certain types of wrongful acts. If the evidence has such probative value, the court must then determine whether its probative value is sufficient to justify its admissibility, notwithstanding the prejudicial tendency of such evidence.

The Court examined *R. v. Ball* and commented:[78]

> In fact, I think it may be said that in all cases in which evidence

---

76   *R. v. D.(L.E.)*, [1989] 2 S.C.R. 111, 50 C.C.C. (3d) 142, 71 C.R. (3d) 1, [1989] 6 W.W.R. 501, 39 B.C.L.R. (2d) 273, 97 N.R. 321.
77   *Ibid.*, at 121 (S.C.R.).
78   *Ibid.*, at 123 (S.C.R.). See *R. v. Ball*, [1911] A.C. 47 (H.L.), discussed in this Chapter, III.A.3.

of prior misconduct is adduced, that evidence to some degree goes to a propensity or disposition of the accused. That, however, cannot be its sole characteristic if it is to be admitted under the similar facts rule.

It is important to note in this case that the acts alleged to have occurred prior to May 1981 bore nearly the entire burden of proving the Crown's case against the appellant on the acts charged. It is a classic case in which the prejudice resulting from the inclination of a trier of fact to punish for past crimes would be at its greatest. The Court held that the trial judge was wrong in admitting this evidence as its probative value was not sufficient to overcome its prejudicial effect.

Accordingly, prior to *C.R.B.*, the Supreme Court was consistent in assessing the relevance of the similar fact evidence from the viewpoint of the facts in issue in the case and the potential for prejudice to the accused. It is submitted that the doctrine has not undergone a radical transformation in *C.R.B.* which was merely an illustration of setting the standard for striking similarity at a low level in view of the special circumstances of the case.

C. *Australian Case Law*

In its recent decision, *R. v. Harriman*,[79] the High Court of Australia grappled with the difficulties of the similar facts rule. The five separate opinions of the justices reflect the different approaches to the similar facts rule. It is significant, however, that of the five justices, only Dawson J. took the view that evidence going to propensity alone may be considered relevant and thereby admissible.

The accused, Harriman, was charged with being knowingly concerned in the importation of heroin into Western Australia. The heroin had been posted by one Martin from London in five parcels addressed to five addresses in Australia. The importation of heroin was not in dispute; what was in dispute was whether the accused, Harriman, had been knowingly concerned in that importation. Martin and Harriman were the principal shareholders of a mining company embroiled in financial troubles. According to Martin, the importation of heroin was the means decided upon to relieve the company's financial situation. The facts disclosed that in March 1987 Harriman

---

79   (1989), 63 A.L.J.R. 694 (H.C.).

went to Thailand, that in April, 1987, Martin travelled to Bangkok where he met Harriman by arrangement, that the two of them travelled together to Chiang Mai by bus overnight and returned by air to Bangkok on the next evening, and that Martin left for London whence he posted the heroin to Australia.

In response to the accused's claim that he had been in Thailand for business and recreational purposes and that he was not a party to the crime eventually committed, the prosecution sought to adduce evidence tending to show the accused to have been both a dealer in and user of heroin before the date of his trip with Martin to Chiang Mai. There were four categories of evidence. The first category consisted of evidence which showed that Martin and the accused had been engaged in a joint enterprise of supplying heroin to others. The second was evidence that the accused alone had supplied heroin. The third was evidence that Harriman himself was a user of heroin. Finally, the prosecution tendered in evidence a number of letters written by the accused while in jail on remand which undoubtedly tended to show a consciousness of guilt on his part with respect to the offence charged, but also demonstrated that he had had prior dealings with heroin. The trial judge admitted all of the above evidence, and the accused was convicted. The Court of Appeal of Western Australia and the High Court of Australia (Gaudron J. dissenting) dismissed his appeals.

All of the justices except Brennan J. considered the evidence of prior use of heroin by the accused as well as certain portions of the letters to be inadmissible. The first two categories of evidence were considered to be admissible notwithstanding that they tended to show propensity because they provided evidence of the accused's previous dealings with and the nature of his relationship with Martin. They provided cogent evidence of his reason for being in Chiang Mai and the only reasonable inference was that he was there with Martin in order to obtain heroin. However, while Gaudron J. also shared the view of the other justices, he was alone in reaching the conclusion that there was a real possibility that the accused lost a real chance of acquittal because of the suspicion generated by the inadmissible evidence. In their separate opinions, the five justices explored the approaches to similar fact evidence thereby refining the analysis of the this rule.[80]

---

80   P. Mirfield, "Similar Facts in the High Court of Australia" (1990), 106 L.Q.R. 199 (April).

Brennan J. proceeded from the principle that evidence is admissible if it is relevant in that it tends to show that the accused is guilty of the crime charged for some reason other than that he has committed crimes in the past or has a criminal disposition. Brennan J. noted that when similar fact evidence is tendered, its admission depends on its "striking similarity" or other distinctive feature to prove a fact in issue in the case in hand. However, while abiding by these principles, Brennan J. appears to have approached dangerously close to the "forbidden analysis" in admitting the evidence:[81]

> A person who is shown to have participated to a substantial degree in that trade — I am not speaking of mere use or of an isolated sale — is likely to have incentives to continue his participation in the trade and, because of the nature of the trade, is more likely to have done so than one who has not been a substantial participant. Evidence of substantial participation in the heroin trade can support an inference of continued participation although, of course, each case depends on its own facts. In determining whether or not evidence of participation can support such an inference, regard must be had to the extent and duration of past participation, the proximity in time between the past participation and the offence charged and the whole of the circumstances of the case.

It is in this light that Brennan J. considered the evidence to be highly probative of the offences charged.

Toohey J. stressed that evidence of propensity is rejected not because it is irrelevant, but because the cost of admitting it is generally thought to be too high, that is, that its probative value is likely to be outweighed by the prejudice it will cause to the accused. He saw the first two categories of evidence as being relevant to the character of the association between the accused and Martin or to the likelihood that the two men acted in concert in Thailand. Its probative force clearly outweighed its prejudicial effect given that the defence of the accused was that Martin was acting independently. Toohey J.'s analysis is unique in suggesting that once probative value is established, there is no valid reason why the evidence should be excluded merely because there may be some prejudice to the accused.

---

81   *Supra*, note 79, at 697.

McHugh J. was of the view that while evidence of disposition alone is not admissible, it will be so admissible if it is "evidence of facts forming a part of the same transaction as that under inquiry". McHugh J. took an interesting approach in stating that circumstantial evidence which directly relates to the facts in issue is so fundamental to the proceedings that its admissibility as a matter of law cannot depend upon a condition that its probative force transcends its prejudicial effect. While a judge always has general discretion to exclude prejudicial evidence, it would be difficult to see how evidence directly related to the very facts in issue can be excluded simply because it would reveal other criminal conduct on the part of the accused. Applying these principles to this case, McHugh J. considered the evidence of past dealings in supplying heroin to be relevant to the critical issue as to whether Martin and the accused acted in concert to import heroin into Australia. Evidence that the applicant used heroin and certain parts of the letters tendered as evidence were, however, considered to be inadmissible. However, McHugh J. also took the view that the admission of such evidence did not result in any miscarriage of justice, as the case against the accused on the admissible evidence was an extremely powerful one.

As stated earlier, Dawson J. took a different approach in reaching the same conclusion. He was of the view that seeing relevance in terms of "categories" was misleading as such categories do not indicate relevance of a different *kind* but are merely examples of the way in which propensity evidence could have a high *degree* of relevance in certain circumstances. This focus on the kind, rather than the degree of relevance, has, in his view, tended to obscure the true test, that propensity evidence must possess the requisite high degree of relevance to justify its admission notwithstanding its prejudicial effect. The test should be that the evidence ought not be admitted if the trial judge is of the opinion that there is a rational view of it which is inconsistent with the guilt of the accused. Applying this criterion to the facts of the case, evidence of the accused's previous relationship with Martin involving dealing in drugs is cogent evidence of his reason for being in Chiang Mai. The only reasonable inference is that he was there with Martin in order to obtain heroin. On the basis of the admissible evidence, Dawson J. reached the conclusion that an appropriately instructed jury, acting reasonably on the evidence before them and applying the correct onus and standard of proof, would inevitably have convicted the accused. It is noteworthy that while Dawson's J.'s statement of the applicable test differs, his reason for admitting the evidence is the same, and it does not rely solely on the general criminal disposition of the accused.

Gaudron J. dissented from the majority in his conclusion. He agreed with the majority that evidence adduced solely to show propensity of an accused to engage in criminal conduct of a particular kind or that the accused is the sort of person likely to commit the offence charged is not admissible to prove that he committed the offence. The probative value of such evidence lies in the evidence "if accepted, not being susceptible of rational explanation on a basis inconsistent with the guilt of the accused". Mere propensity would not meet this test.

Therefore, all of the justices of the Australia High Court, excepting Dawson J., adhered to the notion that there is a difference in kind between evidence adduced solely to show criminal or bad disposition and such evidence which is otherwise relevant to an issue in the case. Brennan J.'s reasons show, however, that the courts must be vigilant to resist the inclination to engage in the "forbidden reasoning".

IV PRINCIPLES GOVERNING ADMISSION OF SIMILAR FACT EVIDENCE IN CRIMINAL CASES

In light of the cases discussed above, the determination as to whether similar fact evidence is admissible in criminal proceedings should be based on the following considerations.

A. *Whether Evidence Relevant to Issue in Case*

The review of the case law reveals two approaches to assessing the relevance of similar fact evidence. The first approach is that evidence of propensity or disposition alone may be relevant, and the test of admissibility is the degree to which such evidence demonstrates the disposition of the accused. This is the approach taken by Dawson J. in *Harriman*.

The second approach requires that evidence of similar facts be relevant to some issue in the case other than the negative disposition or the general criminal propensity of the accused. As the minority in *R. v. B. (C.R.)* wrote:[82]

---

82   [1990] 1 S.C.R. 717, [1990] 3 W.W.R. 385, 109 A.R. 91, at 744 (S.C.R.).

The principal reason for the exclusionary rule relating to propensity is that there is a natural human tendency to judge a person's action on the basis of character. . . . *Yet the policy of the law is wholly against this process of reasoning.* This policy is reflected not only in similar acts cases but as well in the rule excluding evidence of the character of the accused unless placed in issue by him. *The stronger the evidence of propensity, the more likely it is that the forbidden inference will be drawn and therefore the greater the prejudice.* [emphasis added]

In other words, the propensity evidence will be considered relevant only if it has a more specific bearing on some issue in the case than general disposition evidence would have. For example, it may be relevant if it tends to establish identity,[83] to rebut the suggestion of coincidence,[84] or to rebut a defence of innocent association.[85] It may also be relevant in that it sheds light on motive or intent,[86] or because it is viewed as circumstantial evidence tending to prove facts which are the subject of dispute.[87] Past or subsequent similar acts may also be considered relevant if the evidence transcends mere tendency to show disposition and demonstrates "striking similarity" so as to be akin to a "hallmark" of the accused.[88]

It is important to stress that the focus on the relevance of the evidence to some issue in the case does not advocate a return to the category approach to the similar facts rule. In fact, as was made express in *Harris v. D.P.P.*,[89] the situations in which propensity evidence will be considered relevant are not cast in stone, and will depend not only on the defences raised by the accused but on the circumstances of each case. However, while rejecting the category approach, this second view of relevance is consistent with the *raison d'être* of the similar facts rule, in that it is mindful of the unnecessary prejudice which the rule is designed to avoid.

---

83   *R. v. Straffen*, [1952] 2 All E.R. 657, [1952] 2 Q.B.
84   *R. v. Smith* (1915), 11 Cr. App. Rep. 229.
85   *R. v. Ball*, [1911] A.C. 47 (H.L.); *R. v. Harriman, supra,* note 79.
86   *R. v. Robertson, supra,* note 69.
87   *R. v. Morris*, [1983] 2 S.C.R. 190, 7 C.C.C. (3d) 97, 36 C.R. (3d) 1, [1984] 2 W.W.R. 1, 1 D.L.R. (4th) 385, 48 N.R. 341.
88   *R. v. Straffen, supra,* note 83.
89   *Harris v. D.P.P.*, [1952] 1 All E.R. Rep. 1044, [1952] A.C. 694 (H.L.).

B. *Weighing Probative Value Against Prejudicial Effect*

The balancing test comes in once it has been determined that the adduced evidence is relevant on a basis other than to show a general propensity to commit the crime. The probative force of similar fact evidence depends upon three principal factors: (1) the cogency of the evidence showing the accused's disposition; (2) the extent to which such evidence supports the inference sought to be drawn from it; and (3) *the degree of relevance of that inference to some fact in issue in the proceedings.*[90] The view that evidence of disposition alone in the sense that the person has a tendency or is capable of committing the crime charged may be sufficiently probative and thereby admissible fails to take into account the third essential element of probity, the relevance of the inference provided by the evidence to some issue in the case. Relevance in this sense means connection to an issue other than a connection that depends on a general propensity to commit crimes or the type of crime in issue.

The prejudicial effect of bad character fact evidence has been discussed above. The strength of the inference of general criminal disposition to be drawn from the evidence is inevitably concomitant with the potential for prejudice. For the evidence to be admitted, the relevance of the evidence sought to be adduced to some fact in issue in the case must overbear the strength of this inference.

There is some debate as to whether the admission of similar fact evidence leaves any room for further discretion on the part of the judge.[91] It would seem, following *Boardman*, that the judge is bound to exclude evidence whose prejudicial effect outweighs its probative value, and from this perspective, any discretion on the part of the judge would be limited or non-existent.

V   ADMISSION OF SIMILAR FACT EVIDENCE IN CIVIL CASES

As stated earlier, the dangers associated with the admission of similar fact evidence are not present to the same degree in civil cases as in criminal proceedings. However, the same rules apply, and the

---

90   R. Cross and C. Tapper, *Cross on Evidence*, 7th ed. (London: Butterworths, 1990), at 352-56.
91   *Cross on Evidence, ibid.*, at 370-74.

evidence sought to be introduced must possess a sufficient nexus with or display the requisite relevance or materiality to the issues in the case.

The admissibility of similar fact evidence in civil cases was considered by Lord Denning in *Mood Music Publishing Co. v. De Wolfe Ltd.*[92] The plaintiffs, in an action for infringement of copyright, sought to adduce evidence that in three other cases, the defendants had reproduced musical works which were subject to copyright. The defendants conceded that the works now in question were very similar and that their work had been composed after the plaintiffs', but asserted that any similarity was coincidental. Lord Denning stated the test of admissibility of the similar fact evidence in civil cases as follows:[93]

> The criminal courts have been very careful not to admit [similar fact] evidence unless its probative value is so strong that it should be received in the interests of justice: and its admission will not operate unfairly to the accused. In civil cases the courts have followed a similar line but have not been so chary of admitting it. In civil cases the courts will admit evidence of similar facts if it is logically probative, that is, if it is logically relevant in determining the matter which is in issue; provided that it is not oppressive or unfair to the other side; and also that the other side has fair notice of it and is able to deal with it.

It is noteworthy that Lord Denning brings into play notions of oppression and unfairness, perhaps suggesting more flexibility of the rule in civil cases. Lord Denning also noted that these principles have long been applied, as is evidenced by cases such as *Brown v. Eastern & Midlands Railway Co.*,[94] *Moore v. Ransome's Dock Committee*,[95] *Hales v. Kerr*.[96] As the issue in *Mood Music* was whether the resemblances are "mere coincidences" or are due to copying, Lord Denning considered it to be relevant to know that there were other cases in which the defendant had produced musical works bearing a close resemblance to works which were the subject of copyright.

---

92   [1976] 1 All E.R. 763 (C.A.).
93   *Ibid.*, at 766.
94   (1889), 22 Q.B.D. 391 (C.A.).
95   (1898), 14 T.L.R. 539 (C.A.).
96   [1908] 2 K.B. 601 (D.C.).

As in criminal cases, the situations in which similar fact evidence will be considered relevant and thereby admissible are not closed. In *MacDonald v. Canada Kelp Co.*,[97] Bull J.A. of the British Columbia Court of Appeal cited with approval the words of Viscount Simon in *Harris v. D.P.P.*, that evidence of similar facts should be excluded "unless such evidence has a really material bearing on the issues to be decided" and stated the test as follows:[98]

> When there is a real and substantial nexus or connection between the act or allegation made, whether it be a crime or a fraud (but not, of course, limited to those), and facts relating to previous or subsequent transactions are sought to be given in evidence, then those facts have relevancy and are admissible not only to rebut a defence, such as lack of intent, accident, mens rea or the like, but to prove the fact of the act or allegations made.

A. *Evidence of Disposition Alone Not Admissible*

In determining whether the requisite nexus to the issues is present in a particular case, the principle in criminal cases that evidence tending solely to show a general disposition to commit the crime in question is not admissible applies equally in civil cases. For example, in negligence actions the manner in which the defendant or the plaintiff behaved on other occasions is not admissible.[99] Conduct of the defendant, even a short time prior to the accident, is equally inadmissible.[100] In an action for moneys had and received, in which the defendant pleads payment, he cannot, in order to explain the lack of an entry in the plaintiff's books, adduce evidence that in the case of another customer payment was mistakenly not credited.[101] Similarly, the plaintiff, in an assault case, cannot be asked in cross-examination about the number of fights in which he has been involved in order to show a propensity to fight.[102]

---

97   [1973] 5 W.W.R. 689, 39 D.L.R. (3d) 617 (B.C.C.A.).
98   *Ibid.*, at 699 (W.W.R.).
99   *Rock v. Canadian Northern Railway Co.*, [1922] 1 W.W.R. 496, 15 Sask. L.R. 194, 29 C.R.C. 19, 66 D.L.R. 255 (C.A.); *R. v. Royal Bank of Canada*, [1920] 1 W.W.R. 198, 30 Man. R. 104, 50 D.L.R. 293 (C.A.).
100   *Petijevich v. Law*, [1969] S.C.R. 257, 1 D.L.R. (3d) 690; *Ptycia v. Swetlishnoff*, [1971] S.C.R. 670, 16 D.L.R. (3d) 687.
101   *Massey-Harris Co. v. Merrithew* (1910), 39 N.B.R. 544 (C.A.).
102   *Hickey v. Fitzgerald* (1877), 41 U.C.Q.B. 303 (C.A.).

Evidence of disposition has been admitted, however, in divorce cases based on adultery. Previous and subsequent acts of familiarity between the respondents are admissible to prove that, on the occasion in question, an opportunity to have intercourse was probably used.[103] Evidence of disposition with respect to a person not a party to a dispute has also been admitted as circumstantial evidence of the manner in which he or she acted on the occasion in question.[104]

The following is a canvassing of the situations in which similar fact evidence may be considered relevant and admissible.

B. *To Prove a Fact in Issue Where Similar Facts Show "System" or "Scheme"*

Similarity in the *modus operandi* and recurrent instances of the same conduct may be sufficient to render the evidence admissible.[105] In such cases, if the past similar acts constitute a "system", the criterion of materiality will be considered to be fulfilled. In *Blake v. Albion Life Assurance Society*,[106] the plaintiff was induced to purchase a policy of life insurance from the defendant insurer on the false pretense that the plaintiff could thereby obtain a loan from a certain third party. After the policy of insurance was purchased, the said third party refused to go through with the transaction. In an action to set aside the policy and recover the money paid, the plaintiff sought to bring in evidence that other persons had been induced to purchase insurance under similar false pretenses by the same person under various aliases. Although the other judges who decided the case found several different bases on which to consider the evidence receivable, Lindley J. found that it was sufficient that the transaction was one of a class. He wrote:[107]

> The answer to the objection that evidence of frauds on other persons cannot be admitted, is that *this transaction is one of a class*, that *there are features in common*, the features in common being the false pretense and a knowledge of that false pretense on the

---

103   *Shaver v. Shaver*, [1933] O.W.N. 581 (C.A.).
104   *Joy v. Phillips, Mills & Co.*, [1916] 1 K.B. 849 (C.A.).
105   *Kidd v. Henderson* (1889), 22 N.S.R. 57 (C.A.); *Barnes v. Merritt & Co.* (1899), 15 T.L.R. 419 (C.A.).
106   (1878), 4 C.P.D. 94.
107   *Ibid.*, at 107.

part of the defendant company, and *the moment that is shewn the plaintiff's case is established.* [emphasis added]

Two cases of the British Columbia Court of Appeal have stressed that the similar facts must amount to a "system" before they meet the requirement of materiality to the case. In *MacDonald v. Canada Kelp Co.*,[108] the appellants sought to rescind a contract for the sale of shares on the ground of fraudulent misrepresentations made to them by two officers of the company, which, they alleged, induced them to buy the shares. They sought to bring in evidence of witnesses to whom similar representations had been made by the same two officials. This evidence was adduced for the purpose of showing that the alleged representations to the appellants had, in fact, been made. The Court followed *Blake v. Albion Life Assurance Society*,[109] and held that such evidence of similar representations was relevant to the question of whether the respondents actually made the statements to the appellants which were relied upon to prove their case. The Court disagreed with the argument of the respondents that past similar acts are never admissible to prove the doing of the act itself and cited *R. v. Ball*[110] in which the evidence of previous sexual intercourse and its result was allowed in evidence to show that the intercourse charged took place. In admitting the evidence, Bull J.A. stated:[111]

> As I have indicated, the test is relevancy, and relevancy depends largely on nexus or connection of the other transactions with the ones in issue — and a strong connection can well be admissible as relevant to the fact of the actus reus.

The Court also considered the decision of the Supreme Court of Canada in *Larson v. Boyd*,[112] which concerned an action for rescission of a contract for the sale of land by reason of alleged false representations made by the defendant. Evidence was admitted of false representations made by the defendant earlier to other persons, similar in character but with respect to other property. The majority

---

108 *Supra*, note 97.
109 *Supra*, note 106.
110 [1911] A.C. 47 (H.L.).
111 *Supra*, note 97, at 700.
112 (1919), 58 S.C.R. 275, [1919] 1 W.W.R. 808, 46 D.L.R. 126.

of the Supreme Court held that such later acts could not possibly be relevant to the issues of whether or not the earlier statements were made, or as to their materiality and whether or not they induced the plaintiff to purchase the property. In that case, Anglin J. commented with respect to the admissibility of the evidence:[113]

> The evidence of similar misrepresentations made by the plaintiff to other prospective purchasers might have been admissible if his intent in making the misrepresentations as to the defendant . . . had been material to any issue in [the action] . . .

Therefore, the British Columbia Court of Appeal did not consider *Larson* as authority to support the view that evidence of similar facts is never admissible to prove the doing of an act or the making of a statement.[114]

In overruling the trial judge who rejected the evidence, it is not clear that the Court was concerned with whether or not a scheme or system was proven, as it relied on two criminal cases, *R. v. Leforte*[115] and *R. v. Ball*[116] for the proposition that similar acts may be admitted not only to prove intent or motive but also the commission of the act. However, the British Columbia Court of Appeal made clear in *Contini v. Canarim Investment Corp.*,[117] that the decisive factor in *Macdonald* was the existence of a system.

In *Contini*, Bull J.A. noted that *MacDonald v. Canada Kelp Co.* is authority for the proposition that statements made to others similar to those allegedly made by the defendant to a plaintiff are admissible in evidence on the issue of whether or not they were in fact made to the plaintiff *if they have a material bearing on that issue*.[118] Bull J.A. considered the situation in *Contini* to be distinguishable from that in *Macdonald*, as no selling plan or scheme of conduct on the part of the respondents was alleged. Rather, the alleged misrepresentation was said to have been made upon a request for information in somewhat

---

113 *Ibid.*, at 280 (S.C.R.).
114 Robertson J.A., dissenting, considered that the case was concluded by the decision in *Larson v. Boyd* in that there was no attempt to prove a system which would make applicable the principles enunciated in *Blake*.
115 (1962), 31 D.L.R. (2d) 1.
116 *Supra*, note 110.
117 [1974] 5 W.W.R. 709, 49 D.L.R. (3d) 262 (B.C.C.A.).
118 *Ibid.*, at 711 (W.W.R.).

casual circumstances and the evidence did not meet the criterion of materiality.[119] Robertson J.A. was also of the opinion that the evidence was inadmissible for the following reasons:[120]

> In the case before us Shikatani was not trying to sell shares in Northlode to either the appellant or Reed; *there is no evidence that his conversations with Reed and the appellant were "of a class of transactions having common features" or that they formed part of "some mode or system of distribution"* (emphasis added).

It should also be noted that no system can be established on the basis of an isolated act.[121] Furthermore, the situation in which there is a 'system' should be distinguished from past similar acts, as discussed below.

C. To Explain the Animus, Purpose or Object of the Act

In *Blake v. Albion Life Assurance Society* Grove J. stated:[122]

> [W]hen a person is alleged to be guilty of an offence which per se cannot be brought home to him by proving his mere act without explaining his animus, purpose, or object in doing it, the law permits evidence of other acts done by the same person to be given, for the purpose of such explanation.
>
> . . .
>
> There is no difference there that I am aware of between the rule in civil and in criminal cases on this subject.

Thus, in an application for an order of arrest in which expected departure with intent to defraud is an essential ingredient, the former conduct of the debtor with respect to the same debt is a fact to be taken

---

119 MacFarlane J.A. was of the view that the evidence was admissible but would have dismissed the appeal on the basis that there was no reliance even if the representation was actually made.

120 *Supra*, note 117, at 717 (W.W.R.).

121 *Re Controverted Election for Shelburne and Queen's; Cowie v. Fielding* (1906), 37 S.C.R. 604.

122 *Supra*, note 106, at 101-02.

into consideration on the question of intent.[123] So too, in an action to set aside a policy of insurance taken out by A and assigned to B on the grounds that B induced A to take out the policy by fraud, evidence of similar transactions in which B procured policies on the lives of others is admissible to show intent.[124]

Except where a scheme or system is relied upon, similar fact evidence cannot be used to prove that the defendant committed the fraud in question on the basis that he had committed similar frauds on other occasions. Thus, evidence under this heading is not admissible to prove the principal act *but only to show its purpose or object.* The commission of the principal act must be admitted or proved by other evidence. Therefore, as a general rule, evidence of similar facts is only admissible to prove or rebut a defence which can reasonably be anticipated, such as ignorance, accident, a mistake or some innocent motive or intention.[125]

Accordingly, in an action based on fraudulent misrepresentation, if the defendant denies making the statement relied on, the plaintiff cannot adduce evidence that the defendant made similar statements to others.[126] The same rule prevents a defendant, who resists an action for the balance of the purchase price of two lots on the ground of fraudulent representations by the plaintiff, from adducing evidence of other purchasers to whom it is alleged the plaintiff made the same misrepresentations. If the making of the misrepresentations is denied, the representations to others are not admissible. In such circumstances it would not be the intent of the representations that is in issue but whether they were made at all.[127]

D. To Show the State or Condition of Premises, Places or Other Objects

Evidence is admissible to prove that previous accidents have occurred as a result of the physical state of the defendant's premises.[128]

---

123 *Beam v. Beatty* (1901), 2 O.L.R. 362 (C.A.).
124 *Mutual Life Assurance Co. of New York v. Jonah* (1897), 1 N.B. Eq. R. 482.
125 *R. v. Hrechuk* (1950), 98 C.C.C. 44, 10 C.R. 132, [1950] 2 W.W.R. 318, 58 Man. R. 489 (C.A.).
126 *Allen v. Turk* (1911), 20 O.W.R. 627, 3 O.W.N. 364.
127 *Larson v. Boyd, supra,* note 112.
128 *Sims v. Grand Trunk Railway Co.* (1907), 9 O.W.R. 469 (C.A.); *Glidden v. Town of Woodstock* (1895), 33 N.B.R. 388 (C.A.); *Brown v. Eastern and Midland*

Under the same principle, in an action for negligence based on the defective construction of a machine, evidence is admissible that on previous occasions, the machinery acted in the manner complained of.[129]

Similarly, in a nuisance action, the noxious effect of the defendant's premises on the plaintiff's neighbours can be proved in evidence.[130] In an action based on negligence arising out of the explosion of a non-returnable soft drink bottle, the court admitted evidence that other bottles of the same manufacturer burst in similar circumstances.[131] Thus, the evidence need not be confined to the physical state of the place or thing but may include its effect on others.[132] In an action for negligence in which it is alleged that the plaintiff contracted an infectious disease through the negligence of the defendant, a barber, in using razors and other appliances in a dirty and unsanitary condition, evidence is admissible of other customers who contracted a similar disease in the defendant's shop.[133]

While evidence of the general disposition of individuals is not admissible, the lesser species, whose conduct is allegedly more predictable, are subject to the same rule as places and things. Thus, the propensity of an animal to bite people is admissible in order to establish the negligence of the owner.[134]

On the other hand, machinery whose operation is likely to change from day to day by reason of human manipulation is accorded the same respect as a human being. In *Edwards v. Ottawa River Navigation Co.*[135] the defendant's steamboat was alleged to have emitted cinders from the screens of its funnel causing the burning of the plaintiff's premises. It was shown that the screens were open on some days and closed on others. There was no issue as to whether the engine was capable of projecting fire as far as the plaintiff's premises. Evi-

---

Railway Co. (1889), 22 Q.B.D. 391 (C.A.); *Moore v. Ransome's Dock Committee* (1898), 14 T.L.R. 539 (C.A.).
129   *Canada Central Railway Co. v. McLaren* (1883), 8 O.A.R. 564; affd. (1884), 21 C.L.J. 114 (P.C.).
130   *Barlow v. Kinnear* (1843), 4 N.B.R. 94 (C.A.).
131   *Chapman v. Seven-Up Sussex Ltd.* (1970), 2 N.B.R. (2d) 909 (Q.B.).
132   *Brown v. Eastern & Midlands Railway Co.* (1889), 22 Q.B.D. 391 (C.A.); *Zigelstein v. Kent*, [1939] O.W.N. 213.
133   *Hales v. Kerr*, [1908] 2 K.B. 601 (D.C.).
134   *Charlwood v. Greig* (1851), 175 E.R. 457.
135   (1876), 39 U.C.B.Q. 264 (C.A.).

dence, therefore, of fire having been emitted on other occasions was held to be inadmissible. On the same theory, in an action against a railway arising out of an accident at a level crossing, evidence of other accidents is not admissible as such accidents could be occasioned by any number of variables.[136]

E. *To Show Ownership or Title*

Repeated acts of ownership with respect to lands or premises are admissible on the issue of ownership or title.[137]

F. *To Prove Standard Practice or Market Value*

In negligence actions, where the standard of care must be proved, evidence is admitted as to the performance of the act in question by others. If standard practice is proved in a medical malpractice case by reference to the manner in which other practitioners have performed an operation, the defendant may show that he or she performed the operation in the same manner previously with success.[138] Where the value of land or chattels is in question, evidence of comparative sales is admissible.[139]

G. *To Prove Agency*

Evidence that on other occasions a party authorized another to act on his behalf in circumstances similar to the transaction in question is admissible to prove agency on the occasion in question.[140]

H. *To Rebut Other Evidence*

Similar fact evidence may be made relevant and therefore admissible by other evidence presented in the case. An obvious example is presented by the case of *Key v. Thomson*[141] in which evidence of similar

---

136 *Shaver v. Shaver,* [1933] O.W.N. 581 (C.A.); *Wales v. Wales,* [1900] P. 63.
137 *Woodward v. Buchanan* (1870), L.R. 5 Q.B. 285.
138 *Key v. Thomson* (1868), 12 N.B.R. 295 (C.A.).
139 *Stockbridge Mill Co. v. Central Land Board,* [1954] 2 All E.R. 360 (C.A.).
140 *Blake v. Albion Life Assurance Society* (1878), 4 C.P.D. 94; *Woodward v. Buchanan* (1870), L.R. 5 Q.B. 285.
141 *Supra,* note 138.

facts was admitted to rebut other evidence of similar acts. Another example of similar fact evidence being admitted to rebut other testimony is *Cameron v. Moncton (Town)*.[142] This was an action for negligence against the town for non-repair of a sidewalk. The Mayor testified that he routinely inspected the streets and reported anything unusual to the Road Commissioner. Inquiry as to previous similar accidents was held to be admissible to rebut the inference in the Mayor's testimony that every defect was immediately reported to the Commissioner.

VI CONCLUSION

It is apparent from the foregoing that while the rules relating to the admissibility of similar facts in civil cases reflect very strongly the influence of the "category" approach of the earlier criminal cases, they in fact focus on whether the evidence is relevant to the matter in issue. The categories of relevance are not closed and the inquiry should concentrate on determining relevance without the constraint of fitting the evidence into a particular pigeonhole. Moreover, prejudice, which dominates the determination of admissibility of similar fact evidence in criminal cases, plays a significantly lesser role in civil cases, and evidence of similar facts should be admitted if it is logically probative to an issue in the case as long as, to borrow the formula of Lord Denning,[143] it is not unduly "oppressive or unfair" to the other side.

---

142 (1889), 29 N.B.R. 372 (C.A.).
143 *Mood Music Publishing Co. v. De Wolfe Ltd.*, [1976] 1 All E.R. 763, at 766.

CHAPTER 12

OPINION EVIDENCE

I   OPINION OF LAY PERSONS

A. *Rationale and Development of the Rule*

1. Rationale of Exclusion

The development of the modern rule[1] excluding opinion evidence was characterized by Wigmore as "an historical blunder".[2] Reduced to its essentials, it limited a witness to describing precisely and exactly his observations and no more. Any inference to be taken from those observations was a matter for the court and the witness' opinion was not wanted. The exclusion of such opinion evidence was primarily based upon the fear that it would otherwise result in a usurpation of the functions of the judge or jury and that such opinion was irrelevant.[3] Other dangers of such evidence are said to be: that numerous witnesses will be called to give their opinion, resulting in a waste of the court's time and a confusion of issues; that a jury may too readily accept the opinion of influential witnesses without exercising its own independent judgment; and that a witness would be able to testify without any fear of prosecution for perjury. These justifications appear to be mere afterthought to support a rule which is neither sensible nor workable in its strict terms.

---

1   E.W. Cleary (ed.), *McCormick on Evidence*, 3rd ed. (St. Paul: West Publishing, 1984), at 26, note 8, traces the rule beginning in 1801.
2   J. Wigmore, *A Students' Textbook of the Law of Evidence* (Brooklyn: Foundation Press Inc., 1935), at 156.
3   *Law Reform Commission of Canada Report on Evidence* (Ottawa: Information Canada, 1975), at 97.

2. Development of Rule

Originally, only speculation and conjecture not founded upon any observed facts were excluded. However, the modern rule went beyond that to preclude witnesses from stating inferences based upon events that they had personally observed. Wigmore felt that[4]

> ... it is a senseless rule, for not once in a thousand times can the observed data be exactly and fully reproduced in words. Still further, no harm could be done by letting the witness offer his inference, except perhaps the waste of a moment's time, whereas the application of the rule wastes vastly more time. And finally the rule is so pedantically applied by most courts that it excludes the most valuable testimony, such as would be used in all affairs of life outside a court room.

The opinion evidence rule was based upon the assumption that there is a clear demarcation between inferences and the facts which give rise to them. Under the rule, witnesses can testify only to the latter. Its application to particular facts serves to point out the artificiality of the distinction. For example, what if a witness who was a passenger in X's automobile testifies that X was driving at approximately 100 kilometres per hour? Assuming that the witness did not observe the speedometer, is the witness' statement one of fact of which he or she is permitted to testify, or is it an inference drawn from perceived facts? What of statements which indicate distances, the temperature of a room, the age of a man or the identification of a person or handwriting? A witness says that he saw a woman in a store and recognized her as Y. Is that fact or inference? Is the witness' testimony to be restricted to a mere description of the physical features of the woman that he saw in the store? If the witness provides the court with the inference from such facts in those situations, it is apparent that he is just giving a conclusion based upon physical and perceptual sensations that he has experienced in the past and with which he has compared his observations of the events in issue. To rule such testimony inadmissible because it constitutes inference would conflict with the natural mental processes which translate a person's perception into words.[5]

---

4   *Supra*, note 2, at 156.
5   See *R. v. Miller* (1959), 125 C.C.C. 8, 31 C.R. 101, 29 W.W.R. 124, at 136-37 (B.C.C.A.); *Sherrard v. Jacob*, [1965] N.I. 151 (C.A.).

Nevertheless the rule remained but was inconsistently applied. McCormick described its application as a "rule of preference" for primary facts rather than as an exclusionary rule:[6]

> The more concrete description is preferred to the more abstract. Moreover, it seems that the principal impact of the rule is upon the form of examination. The questions, while they cannot suggest the particular details desired, else they will be leading, should nevertheless call for the most specific account that the witness can give ... When recognized as a matter of the form of the examination rather than the substance of the testimony — again, a difference of degree — the opinion rule, like other regulations of form, such as the control over leading questions and questions calling for a free narrative and over the order of proof is seen to fall naturally in the realm of discretion.

Gradually, the courts exercised such discretion thereby permitting some erosion of the rule. They were prepared to give some latitude to statements of inference where practical considerations such as the saving of time justified their reception. Witnesses were permitted to state inferences with respect to perceived facts whenever it would be too difficult or absurd for them to distinguish inference from fact. In such cases, the inference was obvious and the court would not compel the witness to be more specific. To force witnesses in all cases to reduce their testimony to mere verbal description of their mental images devoid of any reasoning or thinking on their part hindered the court's ability to recreate the events in question. Accordingly, in such circumstances of strict necessity, they were permitted to express inferences.[7]

---

6   *McCormick on Evidence, supra*, note 1, at 29.
7   In *Preeper v. R.* (1888), 15 S.C.R. 401, at 418, Gwynne J. indicated by way of example that a lay witness may opine: "that certain hair upon a club was in the opinion of the witness human hair and resembled the hair of the deceased — that a certain substance was hard pan — that a certain person appeared to be in fear — that on being held to answer he looked as if he felt badly — that the appearance of a blood-stain indicated that the [shot] came from below"; *Alexander v. Vye* (1889), 16 S.C.R. 501.

3. Modern Statement of Rule: Helpfulness

Finally, Dickson J. in *R. v. Graat*[8] all but did away with the illogical distinction between so-called fact and opinion. He pointed out the numerous exceptions to the opinion rule that had developed and concluded:[9]

> Except for the sake of convenience, there is little, if any, virtue, in any distinction resting on the tenuous, and frequently false, antithesis between fact and opinion. The line between "fact" and "opinion" is not clear.

Returning to broad principles, Dickson J. put the admissibility of such evidence on a rather simple basis:[10]

> The witnesses had an opportunity for personal observation. They were in a position to give the Court real help.

Couched in these terms, the modern opinion rule should pose few exclusionary difficulties. The real issue will be the assessment and weight to be given to such evidence after it is admitted. Thus, the law has moved away from the requirement of "necessity" whereby opinion evidence was received in the case of a lay witness only if he or she could not "owing to the nature of the matter adequately convey to the jury the data from which such inference is made" and, in the case of an expert witness, if he or she was "owing to his training more competent to draw the inference in question than is the untrained juryman."[11]

One knowledgeable commentator has taken issue with the con-

---

8 [1982] 2 S.C.R. 819, 2 C.C.C. (3d) 365, 31 C.R. (3d) 289, 18 M.V.R. 287, 144 D.L.R. (3d) 267, 45 N.R. 451 (*sub nom. R. v. Gratt*).

9 *Ibid.*, at 835 (S.C.R.).

10 *Ibid.*, at 836 (S.C.R.). In fact, Dickson J.'s approach is in accord with s. 38 of the draft Uniform Evidence Act, *Report of the Federal/Provincial Task Force on Uniform Rules of Evidence* (Toronto: Carswell, 1982), at 541, which also addressed the problem of the difficulty of separating facts from inferences. That section establishes the following basis upon which lay opinion will be received: "A witness who is not testifying as an expert may give opinion evidence where it is based on facts perceived by him, and the evidence would be helpful either to the witness in giving a clear statement or to the trier of fact in determining an issue." *Ibid.*, at 553. This provision follows the recommendations of the Law Reform Commission of Canada in its *Report on Evidence, supra,* note 3.

11 Z. Cowen and P. Carter, *Essays on the Law of Evidence* (Oxford: Clarendon Press, 1956), at 170.

cept of "helpfulness" replacing that of "necessity" as a pre-condition to the admissibility of opinion evidence by lay witnesses.[12] His concern was that a helpfulness test might allow for the admission of too much evidence in the form of inferences and that the underlying facts, particularly if they do not support the inferences, may be successfully concealed from the court. He worried that such a test might lead to endless *voir dires* since the only way to determine whether an opinion is helpful would be to exclude the jury and consider the evidence. Prior to the *Graat* decision, the trial judge would simply stop the witness if he or she began to answer in the form of an opinion and the judge would then determine whether the proffered testimony would be necessary for the trier of fact.

These alleged drawbacks have not prevented others from adopting the "helpful" test. Rule 701 of the United States Federal Rules of Evidence also provides for the admission of opinions or inferences which are "helpful to a clear understanding of [the witness'] testimony or the determination of a fact in issue."[13] As the American Advisory Committee on the Rules of Evidence observed, the courts have made concessions in certain recurring situations such as identification and handwriting, and opinion evidence in these matters is admitted. The Advisory Committee also noted, however, that "necessity as a standard for permitting opinions and conclusions has proved too elusive and too unacceptable to particular situations for purposes of satisfactory judicial administration".[14] The Law Reform Commission of Canada has supported that view and recommended that the present strict necessity test for determining the admissibility of opinion testimony of lay witnesses be altered to a test of whether the opinion would be helpful to the trier of fact.[15] This criterion should have the advantage of being capable of application and permitting witnesses to describe facts not only in a manner in which they are accustomed to speaking but also in a manner which will be most useful to the trier of fact in determining the truth.[16]

---

12   Mr. Justice D.C. McDonald, "Opinion Evidence" (1978), 16 Osgoode Hall L.J. 321, at 322-24.
13   28 U.S.C.A. app. (1976).
14   P. Rothstein, *Rules of Evidence for the United States Courts and Magistrates*, 2nd ed. (New York: C. Boardman Co., c. 1989), at 264.
15   *Supra*, note 3, s. 67 draft Evidence Code, 40.
16   *Report of the Federal/Provincial Task Force on Uniform Rules of Evidence* (Toronto: Carswell, 1982), at 119-20.

Courts now have greater freedom to receive lay witnesses' opinions; but as such evidence approaches the central issues that the courts must decide, one can still expect an insistence that the witnesses stick to the primary facts and refrain from giving their inferences. It is always a matter of degree. As the testimony shades towards a legal conclusion, resistance to admissibility develops.[17]

In view of the "helpfulness" principle enunciated by the Supreme Court of Canada in *R. v. Graat*,[18] the categories of topics about which a lay witness can testify are not limited. However, since lay witnesses traditionally have been allowed to express opinions upon a number of established subjects and a certain amount of protective jurisprudence has developed around them to assure reliability, several illustrations are appropriate.

B. *Illustrations of Lay Opinion*

1. Identity of Persons and Places

Witnesses may state their belief as to the identity of persons or things, whether these are present in court or not. They may also identify absent persons by photographs, produced and proved by any competent testimony to be accurate likenesses.[19] A lay witness may also identify a person by listening to tape-recorded conversations.[20]

---

17 "... the inference may involve a matter of law which is for the court alone and on which the opinion of the witness is plainly irrelevant. A witness, for example, cannot be allowed to say that a defendant was negligent or that the respondent in a divorce suit was guilty of the matrimonial offence of cruelty, for while these issues are issues of fact they necessitate the application of standards determined by law": per Lord MacDermott in *Sherrard v. Jacob*, [1965] N.I. 151, at 156 (C.A.). However, where a testator's competency to make a will is in dispute, lay opinion as to his sanity has been regularly admitted: *Re Fraser* (1911), 26 O.L.R. 508, 8 D.L.R. 955 (C.A.), reversing 24 O.L.R. 222 (Div. Ct.); *Buttrum v. Udell* (1925), 57 O.L.R. 97, [1925] 3 D.L.R. 45 (C.A.), at 103 (O.L.R.); *Robins v. National Trust Co.* (1925), 57 O.L.R. 46 (C.A.), at 58; affd. [1927] A.C. 515, [1927] 1 W.W.R. 692, [1927] 2 D.L.R. 97 (P.C.); *Foothills Pipe Lines (Yukon) Ltd. v. Minister of National Revenue* (1990), 115 N.R. 380 (Fed. C.A.).
18 *Supra*, note 8.
19 M.N. Howard, P. Crane and D.A. Hochberg, *Phipson on Evidence*, 14th ed. (London: Sweet & Maxwell, 1990), § 15-06, at 330.
20 *R. v. Rowbotham* (1988), 41 C.C.C. (3d) 1, 63 C.R. (3d) 113, 25 O.A.C. 321 (S.C.), at 155-58 (C.R.); *R. v. Tarafa* (1990), 53 C.C.C. (3d) 472 (Que. S.C.); see also *R. v. Medvedew* (1978), 43 C.C.C. (2d) 434, 6 C.R. (3d) 185, [1978] 6 W.W.R.

It is common knowledge that identification evidence, because of the frailty of human perception, is fraught with danger. Accordingly, expert evidence is not necessary to establish the generally-held view that human perception and the ability to identify persons may have certain inherent weaknesses.[21] That does not mean that the concern about the probative value of identification evidence is to go unmentioned. In England, it has been held that whenever the case against a defendant depends wholly or substantially on the correctness of one or more identifications which are challenged by the defendant, the judge must warn the jury of the dangers of such identification evidence and draw their attention to the quality of the evidence.[22] Furthermore, in a case in which the quality of the identification is poor, the judge is required to withdraw the case from the jury unless there is other evidence capable of supporting the identification. In Canada, however, a trial judge cannot withdraw a case from the jury unless the identification evidence constitutes "no evidence".[23] In *Joly v. R.*[24] the Court accepted the notion that poor identification evidence can amount to "no evidence" justifying the withdrawal of the case from the jury.[25]

Opinion evidence of lay witnesses is permitted for the purposes of identification of places as well as persons. The Saskatchewan District Court, in *R. v. K & B Ambulance Ltd.*,[26] considered a case which involved illegal possession of radio apparatus and the location of this equipment was crucial to the case at hand. The equipment was stored in a house, apparently a residence, but portions of the house were also the premises of Crescent Ambulance Care. The witness testified that the equipment in question was located in that portion of the house belonging to Crescent Ambulance Care. It was argued by the accused that this evidence, standing alone, was inadmissible as opinion evi-

---

208, 91 D.L.R. (3d) 21 (Man. C.A.) for expert voice identification.

21   *R. v. Audy (No. 2)* (1977), 34 C.C.C. (2d) 231 (Ont. C.A.).

22   *R. v. Turnbull*, [1977] Q.B. 224 (C.A.); *R. v. Barnes* (1989), 112 N.R. 49 (P.C.).

23   *R. v. Mezzo*, [1986] 1 S.C.R. 802, 52 C.R. (3d) 113, 27 C.C.C. (3d) 97, 30 D.L.R. (4th) 161, [1986] 4 W.W.R. 577, 43 Man. R. (2d) 161, 68 N.R. 1; *R. v. Jacobs*, [1988] 2 S.C.R. 1047.

24   (1978), 41 C.C.C. (2d) 538 (Ont. H.C.J.).

25   But *R. v. Sauvé* (1979), 55 C.C.C. (2d) 149, at 169 (Ont. Prov. Ct.) does not accept this position.

26   [1979] 2 W.W.R. 71 (Sask. Dist. Ct.).

dence. The Court noted that the absolute, or strict, opinion rule is, in practice, "all but unworkable" and that the distinction between opinion and fact is often one of degree.[27] The Court stated that:[28]

> The key is that the witness has personal knowledge of the facts on which his opinion is based . . . In the same way as lay witnesses of ordinary intelligence are permitted to give their opinions, based on personal knowledge, of the identity of individuals, they may, it seems to me, be permitted to give it on the identity of places, as here. The area in which non-experts are allowed to give inferential evidence is not closed but, on the authorities, is expanding. Even the rule precluding the expression of a witness upon a matter on which the jury alone has the decision seems less to the fore today in Canadian law.

2. Identification of Handwriting

A lay witness will be allowed to give identification of a person's handwriting if the witness can first establish competence to do so on the basis of having actually watched the person write,[29] or being able to recognize the person's handwriting by reason of a regular exchange of correspondence with that person, or by having seen numerous other examples of the individual's handwriting.[30] In *Alexander v. Vye*,[31] it was held that a witness could identify handwriting even though the witness had received only one letter from the alleged writer and that letter was not produced in court. A stricter test, however, for the foundation of such lay opinion was applied by the Supreme Court of Canada in *Pitre v. R.*[32] in which the witness' alleged receipt of two letters and two postcards from the accused without production thereof was held not to be a sufficient basis to permit the witness to express her opinion on the identification of the handwriting in question.

If a lay witness had seen only one example of the person's handwriting would that be too inadequate a foundation to allow the witness to express an opinion, or should recognition of the unique

---

27   *Ibid.*, at 78.
28   *Ibid.*, at 79.
29   *Phipson on Evidence, supra*, note 19, §§ 32-44, at 837.
30   *Pitre v. R.*, [1933] S.C.R. 69, 59 C.C.C. 148, [1933] 1 D.L.R. 417.
31   (1889), 16 S.C.R. 501.
32   *Supra*, note 30.

writing style suffice to warrant reception of the witness' opinion of identification? The latter view is preferable and the fact that the witness' observations of the handwriting have been few should go only to the weight of the evidence. It has been said that even where the witness has had minimal experience in observing the individual's handwriting on a document, the witness may state an opinion if he or she acted upon the document in some fashion.[33] In addition, handwriting on a disputed document may be proven by a direct comparison with a document that is known to have been written by the person in question. Although originally prohibited, this type of opinion is now expressly permitted by provincial Evidence Acts[34] and the *Canada Evidence Act*.[35]

Either lay or expert testimony as to the genuineness or otherwise of the handwriting is permitted. In such cases, a known sample of the person's handwriting is compared with the disputed writing. The witness indicates in what respects the two handwritings are similar and then gives his or her opinion as to whether they were written by the same person.[36] In the absence of such testimony, the court is entitled

---

33 *Supra*, note 30.
34 Evidence Acts: Ontario, R.S.O. 1980, c. 145, s. 57; Alberta, R.S.A. 1980, c. A-21, s. 59; British Columbia, R.S.B.C. 1979, c. 116, s. 51; Manitoba, R.S.M. 1987, c. E150, s. 56; Newfoundland, R.S.N. 1970, c. 115, s. 22 [am. 1975-76, No. 26, s. 1]; New Brunswick, R.S.N.B. 1979, c. E-11, s. 22; N.W.T., R.O.N.W.T. 1988, E-8, s. 58; Nova Scotia, R.S.N.S. 1989, c. 154, s. 39; Prince Edward Island, R.S.P.E.I. 1988, c. E-11, s. 20; Saskatchewan, R.S.S. 1978, c. S-16, s. 47; Yukon, R.S.Y.T. 1986, c. 57, s. 50.

Section 39 of the draft Uniform Evidence Act (*Report of the Federal/Provincial Task Force on Uniform Rules of Evidence* (Toronto: Carswell, 1982) is identical in content to s. 8 of the *Canada Evidence Act* and reads as follows: "Comparison of a disputed handwriting with another handwriting may be made by witnesses, and such handwritings and the evidence of witnesses with respect to them may be submitted to the trier of fact as proof of the genuineness or otherwise of the handwriting in dispute": *ibid.*, at 554.
35 R.S.C. 1985, c. E-10, s. 8.
36 The statutory provisions do not expressly restrict this kind of testimonial comparison and opinion to expert witnesses alone although F. Auld and C. Morawetz (eds.), *MacRae on Evidence*, 2nd ed. (Toronto: Burroughs and Co., 1952), at 162 indicates, without citing any authority, that the statutory provisions permit the giving of opinion evidence by experts in handwriting. In *R. v. Harvey* (1869), 11 Cox C.C. 546 (Assizes), lay opinion was rejected because, *inter alia*, it was of no probative worth. The case of *Lomas v. DiCecca* (1978), 20 O.R. (2d) 605, 88 D.L.R. (3d) 434 (H.C.J.) considered the standard of proof regarding an

to compare disputed with admitted or proved handwriting, and act upon its own judgment.[37]

3. Mental Capacity and State of Mind

In civil cases a lay witness may express an opinion on the issue of a person's testamentary capacity.[38] Indeed, if the lay person has an opportunity to observe the testator over long periods of time and association, such evidence may be given greater weight than expert testimony.[39] In criminal cases a lay person may testify to facts which circumstantially prove that an accused lacked the requisite mental state by reason of a disease of the mind[40] or of a blow to the head.[41] However, a lay witness is not permitted to testify that an accused was capable of forming the requisite intent, as the jury is able to determine that matter without the assistance of such testimony.[42] Similarly, expert testimony is inadmissible to prove that the accused was normal and acted normally and thus did not have the requisite mental state for the crime.[43] This evidence is outside the area of the witness'

---

allegation of forgery in a civil case. The plaintiff claimed that she had not signed the lease in question and that it was forged. The court held that the seriousness of the consequences flowing from a finding of forgery must be considered when determining whether the plaintiff has met the required standard of proof. In this case, the plaintiff failed to give any expert testimony that the impugned signature was not genuine, whereas the defendant had introduced expert evidence to the contrary. The Court held that the plaintiff had accordingly failed to meet the required standard of proof since such a burden cannot be discharged by "inexact proofs, indefinite testimony or indirect inferences."

37 *Thompson v. Thompson* (1902), 4 O.L.R. 442 (C.A.).

38 *Robins v. National Trust Co.* (1925), 57 O.L.R. 46, at 58 (C.A.); affd. [1927] A.C. 515, [1927] 1 W.W.R. 692, 881, [1927] 2 D.L.R. 97 (P.C.), but see *Wright v. Doe d. Tatham* (1837), 7 Ad. & El. 313, 112 E.R. 488, at 511, 516-17 (E.R.).

39 *Royal Trust Co. v. McClure*, [1945] 3 W.W.R. 641, 61 B.C.R. 544, (*sub nom. McClure v. O'Neil*) [1945] 4 D.L.R. 373 (C.A.); affd. (*sub nom. O'Neil v. Royal Trust Co.*) [1946] S.C.R. 622, [1946] 4 D.L.R. 545; *Re Price; Spence v. Price*, [1946] O.W.N. 80, [1946] 2 D.L.R. 492 (C.A.).

40 *Cooper v. R.*, [1980] 1 S.C.R. 1149, 51 C.C.C. (2d) 129, 13 C.R. (3d) 97, 4 L. Med. Q. 227, 110 D.L.R. (3d) 46, 31 N.R. 234, at 1165, 1170-71 (S.C.R.); however, expert witnesses may often testify if the accused lacked the requisite intent: *ibid.*, at 1168 (S.C.R.).

41 *Bleta v. R.*, [1964] S.C.R. 561, [1965] 1 C.C.C. 1, 44 C.R. 193, 48 D.L.R. (2d) 139 (blow to the head causing automatism).

42 *R. v. Curry* (1980), 38 N.S.R. 575, 69 A.P.R. 575, at 581, 589 (C.A.).

43 This argument presumes that normal persons are incapable of committing

expertise and the jury would not receive appreciable assistance from such evidence.[44]

II THE OPINION OF EXPERTS

A. *General Principles*

1. As an Exception to the General Rule

The testimony of experts is commonplace in Canadian courtrooms. We have come a long way from the early scepticism surrounding such evidence.[45] The concern was that an expert's evidence might well be influenced because the expert is providing testimony to assist one party against another. In this adversarial context there was some fear that an expert called by one side might give his or her evidence in a less than independent fashion. This concern is now a matter of weight rather than of admissibility.[46]

In order to provide the trier of fact with the necessary technical or scientific basis upon which to properly assess the evidence presented, the courts recognized an exception to the opinion rule for expert witnesses.[47] Conceived as a means of assisting jurors in the

---

crimes.

44 *R. v. McMillan* (1975), 23 C.C.C. (2d) 160, 29 C.R.N.S. 191, 7 O.R. (2d) 750 (C.A.); affd. [1977] 2 S.C.R. 824, 33 C.C.C. (2d) 360, 73 D.L.R. (3d) 759, 15 N.R. 20; see also *R. v. Robertson* (1975), 21 C.C.C. 385, 29 C.R.N.S. 141 (Ont. C.A.). Application for leave to appeal to S.C.C. dismissed 21 C.C.C. (2d) 385n — psychiatric evidence to show that a propensity for violence or aggression was not part of an accused's psychological make-up; *R. v. Dubois* (1976), 30 C.C.C. (2d) 412 (Ont. C.A.) — psychiatric evidence of how a person might react to extreme stress resulting from an assault; *Faid v. R.*, 61 C.C.C. (2d) 28, [1981] 5 W.W.R. 349, 30 A.R. 616 (C.A.); revd. on other grounds [1983] 1 S.C.R. 265, 33 C.R. (3d) 1, 2 C.C.C. (3d) 513, [1983] 3 W.W.R. 673, 25 Alta. L.R. (2d) 1, 145 D.L.R. (3d) 67, 46 N.R. 461, 42 A.R. 308 — the accused's disinclination to commit the crime.

45 See R.P. Croom-Johnson and G.F.L. Bridgman, *Taylor on Evidence*, 12th ed. (London: Sweet & Maxwell, 1931), at 59; *Miller (S.S.) Co. Property Ltd. v. Overseas Tankship (U.K.) Ltd.*, [1963] N.S.W.R. 737, at 753; *Tracey Peerage Case* (1843), 10 Cl. & Fin. 154, 8 E.R. 700 (H.L.); *Thorn v. Worthing Skating Rink Co.* (1876), 6 Ch. D. 415, noted in *Plimpton v. Spiller* (1887), 6 Ch. D. 412, at 415.

46 See this Chapter, II.A.2.

47 *Folkes v. Chadd* (1782), 3 Doug. K.B. 157, 99 E.R. 589 (K.B.); *Beckwith v. Sydebotham* (1807), 1 Camp. 116, 170 E.R. 897 (K.B.).

understanding of complex technical issues, expert evidence was permitted only in cases where the subject matter in question was beyond the capabilities of inexperienced persons who could not form a correct judgment without such assistance:[48]

> . . . in other words when it so far partakes of the nature of a science, as to require a course of previous habit or study in order to the attainment of a knowledge of it.

More recently, Dickson J. in *R. v. Abbey*[49] described the role of the expert in the following way:[50]

> With respect to matters calling for special knowledge, an expert in the field may draw inferences and state his opinion. An expert's function is precisely this: to provide the judge and jury with a ready-made inference which the judge and jury, due to the technical nature of the facts, are unable to formulate. "An expert's opinion is admissible to furnish the Court with scientific information which is likely to be outside the experience and knowledge of a judge or jury. If on the proven facts a judge or jury can form their own conclusions without help, then the opinion of the expert is unnecessary": [*R. v.*] *Turner* (1974), 60 Crim. App. R. 80 at p. 83, per Lawton L.J.

It has been said that the hallmark of admissibility simply should be whether the experts' testimony would be helpful to the tribunal. In *R. v. Fisher*[51] Aylesworth J.A. indicated that on some issues such as mental competency and handwriting, a court will admit both lay and expert opinion evidence.[52] It is impossible to delineate the full range of topics about which only experts may testify. The field of matters

---

48 Per Barry C.J.K.B.D. in *Taylor v. Gray* (1937), 11 M.P.R. 588, [1937] 4 D.L.R. 123 (N.B.C.A.), at 599 (M.P.R.).
49 *R. v. Abbey*, [1982] 2 S.C.R. 24, 68 C.C.C. (2d) 394, 29 C.R. (3d) 193, 138 D.L.R. (3d) 202, [1983] 1 W.W.R. 251, 39 B.C.L.R. 201, 43 N.R. 30.
50 *Ibid.*, at 42 (S.C.R.). See also *R. v. Beland*, [1987] 2 S.C.R. 398, at 415, 36 C.C.C. (3d) 481, 43 D.L.R. (4th) 641, 9 Q.A.C. 293, 79 N.R. 263; *Kelliher (Village) v. Smith*, [1931] S.C.R. 672, [1931] 4 D.L.R. 102, at 116 (S.C.R.).
51 [1961] O.W.N. 94, 34 C.R. 320; affd. [1961] S.C.R. 535, 35 C.R. 107, 130 C.C.C. 1.
52 See this Chapter, I.B.2. and 3.

requiring expert assistance is in a state of continual flux. In each case it is a question of fact whether the subject matter under study necessitates comprehension beyond the level of the common person. Some areas are obvious.[53]

> Where expert evidence is tendered in such fields as engineering or pathology, the paucity of the lay person's knowledge is uncontentious. The long-standing recognition that psychiatric or psychological testimony also falls within the realm of expert evidence is predicated on a realization that in some circumstances the average person may not have sufficient knowledge of or experience within human behaviour to draw an appropriate inference from the facts before him or her.

In *R. v. Lavallée*[54] the Supreme Court of Canada held that expert evidence on the psychological effect of wife-battering was both relevant and necessary. Because the battering relationship was subject to a large number of myths, it was considered beyond the ken of the average juror and thus required explanation through expert testimony. Such testimony could assist the jury in determining whether a woman who had killed her partner had had a reasonable apprehension of death because of her heightened sensitivity to her partner's acts, and had thus killed in self-defence.

In *R. v. McMillan*,[55] the Ontario Court of Appeal stated the general criteria for admissibility of expert evidence: (1) the evidence is relevant to some issue in the case, (2) the evidence is not excluded by a policy rule, and (3) the evidence falls within the proper sphere of expert evidence.[56]

Sometimes it is debatable whether the expert testimony would be of value or not. Rejection of expert evidence about whether a common English word used in the ordinary way was generic and what that word meant[57] may be easily justified as not coming within a

---

53   Per Wilson J. in *R. v. Lavallée*, [1990] 1 S.C.R. 852, 76 C.R. (3d) 379, 55 C.C.C. (3d) 97, [1990] 4 W.W.R. 1, 108 N.R. 321, at 111 (C.C.C.).

54   *Ibid.*

55   *Supra*, note 44.

56   *Ibid.*, at 763 (O.R.). Although Martin J.A. was concerned with psychiatric evidence in relation to personality traits or disposition, the comments apply to other fields of expertise.

57   *Aladdin Industries Inc. v. Canadian Thermos Products Ltd.*, [1969] 2 Ex. C.R. 80, 41 Fox Pat. C. 26, 57 C.P.R. 230; affd. [1974] S.C.R. 845, 6 C.P.R. (2d) 1;

subject requiring any special study or experience. The courts, however, have allowed expert testimony about uncommon words or common words used in an unusual manner as, for example, drug slang.[58] Curiously, however, courts have rejected expert evidence in some instances where one would have thought it would have been of value. For example, experts' evidence on the question of whether certain fire prevention facilities should have been provided was held to be inadmissible in a fatal accident action based upon a hotel keeper's negligence.[59]

2. Qualifying the Expert Witness

An expert is usually called for two reasons. The expert provides to the court basic information necessary for its understanding of the scientific or technical issues involved in the case. In addition, because the court is incapable of drawing the necessary inferences on its own from the technical facts presented, an expert is allowed to state his or her opinion and conclusions. The expert's usefulness in this respect is circumscribed by the limits of his or her own knowledge. Before the court will receive the testimony on matters of substance, it must be demonstrated that the witness possesses sufficient background in the area as to be able to assist the court appreciably. The test of expertness so far as the law of evidence is concerned is skill in the field in which the witness' opinion is sought. The admissibility of such evidence does not depend upon the means by which that skill was acquired. As long as the court is satisfied that the witness is sufficiently experienced in the subject-matter at issue, the court will not be concerned with whether his or her skill was derived from specific studies or by practical training, although that may affect the weight to be given to

Home Juice Co. v. Orange Maison Ltée, [1968] 1 Ex. C.R. 163, 36 Fox Pat. C. 111, 52 C.P.R. 175.

58 See R. v. O'Quinn (1976), 36 C.C.C. (2d) 364, [1976] W.W.D. 130 (B.C.C.A.) — "junk" means heroin; R. v. Gladstone (1977), 37 C.C.C. (2d) 185 (B.C. Co. Ct.) — "speed" means methamphetamine. See also B.A. McFarlane, Drug Offences in Canada, 1st ed. (Toronto: Canada Law Book, 1979), at 129-34.

59 Dalton v. Higgins (1964), 51 M.P.R. 52, 43 D.L.R. (2d) 574 (P.E.I.C.A.) and in another case two automotive engineers were prevented from testifying as to human reaction time in highway emergencies because inter alia opinion evidence was stated to be of no value on conjectural issues such as how other persons would probably act in particular situations: Adam v. Campbell, [1950] 3 D.L.R. 449 (S.C.C.).

the evidence. In *Rice v. Sockett*,[60] Falconbridge C.J. quoted the following explanation:[61]

"The derivation of the term 'expert' implies that he is one who by experience has acquired special or peculiar knowledge of the subject of which he undertakes to testify, and it does not matter whether such knowledge has been acquired by study of scientific works or by practical observation. Hence, one who is an old hunter, and has thus had much experience in the use of firearms, may be as well qualified to testify as to the appearance which a gun recently fired would present as a highly-educated and skilled gunsmith."

If opposing counsel wishes to challenge the admission of the expert's testimony, he or she should do so immediately after the expert has stated his or her qualifications and prior to the witness testifying on the matter in issue. If such a challenge is raised, the issue becomes a preliminary question for the judge alone to determine, and opposing counsel can cross-examine the witness as to his or her qualifications. However, if no objection is raised before the expert testifies on substantive matters, then any cross-examination as to qualifications goes only to the weight, not to the admissibility of her or his testimony.[62] This should be distinguished from the situation where an expert gives evidence outside the field in respect of which he or she is qualified. In that instance, it is immaterial that no challenge was made at the time that the witness was qualified. Failure by counsel to object to the expert's qualifications at an early stage is only a bar to a subsequent objection so long as the witness stays within his purported area of expertise.

3. Hypothetical Question

If the expert lacks personal knowledge of the matters in issue, and is called to give an opinion upon certain disputed facts, evidence of

---

60   (1912), 27 O.L.R. 410, 8 D.L.R. 84 (C.A.).
61   *Ibid.*, at 413 (O.L.R.) (from *State v. Davis* (1899), 33 S.E. Repr. 449, cited in *Words & Phrases Judicially Defined*, Vol. 3, p. 2595). To the same effect see *R. v. Silverlock*, [1894] 2 Q.B. 766 (C.C.R.), at 771; *R. v. Bunniss*, [1965] 3 C.C.C. 236, 44 C.R. 262, 50 W.W.R. 442 (B.C. Co. Ct.), at 239 (C.C.C.).
62   *Preeper v. R.* (1888), 15 S.C.R. 401, at 408.

which has been or will be led at trial, the opinion may be elicited only through the vehicle of a hypothetical question.[63] Where the opinion sought is predicated upon facts which are in conflict, the insistence upon the use of a hypothetical question was explained by Ritchie J. in *Bleta v. R.*[64] as follows:[65]

> . . . it is because the opinion of an expert witness on such a question [whether the accused was in a state of automatism] can serve only to confuse the issue unless the proven facts upon which it is based have been clearly indicated to the jury that the practice has grown up of requiring counsel, when seeking such an opinion, to state those facts in the form of a hypothetical question. In cases where the expert has been present throughout the trial and there is conflict between the witnesses, it is obviously unsatisfactory to ask him to express an opinion based upon the evidence which he has heard because the answer to such a question involves the expert in having to resolve the conflict in accordance with his own view of the credibility of the witnesses and the jury has no way of knowing upon what evidence he based his opinion.

A concrete example may be found in *R. v. Swietlinski*[66] in which the accused put forth as a defence to a first-degree murder charge that he had been in a state of drunkenness. A psychiatrist who had previously interviewed the accused and who had been present in the courtroom during the accused's testimony was asked by defence counsel to state an opinion as to whether or not the accused was able to form the requisite specific intent. Martin J.A. agreed with the trial judge that the question in that form was improper. Although the psychiatrist could state an opinion based upon his own personal

---

63　*R. v. Kelly* (1990), 41 O.A.C. 32 (Ont. C.A.), at 37. The formulation and use of the hypothetical question by counsel is discussed by A. Maloney, "Expert Evidence", *Law Society of Upper Canada Special Lectures* (Toronto: Deboo, 1969), at 96 *et seq.*
64　[1964] S.C.R. 561, [1965] 1 C.C.C. 1, 44 C.R. 193, 48 D.L.R. (2d) 139.
65　*Ibid.*, at 564 (S.C.R.). See also M.N. Howard, P. Crane and D.A. Hochberg, *Phipson on Evidence*, 14th ed. (London: Sweet & Maxwell, 1990), § 32-11, at 808.
66　(1978), 44 C.C.C. (2d) 267, 5 C.R. (3d) 324, 22 O.R. (2d) 604, 94 D.L.R. (3d) 218 (C.A.); appeal dismissed on other grounds [1980] 2 S.C.R. 956, 18 C.R. (3d) 231, 55 C.C.C. (2d) 481, 117 D.L.R. (3d) 285, 34 N.R. 569.

interviews, it was not appropriate for him to state an opinion based upon testimony in the courtroom since it required the psychiatrist to assess the truthfulness of the evidence which was a matter exclusively for the jury. It was suggested that the proper approach would have been for the defence counsel to have elicited the psychiatrist's opinion as to the accused's mental state formed on the basis of a psychiatric examination of the accused and then have asked the witness a hypothetical question, whether, assuming the truth of the facts in evidence referred to in the question, they were consistent with or supported the opinion that he had formed from his examination of the accused.

Without a hypothetical question in which the expert is asked to assume that certain disputed facts given in evidence are true, there is the hazard that the premise upon which the opinion is based will be accepted by the jury as conclusive. The expert, in the absence of a hypothesis, would be placed in the untenable position of having to weigh evidence, assess credibility and choose among witnesses in order to determine the premise upon which the opinion is expressed. This power rests with the court, not the witness, and if the trier of fact ultimately rejects the hypothesis as not being accurate, then, of course, the expert's opinion must be rejected as well.[67]

The hypothetical fact situation put to the expert witness must be clear, uncontradictory and proved at trial.[68] The hypothetical question need not include all the facts relevant to the expert's opinion. As long as the question incorporates sufficient assumed facts to enable the witness to give answers of value, it will be proper.[69]

The hypothetical question need not be employed when the factual basis of the expert's opinion is not in dispute. The Supreme Court of Canada has held that where the expert has heard the uncontradicted evidence in the courtroom prior to taking the stand, he or she may state the opinion directly without the aid of a hypothetical question if the previous evidence clearly indicates the foundation of the opinion.[70] The trial judge, however, retains a discretion to require counsel to use the hypothetical question if he or she feels that

---

67 R. v. Kelly, supra, note 63; R. v. Fisher, [1961] O.W.N. 94, 34 C.R. 320, at 97 (O.W.N.); affd. [1961] S.C.R. 535, 35 C.R. 107, 130 C.C.C. 1; 2 Wigmore, Evidence (Chadbourn rev. 1979), § 672, at 932-34.
68 Lindala v. Canadian Copper Co. (1920), 47 O.L.R. 28, 51 D.L.R. 565 (C.A.); 2 Wigmore, Evidence, ibid., § 682, at 947-56.
69 Wilson v. Bell (1918), 45 N.B.R. 442 (C.A.).
70 Bleta v. R., supra, note 64.

it is essential to the jury's understanding of the matter.[71]

B. *Opinion on the Ultimate Issue*

The closer the testimony gets to the ultimate issue the court has to decide, the more inclined it is to reject it. The justification for this prohibition is said to be that such an opinion would "invade the province" or "usurp the function" of the jury. Wigmore has pointed out the fallacy of this reasoning by emphasizing that the jury has the power to accept or reject evidence as it wishes, and, accordingly, it is not obliged to take the expert's opinion on the point as conclusive.[72]

Aylesworth J.A. said in *R. v. Fisher*[73] that it is not because there is encroachment upon the jury's function that expert evidence has been rejected in certain cases, but rather that in those cases the expert opinion was superfluous:[74]

> In some cases where opinion evidence has been rejected, the ground given is that the giving of the witness's opinion usurped the function of the jury. In other decisions it is said that the evidence tendered constituted an opinion upon the very point or issue which the jury had to decide. An examination of these authorities, however, discloses, in my view, that the jury or the Judge, in cases tried without a jury, would have had no difficulty in arriving at a proper conclusion in the absence of the tendered opinion and that this was the true ground for its rejection.

Nevertheless, courts have, from time to time, been guided by the "ultimate issue" doctrine. For example, in *British Drug Houses Ltd. v. Battle Pharmaceuticals*,[75] which was an application to expunge a trademark registration because of its alleged similarity to a previously registered mark, Thorson J. held that a witness could not state his opinion of the impression that the impugned trademark may have on others:[76]

---

71   *Ibid.*, at 567 (S.C.R.).
72   J. Wigmore, *A Students' Textbook of the Law of Evidence* (Brooklyn: Foundation.Press Inc., 1935), at § 1917.
73   *Supra*, note 67, at 95 (O.W.N.).
74   *Ibid.*
75   [1944] 4 D.L.R. 577, 4 Fox Pat. C. 93, [1943] Ex. C.R. 239; affd. [1946] S.C.R. 50, 5 Fox Pat. C. 135, 5 C.P.R. 71, [1946] 1 D.L.R. 289.
76   *Ibid.*, at 580 (D.L.R.).

Kerly on Trade Marks, 6th ed., p. 290, makes the statement that the evidence of persons who are well acquainted with the trade concerned was formerly constantly tendered by the parties to show that in the opinion of such persons, as experts, the alleged resemblance between the contrasted marks was, or was not, calculated to deceive, and it was constantly admitted, but that, since the decision of the House of Lords in *North Cheshire & Manchester Brewery Co. v. Manchester Brewery Co.*, [1899] A.C. 83, such evidence has frequently been disallowed. In that case, Lord Halsbury L.C. said, at p. 85:

> "Upon the one question which your Lordships have to decide, whether the one name is so nearly resembling another as to be calculated to deceive, I am of the opinion that no witness would be entitled to say that, and for this reason: that that is the very question which your Lordships have to decide."

The majority of the Supreme Court of Canada in *R. v. Lupien*[77] dismissed the proposition, and held that a psychiatrist could testify on the very fact in issue which the court had to decide. Having gone that far, it is not surprising to see courts permitting experts to express their opinions in the context of the very words which comprise the legal definition which the court must apply. In fact, this appears to be occurring in practice if not yet in theory. Lord Parker G.J. in *Director of Public Prosecutions v. A. & B.C. Chewing Gum Ltd.*[78] recognized this:[79]

> Those who practise in the criminal courts see every day cases of experts being called on the question of diminished responsibility, and although technically the final question "Do you think he was suffering from diminished responsibility?" is strictly inadmissible, it is allowed time and time again without any objection.

Similarly, in *Cooper v. R.*[80] a psychiatrist testified in relation to an

---

77   [1970] S.C.R. 263, [1970] 2 C.C.C. 193, 9 C.R.N.S. 165, 9 D.L.R. (3d) 1, 71 W.W.R. 110 and 655.

78   [1968] 1 Q.B. 159, [1967] 2 All E.R. 504 (D.C.).

79   *Ibid.*, at 164 (Q.B.); but for a recent case where an English court held that expert evidence as to the histrionic and theatrical nature of the accused was not admissible since it usurped the function of the jury in determining whether or not her confession was true: see *R. v. Weightman* (1990) Times, 8 November (C.A.).

80   [1980] 1 S.C.R. 1149, 13 C.R. (3d) 97, 51 C.C.C. (2d) 129, 4 L. Med. Q. 227, 110 D.L.R. (3d) 46, 31 N.R. 234.

insanity defence that the accused was suffering from a disease of the mind at the relevant period. Dickson J. held:[81]

> As a matter of practice, the trial judge can permit the psychiatrist to be asked directly whether or not the condition in question constitutes a disease of the mind.

Historically, the rule has been ignored by many Canadian and English courts. This is apparent from the authorities canvassed by Aylesworth J.A. in *R. v. Fisher*.[82]

> In many instances opinion evidence is received upon the very issue the Court has to decide, as for example, where the issue is the materiality of a representation in an application for insurance: *Yorke v. Yorks. Ins. Co.*, [1918] 1 K.B. 662, *Sun Ins. Off. v. Roy*, [1927] S.C.R. 8, at p. 13, or where the issue in a marine case is proper seamanship: *Fenwick v. Bell* (1844), 1 C. & K. 311, or in malpractice actions against professional men: *Davy v. Morrison*, [1932] O.R. 1, at p. 9. In *R. v. Mason* (1911), 7 Cr. App. R. 67, the defence to a charge of murder was that the deceased had committed suicide and a doctor who had heard the evidence was asked whether it was his opinion that the fatal wound was inflicted by someone other than the deceased. The Court of Criminal Appeal held that his answer was admissible as an opinion based on an assumed state of facts. In *R. v. Holmes*, [1953] 2 All E.R. 324, the same Court decided that a doctor called in support of the accused's plea of insanity might be asked in cross-examination whether the prisoner's conduct after the crime, indicated that he knew the nature of his act and that it was wrong, although these are, of course, the very points which determine the applicability of the rules in *McNaghten's* case. The decision in the *Holmes* case was approved in the B.C. Court of Appeal in *R. v. Matthews* (1953), 9 W.W.R.N.S. 650. There are numerous other examples of the admission of opinion evidence upon the very point in issue, among which reference may be had to *R. v. Searle* (1831), 1 Mood. & R. 75, *R. v. Francis* (1849), 4 Cox C.C. 57, *R. v. Smith* (1915), 31 T.L.R. 617, *R. v. Rivett* (1950), 34 Cr. App. R. 87.

---

81 *Ibid.*, at 1158 (S.C.R.).
82 *Supra*, note 67, at 95-96 (O.W.N.).

Rule 704 of the United States Federal Rules of Evidence expressly rejects the ultimate issue doctrine. It states:[83]

Testimony in the form of an opinion or inference otherwise admissible is not objectionable because it embraces an ultimate issue to be decided by the trier of fact.

There are, however, numerous examples which appear to apply the ultimate issue doctrine. In *Gorgichuk v. American Home Assurance Co.*,[84] the court was concerned about the interpretation of a coverage provision in an insurance policy. The plaintiff proposed to call the Chairman of the English Department of a Canadian university to give expert opinion as to various matters of English grammar and syntax and specifically as to the applicability of modifiers and various nouns in one of the coverage provisions of the policy. Sutherland J. of the Ontario High Court of Justice held that the interpretation of contractual documents was a core judicial function. He acknowledged that although extrinsic evidence may be admitted to aid in the interpretation of documents which may be ambiguous on their face and to provide background even in the absence of any manifest ambiguity, it would be stretching the doctrine too far to permit the use of expert testimony concerning rules of English grammar and syntax applicable to a contractual document.

In *C. v. M.*,[85] the evidence of a registered nurse who also was a director of a sexual assault centre was ruled inadmissible since her opinion as to the potential social value of making an award of exemplary damages against the defendant was within the competence of the trial judge for which no assistance from an expert was needed.

The assessment of the credibility of witnesses is considered a prime judicial function as well. Unless there is some hidden fact which affects a witness' credibility and which only an expert can reveal, then the jury is not in need of expert assistance in weighing evidence. In *R. v. French*,[86] a psychiatrist was called to give evidence that the principal Crown witness had a character disorder and that she was quite capable

---

83   28 U.S.C.A. app. (1976). Note that Rule 702 imports a helpfulness standard.
84   (1985), 5 C.P.C. (2d) 166, 14 C.C.L.I. 32, [1985] I.L.R. 1-1984 (Ont. H.C.J.); varied [1988] I.L.R. 1-2283, 30 C.C.L.I. 51, 27 O.A.C. 157 (C.R.).
85   (1991), 74 D.L.R. (4th) 129 (Ont. Ct. (Gen. Div.)).
86   (1977), 37 C.C.C. (2d) 201 (Ont. C.A.); affd. [1980] 1 S.C.R. 158, 47 C.C.C. (2d) 411, 98 D.L.R. (3d) 385, 28 N.R. 100.

of lying under oath. He agreed that a layman could come to the same conclusion as he had from observing the witness although it might take a little more effort on the layman's part. In concluding that the evidence should be excluded, MacKinnon J.A. was concerned about the influence that experts may have over juries:[87]

> One can envisage psychiatrists being called on both sides to evaluate the reliability and the evidence of each such witness. The jury, under such circumstances, could be overwhelmed and diverted from its task of assessing the credibility of the witnesses on the basis of its own observations. This is so where the expert acknowledges that the assessment he has made of the witness could be made by a layman, and the ease or rapidity of such assessment was only "a matter of degree", as between himself and a juryman.

> To receive such evidence might, indeed, open a pandora's box, from which there could be no resiling, of confusion and usurpation of function. It does trouble me that the case against the appellant should rest on the evidence of one such as Nadine Deveau, but the members of the jury, properly instructed, are the ones to make the assessment of such a witness when her contradictions are obvious. The Courts must be chary of limiting or usurping the jury's duty and function in this area. It is not "empty rhetoric" to speak of the "usurpation" of the function of the jury in these circumstances. If the evidence were admitted and the jury instructed to weigh it, it would not be surprising if the members of the jury were so impressed by the credentials and knowledge of the expert witness that their own possibly contrary view of the witness' evidence would be overborne by that of the expert. The assessing of a witness' credibility is a matter peculiarly within the province of a jury and it is only in unusual circumstances, which do not obtain here, that the credibility can be attacked by the calling of expert medical evidence.

---

87   *Ibid.*, at 211 (Ont. C.A.). In *R. v. Manahan* (1991), 61 C.C.C. (3d) 139 (Alta. C.A.), a clinical psychologist who was an expert in child sexual abuse was permitted to testify that in her opinion the complainant had not been coached nor made up the incidents of sexual abuse based on the fact that the descriptions of the incidents given by the complainant at different times prior to trial were consistent.

Questions of domestic law as opposed to foreign law are not matters upon which a court will receive opinion evidence. In *R. v. Century 21 Ramos Realty Inc.*,[88] the sole principal of a real estate company was charged with income tax evasion as a result of appropriation of property belonging to the company. An issue at trial was the taxation year when the appropriation took place. The Crown called an employee of Revenue Canada to give expert evidence as to when the accused had appropriated the property. The Ontario Court of Appeal held that such evidence was inadmissible, stating:[89]

> It was a question of law for the judge as to what constitutes an appropriation. It was for the judge to determine, in compliance with the legal definition, if and when an appropriation took place. This was not something on which an expert witness could give evidence.

These cases illustrate that there are certain subject matters which go to the very heart of judicial decision-making and courts remain wary of expert witnesses providing them with advice as to how they should decide issues such as whether a witness is telling the truth or the meaning of English words. Perhaps it is just a matter of sensitivity over the way in which the expert gives his evidence. For example, a court would be loathe to receive explicit evidence from an expert that an accused is guilty or innocent or that a defendant was negligent or not, or that an individual was insane or not. However, it will readily receive evidence which is not so direct but which, if accepted, inescapably leads to that conclusion. For example, it would appear that an expert can testify that the perpetrator of a crime had certain mental or physical characteristics and that the accused matched that description; or that with respect to a particular activity a certain standard of conduct was required and that anything below it amounted to incompetence and that in his opinion the defendant's conduct was substandard; or that the individual's behaving in a certain way exhibited

---

88   (1987), 32 C.C.C. (3d) 353, 56 C.R. (3d) 150, 58 O.R. (2d) 737, 19 O.A.C. 25, 87 D.T.C. 5158, 37 D.L.R. (4th) 649, 29 C.R.R. 320, [1987] 1 C.T.C. 340 (C.A.); leave to appeal to S.C.C. refd. 56 C.R. (3d) xxviii (note).

89   *Ibid.*, at 752 (O.R.). In *Teskey v. Canadian Newspapers Co.* (1989), 68 O.R. (2d) 737, 59 D.L.R. (4th) 709, 33 O.A.C. 383, the Ontario Court of Appeal held that an expert's views on the Rules of Professional Conduct would be admissible since they are not rules of law but rather reflect what members of the profession have decided is proper or improper.

abnormal traits which could lead one to the conclusion that the individual was not mentally balanced.

In the final analysis, the closer the experts' testimony both in opinion and in words comes to the very issue that the court has to decide, the more jittery it becomes in receiving such evidence. This is so because the evidence then begins to overlap not only the fact-finding function of the court but the legal analysis that must be applied to the facts in rendering the ultimate decision.

It is now generally said that if expert testimony is rejected it is excluded not because of any "ultimate issue" doctrine, but because such evidence is superfluous in that the court can just as readily draw the necessary inference without any assistance from an expert.[90] However, even when the evidence may be helpful, courts are still nervous about the extent of the expert's influence over juries, in particular when the expert gives an opinion on the very fundamental issues that they themselves must decide. Much valuable assistance may be lost as a result.[91]

C. Hearsay Issues and Opinion Evidence

1. As a Component of the Expert's Knowledge

Although it has been asserted that the expert's opinion must be based upon either personal knowledge or facts presented at trial, it cannot be completely devoid of a hearsay element. Since the expert by definition possesses a special skill or knowledge in a material area superior to that of the court, the expertise is founded to a large extent

---

90   See Howland C.J.O. in *R. v. Graat* (1980), 55 C.C.C. (2d) 429, 17 C.R. (3d) 55, 30 O.R. (2d) 247, 7 M.V.R. 163, 116 D.L.R. (3d) 143 (C.A.), at 443 (C.C.C.); affd. [1982] 2 S.C.R. 819, 2 C.C.C. (3d) 365, 31 C.R. (3d) 289, 18 M.V.R. 287, 144 D.L.R. (3d) 267, 45 N.R. 451 (*sub nom. R. v. Gratt*); *R. v. Williams* (1985), 50 O.R. (2d) 321, 18 C.C.C. (3d) 356, 44 C.R. (3d) 351, 7 O.A.C. 201, 14 C.R.R. 251; leave to appeal to S.C.C. refd. (1985), 18 C.C.C. (3d) 356n. *R. v. Kelly* (1990), 41 O.A.C. 32, at 37-38 (Ont. C.A.).

91   Lest there be any doubt, s. 40 of the draft Uniform Evidence Act in *Report of the Federal/Provincial Task Force on Uniform Rules of Evidence* (Toronto: Carswell, 1982), at 554, makes it clear that opinion evidence on an ultimate issue should be admissible: "A witness may give opinion evidence that embraces an ultimate issue to be decided by the trier of fact where (a) the factual basis for the evidence has been established; (b) more detailed evidence cannot be given by the witness; and (c) the evidence would be helpful to the trier of fact."

upon hearsay data. An expert's opinion will be based on experience and education received. The latter is naturally comprised of the study and readings of works of authorities in the field and information and data culled from numerous sources.[92]

> An expert in forming an opinion may, of course, draw on works of a general nature which form part of the corpus of knowledge with which an expert in a particular field would be expected to be acquainted . . .

An expert's knowledge is made up of the distilled assertions of others not before the court. Recognition of this hearsay basis of expertise has been acknowledged by Canadian courts for some time.[93] One example is a New Brunswick decision in which it was said:[94]

> A doctor, chemist, professional man or any other person who qualifies as an expert is not confined to opinions based solely on his personal experience of observation, but may draw on information obtained from lectures during his education in his particular field, textbooks, as well as from discussions with other persons learned in the same field. The weight to be given to any opinion is always a matter for the consideration of the trial Judge.

Thus, there is an acceptable hearsay component in the make-up of every expert's knowledge which is drawn upon in formulating the opinion.

2. As a Component of the Expert's Opinion

The more perplexing problem is whether, in addition to the facts before the court, the expert may consider hearsay circumstances and facts not proved in evidence as part of the premise for the opinion. In making their professional decisions experts often rely on such information: for example, psychiatrists rely on medical histories, and

---

92   Per Martin J.A. in *R. v. Valley* (1986), 26 C.C.C. (3d) 207, 13 O.A.C. 89 (C.R.), at 240 (C.C.C.); leave to appeal to S.C.C. refd. (1986), 26 C.C.C. (3d) 207n. See also *Reference re Sections 222, 224 and 224A of the Criminal Code* (1971), 3 C.C.C. (2d) 243, at 569-70 (D.L.R.), 18 D.L.R. (3d) 559 (N.B.C.A.).
93   See *Brownell v. Black* (1890), 31 N.B.R. 594 (C.A.); *C.P.R. v. Jackson* (1915), 52 S.C.R. 281; *R. v. Anderson* (1914), 22 C.C.C. 455, 7 Alta. L.R. 102, 16 D.L.R. 203, 5 W.W.R. 1052, 26 W.L.R. 783 (C.A.).
94   *Reference re Sections 222, 224 and 224A of the Criminal Code, supra*, note 92, at 254 (C.C.C.).

property evaluators rely on records kept in the registry office. In other words, will the court in certain situations relax the rule that the expert must base the opinion either upon personal knowledge of the facts or upon the facts as proved in court, and allow facts learned from hearsay sources to be taken into account?

In 1982, the English Court of Appeal in the case of *R. v. Abadom,*[95] ruled that when an expert is required to contemplate the likelihood of some incident of factual association in arriving at his or her conclusion, it is not only permissible to refer to the statistical results of the work of others but it is essential to do so. The Court held that "... to exclude reliance upon such information on the ground that it is inadmissible under the hearsay rule, might inevitably lead to the distortion or unreliability of the opinion which the expert presents for evaluation by a judge or jury."[96] The Court was further of the view that experts need not limit themselves to published material because "[p]art of their experience and expertise may well lie in their knowledge of unpublished material and in their evaluation of it."[97]

If an expert is entitled to rely on hearsay, may he or she also relate those unproved facts to the court? And what weight should be given to an expert opinion based on unproven facts? A number of Canadian cases have considered these questions in the context of psychiatric evidence.

Wilband v. R.[98] was a case in which the accused was found by the trial judge to be a dangerous sexual offender and was sentenced to preventive detention under s. 661 of the *Criminal Code.*[99] Expert psychiatric evidence was called by the Crown and the opinion of the two psychiatrists rested, in part, on material found in prison files dealing with the accused's background and also on the accused's own admission to the psychiatrists. This evidence was allowed, notwithstanding the absence of formal proof. The rationale for its admissibility was given by Fauteux J. as follows:[100]

Dealing with hearsay: — The evidence, in this case, indicates

---

95   [1983] 1 W.L.R. 126 (C.A.); leave to appeal dismissed, [1983] 1 W.L.R. 405 (H.L.).
96   *Ibid.*, at 129.
97   *Ibid.*, at 131.
98   [1967] S.C.R. 14, 2 C.R.N.S. 29, [1967] 2 C.C.C. 6, 60 W.W.R. 292.
99   Now see s. 753 of the *Criminal Code*, R.S.C. 1985, c. C-46.
100   *Supra*, note 98, at 21 (S.C.R.).

that to form an opinion according to recognized normal psychiatric procedures, the psychiatrist must consider all possible
sources of information, including second-hand source information, the reliability, accuracy and significance of which are within
the recognized scope of his professional activities, skill and
training to evaluate. Hence, while ultimately his conclusion may
rest, in part, on second-hand source material, it is nonetheless
an opinion formed according to recognized normal psychiatric
procedures. It is not to be assumed that Parliament contemplated
that the opinion, which the psychiatrists would form and give to
assist the Court, would be formed by methods other than those
recognized in normal psychiatric procedures. The value of a
psychiatrist's opinion may be affected to the extent to which it
may rest on second-hand source material; but that goes to the
weight and not to the receivability in evidence of the opinion,
which opinion is no evidence of the truth of the information but
evidence of the opinion formed on the basis of that information.

In *R. v. Lupien*,[101] the accused, charged with gross indecency,
testified that he thought the male with whom he was found was a
female, and he attempted, by way of defence, to put forth psychiatric
evidence to the effect that he was not the type to engage knowingly in
homosexual practices. The British Columbia Court of Appeal held
that this psychiatric evidence, which was based upon interviews with
and tests on the accused, was admissible. Although the Supreme Court
of Canada allowed the appeal, a majority of the judges (Hall, Ritchie
and Spence JJ.) thought that this evidence was properly admitted. Hall
J. indicated that the evidence was relevant to the defence being
asserted by the accused and was therefore admissible. He took the view
that "[p]sychiatrists are permitted to testify that from their examination and study, sometimes long after the event, of an accused, including conversations with him and from facts proven in evidence, that the
accused was incapable of forming the intent necessary to constitute
the crime with which he is charged."[102] Ritchie J. (with whom Spence
J. concurred in a dissenting opinion) agreed with Hall J. in holding
that this hearsay evidence was admissible. He added that:[103]

---

101 [1970] S.C.R. 263, 9 C.R.N.S. 165, [1970] 2 C.C.C. 193, 71 W.W.R. 110,
9 D.L.R. (3d) 1.
102 *Ibid.*, at 280 (S.C.R.).
103 *Ibid.*, at 273 (S.C.R.). See also *R. v. Swietlinski* (1978), 44 C.C.C. (2d) 267 at

. . . the fact that the methods pursued by the psychiatrist in reaching his opinion necessitated dependence on information obtained from the respondent and others which was not before the jury, does not make his opinion inadmissible although it may well be a factor to be considered in assessing the weight to be attached to that opinion. If it were otherwise, the Courts would be denied many medical opinions based on clinical methods of diagnosis.

Emerging from those Supreme Court of Canada decisions was the principle that hearsay information upon which the expert relied need not be proven in evidence.[104] But on what basis was this unproven evidence admissible? Professor R. Delisle asked:[105]

Are these three Supreme Court of Canada decisions examples of a growing relaxation of that court's attitude toward the rigours of the hearsay rule? Are they, like the decision in *Ares v. Venner*,[106] a recognition of a Wigmorean approach to the hearsay rule which dictates the reception of out-of-court statements where there are grounds of necessity and circumstantial guarantees of trustworthiness rather than exclusion when such statements cannot be made to fit within pre-recognized pigeonhole exceptions? These grounds of necessity and circumstantial guarantees of trustworthiness appear to justify the reception of the opinions from the particular experts who testified in *Wilband*, *Lupien* and *Irving Oil*. Ought we to approve the reception of opinion evidence from psychiatrists and land valuers without demanding independent proof of the truth of statements relied on by them in arriving at their opinions, *or* ought we to go further

---

302, 5 C.R. (3d) 324, 22 O.R. (2d) 604, 94 D.L.R. (3d) 218 (C.A.), at 302 (C.C.C.); appeal dismissed on other grounds, [1980] 2 S.C.R. 956, 18 C.R. (2d) 231, 55 C.C.C. (2d) 481, 117 D.L.R. (3d) 285; *Lauder v. Lauder* (1970), 12 D.L.R. (3d) 543, 2 R.F.L. 150 (Man. C.A.), at 544 (D.L.R.); *Lenoard v. B.C. Hydro & Power Authority* (1964), 49 D.L.R. (2d) 422, 50 W.W.R. 546, at 424 (D.L.R.).

104 To the same effect in the context of the opinion evidence given by an expert land appraiser see the Supreme Court of Canada decision in *Saint John (City) v. Irving Oil Co.*, [1966] S.C.R. 581, 58 D.L.R. (2d) 404, 52 M.P.R. 126. See also Chapter 6, II.

105 R.J. Delisle, *Evidence: Principles and Problems*, 2nd ed. (Toronto: Carswell, 1989), at 475-76.

106 [1970] S.C.R. 608, 12 C.R.N.S. 349, 73 W.W.R. 347, 14 D.L.R. (3d) 4.

and approve such a practice with respect to *any* expert provided the trial judge is satisfied that there are grounds of necessity and circumstantial guarantees of trustworthiness?

However, the Supreme Court of Canada in *R. v. Abbey*[107] seemed to backtrack on what it had said in these earlier decisions by holding that *all* of the foundational evidence must be proved or else the opinion is valueless. In that case, the accused did not testify at his drug trafficking trial and the only evidence called by the accused was that of a psychiatrist in support of the defence of insanity. The psychiatrist testified that during the course of his interviews the accused had told him of various delusions, visions, hallucinations and sensations which he had experienced in the six months preceding his arrest. The psychiatrist also testified that the accused had described certain symptoms of the disease to his mother several months prior to the commission of the offence. The accused had also told him about several incidents of bizarre and unstable conduct which the psychiatrist recounted in his testimony. The evidentiary value of the events and experiences which were related to the psychiatrist by the accused during several interviews became an issue. In the Supreme Court of Canada, Dickson J. commented on the hearsay element of the psychiatrist's opinion as follows:[108]

An expert witness, like any other witness, may testify as to the veracity of facts of which he has first-hand experience, but this is not the main purpose of his or her testimony. An expert is there to give an opinion. And the opinion more often than not will be based on second-hand evidence. This is especially true of the opinions of psychiatrists.

. . .

The danger, of course, in admitting such testimony is the ever present possibility, here exemplified, that the judge or jury, without more, will accept the evidence as going to the truth of the facts stated in it. The danger is real and lies at the heart of

---

107 [1982] 2 S.C.R. 24, 68 C.C.C. (2d) 394, 29 C.R. (3d) 193, [1983] 1 W.W.R. 251, 39 B.C.L.R. 201, 138 D.L.R. (3d) 202, 43 N.R. 30.
108 *Ibid.*, at 42, 44-45 and 46 (S.C.R.).

this case. Once such testimony is admitted, a careful charge to the jury by the judge or direction to himself is essential . . .

This testimony, while admissible in the context of the opinion, was not in any way evidence of the factual basis of these events and experiences. The trial judge in his decision fell into the error of accepting as evidence of these facts, testimony which if taken to be evidence of their existence would violate the hearsay rule. There was no admissible evidence properly before the Court with respect to [the events and experiences as told to the psychiatrist]

In my view, the trial judge erred in law in treating as factual the hearsay evidence upon which the opinions of the psychiatrist were based.

Counsel for [the accused] said that the passages in which the trial judge seemed to take symptoms as findings of fact were merely "unfortunate language". But it goes further than that . . . It was appropriate for the doctors to state the basis for their opinions and in the course of doing so, to refer to what they were told not only by [the accused] but by others, but it was error for the judge to accept as having been proved the facts upon which the doctors had relied in forming their opinions. While it is not questioned that medical experts are entitled to take into consideration all possible information in forming their opinions, this in no way removes from the party tendering such evidence the obligation of establishing, through properly admissible evidence, the factual basis on which such opinions are based. Before any weight can be given to an expert's opinion, the facts upon which the opinion is based must be found to exist.

The *Abbey* case has been said to stand for the following propositions:[109]

1. An expert opinion is admissible if relevant, even if it is based on second-hand evidence.

2. This second-hand evidence (hearsay) is admissible to show

---

109 Per Wilson J. in *R. v. Lavallée*, [1990] 1 S.C.R. 852, 76 C.R. (3d) 379, 55 C.C.C. (3d) 97, [1990] 4 W.W.R. 1, 108 N.R. 321, at 127-28 (C.C.C.).

the information on which the expert opinion is based, not as evidence going to the existence of the facts on which the opinion is based.

3. Where the psychiatric evidence is comprised of hearsay evidence, the problem is the weight to be attributed to the opinion.

4. Before any weight can be given to an expert's opinion, the facts upon which the opinion is based must be found to exist.

It is this last point which created some controversy. *Abbey* did not make any distinction among the kinds of information that an expert may rely on. Some information may be more trustworthy than others. *Abbey* appeared to say that all such information had to be proven, regardless of its inherent reliability; otherwise, the evidence would be valueless.

The issue was considered in the case of *R. v. Lavallée*.[110] There a psychiatrist testified as to the battered wife-syndrome in support of the accused's defence of self-defence. The expert's evidence was based in part on a conversation between the accused and the accused's mother. However, neither the accused nor her mother testified. The opinion was also based on evidence adduced at trial including a statement given by the accused to the police. The *Abbey* decision had held that there must be admissible evidence to support the facts on which the expert relies before *any* weight can be attributed to the opinion. The majority of the Manitoba Court of Appeal interpreted that requirement as meaning that each and every fact relied upon by the expert must be independently proven and admitted into evidence before the entire opinion can be given any weight. Various facts were referred to in the testimony of the expert for which there was no admissible evidence. The Manitoba Court of Appeal thought that each of those specific facts must be proven in evidence before any weight could be given to the psychiatrist's opinion about the accused's mental state. Wilson J. in the Supreme Court of Canada disagreed and provided the following interpretation of *Abbey*:[111]

---

110 *Ibid.*
111 *Ibid.*, at 130-31 (C.C.C.).

Abbey does not, in my view, provide any authority for that proposition. The court's conclusion in that case was that the trial judge erred in treating as proven the facts upon which the psychiatrist relied in formulating his opinion. The solution was an appropriate charge to the jury, not an effective withdrawal of the evidence. In my view, as long as there is some admissible evidence to establish the foundation for the expert's opinion, the trial judge cannot subsequently instruct the jury to completely ignore the testimony. The judge must, of course, warn the jury that the more the expert relies on facts not proved in evidence the less weight the jury may attribute to the opinion.

. . .

Where the factual basis of an expert's opinion is a mélange of admissible and inadmissible evidence the duty of the trial judge is to caution the jury that the weight attributable to the expert testimony is directly related to the amount and quality of admissible evidence on which it relies.

Alluding to the criticism by academics of the *Abbey* decision on the ground that it appears to set out more restrictive conditions for the use of expert evidence than had been stated in previous decisions of the Supreme Court of Canada, Sopinka J., concurring in the result with Wilson J., pointed out the conundrum arising from *Abbey*:[112]

Upon reflection, it seems to me that the very special facts in *Abbey*, and the decision required on those facts, have contributed to the development of a principle concerning the admissibility and weight of expert opinion evidence that is self-contradictory.

The inherent contradiction in the *Abbey* decision is that it seems to hold that an expert opinion relevant to a material issue in a trial is admissible even though it is based entirely on unproven hearsay (such as statements by an accused who has not testified, as in *Abbey*); but, although admissible, it is entitled to no weight whatsoever. As Sopinka J., asked: "[t]he question that arises is how any evidence can be admissible and yet entitled to no weight."[113] The answer, he said, turns upon whether the hearsay information regularly forms the mass of

---

112 *Ibid.*, at 131 (C.C.C.).
113 *Ibid.*, at 132 (C.C.C.).

material upon which an expert relies in the course of his or her expertise or whether it is hearsay going directly to a matter in issue and comes from a source that is inherently suspect:[114]

> The resolution of the contradiction inherent in *Abbey*, and the answer to the criticism *Abbey* has drawn, is to be found in the practical distinction between evidence that an expert obtains and acts upon within the scope of his or her expertise (as in *City of Saint John*,) and evidence that an expert obtains from a party to litigation touching a matter directly in issue (as in *Abbey*.)

> In the former instance, an expert arrives at an opinion on the basis of forms of enquiry and practice that are accepted means of decision within that expertise. A physician, for example, daily determines questions of immense importance on the basis of the observations of colleagues, often in the form of second or third-hand hearsay. For a court to accord no weight to, or to exclude, this sort of professional judgment, arrived at in accordance with sound medical practices, would be to ignore the strong circumstantial guarantees of trustworthiness that surround it, and would be, in my view, contrary to the approach this court has taken to the analysis of hearsay evidence in general, exemplified in *Ares v. Venner* (1970), 14 D.L.R. (3d) 4, [1970] S.C.R. 608, 12 C.R.N.S. 349. In *R. v. Jordan* (1984), 11 C.C.C. (3d) 565, 39 C.R. (3d) 50 (B.C.C.A.), a case concerning an expert's evaluation of the chemical composition of an alleged heroin specimen, Anderson J.A. held, and I respectfully agree, that *Abbey* does not apply in such circumstances: see also *R. v. Zundel* (1987), 31 C.C.C. (3d) 97 at p. 146, 35 D.L.R. (4th) 338, 56 C.R. (3d) 1 (Ont. C.A.), where the court recognized an expert opinion based upon evidence ". . . of a general nature which is widely used and acknowledged as reliable by experts in that field".

> Where, however, the information upon which an expert forms his or her opinion comes from the mouth of a party to the litigation, or from any other source that is inherently suspect, a court ought to require independent proof of that information. The lack of such proof will, consistent with *Abbey*, have a direct effect on the weight to be given to the opinion, perhaps to the

---

114   *Ibid.*, at 132-33 (C.C.C.).

vanishing point. But it must be recognized that it will only be very rarely that an expert's opinion is entirely based upon such information, with no independent proof of any of it. Where an expert's opinion is based in part upon suspect information and in part upon either admitted facts or facts sought to be proved, the matter is purely one of weight.

When the information comes from an interested party there is great resistance to allowing it to be used for any purpose unless proved in the normal way. With this kind of hearsay in respect of which there is a strong motive to misrepresent, the Supreme Court was not prepared to leave it to the expert to determine its trustworthiness. This type of information often includes facts bearing directly on the innocence or guilt of the accused and experts cannot rely on this type of information at all. It is not a matter of the expert just giving it less weight. If the whole opinion is based on this kind of information it is inadmissible. It may not appear until after the opinion has gone in that the back-up was not proved, in which event the opinion would simply be given no weight. We do not have the concept of striking something from the record that is used in the United States.

When an expert relies on some evidence that is admissible and some that is not, what is the proper instruction to the jury? This issue was considered in *R. v. Lavallée*. The Supreme Court of Canada decided that the admissible evidence must be identified for the jury and that while the opinion is not inadmissible the reliance on information not proven goes to weight. Why does it go to weight? The reason is that without the unsubstantiated material the expert might have qualified his or her opinion or not have given it at all. This brings up a point not dealt with in *Lavallée*. Should the jury not be told to consider first whether in the absence of the unproven matter the expert would have given the opinion at all?

3. Surveys and Polls

Certain hearsay information upon which an expert relies has the hallmarks of necessity and trustworthiness. Surveys and similar statistical data come within this category. The Supreme Court of Canada in *Saint John (City) v. Irving Oil Co.*,[115] considered the admissibility of

---

115 [1966] S.C.R. 581, 58 D.L.R. (2d) 404, 52 M.P.R. 126.

the opinion of an expert land appraiser testifying as to the value of expropriated property. It was argued that his opinion was inadmissible on the ground that it was hearsay based upon calculation made from unrecorded interviews by the expert with forty-seven persons who were involved in land sales in the area, and who were not called as witnesses at trial. Ritchie J., speaking for the Court, feared that if such evidence was excluded because of its hearsay foundation, "then the proceedings to establish the value of land would take on an endless character as each of the appraiser's informants whose views had contributed to the ultimate formation of this opinion would have to be individually called."[116] He then went on to examine the relationship of the interview data to the expert's final opinion and concluded as follows:[117]

> To characterize the opinion evidence of a qualified appraiser as inadmissible because it is based on something that he has been told is, in my opinion, to treat the matter as if the direct facts of each of the comparable transactions which he has investigated were at issue whereas what is in truth at issue is the value of his opinion.
>
> The nature of the source upon which such an opinion is based cannot, in my view, have any effect on the admissibility of the opinion itself. Any frailties which may be alleged concerning the information upon which the opinion was founded are in my view only relevant in assessing the weight to be attached to that opinion . . .

Surveys and public opinion polls conducted by experts have lately been received by Canadian courts even though such evidence consists of data compiled outside the court room. Appellate Courts in Manitoba[118] and Ontario[119] and a District Court in Alberta[120] have

---

116 *Ibid.*, at 592 (S.C.R.).
117 *Ibid.*
118 *R. v. Prairie Schooner News Ltd.* (1970), 1 C.C.C. (2d) 251, 75 W.W.R. 585, 12 Cr. L.Q. 462 (Man. C.A.).
119 *R. v. Times Square Cinema Ltd.* (1971), 4 C.C.C. (2d) 229, [1971] 3 O.R. 688 (C.A.).
120 *R. v. Pipeline News* (1971), 5 C.C.C. (2d) 71, [1972] 1 W.W.R. 241 (Alta. Dist. Ct.).

indicated a willingness to accept expert evidence of surveys relating to community standards in obscenity prosecutions as long as it can be demonstrated that approved statistical methods and social research techniques have been employed. With respect to this kind of evidence, the courts have been more concerned about the procedures and techniques utilized by the experts than they have been about the hearsay aspect of such evidence.[121]

In civil cases in Canada, public opinion poll evidence has been tendered in actions involving trade marks to establish the public's familiarity with them and their association with particular products. In *Aluminum Goods Ltd. v. Canada (Registrar of Trade Marks)*,[122] a petition was issued for a declaration that the mark "Wear-Ever" was generally recognized by dealers and consumers as relating distinctively to the petitioner's cooking utensils and thus was entitled to registration. A survey of over 3,000 lay persons and 500 dealers of such wares in numerous and varied Canadian communities was conducted by a firm employed by the petitioner. Cameron J. admitted this evidence, stating that it was "the most important part of the evidence."[123] In *Building Products Ltd. v. B.P. Canada Ltd.*,[124] however, public opinion poll evidence tendered by both parties on the question of whether the mark in issue would cause confusion in the minds of the consumers, was rejected as being purely hearsay and because the surveys that were conducted could not have created actual "market conditions" in the minds of those interviewed. In light of the decisions in the obscenity cases, the former objection to the evidence on the ground of hearsay would appear to be no longer valid. The second objection to the evidence would now appear to affect only the weight of such evidence. Public opinion polls have also been used as evidence in grievance arbitration proceedings.[125]

---

121 But see *Building Products Ltd. v. B.P. Canada Ltd.* (1961), 36 C.P.R. 121, 21 Fox Pat. C. 130 (Ex. Ct.).

122 [1954] Ex. C.R. 79, 14 Fox Pat. C. 41, 19 C.P.R. 93.

123 *Ibid.*, at 82 (Ex. C.R.).

124 *Supra*, note 122.

125 *Re Canada Safeway Ltd. and Manitoba Food & Commercial Workers Union, Local 82*, [1981] 2 S.C.R. 180, where the employer justified its "no-beard" policy with a survey showing that a demonstrable portion of the public was opposed to food store employees wearing beards. See also *Re Canada Safeway Ltd. and Retail Clerks Union, Local 206* (1982), 7 L.A.C. (3d) 140 (per H.D. Brown); *Re Dominion Stores and United Steelworkers of America* (1976), 11 L.A.C. (2d) 401 (per O.B.

In *R. v. Collins*[126] the Supreme Court of Canada addressed the issue of the admissibility of public opinion poll evidence to demonstrate community standards on the question of what would bring the administration of justice into disrepute within the meaning of s. 24(2) of the *Charter*. In deciding that the evidence should not be used, Mr. Justice Lamer on behalf of the majority wrote:[127]

> The concept of disrepute necessarily involves some element of community views, and the determination of disrepute thus requires the judge to refer to what he conceives to be the views of the community at large. This does not mean that evidence of the public's perception of the repute of the administration of justice, which Professor Gibson suggested could be presented in the form of public opinion polls . . . will be determinative of the issue (see *Therens* . . .). The position is different with respect to obscenity, for example, where the court must assess the level of tolerance of the community, whether or not it is reasonable, and may consider public opinion polls (*R. v. Prairie Schooner News Ltd. and Powers* (1970), 1 C.C.C. (2d) 251 (Man. C.A.), at p. 266, cited in *Towne Cinema Theatres Ltd. v. The Queen*, [1985] 1 S.C.R. 494, at p. 513). It would be unwise in my respectful view, to adopt a similar attitude with respect to the *Charter* . . . The *Charter* is designed to protect the accused from the majority, so the enforcement of the *Charter* must not be left to that majority.

Mr. Justice McIntyre, although dissenting on other issues, wrote:[128]

> I do not suggest that we should adopt the "community shock" test or that we should have recourse to public opinion polls and other devices for the sampling of public opinion. I do not suggest

Shime).
126 [1987] 1 S.C.R. 265, 33 C.C.C. (3d) 1, 56 C.R. (3d) 193, 28 C.R.R. 122, 13 B.C.L.R. (2d) 1, 38 D.L.R. (4th) 508, [1987] 3 W.W.R. 699, 74 N.R. 276.
127 *Ibid.*, at 281-82 (S.C.R.). See A. Bryant, M. Gold, M. Stevenson and D. Northrup, "Public Attitudes Toward the Exclusion of Evidence: Section 24(2) of the Canadian Charter of Rights and Freedoms" (1990), 69 Can. Bar Rev. 1; M. Gold *et al.*, "Public Support for the Exclusion of Unconstitutionally Obtained Evidence" (1990), 1 Sup. Ct. Law Rev. (2d) 555.
128 *Supra*, note 126, at 292 (S.C.R.).

that we should seek to discover some theoretical concept of community views or standards on this question. I do suggest that we should adopt a method long employed in the common law courts and, by whatever name it may be called, apply the standard of the reasonable man. The question should be as stated by Yves-Marie Morissette . . . "Would the admission of the evidence bring the administration of justice into disrepute in the eyes of a reasonable man, dispassionate and fully apprised of the circumstances of the case?"

It appears that the Supreme Court is unwilling to use public opinion poll evidence in *Charter* litigation for determining whether the admission of the evidence could bring the administration of justice into disrepute under the *Charter*, but endorses its use in obscenity cases.

4. Use of Authoritative Literature

Peculiar to the examination of experts is the utilization of textbooks. In support of any theory, an expert is permitted to refer to authoritative treatises and the like, and any portion of such texts upon which the witness relies is admissible into evidence. Moreover, it appears that, if a written work forms the basis of the expert's opinion, then counsel is allowed to read extracts to the expert and obtain his or her judgment on them.[129] The written view of the author thereby becomes the opinion of the witness. If the witness does not adopt the writing as being authoritative and in accord with the witness' own opinion, nothing may be read from the text, for that would be tolerating the admissibility of pure hearsay. Harvey C.J. in *R. v. Anderson*[130] explained why the opinion of an author not present in court and not acknowledged as authoritative by the witness is inadmissible as substantive evidence:[131]

As all evidence is given under the sanction of an oath or its equivalent, it is apparent that textbooks or other treatises as such

---

129 *R. v. Ashe* (1922), 39 C.C.C. 193, 50 N.B.R. 82 (C.A.), at 86 (N.B.R.); *Brownell v. Black* (1890), 31 N.B.R. 594 (C.A.).
130 (1914), 22 C.C.C. 455, 5 W.W.R. 1052, 26 W.L.R. 783, 7 Alta. L.R. 102, 16 D.L.R. 203 (C.A.).
131 *Ibid.*, at 459 (C.C.C.), at 206 (D.L.R.).

cannot be evidence. The opinion of an eminent author may be, and in many cases is, as a matter of fact, entitled to more weight than that of the sworn witness, but the fact is that, if his opinion is put in the form of a treatise, there is no opportunity of questioning and ascertaining whether any expression might be subject to any qualification respecting a particular case.

Beck J., in the same case, indicated the basis for the admissibility of texts as the foundation of the witness' own opinion as follows:[132]

When a medical man or other person professing some science is called as an expert witness, it is his opinion and his opinion only that can be properly put before the jury. Just as in the case of a witness called to prove a fact, it is proper in direct examination to ask him not merely to state the fact, but also how he came by the knowledge of the fact, so in the case of an expert witness called to give an opinion, he may in direct examination be asked how he came by his opinion. An expert medical witness may, therefore, upon giving his opinion, state in direct examination that he bases his opinion partly upon his own experience and partly upon the opinions of text-writers who are recognized by the medical profession at large as of authority. I think he may name the text-writers. I think he may add that his opinion and that of the text-writers named accords. Further, I see no good reason why such an expert witness should not be permitted, while in the box, to refer to such text-books as he chooses, in order, by the aid which they will give him, in addition to his other means of forming an opinion, to enable him to express an opinion; and again, that the witness having expressly adopted as his own the opinion of a text-writer, may himself read the text as expressing his own opinion.

Learned treatises may be used in a similar way in cross-examination of the expert to confront him with an authoritative opinion which contradicts the view expressed by the witness on the stand. The witness can be confronted with such work only if the expert first recognizes it as authoritative. Harvey C.J. put it this way:[133]

---

132 *Ibid.*, at 476 (C.C.C.), at 219-20 (D.L.R.).
133 *Ibid.*, at 459-60 (C.C.C.), at 206-07 (D.L.R.). See also *Brown v. Sheppard* (1856), 13 U.C.Q.B. 178 (C.A.).

On cross-examination the Judge should be careful to see that an improper use is not made of text-books, practically to give in evidence opinions of absent authors at variance with those of the witness. It is quite apparent that if the witness is asked about a text-book and he expresses ignorance of it, or denies its authority, no further use of it can be made by reading extracts from it, for that would be in effect making it evidence, but if he admits its authority, he then in a sense confirms it by his own testimony, and then may be quite properly asked for explanation of any apparent differences between its opinion and that stated by him.

By so doing, the treatise is not used for the hearsay purpose of proving the truth of the opinion contained therein, but as a means of testing the value of the expert witness' conclusion.[134] It becomes not positive evidence, but as in the case of the cross-examining tool of prior inconsistent statements,[135] it is utilized to challenge the expert's credibility; to test whether the witness has intelligently and competently read and applied what has been authoritatively written on the subject. If the witness adopts a passage in the text, it is the expert and not the text writer opinion's that is admitted in evidence.

The Americans have chosen not to limit the evidentiary value of texts to an impeachment purpose on cross-examination, or as demonstrating the basis of the expert's conclusion when examined in chief. Learned treatises, under a number of provisions, are recognized as an exception to the hearsay rule and are received as substantive evidence in their own right, if it is established by the witness, by other expert testimony, or by judicial notice, that the publications are reliable authorities.[136] By eliminating the requirement that the expert witness acknowledge the treatise as authoritative and allowing other experts or the judge by judicial notice to recognize it as such, the hazard of an expert evading a probing cross-examination merely by refusing to acknowledge that a particular work is authoritative, is avoided. Wigmore favoured this exception to the hearsay rule on the basis that the absence of cross-examination of the author of the treatise created no prejudice since the author would obviously possess no bias in the

---

134 *Ibid.*
135 See Chapter 16, VI.D.2.
136 Rule 803(18), Rules of Evidence for United States Courts and Magistrates (1975) 28 U.S.C.A., r. 63(3) of the Uniform Rules of Evidence (1953); r. 529 of the Model Code of Evidence (1942).

particular case and because there would be a strong motivation on his or her part to state the position accurately since the author would be aware that his or her writings would be subject to the scrutiny and criticism of other experts in the field.[137]

5. Cross-Examination of the Expert

A cross-examiner who wishes to challenge an expert's opinion usually attempts to do so by undermining the basis for that opinion. If the basis for his or her opinion is not sound, then the same may be true of the opinion itself. An expert may, therefore, be cross-examined as to whether relevant facts were ignored or disregarded and whether irrelevant facts were taken into account. Such matters relate to the validity of the opinion. However, the Supreme Court of Canada has recently limited the scope of the cross-examination of an expert. In *R. v. Howard*,[138] Howard and Trudel were convicted of first-degree murder. On appeal, new trials were ordered. Prior to the commencement of Howard's re-trial, Trudel pleaded guilty and apparently admitted that certain footprints found near the victim belonged to him. At Howard's re-trial, a defence expert was prepared to testify that the footprints were not those of Trudel. Before the expert testified, the Crown sought permission to cross-examine him as to whether Trudel's admission would change his mind. The purpose of the cross-examination was to attack the expert's credibility by asking whether Trudel's plea was immaterial to his scientific opinion, and secondly, to show that the basis of his opinion was or might not be sound. Although the trial judge and the Ontario Court of Appeal ruled that the proposed question was proper, the Supreme Court of Canada held that the question and answer were inadmissible. Since Trudel's plea and admission were not facts in evidence or going to be adduced in evidence, Lamer J. for the majority held:[139]

> It is not open to the examiner or cross-examiner to put as a fact, or even a hypothetical fact, that which is not and will not become part of the case as admissible evidence. On this ground alone, the question should have been denied.

---

137 6 Wigmore, *Evidence* (Chadbourn rev. 1976), §§ 1690-1708, at 2–73.
138 [1989] 1 S.C.R. 1337, 48 C.C.C. (3d) 38, 69 C.R. (3d) 193, 34 O.A.C. 81, 96 N.R. 81.
139 *Ibid.*, at 1347 (S.C.R.).

L'Heureux-Dubé J. dissented, concluding that such an inflexible approach to cross-examination was unwarranted. Given judicial acknowledgment that expert witnesses benefit from a degree of freedom not enjoyed by ordinary witnesses in that an expert's opinion may be based in whole or in part upon facts not otherwise admissible as evidence at trial, she reasoned that the greater latitude allowed to an expert in examination-in-chief involves a correlative latitude in cross-examination as to the basis of the expert's opinion. One commentator has noted that a rule prohibiting cross-examination unless an evidential foundation is or will be established would foreclose cross-examination on credibility of any witness because the collateral fact rule bars contradicting an opposing party's witness on a collateral matter.[140]

Lamer J. also held that the proposed cross-examination of the expert would establish no more than that he had not considered an irrelevant matter and, therefore, the validity of his opinion would not be impugned. Trudel's admission was a fact for the jury to consider but it was not for the expert to engage in a consideration of Trudel's credibility. Lamer J. put it this way:[141]

> Experts assist the trier of fact in reaching a conclusion by applying a particular scientific skill not shared by the judge or the jury to a set of facts and then by expressing an opinion as to what conclusions may be drawn as a result. Therefore, an expert cannot take into account facts that are not subject to his professional expert assessment, as they are irrelevant to his expert assessment; *a fortiori*, as injecting bias into the application of his expertise, he should not be told of and asked to take into account such a fact that is corroborative of one of the alternatives he is asked to scientifically determine. If the Crown experts had been told by the police when they were retained that Trudel had in fact confessed and that he acknowledged facts that established that it was his footprint, we would be left in doubt as to whether their conclusion is a genuine scientific conclusion. This is so because their expertise does not extend to Trudel's credibility, and what he admits to is totally irrelevant to what they were asked to do to help the Court, that is apply their scientific knowledge to the relevant "scientific facts", i.e., the moulds, etc.

---

140 B. Gover, *Annotation* (1989), 69 C.R. (3d) 194-95.
141 *Supra*, note 138, at 1348 (S.C.R.).

Lamer J. observed that at the new trial, the Crown might call Trudel to testify to this fact in order to prove the expert wrong in his conclusion. However, His Lordship held that these facts would be for the jury's consideration and not the expert "except maybe for the very limited purpose of testing with the expert the degree of certainty to be given to his science of which he will have testified."[142] A commentator suggests that "this concession appears to be at odds with the balance of his judgment on the issue."[143]

D. The Admissibility of New Scientific Evidence

The courts will be presented with the task of determining the admissibility of scientific evidence derived from new principles or techniques.[144] The traditional American standard for admissibility of such evidence was established in *Frye v. United States*:[145]

Just when a scientific principle or discovery crosses the line between the experimental and demonstrable stages is difficult to define. Somewhere in this twilight zone the evidential force of the principle must be recognized, and while courts will go a long way in admitting expert testimony deduced from a well-recognized scientific principle or discovery, the thing from which the deduction is made must be sufficiently established to have gained general acceptance in the particular field in which it belongs.

There are several arguments favouring the *Frye* test. The general acceptance standard provides a uniform test for the courts to assess the reliability of new scientific expert testimony. It guarantees the availability of a pool of qualified experts to testify for the parties and it safeguards against an unproved hypothesis or experimental technique being admitted in court.[146] Critics of the *Frye* standard argue

---

142   *Ibid.*, at 1349 (S.C.R.).
143   B. Gover, *supra*, note 140, at 195.
144   P. Giannelli, "The Admissibility of Novel Scientific Evidence: *Frye v. United States*, a Half-Century Later" (1980), 80 Columbia Law Rev. 1197, at 1198; see also M. McCormick, "Scientific Evidence: Defining a New Approach to Admissibility" (1982), 67 Iowa Law Review 879.
145   293 F. 1013, at 1014 (D.C. Cir. 1923).
146   *United States v. Downing*, 753 F.2d 1224, at 1235 (1985).

that it is difficult to determine the relevant scientific field and the level of acceptance within that community ("scientific nose counting").[147] Also, the test may exclude probative and reliable scientific evidence because the technique has not become sufficiently established in the selected scientific community.[148]

Because of the academic and judicial controversy as to the value of the *Frye* test,[149] numerous variations and alternatives have been suggested.[150] In *United States v. Downing*,[151] the United States Court of Appeal for the Third Circuit held that a particular degree of acceptance of a scientific technique within a scientific community is not a threshold for admissibility for federal courts governed by the Federal Rules of Evidence.[152] Rather, the trial judge's inquiry should focus on the following issues:[153] (1) the soundness and reliability of the process or technique used in generating the evidence; (2) the possibility that admitting the evidence would overwhelm, confuse or mislead the jury; and (3) the proffered connection between the scientific research or test result to be presented and particular disputed factual issues in the case.

The court in *Downing* identified factors to determine the reliability of the scientific evidence: the level of acceptance in the scientific community; the likelihood that the new technique has been exposed to critical scientific scrutiny (the existence of a specialized body of literature is evidence of this factor); the qualifications and stature of the experts; the non-judicial uses of the technique; the frequency of erroneous results; and the type of possible error (whether an error will result in inclusion or exclusion).[154] Other courts and commentators have recognized additional factors of reliability: the existence and maintenance of standards governing the use of the technique; the presence of safeguards in the characteristics of the technique; the availability of other experts to test and evaluate the technique; the relationship of the new technique to more established

---

147 P. Giannelli, *supra*, note 144, at 1208.
148 *United States v. Downing*, *supra*, note 146, at 1235.
149 See authorities cited in Giannelli and McCormick, *supra*, note 144.
150 See authorities cited in Giannelli and McCormick, *supra*, note 144.
151 *Supra*, note 146, at 1237.
152 *Supra*, note 146.
153 *Supra*, note 146, at 1234.
154 *Andrews v. State*, 533 So.2d 841 (Fla. App. 5 Dist. 1988).

modes of scientific analysis; and the care with which the technique was employed in the subject case.[155]

In *Downing* the court proposed that a trial judge must also weigh any danger that the evidence might confuse or mislead the jury.[156] An unwarranted "aura of reliability" and the lack of foundational evidence to allow the jury to verify independently would militate against admission. The court also expressed concern about those scientific techniques where the data was generated by a machine but the expert evidence depended upon subjective evaluations of such data. Finally, the trial judge must balance the reliability of the technique against the danger of confusing or misleading the jury.[157] The court recognized that the balancing exercise may import policy considerations, such as the undue consumption of time and the lack of probative value of the proffered evidence in the subject case.[158]

English and Canadian courts have not attempted to create a single standard of admissibility for novel scientific evidence.[159] Nor has the issue received the considerable amount of judicial and academic attention that it has received in the United States. Recently, however, Canadian courts have examined the admissibility of spectrographic voice analysis,[160] footprint evidence,[161] the testimony of polygraph operators,[162] and 'D.N.A.' fingerprinting.[163] In *R. v. Medvedew*[164] a telephoned bomb threat was tape-recorded. An expert witness used spectrographic voice analysis to identify the accused as the caller. The

---

155 *United States v. Williams*, 583 F.2d 1194 (2d. Cir. 1978), at 1198-99; McCormick, *supra*, note 144 at 911-12.
156 *Supra*, note 146, at 1240-43.
157 *Ibid.*, at 1240.
158 *Ibid.*, at 1243.
159 English and Canadian courts have not applied the exclusionary opinion rule with such strictness as the American courts and thus the rule has been less troublesome: R. Delisle, *Evidence, Principles and Problems*, 2nd ed. (Toronto: Carswell, 1989), at 449-55.
160 *R. v. Medvedew* (1978), 43 C.C.C. (2d) 434, 6 C.R. (3d) 185, 91 D.L.R. (3d) 21, [1978] 6 W.W.R. 208 (Man. C.A.).
161 *R. v. Nielsen* (1984), 16 C.C.C. (3d) 39, 30 Man. R. (2d) 81, 17 C.R.R. 90 (C.A.). Reversed (*sub nom. R. v. Stolar*), [1988] 1 S.C.R. 480, 62 C.R. (3d) 313, 40 C.C.C. (3d) 1, [1988] 3 W.W.R. 193, 52 Man. R. (2d) 46, 82 N.R. 280.
162 *R. v. Béland*, [1987] 2 S.C.R. 398, 60 C.R. (3d) 1, 36 C.C.C. (3d) 481, 43 D.L.R. (4th) 641, 9 Q.A.C. 293, 79 N.R. 263.
163 *R. v. Bourguignon*, unreported, January 14, 1991 (Ont. Ct. (Gen. Div.)); and see *Andrews v. State*, note 154.
164 *Supra*, note 160.

majority found that the trial judge did not err in admitting the "voiceprint" evidence. In dissent, O'Sullivan J.A. held that the expert evidence was inadmissible because the technique was not scientifically established; it depended on the subjective judgment of the expert; the pool of experts was inadequate thereby putting the accused at an intolerable disadvantage; the spectrographs were not adduced in evidence thereby preventing verification of the expert evidence by the jury; and finally, the expert evidence would not assist the jury. Although O'Sullivan J.A. held that the *Frye* test was sound and in accord with the principles of common law,[165] nonetheless he applied a modified *Frye* test, as the latter factors he relied upon are not encompassed within the general acceptance standard.

In *Phillion v. R.*,[166] the accused did not testify. Instead, he attempted to introduce evidence that his confession to the police was false through the testimony of a polygraph operator. The majority of the Supreme Court of Canada excluded this evidence as inadmissible hearsay and because it contravened the rule against self-serving evidence. In a concurring minority judgment, Spence J. stated that such evidence may be admissible in other circumstances.

The issue of the admissibility of polygraph evidence again came before the Supreme Court in *R. v. Béland*.[167] As in *Phillion v. R.*, the lie detector evidence was excluded. In the majority decision, McIntyre J. held that the admission of the polygraph evidence would contravene traditional exclusionary rules: a party is prohibited from bolstering the credibility of its own witness; a witness' prior and subsequent consistent statements are superfluous; and the testimony of character witnesses is limited to the accused's general reputation in the community. McIntyre J. also held that the credibility of an accused was well within the experience of judges and juries and thus the evidence did not pass the "helpfulness" threshold required for expert evidence. The exclusion was also justified on policy grounds because polygraph evidence would disrupt proceedings,[168] it would not improve the fact-finding process of the courts,[169] it would waste time on a collateral

---

165 *Supra*, note 160, at 447 (C.C.C.).
166 [1978] 1 S.C.R. 18, 37 C.R.N.S. 361, 33 C.C.C. (2d) 535, 74 D.L.R. (3d) 136.
167 *Supra*, note 162, at 415 (S.C.R.).
168 *Ibid.*, at 417. Presumably, the test must await the election of the accused to testify.
169 *Ibid.* The results are an interpretation by the operator who is also fallible.

issue, and it would create new procedural problems.[170] In a brief concurring judgment, La Forest J. supported exclusion because of human fallibility in assessing the weight to be given to evidence cloaked under the mystique of science, and because of the inadvisability of expending time on collateral issues.[171]

Wilson J., in dissent, found that the traditional exclusionary rules would not render the opinion of the polygraph operator inadmissible. Her Ladyship questioned whether the fear that the evidence would usurp the role of the jury was well founded.[172] She also stated that the danger of abuse, that the accused will 'expert-shop', should be a factor going to weight and not to admissibility.[173] Wilson J. noted that the *Frye* test had been considerably eroded in the United States and has now given way to a reasonable reliability test.[174] In her view, the traditional tests of helpfulness and relevance retain the value of the *Frye* test without the cost of its disadvantages.[175] Finally, Wilson J. stated that the accused should have been allowed to adduce the evidence in order to make full answer and defence.[176] Although this point was not mentioned in her dissent, one commentator questioned whether exclusion in these circumstances violates s. 7 of the *Charter*.[177]

The judicial experience in the United States demonstrates that a judicial standard for admissibility is problematic. To date, Canadian courts have not attempted to formulate a single rule for the admissibility of new scientific evidence. Rather, the courts first apply the traditional exclusionary rules, the expert evidence rule, and then invoke policy reasons specific to the particular proffered evidence to determine admissibility. This appears to be the preferable route and it accords with the present trend in the American federal courts.[178]

In the context of judicial acceptance of expert evidence, there has been a great deal of discussion lately as to the value of formal

---

170   *Ibid.* E.g., would the Crown be able to require the accused to take a polygraph test or obtain results of other tests?
171   *Ibid.*, at 434 (S.C.R.).
172   *Ibid.*, at 426 (S.C.R.).
173   *Ibid.*, at 424 (S.C.R.).
174   *Ibid.*, at 432-33 (S.C.R.).
175   *Ibid.*, at 433 (S.C.R.).
176   *Ibid.*
177   R. Bessner, "The Road Not Taken" (1988), 60 C.R. (3d) 55, at 58; see also M. McCormick, "Scientific Evidence: Defining a New Approach to Admissibility" (1982), 67 Iowa Law Review 879, at 902-03.
178   *United States v. Downing*, 753 F.2d 1224, at 1235 (1985).

probability statistics.[179] The danger exists, if the courts were to accept probability analysis to help resolve disputes, that undue weight would be attached to mathematical formulae, in search for objectivity, to the neglect of more impressionistic and subjective factors which are important in every case. In *R. v. Bourguignon*,[180] Flanigan J. of the Ontario Court of Justice (General Division) considered the admissibility of evidence of D.N.A. typing and the predictability of identification therefrom. Specifically, the expert witness who had tested semen and blood samples determined that it came from the accused. He then was prepared to give an opinion that the probability figure was that there would not be another such D.N.A. match in more than one person in 23.8 million and in this case he had found two matches. The expert also tested a belt which was alleged to be the murder weapon and he found the presence of D.N.A. of the victim on the belt. He was prepared to give evidence that the probability figure from these tests was one in 55 million. Flanigan J. found that the D.N.A. evidence was relevant, was properly done, met all the technical requirements and would be helpful to the jury and therefore held it to be admissible. He was reluctant, however, to present the jury with the probability figures of one in 23.8 million or one in 55 million. In ruling that the probability evidence was inadmissible, Flanigan J. gave this explanation:[181]

> This Court does not think that the criminal jurisdiction of Canada is yet ready to put such an additional pressure on a jury, by making them overcome such fantastic odds and asking them to weigh it as just one piece of evidence presented. There is a real danger that the jury will use the evidence as a measure of the probability of the accused's guilt or innocence and thereby undermine the presumption of innocence and erode the value served by the reasonable doubt standard. As said in [*State of Minnesota v. Schwartz* 447 N.W. Reporter (2d) 422]: "dehumanize our justice system".

---

179 See E.W. Cleary (ed.), *McCormick on Evidence*, 3rd ed. (St. Paul: West Publishing, 1984), at 650-62.
180 *Supra*, note 163.
181 *Supra*, note 163, at 17. Compare *R. v. Abadom*, [1983] 1 W.L.R. 126 (C.A.); leave to appeal dismissed [1983] 1 W.L.R. 405 (H.L.).

I would therefore, rule admissible the D.N.A. testing evidence but not the statistic probabilities. This restriction can be easily overcome by evidence that "such matches are rare" or "extremely rare" or words to the same effect, which will put the jury in a better position to assess such evidence and protect the right of the accused to a fair trial.

E. *Miscellaneous*

1. Limiting Number of Witnesses and Notice Requirement

There is no restriction on the number of lay witnesses who may, on behalf of a party, give opinion testimony not based upon any particular knowledge or experience. The statutory limitations set out in the *Canada Evidence Act* and the provincial statutes on the number of witnesses entitled according to the law or practice to give opinion evidence refer only to that evidence which is founded on a special or expert knowledge outside the ken of ordinary witnesses.[182]

In some provinces not more than three expert witnesses may be called by either side without leave of the judge.[183] The *Canada Evidence Act* permits a party to call five professional or expert witnesses without leave of the court.[184] These statutory restrictions are meant to save the court's time and acknowledge the fact that the case is not to be decided on the basis of a numerical count of experts called on each side.

Leave to call more than the statutory number of experts can be obtained from the court at any time during the trial and even after one or more of the experts has testified.[185] Until 1969, the *Canada Evidence Act* contained a provision that leave to call more than the set number of experts had to be applied for before the examination of any of the experts who could be examined without such leave.[186] With its repeal

---

182 *Buttrum v. Udell* (1925), 57 O.L.R. 97, [1925] 3 D.L.R. 45 (C.A.); *Robins v. National Trust Co.* (1925), 57 O.L.R. 46 (C.A.); affd. [1927] A.C. 515, [1927] 1 W.W.R. 692 and 881, [1927] 2 D.L.R. 97 (P.C.).
183 *Viz.* Evidence Acts: Ontario, R.S.O. 1980, c. 145, s. 12; Alberta, R.S.A. 1980, c. A-21, s. 10; Manitoba, R.S.M. 1987, c. E150, s. 27; New Brunswick, R.S.N.B. 1979, c. E-11, s. 23; Northwest Territories, R.O.N.W.T. 1988, c. E-8, s. 9; Yukon, R.S.Y.T. 1986, c. 57, s. 9.
184 *Canada Evidence Act*, R.S.C. 1985, c. C-5, s. 7; see also *Saskatchewan Evidence Act*, R.S.S. 1978, c. S-16, s. 48.
185 *Reid v. Watkins*, [1964] 2 O.R. 249 (H.C.J.).
186 R.S.C. 1952, c. 307, s. 7(2). See also *French's Complex Ore Reduction Co. of*

in 1969[187] the discretion of the trial judge can be exercised at any time.[188] Failure to obtain leave of the court will not of itself warrant a new trial if more than the prescribed number of experts gave opinion testimony, unless a substantial wrong or miscarriage of justice resulted.[189]

There are disparate authorities on whether the statutorily prescribed number of experts applies to each fact issue raised in the trial, or whether it represents the total number of such witnesses that a party can call in the entire case. In *Buttrum v. Udell*,[190] the Ontario Court of Appeal construed the relevant provision as permitting each party to call three expert witnesses in the course of the trial. It rejected the earlier Alberta decision of *Scamen v. Canadian Northern Railway Co.*,[191] and concluded that if the number of expert witnesses was limited only by the number of issues of fact in the case,[192]

> a trial Judge could not refuse to hear any such witness, because, before hearing what the witness had to say, he could not satisfactorily determine to just what issue of fact the evidence was applicable, or whether the evidence would amount to "opinion evidence," and thus the statute would . . . either become a dead letter or a new source of trouble, expense, and delay.

The Supreme Court of Canada in *Fagnan v. Ure*,[193] however, without reference to *Buttrum v. Udell*, in considering an Alberta provision identical to the one in Ontario, resurrected the *Scamen* decision and concluded that a proper construction of the section permitted the calling of three witnesses to give expert opinion upon each of the fact issues involved in the trial.

In some provinces, no expert witness may testify except with leave of the trial judge unless the party calling such expert witness has,

---

Canada v. Electrolytic Zinc Process Co., [1930] S.C.R. 462, [1930] D.L.R. 902.
187   S.C. 1968-69, c. 14, s. 1.
188   A similar provision in Ontario was replaced in 1960, c. 31, s. 3.
189   *Leeson v. Darlow* (1926), 59 O.L.R. 421, [1926] 4 D.L.R. 415 (C.A.); *Leadbetter v. Western Shoe Co.*, [1944] O.W.N. 238 (C.A.); *R. v. Barrs* (1946), 86 C.C.C. 9, 1 C.R. 301, [1946] 1 W.W.R. 328, [1946] 2 D.L.R. 655 (Alta. C.A.). But see *Rice v. Sockett* (1912), 27 O.L.R. 410, 8 D.L.R. 84 (Div. Ct.).
190   *Supra*, note 182.
191   (1912), 2 W.W.R. 1006, 5 Alta. L.R. 376, 6 D.L.R. 142 (C.A.).
192   Per Ferguson J.A., in *Buttrum v. Udell*, *supra*, note 182, at 100 (O.L.R.).
193   [1958] S.C.R. 377, 13 D.L.R. (2d) 273.

not less than ten days before the commencement of the trial, served on every other party to the action a report, signed by the expert, setting out his or her name, address and qualifications and the substance of his or her proposed testimony.[194] Other provinces provide for a notice provision of at least 30 days prior to the commencement of the trial.[195]

2. Court-Appointed Experts

The use of experts appointed not by the parties but by the court itself was an early practice. It fell into disuse, however, with the development of the adversarial system whereby parties called witnesses to prove their cases, and the court's intervention in this process diminished.[196]

The rules in Ontario now provide that a judge may appoint, on his or her own initiative, one or more independent experts to inquire into and report on any question of fact or opinion relevant to an issue in the action.[197] A similar rule exists in New Brunswick.[198] These rules now make it clear that the role of the expert is that of a witness, as opposed to one who sits on the Bench with the judge and performs an advisory role.[199] The rule provides that the parties may receive the

---

194 Ontario *Rules of Civil Procedure*, O. Reg. 560/84, r. 53.03; Prince Edward Island *Civil Procedure Rules*, r. 31.08; Newfoundland *Rules of the Supreme Court*, 1986 (Schedule D to *The Judicature Act*, 1986, S.N. 1986, c. 42), r. 46.07; *Saskatchewan Queen's Bench Rules*, r. 284(d). Where the failure to produce the report is that of the expert, and not of counsel, oral testimony of the expert may still be permitted to prevent a substantial wrong or miscarriage of justice: *Gibson v. Toth* (1990), 44 C.P.C. (2d) 137 (Ont. Div. Ct.).

195 Alberta *Rules of Court*, r. 218.1; *Evidence Act*, R.S.B.C. 1979, c. 116, s. 11; The *Queen's Bench Rules of Manitoba*, r. 239.1. In New Brunswick the report must be filed no later than motions day at which the trial date is fixed: *Rules of Court of New Brunswick*, r. 52.01. In Nova Scotia it must be served on each opposite party within 30 days of the filing of the Notice of Trial: Nova Scotia *Civil Procedure Rules*, r. 31.08. *Buttrum v. Udell, supra*, note 182; *Robins v. National Trust Co., supra*, note 182.

196 7 Wigmore, *Evidence* (Chadbourn rev. 1978), § 1917, at 1-11; *Buckley v. Rice Thomas* (1554), 1 Plowd. 118.

197 Ontario *Rules of Civil Procedure*, O. Reg. 560/84, r. 52.03.

198 *Rules of Court of New Brunswick*, r. 54.03.

199 Even under former rules, it had been held that a court-appointed expert was not a judicial officer and that his role was strictly limited to explaining to the judge the evidence addressed by the parties: see *Phillips v. Ford Motor Co. of Canada*,

report of the expert and may cross-examine him or her.

The rules of many other jurisdictions contain similar provisions except that they specify that the court may appoint an independent expert only "where independent technical evidence would appear to be required."[200]

There appears to be no provision for the appointment of experts by a court in British Columbia, Manitoba, Saskatchewan or the Yukon Territories.[201]

[1971] 2 O.R. 637, 18 D.L.R. (3d) 641 (C.A.).

200 Alberta *Rules of Court*, r. 218(1); The *Supreme Court Rules* of Northwest Territories, r. 230; *Nova Scotia Civil Procedure Rules*, r. 23; Prince Edward Island *Civil Procedure Rules*, r. 23; Newfoundland *Rules of the Supreme Court*, 1986, r. 35.

201 The *Queen's Bench Rules of Manitoba* contain, however, a general provision which may be applicable to court appointed experts. Rule 241 provides: "The court may, in any cause or matter where it appears necessary for the purposes of justice, make an order for the examination on oath before an officer of the court, or any other person, and at any place, of any person and may permit such deposition to be given in evidence."

Section III

RULES RELATING TO THE PRODUCTION OF EVIDENCE

CHAPTER 13

COMPETENCE AND COMPELLABILITY OF WITNESSES

I GENERAL

This chapter examines the distinct, but interrelated, matters of competence, compellability and, to a limited extent, evidentiary privilege. Subject to certain common-law and statutory exceptions, every person is competent to give evidence in any civil or criminal case. As a general rule,[1] any competent witness is compellable through the process of the court to come before the court to give evidence.[2] Subject to evidentiary privileges,[3] any competent and compellable witness must answer any questions put by the court or counsel and provide real evidence, so long as it is relevant and otherwise admissible.

II COMPETENCE

A. *General*

The general rule is that every person is competent to testify in any case, civil or criminal. However, by reason of certain disqualifying rules, individuals who possess relevant and primary knowledge may

---

1 Subject to the exceptions noted below.
2 *Tribune Newspaper Co. v. Fort Frances Pulp & Paper Co.*, [1932] 2 W.W.R. 443, 40 Man. R. 401, [1932] 4 D.L.R. 179 (C.A.); *R. v. Barnes* (1921), 49 O.L.R. 374, 36 C.C.C. 40, 61 D.L.R. 623 (C.A.).
3 See Chapter 14.

be precluded from testifying. Any objection to competency should be made at the time the witness is called.[4] Because the issues of competency of an accused and an accused's spouse are integrally related to those of compellability, this subject will be discussed below in the context of compellability.[5]

B. *Witnesses with an Interest in the Proceedings or with a Criminal Record*

Historically, at common law, many factors rendered a potential witness incompetent to testify, with crippling effects upon the court's pursuit of the truth. Almost anyone who was connected with the cause or to the parties to the action was incompetent as a witness. Thus, the parties, their spouses and any persons convicted of crime or possessing a pecuniary interest in the outcome of the litigation were incompetent.[6] The concern was that their evidence would be so tainted and unreliable as to be valueless. Over the course of a century, these general prohibitions eroded to the extent that modern courts are rarely troubled by questions of competency, and any testimonial infirmity which would have been cause for disqualification in the past now merely goes to the question of the witness' credibility.

A series of nineteenth-century statutes wiped away virtually every impediment to a witness giving relevant testimony with respect to matters in issue. It began in 1814 when ratepayers and office holders were made competent witnesses with respect to cases relating to the affairs of their parish or district.[7] In 1833, an individual, even though interested in the result of the litigation, was made competent.[8] The judgment arising in such a case, however, could not be used for or against that interested witness nor anyone claiming under him. Greater reform took place ten years later with the enactment of Lord

---

4   *Prescott v. Jarvis* (1849), 5 U.C.Q.B. 489 (C.A.); *R. v. Schneider*, [1927] 1 W.W.R. 306, 47 C.C.C. 61, [1927] 1 D.L.R. 999 (Sask. C.A.); *R. v. McKevitt*, [1936] 3 D.L.R. 750, 66 C.C.C. 70, 10 M.P.R. 531 (N.S.C.A.).
5   This Chapter, III.A., B. and D.
6   See S. March Phillips, *A Treatise on the Law of Evidence*, 4th ed. (London: Butterworths, 1820) for an exhaustive analysis of the classes of persons incompetent at common law.
7   (1814), 54 Geo. 3, c. 170, s. 9.
8   (1833), 3 & 4 Will. 4, c. 42, s. 26.

Denman's Act,[9] which provided that no person was to be incompetent by reason of crime or interest in any civil or criminal trial. Parties, however, were not allowed to give evidence until the *Small Debts Act*[10] in 1846 made them competent in a limited type of action and until the enactment of Lord Brougham's Act in 1851,[11] which made them competent in all civil proceedings. These statutes, however, did not alter the incompetency of parties in criminal proceedings, or proceedings instituted in consequence of adultery or actions for breach of promise to marry. Moreover, Lord Brougham's Act did not affect the wife's incompetency as a witness in a civil suit in which her husband was a party.[12] Ultimately in 1853, the spouse of either party was made a competent and compellable witness in any civil action except for proceedings arising out of adultery.[13] In 1869 this last restriction was repealed so as to make a spouse competent to give evidence in adultery proceedings as well.[14] This legislative reform also provided that parties could give evidence in actions for breach of promise of marriage.

A similar piecemeal approach to reform took place in Canada. In 1837, interested witnesses were allowed to be examined, but the verdict or judgment was not to be admissible for or against such witnesses.[15] Lord Denman's Act was duplicated in Upper Canada in 1849.[16] In 1859, parties were made competent and compellable in actions other than proceedings arising in consequence of adultery.[17] In 1873, all parties and spouses were made competent and compellable in actions other than proceedings arising in consequence of adultery.[18] Before the century came to a close, however, parties and their spouses were made competent witnesses in adultery proceedings too.[19]

These reforms have been consolidated and are reflected in current Evidence Acts. For example, the Alberta *Evidence Act* does away with the disqualifications as follows:[20]

---

9   (1843), 6 & 7 Vict., c. 85.
10 (1846), 9 & 10 Vict., c. 95, s. 83.
11 (1851), 14 & 15 Vict., c. 99, s. 2.
12 See *Barbat v. Allen* (1852), 7 Ex. 609, 155 E.R. 1092.
13 (1853), 16 & 17 Vict., c. 83, s. 1.
14 (1869), 32 & 33 Vict., c. 68.
15 (1837), 7 Will. 4, c. 3, s. 18.
16 (1849), 12 Vict., c. 70.
17 (1859), 22 Vict., c. 32, s. 5.
18 (1873), 36 Vict., c. 10, ss. 1 and 3.
19 (1882), 45 Vict., c. 10, s. 4.
20 R.S.A. 1980, c. A-21, ss. 3, 4(1), (2). For similar provisions in other provin-

3(1) No person offered as a witness in an action shall be excluded from giving evidence by reason of any alleged incapacity from crime or interest.

(2) A person offered as a witness shall be admitted to give evidence notwithstanding that he has an interest in the matter in question or in the event of the action or that he has been previously convicted of a crime or offence.

4(1) The parties to an action and the persons on whose behalf the action is brought, instituted, opposed or defended are, except as otherwise provided in this Act, competent and compellable to give evidence on behalf of themselves or of any of the parties.

(2) The husbands and wives of the parties and persons mentioned in subsection (1) are, except as otherwise provided in this Act, competent and compellable to give evidence on behalf of any of the parties.

The *Canada Evidence Act* contains similar provisions applicable in the criminal context.[21]

C. Mental, Intellectual and Communicative Deficiencies

1. Mental Impairment

Little authority is required for the proposition that if a person is rendered incapable of interpreting observed events, or of communicating, then that person is incompetent to testify.[22] The difficulty is to

---

cial evidence statutes see Ontario, R.S.O. 1980, c. 145, ss. 6, 8, 10; British Columbia, R.S.B.C. 1979, c. 116, ss. 3, 7 [am. 1985, c. 72, s. 2]; Saskatchewan, R.S.S. 1978, c. S-16, ss. 34, 35 [am. 1988-89, c. 55, s. 28]; New Brunswick, R.S.N.B. 1973, c. E-11, ss. 2, 3, 4, 5 [ss. 3, 4, 5 am. 1990, c. 17, ss. 1, 2, 3]; Nova Scotia, R.S.N.S. 1989, c. 154, ss. 44-48; Prince Edward Island, R.S.P.E.I. 1988, c. E-11, ss. 2, 3, 4, 5, 7, 8, 10; Newfoundland, R.S.N. 1970, c. 115, ss. 2, 2A [en. 1971, No. 48, s. 2; 1971, No. 14, s. 2], 3 [re-en. 1971, No. 48, s. 3], 5, 7; Manitoba, R.S.M. 1987, c. E150, ss. 3, 4, 5.

21   R.S.C. 1985, c. C-5, ss. 3, 4 [am. R.S.C. 1985, c. 19 (3rd Supp.), s. 17]: the subject of the competence and compellability of accused persons and their spouses is considered in this Chapter, III.A. and B.

22   *R. v. Hawke* (1975), 7 O.R. (2d) 145, 29 C.R.N.S. 1, 22 C.C.C. (2d) 19 (C.A.); *Canada Evidence Act, ibid.*, note 21, s. 16(1) [re-en. R.S.C. 1985, c. 19 (3rd Supp.),

determine what degree of mental impairment will warrant the exclusion of the witness' evidence. Should only those handicapped by the most extreme forms of mental disability be precluded from giving evidence? What of lesser forms of psychological abnormalities which may beset a witness? In *R. v. Hill*,[23] the witness was an inmate of a mental hospital when he observed the relevant event. His particular mental affliction was that he believed that spirits were around him and talking to him. The medical evidence, however, indicated that his delusion did not affect his memory and that in all other respects, he was perfectly rational. The Court held that he was qualified and competent to give evidence, rejecting any blanket rule of inadmissibility. Accordingly, not in every case will a person who is mentally incompetent be disqualified from testifying. The witness will be competent if the delusion does not affect perception, memory or articulation of the events in question.

Generally, the mental competency of a witness should be tested at the time the witness is called, and the inquiry should be conducted outside of the presence of the jury.[24] The *Canada Evidence Act* specifically addresses this issue in s. 16, which provides, in part:[25]

(1) Where a proposed witness is a person . . . whose mental capacity is challenged, the court shall, before permitting the person to give evidence, conduct an inquiry to determine

(a) whether the person understands the nature of an oath or a solemn affirmation; and

(b) whether the person is able to communicate the evidence.

. . .

(4) A person referred to in subsection (1) who neither understands the nature of an oath or a solemn affirmation nor is able to communicate the evidence shall not testify.

(5) A party who challenges the mental capacity of a proposed

---

s. 18].
23   (1851), 5 Cox C.C. 259 (C.C.R.).
24   *R. v. Harbuz*, [1979] 2 W.W.R. 105, 45 C.C.C. (2d) 65 (Sask. Q.B.).
25   Re-en. R.S.C. 1985, c. 19 (3rd Supp.), s. 18. See also British Columbia *Evidence Act, supra*, note 20, s. 5 [re-en. 1988, c. 46, s. 25].

witness of fourteen years of age or more has the burden of satisfying the court that there is an issue as to the capacity of the proposed witness to testify under an oath or a solemn affirmation.

If the mental deficiency appears during the course of the witness's examination it is generally a matter of credibility and not competency.[26] However, the judge does have the discretion to stop the giving of testimony and order that the evidence be struck from the record.[27] In certain circumstances it may be appropriate to declare a mistrial. In *R. v. Harbuz*[28] the trial judge declared a mistrial in the proceedings when it became clear during the examination-in-chief that the witness suffered from a mental disease or retardation that affected his competence. By this time the witness had already implicated the accused in a murder but there had not yet been any cross-examination. It would in these circumstances have been unfair to the accused simply to direct the jury not to consider the evidence.[29]

In *R. v. Hawke*[30] the Ontario Court of Appeal confirmed that evidence as to the effect of a mental condition on the ability to perceive events and give an accurate account of them to the court goes not only to credibility, but as an initial matter to the competency of the witness to testify. This is a preliminary matter to be dealt with on a *voir dire*, if raised by counsel. The Court accepted Wigmore's views as to the factors to consider in making such a determination of competency. Wigmore states that the derangement or defect must be such as to substantially negative trustworthiness upon the specific subject of the testimony.[31] Both psychiatric and lay evidence is relevant to the issue of the mental incompetency of a witness.[32]

The testimonial qualifications relating to a witness' ability to observe, record, recall and communicate should be distinguished from the requirement relating to the responsibility to testify truthfully. A

---

26   W.M. Best and A. Russell (eds.), *The Principles of the Law of Evidence*, 6th ed. (London: Sweet, 1875), at §§ 146, 208.
27   *R. v. Steinberg*, [1931] O.R. 222, at 257 (C.A.); affd. [1931] S.C.R. 421, 56 C.C.C. 9, [1931] 4 D.L.R. 8; *R. v. Hawke, supra*, note 22, at 170 (C.C.C.).
28   *Supra*, note 24.
29   See also 11 C.E.D. (Ont. 3rd), Title 57 Evidence, at § 250.
30   *Supra*, note 22.
31   2 Wigmore, *Evidence* (Chadbourn rev. 1979), § 506.
32   *R. v. Hawke, supra*, note 22, at 154-55.

mental condition or belief which affects the witness' moral responsibility to tell the truth is not a defect which affects competency. In *R. v. Walsh*[33] the Crown proffered a witness who, although not suffering from any mental disorder or defect, professed to be a satanist. The trial judge held that he was not competent to testify on the basis that he did not recognize any social duty to tell the truth in court. The Ontario Court of Appeal reversed the ruling of the trial judge holding that a disposition to lie does not disqualify a person from testifying. An adult who does not suffer from intellectual disorders or defects resulting in incompetency pursuant to the test in *R. v. Hill*[34] is not incompetent because he lacks a sense of moral responsibility. Moral defect goes to credibility only. Since the witness appreciated that he was liable to penal sanctions if he gave false evidence he appreciated the duty of speaking the truth in the relevant sense.[35]

2. Children

A related problem is the inherent frailty of the evidence of children.[36] Because of their immaturity they may not perceive events correctly. They may have difficulty in articulating what they have seen. They may be influenced by talking to a parent or friend. There is the danger that they may not comprehend what takes place before their eyes. Notwithstanding that these shortcomings are common to all witnesses, the courts and legislatures have focused on the frailties in the testimony of children. However, an early text on evidence nicely compares the evidence of children and adults:[37]

Independently of the sanction of an oath, the testimony of children, after they have been subjected to cross-examination, is

---

33 (1978), 45 C.C.C. (2d) 199 (Ont. C.A.).

34 *Supra*, note 23.

35 In *R. v. Hawke, supra*, note 22, the trial judge refused to await the testimony of two psychiatrists as to the competency of the witness to testify, because even if the witness was incompetent to take the oath, she could be affirmed pursuant to s. 14 of the *Canada Evidence Act*. The Court of Appeal held such reasoning to be erroneous as there is a difference between competency to take the oath, or alternatively affirm, and general competency to testify.

36 See *Horsburgh v. R.*, [1967] S.C.R. 746, [1968] 2 C.C.C. 288, 2 C.R.N.S. 228, 63 D.L.R. (2d) 699, per Spence J.

37 Best, *supra*, note 26, at §§ 158, 227; for a modern view see M. Mian, K. Haka-Ikse, M. Lefkowitz, C. McGoey, "The Child as Witness", 4 C.R. (4th) 359.

often entitled to as much credit as that of grown persons; and what is wanted in the perfection of intellectual frailties, is sometimes more than compensated by the absence of a motive to deceive.

Where the witnesses were children at the time of the events giving rise to the litigation or charge, their evidence may suffer from the same defects even though they were older children or adults at the time of the trial. Any inaccuracy in their perception of events would not be cured by the passage of time, but more likely compounded. In *Kendall v. R.*,[38] an accused was charged, in 1961, with murder, 9 years after the death of his wife. The evidence against him was given by his children who had witnessed the killing and who, at the time of trial, were aged 21, 19 and 17. At the time that the children observed the event they were 12, 10 and 8 years old. It was argued that the evidence of the children, given when they were grown up, suffered from the same weakness that would have attached to it had they given it as young children and could not at the time of the trial be any stronger. The Court held, however, that the witnesses were of mature intelligence, and thus it was unnecessary to warn the jury of the danger of lack of corroboration, as would have been necessary if unsworn evidence had been given by children of immature years.[39] The tendency of the courts is to permit such witnesses to testify and any defect in their mental or intellectual make-up at the time of the event is a matter going to weight only.[40]

The reception of the evidence of children is, generally, focused on an inquiry into whether the child has the competency to swear an oath or to give unsworn testimony, a matter discussed below.[41]

---

38   [1962] S.C.R. 469, 37 C.R. 179, 132 C.C.C. 216.

39   Corroboration was required by statute for only the unsworn evidence of children; but now see s. 16 of the *Canada Evidence Act, supra*, note 21 [re-en. R.S.C. 1985, c. 19 (3rd Supp.), s. 18].

40   See also *R. v. Budin* (1981), 32 O.R. (2d) 1, 20 C.R. (3d) 86, 58 C.C.C. (2d) 352, 120 D.L.R. (3d) 536 (C.A.); *Re Truscott*, [1967] S.C.R. 309, [1967] 2 C.C.C. 285, 1 C.R.N.S. 1, 62 D.L.R. (2d) 545; *Udy v. Stewart* (1885), 10 O.R. 591 (C.A.); J.A. Andrews, "Issues as to the Credibility of Witnesses," [1965] C.L.R. 461; *R. v. Wallwork* (1958), 42 Cr. App. Rep. 153 (C.C.A.); *R. v. D. (D.)* (1991), 46 O.A.C. 189 (C.A.).

41   This Chapter, II.D.4.

3. Communicative Deficiencies

In *R. v. Imrie*,[42] the witness had been deaf since childhood and was unable to speak intelligibly, although she was able to make herself understood to friends and relations. An attempt was made to put her testimony in through her aunt who acted as interpreter. The evidence proved to be most unsatisfactory, for the witness was unable to respond properly. As a result the accused's counsel could not conduct a proper cross-examination of the witness. The Court of Appeal barred the witness' evidence completely, because the probative value of the evidence that she could give would be slight relative to its prejudicial effect upon the jury. Was the defect in the witness' ability to communicate one going to her incompetency and therefore to be excluded, or merely a factor tending to diminish the probative worth of the evidence? To be consistent with the principle in the *Kendall* case, the evidence of the witness here, providing it possessed some probative value, should not have been looked upon as incompetent; it should have been permitted although given minimal weight because of its inherent frailties.

In *Udy v. Stewart*[43] an Ontario court held that witnesses should not be allowed to give evidence at all, if they lack the intelligence to communicate or are unable to comprehend the questions asked. The probative value of such evidence is said not to outweigh the prejudice to the opposing party who is deprived of a meaningful cross-examination. The court's position on this point was that this defect goes to competency and not just to weight. That result may be too hard. Unless the handicap of the witness is such that his or her mental or intellectual capacity excludes the ability to relate what was observed, then the evidence should be received and any extenuating circumstances should be considered a matter of weight and credibility.[44] At common law deaf-mutes were incompetent to testify.[45] Legislation has altered this position.[46] Such persons can give testimony and be

---

42   (1917), 12 Cr. App. Rep. 282 (C.C.A.).
43   (1885), 10 O.R. 591 (Ont. C.A.).
44   See also *R. v. D. (T.C.)* (1987), 61 C.R. (3d) 168, 38 C.C.C. (3d) 434, 22 O.A.C. 119 (C.A.); *R. v. Harbuz, supra*, note 24; *R. v. Allen (No. 2)* (1979), 46 C.C.C. (2d) 477 (Ont. H.C.).
45   *R. v. Whitehead* (1866), L.R. 1 C.C.R. 33.
46   Evidence Acts: Canada, R.S.C. 1985, c. C-5, s. 6; Alberta, R.S.A. 1980, c. A-21, s. 21; British Columbia, R.S.B.C. 1979, c. 116, s. 17; Saskatchewan, R.S.S. 1978, c. S-16, s. 44; Manitoba, R.S.M. 1987, c. E150, s. 26; Northwest

subjected to cross-examination through interpreters using sign language. Any defects with respect to the testimony go to weight, not to credibility. Some statutes provide that witnesses who are unable to communicate orally may give their evidence in any manner in which it can be made intelligible,[47] but the *Canada Evidence Act* provides that a person who is unable to communicate evidence by reason of mental incapacity shall not testify.[48]

D. The Oath

1. Necessity at Common Law

According to *Omychund v. Barker*,[49] a witness at common law, in order to be competent to give evidence, had to demonstrate a belief in some Supreme Being and had to be sworn according to the witness' own custom. Concomitant with the belief in God was a belief in divine retribution, and thus was created a fear in the witness that lying upon oath would result in punishment in this world[50] or the afterlife.[51] Thus at common law, if the witness refused to take the oath or believed that the oath had no effect on conscience or if there was no belief in spiritual retribution, then the witness was not competent.[52]

2. Form of Oath

In early times, only the Christian ceremony was allowed and, therefore, non-Christians could not testify. As a result of the *Omychund v. Barker*[53] case, all those who believed in a Supreme Being were permitted to give evidence. Now, other ceremonies which bind the consciences of people of different cultures are allowed. So, for example, a ceremony involving the breaking of a saucer or the "chicken oath" or "paper oath" is allowed since it is of moral signifi-

---

Territories, R.S.N.W.T. 1988, c. E-8, s. 26; Yukon Territory, R.S.Y. 1986, c. 57, s. 23.

47   *Ibid.*
48   Section 16(4) [re-en. R.S.C. 1985, c. 19 (3rd Supp.), s. 18].
49   (1744), 1 Atk. 21, 26 E.R. 15 (C.A.).
50   *A.G. v. Bradlaugh* (1885), 14 Q.B.D. 667 (C.A.).
51   *R. v. Tuck* (1912), 19 C.C.C. 471, 2 W.W.R. 605, 5 D.L.R. 629 (Alta. C.A.).
52   Atheists could not be sworn, and a person whose religious beliefs precluded taking an oath could not be sworn: *R. v. Tuck, ibid.*; *Bell v. Bell* (1899), 34 N.B.R. 615 (C.A.); *R. v. Brasier* (1779), 1 Leach 199, 168 E.R. 202 (C.C.A.).
53   *Omychund v. Barker, supra,* note 49.

cance to some Chinese witnesses.[54] In the case of an Indian witness whose tribe had no form of oath, but believed in a Supreme Being and in a future state of rewards and punishments, it was held that the usual form of oath was sufficient.[55] Section 16 of the Ontario *Evidence Act* dictates the manner in which a witness *may* take the oath. The witness is to swear the oath upon the Old or New Testament by holding a copy in hand, or, where the witness objects to this form of oath, the oath can be taken in a manner or form and with such ceremonies as the witness declares binding.[56] Statutory provisions in many jurisdictions codify the common-law rule to the same effect.[57] Therefore, it no longer matters what type of ceremony is used.

The original common-law requirement of belief in a Supreme Being or spiritual retribution is no longer of importance. Nor is it likely any longer that a person will be considered incompetent to swear an oath because of non-recognition of its religious significance.[58] Indeed, a witness may take an oath without knowledge of its consequences.[59] The social reality is that for many adults the swearing of the oath has no religious significance. It is the solemnity of the ceremony which increases the witness' perception of the importance of telling the truth in court. This reality was recognized by MacKinnon J. in *R. v. Fletcher*[60] in the context of considering the competency of a child to give sworn evidence. He stated:[61]

---

54   *R. v. Wooey* (1902), 8 C.C.C. 25, 9 B.C.R. 569 (S.C.); *R. v. Entrehman* (1842), 174 E.R. 493 (N.P.); *R. v. Ping* (1904), 8 C.C.C. 467, 11 B.C.R. 102 (C.A.).

55   *R. v. Pah-Mah-Guy* (1860), 20 U.C.Q.B. 195 (C.A.); see also G.D. Nokes, *An Introduction to Evidence*, 4th ed. (London: Sweet & Maxwell, 1967), at 397-98.

56   R.S.O. 1980, c. 145, s. 16. See also Evidence Acts: Alberta, R.S.A. 1980, c. A-21, ss. 15, 16; Manitoba, R.S.M. 1987, c. E150, ss. 14, 15; Northwest Territories, R.S.N.W.T. 1988, c. E-8, s. 19(a); New Brunswick, R.S.N.B. 1973, c. E-11, s. 13 [re-en. 1983, c. 4, s. 6(1)]; British Columbia, R.S.B.C. 1979, c. 116, s. 23 (as to acceptability of Scottish form of oath); 11 C.E.D. (Ont. 3rd), Title 57 Evidence, at § 239, for a review of statutory provisions.

57   *Ibid.* For an example of the common law, see *R. v. Wooey, supra*, note 54.

58   The witness' competency to swear an oath may become an issue where an objection is raised by the witness.

59   *R. v. Bannerman* (1966), 48 C.R. 110, 55 W.W.R. 257; affd. without reasons [1966] S.C.R. v, 50 C.R. 76, 57 W.W.R. 736.

60   (1982), 1 C.C.C. (3d) 370 (Ont. C.A.); leave to appeal to S.C.C. refd. (1983), 48 N.R. 319.

61   *Ibid.*, at 377.

With deference, I do not think that the understanding of the nature of an oath in any legal proceeding now requires a belief or an expressed belief by the child in God (or another almighty). Nor does it require that the child [understand], in giving the oath, that he is telling such almighty that what he will say will be true.

It is recognized that as society has changed over the years the oath for many has lost its spiritual and religious significance. *Those adults to whom the sanctity of the oath has lost its religious meaning none the less have a sense of moral obligation to tell the truth on taking the oath and feel their conscience bound by it. That is the nature of the oath for many adult witnesses today.* Nor do they object on grounds of conscientious scruples to taking the oath. In my view, a child of tender years is in the same position as an adult witness when the determination is being made whether the child understands the nature of an oath. [emphasis added]

The comments of Laskin J.A. in *Horsburgh v. R.*[62] also question the validity of the religious basis upon which the right to give evidence depends.[63]

. . . at a distance of some 200 years from *Omychund v. Barker* . . . the contention that competency of a witness depends on demonstration that he or she is fearful of divine retribution (as an exclusive test) rather than early justice as the consequences of false testimony, is highly talismanic. The common law deserves better than that at the hands of the judiciary in the 20th century.

In light of these statements the validity of retaining the oath as a precondition of giving testimony is questionable. There is little difference between affirmation and swearing an oath. One can see the value in retaining some form of ceremony to impress the solemnity of the occasion upon the witness, but to retain both the oath and the affirmation could lead to invidious distinctions on issues of credibility

---

62   [1966] 1 O.R. 739, [1966] 3 C.C.C. 240, 47 C.R. 151, 55 D.L.R. (2d) 289 (C.A.); revd. [1967] 1 S.C.R. 746, 2 C.R.N.S. 228, [1968] 2 C.C.C. 288, 63 D.L.R. (2d) 699.
63   *Ibid.*, at 755 (O.R.).

between one witness who swears and another who affirms.[64] Perhaps even a simple reminder by the court to the witness of the obligation to tell the truth and the legal consequences which can result if the truth is not told might be sufficient.

The practice in swearing witnesses reflects the fact that the judiciary is not particularly interested in determining the significance of the oath to the witness. It is up to the witness to raise an objection if he or she has one. The practice is as follows: The trial judge should not raise any questions before swearing the witness. If, however, the witness objects to the form of oath or to taking an oath at all, the trial judge should ask the witness sufficient questions to determine whether any form of oath is binding on his or her conscience, and if the answer is affirmative, the particular oath conforming to the witness' belief should be administered. If the witness objects to an oath on the basis of conscientious scruples, the witness should be asked to affirm to tell the truth.[65] In the absence of objection, the witness is presumed to accept the oath administered. If the witness raises no objections, neither the judge nor counsel should question the witness as to whether the oath is binding.[66] Once the oath is administered and taken, the fact that the person sworn did not believe in the binding effect of the oath does not, for any purpose, affect the validity of the oath.[67]

---

64   For an interesting perspective on the oath requirements see A. Peter Nasmith (His Honour J.), "High Time For One Secular 'Oath'," The Law Society of Upper Canada Gazette, Volume XXIV, Number 3, September 1990, at 230.

65   *R. v. Sveinsson* (1950), 102 C.C.C. 366 (B.C.C.A.); *Roberts v. Poitras* (1962), 133 C.C.C. 86, 32 D.L.R. (2d) 334, 38 W.W.R. 247 (B.C.S.C.).

66   *Ibid.* As to questioning by the trial judge, where a witness objects to the oath, see *R. v. Tuck, supra,* note 51, per Simmons J; although P.K. McWilliams in *Canadian Criminal Evidence,* 3rd ed. (Toronto: Canada Law Book, 1988), at 34-35 expresses the view that if counsel has reason to suspect that a witness does not consider himself bound by the form of oath he should be challenged.

67   Some jurisdictions have a statutory provision to this effect. Canada, R.S.C. 1985, c. C-5, s. 15(2); British Columbia, R.S.B.C. 1979, c. 116, s. 22; Manitoba, R.S.M. 1987, c. E150, s. 18; New Brunswick, R.S.N.B. 1973, c. E-11, s. 15; arguably the common law is to the same effect, see *R. v. Sveinsson, supra,* note 65; *Curry v. R.* (1913), 48 S.C.R. 532, 22 C.C.C. 191, 13 E.L.R. 550, 15 D.L.R. 347; *Ram v. R.* (1915), 51 S.C.R. 392, 25 C.C.C. 69, 8 W.W.R. 613, 26 D.L.R. 267.

3. Affirmation

Today, individuals who object on grounds of conscientious scruples[68] to taking an oath may make an affirmation or declaration that is of the same force as if the individual had taken an oath in the usual form.[69] A witness to whose competence to take an oath objection is taken on the basis of religious belief may affirm.[70] However, the recent developments, suggesting that belief in a Spiritual Being or spiritual retribution is no longer required for a person to be competent to take the oath, may limit the availability of this objection to competency.[71] Generally, unless the requirement is waived,[72] every witness must either be sworn or affirmed to tell the truth before any evidence is taken from her or him. There are exceptions for children of tender years[73] and witnesses called to produce documents. Also, an extradition treaty may permit the reception of unaffirmed or unsworn evidence in extradition proceedings.[74]

An affirmation has the same effect in law as an oath.[75] False testimony given under oath or affirmation is subject to the same penalty.[76] Where an affidavit is affirmed, the fact establishing the right

---

68 Compare the interpretation of conscientious scruples in *R. v. Sveinsson*, *supra*, note 65, at 369 (B.C.C.A.) and *R. v. Leach*, [1966] 1 O.R. 106, 52 D.L.R. (2d) 594 (C.A.), at 111 (O.R.).

69 Evidence Acts: Canada, ss. 14, 15; Alberta, ss. 18, 19; British Columbia, s. 21; Ontario, s. 17; Saskatchewan, ss. 46, 50; New Brunswick, s. 14 [am. 1983, c. 4, s. 6(2)]; Nova Scotia, s. 62; Prince Edward Island, s. 13; Manitoba, s. 16.

70 *Maden v. Catanach* (1861), 7 H. & N. 360, 158 E.R. 512.

71 See this Chapter, II.D.2.

72 *Andrews v. Hopkins*, [1932] 3 D.L.R. 459, 5 M.P.R. 7 (N.S.C.A.).

73 See this Chapter, II.D.4.(b).

74 *Lind v. Sweden (Kingdom)* (1985), 23 C.C.C. (3d) 181, 20 C.R.R. 56 (Ont. H.C.J.); affd. (1987) 36 C.C.C. (3d) 327, 23 O.A.C. 62; leave to appeal to S.C.C. refd. [1987] 2 S.C.R. viii.

75 Evidence Acts: Canada, R.S.C. 1988, c. C-5, s. 14(2); Alberta, R.S.A. 1980, c. A-21, s. 18(2); British Columbia, R.S.B.C. 1979, c. 116, s. 21(4) [s. 21 re-en. 1988, c. 46, s. 27]; Manitoba, R.S.M. 1987, c. E150, s. 18; Saskatchewan, R.S.S. 1978, c. S-16, s. 46; Ontario, R.S.O. 1980, c. 145, s. 17(1); Interpretation Acts: Canada, R.S.C. 1985, c. I-21, s. 35 "oath"; British Columbia, R.S.B.C. 1979, c. 206, s. 29; Manitoba, R.S.M. 1987, c. I80, s. 22(1); Ontario, R.S.O. 1980, c. 219, s. 30(26); Yukon, R.S.Y. 1986, s. 21(1); Northwest Territories, R.S.N.W.T. 1988, s. 28.

76 *Canada Evidence Act, ibid.*, s. 15(2); see also s. 131 of the *Criminal Code*, R.S.C. 1985, c. C-46 [am. R.S.C. 1985, c. 27 (1st Supp.), s. 17].

of the witness to affirm must be set out in the affidavit.[77]

4. Children

(a) *Sworn Evidence*

A child over the age of 14 years is not considered a "witness of tender years" and is presumed to be competent to give sworn testimony.[78] Under the *Canada Evidence Act* a party who challenges the mental capacity of a proposed witness of 14 years of age or more has the burden of satisfying the court that there is an issue as to the capacity of the proposed witness to testify under oath or a solemn affirmation.[79]

Where the witness is under the age of 14 the court must inquire into the child's understanding of the nature of an oath before that child can be sworn. It is not necessary that the child understand that an oath has religious significance. The *Canada Evidence Act* has been amended specifically to require an inquiry into whether a witness under the age of 14 understands the nature of an oath or solemn affirmation, and is able to communicate the evidence. If so, the evidence is to be accepted upon the swearing of the oath or solemn affirmation.[80] In *R. v. Fletcher*, MacKinnon A.C.J.O. quoted:[81]

> The important consideration, we think, when a judge has to decide whether a child should properly be sworn, is whether the child has a sufficient appreciation of the solemnity of the occasion, and the added responsibility to tell the truth, which is

---

77 *Zajac v. Zwarycz*, [1965] 1 O.R. 575, 49 D.L.R. (2d) 52 (C.A.).
78 *R. v. Dyer* (1971), 17 C.R.N.S. 207, 5 C.C.C. (2d) 376, [1972] 2 W.W.R. 1, at 2 (W.W.R.); leave to appeal to S.C.C. refd. 17 C.R.N.S. 233n; *R. v. Bannerman, supra*, note 59; *R. v. Armstrong* (1959), 29 W.W.R. 141, 125 C.C.C. 56, 31 C.R. 127 (B.C.C.A.); *Horsburgh v. R., supra*, note 62, at 746 (O.R.); *Canada Evidence Act, supra*, note 76, s. 16.
79 *Ibid.*, s. 16(5) [re-en. R.S.C. 1985, c. 19 (3rd Supp.), s. 18].
80 *Ibid.*, s. 16(1), (2) [re-en. R.S.C. 1985, c. 19 (3rd Supp.), s. 18].
81 (1982), 1 C.C.C. (3d) 370 (Ont. C.A.), at 380; leave to appeal to S.C.C. refd. (1983), 48 N.R. 319; the quote is from Bridge L.N. in *R. v. Hayes*, [1977] 2 All E.R. 288, at 290-91. See also *R. v. Bannerman* (1966), 48 C.R. 110, 55 W.W.R. 257; affd. without reasons, [1966] S.C.R. v, 50 C.R. 76, 57 W.W.R. 736; *R. v. Horsburgh, supra*, note 62; *Re Truscott*, [1967] S.C.R. 309, [1967] 2 C.C.C. 285, 1 C.R.N.S. 1, 62 D.L.R. (2d) 545, at 368 (S.C.R.); *R. v. Taylor* (1970), 1 C.C.C. (2d) 321, 75 W.W.R. 45 (Man. C.A.); *R. v. Leonard* (1990), 37 O.A.C. 269 (C.A.).

involved in taking an oath, over and above the duty to tell the truth which is an ordinary duty of normal social conduct.

This case constituted a reversal of the previous position taken by the Ontario Court of Appeal requiring an appreciation of the oath's religious significance.[82] Although it may be helpful to inquire into a child's beliefs, it is not necessary.[83] A child under the age of six has been permitted to give sworn testimony.[84]

The trial judge or someone appointed by the judge may instruct the child as to the nature of an oath and may ask leading questions to determine whether or not the child has understood her or his instructions.[85] The same lesson may be administered to a proposed adult witness who is alleged to be incompetent to take the oath because of mental deficiency.[86] The determination of understanding is essentially a matter for the trial judge's discretion.

(b) *Unsworn Evidence*

The significance of swearing an oath, on the Bible or otherwise, is lost on many young children. Some statutory provisions, therefore, allow a child to give unsworn testimony, subject to a corroboration requirement with respect to their evidence.[87] A typical example of such provisions is s. 18 of the Ontario *Evidence Act*, which provides as follows:[88]

---

82 *R. v. Budin* (1981), 32 O.R. (2d) 1, 20 C.R. (3d) 86, 58 C.C.C. (2d) 352, 120 D.L.R. (3d) 356 (C.A.).
83 *R. v. Fletcher, supra*, note 81.
84 *Strachan v. McGinn*, [1936] 1 W.W.R. 412, 50 B.C.R. 394 (S.C.).
85 *R. v. Bannerman, supra*, note 81; *R. v. Brown* (1951), 99 C.C.C. 305, 12 C.R. 388, 27 M.P.R. 315 (N.B.C.A.).
86 See *R. v. Hawke* (1974), 16 C.C.C. (2d) 438, 3 O.R. (2d) 210 (H.C.J.), at 215 (O.R.); revd. on other grounds (1975), 7 O.R. (2d) 145, 29 C.R.N.S. 1, 22 C.C.C. (2d) 19 (C.A.).
87 The scope of the corroboration requirement is considered in Chapter 17, V.B.
88 R.S.O. 1980, c. 145. See also Evidence Acts: Canada, R.S.C. 1985, c. C-5, s. 16; Alberta, R.S.A. 1980, c. A-21, s. 20; British Columbia, R.S.B.C. 1979, c. 116, s. 5 [re-en. 1988, c. 46, s. 25]; New Brunswick, R.S.N.B. 1973, c. E-11, s. 24 [am. 1990, c. 17, s. 5]; Saskatchewan, R.S.S. 1978, c. S-16, s. 42 [re-en. 1989-90, c. 57, s. 4]; Nova Scotia, s. 63; Newfoundland, R.S.N. 1970, c. 115, s. 15A [en. 1972, No. 3, s. 2; 1972, No. 11, s. 2]; Manitoba, R.S.M. 1987, c. E150, s. 24.

18(1) In any legal proceeding where a child of tender years is offered as a witness and the child does not, in the opinion of the judge, justice or other presiding officer, understand the nature of an oath, the evidence of the child may be received though not given upon oath, if, in the opinion of the judge, justice or other presiding officer, as the case may be, the child is possessed of sufficient intelligence to justify the reception of the evidence and understands the duty of speaking the truth.

(2) No case shall be decided upon such evidence unless it is corroborated by some other material evidence.

A child of any age, even a very young age, may give unsworn evidence so long as that child is possessed of sufficient intelligence to justify the reception of the evidence and understands the duty of speaking the truth.[89] Most statutory provisions are framed in this way. Under the provincial statutes, once the requirement of understanding the religious significance of the oath is done away with and the inquiry becomes an understanding of the duty to tell the truth, the difficulty becomes one of differentiating the test for receiving sworn evidence from that for receiving unsworn evidence. This difference was explained recently by the Ontario Court of Appeal in *R. v. Khan*, where the child was four years and eight months old at the time of trial.[90] The difference is that in the case of unsworn testimony, the child need not understand that a moral obligation is being undertaken.[91]

An appreciation of the assumption of "a moral obligation" or a "getting a hold on the conscience of the witness" or (to refer to the factors stressed in *Fletcher, supra*) an "appreciation of the solemnity of the occasion" or an awareness of an added duty to tell the truth over and above the ordinary duty to do so are all matters involving abstract concepts which are not material to a determination whether a child's unsworn evidence may be received.

---

89 *R. v. Khan* (1988), 27 O.A.C. 142, 64 C.R. (3d) 281, 42 C.C.C. (3d) 197 (C.A.), at 148 (O.A.C.); affd. [1990] 2 S.C.R. 531, 79 C.R. (3d) 1, 59 C.C.C. (3d) 92, 41 O.A.C. 353, 113 N.R. 53.
90 *Ibid.* This was a case arising under the former provisions of the *Canada Evidence Act* which were similar to the current provincial statutory provisions.
91 *Supra*, note 89, at 147 (O.A.C.).

Any questions regarding the Bible, religion or the consequences of being in court are irrelevant to an inquiry into whether the child is competent to give unsworn testimony. MacLachlin J. of the Supreme Court of Canada on an appeal from the Ontario court's decision agreed with this analysis.[92] A simpler line of inquiry is sufficient.[93]

To satisfy the less stringent standards applicable to unsworn evidence, the child need only understand the duty to speak the truth in terms of ordinary everyday social conduct. This can be demonstrated through a simple line of questioning directed to whether the child understands the difference between the truth and a lie, knows that it is wrong to lie, understands the necessity to tell the truth, and promises to do so. It is to be borne in mind that under s. 16(2)[94] the child's unsworn evidence must be corroborated by some other material evidence. Any frailties that may be inherent in the child's testimony go to the weight to be given the testimony rather than its admissibility.

The test for the giving of unsworn testimony is whether the child's intellectual attainments are such that he or she is capable of understanding the simpler form of questions that it can be anticipated will be asked, is able to communicate the answer in an understandable manner, and understands the moral obligation to tell the truth. However, with respect to the giving of sworn testimony it will be extremely difficult to determine if the child understands the moral obligation to tell the truth beyond the understanding which questions eliciting whether the child understands the ordinary everyday obligation to tell the truth would demonstrate. It is doubtful whether the courts' statements in *Khan* do much to clarify matters. Further, whether the child gives sworn or unsworn testimony, the inherent weaknesses of the evidence will still be present and the trier of fact will still have to consider the weaknesses as going to the weight of the evidence.[95] Therefore, the distinction between the giving of sworn and unsworn evidence in relation to the evidence of children seems to

---

92   *R. v. Khan* (1990), 113 N.R. 53, at 60 (S.C.C.).
93   *Supra*, note 89, at 147-48 (O.A.C.); see also *R. v. Drolet* (1985), 68 N.S.R. (2d) 78, 159 A.P.R. 78 (N.S.T.D.).
94   This refers to the former s. 16(2), R.S.C. 1970, c. E-10.
95   *Supra*, note 89, at 148 (O.A.C.); *R. v. D. (D.)* (1991), 46 O.A.C. 189 (C.A.), at 196.

serve little purpose in light of the policy that has traditionally caused courts to view it with some scepticism. According to *Khan*, the amendments to s. 16 of the *Canada Evidence Act*, have not altered this distinction.[96]

The requirement of the provincial Evidence Acts that a person under 14 years of age who does not understand the nature of an oath or solemn affirmation but is able to communicate the evidence, may testify on promising to tell the truth, is a necessary step in a finding by the inquiring judge that the child or person understands the duty of speaking the truth.[97] The record should disclose the nature and scope of the judge's inquiry,[98] but if it does not the appellate court will not necessarily assume that it was insufficient.[99]

Section 16 of the *Canada Evidence Act*, as amended, is the exception to the typical statutory scheme. This provision provides, in full:

16(1) Where a proposed witness is a person under fourteen years of age or a person whose mental capacity is challenged, the court shall, before permitting the person to give evidence, conduct an inquiry to determine

(a) whether the person understands the nature of an oath or a solemn affirmation; and

(b) whether the person is able to communicate the evidence.

(2) A person referred to in subsection (1) who understands the nature of an oath or solemn affirmation and is able to communicate the evidence shall testify under oath or solemn affirmation.

(3) A person referred to in subsection (1) who does not understand the nature of an oath or a solemn affirmation but is able to communicate the evidence may testify on promising to tell the truth.

(4) A person referred to in subsection (1) who neither understands the nature of an oath or a solemn affirmation nor is able

---

96   *Ibid.*, at 148 (O.A.C.). The critical difference is corroboration, a matter considered in Chapter 17, V.B.
97   *R. v. Khan, supra,* note 89, at 148 (O.A.C.).
98   *R. v. Duguay* (1966), 48 C.R. 198, [1966] 3 C.C.C. 266 (Sask. C.A.).
99   *R. v. Dunn* (1951), 99 C.C.C. 111 (B.C.S.C.).

to communicate the evidence shall not testify.

(5) A party who challenges the mental capacity of a proposed witness of fourteen years of age or more has the burden of satisfying the court that there is an issue as to the capacity of the proposed witness to testify under an oath or a solemn affirmation.

This section of the *Canada Evidence Act* was considered by the Saskatchewan Court of Appeal in *R. v. D. (R.R.)*,[100] It was held that the procedure of the Act had not been complied with where the trial judge asked the six-year-old witness if she knew what it meant to tell the truth and what would happen if the truth were not told. The fatal omission was in not inquiring as to whether the child understood the solemnity of the occasion and the added responsibility to tell the truth upon taking an oath or making an affirmation. It was also an error to fail to extract from the child a promise to tell the truth. A new trial was ordered on the basis of these omissions. Bayda C.J.S. stated:[101]

> What s. 16 does, in effect, is create three classes of persons under 14 years of age who may testify: (i) those who understand the nature of an oath and are able to communicate the evidence; (ii) those who understand the nature of a solemn affirmation and are able to communicate the evidence; (iii) those who do not understand the nature of an oath or a solemn affirmation but are able to communicate the evidence. Before he may testify, however, a person in any one of these classes must first satisfy a prerequisite; a person in the first class must take an oath; a person in the second class must make a solemn affirmation; and a person in the third class must make a promise. The purposes of an oath, a solemn affirmation and a promise are the same: to put an additional impact on the person's conscience and to give further motivation for the person to tell the truth.

It is difficult to see why the failure to make an inquiry into the child's ability to understand the nature of an oath or affirmation was an error causing such prejudice to the accused as to justify a new trial. The Act abolishes any legal distinction between testifying upon a promise to tell the truth and upon oath or affirmation. The judge might very well

---

100 (1989), 69 C.R. (3d) 267 (Sask. C.A.).
101 *Ibid.*, at 274.

have found that the child had the capacity to testify under oath or upon affirmation if the inquiry had been made, but this would not have assisted the accused in any way.[102]

The Ontario Court of Appeal commented on the new provision in *R. v. Krack*:[103]

> We note that the inquiry is now mandatory, that the statutory requirement of corroboration of the unsworn evidence of a child has been eliminated and that the question whether a particular child is of tender years is no longer left to the discretion of the court.

Unlike the Saskatchewan Court of Appeal in *R. v. D. (R.R.)*, the Ontario Court of Appeal did not believe that the judge's failure to conduct the inquiry mandated by s. 16(1) was an error of substance or such a serious irregularity in procedure as to justify a new trial. This was a matter to be determined on a case-by-case basis.[104]

As noted, the Saskatchewan Court of Appeal held that s. 16 sets out three classes of persons under 14 years of age who may testify. However, there is one common criterion by which testimonial competence is determined for such witnesses and that is whether such person is able to communicate the evidence.[105]

E. Judges, Jurors, Lawyers

A judge or juror may not testify as a witness in a trial in which he or she sits as trier of fact. The reasons for a judge's incompetency are obvious:[106] Who rules on objections? Who compels him or her to answer? Can he or she rule impartially on the weight and admissibility of his or her own testimony? Can a judge, in a jury trial, avoid conferring his or her seal of approval on one side in the eyes of the jury? Can he or she, in a bench trial, avoid an involvement destructive of impartiality? Similar rationales support the incompetency of jurors

---

102　The decision is criticized in a case comment by N. Bala, "D. (R.R.): Too strict interpretation of the New Procedure for the Qualification of Child Witnesses" (1989), 69 C.R. (3d) 276.
103　(1990), 39 O.A.C. 57, 73 O.R. (2d) 480, at 58 (O.A.C.).
104　*Ibid.*, at 61 (O.A.C.).
105　*R. v. D. (D.)*, *supra*, note 95, at 195-96.
106　See the U.S. Federal and Revised Uniform Rules of Evidence, 605, to this effect.

as witnesses.[107] If a juror or judge has relevant personal knowledge of the matters in issue, then the juror or judge should disqualify himself or herself as an arbiter and assume the sole role of witness. Lawyers stand on a somewhat different footing. They are competent in law to appear as witnesses in an action in which they act as counsel.[108] Nevertheless, courts have been reluctant to allow a lawyer who has sworn an affidavit to appear as counsel in that matter.[109] It would place the court in the untenable position of having to assess the credibility of a counsel who has given evidence. Accordingly, the practice has developed of forbidding a lawyer to appear as both counsel and witness in a motion or an action.[110]

F. Burden of Proof on Competency Issues

Section 16 of the *Canada Evidence Act*[111] provides that where a party calls a child under 14 or a person whose mental capacity is challenged as a witness, the court shall conduct an inquiry to determine whether the witness may testify.[112] The legislation provides that if such person swears an oath, affirms, or promises to tell the truth and is able to communicate the evidence, the proposed witness may testify. Section 16(5) of the Act states:

A party who challenges the mental capacity of a proposed witness of fourteen years of age or more has the burden of satisfying the

---

107 See *R. v. Petrie* (1890), 20 O.R. 317, at 320-21 (C.A.). U.S. Federal and Revised Uniform Rules of Evidence, 606(a).

108 *Davis v. Canada Farmers Mutual Insurance Co.* (1876), 39 U.C.Q.B. 452, at 481 (C.A.); *Ward v. McIntyre* (1920), 48 N.B.R. 233, 56 D.L.R. 208 (C.A.); *Grady v. Waite* (1930), 1 M.P.R. 116, [1930] 1 D.L.R. 838 (P.E.I.); *Brett v. Brett*, [1937] 2 W.W.R. 689 (Alta. T.D.); affd. [1938] 2 W.W.R. 372, [1938] 3 D.L.R. 542 (Alta. C.A.).

109 *Williams v. Williams*, [1949] 1 W.W.R. 916 (Sask. K.B.).

110 *Bell Engine etc. Co. v. Gagné* (1914), 7 W.W.R. 62, 7 Sask. L.R. 154, 20 D.L.R. 235 (C.A.); *Parry v. Parry*, [1926] 2 W.W.R. 185 (Sask. C.A.); *Stanley v. Douglas*, [1952] 1 S.C.R. 260, [1951] 4 D.L.R. 689; *A & E Land Industries Ltd. v. Saskatchewan Crop Insurance*, [1988] 3 W.W.R. 590 (Sask. Q.B.).

111 R.S.C. 1985, c. C-5 [re-en. R.S.C. 1985, c. 19 (3rd Supp.), s. 18].

112 In *R. v. D. (R.R.)*, *supra*, note 100, the Saskatchewan Court of Appeal held that an inquiry was mandatory; see also *R. v. Krack*, *supra*, note 103. There are corresponding provisions in Provincial Evidence Acts which distinguish between sworn and unsworn witnesses of children of tender years.

court that there is an issue as to the capacity of the proposed witness to testify under an oath or a solemn affirmation.

The statutory language found in s. 16(5) is ambiguous. Does it mean that the challenging party has an evidential burden to adduce some evidence that the witness lacks the requisite mental capacity or must that party satisfy the court to a balance of probabilities that the witness does not have the capacity to testify? Curiously, the section is silent as to the incidence of the legal burden of proof and the standard of proof where the proposed witness is a child. Perhaps the legislation requires the trial judge to conduct the inquiry as to the competency of the child witness without the assistance of counsel, and thus, it is inappropriate to speak of either burden in these circumstances.

It is observed that the challenged competence of these witnesses relates to the reliability of their evidence. In contrast, spousal competency is justified on grounds of marital harmony, a distinct consideration. In *R. v. Yacoob*,[113] a prosecution for robbery, the accused objected to the competency of a Crown witness on the grounds of spousal immunity. The Court held that the matter should have been raised at the commencement of the trial and that the prosecution had the obligation to prove competency beyond a reasonable doubt![114] In today's society where divorce is commonplace and there are many statutory exceptions to spousal incompetency, the wisdom of requiring the criminal standard of proof for this preliminary fact is questionable. It is submitted that the challenging party should be required to prove incompetency only to a balance of probabilities.

III COMPELLABILITY

A compellable witness is one who may be forced by means of a subpoena to give evidence in court under the threat of contempt proceedings should he or she refuse to comply. Even though a statute makes a witness compellable to testify, the witness may nevertheless

---

113 (1981), 72 Cr. App. Rep. 313 (C.A.), folld. in *R. v. Khan* (1986), 84 Cr. App. R. 44 (C.A.).
114 R. Cross and C. Tapper, *Cross on Evidence*, 7th ed. (London: Butterworths, 1990), at 171-72 suggests that the challenging party bears the evidential burden, but the Court in *R. v. Yacoob* is silent on that issue.

invoke a privilege in certain circumstances of refusing to disclose the information sought by counsel. The law of privileged communications is considered elsewhere in this text.[115]

A. The Accused in Criminal Proceedings

1. General

The accused is not a competent or compellable witness at the behest of the Crown at his or her own criminal trial.[116] At common law the accused was not competent for either the prosecution or the defence. The issue of compellability, therefore, never arose at common law. The accused has been made competent by statute for the defence.[117]

The accused was first made competent in England with the passage of the *Criminal Evidence Act*, 1898. The first legislation in Canada on this subject was the *Criminal Procedure Act*,[118] which entitled the accused to testify for the Crown or the defence in common assault or assault and battery cases. This section was repealed with passage of the *Canada Evidence Act* in 1893,[119] s. 4(1) of which made the accused a competent witness. In *Gosselin v. R.*[120] the Supreme Court of Canada held that the legislative grant of competence necessarily carried with it compellability of the accused as with any other witness. In 1906 section 4(1) was amended to make it clear that the accused was competent only for the defence.[121] Since it is clear that an accused is not competent for the Crown, the issue of compellability does not arise.[122]

---

115 See Chapter 14.
116 *R. v. D'Aoust* (1902), 3 O.L.R. 653, 3 C.C.C. 407 (C.A.).
117 *Canada Evidence Act*, R.S.C. 1985, c. C-5, s. 4(1).
118 R.S.C. 1886, c. 174, s. 216.
119 S.C. 1893, c. 31.
120 (1903), 33 S.C.R. 255, 7 C.C.C. 139.
121 *An Act to Further Amend the Canada Evidence Act, 1893*, S.C. 1906, 6 Edw. VII, c. 10.
122 Recently, in *R. v. Amway Corp.*, [1989] 1 S.C.R. 21, 68 C.R. (3d) 97, 33 C.P.C. (2d) 163, [1989] 1 C.T.C. 255, 23 F.T.R. 160 (note), [1989] 1 T.S.T. 2058, 56 D.L.R. (4th) 309, 37 C.R.R. 235, 2 T.C.T. 4074, 91 N.R. 18 (*sub nom. R. v. Amway of Canada Ltd.*), Sopinka J. remarked that s. 4(1) of the *Canada Evidence Act* left intact the common law with respect to the non-compellability of an accused at the instance of the Crown. *Gosselin, supra*, note 120, was not considered. Although the point is probably academic with respect to an accused person, in

2. Co-Accused

These same common law and statutory rules apply to a co-accused who is being tried jointly at the time that the evidence is required.[123] Such an accused is a competent witness for the co-accused, but he or she is not compellable at the instance of the Crown to testify against the co-accused.[124]

Pre-*Charter*, if an accomplice was charged separately, tried separately or not charged, competence and compellability at the instance of the Crown and the defence existed.[125] Early *Charter* cases held that the privilege against self-incrimination embodied in ss. 7, 11(b) and 13 did not expand the accomplice's rights in this regard.[126] However, with the decision of the Supreme Court of Canada in *R. v. Hebert*[127] explicitly recognizing the embodiment of a right to silence in s. 7, this position may no longer hold. *Hebert* held that a person in the power of the state's criminal process has the right to freely choose whether or not to make a statement to the police. This right may be undermined if a person charged on a separate indictment is compelled to testify at a preliminary inquiry or trial of another person involved in

---

light of s. 11(c) of the *Charter*, it may still have some impact with the spouse of an accused or a co-accused.

123 See *R. v. Connors* (1893), 5 C.C.C. 70, 3 Que. Q.B. 100 (C.A.); *R. v. Blais* (1906), 10 C.C.C. 354, 11 O.R. 345 (C.A.); *Canada Evidence Act, supra*, note 117, s. 4(1).

124 *R. v. McLaughlin* (1974), 2 O.R. (2d) 514, 15 C.C.C. (2d) 562 (C.A.); *R. v. Agawa* (1975), 11 O.R. (2d) 176, 31 C.R.N.S. 293, 28 C.C.C. (2d) 379 (C.A.); R. Delisle, "Compellability of Co-accused" (1976-77), 19 Crim. L.Q. 28.

125 *R. v. Frank* (1910), 16 C.C.C. 237, 21 O.L.R. 196 (C.A.); *Ex parte Ferguson* (1911), 17 C.C.C. 437 (N.S.S.C.); *R. v. Payne* (1872), L.R. 1 C.C.R. 349 (C.C.A.); *R. v. Connors, supra*, note 123; *Winsor v. R.* (1866), L.R. 1 Q.B. 390, affirming L.R. 1 Q.B. 289; *Batary v. Saskatchewan (A.G.)*, [1965] S.C.R. 465, 46 C.R. 34, [1966] 3 C.C.C. 152, 51 W.W.R. 449, 52 D.L.R. (2d) 125; *R. v. Atwood* (1788), 1 Leach 464, 168 E.R. 334; *A.G. v. Bradlaugh* (1855), 14 Q.B.C. 667 (C.A.); *R. v. Blais, ibid.*; *Re Regan* (1939), 71 C.C.C. 221, [1939] 2 D.L.R. 135, 13 M.P.R. 584 (N.S.C.A.); *R. v. Caulfield* (1972), 10 C.C.C. (2d) 539, 10 C.R. (3d) 383 (*sub nom. Caulfield v. R.*) (Alta. C.A.).

126 *R. v. Crooks* (1982), 2 C.C.C. (3d) 57, 143 D.L.R. (3d) 601, 2 C.R.R. 124, 39 O.R. (2d) 193 (H.C.J.); affd. (1982), 2 C.C.C. (3d) 57, at 64n (C.A.); *R. v. Mazur* (1986), 27 C.C.C. (3d) 359, 26 C.R.R. 113, 1 Y.R. 13 (B.C.C.A.); leave to appeal to S.C.C. refd. 27 C.C.C. (3d) 359n.

127 [1990] 2 S.C.R. 151, 77 C.R. (3d) 145. This is discussed in more detail in Chapter 14, IV.E.2.

the same offence.[128] This issue was recently addressed by the General Division of the Ontario Court of Justice in *Praisoody v. R.*[129] Praisoody was charged separately from an alleged co-conspirator, Devasagayam. Praisoody challenged the subpoena issued on behalf of the Crown compelling him to testify at Devasagayam's preliminary inquiry. He argued that he would be obliged to answer questions concerning an agreement between himself and the accused. Although Praisoody would have the protection of s. 13 of the *Charter*, preventing his testimony from being introduced at his own trial,[130] the questioning could reveal possible defences in advance of the Crown establishing that there was a case to meet. The Supreme Court of Canada has recently held, in *R. v. Chambers*,[131] that no adverse comment can be made with respect to the accused's failure to raise alibi defences early when he has relied on the right to remain silent. There the court commented that, as a general rule, there is no obligation resting on the accused to disclose the defence or any details of it prior to the Crown completing its case. The Ontario Court in *Praisoody* concluded that to force Praisoody to testify would deprive him of his right to remain silent in a manner not in accordance with the principles of fundamental justice. Weiler J. did not believe, however, that a person facing separate charges arising out of the same incident could never be lawfully compelled to testify at an inquiry involving the other. She stated:[132]

> I do not wish to suggest that two persons facing separate charges arising out of the same incident will always be deprived of fundamental justice if compelled to testify at an inquiry involving the other. That would place too much emphasis on the rights of the individual and not give due regard to the interests of society

---

128 Watt J. suggested in *R. v. Welton* (1986), 29 C.C.C. (3d) 226 (Ont. H.C.J.) that a subpoena compelling a person to testify at a preliminary inquiry on an accomplice's charge could be questioned on this basis; see also *R. v. Zurlo* (1990), 57 C.C.C. (3d) 407 (Que. C.A.).

129 (1990), 61 C.C.C. (3d) 404 (*sub nom. R. v. Devasagayum*), 3 C.R. (4th) 91, 1 O.R. (3d) 606, 50 C.R.R. 335 (Ont. Gen. Div.) per Weiler J.; see also *R. v. Johnson* (1991), 4 C.R. (4th) 378 (Ont. C.A.).

130 Except for purposes of cross-examination on credibility; see *R. v. Kuldip* (1990), 61 C.C.C. (3d) 385, 1 C.R. (4th) 285, 43 O.A.C. 340, 114 N.R. 284, 1 C.R.R. (2d) 110 (S.C.C.) and Chapter 8, XII.B.

131 (1990), 59 C.C.C. (3d) 321 (S.C.C.).

132 *Supra*, note 129, at 417-18 (C.C.C.).

in uncovering and prosecuting serious crimes. It is apparent that within s. 7 these interests will have to be balanced in considering whether it is contrary to fundamental justice to compel the proposed witness in a particular case to testify. The nature of the proceedings, the history and nature of the charges, whether a charge was laid against the applicant prior to the subpoena to testify being served on him, and whether the Crown is willing to specify in a general way the nature of the questions which would be asked so as to avoid asking for disclosure of the proposed witness' defence or his complicity to the charge he is otherwise facing, or to give any other undertakings, are all factors to consider. The foregoing factors, of course, are far from representing a complete list. They are, however, of relevance to the instant application. The proceedings are criminal in nature; the applicant is jointly charged with Mr. Devasagayam with the identical offence arising out of the same incident; this charge was laid prior to the subpoena to testify being served on him and the Crown is not willing to specify that questions which would require Mr. Praisoody to disclose his defence or complicity will not be asked. Due to the nature of the charge, conspiracy, this would be difficult in any event. Even if the joint charge were withdrawn at this stage, one cannot ignore the history of the matter. Nor does the Crown propose to give an undertaking that it will not jointly indict Mr. Devasagayam and Mr. Praisoody once their separate preliminary inquiries are over. It is for these reasons that I have concluded that to force the applicant to testify would breach his rights under s. 7.

The subpoena was quashed on the basis of s. 24(1) of the *Charter* in order to prevent an anticipated breach of Praisoody's *Charter* rights under s. 7.[133]

3. Provincial Offences

A person charged with a provincial offence may be compellable at the instance of the Crown. The Ontario *Evidence Act*, s. 8(1),[134] for

---

133 See also *R. v. Johnson, supra*, note 129; *R. v. A.*, [1990] 1 S.C.R. 995, 77 C.R. (3d) 219, 55 C.C.C. (3d) 562, 47 C.R.R. 225. For a discussion of compellability before other government investigatory bodies see this Chapter, III.A.4.
134 R.S.O. 1980, c. 145.

example, places parties and their spouses, for the most part, on the same footing as other witnesses. Although the provision was probably intended to apply to civil cases, it is not so limited in its application.[135] Accordingly, a number of provincial statutes expressly provide that a defendant in a prosecution under a provincial statute is not compellable.[136] Even in those provinces which allow the Crown to compel the attendance of the person charged, it is rarely, if ever, that the Crown will violate the accused's right against self-incrimination by forcing the individual's attendance to give evidence. Section 11(c) of the *Charter* may apply to prevent this result.[137]

4. Collateral Administrative Proceedings

(a) Pre-Charter

In the former edition of this text the view was put forth that the principle of non-compellability of an accused also applied to collateral administrative proceedings such as coroners' inquests and investigative public inquiries, where the witness subpoenaed by the tribunal was or was liable to be criminally charged on the same matter into which the tribunal was inquiring. Relied on in support was the decision of the Supreme Court of Canada in *Batary v. Saskatchewan (A.G.).*[138] In *Batary* it was decided that an accused awaiting trial could not be compelled to give evidence at a coroner's inquiry into the death of the person with whose murder the accused had been charged. In rejecting the contention that the accused was a compellable witness before the coroner's inquiry, Cartwright J. said:[139]

---

135 See *Samwald v. Mills* (1977), 12 C.R. (3d) 249, 78 D.L.R. (3d) 219, 4 B.C.L.R. 113, 1 R.F.L. (2d) 292 (S.C.); *R. v. Greenspoon Bros. Ltd.,* [1967] 3 C.C.C. 308, [1967] 2 O.R. 119; but see Evidence Acts: Alberta, R.S.A. 1980, c. A-21, s. 4; Prince Edward Island, R.S.P.E.I. 1988, c. E-11, s. 4; Manitoba, R.S.M. 1987, c. E150, s. 4.

136 Evidence Acts: Newfoundland, R.S.N. 1970, c. 115, s. 3 [am. 1971, No. 48, s. 3]; Nova Scotia, R.S.N.S. 1989, c. 154, s. 48; Saskatchewan, R.S.S. 1978, c. S-16, s. 35(2) [am. 1988-89, c. 55, s. 28]; New Brunswick, R.S.N.B. 1973, c. E-11, s. 5 [am. 1990, c. 17, s. 3]; Ontario *Provincial Offences Act,* R.S.O. 1980, c. 400, s. 47(5).

137 See *R. v. Cohn* (1984), 42 C.R. (3d) 1, 15 C.C.C. (3d) 150, 48 O.R. (2d) 65, 10 C.R.R. 142, 13 D.L.R. (4th) 680, 4 O.A.C. 293 (C.A.), at 14-15 (C.R.). Leave to appeal to S.C.C. refd. (1985), 58 N.R. 160n.

138 *Supra,* note 125; *R. v. Denmark,* [1939] 2 W.W.R. 501 (Man. C.A.).

139 *Supra,* note 125, at 476 (S.C.R.).

It would be a strange inconsistency if the law which carefully protects an accused from being compelled to make any statement at a preliminary inquiry should permit that inquiry to be adjourned in order that the prosecution be permitted to take the accused before a coroner and submit him against his will to examination and cross-examination as to his supposed guilt. In the absence of clear words in an Act of Parliament or other compelling authority I am unable to agree that that is the state of the law.

This principle was extended by a British Columbia court to protect an individual who had been charged not with a crime but with an offence under a provincial statute. In *Re Coroners Act; Re Maddess*,[140] an accused who had been charged with careless driving was held not to be compellable before a coroner's inquest inquiring into the events which gave rise to the charge which was laid against the accused.[141]

However, in the years since *Batary* the common-law principle of non-compellability in collateral proceedings has been significantly eroded. In *R. v. Quebec (Municipal Commission); Ex Parte Longpré*,[142] the Quebec Court of Appeal held that an accused who had been charged with a crime was nevertheless a compellable witness before a provincial administrative commission set up pursuant to the provisions of the Quebec *Public Inquiry Commission Act*.[143] The Court distinguished the *Batary* case on a narrow ground. The latter involved a coroner's inquest and the preliminary inquiry in the related criminal proceeding had not yet been completed, whereas in the case at bar the inquiry was of a more general, administrative nature, and the accused had already been committed for trial at the preliminary inquiry so that his testimony before the provincial tribunal could not have any effect on the outcome of the preliminary inquiry.[144]

The significance of this distinction is elusive. The information forced out of the accused as a witness before the provincial inquiry could lead the police to evidence establishing his guilt, and that

---

140 (1967), 59 W.W.R. 698 (B.C.S.C.).
141 See also the Newfoundland *Evidence (Amendment) Act*, S.N. 1971, No. 48, s. 3 (containing the amendment to s. 3).
142 [1970] 4 C.C.C. 133, 11 D.L.R. (3d) 491 (Que. C.A.).
143 R.S.Q. 1964, c. 11.
144 See also *Re Inquiry re Department of Manpower and Immigration in Montreal* (1974), 22 C.C.C. (2d) 176 (Que. Commn. of Inquiry).

evidence would be admissible at his trial.[145] The limitation by the Quebec Court of Appeal of the *Batary* principle to coroner's inquests arguably emasculated the principle of *nemo tenetur seipsum accusare* in other important areas. As Dean Le Dain commented upon the compellability, generally, of an accused person before administrative tribunals:[146]

> The issue is the extent to which we are going to allow guilt to be determined by an inquisitorial form of justice — the extent to which inquiry may be used to undermine the protection which the accused should have in the criminal law process.
>
> Basically, what is involved here is the right of a man who is liable to criminal prosecution to have his guilt or innocence established through the criminal law process and not through a wide-ranging public inquisition in which he can be compelled to incriminate himself. In this area, inquiry usurps or undermines the function of the judicial process in the ordinary courts.

Another related question is whether a person who has not yet been charged with a crime, but is a prime suspect, should be compelled to testify before a provincial tribunal investigating the circumstances. In *Re Wilson*,[147] the British Columbia Court of Appeal held that such an individual could be compelled to testify before a coroner's inquest. The fact that the protection extends only to those individuals who have been formally charged with a crime or breach of a provincial statute is too technical and encourages the odious practice by the police of not immediately charging a suspect with a crime in the hope that, as a compellable witness before a coroner's inquest, he or she may reveal information which will lead the police to incriminating evi-

---

145 Whether s. 7 of the *Charter* would protect against the subsequent use of derivative evidence is discussed in Chapter 14, IV.E.1.

146 G.E. Le Dain, "The Role of the Public Inquiry in Our Constitutional System", in Jacob S. Ziegel (ed.), *Law and Social Change* (Osgoode Hall Law School of York University, 1973), at 91.

147 [1969] 3 C.C.C. 4 (*sub nom. R. v. McDonald; Ex parte Whitelaw*), 66 W.W.R. 522 (*sub nom. Re Wilson; Whitelaw v. McDonald*), 2 D.L.R. (3d) 298 (B.C.C.A.), reversing (*sub nom. R. v. Coroner of Langley*) [1968] 4 C.C.C. 49, 63 W.W.R. 108, 67 D.L.R. (2d) 541 (B.C.S.C.); see also *Faber v. R.*, [1976] 2 S.C.R. 9, 27 C.C.C. (2d) 171, 32 C.R.N.S. 3, 65 D.L.R. (3d) 423, 6 N.R. 29 and 8 N.R. 29; *Re Morris-Jones and R.* (1975), 28 C.C.C. (2d) 524 (Alta. C.A.).

dence. The rationale underlying the protection provided through the non-compellability of an individual who has been charged with a crime applies as well to those who are likely to be charged with a criminal offence. When it is clear that the individual is the prime suspect and there is a good possibility that he or she will be charged with a criminal offence, then the individual should not be subjected against his or her will to a gruelling examination before a provincial tribunal inquiring into the same matters.

In *Di Iorio v. Montreal Jail*,[148] the Quebec Police Commission launched an inquiry into all aspects of organized crime and it was required to report to the Lieutenant Governor in Council. The inquiry subpoenaed the two appellants who refused to testify and were, consequently, charged with contempt. The Court held that the inquiry did not interfere with the appellants' rights to protection against self-incrimination as they could claim the protection of s. 5(2) of the *Canada Evidence Act*. Again, *Batary* appears to be distinguished on the basis that no charges had been laid at the time of the inquiry.

The Alberta Court of Queen's Bench in *Re Sedlmayr and the Royal Commission into Royal American Shows Inc.*[149] refused to interfere in proceedings under the provincial *Inquiries Act* to look into certain matters which were already the subject of criminal charges. The Court believed that *Batary* did not reflect a general principle of non-compellability, but was to be restricted to coroner's inquests where charges had been laid.[150]

(b) *Post-Charter*

Section 13 of the *Charter*, s. 5(2) of the *Canada Evidence Act* and the various provincial evidence statutes, which prohibit the subsequent use in a criminal trial of the accused's testimony in the previous proceedings, provide some protection for an accused.[151] The extent of any additional protection conferred by s. 7 of the *Charter* is, as yet, not clear. Whether it could provide protection from the subsequent use

---

148 [1978] 1 S.C.R. 152, 33 C.C.C. (2d) 289, 35 C.R.N.S. 57, 8 N.R. 361.
149 [1978] 2 W.W.R. 169 (*sub nom. Royal American Shows Inc. v. Laycraft J.*), 39 C.C.C. (2d) 35 (Alta. S.C.).
150 See also *Re Robinson and R.* (1986), 28 C.C.C. (3d) 489 (B.C.S.C.) where it was held that s. 13 of the *Charter* offered no protection to those compelled to testify before such inquiries.
151 See Chapter 14, IV.

of evidence derived from the compelled testimony is discussed later in this text.[152] But the protection afforded by s. 7 could go so far as to allow certain persons to refuse to testify even before properly constituted investigatory proceedings. In *R. v. Hebert*,[153] the Supreme Court of Canada recognized that a citizen who has been brought under the coercive power of the state, either formally (by arrest or charge) or informally (by detention or accusation), has a right to remain silent. The applicability of this concept to the case of compelled testimony was commented on by the British Columbia Court of Appeal in *Haywood Securities Inc. v. Inter-Tech Resources Group Inc.*[154] The Court stated:[155]

> I agree that if the sole aim and purpose of the proceeding was to obtain evidence to support a charge or to assist the criminal prosecution of the witness, it might be arguable that the witness ought not to be compelled to divulge information which might lead to his conviction. But, in my view, such a result would follow only if the proceedings in which such evidence was given were so devoid of any legitimate public purpose and so deliberately designed to assist the prosecution of the witness that to allow them to continue would constitute an injustice. In such circumstances, the continuance of the proceedings could be said to constitute a violation of the principles of fundamental justice.

The right-to-silence principle was applied by the Federal Court of Appeal in *Tyler v. Minister of National Revenue*.[156] Here it was applied to protect persons who had been charged with offences under the *Narcotic Control Act* and the *Criminal Code* from having to supply information to the Department of National Revenue pursuant to its tax audit power under s. 231.1 of the *Income Tax Act*,[157] where the

---

152 Chapter 14, IV.E.1.
153 [1990] 2 S.C.R. 151, 77 C.R. (3d) 145.
154 (1985), 68 B.C.L.R. 145 (*sub nom. Haywood Securities Inc. v. Brunnhuber*), [1986] 2 W.W.R. 289, 7 C.P.C. (2d) 179, 24 D.L.R. (4th) 724 (C.A.). Leave to appeal to S.C.C. granted (1986), 68 N.R. 319 (note).
155 *Ibid.*, at 153 (B.C.L.R.) and the dissent of Lambert J. See also *R.L. Crain Inc. v. Couture* (1983), 10 C.C.C. (3d) 119, 6 D.L.R. (4th) 478, 9 C.R.R. 287, 30 Sask. R. 191 (Q.B.).
156 (1990), 120 N.R. 140, 91 D.T.C. 5022 (F.C.A.).
157 S.C. 1970-71-72, c. 63 [en. 1986, c. 6, s. 121].

information supplied could be used by the R.C.M.P. on the pending criminal charges. In most circumstances the tax audit power would not amount to a breach of s. 7. However, where concurrent criminal charges are pending, any communication of the signed statements to the police would amount to "conscripting" the declarant against himself in the existing criminal proceedings in a way that would deprive him, as an accused person, of his right to silence.

The Supreme Court of Canada in *Starr v. Ontario (Commissioner of Inquiry)*[158] has also recently limited the jurisdiction of the provinces to establish commissions of inquiry which investigate the criminal conduct of individuals. If such commissions cannot be established, then the citizen is indirectly protected from being compelled to testify against himself or herself.

The context of *Starr v. Ontario (Commissioner of Inquiry)*[159] was as follows: Mrs. Starr, Tridel Corporation and others challenged the jurisdiction of the Commissioner appointed pursuant to the Ontario Public Inquiries Act to inquire into the relationship among certain individuals, corporations and public officials. The terms of reference prohibited the Commissioner from making any findings of criminal or civil responsibility. It was argued that the proceeding was in relation to criminal law and therefore offended the Constitution. The Ontario Divisional Court disagreed.[160]

> It is considered that whether or not there is at the same time a police investigation into matters which may overlap the inquiry, the Commissioner is not concerned with that (he is on record as saying however that the original police investigation has been suspended). It may be, of course, that as the inquiry progresses situations may occur which would require protection of the guaranteed Charter rights of a party or witness; such situations ought to be dealt with as they arise.

This matter was appealed to the Ontario Court of Appeal[161] which confirmed that an inquiry was not invalid merely because it could

---

158 *Starr v. Ontario (Commissioner of Inquiry)*, [1990] 1 S.C.R. 1366, 55 C.C.C. (3d) 472 (*sub nom. Starr v. Houlden*), 41 O.A.C. 161, 68 D.L.R. (4th) 641, 110 N.R. 81; see § 44.
159 *Ibid.*
160 (1989), 70 O.R. (2d) 408, 37 O.A.C. 45, 62 D.L.R. (4th) 702 (Div. Ct.), at 419-20 (O.R.).
161 (1990), 71 O.R. (2d) 161, 64 D.L.R. (4th) 285, 37 O.A.C. 124.

reveal facts upon which criminal charges could be laid. In dealing with the allegation that *Charter* rights were inevitably violated in such an inquiry the Court stated:[162]

> As far as allegations of infringement of the *Canadian Charter of Rights and Freedoms* are concerned, we do not see any at this stage. As far as s. 7 is concerned, the protection of "the principles of fundamental justice" is textually related to *deprivation* of "the right to life, liberty and security of the person": *Reference re: Section 94(2) B.C. Motor Vehicle Act . . .* [1985] 2 S.C.R. 486 [at 500 and 511-13]. Here, as is the practice with inquiries, the commissioner reports and recommends; he does not order. As far as the Charter protections of non-compellability and of the presumption of innocence are concerned, they are both set out in s. 11 — paras. (*c*) and (*d*) respectively — and so are available to "any person charged with an offence", which is not the case with an inquiry, nor can it be. If criminal charges are laid, their protections can be claimed at the trial, as can the protection of s. 13 against self-incrimination. There is no question that the Charter applies to inquiries, but none of the allegations made before us involve a Charter infringement.

The Supreme Court of Canada ultimately held that this inquiry was *ultra vires* the province.[163] It confirmed, however, that if the inquiry were validly constituted the witness could be compelled to testify. The fact, however, that a person could be compelled to submit to questioning under oath with respect to suspected involvement in a criminal offence, for the purpose of gathering sufficient information to lay charges or establish a case, is an important element in determining the validity of the inquiry.[164] The clear implication is that no common-law rule or *Charter* right would prevent compelling the testimony of Patricia Starr or any of the others whose conduct was being investigated by a properly established and conducted inquiry.[165]

---

162 *Ibid.*, at 166-67 (O.R.).
163 [1990] 1 S.C.R. 1366 (*sub nom. Starr v. Houlden*), 55 C.C.C. (3d) 472, 41 O.A.C. 161, 68 D.L.R. (4th) 641, 110 N.R. 81.
164 See Lamer J., at 1409 (S.C.R.).
165 See Chapter 14, IV.E.2.

5. Parallel Civil Proceedings

A parallel problem faces a defendant in a civil action who at the same time is an accused in a pending criminal prosecution arising out of the same set of facts. If the civil action does not await the outcome of the criminal proceeding, he or she faces the prospect of being obliged to disclose the nature of his or her defence in a pleading; by having to produce documents; by being subject to oral examination for discovery; or by being a compellable witness at the civil trial. Nevertheless, Zuber J., in *Stickney v. Trusz*,[166] held that there was no general rule that civil cases should be stayed where criminal proceedings were pending relating to the same facts. Although the judge has a discretion to stay, it was only to be exercised in extraordinary or exceptional circumstances, where the witness proves that the refusal of the stay would affect his or her right to a fair trial.[167] The *Charter* has not affected the applicability of *Stickney*.[168]

B. *Spouse of Accused in Criminal Proceedings*

1. The Common Law Rule

The general law relating to spousal competency and compellability is marked with significant inconsistencies and is in serious need

---

166 (1973), 2 O.R. (2d) 469, 25 C.R.N.S. 257, 16 C.C.C. (2d) 25, 45 D.L.R. (3d) 275 (H.C.J.); affd. (1974), 3 O.R. (2d) 538, 28 C.R.N.S. 125, 17 C.C.C. (2d) 478, 46 D.L.R. (3d) 80 (Div. Ct.); affd. (1974), 3 O.R. (2d), at 539 (C.A.); leave to appeal to S.C.C. refd. (1974), 28 C.R.N.S., at 127*n* (Ont. C.A.).

167 For cases applying *Stickney* see *Haywood Securities Inc. v. Intertech Resources Group Inc.*, *supra*, note 146, per MacFarlane J.A., at 318 (W.W.R.); *Saccomanno v. Swanson* (1987), 49 Alta. L.R. (2d) 327, [1987] 2 W.W.R. 754, 34 D.L.R. (4th) 462, 75 A.R. 392 (*sub nom. Saccomanno v. Berube*) (Q.B.); *Laxton Holdings Ltd. v. Madill*, [1987] 3 W.W.R. 570, 18 C.P.C. (2d) 117, 26 C.C.L.I. 121, 56 Sask. R. 152 (*sub nom. Laxton Holdings Ltd. v. Non-Marine Underwriters*) (C.A.); *Potash Corp. of Saskatchewan Mining, Lanigan Division v. Todd*, [1986] 6 W.W.R. 646, 52 Sask. R. 231 (*sub nom. Potash Corp. of Saskatchewan Mining Ltd. v. Todd*) (Q.B.); *Kendall v. Hunt*, [1978] 3 W.W.R. 295, 9 C.P.C. 146 (B.C.S.C.); *Kay v. McGay Ltd.* (1979), 15 C.P.C. 111, 6 Man. R. (2d) 292, [1979] 5 W.W.R. 279, 101 D.L.R. (3d) 286 (Q.B.); *Event Sales Inc. v. Rommco Group Inc.* (1987), 17 C.P.C. (2d) 318 (Ont. Master); for a case where exceptional circumstances were shown see *Nutting v. Nutting* (1982), 134 D.L.R. (3d) 564 (Sask. Q.B.).

168 *Re Bookman* (1982), 44 C.B.R. (N.S.) 34, 142 D.L.R. (3d) 49 (Ont. S.C.); *Tricontinental Investments Co. v. Guarantee Co. of North America* (1982), 39 O.R. (2d) 614, 141 D.L.R. (3d) 741, 4 C.R.R. 181 (H.C.J.).

of rationalization at the legislative level.[169] The current law is a combination of statutory rules and common-law principles.

At common law the spouse of an accused person is, with one exception, not competent to give evidence either for or against the accused spouse[170] or a co-accused.[171] The policy behind the common-law rule is stated to be the promotion of marital harmony.[172] The rule does not apply, therefore, to divorced spouses[173] or to spouses who are separated with no reasonable prospect of reconciliation.[174] Whether it also applies to separated spouses where there is a prospect of reconciliation has yet to be determined by the courts. The rule also does not apply to common-law spouses.[175] In *R. v. Duvivier*[176] Farley J. of the Ontario Supreme Court considered whether the application

---

169 Per Morden J.A. in *R. v. Czipps* (1979), 25 O.R. (2d) 527, 48 C.C.C. (2d) 166, 12 C.R. (3d) 193, 101 D.L.R. (3d) 323 (C.A.); *R. v. Salituro*, unreported November 28, 1991 (S.C.C.).

170 *Moss v. Moss* (1963), 47 Cr. App. R. 222 (Div. Ct.); *R. v. Bissell* (1882), 1 O.R. 514 (C.A.).

171 Compare *R. v. Thompson* (1872), 12 Cox C.C. 202 (C.C.A.); *R. v. Bartlett* (1844), 1 Cox C.C. 105 (Assizes); *R. v. Thompson* (1870), 13 N.B.R. 71 (C.A.); in *R. v. Salituro* (1990), 38 O.A.C. 241 (Ont. C.A.), Justice Galligan reviews the origins of the rule, at 243-45; see also Justice Lamer's analysis in *R. v. Salituro, supra,* note 169.

172 *R. v. Bailey* (1983), 4 C.C.C. (3d) 21, 32 C.R. (3d) 337 (Ont. C.A.); *R. v. Salituro, ibid.,* at 249 (Blair J.A.); it was offered in *Leach v. R.,* [1912] A.C. 305 (H.L.) that the rationale behind the rule is that spouses are "one" and that there is, therefore, an inherent bias. This reasoning is clearly inapplicable in today's society.

173 *R. v. Bailey, ibid.,* at 23 (C.C.C.); see also *R. v. Marchand* (1980), 55 C.C.C. (2d) 77, 39 N.S.R. (2d) 700, 71 A.P.R. 700, 115 D.L.R. (3d) 403 (C.A.). See also *Police and Criminal Evidence Act, 1984,* 1984 (U.K.), s. 80(5) and *R. v. Cruttenden,* [1991] 3 All E.R. 242 (C.A.) reversing the English common-law position that a divorced spouse was not a competent witness to give evidence for the prosecution about matters which had occurred or been said during the course of the marriage.

174 *R. v. Salituro, supra,* note 169; see also *R. v. Fisher* unreported, July 31, 1986 (Ont. Prov. Ct.); but see *R. v. Pratte* (1975), 24 C.C.C. (2d) 74, [1975] Que. C.A.; *R. v. Wood* (1982), 8 C.C.C. (3d) 217 (Ont. Prov. Ct.).

175 One might, however, question the validity of such a distinction in today's society, which has a policy of not discriminating on the basis of marital status. *Coffin v. R.* (1955), 21 C.R. 333 (Que. C.A.); affd. "in effect" [1956] S.C.R. 191, 23 C.R. 1, 114 C.C.C. 1. *R. v. Cote* (1971), 5 C.C.C. (2d) 49 (*sub nom. Ex parte Cote*), [1972] 1 W.W.R. 737, 22 D.L.R. (3d) 353 (Sask. C.A.); *R. v. Duvivier* (1990), 75 O.R. (2d) 203, 60 C.C.C. (3d) 353 (Ont. Ct. (Gen. Div.)).

176 *Ibid.,* at 207-11 (O.R.).

of s. 15 of the *Charter* required that "common-law" spouses and legally married spouses be treated the same with respect to the compellability rule. The Court held that a common-law spouse was not discriminated against by reason of being compelled to testify against the other spouse. It has also been held that the rule does not apply where the events to which the spouse's evidence relates occurred prior to the marriage.[177]

The above-mentioned exception to the common-law rule is the case where the subject-matter of the charge against the accused is a threat of injury to the 'person, liberty or health' of the spouse.[178] The charge itself need not allege such a threat so long as the evidence does.[179] At common law, such a spouse is a competent witness for the prosecution in these circumstances,[180] but it is unclear whether this exception also renders a spouse compellable. The recent authorities are conflicting.[181] In *R. v. McGinty*[182] the Yukon Territories Court of Appeal found support for its view that compellability was included in the more general principle that a competent witness is a compellable witness.[183] Furthermore, public policy favoured a finding of compellability.[184]

> In my opinion, a rule which leaves to the husband or wife the choice of whether he or she will testify against his aggressor-spouse is more likely to be productive of family discord than to prevent it. It leaves the victim-spouse open to further threats and

---

177 *R. v. Bechard* (1975), 24 C.C.C. (2d) 177 (Ont. Prov. Ct.).
178 For a very early case considering this common-law exception see *The Lord Audley's Case* (1631), 3 State Tr. 401, 123 E.R. 1140 (H.L.).
179 *R. v. Czipps, supra,* note 169; *R. v. Sillars* (1978), 45 C.C.C. (2d) 283, 12 C.R. (3d) 202, [1979] 1 W.W.R. 743 (B.C.C.A.).
180 *R. v. McGinty,* [1986] 4 W.W.R. 97, 52 C.R. (3d) 161, 27 C.C.C. (3d) 36, 1 Y.R. 72, 2 B.C.L.R. (2d) 155 (Y.T.C.A.) per McLachlin J.A.; see also *R. v. Lonsdale* (1974), 15 C.C.C. (2d) 201, 24 C.R.N.S. 255, [1974] 2 W.W.R. 157 (Alta. C.A.); *R. v. Czipps, supra,* note 169; *R. v. Lapworth,* [1931] 1 K.B. 117 (C.C.A.); *R. v. Sillars, ibid.; R. v. Corran* (1978), 45 C.C.C. (2d) 365 (Ont. Prov. Ct.); *R. v. Giroux* (1985), 38 Sask. R. 172 (Q.B.); *Hoskyn v. Metropolitan Police Commissioner,* [1979] A.C. 474, [1978] 2 All E.R. 136 (H.L.).
181 *R. v. McGinty, ibid.;* cases cited *ibid;* see also *R. v. Salituro, supra,* note 169.
182 *Supra,* note 180.
183 *Supra,* note 180, at 100 (W.W.R.); the exception is that a sovereign and foreign diplomats are immune from the process of the court but they may waive their immunity by attending court to answer questions.
184 *Supra,* note 180, at 122 (W.W.R.).

violence aimed at preventing him or her from testifying, and leaves him or her open to recriminations if he or she chooses to testify. It seems to me better to leave the spouse no choice and to extend to married persons the general policy of the law that victims are compellable witnesses against their aggressor.

In *R. v. Czipps*,[185] the Crown sought to compel testimony of the spouse of the accused on a possession of a weapon dangerous to the public peace charge. Morden J.A. considered *Gosselin*[186] authority for the proposition that a competent spouse was also compellable. His Lordship was also of the view that policy considerations favoured compellability. Crimes of violence against spouses are grave offences and successful prosecution should not depend on whether or not the injured spouse is willing to testify against the attacker.[187]

The appropriate rule in terms of public policy considerations is difficult to define. From the point of view of the victim, the result of compellability or non-compellability will most likely turn on the dynamics of the particular family relationship.

The common-law exception was extended to cover a case where the spouse was a principle witness against her husband on a charge of child assault. The justification was that the welfare and protection of the child took precedence over a narrow interpretation of the common-law rule.[188] Otherwise, the common-law position, to the extent that it can be determined, remains intact so far as it has not been modified by statute.[189] Unless the charge involves violence against the spouse or family member, or falls within one of the statutory exceptions, the spouse is neither competent nor compellable for the

---

185 *Supra*, note 169.
186 *Gosselin v. R.* (1903), 33 S.C.R. 255, 7 C.C.C. 139.
187 Morden J.A. adopted the policy reasons given in dissent by Lord Edmund Davies in *Hoskyn v. Metropolitan Police Commissioner, supra*, note 180.
188 See *R. v. McPherson* (1980), 52 C.C.C. (2d) 547, 36 N.S.R. (2d) 674, 64 A.P.R. 674, 110 D.L.R. (3d) 582 (N.S.C.A.). Now see s. 4(4) of the *Canada Evidence Act*. See also *R. v. Fellichle* (1979), 12 C.R. (3d) 207 (B.C.S.C.); *R. v. McNamara* (1979), 48 C.C.C. (2d) 201, 12 C.R. (3d) 210 (Ont. Co. Ct.).
189 Subsection 4(5) of the *Canada Evidence Act* preserves the common-law exception.

prosecution.[190] However, the Ontario Court of Appeal in *R. v. Salituro*[191] exhibited a willingness to extend the common-law exceptions where to do so would conform to the realities of the present age.

2. Statutory Modifications

(a) *General*

The common-law position has been modified by s. 4 of the *Canada Evidence Act*.[192] Under the present Act, a spouse is specifically made competent for the defence. In the context of a predecessor to s. 4(1), the Supreme Court of Canada held that competence carries with it compellability.[193] Recently, however, the Supreme Court of Canada, in *R. v. Amway Corp.*[194] stated that s. 4(1) only addressed itself to competence and not to compellability. The statute was amended in 1906 to make it clear that it applied only on behalf of the defence and subsequent amendments make it clear that incompetence in s. 4(1) does not include compellability.[195] The question is whether a spouse, having been made competent by s. 4(1) for the defence, would be compellable for the defence. The Alberta Court of Appeal indicated in *R. v. Koester*[196] that the spouse could be compelled by the accused. However, if it is accepted that the spouse was neither competent nor compellable at common law, then in light of the comments of the Court in *Amway*, as a matter of statutory interpretation, there would seem to be no basis upon which to make this determination. It is,

---

190 *Ex parte Robichaud* (1925), 45 C.C.C. 181, 39 Que. K.B. 359, [1926] 1 D.L.R. 639 (C.A.); *R. v. Allen* (1913), 22 C.C.C. 124 (N.B.S.C.); *R. v. Pratte, supra,* note 174 (Que. C.A.); *R. v. Dillabough* (1975), 28 C.C.C. (2d) 482 (Ont. C.A.); *Canada Evidence Act,* s. 4(4). Note that the position in England is the opposite. A spouse who is competent by virtue of the common-law rule is not also compellable: *Hoskyn v. Metropolitan Police Commissioner, supra,* note 180.
191 (1990), 38 O.A.C. 241 (S.C.C.).
192 R.S.C. 1985, c. C-5, s. 4(1), as am. R.S.C. 1985, c. 19 (3rd Supp.), s. 17.
193 *Gosselin v. R.* (1903), 33 S.C.R. 285, 7 C.C.C. 139; see also *R. v. Koester* (1986), 70 A.R. 369 (C.A.).
194 *R. v. Amway Corp.,* [1989] 1 S.C.R. 21, 68 C.R. (3d) 97, 33 C.P.C. (2d) 163, [1989] 1 C.T.C. 255, 23 F.T.R. 160 (note), [1989] 1 T.S.T. 2058, 56 D.L.R. (4th) 309, 37 C.R.R. 235, 2 T.C.T. 4074, 91 N.R. 18 (*sub nom. R. v. Amway of Canada Ltd.*), per Sopinka J., but without a consideration of *Gosselin, ibid.,* and other authorities on this issue.
195 In particular see s. 4(2).
196 *Supra,* note 193.

however, not very clear that a spouse was not compellable at common law. A spouse being incompetent it was not necessary for the common law prior to 1883 to consider the issue of compellability. It is still unclear as to whether the common-law position prior to statutory reform was that competence carried with it compellability. This is a matter that the Supreme Court of Canada will have to consider fully and decide.

In any event, the spouse is still not generally competent or compellable on behalf of the Crown.[197] This seems to be an archaic position, at least on the issue of competency. First, there is an anomalous distinction between common-law and legal marital relationships.[198] Secondly, it is paternalistic. If a husband or a wife wishes to testify against the other spouse, why should society determine that it is in the best interests of that relationship that the testimony not be received? As Professor McCormick stated:[199]

The privilege has sometimes been defended on the ground that it protects family harmony. But family harmony is nearly always past saving when the spouse is willing to aid the prosecution. The privilege is an archaic survival of a mystical religious dogma and of a way of thinking about the marital relation that is today outmoded.

(b) *Exceptions*

The *Canada Evidence Act* provides for two exceptions to the general rule against compellability and competency for the Crown. Subsection 4(2) provides:[200]

---

197 R. v. Pratte (1975), 24 C.C.C. (2d) 74, [1975] Que. C.A. 61; R. v. Dillabough (1975), 28 C.C.C. (2d) 482 (Ont. C.A.); although it would appear that a spouse is free to communicate with the Crown out of court, see R. v. McKinnon (1989), 70 C.R. (3d) 10, 33 O.A.C. 114 (C.A.).
198 R. v. Marchand (1980), 55 C.C.C. (2d) 77, 39 N.S.R. (2d) 700, 71 A.P.R. 700, 115 D.L.R. (3d) 403 (C.A.); R. v. Mann, [1971] 5 W.W.R. 84, 4 C.C.C. (2d) 319 (sub nom. Re R. and Mann) (B.C.S.C.).
199 E.W. Cleary (ed.), McCormick on Evidence, 2nd ed. (St. Paul: West Publishing, 1972), § 65, at 145-46. See also Trammel v. U.S., 445 U.S. 40 (1980), where the court articulated that the privilege was no longer appropriate.
200 R.S.C. 1985, c. C-5, as am. R.S.C. 1985, c. 19 (3rd Supp.), s. 17. Originally enacted 1906, c. 10, s. 1, as s. 4(3).

The wife or husband of a person charged with an offence against subsection 50(1) of the *Young Offenders Act* or with an offence against any of sections 151, 152, 153, 155 or 159, subsection 160(2) or (3), or sections 170 to 173, 179, 212, 215, 218, 271 to 273, 280 to 283, 291 to 294 or 329 of the *Criminal Code*, or an attempt to commit any such offence, is a competent and compellable witness for the prosecution without the consent of the person charged.

These offences include sexual offences, bigamy, polygamy, unlawful solemnization of marriage, breach of custody orders, theft by spouses, and the like. Subsection 4(4) states:[201]

(4) The wife or husband of a person charged with an offence against any of sections 220, 221, 235, 236, 237, 239, 240, 266, 267, 268 or 269 of the *Criminal Code* where the complainant or victim is under the age of fourteen years is a competent and compellable witness for the prosecution without the consent of the person charged.

These offences include murder, criminal negligence causing bodily harm or death and sexual assaults against children, among other things.

The present statutory scheme attempts in a rough fashion to balance the competing interests of the need for the court to receive relevant information about a crime and the need to foster marital harmony and to protect a confidential relationship. Also, compelling a person to testify against a spouse may be viewed unfavourably by some persons.[202] Although the inclusion of sexual assault and incest offences in s. 4(4) is understandable, it is not clear why other offences, such as robbery with violence, are excluded from the list. Section 4(4) appears even more arbitrary than s. 4(2). It is difficult to justify on grounds of principle why a spouse is competent and compellable in a murder case where the victim is 13 but not when the victim is 15 years of age. The patchwork approach found in ss. 4(2) and 4(4) adds force to the judicial suggestion that Parliament must comprehensively rationalize the law governing competency and compellability.[203]

---

201 *Ibid.*
202 *R. v. McGinty*, [1986] 4 W.W.R. 97, at 121, 52 C.R. (3d) 161, 27 C.C.C. (3d) 36, 1 Y.R. 72, 2 B.C.L.R. (2d) 155 (Y.T.C.A.).
203 *R. v. Czipps* (1979), 25 O.R. (2d) 527, 48 C.C.C. (2d) 166, 12 C.R. (3d) 193,

C. Parties in Civil Proceedings

As a general rule, all parties to civil proceedings are competent and compellable to give evidence at the instance of any of the other parties.[204] They are also compellable to produce any and all relevant documents.[205]

There was some limited indication in the case law of the recognition of a form of non-compellability in civil cases involving a forfeiture or a penalty. The Supreme Court of Canada recently considered this issue in *R. v. Amway Corp.*[206] The corporate defendant was the subject of an action by the federal government in the Federal Court to enforce a forfeiture of goods and a penalty under the *Customs Act*. The Crown sought an order to compel the defendant to produce an officer for discovery pursuant to the Federal Court *Rules of Practice*. One of the grounds raised to resist the motion was that the officer was not compellable for discovery pursuant to this common-law principle. The Court noted that there may have been a common-law right not to be compelled to testify at trial at the instance of the party seeking to enforce a penalty or forfeiture.[207] Besides noting that these particular common-law rules did not apply to corporations (relying on previous authority to that effect), the Court also took the position that these rules had no place in modern Canadian law. The *Rules of Civil Procedure* and s. 5 of the *Canada Evidence Act* replaced "any shadowy existence . . . these rules may have enjoyed in Canada."[208] These common-law rules were based on a practice in England which applied to trial as well as discovery and the clear implication from *Amway* is that in neither case is it applicable in Canada.

---

101 D.L.R. (3d) 323 (C.A.); see also R. Cross and C. Tapper, *Cross on Evidence*, 7th ed. (London: Butterworths, 1990), at 213-19 for the modern law of England.
204 Evidence Acts: Alberta, R.S.A. 1980, c. A-21, s. 4; British Columbia, R.S.B.C. 1979, c. 116, s. 4(1); New Brunswick, R.S.N.B. 1973, c. E-11, s. 3(1); Nova Scotia, R.S.N.S. 1989, c. 154, s. 45; Newfoundland, R.S.N. 1970, c. 115, s. 2; Manitoba, R.S.M. 1987, c. E150, s. 4; Prince Edward Island, R.S.P.E.I. 1988, c. E-11, s. 4; Saskatchewan, R.S.S. 1978, c. S-16, s. 35(1). See also *R. v. Barnes* (1921), 36 C.C.C. 40, 61 D.L.R. 623, 49 O.L.R. 374 (C.A.).
205 *Hannum v. McRae* (1898), 18 P.R. 185 (Ont. C.A.); the rules of civil procedure in the respective provinces also contain provisions with respect to the production of documents.
206 *Supra*, note 194.
207 *A.-G. v. Radloff* (1854), 10 Exch. 84, 156 E.R. 366.
208 *Supra*, note 194, at 36.

D. Spouses in Civil and Criminal Proceedings[209]

A number of statutes provide that no spouse is compellable to disclose any communication made to him or her by the other spouse during their marriage.[210] It is unclear whether this is properly a matter of privilege or compellability.[211]

E. Judges, Lawyers, Jurors

Judges are not compellable to testify about their decisions or the basis upon which they reached them.[212] This rule also may apply to Justices of the Peace.[213] It has also been held that this rule applies to members of administrative tribunals called to testify in subsequent judicial review proceedings.[214] The principle is not restricted to subsequent proceedings that are to review the actual decision in issue, but applies to any subsequent judicial proceeding in which it is sought to compel the attendance of the judge or tribunal members.

There may be some cases in which members of the judiciary will be compellable. In *Clendenning v. Belleville (Municipality) Commissioners of Police*,[215] the Court held that if the evidence relates to some matter collateral to the decision, that is not inextricably bound up with the decision itself, the decision-maker may be amenable to subpoena. Judge Clendenning had made certain comments during the course of a criminal trial about the demeanour and conduct of two police officers, one of whom was a witness and the other of whom was sitting

---

209 The compellability of spouses of accused persons is considered in this Chapter, III.B.
210 Evidence Acts: Canada, R.S.C. 1985, c. C-5, s. 4(3); Alberta, R.S.A. 1980, c. A-21, s. 8; Prince Edward Island, R.S.P.E.I. 1988, c. E-11, s. 9; Newfoundland, R.S.N. 1970, c. 115, s. 4; Nova Scotia, R.S.N.S. 1989, c. 154, s. 49; Saskatchewan, R.S.S. 1978, c. S-16, s. 36; New Brunswick, R.S.N.B. 1973, c. E-11, s. 10; British Columbia, R.S.B.C. 1979, c. 116, s. 8; Manitoba, R.S.M. 1987, c. E150, s. 8; Ontario, R.S.O. 1980, c. 145, s. 11.
211 It will be dealt with in this text as a matter of privilege. See Chapter 14, II.C.
212 *MacKeigan v. Hickman*, [1989] 2 S.C.R. 796, 50 C.C.C. (3d) 449, 61 D.L.R. (4th) 688; *Clendenning v. Belleville (Municipality) Commissioners of Police* (1976), 15 O.R. (2d) 97, 33 C.C.C. (2d) 236, 75 D.L.R. (3d) 33 (Ont. Div. Ct.).
213 See Martin J.A. in *R. v. Moran* (1987), 36 C.C.C. (2d) 225, 21 O.A.C. 257 (C.A.); *Sirros v. Moore*, [1974] 3 All E.R. 776 (C.A.).
214 *Agnew v. Ont. Assn. of Architects* (1987), 64 O.R. (2d) 8, 30 Admin. L.R. 285 (Div. Ct.).
215 *Supra*, note 212.

in the courtroom waiting to be called as a witness. The Board of Police Commissioners, inquiring into the conduct of these officers on a charge of discreditable conduct, subpoenaed the judge. The Ontario Divisional Court held the judge competent, but not compellable. Steele J. stated:[216]

> Although there is no distinction between a Judge of a superior or inferior Court, I hold that there is a distinction between what happens within the trial and collateral incidents occurring during such trial. In the present case, the one police constable was a witness at the trial and, therefore, was part of that trial and I find that the Judge cannot be compelled to give evidence with respect to this evidence or conduct. The other police constable did not give evidence, but was present in the court-room awaiting his turn to give evidence and therefore, on the surface, was not part of the trial. However, from a review of the transcript, if the Judge were required to appear before the Board of Police Commissioners to give evidence relating to the conduct of the constable who did not give evidence, the conduct was such that it was [inextricably] entwined with the conduct of the constable who did give evidence and therefore the Judge would be subjected to questions relating to matters dealing with the trial. I therefore hold that the Judge is not compelled to give evidence with respect to either of the constables.

Thus, statements or conduct outside the decision-making process might render the decision-maker compellable.[217]

The Supreme Court of Canada has recently considered whether the principle of judicial immunity extends to evidence of administrative functions of the court. In *MacKeigan v. Hickman*[218] the commissioner of a public inquiry sought to compel the attendance of judges who had sat on a criminal appeal to answer questions relating to why the former Attorney-General had been chosen to sit on the panel, what formal record the Court had had before it and why the Court had concluded that there had been no miscarriage of justice. McLaughlin J., for three of five majority members of the Court, held that the *Public Inquiries Act* of Nova Scotia did not contain specific

---

216 *Supra*, note 212, at 102 (O.R.).
217 *Canada Metal Co. v. Heap* (1975), 7 O.R. (2d) 185, 54 D.L.R. (3d) 641 (C.A.).
218 *Supra*, note 212.

enough language to override the fundamental principles of judicial immunity and of protecting the independence of the judiciary. Those principles applied to both administrative and adjudicative decisions. Lamer J. would have permitted an inquiry into the administrative aspects, but only by the Canadian Judicial Council. La Forest J. went further, holding that the province had no constitutional jurisdiction to inquire into matters affecting the independence of the judiciary. The dissenters, Cory and Wilson JJ. would have permitted the subpoena to stand with respect to the giving of evidence as to participation of the Attorney-General and the state of the record, but not with respect to the administration function. It is submitted that if the policy of the rule of judicial non-compellability is to protect the independence of the judiciary then it should apply to administrative as well as adjudicative functions.

F. Foreign Diplomats and the Crown

The Sovereign and heads or agents of foreign states are not compellable witnesses in judicial proceedings.[219] This stems from a general immunity from legal process.[220] Also, other persons such as diplomats and members of their families, consuls and persons connected with various international organizations enjoy immunity, either complete or partial, from the process of the subpoena.[221]

G. Others

1. Illegality of Disclosure Under Foreign Statute

It was held in *R. v. Spencer*[222] that a witness in a libel proceeding could be compelled to disclose information to the court, notwith-

---

219 *State Immunity Act*, R.S.C. 1985, c. S-18.
220 For a general description of the classes of sovereign immunity see J. McLeod, *The Conflict of Laws* (Toronto: Carswell, 1987), at 67-78.
221 See Vienna Convention on Diplomatic Relations, ratified by *Diplomatic Consular Privileges and Immunities Act*, R.S.C. 1985, c. P-22, arts. 31(2) and 37(1) of Schedule I; art. 44 of Schedule II; *Privileges and Immunities (North Atlantic Treaty Organization) Act*, R.S.C. 1985, c. P-24; *Privileges and Immunities (International Organizations) Act*, R.S.C. 1985, c. P-23; refer also to customary principles of International Law.
222 [1985] 2 S.C.R. 278, 48 C.R. (3d) 265, 21 C.C.C. (3d) 385, 11 O.A.C. 207, 85 D.T.C. 5446, [1985] 2 C.T.C. 311, 21 D.L.R. (4th) 756, [1986] D.L.Q. 80, 62 N.R. 81.

standing that a foreign statute made it unlawful for the person to do so. Furthermore, s. 7 of the *Charter* could not avail the witness since it was the foreign law, not the Canadian law, that interfered with the person's liberty and security.

2. Answers to Questions Would be Privileged

In *Mulroney v. Coates*[223] Catzman J. refused to enforce letters of request from the Nova Scotia court asking that Prime Minister Mulroney submit to an examination for discovery in a libel action. It appeared that the line of inquiry to be taken with Mr. Mulroney would have fallen within the public interest immunity enjoyed by the Crown. In the circumstances, Catzman J. exercised his discretion against enforcing the letters of request.[224] In our view, this case should not be viewed as standing for the principle that a witness cannot be compelled to testify where he or she could only testify as to privileged matters. If this were a general principle the line between compellability and evidentiary privilege would be blurred. The decision can be attributed either to the special nature of letters of request or to the judicial reluctance to force a high level politician to testify where the information sought was not crucial to the case.

---

223 (1986), 54 O.R. (2d) 353, 8 C.P.C. (2d) 109 (*sub nom. Southam Inc. v. Mulroney*), 27 D.L.R. (4th) 118 (Ont. H.C.J.).
224 For a discussion of Public Interest Immunity, see Chapter 15.

CHAPTER 14

PRIVILEGE

I INTRODUCTION

Hearsay, opinion and character evidence are barred generally because these types of evidence possess inherent unreliability, lack of probative worth and susceptibility to fabrication. These are all dangers related to the adversarial method of ascertaining the truth. In order to minimize the risk of the trier of fact relying on untested and untrustworthy proof, such evidence is excluded from the fact finding process. The exclusionary rule of privilege, however, rests upon a different foundation. It is based upon social values, external to the trial process.[1] Although such evidence is relevant, probative and trustworthy, and would thus advance the just resolution of disputes, it is excluded because of overriding social interests.[2]

In any discussion about privileges, one must keep in mind the constant conflict between two countervailing policies. On the one hand, there is the policy which promotes the administration of justice requiring that all relevant probative evidence relating to the issues be before the court so that it can properly decide the issues on the merits. On the other hand, there may be a social interest in preserving and encouraging particular relationships that exist in the community at large, the viability of which are based upon confidential communications. Normally these communications are not disclosed to anyone outside that relationship.

Anglo-Canadian law has, for the most part, given priority to the administration of justice over external social values. In fact, the trend

---

1 One branch of solicitor-client privilege, however, is based upon the adversarial nature of our trial process: see this Chapter, II.B.1.
2 *R. v. Gruenke*, not yet reported, October 24, 1991 (S.C.C.), *per* Lamer C.J.C., at 20, and L'Heureux-Dubé J., at 2.

in Canada is to limit the recognition of privileges in favour of the search for truth in the judicial process.[3] The traditional common law has recognized a protective privilege for communications within only the solicitor and client relationship. Statutory law has established a privilege with respect to spousal communications,[4] and in certain jurisdictions, confidences within other relationships such as clergyman and parishioner are also maintained by statutory privilege.[5]

Although there exist numerous other personal and professional relationships, the existence of which turns upon confidentiality of communication, the courts have not recognized an identifiable *prima facie* privilege in their favour. The classic statement in this regard was made in 1881 by Master of the Rolls Jessel in *Wheeler v. LeMarchant*[6] as follows:[7]

In the first place, the principle protecting confidential communications is of a very limited character. It does not protect all confidential communications which a man must necessarily make in order to obtain advice, even when needed for the protection of his life, or of his honour, or of his fortune. There are many communications which, though absolutely necessary because without them the ordinary business of life cannot be carried on, still are not privileged. The communications made to a medical man whose advice is sought by a patient with respect to the probable origin of the disease as to which he is consulted, and which must necessarily be made in order to enable the medical man to advise or to prescribe for the patient, are not protected. Communications made to a priest in the confessional on matters perhaps considered by the penitent to be more important even than his life or his fortune, are not protected. Communications made to a friend with respect to matters of the

---

3   *Per* L'Heureux-Dubé J. in *R. v. Gruenke, ibid.*, at 17.
4   B. McLachlin, "Confidential Communications and the Law of Privilege" (1970), 11 U.B.C.L.R. 266, at 267. There has been some debate as to whether the original privilege for spousal communications is statutory or had its roots in common law. See this Chapter, II.C.1.
5   See this Chapter, II.D.
6   (1881), 17 Ch. D. 675 (C.A.).
7   *Ibid.*, at 681-82. See also *A.G. v. Mulholland; A.G. v. Foster*, [1963] 2 Q.B. 477, [1963] 1 All E.R. 767 (C.A.), at 771 (All E.R.); *W. v. Egdell*, [1990] 1 All E.R. 835, at 848 (C.A.).

most delicate nature, on which advice is sought with respect to a man's honour or reputation, are not protected. Therefore it must not be supposed that there is any principle which says that every confidential communication which it is necessary to make in order to carry on the ordinary business of life is protected. The protection is of a very limited character, and in this country is restricted to the obtaining the assistance of lawyers, as regards the conduct of litigation or the rights to property.

From time to time, however, the courts have shown, albeit hesitantly, a more flexible and pragmatic approach to protecting other specific relationships in certain circumstances. These attempts to expand the doctrine of privilege were bolstered by the Supreme Court of Canada decision in *Slavutych v. Baker*[8] but as yet they have not resulted in the creation of new, identifiable privileges in Canada.

In addition to concerning itself with the protection of confidential communications within certain important societal relationships, privilege may be invoked to preserve society as a whole when disclosure may jeopardize the national security of the country or impair the expeditious administration of the government or hinder police authorities in obtaining information from sources.[9] At a personal level, privilege may serve to shield a witness from his or her own testimonial self-incrimination[10] or to encourage disputing parties to speak openly with a view to reconciling or settling their differences.[11] These categories of privilege are based upon diverse sets of external values worthy of protection even in the face of hindering the effectiveness of the trial process.[12] Accordingly, there always exists a tension when the

---

8   [1976] 1 S.C.R. 254, 38 C.R.N.S. 306, [1975] 4 W.W.R. 620, 75 C.L.L.C. 14,263, 55 D.L.R. (3d) 224.
9   See Chapter 15. In fact, this is not accurately described as privilege, but as an "immunity from disclosure".
10   See this Chapter, IV.
11   See this Chapter, III.
12   Lord Simon in *D. v. National Society for Prevention of Cruelty to Children*, [1978] A.C. 171, [1977] 1 All E.R. 589 (H.L.) who was quoted with approval by the Ontario Court of Appeal in *Reference re Legislative Privilege* (1978), 39 C.C.C. (2d) 226 at 234 stated: "The various classes of excluded relevant evidence may for ease of exposition be presented under different colours. But in reality they constitute a spectrum, refractions of the single light of a public interest which may outshine that of the desirability that all relevant evidence should be adduced to a court of law."

doctrine of privilege is invoked as it consequentially obstructs the truth finding process. That being the natural result, the Courts have not shown great eagerness to proliferate the areas of privilege. Chief Justice Warren Burger put it this way in a celebrated American case:[13]

> Whatever their origins, these exceptions to the demand for every man's evidence are not lightly created nor expansively construed, for they are in derogation of the search for truth.

Accordingly, before consideration is given to broadening the existing limits of the doctrine of privilege it would have to be clearly demonstrated that the external social policy in question is of such unequivocal importance that it cannot be sacrificed before the altar of the courts.[14]

II CONFIDENTIAL COMMUNICATIONS WITHIN SPECIAL RELATIONSHIPS

A. *A Rule of Evidence as Distinct from Ethical or Equitable Principles of Confidence*

Although confidentiality is the cornerstone for the protection of communications within particular relationships, confidentiality alone is not sufficient to attract privilege.[15] Confidentiality may well attract other legal and ethical rights and obligations but it does not have its foundation in the evidentiary doctrine of privilege.

Evidence law does not concern itself with the ethical requirement upon a professional such as a lawyer to hold in strict confidence all information acquired in the course of his or her professional relationship concerning the business and affairs of a client.[16] The

---

13 *United States v. Nixon*, 94 S. Ct. 3090, 3108 (1974).
14 *R. v. Gruenke, supra*, note 2, at 23 *per* L'Heureux-Dubé J.
15 *MacMillan Bloedel Ltd. v. West Vancouver Assessment Area Assessors* (1982), 34 B.C.L.R. 111, 24 C.P.C. 183, 130 D.L.R. (3d) 675, at 681 (B.C.S.C.); *D. v. National Society for Prevention of Cruelty to Children, supra*, note 12.
16 Lord Denning described the distinction in *Parry-Jones v. Law Society*, [1968] 1 All E.R. 177 (C.A.), at 178. Also, see F. Bennett, "Confidentiality in a Solicitor and Client Relationship" (1989), 23 L.S.U.C. Gazette 259. As to the duty of confidentiality between a banker and customer, see *Standard Investments Ltd. v. Canadian Imperial Bank of Commerce* (1983), 45 O.R. (2d) 16, 24 B.L.R. 1, 5 D.L.R. (4th) 452, at 483 (Ont. H.C.J.), revd. on other grounds (1985), 52 O.R. (2d) 473, 30 B.L.R. 193, 11 O.A.C. 318, 22 D.L.R. (4th) 410; leave to appeal to S.C.C. refd.

lawyer has a professional duty not to divulge such information without the client's approval or unless required by law to do so. This ethical rule is wider than the evidentiary solicitor-client privilege and applies without regard to the nature of the source of the information or the fact that others may share the knowledge.[17] Where there is a stronger public interest in disclosure, it will override the professional duties of confidence.[18]

Furthermore, the evidentiary privilege of solicitor-client is different from the principles in equity protecting against breach of confidence. This distinction is best illustrated in the case of *Slavutych v. Baker.*[19] It dealt with the situation where "P" who has received a communication in confidence from "D" attempts to use that confidential information in proceedings against "D". A professor at the University of Alberta was asked to give his candid opinion about a colleague to a tenure committee. There was no question that he was advised that his opinion would be treated confidentially. He gave his opinion but it was somewhat intemperate in language. An arbitration board then used this information against the professor himself as the basis for his own dismissal, holding that he was guilty of a serious misdemeanour in using such language against a fellow faculty member. Other charges were laid by the university against the professor but none of these were found by the arbitration board to be established. The professor appealed on the ground that the tenure form sheet that he filled out was to have been kept strictly confidential and was to have been destroyed after the tenure committee had met. The

---

(1986), 53 O.R. (2d) 663n; and as between physician and patient see *Upham v. You* (1986), 73 N.S.R. (2d) 73, 176 A.P.R. 73, 11 C.P.C. (2d) 83 (*sub nom. You v. Upham*) (C.A.); leave to appeal to S.C.C. refd. October 23, 1986; *Hay v. University of Alberta Hospital*, [1990] 5 W.W.R. 78, at 80-81 (Alta. Q.B.).

17 See, for example, Law Society of Upper Canada, *Professional Conduct Handbook*, Rule 4 and the Commentary. Disclosure by a lawyer of a confidential communication to others without the client's authorization could give rise to a suit for damages by the client: see *Descôteaux v. Mierzwinski*, [1982] 1 S.C.R. 860, 70 C.C.C. (2d) 385, 28 C.R. (2d) 389, 1 C.R.R. 318, 141 D.L.R. (3d) 590, 44 N.R. 462, at 871 (S.C.R.).

18 *W. v. Egdell*, [1990] 1 All E.R. 835 (C.A.); *A.G. v. Guardian Newspapers Ltd. (No. 2)*, [1983] 3 All E.R. 545 (H.L.); *R. v. James Lorimer & Co.*, [1984] 1 F.C. 1065, 77 C.P.R. (2d) 262 (C.A.); *Ontario (A.G.) v. Gowling & Henderson* (1984), 14 C.C.C. (3d) 368, 47 O.R. (2d) 449, 12 D.L.R. (4th) 623 (H.C.J.); *Steintron International Electronics Ltd. v. Vorberg* (1986), 10 C.P.R. (3d) 393 (B.C.S.C.).

19 *Supra*, note 8.

question was whether the University could have used the opinion, written at its request and given on the basis that it was to be confidential, as evidence in the dismissal proceeding. The Supreme Court of Canada held that the tenure form sheet was inadmissible in evidence and accordingly, quashed the decision of the arbitration board.

Spence J. writing for the Court, spoke of protection for confidences as existing apart from the law of evidence. He applied the principle of breach of confidence which does not have its origin in evidence law but rather in equity. Spence J. relied upon the equitable doctrine which may be invoked to prevent a breach of confidence by prohibiting the disclosure of a confidential statement by one of the parties to the communication, or by prohibiting someone who has obtained a copy of it, from using it to the detriment of the party who initially made the statement in confidence. The remedy usually accorded is an injunction to restrain another from using the information in a proceeding or to prevent its general publication in the press.[20] The basis for this equitable principle relates to the general duty to act in good faith. It depends on the broad notion of equity that someone who has received information in confidence shall not take unfair advantage of it. The Supreme Court of Canada has added to that, by holding that where the very parties to the proceedings have agreed in advance that communications or documents exchanged between them would be treated confidentially and not be used for any other purpose, the court will rule against any attempt by a party to introduce any such evidence against the party who made the communication in reliance upon the confidence. That is the basis upon which the Supreme Court of Canada held the confidential statement to be inadmissible as against the professor. This equitable doctrine has empowered courts to enjoin breaches of confidence.[21]

In *obiter dicta* Spence J. went on to say that although the evidence was to be excluded on principles of equity, it would equally be precluded by the evidentiary principles relating to privilege. That was

---

20   See, for example, *Ashburton (Lord) v. Pape*, [1913] 2 Ch. 469 (C.A.); *Calcraft v. Guest*, [1898] 1 Q.B. 759 (C.A.). See also this Chapter, II.B.10.(c).

21   Other remedies may be granted where a party has improperly used confidential information. In *International Corona Resources Ltd. v. LAC Minerals Ltd.*, [1989] 2 S.C.R. 574, 61 D.L.R. (4th) 14, 26 C.P.R. (3d) 97, 69 O.R. (2d) 287, the wrongdoer was required to transfer assets. In *Szarfer v. Chodos* (1986), 27 D.L.R. (4th) 388, 54 O.R. (2d) 663, 36 C.C.L.T. 181 (H.C.J.); affd. (1988), 54 D.L.R. (4th) 383, 66 O.R. (2d) 350 (C.A.), the wrongdoer was required to pay damages.

so because of the applicability of the test propounded by Wigmore. He stated that four fundamental conditions must be met before privilege is extended to any communication and indicated that these four conditions serve as the foundation of policy for determining all relational privileges. They are:[22]

(1) The communications must originate in a *confidence* that they will not be disclosed.

(2) This element of *confidentiality must be essential* to the full and satisfactory maintenance of the relation between the parties.

(3) The *relation* must be one which in the opinion of the community ought to be sedulously *fostered*.

(4) The *injury* that would inure to the relation by the disclosure of the communications must be *greater than the benefit* thereby gained for the correct disposal of litigation.

Spence J. held that this four-fold test applied to the communication in question and, therefore, concluded that it was inadmissible. According to his analysis, the communication from the professor unquestionably originated in confidence, and confidentiality was essential to the operation of a tenure procedure which depended upon university staff giving their opinions frankly and candidly. Moreover, it was in the interest of the university community that the relationship between colleagues be fostered and that proper procedures for granting tenure to members of the university faculty be furthered. As to the final Wigmore condition, all of the factors just mentioned stressed the desirability of the preservation of the confidential nature of the communication. Although it may be recognized that there is some interest in the operation of proper procedures for dismissal, it cannot be said that such interest would be greater than that in the retention of confidentiality of documents which were given upon the firm agreement of both parties that they would remain confidential.

The application of the Wigmore criteria to the particular relationship in the *Slavutych* case has attracted some criticism. As one commentator[23] put it, the Court did not explain how this particular

---

22   8 Wigmore, *Evidence* (McNaughton rev. 1961), § 2285, at 527, quoted by Spence J. in *Slavutych v. Baker, supra*, note 8, at 260 (S.C.R.).

23   See J. Arvay, "*Slavutych v. Baker*: Privilege, Confidence and Illegally Obtained Evidence" (1977), 15 Osgoode Hall L.J. 456.

employee/employer relationship differed from all employment relationships. After all, the common law has never accorded a privilege to communications passing within the master-servant relationship. It could seriously be doubted that other employment relationships would have been treated by the Supreme Court as ones which ought to be sedulously fostered and, therefore, meriting protection for confidential communications made within them.[24] Nor was there any statement by the Court how it concluded that, by disclosure of the confidential information, the injury to the faculty-university relationship would be more serious than the harm to the public in the suppression of important evidence in a public hearing.

Nevertheless, the implications of this *obiter dicta* are clear. This was the first time that a Canadian court adopted Wigmore's four criteria to determine a claim of privilege. The Appellate Division of the Alberta Supreme Court was quick to pick up on the significance of Spence J.'s analysis. In *Strass v. Goldsack*,[25] Clement J.A. in referring to the *Slavutych* decision said:[26]

> To me, the sanction given to these four conditions as the test for a claim of privilege provides a more useful and helpful rationale which should serve well the general public interest in determining such claims. Not only does it provide a rationale: it also leaves room by the third and fourth conditions for adaptation of the principle to changing needs and conditions of society which is essential to the proper function of the common law. Former decisions on privileged documents must now derive their authority or guidance from their apparent conformity to the conditions, and on this view many must be passed over.

McDonald J., sitting *ad hoc* as a member of the Appellate Division, also noted Spence J.'s remarks and stated:[27]

---

24 In this respect, consider that the common-law protection against compellability of employees to testify against their employers was removed by the Supreme Court of Canada. See *R. v. N.M. Paterson & Sons Ltd.*, [1980] 2 S.C.R. 679, 19 C.R. (3d) 164, [1981] 2 W.W.R. 103, 7 Man. R. (2d) 382, 55 C.C.C. (2d) 289, 117 D.L.R. (3d) 517, 34 N.R. 597; *R. v. Amway Corp.*, [1989] 1 S.C.R. 21, 68 C.R. (3d) 97, 56 D.L.R. (4th) 309, (*sub nom. R. v. Amway of Canada Ltd.*) [1989] 1 C.J.C. 255, [1989] 1 T.S.T. 2058, 37 C.R.R. 235, 2 T.C.T. 4074.
25 [1975] 6 W.W.R. 155, 58 D.L.R. (3d) 397 (Alta. C.A.).
26 *Ibid.*, at 160 (W.W.R.).
27 *Ibid.*, at 166 (W.W.R.).

From his approach I draw the clear inference that in deciding whether or not a privilege attaches to a particular communication or class of communication, a Canadian court not only may but ought to consider whether Wigmore's four conditions are satisfied.

The utilization of Wigmore's criteria was again mentioned by Laskin C.J.C. in *Canada (Solicitor General) v. Ontario (Royal Commission of Inquiry into Confidentiality of Health Records)*,[28] where he stated that the *Slavutych* case had established that the categories of privilege are not closed and that the Wigmore criteria are a satisfactory guide for the recognition of a claim of privilege.[29]

A number of cases, particularly in Western Canada, have referred to the principles stated in *Slavutych* in analyzing claims of privilege.[30] Because some of these claims could have been resolved by applying established categories of privilege, these decisions have not expanded the scope of the law of privilege or created new privileges. An example is *Strass v. Goldsack*,[31] a motor vehicle negligence case in which the plaintiff made a statement to an adjuster employed by the defendant's insurer during the course of the investigation of the accident. The majority of the Court held that as Wigmore's four criteria had not

---

28 [1981] 2 S.C.R. 494, 62 C.C.C. (2d) 193, 23 C.R. (3d) 338, 128 D.L.R. (3d) 193, 23 C.P.C. 99, 38 N.R. 588, at 512 (S.C.R.); see also *Reference re Legislative Privilege* (1978), 39 C.C.C. (2d) 226, 18 O.R. (2d) 529, at 537-38, 83 D.L.R. (3d) 161, at 169-70 (C.A.).
29 The Ontario Court of Appeal in *R. v. Church of Scientology* (1987), 31 C.C.C. (3d) 449, at 541 (*sub nom. Church of Scientology v. R. (No. 6); Walsh v. R.*), 18 O.A.C. 321, 30 C.R.R. 238 (*sub nom. R. v. Church of Scientology of Toronto*) (C.A.); leave to appeal to S.C.C. refd. (1987), 23 O.A.C. 320n, stated that with the adoption of Wigmore's criteria, together with *Charter* protection of freedom of conscience and religion, "our courts will be encouraged to recognize the propriety of a priest-and-penitent privilege, if not as a class, at least on a case-by-case basis." See this Chapter, II.D.
30 See *German v. R.* (1978), 45 C.C.C. (2d) 27, (*sub nom. Re Medicine Hat Greenhouses Ltd. and R. (No. 3)*, [1979] 1 W.W.R. 296, 13 A.R. 232, 79 D.T.C. 5091 (C.A.); leave to appeal to S.C.C. refd. 26 N.R. 164; *R. v. Littlechild* (1979), 51 C.C.C. (2d) 406, 11 C.R. (3d) 390, 19 A.R. 395, [1980] 1 W.W.R. 742, 108 D.L.R. (3d) 340 (Alta. C.A.); *R. v. Fehr* (1984), 10 C.C.C. (3d) 321, 37 C.R. (2d) 233, 6 D.L.R. (4th) 281, [1984] 2 W.W.R. 334, 29 Alta. L.R. (2d) 170 (Q.B.); affd. [1985] 2 W.W.R. 287, 35 Alta. L.R. (2d) 96, 14 D.L.R. (4th) 128 (C.A.); *R. v. Morrow* (1990), 52 C.C.C. (3d) 263 (Ont. Dist. Ct.).
31 *Supra*, note 25.

been satisfied, the statement was not privileged. However, the exclusion of such evidence could be explained on the basis of existing principles of privilege pertaining to a solicitor obtaining information in anticipation of litigation without the necessity of invoking Wigmore's criteria.[32]

So, notwithstanding the fanfare accompanying this new flexible approach for the recognition of privileges for other confidential communications, the reality is that apart from the rather rare relationship in the *Slavutych* case,[33] no communications within any other class of identifiable relationship have been explicitly sheltered.[34] Even with respect to relationships that are similar to the one in the *Slavutych* case, other cases have held that when the confidential information sought is that of a committee investigating circumstances that gave rise to the very litigation before the court rather than an "in-house" examination into the qualifications of a member of the professional staff of his or her performance in general, then there is no privilege. Such cases have

---

32   See this Chapter, II.B.8. See also S.N. Lederman, "Comment" (1976), 54 Can. Bar Rev. 422.
33   See also *University of Guelph v. C.A.U.T.* (1981), 29 O.R. (2d) 312, 112 D.L.R. (3d) 692 (H.C.J.). The privilege was held to apply to the relationship between a doctor and a hospital credentials committee inquiring into the suitability of the doctor to become or remain a member of the hospital staff on the ground that it "closely parallels" the *Slavutych* case: *Smith v. Royal Columbian Hospital* (1981), 29 B.C.L.R. 99, 123 D.L.R. (3d) 723 (B.C.S.C.).
34   See B. Cotton, "Is There A Qualified Privilege at Common Law For Non-Traditional Classes of Confidential Communications? Maybe" (1990), 12 The Advocate's Quarterly 195, at 202. The Ontario Court of Appeal in *R. v. Church of Scientology*, *supra*, note 29, did state that there now may be a class privilege for religious communications, but the Supreme Court of Canada in *R. v. Gruenke*, not yet reported, October 24, 1991 (S.C.C.), made it clear that there is not. In *Moysa v. Alberta (Labour Relations Board)*, [1989] 1 S.C.R. 1572, 60 D.L.R. (4th) 1, [1989] 4 W.W.R. 596, 67 Alta. L.R. (2d) 193, 34 C.P.C. (2d) 97, 97 A.R. 368, 89 C.L.L.C. 14,028, 40 C.R.R. 197, 96 N.R. 70, the Supreme Court of Canada held that the Labour Board did not err in concluding that Wigmore's conditions were not satisfied in that case so as to protect as privileged a communication received by a journalist from a source. In *Sharpe Estate v. Northwestern General Hospital* (1991), 2 O.R. (3d) 40 (Ont. Ct. (Gen.Div.)), the Canadian Red Cross failed to satisfy the Wigmore conditions (principally because there was no relationship of confidentiality between it and blood donors) and thus was required to produce the names of blood donors whose blood was given to the plaintiff, a haemophiliac who was suing on the ground that the blood transfusion he received was contaminated by the AIDS virus.

emphasized that the Wigmore rules should not dominate a judge's consideration and the real test should be whether the public interest in the proper administration of justice outweighs in importance any public interests that might be protected by upholding the claim for privilege.[35]

This result might not be so bad as one can readily imagine the adverse impact on the trial process, if the *Slavutych* approach to relationships was applied logically and liberally. Courts would find it most difficult to refuse immunity from disclosure in respect of information given by doctors, clergyman, journalists, bankers, accountants, stockbrokers, social workers, psychologists etc. — in other words, people who regularly provide important evidence to courts. The negative effect upon the administration of justice if such evidence were routinely excluded is obvious.[36] McEachern C.J.S.C., in *F. v. A Psychiatrist*,[37] put it this way:[38]

> ... it is my respectful view that much public mischief is likely to arise if judges are overly astute in developing exceptions to the usual principle that privilege is confined to very special relationships. Society has got along very well with limited privilege and it is not in the public interest, in my view, that the categories of privilege continually be enlarged. If privilege is extended for the medical profession then it must be enlarged for most professions and for many other relationships or functions which one or more parties thought or assumed would be privileged. The question of extending privilege is properly a matter for the legislature, not for judges.

---

35   See *Hacock v. Vaillancourt* (1989), 63 D.L.R. (4th) 205, 40 B.C.L.R. (2d) 83; *Bergwitz v. Fast* (1980), 108 D.L.R. (3d) 732, 18 B.C.L.R. 368 (B.C.C.A.); *Finley v. University Hospital* (1986), 33 D.L.R. (4th) 200, [1987] 2 W.W.R. 40, 14 C.P.C. (2d) 87 (Sask. Q.B.); leave to appeal granted (1986), 14 C.P.C. (2d) 87n (C.A.); *Blais v. Andras*, [1972] F.C. 958, 30 D.L.R. (3d) 287, at 292.

36   McEachern C.J.S.C., in *MacMillan Bloedel Ltd. v. West Vancouver Assessment Area* (1981), 34 B.C.L.R. 111, 24 C.P.C. 183, 130 D.L.R. (3d) 675, at 679 (D.L.R.) was of the view that Wigmore's four tests were developed for the purpose of explaining existing privileged relationships and that other relationships did not qualify because the public interest was against it.

37   (1984), 54 B.C.L.R. 319 (S.C.).

38   *Ibid.*, at 323.

In fact, some judicial doubt has been expressed as to whether Spence J.'s *obiter docta* were ever intended to change the law of privileged communications. In *R. v. Fosty*,[39] the Manitoba Court of Appeal analyzed certain statements, made by the accused to a spiritual adviser, in the context of Wigmore's test and held that none of Wigmore's four conditions were met so as to attract any privilege. However, Twaddle J.A., speaking for the Court, was careful to say that he was doing so[40]

> ... without deciding the extent to which Wigmore's principle is part of the law of Canada. I am not satisfied that the *obiter* comments of Spence J., found in his judgment delivered for the Supreme Court of Canada in *Slavutych v. Baker* ... were intended as an acceptance of Wigmore's principle for all purposes, including the exclusion of confidential communications, otherwise admissible, from evidence in criminal trials. I share the view expressed by Professor McLachlin (now Chief Justice of the Supreme Court of British Columbia) [now Justice of the Supreme Court of Canada] in an article published in the University of British Columbia Law Rev., vol. II, No. 2, p. 266, in which she wrote (p. 273):

> [W]hile Spence, J. approved Wigmore's approach, his reasons do not evince an awareness that the Court was changing the law of evidence on privilege. While this omission is not crucial in itself, it gives rise to doubts how thoroughly the issue was canvassed and how carefully it was considered.

And in *Pryslak v. Anderson*,[41] Killeen L.J.S.C. in speaking of *Slavutych v. Baker* said:[42]

> ... there has been considerable controversy about the reach of this decision in the later case-law and academic literature. In my view, Canadian trial courts should be wary about using the Wigmore doctrine as a basis for creating or identifying new situations of privilege bearing in mind that the Supreme Court

---

39 (1989), 46 C.C.C. (3d) 449, [1989] 2 W.W.R. 193, 55 Man. R. (2d) 289 (C.A.); affd. (*sub nom. R. v. Gruenke*), not yet reported, October 24, 1991 (S.C.C.).
40 *Ibid.*, at 458-59 (C.C.C.), at 296-97 (Man. R.).
41 (1987), 57 O.R. (2d) 788, 15 C.P.C. (2d) 79 (H.C.J.).
42 *Ibid.*, at 792 (O.R.).

has not utilized it in any later case as a basis for analyzing privilege issues. . . .

But when *R. v. Gruenke*[43] came before the Supreme Court of Canada, the Court left no doubt whatsoever that the approach that it took in *Slavutych v. Baker*[44] is *the* legitimate, principled way to analyze the question which takes into account the particular circumstances of each case. Lamer C.J.C. stated:[45]

> This is not to say that the Wigmore criteria are now "carved in stone", but rather that these considerations provide a general framework within which policy considerations and the require-ments of fact-finding can be weighed and balanced on the basis of their relative importance in the particular case before the Court. Nor does this preclude the identification of a new class on a principled basis.

In *Gruenke*, the Court found that religious communications can be excluded in particular cases where the Wigmore criteria are satis-fied but held that they had not been met in the circumstances involved in the case before it.

B. Solicitor and Client

1. Rationale

It has long been established that *prima facie* all four of Wigmore's prerequisites are met in a solicitor and client communication.[46] But its origin and development go back much further in history. The solici-tor-client privilege is the oldest of the privileges for confidential communications with roots in the 16th century. The basis of the early rule was the oath and honour of the solicitor, as a professional man and a gentleman, to keep his client's secret.[47] Thus the early privilege belonged solely to the solicitor,[48] and the client benefited from it only

---

43 Not yet reported, October 24, 1991 (S.C.C.).
44 [1976] 1 S.C.R. 254, 38 C.R.N.S. 306, [1975] 4 W.W.R. 620, 75 C.L.L.C. 14,263, 55 D.L.R. (3d) 224.
45 *Supra*, note 43, at 21-22.
46 See, *e.g.*, *R. v. Fehr*, *supra*, note 30, at 329 (C.C.C.).
47 *Solosky v. Canada*, [1980] 1 S.C.R. 821, 16 C.R. (3d) 294, 50 C.C.C. (2d) 495, 105 D.L.R. (3d) 745, 30 N.R. 380, at 833-35 (S.C.R.), *per* Dickson J.
48 *Geffen v. Goodman Estate* (1991), 81 D.L.R. (4th) 211 (S.C.C.), at 232.

incidentally. By the 18th century, the courts regarded the ascertainment of truth to be more important than professional dignity, and oath and honour alone ceased to excuse lawyers from their civic duty to give testimony. In order to preserve the protection, however, the early rationale gave way to the view that the privilege was necessary, not in order to maintain the solicitor's reputation, but for the protection of the client. Effectual legal assistance, it was assumed, could only be given if clients frankly and candidly disclosed all material facts to their solicitors, which, in turn, was essential to the effective operation of the legal system. It was thought that this would not take place if the possibility existed that their confidences might be revealed.[49]

A complete statement of the privilege has been given as follows:[50]

> That rule as to the non-production of communications between solicitor and client says that where . . . there has been no waiver by the client and no suggestion is made of fraud, crime, evasion, or civil wrong on his part, the client cannot be compelled and the lawyer will not be allowed without the consent of the client to disclose oral or documentary communications passing between them in professional confidence, whether or not litigation is pending.

The Supreme Court of Canada has elevated the privilege to a "fundamental civil and legal right."[51]

---

49   *Geffen v. Goodman Estate, ibid.*, at 231; *R. v. Gruenke, supra*, note 43, *per* Lamer C.J.C., at 20; *Greenough v. Gaskell* (1833), 1 My. & K. 98, 39 E.R. 618 (Ch.); *Anderson v. Bank of British Columbia* (1876), 2 Ch. D. 644, at 649; *Canada (Director of Investigation and Research) v. Shell Canada Ltd.* (1975), 22 C.C.C. (2d) 70, 55 D.L.R. (3d) 713, at 721-22 (Fed. C.A.); *Flack v. Pacific Press Ltd.* (1970), 14 D.L.R. (3d) 334, 74 W.W.R. 275 (B.C.C.A.), at 336-40 (D.L.R.).

50   *Per* Munroe J., in *Canada (Director of Investigation and Research) v. Canada Safeway Ltd.* (1972), 26 D.L.R. (3d) 745, at 746, [1972] 3 W.W.R. 547, 6 C.P.R. (2d) 41 (B.C.S.C.); see also *Greenough v. Gaskell, ibid.; Kulchar v. Marsh*, [1950] 1 W.W.R. 272, at 274 (Sask. Q.B.).

51   *Solosky v. Canada, supra*, note 47, at 760 (D.L.R.); *Geffen v. Goodman Estate, supra*, note 48, at 232.

2. Confidential Nature of the Communication

(a) *General*

A prerequisite for the creation of privilege is that the communication be made in confidence. Although some early Ontario cases have held that the mere fact that the communication was made between solicitor and client was sufficient to raise the privilege,[52] it was subsequently decided that, in addition to the professional character of the communication, it also had to be established that it was made confidentially.[53] The communication need not expressly be made in confidence, so long as the circumstances indicate that the parties intended to keep it secret.

(b) *Presence of and Disclosure to Third Parties*

The presence of unnecessary third parties when the communication was made may serve to vitiate the privilege.[54] When a client or his solicitor admits into the privacy of their relationship an individual whose presence is not essential or of assistance to the consultation, then it may be presumed that the communication was not intended to be made in confidence. If it is reasonably necessary for the conduct of the lawyer's business that a clerk, agent, or secretary be present, then that alone will not destroy the confidential nature of the interview. A more difficult question is whether the presence of a relative or friend of the client militates against confidentiality. That, it would appear, turns upon whether that person's presence at the consultation was required to advance the client's interests and whether there was an

---

52   *Hamelyn v. Whyte* (1874), 6 P.R. 143 (Ch.); *Hoffman v. Crerar* (1897), 17 P.R. 404. In *Minter v. Priest*, [1930] A.C. 558 (H.L.), at 581, Lord Atkin stated that if the communication is made in search of professional legal advice, "it must be deemed confidential". See also *R. v. Bennett* (1963), 41 C.R. 227 (B.C.S.C.).

53   *Zielinski v. Gordon*, [1983] W.W.R. 414, 40 B.C.L.R. 165; *R. v. Bencardino* (1973), 2 O.R. (2d) 351, 15 C.C.C. (2d) 342, 24 C.R.N.S. 173, at 358 (O.R.), at 342 (C.C.C.); *Clergue v. McKay* (1902), 3 O.L.R. 478 (Div. Ct.); *Naujokat v. Bratushesky*, [1942] 2 W.W.R. 97, [1942] 2 D.L.R. 721 (Sask. C.A.), at 107 (W.W.R.), at 731 (D.L.R.); see also *O'Shea v. Wood*, [1891] P. 286 (C.A.), at 289, which followed *Gardner v. Irvin* (1878), 4 Ex. D. 49 (C.A.), at 53, in which the English Court of Appeal stated that: "It is not sufficient for the affidavits to say that the letters are a correspondence between a client and his solicitor; the letters must be professional communications of a confidential character for the purpose of getting legal advice."

54   8 Wigmore, *Evidence* (McNaughton rev. 1961) § 2311, at 601-03.

understanding that what transpired at the meeting would be kept in confidence. If the solicitor is authorized or instructed by the client to transmit a communication to others, then it cannot be said that the client desired it to be confidential. Thus, in *Fraser v. Sutherland*[55] the Court ruled that communications made to a solicitor, which were intended to be and were put before the client's creditors as a compromise proposal, were not privileged. Similarly, in *Conlon v. Conlons Ltd.*,[56] the English Court of Appeal held that privilege did not extend to instructions given by a client to his solicitor for the purpose of presenting an offer of settlement to the opposite party.[57]

(c) *Joint Interests*

Joint consultation with one solicitor by two or more parties for their mutual benefit poses a problem of relative confidentiality. As against others, the communication to the solicitor was intended to be confidential and thus is privileged. However, as between themselves, each party is expected to share in and be privy to all communications passing between either of them and their solicitor, and accordingly, should any controversy or dispute subsequently arise between the parties, then, the essence of confidentiality being absent, either party may demand disclosure of the communication.[58] Moreover, a client cannot claim privilege as against third persons having a joint interest with him in the subject-matter of the communications passing between the client and the solicitor.[59] Thus, in *Hicks v. Rothermel*,[60] the Saskatchewan King's Bench held that communications passing between a trustee and a solicitor were not privileged as against a *cestui que* trust who was claiming under a trust alleged to have been created

---

55   (1851), 2 Gr. 442 (Ch.).

56   [1952] 2 All E.R. 462 (C.A.).

57   See also *Walton v. Bernard* (1851), 2 Gr. 344, at 363-64 (Ch.); *R. v. Prentice* (1914), 23 C.C.C. 436, 20 D.L.R. 791, 7 W.W.R. 271, 7 Alta. L.R. 479 (C.A.), at 796 (D.L.R.); *Doe d. Mariott v. Marquis of Hertford* (1849), 13 Jur. 632; *R. v. Bencardino, supra*, note 53, at 358 (O.R.).

58   *R. v. Dunbar* (1982), 28 C.R. (3d) 324, 68 C.C.C. (2d) 13, 138 D.L.R. (3d) 221 (Ont. C.A.), at 37-38 (C.C.C.); *Lawryshyn v. Aquacraft Products Ltd.* (1963), 42 W.W.R. 340 (B.C.S.C.); *Horowitz v. Rothstein* (1955), 16 W.W.R. 620 (B.C.C.A.); *Wilson v. McLellan*, [1919] 3 W.W.R. 62, 27 B.C.R. 262 (C.A.).

59   *Pax Management Ltd. v. A.R. Ristan Trucking Ltd.*, [1987] 5 W.W.R. 252, (*sub nom. Pax Management Ltd. v. C.I.B.C.*) 14 B.C.L.R. (2d) 257 (B.C.C.A.), at 261-62 (W.W.R.).

60   [1949] 2 W.W.R. 705 (Sask. K.B.).

by the client. In *Platt v. Buck*,[61] correspondence between a solicitor and his client, who was the common grantor of certain land to both the plaintiff and the defendant, was held not to be privileged as against either of the client's successors in title when a dispute over the property arose between them. Similarly, no privilege exists as between partners or as between shareholders and directors where the communication was made by one of them to his solicitor for a reason other than contemplated litigation with those who possess a joint interest.[62]

(d) Subject-Matter

The subject-matter of all communications made by a client to his solicitor may not be confidential. For example, the identification or address of the client are matters which a client would rarely intend to be confidential. Moreover, other considerations bear on the question of whether a solicitor should be compelled to disclose the identity and address of his client in an action or proceeding in which the lawyer purports to represent the client. A litigant against whom allegations are made has the right to be informed of the identity of his adversary. In addition, in order to determine whether a solicitor-client relationship has been entered into, so as to raise the shield of privilege, it is first necessary to disclose the identity of the client. Accordingly, one stream of Canadian cases has maintained that communications showing only the establishment of a solicitor-client relationship or the identity of the client do not constitute privileged communications.[63] Disclosure of the identity of the client takes on a different complexion, however, when the client intended that fact to remain confidential and where its revelation would have the effect of disclosing subject-matter which would otherwise be privileged. Where the identification of the client is closely connected with the confidential legal business in reference to which the solicitor was retained, it should be protected.[64]

---

61   (1902), 4 O.L.R. 421 (Master).
62   *Gourand v. Edison Gower Bell Telephone Co. of Europe* (1888), 57 L.J. Ch. 498; *Dennis (W.) & Sons Ltd. v. West Norfolk Farmers' Manure and Chemical Co-operative Co.*, [1943] 2 All E.R. 94, [1943] 1 Ch. 220; *Woodhouse & Co. v. Woodhouse* (1914), 30 T.L.R. 559 (C.A.).
63   *A. & D. Logging Co. v. Convair Logging Ltd.* (1967), 63 D.L.R. (2d) 618 (B.C.S.C.); *Beamer v. Darling* (1848), 4 U.C.Q.B. 249 (C.A.); see also *Bursil v. Tanner* (1885), 16 Q.B.D. 1 (C.A.) and *Levy v. Pope* (1829), M. & M. 410, 173 E.R. 1206 (N.P.).
64   *United States v. Mammoth Oil Co.* (1925), 56 O.L.R. 635, [1925] 2 D.L.R. 966 (C.A.); *Re Income Tax Act; Solicitor v. M.N.R.*, [1963] C.T.C. 1, 40 W.W.R.

3. Scope of the Privilege

(a) *Within the Professional Relationship*

Although, at one time, the communication had to be made with a view to actual or prospective litigation before the privilege could attach, that is no longer the case. The protection will be afforded so long as the communications fall within the usual and ordinary scope of professional employment. A concise statement of the modern rule is found in Wigmore as follows:[65]

> Where legal advice of any kind is sought from a professional legal adviser in his capacity as such, the communications relating to that purpose, made in confidence by the client, are at his instance permanently protected from disclosures by himself or by the legal adviser except the protection be waived.

The privilege is of considerable breadth and encompasses all information passed within the professional lawyer and client relationship:[66]

> ... a lawyer's client is entitled to have all communications made with a view to obtaining legal advice kept confidential. Whether communications are made to the lawyer himself or to employees, and whether they deal with matters of an administrative nature such as financial means or with the actual nature of the legal problem, all information which a person must provide in order to obtain legal advice and which is given in confidence for that purpose enjoys the privileges attached to confidentiality. This confidentiality attaches to all communications made within the framework of the solicitor-client relationship, which arises as soon as the potential client takes the first steps, and consequently even before the formal retainer is established.

270, 62 D.T.C. 1331 (*sub nom. Re A Solicitor and Income Tax Act*) (B.C.S.C.); appeal quashed (1964), 45 D.L.R. (2d) 134, 48 W.W.R. 213, 64 D.T.C. 5107 (B.C.C.A.); application for leave to appeal dismissed (*sub nom. Canada (Dep. A.G.) v. Brown*), [1965] S.C.R. 84, [1964] C.T.C. 483, 64 D.T.C. 5296, 47 D.L.R. (2d) 402; *Thorson v. Jones* (1973), 38 D.L.R. (3d) 312, [1973] 4 W.W.R. 437 (B.C.S.C.).

65   8 Wigmore, *supra*, note 54, § 2292, at 554, quoted by the Supreme Court of Canada in *Solosky v. Canada*, *supra*, note 47, and *Descôteaux v. Mierzwinski*, [1982] 1 S.C.R. 860, 70 C.C.C. (2d) 385, 28 C.R. (3d) 289, 1 C.R.R. 318, 141 D.L.R. (3d) 590, 44 N.R. 462, at 873 (S.C.R.).

66   *Descôteaux v. Mierzwinski, ibid.*, at 892-93 (S.C.R.).

Disclosure of a communication will not be compelled even though it was made at a time when the relationship between solicitor and client had not been formally established by either retainer or payment of fees. Preliminary communications made by a person to a solicitor, with the view to retaining him or her to act on his or her behalf, establishes a sufficient relationship to which privilege will attach. It is immaterial whether the solicitor agrees to take the brief and represent the client.[67] An individual should be encouraged to approach a solicitor of his or her choice, but in so doing, there can be no guarantee that the solicitor will accept employment. Therefore, the right to privilege turns not upon the existence of a contract but upon the relationship or its potential existence when an individual seeks professional advice from the solicitor.

(b) *For Communications Only*

The protection is for communications only and facts that exist independent of a communication may be ordered to be disclosed.[68] In *Ontario (Securities Commission) v. Greymac Credit Corp.*,[69] the Ontario Divisional Court held that the solicitor, and indeed the client, could be compelled to answer questions about funds passing into and out of the solicitor's trust account. These were regarded as information about events or transactions which the solicitor possessed apart from any communication. The Court said:[70]

> The fact that a client has paid to, received from, or left with his solicitor a sum of money involved in a transaction is not a matter as to which the client himself could claim the privilege, because it is not a communication at all. It is an act. The solicitor-and-client privilege does not enable a client to retain anonymity in transactions in which the identity of the participants has become relevant in properly constituted proceedings.

---

67 *Shedd v. Boland*, [1942] O.W.N. 316, affd. without written reasons, [1942] O.W.N. 346 (C.A.); *Descôteaux v. Mierzwinski, supra*, note 65; *Minter v. Priest, supra*, note 52.

68 *Dusik v. Newton* (1983), 48 B.C.L.R. 111, 38 C.P.C. 87, 1 D.L.R. (4th) 568 (C.A.).

69 (1983), 41 O.R. (2d) 328, 146 D.L.R. (3d) 73, 21 B.L.R. 37, 33 C.P.C. 270 (Div. Ct.).

70 *Ibid.*, at 337 (O.R.).

The distinction between "fact" and "communication" is often a difficult one and courts should be wary of drawing the line too fine lest the privilege be seriously emasculated.[71]

(c) Purpose of the Communication

(i) Seeking Legal Advice

However, not all communications passing between the lawyer and a client are privileged. In order to be considered such, the communication must be made in the course of seeking legal advice and with the intention that it be confidential.[72] An illustration is afforded by R. v. Bencardino.[73] In this case, a Crown witness incriminated the accused, but subsequently changed his evidence when called as a witness by the defence in order to exculpate the accused. It was the opinion of the Crown that he had done so due to threats made on his life while he was an inmate in a penitentiary. However, the witness denied this upon direct questioning by the Crown. The Crown then sought to call the lawyer that represented the witness during his own trial to prove certain statements made by the lawyer to the Crown as a result of what the witness had told his own lawyer. It was then claimed that such information was privileged as being between solicitor and client. The trial judge held, after conducting a voir dire, that the lawyer could not be asked what the witness had told him but could be asked about the conversation that he had with the Crown. Jessup, J.A. of the Ontario Court of Appeal held that the trial judge had erred. What the lawyer had said to the Crown was not evidence of anything; but what the witness said to his lawyer might be evidence to show a state of mind of fear and might have been made not for the purpose of seeking legal advice but to obtain relief from intimidation in prison or to have his plight divulged to the authorities. The Court stated that not every communication by a client to his solicitor was privileged. To

---

71 In *Madge v. Thunder Bay (City)* (1990), 44 C.P.C. (2d) 186 (Ont. H.C.J.), the Court did limit *Greymac* to its special facts and refused to extend it to force a party to disclose whether she had delivered certain minutes of a meeting to her solicitor.

72 *Solosky v. Canada*, [1980] 1 S.C.R. 821, 16 C.R. (3d) 294, 50 C.C.C. (2d) 495, 105 D.L.R. (3d) 745, 30 N.R. 380, at 755-57 (D.L.R.); *Descôteaux v. Mierzwinski, supra*, note 65, at 585; *Naujokat v. Bratushesky*, [1942] 2 D.L.R. 721, [1942] 2 W.W.R. 97, at 107 (Sask. C.A.).

73 (1973), 24 C.R.N.S. 173, 15 C.C.C. (2d) 342, 2 O.R. (2d) 351 (C.A.).

be privileged, a communication must be made in the course of seeking legal advice and with the intention of confidentiality. Accordingly, the trial judge should have held a *voir dire* to examine the circumstances under which the statement was made by the witness to his lawyer to ascertain whether or not it was privileged. If it was not then the lawyer could be called to testify as to it.

Furthermore, the communication must be made in order to elicit professional advice from the lawyer based upon his or her expertise in the law. If the communication was made in a personal capacity rather than being referable to the professional relationship, no privilege will attach. As Wigmore suggests:[74]

> Such a conversation is not privileged, because the reason of the privilege designs to secure only the freedom of resort to attorneys where some appreciable interest of the client is to be protected and the advice is sought and given with a view to its protection.

Thus, in *Rudd v. Frank*[75] the Ontario Divisional Court characterized the communication to solicitors in that case as one which was made to them in their capacity as friends, rather than legal advisers, and held that no privilege attached.[76] In *S. Fremes & Co. v. Neima*,[77] it was held that a request to a solicitor by an individual to register a business in his wife's name, although he owned and carried it on for his own personal interest, did not fall within the normal scope of a solicitor's work and thus no privilege protected any communications passing between them.[78]

---

74   8 Wigmore, *Evidence* (McNaughton rev. 1961), § 2303, at 584.

75   (1889), 17 O.R. 758 (C.A.).

76   To the same effect, see *Smith v. Daniell* (1874), 44 L.J. Ch. 189; see also *Wilson v. Rastall* (1792), 4 Term Rep. 753, 100 E.R. 1283 (K.B.), at 758 Term Rep., at 1286 (E.R.), in which letters given to a solicitor, but not in his character as a legal adviser, were held to be not privileged. Similarly, in *Greenlaw v. King* (1838), 1 Beav. 137, 48 E.R. 891 (Ch.), at 145 (Beav.), at 894 (E.R.), the Court held that correspondence to a solicitor, but only as "agent and confidential friend" was not privileged.

77   [1939] 2 D.L.R. 581, 14 M.P.R. 153 (N.S.C.A.).

78   See also *Missiaen v. Minister of National Revenue* (1967), 61 W.W.R. 375 at 377, 68 D.T.C. 5039, [1967] C.T.C. 57; *Hicks v. Rothermel*, [1949] 2 W.W.R. 705 (Sask. K.B.); *Minter v. Priest*, [1930] A.C. 558, at 580-81, 99 L.J.K.B. 391 (H.L.).

(ii) In Furtherance of Unlawful Conduct

Accordingly, the reason for which a client seeks advice from a lawyer may be decisive as to whether privilege attaches to the communication. If a client seeks out a lawyer for the purpose of assisting him or her to perpetrate a crime or fraud there can be no privilege, whether or not the solicitor is aware of the client's motive in consulting him or her. As stated by Dickson J. in *Solosky v. Canada*[79]

> . . . if a client seeks guidance from a lawyer in order to facilitate the commission of a crime or a fraud, the communication will not be privileged and it is immaterial whether the lawyer is an unwitting dupe or knowing participant. The classic case is *R. v. Cox and Railton* (1884), 14 Q.B.D. 153, in which Stephen, J., had this to say (p. 167): "A communication in furtherance of a criminal purpose does not 'come in the ordinary scope of professional employment'."

A *fortiori*, a solicitor cannot invoke the privilege for the purpose of assisting his client to suppress real evidence of a crime.[80]

There is no reason why this exception to the solicitor-client privilege should not also include those communications made with a view to perpetrating tortious conduct which may not become the subject of criminal proceedings.[81]

In order for the privilege to be displaced on the grounds that the communication for which privilege is claimed was made in connection with fraudulent conduct, there must be more than a mere allegation

---

79   *Supra*, note 72, at 757 (D.L.R.). See also *Descôteaux v. Mierzwinski, supra,* note 65, at 881 (S.C.R.).

80   In *Re Ryder*, 263 F. Supp. 360 (1967), it was held to be improper for a lawyer to take into his possession stolen money and a weapon used in a robbery for the purpose of preventing their detection. Not only was such activity outside the ambit of solicitor-client privilege but the lawyer was thereby liable to professional discipline.

81   *Williams v. Quebrada Railway, Land and Copper Co.*, [1895] 2 Ch. 751; *O'Rourke v. Darbishire*, [1920] A.C. 581 (H.L.); *R. v. Church of Scientology (No. 3)* (1984), 47 O.R. (2d) 90, 13 C.C.C. (3d) 353, 10 D.L.R. (4th) 711, (*sub nom. R. v. Church of Scientology (No. 2)*) 44 C.P.C. 87 (H.C.J.), at 93 (O.R.); but see *Rocking Chair Plaza (Bramalea) Ltd. v. Brampton (City)* (1988), 29 C.P.C. (2d) 82 (Ont. H.C.J.), holding that the exception could not be extended to allegations of bad faith or indeed tortious conduct or breach of contract.

of fraud.[82] Some cases have suggested that a *prima facie* case of fraud must first be made out.[83] Another test which is perhaps more workable is for the court to inquire whether there is "something to give colour to the charge."[84] Some controversy has arisen as to whether this necessitates an examination by the trial judge of the very statement or documents for which privilege is claimed. In *K-West Estates Ltd. v. Linemayr*[85] the Court held that the circumstances disclosed by the material including the documents for which privilege was claimed indicated matters requiring exploration and explanation and concluded that there was sufficient evidence of fraudulent conduct to negate the claim. In that sense there was sufficient evidence of fraudulent conduct and accordingly, the claim for privilege failed. Moreover, in *R. v. Bencardino*[86] the Court required the solicitor to reveal the contents of the communication on a *voir dire* to determine whether it fell within the criminal purpose exception to solicitor-client privilege. However, in *R. v. Giguere*[87] the Quebec Superior Court explicitly rejected the suggestion in *Bencardino* that the communication itself could be examined to determine whether the privilege had been lost. There had to be extrinsic evidence independent of the communication itself.

4. When the Privilege May be Asserted

It had been long considered that solicitor-client privilege was a testimonial privilege in that it could only be asserted at trial and could not be dealt with, for example, on a motion to quash a search warrant.

---

82   *O'Rourke v. Darbishire, ibid.*, at 604. *Finers (a firm) v. Miro*, [1990] 2 W.L.R. 35, [1990] N.L.J.R. 1387 (C.A.); *Borden & Elliott v. R.* (1975), 30 C.C.C. (2d) 337, 13 O.R. (2d) 248, 70 D.L.R. (3d) 579 (C.A.).

83   *Canada (Director of Investigation and Research) v. Shell Canada Ltd.* (1975), 22 C.C.C. (2d) 70, 55 D.L.R. (3d) 713 (Fed. C.A.); *Re Bowlen*, [1971] C.T.C. 682, 71 D.T.C. 5407 (B.C.S.C.); *Re Income Tax Act; Re Milner* (1968), 70 D.L.R. (2d) 429, 66 W.W.R. 129 (B.C.S.C.); *Goodman & Carr v. Minister of National Revenue*, [1968] 2 O.R. 814, at 819, 70 D.L.R. (2d) 670, [1968] C.T.C. 484 (*sub nom. Re Goodman & Carr*), 68 D.T.C. 5288 (H.C.J.); *Butler v. Board of Trade*, [1971] Ch. 680.

84   *K-West Estates Ltd. v. Linemayr*, [1984] 4 W.W.R. 375, 54 B.C.L.R. 60 (S.C.), at 380 (W.W.R.); *Missiaen v. M.N.R.*, *supra*, note 78.

85   *Ibid.* See also *R. v. Governor of Pentenville Prison, ex p. Osman*, [1989] 3 All E.R. 701 (Q.B.).

86   *Supra*, note 73.

87   (1978), 44 C.C.C. (2d) 525.

This view was expressed by Osler J. in *R. v. Colvin*[88] as follows:[89]

... the rule is a rule of evidence, not a rule of property ... The only way, as I see it, in which the privilege can be asserted is by way of objection to the introduction of any allegedly privileged material in evidence at the appropriate time.

A rash of subsequent decisions[90] has extended the time when privilege may be claimed, and has recognized that it is deserving of protection not only when the issue of admissibility arises (namely, trial and discovery), but can be asserted even in the early investigative stages when a solicitor is confronted by a search warrant. Dickson J. alluded to this development in *Solosky v. Canada*:[91]

Recent case law has taken the traditional doctrine of privilege and placed it on a new plane. Privilege is no longer regarded merely as a rule of evidence which acts as a shield to prevent privileged materials from being tendered in evidence in a court room. The courts, unwilling to so restrict the concept, have extended its application well beyond those limits.

This is really part of the trend towards a broader concept of solicitor-client privilege. In *Descôteaux v. Mierzwinski*,[92] Lamer J. indicated that the privilege was to be considered a substantive rule and not just a rule

---

88 [1970] 3 O.R. 612, 1 C.C.C. (2d) 8 (H.C.J.).
89 *Ibid.*, at 617 (O.R.).
90 Including one of Osler J. in which he reversed his earlier position: see *Presswood v. International Chemalloy Corp.* (1975), 36 C.R.N.S. 322, 65 D.L.R. (3d) 228, 11 O.R. (2d) 164, 25 C.P.R. (2d) 33 (H.C.J.).
91 [1980] 1 S.C.R. 821, 50 C.C.C. (2d) 495, 16 C.R. (3d) 294, 105 D.L.R. (3d) 745, 30 N.R. 380, at 836 (S.C.R.), at 745 (D.L.R.). Dickson J. relied on the following authorities: *Canada (Director of Investigation and Research) v. Canada Safeway Ltd.* (1972), 26 D.L.R. (3d) 745, 6 C.P.R. (2d) 41, [1972] 3 W.W.R. 547 (B.C.S.C.); *Canada (Director of Investigation and Research) v. Shell Canada Ltd.* (1975), 22 C.C.C. (2d) 70, 55 D.L.R. (3d) 713 (Fed. C.A.); *Presswood v. International Chemalloy Corp., ibid.* (Ont. H.C.J.); *Borden & Elliott v. R., supra*, note 82, at 337 (C.C.C.), at 580 (D.L.R.); *B.X. Development Ltd. v. R.* (1976), 31 C.C.C. (2d) 14, 70 D.L.R. (3d) 366, [1976] 4 W.W.R. 364 (B.C.C.A.); *B. v. R.* (1977), 36 C.C.C. (2d) 235 (Ont. Prov. Ct.); see also *Descôteaux v. Mierzwinski*, [1982] 1 S.C.R. 860, 70 C.C.C. (2d) 385, 28 C.R. (3d) 289, 141 D.L.R. (3d) 590, 1 C.R.R. 318, 44 N.R. 462.
92 *Ibid.*, at 875 (S.C.R.).

of evidence which would be asserted only at the time that testimony is sought in court. Privilege may therefore be asserted when police authorities are attempting to execute upon a search warrant. Parliament has provided a procedure to determine claims of solicitor-client privilege in relation to documents in the possession of a lawyer which are seized by a peace officer or public officer under a federal statute other than the *Income Tax Act*.[93] Section 488.1 of the *Criminal Code* sets out a speedy procedure for the assertion and summary determination of such claims for such documents.[94]

However, the Supreme Court of Canada in *Solosky v. Canada*[95] emphasized that although the notion of privilege has been broadened by shifting the time at which the privilege can be asserted, it must be kept in mind that privilege is not a rule of property and there should be an evidentiary connection. In that case, an inmate in a prison complained about his mail being opened and read. There was no suggestion that the authorities intended to employ the letters or extracts obtained therefrom as evidence in any proceeding of any kind. His mail was being opened as a means of preserving institutional security. The inmate, however, sought a declaration that correspondence between himself and a solicitor was to be regarded as privileged and forwarded unopened. Since the assertion of the privilege here was aimed at the mere opening of the inmate's mail and not at any improper use or disclosure, the Supreme Court of Canada concluded that there was no evidentiary connection and that what the inmate was seeking here was well beyond the limits of the privilege even as amplified in modern cases:[96]

> All of this occurs within prison walls and far from a court or quasi-judicial tribunal. It is difficult to see how the privilege can be engaged, unless one wishes totally to transform the privilege into a rule of property, bereft of an evidentiary basis.

---

93 R.S.C. 1985, c. 27 (1st Supp.), s. 71. Similar statutory provisions are set out in s. 232 of the *Income Tax Act*, 1970-71-72, c. 63, as amended, and s. 19 of the *Competition Act*, R.S.C. 1985, c. C-34 [re-en. 1985, c. 19 (2nd Supp.), s. 24].
94 *Criminal Code*, R.S.C. 1985, c. C-46. See D. Watt, *Tremeear's Criminal Code 1990* at 674-75 for an explanation of the mechanics of the section.
95 *Supra*, note 91.
96 *Per* Dickson J., *supra*, note 91, at 838 (S.C.R.).

While recognizing the importance of privacy (as opposed to a privilege) in solicitor-client correspondence, the Court said that had to be balanced against the public interest in maintaining safety and security within a penal institution. The difficulty is ensuring that the correspondence between the inmate and his solicitor is not used as an improper means to pass drugs, weapons or escape plans. The Court felt there must be some mechanism for verification of the authenticity of a true solicitor-client communication. Thus, the Court concluded that the penitentiary authorities could censor the inmate's mail but only to the extent necessary to establish whether it is properly the subject-matter of solicitor-client contact. In so doing, the prison regulations permitting censoring of mail were to be interpreted to minimize interference with legitimate solicitor-client communications.

5. What Legal Advisers are Included

Many years ago, the Ontario Court of Appeal held that the lawyer must be competent to practise in the jurisdiction, the law of which is relevant to the issues in question. In *United States v. Mammoth Oil Co.*,[97] it was held in circumstances where an American citizen consulted a Canadian lawyer on American law that no privilege attached to the communication as a Canadian lawyer was not qualified to practise in the United States.[98] This decision could create problems for a corporate counsel particularly where the corporation is a multinational or carries on business in more than one province. If, for example, a problem arises outside of Ontario but the corporate counsel who is a member of the Ontario Bar only is consulted at the corporation's head office in Toronto, should that communication not be privileged? More recent authority suggests that the protection should not be so limited and that as long as one of the parties to the communication is a lawyer, though perhaps not called to the bar of the jurisdiction in which the issue arises, then the umbrella of privilege should cover it.[99] At the very least, it could be said that such a

---

97   (1925), 56 O.L.R. 635, [1925] 2 D.L.R. 966 (C.A.).
98   See also *Procter & Gamble Co. v. Calgon Interamerican Corp.* (1980), 48 C.P.R. (2d) 63 (Fed. Ct.).
99   *Mutual Life Assurance Co. of Canada v. Canada (Deputy Attorney General)* (1989), 28 C.P.C. (2d) 101, at 104 (Ont. H.C.J.); *Hartz Canada Inc. v. Colgate-Palmolive Co.* (1987), 27 C.P.C. (2d) 152 (Ont. H.C.J.); *Re Duncan; Garfield v. Fay*,

consultation is preparatory to the foreign lawyer providing information or instructions to a lawyer who is in fact licensed to practise in the relevant jurisdiction. This would be in keeping with the fact that the privilege arises, as Lamer J. said "as soon as the potential client takes the first steps, and consequently even before the formal retainer is established."[100]

The protection, however, does not extend to communications with persons who are not duly qualified legal advisers even though the advice they might give is legal in nature. Thus, a newspaper service providing legal advice to subscribers was denied privilege.[101] Nor does privilege apply to communications with patent agents who are not lawyers even though they may be rendering legal advice or assistance.[102] There is jurisprudence to the effect that privilege attaches in cases where the adviser falsely holds himself out to be a duly qualified professional lawyer or his agent, and the client reasonably assumes that he is such. In the case of *R. v. Choney*,[103] the Manitoba Court of Appeal held that conversations between an accused and a police officer pretending to be an agent of the accused's solicitor were privileged.[104] Since the privilege of confidential communication is that of the client and not that of the solicitor, it would appear to be quite consistent with the concept of encouraging confidence and openness in speaking to legal advisers, that conversations with persons holding themselves out to be duly qualified solicitors should be protected, provided that the

---

[1968] 2 All E.R. 395, [1968] 2 W.L.R. 1479; *Morrison-Knudsen Co. Inc. v. British Columbia Hydro & Power Authority* (1971), 19 D.L.R. (3d) 726, [1971] 3 W.W.R. 71 (B.C.S.C.).
100 *Descôteaux v. Mierzwinski, supra*, note 91, at 893 (S.C.R.).
101 *Naujokat v. Bratushesky*, [1942] 2 W.W.R. 97, [1942] 2 D.L.R. 721 (Sask. C.A.).
102 *Lumonics Research Ltd. v. Gould*, [1983] 2 F.C. 360, 33 C.P.C. 230, 70 C.P.R. (2d) 11, 46 N.R. 483 (C.A.), at 366 (F.C.). The situation is otherwise if the patent agent is merely acting as an intermediary in passing on a solicitor's opinion to a client: *Sunwell Engineering Co. v. Mogilevsky* (1986), 8 C.P.C. 14, 8 C.I.P.R. 144 (Ont. H.C.J.); leave to appeal to Div. Ct. refd. (1986), 8 C.P.C. (2d) 14n.
103 (1908), 13 C.C.C. 289, 7 W.L.R. 537, 17 Man. R. 467 (C.A.).
104 See also the American decision of *People v. Barker*, 60 Mich. 277, 27 N.W. 539 (1886), in which a confession made to a detective fraudulently pretending to be an attorney, was held privileged. To the same effect, see *State v. Russell*, 83 Wis. 330, 53 N.W. 441 (1892). But see *contra*, *Fountain v. Young* (1807), 6 Esp. 113, 170 E.R. 846 (N.P.); *Feuerheerd v. London General Omnibus Co.*, [1918] 2 K.B. 565 (C.A.).

client *bona fide* and reasonably believes that the adviser possesses such status. To hold otherwise, of course, would be to require the prospective client to investigate the professional qualifications of persons appearing to be solicitors before disclosing any information — a requirement which would surely not be such as to inspire confidence and frankness between a solicitor and his client.

6. Use of Agents

The lawyer in the ordinary course of his practice utilizes employees such as articling students, law clerks and secretaries. Communication to such agents for the purpose of facilitating the obtaining of legal advice is equally protected.[105] The same can be said about the client's agents so long as they are employed as his agents for the purpose of obtaining legal advice.[106] That is so, notwithstanding that the agent may add something to the communication as a product of his own skill. Accordingly, communications by a client to an accountant who then lays the matter before a solicitor with his own comments or advice are protected.[107] If, however, the communication is made to a person who must himself consider and act upon it, no privilege arises even though the result of the decision may necessarily be the retention of a solicitor. In *Goodman & Carr v. Minister of National Revenue*[108] an accountant's opinion was sent to the client's lawyer at the client's request. It was held not to be privileged because the agent was not an agent for the client seeking legal advice but really offering his own opinion. Because these communications through agents are not normally made in a litigious atmosphere, this situation must be distinguished from the case where a third party is retained to obtain facts or to make a report to assist the client or his solicitor in litigation.[109]

---

105 *Descôteaux v. Mierzwinski, supra,* note 91; *Alcan-Colony Contracting Ltd. v. Minister of National Revenue,* [1971] 2 O.R. 365, 18 D.L.R. (3d) 37, 71 D.T.C. 5082 (H.C.J.); *Susan Hosiery Ltd. v. Minister of National Revenue,* [1969] 2 Ex. C.R. 27, [1969] C.T.C. 353, 69 D.T.C. 5278.
106 *Wheeler v. Le Marchant* (1881), 17 Ch. D. 675, at 684 (C.A.).
107 *Susan Hosiery Ltd. v. M.N.R., supra,* note 105; *Sunwell Engineering Co. v. Mogilevsky, supra,* note 102.
108 [1968] 2 O.R. 814, 70 D.L.R. (2d) 670, [1968] C.T.C. 484, (*sub nom. Re Goodman & Carr*) 68 D.T.C. 5288 (H.C.J.).
109 See this Chapter, II.B.8.

7. Corporations as Clients

(a) Corporate Counsel

Lawyers who are employed by a corporation and therefore have only one client are covered by the privilege provided that they are performing the function of a solicitor.[110] Lawyers, however, whether in house or not, often occupy a dual function and only the portions of the communication made in the capacity of solicitor are protected. In *Presswood v. International Chemalloy Corp.*[111] an inspector appointed pursuant to the Ontario *Business Corporations Act* had wide powers of examination of the company's affairs. However, the company claimed privilege from examination for certain documents that were in the possession of the company's solicitor who was also a director of the corporation. The company argued that the particular provision of the Ontario *Business Corporations Act* did not override the privilege for communications between a solicitor and client. The Court recognized the fact that the company solicitor in this case was also a director and stated that any work done for the employer in a capacity other than that of solicitor could not be the subject of any legal professional privilege. Bearing this in mind the Court held that the company could claim privilege for any particular letter, document or record in the files in the possession of the solicitor/director. Any disputes as to whether the privilege applied to a particular document were to be referred to the Master. Thus, the character of the activity carried on by the individual in question must be scrutinized to determine its nature. If the solicitor has information as a result of communications in his professional capacity as a lawyer, privilege will attach but not otherwise.[112]

(b) Corporate Client

Canadian courts have never been troubled with the question of identifying which individuals in the corporation are the client for the purpose of determining whose communications are protected by

---

110 *IBM Canada Ltd. v. Xerox of Canada Ltd.*, [1978] 1 F.C. 513, at 516 (C.A.).
111 (1975), 36 C.R.N.S. 322, 65 D.L.R. (3d) 228, 11 O.R. (2d) 164, 25 C.P.R. (2d) 33 (H.C.J.).
112 *Crompton (Alfred) Amusement Machines Ltd. v. Customs and Excise Commissioners (No. 2)*, [1972] 2 All E.R. 353; revd. [1972] 2 All E.R. 371 (C.A.); affd. [1973] 2 All E.R. 1169 (H.L.); *Canary v. Vested Estates Ltd.*, [1930] 3 D.L.R. 989, [1930] 1 W.W.R. 996, 43 B.C.R. 1 (S.C.), at 990 (D.L.R.), at 997-98 (W.W.R.).

solicitor-client privilege. On the other hand, there has been considerable jurisprudence in the United States on this subject. At one time only that small group of individuals who could be in a position to control or even to take a substantial part in a decision about any action which the corporation may take upon the advice of attorneys would have the protection of the privilege.[113] Another test that had gained some favour in the U.S. was known as the (subject-matter test) which recognized that an employee outside of the control group would have his or her communications protected by legal privilege but only if the communication was at the direction of his or her superiors and where the subject-matter for which legal advice was sought fell within the performance by the employee of the duties of his or her employment.[114] The U.S. Supreme Court reviewed the issue of corporate privilege in *Upjohn v. United States*[115] and rejected the control group test. It stressed that it was essential for counsel to be able to communicate with the lower levels of the company without fear of disclosure. Chief Justice Burger in a separate judgment put forth a test which has similar hallmarks to the subject-matter test in that the communication of the employee must concern a matter within the scope of his or her employment and must be made at the bidding of a superior for the purpose of obtaining legal advice.

In Canada there has been broad protection for confidential communications emanating from an employee regardless of the level of his or her position in the corporate hierarchy provided the objective was to obtain legal advice. Moreover, as long as the statement was made generally in the course of his or her employment, no specific inquiry need be made of the subject-matter to ensure that it fell squarely within the scope of his or her duties. For the most part, the issue has been treated by Canadian courts as one coming within the agency theory of privilege; that is, any employee can be engaged by the corporate client to pass on information to solicitors for the purpose of receiving legal advice.[116]

---

113 *City of Philadelphia v. Westinghouse Electric Corp.*, 210 F. Supp. 483 (1962).
114 *Harper & Row v. Decker*, 423 F. (2d) 487 (1970).
115 449 U.S. 383 (1981).
116 G. Grenier, "Solicitor-Client Privilege and the Ontario Loan and Trust Corporations Act" (1989), 15 Can. Bus. L.J. 129 at 140-41.

8. Materials Obtained and Prepared
in Anticipation of Litigation

As the principle of solicitor-client privilege developed, the breadth of protection took on different dimensions. It expanded beyond communications passing between the client and solicitor and their respective agents, to encompass communications between the client or his solicitor and third parties if made for the solicitor's information for the purpose of pending or contemplated litigation.[117] Although this extension was spawned out of the traditional solicitor-client privilege, the policy justification for it differed markedly from its progenitor. It had nothing to do with clients' freedom to consult privately and openly with their solicitors; rather, it was founded upon our adversary system of litigation by which counsel control fact-presentation before the Court and decide for themselves which evidence and by what manner of proof they will adduce facts to establish their claim or defence, without any obligation to make prior disclosure of the material acquired in preparation of the case.[118] Accordingly, it is somewhat of a misnomer to characterize this aspect of privilege under the rubric, (solicitor-client privilege), which has peculiar reference to the professional relationship between the two individuals.[119] The policy behind this aspect of the privilege was expressed in *Ottawa-Carleton (Regional Municipality) v. Consumers' Gas Co.*[120]

---

117 *Anderson v. Bank of British Columbia* (1876), 2 Ch. D. 644, at 649-50 (C.A.); *Southwark Water Co. v. Quick* (1878), 3 Q.B.D. 315, at 321-23 (C.A.); *Re Strachan*, [1895] 1 Ch. 439 at 444-45 (C.A.); *Wheeler v. Le Marchant, supra*, note 97, at 682; *Susan Hosiery Ltd. v. M.N.R., supra*, note 105, at 31, 33-34; *Flack v. Pacific Press Ltd.* (1970), 74 W.W.R. 275, 14 D.L.R. (3d) 334, at 336 (B.C.C.A.).
118 C. Tapper and R. Cross, *Cross on Evidence*, 7th ed. (London: Butterworths, 1990), at 433; R.J. Sharpe, "Claiming Privilege in The Discovery Process" (1984) L.S.U.C. Special Lectures 163, at 165-68.
119 *Warunki v. Warunki* (1983), 24 Alta. L.R. (2d) 266, 36 C.P.C. 199, 44 A.R. 135 (Q.B.); *Steeves v. Rapanos* (1982), 29 C.P.C. 41, 39 B.C.L.R. 60, [1982] 6 W.W.R. 244, 29 C.P.C. 41, 140 D.L.R. (3d) 121, [1983] I.L.R. 1-1624 (S.C.), at 157 (C.P.C.), affd. [1983] 2 W.W.R. 380, 41 B.C.L.R. 312, [1983] I.L.R. 1-1626, 33 C.P.C. 70, 142 D.L.R. (3d) 556 (C.A.); McEachern C.J.B.C. in *Hodgkinson v. Simms*, [1989] 3 W.W.R. 132, 33 B.C.L.R. (2d) 129, 55 D.L.R. (4th) 577 (C.A.), at 136-37, 139 (W.W.R.) views it as part of an all embracing privilege and states that it is not helpful to attempt a distinction between solicitor-client privilege and the lawyer's work product.
120 (1990), 74 O.R. (2d) 637 at 643, 74 D.L.R. (4th) 742 at 748 (Ont. Div. Ct.); see also *Ocean Falls Corp. v. Worthington (Can.) Inc.* (1985), 69 B.C.L.R. 124 at 126

The adversarial system is based on the assumption that if each side presents its case in the strongest light the court will be best able to determine the truth. Counsel must be free to make the fullest investigation and research without risking disclosure of his opinions, strategies and conclusions to opposing counsel. The invasion of the privacy of counsel's trial preparation might well lead to counsel postponing research and other preparation until the eve of or during the trial, so as to avoid early disclosure of harmful information. This result would be counter-productive to the present goal that early and thorough investigation by counsel will encourage an early settlement of the case. Indeed, if counsel knows he must turn over to the other side the fruits of his work, he may be tempted to forgo conscientiously investigating his own case in the hope he will obtain disclosure of the research, investigations and thought processes compiled in the trial brief of opposing counsel . . .

Although long steeped in Anglo-Canadian jurisprudence, it was only in 1947, in the case of *Hickman v. Taylor*,[121] that the Americans firmly developed something comparable to this second branch of the legal professional privilege, which they termed the 'work-product' doctrine. Murphy J. explained its basis in the following oft-quoted passage:[122]

In performing his various duties . . . it is essential that a lawyer work with a certain degree of privacy, free from unnecessary intrusion by opposing parties and their counsel. Proper preparation of a client's case demands that he assemble information, sift what he considers to be the relevant from the irrelevant facts, prepare his legal theories and plan his strategy without undue and needless interference. . . . This work is reflected, of course, in interviews, statements, memoranda, correspondence, briefs, mental impressions, personal beliefs, and countless other tangi-

---

(S.C.).
121 67 S.Ct. 385, 329 U.S. 495 (1947).
122 *Ibid.*, at 510-11 (U.S.). Some judges have imported the "work-product" rule into the Canadian context although the "anticipation-of-litigation" privilege is sufficiently broad to envelop all the material protected by the *Hickman* doctrine: see *Evans v. Banffshire Apartments Ltd.* (1968), 70 D.L.R. (2d) 226 at 228 (B.C.S.C.).

ble and intangible ways — aptly though roughly termed by the Circuit Court of Appeals in this case as the "work product of the lawyer". Were such materials open to opposing counsel on mere demand, much of what is now put down in writing would remain unwritten. An attorney's thoughts, heretofore inviolate, would not be his own. Inefficiency, unfairness and sharp practices would inevitably develop in the giving of legal advice and in the preparation of cases for trial. The effect on the legal profession would be demoralizing. And the interests of the clients and the cause of justice would be poorly served.

It must be recognized that the protection given by the United States federal courts to a lawyer's work product arose in the context of the procedural principles of discovery and did not fall under the umbrella of the traditional attorney-client privilege.[123] The Supreme Court of the United States in *Hickman v. Taylor*, while acknowledging that information obtained by an attorney in preparation of his or her case was outside the limited scope of the American attorney-client privilege, held that such information may nevertheless have a qualified immunity from discovery under this newly articulated doctrine. The protection was qualified in that such material would be discoverable only upon a substantial showing of necessity or justification.[124]

In Canada, the 'anticipation of litigation' privilege is without such qualification. However, there are two other conditions that must be met. First, such communications with third parties must have been made specifically with existing or contemplated litigation in mind and not just in the context of general legal professional advice.[125] Secondly, special regard must be had to situations where the creation of a document or report has a two-fold purpose, one of which is to assist

---

123 ". . . the protective cloak of [attorney-client privilege] does not extend to information which an attorney secures from a witness while acting for his client in anticipation of litigation. Nor does this privilege concern the memoranda, briefs, communications and other writings prepared by counsel for his own use in prosecuting his client's case; and it is equally unrelated to writings which reflect an attorney's mental impressions, conclusions, opinions or legal theories . . ." *per* Murphy J. in *Hickman v. Taylor, supra,* note 121, at 508 (U.S.).
124 *Supra*, note 121, at 509-510 (U.S.). Now see R. 26(b)(3) of the Federal Rules of Civil Procedure, as set out in 48 F.R.D. 457 (1970).
125 *Goodman & Carr v. M.N.R., supra,* note 108; *Marlborough Hotel Co. v. Parkmaster (Canada) Ltd.* (1959), 28 W.W.R. 49, 17 D.L.R. (2d) 720 (Man. C.A.).

counsel in litigation. In such cases, it has been held in England that the privilege will only attach if the dominant purpose for the third party communication was to assist in possible forthcoming litigation. In *Waugh v. British Railways Board*[126] the House of Lords ordered production of an accident report which had been commissioned for both safety purposes and for the purpose of obtaining litigation advice. In discussing the use of this test, Lord Wilberforce stated:[127]

> It is clear that the due administration of justice strongly requires disclosure and production of this report: it was contemporary; it contained statements by witnesses on the spot; it would be not merely relevant evidence, but almost certainly the best evidence as to the cause of the accident. If one accepts that this important public interest can be overridden in order that the defendant may properly prepare his case, how close must the connection be between the preparation of the document and the anticipation of litigation? On principle I would think that the purpose of preparing for litigation ought to be either the sole purpose or at least the dominant purpose of it: to carry the protection further into cases where that purpose was secondary or equal with another purpose would seem to be excessive, and unnecessary in the interest of encouraging truthful revelation. At the lowest such desirability of protection as might exist in such cases is not strong enough to outweigh the need for all relevant documents to be made available.

Although the 'dominant purpose' test has been adopted by many courts in Canada,[128] Ontario courts have been divided, some holding that so long as a "substantial" purpose for the creation of the document

---

126 [1980] A.C. 521, [1979] 2 All E.R. 1169, [1979] 3 W.L.R. 150 (H.L.).
127 *Ibid.*, at 531-32 (A.C.).
128 *New West Construction Co. v. R.*, [1980] 2 F.C. 44, 106 D.L.R. (3d) 272 (T.D.); *Davies v. Harrington* (1980), 39 N.S.R. (2d) 258, 71 A.P.R. 258, 115 D.L.R. (3d) 347 (C.A.); *Voth Brothers Construction (1974) Ltd. v. North Vancouver School District No. 44*, [1981] 5 W.W.R. 91, 29 B.C.L.R. 114, 23 C.P.C. 276 (B.C.C.A.); *Nova, an Alberta Corp. v. Guelph Engineering Co.* (1984), 42 C.P.C. 194 (Alta. C.A.); *Levin v. Boyce*, [1985] 4 W.W.R. 702, 19 D.L.R. (4th) 128, 34 Man. R. (2d) 1, 34 M.V.R. 55, 12 C.C.L.I. 119 (C.A.); *McCaig v. Trentowsky* (1983), 148 D.L.R. (3d) 724, 47 N.B.R. (2d) 71, 124 A.P.R. 71 (C.A.); *Sauder Industries Ltd. v. The Molda* (1986), 3 F.T.R. 190 (Fed. T.D.).

was for litigation that will suffice to invoke the privilege.[129]

The privilege also protects communications from a solicitor to a third party. It will often be necessary for a solicitor to convey privileged information, either oral or written, to third parties, such as potential experts or others with special knowledge, in order to obtain their advice or assistance. The instructions or communications are themselves privileged.[130]

In some circumstances the solicitor can delegate the communication to an interpreter, messenger or other agent for transmission to the expert. In *R. v. Perron*,[131] the Quebec Court of Appeal held that where counsel requires the services of an expert in order to help in the preparation of the defence, communications between the accused and the expert are covered by the privilege; and there is no requirement that counsel be present during such discussions.[132]

As long as they were made for the purpose of litigation, it would appear that the protection is sufficiently wide to cover copies of non-privileged documents that a lawyer has made for his brief.[133] However, it would be a matter of concern, as one judge expressed it,[134] that original documents which were not privileged could in effect become so merely because counsel has photocopied them for litiga-

129 *Blackstone v. Mutual Life Insurance Co. of New York*, [1944] 3 D.L.R. 147, [1944] O.R. 328, 11 I.L.R. 97 (C.A.), at 333 (O.R.); *Delta-Benco-Cascade Ltd. v. Lakes Cablevision Inc.* (1982), 26 C.P.C. 145 (S.C.); *Ilich v. Hartford Fire Insurance Co.* (1980), 20 C.P.C. 8 (Ont. H.C.J.); *Schonberger v. Toronto Transit Commission* (1981), 43 C.P.C. 215 (Ont. H.C.J.); *Armak Chemicals v. Canadian National Railway* (1984), 48 O.R. (2d) 381, 47 C.P.C. 219 (H.C.J.); *McIntyre v. Canadian Pacific Ltd.* (1984), 43 C.P.C. 59 (Ont. H.C.J.); *Falconbridge Ltd. v. Hawker Siddeley Diesels & Electronics Ltd.* (1985), 50 O.R. (2d) 794, 3 C.P.C. (2d) 133 (H.C.J.); *Walters v. Toronto Transit Commission* (1985), 50 O.R. (2d) 635, 4 C.P.C. (2d) 66 (H.C.J.); *Werner v. Warner Auto-Marine Inc.* (1990), 73 O.R. (2d) 59 (H.C.J.).
130 *Bell Canada v. Olympia & York Developments Ltd.* (1989), 68 O.R. (2d) 103, 36 C.P.C. (2d) 193, 33 C.L.R. 258 (H.C.); *Bombardier Ltd. v. Canada (Restrictive Trade Practices Comm.)* (1980), 113 D.L.R. (3d) 295 (*sub nom. Re A.G. Can. and Restrictive Trade Practices Comm.*) 48 C.P.R. (2d) 248 (Fed. Ct.); *Farhat v. Travelers Indemnity Co. of Canada* (1985), 12 C.C.L.T. 115, 61 A.R. 248 (Master).
131 (1990), 54 C.C.C. (3d) 108 (Que. C.A.).
132 See also *Bombardier Ltd. v. Canada (Restrictive Trade Practices Comm.)*, *supra*, note 130 at 255 (C.P.R.).
133 *Hodgkinson v. Simms*, [1989] 3 W.W.R. 132, 33 B.C.L.R. (2d) 129, 55 D.L.R. (4th) 577 (C.A.).
134 *Ibid.*, at 147 (W.W.R.), Craig J.A., dissenting; see also *Dubai Bank Ltd. v. Galadari*, [1989] 3 All E.R. 769 (C.A.).

tion purposes. But as was made clear in *Ottawa-Carleton (Regional Municipality) v. Consumers' Gas Co.*,[135] the making of a copy and the giving of it to a solicitor does not clothe the original document with privilege. If the copy has been prepared with the requisite dominant purpose, then the copy, but not the original, is privileged.[136] The English Court of Appeal, however, in *Ventouris v. Mountain*[137] was of the view that if the original was not privileged, then neither was a copy, even if it had been made by a solicitor for litigation purposes.[138]

9. Duration of Privilege

(a) *In Other Proceedings*

When a solicitor-client communication is once privileged it is "always privileged."[139] The privilege continues to subsist even with respect to other litigation that may arise in the future.[140] That is so even if the solicitor has been disbarred,[141] or if the client has changed solicitors. A case in point is *Bell v. Smith*,[142] In that case, the defendants brought an application for judgment in accordance with an alleged settlement with the plaintiffs for claims made in an action arising out of a motor vehicle accident. Before the motion for judgment came on for hearing, however, the plaintiffs had changed their solicitors, and at the hearing, the former solicitor appeared under subpoena and gave

---

135 *Supra*, note 120.
136 *Supra*, note 120 at 642 (O.R.), at 747 (D.L.R.).
137 [1991] 1 W.L.R. 607, at 619 (C.A.).
138 To the same effect, see *Buttes Gas and Oil Co. v. Hammer (No. 3)*, [1981] Q.B. 223 (C.A.); vard. for other reasons [1982] A.C. 888, [1981] 3 All E.R. 616 (H.L.).
139 *Calcraft v. Guest*, [1898] 1 Q.B. 759 (C.A.) at 761, per Lindley M.R.; *Mann v. American Automobile Insurance Co.*, [1938] 1 W.W.R. 538, [1938] 2 D.L.R. 261, 52 B.C.R. 460, 5 I.L.R. 125 (C.A.), at 542 (W.W.R.); *Bullock & Co. v. Corry & Co.* (1878), 3 Q.B.D. 356; *per* Cockburn C.J.; *Pearce v. Foster* (1885), 15 Q.B.D. 114 at 119 (C.A.).
140 *Small v. Nemez*, [1963] 1 O.R. 91 (Master); but see *Boulianne v. Flynn*, [1970] 3 O.R. 84 (Co. Ct.), in which it was held that communications between a solicitor and a third party for the purposes of earlier litigation are to be contrasted with communications passing between the solicitor and his client and that the privilege attached to the former disappears once the earlier litigation has been completed; *Bullock & Co. v. Corry & Co.*, *ibid.*
141 *Cholmondeley (Earl) v. Lord Clinton* (1815), 19 Ves. 261, 34 E.R. 1231 (Ch.).
142 [1968] S.C.R. 664, 68 D.L.R. (2d) 751.

evidence on behalf of the defendants and related the settlement discussions that he had had with his former clients. The Supreme Court of Canada held that it was most improper to put to a solicitor questions involving disclosure of confidential information without evidence of proper waiver by his former client. Spence J. in expressing that there had been a violation of a solicitor-client privilege, had this to say:[143]

> It is rather astounding that Mr. Schreiber should be subpoenaed to give evidence on behalf of the defendants as against his former clients and that he should produce his complete file including many memoranda and other material all of which were privileged as against the plaintiffs and whether the plaintiffs' counsel objected or not that he should be permitted to so testify and so produce without the consent of the plaintiffs being requested and obtained.

Lord Chancellor Eldon said, in *Beer v. Ward* [(1821), Jacob 77], at p. 80:

> . . . it would be the duty of any Court to stop him if he was about to disclose confidential matters . . . the Court knows the privilege of the client, and it must be taken for granted that the attorney will act rightly, and claim that privilege; or that if he does not, the Court will make him claim it.

The Court went on to add that it was improper for the solicitor not to claim the privilege when there had been no waiver by the client.[144] Moreover, it is irrelevant whether the client's present counsel objected to the introduction of such evidence because, as Spence J. indicated, the client's privilege is a duty owed to the court and thus no objection is necessary to exclude it.[145]

Unlike solicitor-client communications, the privilege for third party communications in preparation for litigation does not last indefinitely. It ends with the litigation for which the reports or other

---

143 *Ibid.*, at 671 (S.C.R.). See also *Geffen v. Goodman Estate* (1991), 81 D.L.R. (4th) 211 at 232 (S.C.C.).
144 To the same effect see *Kulchar v. Marsh*, [1950] 1 W.W.R. 272 at 276 (Sask. K.B.); *Livingstone v. Gartshore* (1863), 23 U.C.Q.B. 166 (C.A.).
145 *Bell v. Smith, supra*, note 142, at 671 (S.C.R.).

communications were prepared subject to any undertaking of confidentiality.[146]

Although the authorities are few and provide little explanation, it has been held that any recognized privilege would have to give way where necessary to establish the innocence of an accused in criminal proceedings.[147]

(b) After Death

The privilege against non-disclosure of solicitor-client communications will continue even after the client dies.[148] An exception to this latter principle has been made in cases in which the succession to property turned upon some question of will interpretation or where the existence or validity of a will was in issue. It was Wigmore's belief that a client's discussions with his or her solicitor with respect to the drafting of a will were intended to be only temporarily confidential during the lifetime of the testator, and that after his or her death, the solicitor was free to disclose all those facts that related to the execution and contents of the will.[149] Phipson's explanation for the exception is based on the fact of the claimants having a joint interest with the client in the subject-matter of the communication. Thus, he concludes that as between joint claimants under a testator as to communications between the latter and his solicitor, no privilege applies.[150]

Canadian courts, however, have founded the right of disclosure in wills cases upon a different basis. The leading case in this regards is *Stewart v. Walker*[151] in which the issue was whether the deceased had died intestate. No original will was found, but a document purporting to be a copy of the will and sworn by the plaintiff to have been made

---

146 *Meaney v. Busby* (1977), 15 O.R. (2d) 71, 2 C.P.C. 340 (H.C.J.); *Boulianne v. Flynn, supra,* note 140.

147 *R. v. Seaboyer* (1991), 66 C.C.C. (3d) 321, 4 O.R. (3d) 383*n*, 128 N.R. 81, 83 D.L.R. (4th) 193 at 260 (S.C.C.); *R. v. Morrow* (1989), 52 C.C.C. (3d) 263 (Ont. Dist. Ct.); *R. v. Delong* (1989), 47 C.C.C. (3d) 402, 31 O.A.C. 339 (C.A.); *R. v. Dunbar* (1982), 68 C.C.C. (2d) 13, 28 C.R. (3d) 324, 138 D.L.R. (3d) 221 (Ont. C.A.); *R. v. Barton,* [1972] 2 All E.R. 1192 (Eng. Crown Ct.).

148 *Bullivant v. A.G. for Victoria,* [1901] A.C. 196 at 206 (H.L.); *Re Cirone* (1965), 8 C.B.R. (N.S.) 237 (Ont. S.C.); *Langworthy v. McVicar* (1913), 25 O.W.R. 297, 5 O.W.N. 345 (S.C.).

149 8 Wigmore, *Evidence* (McNaughton rev. 1961), § 2314, at 612-16.

150 J. Buzzard *et al., Phipson on Evidence,* 13th ed. (London: Sweet & Maxwell, 1982) at 300.

151 (1903), 6 O.L.R. 495, 2 O.W.R. 990 (C.A.).

by him on the day of the execution of the original was produced. The Attorney-General, who was alleging an intestacy, called the deceased's solicitor as a witness at trial to testify with respect to certain communications that passed between them during the existence of the professional relationship, although he did not draft the will. Those who were named as beneficiaries in the purported copy of the will claimed the right to exclude the solicitor's testimony on the ground that the communications that passed between him and the deceased were privileged. The Ontario Court of Appeal indicated that the solicitor-client privilege does not necessarily die with the client. It may continue on and be exercised by the deceased's heirs, or next of kin. The problem in this case was that the client died without leaving any successors to stand in his place. The plaintiff had claimed that the benefit of the privilege had devolved upon him as executor of the will; however, the very issue in this case was whether there was a will in existence or not. The Court held that the question of privilege did not arise at all, because the permitting of the solicitor to give testimony would advance the client's interest and not defeat it.[152] Moss C.J.O. explained it as follows:[153]

> The nature of the case precludes the question of privilege from arising. The reason on which the rule is founded is the safeguarding of the interests of the client, or those claiming under him when they are in conflict with the claims of third persons not claiming, or assuming to claim, under him. And that is not this case, where the question is as to what testamentary dispositions, if any, were made by the client. As said by Sir George Turner, Vice-Chancellor, in *Russell v. Jackson* (1851), 9 Ha. 387, at p. 392: "The disclosure in such cases can affect no right or interest of the client. The apprehension of it can present no impediment to the full statement of his case to his solicitor . . . and the disclosure when made can expose the Court to no greater difficulty than presents itself in all cases where the Courts have to ascertain the views and intentions of parties, or the objects and purposes for which dispositions have been made." It has been the constant practice to apply the rule here stated in cases of contested wills and where the evidence of the solicitors by whom the wills were

---

152 See Wigmore, *supra*, note 149.
153 *Supra*, note 151, at 497-98 (O.L.R.).

prepared, as to the instructions they received, is always received. And the application of a different rule in this action would deprive the plaintiff of a considerable part of the proof of his case. On these grounds we held that the evidence should have been received . . .

So, in a will's case where the court is seeking to implement the testator's intention, and it thereby becomes important to know what instructions were given to his or her solicitor, the question of privilege does not even arise. The disclosure by the solicitor, in fact, affords protection to the client's interests. This was emphasized by Anderson, Surr. Ct. J. in *Re Ott*,[154] who had before him the question whether the testator destroyed a will in the mistaken belief that its destruction revived a prior will or whether by its destruction he intended unconditional revocation. As to whether communications between the testator and his solicitor should be admitted on this point, he said:[155]

> . . . since it is of essence to the case to find out the intention of the testator when he destroyed the will whether or not he was revoking his will unconditionally or whether he was only tearing it up on condition that an earlier will was thus revived, the whole issue turns on this question and it would seem to me that to invoke the privilege of the client, after the client is deceased would make it impossible for the Court to determine the intention of the testator in tearing up the will. In the interests of justice, it is more important to find out the true intention of the testator.

There is no logical reason why this exception to the solicitor-client privilege which was developed in cases where the succession of property turned on the validity of a will would not also apply to *inter vivos* trust agreements when the settlor has died. In both cases, it is the duty of the court to ascertain the true intention and capacity of the deceased and it is in both the interest of the client and the interest of justice that the relevant evidence of the solicitor be admitted in evidence.

---

154 [1972] 2 O.R. 5, 24 D.L.R. (3d) 517, 7 R.F.L. 196 (Surr. Ct.).
155 *Ibid.*, at 11 (O.R.).

In *Geffen v. Goodman Estate*,[156] the Supreme Court of Canada did in fact extend the exception to actions involving the validity of a trust agreement after the death of the settlor. Wilson J. explained the reason for so doing as follows:[157]

In my view, the considerations which support the admissibility of communications between solicitor and client in the wills context apply with equal force to the present case. The general policy which supports privileging such communications is not violated. The interests of the now deceased client are furthered in the sense that the purpose of allowing the evidence to be admitted is precisely to ascertain what her true intentions were.

10. Loss of Privilege

(a) *Who May Waive the Privilege*

The privilege which arises out of the professional legal relationship is that of the client and does not belong to the solicitor.[158] This is also the case with respect to the 'anticipation of litigation' privilege although it has its origin in the protection of the solicitor's brief rather than client communications.[159]

Only the client or his or her successors in interest,[160] if so predisposed, may waive the solicitor-client privilege.[161] Still, legal advisors do have ostensible authority to bind the client to any matter which arises in or is incidental to the litigation and that ostensible authority extends to waiver of the client's privilege.[162] In circum-

---

156 *Supra*, note 143.
157 *Supra*, note 143, at 235.
158 *Geffen v. Goodman Estate* (1991), 81 D.L.R. (4th) 211 (S.C.C.); *Stewart v. Walker, supra*, note 151; *Shedd v. Boland*, [1942] O.W.N. 316 (Master); affd. without written reasons, [1942] O.W.N. 346.
159 In *Hodgkinson v. Simms*, [1989] 3 W.W.R. 132, 33 B.C.L.R. (2d) 129, 55 D.L.R. (4th) 577 (C.A.), at 139 and 145 (W.W.R.), it was held that disclosure of this kind of information required the consent of the client.
160 *Geffen v. Goodman Estate, supra*, note 143; *Langworthy v. McVicar* (1913), 25 O.W.R. 297, 5 O.W.N. 345.
161 *Stewart v. Walker, supra*, note 151, at 497 (O.L.R.); see also *Bell v. Smith, supra*, note 142, in which the Supreme Court of Canada held that it was a solicitor's obligation to refuse disclosure of confidential communications passing between him and his client where the client has not waived the privilege.
162 *Derby & Co. Ltd. v. Weldon (No. 8)*, [1991] 1 W.L.R. 73 (C.A.) at 87; *Great Atlantic Insurance Co. v. Home Insurance Co.*, [1981] 1 W.L.R. 529 (C.A.) at 540.

stances where it cannot be said that there was waiver, courts are obliged to step in to prevent a solicitor from making the disclosure.[163] This demonstrates how important the right to communicate in confidence with one's lawyer is. In fact, the Supreme Court of Canada has described the privilege as "a fundamental civil and legal right"[164] which should not lightly be abrogated. In *Descôteaux v. Mierzwinski*,[165] the Supreme Court laid down the following rules when there is an attempt to interfere with the privilege:[166]

1. The confidentiality of communications between solicitor and client may be raised in any circumstances where such communications are likely to be disclosed without the client's consent.

2. Unless the law provides otherwise, when and to the extent that the legitimate exercise of a right would interfere with another person's right to have his communications with his lawyer kept confidential, the resulting conflict should be resolved in favour of protecting the confidentiality.

3. When the law gives someone the authority to do something which, in the circumstances of the case, might interfere with that confidentiality, the decision to do so and the choice of means of exercising that authority should be determined with a view to not interfering with it except to the extent absolutely necessary in order to achieve the ends sought by the enabling legislation.

4. Acts providing otherwise in situations under paragraph 2 and enabling legislation referred to in paragraph 3 must be interpreted restrictively.

(b) *Voluntary Waiver*

It was once thought that certain requirements should be established in order for waiver of the privilege to be established, e.g., the holder of the privilege must possess knowledge of the existence of the

---

163 *Geffen v. Goodman Estate, supra*, note 158 at 232.
164 *Solosky v. Canada*, [1980] 1 S.C.R. 821, 16 C.R. (3d) 294, 50 C.C.C. (2d) 495, 105 D.L.R. (3d) 745, 30 N.R. 380, at 760 (D.L.R.).
165 [1982] 1 S.C.R. 860, 70 C.C.C. (2d) 385, 28 C.R. (2d) 389, 1 C.R.R. 318, 141 D.L.R. (3d) 590, 44 N.R. 462.
166 *Ibid.*, at 875 (S.C.R.).

privilege which he or she is foregoing, have a clear intention of waiving the exercise of his or her right of privilege, and a complete awareness of the result.[167] But, as will be pointed out, other considerations unique to the adversarial system, such as fairness to the opposite party and consistency of positions have overtaken these factors.

An obvious scenario of waiver is if the holder of the privilege makes a voluntary disclosure or consents to disclosure of any material part of a communication.[168] Thus the Court in *Frind v. Sheppard*[169] held that a client had waived the privilege which attached to letters passing between himself and his solicitor because they had been read into the record in a previous proceeding. In other cases, waiver was said to have taken place when documents over which privilege was claimed had been disclosed in proceedings in another jurisdiction[170] or were referred to in an Affidavit of Documents and had been inspected.[171] Similarly, if a client testifies on his or her own behalf and gives evidence of a professional, confidential communication, he or she will have waived the privilege shielding all of the communications relating to the particular subject-matter.[172] Moreover, if the privilege is waived, then production of all documents relating to the acts contained in the communication will be ordered.[173]

If the communication is elicited in cross-examination of the client, it seems that unless it can be shown that the witness was misled or did not comprehend what was being asked of him or her, the assertion of the communication would amount to a waiver.[174] Of

---

167 *Per* Lamont J.A., in *Western Canada Investment Co. v. McDiarmid*, [1922] 1 W.W.R. 257, 15 Sask. L.R. 142, 66 D.L.R. 457 (C.A.) at 261 (W.W.R.); see also *R. v. Perron* (1990), 54 C.C.C. (3d) 108 at 120 (Que. C.A.).

168 There will be waiver if one simply asserts an intention to disclose an otherwise privileged document for settlement purposes: see *Marlborough Hotel Co. v. Parkmaster (Canada) Ltd.* (1959), 28 W.W.R. 49, 17 D.L.R. (2d) 720 (Man. C.A.).

169 [1940] O.W.N. 135 (Master).

170 *Western Assurance Co. v. Canada Life Assurance Co.* (1987), 63 O.R. (2d) 276, 23 C.P.C. (2d) 207 (Master).

171 *Re Briamore Manufacturing Ltd.*, [1986] 1 W.L.R. 1429 (Ch.); *Kennedy v. Diversified Mining Interests (Can.) Ltd.*, [1948] O.W.N. 798 (H.C.J.).

172 *Smith v. Smith*, [1958] O.W.N. 135 (H.C.J.).

173 *Doland (George) Ltd. v. Blackburn, Robson, Coates & Co. (a firm)*, [1972] 3 All E.R. 959 (Q.B.).

174 E.W. Cleary, (ed.), *McCormick on Evidence*, 3rd ed. (St. Paul: West Publishing, 1984) at 227.

665

course, if the client merely testifies as a witness to the facts in issue, that will not constitute a waiver of privilege. Nor would solicitor-client privilege be lost by an accused merely because his or her memory was refreshed from notes made by him or her for counsel in preparation for trial.[175]

(c) *Waiver by Implication*

It has also been said that clear intention is not in all cases an important factor. In some circumstances, waiver may occur even in the absence of any intention to waive the privilege. There may also be waiver by implication only.

As to what constitutes waiver by implication, Wigmore said:[176]

> Judicial decision gives no clear answer to this question. In deciding it, regard must be had to the double elements that are predicated in every waiver, i.e., not only the element of implied intention, but also the element of fairness and consistency. A privileged person would seldom be found to waive, if his intention not to abandon could alone control the situation. There is always also the objective consideration that when his conduct touches a certain point of disclosure, fairness requires that his privilege shall cease whether he intended that result or not. He cannot be allowed, after disclosing as much as he pleases, to withhold the remainder. He may elect to withhold or to disclose, but after a certain point his election must remain final.

Whether intended or not, waiver may occur when fairness requires it, for example, if a party has taken positions which would make it inconsistent to maintain the privilege. In *Land v. Kaufman*,[177] solicitor-client privilege was held to have been waived by a solicitor, who filed an affidavit in support of the plaintiff's motion to withdraw admissions made in the Statement of Claim where the affidavit referred to the very instructions which the plaintiff now sought to protect from disclosure. The defendants contended that the admis-

---

175 *R. v. Parker* (1985), 10 O.A.C. 156 (C.A.), referred to in *R. v. Ticchiarelli*, unreported, May 3, 1990 (Ont. Dist. Ct.).
176 8 Wigmore, *Evidence* (McNaughton rev. 1961), at § 2327, at 635-36, quoted in *Hunter v. Rogers*, [1982] 2 W.W.R. 189, (*sub nom. Rogers v. Hunter*) 34 B.C.L.R. 206 (S.C.), at 191 (W.W.R.).
177 (1991), 2 W.D.C.P. (2d) 259 (Ont. Ct. (Gen. Div.)).

sions had been crucial to their defence and they could not explore whether the admissions were inadvertent or resulted from wrong instructions without knowing the content of the instructions. The Court concluded that fairness demanded that the defendants be entitled to that disclosure, especially where discoveries had already been completed and the positions of the parties had been revealed by their pleadings and their evidence on discovery.

The notion of fairness has also been invoked as a basis for waiver when the party directly raises in a pleading or proceeding the legal advice that he or she received, thereby putting that advice in issue.[178] Similarly, if a client denies that he or she gave instructions to the lawyer to settle a debt, the other party who is seeking to enforce the settlement is free to examine the lawyer on what was said between the lawyer and the client.[179]

The extent and nature of legal advice received by a party can be put in issue when that party alleges that he or she possessed a particular state of mind as, for example, reliance upon the defendant's representations. If the defence is that the plaintiff had relied upon his or her own legal advice on the question, then such legal advice must be disclosed. In *Lloyds Bank Canada v. Canada Life Assurance Co.,*[180] the plaintiff pleaded in its Statement of Claim that it was induced by the defendants to make a loan and that it relied upon the defendant's representations in deciding to advance the funds. The defendants alleged that such reliance was unreasonable and that the plaintiff had received its own legal advice before committing to loan the funds. Van Camp J. held that because the plaintiff had pleaded reliance upon the defendant's representations, it had waived the privilege insofar as it had to divulge whether it had obtained legal advice as to the value of the representation before authorizing the loan. She quoted the Wigmore passage above and drew upon the words of McLachlin J., then a member of the British Columbia Supreme Court in *S. & K. Processors Ltd. v. Campbell Avenue Herring Producers Ltd.*:[181]

178 *Nowak v. Sanyshyn* (1979), 23 O.R. (2d) 797, 9 C.P.C. 303 (H.C.J.); *Harich v. Stamp* (1979), 59 C.C.C. (2d) 87, 27 O.R. (2d) 395, 106 D.L.R. (3d) 340, 14 C.P.C. 246, 11 C.C.L.T. 49 (C.A.); leave to appeal to S.C.C. refd. (1980), 59 C.C.C. (2d) 87n; *Lev v. Lev*, [1990] 4 W.W.R. 130, 26 R.F.L. (3d) 86, 64 Man. R. (2d) 306 (Q.B.).
179 *Newman v. Nemes* (1979), 8 C.P.C. 229 (Ont. H.C.J.).
180 (1991), 47 C.P.C. (2d) 157 (Ont. Ct. (Gen. Div.)).
181 (1983), 35 C.P.C. 146, [1983] 4 W.W.R. 762, 45 B.C.L.R. 218 (S.C.) at

In the cases where fairness has been held to require implied waiver, there is always some manifestation of a voluntary intention to waive the privilege at least to a limited extent. The law then says that in fairness and consistency, it must be entirely waived.

But what if one party puts in issue the knowledge and intent of the *other party*? Does the latter lose the privilege because of the position taken by the opposing party? Van Camp J. in the *Lloyds Bank Canada* case[182] said:

> . . . [T]here is not waiver in every instance where the state of mind is in issue. Certainly it will not be waived where it is the person who seeks the information that has raised the question of reliance.

Professor Gary D. Watson has suggested that future cases may view the issue differently:[183]

> It seems reasonably clear that the "fairness" test has emerged as the relevant principle for determining when solicitor and client privilege is waived by conduct in the course of the litigation. While the courts have not yet clearly embraced the view that the unilateral assertion of an issue by one party can lead to compulsory disclosure of the adverse party's solicitor-client communications, do not be surprised if the law moves in this direction; ultimately, the fairness test may be interpreted as meaning that solicitor-client privilege is waived whenever the communications between the solicitor and the client are legitimately brought in issue in the action.

149-50 (C.P.C.). See also *Rogers v. Bank of Montreal*, [1985] 4 W.W.R. 503, 61 B.C.L.R. 239, 57 C.B.R. (N.S.) 251 (S.C.); affd. [1985] 4 W.W.R. 508, 62 B.C.L.R. 387, 57 C.B.R. (N.S.) 256 (C.A.); *Petro Can Oil & Gas Corp. Ltd. v. Resource Service Group Ltd.* (1988), 59 Alta. L.R. (2d) 34, 32 C.P.C. (2d) 50 (Q.B.).
182 *Supra*, note 180, at 167-68.
183 G.D. Watson, "Solicitor-client Privilege in Litigation: Current Developments and Future Trends", Canadian Bar Association, Ontario Continuing Legal Education, October 19, 1991. See also E.A. Dolden, "Waiver of Privilege: The Triumph of Candor Over Confidentiality", (1990) 36 C.P.C. (2d) 56.

Generally disclosure to outsiders of privileged information would constitute waiver of the privilege.[184] However, it may be necessary for certain outsiders such as a co-accused and their counsel to be present to assist in the preparation of a client's defence.[185] Indeed, an exchange of confidential information between individuals who have a common interest in anticipated litigation is within the context of this privilege. Lord Denning described the nature of this common interest in *Buttes Gas and Oil Co. v. Hammer (No. 3)*[186] as follows:[187]

That is a privilege in aid of anticipated litigation in which several persons have a common interest. If often happens in litigation that a plaintiff or defendant has other persons standing alongside him who have the selfsame interest as he and who have consulted lawyers on the selfsame points as he but who have not been made parties to the action. Maybe for economy or for simplicity or what you will. All exchange counsels' opinions. All collect information for the purpose of litigation. All make copies. All await the outcome with the same anxious anticipation because it affects each as much as it does the others. Instances come readily to mind. Owners of adjoining houses complain of a nuisance which affects them both equally. Both take legal advice. Both exchange relevant documents. But only one is a plaintiff. An author writes a book and gets it published. It is said to contain a libel or to be an infringement of copyright. Both author and publisher take legal advice. Both exchange documents. But only one is made a defendant.

In all such cases I think the courts should, for the purposes of discovery, treat all the persons interested as if they were partners in a single firm or departments in a single company. Each can avail himself of the privilege in aid of litigation. Each can collect information for the use of his or the other's legal adviser. Each can hold originals and each make copies. And so forth. All are the

---

184 *Wellman v. General Crane Industries Ltd.* (1986), 20 O.A.C. 384; *R. v. Kotapski* (1981), 66 C.C.C. (2d) 78 (Que. S.C.).

185 *R. v. Dunbar* (1982), 68 C.C.C. (2d) 13, 28 C.R. (3d) 324, 138 D.L.R. (3d) 221 (Ont. C.A.).

186 [1980] 3 All E.R. 475 (C.A.); vard. for other reasons [1982] A.C. 888, [1981] 3 All E.R. 616 (H.L.).

187 *Ibid.*, at 483-84.

subject of the privilege in aid of anticipated litigation, even though it should transpire that, when the litigation is afterwards commenced, only one of them is made a party to it. No matter that one has the originals and the other has the copies. All are privileged.

Moreover, where the communication to the third person is itself subject to privilege, such as the 'anticipation of litigation privilege', the original privilege is not waived.[188] The same rule would apply where the second communication was privileged on some other basis, such as marital communications privilege.[189]

Although the actual disclosure to the third person made in anticipation of litigation would not waive the original privilege, there is some debate over whether the privilege is waived where the third person takes the stand at trial and gives testimony. In *Bell Canada v. Olympia & York Developments Ltd.*,[190] Justice Eberle of the Ontario Supreme Court held that there was no waiver of privilege with respect to documents disclosed to an expert witness even when that witness testified at trial. The position is no different than if the client takes the stand. Disclosure of confidential communications between the client and the lawyer is not required in such a case. In *Bombardier v. Canada (Restrictive Trade Practices Comm.)*,[191] on the other hand, the Federal Court stated, *in dicta*, that the privilege might be waived where experts testify at trial and have founded their opinions on confidential communications. In fact, it was so held by the British Columbia Supreme Court in *Vancouver Community College v. Phillips Barratt*[192] and the following rationale was given:

---

188 *Wellman v. General Crane Industries Ltd., supra*, note 184; *Bell Canada v. Olympia & York Developments Ltd.* (1989), 68 O.R. (2d) 103, 36 C.P.C. (2d) 193, 33 C.L.R. 258 (H.C.J.); *Bombardier Ltd. v. Canada (Restrictive Trade Practices Comm.)* (1980), 48 C.P.R. (2d) 248 (*sub nom. Re A.G. Can. and Restrictive Trade Practices Comm.*) 113 D.L.R. (3d) 295 (Fed. Ct.).

189 *R. v. Kotapski, supra*, note 184.

190 *Supra*, note 188. See also *Highland Fisheries Ltd. v. Lynk Electric Ltd.* (1989), 63 D.L.R. (4th) 493 (N.S.T.D.); *Kelly v. Kelly* (1990), 42 C.P.C. (2d) 181 (Ont. U.F.C.).

191 *Supra*, note 188. See also *Delgamuukw v. British Columbia* (1988), 32 B.C.L.R. (2d) 156, 55 D.L.R. (4th) 73 (S.C.).

192 (1987), 20 B.C.L.R. (2d) 289, 27 C.L.R. 11, 38 L.C.R. 30 (S.C.) at 296-97 (B.C.L.R.).

So long as the expert remains in the role of a confidential advisor, there are sound reasons for maintaining privilege over documents in his possession. Once he becomes a witness, however, his role is substantially changed. His opinions and their foundation are no longer private advice for the party who retained him. He offers his professional opinion for the assistance of the court in its search for the truth. The witness is no longer in the camp of a partisan. He testifies in an objective way to assist the court in understanding scientific, technical or complex matters within the scope of his professional expertise. He is presented to the court as truthful, reliable, knowledgeable and qualified. It is as though the party calling him says: "Here is Mr. X, an expert in an area where the court needs assistance. You can rely on his opinion. It is sound. He is prepared to stand by it. My friend can cross-examine him as he will. He won't get anywhere. The witness has nothing to hide."

It seems to me that in holding out the witness's opinion as trustworthy, the party calling him impliedly waives any privilege that previously protected the expert's papers from production. He presents his evidence to the court and represents, at least at the outset, that the evidence will withstand even the most rigorous cross-examination. That constitutes an implied waiver over papers in a witness's possession which are relevant to the preparation or formulation of the opinions offered, as well as to his consistency, reliability, qualifications and other matters touching on his credibility.

No doubt the witness should be subject to cross-examination on the factual basis of the opinion. But since an expert usually gives an opinion on the basis of hypothetical facts and is not generally offering the facts as proof thereof, there would seem to be little reason for compelling disclosure of the source of those facts if that source is otherwise a privileged communication or document. As to the expert's credibility, caution should be exercised before that becomes the basis for wide-ranging disclosure of all solicitor-expert communications and drafts of reports. In any event, it might just lead to a general practice among solicitors of destroying drafts after they are no longer needed just to avoid the problem.

(d) By Legislation

It has been held that if the solicitor-client privilege is to be abrogated by legislation, it must be done in clear and in unambiguous terms.[193] However, s. 10(b) of the *Charter* may put the protection of the solicitor-client privilege which is implicit in any right of an accused to instruct counsel completely beyond the reach of Parliament or the provincial legislatures.[194] The privilege may also be part of the guarantee against deprivation of liberty or security of the person except in accordance with fundamental justice as set out in s. 7 of the *Charter* and thus may be immune from any legislation that would have the effect of undermining it.

(e) Inadvertent Disclosure or Intercepted Communications

Occasionally, the disclosure by the client, or the solicitor, is totally inadvertent without any intention of waiver, deliberate or implied. The communication may have come into a third party's possession by accident or by stealth. Is the manner by which disclosure occurred significant? Or is the mere loss of confidentiality, whether accidental or by design, sufficient to constitute a loss of the privilege? The traditional common law has said it does not matter. In either circumstance, the privilege is lost and the communication is admissible.

This rule was authoritatively established by the English Court of Appeal in *Calcraft v. Guest*.[195] In that case, the Court rejected the argument that the solicitor-client privilege which protected certain documents could be extended to preclude the admissibility of secondary evidence by way of copies thereof. The Court added that they were admissible irrespective of how they had been acquired.

Almost a century later, Lamer J. in *Descôteaux v. Mierzwinski* stated:[196]

---

193 *Canada (Director of Investigation and Research) v. Canada Safeway Ltd.* (1972), 26 D.L.R. (3d) 745, [1972] 3 W.W.R. 547, 6 C.P.R. (2d) 41 (B.C.S.C.); *Descôteaux v. Mierzwinski*, [1982] 1 S.C.R. 860, 70 C.C.C. (2d) 385, 28 C.R. (2d) 389, 1 C.R.R. 318, 141 D.L.R. (3d) 590, 44 N.R. 462, at 875 (S.C.R.).

194 *R. v. Wilson* (1982), 38 O.R. (2d) 240 (Prov. Ct.).

195 [1898] 1 Q.B. 759 (C.A.). Even earlier nineteenth-century English cases had stated the same proposition: see *Lloyd v. Mostyn* (1842), 10 M. & W. 478; *Phelps v. Prew* (1854), 3 E. & B. 430, 118 E.R. 1203 (Q.B.); *Stockfleth v. De Tastet* (1814), 4 Camp. 10, 171 E.R. 4.

196 *Supra*, note 193, [1982] 1 S.C.R. 860 at 871 (note) (S.C.R.).

In its present state, the rule of evidence . . . would not prohibit a third party [who has come into possession of the communication] from making such a disclosure.

Therefore, if a third party overhears the communication, with or without the client's consent, no privilege can be claimed and that person may be forced to reveal the conversation. Similarly, if a third party, openly or covertly, secures a document or makes a copy thereof, he may produce it, notwithstanding that it would have otherwise been privileged in the solicitor's possession.

If the rationale behind the solicitor-client privilege is to encourage people to speak frankly with their solicitors, the concern that someone may be overhearing, or that a communication may be intercepted, does not promote that end. Nevertheless, the courts have placed greater weight upon the competing policy interest that all relevant facts be disclosed to the court and have not extended the protection of the privilege to communications intended to be passed between a solicitor and his client, but which have gone astray and have fallen into the hands of another.

In certain circumstances, however, equity may be invoked to restrain an individual, who has unlawfully or improperly obtained evidence, from introducing it in a civil proceeding. This equitable principle emerges from the famous case of *Ashburton (Lord) v. Pape.*[197] In that case, Lord Ashburton attempted to enjoin the defendant from putting into evidence copies of letters which he obtained in a dishonest manner from Lord Ashburton's solicitor. The original letters were protected from disclosure by legal-professional privilege. The defendant hoped to use copies of these letters as secondary evidence in a bankruptcy proceeding in which he was seeking a discharge of his bankrupt status, and which, in turn, was opposed by the plaintiff, one of his creditors. Cozens-Hardy M.R. reaffirmed the principle that illegally obtained evidence is admissible in civil proceedings and explained it this way.[198]

The rule of evidence as explained in *Calcraft v. Guest* merely amounts to this, that if a litigant wants to prove a particular document which by reason of privilege or some circumstance he

---

197 [1913] 2 Ch. 469 (C.A.).
198 *Ibid.*, at 473.

cannot furnish by the production of the original, he may produce a copy as secondary evidence although that copy has been obtained by improper means, and even, it may be, by criminal means. The Court in such an action is not really trying the circumstances under which the document was produced. That is not an issue in the case and the Court simply says: "Here is a copy of a document which cannot be produced; it may have been stolen, it may have been picked up in the street, it may have improperly got into the possession of the person who proposes to produce it, but that is not a matter which the Court in the trial of the action can go into."

Notwithstanding the fact that the copies of the letters in question could accordingly have been introduced as evidence, the Court granted an injunction to restrain the defendant from introducing that evidence in the bankruptcy proceeding. The Court thereby recognized that the equitable remedy of injunction would be available to prevent confidential material, which had been unlawfully acquired or copied, from being used in a proceeding against the lawful owner of such material or to prevent its general publication.[199] The following words of Swinfen Eady L.J. perhaps best illustrate the Court's reasoning on the matter:[200]

There is here a confusion between the right to restrain a person from divulging confidential information and the right to give secondary evidence of documents where the originals are privileged from production, if the party has such secondary evidence in his possession. The cases are entirely separate and distinct. If a person were to steal a deed, nevertheless in any dispute to which it was relevant the original deed might be given in evidence by him at the trial. It would be no objection to the admissibility of the deed in evidence to say you ought not to have possession of it. His unlawful possession would not affect the admissibility of the deed in evidence if otherwise admissible. So again with regard to any copy he had. If he was unable to obtain or compel

---

199 For an instance in which a court granted an injunction to restrain the publication of confidential information, see *Argyll (Duchess) v. Argyll (Duke)*, [1965] 2 W.L.R. 790, [1965] All E.R. 611.
200 *Supra*, note 197, at 476-77.

production of the original because it was privileged, if he had a copy in his possession it would be admissible as secondary evidence. The fact, however, that a document, whether original or copy, is admissible in evidence is no answer to the demand of the lawful owner for the delivery up of the document, and no answer to an application by the lawful owner of confidential information to restrain it from being published or copied.

The remedy of injunction, therefore, may be invoked by a party to a confidence in order to restrain the use of confidential material by another in a subsequent proceeding to prevent a breach of that confidence.[201] The decision is confusing in that it both affirms the principle in *Calcraft v. Guest* and at the same time appears to undermine it. The reasoning in the *Ashburton* case leads to the anomalous result that if a party prior to trial seeks an injunction he or she will be successful in preventing a copy of a document which has been improperly obtained by a breach of confidence from being used at trial. Yet if the party waits until trial and objects to the admissibility of the illegally obtained evidence, the court will be bound to apply the rule in *Calcraft v. Guest* and permit its admission into evidence. Unfortunately, this distinction in procedure is one that is not "logically satisfactory".[202]

Notwithstanding this, English and Canadian cases continue to abide by this dichotomous rule. In England in *Derby & Co. Ltd. v. Weldon (No. 8)*,[203] the Court of Appeal upheld an injunction against the use of documents inadvertently disclosed by the defendant's solicitors, yet at the same time asserting that *Calcraft v. Guest* was still the law to be applied when the court is dealing with admissibility of the evidence at trial. In Canada, in *Pfiel v. Zinc*,[204] a British Columbia court allowed cross-examination on notes of an interview between a solicitor-client which had inadvertently been sent to the opposite party. And in *McPherson v. Institute of Chartered Accountants (British Columbia)*[205] another British Columbia court invoked the *Ashburton*

---

201 *Descôteaux v. Mierzwinski, supra*, note 193, at 871 (S.C.R.); *Slavutych v. Baker*, [1976] 1 S.C.R. 254, 38 C.R.N.S. 306, [1975] 4 W.W.R. 620, 75 C.L.L.C. 14,263, 55 D.L.R. (3d) 224.
202 *Goddard v. Nationwide Building Society*, [1986] 3 All E.R. 264 (C.A.), at 270.
203 [1991] 1 W.L.R. 73 (C.A.).
204 (1984), 60 B.C.L.R. 32 (S.C.).
205 (1988), 32 B.C.L.R. (2d) 328, [1989] 2 W.W.R. 649 (C.A.).

doctrine to enjoin the use of a privileged legal opinion that somehow had come into the possession of the other side.

However, more recently, there has been resistance by some courts to slavishly follow the rule of admissibility laid down by *Calcraft v. Guest* in situations where the privileged information has come into a third party's hands by non-innocent means. In *Re Markovina*,[206] Skipp J. of the British Columbia Supreme Court ruled inadmissible an affidavit containing privileged information, holding that the *Calcraft* rule did not apply where the third party is not an innocent bystander. Here, the party seeking to introduce the information actively sought to obtain the evidence when that party knew or ought to have known it was privileged. And in *Double-E Inc. v. Positive Action Tool Western Ltd.*,[207] Muldoon J. of the Federal Court, Trial Division, refused to countenance the admissibility of privileged documents which had been inadvertently disclosed.

In criminal proceedings, if the privileged information is sought pursuant to a search warrant or a subpoena, an application may be brought prior to trial to quash the warrant or subpoena on that ground.[208] Alternatively, a summary application may be made to a superior court judge for an order for the return of documents seized from the possession of a lawyer by a warrant issued under a federal statute if the judge determines that a named client has a solicitor-client privilege in the document.[209]

In situations where the communications come into possession of a third party not by innocent means but by trickery, there may be another basis upon which to seek protection from disclosure of such evidence. This is to rely upon notions of public policy precluding a party who has acted improperly in the proceedings from making use of such evidence. There is some authority that courts do have a discretion to balance the public interest that the truth should be

---

206 (1991), 57 B.C.L.R. (2d) 73 (B.C.S.C.). See also *Vancouver Hockey Club Ltd. v. National Hockey League* (1987), 18 B.C.L.R. (2d) 91, 44 D.L.R. (4th) 139 (S.C.), at 91 (B.C.L.R.).

207 [1989] 1 F.C. 163, 21 F.T.R. 121, 21 C.P.R. (3d) 195, 20 C.I.P.R. 109.

208 *R. v. Logan* (1988), 65 O.R. (2d) 717 (C.A.); *R. v. Westmoreland* (1985), 15 C.C.C. (3d) 340, 48 O.R. (2d) 377, [1984] I.L.R. 1-1829, 14 D.L.R. (4th) 112 (H.C.J.).

209 *ITC Film Distributors v. Video Exchange Ltd.*, [1982] 2 All E.R. 241 (Ch. D.). In England, this discretion upon public policy grounds does not exist in criminal cases; see *R. v. Uljee*, [1982] 1 N.Z.L.R. 561 (C.A.).

ascertained against the public interest that a solicitor should be able to deal with the client confidentially without fear that their communications will be intercepted by stealth or trick and then used against the client in evidence.[210] In Canada it is open to question whether such a discretion exists in the trial judge.[211] At least that was so prior to the existence of the *Charter*. It can now be argued that in criminal cases the interception of solicitor-client communication amounts to an unreasonable search or seizure or interference with an accused's right to retain and instruct counsel and as such should be excluded under s. 24 (2).[212] Furthermore, if a solicitor-client communication is intercepted pursuant to a judicially authorized interception, "[a]ny information obtained by an interception that, but for the interception, would have been privileged remains privileged and inadmissible as evidence without the consent of the person enjoying the privilege."[213] Thus, the section preserves the privileged character of the communication notwithstanding it was intercepted by lawful means.

C. Husband and Wife Communications

1. Origin and Rationale

Unlike solicitor-client privilege, the privilege for marital communications is expressly set out in statute. Section 4(3) of the *Canada Evidence Act [CEA]*[214] provides:

> No husband is compellable to disclose any communication made to him by his wife during their marriage, and no wife is compellable to disclose any communication made to her by her husband during their marriage.

---

210 *Criminal Code*, R.S.C. 1985, c. C-46, s. 488.1 [en. R.S.C. 1985, c. 27 (1st Supp.), s. 71].
211 *R. v. Dunbar* (1982), 62 C.C.C. (2d) 13, 28 C.R. (3d) 324, 138 D.L.R. (3d) 221 (Ont. C.A.), at 42 (C.C.C.).
212 *R. v. Manninen*, [1987] 1 S.C.R. 1233, 34 C.C.C. (3d) 385, 58 C.R. (3d) 97, 21 O.A.C. 192, 41 D.L.R. (4th) 301, 61 O.R. (2d) 736n, 76 N.R. 198; *R. v. Playford* (1987), 40 C.C.C. (3d) 142, 61 C.R. (3d) 101, 63 O.R. (2d) 289, 24 O.A.C. 161 (C.A.); *R. v. Longaphie* (1988), 35 C.R.R. 167 (Ont. Dist. Ct.); see also Chapter 9.
213 *Criminal Code*, R.S.C. 1985, c. C-46, s. 189(6); *R. v. Lloyd*, [1981] 2 S.C.R. 645, 64 C.C.C. (2d) 169, 31 C.R. (3d) 157, 35 B.C.L.R. 145, 131 D.L.R. (3d) 112, 39 N.R. 474.
214 R.S.C. 1985, c. C-5.

The provincial Evidence Acts contain similarly worded provisions:[215]

At common law, spouses were disqualified from testifying on behalf of or against each other on the ground that they were so closely identified with each other that an aura of bias would surround any evidence that they might give.[216] Other justifications for the rule of incompetency of spouses were the promotion of conjugal confidences and the preservation of matrimonial harmony.[217] Although there was some recognition in the early 19th century of the fact that the disclosure of communications between married persons would jeopardize mutual confidence and trust which are basic to the maintenance of the relationship, no separate and distinct privilege protected such communications.[218] In any event, there was no necessity for such protection, because the general rule of disqualification of spouses was sufficient to ensure the sanctity of confidences between them. If a spouse was incompetent to testify as a witness, there could be no issue as to the revelation of any communication with his or her spouse. When the rule of incompetency of spouses was abolished and husbands and wives were made competent and compellable as witnesses in civil cases[219] and the accused and his or her spouse were made competent witnesses in criminal cases,[220] the legislators at the same time created a privilege against disclosure of communications made between spouses during the marriage.

Ambiguities abound in the interpretation and application of the privilege. For example, does the privilege protect only verbal commu-

---

215 Evidence Acts: Alberta, R.S.A. 1980, c. A-21, s. 8; British Columbia, R.S.B.C. 1979, c. 116, s. 8; Manitoba, R.S.M. 1987, c. E150, s. 8; New Brunswick, R.S.N.B. 1973, c. E-11, ss. 5 [am. 1990, c. 17, s. 3] and 10; Newfoundland, R.S.N. 1970, c. 115, s. 4; Northwest Territories, R.S.N.W.T. 1988, c. E-8, s. 6; Nova Scotia, R.S.N.S. 1989, c. 154, s. 49; Ontario, R.S.O. 1980, c. 145, s. 11; Prince Edward Island, R.S.P.E.I. 1988, c. E-11, s. 9; Saskatchewan, R.S.S. 1978, c. S-16, s. 36; Quebec, *Code of Civil Procedure*, R.S.Q. 1977, c. C-25, s. 307; Yukon Territory, R.S.Y. 1986, c. 57, s. 6.
216 *Davis v. Dinwoody* (1792), 4 Term Rep. 678, at 679, 100 E.R. 1241 (K.B.). See also, Chapter 13, III.B.
217 *Woods v. Mackey* (1881), 21 N.B.R. 109 (C.A.); *Rumping v. Director of Public Prosecutions*, [1962] 3 All E.R. 256 (H.L.).
218 *Rumping v. Director of Public Prosecutions, ibid.*, at 258-59.
219 English *Evidence Amendment Act, 1853* (16 and 17 Vict.), c. 83, s. 3. A similar provision was adopted in Ontario in 1869: S.O. 1869, c. 13.
220 English *Criminal Evidence Act*, 1898 (61 & 62 Vict.), c. 36, s. 1(d); *Canada Evidence Act, 1893*, S.C. 1893, c. 31.

nications between spouses, or does it encompass non-verbal communication, or for that matter, observations by one spouse of the conduct or acts of his or her mate? Does the privilege shield only those communications which were intended to be confidential? Are communications which were made prior to marriage privileged? If one of the spouses dies or if they become divorced, does the privilege continue? Much turns upon the policy rationale behind the privilege; and it would be best to examine each of the problems in turn.

2. Subject-Matter of the Privilege

The subject-matter of the statutory privilege includes "any communication". Communication is the act of imparting information and thus logically should include all conduct, oral, written or otherwise which is intended to convey a thought or message to one's spouse. That is clear. But should the phrase "any communication" be construed to include observations of facts or events which were not intended by a spouse to be expressive, but which information was learned only because of the intimacy and privacy of the marital relationship? The Supreme Court of Canada examined this problem in the context of a criminal proceeding. In *Gosselin v. R.*,[221] a murder prosecution, the wife of the accused was, notwithstanding her claim of privilege, forced to disclose that she saw her husband's blood-spattered clothes shortly after he left the premises. A majority of the Court held that the observation of this non-communicative fact did not constitute a "communication" within the meaning of the relevant provision of the *CEA*.[222] The dissenting judges, Girouard and Mills JJ., took a more liberal view of the word "communication" and were prepared to extend the protection to all kinds of relations between the spouses and to any information which was secured from a spouse as a result of the marital relationship. The restrictive interpretation by the majority of the Supreme Court of Canada is consistent with the limitation of the solicitor-client privilege to communications only.[223] It is also in accord with the overall policy that there be few restrictions on the power of the court to enquire into all relevant facts. Nevertheless, if one of the justifications for the existence of the privilege is to ensure candour in marital relations, then any act, whether intended to

---

221 (1903), 33 S.C.R. 255, 7 C.C.C. 139 [Que.].
222 Now see R.S.C. 1985, c. C-5, s. 4(3).
223 See this Chapter, II.B.3.(b).

be communicative or not, taking place within the intimacy of the marital relationship should be protected. Is there any reason why the court should be prepared to cloak with privilege an admission of guilt that may be made by an accused to his wife, but not her discovery of tell-tale clothes? Both events would have taken place within the privacy and confidence of the conjugal relationship.

The protection given to the communication does not shield disclosure of material facts upon which the litigant relies. In *Ostrom v. Henders*,[224] Master Barlow drew a distinction between communications made between spouses and the facts upon which a party relies for the allegations made in his pleading.[225]

> The cases which have been quoted in support of the contention that the adult plaintiff is not compelled to answer all deal with such questions as, "What did your wife tell you?" or, "What was said to you by your wife?" These are communications. The facts upon which the allegations in the statement of claim are based are admittedly known to the adult plaintiff. The fact that he may have obtained some of them from his wife and the others from the infant plaintiff who is some thirteen years of age, does not relieve him from disclosing to the defendant upon examination for discovery the facts upon which he relies . . .

If the sanctity of the marriage bond is dependent upon the protection of confidences, it would be logical to insist that the right to claim privilege does not attach to all the usual and ordinary exchanges between a husband and wife in their daily lives, but only to those communications which were induced by the existence of the marital relationship and which were intended to be confidential. The governing legislation, however, imposes no such requirement, and would allow the privilege to attach to "any communication". Nor have Canadian courts shown a propensity to interpret the provision narrowly so as to limit privilege to confidential communications only.[226]

---

224 [1939] O.W.N. 594 (H.C.J.).
225 *Ibid.*, at 595.
226 *Connolly v. Murrell* (1891), 14 P.R. 187, at 188 (Practice Ct.); affd. 14 P.R. 270; *MacDonald v. Bublitz* (1960), 31 W.W.R. 478, 24 D.L.R. (2d) 527 (B.C.S.C.). Wigmore, however, argues that because the basis of the immunity given to marital

Thus, discussions between husband and wife about ordinary business matters would be privileged, notwithstanding that they would have been more than willing to discuss the subject-matter in the presence of other persons, or would have consented to a repetition of the conversation by others.

3. Marital Status

Another problem of statutory interpretation relates to the marital status at the time that the communication was made. The legislation provides that the spouses are not compellable to disclose any communication made between them "during the marriage". Is this to be interpreted to mean that the parties must be married at the time that the communication was made, or at the time that disclosure is sought, or both? Would the policy justification for protection of marital communications be met if the privilege was extended to: (1) conversations between a man and a woman who at the time, although not married, are intimate with each other and intend to and subsequently do marry; and (2) conversations between a husband and wife, one of whom has died prior to the time of disclosure, or who, prior to trial, have divorced or are living separate and apart? If the desire is paramount to prevent interference with matrimonial harmony by forcing one of the spouses to make disclosure which may have the effect of impairing the relationship, then it follows that the privilege can be invoked only if there is a subsisting marriage at the time that disclosure is sought; however, it need not necessarily be in existence when the communication took place. On the other hand, if the rationale for the privilege lies not in the danger of embarrassing or disturbing the parties in their marital relations, but in the protection of confidences so that parties will be encouraged to communicate freely with each other without the fear of subsequent publicity, then it is of importance that the parties be married when the communica-

---

communications is the protection of spousal confidences, only communications which were intended to be private would be privileged. Accordingly, he would construe the phrase "any communication" as possessing the implied limitation of confidentiality. Wigmore would presume that all marital communications were, by implication, intended to be confidential unless negatived by circumstances, such as the known presence of a third party or the obvious intention to convey the message to a third party, which indicate the contrary: 8 Wigmore, *Evidence* (McNaughton rev., 1961), § 2336.

tion was made, but of no consequence that at the time of disclosure the relationship had been terminated by reason of divorce or death, or the spouses are separated without any reasonable possibility of reconciliation.[227]

The courts, however, have not consistently adhered to one policy over the other, particularly on the question of whether the privilege continues after the termination of the marital relationship. Yet they have been steadfast in one respect. They all maintain that a valid and subsisting marriage had to be in existence at the time that the communication was made. Thus, discussions between parties living together in a common-law relationship will not be protected, "since the relation is not one in which the law wishes to foster confidence."[228] Similarly, the privilege will not apply if the marriage was bigamous. Accordingly, in *Wells v. Fisher*[229] the Court denied privilege to communications between a wife and her second husband whom she married believing, erroneously, that her first husband had died. It is suggested that the requirement that there be an existing marriage between the parties at the time of the communication should not be strictly applied in all situations. For example, where the parties intend to wed and make communications within the framework of that relationship, then the fact that no marriage existed at the time of the communications should not bar the exercise of privilege. The contemplation of a marital relationship and the commitment to become married should suffice.

What of the situation in which the husband and wife were living separate and apart at the time that the communication was made? Although the parties were legally married at the relevant time, there

---

227 In *R. v. Salituro*, not yet reported, November 28, 1991 (S.C.C.), the Supreme Court of Canada changed the common-law rule to make spouses who are irreconcilably separated competent witnesses for the prosecution.
228 8 Wigmore, *Evidence, supra*, note 199, § 2335, at 637; *R. v. Coffin* (1954), 19 C.R. 222 (Q.B.) is a case in which a woman who was cohabiting with the accused, but not married to him, was forced to reveal communications passing between them. More recently, see *R. v. Andrew* (1986), 26 C.C.C. (3d) 111, at 121-22 (B.C.S.C.). In light of provincial family law legislation (for example, Ontario *Family Law Act*, 1986, S.O. 1986, c. 4, ss. 29, 30) which now provide support rights and obligations for separated common-law spouses who had cohabited for a specific period of years, can it not be said that there is a public interest in the recognition and maintenance of such relationships?
229 (1831), 1 M. & Rob. 99, 174 E.R. 34 (N.P.).

would in all likelihood be no confidences exchanged in this setting of estrangement and no marital harmony to be preserved. No Canadian court has dealt with this point,[230] but American authors support the view that privilege would not apply.[231] If, however, the communication took the form of an attempted reconciliation between the spouses, then privilege of a different kind would apply.[232]

The courts have not taken a uniform position on the question as to whether a marriage must be subsisting at the time that disclosure is demanded. The few Canadian authorities that exist have gone in opposite directions. Street J. in *Connolly v. Murrell*,[233] referring to a predecessor section of the present Ontario provision, stated, without elaboration, that ". . . the death of the husband or the wife did not remove the seal from the lips of the survivor; even their divorce did not compel them to break their silence."[234] A conflicting viewpoint was expressed in *obiter dicta* by the British Columbia Court of Appeal in a criminal case, *R. v. Kanester*,[235] which, in following the English Court of Appeal decision in *Shenton v. Tyler*,[236] accepted the reasoning that a divorced woman could not claim privilege with respect to communications made between herself and her former husband while they were married. In *Layden v. North American Life Assurance Co.*,[237] the plaintiff brought an action upon an insurance policy on her husband's life. The defendant denied liability on the ground that the husband had committed suicide within two years after taking out the policy. On discovery, the plaintiff wife claimed the protection of s. 10

---

230 Master Drew in *Jackson v. Boyes* (1930), 37 O.W.N. 458 (Master), at 459, did state in *dicta*, however: "Even where the spouses are estranged, and the wife is on the point of permanently leaving her husband . . . statements made by one to the other do not lose their privilege as matrimonial communications, unless the privilege is removed on some other ground." To be consistent with the rules on spousal competency the privilege should not apply in such circumstances. See *R. v. Salituro, supra*, note 227 and Chapter 13, III.B.
231 8 Wigmore, *Evidence, supra*, note 226, § 2335, at 647; E.W. Cleary (ed.), *McCormick on Evidence*, 3rd. ed. (St. Paul: West Publishing, 1984), at 195.
232 See this Chapter, II.C.2.
233 (1891), 14 P.R. 187; affd. 14 P.R. 270.
234 *Ibid.*, at 188.
235 [1966] 4 C.C.C. 231, 48 C.R. 352, 55 W.W.R. 705 (B.C.C.A.) (MacLean J.A. dissenting on another issue); revd. [1966] S.C.R. v, [1967] 1 C.C.C. 97, 49 C.R. 402, 57 W.W.R. 576 (adopting the reasons of MacLean J.A.).
236 [1939] Ch. 620, [1939] 1 All E.R. 827 (C.A.).
237 (1970), 74 W.W.R. 266, [1970] I.L.R. 1-372 (Alta. Master).

THE LAW OF EVIDENCE IN CANADA

of the *Alberta Evidence Act*[238] and refused to disclose the details of any communications made to her by her husband prior to his death. Master Hyndman, in ordering that the wife reattend on discovery and answer questions concerning such communications as would have any relevance to motive or facts relating to the issue of suicide, stated that *Shenton v. Tyler*[239] should be accepted in preference to *Connolly v. Murrell*, and thus held that the death of one of the spouses terminated the privilege. The English Court of Appeal in *Shenton v. Tyler* gave a narrow interpretation to the relevant statutory provision and concluded that the privilege lasted only so long as the parties remained married. Accordingly, privilege cannot be claimed where the marriage has been dissolved by reason of divorce, or terminated by reason of the death of one of the spouses.[240] In the *Shenton* case, the Court ruled that a widow had to disclose communications which her deceased husband had made to her with respect to the alleged establishment of a secret trust. The fact that the relevant statutory provision refers to "husband" and "wife" only, and not to widows or widowers or divorced persons, is consistent with the *Shenton* decision.

4. Intercepted or Overheard Communications Between Spouses

Consistent with the solicitor-client privilege, the privilege relating to matrimonial communications is limited to the spouses themselves. Third persons, who have either intentionally or accidentally overheard or intercepted a communication passing between a husband and wife, by means other than electronic surveillance by some agency of the state.[241] are allowed to and may be compelled to testify

---

238 Now R.S.A. 1980, A-21, s. 8.
239 *Supra*, note 238.
240 See also *R. v. Baker* (1984), 34 Sask. R. 49 (C.A.). Section 179 of draft *Uniform Evidence Act*, Bill S-33, 1980-81-82, provides that the privilege subsists for the lifetime of the declarant; notwithstanding any dissolution of the marriage.
241 In which case the recorded communication may be inadmissible: *R. v. Duarte*, [1990] 1 S.C.R. 30, 53 C.C.C. (3d) 1, (*sub nom. R. v. Sanelli*) 74 C.R. (2d) 281, 37 O.A.C. 322, 103 N.R. 86, 65 D.L.R. (4th) 240, 71 O.R. (2d) 575, 45 C.R.R. 278, in which the Supreme Court of Canada held that electronic surveillance conducted by the police without judicial authorization is contrary to s. 8 of the *Charter* even if the consent of one of the participants to the conversation had been obtained. The communication was nevertheless held to be admissible as the Court was of the view that, in the circumstances, its admission would not bring the

with respect to the communication. In *Jackson v. Boyes*[242] the defendant made an alleged slanderous statement to her husband in the hearing of a number of persons. Master Drew put the point succinctly:[243]

> The fact that remarks might be privileged as between husband and wife does not extend that privilege to remarks heard by third persons: *R. v. Simons* (1834), 6 C. & P. 540; *R. v. Bartlett* (1837), 7 C. & P. 832; nor can the fact that the remarks were not necessarily intended to be heard by the third persons possibly affect the situation.

The leading case on disclosure by third parties of matrimonial communications is *Rumping v. Director of Public Prosecutions*,[244] which involved the murder of a young woman. Shortly after the woman's death, the accused, who was a seaman on a Dutch ship, handed to a shipmate a sealed letter addressed to his wife, and asked him to post it in a foreign port. When the ship reached Liverpool, the accused was arrested, and the letter came into the possession of the police. The letter contained a statement tantamount to a confession. At the trial, objection was made by the accused's counsel that the letter was inadmissible since it was a privileged communication between a husband and wife. The House of Lords disagreed. It held that the wording of the relevant section did not prohibit proof of the communication by other evidence such as the testimony of a person who intercepted a letter between a husband and wife, or by a person who overheard a conversation between the spouses. Lord Morris of Borthy-Gest balanced the policy considerations and came to the following conclusion:[245]

---

administration of justice into disrepute.
242 (1930), 37 O.W.N. 458 (Master).
243 *Ibid.*, at 460.
244 [1962] 3 All E.R. 256, [1964] A.C. 814 (H.L.).
245 *Ibid.*, at 276 (All E.R.), and at 860-61 (A.C.). See also *R. v. Kopinsky* (1985), 39 Alta. L.R. 150, at 152 (Q.B.); *R. v. Armstrong* (1970), 1 C.C.C. (2d) 106, 11 C.R.N.S. 384, 2 N.S.R. (2d) 204; motion for leave to appeal dismissed 4 N.S.R. (2d) 248 (Can.). The policy considerations articulated by Lord Morris of Borthy-Gest are subject in Canada to constitutional protection of a person's reasonable expectation of privacy; see *R. v. Duarte, supra*, note 241; *Thomson Newspapers Ltd. v. Canada (Director of Investigation and Research, Restrictive Trade Practices Commission)*, [1990] 1 S.C.R. 425, 76 C.R. (3d) 129, 54 C.C.C. (3d) 417, 39 O.A.C. 161, 67 D.L.R. (4th) 161, 47 C.R.R. 1, 29 C.P.R. (3d) 97, 106 N.R. 161.

Respect is due to the confidences of married life: but so is respect due to the ascertainment of the truth. Marital accord is to be preserved: but so is public security. If the police found stolen goods in a house and saw on a table a note from a husband to his wife clearly indicating that it was he who had stolen the goods and directing her as to their disposal I cannot think that public policy would require that in court proceedings against the husband no evidence as to the note should be given. If after a murder a dangerous murderer were at large and if what was intended by a husband to be a private admission to his wife of guilt of the murder was by chance overheard by a third person I cannot think that public policy would demand that the third person should be excluded from giving evidence as to what he had heard. Public policy and public safety would alike require that vital evidence should not be withheld.

In addition, the Court held that the stage of confidence between a husband and wife had not been reached in the circumstances of that case, because the letter was never communicated to the wife. More important, the wife was not called as a witness and so no question of statutory privilege ever arose.

If private communications between husband and wife are intercepted by an authorized wire tap the privilege can still be asserted. The Supreme Court of Canada in *R. v. Lloyd*[246] held that such intercepted conversations should be excluded because of the conjoint effect of s. 178.16(5) [now s. 189(6)] of the *Criminal Code* and s. 4(3) of the *Canada Evidence Act*. This decision makes no distinction between those conversations in which a crime that has already been committed is discussed and those conversations in which the commission of a crime is being planned. It should be noted that solicitor-client privilege does not protect conversations in furtherance of a crime.[247] Should the marital privilege not be so limited, as well?[248]

---

246 [1981] 2 S.C.R. 645, 64 C.C.C. (2d) 169, 31 C.R. (3d) 157, 35 B.C.L.R. 145, 131 D.L.R. (3d) 112, 39 N.R. 474.
247 See this Chapter, II.B.3(c).
248 R.J. Delisle, *Evidence: Principles and Problems*, 2nd ed. (Toronto: Carswell, 1990) at 508.

5. Who May Exercise the Privilege

For some inexplicable reason, the privilege rests only with the spouse who has received the communication, and not with the spouse who has made it.[249] Lord Reid in *Rumping v. Director of Public Prosecutions*[250] was at a loss to elucidate any justification for giving the privilege to only the recipient spouse.[251]

> It is a mystery to me why it was decided to give this privilege to the spouse who is a witness: it means that if the spouse wishes to protect the other he or she will disclose what helps the other spouse but use this privilege to conceal communications if they would be injurious, but on the other hand a spouse who has become unfriendly to the other spouse will use this privilege to disclose communications if they are injurious to the other spouse but conceal them if they are helpful.

A literal interpretation of the statutory privilege, however, may not be appropriate. In *Moore v. Whyte (No. 2)*[252] Street C.J. in reviewing legislation in New South Wales, which conferred a privilege upon a

---

249 "A privilege against disclosure was given but it was one that could be waived: if waived it would be waived not by the spouse making the communication but by the spouse to whom it was made . . . the enactment would protect a husband or wife from being obliged to disclose a communication made to him or her by the other but would not protect him or her from being obliged to disclose a communication made by him or her to the other.": *per* Lord Morris of Borth-y-Gest in *Rumping v. Director of Public Prosecutions, supra*, note 244, at 275 (All E.R.), at 858-59 (A.C.). See also *Williamson v. Merrill* (1905), 5 O.W.R. 64 (Master); *McBay v. Merritt* (1946), 11 M.P.R. 20, [1936] 4 D.L.R. 319 (C.A.). In *Jackson v. Boyes, supra*, note 242, however, a communicating spouse was not compelled to disclose on discovery a statement made by her to her husband.
250 *Supra*, note 244.
251 *Supra*, note 244, at 259 (All E.R.), at 833-34 (A.C.). In referring to the English equivalent of the provincial statutory marital privilege, the *16th Report of the English Law Reform Committee on Privilege in Civil Proceedings*, 1967, Cmnd. 3472, stated, at 17-18, as follows: "This curious provision . . . was presumably intended to prevent use being made of admissions made by one spouse to the other, but if so it gives the liberty to disclose to the spouse in whom confidence was reposed and not to the spouse who reposed the confidence. The communicator has no right to prevent the spouse to whom the communication was made from waiving the privilege. This does not make sense."
252 (1922), 22 S.R. (N.S.W.) 570 (C.A.).

spouse in respect of the communication to that spouse, stated:[253]

> The word "communication" is a comprehensive word of very wide meaning and ... it is clear that the intention of the Legislature was to place the seal of the law upon all communications of any kind passing between them during marriage. To purport to observe the strict meaning of the words used, while so interpreting them as completely to nullify this intention is not permissible in our opinion.

If privilege is designed to encourage spouses to confide in one another, then surely waiver of the privilege should not belong only to the recipient of the communication. The statutes do not expressly protect the person who makes the communication and it is clear that an amendment is desirable to make only the communicating spouse the holder of the privilege.[254]

6. Loss of Privilege

As with the solicitor-client privilege, a spouse who has the right to waive the privilege may do so expressly or implicitly by disclosing the communication in an earlier proceeding, or by failing to object to the introduction of the confidential communication in the first instance.

In *Ostrower v. Genereux*[255] the plaintiff alleged a conspiracy to defraud by husband and wife who were both solicitors. On a motion for an interlocutory injunction, the wife filed an affidavit denying

---

253 *Ibid.*, at 583. New South Wales legislation now specifically extends the privilege to communication "made between" spouses: see *Australian Law Reform Commission Report*, (Vol. 2, Interim Report) at 245. In a different context, see *Goldman v. R.*, [1980] 1 S.C.R. 976, 51 C.C.C. (2d) 1, 13 C.R. (3d) 228, 30 N.R. 453 (*sub nom. R. v. Goldman*), 108 D.L.R. (3d) 17, and *R. v. Rosen*, [1980] 1 S.C.R. 961, 51 C.C.C. (2d) 65, 13 C.R. (3d) 215, 108 D.L.R. (3d) 60, 30 N.R. 483.

254 See s. 178 of draft *Uniform Evidence Act*; 8 Wigmore, *Evidence* (McNaughton rev. 1961), § 2340 at 670; E.W. Cleary (ed.), *McCormick on Evidence*, 3rd. ed. (St. Paul: West Publishing, 1984), at 198. The forerunner of s. 4(3) of the *CEA* specifically made the spouse to whom the communication was made incompetent as a witness and he or she could not reveal it; but this section was changed by S.C. 1906, c. 10, s. 1 and was made to conform with the provision in the provincial Evidence Acts.

255 (1985), 5 C.P.C. (2d) 35 (Ont. H.C.J.).

knowledge of the transaction in issue or other transactions conducted by the husband's law firm. The affidavit stated facts from which inferences as to the wife's knowledge of the business of the law firm could be drawn. It was held that the filing of such evidence constituted a waiver of any husband and wife privilege that may have existed with respect to conversations between her and her husband relating to the business of the law firm.

In *Whyte v. Armstrong*[256] the British Columbia Supreme Court held that a spouse who elects to be a plaintiff and raise certain issues cannot then elect to call upon a privilege to resist disclosure of relevant communications.

Apart from waiver of privilege by a spouse, it is unclear whether the court has any discretion in certain circumstances to disallow a claim of privilege. American jurisprudence suggests that the husband and wife privilege should be inapplicable in actions by one spouse brought against the other. The rationale for exclusion of the privilege in such cases is similar to the reasoning supporting disclosure of communications between a solicitor and joint clients in disputes or controversies arising between the two clients.[257] A husband and wife would reasonably anticipate that the communication made between them would not be used to their mutual disadvantage by a stranger; but, as between themselves, there would probably be no intention that the communication remain suppressed.[258]

The Quebec Court of Appeal has held that a spouse who is a compellable witness for the Crown because of the nature of the charge against her husband cannot assert the privilege to suppress a communication made to her by the accused. Kaufman J.A. in *R. v. St. Jean*[259] gave the following explanation:

It seems to me that it would not make sense to make a spouse competent and compellable, only to put severe restrictions on the scope of his or her testimony. Take, for instance, the case of *R. v. Lonsdale* (1973), 15 C.C.C. (2d) 201, 24 C.R.N.S. 225, [1974] 2 W.W.R. 157, where a husband was charged with the attempted murder of his wife. The Alberta Court of Appeal, in a

---

256 (1990), 42 C.P.C. (2d) 97 (B.C.S.C.).
257 See this Chapter, II.B.2.
258 See *McCormick on Evidence, supra*, note 254 at 199-200.
259 (1976), 32 C.C.C. (2d) 438, at 441, 34 C.R.N.S. 378 (Que. C.A.).

clear and succinct opinion (given by Sinclair, J.A.) held that by virtue of s. 4(4) of the Act the wife was a competent and compellable witness against the accused. No conversations between husband and wife appear to have taken place at the time of the incident, but supposing the husband, while pointing a gun at his wife, would have made certain remarks indicative of his intent to kill her, could it be seriously said that while the wife could describe her husband's actions she could not repeat his words? I think not.

Other appellate courts, however, have taken a different view and have held that even in situations where the witness spouse is compellable by the Crown then he or she may claim the privilege.[260]

7. Abolition of the Privilege

Two reasons have been given for the existence of the marital privilege rule:

(1) It encourages candour and frankness in communications between husband and wife;

(2) It avoids the embarrassment and indelicacy of forcing one spouse to reveal conversations with the other and the attendant risk of matrimonial discord.

One must seriously question, however, whether these objectives are satisfied by the privilege. It is doubtful that a spouse is deterred from communicating with his or her mate because of the possibility that at some future time the conversation may be disclosed in court. Few people anticipate that they will be involved in litigation and thus it is difficult to believe that spousal communications will be influenced in any material way by the fact that disclosure cannot be compelled in courts. Husbands and wives communicate with each other not because of the privilege but because of a basic trust in their relationship. In any event, few people would be aware of the existence of the privilege and

---

260   *R. v. Jean* (1979), 46 C.C.C. (2d) 176, 7 C.R. 338, 15 A.R. 147 (Alta. C.A.) at 185 (C.C.C.); affd. [1980] 1 S.C.R. 400, 51 C.C.C. (2d) 192, 16 C.R. (3d) 193, 20 A.R. 360, 31 N.R. 410; *R. v. Mailloux* (1980), 30 C.R. (3d) 121, 55 C.C.C. (2d) 193 at 196 (Ont. C.A.).

thus it cannot be said to affect their conduct.[261] The English Law Reform Committee agreed that the privilege does not promote confidences between spouses, and is therefore of little value. It concluded as follows:[262]

> ... there is, we think, great force in the contention that such a privilege in civil actions other than actions between spouses is of little practical importance and would have a minimal effect upon marital relations. It is unrealistic to suppose that candour of communication between husband and wife is influenced today by section 3 of the *Evidence (Amendment) Act*, 1853, which, as we have pointed out, does not ensure that marital confidences will be respected ...

With respect to the second rationale for the existence of the privilege, i.e., that the court does not wish to interfere with marital harmony, it is submitted that this is not of such a high policy interest so as to warrant the exclusion of relevant, probative evidence bearing on the issues of the case. The necessity for disclosure of material facts in court should override any desire to avoid marital embarrassment. It is suggested, therefore, that the husband-wife privilege with respect to marital communications be abolished altogether.[263] At the least, only a qualified privilege should apply and the trial judge should be given discretion to determine whether disclosure is absolutely essential in the particular circumstances, or whether the subject-matter may be proved by other evidence, thus avoiding any trespass upon the matrimonial relationship. This was the recommendation of the English Law Reform Committee which stated:[264]

---

261 R. Hutchins and D. Slesinger in "Some Observations on the Law of Evidence: Family Relations" (1929), 13 Minn. L. Rev. 675, at 682 indicate that: "... practically no one outside the legal profession knows anything about the rules regarding privileged communications between spouses. As far as the writers are aware (though research might lead to another conclusion) marital harmony among lawyers who know about privileged communications is not vastly superior to that of other professional groups."

262 *16th Report of the English Law Reform Committee on Privilege in Civil Proceedings, supra*, note 251, at 18.

263 *The Report of the Federal/Provincial Task Force on Uniform Rules of Evidence, 1982*, at 416, recommended abolition of the privilege in all cases.

264 *Supra*, note 251. The statutory privilege of a husband or wife to refuse to disclose communications received from his or her spouse during the marriage was repealed, except in relation to criminal proceedings, in England by the *Civil*

On the whole, we think that the reasonable protection of the confidential relationship between husband and wife is best left to the discretion of the judge and, we may add, the good taste of counsel.

8. Privilege Respecting Evidence of Sexual Intercourse Between Spouses

A related privilege is that which allows spouses to decline to give evidence of sexual intercourse between themselves or its abstinence. As pointed out elsewhere,[265] the provincial Evidence Acts made parties and the husbands and wives of such parties competent and compellable witnesses in civil cases. The Acts in a second subsection went on to provide for a privilege.[266] In Ontario, for example, it reads:

Without limiting the generality of subsection (1), a husband or a wife may in an action give evidence that he or she did or did not have sexual intercourse with the other party to the marriage at any time or within any period of time before or during the marriage.

This enactment came into effect in 1946[267] for the purpose of abrogating the rule in *Russell v. Russell.*[268] The House of Lords held in that case that when a child is born during the period of wedlock, both the husband and wife are incompetent to give evidence of their non-access during the marriage to bastardize the child.[269] Statutory reform eliminated the incompetency of the spouses and created a privilege in its place which either spouse can waive. The statute went further than merely abolishing the rule in *Russell v. Russell,* for it allows both party

---

Evidence Act 1968, c. 64, s. 16(3).
265 See Chapter 13, III.B.
266 Evidence Acts: Alberta, R.S.A. 1980, c. A-21, s. 5; British Columbia, R.S.B.C. 1979, c. 116, s. 7(2); Manitoba, R.S.M. 1987, c. E150, s. 5; Nova Scotia, R.S.N.S. 1989, c. 154, s. 47; Northwest Territories, R.S.N.W.T. 1988, c. E-8, s. 4; Ontario, R.S.O. 1980, c. 145, s. 8(2); Prince Edward Island, R.S.P.E.I. 1988, c. E-11, s. 5; Saskatchewan, R.S.S. 1978, c. S-16, s. 35(3); Yukon Territory, R.S.Y. 1986, c. 57, s. 4. New Brunswick and Quebec have not enacted such provisions.
267 *The Evidence Amendment Act,* S.O. 1946, c. 25, s. 1.
268 [1924] A.C. 687 (H.L.).
269 See also *Brown v. Argue* (1925), 57 O.L.R. 297, [1925] 3 D.L.R. 873 (C.A.); *Myers v. Myers,* [1945] O.W.N. 429, [1945] 4 D.L.R. 523 (H.C.J.).

and non-party witnesses to claim the privilege. Moreover, the privilege may be claimed in proceedings involving other than matrimonial matters and is not limited to evidence which has the effect of bastardizing a child.

The statute clearly makes the direct evidence of a husband or wife as to access or non-access admissible. The English Court of Appeal in *Re Jenion; Jenion v. Wynne*[270] held that the statute also permitted indirect or secondary evidence, such as extra-judicial statements to like effect made by a husband or wife, since deceased, provided they were otherwise admissible. The Court reasoned that inasmuch as the rule in *Russell v. Russell* was abrogated in relation to direct evidence, there was no justification for its retention with respect to indirect evidence.

The justification for this privilege is founded in considerations of decency and morality.[271] But it is difficult to imagine that questions of delicacy and embarrassment play any significant role. For, as the English Law Reform Committee pointed out:[272]

> . . . if either spouse is indelicate enough to give evidence on the topic, as is common in matrimonial causes, it is not much use for the other to refuse to give evidence about it, for this would leave the evidence of the first spouse uncontradicted.

In any case, in this day and age, embarrassment is not an appropriate reason to preclude this kind of evidence. Moreover, it is of little value even in legitimacy proceedings. If, in such cases, one spouse testifies that marital intercourse did not take place at the time when the child must have been conceived, a claim of privilege by the other spouse affords only chimerical protection. The evidence of the first spouse stands uncontradicted and there is the danger that the failure to raise a denial will lead to the inference that the testimony of the first spouse was true, when in fact it may have been false. Therefore, nothing is to be gained by a spouse claiming privilege in such circumstances and it is the child who may suffer by its exercise.[273] Because of the absence

---

270   [1952] Ch. 454, [1952] 1 All E.R. 1228 (C.A.).
271   *Goodright & Stevens v. Moss* (1777), 2 Cowp. 591, 98 E.R. 1257.
272   *16th Report of the English Law Reform Committee on Privilege in Civil Proceedings*, 1967, Cmnd. 3472, at 19.
273   The English Law Reform Committee concluded that ". . . the privilege is illusory and may in some cases result in injustice to the child of the marriage. For our part, we would recommend the abolition of the privilege.": *16th Report of the*

of any practical justification for its retention, this privilege was abolished in England in 1968,[274] and in Newfoundland in 1971.[275] Similar reform should be initiated in the other provinces.[276] Spouses should be both competent and compellable to testify that marital intercourse did or did not take place between them at any time.

D. Spiritual Advisers

Until recently, the question of whether there is an absolute common-law privilege for communications made to spiritual or religious advisers has been largely academic. It appears that there has been a practice in English and Canadian courts not to compel members of the clergy to disclose confidential religious communications without regard to whether a privilege for such communications actually existed.[277] In fact, neither in Canada nor in England has there been a single reported case in which a priest has been forced to disclose what was said to him in the confessional.[278] In any event, the threat of

---

Law Reform Committee on Privilege in Civil Proceedings, 1967, Cmnd. 3472 at 19.

274 Civil Evidence Act, 1968, c. 64, s. 16(4).

275 The Evidence (Amendment) Act, 1971, S.N. 1971, No. 48, s. 2.

276 The Ontario Law Reform Commission recommended its abolition (Report on the Law of Evidence) (Ontario: Ministry of the Attorney General, 1976), at 144) as did the Report of the Federal/Provincial Task Force on Uniform Rules of Evidence (Toronto: Carswell, 1982), at 414.

277 R. v. Gruenke, not yet reported. October 24, 1991 (S.C.C.) at 19.

278 "In . . . the 20th century, no English decisions have dealt with the privilege as it appears that the discretion of the prosecutors and the courts have avoided any necessity for such determination. The Ontario practice has similarly been for the trial judge to suggest that questions that would require a violation of priest-and-penitent confidence not be pressed. . .", in R. v. Church of Scientology, supra, note 29, at 537-38 (C.C.C.). See also, Report of the Royal Commission Inquiry into Civil Rights in Ontario, 1968, Vol. 2, at 820-21; 16th Report of the English Law Reform Committee on Privilege in Civil Proceedings, 1967, Cmnd. 3472 at 19-20. Ontario Law Reform Commission, Report on the Law of Evidence (Ontario: Ministry of the Attorney General, 1976) at 145-46; Report of the Federal/Provincial Task Force on Uniform Rules of Evidence (Toronto: Carswell, 1982), at 417-23. In Broad v. Pitt (1828), 3 Car. & P. 518, 172 E.R. 528 (C.P.), Best C.J. stated (at 519, C. & P.): "I, for one, will never compel a clergyman to disclose communications, made to him by a prisoner . . .". R. v. Hay (1860), 2 F. and F. 4, 175 E.R. 933 (N.P.), appears to be the only case in which a court held a priest in contempt for refusal to disclose what transpired between him and his communicant, but it should be noted that the facts which were sought to be disclosed were not communicated to him in the nature of a confession.

temporal sanctions is not generally viewed as an effective means of forcing disclosure because it is doubtful that many members of the clergy would violate what they consider to be a sacred trust even in the face of contempt proceedings.

Only Newfoundland and Quebec have found it necessary to legislate a class privilege to protect the clergy-parishioner relationship.[279] That fact alone might suggest that the common law did not protect religious communications — thus necessitating the statutory protection.[280]

The fundamental question of whether a common-law privilege does exist, however, has become a real issue in Canadian courts lately in situations where the communications in question were made not to priests, but to pastors and lay counsellors of non-mainstream religious organizations and in situations where trial judges have shown less reluctance to compel disclosure. In *R. v. Gruenke*,[281] the trial judge ordered a pastor and lay counsellor of the Victorious Faith Centre (a born-again Christian group) to disclose statements made to them by the accused. They provided such testimony at trial. The accused were convicted and ultimately, the issue was appealed to the Supreme Court of Canada. The Court took the occasion to decide whether there is a common-law privilege for religious communications. Lamer C.J.C. said whether there was such a privilege was essentially one of policy and in his view (supported by six other Judges) it did not favour the recognition of a *prima facie* common-law privilege for this class of communications:[282]

---

279 Newfoundland *Evidence Act*, R.S.N. 1970, c. 115, s. 6; Quebec *Charter of Human Rights and Freedoms*, R.S.Q. 1977, c. C-12, s. 9. Law reform bodies in Canada, Ontario and England have expressly recommended against the enactment of a clerical privilege: see *R. v. Church of Scientology, supra*, note 29, at 539-40 (C.C.C.). A literal interpretation of the statutory privilege in each case suggests that it is reposed not in the communicant but in the cleric, and accordingly, he is not compellable to disclose the communication even in the situation where the parishioner is willing to waive the privilege. Because the privilege belongs to the cleric, only he would have the power to waive it. A more purposive interpretation would vest the privilege in both parties. Moreover, the Newfoundland provision grants privilege only to communications made by way of confession, whereas the Quebec enactment allows a cleric to decline to divulge any information received by reason of his or her status or profession.

280 *Per* Lamer C.J.C. in *R. v. Gruenke, supra*, note 277 at 19.

281 *Supra*, note 277.

282 *Supra*, note 277, at pp. 20-21.

Unless it can be said that the policy reasons to support a class privilege for religious communications are as compelling as the policy reasons which underlay the class privilege for solicitor-client communications, there is no basis for departing from the fundamental "first principle" that all relevant evidence is admissible until proven otherwise.

In my view, the policy reasons which underlay the treatment of solicitor-client communications as a separate class from most other confidential communications, are not equally applicable to religious communications. . . In my view, religious communications, notwithstanding their social importance, are not inextricably linked with the justice system in the way that solicitor-client communications surely are.

While the value of freedom of religion, embodied in section 2(a) [of the Charter], will become significant in particular cases, I cannot agree with the appellant that this value must necessarily be recognized in the form of a *prima facie* privilege in order to give full effect to the *Charter* guarantee.

The extent (if any) to which disclosure of communications will infringe on an individual's freedom of religion will depend on the particular circumstances involved, for example: the nature of the communication, the purpose for which it was made, the manner in which it was made, and the parties to the communication.

L'Heureux-Dubé J. was more inclined to find that religious communications should be accorded a class privilege because of their societal importance even though they stood on a different footing than the solicitor-client relationship. She stated:[283]

In my view, it is more in line with the rationales identified earlier, the spirit of the *Charter* and the goal of assuring the certainty of the law, to recognize a pastor-penitent category of privilege in this country. If our society truly wishes to encourage the creation and development of spiritual relationships, individuals must have a certain amount of confidence that their religious confessions, given in confidence and for spiritual relief, will not be disclosed.

---

283 *Supra*, note 277 at 23.

Not knowing in advance whether his or her confession will be afforded any protection, a penitent may not confess, or may not confess as freely as he or she otherwise would. Both the number of confessions and their quality will be affected . . . The special relationship between clergy and parishioners may not develop, resulting in a chilling effect on the spiritual relationship within our society. In that case, the very rationale for the pastor-penitent privilege may be defeated. The lack of a recognized category also has ramifications for freedom of religion. Concerns about certainty apply as much to the development of specific religions as to spiritual practices in general.

However, unlike a solicitor-client relationship which can be easily identified with very little inquiry (i.e. is the solicitor licensed to practise law and was the communication made for professional reasons?),[284] considerably more analysis into the specific nature of the religious relationship would have to be made to ensure that it fits the category. Moreover, that would not end the inquiry as the creation of a category of privilege would simply acknowledge that society recognizes that the relationship should be fostered and that disclosure of communications will generally do more harm than good. In each situation, it would still have to be established that the communication was made in confidence and that confidentiality is essential to the maintenance of that particular spiritual relationship.

Either way, the Supreme Court of Canada reinforced the notion that religious communications should be examined on a case-by-case basis in accordance with the Wigmore test.[285] This approach to religious communications was first suggested by the Ontario Court of Appeal in *R. v. Church of Scientology*:[286]

In our view, however, while section 2 of the Charter enhances the claim that communications made in confidence to a priest or ordained minister should be afforded a privilege, its applicability must be determined on a case-by-case basis. The freedom is not absolute.

---

284 See Lamer C.J.C. at 20.
285 This four-fold test is set out in this Chapter, II, *supra*, at note 22.
286 *Supra*, note 29, at 540 (C.C.C.).

This pragmatic approach to the identification of privilege by utilizing the Wigmore criteria finds its roots in the Supreme Court of Canada decision in *Slavutych v. Baker*.[287] Lamer C.J.C., in *R. v. Gruenke*[288] explained how both the Wigmore criteria and the *Charter* will assist a court in determining whether it should recognize a religious communication privilege in any particular circumstance:

> This [case-by-case] approach is consistent with the approach taken by this Court in *Slavutych v. Baker, supra*, and is, in my view, consistent with a principled approach to the question which properly takes into account the particular circumstances of each case. This is not to say that the Wigmore criteria are now "carved in stone", but rather that these considerations provide a general framework within which policy considerations and the requirements of fact-finding can be weighed and balanced on the basis of their relative importance in the particular case before the court. Nor does this preclude the identification of a new class on a principled basis.

> Furthermore, a case by case analysis will allow courts to determine whether, in the particular circumstances, the individual's freedom of religion will be imperilled by the admission of the evidence.

> . . .

> The Wigmore criteria will be informed both by the *Charter* guarantee of freedom of religion and by the general interpretative statement in s. 27 of the *Charter*:

>> This Charter shall be interpreted in a manner consistent with the preservation and enhancement of the multicultural heritage of Canadians.

> . . .

> In applying the Wigmore criteria to particular cases, both s. 2(a) and s. 27 must be kept in mind. This means that the case by case analysis must begin with a "non-denominational" approach. The

---

287 [1976] 1 S.C.R. 254, 38 C.R.N.S. 306, [1975] 4 W.W.R. 620, 75 C.L.L.C. 14,263, 55 D.L.R. (3d) 224. See this Chapter, II.
288 *Per* Lamer C.J.C., *supra*, note 277 at 21, 22 and 23.

fact that the communications were not made to an ordained priest or minister or that they did not constitute a formal confession will not bar the possibility of the communications being excluded. All of the relevant circumstances must be considered and the Wigmore criteria applied in a manner which is sensitive to the fact of Canada's multicultural heritage. This will be most important at the second and third stages of the Wigmore inquiry.

A consideration of the Wigmore criteria as applied to the facts of the case led the Court to the conclusion that the communications did not attract privilege. The communications in question did not even satisfy the first requirement: namely, that they originate in confidence that they will not be disclosed. "Without this expectation of confidentiality, the *raison d'être* of the privilege is missing."[289] The communications in question were described as being made more to relieve the accused's emotional stress than for a religious or spiritual purpose. The Court did note that nothing of significance turned on the fact that there was a lack of a formal practice of "confession" in the Victorious Faith Centre Church. While the existence of such a practice might indicate that the parties expected the communication to be confidential, the lack of such a formal confession practice was not in and of itself determinative. Moreover, the Court found that the admission into evidence of the communications did not infringe the accused's freedom of religion.

The issue of privilege, when raised at trial, should be determined within a formal *voir dire* in which evidence can be heard and argument submitted in the absence of the jury. This also provides the accused an opportunity to testify for a limited purpose without being subject to general cross-examination. The trial judge is then best equipped to apply the Wigmore criteria and to rule on the admissibility of the communication in question.[290]

The case-by-case approach was taken by Campbell J. in *R. v. Medina*[291] when faced with the assertion of clerical privilege. He carefully applied Wigmore's four criteria to the facts surrounding the communication in question. He found that the circumstances did not give rise to a privilege since the conversation in question took place

---

289 *Supra*, note 277, at 24.
290 *Supra*, note 277, at 26-27.
291 Unreported, October 12, 1988, Ont. H.C.J.

between the accused and the pastor in a casual way. Also, there was no indication of penitence shown by the accused. Although the statement was made in a religious context, there was real doubt that it was intended to be confidential and it was unclear whether the pastor was being consulted as a minister of religion rather than as someone who might help the accused escape criminal justice. Accordingly, Campbell J. concluded that none of the four Wigmore criteria had been satisfied.

E. *Journalists*

1. Identity of News Sources

Occasionally, journalists are called upon in court proceedings to disclose the identity of a source of information to whom they have promised confidentiality. Proponents of a privilege for this information argue that the threat of disclosure of the sources of information obstructs the press' ability to gather news. It is argued that public policy demands that the press have total freedom to uncover and report wrongdoing. The hazard of disclosure would deter informants from going to the press, thereby depriving the public of important information.[292]

However, courts have not recognized the journalist-source relationship as being a category of relationship entitled to absolute privilege. Two cases coming out of a 1963 inquiry in England into circumstances surrounding breach of the *Official Secrets Act*, relating to stories about British spying activity, accurately summarize the traditional attitude of the Commonwealth courts to the assertion of such a privilege. In *Attorney General v. Clough*[293] Lord Parcker C.J. expressed

---

292 Lord Denning explained the argument in favour of such a privilege in *A.G. v. Mulholland*; *A.G. v. Foster*, [1963] 2 Q.B. 477, [1963] 2 W.L.R. 658, [1963] 1 All E.R. 767, at 771, as follows: "The journalist puts forward as his justification the pursuit of truth. It is in the public interest, he says, that he should obtain information in confidence and publish it to the world at large, for, by so doing, he brings to the public notice that which they should know. He can expose wrongdoing and neglect of duty which would otherwise go unremedied. He cannot get this information, he says, unless he keeps the source of it secret. The mouths of his informants will be closed to him, if it is known that their identity will be disclosed. So he claims to be entitled to publish all his information without ever being under any obligation, even when directed by the court or a judge, to disclose whence he got it."

293 [1963] 1 All E.R. 420, at 427-28 (Q.B.D.).

the state of the law as follows:

> ... I have without the slightest hesitation come to the conclusion that, in regard to the press, the law has not developed and crystallised the confidential relationship in which they stand to an informant into one of the classes of privilege known to the law.

Lord Denning, in the other case arising out of this inquiry, was more expansive in his reasons for the denial of the privilege for this class. In *A.G. v. Mulholland; A.G. v. Foster*[294] he stated:

> [T]he authorities are all one way. There is no privilege known to the law by which a journalist can refuse to answer a question which is relevant to the inquiry, and is one which, in the opinion of the judge, it is proper for him to be asked. I think it is plain that, in this particular case, it is in the public interest for the tribunal to inquire as to the sources of information. How is anyone to know that this story was not a pure invention, if the journalist will not tell the tribunal its source? Even if it was not invention, how is anyone to know that it was not the gossip of some idler seeking to impress? It may be mere rumour unless the journalist shows that he got it from a trustworthy source. And, if he has got it from a trustworthy source (as I take it on his statement he has, which I fully accept), then, however much he may desire to keep it secret, he must remember that he has been directed by the tribunal to disclose it as a matter of public duty, and that is justification enough.

Canadian courts too have refused to recognize a privilege for this category of relationship.[295] The position in England has been changed somewhat by s. 10 of the *Contempt of Court Act, 1981* which states:[296]

> No Court may require a person to disclose, nor is any person guilty of contempt of court for refusing to disclose, the source of

---

294 [1963] 1 All E.R. 767, at 772 (C.A.); see also *McGuinness v. Attorney-General of Victoria* (1940), 63 C.L.R. 73 (Aust. H.C.).
295 *Crown Trust Co. v. Rosenberg* (1983), 38 C.P.C. 109, at 117-18 (Ont. H.C.J.)
296 (Eng.), c. 49. For a recent case applying this provision see *"X" Ltd. v. Morgan Grampian Publishers Ltd.* (1990), 110 N.R. 367 (H.L.).

information contained in a publication for which he is responsible, unless it be established to the satisfaction of the court that disclosure is necessary in the interests of justice or national security or for the prevention of disorder or crime.

Similar "shield laws" exist in many American states. The Canadian position remains governed by the common law.

2. Newspaper Rule

A very limited form of protection from disclosure of the identity of news sources may be applied during the discovery process of a defamation action against the journalist or publisher.[297] This limited protection is referred to as the 'newspaper rule'. It provides that a court has a discretion to not order a journalist to reveal his or her source (or any information that would effectively disclose the identity) in discovery proceedings, even if the information is relevant.[298] However, if the matter proceeds to trial and the identity of the source is still a relevant issue disclosure may be made at that stage.[299] It was

---

297 It also seems to have been applied in a non-libel case in *Crown Trust Co. v. Rosenberg, supra*, note 295, at 118.

298 This issue normally arises where the journalist or representative of the newspaper or magazine, upon being examined for discovery, refuses to answer questions relating to the identity of the source. The plaintiff then brings a motion to compel reattendance to answer the questions refused. Upon this motion the master or judge may refuse to make the order requested.

299 Referred to in *Wasylyshen v. Canadian Broadcasting Corp.* (1989), 32 C.P.C. (2d) 237, at 254 (Sask. C.A.); applied in *McInnis v. University Students' Council of University of Western Ontario* (1984), 47 O.R. (2d) 663, 12 D.L.R. (4th) 457, 46 C.P.C. 93, 31 C.C.L.T. 95 (Co. Ct.); affd. with variance (1984), 48 O.R. (2d) 542, 14 D.L.R. (4th) 126 (H.C.J.); leave to appeal to Div. Ct. refd. (1984), 48 O.R. (2d) 542, at 544 (H.C.J.); *Reid v. Telegram Publishing Co.*, [1961] O.R. 418, 28 D.L.R. (2d) 6 (H.C.); *Red Deer Nursing Home Ltd. v. Taylor* (1968), 67 W.W.R. 1, 1 D.L.R. (3d) 491 (Alta. T.D.); *Baxter v. Canadian Broadcasting Corp.* (1978), 22 N.B.R. (2d) 307, 39 A.P.R. 307 (Q.B.); *Drabinsky v. Maclean-Hunter Ltd.* (1980), 28 O.R. (2d) 23, 16 C.P.C. 280, 108 D.L.R. (3d) 391 (H.C.J.); *Hennessy v. Wright (No. 2)* (1888), 24 Q.B.D. 445n (C.A.); *Hope v. Brash*, [1897] 2 Q.B. 188 (C.A.); *Schmuck v. McIntosh* (1903), 2 O.W.R. 237 (Master); *Marsh v. McKay* (1904), 3 O.W.R. 48; *Sangster v. Aikenhead* (1905), 5 O.W.R. 438; affd. 5 O.W.R. 495; *Hays v. Weiland* (1918), 42 O.L.R. 637, 43 D.L.R. 137 (C.A.). The protection is one granted to the media only. It cannot be claimed by other defendants in libel actions: *Massey-Harris Co. v. DeLaval Separator Co.* (1906), 11 O.L.R. 227; affd. 11 O.L.R. 591 (C.A.); *Dennison v. Sanderson*, [1944] O.W.N. 606; *de Schelking v. Cromie*, [1918]

702

explained by Mr. Justice Wells in *Reid v. Telegram Publishing Co.*[300] as follows:[301]

> ... it ... appears from the cases that when the defendant is a newspaper or journal of some description or reporter therefor, there has, over a long time, developed a rule of practice which is based substantially on grounds of public policy, which has led to the refusal of such information as the plaintiff is now seeking in discovery. It is quite clear, I think, that this is not too great a hardship on the plaintiff because any perusal of the pleadings would, I think, indicate that to establish the defences which are pleaded it will be necessary for the defendant company to call Mr. Drea's informants and through them to not only prove the *bona fides* under which their information was given but also its truth in fact.

In exercising the judicial discretion the court considers whether the sources of information in fact asked for confidentiality, the scope of disclosure requested, how necessary the information is to the case, and whether the information could be obtained by alternate means.[302]

In Ontario, this rule evolved at a time when the general discovery rules imposed significant limits on the scope of discovery. The Canadian application of the rule was also developed with reference to the English cases. In England the scope of allowable pre-trial interrogatories is very limited and, in fact, the newspaper privilege at this stage of proceedings has been codified.[303] Many of the provincial court rules, including those of Ontario, now allow for broad ranging discovery. This has led the courts in other provinces to reject the recognition of a pre-trial privilege.[304] In *Wismer v. MacLean-Hunter Publishing Co.*

---

3 W.W.R. 1038 (B.C.S.C.).

300 *Ibid.*, at 422 (O.R.), and at 10 (D.L.R.).

301 See also *A.G. v. Mulholland, supra,* note 294, at 771, *per* Lord Denning.

302 *Wasylyshen v. C.B.C., supra,* note 299, at 257.

303 Supreme Court Practice, O. 82, r. 6, which prohibits interrogatories with respect to the defendant's sources of information and grounds of belief in defamation actions.

304 *Wasylyshen v. C.B.C., supra,* note 299; *McConachy v. Times Publishers Ltd.* (1964), 50 W.W.R. 389, 49 D.L.R. (2d) 349 (B.C.C.A.); *Price v. Richmond Review (The)* (1965), 54 W.W.R. 378 (B.C.S.C.); *Wismer v. Maclean-Hunter Publishing Co. (No. 2),* [1954] 1 D.L.R. 501, 10 W.W.R. (N.S.) 625 (B.C.C.A.); *Tisman v. Rae,* [1946] 2 W.W.R. 641, 62 B.C.R. 477, [1946] 4 D.L.R. 78 (C.A.); *Maloney v. Winnipeg Free Press Co.,* [1976] 4 W.W.R. 292 (Man. Q.B.); *Savage v. Futcher*

(No. 2),[305] a political commentator, who was being sued in a libel action, was ordered to reveal on discovery the sources of information on which his impugned newspaper article was based. The majority of the British Columbia Court of Appeal in that case felt that the earlier English decision which granted to newspapers immunity from making disclosure of the identity of their informants propounded merely a rule of practice which turned upon the limits of the English system of interrogatories. In contrast, the nature of oral examination for discovery in British Columbia afforded a wider latitude to the examiner who may cross-examine on the issues raised by the pleadings and any matter relevant to those issues. Since the pleadings in the *Wismer* case disclosed a defence of justification, and because malice was put in issue by reason of the defences of qualified privilege and fair comment, the Court held that the identity of the informants was relevant and therefore, could properly form the subject-matter of discovery. Eleven years later, the same court, differently constituted, reiterated the distinction between the English and British Columbia practice of pre-trial discovery. In *McConachy v. Times Publishers Ltd.*,[306] Norris J.A., after acknowledging the non-existence of any "newspaper privilege", went on to add that whatever may be the English practice with regard to the limits of interrogatories, it was clear that such practice had no application to an examination for discovery in British Columbia which allowed for a searching cross-examination into any area relevant to the issues raised in the pleadings.[307] One court has also noted that the application of the 'newspaper rule' could result in the fragmentation of trials if it subsequently turns out that the information as to the identity of the source is still relevant at the time the case comes on for trial.[308]

Although the discovery rules have been liberalized in Ontario, *Reid* has not been overruled, despite some opportunity to do so.[309] In

(1956), 17 W.W.R. 621 (B.C.S.C.); *Hopper v. Dunsmuir (No. 2)* (1903), 10 B.C.R. 23, 23 C.C.L.T. 275 (C.A.); *Ansley v. Ansley*, [1973] 5 W.W.R. 181, 12 R.F.L. 93 (B.C.S.C.); *Richards v. Watch Lake Development Co.* (1978), 9 B.C.L.R. 215, 10 C.P.C. 82 (S.C.).

305   [1954] 1 D.L.R. 501, 10 W.W.R. (N.S.) 625 (B.C.C.A.).
306   (1964), 49 D.L.R. (2d) 349, 50 W.W.R. 389 (B.C.C.A.).
307   See also *Price v. Richmond Review (The)* (1965), 54 W.W.R. 378 (B.C.S.C.).
308   *Wasylyshen v. C.B.C.*, *supra*, note 299, at 258.
309   *Reichmann v. Toronto Life Publishing Co.* (1988), 28 C.P.C. (2d) 11 (Ont. H.C.J.) at 16; leave to appeal refd. 28 C.P.C. (2d) 11n.

McInnis v. University Students' Council of University of Western Ontario[310]
Killeen Co. Ct. J. decided that it was time to put the 'newspaper rule'
to rest, given the expanded range of discovery available in Ontario.[311]
On appeal, J. Holland J. disagreed with Judge Killeen holding that the
fact that the English position was based on particular practice rules
was not relevant. He stated:[312]

> At the discovery stage, the purpose of the rule in a libel action is
> to protect the source of the information, not the information
> itself. The difference between the discovery procedure here and
> in England does not affect this fundamental basis. In *Reid*, above,
> Wells J. expressly did not follow the British Columbia case,
> referred to with approval by the judge below. *Reid* was binding
> authority on that judge and he was required to follow it in so far
> as it dealt with disclosure of the source of information at the
> discovery stage.
>
> While it is unnecessary that I go further, I add that I am in
> agreement with the comments of Wells J. in *Reid* relating to the
> issue of source disclosure.

Leave to appeal to the Divisional Court was refused by Krever J.[313] on
the basis that Judge Killeen was not free to disagree with the *Reid*
decision because of the principle of *stare decisis*. His Lordship made no
comment on the appropriateness of the decision in *Reid*. It would
appear then that in an appropriate case the Ontario court may recon-
sider the decision in *Reid*, but that it is not a foregone conclusion that
it will be overruled. It is suggested that the decision in *Reid* be
reconsidered, particularly in light of the expanded scope of discovery
in Ontario. There is neither a practice nor a policy in law in Ontario
which grants a privilege or immunity to newspapers from disclosing
the identity of the source at discovery. The practice is different in
England where a specific rule of practice, not a rule of policy,[314] grants
such immunity at the interlocutory level.

---

310 *Supra*, note 299.
311 *Ibid.*, at 667 (47 O.R.).
312 *Ibid.*, at 543 (48 O.R.).
313 *Ibid.*, at 544 (48 O.R.).
314 Despite the comments of Holland J. to the contrary, quoted *supra*, at note
312.

The 'newspaper rule', to the extent that it exists, applies only to the identity of the source and not the information provided by the source.[315]

3. Qualified Privilege

(a) Overriding Judicial Discretion

In England, there are dicta in cases dealing with claims of privilege by newspaper reporters to the effect that the court has a discretion to exclude relevant evidence where public policy demands it. Thus in *Attorney-General v. Mulholland; Attorney-General v. Foster*,[316] in an appeal by a journalist from an order committing him for contempt for refusing to disclose his sources of information, the Court of Appeal upheld the order of committal, but Donovan L.J. referred to the need for some residual discretion not only in cases where a journalist asserts a privilege but in situations, ". . . arising out of the infinite variety of fact and circumstances which a court encounters, which may lead a judge to conclude that more harm than good would result from compelling a disclosure or punishing a refusal to answer."[317]

In *Secretary of State for Defence v. Guardian Newspapers Ltd.*,[318] Lord Diplock commented on the common-law position prior to the enactment of s. 10 of the *Contempt of Court Act, 1981*, stating:[319]

The rationale of the existence of this discretion was that unless informants could be confident that their identity would not be disclosed there was a serious risk that sources of information would dry up. So the exercise of the discretion involved weighing the public interest in eliminating this risk against the conflicting public interest that information which might assist a judicial tribunal to ascertain facts relevant to an issue on which it is required to adjudicate should not be withheld from that tribunal. Unless the balance of competing public interest tilted *against* disclosure, the right to disclosure of sources of information in

---

315 *Reichmann v. Toronto Life Publishing Co.*, *supra*, note 309.
316 [1963] 2 Q.B. 477, [1963] 1 All E.R. 767 (C.A.).
317 *Ibid.*, at 772-73 (All E.R.).
318 [1984] 3 W.L.R. 986 (H.L.).
319 *Ibid.*, at 991; see also *British Steel Corp. v. Granada Television Ltd.*, [1981] 1 All E.R. 417, [1981] A.C. 1096 (H.L.).

cases where this was relevant prevailed.

In the exercise of this common law discretion, the protection of some general right, albeit of imperfect obligation, which members of the public had to be informed of reprehensible conduct by persons in responsible positions or of future action intended to be taken by government and other bodies entitled to exercise executive powers, does not appear to have been treated as a factor to be put into the balance when weighing the competing public interests in favour of and against disclosure of sources of information.

Some support for the existence of a judicial discretion to protect the confidentiality of news sources can be found in the decision of Saunders J. in *Crown Trust Co. v. Rosenberg*.[320] In that case the Ontario government had seized the assets of three trust companies and commenced a number of actions against various persons involved with the companies. A defendant sought to set aside an *ex parte* Mareva injunction order and an order appointing a receiver. To obtain evidence in support of the motion the defendant subpoenaed a journalist who had written an article on the Crown Trust affair indicating that the government had not disclosed important information in the affidavit filed in support of its motion for the Mareva and receiver. The journalist declined to answer questions about his government source and the defendant brought a motion to compel him to answer. After determining that no absolute privilege for journalists existed, Saunders J. took a cautious approach to ordering disclosure:[321]

> It seems to me that Stewart must answer questions relating to what he was told by government officials. I go no farther than that at present. I do not order that he answer questions relating to the identity of the government officials. That may not become necessary. It may be that the information will turn out not to be relevant. It may be that once it is known it can be readily made available from other sources. It may be that the plaintiffs will admit its truth for the purposes of the motion. There may be other developments. I recognize that by possibly limiting the

---

320 (1983), 38 C.P.C. 109, at 117-18 (Ont. H.C.J.).
321 *Ibid.*, at 118; see also *Jackson v. Belzberg*, [1981] 6 W.W.R. 273, 31 B.C.L.R. 140 (B.C.C.A.) reversing (*sub nom. Belzberg v. B.C.T.V. Broadcasting System Ltd.*), [1981] 3 W.W.R. 85, at 89 (B.C.S.C.).

initial scope of the examination there will be a further prolongation of proceedings that are already protracted. In my view, proceeding carefully and in a step-by-step fashion in this matter is justified in the interest of preserving the confidentiality of the sources if it is at all possible to do so.

The discretionary approach in this context appears to be an example of a more generally recognized residual discretion to exclude relevant evidence where there are alternative sources for the information and where the interests of uninvolved third parties outweigh the value of the evidence in the particular case.[322]

(b) Application of Wigmore's Four Conditions

The application of Wigmore's four conditions for the judicial recognition of confidentiality,[323] accepted in *Slavutych v. Baker*,[324] could form the basis for the recognition of a qualified privilege for the news media in individual cases.[325] The first two conditions[326] are often met with a communication between a journalist and source. Good arguments can also be made to support the view that the relationship is one which it is in the public interest to foster. The contentious element will be whether the injury that would inure to the relation by the disclosure of the communications is greater than the benefit gained for the correct disposal of litigation.[327] Some guidance for a court on this particular issue can be found in the reasons of Lord

---

322 For example, see *Canadian Broadcasting Corp. v. Lessard*, not yet reported, November 14, 1991 (S.C.C.); *Canadian Broadcasting Corp. v. New Brunswick (Attorney General)*, not yet reported, November 14, 1991 (S.C.C.); *Descôteaux v. Mierzwinski*, [1982] 1 S.C.R. 860, 70 C.C.C. (2d) 385, 28 C.R. (3d) 289, 141 D.L.R. (3d) 590, 1 C.R.R. 318, 44 N.R. 462; *Pacific Press Ltd. v. R.* (1977), 37 C.C.C. (2d) 487, 38 C.R.N.S. 295, [1977] 5 W.W.R. 507 (B.C.S.C.); see also sources cited in S.N. Lederman *et al.*, "Confidentiality of News Sources" in *The Media, the Courts and the Charter* (Toronto: Carswell, 1986), at 246-47.
323 For a general discussion of these four conditions see this Chapter, II.A.
324 [1976] 1 S.C.R. 254, 38 C.R.N.S. 306, [1975] 4 W.W.R. 620, 55 D.L.R. (3d) 224, 75 C.L.L.C. 14,263.
325 Professor Goldsworthy favours such a qualified privilege. See "The Claim to Secrecy of News Sources: A Journalistic Privilege?" (1970), 9 Osgoode Hall L.J. 157.
326 That the communication originates in confidence that it will not be disclosed and that the element of confidentiality is essential to the full and satisfactory maintenance of the relationship.
327 Goldsworthy, *supra*, note 325, at 158-59.

Bridge in *"X" Ltd. v. Morgan Grampian Publishers Ltd.*[328] Although the case considers the application of s. 10 of the *Contempt of Court Act, 1981*,[329] it also deals with the various conflicting public interests in cases of this nature and how it might be determined if one is to take precedence over another in any particular case. Lord Bridge states:[330]

> It would be foolish to attempt to give comprehensive guidance as to how the balancing exercise should be carried out. But it may not be out of place to indicate the kind of factors which will require consideration. In estimating the importance to be given to the case in favour of disclosure there will be a wide spectrum within which the particular case must be located. If the party seeking disclosure shows, for example, that his very livelihood depends upon it, this will put the case near one end of the spectrum. If he shows no more than that what he seeks to protect is a minor interest in property, this will put the case at or near the other end. On the other side the importance of protecting a source from disclosure in pursuance of the policy underlying the statute will also vary within a wide spectrum. One important factor will be the nature of the information obtained from the source. The greater the legitimate public interest in the information which the source has given to the publisher or intended publisher, the greater will be the importance of protecting the source. But another and perhaps more significant factor which will very much affect the importance of protecting the source will be the manner in which the information was itself obtained by the source. If it appears to the court that the information was obtained legitimately this will enhance the importance of protecting the source. Conversely, if it appears that the information was obtained illegally, this will diminish the importance of protecting the source unless, of course, this factor is counterbalanced by a clear public interest in publication of the information, as in the classic case where the source has acted for the purpose of exposing iniquity. I draw attention to these considerations by way of illustration only and I emphasize once again that they are in no way intended to be read as code.

---

328 (1990), 110 N.R. 367 (H.L.).
329 See this Chapter, II.E.1.
330 *Supra*, note 328, at 375.

In *Moysa v. Alberta (Labour Relations Board)*[331] a reporter sought to quash a decision of the Alberta Labour Relations Board ordering her to disclose the identity of and information obtained from members of management of the Hudson's Bay Company during a union organizing campaign. The evidence sought would have supported the union's allegation of unfair labour practices. The reporter argued that she was entitled to a qualified privilege on the basis of the application of Wigmore's four conditions.[332] The Board considered that a qualified privilege might be recognized on the basis of these four criteria, but held that they were not satisfied in this case given that the element of confidence was not part of the maintenance of a continuing relationship between the reporter and the managers and that the injury resulting from disclosure would not be greater than the benefit. The Supreme Court of Canada declined to state whether a qualified testimonial privilege on the basis of the application of these criteria existed in Canada.[333] Sopinka J. agreed with the Board that any such privilege would not be applicable on the facts of this case. Therefore, it remains an open question in Canada whether the application of Wigmore's four conditions could offer any limited protection from the disclosure of the informant's identity or information received from the informant.

(c) Charter, Section 2(b)

It has also been argued that s. 2(b) of the *Charter*, recognizing the freedom of the press, applied to protect a journalist or newspaper from compelled disclosure.[334] In *Moysa v. Alberta (Labour Relations Board)*[335] the reporter argued that s. 2(b) protected the press's right to gather news and that if journalists were compelled to disclose sources then they would lose access to information as news sources "dry up". The

---

331 [1989] 1 S.C.R. 1572, 67 Alta. L.R. (2d) 193, 34 C.P.C. (2d) 97, [1989] 4 W.W.R. 596, 97 A.R. 368, 84 C.L.L.C. 14,028, 40 C.R.R. 197, 60 D.L.R. (4th) 1, 96 N.R. 70; affg. (1987), 52 Alta. L.R. (2d) 193, 79 A.R. 118, 43 D.L.R. (4th) 159, 17 C.P.C. (2d) 91 (C.A.), affg. (1986), 45 Alta. L.R. (2d) 37, 71 A.R. 70, 28 D.L.R. (4th) 140, 25 C.R.R. 346 (Q.B.).

332 8 Wigmore, *Evidence* (McNaughton rev. 1961), § 2285 at 527.

333 *Supra*, note 331 at 157 (S.C.R.).

334 See M. Doody, "Freedom of the Press, the Canadian Charter of Rights and Freedoms, and a New Category of Qualified Privilege" (1983), 61 Can. Bar Rev. 124.

335 *Supra*, note 331.

Supreme Court of Canada declined to decide whether or not s. 2(b) protected the news-gathering function of the press. However, Sopinka J. held that even if it did there would be no right to protection in this case. The reporter's evidence was not sufficient to demonstrate any link between testimonial compulsion and a "drying-up" of news sources. Furthermore, the reporter had not promised her sources confidentiality and this was fatal to her claim that disclosure would constitute a violation of s. 2(b).

In *Coates v. Citizen (The)*[336] Grant J. appears to have recognized the applicability of the *Charter* in cases of this nature. He held, however, that in the circumstances of this case there was no infringement of the press freedom. On appeal to the Nova Scotia Court of Appeal the Court made no comment as to the applicability of the *Charter*.[337]

Subsequently, the Supreme Court of Canada in *Canadian Broadcasting Corp. v. Lessard*[338] considered the impact of s. 2(b) of the *Charter* on the validity of a search warrant issued for the premises of a media organization. La Forest J., who delivered a concurring majority judgment, rejected the argument that there should be a general restriction against searches of the press for fear that it would lose its access to sources:[339]

Another matter requiring consideration is the possibility that the police will uncover other confidential sources in the course of searching for the relevant material. This arguably would point towards adding restrictions against searches of press organizations under all circumstances. While the C.B.C. argues that the possibility of this occurring will also render people less likely to provide the press with information, I am, on the whole, of the opinion that this connection is simply too attenuated; see *Moysa v. Alberta (Labour Relations Board)*, [1989] 1 S.C.R. 1572, at p. 1581, where compulsion of testimony from a journalist was held not to violate s. 2(b) in the absence of evidence that such

---

336 (1986), 72 N.S.R. (2d) 116, 173 A.P.R. 116 (T.D.); affd. in part (1986), 74 N.S.R. (2d) 143, 180 A.P.R. 143, 29 D.L.R. (4th) 523, 11 C.P.C. (2d) 96 (C.A.).
337 *Ibid.*
338 Not yet reported, Nov. 14, 1991 (S.C.C.). See also the companion decision in *Canadian Broadcasting Corp. v. New Brunswick (Attorney General)*, not yet reported, November 14, 1991 (S.C.C.).
339 *Ibid.*, La Forest J. judgment at 5-6.

compulsion would detrimentally affect the journalist's ability to gather information. Should there be evidence in a future case that this does indeed give rise to a real problem, the issue can be addressed at that time. In the meantime, this concern can probably best be addressed by limiting the warrant to specifically delineated items.

The American experience with the comparable First Amendment[340] has offered some protection for journalists.[341] The United States Supreme Court rejected that the First Amendment supported an absolute constitutional privilege in *Branzburg v. Hayes*.[342] However, the majority of judges recognized a limited qualified privilege to be applied on a case-by-case basis. This case-by-case balancing approach has been adopted in many subsequent U.S. cases and appears to be coextensive with a recognized common-law privilege.[343] The relevance of the U.S. experience was apparently recognized by the Nova Scotia court in *Coates v. Citizen (The)*.[344] It will no doubt prove to be an important source of guidance as this matter is more fully considered by the Canadian courts in the future. In light of the Supreme Court of Canada's comments in *Moysa* and *Lessard*, courts in hearing arguments for the application of the *Charter* will expect empirical evidence of the extent of use of confidential sources by journalists. It will not simply be assumed that forced disclosure will affect newsgathering.

F. Doctor and Patient

Notwithstanding the acknowledgement that it is dishonourable and indiscreet for a physician to reveal professional confidences, Anglo-Canadian courts for almost two centuries have steadfastly maintained that a doctor is compellable to divulge such information in a court of justice.[345] The reluctance to extend the privilege, which

---

340 "Congress shall make no law . . . abridging freedom of speech or of the press."
341 For a discussion of the American experience see S.N. Lederman *et al.*, "Confidentiality of News Sources", *supra*, note 322, at 248-54.
342 408 U.S. 665 (1972).
343 For a review of these cases see S.N. Lederman *et al.*, "Confidentiality of News Sources" *supra*, note 322.
344 *Supra*, note 336.
345 *D. v. National Society for the Prevention of Cruelty to Children*, [1978] A.C. 171,

heretofore has been limited to the solicitor-client relationship, may have been based on the feeling that a patient who is obsessed with his or her illness or injury, in seeking medical treatment, gives no thought to the possibility that any disclosure that he or she may make to the physician may subsequently be revealed in the courtroom. In other words, the lack of privilege for medical advisers does not discourage patients from confiding in them, whereas consultation with a solicitor usually implies an awareness of the necessity that the communications be kept in confidence; thus, the policy justification for the protection of solicitor-client communications does not necessarily apply to the doctor-patient relationship.[346]

1. Psychiatric Consultations

Nevertheless, there has been a tendency to recognize the importance of protecting confidentiality in psychiatric treatment. In *Dembie v. Dembie*[347] Stewart J. indicated that he would not compel a psychiatrist-witness to reveal statements made to him by his patient during his examination. He stated:[348]

. . . I think it is inimical to a fair trial to force a psychiatrist to disclose the things he has heard from a patient, and, in addition to that, I think it rather shocking that one profession should attempt to dictate the ethics of another, which the courts are doing when they see fit to state what a doctor will say and what he will not. They are forcing a breach of [the Hippocratic] oath, and the legal concept that the doctor is not breaching it, that he

---

[1977] 1 All E.R. 589 (H.L.), at 244-45 (A.C.); *Hunter v. Mann*, [1974] 2 All E.R. 414, [1974] Q.B. 767 (D.C.); *R. v. Duchess of Kingston* (1776), 20 State Tr. 355, at 537; *Garner v. Garner* (1920), 36 T.L.R. 196; *Halls v. Mitchell*, [1928] S.C.R. 125, [1928] 2 D.L.R. 97, at 136 (S.C.R.); *R. v. Burgess*, [1974] 4 W.W.R. 310 (B.C. Co. Ct.), at 312-13; *Torok v. Torok* (1983), 44 O.R. (2d) 118, 38 C.P.C. 52 (Master).
346 S. Freedman, "Medical Privilege" (1954), 32 Can. Bar Rev. 1, at 5; M.N. Howard, P. Crane and D. Hochberg, *Phipson on Evidence*, 14th ed. (London: Sweet & Maxwell, 1990) at 502; E.W. Cleary (ed.), *McCormick on Evidence*, 3rd. ed. (St. Paul: West Publishing, 1984) at 244; see also *Upham v. You* (1986), 73 N.S.R. (2d) 73, 176 A.P.R. 73, 11 C.P.C. (2d) 83 (C.A.); leave to appeal to S.C.C. refd. (1986), 76 N.S.R. (2d) 180. But see H. Hammelman, "Professional Privilege: A Comparative Study" (1950), 28 Can. Bar Rev. 750, at 753.
347 (1963), 21 R.F.L. 46 (Ont. S.C.).
348 *Ibid.*, at 50.

shall not disclose anything a patient shall tell him unless mete to do so, the idea that it is mete when he gets in the witness box is nonsense, and I have no intention of forcing Doctor Kyne to repeat what his patient told him.

Although *Dembie v. Dembie* was a case in which it could be suggested that the privilege which protected the psychiatrist from making disclosure was one not protecting him in his capacity as a psychiatrist *per se*, but in his capacity as mediator consulted by one spouse in an honest effort to reconcile her marital difficulties with her husband,[349] the importance of protecting the psychiatrist-patient relationship as an entity independent of any matrimonial dispute was emphasized.

Subsequently, in *G. v. G.*,[350] a case in which disclosure was sought of a communication made to a marriage counsellor in an attempt to settle matrimonial differences, Landreville J. in *dicta* stressed the necessity of full and frank disclosure between a patient and his psychiatrist:[351]

Most generally and fundamental to the practice of psychiatry is the fact that the patient seeking medical help must give a detailed picture of his past life. A full statement can only be obtained if the patient knows that what he is to say and hear will be of strict confidential nature. . . .

Legislative action to bring unequivocal recognition of medical privilege would obviously be the rapid answer. But as statutory enactments normally come into existence after *fait accompli* and

---

349 See this Chapter, IV.G.2.
350 [1964] 1 O.R. 361 (H.C.J.).
351 *Ibid.*, at 365-66. In *Nuttall v. Nuttall* (1964), 108 Sol. Jo. 605, a husband in a divorce proceeding against his wife, subpoenaed as a witness a psychiatrist who had been consulted by the wife and the co-respondent. The doctor claimed privilege. The presiding Divorce Commissioner held that "what a person said to a doctor in a professional consultation was not privileged" and the witness was instructed to give his evidence under threat of being committed to prison for contempt of court. The brief report of this decision gives no indication of whether the wife's mental condition was an issue. The *16th Report of the English Law Reform Committee on Privilege in Civil Proceedings*, 1967, Cmnd. 3472, at 22, stated that "in the absence of some issue of this kind, we think it likely that, if the psychiatrist had persisted in his refusal, the Commissioner's exercise of his discretion in insisting on an answer would have been reversed by the Court of Appeal."

accepted, laxity in admitting evidence pertaining to what the laymen believes is privileged communication, is to be resisted.

But, in *R. v. Hawke*,[352] the Ontario Court of Appeal stated that there was no such judicial discretion to exclude this kind of psychiatric evidence unless it is of only slight probative value and gravely prejudicial to the accused.

Although a qualified privilege for psychiatric communications gained a tentative foothold in Canada, only the Province of Quebec has extended the privilege by legislation to the general physician-patient relationship.[353] The Common Law provinces have been reluctant to expand the privilege to protect communications between physician and patient for two reasons. First, it is doubtful that such an extension of privilege would further inspire confidence in the patient and encourage him to make a full disclosure to his doctor as to his symptoms and condition. Secondly, it would serve to suppress highly relevant and probative evidence which would otherwise shed some light on the patient's mental or physical condition. These two factors were mentioned in the *Report of the Royal Commission into Civil Rights in Ontario*[354] as follows:[355]

We have had no representations made to us by members of the medical profession or others, from which a conclusion could reasonably be drawn that patients have received inadequate medical advice because they feared the attending physician might be called upon to testify as to communications made to him during a medical examination. Such a restriction could obviously cause great injustice to litigants. For example, in a personal injury case the previous history of the patient is very important. The patient may deny previous complaints of disability, which available medical testimony could prove without difficulty. The exclusion of such evidence would be an exclusion of the truth. Likewise the most cogent evidence of testamentary

---

352 (1975), 7 O.R. (2d) 145, 22 C.C.C. (2d) 19, 29 C.R.N.S. 1 (C.A.), at 181 (O.R.).
353 *Medical Act*, R.S. Que. 1977, c. M-9, s. 42. In British Columbia, statements made to a medical research group are treated as privileged communications: The British Columbia *Evidence Act*, R.S.B.C. 1979, c. 116, s. 57(4).
354 Report No. 1, Vol. 2 (Ontario Ministry of the Attorney General, 1988).
355 *Ibid.*, at 822.

disability may be evidence of the attending physician based on communications with the patient.

Furthermore, although a number of American states have by statute enshrouded the doctor-patient relationship with privilege, Wigmore felt that its adoption in other jurisdictions should be deprecated.[356] In examining the types of cases in which the doctor-patient privilege had been invoked, Wigmore concluded that 99 per cent of the litigation consisted of three classes of cases:

(1) Actions on life insurance policies where the deceased's representations of his health were involved;

(2) Actions for bodily injury;

(3) Testamentary actions in which the testator's mental capacity was in dispute.

He went on to add:[357]

In all of these the medical testimony is absolutely needed for the purpose of learning the truth. In none of them is there any reason for the party to conceal the facts, except as a tactical manoeuvre in litigation. . . . In none of these cases need there be any fear that the absence of the privilege will subjectively hinder people from consulting physicians freely. The actually injured person would still seek medical aid, the honest insured would still submit to medical examination, and the testator would still summon physicians to his cure.

Compelling reasons, therefore, militate against the extension of the privilege to the general physician-patient relationship, other than one which is psychiatric in nature.[358] The English Law Reform Committee, although not prepared to recommend the creation of a statutory

---

356 8 Wigmore, *Evidence* (McNaughton rev. 1961), § 2380a, at 831.
357 *Ibid.*, at 831-32.
358 Disclosure by physicians is specifically compelled by statute in certain circumstances: for example, in Ontario see *The Highway Traffic Act*, R.S.O. 1980, c. 198, s. 177; *The Vital Statistics Act*, R.S.O. 1980, c. 524, ss. 5, 14 [am. 1990, c. 12, s. 8], 17 [am. 1990, c. 12, s. 9]; *Workers' Compensation Act*, R.S.O. 1980, c. 539, s. 53 [am. 1989, c. 47, s. 18].

privilege, concluded that whether there be disclosure or not was best left to the discretion of the trial judge in the circumstances of each case.[359]

2. Application of Wigmore's Four Criteria

Of course, in view of the Supreme Court of Canada decision in *Slavutych v. Baker*[360] the courts now have a judicial discretion to recognize and give effect to new categories of privilege on a case-by-case basis provided that the four criteria as enunciated in that case are satisfied.[361] In *R. v. S. (R.J.)*[362] the Ontario Court of Appeal considered such criteria in the context of communications taking place within a group therapy session. There, the accused was charged with a number of sexual offences involving allegations of sexual abuse of his young step daughters. After a complaint was made by the victims to their mother and to physicians, the family was referred to a family clinic for counselling sessions. The Crown sought to introduce at trial a tape recording of one of the sessions which had been made by the clinic's resident in family therapy. The Court of Appeal held that two of Wigmore's four criteria had not been met and, therefore, the evidence should be admitted. The Court recognized that there was a therapeutic relationship between the accused and the psychiatrist inasmuch as the accused was a participant in the group therapy session and it was clear that the session itself was confidential. It was also acknowledged that group therapy for the purpose of family counselling in cases of child abuse is one which meets the community approval and it should be encouraged. However, the Court concluded that the fourth criterion which was that the injury that would inure to the relation by the

---

359 *16th Report of the English Law Reform Committee on Privilege in Civil Proceedings, supra,* note 351, at 21-22.
360 [1976] 1 S.C.R. 254, 38 C.R.N.S. 306, [1975] 4 W.W.R. 620, 75 C.L.L.C. 14,263, 55 D.L.R. (3d) 224.
361 In *Upham v. You, supra,* note 346, it was held that the criteria were not satisfied in a situation where the plaintiff had brought a malpractice action against the doctor for negligence in the performance of a varicose vein operation. She successfully obtained production of a list of the doctor's patients upon whom he had performed similar operations on the basis that the information was relevant regarding procedures carried out by the doctor and the scarring to be expected as a result.
362 (1985), 19 C.C.C. (3d) 115 (*sub nom. R. v. R.S.*), 45 C.R. (3d) 161, 8 O.A.C. 241; leave to appeal to S.C.C. refd. (1985), 61 N.R. 266n.

disclosure of the communications must be greater than the benefit thereby gained for the correct disposal of the litigation was not met here since the search for truth in the criminal process outweighed the need for family counselling at least in cases of suspected child abuse. The Court was of the view that the vital interest of society in protecting children from abuse must be superior to the encouragement of patients to seek therapy from psychiatrists with the assurance that their confidential communications will be protected. Society considers the detection and prevention of child abuse more important than the confidentiality of psychiatric counselling. In view of its holding that the fourth criterion had not been met, the Court of Appeal found it unnecessary to decide whether the confidentiality element was or was not essential to the full and satisfactory maintenance of the relationship between a psychiatrist and his patient in group therapy sessions.

3. Court-Ordered Psychiatric Assessments

In the context of criminal cases, accused are often ordered by the court to be interviewed and assessed by a psychiatrist during a remand for observation. Under the present law, any statements made during this process are not privileged. A majority of the Federal/Provincial Task Force on the Uniform Rules of Evidence[363] recommended that a privilege be enacted for communications made between an accused and an assessing physician during a remand for observation. Such communications would be inadmissible against the accused at any criminal proceeding other than a fitness hearing except where the accused waives the privilege by putting his or her mental state in issue. The rationale for creating such a privilege is that the object of a remand for assessment is to determine if the accused is fit to stand trial. In some provinces, defence counsel instruct their clients not to speak with the assessing psychiatrist because if the court decides that the accused is fit to stand trial, the Crown may call the psychiatrist to introduce into evidence the accused's statements concerning the incident in question.

---

363 *Federal/Provincial Task Force on the Uniform Rules of Evidence* (Toronto: Carswell, 1982) at 422-23.

III COMMUNICATIONS IN FURTHERANCE OF SETTLEMENT

A. Policy and General Rule

It has long been recognized as a policy interest worth fostering that parties be encouraged to resolve their private disputes without recourse to litigation, or if an action has been commenced, encouraged to effect a compromise without a resort to trial.[364] In furthering these objectives, the courts have protected from disclosure communications, whether written or oral, made with a view to reconciliation or settlement. In the absence of such protection, few parties would initiate settlement negotiations for fear that any concession that they would be prepared to offer could be used to their detriment if no settlement agreement was forthcoming. The principle of exclusion was enunciated in two early Ontario cases. In *York (County) v. Toronto Gravel Road & Concrete Co.*[365] Proudfoot J. said:[366]

> The rule I understand to be that overtures of pacification, and any other offers or propositions between litigating parties, expressly or impliedly made without prejudice, are excluded on grounds of public policy.

Four years later, in *Pirie v. Wyld*,[367] Cameron C.J. confirmed the rule as follows:

> The authorities seem, though not very numerous, to be clear upon the first point, that letters written or communications made without prejudice, or offers made for the sake of buying peace, or to effect a compromise, are inadmissible in evidence. It seemingly being considered against public policy as having a tendency to promote litigation, and to prevent amicable settlements.

---

364 *16th Report of the English Law Reform Committee on Privilege in Civil Proceedings*, 1967, Cmnd. 3472, at 14.
365 (1882), 3 O.R. 584; affd. without reference to this point (1885), 11 O.A.R. 765; affd. (1885), 12 S.C.R. 517.
366 *Ibid.*, at 593-94 (O.R.).
367 (1886), 11 O.R. 422 at 427 (C.A.).

Many other authorities have expressed this public policy to be the justification for the recognition of the privilege.[368] However, there are a number of competing theories which are discussed in Wigmore on Evidence:[369]

1. That admissions in settlement negotiations are likely to be hypothetical or conditional only, as a supposition on which a settlement might rest, whether that supposition is true or false, and that such an admission has no relevance and is inadmissible on that ground, though if an admission is clearly an unqualified admission of fact, it would be admissible;

2. That all admissions in the course of negotiations towards settlement are without prejudice, whether those words are used or not, and are protected by a privilege based on public policy, and are not admissible in evidence;

3. That settlement negotiations are conducted on the normal contractual basis of offer and acceptance and with an express reservation of secrecy, and that, if a contract is reached, the negotiations are superseded by the contract itself, and become irrelevant and inadmissible, and if no contract is reached, then the negotiations are, for that reason, irrelevant;

4. That admissions made in the course of settlement negotiations may not be concessions of wrongs done, but merely an expres-

---

368 For example, *Paddock v. Forrester* (1842), 3 Man. & G. 903; *Re Daintrey; Ex parte Holt*, [1893] 2 Q.B. 116; *Stewart v. Muirhead* (1890), 29 N.B.R. 273 at 279 (C.A.); *I. Waxman & Sons Ltd. v. Texaco Canada Ltd.*, [1968] 1 O.R. 642, 67 D.L.R. (2d) 295 (H.C.J.); affd. [1968] 2 O.R. 452, 69 D.L.R. (2d) 543 (C.A.); *Thibodeau v. Thibodeau* (1984), 65 N.S.R. (2d) 442, 147 A.P.R. 442, 47 C.P.C. 224 at 226 (T.D.); *Canadian Imperial Bank of Commerce v. Val-Del Construction Ltd.* (1987), 63 O.R. (2d) 283 at 287 (Ont. Master); *Excelsior Life Insurance Co. v. Saskatchewan* (1987), 63 Sask. R. 35 (Q.B.); *Cutts v. Head*, [1984] 1 Ch. 290 at 306, [1984] 2 W.L.R. 349, [1984] 1 All E.R. 597 (C.A.); *Rush & Tompkins Ltd. v. Greater London Council*, [1988] 3 W.L.R. 939 (H.L.), reversing [1988] 2 W.L.R. 533, [1988] 1 All E.R. 549; *Ed Miller Sales & Rental Ltd. v. Caterpillar Tractor Co.* (1990), 72 Alta. L.R. (2d) 330, [1990] 4 W.W.R. 39, 105 A.R. 4 (Q.B.); affd. (1990), 74 Alta. L.R. (2d) 271, [1990] 5 W.W.R. 377 (C.A.).
369 4 Wigmore, *Evidence* (Chadbourn rev. 1972), § 1061, at 33-47, as cited in *Derco Industries Ltd. v. A.R. Grimwood Ltd.*, [1985] 2 W.W.R. 137, 47 C.P.C. 82, 57 B.C.L.R. 395 (C.A.) at 139-140 (W.W.R.).

sion of a desire to purchase peace, and as such irrelevant and inadmissible.

The second theory is clearly the one that is accepted in Ontario.[370] It is unclear however whether the law in British Columbia is to the same effect. It was suggested by Spencer J. in *Derco Industries Ltd. v. A.R. Grimwood Ltd.*[371] that the British Columbia Court of Appeal in *Schetky v. Cochrane*[372] preferred Wigmore's first "conditional admissibility" theory. Lambert J.A. on the appeal of *Derco* left the question of the basis of the "privilege" open,[373] but commented that no *ratio decidendi* could be determined from *Schetky* that was binding on the British Columbia courts. Other courts have applied the express or implied agreement theory.[374] The undesirability of different theories applying in different provinces is patent.

Where the privilege theory applies it is true that the overriding policy interest may justify the exclusion of evidence which may otherwise be relevant and probative. An offer to pay a sum of money to settle a dispute, for example, may be relevant as suggesting a weak case on liability, and, but for the privilege, be tendered as an admission of such by the opposing party should the offer not be accepted.[375]

The privilege applies to oral or written communications. It also applies at either the discovery or the trial stage.[376] The judge, however,

---

370   *I. Waxman & Sons Ltd. v. Texaco Canada Ltd.*, *supra*, note 368.
371   (1984), 57 B.C.L.R. 390, [1985] 1 W.W.R. 541, 46 C.P.C. 263 (S.C.); affd. [1985] 2 W.W.R. 137, 57 B.C.L.R. 395, 47 C.P.C. 82 (C.A.).
372   [1918] 1 W.W.R. 821, 24 B.C.R. 496 (C.A.).
373   *Supra*, note 369, at 141 (W.W.R.).
374   *Rabin v. Mendoza & Co.*, [1954] 1 W.L.R. 271, [1954] 1 All E.R. 247 (C.A.); *Re River Steamer Co.; Mitchell's Claim* (1871), 6 L.R. Ch. App. 822; *Whiffin v. Hartwright* (1848), 11 Beav. 111, 50 E.R. 759; see Eberts J.A. in *Schetky v. Cochrane*, *supra*, note 372, at 830 (W.W.R.).
375   Once an action has been commenced, Rules of Court provide that the fact that the defendant has made a formal offer to settle the plaintiff's claim does not constitute an admission of the cause of action: see, for example, Alberta *Rules of Court*, Alta. Reg. 84/84, s. 2, Rules 171, 173; British Columbia *Supreme Court Rules*, B.C. Reg. 310/760, Rules 37(5), (21), 57(19), (20); Manitoba *Queen's Bench Rules*, Man. Reg. 553/88, Rule 49.05; Saskatchewan *Queen's Bench Rules*, Rule 181(3); Ontario *Rules of Civil Procedure*, O. Reg. 560/84, Rules 49.05, 49.06 as amended by O. Reg. 221/86.
376   *Rush & Tompkins Ltd. v. Greater London Council*, *supra*, note 368; *I. Waxman & Sons Ltd. v. Texaco Canada Ltd.*, *supra*, note 368, at 656 (O.R.), and 453 (O.R.) on appeal. Although at the discovery stage the questions may be allowed or

may examine the documents to determine if the privilege should apply.[377]

B. Conditions for Recognition of the Privilege

There are a number of conditions that must be present for the privilege to be recognized:

(a) a litigious dispute must be in existence or within contemplation;

(b) the communication must be made with the express or implied intention that it would not be disclosed to the court in the event negotiations failed; and

(c) the purpose of the communication must be to attempt to effect a settlement.

1. Litigious Disputes in Existence

A litigious dispute must be in existence or at least contemplated for this privilege to be recognized. It is not necessary that proceedings have commenced.[378]

2. Made with Intention of Non-Disclosure

A second condition is that the communication be made with the intention that should negotiations fail, it would not be disclosed without consent. This intention may be implied from the use of the phrase "without prejudice" at the head of the correspondence. Sopinka J. in *Maracle v. Travelers Indemnity Co. of Canada*[379] in referring to a letter written 'without prejudice' stated:[380]

The use of this expression is commonly understood to mean that if there is no settlement, the party making the offer is free to

---

disclosure ordered if it can be shown that an exception to the privilege might be proved at trial. Producibility does not assure admissibility at trial.

377 *Re Daintrey, supra,* note 368; *Bank of Ottawa v. Stamco Ltd.* (1915), 8 W.W.R. 574, 22 D.L.R. 679 (Sask. S.C.).

378 *Warren v. Gray Goose Stage Ltd.,* [1937] 1 W.W.R. 465, at 472 (Sask. S.C.); revd. on other grounds [1938] S.C.R. 52, [1938] I.L.R. 104, 47 C.R.C. 214, [1938] 1 D.L.R. 104.

379 (1991), 80 D.L.R. (4th) 652, 3 O.R. (3d) 510*n* (S.C.C.).

380 *Ibid.,* at 658.

assert all its rights, unaffected by anything stated or done in the negotiations.

Although the use of this phrase is not conclusive of the intention, it may constitute some, if not *prima facie*, evidence of it and thus its use is of value.[381] Moreover, in the course of negotiations, if a letter has been written by one party "without prejudice", then an intention to maintain the privilege with respect to the whole of the correspondence of which the letter forms a part may be inferred.[382]

Absence of the phrase as part of the correspondence or discussion does not mean that there is no intention of confidentiality. The intention may be implicit in the circumstances, and accordingly the words would be superfluous. Although opposing solicitors engaged in negotiations on behalf of their clients are usually vigilant in ensuring that their correspondence is appropriately marked, in most cases it could be implied from the very involvement of the lawyers.[383] Furthermore, many of the cases in this area seem to pay little attention to the question of intention, and focus instead on the other conditions for application of the privilege.[384] In *Excelsior Life Insurance Co. v. Saskatchewan*[385] the Court appears to have inferred the requisite intention from the intention to avoid litigation. This essentially means that the intention can be implied from the fact that the parties are engaged in settlement negotiations and it would, therefore, seem to diminish the importance of intention as a separate element for application of the privilege. In fact, in *William Allan Real Estate Co. v. Robichaud*,[386]

---

381 *Hartney v. Northern British Fire Insurance Co.* (1887), 13 O.R. 581; *Peel Condominium Corp. No. 199 v. Ontario New Home Warranties Plan* (1988), 30 C.P.C. (2d) 118 (Ont. Div. Ct.); *Flegel Construction Ltd. v. Cambac Financial Projects Ltd.*, [1983] 3 W.W.R. 405, 24 Alta. L.R. (2d) 340, 44 A.R. 181 (Q.B.), at 413 (W.W.R.).

382 *Paddock v. Forrester* (1842), 3 Man. & G. 903; *Denovan v. Lee* (1990), 40 C.P.C. (2d) 54 (B.C. Master).

383 But see *Podovinikoff v. Montgomery* (1984), 14 D.L.R. (4th) 716, 58 B.C.L.R. 204, 30 M.V.R. 19, 46 C.P.C. 77, 10 C.C.L.I. 169 (C.A.), at 207 (B.C.L.R.), where the failure of an experienced insurance adjuster to mark his letter without prejudice operated against him.

384 See, for example, *Phillips v. Rodgers* (1988), 62 Alta. L.R. (2d) 146, 29 C.P.C. (2d) 193, 92 A.R. 253 (Q.B.).

385 (1987), 63 Sask. R. 35 (Q.B.).

386 (1987), 17 C.P.C. (2d) 138, 37 B.L.R. 286 (H.C.J.); leave to appeal granted (1987), 28 C.P.C. (2d) 47 (H.C.J.).

Campbell J., relying on *Pirie v. Wyld*,[387] held that the privilege arises if the communication is made for the sake of buying peace or to effect a compromise, without more. As His Lordship stated:[388]

> What sensible man would attempt settlement if it could be used against him at trial?

Other courts have required something more to show an implied without prejudice.[389]

If the parties are clearly involved in negotiating a settlement or buying peace the intention should be inferred in the absence of anything to suggest otherwise. Where it is less clear that settlement negotiations are involved a closer scrutiny may be required.

3. Purpose of Communication

The communication must have been written for the purpose of attempting to effect a settlement. If the circumstances reveal otherwise, then neither the presence of the words "without prejudice" nor the fact that a dispute existed will avail to confer a privilege.[390] For example, in *William Allan Real Estate Co. v. Robichaud*,[391] a case of an agent claiming commission, the trial judge denied the privilege claim after examining all the circumstances surrounding a decision to pay the agent an amount of money and determined that the amount was not offered to buy peace or settle a dispute, but in the course of negotiating an actual commission agreement.[392]

The communication does not have to contain an actual settle-

---

387 *Supra*, note 367.

388 *Supra*, note 386 at 141 (C.P.C.); the issue of privilege was considered again by Arbour J. at trial, *William Allan Real Estate Co. v. Robichaud* (1990), 72 O.R. (2d) 595 (H.C.J.), *infra*, note 391, but there was no disagreement with Campbell J.'s statement of the law.

389 For example, *Podovinikoff v. Montgomery, supra*, note 383.

390 *Bank of Ottawa v. Stamco Ltd., supra*, note 377; *Phillips v. Rodgers, supra*, note 384; *Cameron Packaging Ltd. v. Ruddy* (1983), 41 C.P.C. 154 (Ont. H.C.J.); affd. (1984), 41 C.P.C. 154n (Ont. C.A.); *Belanger v. Gilbert*, [1984] 6 W.W.R. 474, 58 B.C.L.R. 191, 14 D.L.R. (4th) 428, 9 C.C.L.I. 244 (C.A.); *Sidhu v. Grewal* (1986), 70 B.C.L.R. 128, 24 D.L.R. (4th) 467 (S.C.).

391 (1990), 72 O.R. (2d) 595, 68 D.L.R. (4th) 37, 9 R.P.R. (2d) 48 (H.C.J.); additional reasons at (1990), 72 O.R. (2d) 595 at 615, 68 D.L.R. (4th) 37 at 57.

392 *Ibid.*, at 607-08 (O.R.).

ment offer in order to attract the privilege. In *Pirie v. Wild*[393] the Court held that the rule "should be held to cover and protect all communications expressed to be without prejudice and fairly made for the purpose of expressing the writer's views on the matter of litigation or dispute, as well as overtures for settlement or compromise".[394] In *Phillips v. Rodgers*[395] a letter written by the defendant's insurance adjuster to the defendant inquiring whether a claim would be made was considered as part of the process of negotiating a settlement as it opened the door to the actual negotiation.

Other cases suggest, however, that an offer of settlement must be found within the document in order to attract the privilege.[396]

A reasonable reconciliation of these apparently different approaches and cases is that the communication must be part of a correspondence which the parties intend will reasonably lead to a compromise or settlement of the dispute. Hence, letters designed to open such negotiations, or letters or discussions which attempt to convince the opponent of the strengths of the other's position, but which also recognizes weaknesses, in the hope that some settlement can be effected once each other's positions are on the table, should be subject to the privilege whether or not they contain an actual offer of settlement.

C. *Application of the Privilege in Subsequent Proceedings Between Different Persons*

If it is accepted that the basis of the privilege is a public policy to encourage settlement, then it follows that the privilege should extend to subsequent proceedings not related to the dispute which the parties attempted to settle. Any possibility of subsequent adverse use could

---

393 (1886), 11 O.R. 422 at 429 (C.A.).
394 See also *Abrams v. Grant* (1978), 5 C.P.C. 308 (Ont. H.C.J.).
395 *Supra*, note 384.
396 For example *Drabinsky v. Maclean-Hunter Ltd.* (1980), 28 O.R. (2d) 23, 16 C.P.C. 280, 108 D.L.R. (3d) 391 (H.C.J.), at 26 (O.R.); *Re Daintrey; Ex parte Holt*, [1893] 2 Q.B. 116, at 119; *Lamoureux v. Smit*, [1983] 1 W.W.R. 373, 40 B.C.L.R. 151, 30 C.P.C. 287, [1983] I.L.R. 1-1636 (S.C.), at 378 (W.W.R.); *Belanger v. Gilbert*, *supra*, note 390, at 476 (W.W.R.); *Farrell v. Tisdale* (1987), 16 B.C.L.R. (2d) 230 (C.A.); *Flegel Construction Ltd. v. Cambac Financial Projects Ltd.*, *supra*, note 381 at 411 (W.W.R.); *Warren v. Gray Goose Stage Ltd.*, *supra*, note 378, at 472 (W.W.R.).

deter full and frank discussion.[397] The principle 'once privileged, always privileged' applies.[398] This is illustrated in *I. Waxman & Sons Ltd. v. Texaco Canada Ltd.*[399] The issue in that proceeding was whether or not production could be compelled of letters, written "without prejudice" and with a view to settlement of the issue between A and C, upon the demand of B, in subsequent litigation between A and B on the same subject-matter. Fraser J., whose decision was affirmed by the Ontario Court of Appeal, concluded that a party to a correspondence within the 'without prejudice' privilege is protected from being required to disclose it on discovery or at trial in proceedings by or against a third party. He went on to add in *obiter dicta* that the correspondence would be no less inadmissible if there had been secondary evidence to prove its contents. He stated:[400]

> In the case of a without prejudice privilege I am tentatively of opinion that a party to the negotiations is entitled to the privilege against all persons unless it is waived or brought within some recognized exceptions. To permit a third party to use an otherwise privileged document because he can prove it or its contents otherwise than by a party to the negotiation would greatly weaken the efficacy of the privilege.

The position may not be the same in British Columbia where there is some suggestion that the conditional admissibility theory governs in this area.[401] *Derco Industries Ltd. v. A.R. Grimwood Ltd.*[402] involved two separate actions arising from one construction project. In the first action the contractor (Grimwood) brought an action against the owner (I.C.B.C.), the construction manager (PCL) and one other claiming damages for construction delays. In the second action Derco, a supplier to the project, claimed damages for delay

---

397 See the comments on Wachowich J. in *Ed Miller Sales & Rentals Ltd. v. Caterpillar Tractor Co.* (1990), 72 Alta. L.R. (2d) 330, [1990] 4 W.W.R. 39, 105 A.R. 4 (Q.B.), at 340-41 (Alta. L.R.); affd. (1990), 74 Alta. L.R. (2d) 271, [1990] 5 W.W.R. 377 (C.A.).

398 See this Chapter, II.B.9(a).

399 [1968] 1 O.R. 642, 67 D.L.R. (2d) 295 (H.C.J.); affd. [1968] 2 O.R. 452, 69 D.L.R. (2d) 543 (C.A.).

400 *Ibid.*, (H.C.J.) at 657 (O.R.).

401 See this Chapter, III.A.

402 [1985] 2 W.W.R. 137, 57 B.C.L.R. 395, 47 C.P.C. 82 (C.A.).

negligently caused by I.C.B.C., PCL and Grimwood. It further alleged that Grimwood was unjustly enriched because it had received settlement payments in the first action which it did not share with Derco. Derco demanded production during the discovery process of the settlement agreement and the documents leading to the settlement. Spencer J. ordered production because in his view the privilege theory of settlement negotiations applicable in Ontario did not apply in British Columbia. Since the conditional admissibility theory governed they could be ordered to be produced with the question of admissibility being dealt with at trial. Grimwood appealed. On the appeal Lambert J.A. upheld Spencer J.'s decision, but for different reasons. He decided that in this case, given that settlement had been reached and that it could operate to the detriment of Derco or influence the outcome of the litigation itself, it should be produced.[403] His Lordship was careful to restrict his decision to the particular circumstances of the case and to documents demanded by a third party arising in the course of settlement negotiations leading to a completed settlement and to issues of producibility and not admissibility (although the issue of admissibility would be restricted to relevance only).[404] In different circumstances the British Columbia court may recognize the application of the privilege in proceedings involving third parties.

This issue was first considered in Alberta in *Ed Miller Sales & Rentals Ltd. v. Caterpillar Tractor Co.*[405] There the plaintiff brought suit against two defendants. During the course of the action the plaintiff and the first defendant entered into 'without prejudice' negotiations for an amalgamation of the two corporations. No settlement was made and the second defendant sought to examine the representative of the plaintiff as to the content of the discussions. Wachowich J. preferred the *I. Waxman* position and held that "the better position in law is that a stranger to 'without prejudice' negotiations for settlement is not entitled to disclosure of the content of such discussions during examination for discovery in the circumstances of this case."[406]

403 *Ibid.*, at 142 (W.W.R.).
404 *Supra*, note 402; *Derco* may have been misunderstood in *Mueller Canada Inc. v. State Contractors Inc.* (1989), 35 C.P.C. (2d) 175 at 176 (Ont. Master); affd. on other grounds (1989), 71 O.R. (2d) 397, 41 C.P.C. (2d) 291 (Ont. H.C.J.).
405 *Supra*, note 397.
406 *Supra*, note 397, at 338.

It is also worthy of comment that this is the preferred position of the English House of Lords.[407]

D. Exceptions to the Privilege

1. Introduction

It is not an absolute rule that communications made *bona fide* to induce the settlement of litigation are never to be disclosed. Fraser J., in *I. Waxman & Sons Ltd. v. Texaco Canada Ltd.*, tersely listed the exceptions:[408]

> There are, of course, exceptions to that rule [*Underwood v. Cox*][409] ... exemplified one of them, *i.e.*, where there were threats — *Re Daintrey*[410] exemplified another, *i.e.*, where it is highly prejudicial to the recipient and constituted an act of bankruptcy. Also it would seem that where the correspondence constitutes or leads up to a new contractual relation, which is in issue, in some or all cases, it ceases to be privileged. In this connection I refer to *Hutchinson v. Glover* (1875), 1 Q.B.D. 138, and *Pearlman v. National Life Ass'ce Co. of Canada* (1917), 39 O.L.R. 131. It would seem that there may be a further exception in some circumstances where fraud is in issue.

Statutes may also abrogate the privilege.[411] The exceptions to the rule of privilege find their rationale in the fact that the exclusionary rule was meant to conceal an offer of settlement only if an attempt was made to establish it as evidence of liability or a weak cause of action, not when it is used for other purposes.

2. Unlawful Communications

Communications which contain unlawful threats toward the recipient which are designed to intimidate may be admitted to prove not only the threat, but also the admission of liability. In *Greenwood v.*

---

407 *Rush & Tompkins Ltd. v. Greater London Council*, [1988] 3 W.L.R. 939, reversing [1988] 2 W.L.R. 533, [1988] 1 All E.R. 549 (H.L.).
408 *Supra*, note 399 at 656 (O.R.).
409 (1912), 26 O.L.R. 303, 4 D.L.R. 66 (C.A.).
410 *Re Daintrey; ex parte Holt*, [1893] 2 Q.B. 116.
411 *Re Erinco Homes Ltd.* (1977), 3 C.P.C. 227 (Ont. Master).

Fitts,[412] the defendant, during the course of settlement negotiations with the plaintiff, attempted to undermine the administration of justice by threatening the plaintiffs that if the action proceeded to trial, he would perjure himself and would suborn witnesses in order to be successful at trial, and further, that he would flee from the jurisdiction in order to avoid execution of any judgment against him. The British Columbia Court of Appeal held that the privilege was never intended to protect this type of threatening communication and held that the statements were admissible as evidence of the defendant's admission of liability. In *Kurtz & Co. v. Spence & Sons*,[413] a 'without prejudice' letter which contained a threat of legal proceedings, in breach of English patent legislation, if the offer was not accepted, was held to be subject to disclosure on the ground that the phrase could not be used to mask the contravention of the statute.

3. Communications Prejudicial to the Recipient

If the recipient would be prejudiced by his rejection of an offer contained in a letter or document, then no privilege arises.[414] Thus, in *Re Daintrey; ex parte Holt*[415] statements in a debtor's letter, admitting that he was incapable of meeting his debts as they fell due, was held to constitute an act of bankruptcy and notice to the creditor of such an act. As a result, it was held that it could not be given "without prejudice", even though expressly stated to be so made, because the letter by its very character was one which could prejudicially affect the recipient whether or not he agreed to the terms offered therein. The privilege cannot be used as a means to deceive the courts as to the facts, by excluding evidence which would repel a charge of fraud made by a party or who is shown by the impugned communication to have effected a waiver or made an election.[416]

---

412 (1961), 29 D.L.R. (2d) 260 (B.C.C.A.); see also *Underwood v. Cox* (1912), 26 O.L.R. 303, 4 D.L.R. 66 (C.A.) at 315, 323 (O.L.R.).
413 (1887), 58 L.T. 438.
414 *Clark v. Grand Trunk Railway* (1869), 29 U.C.Q.B. 136 at 147 (C.A.); *Ussher v. Simpson* (1909), 13 O.W.R. 285, at 293-94 (C.A.); *Côté v. Rooney* (1982), 137 D.L.R. (3d) 371, 29 C.P.C. 261 (Ont. S.C.).
415 *Supra*, note 410.
416 *Derco Industries Ltd. v. A.R. Grimwood Ltd.*, *supra*, note 402; *Schetky v. Cochrane*, [1918] 1 W.W.R. 821, 24 B.C.R. 496 (C.A.).

4. Concluded Settlement Agreement in Issue

If the negotiations are successful and result in a consensual agreement, then the communications may be tendered in proof of the settlement where the existence or interpretation of the agreement is itself in issue. Such communications form the offer and acceptance of a binding contract, and thus may be given in evidence to establish the existence of a settlement agreement.[417] Some courts have made the overly broad statement that once a concluded settlement is reached the privilege is lost.[418] This suggests that it is lost for the purpose of any subsequent suit whether between the parties or strangers, no matter whether the agreement itself is put in issue in subsequent proceedings.

However, the better view is that the privilege applies not only to failed negotiations, but also to the content of successful negotiations, so long as the existence or interpretation of the agreement itself is not in issue in the subsequent proceedings and none of the exceptions is applicable.[419] The rationale behind the privilege supports this position. If parties to settlement negotiations believed that their state-

---

417 *Pearlman v. National Life Assurance Co. of Canada* (1917), 39 O.L.R. 141 at 142; *McLeod v. Pearson*, [1931] 3 W.W.R. 4, [1931] 4 D.L.R. 673 at 684 (Alta. T.D.); *Fischer v. Robert Bell Engine & Thresher Co.*, [1923] 3 W.W.R. 320 at 328; revd. on other grounds [1924] 2 W.W.R. 725, [1924] 3 D.L.R. 545, 18 Sask. L.R. 330; *Vardon v. Vardon* (1883), 6 O.R. 719 (C.A.); *Omnium Securities Co. v. Richardson* (1884), 7 O.R. 182 (Ch.); *Tomlin v. Standard Telephones and Cables Ltd.*, [1969] 1 W.L.R. 1378 (C.A.); *Re River Steamer Co.; Mitchell's Claim* (1871), 6 L.R. Ch. App. 822; C. Tapper and R. Cross, *Cross on Evidence*, 7th ed. (London: Butterworths, 1990) at 273-74; *Cameron Packaging Ltd. v. Ruddy* (1983), 41 C.P.C. 154 (Ont. H.C.); affd. (1984), 41 C.P.C. 154n (Ont. C.A.).

418 *Begg v. East Hants (Municipality)* (1986), 75 N.S.R. (2d) 431, 186 A.P.R. 431, (*sub nom. Director of Assessment v. Begg*) 33 D.L.R. (4th) 239 (C.A.), at 242 (D.L.R.), although the agreement itself was in issue; *Omnium Securities Co. v. Richardson* (1884), 7 O.R. 182 at 183; *Derco Industries Ltd. v. A.R. Grimwood Ltd.*, *supra*, note 402; *Thibodeau v. Thibodeau* (1984), 65 N.S.R. (2d) 442, 147 A.P.R. 442, 47 C.P.C. 244 (T.D.) at 226, 228 (C.P.C.); *Ed Miller Sales & Rental Ltd. v. Caterpillar Tractor Co.* (1990), 72 Alta. L.R. (2d) 330, [1990] 4 W.W.R. 39, 105 A.R. 4 (Q.B.); affd. (1990), 74 Alta. L.R. (2d) 271, [1990] 5 W.W.R. 377 (C.A.).

419 This is the position accepted by the House of Lords in *Rush & Tompkins v. Greater London Council*, *supra*, note 407; See M.N. Howard, P. Crane and D. Hochberg, *Phipson on Evidence*, 14th ed. (London: Sweet & Maxwell, 1990) at 555, § 20-67.

ments might be used by a third party in subsequent proceedings, whether or not they reached agreement, they might be less frank in those discussions.

5. Limitation Periods

Settlement negotiations conducted without prejudice may be taken into account by the court where a question of laches is raised as a defence. The fact that compromise negotiations took place and the dates upon which they occurred may be admitted to explain away an allegation of delay in bringing an action.[420] It is not usually necessary to disclose the content of the communications.

Section 5 of the British Columbia *Limitation Act*[421] extends the limitation period in the Act where during the specified limitation period there has been written confirmation of the existence of the cause of action. The question of how this provision operates where the written confirmation is found in a without prejudice communication has been considered several times.[422] Lambert J.A. has commented[423] that a letter could be privileged for trial purposes, but admissible for the purpose of s. 5.

6. Costs

Although an early Ontario case held that a letter written "without prejudice" could be admitted on the question of costs,[424] the prevailing view in Canada appears to be that it cannot.[425]

---

420 *Schetky v. Cochrane, supra*, note 416 at 826 (W.W.R.); *Walker v. Wilsher* (1889), 23 Q.B.D. 335 (C.A.) at 328; *Jones v. Foxall* (1852), 21 L.J. Ch. 725 at 729; *Lev v. Lev*, [1990] 4 W.W.R. 130, 26 R.F.L. (3d) 86, 64 Man. R. (2d) 306 (Q.B.); *Simaan General Contracting Co. v. Pilkington Glass Ltd.*, [1987] 1 All E.R. 345 (Q.B.).
421 R.S.B.C. 1979, c. 236 [s. 5(2) am. 1990, c. 33, s. 8].
422 *Podovinikoff v. Montgomery* (1984), 58 B.C.L.R. 204, 14 D.L.R. (4th) 716, 30 M.V.R. 19, 46 C.P.C. 77, 10 C.C.L.I. 169 (C.A.); *Lamoureux v. Smit*, [1983] 1 W.W.R. 373, 40 B.C.L.R. 151, 30 C.P.C. 287, [1983] I.L.R. 1-1636 (S.C.); *Farrell v. Tisdale* (1987), 16 B.C.L.R. (2d) 230 (C.A.); *Belanger v. Gilbert*, [1984] 6 W.W.R. 474, 14 D.L.R. (4th) 428, 58 B.C.L.R. 191, 9 C.C.L.I. 244 (B.C.C.A.); *Derco Industries Ltd. v. A.R. Grimwood Ltd.*, [1985] 2 W.W.R. 137, 57 B.C.L.R. 395, 47 C.P.C. 82 (C.A.).
423 *Belanger v. Gilbert, ibid.*, at 476 (W.W.R.).
424 *Boyd v. Simpson* (1879), 26 Gr. 278.
425 *I. Waxman & Sons Ltd. v. Texaco Canada Ltd.*, [1968] 1 O.R. 642, 67 D.L.R. (2d) 295 (H.C.J.), at 649 (O.R.); affd. [1968] 2 O.R. 452, 69 D.L.R. (2d) 543 (C.A.);

E. *Involvement of Mediators*

Negotiations conducted directly between the parties themselves rarely achieve success. The usual practice is for the parties to engage professional advisers (legal, spiritual, medical, or social) to assist them with their differences. This is particularly true in cases of matrimonial difficulty in which the parties may wisely seek help from a number of disciplines to resolve their conflicts. Consequently, some courts have recognized reconciliation discussions involving a third party mediator as privileged. The fact that a mediator has been requested by one or both of the parties to try to settle their differences raises the presumption that communications made to him or her were expressed at a time when matrimonial proceedings were contemplated.[426]

In *Porter v. Porter*,[427] spouses agreed to a mediation of their custody and access dispute by a psychologist. The psychologist had prepared a report which contained some adverse discussion with respect to the husband. The wife sought to admit the report into evidence. The Court found that a privilege existed based on Wigmore's four conditions.[428] The Court also determined that the privilege attaching to without prejudice negotiations applied as an alternative and separate ground for recognizing the existence of a privilege.[429] Some other courts do not appear to have recognized communications made through a mediator as a privileged situation apart from the application of Wigmore's four conditions.[430]

Walker v. Wilsher, supra, note 420; *Stotesbury v. Turner*, [1943] K.B. 370; *Cominco Ltd. v. Westinghouse Canada Ltd.*, [1982] 1 W.W.R. 640, 33 B.C.L.R. 202, 25 C.P.C. 12 (S.C.). In England, it appears that the issue has been reconsidered and settlement offers now appear to be admissible for the purposes of costs: *Cutts v. Head*, [1984] 1 Ch. 290 (C.A.); *Computer Machinery Co. Ltd. v. Drescher*, [1983] 1 W.L.R. 1379 (C.A.).

426 *16th Report of the English Law Reform Committee on Privilege in Civil Proceedings*, 1967 Cmnd. 3472 at 15.

427 (1983), 40 O.R. (2d) 417, 32 R.F.L. (2d) 413 (Fam. Ct.).

428 See this Chapter, II.A for a discussion of these factors.

429 *Supra*, note 427, at 423 (O.R.); see also *Vickers v. Vickers*, per Stewart J., unreported, November 20, 1963 (Ont. S.C.); *Keizars v. Keizars* (1982), 29 R.F.L. (2d) 223 (Ont. U.F.C.); *Hillesheim v. Hillesheim* (1974), 6 O.R. (2d) 647, 19 R.F.L. 42 (Master).

430 See for example, *Mortlock v. Mortlock* (1980), 17 R.F.L. (2d) 253 (N.S. Fam. Ct.); *Dembie v. Dembie* [1963] 21 R.F.L. 46 (Ont. H.C.J.), discussed in A.M. Kirkpatrick, "Privileged Communication in the Correction Services" (1964-65), 7 Crim. L.Q. 305 at 316-18; *G. v. G.*, [1964] 1 O.R. 361 (H.C.J.).

The cases do not purport to create a new privilege but are a logical extension of the privilege attaching to communications made in furtherance of settlement. The courts in England have had no hesitation in so extending the privilege. Thus in *McTaggart v. McTaggart*,[431] the Court of Appeal, although holding that the privilege had been waived, recognized that a probation officer who had interviewed the spouses was not free to divulge the evidence unless the parties consented or waived the privilege. In *Mole v. Mole*[432] it was held that the privilege attached when one of the parties obtained the assistance of a probation officer who communicated with the other spouse in an attempt to effect a reconciliation. The Court stressed the fact that the same would apply to a doctor, clergyman or other marriage guidance counsellor who was approached by the parties with a view to reconciling marital differences. The rationale of the privilege was stated to be a tacit understanding that negotiations were to be without prejudice.[433]

In *McTaggart v. McTaggart*[434] Denning L.J. said:

> It seems to me that negotiations which take place in the presence of the probation officer with a view to reconciliation are on the understanding, by all concerned, that they are to be without prejudice to the rights of the parties. The rule as to "without prejudice" communications applies with especial force to negotiations for reconciliation.

Statutory privilege now expressly protects communications made between spouses and a mediator appointed by the court under ss. 10(4), (5) of the *Divorce Act*,[435] and under s. 31 of the *Children's Law Reform Act*.[436] It is interesting to note that the *Divorce Act* provision confers an absolute privilege which cannot be waived by any party. If the mediator is not court-appointed under the *Divorce Act*, or if the matrimonial proceedings are not pursuant to the *Divorce Act*, then it appears that the privilege belongs to the spouse and not the concilia-

---

431 [1949] P. 94, [1948] 2 All E.R. 754 (C.A.).
432 [1951] P. 21, [1950] 2 All E.R. 328 (C.A.).
433 See also *Theodoropoulas v. Theodoropoulas*, [1964] P. 311, [1963] 2 All E.R. 772; *Henley v. Henley*, [1955] P. 202, [1955] 1 All E.R. 590n.
434 *Supra*, note 431 at 97 (P.), at 755 (All E.R.).
435 R.S.C. 1985, c. 3 (2nd Supp.).
436 R.S.O. 1980, c. 68 [s. 31 en. S.O. 1982, c. 20, s. 1; am. 1989, c. 22, s. 6].

tor. Accordingly, in those situations both spouses together may waive the privilege and if they do so, the mediator must disclose the communications that occurred.[437]

IV PRIVILEGE AGAINST SELF-INCRIMINATION

A. *Introduction*

Social policies distinct from those related to the protection of private communications have been asserted for the protection of the witness who is asked questions, the answers to which may be prejudicial to the witness' interests. Here the law is not concerned with fostering the confidential relationship between the communicants, but attempts to define, in part, the appropriate balance between the interest of the state in law enforcement and the interest of the citizen in freedom from interference by the state. The privilege is founded on the concept of fundamental fairness which is opposed to forcing a person to be the source of proof against himself or herself. This privilege finds expression in the maxims, "*Nemo tenetur seipsum prodere*" and "*nemo tenetur seipsum accusare*".[438]

The privilege against testimonial self-incrimination, which is constitutionalized by s. 13 of the *Charter*, is closely related to other fundamental protections such as the presumption of innocence,[439] the right of an accused not to be compelled to testify,[440] the confessions rule[441] and the right to remain silent in the face of state interrogations into criminal activity.[442] Each of such rights recognizes to some extent

---

437 *Pais v. Pais*, [1971] P. 119, [1970] 3 All E.R. 491.

438 In *Re Worrall; ex parte Cossens* (1820), Buck 531, Lord Elson was moved to say at 540 that: "this precept is one of the most sacred principles in the law". The rights developed out of a revulsion against the practices of the courts of the Star Chamber and the High Commission in the seventeenth century: see Professor E. Ratushny, *Self-Incrimination in the Canadian Criminal Process* (Toronto: Carswell, 1979) and the discussion by Wilson J. in *Thomson Newspapers Ltd. v. Canada (Director of Investigation and Research, Restrictive Trade Practices Commission)*, [1990] 1 S.C.R. 425, 76 C.R. (3d) 129, 54 C.C.C. (3d) 417, 39 O.A.C. 161, 67 D.L.R. (4th) 161, 47 C.R.R. 1, 29 C.P.R. (3d) 97, 106 N.R. 161, at 471-72 (S.C.R.).

439 Subsection 11(d).

440 Subsection 11(c).

441 See Chapter 8.

442 *Charter*, s. 7; see also *R. v. Hebert*, [1990] 2 S.C.R. 151, 57 C.C.C. (3d) 1, 77 C.R. (3d) 145, [1990] 5 W.W.R. 1, 47 B.C.L.R. (2d) 1, 49 C.R.R. 114, 110 N.R. 1.

that a citizen should not be condemned from his or her own mouth. It is up to the state to investigate and prove its own case.[443] As Wigmore states "[t]he privilege contributes to a fair state-individual balance by requiring the government to leave the individual alone until good cause is shown for disturbing him . . .".[444] Using a witness' previous compelled testimony or statements to incriminate him or her in a subsequent proceeding indirectly conscripts the persons as witness against himself or herself.[445]

B. Recognition of the Privilege at Common Law

At common law, no witness, whether a party or otherwise, was compellable to answer any question, the tendency of which was to expose the witness to any criminal charge, penalty or forfeiture of property[446] or to any ecclesiastical punishment or censure.[447] The oath of the witness that he or she believed that the answer would or might tend to incriminate him or her was necessary.[448] The court had to be

---

443 This is known as the "case to meet" principle.

444 8 Wigmore, *Evidence* (McNaughton rev. 1961), § 2251.

445 *R. v. Dubois*, [1985] 2 S.C.R. 350 (*sub nom. Dubois v. R.*), 22 C.C.C. (3d) 513, 48 C.R. (3d) 193, 23 D.L.R. (4th) 503, [1986] 1 W.W.R. 193, 41 Alta. L.R. (2d) 97, 18 C.R.R. 1, 66 A.R. 202, 62 N.R. 50, motion requesting rehearing refd. (1986), 41 Alta. L.R. (2d) liv (note) (S.C.C.).

446 For a discussion of the common-law right to remain silent in the face of any question tending to subject the witness to a forfeiture or penalty, see *R. v. Amway Corp.*, [1989] 1 S.C.R. 21, 68 C.R. (3d) 97, 56 D.L.R. (4th) 309, (*sub nom. R. v. Amway of Canada Ltd.*) [1989] 1 C.T.C. 255, [1989] 1 T.S.T. 2058, 37 C.R.R. 235, 2 T.C.T. 4074. Of note are Sopinka J.'s comments that the common-law rules relating to forfeitures and penalties are grounded in a policy from a bygone era, which does not exist in Canada today. The rule with respect to forfeitures only applied to forfeiture of land or an interest in land. Now any policy against actions for forfeiture is contained in various statutory provisions empowering the Court to grant relief from forfeiture and penalties. Section 5 of the *Canada Evidence Act* replaced any common-law testimonial privilege.

447 The reference to ecclesiastical censure is of historical reference only as the English Court of Appeal, in *Blunt v. Park Lane Hotel Ltd.*, [1942] 2 K.B. 253, [1942] 2 All E.R. 187 (C.A.), stated that the privilege no longer applied as the jurisdiction of the ecclesiastical courts had become obsolete. See *R. v. Boyes* (1861), 1 B. & S. 311; *Lamb v. Munster* (1882), 10 Q.B.D. 110; *Redfern v. Redfern*, [1891] P. 139 (C.A.); and *Doe d. Marr v. Marr* (1853), 3 U.C.C.P. 36 (C.A.) for cases recognizing this privilege.

448 *Ellis v. Power* (1882), 6 S.C.R. 1, at 7; *Lockett v. Solloway, Mills & Co.*, [1932] 1 W.W.R. 886, [1932] 3 D.L.R. 600, 45 B.C.R. 375 (C.A.).

satisfied from the circumstances of the case and the nature of the evidence that the witness was to give, that there were reasonable grounds for apprehending danger of a prosecution arising from his or her compulsion to answer the question.[449] With respect to civil cases, although the common-law privilege protected against answers which might subject the witness to penalties or forfeitures,[450] the witness could not decline or refuse to answer a relevant question on the ground that the answer would tend to show that the witness owed a debt, or would otherwise expose the witness to a civil action.[451]

It is unclear whether the common-law privilege applied with respect to the discovery or production of documents. While some cases suggested that it did,[452] others did not recognize the privilege.[453] This is now irrelevant, given that the federal and provincial Evidence Act provisions have abolished any such privilege and neither s. 13 nor s. 7 of the *Charter* require the recognition of any such privilege for documents.[454]

C. *Statutory Modification of the Common-Law Rule*

As the sanctions of the criminal law eased, it was no longer felt necessary to protect witnesses to such an extent, and accordingly, in

---

449 *Bell v. Klein*, [1955] S.C.R. 309, [1955] 2 D.L.R. 513, at 316 (S.C.R.); *Lamb v. Munster, supra*, note 447; *Mills v. Mercer Co.* (1893), 15 P.R. 276 (C.A.).

450 *Mexborough (Earl) v. Whitwood Urban District Council*, [1897] 2 Q.B. 111 (C.A.). Section 16(1)(a) of the English *Civil Evidence Act 1968*, c. 64 abolished the witness' privilege to decline to answer questions tending to expose him or her to a forfeiture. Now see *R. v. Amway Corp., supra*, note 446.

451 *Hannum v. McRae* (1898), 18 P.R. 185, at 191 (Ont. C.A.); *Melville's (Viscount) Case* (1806), 29 St. Tr. 549; *R. v. Doull*, [1931] Ex. C.R. 159.

452 *Hunnings v. Williamson* (1883), 10 Q.B.D. 459; *Bell v. Klein, supra*, note 449; *Attorney General v. Kelly* (1916), 10 W.W.R. 131, 28 D.L.R. 416 (Man. C.A.); affirming 9 W.W.R. 863 (K.B.).

453 *R. v. Simpson* (1943), 79 C.C.C. 344, [1943] 2 W.W.R. 426, 59 B.C.R. 132, [1943] 3 D.L.R. 355 (C.A.); leave to appeal to S.C.C. refd. (*sub nom. Walsh v. R., Simmons v. R; Hall v. R*), [1943] 3 D.L.R. 367, 79 C.C.C. 344; and see *Ziegler v. Canada (Director of Investigation & Research)* (1983), 8 D.L.R. (4th) 648 (*sub nom. Re Ziegler and Hunter*), 39 C.P.C. 234, 8 C.R.R. 47, 81 C.P.R. (2d) 1, 51 N.R. 1 (Fed. C.A.); leave to appeal to S.C.C. refd. 8 D.L.R. (4th) 648n, considering whether s. 2(d) of the *Canadian Bill of Rights* required the recognition of such a privilege.

454 See this Chapter, IV.D.2.

1893, the *CEA* was amended to abolish the right of a witness to refuse to answer questions which might tend to criminate him or her.[455] Although, as has been stated, there was no privilege at common law affording a witness the right to decline to answer questions which tended to establish civil liability (other than liability to a penalty or forfeiture), nevertheless, both the Federal Parliament and the Ontario Legislature took it upon themselves to abrogate a non-existent privilege and enacted legislation that provided that a witness was not excused from answering questions upon the ground that the answer might tend to establish liability to a civil proceeding at the instance of the Crown or of any person.[456] Thus, a witness, in both criminal and civil cases, lost the right to claim this protection, if it had indeed ever existed.

In addition to abolishing a non-existent civil privilege, the evidence statutes also abolished the recognized privileges with respect to criminal proceedings and for a forfeiture or penalty.[457] In its place was a limited protection from the use of prior testimony in a subsequent proceeding.[458] Typical of such provisions is the federal provision which reads as follows:[459]

5. (1) No witness shall be excused from answering any question on the ground that the answer to the question may tend to criminate him, or may tend to establish his liability to a civil proceeding at the instance of the Crown or of any person.

(2) Where with respect to any question a witness objects to answer on the ground that his answer may tend to criminate him,

---

455 S.C. 1893, c. 31, s. 5.
456 *Re Ginsberg* (1917), 40 O.L.R. 136, 38 D.L.R. 261 (C.A.).
457 Evidence Acts: Canada, R.S.C. 1985, C-5, s. 5(1); Alberta, R.S.A. 1980, A-21, s. 6(1); British Columbia, R.S.B.C. 1979, c. 116, s. 4(1); Manitoba, R.S.M. 1987, c. E150, s. 6(1); New Brunswick, R.S.N.B. 1973, c. E-11, s. 7; Newfoundland, R.S.N. 1970, c. 115, s. 3A(1) [en. 1971, No. 48, s. 4]; Northwest Territories, R.S.N.W.T. 1988, c. E-8, s. 7(2); Nova Scotia, R.S.N.S. 1989, c. 154, s. 59(1); Prince Edward Island, R.S.P.E.I. 1988, c. E-11, s. 6; Ontario, R.S.O. 1980, c. 145, s. 9(1); Saskatchewan, R.S.S. 1978, c. S-16, s. 37(1); Yukon Territory, R.S.Y. 1986, c. 57, s. 7(2).
458 Thereby clearly abolishing any privilege that might have existed at common law for documents.
459 *Canada Evidence Act*, R.S.C. 1985, c. C-5, s. 5. For a review of the history of s. 5 see *Bell v. Klein, supra*, note 449.

or may tend to establish his liability to a civil proceeding at the instance of the Crown or of any person, and if but for this Act, or the Act of any provincial legislature, the witness would therefore have been excused from answering the question, then although the witness is by reason of this Act or the provincial Act compelled to answer, the answer so given shall not be used or admissible in evidence against him in any criminal trial or other criminal proceeding against him thereafter taking place, other than a prosecution for perjury in the giving of that evidence.

The provincial Evidence Acts contain similar protections that apply to subsequent use with respect to provincial offences.[460]

In order for the protection to apply it was necessary for the witness to expressly claim its protection in the first proceeding.[461] A witness could not avail him or herself of this protection if the privilege to refuse to answer did not previously exist at common law and, therefore, use could be made of the answer in subsequent civil proceedings even if the claim for protection was made.

Although this statutory protection remains in place in the post-*Charter* era, it has largely been superseded by s. 13 of the *Charter*, which in certain respects provides a wider protection.[462] The case law dealing with the scope of the statutory protection may still be relevant in defining the scope of the *Charter* protection since some judicial reluctance to hold that the provincial Acts or s. 5(2) of the *CEA* provide greater protection than the *Charter* is likely.[463] Because many of the

---

460 Alberta, R.S.A. 1980, c. A-21, s. 6(2) [am. S.A. 1985, c. 15, s. 1]; British Columbia, R.S.B.C. 1979, c. 116, s. 4(2); Manitoba, R.S.M. 1987, c. E150, s. 6(2); New Brunswick, R.S.N.B. 1973, c. E-11, s. 7; Newfoundland, R.S.N. 1970, c. 115, s. 3A(2) [en. 1971, No. 48, s. 4]; Northwest Territories, R.S.N.W.T. 1988, c. E-8, s. 7(3); Nova Scotia, R.S.N.S. 1989, c. 154, s. 59(2); Ontario, R.S.O. 1980, c. 145, s. 9(2); Prince Edward Island, R.S.P.E.I. 1988, c. E-11, s. 6; Saskatchewan, R.S.S. 1978, c. S-16, s. 37(2). The Yukon Act provides no subsequent use protection.
461 *R. v. Tass*, [1947] S.C.R. 103, 87 C.C.C. 97, 2 C.R. 503, [1947] 1 D.L.R. 497; *Boulet v. R.*, [1978] 1 S.C.R. 332, 34 C.C.C. (2d) 397, 40 C.R.N.S. 158, 75 D.L.R. (3d) 223, 15 N.R. 541.
462 Discussed this Chapter, IV.D. The most notable difference is that to claim the protection of s. 13 the witness need not have claimed the protection during the first proceeding: see IV.D.1.
463 See the policy argument made by Martin J.A. in *R. v. Kuldip* (1988), 40 C.C.C. (3d) 11, 62 C.R. (3d) 336, 24 O.A.C. 393 (C.A.); revd. (1990), 61 C.C.C.

same issues arise in a consideration of s. 13 and provisions such as s. 5(2),[464] the privilege against self-incrimination will be discussed in the context of s. 13.

D. *Charter, Section 13*

Section 13 of the *Charter* provides as follows:

13. A witness who testifies in any proceedings has the right not to have any incriminating evidence so given used to incriminate that witness in any other proceedings, except in a prosecution for perjury or for the giving of contradictory evidence.

1. Automatic Protection

Unlike s. 5(2) of the *CEA* and many provincial provisions,[465] the protection from the subsequent incriminating use provided by s. 13 is automatic. There is no need, as there is with the statutory provisions, for the witness to specifically claim the protection when the testimony in the first proceeding is given. If a witness did not claim the statutory protection, for whatever reason, such testimony would be admissible in a subsequent proceeding without the necessity of a voir dire.[466] Because the trial judge or other presiding official in the first proceeding was under no obligation to inform a witness of this right, there was a premium on knowledge of this proviso. Section 13 is, therefore, an improvement in the law because, in some cases, the suspect or the accused was subpoenaed to testify in a collateral proceeding, such as a coroner's inquest, where he or she was subject to discovery by the Crown. An unrepresented person who was unaware of his or her rights was put in an unfair position.

Also, the protection of s. 13 applies whether the witness testified voluntarily or under compulsion in the first proceedings. Therefore, even an accused who testifies voluntarily at his or her first trial (where

---

(3d) 385 (S.C.C.). Although on appeal, Lamer J. did not completely accept this approach, he did not reject the idea that cases defining the scope of s. 5(2) would have some probative value: at 410 (C.C.C.).

464 For example, the question of who is a "witness".

465 Except Alberta: s. 6(2) [am. S.A. 1985, c. 15, s. 1].

466 *Bell v. Klein, supra,* note 449.

there could have been no compulsion by the Crown) could not have the answers used to incriminate him or her in a second trial.[467] As Lamer J. explained in *R. v. Dubois*:[468]

> The focus on the subsequent proceedings is even more pronounced in s. 13 of the *Charter*, which does not refer to any compulsion to answer at the time of the testimony nor to any objection to answer on the part of the accused. Consequently, although s. 13 refers to "A witness who testifies", it is, like its predecessor, designed to be operative and to protect the interests of the person in the subsequent proceedings. Indeed, it is even clearer in s. 13 that the right functions at the level of the "other proceedings".

Arguably, conferring the protection of s. 13 on a witness who could not have been compelled in the first proceeding and who voluntarily testified at such a proceeding, goes beyond what is required to promote the 'case to meet' principle. The accused has not been compelled to assist the police or the Crown in making out their case.[469] Nevertheless, the wider protection is provided. By contrast, under the broad concept of self-incrimination in the United States, compulsion is a requirement to trigger the right.[470]

Since the right to the protection against subsequent use arises at the time the statements are sought to be used and since the protection is automatic it would seem that no effective waiver of the s. 13 rights could occur until that time. It is difficult to imagine what could constitute an effective waiver of this right beyond an express waiver at the time of the trial.

---

467   *R. v. Dubois*, [1985] 2 S.C.R. 350 (*sub nom. Dubois v. R.*), 22 C.C.C. (3d) 513, 48 C.R. (3d) 193, 23 D.L.R. (4th) 503, [1986] 1 W.W.R. 193, 41 Alta. L.R. (2d) 97, 18 C.R.R. 1, 66 A.R. 202, 62 N.R. 50, *per* Lamer J. Motion requesting rehearing refd. (1986), 41 Alta. L.R. (2d) liv (note) (S.C.C.).

468   *Ibid.*, at 526 (D.L.R.), at 362-63 (S.C.R.), at 534 (C.C.C.), 218 (W.W.R.). In *R. v. Kuldip* (1990), 61 C.C.C. (3d) 385 (S.C.C.), Lamer J. noted that s. 5(2) and s. 13 provided virtually identical protection, the difference being that s. 5(2) requires an objection at the first proceeding while s. 13 does not.

469   For an argument to this effect see D. Paciocco, "Self-Incrimination: Removing the Coffin Nails" (1989), 35 McGill L.J. 74, at 92-93.

470   *Schemerber v. State of California*, 86 S.Ct. 1826 (1966). See D. Doherty (now Doherty J.), *Annotation*, 48 C.R. (3d) 194. For a different justification for the result in *Dubois* see L. Arbour (now Arbour J.) *Annotation* (1988), 61 C.R. (3d) 158.

2. To What Evidence Does Section 13 Apply?

Section 13 provides protection against testimonial compulsion only. L'Heureux-Dubé J. in *Thomson Newspapers Ltd. v. Canada (Director of Investigation and Research, Restrictive Trade Practices Commission)*[471] made this clear where she stated:[472]

> When one considers the carefully formulated wording of s. 13, especially in light of the narrow privilege against self-incrimination as it existed prior to the *Charter*, the drafters could not have made any clearer their intention to restrict the scope of the immunity to "testimonial" evidence. The word "testify" connotes the giving of evidence by means of oral communication in a proceeding. A witness "testifies" in recounting his or her version of events. This common sense meaning is simply not involved by the act of producing documents to the court.

Not only does s. 13 not apply to the production of documents, it also does not apply to the provision of compulsory breath samples or other "real evidence". As stated by Zuber J.A. in *R. v. Altseimer*:[473]

> It is plain that the protection continues to be protection against testimonial compulsion and nothing else. The protection afforded to the witness (s. 13) is enhanced since the witness need no longer claim protection as he had to do pursuant to s. 5 of the *Canada Evidence Act*, R.S.C. 1970, c. E-10. Section 11(c) con-

---

471 [1990] 1 S.C.R. 425, 54 C.C.C. (3d) 417, 76 C.R. (3d) 129, 39 O.A.C. 161, 67 D.L.R. (4th) 161, 47 C.R.R. 1, 29 C.P.R. (3d) 97, 106 N.R. 161.

472 At 587 (S.C.R.). Dealing with whether s. 7 of the *Charter* provides any additional protection from the use of documents, see the reasons of Sopinka J. at 607-608 (S.C.R.), Wilson J. at 480 (S.C.R.) and to a certain extent La Forest J. who recognizes the validity of the distinction between real evidence previously existing and compelled testimony. For a similar decision in the context of s. 2(d) of the *Canadian Bill of Rights* see *Ziegler v. Canada (Director of Investigation & Research)* (1983), 39 C.P.C. 234, (*sub nom. Re Zeigler and Hunter*) 8 D.L.R. (4th) 648, 81 C.P.R. (2d) 1, 51 N.R. 1, 8 C.R.R. 47 (*sub nom. Director of Investigation & Research v. Ziegler*) (Fed. C.A.). Leave to appeal to S.C.C. refd. (1984) 8 D.L.R. (4th) 648n.

473 (1982), 1 C.C.C. (3d) 7, 29 C.R. (3d) 276, 38 O.R. (2d) 783, 2 C.R.R. 119, 17 M.V.R. 8, 142 D.L.R. (3d) 246 (C.A.), at 787 (O.R.). L'Heureux-Dubé J. in *Thomson Newspapers Ltd.*, *supra*, note 471, at 587 (S.C.R.), noted that she had considerable sympathy for this view.

tinues to protect an accused from being compelled to enter a witness-box. The protection against testimonial compulsion, in my view, simply has nothing to do with compulsory breath tests pursuant to the *Criminal Code*.

3. "In Any Proceeding"

The incriminating statement must be made in the context of a "proceeding" for the protection of s. 13 to apply. The word "proceedings" should be given a large and liberal interpretation so as to cover any kind of proceeding, whether adjudicative or investigative and so would include an inquiry by a government agency[474] or a disciplinary proceeding before a statutory tribunal.[475] An examination for discovery would also be included, as it has been under s. 5(2) and the similar provincial Acts.[476] Similarly, a judgment debtor being examined in aid of execution is a "witness" and is entitled to like protection.[477] The privilege can also be claimed by a witness on an

---

474 See the statements of Wilson J. in *Thomson Newspapers Ltd., supra*, note 471, at 481 (S.C.R.).

475 *Donald v. Law Society (British Columbia)* (1983), 48 B.C.L.R. 210, 2 D.L.R. (4th) 385, [1984] 2 W.W.R. 46 (C.A.), additional reasons at [1985] 2 W.W.R. 671; leave to appeal to S.C.C. refd (1984), 7 C.R.R. 305, 55 N.R. 237; *Johnstone v. Law Society (British Columbia)* (1987), 40 D.L.R. (4th) 550, [1987] 5 W.W.R. 637, 15 B.C.L.R. (2d) 1 (C.A.); leave to appeal to S.C.C. refd. [1988] 1 S.C.R. x.

476 *Bank of Nova Scotia v. MacBrien*, [1953] O.W.N. 406; *Chambers v. Jaffray* (1906), 12 O.L.R. 377 (Div. Ct.); *Bell v. Klein*, [1955] S.C.R. 309; *C.M. Oliver & Co. v. Gilroy*, [1959] O.R. 316, 18 D.L.R. (2d) 280; *R. v. Fox* (1899), 18 P.R. 343; *Biss v. Biss*, [1942] 1 W.W.R. 224, [1942] 1 D.L.R. 264. It was originally held in Alberta that a person being examined for discovery was not a "witness": *Harrison v. King*, [1925] 3 D.L.R. 395, [1925] 2 W.W.R. 407, 21 Alta. L.R. 381 (C.A.); *Webster v. Solloway Mills & Co. (No. 2)*; [1930] 3 W.W.R. 445, 25 Alta. L.R. 8, [1931] 1 D.L.R. 831, but this was changed by statute, S.A. 1931, c. 23, s. 2, and it was subsequently held in *Campbell v. Aird*, [1941] 2 D.L.R. 807, [1941] 1 W.W.R. 645 (T.D.), that a person being examined for discovery was a witness within the meaning of the *Alberta Evidence Act*. Now see Alberta, R.S.A. 1980, c. A-21, s. 1(c); Manitoba, R.S.M. 1987, c. E150, s. 6(3); Northwest Territories, R.S.N.W.T. 1988, c. E-8, s. 7(1); Yukon Territory, R.S.Y. 1986, c. 57, s. 7(1). Although answers given on discovery cannot be used to incriminate an accused in subsequent criminal proceedings, s. 13 does not entitle a party to a stay of discoveries in a civil action on the speculative basis that his answers could influence the Crown's case against him in criminal proceedings: *Schwartz v. Stinchcombe* (1990), 44 C.P.C. (2d) 251 (Alta. Q.B.).

477 *C.M. Oliver & Co. v. Gilroy, ibid.; R. v. Nozaki*, 46 C.C.C. 168, [1926] 3

examination for a pending motion in an action.[478] It may be claimed as well by a person who is being examined by the Superintendent in Bankruptcy or official receiver in the course of an investigation into the possible commission of an offence in connection with a bankruptcy.[479] It would not, however, include an informal police investigation.[480] Whether s. 7 of the *Charter* provides protection against the use of information provided in less formal settings is considered below.

The wording of s. 13 also makes it quite clear that any evidence derived from the testimonial evidence given in the first proceeding is not afforded use immunity in subsequent proceedings.[481]

4. Incriminating Use

(a) *Time of Assessment of Nature of Use*

The incriminating nature of the evidence in issue is to be assessed at the time of its attempted use in the second proceeding and not at the time of its use in the first proceeding. As stated by Lamer J. in *R. v. Dubois*[482] responding to the Crown's argument that the nature of the evidence should be assessed at both the first and second proceeding:

> Although a literal reading of the section supports the position of the Crown, I am nevertheless of the view that s. 13 does not require that the incriminating character of the evidence be evaluated in the first proceedings as well as in the second. Indeed the literal approach defeats the nature and purpose of the section

W.W.R. 332, [1926] 4 D.L.R. 955, 37 B.C.R. 305 (C.A.).

478 *Mackell v. Ottawa Separate School Trustees* (1917), 40 O.L.R. 272, 12 O.W.N. 401.

479 *Bankruptcy Act*, R.S.C. 1985, c. B-3, s. 10(5).

480 *Thomson Newspapers Ltd. v. Canada (Director of Investigation and Research)*, *supra*, note 471, at 482 (S.C.R.). See also *R. v. Metcalfe*, unreported, February 3, 1990 (Alta. Prov. Ct.); *Prousky v. Law Society (Upper Canada)* (1987), 61 O.R. (2d) 37, 41 D.L.R. (4th) 565 (H.C.J.); affd. on other grounds (1987), 62 O.R. (2d) 224, 45 D.L.R. (4th) 640 (note) (C.A.).

481 *Thomson Newspapers Ltd. v. Director of Investigation and Research*, *supra*, note 471, explores whether s. 7 of the *Charter* could provide such derivative use immunity. See this Chapter, IV.E.2.

482 [1985] 2 S.C.R. 350 (*sub nom. Dubois v. R.*), 22 C.C.C. (3d) 513, 48 C.R. (3d) 193, 23 D.L.R. (4th) 503, [1986] 1 W.W.R. 193, 41 Alta. L.R. (2d) 97, 18 C.R.R. 1, 66 A.R. 202, 62 N.R. 50, at 363 (S.C.R.), at 526 (D.L.R.), at 218 (W.W.R.). Motion requesting rehearing refd. (1986), 41 Alta. L.R. (2d) liv (note) (S.C.C.).

and furthermore leads to absurdity. When such is the case, the literal approach should not prevail unless the language used is of "absolute intractability", which is not the case here.

(b) Forfeitures and Penalties

An issue that has received much attention in the case law is what the word "incriminate" means. Both pre- and post-*Charter*, it is clear that no protection from use of the evidence in civil proceeding exists, including proceedings for a forfeiture or penalty.[483]

(c) Use During Crown's Case in Chief

It is also the case that any use of the prior statements by the Crown during its case in chief in a criminal prosecution would be an incriminating use.[484]

(d) Crown's Use in Cross-Examination

Prior to the enactment of the *Charter* it was somewhat unclear whether s. 5(2) provided a blanket protection against any use of the testimony from prior proceedings or whether certain forms of cross-examination by the Crown on the previous inconsistent statements would be permitted.[485] The same issue arose with respect to s. 13 of the *Charter*. This issue was laid to rest by Lamer J. speaking for the majority of the Supreme Court of Canada in *R. v. Kuldip*.[486] Lamer J. drew a distinction between cross-examination for the purpose of undermining the credibility of the accused and cross-examination to prove the truth of the previous statements, holding that s. 13 was not implicated in the former case. In *Kuldip* the accused was convicted of failing to remain at the scene of an accident with intent to escape civil or criminal liability. A Summary Conviction Appeal Court allowed his

---

483 For a post-*Charter* example see *McClure v. Backstein* (1987), 17 C.P.C. (2d) 242 (Ont. H.C.J.). Any vestiges of the civil privilege were removed in *R. v. Amway Corp.*, [1989] 1 S.C.R. 21, 68 C.R. (3d) 97, 56 D.L.R. (4th) 309, (*sub nom. R. v. Amway of Canada Ltd.*) [1989] 1 C.T.C. 255, 37 C.R.R. 235, [1989] 1 T.S.T. 2058, 2 T.C.T. 4074, at 35-36 (S.C.C.).

484 *R. v. Dubois, supra*, note 482, at 528 (D.L.R.), *per* Lamer J.

485 *R. v. Wilmot* (1940), 74 C.C.C. 1, [1940] 2 W.W.R. 401 (Alta. C.A.); appeal dismissed for want of jurisdiction, [1941] S.C.R. 53, 75 C.C.C. 161, [1941] 1 D.L.R. 689; *R. v. Côté* (1979), 50 C.C.C. (2d) 564 (Que. C.A.). Leave to appeal to S.C.C. refd. (1979), 50 C.C.C. (2d) 564n.

486 *R. v. Kuldip* (1990), 61 C.C.C. (3d) 385 (S.C.C.).

appeal and a new trial was ordered. At the second trial the accused testified in his own defence once again and the Crown sought to cross-examine him on his previous testimony (to the effect that he had seen a particular officer at the police station on the day of the accident) in order to prove that he had changed his evidence with respect to the presence of the officer on that day. The accused had discovered just prior to the second trial that this officer had not been on duty on the day of the accident. There was no record that the accused had reported the accident on the day of its occurrence.

To Justice Lamer it was clear that the purpose for the use of the accused's testimony from the first trial was to impeach the credibility of the accused's testimony at the second trial with respect to his allegation that he had reported the accident in which he was involved. However, the content of a statement from a first proceeding could, in addition to being an inconsistent statement capable of forming the basis of a cross-examination on credibility, also be relevant evidence against an accused. His Lordship explained how the distinction between purposes would operate in such a situation:[487]

> Using a prior inconsistent statement from a former proceeding during cross-examination in order to impugn credibility of an accused does not, in my view, incriminate that accused person. The previous statement is not tendered as evidence to establish the proof of its contents, but rather is tendered for the purpose of unveiling a contradiction between what the accused is saying now and what he or she has said on a previous occasion. For example, a situation could arise where A. is charged with murder and B. gives testimony at A.'s trial that B. was with A. in Montreal on the day of the alleged murder committing a bank robbery. B. may subsequently become the accused in a trial for robbery and choose to take the stand in his defence. If B. then testifies that he was in Ottawa on the day of the alleged robbery, the Crown is entitled to cross-examine B. with respect to the discrepancy

---

487   *Ibid.*, at 397-98. One might wonder how any sensible juror would not use such a statement as an express admission of the crime. Other cases which have held cross-examination on credibility to be permissible are *R. v. Langille* (1986), 73 N.S.R. (2d) 262, 176 A.P.R. 262, 60 C.B.R. (N.S.) 55 (C.A.); *R. v. B. (W.D.)* (1987), 38 C.C.C. (3d) 12, (*sub nom. R. v. B.*) 59 Sask. R. 220, 45 D.L.R. (4th) 429 (C.A.) and *Johnstone v. Law Society (British Columbia), supra*, note 475. *R. v. Dhaliwal* (1990), 60 C.C.C. (3d) 302 (B.C.C.A.).

between his current testimony and his previous testimony. The previous statement is used only to impeach the accused's credibility with respect to his current testimony that he was in Ottawa on the day of the alleged robbery. The previous statement may not be used, however, to establish the truth of its contents; it may not be used to establish that the accused was, in fact, in Montreal on the day of the alleged bank robbery nor can it be used to establish that the accused did, in fact, commit the alleged bank robbery. In the situation just described, it would be incumbent upon the trial judge to give a warning to the jury that it would not be open to it to conclude, on the basis of his previous statement, that the accused was in Montreal on the day of the alleged bank robbery nor to conclude that the accused did, in fact, commit the bank robbery. The jury would have to be warned that the only possible conclusion open to it from such cross-examination would be that the accused was not telling the truth when he said that he was in Ottawa on the day of the robbery and that he was not, in fact, in Ottawa on that day. Of course, this in turn might well enable it to conclude, beyond a reasonable doubt, that B. *was* in Montreal committing the robbery; but this conclusion could only be reached as a result of *other* evidence which will have become uncontradicted evidence as a result of the cross-examination which has impeached the credibility of the accused and thereby caused the injury to disbelieve the accused's current testimony.

Lamer J. agreed that it would often be difficult to draw the distinction between cross-examination for purpose of impeaching credibility and cross-examination for the purpose of incrimination. He was of the view that any concerns in this regard could be appropriately taken care of through an appropriate warning to the jurors as to the use they could make of the evidence. Similar warnings are accepted in the case of cross-examination of an accused on a previous record. Any other interpretation would in Lamer J.'s view tip the balance between the state and the individual too far in favour of the individual:[488]

> An accused has the right to remain silent during his or her trial. However, if an accused chooses to take the stand, that accused is implicitly vouching for his or her credibility. Such an accused,

---

488 *Ibid.*, at 398-99.

like any other witness, has therefore opened the door to having the trustworthiness of his/her evidence challenged. An interpretation of s. 13 which insulates such an accused from having previous inconsistent statements put to him/her on cross-examination where the only purpose of doing so is to challenge that accused's credibility, would, in my view, "stack the deck" too highly in favour of the accused.

It is interesting to distinguish *Kuldip* with the Supreme Court of Canada's prior decision in *R. v. Mannion*.[489] This again was a case of cross-examination on a statement made by the accused at a previous trial on the same charge. The central issue in the second trial was the inference to be drawn from the accused's departure from Edmonton to Vancouver after the alleged crime. It could have indicated a consciousness of guilt if the accused was aware of the charge prior to his departure. The accused testified at both trials and at the first trial testified that he had had a conversation with a police detective prior to the departure where the police officer told him that he wanted to see him concerning a rape. At the second trial on the same indictment the accused admitted the conversation with the police officer, but testified that there had been no mention of the specific reason, only that it was a serious matter. The police detective testified that he had not mentioned rape to the accused. McIntyre J. was of the view that the cross-examination on the prior inconsistent statement was in this case for the purpose of incrimination:[490]

> The Crown adduced evidence at both trials that, prior to the arrest of the respondent at Hinton on his way to Vancouver, no police officer had communicated to him that they were investigating his involvement in a rape. Mannion had earlier mentioned that he knew a rape was involved in his earlier trial and this fact was put to him in cross-examination in the second. The Crown argued in each trial that Mannion knew that a rape was involved before the police told him and that his precipitate flight from Edmonton when he became aware that the police wanted to see him displayed a consciousness of guilt. It is clear then that the

---

489 [1986] 2 S.C.R. 272, 28 C.C.C. (3d) 544, 53 C.R. (3d) 193, [1986] 6 W.W.R. 525, 47 Alta. L.R. (2d) 177, 31 D.L.R. (4th) 712, 75 A.R. 16, 25 C.R.R. 182, 69 N.R. 189.
490 *Ibid.*, at 550-51 (C.C.C.).

purpose of the cross-examination, which revealed the inconsistent statements, was to incriminate the respondent. This evidence was relied upon by the Crown to establish the guilt of the accused.

It would appear that the same evidence could have been admitted if the Crown had not suggested to the jury that they use it to establish a consciousness of guilt and if appropriate warnings had been given to the jury.

An argument of the accused that had found favour with Martin J.A. of the Ontario Court of Appeal in *Kuldip* was that to give s. 13 this narrow interpretation would result in s. 5(2) of the *CEA* giving wider protection as it provided protection against *any* subsequent use of the prior testimony. As a matter of policy this was to be avoided. Although Lamer J. did not deny the relevance of the s. 5(2) jurisprudence, he did not find this policy argument compelling. The legislature was quite capable if it so chose of conferring greater protections than those afforded by the *Charter*. However, there was no need to consider this argument, given Lamer J.'s view that s. 5(2) did not provide protection against all subsequent use of the prior testimony.[491]

> Secondly, and I say this with the utmost respect, I cannot accept the Ontario Court of Appeal's interpretation of s. 5(2) of the *Canada Evidence Act*. In my opinion, the protection offered by s. 5(2), namely, the guarantee that "the answer so given [by the witness] shall not be used or receivable in evidence against him in any criminal trial, or other criminal proceeding against him thereafter taking place . . .", must be interpreted in consideration of the express purpose of allowing the witness to make an objection under s. 5(2). This purpose is expressed clearly in the opening words of s. 5(2) that impose the substantive condition to be fulfilled before the section is made operative: a witness is entitled to object to a question on the grounds that "his answer may tend to criminate him, or may tend to establish his liability to a civil proceeding at the instance of the Crown or of any person . . .". Since the witness is only entitled to object to a question on the grounds that the answer to the question will tend to criminate him, it is only logical that he be guaranteed, in exchange for compelling him to answer the question, that his answer will not

---

491   *R. v. Kuldip, supra,* note 486 at 401.

be used to criminate him in a subsequent proceeding. A further guarantee that such answer will not be used in cross-examination to challenge the witness's credibility at a later proceeding would extend beyond the purpose of s. 5(2). With respect for contrary views, testimony given by a witness at a proceeding may, notwithstanding an objection under s. 5(2), be used at a subsequent proceeding in cross-examining the witness if the purpose of such use is to impeach his credibility and not to incriminate the witness.

5. "Any Other Proceedings"

Under s. 5(2) of the *CEA* the privilege could not be claimed for the very proceeding in which the objection to answering the question was made.[492] The same position holds with respect to s. 13.

The phrase "any other proceedings" must of course be read in light of the word "incriminate", so that the protection would not apply to proceedings other than those where the person seeking the protection was subject to a criminal prosecution or analogous penalty. Therefore, even if the protection is taken by a witness being examined for discovery, the answers could clearly be used in the subsequent civil trial.[493]

The protection afforded by s. 13 applies to administrative proceedings only if they expose the individual to true penal consequences such as imprisonment or a fine which by its magnitude would appear to be imposed for the purpose of redressing the wrong done to society at large rather than to maintain internal discipline within a limited sphere of activity. In *Donald v. Law Society (British Columbia)*,[494] a solicitor at a disciplinary hearing was given the protection of s. 13 since he faced liability to fines of up to $10,000 for each offence in addition

---

492 *Chambers v. Jaffray, supra,* note 476; *R. v. Anderson,* [1976] 2 W.W.R. 93 (Alta. S.C.); revd. without written reasons, [1976] 2 W.W.R. 672 (C.A.), *per* Sopinka J. in *R. v. Amway Corp., supra,* note 483, at 31 (S.C.R.).
493 Except if the proceeding was for a penalty or forfeiture, in which case the discovery transcript could be used on the basis that it was testimony in the same proceeding.
494 (1983), 2 D.L.R. (4th) 385, [1984] 2 W.W.R. 46, 48 B.C.L.R. 210, 7 C.R.R. 305n, additional reasons at [1985] 2 W.W.R. 671 (C.A.); leave to appeal to S.C.C. refd. (1984), 7 C.R.R. 305, 55 N.R. 237.

to reprimand, suspension and disbarment. But in *Knutson v. Sask. Registered Nurses' Assn.*,[495] s. 13 was held not to apply to the proceedings of the discipline committee of the Nurses' Association since there was no liability to imprisonment or fine, and therefore no element of punishment.

The interesting issues in this context relate to the different proceedings involved in a single criminal prosecution. Are the voir dire with respect to the admissibility of a confession, a bail hearing, the preliminary hearing and a re-trial on the same indictment "other proceedings"?

In *R. v. Dubois*[496] it was held that a re-trial on the same charge or an included offence constituted another proceeding for the purpose of s. 13:

> I do not see how the evidence given by the accused to meet the case as it was in the first trial could become part of the Crown's case against the accused in the second trial, without being in violation of s. 11(*d*), and to a lesser extent of s. 11(*c*). For, the accused is being *conscripted* to help the Crown in discharging its burden of *a case to meet*, and is thereby denied his or her right to stand mute until a case has been made out.

To allow the prosecution to use, as part of its case, the accused's previous testimony would, in effect, allow the Crown to do indirectly what it is estopped from doing directly by s. 11(c), i.e., to compel the accused to testify. It would also permit an indirect violation of the right of the accused to be presumed innocent and remain silent until proven guilty by the prosecution, as guaranteed by s. 11(d) of the *Charter*.[497]

With respect to statements made by the accused at the preliminary hearing, the Ontario Court of Appeal in *R. v. Yakeleya*[498] has held

---

495 [1991] 2 W.W.R. 327 (Sask. C.A.).

496 *Supra*, note 482, at 465 (S.C.R.).

497 *R. v. Dubois, supra*, note 482, at 537-38 (C.C.C.). *Dubois* overrides the Court's previous ruling in *R. v. Brown (No. 2)*, [1963] 3 C.C.C. 341n, [1963] S.C.R. vi (note), 40 C.R. 105, 42 W.W.R. 448, affirming the judgment of Johnson J.A. at [1963] 3 C.C.C. 326, 40 C.R. 90, 41 W.W.R. 129 (N.W.T.C.A.), to the extent that *Brown* could be taken to have endorsed that a re-trial was not a subsequent proceeding for the purpose of s. 5(2) and *R. v. Sophonow*, [1984] 2 S.C.R. 524, 17 C.C.C. (3d) 128, 15 D.L.R. (4th) 480, 57 N.R. 13. *Dubois* was followed on this point in *R. v. Mannion, supra*, note 489.

498 (1985), 20 C.C.C. (3d) 193, 46 C.R. (3d) 282, 9 O.A.C. 284, 14 C.R.R. 381.

that the preliminary hearing and the trial constitute the same proceedings.[499]

The search for truth is not, of course, an absolute value in a criminal trial and must sometimes yield to other values recognized by the criminal justice system, such as, fairness, openness and protection from oppressive questioning. It would, however, be anomalous, in our view, if an accused could testify under oath as a witness at his preliminary hearing in respect of the charge against him, in order to exculpate himself from the charge and upon ascertaining that his first story did not fit the facts, could then tell a different story under oath at his trial, and rely on s. 13 of the Charter to insulate his first story from exposure at his trial. This would mean that the jury would be required to try an artificial case rather than the real case. We cannot think that s. 13 of the Charter in those circumstances precludes the exposure to the jury of the accused's first story when he takes the stand in his own defence at his trial.

Of course, the same could be said of the statements given by an accused at a first trial. Furthermore, the Court of Appeal's concern that too much protection would be afforded to the accused is now addressed to some extent by the narrowing of s. 13 by the Supreme Court of Canada in *R. v. Kuldip*.[500] In *R. v. Dubois* Lamer J. intimated (although he certainly did not decide) that his reasoning may apply to the statements made on a preliminary inquiry. However, he also indicated that a s. 1 analysis could result in a different position with respect to preliminary hearings.[501]

Concern has been expressed as regards the logical extension of this reasoning to the admissibility of evidence given by an accused at the preliminary inquiry under s. 469 of the *Criminal Code*. The matter is not raised on this appeal. But, even assuming without deciding that a preliminary inquiry is another proceeding, the question then to be addressed is whether s. 469 would be, under s. 1 of the *Charter*, an unreasonable limit to the protections afforded by s. 13. Relevant to this determination

---

499 *Ibid.*, at 195 (C.C.C.).
500 (1990), 61 C.C.C. (3d) 385 (S.C.C.). See discussion this Chapter, IV.D.4(d).
501 *Supra*, note 482, at 366 (S.C.R.).

would, amongst other considerations, be the nature of the jeopardy in which an accused is placed, at that stage, if he chooses not to testify at the preliminary to rebut the *"prima facie* case".

A bail hearing has been held to be an "other proceeding",[502] as has a voir dire.[503] A contempt hearing resulting from non-compliance of an order compelling a party to answer questions during a proceeding such as a discovery, cross-examination on an affidavit or an examination in aid of execution is an integral part of the entire civil action from its commencement to judgment, and to enforcement thereof, and therefore constitutes the same proceeding as the civil action (even if the use of evidence given in a civil proceeding could be characterized as incriminating).[504]

6. Who Can Claim the Protection?

The protection given by the statutes and s. 13 can be claimed only by the witness for his or her own benefit and not the protection of a third person.[505] This raises interesting issues in the context of corporations. In *R. v. Amway Corp.*[506] a unanimous Supreme Court of

---

502 *R. v. Buxbaum* (1989), 70 C.R. (3d) 20, 33 O.A.C. 1 (C.A.).

503 *R. v. Tarafa* (1989), 53 C.C.C. (3d) 472, [1990] R.J.Q. 427 (S.C.). The pre-*Charter* decision of the Ontario Court of Appeal in *R. v. Tarrant* (1981), 25 C.R. (3d) 157, 63 C.C.C. (2d) 385, 34 O.R. (2d) 747, holding that an accused could be cross-examined on statements made during the *voir dire* if the confession was held to be admissible is to be read in light of *R. v. Dubois*, [1985] 2 S.C.R. 350, 22 C.C.C. (3d) 513, 48 C.R. (3d) 193, 23 D.L.R. (4th) 503, [1986] 1 W.W.R. 193, 41 Alta. L.R. (2d) 97, 18 C.R.R. 1, 66 A.R. 202, [1986] D.L.Q. 87n, 62 N.R. 50, and *R. v. Kuldip* (1990), 61 C.C.C. (3d) 385 (S.C.C.) and should be modified to the extent that cross-examination would not be permitted if the purpose was to incriminate the accused. It should also be noted that if the confession was ruled to be inadmissible the statements made on the voir dire could not be used in evidence at the trial for any purpose: see *R. v. Magdish* (1978), 41 C.C.C. (2d) 449, 3 C.R. (3d) 377 (Ont. C.A.); *Wong Kam-ming v. R.*, [1979] 2 W.L.R. 81, [1979] 1 All E.R. 939, [1980] A.C. 247 (P.C.); *R. v. Erven*, [1979] 1 S.C.R. 926, 44 C.C.C. (2d) 76, 6 C.R. (3d) 97, 30 N.S.R. (2d) 89, 49 A.P.R. 89, 92 D.L.R. (3d) 507, 25 N.R. 49.

504 *McClure v. Backstein, supra*, note 483.

505 *R. v. Mayflower Bottling Co.* (1909), 44 N.S.R. 417 (C.A.); *Re Jenkins* (1910), 7 E.L.R. 543 (P.E.I.S.C.).

506 [1989] 1 S.C.R. 21, 68 C.R. (3d) 97, 56 D.L.R. (4th) 309, (*sub nom. R. v. Amway of Canada Ltd.*) [1989] 1 C.T.C. 255, 37 C.R.R. 235, [1989] 1 T.S.T. 2058, 2 T.C.T. 4074.

Canada held that a corporation could not be a "witness" within the meaning of s. 11(c) of the *Charter*. Presumably this reasoning would apply to s. 13 and also to s. 5(2) of the *CEA* and the similar provincial statutes. An officer or director or employee of a corporation who testifies in criminal proceedings is the witness, not the corporation itself.[507] Similarly, if an officer, director or employee is asked a question on an examination for discovery, the answers given cannot be used against the officer, director or employee in a subsequent criminal proceeding against that person, but they could be used in a subsequent criminal proceeding against the corporation. This is the case notwithstanding that the witness being examined for discovery is being examined as a representative of the corporation.[508] The common law provided that the privilege could be claimed on behalf of the corporation where the information being supplied, whether in the form of documents or otherwise, belonged to the corporation.[509] This privilege is now replaced by s. 5 of the *CEA* and s. 13 of the *Charter*. Since these apply only to testimonial privilege and can be claimed only by a witness there is no longer any protection against self-incrimination for a corporation.

E. *Charter, Section* 7

1. Derivative Use Immunity

It has been argued that s. 13 of the *Charter* does not exhaust the scope of the self-incrimination principle. On a number of occasions it has been submitted that s. 7 of the *Charter* provides a wider protection. Section 7 reads:

> 7. Everyone has the right to life, liberty and security of the person and the right not to be deprived thereof except in accordance with the principles of fundamental justice.

---

507   *Ibid.*, at 37; *R. v. N.M. Paterson & Sons Ltd.*, [1980] 2 S.C.R. 679, 19 C.R. (3d) 164, 55 C.C.C. (2d) 289, [1981] 2 W.W.R. 103, 7 Man. R. (2d) 382, 117 D.L.R. (3d) 517, 34 N.R. 597; and see *R. v. General Sessions of the Peace for York County* (1970), 3 C.C.C. (2d) 204, 16 C.R.N.S. 329, [1971] 2 O.R. 3, 16 D.L.R. (3d) 609, 65 C.P.R. 250 (*sub nom. Corning Glass Works of Canada Ltd. v. R.*) (C.A.).
508   *R. v. Amway Corp., supra*, note 506, at 37-39 (S.C.R.).
509   *Bell v. Klein*, [1955] S.C.R. 309, [1955] 2 D.L.R. 513.

In *Thomson Newspapers Ltd. v. Canada (Director of Investigation and Research, Restrictive Trade Practices Commission)*,[510] the issue was whether s. 7 conferred an additional immunity against the use of evidence discovered as a result of testimony in prior proceedings. This was referred to in the case as a "derivative use immunity". Section 20 of the *Combines Investigation Act*, the statute in issue in *Thomson*, provided a testimonial use immunity co-extensive with that in s. 5(2) of the *CEA*. It was argued that s. 17 of the *Combines Investigation Act* was in conflict with the *Charter* since it provided that a person could be punished for contempt for refusing to answer questions put by a Commissioner conducting an investigation under the Act on the ground that the answers could incriminate. Although s. 13 of the *Charter* (and s. 20 of the Act) would provide protection against the subsequent use of the oral testimony given before the Commissioner, no protection against the use of the evidence discovered from the oral testimony was provided.

Lamer J. refused to answer the question put with respect to s. 7 on the basis that, given the similarity between s. 5(1) of the *CEA* and s. 20 of the *Combines Investigation Act*, it inferentially required a finding that s. 5(1) of the *CEA* was unconstitutional. Section 5(1) would have the effect of removing a constitutional privilege if s. 7 were found to provide greater protection than a testimonial use immunity. Since the appellants had challenged the validity of s. 17 and not s. 20 it was Lamer J.'s view that it was not appropriate to answer the question. As the other four of the five judges hearing the appeal split on the issue of whether s. 7 provided a derivative use immunity, it would seem that the issue is unresolved.

Wilson J. dissented on the s. 7 issue. She found that one of the purposes of the investigatory powers of the Commissioner was the collection of information that could form the basis of a criminal prosecution under the Act. In this context it was her view that, to be meaningful, the privilege against self-incrimination had to also protect against the subsequent use of evidence derived from "compelled testimony". Because the derivative evidence could pursuant to the Act be forwarded to the Attorney General to form the basis of a prosecution, Wilson J. would have held that s. 17 infringed s. 7. She in effect recognizes a right to remain silent where a privilege protecting the

---

510   [1990] 1 S.C.R. 425, 54 C.C.C. (3d) 417, 76 C.R. (3d) 129, 39 O.A.C. 161, 67 D.L.R. (4th) 161, 47 C.R.R. 1, 29 C.P.R. (3d) 97, 106 N.R. 161.

witness from the use of derivative evidence is not provided. If the protection from subsequent use had been afforded she might have held that the witness had no right to refuse to answer the questions. It is not clear from the judgment whether she would or would not have done so. The reasoning is, therefore, more consistent with an extension of the testimonial self-incrimination privilege than with a more general right to remain silent.

Sopinka J., on the other hand, agreed in the result with Wilson J. on the s. 7 issue, but based his reasoning on the recognition of a right to remain silent (of which the testimonial privilege in s. 13 is but an aspect) and not an extension of the right not to answer questions that incriminate or tend to incriminate the person being examined.[511] He distinguished modern usage of the terms 'privilege against self-incrimination' and 'the right to remain silent'.[512]

> The privilege against self-incrimination is often used as a general term embracing aspects of the right to remain silent. In origin they derive from the principle *nemo tenetur seipsum accusare*. Nevertheless, in modern usage, the privilege against self-incrimination is limited to the right of an individual to resist testimony as a witness in a legal proceeding. A privilege is an exclusionary rule of evidence which is appropriately asserted in court.
>
> . . .
>
> The right to remain silent is the basis for the non-compellability of the accused as a witness at trial but it extends beyond the witness box.

La Forest and L'Heureux-Dubé JJ. disagreed that s. 7 afforded any protection in this situation. However, La Forest J. adopted a more flexible approach than any of the other justices, but one that also recognized that the general principle against self-incrimination could afford some protection against the use of derivative evidence. He stated[513] that although to use such evidence might be equivalent to direct reliance on the compelled testimony, there were important differences between the type of prejudice suffered by the accused in

---

511 *Ibid.*, at 603 (S.C.R.).
512 *Ibid.*, at 599 (S.C.R.).
513 *Ibid.*, at 548-49 and 555 (S.C.R.).

each case. The compelled testimony is evidence that would not exist independently of the power to compel it and could, therefore, be obtained only from the accused. Derivative evidence does have an independent existence, although it may go undetected without the compelled statements. If the probability of independent discovery is very low its use may be equivalent in effect to the use of the testimony. In most cases, however, the derivative evidence could have been discovered without any reliance on the compelled testimony.

Viewed in this light, it was apparent that to La Forest J. derivative evidence could only be *self*-incriminatory by virtue of the circumstances surrounding its discovery in a particular case. Compelled testimony on the other hand is by definition *self*-incriminatory, since testimony is a form of evidence necessarily unique to the party giving it. On the basis of the accused's right to a fair trial encapsulated in s. 11(d) La Forest J. would leave it up to the trial judge to determine whether fairness required the exclusion of the evidence in any particular case.

L'Heureux-Dubé J. expressly disagreed with Sopinka J.'s approach. She did not believe that s. 7 recognized any general right to remain silent in the face of a statutory obligation to testify before a properly constituted tribunal. Nor did she agree with Wilson J. that s. 7 required a derivative use immunity to be provided.[514]

> To state my views positively, I agree that s. 7 may offer residual protection in commanding some type of immunity in respect of the testimony given by individuals during an investigation. In my view, "fundamental justice" requires protection coextensive with the individual's testimonial participation in the investigation, that is, use immunity. Such protection serves the end of preventing the state from using incriminating evidence which was obtained from the individual himself, while at the same time tailoring the protection to what our system considers to be the appropriate boundary of fairness in the judicial process. Once it is established that our legal tradition recognizes the usefulness of commissions of inquiry and other investigative agencies such as the Commission, the question of the correct amount of protection to be given to witnesses must leave some room for the purpose of proper law enforcement to be served.

---

514 *Ibid.*, at 583-84 (S.C.R.).

She concluded:[515]

Derivative evidence, which consists mainly of real evidence, cannot be assimilated to self-incriminating evidence and does not go to the fairness of the judicial process which is what, in the end, fundamental justice is all about.

Although the judgment in *Thomson* does not arrive at a consensus as to the appropriate analysis to apply in determining the scope of the testimonial immunity found in s. 7, the majority agreed that it existed. Wilson J. and La Forest J. would give protection from the use of derivative evidence, and in the right case Lamer J. might do so also. Sopinka J. expressly recognized a right to remain silent in s. 13 of the *Charter* and s. 5(2) of the *Canada Evidence Act*. In the subsequent case of *R. v. Hebert*[516] the Supreme Court of Canada confirmed the existence of such a right extending beyond the protection of the testimonial privilege.

2. Right of Silence

As suggested at the beginning of this chapter, the privilege against self-incrimination is also reflected in s. 11(c) of the *Charter* which protects an accused from being compelled to be a witness against him or herself. Here the *Charter* recognizes a right co-extensive with the rights which an accused had at common law. The question is whether s. 7 of the *Charter* encompasses any further right to remain silent that cannot be abrogated by statute. As discussed above, Sopinka J. in *Thomson Newspapers Ltd.*[517] took the position that such a right of silence could exist beyond that recognized in s. 11(c). It is submitted that this was also the basis of the judgment of Wilson J. as confirmed by the position which she took in *Hebert*.[518] La Forest J. indicated that he would give it some scope, but disagreed that it applied in the context of the investigation provisions of the *Combines*

---

515 *Ibid.*, at 585 (S.C.R.).
516 [1990] 2 S.C.R. 151, 57 C.C.C. (3d) 1, 77 C.R. (3d) 145, [1990] 5 W.W.R. 1, 47 B.C.L.R. (2d) 1, 49 C.R.R. 114, 110 N.R. 1.
517 *Supra*, note 510.
518 Discussed below.

Investigation Act. L'Heureux-Dubé J. did not believe that it had any scope, at least where the investigatory tribunal was properly constituted.

The Supreme Court of Canada subsequently considered the issue in more detail in *R. v. Hebert.*[519] It is clear from this decision that s. 7 does not reinstate the common law privilege against self-incrimination or grant an absolute right of silence. McLachlin J. gave the judgment for the majority. She explained the relationship between the confessions rule, the privilege against self-incrimination (as encompassed in s. 11(c)) and the right to silence as deriving from two common-law concepts; the confessions rule and the privilege against self-incrimination. The common theme uniting these two separate rules was the idea that a person in the power of the state in the course of the criminal process has the right to choose whether to speak to the police or remain silent.[520] Her review of the case law with respect to the confessions rule confirmed that this was indeed a common theme running through the jurisprudence, accompanied by a correlative concern with the repute and integrity of the judicial process.

With respect to the privilege against self-incrimination she noted that it was[521] rooted in an abhorrence of the interrogation practised by the old ecclesiastical courts and the Star Chamber and the notion, which grew out of that abhorrence, that the citizen involved in the criminal process must be accorded procedural protections against the overweening power of the state.[522] It shared with the confessions rule the notion that an accused person has no obligation to give evidence against him or herself, that he or she has the right to choose whether to make a statement to the police or not.[523] The principle difference between McLachlin J. and Sopinka J.[524] was as to when the right was attracted and how it could be lost. Sopinka and Wilson JJ. agreed that the right would arise whenever the coercive power of the state was brought to bear on the individual, which could predate detention, whereas McLachlin J. viewed detention as the relevant time.[525] McLachlin J. was of the view that the right to remain

---

519 *Supra*, note 516.
520 *Supra*, note 516, at 164 (S.C.R.).
521 *Supra*, note 516, at 33 (C.C.C.).
522 *Ibid.*, at 180 (S.C.R.).
523 *Ibid.*
524 With whom Wilson J. agreed.
525 *Ibid.*, McLachlin J. at 184 (S.C.R.); Wilson J. at 190 (S.C.R.); Sopinka J. at

silent was not an absolute right and, therefore, it was unnecessary to consider the application of the concept of waiver.[526] Sopinka and Wilson JJ. disagreed with this, holding that the right would be waived if, with full knowledge of his or her rights, the accused voluntarily spoke to the authorities.[527]

In the result it was held that a person as a right to remain silent in the face of police interrogation of his or her suspected criminal activity. Placing an undercover police officer in the cell with a suspect who has expressly stated that he does not wish to speak to the police in order to solicit admissions, infringes that right.[528] The Supreme Court of Canada extended the principle in *R. v. Broyles*[529] to a situation where the individual who elicited the admissions from the accused was not an undercover police officer but rather a friend of the accused who was asked by the police to visit the accused and whose visit was facilitated by them. Admissibility of any statement resulting from the infringement of such right would depend on the application of s. 24(2) of the *Charter*.

Could this right of silence apply to investigations of activity by other state agencies? It is unclear from *Thomson* whether it would apply to investigations under the *Competition Act*. If characterized essentially as an investigation into criminal conduct, then it could very well apply.[530] Where the investigatory proceedings are administrative

---

200 (S.C.R.).
526 *Ibid.*, at 183-85 (S.C.R.).
527 *Ibid.*, Sopinka J. at 203-04 (S.C.R.) and Wilson J. at 191 (S.C.R.).
528 See *R. v. Graham* (1991), 1 O.R. (3d) 499, 62 C.C.C. (3d) 128 (C.A.), where the evidence of statements made to an undercover police officer placed in the accused's cell was admitted. *Hebert* was distinguished on the basis that the accused had never stated that he did not want to give a statement to the police and he had spoken to the officers without solicitation. Similarly, in *R. v. Johnston* (1991), 2 O.R. (3d) 771 (C.A.), it was held that the use of the informer's testimony did not violate the accused's right to silence since he spoke freely with him and the impugned statements were not the product of any actively eliciting conduct by the informer.
529 Not yet reported, November 28, 1991 (S.C.C.).
530 See the reasoning of the majority of the British Columbia Court of Appeal in *Haywood Securities Inc. v. Inter-Tech Resource Group Inc.* (1985), 68 B.C.L.R. 145 (*sub nom. Haywood Securities Inc. v. Brunnhuber*), [1986] 2 W.W.R. 289, 7 C.P.C. (2d) 179, 24 D.L.R. (4th) 724 (C.A.), at 152 (B.C.L.R.). See also *R. L. Crain Inc. v. Couture* (1983), 10 C.C.C. (3d) 119, 6 D.L.R. (4th) 478, 9 C.R.R. 287, 30 Sask. R. 191 (Q.B.).

in nature, such as the audit power under the *Income Tax Act*,[531] compelled testimony would not likely in itself be enough to give rise to a right of silence. On the other hand, if charges of tax fraud are pending and there is a significant probability that the state would use the power to obtain additional information for the charge, then the section would be implicated.[532]

The danger of provincial inquiries infringing the right of silence is much reduced by the recent decision of the Supreme Court of Canada in *Starr v. Ontario (Commissioner of Inquiry)*[533] restricting the right of the province to enact a public inquiry with all its coercive powers as a substitute for an investigation and preliminary inquiry into specific individuals in respect of specific criminal offences.

F. Protecting the Accused's Privilege Against Self-Incrimination and Right of Silence

1. Commenting on the Accused's Failure to Testify

Section 4(6) (formerly s. 4(5)) of the *Canada Evidence Act* prohibits a judge or counsel for the prosecution from commenting to the jury[534] on the failure of the accused (or the accused's spouse) to testify. The section is intended to prevent comments to the effect that an innocent person could have been expected to take the stand in his or her own defence. Commentary to this effect would seriously erode the accused's privilege against self-incrimination. The section does not prevent the court or prosecution from commenting that the Crown's evidence is uncontradicted or is the only evidence on the matter or is undenied.[535] Crown counsel might even comment that the defence did

---

531 Section 231.3(1)(a).
532 See *Tyler v. Minister of National Revenue*, not yet reported, November 19, 1990 (Fed. C.A.).
533 (*sub nom. Starr v. Houlden*), [1990] 81 S.C.R. 1366, 55 C.C.C. (3d) 472, 41 O.A.C. 161, 68 D.L.R. (4th) 641, 110 N.R. 81.
534 The section only applies to jury trials. See *R. v. Binder* (1948), 92 C.C.C. 20, 6 C.R. 83, [1948] O.R. 607 (C.A.); *Pratte v. Maher*, [1965] 1 C.C.C. 77 (Que. C.A.); *R. v. Clark* (1901), 5 C.C.C. 235, 3 O.L.R. 176 (C.A.); *R. v. MacLeod*, [1968] 2 C.C.C. 365 (P.E.I.C.A.); *Tilco Plastics Ltd. v. Skurjat; Ontario (A.G.) v. Clark*, [1967] 1 C.C.C. 131, 49 C.R. 99, [1966] 2 O.R. 547, 57 D.L.R. (2d) 596, 66 C.L.L.C. 14,138 (Ont. H.C.J.); affd. [1967] 2 C.C.C. 196n; leave to appeal to S.C.C. refd. [1967] 2 C.C.C. 196n.
535 *Wright v. R.*, [1945] S.C.R. 319, 83 C.C.C. 225, 1 C.R. 43, [1945] 2 D.L.R.

not see fit to contradict the evidence.[536] It has also been held that counsel for a co-accused may comment on the failure of the accused to testify.[537]

But because s. 4(6) prevents the judge from making *any* comment on the accused's failure to testify it also prevents any warning to the jury members not to draw any adverse inference from the failure. This was determined by the Supreme Court of Canada in *R. v. Vezeau*.[538] It was there held that the jury is entitled to draw such an inference of its own accord. As Justice Martland stated:[539]

> It was part of the appellant's defence to the charge that he could not have committed the offence because he was in Montreal when the murder occurred. Proof to this alibi was tendered by a witness who claimed to have been with the appellant in Montreal. The direction of the trial Judge precluded the jury, when considering this defence, from taking into consideration the fact that the appellant had failed to support his alibi by his own testimony. *The failure of an accused person, who relies upon an alibi, to testify and thus to submit himself to cross-examination is a matter of importance in considering the validity of that defence.* The jury, in this case, was instructed that they could not take that fact into account in reaching their verdict. [emphasis added]

In *R. v. Boss*[540] Cory J.A. of the Ontario Court of Appeal held that the *Charter* had not changed the law in this regard. The accused argued that the inability of the trial judge to direct the jury that an

---

523; *R. v. MacLean* (1906), 11 C.C.C. 283 (N.S.S.C.); *R. v. Guerin* (1909), 14 C.C.C. 424, 18 O.L.R. 425.

536 *R. v. Schmidt* (1948), 90 C.C.C. 297, 5 C.R. 165, [1948] O.R. 198, [1948] 2 D.L.R. 826 (Ont. C.A.); revd. on other grounds, [1948] S.C.R. 333, 92 C.C.C. 53, 6 C.R. 317, [1948] 4 D.L.R. 217. However, the judge and the Crown must be careful here: see *R. v. Jacobs* (1953), 106 C.C.C. 288, [1953] O.W.N. 656 (C.A.); *R. v. Zicari* (1936), 65 C.C.C. 386, [1936] 2 D.L.R. 542 (Ont. C.A.); *Vigeant v. R.*, [1930] S.C.R. 396, 54 C.C.C. 301, [1931] 3 D.L.R. 512.

537 *R. v. Naglik* (1991), 3 O.R. (3d) 385 (C.A.); leave to appeal to S.C.C. granted December 4, 1991.

538 [1977] 2 S.C.R. 277, 28 C.C.C. (2d) 81, 34 C.R.N.S. 309, 66 D.L.R. (3d) 418, 8 N.R. 235.

539 *Ibid.*, at 87-88 (C.C.C.). Dickson and Laskin JJ. also were of the view that the judge was in error in giving such an instruction.

540 (1988), 46 C.C.C. (3d) 523, 68 C.R. (3d) 123, 30 O.A.C. 184.

adverse inference should not be drawn resulted in a practical compulsion to testify, thereby infringing the privilege against self-incrimination and the right to be presumed innocent. Cory J.A. commented as follows:[541]

> . . . in my view, it could be said that s. 4(5) [now s. 4(6)] of the *Canada Evidence Act* constitutes a reasoned and considered legislative attempt to protect in a measured way the rights of the accused. By its provisions neither the judge nor the prosecutor can make any comment pertaining to the failure of the accused to testify if the accused has made such a decision. However, counsel for the accused is entitled to make an appropriate comment on the issue. For example, it might be explained to the jury that the case against the accused must be made out by the Crown which must bear the burden of proving all the essential elements of the offence beyond any reasonable doubt. Counsel can stress that there is no duty upon the accused to testify and that, rather, the obligation rests upon the Crown throughout the case to satisfy them beyond all reasonable doubt that the accused has indeed committed the crime with which he or she is charged. In pre-Charter times the section certainly constituted a fair approach which eliminated any comment from the judge and prosecutor. Such legislation is, I think, entitled to some deference requiring careful judicial consideration before it is held to be invalid.

Cory J.A. went on to consider whether the inability of the judge to comment resulted in any practical compulsion to testify such as to infringe s. 11(c). In holding that it did not he stated:[542]

> In Canada, while both the prosecutor and judge are prohibited from making any comment on the failure to testify, counsel for the accused may make appropriate submissions to the jury on the issue. In those circumstances, and in light of the trial judge's

---

541 *Ibid.*, at 538-39 (C.C.C.). As to the ability of defence counsel to comment see also, *R. v. McConnell*, [1968] 1 C.C.C. 368, 2 C.R.N.S. 50, [1967] 2 O.R. 527 (Ont. C.A.); affd. [1968] S.C.R. 802, [1968] 4 C.C.C. 257, 4 C.R.N.S. 269, 69 D.L.R. (2d) 149.
542 *Ibid.*, at 541-42 (C.C.C.).

discretion to restrict cross-examination of the accused as to prior conviction,[543] it cannot be said that, in the absence of a trial judge's instruction on the issue, the accused is being penalized for exercising his constitutional right. An accused who decides to remain silent in the face of a case presented by the Crown that cries out for an explanation must accept the consequences of that decision. An accused who remains silent cannot be said to have been penalized by the provisions of s. 4(6) of the *Canada Evidence Act*.

In any event, s. 4(6), even if it did constitute a tactical compulsion, did not constitute a legal compulsion and could not, therefore, infringe the privilege against testimonial self-incrimination enshrined in s. 11(c).[544]

An example of the trial judge considering drawing an adverse inference from the failure of an accused to testify is found in *R. v. Manchev*.[545] Bobby Manchev was charged with a number of offences relating to a shooting incident. It was alleged that he had shot at a car containing two persons with whom the Manchev family were feuding. The "victims" testified that they saw Bobby Manchev shoot at them. Bobby's father testified that he, and not his son, was the person who shot at them. The trial judge felt that the credibility of all of the witnesses was in question. Bobby did not take the stand in his own defence. Doherty J. considered that the failure to testify could potentially have some relevance. He stated:

> I must also consider the effect, if any, of Bobby Manchev's failure to testify. Even on the defence account of events, Bobby Manchev was an eyewitness to the shooting. This is not a case where Bobby Manchev's version of the events is before the court in the form of a statement. His statement, while it is a denial of his involvement as the shooter, does not place any account of the shooting before me. Finally, I note that the evidence adduced by the defence and the Crown makes it clear that Bobby Manchev has a criminal past. This is, consequently, not a case where the

---

543 Now recognized by the Supreme Court of Canada in *R. v. Corbett*, [1988] 1 S.C.R. 670, 41 C.C.C. (3d) 385, 64 C.R. (3d) 1, [1988] 4 W.W.R. 481, 28 B.C.L.R. (2d) 145, 85 N.R. 81.
544 See also *R. v. Naglik, supra*, note 537, at 395-96.
545 Unreported, August 23, 1990 (Ont. H.C.J.), *per* Doherty J.

spectre of cross-examination under s. 12 of the *Canada Evidence Act* looms large and may have kept the accused out of the witness stand.

Doherty J. recognized, on the basis of *Boss*, that he was entitled to draw an adverse inference from the failure to testify, although he had to be careful in doing so. A failure to testify was not to be treated as independent evidence of guilt.

> Bobby Manchev's failure to testify is not an independent piece of evidence to be placed on the evidentiary scale and weighed like evidence given by various witnesses. It is, rather, a feature of the trial which I may look to in deciding what inferences can reasonably be drawn from the evidence adduced before me. In a case where the totality of the evidence suggests various inferences, the accused's failure to testify can assist in determining the appropriate inference. It can tip the scales in favour of an inference which is less favourable to the accused than others which may have been available. Even in such situations, however, the failure of the accused to testify is not conclusive, and the extent to which it will weigh against the accused will vary with the evidence adduced in any particular case and the issues raised. Where the issue is not what inference should be drawn, but whether direct evidence tendered by the Crown is sufficiently reliable to justify a conviction, the accused's failure to testify does not assist. If the Crown witness cannot be believed, or if one cannot be satisfied to the necessary degree based on their evidence, then they do not become more believable because the accused did not testify. Similarly, the accused's failure to testify cannot detract from the credibility of other defence witnesses. If a defence witness's evidence leaves a trier of fact with a reasonable doubt, then that doubt does not disappear because the accused, who was in a position to corroborate that person's evidence, does not testify. The accused's failure to testify, in my view, has no role to play in judgments of credibility of other, particularly Crown witnesses, although it clearly has a role to play in determining what inferences should be drawn after assessments of credibility have been made.

Doherty J.'s analysis illustrates the acceptable approach for a jury in considering the accused's failure to testify. However, *Boss* and *Vezeau* dealt only with inferences that a jury could draw, not a trial judge. Short of raising the subject, there is no way of preventing the jury from employing the analysis. It is doubtful that a judge should be able to expressly direct him or herself to employ this analysis. Despite some earlier cases that contain suggestions otherwise, the failure to testify is not direct evidence of guilt. However, if the Crown has established a case to meet and the accused is in the best position to establish his or her defence, then the trier of fact may reasonably consider the failure to testify as rendering the defence theory less plausible.[546]

2. Evidentiary Effect of the Accused's Silence in the Face of an Accusation from a Person in Authority

Just as commenting adversely on the failure of the accused to testify impairs the accused's privilege against self-incrimination, allowing direct evidence on the accused's failure to assist the police in their investigation or failing to give a timely explanation to the police can compromise the accused's right to remain silent.[547] Therefore, as a general rule such evidence is not permitted. This was established recently by the Supreme Court of Canada in *R. v. Chambers*.[548] The charge against the accused was conspiracy to import cocaine into British Columbia. The accused admitted that he had agreed to assist in such an endeavour but argued that he had no intention to carry out the agreement. He had only agreed to assist in order to win back the affections of his former girlfriend, a co-conspirator. The defence put forth evidence that the accused had tried to stop the importation by arranging for a third person, Kuko, to steal the drugs from the person who was to bring the drugs into Canada. Chambers did not raise this defence until his second trial which was held over five years after the charge was laid. The trial judge allowed Crown counsel to cross-examine the accused as to why he had not raised the defence prior to

---

546 See *Kolnberger v. R.*, [1969] S.C.R. 213, [1969] 3 C.C.C. 241, 66 W.W.R. 560, 2 D.L.R. (3d) 409; *R. v. Jacquard* (1950), 98 C.C.C. 72, 10 C.R. 155, 25 M.P.R. 149 (N.S.C.A.); *R. v. Patrick* (1982), 63 C.C.C. (2d) 1, 28 B.C.L.R. 244, 128 D.L.R. (3d) 496 (C.A.); affd. 66 C.C.C. (2d) 575, 40 B.C.L.R. 173, 138 D.L.R. (3d) 384 (S.C.C.). See also the discussion of this issue in P. K. McWilliams, *Canadian Criminal Evidence*, 3rd ed. (Toronto: Canada Law Book, 1988) at § 30:10700.
547 See this Chapter, IV.E.2.
548 [1990] 2 S.C.R. 1293, 59 C.C.C. (3d) 321, [1990] 6 W.W.R. 554.

that time and in particular at the time of his arrest. Objections were taken to this line of questioning and both counsel subsequently agreed that the trial judge would direct the jury to ignore the questions and answers. Consequently, defence counsel did not re-examine the accused as to when he had first raised the defence. The trial judge, however, neglected to so charge the jury and neither counsel reminded him of his duty in this regard. After noting that the right of silence was now recognized as a basic tenet of our legal system, Cory J. remarked that:[549]

> ... it would be a snare and a delusion to caution the accused that he need not say anything in response to a police officer's question but none the less put in evidence that the accused clearly exercised his right and remained silent in the face of a question which suggested his guilt.

Justice Cory accepted the opinion of Dubin J.A. in *R. v. Robertson*[550] to the effect that:

> ... the purported resumé of the facts as stated by Inspector Lyle, coupled with the response of "nothing", after being cautioned, was so highly prejudicial that I am not satisfied that the learned trial Judge's instructions to the jury could erase the prejudicial effect which that evidence would have on the jury. I cannot help but feel that most juries would assume that an innocent man would be prompted to deny any false accusations against him and his failure to do so would tend to prove belief in the truth of the accusations.

Dubin J.A. later stated:[551]

> In the absence of any issue raised by the defence, the mere silence of an accused during police interrogation cannot be said to advance the case for the Crown. It cannot be a step on the way to the proof of the accused's guilt. It, therefore, becomes, in my opinion, irrelevant to any issue at trial. To prove as part of the Crown's case the fact that the accused has exercised his common

---

549 *Ibid.*, at 341 (C.C.C.).
550 (1975), 21 C.C.C. (2d) 385, at 395, 29 C.R.N.S. 141 (Ont. C.A.).
551 *Ibid.*, at 400 (C.C.C.), quoted in *R. v. Chambers, supra*, note 548, at 341 (C.C.C.).

law right to remain silent would constitute silence a trap if his silence is placed in evidence against him at his trial.

In *Robertson* Dubin J.A. was in dissent, but Martin J.A. for the majority agreed with the basic principle that such evidence could not be admitted unless it was relevant to an issue. On the facts Martin J.A. felt that the evidence was relevant since the trial judge had ruled that statements made by the accused subsequent to the caution were voluntary, and, therefore, evidence of the caution was relevant to the voluntariness issue. The trial judge had given the jury a very clear direction that they were not going to consider the accused's failure to speak to the police as evidence of guilt.[552]

In *R. v. Chambers* Cory J. affirmed this view that questions by investigating officers and evidence as to the ensuing silence of the accused could not be put before the jury unless the Crown could establish a "real relevance" and a "proper basis" for the evidence. Cory J. concluded by stating:[553]

> As a result of the Crown's cross-examination, the jury could well have been left with the erroneous impression that Chambers was under a duty to disclose the Kuko story to a person in authority. The failure to disclose a defence of alibi in a timely manner may be considered in assessing the credibility of that defence but that is a unique situation. As a general rule there is no obligation resting upon an accused person to disclose either the defence which will be presented or the details of that defence before the Crown has completed its case. There was clearly no obligation resting upon the appellant to disclose either his defence of double intent or the Kuko story to the Crown or anyone in authority. The failure to correct such an impression by direction from the trial judge rendered the right to silence a snare of silence for the appellant.

As a matter of logic, failure to raise a defence until the "eleventh hour" is relevant in assessing its merit. Obviously the evidence of the accused's delay in putting forth a defence in *Chambers* was sought to be used for that purpose. Yet it seems implicit in the reasoning of Cory

---

552 See also *R. v. Symonds* (1983), 9 C.C.C. (3d) 225, 38 C.R. (3d) 51, 11 W.C.B. 163, 11 O.A.C. 103, at 227 (C.C.C.).
553 *Supra*, note 548 at 343 (C.C.C.).

J. that the questions should never have been asked.[554] Unlike the case where the failure of the accused to testify will be obvious to the jury, in this case they have no way of knowing that the alibi is not timely unless the Crown can adduce evidence to this effect. An exception has been made with respect to alibi evidence which, while unique in this respect, is difficult to justify on a principal basis.

It has been held that the failure of the accused to participate in a police line-up or provide a bodily sample by virtue of an unauthorized search and seizure should not be admissible.[555]

G. Privilege Against Disclosing Adulterous Conduct

1. General

Another privilege afforded to a witness, which was originally part of the common-law privilege against self-incrimination,[556] is the right in certain proceedings to decline to answer questions relating to his or her adultery. The common-law privilege is now preserved in many provincial statutes. Section 10 of the Ontario *Evidence Act*[557] is an example:

---

554 However, both Crown and defence counsel agreed that the questions and answers were not relevant to any issue and therefore Cory J. may have felt that he did not have to consider the evidence on this basis.

555 *Marcoux v. R.*, [1976] 1 S.C.R. 763, 24 C.C.C. (2d) 1, 29 C.R.N.S. 211, 60 D.L.R. (3d) 119, 4 N.R. 64.

556 At common law the privilege arose out of the fact that ecclesiastical courts were empowered to impose punishment for the offence of adultery: *Redfern v. Redfern*, [1891] P. 139. The common-law protection, however, has been abrogated and has fallen into disuse because of the recognition that ecclesiastical courts no longer have any jurisdiction over such matters: *Blunt v. Park Lane Hotel Ltd.*, [1942] 2 K.B. 253 (C.A.); *Minaker v. Minaker*, [1959] O.R. 545, 18 D.L.R. (2d) 695 (C.A.).

557 R.S.O. 1980, c. 145. British Columbia does not have such a statutory privilege. Newfoundland removed the statutory privilege in 1971: S.N. 1971, No. 48, s. 2 and New Brunswick in 1990, S.N.B. 1990, c. 17, s. 4. Other similarly worded provincial enactments are Evidence Acts: Alberta, R.S.A. 1980, c. A-21, s. 7; Manitoba, R.S.M. 1987, c. E150, s. 7; Northwest Territories, R.S.N.W.T. 1988, c. E-8, s. 5; Nova Scotia, R.S.N.S. 1989, c. 154, s. 46; Prince Edward Island, R.S.P.E.I. 1988, c. E-11, s. 8; Saskatchewan, R.S.S. 1978, c. S-16, s. 35 [am. 1988-89, c. 55, s. 28; 1990-91, c. F-6.1, s. 33; Yukon Territory, R.S.Y.T. 1986, c. 57, s. 5.

10. The parties to a proceeding instituted in consequence of adultery and the husbands and wives of such parties are competent to give evidence in such proceedings, but no witness in any such proceeding, whether a party to the suit or not, is liable to be asked or bound to answer any question tending to show that he or she is guilty of adultery, unless such witness has already given evidence in the same proceeding in disproof of his or her alleged adultery.

The protection applies both in court and on discovery.[558]

Although in Ontario the protection is limited to witnesses in proceedings instituted in consequence of adultery, no similar restriction exists in Alberta, Manitoba, the Northwest Territories or the Yukon.[559] In these regions, all witnesses in *any* action may claim the protection of the statute. In New Brunswick, Nova Scotia and Prince Edward Island, the protection applies to any party to a proceeding instituted in consequence of adultery and to the husband and wife of such party. In Saskatchewan the privilege can be claimed by any party in a matrimonial proceeding and expressly extends to examination for discovery.

2. Proceedings in Consequence of Adultery

In the past, this privilege was typically raised in proceedings for divorce on the ground of adultery. Now adultery has been removed as a specific ground for divorce and replaced with the concept of marriage breakdown.[560] The marriage breakdown may have been contributed to by the adulterous conduct of a party and it is possible that a court would consider such a proceeding to be one in consequence of adultery. However, this privilege has been subject to much criticism[561]

---

558 *Livingstone v. Livingstone*, [1945] O.W.N. 623, [1945] 4 D.L.R. 121 (Ont. C.A.); *Gentle v. Gentle* (1974), 3 O.R. (2d) 544, 15 R.F.L. 373, 46 D.L.R. (3d) 164 (H.C.J.).
559 *Supra*, note 557.
560 *Divorce Act*, S.C. 1986, c. 4 [now R.S.C. 1985, c. 3 (2nd Supp.)].
561 J.D. Payne, "The Privilege Against Self-Crimination" (1968), 2 Ottawa L. Rev. 461; L. Rosen, "The Privilege Against Self-Incrimination as to Adultery. Should it be Abolished?" (1960), 23 Mod. L. Rev. 275; Z. Cowen, "Adultery and the Privilege against Self-Crimination" (1949), 65 Law. Q. Rev. 373; K.G. Morden, "Case Comment" (1949), 27 Can. Bar Rev. 468; H.R. Ryan, "Case Comment" (1949), 27 Can. Bar Rev. 851; *16th Report of the English Law Reform*

and therefore, there may be a great deal of judicial reluctance to extend it to such proceedings.[562] A number of other factors may contribute to the practical demise of the privilege. Now that a divorce can be obtained on the ground of one year's separation, the cases where adulterous conduct forms the basis of an application for divorce based on marriage breakdown are much fewer than under the previous divorce legislation. Furthermore, as discussed earlier,[563] the common-law actions for criminal conversation and alienation of affections have been abolished in many provinces. This privilege has, therefore, already lost much of its significance.

In any event, what constituted "proceedings in consequence of adultery" was interpreted fairly narrowly in Ontario.[564] Filiation proceedings against a married man were held not to be based on adultery since it was irrelevant to the cause of action that the witness had committed adultery.[565] The privilege was denied where the issue of adultery was raised in an alimony proceeding,[566] in a case where it was relevant only to damages[567] and in a case where a decree *nisi* tied the receipt of maintenance payments to the chastity of the wife and where the ex-husband was alleging that she had not been chaste.[568] On the other hand, in custody proceedings where an allegation of adultery is made to show that a spouse is unfit to have custody, it has been held that these are proceedings in consequence of adultery.[569]

Committee on Privilege in Civil Proceedings, 1967 Cmnd. 3472, at 19. England abolished the privilege in 1968 in the *Civil Evidence Act, 1968*, c. 64, s. 16(5).

562   But see *King v. King* (1975), 20 N.S.R. (2d) 260, 25 R.F.L. 232 (T.D.).

563   See Chapter 10, II.A.2.

564   For a more detailed discussion of this issue see J. Sopinka and S.N. Lederman, *The Law of Evidence in Civil Cases* (Toronto: Butterworths, 1974), at 228-37.

565   *Re Hollum*, [1960] O.W.N. 281.

566   *Minaker v. Minaker*, [1959] O.R. 545, 18 D.L.R. (2d) 695 (C.A.). In *Rayner v. Rayner*, [1972] 2 O.R. 588, 26 D.L.R. (3d) 169, 7 R.F.L. 103, the Ontario Court of Appeal held that an allegation contained in a plaintiff's statement of claim in an action for alimony to the effect that the defendant cohabited with another woman in circumstances supporting actual and reasonable belief of adultery was insufficient to make the claim one "instituted in consequence of adultery".

567   *McCarthy v. Morrison-Lamothe Bakery Ltd.*, [1956] O.W.N. 690, 5 D.L.R. (2d) 645.

568   *Heal v. Heal* (1974), 3 O.R. (2d) 177, 45 D.L.R. (3d) 10, 14 R.F.L. 279 (C.A.).

569   *Bradburn v. Bradburn*, [1953] O.R. 882, [1953] O.W.N. 818 (C.A.).

The issue is more complicated where there are multiple causes of action, only one of which is founded on adultery. The authorities are somewhat conflicting, but tend towards protecting the witness from disclosure.[570]

3. Waiver of the Privilege

As a matter of practice, both the court and counsel should forewarn the witness of his or her right to refuse to be questioned on the issue of adultery.[571] However, it is not an error of law for the judge to fail to do so.[572]

As with other privileges, a witness may waive the protection afforded by the Act and elect to testify as to his or her adultery.[573] The privilege may also be waived by the witness leading evidence in disproof of his or her alleged adultery. A denial of the adultery in an affidavit in interim or collateral proceedings will not waive the privilege.[574] Nevertheless, the waiver of the privilege by producing evidence of non-adultery is not limited to trials, but would, in addition, "include any sworn evidence taken on commission or otherwise as long as it is receivable for the purpose of determining the issue."[575] Therefore, in theory a party could waive the privilege by giving evidence of disproof upon the examination for discovery. However,

---

570 See *White v. White*, [1951] O.W.N. 439; *Booth v. Booth*, [1949] O.R. 80, [1949] O.W.N. 50; *Bradburn v. Bradburn, ibid.*; *Lock v. Lock*, [1955] O.W.N. 372; *Lichtenberg v. Lichtenberg*, [1966] 1 O.R. 585 (Master); *Livingstone v. Livingstone, supra*, note 558; *Hunter v. Hunter*, [1973] 1 O.R. 162, 11 R.F.L. 94.

571 *Elliot v. Elliot*, [1933] O.R. 206, at 211, [1933] 2 D.L.R. 40; *Welstead v. Brown*, [1952] 1 S.C.R. 3, 102 C.C.C. 46, [1952] 1 D.L.R. 465; *Lang v. Lang*, [1951] O.W.N. 389 (Ont. H.C.J.).

572 *Alberta (A.G.) v. Shepherd* (1965), 53 W.W.R. 318, [1965] 4 C.C.C. 257 (Alta. C.A.); in *Dobbs v. Dobbs*, [1962] 1 W.L.R. 914, at 919 it was described as a practice only. But see *Enns v. Enns* (1967), 61 W.W.R. 462, at 466 (Man. Q.B.).

573 *Woodcock v. Woodcock*, [1941] 2 W.W.R. 111, [1941] 3 D.L.R. 207, 49 Man. R. 113 (C.A.); *Rosenberg v. Rosenberg* (1964), 50 W.W.R. 257, 49 D.L.R. (2d) 401, at 404; *Enns v. Enns, ibid.*

574 *A. v. A.*, [1962] P. 196; *Livingstone v. Livingstone, supra*, note 558; *Saunders v. Saunders*, [1947] O.W.N. 8; *Battersby v. Battersby*, [1948] 2 W.W.R. 623, at 627 (Man.); *Enns v. Enns, supra*, note 572; *Martin v. Martin* (1923), 24 O.W.N. 323 (H.C.J.); *Guiry v. Wheeler*, [1952] O.W.N. 657 (H.C.J.); *Rosenberg v. Rosenberg, ibid.*

575 *Livingstone v. Livingstone, supra*, note 558, at 126 (D.L.R.) *per* McRuer J.A.

since the examination for discovery is not receivable in evidence at the option of the party being discovered, the privilege has been held not to be waived by such a denial.[576]

---

576 *McIvor v. McIvor* (1953), 8 W.W.R. 92 (Man. Q.B.).

CHAPTER 15

PUBLIC INTEREST IMMUNITY

I INTRODUCTION

In many lawsuits, both civil and criminal, documents and information in the possession and control of the executive branch of government and various government agencies and employees are relevant to the issues in dispute. Claims for the disclosure of such documents and information can involve a conflict between public interests. The public interest in the administration of justice is promoted through full access of litigants to relevant information. The public also has an interest in protecting the country from the damage to national security and international relations that could be caused by the disclosure of state secrets.[1] Also, damage to the process of government decision making and functioning may be caused by disclosure of other government documents. In those areas where the public interest favours non-disclosure the government may assert an immunity from disclosure.

This government right, where it can be successfully asserted, is more appropriately labelled an "immunity" rather than a privilege.[2]

---

1   *Carey v. R.*, [1986] 2 S.C.R. 637, at 639, 30 C.C.C. (3d) 498, 35 D.L.R. (4th) 161, 58 O.R. (2d) 352 (Digest), 20 O.A.C. 81, 72 N.R. 81, 22 Admin. L.R. 236, 14 C.P.C. (2d) 10.
2   Lord Reid in *Rogers v. Secretary of State for the Home Department*, [1972] 2 All E.R. 1057, at 1060, [1972] 3 W.L.R. 279 (H.L.) took issue with the use of the phrase "Crown privilege" as follows: "I think that the expression is wrong and may be misleading. There is no question of any privilege in the ordinary sense of the word. The real question is whether the public interest requires that the letter shall not be produced and whether that public interest is so strong as to override

The assertion of an immunity claim may result in the non-disclosure of reports, memoranda and communications, just as in the case of a traditional privilege. However, unlike the private privileges, such as that relating to communications passing between solicitor and client, this public immunity belongs not to any private party, nor to any witness.[3] It is most often asserted by government, either during the discovery process, where the government is a party to the action, or at trial where the government has been served with a *subpoena duces tecum*.[4] It applies whether or not the government is a party to the litigation.

Even in the absence of the Crown's objection the judge should prohibit disclosure if he or she feels that disclosure will be harmful to the state.[5] Moreover, any party or witness may draw the court's attention to the nature of the evidence with a view to its exclusion,[6]

---

the ordinary right and interest of a litigant that he shall be able to lay before a court of justice all relevant evidence." Lords Pearson, Simon and Salmon, *ibid.*, [1972] 2 All E.R., at 1066 and 1070, were of the same view. Canadian courts, however are still content to use the word "privilege": see *Churchill Falls (Labrador) Corp. v. R.* (1972), 28 D.L.R. (3d) 493 (Fed. T.D.); *Blais v. Andras*, [1972] F.C. 958, 30 D.L.R. (3d) 287 (C.A.); *Huron Steel Fabricators (London) Ltd. v. M.N.R.; Fratschko v. M.N.R.*, [1972] F.C. 1007, 31 D.L.R. (3d) 110, [1972] C.T.C. 506, 72 D.T.C. 6426 (T.D.); affd [1973] F.C. 808 (*sub nom. Minister of National Revenue v. Huron Steel Fabricators (London) Ltd.*), 73 D.T.C. 5347, 41 D.L.R. (3d) 407, [1973] C.T.C. 422 (C.A.); *Smerchanski v. Lewis; Smerchanski v. Asta Securities Corp.* (1981), 58 C.C.C. (2d) 328, 31 O.R. (2d) 705, at 708, 120 D.L.R. (3d) 745, 21 C.P.C. 105 (C.A.); and see also *Evans v. Chief Constable of Surrey Constabulary*, [1989] 2 All E.R. 594 (Q.B.), [1988] Q.B.D. 588; *Air Canada v. Secretary of State for Trade (No. 2)*, [1983] 2 A.C. 394, at 436, [1983] 1 All E.R. 910, at 917 (H.L.). See the discussion in T.G. Cooper, *Crown Privilege* (Aurora: Canada Law Book, 1990), at 1-5.

3   *Carey v. R., supra*, note 1, [1986] 2 S.C.R., at 653.

4   *Duncan v. Cammel, Laird & Co.*, [1942] A.C. 624, at 638, [1942] 1 All E.R. 587 (H.L.); *United States v. Reynolds*, 345 U.S. 1 (1953).

5   *Carey v. R., supra*, note 1, [1986] 2 S.C.R., at 653; *R. v. Governor of Brixton Prison*, [1991] 1 W.L.R. 281 (Q.B.D.), at 290; C. Tapper and R. Cross, *Cross on Evidence*, 7th ed. (London: Butterworths, 1990), at 456; *Conway v. Rimmer*, [1968] A.C. 910, [1968] 1 All E.R. 874 (H.L.), at 887; *Rogers v. Secretary of State for the Home Department, supra*, note 2, [1972] 2 All E.R., at 1060; *Hennesy v. Wright* (1888), 21 Q.B.D. 509, at 521 (D.C.); *Alfred Crompton Amusement Machines Ltd. v. Customs and Excise Commissioners (No. 2)*, [1972] 2 All E.R. 353 (C.A.), at 380; affd [1973] 3 W.L.R. 268, [1973] 2 All E.R. 1169 (H.L.).

6   *Rogers v. Secretary of State, supra*, note 2, [1972] 2 All E.R., at 1066; *Smerchanski v. Lewis, supra*, note 2, 31 O.R. (2d), at 710; but see *Thornhill v.*

whether or not the Crown has raised an objection.[7] However, the court may not be under a duty to raise the objection if the government is a party and has clearly waived the privilege.[8] Generally, however, this immunity cannot be "waived" by the Crown in the same way as a traditional privilege may be waived.[9] Furthermore, secondary evidence of a document or communication covered by this immunity is inadmissible.[10]

The trend in the application of this immunity is to treat the government no differently than any other litigant or witness. The immunity should not be invoked unless clearly warranted by the circumstances.[11]

Dartmouth Broadcasting Ltd. (1981), 45 N.S.R. (2d) 111 (S.C.T.D.), at 130 and *R. v. Lines* (1986), 27 C.C.C. (3d) 377 (N.W.T.C.A.), where an accused argued that the disclosure of certain information would be contrary to the public interest. The court dismissed the objection to the evidence since the accused was not an interested member of the government within the meaning of s. 36.1 of the *Canada Evidence Act*, R.S.C. 1970, c. E-10 [now R.S.C. 1985, c. C-5].

7   *R. v. Snider*, [1954] S.C.R. 479, 109 C.C.C. 193, 54 D.T.C. 1129, [1954] C.T.C. 255.

8   *Leeds v. Alberta (Minister of the Environment)* (1990), 69 D.L.R. (4th) 681, at 695, 43 L.C.R. 145 (Alta. Q.B.).

9   *Rogers v. Secretary of State, supra*, note 2; *Burmah Oil Co. v. Bank of England*, [1979] 3 W.L.R. 722 (H.L.); *Air Canada v. Secretary of State for Trade, supra*, note 2; *Science Research Council v. Nassé, B.L. Cars Ltd. (Formerly Leyland Cars) v. Vyas*, [1979] 3 All E.R. 673, [1979] 3 W.L.R. 762 (H.L.). But see *Leeds v. Alberta (Minister of the Environment), ibid.*, where Miller A.C.J.Q.B. held that the Crown had waived the immunity by disclosing the documents in a proceeding in which it was a party (see at 694). See also *R. v. Meuckon* (1990), 57 C.C.C. (3d) 193, 78 C.R. (3d) 196 (B.C.C.A.), at 203 where the court noted that the Crown could withdraw the privilege claim.

10   *Cooke v. Maxwell* (1817), 2 Stark 183, at 186 (N.P.); *Air Canada v. Secretary of State for Trade (No. 2), supra*, note 2, [1983] 2 A.C., at 442, and [1983] 1 All E.R., at 920.

11   *Carey v. R., supra*, note 1; *Leeds v. Alberta, supra*, note 8, at 688; as Angers J. stated in *Dufresne Construction Co. v. R.*, [1935] Ex. C.R. 77 at 88: "The privilege of exclusion of documents as evidence at the request of the Crown must not be extended beyond the requirements of public safety or convenience." In the United States, the constitutional right of freedom of speech and the right of the people to know what their government is doing moved the Supreme Court of the United States in *New York Times Co. v. United States*, 403 U.S. 713 (1971), 91 S. Ct. 2140 (1971), to refuse to prevent the publication in American newspapers of military secrets which were stolen from the Department of Defense in the Pentagon and which related to the Vietnam War.

II   BASIS OF CROWN IMMUNITY

At common law the government possessed a prerogative right to refuse to produce documents. This right was invoked in one of two ways. If the Crown was a party to a proceeding, it was immune from discovery and therefore could not be forced to produce official documents.[12] If the proceeding was between private litigants and production of a relevant official document was sought, the Crown could refuse production on the ground that it would be contrary to public interest. Statutory reform now makes the Crown in any civil proceeding subject to discovery and inspection of documents and examination for discovery.[13] The legislation is applicable only in those cases where the Crown is a party and thus the Crown's common law rights in proceedings between private parties remain unchanged.[14] Crown ministers and officials are not immune from the power of the subpoena at trial.[15]

---

12   *Southam Inc. v. Theriault* (1988), 61 O.R. (2d) 758, 23 C.P.C. (2d) 133, at 138 (Ont. H.C.J.). See S.G. Linstead, "The Law of Crown Privilege in Canada and Elsewhere" (1968-1969), 3 Ottawa L. Rev. 79, at 86-89, and Williston and Rolls, *The Law of Civil Procedure* (Toronto: Butterworths, 1970), Vol. 2, at 774. For a history of the development of Crown immunity see T.G. Cooper, *Crown Privilege, supra*, note 2, at 8-16.
13   Alberta, *Proceedings Against the Crown Act (PAC)*, R.S.A. 1980, c. P-18, s. 11; British Columbia, *Crown Proceedings Act*, R.S.B.C. 1979, c. 86, s. 9; Manitoba, *PAC*, R.S.M. 1987, c. P140, s. 9(1); New Brunswick, *PAC*, R.S.N.B. 1973, c. P-18, s. 10; Newfoundland, *PAC, 1973*, S.N. 1973, no. 59, s. 11; Nova Scotia, *PAC*, R.S.N.S. 1989, c. 360, s. 11; Ontario, *PAC*, R.S.O. 1980, c. 393, s. 12; P.E.I., *Crown Proceedings Act*, R.S.P.E.I. 1988, c. C-32, s. 8; Saskatchewan, *PAC*, R.S.S. 1978, c. P-27, s. 13.
14   *Thornhill v. Dartmouth Broadcasting Ltd.* (1981), 45 N.S.R. (2d) 111, 86 A.P.R. 111 (S.C.T.D.), at 128-129; *Quebec (Attorney-General) v. Canada (Attorney-General)*, [1979] 1 S.C.R. 218, at 245; *Re Canadian Javelin Ltd.* (1980), 55 C.P.R. (2d) 72, [1981] 2 F.C. 521, 118 D.L.R. (3d) 143, 34 N.R. 460 (C.A.); affd [1982] 2 S.C.R. 686, 141 D.L.R. (3d) 395 (*sub nom. Smallwood v. Sparling*, 44 N.R. 571, 68 C.P.R. (2d) 145. But see *Marek v. Cieslak* (1974), 4 O.R. (2d) 348, 48 D.L.R. (3d) 39 (H.C.J.), where Goodman J. held that there was no Crown prerogative recognized at common law in cases where the Crown was not a party to the proceedings and therefore with the amendments to the rules of practice making third parties compellable to discovery the Crown could not rely on the prerogative. See also the *Federal Court Rules*, C.R.C. 1978, c. 663, r. 464(2) which does provide for discovery and inspection of Crown documents even if it is not a party.
15   *Re Canadian Javelin Ltd., ibid.*

The effect of the legislation where the government is a party is simply to make the government compellable to the process of discovery or before the court. It does not remove the common law immunity from disclosure on the basis of the public interest. For example, s. 11 of the Nova Scotia *Proceedings Against the Crown Act*[16] provides as follows:

> In proceedings against the Crown, the rules of the court in which the proceedings are taken as to discovery and inspection of documents, examination for discovery and interrogatories apply in the same manner as if the Crown were a corporation, except that the Crown may refuse to produce a document or to make answer to a question on discovery or interrogatories on the ground that the production thereof or the answer would be injurious to the public interest.

No definition of "public interest" is set out. As one author has stated in discussing a similar English statute:

> Thus, with the express preservation of the common law privilege, the position is not very different from what it was before — or, if there is any difference, it is merely procedural and is of dubious advantage to the subject. Formerly, in a suit against the Crown — say, a petition of right on a contract — the plaintiff knew that he could not get discovery and he had to rely on the common honesty of the Crown to put in evidence relevant documents, which it was always prepared to do once the Attorney-General's fiat had been obtained and provided that no issue of public interest was involved . . . If privilege is claimed for essential documents [today], he may find that his case collapses for lack of them, and all that the Crown Proceedings Act has conferred upon him is additional interlocutory costs.[17]

Under the *Canada Evidence Act*,[18] the common law concept of public interest immunity is also relevant. Section 37 provides, in part, as follows:

---

16 *Supra*, note 13.
17 C.K. Allen, *Law and Orders*, 3rd ed. (London: Sweet & Maxwell, 1965), at 331.
18 R.S.C. 1985, c. C-5.

(1) A minister of the Crown in right of Canada or other person interested may object to the disclosure of information before a court, person or body with jurisdiction to compel the production of information by certifying orally or in writing to the court, person or body that the information should not be disclosed on the grounds of a specified public interest.

(2) Subject to sections 38 and 39, where an objection to the disclosure of information is made under subsection (1) before a superior court, that court may examine or hear the information and order its disclosure, subject to such restrictions or conditions as it deems appropriate, if it concludes that, in the circumstances of the case, the public interest in disclosure outweighs in importance the specified public interest.[19]

Generally, therefore, the common law concept of Crown immunity is relevant in cases where the federal Crown is a party or where the federal Crown submits or is submitted to the discovery or trial process.[20] The common law position also applies to the provincial Crown, except in Quebec.[21]

III THE DETERMINATION OF IMMUNITY

A. *General*

An important issue in this area is whether the court or the government has the last word on the applicability of the public interest immunity. In most cases the objection to production will be raised by the government. In support of the objection, the Minister or some other high level government official will file an affidavit with the court that deposes to the government's opinion that the document is subject

---

19   The "public interest" was also left undefined by former s. 41 [rep. 1980-81-82-83, c. 111] of the *Federal Court Act*, R.S.C. 1970, c. 10 (2nd Supp.) [now R.S.C. 1985, c. F-7].

20   Subject to what will be said below with respect to confidences of the Queen's Privy Council, see this Chapter, III.B.

21   Article 308 of the *Code of Civil Procedure*, L.R.Q., c. C-25, governs in Quebec and is purportedly a codification of the common law; see *Bisaillon v. Keable*, [1983] 2 S.C.R. 60, 7 C.C.C. (3d) 385, at 418, 37 C.R. (3d) 289, 2 D.L.R. (4th) 193, 51 N.R. 81 *per* Beetz J.

to public interest immunity on some particular specified basis. The issue is whether the court must give that opinion conclusive weight or whether it can consider it as one factor in its own balancing of the interests that favour disclosure and those that favour non-disclosure.

B. *Statutory Provisions that Give Conclusive Weight to Government Opinion*

Section 39 of the *Canada Evidence Act* provides an absolute immunity from disclosure of certain Cabinet documents upon objection by a Minister of the Crown or the Clerk of the Privy Council. Section 39(1) provides as follows:

> 39.(1) Where a minister of the Crown or the Clerk of the Privy Council objects to the disclosure of information before a court, person or body with jurisdiction to compel the production of information by certifying in writing that the information constitutes a confidence of the Queen's Privy Council for Canada, disclosure of the information shall be refused without examination or hearing of the information by the court, person or body.[22]

A "confidence of the Queen's Privy Council" is defined in s. 39(2) to include information contained in various types of communications such as:

> (a) a memorandum the purpose of which is to present proposals or recommendations to Council;

> (b) a discussion paper the purpose of which is to present background explanations, analyses of problems or policy options to

---

22   In *Human Rights Commission v. Canada (Attorney-General)*, [1982] 1 S.C.R. 215, the Supreme Court of Canada held that a similar section (now repealed) in the *Federal Court Act* did not offend section 1(b) of the *Canadian Bill of Rights*, R.S.C. 1985, App. III, the right to equality before the law, and was not *ultra vires* the federal Parliament. In *Canada (Ministry of Industry, Trade & Commerce) v. Central Cartage Co. (No. 1)* (1990), 71 D.L.R. (4th) 253, [1990] 2 F.C. 641, 109 N.R. 357, 32 C.P.R. (3d) 308, 2 C.R.R. (2d) D-5; leave to appeal to S.C.C. dismissed January 17, 1991 (F.C.A.) it was held that s. 15 of the *Canadian Charter of Rights and Freedoms*, R.S.C. 1985, App. II, No. 44, was not infringed by s. 36.3 of the *Canada Evidence Act*, R.S.C. 1970, c. E-10 [now R.S.C. 1985, c. C-5, s. 39]. Nor did it infringe the right to a fair hearing in accordance with the principles of fundamental justice.

Council for consideration by Council in making decisions [unless the decisions to which the discussions relate have already been made public or if the decision has not been made public four years have passed from the date of the decision[23]];

(c) an agendum of Council or a record recording deliberations or decisions of Council;

(d) a record used for or reflecting communications or discussions between ministers of the Crown on matters relating to the making of government decisions or the formulation of government policy;

(e) a record the purpose of which is to brief Ministers of the Crown in relation to matters that are brought before, or are proposed to be brought before, Council or that are the subject of communications or discussions referred to in paragraph (d); and

(f) draft legislation.

If the confidences are greater than twenty years old the absolute immunity does not apply.[24] "Council" is defined to mean the Queen's Privy Council for Canada, committees of that Council, Cabinet and committees of Cabinet.[25]

It should be noted that it is any information contained in these documents that is subject to the immunity and not simply information that would damage national security or international diplomatic relations if disclosed. It is an immunity granted to a class of documents. The policy behind the immunity is to promote candour in such communications and protect the government against harassment in its decision and policy making process.[26]

At issue in *Canada (Ministry of Industry, Trade & Commerce) v. Central Cartage Co. (No. 1)*[27] was the degree of disclosure required by

---

23 Section 39(4)(b) of the *Canada Evidence Act, supra,* note 18.
24 It is also doubtful whether any common law immunity would apply to such dated communications.
25 Section 39(3) of the *Canada Evidence Act, supra,* note 18.
26 Although one might question whether the government should be protected from harassment, and particularly, whether the government should be the body that can decide when it should be protected from harassment.
27 *Supra,* note 22.

the Clerk of the Privy Council in attempting to invoke the protection of this provision. The trial judge had struck out the certificate of the Clerk on the basis that it did no more than track the language of the section. It should have stated the date of the document, from whom and to whom it was sent and its subject matter. Iacobucci J. in the Federal Court of Appeal disagreed holding that the section required only that the Clerk track the statutory language. Although this might be rather formalistic, the courts could take some comfort from the fact that the Clerk directed his mind to the criteria and limitations specified.[28]

C. Judge's Determination of Privilege

In all cases not governed by s. 39 of the *Canada Evidence Act*, it is for the court to determine whether or not immunity should be granted for a particular document or communication.[29] The court may inspect the documents in question, although there may be circumstances in which the decision can be made without such an inspection. Section 37(2) of the *Canada Evidence Act* specifically provides for court inspection of documents for which a claim of public interest immunity has been made.[30] Where the government's objection to disclosure is on

---

28 See also *Landreville v. R.*, [1977] 1 F.C. 419, at 422-423, 70 D.L.R. (3d) 122 (T.D.); *Human Rights Commission v. Canada (Attorney-General)*, *supra*, note 22; *Smith, Kline & French Laboratories Ltd. v. Canada (Attorney-General)*, [1983] 1 F.C. 917, 38 C.P.C. 182, 76 C.P.R. (2d) 192 (T.D.); *I.L.W.U. v. Canada*, [1989] 1 F.C. 444 (T.D.).

29 *Carey v. R.*, [1986] 2 S.C.R. 637, at 653, 30 C.C.C. (3d) 498, 35 D.L.R. (4th) 161; *Re Canadian Javelin Ltd.*, *supra*, note 14.

30 Subsections 37(1) and (2) provide as follows:

37. (1) A minister of the Crown in right of Canada or other person interested may object to the disclosure of information before a court, person or body with jurisdiction to compel the production of information by certifying orally or in writing to the court, person or body that the information should not be disclosed on the grounds of a specified public interest.

(2) Subject to sections 38 and 39, where an objection to the disclosure of information is made under subsection (1) before a superior court, that court may examine or hear the information and order its disclosure, subject to such restrictions or conditions as it deems appropriate, if it concludes that, in the circumstances of the case, the public interest in disclosure outweighs in importance the specified public interest.

Section 37(3) deals with the body before whom the application is to be heard if

grounds that the disclosure would be injurious to international relations or national defence or security, the objection may be determined on application only by the Chief Justice of the Federal Court or his or her designate.[31] Such applications are to be heard *in camera*.[32]

In the usual case a Minister of the government or a senior public official will certify, in affidavit form, his or her opinion that the documents should be immune from disclosure. The opinion of the Minister or official must be given due consideration by the court, but its weight will vary with the nature of the public interest sought to be protected.[33] Generally, where the matter involves issues of national security or international relations the court will give great weight to the affidavit of the minister or government official. In such circumstances the court may choose not to inspect the documents in question. Section 37(2) of the *Canada Evidence Act* permits inspection, but does not mandate it.[34]

The common law position is the same. In considering this issue La Forest J., in *Carey v. R.*,[35] noted that the decision of the House of Lords in *Duncan v. Cammell, Laird & Co.*,[36] holding that the court was not bound to look behind the Minister's opinion, was rightly decided in the circumstances. In *Duncan* actions in negligence were commenced by the estates of deceased seamen against the manufacturer of a British submarine which had been lost at sea. The defendants refused to produce a number of documents relating to the structure of the submarine on the ground of Crown immunity. The First Lord of the "Admiralty" had sworn an affidavit in which he stated that upon a personal consideration of the documents in question, he formulated the opinion that disclosure of the documents would be injurious to the public interest. The House of Lords accepted that statement and held that since these documents affected a matter of national security, especially at a time of war, the privilege should attach. Although the

---

the objection is not originally made in a superior court. Section 39(4), (5), (6) and (7) deal with various procedural and appeal rights for such applications.

31   *Canada Evidence Act*, R.S.C. 1985, c. C-5, s. 38(1).
32   *Ibid.*, s. 38(5).
33   *Carey v. R.*, *supra*, note 29; and subject to s. 39 of the *Canada Evidence Act* discussed above.
34   *Goguen v. Gibson* (1984), 10 C.C.C. (3d) 492, [1983] 2 F.C. 463, 7 D.L.R. (4th) 144, 50 N.R. 286, 3 Admin. L.R. 225, 40 C.P.C. 295 (C.A.).
35   *Supra*, note 29.
36   [1942] A.C. 624, [1942] 1 All E.R. 587 (H.L.).

court gave lip service to the principle that in the final result it is for the judge to determine whether the privilege is available,[37] it went on to add that if the Minister swears that the disclosure of the documents would be contrary to the public interest, the court will, without question, abide by that ministerial decision and will not allow production.[38]

As Dean Wright has pointed out:

> That judgment seems to amount to an abdication by the courts of their proper function of determining what is admissible or inadmissible evidence in leaving to the Executive an unlimited power of refusing to produce evidence on its mere say-so concerning public interest.[39]

The justification for the ruling is that the Minister is in the best position to know if the disclosure of the documents would be deleterious to the public interest. In *Carey*, La Forest J. commented:

> The case was undoubtedly correctly decided. A properly framed affidavit by a Minister of the Crown objecting to giving information about the structure of equipment intended for the defence of the country must surely be treated with the utmost deference, especially in wartime. Lord Blanesburgh in *Robinson's* case had noted that the documents should not be inspected where this could have the effect of itself defeating the reasons for which a privilege was claimed.[40]

---

37   *Ibid.*, [1942] A.C., at 642.
38   *Ibid.*, at 633. To the same effect, see *Bradley v. McIntosh* (1884), 5 O.R. 227 (C.A.); *Murray v. Murray*, [1947] 3 D.L.R. 236 (B.C.S.C.); *Minister of National Revenue v. Die-Plast Co.* (1952), 32 C.B.R. 241, [1952] 2 D.L.R. 808, [1952] Que. Q.B. 342, [1952] C.T.C. 175, 52 D.T.C. 1082 (C.A.); *Weber v. Pawlik* (1952), 5 W.W.R. 49, [1952] 2 D.L.R. 750, [1952] C.T.C. 32, 52 D.T.C. 1059 (B.C.C.A.); *Clemens v. Crown Trust Co.*, [1952] O.W.N. 434, [1952] 3 D.L.R. 508, 52 D.T.C. 1128 (H.C.J.); *R. v. Reese*, [1955] Ex. C.R. 187, [1955] 3 D.L.R. 691; *Re Lew Fun Chaue* (1955), 112 C.C.C. 264, [1955] O.W.N. 821, [1955] 5 D.L.R. 513 (Master); *Miles v. Miles*, [1960] O.W.N. 23, 24 D.L.R. (2d) 228, [1960] C.T.C. 37, 60 D.T.C. 1035 (H.C.J.).
39   C.A. Wright, "Case and Comment" (1942), 20 Can. Bar Rev. 805, at 805-806.
40   *Carey, supra*, note 29, [1986] 2 S.C.R., at 650-51.

Canadian courts have generally disagreed with the view taken in *Duncan* regarding the respective roles of the courts and the government in determining whether the ministerial objection should prevail. In *Carey v. R.*,[41] La Forest J. also disagreed with the absolute nature of the statement in *Duncan*. In *Gagnon v. Quebec Securities Commission*,[42] the Supreme Court of Canada considered the question of whether the court had the right to go behind a ministerial claim of Crown privilege. Production of a letter, alleged to have been written to the Quebec Securities Commission, was sought from the Secretary of the Commission during the course of a bankruptcy proceeding. The Secretary refused to disclose whether or not the Securities Commission possessed such a letter, claiming that Crown privilege was embodied in art. 332 of the Quebec *Code of Civil Procedure*.[43] In support of that claim the Secretary produced a letter from the Attorney-General of Quebec which stated that it was in the public interest that there be no disclosure of facts and documents assembled in the course of inquiries by the Securities Commission. The Supreme Court of Canada held that the Attorney-General's certificate was not conclusive on the matter, and that it was open to the court to examine the circumstances to decide if the public interest would be threatened by production. The court held that the certificate in question was not related to the particular facts to which the examination of the Secretary of the Securities Commission was directed, but merely constituted a blanket claim capable of serving in all cases regardless of the facts.

This ruling was consistent with the Supreme Court of Canada's earlier decision in a criminal case, *R. v. Snider*,[44] in which the Minister of National Revenue objected by way of affidavit to the production of the income tax returns of the accused and the giving of oral evidence on the ground that such production would be injurious to the public interest. The court held that the Minister's affidavit was not conclusive on the issue.[45] The court had the discretion to determine whether the Minister's view would prevail or not, and the court was not prepared

---

41   [1986] 2 S.C.R. 637, 30 C.C.C. (3d) 498, 35 D.L.R. (4th) 161.
42   [1965] S.C.R. 73, 50 D.L.R. (2d) 329.
43   L.R.Q., c. C-25, s. 332 [rep. 1976, c. 9, s. 56].
44   [1954] S.C.R. 479, 109 C.C.C. 193, 54 D.T.C. 1129, [1954] C.T.C. 255.
45   Rand, Kellock, Locke, and Cartwright JJ., *ibid.*, however, indicated that as between criminal and civil proceedings, there may be some distinction in the practice to be followed as to whether a Ministerial affidavit is to be treated as being conclusive of the issue.

to substitute the Minister's opinion for its own. The court would refuse the privilege unless it was shown clearly that revelation of the facts or documents might prejudice the public interest. Although the *Income Tax Act*[46] forbids the disclosure of information to persons not legally entitled thereto, that prohibition is directed only against voluntary disclosure and is irrelevant to judicial proceedings in which production is sought. The interest of an individual in keeping secret his tax returns is far outweighed by the necessity for a fair trial in criminal proceedings, and, accordingly, no Crown privilege attaches.[47] Moreover, the mere possession of the documents by the agency of the Crown is not sufficient to warrant any claim of state or Crown privilege. As Rand J. suggested:

> Neither the prerogative nor any constitutional or political function is involved. To suggest that either in the case of protecting or attacking the private interest of the taxpayer the custody of tax returns rendered to the department can be refused production on the ground of the nature of the possession is to attract some vague magic sensed or associated with the prerogative to the routine of administrative government. All governmental and administrative activity may be said to be carried out by the Executive, but it is not in these levels of administration, which might extend to every clerk, say, of a government railway, that any degree or shade of possession in the course of executive action is, by a reference to the Crown, to be placed beyond the reach of the courts.[48]

Even if it could be said that the decision in the *Snider* case is referable to criminal proceedings,[49] at least one judge of the British

---

46 S.C. 1970-71-72, c. 63.

47 See also *Re Lew Fun Chaue, supra,* note 38.

48 *R. v. Snider, supra,* note 44, [1954] S.C.R., at 484-85; see also *McDougall v. Dominion Iron & Steel Co.* (1902), 40 N.S.R. 333 (C.A.). On the other hand, the Crown need not have possession in order to claim privilege. The privilege may attach to a document whosoever has possession of it and from wherever it has been unearthed; see *R. v. Lewes JJ.,* [1971] 2 All E.R. 1126, [1971] 2 W.L.R. 1466 (D.C.), at 1471; affd [1972] 3 W.L.R. 279, [1972] 2 All E.R. 1057 (H.L.); *Conway v. Rimmer,* [1968] 1 All E.R. 874, at 887, [1968] A.C. 910 (H.L.).

49 The trial judge in *Miles v. Miles,* [1960] O.W.N. 23 (H.C.J.), a civil action, distinguished *R. v. Snider, supra,* note 44, on this basis and accepted the principle

Columbia Court of Appeal subsequently confirmed, in *Gronlund v. Hansen*,[50] that a Minister's affidavit in support of a claim for privilege is not to be treated as being conclusive in civil cases.

There is no discernible reason why a claim for public interest immunity should be treated any differently in a criminal case than in a civil case.[51] The application of the public immunity doctrine in criminal proceedings, however, will involve a different balancing exercise to that in a civil proceeding in that in the former there exists the important public interest that the administration of justice should not be frustrated by the withholding of documents that might assist an accused to establish his or her innocence.[52]

The English courts also eventually moved away from the strict view of *Duncan*. In the face of mounting criticism of the *Duncan* position[53] the House of Lords recanted. In *Conway v. Rimmer*,[54] it refused to adhere to the principle that a statement by a Minister of the Crown should be accepted by the court as conclusively foreclosing any right to production. Lord Reid indicated that the *Duncan* decision was cast too broadly. At stake in the *Duncan* case was clearly the national security of the country which was embroiled at the time in a world war.[55] The same considerations did not apply in circumstances where injury to the national interest was not readily apparent.[56] The *Conway* case was an action for malicious prosecution against the superintendent of a police force by a probationary police constable who pre-

---

of conclusiveness of the Minister's affidavit as enunciated in *Duncan v. Cammell, Laird & Co.*, *supra*, note 36, and thus accorded Crown privilege to certain income tax returns, the production of which had been objected to by the Minister of National Revenue. The same result was reached in a bankruptcy proceeding in Quebec in *Re Mercier*, [1964] B.R. 349 (C.A.).

50   (1968), 64 W.W.R. 74, 68 D.L.R. (2d) 223 (B.C.C.A.) per Robertson J.A.

51   *R. v. Governor of Brixton Prison*, [1991] 1 W.L.R. 281 (Q.B.D.), at 290.

52   *Ibid.*, at 289.

53   *Merricks v. Nott-Bower*, [1965] 1 Q.B. 57, [1964] 1 All E.R. 717 (C.A.); *Re Grosvenor Hotel, London (No. 2)*, [1965] Ch. 1210 (C.A.); *Wednesbury Corp. v. Ministry of Housing*, [1965] 1 W.L.R. 261, [1965] 1 All E.R. 186 (C.A.); *Ellis v. Home Office*, [1953] 2 Q.B. 135, [1953] 2 All E.R. 149 (C.A.).

54   [1968] 1 All E.R. 874, [1968] A.C. 910 (H.L.). See D.H. Clark, "The Last Word on the Last Word" (1969), 32 M.L.R. 142.

55   See the remarks of Karminski L.J. in *Alfred Crompton Amusement Machines v. Customs and Excise Commissioners (No. 2)*, [1972] 2 All E.R. 353 (C.A.), at 383; affd [1973] 3 W.L.R. 268, [1973] 2 All E.R. 1169 (H.L.).

56   *Conway v. Rimmer*, *supra*, note 52, [1968] 1 All E.R., at 879-880.

viously had been acquitted on a charge of theft of another constable's flashlight. The Home Secretary, invoking Crown privilege, refused to produce, on discovery, routine internal police reports on the probationary constable. The House of Lords did not accept this claim of privilege as being conclusive. Although the court was prepared to concede that there exist certain classes of documents which should never be disclosed whatever their content may be, the same could not be said with respect to routine reports or memoranda. The latter may attract special reasons for the withholding of its disclosure if it can be demonstrated that secrecy is necessary for the proper functioning of the public service. But that is a matter within the discretion of the judge who will have to consider whether production will be harmful to the public interest. In rejecting the conclusiveness of a Minister's opinion, Lord Reid put forth the following rule:

> I would therefore propose that the House ought now to decide that courts have and are entitled to exercise a power and duty to hold a balance between the public interest, as expressed by a minister, to withhold certain documents or other evidence, and the public interest in ensuring the proper administration of justice. That does not mean that a court would reject a Minister's view: full weight must be given to it in every case, and if the Minister's reasons are of a character which judicial experience is not competent to weigh then the Minister's view must prevail; but experience has shown that reasons given for withholding whole classes of documents are often not of that character.[57]

Ultimately, it is for the judge to decide what weight to give the Minister's statement. In some cases the court could come to a decision on the basis of a ministerial statement alone. In cases of doubt, the court could inspect the documents.[58]

In *Goguen v. Gibson*[59] the Federal Court of Appeal considered the

---

57   *Ibid.*, at 888. See also *Moosomin (School Board) v. Gordon*, [1972] 3 W.W.R. 380, at 386, 24 D.L.R. (3d) 505 (Sask. Q.B.); revd on another point [1972] 5 W.W.R. 375, 26 D.L.R. (3d) 510 (*sub nom. Re Moosomin School Board and Gordon* (Sask. C.A.).
58   *Carey v. R.*, [1986] 2 S.C.R. 637, 30 C.C.C. (3d) 498, 35 D.L.R. (4th) 161, 58 O.R. (2d) 352 (Digest), 20 O.A.C. 81, 72 N.R. 81, 22 Admin. L.R. 236, 14 C.P.C. (2d) 10.
59   (1984), 10 C.C.C. (3d) 492, [1983] 2 F.C. 463, 7 D.L.R. (4th) 144, 50 N.R.

circumstances where inspection might not be necessary. LeDain and Ryan JJ. were of the view that inspection would be unproductive. The government's affidavit materials were quite extensive and clearly set out the claim for immunity based on national security and international relations as that claim related to the particular documents of which disclosure was sought. Marceau J. expressed his views on when inspection would be appropriate as follows:

> That, in the case of a request for disclosure of information in respect of which an objection has been raised under ss. 36.1 and 36.2 [now s. 39] of the Act, the Court must proceed by way of a potential two-stage determination of the application is to me quite clear. Authority to inspect the documents is vested in the Court, but no duty is imposed on it to do so, and it seems to me that an authority of that kind would be abused if it were exercised unreservedly, uselessly and for any other reason than because it is required to arrive at a conclusion. This observation, to me, not only confirms the inevitability of the two-stage approach but, at the same time, indicates the nature of the so-called test that is implied in it. The Court will proceed to the second stage and examine the documents if, and only if, it is persuaded that it must do so to arrive at a conclusion or, put another way, if, and only if, on the sole basis of the material before it, it cannot say whether or not it will grant or refuse the application. Now, many reasons may be thought of that may lead the Court to reach a conclusion on the sole basis of the material before it. An easy possibility is a lack of seriousness in the contention that, in the circumstances, some public interest requires immunity; another is the frivolity of the request for disclosure, because the information sought would likely have no bearing on the litigation in which the applicant is involved; still another is the unreasonableness of the application, it being clearly of the nature of a fishing expedition. But the reason most likely to come to the fore is certainly the acquired certitude in the mind of the Judge that even if the information sought is of the nature or to the effect expected by the applicant, there is no possibility that the importance of the public interest in keeping the information secret be outweighed by the importance of the public interest in disclosing it. To me,

---

286, 3 Admin. L.R. 225, 40 C.P.C. 295 (C.A.).

all that is common sense, and I do not read the Chief Justice's comments in support of the approach he was adopting as meaning anything beyond that.[60]

D. *Application to Oral Evidence*

In *Re Canadian Javelin Ltd.*,[61] the Supreme Court of Canada confirmed that the principles that apply to the production of documents apply equally to the giving of oral testimony.[62]

E. *The Government's Affidavit*

Since the court may decide whether to grant immunity on the basis of the government's affidavit alone, it is in the government's interest to make that affidavit as complete as possible without disclosing the sensitive information. In *Carey v. R.*,[63] La Forest J. remarked that the Minister should be as helpful as possible in identifying the interest sought to be protected and should go as far as possible without disclosing what is sought to be protected.[64] If the affidavit is insufficient, the court may decline the claim of immunity or inspect the documents in issue.[65]

In *Gold v. Canada*,[66] the trial judge did not inspect the documents for which the Crown claimed immunity from disclosure. The Court of Appeal upheld the trial judge's decision but disagreed that the information sought had to be absolutely essential to the plaintiff's case in order for inspection to be warranted. The factors that were to be taken into account in determining whether to inspect were the probable relevance of the information, its admissibility and the availability of some alternative proof.

---

60   *Ibid.*, 40 C.P.C., at 313-14.
61   [1982] 2 S.C.R. 686, 141 D.L.R. (3d) 395 (*sub nom. Smallwood v. Sparling*), 68 C.P.R. (2d) 145.
62   See also *Gain v. Gain*, [1962] 1 All E.R. 63, [1961] 1 W.L.R. 1469 (*sub nom. Gane v. Gane*) (P.D. & A.) and *R. v. Meuckon* (1990), 57 C.C.C. (3d) 193, 78 C.R. (3d) 196 (B.C.C.A.).
63   *Supra*, note 58, [1986] 2 S.C.R., at 656.
64   For examples of how this should be done see *Burmah Oil Co. v. Bank of England*, [1979] 3 All E.R. 700, [1979] 3 W.L.R. 722 (H.L.) and *Goguen v. Gibson*, *supra*, note 59.
65   *Gloucester Properties Ltd. v. R.* (1981), 129 D.L.R. (3d) 275, [1982] 1 W.W.R. 449, 32 B.C.L.R. 61, 24 C.P.C. 82 (C.A.).
66   [1986] 2 F.C. 129, 25 D.L.R. (4th) 285, 64 N.R. 260 (C.A.).

IV CRITERIA FOR GRANT OF IMMUNITY

A. *General*

Whether the balance falls in favour of disclosure or immunity depends on the circumstances of the particular case. The judge must weigh the competing public interests[67] by considering such factors as: (a) the probative value of the evidence in the particular case and how necessary it will be for a proper determination of the issues,[68] (b) the subject matter of the litigation,[69] (c) the effect of non-disclosure on the public perception of the administration of justice, (d) whether the claim or defence involves an allegation of government wrongdoing (in which case the claim for immunity may be motivated by self-interest and not a genuine concern for the secrecy of the information),[70] (e) the length of time that has passed since the communication was made,[71] (f) the level of government from which the communication emanated, and (g) the sensitivity of the contents of the communication (including whether and the extent to which there has been prior publication of the information).[72] In the criminal context the accused's right to a fair hearing and to make full answer and defence can require the disclosure of the information.[73]

Recently, the Supreme Court of Canada reviewed the policy considerations concerning disclosure in criminal cases and concluded that there was a duty on the Crown to disclose all relevant information

---

67 For a review of the various factors see *Leeds v. Alberta (Minister of the Environment)* (1990), 69 D.L.R. (4th) 681, 43 L.C.R. 145 (Alta. Q.B.).

68 *R. v. Meuckon* (1990), 57 C.C.C. (3d) 193, 78 C.R. (3d), at 203.

69 *Gold v. Canada, supra,* note 66. For example, in *Mickle v. R.* (1987), 19 B.C.L.R. (2d) 266 (S.C.), the court was clearly influenced by the fact that the party wanting disclosure was applying for a firearms permit and was not the subject of a criminal prosecution. Disclosure will be warranted more often in criminal than in civil cases: See C. Tapper and R. Cross, *Cross on Evidence,* 7th ed. (London: Butterworths, 1990), at 473; T.G. Cooper, *Crown Privilege* (Aurora: Canada Law Book, 1990), at 76 and following.

70 *Carey v. R., supra,* note 58.

71 *Carey v. R., supra,* note 58; *Canada Evidence Act,* R.S.C. 1985, c. C-5, s. 38.

72 *Carey v. R., supra,* note 56, [1986] 2 S.C.R., at 673-674; *R. v. Governor of Brixton Prison,* [1991] 1 W.L.R. 281 (Q.B.D.), at 290-91.

73 *R. v. Meuckon, supra,* note 68; *Tatham v. Canada (National Parole Board)* (1990), 77 C.R. (3d) 209 (B.C.S.C.); *R. v. Stinchcombe,* unreported, November 7, 1991 (S.C.C.).

to an accused.[74] The Court recognized the ". . . overriding concern that failure to disclose impedes the ability of the accused to make full answer and defence".[75] This common law right to full disclosure is now guaranteed by s. 7 of the *Charter* as a principle of fundamental justice. A decision by the Crown not to disclose all relevant evidence to an accused is reviewable by the courts and the Crown must bring itself within any recognized exception, such as the identity of an informer.

B. *Contents Claims*

Traditionally, government claims for immunity have fallen into two broad categories, which can be conveniently described as contents claims and class claims. In terms of the evidentiary principles there is no distinction between the two. The same balancing exercise is undertaken in each case. In practice, it is more likely that a contents claim for immunity will be successful than will a class claim, for it is with the former type of documents or information that more judicial deference will be accorded the executive's claim for immunity.

Contents claims are based on the substance or the actual content of the document or communication. A document may contain information that could compromise national security[76] or detrimentally affect international or intergovernmental relations,[77] if publicly disclosed. In these types of cases the court will generally give substantial weight to the opinion of the Minister or official.[78]

An example of significant weight being given to the Minister's opinion is the case of *Goguen v. Gibson*.[79] The appellants sought disclosure from the Deputy Solicitor-General to assist in their defence on charges of theft and breaking and entering to commit theft of

---

74   *Ibid.*, *R. v. Stinchcombe.*
75   *Ibid.*, at 10.
76   As in *Duncan v. Cammell, Laird & Son Ltd.*, [1942] A.C. 624, [1942] 1 All E.R. 587 (H.L.), and *Goguen v. Gibson, supra,* note 59; *Asiatic Petroleum Co. v. Anglo-Persian Oil Co.*, [1916] 1 K.B. 822, [1916-17] All E.R. 637 (C.A.); *R. v. Governor of Brixton Prison; Ex parte Soblen v. Secretary of State, Ex Parte Lees*, [1941] 1 K.B. 72 (C.A.); *Beatson v. Skene* (1860), 5 H. & N. 838; *Home v. Bentinck* (1820), 2 Brod. & Bing. 130 (Ex. Ch.); and see section 39 of the *Canada Evidence Act.*
77   *Goguen v. Gibson, supra,* note 59.
78   See also *Carey v. R., supra,* note 58 at 653 (S.C.R.).
79   *Supra,* note 59.

information contained in documents and files of the security service of the R.C.M.P. The appellants' defence was that they had been engaged on R.C.M.P. business in the taking of the tapes alleged to have been stolen. The Deputy Solicitor-General's filed affidavit indicated that disclosure:[80]

> . . . would identify or tend to identify (a) human sources and technical sources of the Security Service; (b) targets of the Security Service; (c) methods of operation and the operational and administrative policies of the Security Service, including the specific methodology and techniques used in the operations of the Security Service and in the collection, assessment and reporting of security intelligence; and (d) relationships that the Security Service maintains with foreign security and intelligence agencies and information obtained from said foreign agencies.

A secret affidavit explained in more detail how national security and international relations could be affected by the particular documents. The trial court refused to inspect the documents on the basis that it could make a decision that the public interest in immunity outweighed the public interest in disclosure without such an inspection. The appeal court agreed with this approach.

C. Class Claims

The class claim for immunity does not depend on the actual content of the communication, but on the fact that it is a document or communication of a particular type, such as a report of Cabinet or other high level official or a report of a police informer. Two rationales have been expressed to support the class claim, those being the candour argument and the interference or harassment argument.

1. The Candour Argument

Government often argues that disclosure of a certain class of communications would have a chilling effect on the candour and frankness of discussion and debate between members of the government. Particularly at high government levels, this could negatively affect government policy and decision making.[81] Furthermore, disclo-

---

80   *Goguen v. Gibson, supra,* note 59, at 467 (F.C.).
81   See *South-West Oxford (Corp. of the Twp.) v. Ontario (Attorney-General)*

sure of names of informants or of information supplied during police or other government investigations could stifle communications from third persons and thereby have a negative effect on the administration of justice or the workings of government agencies. The candour argument, appears acceptable enough at first glance, but upon further consideration one quickly realizes that it is applicable to most government reports.

In *Carey v. R.*,[82] the government attempted to justify a class claim on the basis of the candour argument. The plaintiff alleged that the Ontario government had breached an agreement to provide financial support for the Minaki Lodge, a tourist retreat in Northern Ontario. The documents which were sought to be disclosed emanated from or were records of discussions of the Cabinet secretary and others. In assessing the candour argument La Forest J. stated:[83]

> I am prepared to attach some weight to the candour argument but it is very easy to exaggerate its importance. Basically, we all know that some business is better conducted in private, but generally I doubt if the candidness of confidential communications would be measurably affected by the off-chance that some communication might be required to be produced for the purposes of litigation. Certainly the notion has received heavy battering in the courts.

The candour argument has also been put forward to support a claim for immunity at lower government levels. *Conway v. Rimmer*[84] involved routine police investigation reports, such as probation reports. In *Carey* La Forest J. reviewed the views of members of the House of Lords and synthesized them as follows:[85]

> The House of Lords had occasion to deal with the candour argument in *Conway v. Rimmer*, albeit at a lower level of govern-

---

(1985), 49 C.P.C. 233 (Ont. S.C.); leave to appeal granted, 1 W.D.C.P. 517 (Ont. S.C.).

82   [1986] 2 S.C.R. 637, at 662, 30 C.C.C. (3d) 498, 35 D.L.R. (4th) 161, 58 O.R. (2d) 352 (Digest), 20 O.A.C. 81, 72 N.R. 81, 22 Admin. L.R. 236, 14 C.P.C. (2d) 10.

83   *Ibid.*, [1986] 2 S.C.R., at 657; see also the views of Gibbs J. in *Sankey v. Whitlam* (1978), 21 A.L.R. 505 (H.C.).

84   [1968] 1 All E.R. 874, [1968] A.C. 910.

85   *Carey v. R.*, *supra*, note 82, [1986] 2 S.C.R., at 657.

ment. Lord Reid dismissed it so far as it concerned routine documents like the probation and other reports in question in that case. He failed to see how such an argument could apply to such communications within a government department when similar communications within public corporations would not be so protected. Lord Morris of Borth-Y-Gest found the proposition that candour would be affected by the knowledge that by some remote chance a document might be the subject of possible enforced production one of "doubtful validity" (p. 957). To Lord Hodson, it seemed strange that civil servants alone are supposed to be unable to be candid without the protection denied other people (p. 976). Lord Pearce indicated that there were many circumstances where the possibility of disclosure would make the writer more candid (p. 987). And Lord Upjohn found it difficult to justify non-disclosure of class documents simply on the basis of the candour argument when equally important matters of confidence in relation to security and personnel matters in other walks of life were not similarly protected (p. 995).

All in all, the candour argument is not a particularly compelling one.

2. The Interference or Harassment Argument

In *Carey*, La Forest J. considered that another rationale for class claims was more compelling. His Lordship accepted that disclosure of Cabinet correspondence, before it became of historical interest only, could result in harassment of Cabinet and thereby make government unmanageable. Lord Reid in *Conway v. Rimmer* expressed the same rationale:[86]

I do not doubt that there are certain classes of documents which ought not to be disclosed whatever their contents may be. Virtually everyone agrees that Cabinet minutes and the like ought not to be disclosed until such times as they are only of historical interest. But I do not think that many people would give as the reason that premature disclosure would prevent candour in the Cabinet. To my mind the most important reason is that such disclosure would create or fan ill-informed or

---

86   *Supra*, note 84, [1968] A.C., at 952; cited with approval in *Carey v. R.*, *ibid.*, at 658-659.

captious public or political criticism. The business of government is difficult enough as it is, and no government could contemplate with equanimity the inner workings of the government machine being exposed to the gaze of those ready to criticise without adequate knowledge of the background and perhaps with some axe to grind. And that must, in my view, also apply to all documents concerned with policy making within departments including, it may be, minutes and the like by quite junior officials and correspondence with outside bodies. Further it may be that deliberations about a particular case requires protection as much as deliberations about policy. I do not think that it is possible to limit such documents by any definition.

La Forest J. disagreed, however, with the absolute character of the protection accorded their deliberations or policy formulation. Other factors could outweigh the public interest based on this argument. The candour and political disruption arguments are single factors favouring immunity which must be weighed in the balance with all the rest. Generally, the class claim will be less compelling than a *bona fide* contents claim.

The self-interest of members of government in asserting a class claim is evident and warrants close scrutiny. Self-interest is not so apparent in a contents claim. The class claim has a greater chance of success if the government identifies that the documents specifically relate to the formulation of government policy on important economic and financial matters demonstrating the sensitivity of disclosure in the particular case.[87]

D. *Level of Government Involved*

The candour argument and the political harassment arguments can be applied to any level of government. If the arguments were accepted without much probing there would be few government reports or documents that would not be immune from disclosure. It is, therefore, most important that the courts closely examine the merits of the claim, particularly where lower levels of government or government agencies are involved. Governmental demands for privilege over official domestic information cannot be justified as readily

---

87   *Carey v. R., ibid.*

as being in the interest of the public.[88] The identification of public interest in such cases becomes more amorphous. The increasing and expanding activities of government have created a corresponding demand by litigants for disclosure of documents and reports in the custody and control of governmental departments. When this demand is repelled by the assertion of Crown privilege, then, as McCormick suggests:[89]

> . . . the resultant question requires a delicate and judicious balancing of the public interest in the secrecy of "classified" official information against the public interest in the protection of the claim of the individual to due process of law in the redress of grievances.

In *Carey v. The Queen* it was noted that the level of decision making process concerned is one of the variables to be taken into account, but is not as important a factor as the particular policy concerned and the actual contents of the documents.[90] Courts have generally urged that in situations where civil servants are duty-bound to furnish information or reports, they are not likely to be influenced in their candour by the threat of disclosure.[91]

E. *Information Supplied to Government by Outside Sources*

Where the information is provided to government agencies by outsiders there is a greater prospect that the providers of that information may be less frank or will not provide the information at all if there is a prospect of disclosure. Of course, where no expectation of

---

88 See R. Thompson, "Case Comment on *Conway v. Rimmer*" (1968), 46 Can. Bar Rev. 482, at 484.

89 E.W. Cleary (ed.), *McCormick on Evidence*, 3rd ed. (St. Paul: West Publishing, 1984), at 262.

90 See also *Nova Scotia (Attorney-General) v. Royal Commission (Marshall Inquiry)*, [1989] 2 S.C.R. 788, at 790-91, 50 C.C.C. (3d) 486, 93 N.S.R. (2d) 271, 62 D.L.R. (4th) 354, 100 N.R. 73.

91 *Conway v. Rimmer, supra*, note 84; *R. v. Lewes JJ.*, [1971] 2 All E.R. 1126, [1971] 2 W.L.R. 1466 (D.C.), at 1471; affd [1972] 3 W.L.R. 279, [1972] 2 All E.R. 1057 (H.L.); *Blais v. Andras*, [1972] F.C. 958, 30 D.L.R. (3d) 287 (C.A.).

confidentiality exists the candour argument is without merit.[92] In *Re Lew Fun Chaue*,[93] the applicant, whose application to the Department of Citizenship and Immigration for admission to Canada was refused, brought *mandamus* proceedings in which he sought production of two classes of documents: (i) inter-departmental and intra-departmental communications, and (ii) communications received by the Department of Citizenship and Immigration from outside sources other than the applicant or other governmental departments. The Master treated the Minister's objecting affidavit as being conclusive with respect to the first mentioned class of documents and refused disclosure thereof. With respect to the second class of documents, the Master weighed the necessity for secrecy surrounding the acquisition of information by the Department of Citizenship and Immigration for the purpose of deciding whether an alien should be admitted to Canada, and he concluded that this was more important than enabling the applicant to present to the court all relevant facts upon which the Department may have made its decision. The Master held that the Minister, in carrying out his function with respect to the admission of foreign nationals to Canada, would be hampered if the documents in question were ordered to be produced, by reason of the fact that if persons supplying the Department of Citizenship and Immigration with information knew that there was a possibility of disclosure, they might refuse, or be reluctant to provide the true facts, or complete facts on the ground that such disclosure might jeopardize their position.

In *R. v. Snider*[94] the Minister of National Revenue sought immunity for tax returns filed by individuals. The court held that the mere possession of documents by an agency of the Crown was clearly not sufficient to warrant any claim to immunity. As Rand J. suggested:[95]

> Neither the prerogative nor any constitutional or political function is involved. To suggest that either in the case of protecting

---

92   *Norwich Pharmacal Co. v. Customs & Excise Commissioners*, [1974] A.C. 133, [1973] 2 All E.R. 943 (H.L.).
93   (1955), 112 C.C.C. 264, [1955] O.W.N. 821, [1955] 5 D.L.R. 513 (Master).
94   [1954] S.C.R. 479, 109 C.C.C. 193, 54 D.T.C. 1129, [1954] C.T.C. 255.
95   *Ibid.*, [1954] S.C.R., at 484-85; see also *McDougall v. Dominion Iron and Steel Co.* (1902), 40 N.S.R. 333 (C.A.). On the other hand, the Crown need not have possession in order to claim privilege. The privilege may attach to a document whosoever has possession of it and from wherever it has been unearthed; see *R. v. Lewes JJ., supra*, note 91, at 1471; *Conway v. Rimmer, supra*, note 84.

or attacking the private interest of the taxpayer the custody of tax returns rendered to the department can be refused production on the ground of the nature of the possession is to attract some vague magic sensed or associated with the prerogative to the routine of administrative government. All governmental and administrative activity may be said to be carried out by the Executive but it is not in these levels of administration, which might extend to every clerk, say, of a government railway, that any degree or shade of possession in the course of executive action is, by a reference to the Crown, to be placed beyond the reach of the courts.

In *Gronlund v. Hansen*,[96] the dependents of a deceased seaman brought an action against the master of a fishing vessel whose negligence was alleged to have caused a collision with another ship thereby causing the death of a seaman. Under the *Canada Shipping Act*,[97] the Minister of Transport was empowered to and did appoint a one-man board to make a preliminary inquiry respecting the shipping casualty that was alleged by the plaintiffs to have been caused by the negligence of the ship's captain. Following the inquiry, the Board forwarded to the Minister a report containing its statement of the case and opinion with respect to the cause of the accident. In response to the motion requesting an order compelling production of the report, the Minister of Transport filed an affidavit in which he deposed that it was his opinion that the production of the report would prejudice the candour and completeness of the information that would be furnished in the course of preliminary inquiries respecting shipping casualties, that it is essential to the proper conduct of such inquiries that such documents remain unproduced, and that it would be contrary to the public interest to produce them. Davey C.J.B.C. gave effect to the Minister's objection, holding that disclosure of information secured at the preliminary inquiry would discourage junior officers and members of a ship's crew from giving candid and truthful information as to the cause of marine casualties for fear of reprisals from owners and senior officers of the ship. It is difficult to understand how Davey C.J.B.C. came to this conclusion in face of the reservation which he himself expressed over the soundness of this rationale. He pointed out that if

---

96 (1968), 68 D.L.R. (2d) 223, 64 W.W.R. 74 (B.C.C.A.).
97 R.S.C. 1952, c. 29 [now R.S.C. 1985, c. S-9].

the Minister of Transport ordered a formal inquiry, the informants would have to give evidence in public and face cross-examination and this might, accordingly, incur the hostility of owners or senior officers in any event. Moreover, he added that if the evidence of a witness on a formal inquiry departed from a previous statement given on the preliminary inquiry, it would be desirable to cross-examine her or him upon the former statement. The absence of Crown privilege would thereby tend to ensure that informants would take more care to speak truthfully on the preliminary inquiry for fear of possible cross-examination on a later occasion upon an inconsistent statement. Although acknowledging the House of Lords' decision in *Conway v. Rimmer*,[98] to the effect that the objection of the Minister was not conclusive, Davey C.J.B.C. in the circumstances of this case, chose to follow the Minister's advice notwithstanding his doubts that the public interest would be impaired by disclosure. Robertson J.A. came to the same conclusion even though he too felt that the Minister's affidavit was "rather slim".[99] Branca J.A. thought that Crown privilege was properly invoked in this case in that the affidavit of the Minister satisfied the court that there might be prejudice to the public welfare which required, in the interest of candour and completeness of communications within a public department, that this particular class of communications should not be open to general scrutiny. In light of the grave reservations possessed by both Davey C.J.B.C. and Robertson J.A., one must question whether there existed reasonable grounds for the application of the privilege in this case.

In this regard, it should be noted that in *Conway v. Rimmer*, Lord Reid, in reviewing the case of *H.M.S. Bellerophon*,[100] which involved a collision between two ships, said that he found it difficult to believe that the candour of naval officers in preparing a purely factual report would be inhibited by any fear of publication of the report.[101] The conclusion that the proper functioning of the public service would be impaired by the disclosure of the reports in question is therefore suspect and it is doubtful the case would be decided the same way today. This is particularly true upon a consideration of the House of Lords' holding in *Conway v. Rimmer*, and the Supreme Court of

---

98   [1968] 1 All E.R. 874, [1968] A.C. 910.
99   *Supra*, note 95, at 239 (D.L.R.).
100   (1874), 44 L.J. Adm. 5, 31 L.T. 756 (Adm.).
101   *Conway v. Rimmer*, *supra*, note 98.

Canada in *Carey v. R.*,[102] that there is a heavy burden of proof on any public authority asserting a claim for class privilege.[103]

The House of Lords, in *Rogers v. Secretary of State for the Home Department*,[104] though acceding to the Crown's claim for privilege, religiously applied the principles of *Conway* in coming to its conclusion to deny production. In that case, the applicant sought the consent of the Gaming Board for Great Britain which was required as a precondition to the granting of a gaming licence. His application was refused following an investigation by the Board. In pursuance of its duty, the Board had made certain inquiries of the police and received a written response from the chief constable of Sussex. The applicant, who had received a copy of the letter from an anonymous source, laid an information against the chief constable for criminal libel, alleging that libel was contained in the letter forwarded to the Gaming Board. The applicant sought an order for production of the original letter and, by way of defence to the motion, a claim for Crown privilege was asserted on the ground that the Gaming Board could not satisfactorily perform its statutory duty unless it could preserve the confidentiality of all communications to it regarding the character, reputation or antecedents of applicants.

Lord Reid acknowledged the "heavy burden of proof on any authority which makes such a claim",[105] but thought that, in the unusual circumstances of the case, the Crown's assertion was forceful. It was the duty of the Gaming Board to make extensive inquiries to ensure that those of unsavoury and disreputable character not obtain gaming club licences. Who but those of similar background would best know whether an applicant is of such ilk? As Lord Reid said, "...

---

102 [1986] 2 S.C.R. 637, 30 C.C.C. (3d) 498, 35 D.L.R. (4th) 161, 58 O.R. (2d) 352 (Digest), 20 O.A.C. 81, 72 N.R. 81, 22 Admin. L.R. 236, 14 C.P.C. (2d) 10.
103 *Per* Lord Reid in *Rogers v. Secretary of State for the Home Department*, [1972] 2 All E.R. 1057, at 1060, [1972] 3 W.L.R. 279 (H.L.). However, Lord Cross in *Alfred Compton Amusement Machines Ltd. v. Commissioners of Customs & Excise (No. 2)*, [1973] 2 All E.R. 1169 at 1185, [1973] 3 W.L.R. 268, retracted from this position for he held that "[i]n a case where the considerations for and against disclosure appear to be fairly evenly balanced the courts should ... uphold a claim to privilege on the ground of public interest and trust to the head of the department concerned to do whatever he can to mitigate the ill-effects of non-disclosure".
104 *Ibid.*
105 *Supra*, note 103, [1972] 2 All E.R., at 1060.

it is obvious that the best source of information about dubious characters must often be persons of dubious character themselves".[106] That fact is the significant feature which warranted the invocation of Crown privilege. One could not expect those who haunt the fringes of the criminal underworld to volunteer frankly and candidly such information to the Gaming Board without a guarantee of total confidentiality. Although Lord Morris thought that such informants might be inhibited in the future for fear that they, as a result of disclosure, might be prosecuted or sued themselves,[107] Lord Salmon's suggestion that such informants would be reluctant to come forth because their very lives would be imperilled[108] is more convincing. The threat of danger to one's safety and life would be a considerable deterrent to providing the Gaming Board with the kind of information it seeks.

In *R. v. Homestake Mining Co.*[109] the Minister of Mineral Resources claimed immunity from disclosure in proceedings brought by a former employee of the Ministry of information supplied to the Ministry under compulsion of law for the purpose of administering the potash prorationing program. The court weighed the need for the evidence against the public interest. Because there was no need to disclose the actual content of the findings there was no threatened injury to the public interest. It was in this court's view clear that the doctrine of absolute Crown privilege was not part of the law of Canada.

An interesting English decision is that of the House of Lords in *D. v. National Society for Prevention of Cruelty to Children.*[110] It is difficult to decide whether to treat this case as an expansion of the categories of privilege or as an example of public interest immunity. In a negligence action against the N.S.P.C.C., a children's aid organization, a mother sought disclosure of documents that would reveal the source

---

106 *Ibid.*, at 1061. Lord Salmon, *ibid.*, at 1071, said, "some . . . [of the Board's information] no doubt comes from the underworld", and later added, at 1071, "It must be remembered that if an applicant who has never or seldom been convicted happens to be a crony of gangsters, it is from the underworld that information may come which will enable the true facts about him to be discovered."
107 *Ibid.*, at 1065.
108 *Ibid.*, at 1069, 1071.
109 [1977] 3 W.W.R. 198, 76 D.L.R. (3d) 521 (*sub nom. Homestake Mining Co. v. Texasgulf Potash Co.* (Sask. Q.B.); affd [1977] 3 W.W.R. 629, 3 C.P.C. 110, 38 C.R.N.S. 214 (Sask. C.A.).
110 [1978] A.C. 171, [1977] 1 All E.R. 589 (H.L.).

of a complaint of ill-treatment by her of her children. The N.S.P.C.C. had given an express pledge of confidentiality to the source. The House of Lords unanimously held that this class of documents need not be disclosed. Each member of the court agreed that a relationship of confidentiality was not itself sufficient to justify non-disclosure. Their Lordships also agreed that there was no reason to confine the public interest to that of the central organs of government. The analogy to the police/informant privilege was noted, but it is clear from the reasoning of the members of the court that their decision was based on general principles and not on the creation of a new category of confidentiality. Lord Diplock expressed the view that a private promise of confidentiality would yield to the general public interest in the administration of justice, unless by reasons of the character of the information or the relationship of the recipient to the informant a more important public interest would be served by protecting the information or the identity of the informer. Here that more important public interest was identified by analogy to the police/informer privilege.[111] Lord Hailsham rejected that the court was to balance in each case the competing public interests. He reasoned that the court should move by extension from existing categories of privilege. The issues of waiver and the use of secondary evidence were questions to be dealt with on a case by case basis.[112] This feature makes it particularly difficult to categorize the claim as either a privilege or an example of public interest immunity. The other judges took an approach similar to Lord Diplock's.

F. Statements to Police and Police Reports

Following *Conway v. Rimmer*,[113] Canadian courts have generally held that statements given to the police and police reports prepared during the course of an investigation are not as a class immune from disclosure.[114]

---

111 *Ibid.*, [1978] A.C., at 218.
112 *Ibid.*, at 230.
113 *Supra*, note 98.
114 The question of police/informant privilege is considered in this Chapter, V.

In *Smerchanski v. Lewis; Smerchanski v. Asta Securities Corp.*,[115] the respondent sought to quash a subpoena requiring the disclosure of statements made to the police during an investigation of securities legislation violations. Cromarty J. at trial had ruled against disclosure stating:[116]

> It seems to me very clear that in these circumstances, where there are criminal charges upon which a preliminary inquiry has commenced, the public policy most certainly requires that the Crown should not be compelled to disclose its case in those proceedings in this way.

The Court of Appeal held that the trial judge erred in failing to inspect the documents to consider whether the contents of all or part of the statements might be admissible.[117] Although the court noted the need for caution in disclosing the contents of any document in the possession of the police, it stated that this was never a reason for recognizing a class claim. The court stated:[118]

> So I think that if privilege is claimed for a document upon the ground of "class," the judge, if he feels any doubt about the reason for its inclusion as a class document, should not hesitate to call for its production for his private inspection, and to order its production if he thinks fit. [Quoting from *Conway v. Rimmer*]

> Lord Reid in *Conway v. Rimmer* dealt more specifically with the privilege to be accorded to documents which "might be material in a pending prosecution" in the following passage at pp. 953-4:

> The police are carrying on an unending war with criminals many of whom are today highly intelligent. So it is essential that there should be no disclosure of anything which might give any useful

---

115 (1981), 58 C.C.C. (2d) 328, 31 O.R. (2d) 705, 120 D.L.R. (3d) 745, 21 C.P.C. 105 (C.A.); See also *Bailey v. R.C.M.P.* (1990), 12 W.C.B. (2d) 22 (F.C.T.D.), where the court refused to order production of a police report in applying s. 37 of the *Canada Evidence Act*, R.S.C. 1985, c. C-5.

116 *Smerchanski, ibid.*, at 708 (O.R.).

117 *Ibid.*, 31 O.R. (2d), at 711-12 (O.R.); see also Lord Upjohn's Speech in *Conway v. Rimmer*, [1968] 1 All E.R. 874, [1968] A.C. 910 (H.L.), at 995; *R. v. Stinchcombe*, unreported, November 7, 1991 (S.C.C.).

118 *Smerchanski, supra*, note 115, 31 O.R. (2d), at 712.

information to those who organise criminal activities. And it would *generally* be wrong to require disclosure in a civil case of anything which might be material in a pending prosecution: but after a verdict has been given or it has been decided to take no proceedings there is not the same need for secrecy. [emphasis added]

It seems to me that in this passage Lord Reid has merely made the sensible observation that even greater caution must be used in deciding whether to disclose documents material to a pending prosecution. This, as he points out, is a sound general rule but its application in any case must depend upon the proper exercise of the discretion of the Judge. There is no established rule of law which accords automatic protection from production as a "class" to the statements given to the police in issue in this case.

The Court of Appeal saw no reason to extend the protection of class privilege to the statements. The fact that the statements related to a pending criminal proceeding was only one of the factors that should have been taken into account.[119]

This does not mean that the court must always inspect the documents where a claim for immunity from disclosure is made by the police. In *Mickle v. R.*,[120] a member of the Hell's Angels motorcycle gang was denied a firearms permit by the designated firearms officer. On appeal of the denial to a magistrate of the denial, the applicant demanded that the police witness disclose the files in the possession of the R.C.M.P. upon which he had relied in making various statements about the criminal activities of the organization. The R.C.M.P. alleged that disclosure of these files would reveal important and confidential police procedures and information systems which would damage future investigations, would reveal the *modus operandi* of police agents and agencies and would reveal the names of persons currently under investigation. Without examining the documents the court held that the public interest in maintaining the strict confidentiality of police investigations outweighed the public interest in ensuring the highest possible standards of justice in processing the firearms certificate. Nor has the candour argument assured success in this

---

119 *Ibid.*, at 713.
120 (1987), 19 B.C.L.R. (2d) 266 (S.C.).

context.[121] The doctrine of Crown immunity has also been applied to information with respect to police methodology.[122]

V PROTECTION OF INFORMANT'S IDENTITY[123]

A. *Statement of the General Rule*

The court cannot compel the disclosure of the identity, or information which might disclose the identity of persons who have given information to the police acting in the course of their investigative duties.[124] The rule does not protect any other information communicated by the informant (although a more general claim for Crown immunity may apply). This so-called "secrecy rule"[125] or "police informant privilege" applies not only where a person with knowledge of the identity is testifying, such as the police officer, but also where the witness himself or herself is the informant.[126] The rule applies in criminal, civil and administrative proceedings.[127] It applies

---

121 *Basse v. Toronto Star Newspapers Ltd.* (1985), 1 C.P.C. (2d) 105 (Ont. Master); *Benoit v. Higgins* (1987), 16 C.P.C. (2d) 15 (Ont. Master); *Thornhill v. Dartmouth Broadcasting Ltd.* (1981), 45 N.S.R. (2d) 111 (S.C.); *Augustine v. St. John (City)* (1975), 12 N.B.R. (2d) 59 (Q.B.); *Pavey v. Furrie* (1979), 13 C.R. (3d) 79, [1980] 1 W.W.R. 441, 22 A.R. 615, 106 D.L.R. (3d) 425 (Q.B.); *Campbell v. Paton* (1979), 26 O.R. (2d) 14, 104 D.L.R. (3d) 428, 10 C.P.C. 229 (H.C.J.); leave to appeal to Ont. C.A. denied (1980), 12 C.P.C. 133 (H.C.J.); but see *Evans v. Chief Constable of Surrey Constabulary*, [1989] 2 All E.R. 594 (Q.B.).
122 *R. v. Meuckon* (1990), 57 C.C.C. (3d) 193, 78 C.R. (3d) 196 (B.C.C.A.).
123 For an article examining the Canadian law on police/informant privilege see L.E. Lawler, "Police Informer Privilege: A Study for the Law Reform Commission of Canada" (1985-86), 28 C.L.Q. 92. See also T.G. Cooper, *Crown Privilege* (Aurora: Canada Law Book, 1990), at 183ff.
124 The genesis of this rule is the decision in *Marks v. Beyfus* (1890), 25 Q.B.D. 494, 17 Cox C.C. 196 (C.A.).
125 This is how it is described in *Bisaillon v. Keable*, [1983] 2 S.C.R. 60, at 96-97, 7 C.C.C. (3d) 385, 37 C.R. (3d) 289, 2 D.L.R. (4th) 193 per Beetz J.
126 *Bisaillon v. Keable, ibid.*, 7 C.C.C. (3d), at 412; *Canada (Solicitor-General) v. Ontario (Royal Commission of Inquiry into Confidentiality of Health Records*, [1981] 2 S.C.R. 494, at 527-30, 62 C.C.C. (2d) 193, 23 C.R. (3d) 338, 128 D.L.R. (3d) 193, 38 N.R. 588, 23 C.P.C. 99, per Martland J. (the "Health Records Case"); *A.-G. v. Briant* (1846), 15 M. & W. 169, 15 L.J. Ex. 265, at 274.
127 *Bisaillon v. Keable, ibid.*; *Health Records Case, ibid.*; *Marks v. Beyfus, supra*, note 120; *Humphrey v. Archibald* (1893), 20 O.A.R. 267.

to both documentary evidence and oral testimony. No judicial balancing exercise takes place where the rule applies. However, it apparently does not apply where the informant is an "agent provocateur".[128] The policy behind the rule was expressed by Cory J.A. (as he then was) in *R. v. Hunter*:[129]

> The rule against the non-disclosure of information which might identify an informer is one of long standing. It developed from an acceptance of the importance of the role of informers in the solution of crimes and the apprehension of criminals. It was recognized that citizens have a duty to divulge to the police any information that they may have pertaining to the commission of a crime. It was also obvious to the courts from very early times that the identity of an informer would have to be concealed, both for his or her own protection and to encourage others to divulge to the authorities any information pertaining to crimes. It was in order to achieve these goals that the rule was developed.

The importance of the rule with respect to informants in drug trafficking cases was emphasized by Cory J. in the recent Supreme Court of Canada decision in *R. v. Scott*.[130]

Although it is often described as such, this rule of non-disclosure is not an evidentiary privilege. Nor is it a facet of Crown immunity. The informant alone cannot "waive" the privilege[131] and neither can the party to the civil proceeding or the Crown in the criminal proceeding.[132] The distinguishing features were described by Justice Beetz in *Bisaillon v. Keable*:[133]

---

128 *R. v. Davies* (1982), 1 C.C.C. (3d) 299, 31 C.R. (3d) 88 (Ont. C.A.). Although who is an "agent provocateur" and why the rule should not apply in such cases is unclear. See annotation, *ibid.*, 31 C.R. (3d), at 89; *R. v. Scott*, [1990] 3 S.C.R. 979.
129 (1987), 34 C.C.C. (3d) 14, 57 C.R. (3d) 1, 59 O.R. (2d) 364, 19 O.A.C. 131 (C.A.); see also *D. v. N.S.P.C.C.*, *supra*, note 110, [1978] A.C., at 218-19.
130 *Supra*, note 128.
131 *Bisaillon v. Keable*, *supra*, note 126; *Health Records Case*, *supra*, note 125.
132 *Bisaillon v. Keable*, *ibid.*; *Newfoundland (Attorney-General) v. Trahey* (1984), 51 Nfld. & P.E.I.R. 203 (S.C.). Although if the Crown and informant both agree the rule will not apply: *R. v. Hunter*, *supra*, note 129.
133 *Bisaillon v. Keable*, *supra*, note 125, [1983] 2 S.C.R., at 96-98; see also *Rogers v. Secretary of State for the Home Department*, [1972] 2 All E.R. 1057, at 1066, [1972] 3 W.L.R. 279 (H.L.).

The secrecy rule regarding police informers' identity has been confused with Crown privilege, but this in my view is a mistake.

The reason for the mistake may be that the secrecy rule regarding police informers' identity and Crown privilege have several points in common: in both cases relevant evidence is excluded in the name of a public interest regarded as superior to that of the administration of justice; in both cases the secrecy cannot be waived; finally, in both cases it is illegal to present secondary proof of facts which in the public interest cannot be disclosed. However, these points in common should not be allowed to hide the specificity of the set of common law provisions applicable to secrecy regarding police informers' identity, which distinguishes it from the set of rules governing Crown privilege.

In both cases, it is public interest which makes secrecy necessary, but this public interest, which takes priority over that of the administration of justice, differs depending on whether Crown privilege or secrecy regarding police informers' identity is concerned. The public interest which is the reason behind the Crown privilege lies either in national security or in the effective conduct of government. The public interest which requires secrecy regarding police informers' identity is the maintenance of an efficient police force and an effective implementation of the criminal law.

In addition, the kind of secrecy affects procedure. There is no question of a sworn statement by the Minister involved as a basis for secrecy regarding police informers' identity. There is also no question of the court itself examining what is secret to decide whether it should be disclosed or, for example, inspecting a list of informers to determine whether producing it would be contrary to the public interest.

However, what is of primary importance is the reason why the procedure differs, or more specifically, the reason why application of the rule regarding police informers is not, unlike Crown privilege, subject to any kind of procedure.

The Crown has a vast store of information and its interest in keeping this secret may be infinitely variable depending on the type of information or documents and their content. There are cases in which the information is not confidential or its confidential nature is of minor importance from the standpoint of the public interest. There are cases in which the public interest obviously demands secrecy; and there are borderline cases. The common law allows a member of the executive to make the initial decision; if he decides in favour of secrecy and states his reason for doing so in a sworn statement, the law empowers the judge to review the information and in the last resort to revise the decision by weighing the two conflicting interests, that of maintaining secrecy and that of doing justice.

This procedure, designed to implement Crown privilege, is pointless in the case of secrecy regarding a police informer. In this case, the law gives the Minister, and the Court after him, no power of weighing or evaluating various aspects of the public interest which are in conflict, since it has already resolved the conflict itself. It has decided once and for all, subject to the law being changed, that information regarding police informers' identity will be, because of its content, a class of information which it is in the public interest to keep secret, and that this interest will prevail over the need to ensure the highest possible standard of justice.

Accordingly, the common law has made secrecy regarding police informers subject to a special system with its own rules, which differ from those applicable to Crown privilege.

As a "rule" of criminal law, the provincial government cannot legislate so as to abrogate the rule in criminal cases.[134] Nor does the court have any discretion to decide on a case by case basis whether the public interest favours application of the rule.[135]

---

134 *Bisaillon v. Keable, supra*, note 125.
135 *Health Records* case, *supra*, note 126; but see *Mickle v. R., supra*, note 120, where the court appears to have taken this approach. Determining whether the exceptions applicable in criminal cases apply is however done on a case by case basis. See this Chapter, V.C.

B. *Extension of the Rule Beyond the Police Informant Relationship*

The rule has been extended to statements made by informants to the National Parole Board[136] and in England to statements made to the children's aid society.[137] Where the court is asked to extend the rule beyond the traditional parameters, a careful inquiry into the public policy aspects is required. Society's need to foster the informal relationship must be clearly evidenced. The lack of such a need led the court to deny the existence of the privilege in *Reference re Legislative Privilege*.[138] The Court of Appeal held that society did not require that the relationship between a member of the legislature and an informant with respect to criminal activities be "sedulously fostered". Rather informants should be encouraged to go with such information to the police who are charged with the duty to investigate crime.

C. *Exception to the General Rule*

The rule admits of no exception in the civil context. However, it can in certain circumstances be excepted in criminal proceedings where its application may conflict with an accused's right to make full answer and defence. The exception is difficult to state for it has been judicially expressed in many, arguably inconsistent, ways.

1. Criminal Proceedings in General

In criminal proceedings the identity of the informant could be critical evidence in the accused's defence, particularly if the informant is a material witness to the crime. Since *Marks v. Beyfus*,[139] it has been recognized that disclosure of the informant's identity might be ordered where the information was necessary for the accused's defence. The necessity for disclosure in some cases is reinforced by s. 7 of the *Charter*.[140] What is not clear from the case law is the required

---

136 .*Rice v. Canada (National Parole Board)* (1985), 16 Admin. L.R. 157 (Fed. T.D.); *R. v. Robinson* (1986), 39 Man. R. 289 (Q.B.).
137 *D. v. N.S.P.C.C.*, [1978] A.C. 171, [1977] 1 All E.R. 589 (H.L.).
138 (1978), 39 C.C.C. (2d) 226, 18 O.R. (2d) 529, 83 D.L.R. (3d) 161 (C.A.).
139 (1890), 25 Q.B.D. 494, 17 Cox C.C. 196 (C.A.).
140 Although it is not likely that s. 7 changes the pre-*Charter* law (see *R. v. Archer* (1989), 47 C.C.C. (3d) 567, 65 Alta. L.R. (2d) 183 (C.A.)), "... has acquired new vigour by virtue of its inclusion in s. 7 of the *Charter* as one of the principles of

degree of materiality to justify disclosure. To state that disclosure will be ordered where it is "essential" or "necessary to show the innocence of an accused"[141] or where it "could help to show that the defendant was innocent of the offence" is not a very helpful formulation of a test.[142] Given that the accused is entitled to the benefit of any doubt, it could be argued that even evidence with the slightest potential evidential value in favour of the accused should be admitted. Such evidence is no doubt "essential" although lacking in any strong probative value. But such a wide exception would completely emasculate the exclusionary rule in criminal cases and would fail to balance the public interest in non-disclosure of an informant's identity with the accused's interest in a fair trial.

However, despite these rather broad expressions of the exception, the courts have not held that disclosure is required for the defence in all cases where the accused has simply alleged that the information could potentially assist in the defence.[143] In many of those cases where disclosure has been required the informant had witnessed or been involved in the commission of the offence.[144] An informant who participates, even inactively, in the offence should be available for the accused. In *R. v. Davies*,[145] a long time informant for the R.C.M.P. told the accused that because he was up on cocaine charges he was not able to supply one of his regular customers with cocaine. The informant asked whether the accused could find a new source of supply for the customer. The informant, after agreeing to pay the accused for the supply, informally introduced the accused to an undercover R.C.M.P. officer. Men connected with the accused sold cocaine to the officer.

---

fundamental justice." per Sopinka J. in *R. v. Stinchcombe*, unreported, Nov. 11, 1991 (S.C.C.).

141 *Health Records Case*, [1981] 2 S.C.R. 494, at 527-530, 62 C.C.C. (2d) 193, 23 C.R. (3d) 338, 128 D.L.R. (3d) 193, 38 N.R. 588, 23 C.P.C. 99 per Martland J.; *R. v. Davies* (1982), 1 C.C.C. (3d) 299, 31 C.R. (3d) 88 (Ont. C.A.).

142 *D. v. N.S.P.C.C.*, *supra*, note 137; *R. v. Hunter* (1987), 34 C.C.C. (3d) 14, 57 C.R. (3d) 1, 59 O.R. (2d) 364, 19 O.A.C. 131 (C.A.).

143 See, for example, *R. v. Blain* (1960), 127 C.C.C. 267, 33 C.R. 217, 1 W.W.R. 145 (Sask. C.A.).

144 *R. v. Farrer* (1975), 32 C.C.C. (2d) 84 (Ont. Co. Ct.); *Ferrero v. R.* (1981), 59 C.C.C. (2d) 93 (*sub nom. Re Ferrero and R.*), 21 C.R. (3d) 376, 29 A.R. 469 (C.A.); *Quebec (Liquor Commission) v. Goulet* (1929), 52 C.C.C. 392 (Que. S.P.); see the comments of Martin J.A. in the Ontario Court of Appeal in *R. v. Chambers* (1985), 20 C.C.C. (3d) 440 (Ont. C.A.), at 451.

145 *Supra*, note 141.

The accused's defence was that he was acting as an "agent" for the informant.[146] The trial judge refused to order disclosure of the name and last known whereabouts of the informant and the accused appealed on the ground that this prevented him from making full answer and defence. The Ontario Court of Appeal agreed and ordered a new trial. Lacourcière J.A. stated:[147]

> In the present case Bud was the only witness who could corroborate the testimony of the appellant that any vendors he introduced to Bud would have to make their own deals and that the appellant had no interest in any further participation, wanting only enough money to move to a larger apartment. I am unable to say that, if Bud's testimony had corroborated the appellant's in those respects, the jury would not have been left with a reasonable doubt as to whether the appellant had acted as agent for the vendors. I cannot assume that Bud's testimony would not have supported the appellant. Indeed, the Crown conceded that Bud's testimony might have been helpful.
>
> Fairness required that the full name and whereabouts of Bud should have been made available to defence counsel notwithstanding the delay in making the request. While the Crown may not be faulted for not producing it at an earlier stage in view of their perception of Bud as a police informant, it is my view that the learned trial judge had a duty to enforce his order of disclosure once he had been apprised of all the relevant facts which came out in the voir dire. This information was potentially necessary to the appellant in order to establish his status in the transactions upon which pivoted his guilt or innocence: the failure to provide it had, in my opinion, the result of preventing him from making full answer and defence.

The Supreme Court of Canada has referred to this as the "material witness" exception to the police/informant rule.[148]

---

146 A defence that now rarely succeeds, see *Poitras v. R.*, [1974] S.C.R. 649, 12 C.C.C. (2d) 337, [1973] 6 W.W.R. 183, 37 D.L.R. (3d) 411, 24 C.R.N.S. 159.
147 *R. v. Davies* (1982), 1 C.C.C. (3d) 299, 31 C.R. (3d) 88 (Ont. C.A.), at 96. See also the discussion below of *R. v. Garofoli*, [1990] 2 S.C.R. 1421, 60 C.C.C. (3d) 161, 80 C.R. (3d) 317, 43 O.A.C. 1, 116 N.R. 241, 50 C.R.R. 206, as applied to the opening of the sealed packet used to authorize wiretap.
148 *R. v. Scott* (1990), 11 W.C.B. (2d) 358 (S.C.C.), per Cory J.

In considering the "innocence at stake" exception to the rule, in *R. v. Garofoli*[149] Justice Sopinka indicated that the exception is quite broad:[150]

> The identity of informers is generally not relevant. When a trial judge is engaged in the editing process, he or she must consider the "innocence at stake" exception. In *Re Rideout and The Queen* (1986), 31 C.C.C. (3d) 211 at p. 220, 61 Nfld. & P.E.I.R. 160 (S.C.), Goodridge J. took the following view of the exception:
>
> > The rule against the identification of police informants is only made possible because, in almost every case, it will not be relevant... Where it is relevant, it will be admitted for that was the one exception mentioned by Beetz J. in the passage set forth above — the situation where disclosure was needed to demonstrate the innocence of an accused person.
>
> In *Roviaro v. United States*, 353 U.S. 53 at pp. 60-1 (1957) (7th Cir.), Justice Burton wrote:
>
> > Where the disclosure of an informer's identity, or of the contents of his communication, is relevant and helpful to the defence of an accused, or is essential to a fair determination of a cause, the privilege must give way. In these situations the trial court may require disclosure and, if the Government withholds the information, dismiss the action.
>
> In *R. v. Chambers* (1985), 20 C.C.C. (3d) 440 at p. 451, 14 W.C.B. 268 (Ont. C.A.), Martin J.A. pointed out that the exception was "more likely to apply where the informer is a witness to material facts".
>
> The determination in each case will require the balancing of the relevance of the identity of the informer to the accused's case against the prejudice to the informer and to the public interest in law enforcement which disclosure would occasion. The issue does not arise in this appeal since it is not contended that the identity of the informer is relevant. It is undesirable, therefore,

---

149 (1990), 60 C.C.C. (3d) 161 (S.C.C.).
150 *Ibid.*, at 193.

to delve further into the process of weighing these interests in determining whether an exception has been made out. Suffice it to say that it is very much a determination to be made by the trial judge.

Reference to the statements from *Rideout* and *Roviaro* suggests that whenever the information is "relevant" to the defence the evidence would be necessary for the full defence of the accused. On the other hand, the last paragraph of Sopinka J.'s comments retreats from the view that the exception would always apply in such cases. He suggests that even if the information is relevant some weighing of the accused's need for the evidence against the public interest in law enforcement would have to be made by the trial judge.[151] If relevance were the only criterion then there really would be no special police/informant rule in criminal cases. An accused should not be entitled to the information simply on the basis that it is relevant.

Where the evidence is required in order for the accused to make full answer and defence, the Crown must decide whether to call the informant as a witness or drop the charges. Because the "privilege" is not one that either the Crown or the informant alone can waive, the co-operation of any police officer having the knowledge of identity must be obtained if the Crown decides to proceed with disclosure. *R. v. Davies*[152] suggests that the Crown or its witness can be ordered to make the information available, and that the trial judge erred in not so ordering where the information is necessary for the accused's defence. However, the better approach would be not to order disclosure, but to indicate to the Crown that it risks a judicial stay of proceedings if the information is not disclosed. This would encourage the Crown to seek the cooperation and opinion of the witness and the informant. These persons are generally in a better position than the trial judge to determine whether disclosure would compromise their operations or put the informant's safety at risk.

2. Informant's Evidence as Basis of Search Warrant

This approach is also consistent with the approach taken in cases where the informant's evidence has contributed to an order for a search warrant or wiretap authorization. In these cases, the informant

---

151 *Ibid.*, at 194.
152 *Supra*, note 147.

is not necessarily involved either directly or indirectly in the commission of the offence and may not have witnessed the offence. The evidence which they could give may not relate at all to the elements of the offence. However, the accused's right to protection against unreasonable search and seizure, recognized in s. 8 of the *Charter*,[153] requires that the accused be able to fully investigate the grounds upon which a warrant is ordered.[154] Reasonable disclosure of the information used to obtain the warrant should be made.[155] Here two important policies of criminal law reflected in the police-informant rule and in the jurisprudence regarding s. 8 may conflict.

The courts have responded to this conflict by introducing a procedure of editing the information to delete references to the informant's name or other information that could reveal the identity.[156] The edited information, after a review of the material by the Crown, is then disclosed to the accused. The procedure was described by the Ontario Court of Appeal in *R. v. Hunter*:[157]

> Upon receipt of such a request the trial judge should review the information with the object of deleting all references to the identity of the informer. The information so edited should then be made available to the accused. However, if at the conclusion of the editing procedure the Crown should still be of the opinion that the informer would become known to the accused upon production of the information then a decision would have to be made by the Crown. The informer might by this time be willing to consent to being identified. Alternatively, the informer's identity might have become so notorious in the community or become so well-known to the accused that his or her identification would no longer be a significant issue.

---

153   *Charter*, s. 8 reads: "Everyone has the right to be secure against unreasonable search or seizure."

154   *MacIntyre v. Nova Scotia (Attorney-General)*, [1982] 1 S.C.R. 175, 65 C.C.C. (2d) 129, 26 C.R. (3d) 193, 132 D.L.R. (3d) 385 (*sub nom. Nova Scotia (Attorney-General v. MacIntyre*), 40 N.R. 181, 49 N.S.R. (2d) 609.

155   *Ibid.*; see also *R. v. Scott, supra*, note 148.

156   *R. v. Parmar* (1987), 34 C.C.C. (3d) 260 (Ont. S.C.) at 280-83.

157   (1987), 34 C.C.C. (3d) 14, at 26-27, 57 C.R. (3d) 1, 59 O.R. (2d) 364, 19 O.A.C. 131 (C.A.); but see *R. v. Archer* (1989), 47 C.C.C. (3d) 567, 65 Alta. L.R. (2d) 183 (C.A.), where the Alberta Court of Appeal did not recognize this special procedure in a search and seizure case, but asked whether the information was necessary for the accused's substantive defence.

It must be remembered that the object of the procedure is to make available to an accused enough information to enable the court to determine whether reasonable and probable grounds for the issuance of the warrant have been demonstrated. Most informations should lend themselves to careful editing. It would always be preferable to have the validity of the warrant determined on its merits.

This procedure should protect the rights both of the accused and of the informer, and ensure that in most cases the issue is determined on its merits. If the Crown is of the view that to produce the informant would be prejudicial to the administration of justice, the Crown may elect not to proceed or to proceed on the basis of a warrantless search. In those circumstances the trial judge will have to consider s. 24(2) of the Charter and determine whether the admission of the evidence would bring the administration of justice into disrepute. There is no way of knowing whether that situation will ever arise in this case, consequently nothing should be said about the possible result.

The same procedure would apply on a pre-trial discovery motion.[158]

3. Informant's Evidence as Basis of Wiretap

A similar procedure is mandated where the accused seeks access to the sealed packet upon which a wiretap authorization is based. In *R. v. Parmar*,[159] the court applied the *Hunter* editing process to the sealed packet materials. The court also clarified that it is still open for the court to find that a search was made subject to a valid warrant where the identity information is excised so long as what information remains can reasonably support the issuance of the warrant. It is only where the editing process fails to leave information demonstrating a reasonably grounded belief that the Crown would have to decide

---

158 *R. v. Den Hollander*, [1989] N.W.T.R. 343 (S.C.); but see *Canada (Attorney-General) v. Andrychuk*, [1980] 6 W.W.R. 231 (Sask. C.A.).
159 *Supra*, note 152; *R. v. Parmar* (1987) 31 C.R.R. 256 (Ont. S.C.). There are two rulings of Watt J. dealing with the editing of the sealed packet and disclosure to the accused to give substance to the accused's right to make fair answer and defence.

whether or not to proceed on the basis of a warrantless search:[160]

The recognition of such a middle ground is not only consistent with the teachings of *Hunter, supra*, but equally compatible with the basic principles it finds applicable. To determine the validity of a warranted search exclusive of the grounds supplied by an informer is to, nonetheless, permit impeachment and furnish reasonable information therefore to an accused. It requires the prosecution to make its case apart from material which it is not at liberty to disclose, thereby ensuring anonymity without conferring unfair advantage on the party seeking to preserve it. Further, the preservation of anonymity, together with its control by the informer, leaves at least some vestige of protection to confidential police sources thereby not wholly discouraging their involvement in law enforcement as would a rule of absolute disclosure. In addition, the law enforcement community will be fully cognizant of the need to investigate beyond the four corners of the former's [*sic*] information to provide confirmation and additional material where applicable.

In summary, in my respectful view, in cases wherein the reasonable and probable grounds alleged in an information to obtain a search warrant are dependent in part upon information provided by an informer whose identity Crown counsel does not wish to disclose, but which will be disclosed by production of the information sought, the reasonableness of the search conducted or seizure effected may fall to be determined.

(i)   as a warranted search with full disclosure of the information to obtain including such portions of it as may directly or by necessary implication reveal the identity of the informer;

(ii)   as a warranted search without full disclosure of the matters described in paragraph (i), *supra*, but with the determination of its reasonableness to be made without reference to such matters as are not disclosed; and,

(iii)   as a warrantless search without full disclosure of such matters.

---

160 *Ibid.*, 31 C.R.R., at 276-77.

It is perhaps unnecessary to add that in the event that what constitutes the informer's material is so critical to a determination of the reasonableness and probable grounds that it cannot be separated out, the middle alternative may not, in such cases, be available.

In this particular case the Crown conceded that the issuance of the authorization could not be sustained without reference to the undisclosed material. The Crown's case failed on this basis.

This issue has recently been dealt with by the Supreme Court of Canada. In *Dersch v. Canada (Attorney-General)*,[161] it was held that, on the basis of the right to make full answer and defence embodied in s. 7 of the *Charter*, the accused is entitled to have the sealed packet opened and, subject to editing, have its contents produced. In *R. v. Garofoli*,[162] a case heard together with *Dersch*, Sopinka J. reviewed the principles and procedures applicable to the editing of the contents of the sealed packet. In determining the procedure regard was to be had to the competing interests of law enforcement, namely, the protection of the identity of informers and police techniques, on the one hand, and the right of the accused to make full answer and defence on the other.[163] Regard was to be had to the rule against disclosure of police informants and the "innocence at stake" exception to that rule[164] which was expressed by Beetz J. in *Bisaillon v. Keable*.[165] In deciding what to edit, Sopinka J. thought that the trial judge should have regard to the factors outlined by Watt J. in *R. v. Parmar*, namely:[166]

(a) whether the identities of confidential police informants, and consequently their lives and safety, may be compromised, bearing in mind that such disclosure may occur as much by reference to the nature of the information supplied by the confidential source as by the publication of his or her name;

---

161 [1990] 2 S.C.R. 1505, 60 C.C.C. (3d) 132, 80 C.R. (3d) 299, [1991] 1 W.W.R. 231, 77 D.L.R. (4th) 473, 116 N.R. 340 (*sub nom. R. v. Dersch*), 51 B.C.L.R. (2d) 145, 50 C.R.R. 272, 43 O.A.C. 256.
162 (1990), 60 C.C.C. (3d) 161 (S.C.C.).
163 *Ibid.*, at 192.
164 *Ibid.*, at 192-93.
165 [1983] 2 S.C.R. 60, at 96-97, 7 C.C.C. (3d) 385, 37 C.R. (3d) 289, 2 D.L.R. (4th) 193; see also *Rideout v. R.* (1986), 31 C.C.C. (3d) 211 (S.C.C.), at 220.
166 *Supra*, note 153, at 194 (C.C.C.), quoting Watt J. in *Parmar* (1987), 34 C.C.C. (3d) at 281-82.

(b) whether the nature and extent of ongoing law enforcement investigations would thereby be compromised;

(c) whether disclosure would reveal particular intelligence-gathering techniques thereby endangering those engaged therein and prejudicing future investigation of similar offences and the public interest in law enforcement and crime detection; and

(d) whether the disclosure would prejudice the interests of innocent persons.

The procedure which commended itself to Sopinka J. was as follows:[167]

1. Upon opening of the packet, if the Crown objects to disclosure of any of the material, an application should be made by the Crown suggesting the nature of the matters to be edited and the basis therefor. Only Crown counsel will have the affidavit at this point.

2. The trial judge should then edit the affidavit as proposed by Crown counsel and furnish a copy as edited to counsel for the accused. Submissions should then be entertained from counsel for the accused. If the trial judge is of the view that counsel for the accused will not be able to appreciate the nature of the deletions from the submissions of Crown counsel and the edited affidavit, a form of judicial summary as to the general nature of the deletions should be provided.

3. After hearing counsel for the accused and reply from the Crown, the trial judge should make a final determination as to editing, bearing in mind that editing is to be kept to a minimum and applying the factors listed above.

4. After the determination has been made in step 3, the packet material should be provided to the accused.

5. If the Crown can support the authorization on the basis of the material as edited, the authorization is confirmed.

---

167 *Ibid., Garfoli*, at 194-95.

6. If, however, the editing renders the authorization insupportable, then the Crown may apply to have the trial judge consider so much of the excised material as is necessary to support the authorization. The trial judge should accede to such a request only if satisfied that the accused is sufficiently aware of the nature of the excised material to challenge it in argument or by evidence. In this regard, a judicial summary of the excised material should be provided if it will fulfill that function. It goes without saying that if the Crown is dissatisfied with the extent of disclosure and is of the view that the public interest will be prejudiced, it can withdraw tender of the wiretap evidence.

VI CONCLUSION

The full discovery of all documents and the examination of witnesses in civil cases is the predominant rule. In most circumstances, a claim for non-disclosure based on public interest immunity is reviewable by the courts.[168] The legislative and judicial trend is that litigants should have full access to all relevant information in order to have a fair trial. On a case by case basis, the courts may recognize that a particular document should not be disclosed because it relates to national defence or security or to international relations.

In criminal cases, there is an overriding obligation on the Crown to disclose all relevant information to the accused, subject to a few recognized exceptions.[169] The failure to disclose such information impedes the accused's right to make full answer and defence as guaranteed under s. 7 of the *Charter*, one of the pillars of criminal justice ensuring that the innocent are not convicted.[170] A decision by Crown counsel not to disclose information to an accused, for example, to protect the identity of informers or to protect a witness from harm is subject to judicial review. However, even the informer privilege is subject to the "innocence exception" and with respect to other persons who have relevant information, it may merely be a matter of timing rather than whether disclosure will be made at all.

---

168 See this Chapter, III.
169 *R. v. Stinchcombe*, unreported, November 7, 1991.
170 *Ibid.*

CHAPTER 16

THE EXAMINATION
OF WITNESSES

I GENERALLY

The adjudicative process in our adversarial system relies over-
whelmingly on *viva voce* testimony adduced from witnesses examined
before the trier of fact. This chapter analyses the permissible scope
and manner of the examination of witnesses before the court.

In general terms, it is the role of the parties, not the court, to call
and examine witnesses. At common law counsel have wide latitude to
determine what witnesses to call,[1] in what order,[2] and what evidence
to adduce from them. There are no witnesses which a party must call.[3]
The plaintiff, or prosecution, calls its witnesses first. Parties in the
same interest then have the right to examine the witness, but not to
cross-examine. Parties adverse in interest have the right to cross-
examine, a right of fundamental importance. Finally, the party producing the witness may re-examine the witness.

The parties have a right to be present at trial. In civil cases,

---

1   *Lemay v. R.*, [1952] 1 S.C.R. 232, 102 C.C.C. 1, 14 C.R. 89; *Harwood v.
Wilkinson* (1929), 64 O.L.R. 658, [1930] 2 D.L.R. 199 (C.A.). There is no duty
on the Crown to call witnesses listed on the back of the indictment.
2   *Briscoe v. Briscoe*, [1966] 1 All E.R. 465, [1966] 2 W.L.R. 205.
3   In England there is a duty on the Crown to call all witnesses whose
testimony is essential to the narrative of the case: R. Cross and C. Tapper, *Cross
on Evidence*, 7th ed. (London: Butterworths, 1990), at 243. In Canada: (*Lemay,
supra*, note 1) and in Australia see (*R. v. Apostilides* (1984), 53 A.L.R. 445) there is
no such obligation, but the verdict can be set aside on general grounds if the failure
to call a witness led to a substantial miscarriage of justice.

however, the trial judge has the authority to order any or all witnesses out of the courtroom until called to testify. It is doubtful that the trial judge has the power at common law to exclude a party. In civil cases, however, the trial judge has a discretion to order that a party who wishes to be present in the courtroom during the examination of witnesses testify first. There is no such discretion in criminal cases as the accused is entitled to be present at all stages of the trial.

Furthermore, witnesses must generally testify in court before the parties. In civil cases, however, the trial judge can interview children in chambers in the presence of counsel, and in the absence of counsel if all parties consent. In the latter situation, the trial judge should divulge the information so that the parties may controvert the evidence received.[4] In criminal trials, it is impermissible for the judge to hear evidence in private. A rare exception to the general rule of testimony before the parties is provided by ss. 486(2.1) and (2.2) of the *Criminal Code* which permit the complainant in some sexual cases to testify out of court if, in the trial judge's discretion, this step is necessary to produce a full and candid account of the acts complained of. Provided that full rights of cross-examination are retained, it is unlikely that these provisions could be successfully attacked under the Charter as the right to physical confrontation of the witness at trial by the accused is not a requisite component of fundamental justice.[5]

Once a witness has testified in chief, fundamental rules of fairness dictate that the parties adverse in interest have the right to cross-examine the witness. In criminal cases, the opportunity to cross-examine the maker of a statement adverse to the accused admitted into evidence is guaranteed,[6] with the possible exception of a child of tender years whose out-of-court statement in some circumstances is admissible as an exception to the hearsay rule.[7] It is opportunity to cross-examine, not the fact of cross-examination, that is crucial to the fairness of the proceedings.[8] Notwithstanding that cross-examination is critical in assessing credibility, it is not necessary that this take place in front of the trier of fact, but it is highly desirable that the jury be

---

4   *Re Allan and Allan* (1958), 16 D.L.R. (2d) 172 (B.C.C.A.).
5   *R. v. Potvin*, [1989] 1 S.C.R. 525, 47 C.C.C. (3d) 289, 68 C.R. (3d) 193, 21 Q.A.C. 258, 93 N.R. 42 (S.C.C.).
6   *Ibid.*, at 301. *R. v. Davidson* (1988), 42 C.C.C. (3d) 289 (Ont. C.A.).
7   *R. v. Khan*, [1990] 2 S.C.R. 531, at 544, 59 C.C.C. (3d) 92, 79 C.R. (3d) 1, 41 O.A.C. 353, 113 N.R. 53.
8   *Potvin, supra*, note 5, and *Davidson, supra*, note 6, *per* Martin J.A., at 298.

warned of the dangers of accepting testimony in the absence of live cross-examination.[9]

Trials must ordinarily be open to the public. In civil cases, the trial judge has the power in exceptional circumstances to hear witnesses *in camera*. This discretion is frequently exercised with respect to children of tender years testifying in custody cases. Nevertheless, any restriction of public access, judicial or statutory, must be done with restraint. The right to open and reported trials, which belongs to the public at large as well as to the parties, is embodied in the freedom of the press.[10] The statutory judicial discretion to hold hearings *in camera*[11] must be exercised in light of the public interest to have information. Regard must also be had for the fact that confidence in the judicial system is fostered by open public hearings. Thus, the *Criminal Code* provisions which permit the complainant in sexual assault cases to apply for a mandatory order prohibiting publication of the victim's name violate freedom of the press under the *Charter*, but the limit so imposed is reasonable in light of the fact that sexual assaults are under-reported because of fear of publicity.[12]

The trial judge's judicial discretion to exclude unduly prejudical but relevant evidence should also be kept in mind as an overriding principle applicable to the examination of witnesses.[13]

---

9   *Potvin, supra,* note 5, at 310 (C.C.C.). This requirement may apply to commissioned evidence introduced at a trial.

10   *The Edmonton Journal v. Alberta (A.G.),* [1989] 2 S.C.R. 1326, [1990] 1 W.W.R. 577, 102 N.R. 321, 64 D.L.R. (4th) 577, 71 Alta. L.R. (2d) 273, 103 A.R. 321, 45 C.R.R. 1.

11   *Criminal Code,* R.S.C. 1985, c. C-46, s. 486(1). In civil cases in Ontario, *Courts of Justice Act, 1984,* S.O. 1984, c. 11, s. 145(2).

12   *Canadian Newspapers Co. v. Canada (A.G.),* [1988] 2 S.C.R. 122, 43 C.C.C. (3d) 24, 65 C.R. (3d) 50, 87 N.R. 163, 65 O.R. (2d) 637, 52 D.L.R. (4th) 690, 32 O.A.C. 259, 38 C.R.R. 72 (S.C.C.).

13   See Chapter 2, II.C.1.(a).

II THE EXAMINATION OF WITNESSES BY THE TRIAL JUDGE

A. *Judge's Right to Examine Witnesses*

While the presentation of evidence is left to the parties and their counsel, the trial judge has the right to question the witnesses. In fact, it is the duty of the trial judge to question a witness[14] if, in the judge's view, examination is necessary in order to properly evaluate the witness' evidence.[15] The trial judge's power, however, is not limited to questions designed to clear up doubtful points, but extends to questions on matters not dealt with in counsel's examination.[16] Furthermore, the trial judge is not subject to the limitation against leading questions.[17]

B. *Limits on the Judge's Right*

However, in order to ensure that the accused has a fair trial, questions by the trial judge, should not disrupt examination by counsel or display bias. The test to be applied is not one of bias or disruption in fact, but reasonable apprehension of unfairness. As Martin J.A. said in *R. v. Valley*:[18]

---

14 *R. v. Brouillard*, [1985] 1 S.C.R. 39, 17 C.C.C. (3d) 193, 44 C.R. (3d) 124 (*sub nom. Brouillard (Chatel) c. R.*), [1985] R.D.J. 38 (*sub nom. Brouillard c. R.*) 16 D.L.R. (4th) 447, 57 N.R. 168.

15 *Nelson v. Murphy* (1957), 65 Man. R. 252, 22 W.W.R. 137, 9 D.L.R. (2d) 195 (C.A.); *R. v. Torbiak* (1974), 18 C.C.C. (2d) 108, 26 C.R.N.S. 108 (Ont. C.A.).

16 *Connor v. Brant (Township)* (1914), 31 O.L.R. 274 (C.A.).

17 *French v. McKendrick* (1930), 66 O.L.R. 306, [1931] 1 D.L.R. 696 (C.A.).

18 (1986), 26 C.C.C. (3d) 207 (Ont. C.A.), at 231-32. See also *Majcenic v. Natale*, [1968] 1 O.R. 189, 66 D.L.R. (2d) 50 (C.A.), where Evans J.A. said: "When a Judge intervenes in the examination or cross-examination of witnesses to such an extent that he projects himself into the arena, he of necessity, adopts a position which is inimical to the interests of one or other of the litigants. His action, whether conscious or unconscious, no matter how well intentioned or motivated, creates an atmosphere which violates the principle that 'justice not only be done, but appear to be done'. Intervention amounting to interference in the conduct of a trial destroys the image of judicial impartiality and deprives the Court of jurisdiction. The right to intervene is one of degree and there cannot be a precise line of demarcation but it can be fairly said that it amounted to the usurpation of the function of counsel and is not permissible." See also J. Sopinka, *Trial of an*

The ultimate question to be answered is not whether the accused was in fact prejudiced by the interventions but whether he might *reasonably* consider that he had not had a fair trial or whether a reasonably minded person who had been present throughout the trial would consider that the accused had not had a fair trial.

The trial judge should give counsel for the parties an opportunity to examine a witness further on any matter arising out of questions put by the judge. Excessive participation by the trial judge may be tempered by this practice.[19]

Although the trial judge's role is no longer considered to be that of a mere umpire,[20] there are limitations with respect to his or her involvement in the trial. Accordingly, if the trial judge takes over the examination of witnesses to the extent of descending into the arena, a new trial may be ordered.[21] Furthermore, subject to the power to recall a witness,[22] the trial judge should leave the leading of evidence to the parties. A new trial may also be ordered if the trial judge conducts an inquisitorial type of proceeding.[23]

C. *Judge's Right to Call Witnesses*

The trial judge may recall any witness who has given evidence and examine the witness on matters not dealt with in the witness' previous examination.[24] However, except with the consent of the parties,[25] the trial judge has no power in civil matters to call a witness who has not been previously examined. This restriction applies to an appellate court with equal or greater force.[26]

Action (Toronto: Butterworths, 1981), at 118-21.
19 *Boran v. Wenger*, [1942] O.W.N. 185, [1942] 2 D.L.R. 528 (C.A.).
20 *Jones v. National Coal Board*, [1957] 2 All E.R. 155, [1957] 2 Q.B. 55, *per* Lord Denning, at 158-59 All E.R.
21 *Magel v. Krempler* (1970), 75 W.W.R. 37, 14 D.L.R. (3d) 593 (Man. C.A.).
22 Discussed in this chapter at II.C.
23 *Phillips v. Ford Motor Co. of Canada Ltd.*, [1971] 2 O.R. 637, 18 D.L.R. (3d) 641 (C.A.).
24 *French v. McKendrick, supra*, note 17.
25 *Lindsay v. Imperial Steel & Wire Co.* (1910), 21 O.L.R. 375 (C.A.); *Fowler v. Fowler*, [1949] O.W.N. 244 (C.A.); *Briscoe v. Briscoe*, [1966] 1 All E.R. 465, [1966] 2 W.L.R. 205; *Enoch and Zaretsky, Bock and Co., Re*, [1910] 1 K.B. 327, [1908-10] All E.R. Rep. 625 (C.A.).
26 *Fraser, Re* (1911), 26 O.L.R. 508, 8 D.L.R. 955 (C.A.).

In criminal trials[27] the trial judge has a limited discretion to call a witness not called by the parties and without their consent. Because the liberty of the accused is at stake and the object of the proceedings is to see that justice be done as between the accused and the state, such a discretion is justified in criminal cases. The discretion, however, must be exercised infrequently and with great care so as not to prejudice the accused or usurp the role of counsel[28] and it is particularly important that the testimony should not be such as to alter the course of the trial or the conduct of the defence.[29] Accordingly, the gravest concern is reserved for the impact of a witness called after the close of the case for the defence; such a witness may only be called if the need to call the witness arose unexpectedly.[30]

III THE EXCLUSION OF WITNESSES AND PARTIES BY THE TRIAL JUDGE

A. *Reason for Discretion*

In both civil and criminal proceedings the trial judge has discretionary power to exclude witnesses from the courtroom until such time as it is necessary for them to give their evidence.[31] Moreover, a special examiner possesses a similar power to exclude a party during the examination for discovery of the opposite party.[32] Upon the request of a party, the judge will, as a matter of course, grant such an order. The purpose of excluding witnesses is to preserve a witness' testimony in its original state. A witness listening to the evidence given

---

27   The Canadian position parallels the English and Australian: *R. v. Apostilides* (1984), 53 A.L.R. 445.

28   *R. v. Cleghorn*, [1967] 2 Q.B. 584.

29   But see *R. v. Bouchard* (1973), 24 C.R.N.S. 31, 12 C.C.C. (2d) 544 (N.S. Co. Ct.).

30   *R. v. Harris*, [1927] 2 K.B. 587; *R. v. MacPhee* (1985), 37 Alta. L.R. (2d) 15, 19 C.C.C. (3d) 345, 59 A.R. 314 (Q.B.).

31   The criminal power is not codified: see *Dobberthien v. R.*, [1975] 2 S.C.R. 560, 18 C.C.C. (2d) 449, [1975] 2 W.W.R. 645, 30 C.R.N.S. 100, 3 N.R. 1, 50 D.L.R. (3d) 305 (S.C.C.). The civil power is often recognized in the Rules of Court: see, for example, Ontario Rules of Civil Procedure, O. Reg 560/84, r. 52.06. But it would appear that this discretion exists in the absence of statutory authority: *Moore v. Lambeth Co. Ct. Registrar*, [1969] 1 W.L.R. 141.

32   *Berndt v. A.H. Rushforth Sec. Ltd.*, [1961] O.W.N. 127.

by another may be influenced by the latter's testimony, and accordingly change his evidence to conform with it. Also, by being present in the courtroom and listening to testimony prior to giving his evidence, he or she may be able to anticipate, and thereby reduce the effectiveness of, the cross-examination that will ultimately be faced. It may also facilitate collusion by allowing a witness to tailor the evidence to fit that of another. An order excluding witnesses seeks to eliminate this potential unfairness. Moreover, exclusion of witnesses may reveal earlier collusion. The similarity of language and phrases used may expose the fact that the witnesses had compared their version of events and memorized consistent stories.

B. *Discretion to Exclude Parties*

The trial judge has no authority to order the exclusion of a party to the proceedings.[33] There is however, limited authority in civil matters to affect the order of witnesses by requiring a party to testify before calling other witnesses.[34] No such authority exists in criminal trials with respect to the accused. Exemptions to a general exclusion order are possible for witnesses other than a party whose presence is essential to instruct counsel for the calling party, though the exemption may be coupled with an order to testify before other witnesses for the calling party.

C. *Effect of Breach of Order*

At common law a breach by an individual of a court order excluding witnesses would not result in that witness being prohibited from giving his or her testimony. This was grounded on the principle that a party should not be prejudiced and totally deprived of the witness's evidence because of the latter's conduct.[35] However, the evidence of a witness who has remained in the courtroom during the giving of other evidence or has consulted with other witnesses before

---

33   The presence of the accused is of course mandatory. In civil actions, the presence of a party is a common law requirement. The Rules of Practice are generally consonant with this: see, for example, Ontario r. 52.06(2).

34   In Ontario, *supra*, note 31, r. 52.06(2).

35   See the authorities cited by Ritchie J. in *Dobberthein v. R.*, *supra*, note 31; cf. the express position in the dissent of Spence J. (Laskin C.J.C. concurring).

he or she has testified in the face of an exclusionary order may be less credit worthy. She or he also may be subjected to a prosecution for contempt.[36]

A distinction must be drawn between witnesses called in reply and those who have testified in chief. There is no certainty that specific witnesses will be called to give rebuttal evidence. Such witnesses only become aware of this fact at the close of the evidence for the defence, and, if called, it is in the expectation that they will contradict or refute the testimony given by witnesses for the defence. Accordingly, courts have not strictly applied any sanction with respect to witnesses called in reply who have breached an exclusion order.[37]

IV INTERPRETERS AND THE LANGUAGE OF PROCEEDINGS

A. *Translation of the Proceedings*

Comprehension of the proceedings by the parties is a component of fair trial rights. The proceedings cannot meet the dictates of natural justice if a party cannot understand the language employed. Accordingly, s. 14 of the *Charter* affords the accused *qua* party the right to have the entire proceedings translated into a language which the accused understands. In civil cases, because translation prolongs the proceeding and adds to its cost, the discretion to allow the whole of the proceedings to be interpreted is one that is sparingly exercised.[38]

B. *Translation of a Witness' Evidence*

A witness unable to communicate in the language of the proceedings has the right to the assistance of an interpreter.[39] In both civil and criminal cases, translation inures to the benefit of the parties who have an interest in having the court fully understand the case and defence

---

36   *R. v. Carefoot*, [1948] O.W.N. 281, 90 C.C.C. 331, at 335, 5 C.R. 215, [1948] 2 D.L.R. 22 (H.C.).
37   *Dobberthien v. R., supra*, note 31; *R. v. Carefoot, ibid.*
38   *Fuld, Re, Hartley v. Fuld (Fuld intervening)*, [1965] 2 All E.R. 653 at 656, [1965] 1 W.L.R. 1336.
39   Section 14 of the *Canadian Charter of Rights and Freedoms*, App. II, No. 44. Ont. r. 53.01(5). At common law in civil cases the matter was solely within the discretion of the trial judge: *Fuld, ibid.; Filios v. Morland*, [1963] N.S.W.R. 331.

put forward. If use of an interpreter is opposed, the trial judge must make a finding on whether the witness possesses sufficient knowledge of the language of the proceedings to really understand and answer the questions put to him or her. In arriving at this decision, the trial judge is not bound to accept the statement of counsel producing the witness as to the linguistic ability of the witness, but may allow the examination to proceed to make an independent determination.[40] The trial judge may also allow counsel opposing the use of an interpreter to question the witness in order to test the witness's language skills.[41] Also, the trial judge may put questions to the witness directly. If, however, the witness persists in stating his or her ignorance of the relevant language and apparently fails to understand the questions, the witness should be permitted to give the evidence in a language he or she understands.

The primary consideration for the trial judge should be that a witness, especially a party, should be permitted to put before the court his or her evidence as fully and accurately and as fairly and effectively as all the circumstances permit.[42] However, the trial judge should also bear in mind that it is desirable that evidence should be given in the language of the proceedings by a witness who has sufficient knowledge of that language to understand the questions and to answer them. A dishonest witness enjoys a great advantage in being allowed to give evidence through an interpreter, because answers may be formulated while the interpreter performs the superfluous function of furnishing the witness with a needless translation.[43] Furthermore, the trial judge should consider the disadvantageous impact of translation on a cross-examiner. It is much more difficult to assess the credibility of evidence given through an interpreter:[44]

> ... it is especially important with reference to cross-examination, the great value of which arises from the demeanour of the witness, and the hesitation or fairness with which he answers questions unexpected by him, and put suddenly to him, and his demeanour while being so cross-examined is powerful with the

40   *Filios v. Morland, ibid.*
41   *R. v. Wong On (No. 2)* (1904), 8 C.C.C. 343 (B.C.S.C.).
42   *Filios v. Morland, supra,* note 39, at 332.
43   *Ponomoroff v. Ponomoroff,* [1925] 3 W.W.R. 673 (Sask. C.A.).
44   *R. v. Burke* (1858), 8 Cox. C.C. 44, at 46-47.

jury to judge of the credit which they ought to give to his testimony; and it is plain that the value of this test is very much lessened in the case of a witness having sufficient knowledge of the English language to understand the questions put by counsel, pretending ignorance of it, and gaining time to consider answers while the interpreter is going through the useless task of interpreting the question which the witness already perfectly understands. To anyone who has been conversant with trials, whether criminal or civil, the importance of this, and the materiality of the fact as the language in which the witness is being examined, is so well known that it is unnecessary for me to make any further observations on it.

In the result, the task before the trial judge is to accommodate the calling party's interest in having the evidence of the witness before the court without causing undue prejudice to the adverse party. Although the exercise of the judge's discretion may be reviewed on appeal,[45] a court of appeal is unlikely to interfere except for extremely cogent reasons.[46]

C. Choice of Interpreter

The trial judge should not allow an interpreter to be used who does not possess the necessary facility in the language of the witness.[47] The interpreter should be impartial and should not be identified with a party to the litigation by relationship or interest. In *Udy v. Stewart*,[48] an action for damages for seduction, it was pointed out that in criminal cases it is common for a relative to interpret for a person who cannot hear or speak. The trial judge allowed the alleged victim of the seduction, a severely retarded girl, to give evidence through her sister who was able to understand the utterances of the former which were not always intelligible to the court. The Court of Appeal, after referring to the practice in criminal cases, implied that, had it not been

---

45 *Ponomoroff v. Ponomoroff, supra,* note 43.
46 *Filios v. Morland, supra,* note 39.
47 *R. v. Walker* (1910), 15 B.C.R. 100, 13 W.L.R. 47, 16 C.C.C. 77 (C.A.); see also Kenneth Polack and Ann Corsellis, "Non-English speakers and the criminal justice system" (1990), 140 N.L.J. 1634.
48 (1885), 10 O.R. 591 (C.A.).

the court's view that the child should not have been sworn at all, it would not have found the use of the interpreter objectionable. Cameron J. said:[49]

> The objection to the daughter of the plaintiff being allowed to act as interpreter is one that I should have much difficulty in dealing with if the case depended upon that alone. The works of evidence that I have had access to do not treat of the question.
>
> In criminal cases, it is a common thing for the relative of a deaf and dumb witness to interpret for him; but in that case the witness, though the principal one for the Crown, is not a party to the suit. And if the interpreter is performing a quasi-judicial function his relationship to either of the litigants would be a disqualification.
>
> Then again, in a case like the present, it may be that no one except a relative would be capable of interpreting. . . .

In *Mann v. Balaban*,[50] the plaintiff, who had been rendered totally deaf as a result of an alleged assault, was able to communicate by lip reading with the woman with whom he was living as man and wife. She was allowed to act as his interpreter and the evidence was taken in the manner described in the following passage from the opening address of counsel for the plaintiff:

> Members of the jury, I should advise you at this time that we are introducing the evidence of Mr. Mann, because he is deaf, we are introducing this evidence by addressing questions to him through Mrs. Mann and she is going to attempt to mouth the words for him and then he will repeat the question that is asked of him.

D. *Official Languages*

There is no general right to have proceedings carried on in the language of choice; there is no broad right to make submissions in the language of choice or to demand that submissions are understood by

---

49   *Ibid.*, at 607-08.
50   [1970] S.C.R. 74, 8 D.L.R. (3d) 548, unreported on this point.

the court without the aid of translation. Such rights extend well beyond what are considered the requirements for a fair trial and hence the role of s. 14 of the *Charter*. However, by virtue of political compromise, in some jurisdictions there are constitutional,[51] quasi-constitutional,[52] and legal rights along these lines with respect to the two official languages in both criminal[53] and civil matters.[54] The various provisions enacting language rights have been given substantially similar interpretations.[55] Though there is a general principle of evolutionary development in the interpretation of linguistic rights, this must be balanced against the fact that they are the result of political compromise, not the dictates of natural justice.[56] Where the right to plead in the official language of choice is granted, this has not been extended to encompass the right to be understood in that language.[57]

V   EXAMINATION IN CHIEF

A. *General*

A party who calls a witness examines that witness in-chief. Evidence adduced in examination-in-chief is generally designed to serve one of the following purposes, which are not mutually exclusive:

---

51   In the Federal Court: s. 133 of the *Constitution Act, 1867* (U.K.), 30 & 31 Vict., c. 3; in New Brunswick: s. 19(2) of the *Charter*, discussed in *Société des Acadiens c. Association of Parents*, [1986] 1 S.C.R. 549, 69 N.B.R. (2d) 271, 177 A.P.R. 271, 27 D.L.R. (4th) 406, 66 N.R. 173, 23 C.R.R. 119; in Quebec: s. 133 of the *Constitution Act of 1867*, discussed in *MacDonald v. Montreal (City)*, [1986] 1 S.C.R. 460, 25 C.C.C. (3d) 481, 67 N.R. 1, 27 D.L.R. (4th) 321; in Manitoba: s. 23 of *The Manitoba Act, 1870*, 33 Vict., c. 3 (Can.).
52   Section 110 of the *Northwest Territories Act*, R.S.C. 1886, c. 50 (am. S.C. 1891, c. 22, s. 18): *R. v. Mercure*, [1988] 1 S.C.R. 234, 39 C.C.C. (3d) 385, 48 D.L.R. (4th) 1, 83 N.R. 81, 65 Sask. R. 1.
53   Section 530 of the *Criminal Code*.
54   For example, in Ontario ss. 135-36 of the *Courts of Justice Act, 1984*, S.O. 1984, c. 11.
55   *R. v. Mercure*, *supra*, note 52, *per* LaForest J. at 273.
56   *MacDonald v. Montreal (City)*, *supra*, note 51.
57   *Société des Acadiens, supra*, note 51; *R. v. Mercure, supra*, note 52; *R. v. Paquette*, [1990] 2 S.C.R. 1103 (appeal dismissed October 2, 1990, by the Supreme Court of Canada for the reasons given in *Mercure, supra*, note 52).

(1) build or support the calling party's case;

(2) weaken the opponent's case;

(3) strengthen the credibility of the witness;

(4) strengthen or weaken the credibility of other witnesses.

There are constraints on the form of the examination-in-chief, most importantly, in the rule against leading questions. The content of the examination-in-chief is controlled by the issues in the case as set out in the pleadings, as well as by the rules of evidence governing admissibility. The latter are dealt with elsewhere in this work.

B. Leading Questions

1. Reasons for the Rule

Of all the rules of evidence, perhaps the best known, and yet most often breached, is that a party calling a witness ought not to ask leading questions.

The following are the reasons most commonly cited for the existence of the rule:[58]

(1) The bias of the witness in favour of the examiner;

(2) The advantage the examiner has over his adversary in knowing what the witness' evidence is; this creates a danger that leading questions will only bring out what is helpful to the party calling the witness rather than a balanced version of the witness' knowledge;

(3) The propensity of a witness to assent readily to suggestions put to him by the party calling the witness.

2. Form of Leading Questions

The most common form of a leading question is one which suggests the answer. For example, in an action to set aside the transfer by the deceased on the grounds of his incapacity, the following

---

58   *Maves v. Grand Trunk Pacific Rly. Co.* (1913), 6 Alta. L.R. 396, 5 W.W.R. 212, 14 D.L.R. 70, 25 W.L.R. 503 (C.A.); *Connor v. Brant (Township)* (1914), 31 O.L.R. 274, at 285 (C.A.).

question was held to be leading: "Did you observe a gradual failing of the mind?"[59] Even more objectionable is a question which invites a witness to corroborate the evidence of another witness or which seeks the witness' assent to the contents of a document.[60]

Another equally objectionable form of leading question, (although often unrecognized as such) is one which assumes a fact or a state of facts which is in dispute. Accordingly, in a case in which a witness' presence at the scene of an accident or crime is in dispute, it would be objectionable to ask the witness to describe what he or she saw at the scene before it is established by preliminary questions that the witness was there.

It has been said that the test of a leading question is whether an answer to it by "yes" or "no" would be conclusive upon the matter in issue.[61] The test apparently originated in a case decided by Lord Ellenborough,[62] but it has been characterized as untenable in *Cross on Evidence*.[63] This criticism loses some of its force if the words, "upon the matter in issue" are given their proper emphasis. Certainly, many questions can be answered by "yes" or "no" that are not leading. A question, however, which enables the witness to dispose of an issue by the answer "yes" or "no" will be leading in most cases. This test, however, is rather a difficult one to apply and is not generally used in practice.

3. Exceptions to the Rule

The rule against "leading" is not an absolute prohibition. It is a relative term. There is no such thing as leading in the abstract.[64] Accordingly, it is not only permissible but desirable to lead a witness on introductory matters. It is, therefore, usual to begin any examination-in-chief as follows:

---

59   *Bradshaw v. Baptist Foreign Mission* (1896), 1 N.B. Eq. 346.
60   *R. v. Legge* (1936), 11 M.P.R. 144 (N.S.C.A.).
61   See W.M. Best, *Best on Evidence*, 11th ed. (London: Sweet & Maxwell, 1911), at 625, quoted in *Maves v. Grand Trunk Rly. Co., supra*, note 58.
62   *Nicholls v. Dowding and Kemp* (1815), 1 Stark. 81.
63   R. Cross and C. Tapper, *Cross on Evidence*, 7th ed. (London: Butterworths, 1990), at 269.
64   *Maves v. Grand Trunk Pacific Rly. Co., supra*, note 58, at 219, quoting from *Best on Evidence* (11th ed.), at 625.

Your name is John Doe and you reside at 1 Toronto Street. On November 1, 1972, I understand that you were operating your motor vehicle in a northerly direction on Toronto Street.

In the case of expert witnesses, it is common to lead the witness through his or her qualification. In most cases, a written statement of the witness' qualification filed with the court is welcomed. The witness can then be questioned on the highlights of the statement.

Similarly, there is no objection to leading questions with respect to matters that are not in dispute. An examination-in-chief, which is made up of questions which assume undisputed matters to be established, is more orderly and saves the court's time.[65]

It is necessary to lead a witness, to some extent, in order to direct his attention to the subject matter. A question designed for this purpose can suggest the answer to the extent of identifying the subject matter in order to "lead the mind of the witness to the subject of the enquiry".[66] It is quite common, therefore, to ask a witness, "Did you have a conversation with the defendant on the day in question?" even though the question contains a suggestion that there was such a conversation.

Although it is neither desirable nor possible to give an exhaustive list of the exceptions to the rule against leading, the following are the most common:

(1) For the purpose of identifying persons or things, the attention of the witness may be directly pointed to them;[67]

(2) where a witness is called to deny that a particular statement was made by the witness to a previous witness, the witness in the witness box may be asked whether he made the statement and the statement may be quoted;[68]

(3) To establish time;[69]

(4) In certain circumstances the trial judge may relax the rule when the inability of the witness to answer questions put in the regular

---

65 *Maves v. Grand Trunk Pacific Rly. Co., supra,* note 58, at 220.
66 *Ibid.*
67 *Ibid.*
68 *McMillan v. Walker* (1881), 21 N.B.R. 31; affd. 6 S.C.R. 241.
69 *Oliphant v. Alexander* (1913), 27 W.L.R. 56, 15 D.L.R. 618 (B.C.C.A.).

way arises from defective memory, or where the complicated nature of the matter to be dealt with makes it difficult to examine without leading.[70]

With respect to a witness with defective memory, the Supreme Court of Alberta *en banc* in *Maves v. Grand Trunk Pacific Railway Co.*,[71] took what appears to be a rather liberal view as to the extent of permissible leading. Beck J. explained the procedure he would follow:[72]

A case which not infrequently arises in practice is that of a witness who recounts a conversation and in doing so omits one or more statements, which counsel examining him is instructed formed part of it. The common and proper practice is to ask the witness to repeat the conversation from the beginning. It is often found that in his repetition he gives the lacking statement — possibly omitting one given the first time. This method may be tried more than once and as a matter of expediency — so as to have the advantage of getting the whole story on the witness' own unaided recollection — counsel might pass on to some other subject and later revert to the conversation, asking him to again state it. But when this method fails, the trial Judge undoubtedly ought to permit a question containing a reference to the subject matter of the statement which it is supposed has been omitted by the witness. If this method fails, then and not till then — that is when his memory appears to be entirely exhausted, the trial Judge should allow a question to be put to him containing the supposedly omitted matter. It will be, of course, for the jury, or the judge if there be no jury, to draw a conclusion as to the truthfulness of the witness; but although the permitting of a question in a certain form is largely — though I think not wholly — in the discretion of the trial Judge.

Several examples are given by Beck J. in support of the above statement. He refers to the case of *Rivers v. Hague*,[73] in which the

---

70   *Maves v. Grand Trunk Pacific Rly. Co.*, *supra*, note 58; *R. v. Coffin*, [1956] S.C.R. 191, 114 C.C.C. 1, 23 C.R. 1.
71   *Supra*, note 58.
72   (1913), 5 W.W.R. 212, at 222.
73   Unreported (1837), cited in *Best on Evidence*, *supra*, note 61, at 626.

plaintiff complained about the following slanderous statement alleged to have been made about him by the defendant:

... he [the plaintiff] was in bankrupt circumstances, that his name had been seen in a list in the Bankruptcy Court, and would appear in the next *Gazette*. . . .

The witness was asked about the conversation with the defendant and gave the first two parts of the statement but not the last. The following question was ruled proper: "Was anything said about the *Gazette*?" In *Acerro v. Petroni*,[74] a witness was called to prove the composition of a partnership. He could not recall the names of the partners. He said, however, that if he could see a list, he would be able to pick them out. The witness was allowed to read a written list.

It is difficult to define accurately the extent of the trial judge's discretion to allow leading questions by multiplying examples. What can be said, however, as the court did in *R. v. Coffin*,[75] is that there is a general rule against leading questions, but the court has a discretion, not open to review, to relax it whenever necessary in the interests of justice. A witness may be allowed to have his memory refreshed by leading questions. Leading questions may also be allowed if the witness is unwilling to give evidence or otherwise appears unfavourable. Where, however, the object of the examination is to discredit or contradict a party's own witness, it is necessary to have the witness declared hostile or adverse.[76]

It appears that a party who calls the opposite party as a witness is subject to the same restrictions as to leading as in the case of any other witness, although provincial rules of civil procedure may permit cross-examination of a party witness.[77] In such a case, however, it would be the proper exercise of the trial judge's discretion to relax the rules against leading.

Counsel for a party who elicits the evidence of his own witnesses by leading questions with respect to matters on which the witness should not be led impairs the persuasive value of the evidence. The

---

74   (1815), 1 Stark. 100 (N.P.).
75   *Supra*, note 70.
76   Discussed this Chapter, V.B.2.
77   *Price v. Manning* (1889), 42 Ch.D. 372, 37 W.R. 785. In Ontario see Ontario, Rules of Civil Procedure, r. 53.07(3).

court is justified in according slight weight to evidence which is brought out in this manner.[78]

C. Bolstering, Contradicting and Discrediting One's Own Witness

1. Bolstering

Subject to the rules against the admission of self-serving evidence,[79] it is permissible to attempt to bolster testimony of a witness by examination of that witness, but direct testimony from the witness as to his or her own veracity is unlikely to be persuasive and is rarely employed. A witness may be asked, for example, whether he or she is telling the truth. However, indirect evidence of trustworthiness is frequently a powerful and persuasive tool. Accordingly, it is frequent practice to emphasize the stature of the witness in the community, or to draw attention to the demeanour, uniform, title, or profession of the witness.[80]

Another technique is to attempt to immunize the witness against damaging impeachment. The credibility of a witness is less impaired by the candid admission of personal weaknesses than it is by the apparent revelation of an attempt to dupe the trier. Accordingly, it is frequent practice for counsel to bring out the prior convictions of a witness in-chief and thereby reduce the impact of the impeaching evidence.

2. Contradicting and Discrediting

(a) General Rule at Common Law

At common law, it was well established that one's own witness could always be contradicted by other evidence, but not by general evidence of bad character.[81] The cases conflicted, however, as to

---

78 *Calgary Grain Co. v. Nordness* (1917), 35 D.L.R. 794, at 795, [1917] 2 W.W.R. 713, at 714, 12 Alta. L.R. 203 (C.A.); *Smith v. Transcona (Town)*, [1923] 2 W.W.R. 995 (Man. K.B.).
79 See Chapter 7.
80 *Meek v. Fleming*, [1961] 2 Q.B. 366: it is indicative of the power of this form of bolstering that deliberately misleading the court in this regard is a very serious breach of counsel's duty.
81 *R. v. Duckworth* (1916), 26 C.C.C. 314, 37 O.L.R. 197 (C.A.); *Cariboo*

whether or not a party had the right to prove at trial that one of his or her own witnesses, who was found to be hostile, had made a prior inconsistent statement.[82]

(b) Statutory Reform

In 1854, the English Parliament enacted s. 22 of *The Common Law Procedure Act*.[83] The wording of the English Act was reproduced in the *Canada Evidence Act* and in all of the Evidence Acts of the common law provinces. Section 9 of the *Canada Evidence Act*, until its amendment in 1969,[84] provided as follows:

> A party producing a witness shall not be allowed to impeach his credit by general evidence of bad character, but if the witness, in the opinion of the court, proves adverse, such party may contradict him by other evidence, or, by leave of the court, may prove that the witness made at other times a statement inconsistent with his present testimony; but before such last mentioned proof can be given the circumstances of the supposed statement, sufficient to designate the particular occasion, shall be mentioned to the witness, and he shall be asked whether or not he did make such statement.

The insertion of the words "if the witness, in the opinion of the court, proves adverse" before the words "such party may contradict him by other evidence" did not have the effect of abrogating the common law rule, and the section was interpreted as if the requirement as to proof of adversity followed, rather than preceded, the words "may contradict him by other evidence".[85]

(c) Provincial Evidence Acts

The corrected version is the same as that now contained in s. 23 of the Ontario *Evidence Act*, which provides as follows:[86]

Observer Ltd. v. Carson Truck Lines Ltd. (1961), 32 D.L.R. (2d) 36, 37 W.W.R. 209 (B.C.C.A.).
82   See 11 C.E.D. (Ont. 3rd) Title 57, *Evidence* § 437, at 285-86, where the cases are collected.
83   (1854), 17 & 18 Vict., c. 125.
84   R.S.C. 1952, c. 307, s. 9 [am. 1968-69, c. 14, s. 2]. For a discussion of the revised version of this section, see below, V.C.2.(d).
85   *Greenough v. Eccles* (1859), 141 E.R. 315, 5 C.B. N.S. 786, at 806.
86   R.S.O. 1980, c.145; Evidence Acts: Alta., R.S.A. 1980, c. A-21, s. 26; B.C.,

A party producing a witness shall not be allowed to impeach his credit by general evidence of bad character, but he may contradict him by other evidence, or, if the witness in the opinion of the judge or other person presiding proves adverse, such party may, by leave of the judge or other person presiding, prove that the witness made at some other time a statement inconsistent with his present testimony, but before such last-mentioned proof is given the circumstances of the proposed statement sufficient to designate the particular occasion shall be mentioned to the witness and he shall be asked whether or not he did make such statement.

The extent of the right to confront one's own witness with a prior inconsistent statement turns on the meaning to be ascribed to the word "adverse". Prior to the enactment of this section, a witness could be cross-examined by counsel for the party who had called him:[87]

. . . if the trial Judge was of the opinion that the witness was hostile in the sense that he showed a mind hostile to the party calling him and by his manner of giving evidence betrayed a desire not to tell the truth, and he declared that in his opinion the witness was hostile.

In *Wawanesa Mutual Insurance Co. v. Hanes*,[88] it was held that the word "adverse" is not restricted to cases where a witness is "hostile", but includes any case in which the witness, by his or her evidence, assumes a position opposite to that of the party calling him or her, and it is shown that he or she had made a former inconsistent statement. The court held that, in arriving at this opinion with respect to adversity, the trial judge ought to consider the statement alleged to be inconsistent. In summarizing the impact of the *Wawanesa* case,

---

R.S.B.C. 1979, c. 116, s. 16; Man., R.S.M. 1987, c. E150, s. 19; N.B., R.S.N.B. 1973, c. E11, s. 17; Nfld., R.S. Nfld. 1970, c. 115, s. 8; N.S., R.S.N.S. 1989, c. 154, s. 55; N.W.T., R.S.N.W.T. 1988, c. E-8; P.E.I., R.S.P.E.I. 1989, c. E-11, s. 15; Sask., R.S.S. 1978, c. S-16, s. 38; Yukon, R.S.Y.T. 1986, c. E-6., s. 27.
87   *Per* Schroeder J.A., in *Boland v. The Globe & Mail Ltd.*, [1961] O.R. 712, 29 D.L.R. (2d) 401, at 421-22 (C.A.).
88   [1963] 1 C.C.C. 176, [1961] O.R. 495, 28 D.L.R. (2d) 386, revd. on other grounds without dealing with this point, [1963] S.C.R. 154, [1963] 1 C.C.C. 321, 36 D.L.R. (2d) 718.

Schroeder J.A., in *Boland v. The Globe and Mail Ltd.*,[89] said:

> There is a respectable body of judicial opinion which supports the view that "adverse" extends to and includes a case where a witness' testimony merely contradicts his proof. The authorities upon this point were exhaustively reviewed in the very recent judgment of this Court in *Wawanesa Mutual Ins. Co. v. Hanes*, 28 D.L.R. (2d) 386, [1961] O.R. 495 and it is needless to refer to them here.

Despite the circularity of the reasoning, the effect of the *Wawanesa* case is that proof of a prior inconsistent statement is sufficient evidence of adversity and without more, the trial judge can, in the exercise of his or her discretion, allow the witness to be contradicted by the statement. It is, however, a matter of the exercise of the judge's discretion in each case. The judge should examine the statement to determine whether it is indeed inconsistent.[90] The exercise of the trial judge's discretion will not be interfered with lightly.[91]

The procedure to be followed when an application is made under s. 24 was described by MacKay J.A. in *Wawanesa Mutual Insurance Co. v. Hanes*[92] as follows:

> 1. That if "adverse" as used in s. 29 [now s. 24] of *The Evidence Act* is to be treated as meaning "hostile" it means "hostility of mind".

> 2. Whether a witness is hostile in mind is a question of fact. To determine this collateral issue a trial Judge should hear all and any evidence relevant to that issue. The fact that a witness has made a previous contradictory statement is relevant, admissible and most cogent evidence on that issue and that evidence alone may be accepted by the Judge as sufficient proof of the hostility of the witness irrespective of the demeanour and manner of the

---

89   *Supra*, note 87, at 423.
90   *Per* Porter C.J.O., dissenting in *Boland v. The Globe & Mail Ltd., supra*, note 87, at 409; *Wawanesa Mutual Insurance Co. v. Hanes, supra*, note 88, *per* Porter C.J.O., at 503.
91   *Per* Schroeder J.A., in *Boland v. The Globe & Mail Ltd., supra*, note 87, at 421.
92   [1961] O.R. 495, at 534-35.

witness in the witness-box. (It is also of course, open to a trial Judge to rule that a witness is hostile solely by reason of his manner of giving evidence and demeanour in the witness-box.)

3. That if the case is being tried with a jury, the evidence relevant to the issue of hostility should be heard in the absence of the jury.

4. If the prior contradictory statement is to be proved by oral evidence, the Judge may hold a *voir dire* to determine this issue.

5. If the prior contradictory evidence is to be proved by written statement signed by the witness, the witness may be asked if he signed the statement and if he admits having signed it, the Judge may look at the statement for the purpose of arriving at a decision as to the adverseness or hostility of the witness.

If the trial judge exercises his discretion in favour of giving leave to contradict the witness with the statement, he or she should, in the presence of the jury (where a jury is present), direct that the circumstances of the making of the statement be put to the witness, and that the witness be asked whether he or she made the statement. If, of course, the witness admits the making of the statement, no further proof is required. Otherwise, the statement must be proved.

(d) *Canada Evidence Act*

In criminal cases and civil cases governed by the *Canada Evidence Act*, the evolution of this branch of the law took a somewhat different course from that developed under s. 24 of the Ontario *Evidence Act*. Section 9 of the *Canada Evidence Act* was considered in *R. v. Wyman*[93] and "adverse" was interpreted to mean "hostile". Notwithstanding the *Wawanesa* case, a number of criminal cases adhered to the notion that the previous inconsistent statement was not admissible to establish hostility.[94] To overcome the rigours of this interpretation, the *Canada Evidence Act* was amended in 1969 by adding subs. (2) to s. 9 which permits a party to cross-examine his or her own witness on a prior inconsistent statement.[95] Section 9(2) provides:

---

93   (1958), 122 C.C.C. 65, 28 C.R. 371 (N.B.C.A.).
94   *R. v. McIntyre*, [1963] 2 C.C.C. 380, 43 C.R. 262 (N.S.C.A.); *R. v. Collerman*, [1964] 3 C.C.C. 195, 43 C.R. 118, 46 W.W.R. 300 (C.A.); *R. v. Brennan*, [1963] 3 C.C.C. 30, 40 C.R. 329 (P.E.I.S.C.).
95   *R. v. Marshall* (1972), 8 C.C.C. (2d) 239, 4 N.S.R. (2d) 517 (C.A.); S.C.

(2)   Where the party producing a witness alleges that the witness made at other times a statement in writing, or reduced to writing, inconsistent with his present testimony, the court may, without proof that the witness is adverse, grant leave to that party to cross-examine the witness as to the statement and the court may consider the cross-examination in determining whether in the opinion of the court the witness is adverse.

This subsection creates a right to cross-examine which, subject to the exercise of judicial discretion, is independent of a showing of adversity.[96] The prior inconsistent statement must have been reduced to writing but there is no requirement that it be signed or acknowledged by the maker of the statement.[97] This requirement is apparently designed to limit the section to statements that are verifiable by objective indicia of accuracy. While a verbatim transcript would probably qualify, notes of a conversation made by someone other than the speaker apparently do not.[98]

The procedures to be followed in application of this provision were laid out in *R. v. Milgaard*:[99]

(1)   Counsel should advise the Court that he desires to make an application under s. 9(2) of the *Canada Evidence Act*.

(2)   When the Court is so advised, the Court should direct the jury to retire.

(3)   Upon retirement of the jury, counsel should advise the learned trial Judge of the particulars of the application and produce for him the alleged statement in writing, or the writing to which the statement has been reduced.

1968-69, c. 14, s. 2 [now R.S.C. 1985, c. C-5].
96   *McInroy v. R.*, [1979] 1 S.C.R. 588, 42 C.C.C. (2d) 481, 5 C.R. (3d) 125, [1978] 6 W.W.R. 585, 89 D.L.R. (3d) 609, 23 N.R. 589, *per* Martland J. at 494, and *per* Estey J. at 500. See also *R. v. Cassibo* (1982), 70 C.C.C. (2d) 498, 39 O.R. (2d) 288 (C.A.), *per* Martin J.A.
97   *R. v. Carpenter (No. 2)* (1982), 142 D.L.R. (3d) 237.
98   *R. v. Cassibo, supra*, note 96.
99   (1971), 2 C.C.C. (2d) 206, at 221, 14 C.R.N.S. 34, [1971] 2 W.W.R. 266. Leave to appeal to S.C.C. refused (1971), 4 C.C.C. (2d) 566n (S.C.C.), adopted in *McInroy v. R., supra*, note 96.

(4) The learned trial Judge should read the statement, or writing, and determine whether, in fact, there is an inconsistency between such statement or writing and the evidence the witness has given in Court.[100] If the learned trial Judge decides that there is no inconsistency, then that ends the matter. If he finds there is an inconsistency, he should call upon counsel to prove the statement or writing.

(5) Counsel should then prove the statement, or writing. This may be done by producing the statement or writing to the witness. If the witness admits the statement, or the statement reduced to writing, such proof would be sufficient. If the witness does not so admit, counsel then could provide the necessary proof by other evidence.

(6) If the witness admits making the statement, counsel for the opposing party should have the right to cross-examine as to the circumstances under which the statement was made. A similar right to cross-examine should be granted if the statement is proved by other witnesses. It may be that he will be able to establish that there were circumstances which would render it improper for the learned trial Judge to permit the cross-examination, notwithstanding the apparent inconsistencies. The opposing counsel, too, should have the right to call evidence as to factors relevant to obtaining the statement, for the purpose of attempting to show that the cross-examination should not be permitted.

---

100 Whether or not inconsistency has been established may be a difficult judgment. For instance, present failure to recall events may be truthful. In such a case confronting a witness with a prior statement may only invoke the doctrine of past memory recorded, discussed *infra*. Alternatively, the professed lack of recall may be inconsistent with a detailed prior statement. For this to be the case, however, the witness must lie while testifying. In *McInroy v. R.*, *supra*, note 96, the unanimous British Columbia Court of Appeal characterized the relationship between the prior statements and the in-court testimony as one of past recollection recorded. The unanimous Supreme Court of Canada held that the relationship was one of prior inconsistent statements. A similar divergence existed between the majority and minority views in *R. v. Coffin*, [1956] S.C.R. 191, 114 C.C.C. 1, 23 C.R. 1 *per* Taschereau J. and *per* Cartwright J.

(7) The learned trial Judge should then decide whether or not he will permit the cross-examination. If so, then the jury should be recalled.

These procedures, although expressed in greater detail, are substantially the same as those set out in *Wawanesa*, with the following exception. In *Wawanesa*, step two seems to permit a full cross-examination on the issue prior to a ruling of adversity, while in *Milgaard*, step five limits counsel producing the witness to "producing the statement or writing to the witness". By virtue of step six, opposing counsel can cross-examine as to the circumstances under which the statement was made. The limit on counsel producing the witness was confirmed by Martin J.A. in *R. v. Cassibo*,[101] albeit a case dealing with s. 9(1). Where the statement is oral, it would appear to accord with the above procedure to allow the witness to be questioned about the oral statement, and if the making of the statement is admitted then step six is permitted to be carried out. If the making of the statement is denied, independent proof of the statement is required before step six.

The result of *Wawanesa* and *Milgaard* is that the distinction between subss. (1) and (2) of s. 9 has been blurred. There is still a distinction in that subs. (2) is limited to statements "in writing or reduced to writing". Proof of a prior inconsistent statement will in most cases be sufficient under both sections notwithstanding that a finding of adversity is required only under subs. (1). In both cases, however, the trial judge has a discretion to refuse leave to cross-examine.[102] Furthermore, the trial judge may have a discretion to relax the strict application of these principles if strict application would deprive the accused of the right to make full answer and defence under s. 7 of the *Charter*.[103]

While a trial judge must still make a finding of adversity when called upon to apply subs. (1), the test set out in *Wawanesa* appears to have general acceptance. Accordingly, it is sufficient if the witness is

---

101 *Supra*, note 96.
102 *McInroy v. R.*, *supra*, note 96, and *Cassibo*, *supra*, note 96.
103 *R. v. Williams* (1985), 18 C.C.C. (3d) 356, 44 C.R. (3d) 351, 50 O.R. (2d) 321, 7 O.A.C. 201, 14 C.R.R. 251 (Ont. C.A.), leave to appeal to S.C.C. refused (1985), 18 C.C.C. (3d) 356n, 44 C.R. (3d) 351n, 50 O.R. (2d) 321n, 10 O.A.C. 319n, 59 N.R. 160 (S.C.C.).

unfavourable in the sense of assuming a position opposite to that of the party calling him.[104] The previous statement itself is admissible to establish adversity.[105] Furthermore, if cross-examination is permitted under s. 9(2) and the cross-examiner seeks a declaration that the witness is adverse, the trial judge may consider the cross-examination under s. 9(2) in deciding the question of adversity.[106] A declaration of adversity would widen the avenues of cross-examination to permit not only impeachment by previous inconsistent oral statement as provided by s. 9(1), but the wider right of impeachment of a hostile witness accorded by the common law. This is a right which has not been taken away by the statutory provisions. It is arguable that this right is available only if hostility is established in its common law sense and not in its watered down version based on judicial interpretation of adversity. Certainly something more than a "bad answer" on examination-in-chief ought to be required before the party calling the witness is allowed to cross-examine. It seems quite plausible to allow contradiction by a previous inconsistent statement, but not to allow full cross-examination simply because the witness has given evidence that is unfavourable to the party calling the witness. In the former case, the change of posture warrants explanation by cross-examination. The latter case is just one of the hazards of litigation. It is a truism that every witness can be a double-edged sword. The Federal/Provincial Task Force on Uniform Rules of Evidence[107] recommended that the test in *Wawanesa* be adopted and that the witness must be shown to be opposed in interest to the party calling him or her. A prior inconsistent statement may be sufficient to establish this precondition, but this will not invariably be the case.

The scope of the cross-examination of a hostile witness is not unlimited. First, the common law imposed a restriction, which is now preserved by statute,[108] which precludes contradiction by general evidence of bad character. The term "general evidence of bad character" was treated at common law as evidence of reputation.[109] It is by no means clear why, subject to this limitation, cross-examination

104 *Per* Martin J.A. in *Cassibo, supra,* note 96, at 514.
105 *Ibid.,* at 521.
106 *Ibid.,* at 520.
107 *Report of the Federal/Provincial Task Force on Uniform Rules of Evidence* (Toronto: Carswell, 1982), at 327-31.
108 See s. 9 of the *Canada Evidence Act,* and s. 23 of the Ontario *Evidence Act.*
109 *R. v. Rowton* (1865), L. & C. 520, 10 Cox. C.C. 25, 169 E.R. 1497.

should not be permitted as in the case of a witness called by an opposite party.[110]

D. Evidential Value of a Previous Inconsistent Statement

The Evidence Acts have settled the question which existed at common law as to whether a previous inconsistent statement could be proved against one's own witness. Under both branches of s. 9 of the *Canada Evidence Act* the statement can be proved.[111]

An issue of considerable controversy is the evidential value of a proved prior inconsistent statement. If the witness admits the truth of the statement, then it is available to impeach the witness's credibility and it is evidence of the truth of its contents.[112] If its truth is not admitted, then its only permissible use is to impeach credibility. This rule is settled, regardless of whether the statement is by a party's[113] or opponent's[114] witness, (except where the witness is a party,[115]). At a minimum the inconsistent testimony may be nullified. Potentially all of the witness' testimony is discredited, but under no circumstances can the prior statement be employed for proof of the truth of the contents. Academic condemnation of this position is nearly universal, and the best known judicial attack is Estey J.'s stinging dissent in *McInroy and Rouse*.[116]

The argument most often cited to support the restricted use of

---

110 It is suggested by the author of R. Cross and C. Tapper, *Cross on Evidence*, 7th ed. (London: Butterworths, 1990), at 313, that "the witness cannot be impeached by evidence of convictions or discreditable acts unconnected with his testimony."

111 *Cassibo, supra*, note 96, at 520.

112 *R. v. Moore* (1956), 25 C.R. 159, [1956] O.W.N. 877 (C.A.); *R. v. Deacon*, [1947] S.C.R. 531, at 534, 89 C.C.C. 1, 3 C.R. 265, [1947] 3 D.L.R. 772; *R. v. Kadeshevitz* (1933), 61 C.C.C. 193, [1934] O.R. 213 (C.A.); *R. v. Deacon (No. 2)* (1948), 91 C.C.C. 1, [1948] 3 D.L.R. 93 (C.A.).

113 Section 9(1): *R. v. Deacon, ibid.*, s. 9(2): *McInroy v. R., supra*, note 96.

114 Section 10(1): *R. v. Campbell* (1977), 38 C.C.C. (2d) 6, 1 C.R. (3d) S-49, 1 C.R. (3d) 309, 17 O.R. (2d) 673 (C.A.). See the discussion this Chapter, VI.D.

115 In which case the statement would be an admission against interest and admissible as substantive evidence: *R. v. Mannion*, [1986] 2 S.C.R. 272, 28 C.C.C. (3d) 544, 53 C.R. (3d) 193, [1986] 6 W.W.R. 525, 47 Alta. L.R. (2d) 177, 69 N.R. 189, 31 D.L.R. (4th) 712, 75 A.R. 16, 25 C.R.R. 182. See Chapter 6, II.K.

116 *Supra*, note 96.

the statement is that it is hearsay, and that the maker swears that it is untrue. This argument is unpersuasive. The rule against hearsay protects against the dangers inherent in admission of out-of-court statements by non-witnesses.[117] Here, the maker of the statement is present before the trier of fact and subject to extensive cross-examination. Furthermore, it is suggested that it offends against common sense that any trier of fact is capable of compartmentalizing the mind in the manner required.[118] Accordingly, the trier of fact should be entitled to decide which, if either, statement to accept and to rely on the version that is accepted for proof of the truth of the contents of the statement.

The restrictive use of the statement in civil cases has been abolished by statute in England. Section 3(1)(a) of the *Civil Evidence Act, 1968* provides as follows:

Where in any civil proceedings—(a) a previous inconsistent or contradictory statement made by a person called as a witness in those proceedings is proved by virtue of section 3 of the *Criminal Procedure Act* 1865, that statement shall, by virtue of this subsection be admissible as evidence of any fact stated therein of which direct oral evidence by him would be admissible.

The continued existence of the rule in Canada, particularly in criminal cases, is supported both by practical consideration and the fact that use of previous inconsistent statements is likely to be of more assistance to the crown than the defence.[119] Furthermore, it can be justified on the basis that unsworn statements that may have been induced by a clever or over-enthusiastic interviewer should not be regarded as sworn evidence.[120] Concern for the dangers in the indiscriminate use of prior statements has been expressed by Saltzburg and Redden, the drafters of the *Model Code*.[121]

---

117 See, for example, The Advisory Committee's Note to R. 801(d)(1) of the Proposed Rules of Evidence for the United States Courts and Magistrates (1973).
118 Although some rules of evidence presuppose that this exercise is impossible. See, for example, the rules on cross-examining an accused on a previous criminal record pursuant to s. 12 of the *Canada Evidence Act*, Chapter 10, III.B.1.(b).(v) and Cory J.'s analysis in *R. v. Corbett*, [1988] 1 S.C.R. 670.
119 *R. v. Cassibo* (1982), 70 C.C.C. (2d) 498, 39 O.R. (2d) 288 (Ont. C.A.).
120 See *Cross on Evidence, supra*, note 110, at 302, where the author provides the arguments both pro and con.
121 Referred to in *R. v. Williams* (1985), 18 C.C.C. (3d) 356, at 379, 44 C.R.

The Federal/Provincial Task Force[122] recommended, by a majority, that:[123]

... a prior inconsistent statement, given under oath and subject to cross-examination at the time it was made, be admissible for all purposes in a civil or criminal proceeding.

The recommendation was based on concerns about the admission of hearsay evidence and the creation of an incentive for the police to coerce statements. The Task Force also worried about the effect on civil cases, in particular forcing parties to find not only the witnesses who had witnessed the events, but also those to whom they had spoken.[124] In the view of the Task Force, an exception to the general rule against admissibility could be made only in the case of statements made in circumstances guaranteeing their reliability.[125] Section 121 of the *Draft Uniform Evidence Act* implemented this recommendation.

E. Refreshing a Witness' Memory

1. General

A witness may refresh his or her memory for the purpose of testifying at trial from:

(1) A writing made by the witness at or near the time of the occurrence of the event or matter recorded;[126] and

(2) a writing made by a person other than the witness, recording events or matters observed or heard by the witness, which the witness verified as an accurate account when the facts were fresh in the memory of the witness.[127]

(3d) 351, 50 O.R. (2d) 321, 7 O.A.C. 201, 14 C.R.R. 251; leave to appeal to S.C.C. refused (1985), 18 C.C.C. (3d) 356n, 44 C.R. (3d) 351n, 50 O.R. (2d) 321n, 10 O.A.C. 319n, 59 N.R. 160 (S.C.C.).

122 *Supra*, note 107, at 330, para. 24.11.

123 This recommendation was implemented in Bill S-33 as s. 120. Bill S-33 did not pass into law.

124 *Ibid.*, at 315.

125 *Ibid.*, at 315.

126 *Fraser v. Fraser* (1864), 14 U.C.C.P. 70 (C.A.).

127 *Fleming v. Toronto Ry. Co.* (1911), 25 O.L.R. 317 (C.A.), ordering new trial

Accordingly, a witness to a deed may refresh his memory by referring to the deed,[128] a lawyer by referring to his or her notes,[129] an agent who has made a memorandum as to the terms of the lease by referring to the memorandum,[130] and a breathalyzer technician who fills in a check sheet as each step of the test is made by referring to the check sheet.[131] A clerk who entered transactions into a book as they occurred, which were then copied into a ledger by the clerk's employer and checked by the clerk, was allowed to refer to the ledger to refresh his memory.[132] A witness who verified the accuracy of a newspaper article read by him, when the events were fresh in his mind, was able to use the article to refresh his memory when testifying as to the events recorded.[133]

2. Contemporaneity of Record

The record which the witness is allowed to consult must have been made or verified by the witness at or near the time that the matters recorded were observed by the witness. In deciding whether the record was made or verified with the requisite contemporaneity, it is insufficient to accept the assertions of the witness that his or her recollection was still fresh when he or she made or verified the record. While a finding that the witness did not have a fresh recollection at the time of the making of the record is fatal to its use, the court, in each case, imposes a time limit beyond which the memory of the witness will not be trusted.[134] This period varies depending on the circumstances of the case and the court's interpretation of what is meant by the words "at or near the time" of the events recorded. In *Clarke v. British Columbia Electric Railway Co.*,[135] a record, made two months after the events, was rejected. In *Archibald v. R.*,[136] several

---

which was affd, 27 O.L.R. 332, 15 C.R.C. 17; *R. v. Skwarchuk*, [1942] 3 W.W.R. 309, [1943] 1 D.L.R. 354.

128 *Ibid.*, at 323.

129 *Ibid.*

130 *Ibid.*

131 *Reference re Sections 222, 224 and 224A of the Criminal Code* (1971), 3 N.B.R. 511, 18 D.L.R. (3d) 559 (C.A.).

132 *Burton v. Plummer* (1834), 111 E.R. 132, 2 Ad. & El., 4 L.J.K.B. 53.

133 *Dyer v. Best* (1866), L.R. 1 Exch. 152, 4 H. & C. 189; see also *Taylor v. Massey* (1891), 20 O.R. 429 (C.A.).

134 *Fraser v. Fraser, supra*, note 126, at 80.

135 [1949] 1 W.W.R. 977 (B.C.S.C.).

136 (1956), 116 C.C.C. 62, 24 C.R. 50 (Que. S.C.).

weeks was considered to be too long. The use of an arbitrary time limit is justified on the ground that the assertions of a witness, whose memory is admittedly faulty with respect to the period of time in question, should be tested with reference to objective criteria.

The requirement of contemporaneity must be more strictly enforced in the case of a witness who has no independent recollection. In such a case, the witness' evidence is of little or no assistance with regard to the acuity of his or her recollection at the relevant time. It is, therefore, proper for the court to insist on a prompt recording of events as the only guarantee of accuracy.

3. Absence of Independent Recollection

It is not essential that the witness have any independent recollection of the events recorded. If, after consulting a record to which he may properly refer, the witness can say that he made it or verified it when the facts were fresh in his memory, and that he has no reason to doubt that the facts are correctly stated, the witness' statement is evidence of the facts recorded in the writing. In *Fleming v. Toronto Railway Co.*,[137] Meredith J.A. put the test thus:

> If, looking at the report, the witness could have said, 'That is my report, it refers to the car in question, and shews that it was examined at that time, and, though I cannot from memory say that it was then examined, I can now swear that it was, because I signed no report that was untrue, and at the time I signed this report I knew that it was true,' that would, of course, be very good evidence. . . .

When a witness who has no independent recollection, bases his evidence on a document in the manner described by Meredith J.A., difficult questions arise as to whether the document itself is evidence. In such a case, the witness is not refreshing his memory at all because the writing has failed to stimulate any memory. The witness affirms the making of the document and expresses his faith in its accuracy. Should not the document, then, be the evidence rather than the witness' paraphrase of it? The jurisprudence on this point is not uniform in common law jurisdictions. In England the rule is clear that

---

137 (1911), 25 O.L.R. 317, at 325-26, ordering new trial which was affd. 27 O.L.R. 332, 15 C.R.C. 17, 8 D.L.R. 507, which was affd. 47 S.C.R. 612, 15 C.R.C. 386, 12 D.L.R. 249.

the writing is not evidence.[138] On the other hand, the opposite conclusion has been adopted by the New Zealand Court of Appeal in *R. v. Naidanovici*.[139] An entry in a sales book and a duplicate sales invoice, both prepared by a sales clerk, were admitted as evidence of the facts when the clerk testified that he made them, but had no independent recollection of the matters recorded. In Canada, a number of cases have enunciated the general proposition that a writing used to refresh memory is not evidence, but few cases have specifically addressed the distinction between reviving faulty memory and affirming past recollection recorded.[140] In *Young v. Denton*,[141] a record made by the defendant and used to refresh his memory was treated as evidence by the trial judge. The Saskatchewan Court of Appeal ordered a new trial on the ground that the record was not evidence. The report of the case does not disclose whether the defendant had any independent recollection of the matters recorded. *Fleming v. Toronto Railway Co.*,[142] which is the principle authority on the use of a writing in the case of a witness without independent recollection, does not consider whether the writing itself is evidence.

The arguments in favour of making the writing evidence outweigh those against its admission. It makes little sense to treat the assertions of the witness as evidence when the witness adds little to what is stated in the writing. It is said that the writing is self-serving and should not be admitted because "a man cannot make evidence for himself".[143] The witness' paraphrase of the document, however, is subject to the same criticism.

Whether the document is admitted as evidence or the witness is allowed to read it or paraphrase it, one thing is clear: the evidence is based entirely on the document. The law should favour the reception of the evidence. If the document is not treated as evidence, then in a case in which the document has been lost but an exact copy, not verified by the witness, has been made by another person, the copy

---

138 R. Cross and C. Tapper, *Cross on Evidence*, 7th ed. (London: Butterworths, 1990), at 279.

139 [1962] N.Z.L.R. 334.

140 *R. v. Bengert (No. 2)* (1978), 15 C.R. (3d) 21, [1979] 1 W.W.R. 472 (B.C.S.C.); affd. (1980), 53 C.C.C. (2d) 481, at 522, 15 C.R. (3d) 114 (B.C.C.A.).

141 [1927] 1 W.W.R. 75, 21 Sask. L.R. 319, [1927] 1 D.L.R. 426 (Sask. C.A.).

142 *Supra*, note 137.

143 *Young v. Denton*, *supra*, note 141, at 79 (W.W.R.). Prior Consistent Statements are dealt with in Chapter 7.

could not be received. In such a situation valuable evidence might be excluded. On the other hand, if the document is treated as evidence, secondary evidence may be given of its contents once its absence has been accounted for.[144] In *R. v. Kearns*,[145] the British Columbia Court of Appeal dealt with this very problem. The appellant was charged with retaining stolen goods which were not proved to have been taken from a shop window. A shop employee made a list of the goods and their serial numbers. The list was given to a policeman who made a typewritten copy of it but lost the original. The Court of Appeal held that the copy was admissible as secondary evidence of the original. The typewritten copy, which was admitted, possessed a high degree of reliability. It would be unfortunate if such evidence were rejected. To admit the evidence, however, without doing violence to the principles under which documents may be used to refresh memory, it is necessary to reject the English view.

If the record used to refresh memory has not been made evidence in the examination-in-chief, it does not necessarily become evidence if it is dealt further with in cross-examination. If counsel cross-examine on the parts used for refreshment, then there is still no reason to make it evidence.[146] As a general rule, when a party calls for and inspects a document that they are not entitled to, the producing party may compel the inspecting party to enter the document into evidence.[147] As the law now stands, when cross-examination on an aide memoire goes beyond the parts relied on to refresh memory, then the party cross-examining may be compelled by the calling party to make the document evidence.[148] Strictly speaking this should only apply to instances of past recollection recorded since a spark which truly refreshes latent memory is of no evidential value itself, but is merged

---

144 See Chapter 18.
145 84 C.C.C. 357, [1945] 3 D.L.R. 645, [1945] 2 W.W.R. 477, 61 B.C.R. 278 (C.A.).
146 *Young v. Denton, supra*, note 141.
147 *Armak Chemicals Ltd. v. Cdn. National Rly. Co.* (1985), 7 C.P.C. (2d) 273 (Ont. H.C.J.); *McLean v. Merchants Bank of Canada* (1916), 10 W.W.R. 191, 9 Alta. L.R. 471, 27 D.L.R. 156 (C.A.); *Morrison-Knudsen Co. v. British Columbia Hydro & Power Authority* (1972), 31 D.L.R. (3d) 633, [1972] 6 W.W.R. 254. A passage from *Cross on Evidence, supra*, note 138, is routinely cited for this proposition without further authority. In view of the modern practice which requires production of all documents by way of discovery, this rule is anachronistic.
148 *R. v. Britton*, [1987] 2 All E.R. 412 (C.A.).

in the oral testimony of the witness. If the cross-examiner strays beyond the parts of the aide memoire not for the purpose of further refreshing the witness' memory on the point dealt with in-chief, but to contradict the witness on a previous inconsistent statement, different considerations apply.[149]

4. What Records or Devices May be Used to Refresh Memory

The use of a copy of the record, when the original is unavailable has been judicially frowned on, unless the copy itself satisfies the test applicable to the original. In *R. v. Elder*,[150] the court refused to allow a policeman to use a typewritten copy of his notes, because the copy was prepared when the facts were no longer fresh in his mind. The better view, however, is that a copy may be used if the absence of the original is accounted for, and a witness proves that the copy is a true reproduction of the original.[151] If the copy contains changes or is a distillation or summary of the original, its use should be disallowed unless the witness had a fresh recollection of the facts when the changes were made.

Some more recent cases have considered the question of whether a record made by means other than writing can be used to refresh memory. In *R. v. Mills*,[152] Winn J. allowed a police officer, who had overheard statements made by the two accused confined in separate cells, to refresh his memory from a tape recording which had been placed in the corridor, and on which the accused's statements were recorded. The use of the tape was supported on the basis that the recording device merely took the place of a pen or pencil, and, alternatively, that the machine was set by the policeman to perform the function of making the record, and its accuracy was verified by the policeman while the statements by the accused were fresh in his memory. In this regard, the tape was comparable to a record made by

---

149 See this Chapter, VI.D.2.
150 (1925), 44 C.C.C. 75, [1925] 3 D.L.R. 47, 35 Man. R. 161, [1925] 2 W.W.R. 545 (C.A.).
151 *Daynes v. British Columbia Electric Ry. Co.* (1912), 3 W.W.R. 193, 17 B.C.R. 498, 14 C.R.C. 309, 7 D.L.R. 767; revd. other grounds (1914), 49 S.C.R. 518, 6 W.W.R. 512, 18 C.R.C. 146, 19 D.L.R. 266; *Stovel v. Allen* (1851), 1 U.C.C.P. 300 (C.A.); *Topham v. McGregor* (1844), 1 Car. & Kir. 320; *Doe d. Church and Phillips v. Perkins* (1790), 3 Term. Rep. 749, 100 E.R. 838.
152 [1962] 3 All E.R. 298, [1962] 1 W.L.R. 1152 (C.C.A.).

a person other than the witness and verified by the latter.

In *R. v. Davey*,[153] a witness had recorded the licence number of the accused's automobile upon seeing it leave the scene of an accident. The witness immediately reported the incident orally to a patrolling policeman who wrote it down, and then broadcast it correctly over a radio with which the police car was equipped. The broadcast was made in the presence of the witness who confirmed the accuracy of the number. The witness at no time saw the policeman's note. At the trial, the witness had lost her note and sought to refresh her memory from the policeman's note. Aikins J. upheld the magistrate's ruling which allowed the note to be used. The decision was based on the ground that the witness had effectively verified the accuracy of the policeman's note while the events were fresh in her memory. This case illustrates the proposition that a record need not be verified directly by having the witness actually read it. Its accuracy may be verified by indirect means.

Several cases have allowed the previous depositions of a witness to be used to refresh the witness' memory at a subsequent trial.[154] The use of these documents to refresh memory is difficult to reconcile with the principles outlined above. The previous testimony of a witness is recorded by the court reporter and its accuracy is not verified by the witness. The matters recorded may not satisfy the requirement of contemporaneity because the witness is usually testifying long after the events took place.

The leading Canadian case on the point is *R. v. Laurin*,[155] which follows an English case, *R. v. Williams*.[156] In *R. v. Williams*, however, the depositions used had been signed by the witness, thus satisfying the requirement that the record be verified. The court in *R. v. Laurin* affirmed the principle that the record must have been verified by the witness, but failed to explain how the requirement was satisfied in the case at bar. Modern practice does not require witnesses to sign the transcript of their evidence taken in court proceedings. In any event, the transcript is not available until some time after the evidence is

---

153 [1970] 2 C.C.C. 351, 6 C.R.N.S. 288, 68 W.W.R. 142 (B.C.S.C.).
154 *R. v. Laurin* (1902), 6 C.C.C. 135 (Que.); *R. v. Marshall*, [1965] 4 C.C.C. 35, 51 W.W.R. 185 (Alta.).
155 *Laurin, ibid.*
156 (1985), 18 C.C.C. (3d) 356, 44 C.R. (3d) 351, 50 O.R. (2d) 321, 7 O.A.C. 201, 14 C.R.R. 251; leave to appeal to S.C.C. refused (1985), 18 C.C.C. (3d) 356n, 44 C.R. (3d) 351, 50 O.R. (2d) 321n, 10 O.A.C. 319n, 59 N.R. 160 (S.C.C.).

given. The requirement of verification, therefore, could not be followed in the recent decision in England of *R. v. Woodcock*.[157]

Finally, in *R. v. Pitt*,[158] a completely novel method of refreshing memory was permitted. During the trial of an accused on a charge of attempted murder, it was shown that the accused suffered from functional amnesia with respect to a period of time which was material. Two psychiatrists gave evidence that hypnosis is regarded as a useful and efficacious method of enabling a person who has functional amnesia, to bring back to conscious recollection those events which have been forgotten. The witness was allowed to be hypnotized in court in the presence of the jury. While in the hypnotic trance, she was requested by a psychiatrist to recall all that she could about the period in question but not to relate it while in the trance. The accused was then brought out of the trance and allowed to testify as to her recollection. This case may be regarded as the precursor to the judicial sanction of the use of artificial stimulae to revive memory.

5. Procedural Matters

A witness who is called to testify and who wishes to refer to a record for the purpose of refreshing memory, should request the permission of the court to do so. Counsel calling the witness should lay a foundation for the use of the record. Failure to obtain the permission of the court and to lay a foundation for the use of the record does not vitiate the evidence, provided that the record satisfies the conditions under which a document may be used to refresh memory.[159] If, however, a document is used which does not satisfy the requirements, the evidence of the witness may be rejected.[160]

Counsel for the opposite party is entitled to inspect the record relied on by the witness.[161] It has been held that a writing used by the witness to refresh his recollection prior to giving evidence may, in the

---

157 [1963] Crim. L.R. 273 (C.A.). The practice of refreshing memory from the previous testimony appears to have received the blessing of Taschereau J. in *R. v. Coffin*, [1956] S.C.R. 191, 114 C.C.C. 1, at 19-20.

158 [1968] 3 C.C.C. 342, 66 W.W.R. 400, 68 D.L.R. (2d) 513 (B.C.S.C.).

159 *R. v. Fleming* (1972), 18 C.R.N.S. 93, 7 C.C.C. (2d) 57.

160 *Mutual Life Assur. Co. v. Lamarche* (1942), 9 I.L.R. 346, affd. without reference to this point (1943), 10 I.L.R. 37 (*sub nom. Mutual Life Assur. Co. v. Jeannotte*); *Young v. Denton, supra,* note 141, at 83 (W.W.R.).

161 *Beech v. Jones*, [1848] 5 C.B. 696.

discretion of the trial judge be ordered to be produced.[162] There is, however, strong authority to the contrary.[163] There is no valid reason why the trial judge's discretion should be fettered. As pointed out in *R. v. Lewis*,[164] notes used five to ten minutes before testifying in court are just as much a refreshing of memory at trial as they are when used in the courtroom.

VI CROSS-EXAMINATION

A. *Scope*

The oft-quoted words of Wigmore that cross-examination is "beyond any doubt the greatest legal engine ever invented for the discovery of truth"[165] indicate its great value in the conduct of litigation. Three purposes are generally attributed to cross-examination:

(1) To weaken, qualify or destroy the opponent's case;

(2) To support the party's own case through the testimony of the opponents witnesses;[166]

(3) To discredit the witness.

To accomplish these ends, counsel is given wide latitude and there are, accordingly, very few restrictions placed on the questions that may be asked or the manner in which they may be put. Any question which is relevant to the substantive issues or to the witness' credibility is allowed.[167] It appears that the scope of cross-examination is wide enough to permit questions which suggest facts which cannot be

---

162 *R. v. Lewis*, [1969] 3 C.C.C. 235, 67 W.W.R. 243 (B.C.S.C.); *R. v. Monfils* (1972), 4 C.C.C. (2d) 163, [1972] 1 O.R. 11 (C.A.).

163 *R. v. Bonnycastle*, [1970] 4 C.C.C. 382, 3 D.L.R. (3d) 288 (Sask. Q.B.); *R. v. Kerenko*, [1965] 3 C.C.C. 52, 45 C.R. 291, 51 W.W.R. 53, 49 D.L.R. (2d) 760 (Man. C.A.).

164 *Supra*, note 162.

165 3 Wigmore, *Evidence*, § 1367 (Chadbourn rev. 1970).

166 See *Jones v. Burgess* (1914), 43 N.B.R. 126 (C.A.), *per* Barry J. dissenting on other grounds at 151-52; revd. in part by the Supreme Court of Canada (unreported, March 3, 1916).

167 *Hickey v. Fitzgerald* (1877), 41 U.C.Q.B. 303 (C.A.).

proved by other evidence. Lord Radcliffe in *Fox v. General Medical Council*[168] put the point as follows:[169]

> ... An advocate is entitled to use his discretion as to whether to put questions in the course of cross-examination which are based on material which he is not in a position to prove directly. The penalty is that, if he gets a denial or some answer that does not suit him, the answer stands against him for what it is worth.

This statement was made in the context of disciplinary proceedings taken against a physician in which the following exchange took place on cross-examination:

> Q: Did you seduce her in surgery very soon after that ... ?
>
> A: I did not.

The question was considered proper even though counsel did not subsequently lead any evidence to establish the fact of seduction.[170] This principle runs counter to what is the established practice in trials in some jurisdictions.[171] Furthermore, it accords a power to cross-examining counsel that does not appear warranted in the interest of justice and it may be the subject of considerable abuse. Juries, in particular, could be influenced by suggestions made in cross-examination, but not subsequently proved. Most juries would assume that a responsible counsel would not put such suggestions unless there was some justification for them in his other brief. It is preferable to treat a breach of this rule as an ethical problem rather than a matter of

---

168 [1960] 3 All E.R. 225, 1 W.L.R. 1017 (P.C.).

169 *Ibid.*, at 1023.

170 Also see *R. v. Bencardino* (1973), 11 C.C.C. (2d) 549, 2 O.R. (2d) 351, at 356 (C.A.).

171 Haines J. thought that some control over this kind of questioning was necessary and in *R. v. Hawke* (1974), 16 C.C.C. (2d) 438, 3 O.R. (2d) 210, at 229 [revd. on other grounds (1975), 22 C.C.C. (2d) 19], said: ". . . I would think that in appropriate situations, any trial Judge would at least protect the witness who was asked a demeaning question where the Judge has reason to believe it is without foundation or for some ulterior motive. All the Judge need say to counsel is: 'Are you prepared to call evidence in support of your question?' and if the answer is 'No', to direct the witness not to reply. In my opinion, fairness demands nothing less." And see *Hey v. Huss* (1957), 165 N.Y.S. (2d) 159, at 162 (N.Y. City C.).

admissibility or weight of evidence. To enforce it as a rule of evidence would require the cross-examiner to satisfy the judge that there is a foundation for the question which would be unduly restrictive.[172]

Cross-examination is not restricted, as it is in the United States Federal Courts and many state courts, to matters raised in the examination-in-chief.[173] "The slightest direct examination, even for formal proof, opens up the whole of the cross-examiner's case."[174] Moreover, the cross-examining counsel is permitted to pose leading questions to the witness even on material points, a privilege designed to offset the bias that a witness is assumed to possess in favour of the party calling him and to overcome the advantage held by a party calling a witness who knows beforehand what the witness is expected to say.[175]

Although counsel's licence to cross-examine is a broad one, it is not without limitation. Counsel cannot, under the guise of cross-examination, circumvent other rules of evidence by asking a question, the answer to which would be inadmissible if offered in-chief.[176] Similarly, the trial judge has a discretion to disallow relevant cross-examination as to credibility where the evidence elicited constitutes inadmissible bad character evidence of the accused.[177] In addition, regard must be given to a trial judge's discretion, rooted in the common law, to disallow a question which in his opinion is merely

---

172 See J. Sopinka, *Trial of an Action* (Toronto: Butterworths, 1981), at 80.

173 E.W. Cleary (ed.), *McCormick on Evidence*, 3rd ed. (St. Paul: West Publishing, 1984), at 52: see r. 611(b) of the Federal Rules of Evidence (1974), which allows a witness to be cross-examined on any matter raised in the direct examination and on matters affecting credibility, subject to a residual discretion in the trial judge to permit cross-examination into new matters not covered in direct examination.

174 *Per* Barry J., in *Jones v. Burgess* (1914), 43 N.B.R. 126 (C.A.), at 152.

175 See *Maves v. Grand Trunk Pacific Rly. Co.* (1913), 6 Alta. L.R. 396, 5 W.W.R. 212, 14 D.L.R. 70, 25 W.L.R. 503 (C.A.). But see *Stewart v. Walker* (1903), 6 O.L.R. 495, at 506 (C.A.) in which Moss C.J.O. suggests that a trial judge has a discretion to prohibit a cross-examining counsel from asking leading questions of a witness who appears to be overly favourable to his case.

176 *Cherniak v. Kurchaba* (1958), 24 W.W.R. 270 (Man.); *Doe d. Wetmore v. Bell* (1890), 30 N.B.R. 83 (C.A.); *R. v. Drew (No. 2)* (1933), 60 C.C.C. 229, [1933] 2 W.W.R. 243, [1933] 4 D.L.R. 592 (Sask. C.A.); but see *Dudas v. Eagle Star Insurance Co.* (1965), 51 D.L.R. (2d) 526, 52 W.W.R. 48, in which the British Columbia Court of Appeal ruled that hearsay given in response to questions asked in cross-examination was admissible.

177 See *R. v. Belanger*, (1975), 24 C.C.C. (2d) 10 (Ont. C.A.) discussed in Chapter 10, III.B.1.(b).(i).

vexatious. The Supreme Court of Canada, in *Brownell v. Brownell*,[178] held that the trial judge had not erred in refusing to allow the witness to give the name of his wife in a bigamous marriage when this information was sought in cross-examination. As was stated by Anglin J.:[179]

> No doubt the limits of relevancy must be less tightly drawn upon cross-examination than upon direct examination. The introduction upon cross-examination of the issue of the witness's credibility necessarily enlarges the field. But it does not follow that all barriers are therefore thrown down. That which is clearly irrelevant to this issue or the issues raised in the pleadings is no more admissible in cross-examination than in examination in chief.

This common law discretion is presently entrenched in provincial regulations governing the rules of court. For example, in Ontario, r. 53.01(2) provides:[180]

> The trial judge shall exercise reasonable control over the mode of interrogation of a witness so as to protect the witness from undue harassment or embarrassment and may disallow a question put to a witness that is vexatious or irrelevant to any matter that may properly be inquired into at the trial.

The court also has a discretion to deny counsel the right to recall a witness, whom counsel has already cross-examined, merely to review testimony previously elicited.[181]

The corollary of this proposition is that the trial judge may compel a witness to answer a relevant question, even one relevant only to the witness' credibility, under pain of contempt. Counsel or the witness may object to an irrelevant question, and where an objection is taken the trial judge should require counsel to indicate the basis on

---

178 (1909), 42 S.C.R. 368.
179 *Ibid.*, at 374. See also *N.B. Electric Power Comm. v. Barderie* (1968), 70 D.L.R. (2d) 492 (N.B.C.A.); *Geddie v. Rink*, [1935] 1 W.W.R. 87 (Sask. C.A.); *Murray v. Haylow* (1926-27), 60 O.L.R. 629, [1927] 3 D.L.R. 1036 (C.A.); *R. v. Rowbotham (No. 5)* (1977), 2 C.R. (3d) 293, at 296 (Ont. G.S.P.); *R. v. Fields* (1986), 28 C.C.C. (3d) 353, 53 C.R. (3d) 260, 56 O.R. (2d) 213, 16 O.A.C. 286.
180 *Rules of Civil Procedure*, O. Reg. 560/84.
181 *Graham v. Graham* (1876), 11 N.S.R. 265 (C.A.).

which it is relevant.[182] When the trial judge compels the witness to answer, the judge should indicate what the relevance of the question is.[183]

Not all witnesses are subject to cross-examination. In *Lyone v. Long*,[184] McKay J., citing *Phipson on Evidence*, gave two such examples:

(1) a witness called merely to produce a document where the document requires no proof or is to be proved by other means; and

(2) a witness sworn by mistake and whose examination has not substantially commenced.

It should be noted, however, that with regard to the latter exception, the mistake must arise from the inability of the witness to speak to the matter and not from the imprudence of counsel in having called him to give evidence. Moreover, a witness who has been called to the stand by the trial judge is not subject to cross-examination by a party, unless leave is granted by the judge, which is generally given if the witness' evidence is adverse to that party.[185]

While it used to be the law that a party could not prove his case by cross-examination,[186] that rule has since been relaxed, for, as Barry J. stated in *Jones v. Burgess*:[187]

If a plaintiff calls a witness to prove the simplest fact connected with his case, the defendant is at liberty to cross-examine him on every issue, and by putting leading questions, establish if he can, his entire defense. . . .

If a cross-examination is interrupted by an adjournment or a recess, it is improper for counsel to communicate directly or indirectly with the witness. Once the cross-examination of a witness has commenced, counsel should not converse with him until it is concluded,

---

182 *R. v. Fields, supra*, note 179. See also Chapter 2, II.E.4.(a).
183 *Ibid.*
184 [1917] 3 W.W.R. 139, 10 Sask. L.R. 343, 36 D.L.R. 76 (C.A.) citing *Phipson on Evidence*, 4th ed. (London: Stevens & Haynes, 1907), at 459.
185 *Coulson v. Disborough*, [1894] 2 Q.B. 316, 42 W.R. 449 (C.A.).
186 *Atkinson v. Smith* (1859), 9 N.B.R. 309.
187 (1914), 43 N.B.R. 126, at 151. Also see *Lamb v. Ward* (1860), 18 U.C.Q.B. 304 (C.A.); *Dickson v. Pinch* (1861), 11 U.C.C.P. 146 (C.A.).

unless leave is obtained.[188] It is questionable whether, in addition to being a rule of ethical conduct, this rule is one of evidence which can result in rejection of evidence. Breach of the rule may, however, affect the weight to be given to the evidence.

There are further restraints imposed on counsel in the cross-examination of witnesses, but these are better canvassed under the specific headings that follow.

B. Cross-Examination Where there are Multiple Parties

1. Civil Cases

Where a number of defendants have appeared and pleaded by the same lawyer and their defence is substantially the same, but they are represented at trial by separate counsel, only one counsel will be permitted to cross-examine the plaintiff's witnesses.[189] In cases where there are co-defendants with similar interests who have pleaded separately and are represented by different counsel, a trial judge has a discretion to refuse to allow counsel for one defendant to cross-examine a co-defendant's witnesses. If, however, the interests of the parties are not similar, separate counsel are usually allowed to cross-examine a co-defendant or that co-defendant's witnesses.[190] In *Losier v. Clement*,[191] a plaintiff brought an action against the driver of a vehicle in which she was a passenger, and another action against an unknown motorist. The plaintiff's allegation against the unknown motorist was that he had forced the vehicle in which she was a passenger off the road. The actions were consolidated and, at trial, counsel for the unknown motorist and for the host driver were permitted to cross-

---

188 Law Society of Upper Canada: Rules of Professional Conduct; J. Sopinka: *Trial of an Action, supra,* note 172, at 103-07; Orkin, M., *Legal Ethics* (Toronto: Cartwright, 1957), at 52-53; 3 *Halsbury's Laws of England,* 4th ed. (London: Butterworths, 1976), § 1186, at 653. Boulton, Sir W., *A Guide to Conduct and Etiquette at the Bar of England and Wales* (5th ed.) (London: Butterworths, 1975), at 12.

189 *Walker v. McMillan* (1882), 6 S.C.R. 241.

190 *Millar v. B.C. Rapid Transit Co.,* [1926] 1 W.W.R. 543, 36 B.C.R. 345, [1926] 1 D.L.R. 1171 (C.A.).

191 (1970), 3 N.B.R. (2d) 317, 18 D.L.R. (3d) 185 (C.A.).

examine each other's witnesses as if they were defendants adverse in interest even though no issue existed between them.[192]

If several counsel represent a number of defendants, each counsel will not be permitted in cross-examination to cover all of the ground which is common to co-defendants. The counsel who cross-examines first can probe into all issues at large, and if this cross-examination encompasses the whole field, another counsel with the same interest will not be allowed to go over it once again, but will be confined to new matters or issues which have a special bearing upon his or her client.[193] Similar considerations apply if more than one counsel represent one client.[194] As held in *Stewart v. Walker*,[195] the order in which parties in an action can cross-examine witnesses lies within the discretion of the trial judge.

2. Criminal Cases

In criminal cases the accused has a constitutional right to make full answer and defence. A pre-*Charter* case, *R. v. McLaughlin*,[196] held that an accused had an absolute right to cross-examine a co-accused whether the latter's evidence is favourable or unfavourable. The right extends to witnesses called by a co-accused. While the trial judge's discretion to control the cross-examination is much more limited than in criminal cases, it would seem that if the co-accused or a witness called by the co-accused has not given any adverse evidence against the accused, questions seeking to impugn the credibility of the witness could be ruled out.[197]

---

192 See also *Standard International Corp. v. Morgan*, [1967] 1 O.R. 328 (Master).
193 *Graydon v. Graydon* (1921), 51 O.L.R. 301, at 302-03, 67 D.L.R. 116. See also *Wingold v. W. B. Sullivan Const. Ltd.* (1980), 20 C.P.C. 76 (Ont. H.C.J.) where the general proposition was stated that unless the parties are adverse, there is no right to cross-examine.
194 *Omnia Pelts v. C.P. Airlines Ltd.* (1986), 57 O.R. (2d) 568, 15 C.P.C. (2d) 99 (H.C.J.).
195 (1903), 6 O.L.R. 495, at 506 (C.A.).
196 (1974), 15 C.C.C. (2d) 562, 25 C.R.N.S. 362, 2 O.R. (2d) 514 (C.A.).
197 See R. Cross and C. Tapper, *Cross on Evidence*, 7th ed. (London: Butterworths, 1990), at 304.

C. Cross-Examination on Documents Generally

Guidelines for cross-examining on documents were laid down by the House of Lords in 1820 in *Queen Caroline's Case*.[198] In that case, a witness who was called for the Crown was cross-examined as to the contents of a letter that she had allegedly written to her sister. Objection was taken by the Attorney-General to this line of cross-examination, and it was insisted that the letter had to be admitted into evidence before any use could be made of it by way of cross-examination. The court took the opportunity to consider the whole question of cross-examination on documents and laid down the principles that a witness could not be cross-examined on his or her own document, unless that document was first shown to him or and that the cross-examiner was obliged to tender it into evidence. The rule that the examiner must show the document to the witness before questioning him about its contents appears to have been erroneously derived from the best evidence rule, which required the production of the original document when it is tendered for the purpose of proving its contents.[199] It is apparent, however, that the document is not being tendered for this purpose at all. Counsel is putting it forth to discredit the witness in anticipation that the witness will deny the truth of the contents of the document. Moreover, the best evidence rule was established to ensure that the trier of fact had before him the most trustworthy and primary evidence possible. It was not created so that the witness would have the best possible proof of the contents of the document. The rule served as a great impediment to cross-examining counsel who could not lay an appropriate foundation for effective confrontation. Accordingly, Wigmore denounced it as a rule, "which for unsoundness of principle, impropriety of policy, and practical inconvenience in trials committed the most notable mistake that can be found among the rulings upon the present subject."[200] Requiring counsel to produce the document to the witness for his or her inspection prior to cross-examining him or her on it afforded the witness an opportunity to escape the grasp of contradiction. McCormick described it as follows:[201]

---

198 (1820), 2 Brod. & B. 284, 129 E.R. 976 (H.L.).
199 As to the current status of the best evidence rule, see Chapter 18, II.
200 4 Wigmore, *Evidence* (Chadbourn rev. 1972), § 1259, at 610.
201 E.W. Cleary (ed.), *McCormick on Evidence*, 2nd ed. (St. Paul: West Publishing, 1972), at 56.

Thus, in vain is the potential trap laid before the eyes of the bird. While reading the [document] . . . the witness will be warned by what he sees not to deny it and can quickly weave a new web of explanation.

Opposition to the rule grew in intensity until 1854 when Parliament abrogated it and enacted legislation providing that "a witness may be cross-examined as to previous statements made by him in writing or reduced to writing, relative to the subject matter of the cause, without such writing being shown to him . . ."[202] Similar provisions were incorporated in the *Canada Evidence Act*[203] and the provincial Evidence Acts.[204] If, however, the cross-examiner intends to use the document for the purposes of contradiction, compliance with other procedures must be followed and these are discussed in the next sub-chapter. Although the legislation dispensed with the necessity of showing the writing to the witness, it also implied that it need not be read to the witness either, nor produced subsequently unless counsel intended to contradict the witness.

The value of the legislation, referred to in the preceding paragraph, as an instrument of cross-examination, is substantial. While under the rule in *Queen Caroline's Case* ("*The Queen's Case*"), the witness is merely shown to have made a previous contradictory statement, under the present legislation, if the witness lies about making the statement or cannot remember having made it, the whole of the witness' evidence may be neutralized. The technique by which this may be done is illustrated in a number of cases collected by Wigmore.[205] These cases support the view that a witness may be asked generally whether he or she ever made a previous statement which contradicts his or her present testimony on the matter. The cross-examiner does not initially furnish any particulars as to time, place or the person to whom the previous statement was made. When the witness' denials have been firmly secured, he is then confronted with the statement. As a matter of fairness, and therefore effectiveness as well, some particulars of the previous statement would have to be given to the witness in a modern trial. Thus the witness might be asked: "Did you write the letter to the defendant in which, contrary

---

202 *Common Law Procedure Act* (1854), 17 & 18 Vict., c. 125, s. 24.
203 1985, c. C-5, ss. 10 and 11.
204 See, for example, the Ontario *Evidence Act*, R.S.O. 1980, c. 145, s. 21.
205 4 Wigmore, *Evidence* (Chadbourn revision 1972), § 1260.

to your present testimony, you stated that you had not witnessed the accident?" No further particulars need be given to the witness until an answer to the question is obtained. To require greater particularity to identify the statement would be to re-establish the rule in *The Queen's Case* which the legislation was designed to abolish.

The legislation which abrogated the rule in *The Queen's Case* relates only to the cross-examination of the author of the document. No mention is made about cross-examining a witness on a document that was written or prepared by another. It would appear that in such circumstances the principles enunciated in *The Queen's Case* must be adhered to.[206] Accordingly, if counsel wishes to cross-examine the witness upon such a document, counsel would first have to prove the other person's statement by proper means or undertake to prove it. Notwithstanding that the object of such questioning is merely to test the witness' credibility, and not to prove the truth of the contents of the document, the rule in *The Queen's Case* prohibits the use of such a document which has not been put into evidence or which counsel cannot undertake to prove in due course. In this context, the rule prevents any surreptitious attempt to adduce evidence of the contents of a written document without putting it in the document itself.

Where counsel cross-examines a witness on a document used by that witness to refresh his memory, he does not thereby make that document his evidence nor does it entitle the opposite party to put the document in as evidence, so long as the cross-examining counsel refers only to those parts of the document which were the subject of examination-in-chief.[207] If, however, counsel cross-examines the witness in relation to the whole of the document including matters beyond those discussed by the witness in-chief, different considerations may apply.[208]

D. *Impeachment of a Witness' Credibility*

1. Testing Testimonial Capabilities

The evidence of a witness is acceptable as general rule only if the witness perceived the fact about which he or she is testifying with his

---

206 See *Darby v. Ouseley* (1856), 1 H. & N. 1, 156 E.R. 1093; *R. v. Tower* (1880), 20 N.B.R. 168.

207 *Young v. Denton*, [1927] 1 W.W.R. 75, 21 Sask. L.R. 319, [1927] 1 D.L.R. 426 (C.A.).

208 But see the discussion this Chapter VI.D.2.

or her own senses. This requirement has been the basis of exclusionary rules such as those relating to hearsay and opinion.[209] Perception includes more than merely observing an event. A counsel cross-examining with respect to a witness' perception may inquire into the witness' powers of observation. A witness may be suffering from some physical or mental impairment that may have diminished his ability to observe accurately. Similarly, environmental conditions such as a dark night, or the placement of tangible obstacles, may also affect the witness' visual acuity. Moreover, a cross-examiner can attempt to demonstrate, through questioning, that the witness was not really physically in a position to observe the event. All questions directed toward showing that the witness lacked the opportunity to observe the event, or that his observations were less acute than they might have been, are clearly proper in cross-examination. The vagaries of perception extend beyond a witness' capacity and opportunity to observe, for individuals may interpret the same event differently. Accordingly, the accuracy of a witness' interpretation of an event that he perceived is properly the subject matter of cross-examination as well.

A witness' memory or ability to recall an event may be tested by cross-examination. The time lag between the event and the testimony may be tested by cross-examination. The time lag between the event and its recounting by the witness may result in a distortion in the recollection of the event. Furthermore, the witness may have been susceptible to other influences which permitted his mental reconstruction of the event to be altered. Therefore, a cross-examiner is free to probe the stresses and other factors which may have had some impact upon the accuracy of the witness' impression.

Another factor which could affect the trustworthiness of the testimony is the witness' articulation of the events in the witness box. Testimonial narration results from translation of impressions into language. In relating what he or she saw, the witness may be confusing inference with actual fact. In addition, distortion may arise if the witness uses a word improperly or otherwise conveys thoughts inaccurately.

---

209   See Chapters 6 and 11.

All human testimony is subject to these frailties and thus, cross-examination can be most instrumental in bringing them to light so that the proper weight may be given to the evidence. The following statement by Morgan is apt:[210]

> The judicial device for exposing these weaknesses is cross-examination. Its most dramatic quality is its power to detect wilfully false testimony, but more valuable is its capacity for bringing to light errors of perception, defects of memory and deficiencies of narration. It requires no extended trial experience to demonstrate that for every perjurer there are scores of honest witnesses whose direct examination produces the effect of falsehood because its subject-matter was incorrectly or incompletely observed or inaccurately remembered or inadequately narrated. It might, then, be argued that in a judicial investigation no testimony should be received which is not tested in the fire of cross-examination.

Apart from the subconscious errors attributable to the human condition, an effective cross-examination may also expose bias, detect falsehood, and generally reveal the witness's mental and moral condition and whether his or her evidence is tainted by enmity towards a party to the litigation.[211]

2. Previous Inconsistent Statements

The most common method of impeaching the credit of an opponent's witness is that of self-contradiction by means of a prior inconsistent statement written or uttered by the witness. The prior statement may take one of many forms. It may be a statement given by a party under oath, in examination for discovery, or in an earlier trial, or in an affidavit; it may have been unsworn, as for example, a statement given by a witness to an investigator, it may be a statement made orally, or written in correspondence by the witness to another. The authority under, and method by which a witness' credibility may be impeached by a prior inconsistent statement is prescribed by

---

210 E.M. Morgan, "The Relation Between Hearsay and Preserved Memory" (1927), 40 Harv. L. Rev. 712.
211 See the remarks of E.F.B. Johnston, K.C. in "The Art of Cross-Examination", [1936] 2 D.L.R. 673.

legislation. Section 20 of the Ontario *Evidence Act,* and s. 10 of the *Canada Evidence Act* deal with situations where the prior statement is written,[212] whereas s. 21 of the Ontario *Evidence Act* and s. 11 of the *Canada Evidence Act* deal with prior inconsistent statements made orally.[213] Although a counsel embarking upon the cross-examination of a witness need not at the outset reveal the document containing the contradictory statement, counsel must, prior to introducing the statement for the purpose of contradicting the witness, call the witness' attention to the contradicting parts of the document. Even at this stage, the statement need not be shown to the witness unless the trial judge, who may require its production for his or her own inspection, requires that the statement be shown to the witness. A witness can also be cross-examined as to the making of a prior inconsistent oral statement.[214] If the witness denies making it, then proof can be given that it was in fact made; but, before evidence thereof can be led, counsel must sufficiently relate to the witness the circumstances surrounding the making of the statement, and the witness must be expressly asked whether or not he or she did make the statement.

A special species of previous statement is the transcript of an examination for discovery. In civil cases, Rules of Court generally permit questions and answers to be read by a party adverse in interest as an admission.[215] When used as previous inconsistent statements to impeach the credibility of a party, it would appear that the statutory requirements must be complied with. Accordingly, if a party testifies, the opposite party is obliged to put the relevant passages from the examination for discovery to the party-witness.[216]

---

212   Similar provisions in other provincial Evidence Acts: Alta, R.S.A. 1980, c. A-21, s. 23; B.C., R.S.B.C. 1979, c. 116, s. 13; Man., R.S.M. 1987, c. E-150, s. 20; N.B., R.S.N.B. 1973, c. E-11, s. 19; Nfld., R.S. Nfld. 1970, c. 115, s. 10; N.S., R.S.N.S. 1989, c. 154, s. 55; P.E.I., R.S.P.E.I. 1989, c. E-11, s. 17; Sask., R.S.S. 1978, c. B-16, s. 40.

213   Similar provisions in other provincial Evidence Acts: Alta., *ibid.,* s. 24; B.C., *ibid.,* s. 14; Man. *ibid.,* s. 21; N.B. *ibid.,* s. 18; Nfld. *ibid.,* s. 9; N.S. *ibid.,* s. 57; P.E.I., *ibid.,* s. 16; Sask. *ibid.,* s. 39.

214   *Canada Evidence Act,* s. 11.

215   See Ontario Rules of Practice, O. Reg. 560/84, r. 31.11.

216   It is submitted that rules applied by some trial judges which required this to be done irrespective of the purpose of the use of the discovery, went too far. See *Sterling Trusts Corp. v. Postma,* [1965] S.C.R. 324, at 346, 48 D.L.R. (2d) 423; also see Williston and Rolls, *The Law of Civil Procedure* (Toronto: Butterworths, 1970), Vol. 2, at 884-87.

Certain restrictions circumscribe the independent proof of prior inconsistent statements for cross-examination purposes. It is clear that before the statement can be proved it must be inconsistent. This is a restriction that also applies before counsel embarks on any cross-examination on a previous statement as counsel has no greater right to introduce inadmissible previous consistent statements in cross-examination than exist for examination in-chief. If lack of inconsistency is obvious, cross-examination on the statement ought not to proceed. At the outset, however, the presence or absence of inconsistency may not be clear, and counsel may examine the witness in order to lay a foundation from which to demonstrate inconsistency.

McCormick states that the test of "inconsistent" should be:[217]

> . . . could the jury find that a witness who believed the truth of the facts testified to would have been unlikely to make a prior statement of this tenor?

Some courts have adopted a liberal interpretation of "inconsistent" and applied the section when, for example, the witness admitted the statement "in a slightly different form".[218] Certainly this would appear to comply with the meaning of the phrase "Where a witness . . . does not distinctly admit that he did make the statement" in s. 11 of the *Canada Evidence Act.* The policy underlying the section appears to be that the statement should generally be permitted to be proved when such proof would aid the trier of fact to assess credibility and would not cause undue prejudice to the witness or calling party.[219] When a prior inconsistent statement is independently proved, this should be done during the cross-examining party's case.[220]

The admissibility of previous inconsistent statements is governed, to some degree, by the traditional collateral fact rule which limits the adducement of extrinsic evidence by way of rebuttal to an answer given by a witness in cross-examination to matters which are

---

217 E.W. Cleary (ed.), *McCormick on Evidence*, 3rd ed. (St. Paul: West Publishing, 1984), at 75.
218 See *R. v. Moore* (1980), 36 N.S.R. (2d) 228. This contrasts with the very narrow interpretation of "inconsistent" in s. 9: *R. v. Cassibo* (1982), 70 C.C.C. (2d) 498, 39 O.R. (2d) 288 (C.A.).
219 A.W. Bryant, "The Adversary's Witness: Cross-Examination and Proof of Prior Inconsistent Statements" (1984), 62 Can. Bar Rev. 43.
220 *Ibid.*; J. Sopinka, *The Trial of an Action* (Toronto: Butterworths, 1981).

relevant only to the substantive issues in the case. Consequently, a previous contradictory statement, the making of which has been denied by the witness in cross-examination, will be admitted only if it relates to matters of substance and not to collateral issues. If it relates to the latter, the cross-examiner must accept the witness' statement as final and is precluded from adducing the contradictory statement in evidence. Sections 21 and 22 of the Ontario *Evidence Act* specifically incorporate this restriction for they provide that the statements must be "relative to the subject matter in question." Sections 10 and 11 of the *Canada Evidence Act* use the phrase "relative to the subject matter of the case". Accordingly, prior oral or written statements made by a witness relating to collateral matters cannot be proved under these provisions.[221]

When a prior inconsistent statement is proved after the witness has denied making it, it has only limited evidential value. Unless the witness concedes the truth of the contents of the previous statement, it does not become evidence of the truth of the facts contained therein.[222] Its only purpose is to impair the witness' credibility and thereby may have the effect of neutralizing the witness' testimony.[223] It only goes to show that the witness is not one who should be believed. The reasons advanced for and against the preservation of this rule are the same as in the case of a previous inconsistent statement that is proved on the examination of a party's own witness.[224] Given the fact that the inconsistent statement is admissible only as evidence of the witness' lack of credibility, the judge or jury are not obliged to disregard all of the witness' testimony because of the contradiction, but they may give whatever weight to the evidence that they feel is appropriate in light of the contradiction.[225]

---

221 See I. Levinter, "Cross-Examination on Previous Contradictory Statements" (1955), *Special Lectures of the Law Society of Upper Canada on Evidence*, at 47, 48.
222 *R. v. Deacon*, [1947] S.C.R. 531, 89 C.C.C. 1, 3 C.R. 265, [1947] 3 D.L.R. 772; *R. v. Deacon (No. 2)* (1948), 91 C.C.C. 1, 5 C.R. 356, [1948] 1 W.W.R. 705, [1948] 3 D.L.R. 93, 56 Man. R. 1 (C.A.); *Royal Bank v. Sullivan*, [1957] O.W.N. 520, 10 D.L.R. (2d) 494.
223 *Zwicker v. Young* (1929), 60 N.S.R. 233, [1929] 1 D.L.R. 62 (C.A.); *Ontario Gravel Freighting Co. v. Mathews SS. Co.*, [1927] 2 S.C.R. 92, [1927] 1 D.L.R. 1045.
224 See this Chapter, V.C.
225 *Weston v. Middlesex (County)* (1913), 30 O.L.R. 21, 16 D.L.R. 325; affd. (1914), 31 O.L.R. 148, 19 D.L.R. 646 (C.A.); *Stenhouse v. Wright*, [1950] 2

When counsel has cross-examined on a previous inconsistent statement, or a statement which was used by the witness to refresh memory, questions arise as to whether the statement should be entered as an exhibit if it was not so entered during the examination-in-chief. If the cross-examination merely extends the memory refreshing by reference to other parts of the document, the same rules should apply as in the case of examination-in-chief. Only such portions of past recollection recorded adopted by the witness become evidence.[226] If, however, the witness' evidence is impeached or sought to be impeached by a statement or parts of a statement not dealt with in-chief, two questions arise: i) should the document be made an exhibit; and ii) if it is, to what extent is it evidence of the truth of the contents?

With respect to the first question, the trial judge has a discretion codified in s. 10 of the *Canada Evidence Act* to "make such use of [the document] for the purposes of the trial as he sees fit."[227] This discretion should be exercised to admit portions of the document if the presence of these portions in the record is necessary to fully appreciate the evidence of the witness or if they are otherwise relevant.[228] In exercising this discretion the trial judge should not introduce the document as an exhibit if the prejudice to the accused will overbear the usefulness of the exhibit. While the whole statement need not go in as a general rule, those parts admitted to be true or proved will be entered as an exhibit. In addition, other parts which explain or throw light on the witness' evidence may be admitted. Thus, where, for instance, it is suggested that inconsistency arises because the witness failed to raise a particular matter when making the previous statement, the jury may need to examine the entire previous statement in order to assess this ground of impeachment.[229]

With respect to the second question, the fact that the statement is introduced as an exhibit does not make it evidence of the facts contained therein.[230] Whether it is evidence will depend on other rules

---

W.W.R. 481 (Man. K.B.).

226 See this Chapter, V.D.

227 Note that no such discretion exists in s. 9 of the *Canada Evidence Act*, R.S.C. 1985, c. C-5.

228 *R. v. Rodney* (1988), 46 C.C.C. (3d) 323, 33 B.C.L.R. (2d) 280 (B.C.C.A.); *R. v. Rowbotham* (1988), 41 C.C.C. (3d) 1 (Ont. C.A.).

229 *R. v. Newall* (1983), 9 C.C.C. (3d) 519, 5 D.L.R. (4th) 352, [1984] 2 W.W.R. 131 (B.C.C.A.).

230 *R. v. Deacon, supra*, note 222.

of admissibility as, for example, whether the witness admitted the facts in the statement, or adopted the statement as past recollection recorded, or whether it remains simply a previous inconsistent statement relevant only to credibility.

3. Prior Convictions

A rather odd method of impeaching the credibility of a witness, which unfortunately has lingered on in this jurisdiction, is the right of counsel to cross-examine a witness with respect to any previous conviction. The rationale for this mode of impeachment is based on the presumption that a person who has been convicted of a crime is of more doubtful veracity than one who possesses no criminal record. Statutory authorization is given to this form of impeachment in the various provincial Evidence Acts. For example, s. 22(1) of the Ontario *Evidence Act* provides as follows:[231]

> A witness may be asked whether he has been convicted of any crime, and upon being so asked, if he either denies the fact or refuses to answer, the conviction may be proved.

The *Canada Evidence Act* contains a similar provision except that the word "offence" is substituted for the word "crime". Considerable controversy has surrounded the operation of, and even more basically, the justification for these impeaching provisions.

What types of convictions may form the subject matter of cross-examination? Clearly all convictions under the *Criminal Code* and related statutes are included. The matter is less clear with respect to provincial offences. In *Street v. Guelph (City)*[232] the court held that the Ontario provision does not permit counsel to cross-examine a witness as to an offence under the *Highway Traffic Act* or the *Liquor Control Act*. Grant J. stated:[233]

> I am guided in my decision herein by the fact that the commission of an offence under the *Highway Traffic Act* usually carries with it no particular moral turpitude while an offence

---

231 R.S.O. 1980, c. 145. Similar provisions in other provincial Evidence Acts, *supra*, note 49: Alta., s. 25(2); B.C. s. 15(1); Man., s. 22(1); N.B., s. 20(1); Nfld., s. 11; N.S., s. 55; P.E.I., s. 18; Sask., s. 41 [am. 1979-80, c. 92, s. 86].
232 [1965] 2 C.C.C. 215, [1964] 2 O.R. 421, 45 D.L.R. (2d) 652.
233 *Ibid.*, at 653 (D.L.R.).

under the *Criminal Code* usually does, and the perpetration of the latter is of assistance in determining credibility . . .

But, is that necessarily true of all provincial offences? For example are not convictions for making false statements contrary to the provisions of the *Securities Act*,[234] matters of moral turpitude? By the same token, it is apparent that not all crimes under the *Criminal Code* reflect upon the dishonesty or lack of truthfulness of the witness.[235] On the question as to whether a counsel can cross-examine a witness with respect to his or her previous convictions for provincial offences generally, it is interesting to note that some Canadian courts have taken a different view than Grant J. In *Clarke v. Holdsworth*,[236] a British Columbia court held that a provision of its provincial *Evidence Act*, identical in wording to the Ontario section, permitted the questioning of a witness with regard to a prior conviction for an offence against a provincial statute. The Supreme Court of Canada in *Telford v. Secord*[237] which was decided much earlier than the *Street* case, insinuated in *obiter dicta* that convictions for offences under the *Highway Traffic Act* might fall within the purview of s. 23 of the Ontario *Evidence Act*. Much more recently, commenting on the above quoted statement in the *Street* case, Lacourcière J.A. said:[238]

> . . . I do not wish to be taken as adopting the passage as a correct statement of the law. The statement may be too broad in that certain provincial offences may reflect upon the dishonesty or lack of truthfulness of a witness while certain crimes under the *Criminal Code* may not have that effect.

Should not cross-examination on convictions or offences be limited to only those involving characteristics of moral turpitude? Dean Wright was of the opinion that only convictions which intimated a propensity to lie, such as perjury or false pretenses, were relevant.[239] The American Revised Uniform Rules of Evidence limit

---

234 For example, R.S.O. 1980, c. 466, s. 118(1) [am. 1987, c. 7, s. 10(1)].
235 See the remarks of O Hearn Co. Ct. J. in *Levin v. Willis* (1969), 9 D.L.R. (3d) 536 (N.S. Co. Ct.), at 540.
236 (1967), 62 W.W.R. 1.
237 [1947] S.C.R. 277, [1947] 2 D.L.R. 474.
238 *Deep v. Wood* (1983), 33 C.P.C. 256, 143 D.L.R. (3d) 246, at 249 (Ont. C.A.).
239 C.A. Wright, "Case Comment" (1940), 18 Can. Bar Rev. 808.

the admissibility of criminal convictions for the purpose of impairing credibility to those involving dishonest or false statements.[240] The Federal Rules of Evidence adopted this provision, but added thereto evidence of convictions for crimes punishable by death or imprisonment in excess of one year, following the tradition that permitted use of felonies generally without regard to the nature of the offence.[241] The Federal Rules have also incorporated a time limitation, precluding the use of a conviction for impeachment purposes if a time period of more than ten years has elapsed since the date of the witness' release from imprisonment or the expiration of his parole, probation, or sentence, whichever is the later date.[242]

Although no jurisdiction, as yet, appears to have abolished entirely the right to utilize previous convictions for cross-examination purposes, serious doubt as to its value has arisen. The principle that a person with a criminal record is deserving of a standard of belief less than one with no criminal record cannot be accepted as a general principle. Cross-examination on previous convictions should not, however, be prohibited in cases in which the previous conviction is relevant, either to an issue or to credibility. This result may now be achieved, at least in cross-examination of the accused in cases governed by s. 12 of the *Canada Evidence Act* by reason of the decision of the Supreme Court of Canada in *R. v. Corbett*.[243]

E. Witness Tendered for Cross-Examination

A party may call a witness to the stand and, without asking any questions in-chief, make the witness available for cross-examination. This may be done to avoid the court drawing an adverse inference from the failure of the party to call a witness who is presumed to possess relevant information. Although such a witness can then be subjected to cross-examination on the substantive issues, the witness cannot be attacked on his or her credit on the ground that, because he or she has given no testimony, his or her credibility is not in issue.[244]

---

240 The Uniform Rules of Evidence, r. 21.
241 The Federal Rules of Evidence (1974), r. 609(a).
242 *Ibid.*, r. 609(b).
243 [1988] 1 S.C.R. 670, 41 C.C.C. (3d) 385, 64 C.R. (3d) 1, [1988] 4 W.W.R. 481, 28 B.C.L.R. (2d) 145. This case is discussed more fully in Chapter 10, III.B.1.(b).(x).
244 *Bracegirdle v. Bailey* (1859), 1 F. & F. 536, 175 E.R. 842.

F. *The Rule in* Browne v. Dunn

It appears that if the cross-examiner intends to impeach the credibility of a witness by means of extrinsic evidence, he must give that witness notice of his intention. This was the rule laid down in *Browne v. Dunn* in which Lord Herschell explained the reason for it as follows:[245]

> Now, my Lords, I cannot help saying that it seems to me to be absolutely essential to the proper conduct of a cause, where it is intended to suggest that a witness is not speaking the truth on a particular point, to direct his attention to the fact by some questions put in cross-examination showing that that imputation is intended to be made, and not to take his evidence and pass it by as a matter altogether unchallenged, and then, when it is impossible for him to explain, as perhaps he might have been able to do if such questions had been put to him, the circumstances which it is suggested indicate that the story he tells ought not to be believed, to argue that he is a witness unworthy of credit. My Lords, I have always understood that if you intend to impeach a witness you are bound, whilst he is in the box, to give him an opportunity of making any explanation which is open to him; and, as it seems to me, that is not only a rule of professional practice in the conduct of a case, but is essential to fair play and fair dealing with witnesses. Sometimes reflections have been made upon excessive cross-examination of witnesses, and it has been complained of as undue; but it seems to me that a cross-examination of a witness which errs in the direction of excess may be far more fair to him than to leave him without cross-examination, and afterwards to suggest that he is not a witness of truth, I mean upon a point on which it is not otherwise perfectly clear that he has had full notice beforehand that there is an intention to impeach the credibility of the story which he is telling.

Accordingly, if counsel is considering the impeachment of the credibility of a witness by calling independent evidence, the witness must be confronted with this evidence in cross-examination while he or she is still in the witness-box.[246]

---

245 (1893), 6 R. 67 (H.L.), at 70-71.
246 See also *Peters v. Perras* (1909), 42 S.C.R. 244, 13 Alta. L.R. 80; *New Hamburg Mfg. Co. v. Webb* (1911), 23 O.L.R. 44 (C.A.); *United Cigar Stores Ltd.*

The rule applies not only to contradictory evidence but to closing argument as well. In *Browne v. Dunn* Lord Halsbury added:[247]

To my mind nothing would be more absolutely unjust than not to cross-examine witnesses upon evidence which they have given, so as to give them notice, and to give them an opportunity of explanation, and an opportunity very often to defend their own character, and, not having given them such an opportunity, to ask the jury afterwards to disbelieve what they have said, although not one question has been directed either to their credit or to the accuracy of the facts they have deposed to.

Accordingly, there has been some suggestion that a presumption of truth attaches to the testimony of a witness not subjected to cross-examination.[248] It is questionable, however, whether the principle in *Browne v. Dunn* can extend that far, particularly in cases where the evidence which has not been cross-examined upon is inconsistent with other evidence. In *R. v. Mete*, Bull J.A. rejected this proposition:[249]

In default of authority binding on me . . . I can see no reason or logic in any view that a judge may not reject evidence which he disbelieves merely because it has not been cross-examined upon. The usefulness of cross-examination in like circumstances has been a subject of comment in a civil case by Lord Halsbury, the

v. Buller, [1931] 2 D.L.R. 144, 66 O.L.R. 593 (C.A.); *Union Carbide Canada Ltd. v. Trans-Canadian Feeds Ltd.* (1966), 32 Fox Pat. C. 17, 49 C.P.R. 7 (Ex. Ct.); *Stewart v. Royal Bank*, [1930] 2 D.L.R. 617, at 623; revd. on other grounds, [1930] S.C.R. 544, [1930] 4 D.L.R. 694; *R. v. Hawke* (1974), 16 C.C.C. (2d) 438, 3 O.R. (2d) 210, at 225; revd. on other grounds 22 C.C.C. (2d) 19, 29 C.R.N.S. 1, 7 O.R. (2d) 145.

247 *Supra*, note 245, at 76-77.

248 *R. v. Dyck* (1969), 8 C.R.N.S. 191, [1970] 2 C.C.C. 283, 70 W.W.R. 449 (B.C.C.A.); *Peters v. Perras*, *supra*, note 246; *R. v. Hart* (1932), 23 Cr. App. Rep. 202; *Jarvis v. Connell* (1918-19), 44 O.L.R. 264, at 267; *Jarvis v. Hall* (1912), 4 O.W.N. 232, at 235, 8 D.L.R. 412, 23 O.W.R. 282 (C.A.); *Horner v. Canadian Northern Ry.*, [1920] 3 W.W.R. 909 (but see the remarks of Stuart J. at 929), 55 D.L.R. 340; affd. without reference to this point, 61 S.C.R. 547, 58 D.L.R. 154, [1921] 1 W.W.R. 969; *Seymour v. Arrowsmith*, [1931] 3 W.W.R. 561, at 563, 567 (Sask. C.A.); *R. v. Bedere* (1891), 21 O.R. 189 (C.A.), at 192; *R. v. Hawke*, *supra*, note 246, at 225-26.

249 (1973), 22 C.R.N.S. 387, [1973] 3 W.W.R. 709, at 712.

Lord Chancellor, in *Aaron's Reefs Ltd. v. Twiss*, [1896] A.C. 273, an outstanding authority which has been long followed, in which the Lord Chancellor had these very pithy comments to make in dealing generally with this subject. At pp. 282-3 he said:

> Some comment has been made upon the absence of cross-examination on the subject. I should have thought for myself that it would have been very rash for those who had no means of contradicting anything that was said to cross-examine persons who had, by the hypothesis, not many scruples as to what they might say, and that it was far wiser (it seems to have been successful) to leave the statements which they chose to make to be judged of by the jury.

As I say, that was stated in a civil case and it may perhaps have not too much direct bearing on this case; but the thought that the Lord Chancellor enunciated, to my mind, is apt. I just add that I find it hard to think that, if this were a jury case, a judge charging a jury would have to direct the jury that, although they disbelieved the evidence of an un-cross-examined witness, they must accept that evidence notwithstanding and acquit the accused.

The rule is one designed to accord fairness to witnesses and to the parties. It is, therefore, not absolute, and the extent and manner of its application will be determined by the trial judge in all the circumstances of the case.[250] The factors which may be taken into account include:[251]

(1) notice beforehand to the witness that her credibility is in issue;

(2) the testimony is of such a nature that it is obvious that credibility is in issue;

(3) failure to cross-examine is based on concern for the witness as in the case of children of tender years.

---

250 *Palmer v. R.*, [1980] 1 S.C.R. 759, 50 C.C.C. 193, at 210, 14 C.R. (3d) 22, 17 C.R. (3d) 34, 106 D.L.R. (3d) 212, 30 N.R. 181.
251 M.N. Howard, P. Crane, and D.A. Hochberg, *Phipson on Evidence*, 14th ed. (London: Sweet & Maxwell, 1990), § 12-13.

If the trial judge's discretion is exercised to enforce the rule, it would follow, logically, that it be applied throughout the adjudicative process. Credibility should therefore not be subject to attack by evidence or argument. Furthermore, the trier of fact should not consider credibility as a factor. To do so would be to decide a matter in the absence of an explanation of the matter by evidence and argument.

VII RE-EXAMINATION

The purpose of re-examination is to enable the witness to explain and clarify relevant testimony which may have been weakened or obscured in cross-examination. The witness is not ordinarily allowed to supplement the examination-in-chief by introducing new facts which were not covered in cross-examination.[252] The general rule is that re-examination must be confined to matters which arose out of cross-examination.[253] The right to re-examine, however, extends to rehabilitation of the credibility of the witness which may have been impaired in cross-examination. This includes the right to ask the witness to explain or clarify discrepancies between the witness' evidence-in-chief and in cross-examination.[254] In addition, this may entail the introduction of a previous consistent statement to rebut the suggestion that the witness' evidence was a recent contrivance.[255]

In addition to the right to re-examine, the trial judge has a discretion to permit re-examination in circumstances that do not accord with the principles stated above. It is a discretion that is to be exercised sparingly but extends to permit re-examination on matters not touched on in cross-examination which may, through oversight, have been omitted in chief. In such cases, the opposing party will have a further right to cross-examine the witness.[256] As with examination-in-chief, leading questions may not be posed.[257] Inadmissible evidence which was improperly elicited in cross-examination may be the subject of re-examination, for, if a party is initially prejudiced by the intro-

---

252 *Doe d. Wetmore v. Bell* (1890), 30 N.B.R. 83 (C.A.), at 89.
253 *Prince v. Samo* (1838), 7 Ad. & El. 627, 3 Nev. & P.K.B. 139.
254 *The Federal/Provincial Task Force on Uniform Rules of Evidence* (Toronto: Carswell, 1982), para. 21.10, at 272.
255 *R. v. Wannebo* (1972), 7 C.C.C. (2d) 266, [1972] 5 W.W.R. 372 (B.C.C.A.).
256 6 Wigmore, *Evidence* (Chadbourn rev. 1976), § 1899.
257 *Ireland v. Taylor*, [1949] 1 K.B. 300, at 313, [1948] 2 All E.R. 450.

duction of such evidence in cross-examination, the party should have an opportunity to qualify or explain it.[258]

VIII REPLY EVIDENCE

There are important restraints on the right of a party to call evidence to rebut the testimony of a previous witness. The primary restrictions are:

(1) the limits of permissible reply evidence;

(2) effect of the failure to cross-examine; and,

(3) the collateral fact rule.

A. *Limits on Reply Evidence*

At the close of the defendant's case, the plaintiff or Crown has a right to adduce rebuttal evidence to contradict or qualify new facts or issues raised in defence.[259] The general rule in civil cases is that matters which might properly be considered to form part of the plaintiff's case in chief are to be excluded.[260] As for criminal cases, Martin J.A. said in *R. v. Campbell*:[261]

> The general rule with respect to the order of proof is that the prosecution must introduce all the evidence in its possession upon which it relies as probative of guilt, before closing its case.

Two very practical rationales for this rule were articulated by Wigmore:[262]

---

258 *R. v. Noel* (1903), 7 C.C.C. 309, 6 O.L.R. 385 (C.A.); *Blewett v. Tregonning* (1835), 3 Ad. & El. 554, [1835-42] All E.R. Rep. 83.

259 6 Wigmore, *Evidence* (Chadbourn rev. 1976), § 1873 at 672.

260 The rule "will exclude *all evidence which has not been made necessary by the opponent's case in reply*": 6 Wigmore, *Evidence* (Chadbourn rev. 1976), § 1873.

261 (1977), 38 C.C.C. (2d) 6, at 26, 1 C.R. (3d) S-49, 1 C.R. (3d) 309, 17 O.R. (2d) 673.

262 6 Wigmore, *Evidence* (Chadbourn rev. 1976), § 1873, at 672.

... first, the possible unfairness of an opponent who has unjustly supposed that the case in chief was the entire case which he had to meet, and, second, the interminable confusion that would be created by an unending alternation of successive fragments of each case which could have been put in at once in the beginning.

Martin J.A. articulated slightly different purposes in *Campbell* relevant to criminal trials:[263]

The rule prevents the accused being taken by surprise, and being deprived of an adequate opportunity to make proper investigation with respect to the evidence adduced against him. The rule also provides a safeguard against the importance of a piece of evidence, by reason of its late introduction, being unduly emphasized or magnified in relation to the other evidence.

The Ontario Court of Appeal held in *Allcock, Laight & Westwood Ltd. v. Patten*,[264] that the trial judge had erred in permitting the plaintiff to adduce evidence, ostensibly as rebuttal, when the evidence was in effect confirmatory only of the plaintiff's case. Shroeder J.A., noting with approval an earlier decision of the Court of Appeal, *R. v. Michael*,[265] stated:[266]

It is well settled that where there is a single issue only to be tried, the party beginning must exhaust his evidence in the first instance and may not split his case by relying on *prima facie* proof, and when this has been shaken by his adversary, adducing confirmatory evidence: *Jacobs v. Tarleton* (1848), 11 Q.B. 421, 116 E.R. 534. ... The rule is now so well settled that it requires no further elaboration. It is important in the trial of actions, whether before a jury or a Judge alone, that this rule should be observed. A defendant is entitled to know the case which he has to meet when he presents his defence and it is not open to a plaintiff under the guise of replying to reconfirm the case which he was

---

263 *Supra*, note 261, at 26 (C.C.C.).
264 [1967] 1 O.R. 18 (C.A.).
265 (1954), 110 C.C.C. 30, 20 C.R. 18, [1954] O.R. 926 (C.A.).
266 [1967] 1 O.R. 18, at 21. See also *B.F. Goodrich Canada Ltd. v. Mann's Garage Ltd.* (1959), 21 D.L.R. (2d) 33.

required to make out in the first instance or take the risk of non-persuasion.

Should reply evidence be excluded if the point in respect of which contradictory evidence is sought to be adduced in reply arose in cross-examination of the other parties' witnesses rather than their evidence-in-chief? In *Mersey Paper Co. v. Queens (County)*,[267] the Nova Scotia Court of Appeal considered this to be an unjustifiable technical distinction. It is submitted that, at least in civil cases, it would depend on whether the matter was part of the plaintiff's case and one which might have been adduced in the plaintiff's case in-chief. A plaintiff cannot leave part of its case until cross-examination of the defendant's witnesses and then when that goes badly make up for it in reply. In criminal cases the question must be resolved by determining whether the matter was in the possession of the Crown and is relied on as probative of guilt.

Although the authorities are not entirely clear on this point, the better view is that reply evidence that conforms with the principles stated above can be adduced as of right. There is, however, a discretionary power vested in the trial judge to admit such evidence, notwithstanding that it may not be the proper subject of reply.[268]

A widely accepted formulation of the extent of the discretion in criminal cases was made in *R. v. Coombs*,[269] where Robertson J.A. said:

> From these authorities and others I think that it is clear that the Judge in each case has a discretion with regard to the admission of evidence in rebuttal and that in exercising his discretion he should not generally allow such evidence to be given when it has before or during the presentation of the Crown's case been both within the possession of the Crown and clearly relevant to the issue.

---

267 (1959), 18 D.L.R. (2d) 19, 42 M.P.R. 397.
268 *B.F. Goodrich Canada Ltd. v. Mann's Garage Ltd., supra*, note 266; *Devlin v. Crocker* (1850), 7 U.C.Q.B. 398 (C.A.); *R. v. Markadonis*, [1935] S.C.R. 657, 64 C.C.C. 41, [1935] 2 D.L.R. 105, at 112; *R. v. Parkin* (1922), 37 C.C.C. 35, 66 D.L.R. 175, at 201, [1922] 1 W.W.R. 732 (C.A.); *Williams v. Davies* (1833), 1 Cr. & M. 464, 149 E.R. 481; *Neary v. Fowler* (1869), 7 N.S.R. 495 (C.A.); *R. v. Crippen*, [1911] 1 K.B. 149, [1908-10] All E.R. Rep. 390 (C.C.A.); *R. v. Briden* (1960), 127 C.C.C. 154, 33 C.R. 159, [1960] O.R. 362 (C.A.), at 365.
269 (1977), 35 C.C.C. (2d) 85, at 92, 2 B.C.L.R. 1 (C.A.).

Appellate review adjusting the parameters of the trial judge's discretion has been quite vigourous. At one time the rule was very restrictive. The Crown had to adduce all evidence-in-chief unless the matter arose *ex improviso*, and could not have been foreseen.[270] However, it has been pointed out that *ex improviso* simply means "unexpectedly" or "suddenly", and that the phrase "no human ingenuity could foresee" is not to be found in the report of the case often cited in support of the rule.[271] On occasion, the rule became more flexible, and evidence which tended to link the accused with the crime could be admitted subject to the proviso that the prosecution must not have acted unfairly.[272] Now, it is clear that the courts are willing to apply a somewhat more restrictive test which balances relevance and prejudice.[273] The exercise of the discretion is very much a function of the issues and facts of the particular case. It is preferable, therefore, not to attempt to lay down precise rules with respect to its exercise. It will be exercised more sparingly in criminal cases because of the importance of avoiding prejudice to the accused. In civil cases the discretion is wider and should be exercised in light of the broad principles which are the basis for the restriction on reply evidence. These principles are designed to ensure that the defendant knows the case to be met and that the plaintiff not be permitted to split his or her case. The rationale for the latter principle is that trials should not be unduly prolonged by creating a need for surrebuttal.[274] Within these broad parameters the trial judge has a discretion to permit reply evidence when it is the reasonable and proper course to follow.[275]

B. *The Collateral Fact Rule*

There is a general rule that answers given by a witness to questions put to him or her on cross-examination concerning collateral facts are treated as final, and cannot be contradicted by extrinsic evidence. Without such a rule, there is the danger that litigation will otherwise be prolonged and become sidetracked and involved in

---

270 *R. v. Frost* (1840), 9 Car. & P. 129, [1835-42] All E.R. Rep. 106.

271 *Shaw v. R.* (1952), 85 C.L.R. 365, at 379.

272 *R. v. Crippen, supra,* note 268.

273 *R. v. Perry* (1977), 36 C.C.C. (2d) 209 (Ont. C.A.); *R. v. Levy* (1966), 50 Cr. App. R. 198 (C.C.A.).

274 *Erco Industries Ltd. v. Allendale Mutual Insurance Co.* (1987), 62 O.R. (2d) 766, at 772-74, 25 O.A.C. 130, 29 C.C.L.I. 4.

275 *Mersey Paper Co. v. Queens (County), supra,* note 267.

numerous subsidiary issues. The rule does permit the use of extrinsic evidence to contradict a witness who has made a statement in cross-examination which is relevant to the substantive issue; but, with respect to questions which are directed solely to impeaching a witness' credibility, the answers must, save for certain common law and statutory exceptions, be accepted as final.[276] Difficulties have arisen, however, because of uncertainty as to whether a question merely goes to a collateral issue or whether it goes to a substantive one. Pollock C.B. attempted to articulate the distinction in *A.G. v. Hitchcock*,[277] as follows:

> ... the test, whether the matter is collateral or not, is this: if the answer of a witness is a matter which you would be allowed on your part to prove in evidence — if it have such a connection with the issue, that you would be allowed to give it in evidence — then it is a matter on which you may contradict him.

The collateral fact rule applies to parties as well as to ordinary witnesses.[278] Certain exceptions to the rule have developed. The generally recognized categories are both common law and statutory. They are:

(1) To prove a charge of bias or partiality in favour of the opposite party;

(2) To prove that the witness has previously been convicted of a criminal offence;

(3) Where the proper foundation has been laid, a previous inconsistent statement may be proved to contradict a witness;

(4) Medical evidence to prove that by reason of a physical or mental condition the witness is incapable of telling or unlikely to tell the truth; and

(5) Independent evidence that an adverse witness has a general reputation for untruthfulness and that the witness testifying to such reputation would not believe the impugned witness under oath.

---

276 *R. v. Rafael* (1972), 7 C.C.C. (2d) 325, [1972] 3 O.R. 238 (Ont. C.A.).
277 (1847), 1 Exch. 91, at 99, 16 L.J. Ex. 259, 154 E.R. 38, at 42.
278 *Hickey v. Fitzgerald* (1877), 41 U.C.Q.B. 303 (C.A.).

1. Bias or Partiality

At common law, it was permissible to discredit a witness by introducing contradicting evidence to show that the witness was biased, possessed a real interest in the outcome of the litigation, or was corrupt or unscrupulous in the giving of his testimony. The introduction of such evidence is predicated on a denial from the witness that he is not biased or partial.[279] This exception encompasses extrinsic evidence showing that the witness bears a family, intimate or employment relationship with one of the parties, or evidence that the witness has recently quarreled with one of the parties, or evidence of conduct which suggests that the witness possesses partisan feelings towards one of the parties, or evidence that the witness has accepted a bribe or that his testimony has otherwise been suborned.[280]

Under this exception it is possible to introduce specific acts of bad character, for instance, that the witness is a kept mistress of the party calling her,[281] or that a witness for the defendant attempted to induce a stranger to the action to break his contract with the plaintiff by deceitful means.[282]

2. Previous Convictions

This is a statutory exception to the rule that answers to collateral matters are conclusive.[283] While this exception allows a specific act tending to show bad character to be introduced, it is a tactic that is seldom used and is unpopular with trial judges in civil cases.

However, though previous convictions are potentially of tenuous relevance to credibility, it is clear that whatever value they have would be nullified if the witness could deny them with impunity. They are so readily proved, and denial so unprofitable, that resort to their proof in reply is rarely required.

3. Previous Inconsistent Statements

While this is stated to be an exception to the rule that a cross-examiner is bound by answers to collateral matters,[284] it is not univer-

---

279 *General Films Ltd. v. McElroy*, [1939] 4 D.L.R. 543, [1939] 3 W.W.R. 491.
280 *R. v. Bencardino* (1973), 15 C.C.C. (3d) 342, 24 C.R.N.S. 173, 2 O.R. (2d) 351 (C.A.), at 359 (O.R.); *A.G. v. Hitchcock, supra*, note 277.
281 *Thomas v. David* (1836), 7 C. & P. 350 (N.P.).
282 *General Films v. McElroy, supra*, note 279.
283 *Canada Evidence Act*, R.S.C. 1985, c. C-5, s. 12.
284 R. Cross and C. Tapper, *Cross on Evidence*, 7th ed. (London: Butterworths,

sally accepted as such.[285] The statutory provision permitting cross-examination on a previous inconsistent statement does not apply where the witness' testimony does not relate to a fact in issue but to collateral matters.[286] The statutory provision is merely declaratory of the common law,[287] and applies where the present testimony and previous inconsistent statement relate to the matter in question.[288]

4. Physical or Mental Condition for Untruthfulness

Under this exception, medical evidence has been permitted to attack the credibility of a witness by showing that the witness was beset with psychological problems which cast doubt upon the witness' testimonial reliability. In *Toohey v. Metropolitan Police Commissioner*,[289] the accused was charged and convicted of assaulting a young man who alleged that the accused and two other men had beaten and attempted to rob him. The defence of the accused was to the effect that the complainant's story was an "hysterical invention", and to establish this, the accused attempted to introduce evidence of a medical report indicating that the complainant was hysterical, prone to exaggerate and even imagine events that had not taken place, and whose testimony was therefore untrustworthy. The House of Lords held that such medical evidence was admissible to impeach the complainant's credibility. Such evidence is not confined to general opinion of unreliability of the witness but evidence may be given of all matters necessary to show not only the foundation of and reason for the diagnosis, but also the extent to which the credibility of the witness is affected.[290] This rule does not appear to operate in reverse so as to admit similar evidence to show that the witness is credible.[291]

1990), at 311.
285 M.N. Howard, P. Crane and D.A. Hochberg, *Phipson on Evidence*, 14th ed. (London: Sweet & Maxwell, 1990), at paras. 12-34 to 12-37.
286 See this Chapter, V.C.2.(d).
287 *Crowley v. Page* (1837), 7 C. & P. 789.
288 See *Zwicker v. Young*, [1929] 1 D.L.R. 602, 60 N.S.R. 233.
289 [1965] A.C. 595, [1965] 1 All E.R. 506.
290 *Ibid.*; *R. v. Hawke* (1974), 16 C.C.C. (2d) 438, 3 O.R. (2d) 210 (H.C.J.); revd. on other grounds (1975), 22 C.C.C. (2d) 19, 29 C.R.N.S. 1, 7 O.R. (2d) 145 (C.A.).
291 *R. v. Burkart*, [1965] 3 C.C.C. 210, 45 C.R. 383, 50 W.W.R. 515 (*sub nom. R. v. Sawalsky*). However, conflict may arise with this rule when an accused attempts to adduce exculpatory expert evidence of disposition: see *R. v. Lupien*, [1970] S.C.R. 263, [1970] 2 C.C.C. 193, 9 C.R.N.S. 165, 71 W.W.R. 110, 71 W.W.R. 655, *per* Martland J.

Before admission, such evidence must overcome the threshold of admissibility applicable to all expert testimony:[292]

> [W]hen a witness through physical (in which I include mental) disease or abnormality is not capable of giving a true or reliable account to the jury it must surely be allowable for medical science to reveal this vital hidden fact to them.

5. Evidence of Reputation for Untruthfulness

While this is treated as an exception to the rule, the case which appears to have originated the practice, *Mawson v. Hartsink*,[293] does not indicate that it is a condition precedent to the introduction of this contradictory evidence that the subject of the contradictory evidence be put to the witness. The case was brought on an *assumpsit* against defendants who pleaded bankruptcy and produced certificates. One, Stanley Leathes, was called by the plaintiff to impeach the certificates on the grounds that they were improperly obtained. The defendants then called several witnesses to impeach the credit of Leathes. The chief clerk of the Magistrates Court at Bow Street attempted to testify that Leathes had been before the justices and from what transpired, he (the clerk) would be unwilling to believe Leathes. Lord Ellenborough rejected this evidence as well as the evidence of Leathes' general character gained as a result of particular enquiries made by the clerk. Questions, however, were allowed in this form: "Have you the means of knowing what the general character of this witness was? And from such knowledge of his general character would you believe him under oath?" It was held that in cross-examination the witness could be asked as to his means of knowing Leathes' character. In reply to this question, presumably specific instances of bad conduct could be given.[294]

Of all the so-called exceptions to the rule, this is the only one that allows evidence of reputation to be adduced. While the other exceptions permit specific acts of conduct to be introduced, evidence of a witness' reputation is not allowed.

In cases in which the technique in *Mawson v. Hartsink*[295] has been

---

292   *Toohey, supra*, note 289, at 608 (A.C.).
293   (1802), 4 Esp. 102 (N.P.).
294   *Phipson on Evidence, supra*, note 285, at 26, § 12-36.
295   *Supra*, note 293.

employed, the party producing the witness, whose credit has been impeached, can in turn lead independent evidence that the impeaching witness is unworthy of credit. The exercise, however, cannot be repeated.[296]

The basis for the restriction of character evidence to the general reputation of the witness in the community articulated in *R. v. Rowton*,[297] has been the subject of considerable adverse comment.[298] The common law did not, however, restrict the evidence of the impeaching witness to evidence of reputation, but permitted the witness to express a personal opinion. In *R. v. Gonzague*,[299] the Ontario Court of Appeal endorsed the reception of a personal opinion of a non-expert of the lack of veracity of a previous witness. The trial judge had excluded the proposed evidence. Martin J.A. said:[300]

> [T]he English Court of Appeal in *R. v. Gunewardene* (1951), 35 Cr. App. R. 80, held that the impeaching witness is . . . not confined to expressing an opinion of the lack of veracity of the witness based upon the latter's general reputation (at p. 88). . . .
>
> . . .
>
> Although the matter is not free from doubt, because of the views expressed by the House of Lords in *Toohey v. Metropolitan Police Com'r*, . . . and, in view of the opinion expressed by Professor Cross in his well-known work *Cross on Evidence*, 2nd ed. (1963), which was also quoted with approval in the *Toohey* case, we think that it would have been preferable if the defence had been allowed to elicit the evidence which it desired.

In the circumstances, however, as the evidence had little weight, its exclusion was an insufficient ground to interfere with the verdict of the jury.

---

296   *R. v. Whelan* (1881), 14 Cox C.C. 595 (Ir.).
297   (1865), L. & C. 520, 169 E.R. 1497, [1861-73] All E.R. Rep. 549.
298   Wigmore described reputation evidence as ". . . the second hand, irresponsible product of multiplied guesses and gossip . . .", 7 Wigmore, *Evidence*, § 1986 (Chadbourn rev. 1978).
299   (1983), 4 C.C.C. (3d) 505, 34 C.R. (3d) 169 (Ont. C.A.).
300   *Ibid.*, at 512 (C.C.C.).

The Task Force[301] recommended that the use of evidence of general reputation be abolished. Its report stated:

> Bad reputation evidence of witnesses is seldom called. Such evidence could embarrass the non-party witness and could prejudice the party witness especially an accused. Because such evidence is seldom called, the rules governing its admissibility are unclear.

The use of this evidence is an anachronism and should be discontinued. It was appropriate when persons lived in smaller communities and each person had a well-defined reputation. This is no longer the case in modern society and the recommendation of the Task Force should be adopted.

The wisdom in maintaining a limited list of exceptions to the collateral fact rule is challenged when the admissibility of evidence highly relevant to credibility and easily proved, is excluded. Facts relating to a witness' opportunity or ability to observe or communicate have been excluded although they would have been of considerable assistance in assessing the credibility of the witness and would not have prolonged the proceedings unduly. In *Piddington v. Bennet and Wood Pty Ltd.*,[302] an Australian case, a witness in a motor accident case was asked how he happened to be present at the scene. The witness replied that he had been to the bank for a named person. A new trial was ordered on the ground that the trial judge had improperly admitted the evidence of the bank manager that no such transaction had been completed that day.

Furthermore, in *R. v. Burke*,[303] a case in which a witness gave evidence through an interpreter, evidence contradicting the witness' assertion in cross-examination that he was ignorant of the English language, was excluded. On the other hand, in *Tzagarakis v. Stevens*,[304] the Nova Scotia Court of Appeal admitted evidence that contradicted the testimony of an eye witness that she had made her presence known at the scene of the accident. It did so, however, on the dubious basis

---

301 *Report of the Federal/Provincial Task Force on Uniform Rules of Evidence* (Toronto: Carswell, 1982), at 333.
302 (1940), 63 C.L.R. 533.
303 (1858), 8 Cox C.C. 44.
304 (1968), 69 D.L.R. (2d) 466 (N.S.C.A.).

that the question was relevant not only to credibility but to negligence. Were it not for the closed list of exceptions to the rule, a more forthright basis of admission of the evidence would have been its obvious probative value weighed against the minimal import on the prolongation of the trial process.

As in the case of evidence of similar acts,[305] it may be time to liberate trial judges from the specific exceptions to the rule by treating them as illustrations in respect of which its basic rationale does not apply. Accordingly, evidence that does not come within a specific exception may yet be admitted if its probative value overbears the public interest in achieving a finality to legal proceedings.[306]

---

305 See Chapter 10.
306 For a criticism of the finality rule, see S. Schiff, *Evidence in the Litigation Process*, 3rd ed. (Toronto: Carswell, 1988) at 534-35; R. Cross and C. Tapper, *Cross on Evidence*, 7th ed. (London: Butterworths, 1990), at 310.

CHAPTER 17

CORROBORATION

I INTRODUCTION

The general rule is that the testimony of a single witness, if believed to the requisite degree of certainty, is sufficient to found a conviction or civil judgment.[1] Because there may be concerns about the reliability of a witness' testimony, for example, the witness has a financial interest in the outcome of the proceedings or he or she is an accomplice, the trier of fact may search for supporting evidence to confirm that witness' testimony. This search for confirmatory evidence is a matter of common sense.

From early times however, there existed certain types of cases or categories of witnesses that required confirmatory evidence of a particular kind. An extreme illustration is found in a small number of statutes, some of which still survive in England today, requiring the evidence of two or more witnesses for a conviction.[2] The need for a plurity of witnesses was refined into rules of practice which evolved into common law and statutory rules of law. There were two types of corroboration rules. The first type consisted of common law and statutory rules governing criminal proceedings that required the trial judge to warn the trier of fact of the danger of convicting on the uncorroborated evidence of particular categories of witnesses. However, the trial judge also directed the jury that they were free to convict the accused if they were satisfied of his or her guilt beyond a reasonable

---

1   In *Radford v. MacDonald* (1891), 18 O.A.R. 167 (Ont. C.A.), at 171, Osler J.A. stated: "The common law rule is: 'The testimony of a single witness, relevant for proof of the issue in the judgment of the judge, and credible in that of the jury, is a sufficient basis for decision both in civil and criminal cases' ".
2   See R. Cross and C. Tapper, *Cross on Evidence*, 7th ed. (London: Butterworths, 1990), at 225-27.

doubt. Thus, provided that the trial judge properly warned the jury of the danger of acting on uncorroborated evidence, a conviction could be found in the absence of corroboration.[3] The common law accomplice corroboration rule[4] and the statutory rule in relation to the testimony of complainants in sexual cases[5] belonged to this class of corroboration rule; however, this type of rule no longer exists in Canada by reason of judicial[6] and Parliamentary[7] reform of the law.

The second type of corroboration rule, imposed by statute, made corroboration mandatory. These rules require additional evidence beyond that of an interested party or potentially unreliable witness. A conviction or civil judgment founded on uncorroborated evidence constituted an error of law that would be overturned on appeal. As noted, many of these statutory provisions codified former rules of practice.[8] An illustration of this type of corroboration rule is found in several provincial Evidence Acts that admit the reception of unsworn evidence of a child of tender years, but provide that "[n]o case shall be decided upon such evidence unless it is corroborated by some other material evidence".[9]

In this chapter, we will examine the modern common law governing the testimony of potentially unreliable witnesses in criminal cases. Before we examine the nature of corroboration, we will describe the reform of the law of corroboration by Canadian legislatures that now applies to a limited number of criminal prosecutions and several civil actions. We will conclude by illustrating how the courts have applied the doctrine of corroboration in relation to a cause of action and to potentially unreliable witnesses.

---

3   *R. v. Baskerville*, [1916] 2 K.B. 658, at 663, 12 Cr. App. Rep. 81, [1916-17] All E.R. Rep. 38 (C.C.A.).
4   *R. v. Baskerville, ibid.*
5   R.S.C. 1970, c. C-34, s. 142 [rep. and sub. 1974-75-76, c. 93, s. 8]. This was formerly a rule of practice, see *R. v. Firkins* (1979), 37 C.C.C. (2d) 227, 39 C.R.N.S. 178, 80 D.L.R. (3d) 63 (B.C.C.A.); leave to appeal to S.C.C. refd. 37 C.C.C. (2d) 227*n*, 80 D.L.R. (3d) 63*n*.
6   *R. v. Vetrovec*, [1982] 1 S.C.R. 811 (*sub nom. R. v. Vetrovec: R. v. Gaja*), 27 C.R. (3d) 304, 67 C.C.C. (2d) 1, 136 D.L.R. (3d) 89, [1983] 1 W.W.R. 193.
7   See this Chapter, III.
8   *Groat v. Kinnaird* (1914), 7 W.W.R. 264, 20 D.L.R. 421, 7 Alta. L.R. 390 (C.A.); *Re Jackson* (1929), 64 O.L.R. 215, [1929] 4 D.L.R. 213 (C.A.).
9   Ontario *Evidence Act*, R.S.O. 1980, c. 145, s. 18(1); see this Chapter, III.

II *VETROVEC*: THE MODERN COMMON LAW

In the landmark decision of *R. v. Vetrovec*,[10] the Supreme Court of Canada eliminated the common law rule requiring corroboration for particular categories of witnesses.[11] In *Vetrovec*, the accused appealed their convictions on the ground that the trial judge incorrectly directed the jury as to the evidence that was capable of corroborating the testimony of an accomplice. After thoroughly reviewing the development of the accomplice corroboration rule and its rationale, Dickson J. (as he then was) held that the law had become unduly and unnecessarily complicated and technical and that it was in need of reform.[12] Quoting from a Law Reform Commission of Canada paper,[13] Dickson J. stated that an ". . . enormous superstructure . . . has been erected on the original basic proposition that the evidence of some witnesses should be approached with caution".[14] He observed that corroboration had become a legal term of art wholly unconnected with its original justification as to whether there existed evidence that bolstered the credibility of the potentially unreliable witness.[15] He suggested that a legally correct summing-up on the law of corroboration may tend to confuse a jury[16] and that recent pronouncements by the Supreme Court of Canada and the House of Lords[17] had departed from the formal requirements of what had become known as the *Baskerville* rule.[18] In rejecting the formal common law rule Dickson J. stated:[19]

> Rather than attempting to pigeon-hole a witness into a category and then recite a ritualistic incantation, the trial judge might

---

10   *Supra*, note 6.
11   *R. v. B. (G.) (No. 1)*, [1990] 2 S.C.R. 3, at 25, 77 C.R. (3d) 327, 56 C.C.C. (3d) 200, 111 N.R. 1.
12   *Vetrovec v. R.*, *supra*, note 6, at 816 (S.C.R.).
13   Law Reform Commission of Canada, *Evidence: 11 Corroboration* (Study Paper) (Ottawa: Law Reform Commission of Canada, 1975), at 7.
14   *Supra*, note 6, at 818 (S.C.R.).
15   *Ibid.*, at 825-26 (S.C.R.).
16   *Ibid.*, at 829 (S.C.R.) (citing with approval Lord Diplock in *D.P.P. v. Hester*, [1972] 3 All E.R. 1056, at 1075, [1973] A.C. 296, 57 Cr. App. R. 212 (H.L.)).
17   *D.P.P. v. Hester*, *ibid.*; *D.P.P. v. Kilbourne*, [1973] 1 All E.R. 440, [1973] A.C. 729, [1973] 2 W.L.R. 254. For more recent English authority see *R. v. Spencer*, [1986] 2 All E.R. 928, at 937 (H.L.).
18   *Supra*, note 6, at 819 (S.C.R.).
19   *Ibid.*, at 823 (S.C.R.).

better direct his mind to the facts of the case, and thoroughly examine all the factors which might impair the worth of a particular witness. If, in his judgement, the credit of the witness is such that the jury should be cautioned, then he may instruct accordingly. If, on the other hand, he believes the witness to be trustworthy, then, regardless of whether the witness is technically an "accomplice", no warning is necessary.

Dickson J. emphasized that this common sense approach to potentially suspect witnesses existed long before the English Court of Criminal Appeal, in *R. v. Baskerville*,[20] converted the rule of practice of warning a jury as to the danger of convicting on the uncorroborated evidence of an accomplice into a rule of law.[21]

The Supreme Court reduced the technical common law accomplice rule to a judicial discretion to warn a jury, if necessary, on the dangers of reaching a conclusion of guilt based on the testimony of a suspect witness:[22]

1. It is within the discretion of the trial judge, depending upon his view as to the trustworthiness of the witness, whether to warn the jury as to the risk of convicting, without more, on the testimony of a witness whose evidence occupies a central position in the proof of guilt, but who may be suspect by reason of being an accomplice or a person of unsavoury character.

Where circumstances warrant the need for the jury to approach particular evidence with caution, the trial judge may give ". . . a clear sharp warning to attract the attention of the juror to the risks of adopting, without more, the evidence of the witness."[23] The trial judge

---

20   *Supra*, note 3.

21   *Supra*, note 6, at 819-20 (S.C.R.). In *Gouin v. R.*, [1926] S.C.R. 539, 46 C.C.C. 1, [1926] 3 D.L.R. 649 the *Baskerville* direction was adopted as a rule of law in Canada.

22   *R. v. Yanover (No. 1)* (1985), 20 C.C.C. (3d) 300, 9 O.A.C. 93, at 109 (C.A.), folld. in *R. v. Vautour* (1987), 198 A.P.R. 84, 78 N.B.R. (2d) 84 (C.A.). See also *Vetrovec, supra*, note 6, at 831 (S.C.R.).

23   *Supra*, note 6, at 831 (S.C.R.); see *R. v. Bevan* (1991), 4 C.R. (4th) 245, 63 C.C.C. (3d) 333, 44 O.A.C. 53, 2 O.R. (3d) 381 (*sub nom. R. v. Griffith*) (O.C.A.) and *R. v. K. (V.)* (1991), 4 C.R. (4th) 338 (B.C.C.A.) for illustrations where the trail judges did not give such a warning. The "Vetrovec" warning should not be given in relation to the testimony of the accused, *R. v. Hoilett* (1991), 4 C.R. (4th) 372, 3 O.R. (3d) 449 (Ont. C.A.).

need not use the word corroboration or other comparable expressions such as "confirmation" or "support" in the summing-up, nor express the warning according to a particular form of words.[24] The judge may assist the jury by indicating the item(s) of evidence that may confirm the suspect witness' testimony,[25] but she or he is no longer required to exhaustively identify the evidence that is capable of supporting the witness.[26]

Although *Vetrovec* focused on the common law corroboration rule for accomplices, the court's analysis applied to the other common law corroboration rules.[27] Thus, it is no longer necessary to caution a jury about testimony according to an arbitrary classification of witnesses. The old rigid rules requiring corroborative evidence to be independent and implicate the accused in a material particular are no longer determinative as to the correctness of a trial judge's summing-up.[28] Even the use of the word "corroboration", being a term not heard or used outside of a courtroom, is unnecessary.[29] In *R. v. Hayes*[30] the Supreme Court of Canada stated:[31]

> The decision of this court in *Vetrovec v. The Queen* . . . stands for the proposition that there was no "fixed and invariable rule" regarding the appropriate charge with respect to the testimony of accomplices. Instead of assuming that all accomplices are inherently untrustworthy as witnesses, Dickson J. (as he then

---

24 *Supra*, note 22, at 110 (O.A.C.).
25 *Ibid.*
26 *Ibid.*
27 *Supra*, note 11, at 24-26 (S.C.R.).
28 In *R. v. B. (G.) (No. 1)*, *ibid.*, at 26 (S.C.R.), after considering *Vetrovec*, Wilson J. stated that "this Court has clearly rejected an ultra technical approach to corroboration and has returned to a common sense approach which reflects the original rationale for the rule and allows cases to be determined on their merits".
29 Dickson J.'s dissatisfaction with the term is expressed in *R. v. Vetrovec*, [1982] 1 S.C.R. 811, at 829, 27 C.R. (3d) 304, 67 C.C.C. (2d) 1, 136 D.L.R. (3d) 89. See *R. v. Ertel* (1987), 58 C.R. (3d) 252, 35 C.C.C. (3d) 209, 20 O.A.C. 257 (Ont. C.A.); leave to appeal to S.C.C. refd. (1987), 24 O.A.C. 320n, 30 C.R.R. 209n, 86 N.R. 266n; *R. v. MacKinlay* (1987), 191 A.P.R. 232, 77 N.S.R. (2d) 294 (N.S.C.A.) for non-jury cases. Also note that merely substituting some other term for the word corroboration (e.g., "supporting evidence"), will not necessarily comply with the Supreme Court's ruling in *Vetrovec*, *ibid.*: *R. v. Rodgers* (1987), 82 A.R. 319 (C.A.).
30 [1989] 1 S.C.R. 44, 68 C.R. (3d) 245, 89 N.R. 138.
31 *Ibid.*, at 49 (S.C.R.).

was) advocated an approach tailored to the particular case.

In *Vetrovec*, the Supreme Court expressly pointed out, however, that the statutory rules survived its decision.[32]

The common sense rule may be described as simply looking for evidence in relation to a material issue which confirms the story of the witness who potentially may lack credibility. Wigmore states the justification for this approach:[33]

> ... whatever restores our trust in him personally restores it as a whole; if we find that he is desiring and intending to tell a true story, we shall believe one part of his story as well as another; whenever, then, by any means, that trust is restored, our object is accomplished, and it cannot matter whether the efficient circumstances related to the accused's identity or to any other matter. The important thing is, not *how* our trust is restored, but whether it *is* restored at all.

III LEGISLATIVE DEVELOPMENTS

A. *The Criminal Law*

1. Legislative Repeals

Parliament repealed several legislative provisions that required the trial judge to give a corroboration warning for some offences or that prohibited a conviction upon the uncorroborated evidence of only one witness. First, the former *Criminal Code* provision that mandated a corroboration warning for five sexual offences was repealed in 1975.[34] Then in 1982, as part of substantial revisions to

---

32 "I would point out that my comments have been limited to situations in which corroboration is required as a matter of common law. The *Criminal Code* specifies a number of instances in which corroboration is required, and defines the nature of the corroboration which must be supplied . . . . The statutory requirements would, of course, be controlling in cases coming under any of those sections" per Dickson J., *supra*, note 29, at 832 (S.C.R.).

33 7 Wigmore, *Evidence* (Chadbourn rev. 1978), § 2059, at 424. The last sentence of this paragraph has been frequently cited subsequent to *Vetrovec*; e.g., *R. v. Gervais* (1988), 42 C.C.C. (3d) 352, at 366 (Que. S.C.); *R. v. Williams* (1987), 46 Man. R. 105, at 107 (Man. C.A.).

34 Rep. & sub. 1974-75-76, c. 93, s. 8. The former s. 142 (R.S.C. 1970,

the criminal law in relation to sexual offences, Parliament repealed the provision that required corroboration for several other sexual crimes.[35] Indeed, the legislation expressly prohibits a corroboration warning for some offences.[36] Nonetheless, a trial judge is not prohibited from commenting, in his or her summing-up, as to the weight to be given to the unsupported evidence of a complainant.[37]

The other significant legislative initiative in the criminal area was

---

c. C-34) read: "Notwithstanding anything in this Act or any other Act of the Parliament of Canada, where an accused is charged with an offence under section 144 [rape], 145 [attempt rape], subs. 146(1) [sexual intercourse with female under 14 years] or (2) [sexual intercourse with female 14-16] or subs. 149(1) [indecent assault on female], the judge shall, if the only evidence that implicates the accused is the evidence, given under oath, of the female person in respect of whom the offence is alleged to have been committed and that evidence is not corroborated in a material particular by evidence that implicates the accused, instruct the jury that it is not safe to find the accused guilty in the absence of such corroboration, but that they are entitled to find the accused guilty if they are satisfied beyond a reasonable doubt that her evidence is true".

35 R.S.C. 1970, c. C-34, s. 139(1) [rep. & sub. 1980-81-82-83, c. 125, s. 5]. Section 139(1) read: "No accused shall be convicted of an offence under ss. 148 [sexual intercourse with a feeble minded], 150 [incest], 151 [seduction of female aged 16-18 years], 152 [seduction under promise of marriage], 153 [sexual intercourse with a step-daughter or female employee], 154 [seduction of female passengers on vessels] or 166 [parent or guardian procuring defilement] upon the evidence of only one witness unless the evidence of the witness is corroborated in a material particular by evidence that implicates the accused". Additionally 1980-81-82-83, c. 125, s. 13 removed the requirement for corroboration for the offence of procuring (R.S.C. 1970, c. C-34, s. 195).

36 Now see s. 274 of the *Criminal Code*, R.S.C. 1985, c. C-46 [rep. & sub. 1985, c. 19 (3rd Supp.), s. 11]. The prohibition against a corroboration warning was expanded by listing additional crimes and including some newly enacted offences. Offences now included within the current s. 274 are: ss. 151 (sexual interference), 152 (invitation to sexual touching), 153 (sexual exploitation), 155 (incest), 159 (anal intercourse), 160 (bestiality), 170 (parent or guardian procuring sexual activity), 171 (householder procuring sexual activity), 172 (corrupting children), 173 (indecent acts), 212 (procuring), 271 (sexual assault), 272 (sexual assault with a weapon, threats to a third party or causing bodily harm), and 273 (aggravated sexual assault).

37 *R. v. Boss* (1988), 68 C.R. (3d) 123, 30 O.A.C. 184 (C.A.), at 190 (O.A.C.); *R. v. K. (V.)*, *supra*, note 23. See also D. Watt, *The New Offences Against the Person: the Provisions of Bill C-127* (Toronto: Butterworths, 1984), at 176. However the trial judge must be careful not to parallel the old requirement for corroboration in his or her charge to the jury by merely replacing the word "corroboration" with some other synonym, see *R. v. Rodgers*, *supra*, note 29.

the repeal of s. 659 of the *Criminal Code* which prohibited a conviction upon the unsworn evidence of a child "... unless the evidence of the child is corroborated in a material particular that implicates the person".[38] The related provisions of s. 16(2) of the *Canada Evidence Act* and s. 61(2) of the *Young Offender's Act* to the same effect were also repealed.[39]

These substantial changes to the law posed several new issues. One of the first questions was whether the repeal of these statutory provisions revived the former rules of practice. In *R. v. Firkins*[40] and *R. v. Camp*[41] the courts considered the effect of the repeal of s. 142 of the *Criminal Code*[42] that had required a corroboration warning for complainants in rape cases. It was argued that since the statutory corroboration provisions did not "alter, vary or modify" but rather only codified the common law, the old corroboration rules of practice were revived under s. 8(2) of the *Criminal Code*.[43]

Provincial appellate courts rejected this argument on two grounds. First, the codification was an alteration or modification of the common law rule and thus s. 8 did not apply.[44] Secondly, the courts applied the federal *Interpretation Act* which states that:[45] "[w]here an enactment is repealed in whole or in part, the repeal does not ... revive any enactment or anything not in force or existing at the time when the repeal takes place". Recently, in *R. v. Potvin* Wilson J. stated:[46]

---

38 Repealed R.S.C. 1985, c. 19 (3rd Supp.), s. 15.

39 By R.S.C. 1985, c. 19 (3rd Supp.), s. 18 and R.S.C. 1985, c. 24 (2nd Supp.), s. 40 respectively.

40 (1977), 37 C.C.C. 227, 39 C.R.N.S. 178, 80 D.L.R. (3d) 63 (B.C.C.A.); leave to appeal to S.C.C. refd. (1978), 37 C.C.C. (2d) 227n, 80 D.L.R. (3d) 63n.

41 (1977), 36 C.C.C. (2d) 511, 39 C.R.N.S. 164, 17 O.R. (2d) 99, 79 D.L.R. (3d) 462 (C.A.); folld. in *R. v. Daigle* (1977), 37 C.C.C. (2d) 386, 18 N.B.R. (2d) 658 (C.A.).

42 R.S.C. 1970, c. C-34, s. 142 [rep. 1974-75-76, c. 93, s. 8].

43 "The criminal law of England that was in force in a province immediately before April 1, 1955 continues in force in the province except as altered, varied, modified or affected by this Act or any other Act of the Parliament of Canada", R.S.C. 1985, c. C-46.

44 *R. v. Firkins, supra,* note 40 and *R. v. Camp, supra,* note 41.

45 Now R.S.C. 1985, c. I-21, s. 43(a).

46 [1989] 1 S.C.R. 525, at 557, 47 C.C.C. (3d) 289, 68 C.R. (3d) 193, 93 N.R. 42, 21 Q.A.C. 258. This position has been recently affirmed in *R. v. B. (G.) (No. 1),* [1990] 2 S.C.R. 3, 77 C.R. (3d) 327, 56 C.C.C. (3d) 200, 111 N.R. 1; see also *R. v. Bevan, supra,* note 23 and *R. v. K. (V.), supra,* note 23.

Vetrovec, in my view, represents a rejection of the formalistic and *a priori* categories concerning the trustworthiness of evidence both with regard to warnings and corroboration. In every case, it is for the trial judge on the basis of his or her appreciation of all circumstances and, may I add, on the basis of the application of sound common sense, to decide whether a warning is required.

It seems unlikely that the courts will revive the old rules of practice in the near future.

A different issue was whether the repeal of the rules was retroactive. For example, where an offence occurred prior to the repeal but the trial took place after the repeal of the statutory provision the question arose whether the corroboration rule applied at the accused's trial. Because rules of corroboration relate to procedural and evidentiary matters, appellate courts have held that the presumption against the retrospective operation of statutes does not apply.[47] The courts have also held that the alteration of an evidentiary rule, that is abolishing the requirement of corroboration, does not violate s. 7 of the *Canadian Charter of Rights and Freedoms*.[48]

2. Statutory Corroboration Requirements

The *Criminal Code* and *Canada Evidence Act* no longer contain any general provision mandating corroboration for particular categories of witnesses.[49] Rules of corroboration are now restricted to five *Criminal Code* offences: high treason,[50] treason,[51] procuring a feigned marriage,[52] perjury,[53] and forgery.[54] Each of these offences contain an

---

47 *R. v. Bickford* (1989), 34 O.A.C. 34, 51 C.C.C. (3d) 181, 48 C R.R. 194 (C.A.); *R. v. Inkster* (1988), 69 Sask. R. 1 (Q.B.).
48 R.S.C. 1985, App. II, No. 44. *R. v. Bickford, ibid.*, at 38-42 (O.A.C.).
49 Note that R.S.C. 1985, c. C-46, s. 658(2) mentions corroboration but does not require it.
50 R.S.C. 1985, c. C-46, s. 47(3).
51 *Ibid.*
52 *Ibid.*, s. 292(2).
53 *Ibid.*, s. 133. The corroboration requirement includes subornation of perjury (*R. v. Doz* (1984), 12 C.C.C. 200, at 210, 52 A.R. 321 (C.A.)) but not incitement to commit perjury (*R. v. Kyling*, [1970] S.C.R. 953, at 956-57, 2 C.C.C. (2d) 79, 14 C.R.N.S. 257, 15 D.L.R. (3d) 351).
54 *Ibid.*, s. 367.

almost identically worded corroboration provision. For example, the forgery provision provides:[55]

> No person shall be convicted of an offence under this section [forgery] on the evidence of only one witness, unless the evidence of that witness is corroborated in a material particular by evidence that implicates the accused.

A prosecution would be rare for some of these remaining offences and it is difficult to justify their continued existence on grounds of policy.[56] Take for example the requirement for corroboration for the crime of forgery. Professors Wakeling[57] and Delisle[58] explain that the provision originated in the *Forgery Act* of 1869[59] which made a party to the litigation competent to testify when parties were generally incompetent. The corroboration requirement was enacted as a matter of caution. Thus, its justification is a historic anomaly.[60] As illustrated in the recent case of *R. v. Ookpik*,[61] the corroboration requirement for forgery may be logically unsound. In *Ookpik*, four bank withdrawal slips were allegedly forged in order to withdraw monies from the victim's account. The accused was charged in a single information with four counts of forgery and four counts of uttering in relation to the forged bank withdrawal documents. The trial judge, sitting without a jury, was required to apply the corroboration rule to the testimony of the handwriting expert on the forgery counts but not on the uttering charges. It also is observed that for crimes similar to forgery, for example counterfeiting, there is no requirement for corroboration.

---

55 *Ibid.*, s. 367(2).
56 For a review of their original justification, see *Report of the Federal/Provincial Task Force on Uniform Rules of Evidence* (Toronto: Carswell, 1982), at 365-68; Audrey A. Wakeling, *Corroboration in Canadian Law* (Toronto: Carswell, 1977), at 11-13, 128-31; R. Delisle, *Evidence, Principles and Problems*, 2nd ed. (Toronto: Carswell, 1989), at 311-18.
57 Wakeling, *ibid.*, at 12 and 131.
58 Delisle, *supra*, note 56, at 311.
59 S.C. 1869, c. 19, s. 54.
60 See *Task Force Report, supra*, note 56, at 366. Additionally it should be noted that requiring confirmation of the testimony of a competent witness is in itself anomalous, see *R. v. Baskerville*, [1916] 2 K.B. 658, at 664, 12 Cr. App. Rep. 81 (C.C.A.).
61 *R. v. Ookpik*, [1988] N.W.T.R. 67*n* (C.A.).

B. *The Civil Law*

1. General

There have also been significant legislative developments in the civil field. Traditionally, there were four causes of action for which corroboration was mandatory in many provincial jurisdictions: breach of promise to marry; affiliation proceedings; actions by or against a mentally incompetent person; and, actions by or against the heirs, executors or assigns of a deceased person. Also, the unsworn testimony of a child required corroboration. In Canada, the corroboration requirement governing these causes of action resembles a checkerboard since the provincial legislatures did not uniformly codify the rules of practice and some of the legislatures that did so, have now repealed their statutory provisions. We will now review the status of these corroboration provisions in the provincial jurisdictions.

2. Breach of Promise to Marry

The cause of action for a breach of promise to marry was abolished in Ontario,[62] British Columbia[63] and Manitoba[64] and New Brunswick and Nova Scotia have never had a corroboration requirement for this cause of action. Only the Evidence Acts of Alberta, Newfoundland, Prince Edward Island, Saskatchewan, and the Yukon and Northwest Territories currently maintain this provision.[65] These statutory corroboration rules require that the plaintiff's testimony be corroborated in relation to the promise to marry. For example, the *Alberta Evidence Act* states:[66]

> The plaintiff in an action for breach of promise of marriage shall not succeed in the action unless the plaintiff's testimony is corroborated by some other material evidence in support of the promise.

---

62   *Marriage Act*, R.S.O. 1980, c. 256, s. 32.
63   *Family Relations Act*, R.S.B.C. 1979, c. 121, s. 75(2)(c) [new 1985, c. 72, s. 36].
64   *Equality of Status Act*, R.S.M 1987, c. E130, s. 4(1) [new R.S.M. 1987, c. 16 (supp.), s. 3].
65   Evidence Acts: Alberta, R.S.A. 1980, c. A-21, s. 11; Newfoundland, R.S.N. 1970, c. 115, s. 5; Prince Edward Island, R.S.P.E.I. 1988, c. E-11, s. 7; Saskatchewan, R.S.S. 1978, c. S-16, s. 43; Yukon, R.S.Y. 1986, c. 57, s. 13; Northwest Territories, R.S.N.W.T. 1988, c. E-8, s. 16.
66   *Ibid.*

3. Affiliation Proceedings

The requirement for corroboration in affiliation proceedings is almost extinct. For example, Ontario replaced the affiliation provisions contained in the former *Child Welfare Act*,[67] including the requirement for corroboration,[68] with the *Children's Law Reform Act*.[69] The latter Act does not require corroboration. British Columbia, Manitoba and Newfoundland have repealed the statutory corroboration requirement in affiliation proceedings[70] and Alberta and Saskatchewan have recently done the same.[71] Prior to its repeal in some jurisdictions, courts held that the corroboration provision contravened s. 15 of the *Charter* and could not be saved by s. 1.[72] The rule of practice does not exist in New Brunswick,[73] Prince Edward Island, or Nova Scotia. Thus, the rule is now restricted to the Northwest Territories.[74]

---

67 R.S.O. 1970, c. 64.

68 *Ibid.*, s. 56.

69 R.S.O. 1980, c. 68. See *Re Ruby* (1983), 43 O.R. (2d) 277, at 283 (Ont. Surr. Ct.).

70 In British Columbia s. 13(1) of the *Child Paternity and Support Act*, R.S.B.C. 1979, c. 49 was repealed by the *Family Relations Amendment Act*, S.B.C. 1988, c. 36, s. 9; in Manitoba the repealing legislation was the *Child and Family Services Act*, S.M. 1985-86, c. C-80, s. 87(1); and, in Newfoundland: *The Children's Law Act*, S.N. 1988, c. 61, s. 89(1).

71 In Alberta, s. 29 of the *Parentage and Maintenance Act*, S.A. 1990, P-0.7 repeals s. 19 of the *Maintenance and Recovery Act*, R.S.A. 1980, c. M-2. In Saskatchewan, s. 29(2) of the *Family Maintenance Act*, S. Sask. 1990, c. F-6.1 repeals *Children of Unmarried Parents Act*, R.S.S. 1978, c. C-8.

72 *Bomboir v. Harlow* (1987), 58 Sask. R. 212, [1987] 5 W.W.R. 55 (Sask. U.F.C.) (*sub nom. B. (L.M.) v. H. (T.)*); *G. (T.L.) v. L. (D.)* (1988), 66 Sask. R. 211, [1988] 4 W.W.R. 763, 50 D.L.R. (4th) 758, 14 R.F.L. (3d) 288 (C.A.); *W. (D.S.) v. H. (R.)*, [1989] 2 W.W.R. 481, 71 Sask. R. 66, 55 D.L.R. (4th) 720, 18 R.F.L. (3d) 162 (Sask. C.A.); *K. (L.) v. L. (T.W.)* (1988), 31 B.C.L.R. (2d) 41 (B.C. Prov. Ct.).

73 For historical interest it may be noted that 1854, s. 7, *The Bastardy Act* (R.S.N.B., c. 57), stated: "If the [affiliation] order be made on evidence of the mother it shall be corroborated in some material particular by other evidence if the Sessions deem necessary". This provision disappeared in a subsequent revision of the statute.

74 Northwest Territories: *The Child Welfare Act*, R.S.N.W.T. 1988, c. C-6, s. 60.

4. Actions Involving the Estate of Deceased Persons

Provisions requiring corroboration for actions involving the estate of a deceased person currently exist in Ontario, Alberta, Newfoundland, Nova Scotia, Prince Edward Island, the Yukon and Northwest Territories.[75] These provisions are worded similarly to s. 11 of the Prince Edward Island statute, which reads:[76]

> In any action or proceeding by or against the heirs, or personal representatives or their assigns of a deceased person, an opposite or interested party to the action shall not obtain a verdict, judgement or decision therein on his own evidence in respect of any matter occurring before the death of the deceased person, unless the evidence is corroborated by some other material evidence.

British Columbia repealed the legislative rule in 1976,[77] and there is no such requirement in Manitoba, Saskatchewan and New Brunswick.

5. Actions Against Mental Incompetents

In actions against mentally incompetent persons there is a similar lack of unanimity amongst the various provincial jurisdictions. There is a corroboration requirement in Ontario,[78] Alberta, British Columbia, Newfoundland, Prince Edward Island, and the Yukon and Northwest Territories,[79] but there is no requirement in the remaining jurisdictions.

---

75 Evidence Acts: Ontario, R.S.O. 1980, c. 145, s. 13; Alberta, R.S.A. 1980, c. A-21, s. 12; Newfoundland, R.S.N. 1970, c. 115, s. 14; Nova Scotia, R.S.N.S. 1989, c. 154, s. 45; Prince Edward Island, S.P.E.I. 1988, c. E-11, s. 11; Yukon, R.S.Y. 1986, c. 57, s. 14; Northwest Territories, R.S.N.W.T. 1988, c. E-8, s. 17.
76 R.S.P.E.I. 1988, c. E-11.
77 S.B.C. 1976, c. 2, s. 20(a), repealing R.S.B.C. 1960, c. 134, s. 11.
78 The *Evidence Act*, R.S.O. 1980, c. 145, s. 14 reads: "In an action by or against a mentally incompetent person so found, or a patient in a psychiatric facility, or a person who from unsoundness of mind is incapable of giving evidence, an opposite or interested party shall not obtain a verdict, judgment or decision on his own evidence, unless such evidence is corroborated by some other material evidence.
79 Evidence Acts: Alberta, R.S.A. 1980, c. A-21, s. 13; British Columbia, R.S.B.C. 1979, c. 116, s. 9; Newfoundland, R.S.N. 1970, c. 115, s. 15; Prince Edward Island, R.S.P.E.I. 1988, c. E-10, s. 12; Yukon, R.S.Y. 1986, c. 57, s. 15; Northwest Territories, R.S.N.W.T. 1988, c. E-8, s. 18.

6. Unsworn Evidence of Children

Most provincial Evidence Acts contain a provision for the reception of the unsworn evidence of children of tender years,[80] if ". . . the child is possessed of sufficient intelligence to justify the reception of the evidence and understands the duty of speaking the truth."[81] These acts also provide that "[n]o case shall be decided upon such evidence unless it is corroborated by some other material evidence".[82] In accordance with the general legislative trend to repeal corroboration rules, New Brunswick recently repealed the provision from its *Evidence Act*,[83] while British Columbia has amended its legislation to mirror s. 16 of the *Canada Evidence Act*.[84] Interestingly, there has never been a corroboration requirement in Prince Edward Island.

7. Effect of Repeal on Common Law Rules of Practice

Like the criminal law, the repeal of these statutory provisions does not revive the earlier common law rules of practice.[85] In some situations where rules of practice have not been codified by statute, suspect evidence is required to be subjected to special scrutiny. For example, in actions to set aside a conveyance between near relatives as being in fraud of creditors, an old rule of practice made corroboration desirable,[86] but not mandatory.[87] This reasoning seems remarkably

---

80   Evidence Acts: Ontario, R.S.O. 1980, c. 145, s. 18(1); Alberta, R.S.A. 1980, c. A-21, s. 20(1); Manitoba, R.S.M. 1987, c. E150, s. 24(1); Saskatchewan, R.S.S. 1978, c. S-16, s. 42(1); Nova Scotia, R.S.N.S. 1989, c. 154, s. 63(1); New Brunswick, R.S.N.B. 1973, c. E-11, s. 24(1); Newfoundland, R.S.N. 1970, c. 115, s. 15A(1) [new S.N. 1972, No. 3, s. 2; 1972, No. 11, s. 2]; Northwest Territories R.S.N.W.T. 1988, c. E-8, s. 25; Yukon, R.S.Y. 1986, c. 57, s. 22.
81   The *Evidence Act*, R.S.O. 1980, c. 145, s. 18(1).
82   *Evidence Act*, R.S.O. 1980, c. 145, s. 18(2); see also Alberta, R.S.A. 1980, c. A-21, s. 20(2); Manitoba, R.S.M. 1987, c. E150, s. 24(2); Saskatchewan, R.S.S. 1978, c. S-16, s. 42(2); Nova Scotia, R.S.N.S. 1989, c. 154, s. 63(2); Newfoundland, R.S.N. 1970, c. 115, s. 15A(2) [new S.N. 1972, No. 3, s. 2; 1972, No. 11, s. 2]; Northwest Territories, R.S.N.W.T. 1988, c. E-8, s. 19; Yukon, R.S.Y. 1986, c. 57, s. 16.
83   S.N.B. 1990, c. 17, s. 5.
84   S.B.C. 1988, c. 46, s. 25.
85   *McLeod v. MacLeod* (1980), 22 B.C.L.R. 51 (S.C.) appd. in *Shiell v. Coach House Hotel Ltd.* (1982), 37 B.C.L.R. 254, 136 D.L.R. (3d) 470, 27 C.P.C. 78 (C.A.).
86   *Hawley v. Hand* (1921), 50 O.L.R. 444, (1922), 64 D.L.R. 504 (C.A.).
87   *Koop v. Smith* (1915), 51 S.C.R. 554, 25 D.L.R. 335, 8 W.W.R. 1203. See

similar to the *Vetrovec* approach that if circumstances warrant, the trial judge has a discretion to scrutinize the evidence[88] or to warn a jury of potentially unreliable evidence. A civil action based on acts amounting to a criminal offence, which would require corroboration if charged as a crime, is not subject to the rules governing criminal cases.[89] No corroboration is required unless the case falls within one of the statutory rules, such as those described above.[90]

IV THE NATURE OF CORROBORATION

A. *General Requirements*

The statutory provisions requiring confirmatory evidence are not identically worded and it is understandable that questions arose as to *what* that confirmatory evidence must be.[91] There have been numerous attempts to explain the meaning of corroboration by many learned jurists and scholars. The Supreme Court's decision in *Vetrovec* focused the debate upon two competing interpretations of statutory corroboration provisions. One construction was labelled the *Baskerville* or technical corroboration rule while the alternate interpretation was called the common sense approach.[92] We will now examine some of the more prominent authorities in the context of the criminal and civil law.

The traditional definition of corroboration is found in Lord

---

also *Adamson v. Vachon* (1914), 6 W.W.R. 114, and *Re Riffel Estate* (1987), 28 E.T.R. 1, 64 Sask. R. 190 (Sask. Q.B.).

88   *Miller v. Miller Estate* (1987), 14 B.C.L.R. (2d) 42, 26 E.T.R. 243 (S.C.); see also *Re Murray* (1966), 60 D.L.R. (2d) 76 (B.C.S.C.).

89   *Dunn v. Gibson* (1912), 20 C.C.C. 195, 8 D.L.R. 297, 4 O.W.N. 329, 23 O.W.R. 356 (C.A.). See also *Mattouk v. Massad*, [1943] A.C. 588, [1943] 2 All E.R. 517, [1944] 3 W.W.R. 169 (C.A.).

90   Subject to occasional statutory exceptions, e.g., in *Paquette v. Chubb* (1988), 65 O.R. (2d) 321, 52 D.L.R. (4th) 1, 29 O.A.C. 243, 31 C.P.C. (2d) 87 corroboration was not required under the Ontario *Evidence Act*, R.S.O. 1980, c. 145, but was required under the Ontario *Mining Act*, R.S.O. 1980, c. 268.

91   It is unclear whether the corroboration rule applies at the preliminary enquiry: *R. v. McKay* (1987), 81 N.S.R. (2d) 320 (N.S.T.D.); *Re Smith* (1974), 15 N.S.R. (2d) 540 (N.S.T.D.); *Poirier v. R.* (1974), 62 C.C.C. (2d) 452 (Que. C.A.): *Contra: Stillo v. R.* (1981), 22 C.R. (3d) 224, 60 C.C.C. (2d) 243 (Ont. C.A.).

92   *R. v. B. (G.) (No. 1)*, [1990] 2 S.C.R. 3, at 25-26, 77 C.R. (3d) 327, 56 C.C.C. (3d) 200, 111 N.R. 1.

Reading's reasons for judgment in *R. v. Baskerville*:[93]

> We hold that evidence in corroboration must be independent testimony which affects the accused by connecting or tending to connect him with the crime. In other words, it must be evidence which implicates him, that is, which confirms in some material particular not only evidence that the crime has been committed, but also that the prisoner committed it. . . . The language of the statute, "implicates the accused" compendiously incorporates the test applicable at common law in the rule of practice. . . . [C]orroborative evidence is evidence which shows or tends to show that the story of the accomplice that the accused committed the crime is true, not merely that the crime has been committed, but that it was committed by the accused.

Thus, corroboration was required as to a material circumstance of the crime *and* the identity of the accused in relation to that crime.[94] A concise summary of many of the aspects of this definition of corroboration is found in the decision of the Ontario Court of Appeal in *R. v. McNamara (No. 1)*:[95]

> 1. Corroborative evidence is independent evidence which shows or tends to show that the story of the accomplice that the accused committed the crime, is true, not merely that the crime was committed but that it was committed by the accused.

> 2. An elaboration of the *Baskerville* rule, where circumstantial evidence is relied upon as corroborative, is that evidence to be corroborative must be more consistent with the truth than with the falsity of the accomplice's evidence on the vital issue or issues, and if in the view of the jury the facts, even though independently proved, are equally consistent with the truth as with the falsity of the accomplice's evidence on the vital issue or issues, they are not corroborative. Another and, perhaps, preferable way of stating the *Baskerville* rule, where circumstantial evidence is relied on as corroborative, is that corroboration is independent evidence

---

93   [1916] 2 K.B. 658, at 667, 12 Cr. App. Rep. 81, [1916-17] All E.R. Rep. 38.
94   *R. v. B. (G.)*, *supra*, note 92.
95   (1981), 56 C.C.C. (2d) 193, at 278-79 (C.A.).

which makes it probable that the accomplice's testimony with respect to the vital issue or issues is true.

3. It is the function of the Judge to instruct the jury what evidence is capable of constituting corroboration; it is for the jury to say whether the evidence, in fact, is corroborative.

4. It would seem axiomatic that since guilt may be established by circumstantial evidence, a number of circumstances collectively may constitute corroboration, provided that viewed together the circumstances satisfy the test of corroborative evidence. Accordingly, circumstances which, viewed in isolation, are incapable of constituting corroboration may, when considered together, be of sufficient strength to corroborate the commission of the offence and to connect the accused with its commission and, hence, be capable of being corroborative. It is proper for the Judge to leave with the jury a number of items of evidence, which viewed together, are capable of constituting corroboration provided that, viewed cumulatively, the circumstances meet the test required for evidence to be capable of being corroborative.

5. In considering whether evidence is capable of being corroborative it must be viewed against the total picture of all the evidence.

6. Whether a fact independently proved is capable of being corroborative must be determined without reference to the defence evidence. Where the accused offers an explanation of a fact capable of being corroborative, it is for the jury to accept or reject the accused's explanation. If they reject the explanation the fact retains its corroborative quality.

7. Where there is any independent evidence of facts relied upon as corroboration, it is for the jury to say whether those facts are more consistent with the truth than the falsity of the accomplice's testimony on the vital issue or issues, provided the facts are of such probative quality that if accepted by the jury as proved, and any evidence given by the defence explaining those facts rejected, a reasonable jury would be warranted in concluding that they are

more consistent with the truth than the falsity of the accomplice's evidence on the vital issue or issues. It is a question for the Judge whether the facts are *capable* of being corroborative; it is for the jury to consider whether to *accept* the facts as corroborative.

8. The Judge must specify for the jury which items are capable of being corroborative. If corroborative evidence is left to the jury on the basis that it is capable of affording corroboration when viewed cumulatively, the Judge should instruct the jury which items of evidence can be considered as part of the cumulative package. These items, of course, should be confined to items which have substantial probative value considered collectively on the vital issue or issues in the particular case.[96]

This summary demonstrates the legal complexity of the *Baskerville* rule which imposes constraints on the trial judge in his or her summing-up to the jury. Also, as the case law demonstrates, it may be a nice question whether evidence, especially circumstantial evidence, meets the test of independence and materiality in order to qualify as being corroborative. We will now review the development of the corroboration rule in the civil context.

B. *Degree and Extent of Corroboration*

Like the provisions governing criminal proceedings, the statutory civil corroboration provisions do not specify the degree or extent to which evidence needs to be corroborated.[97] In those statutes which require the evidence to be corroborated "by some other material evidence",[98] the Supreme Court of Canada in *Smallman v. Moore*[99] held that the word "material" is not synonymous with every fact required to be proved in order to establish a cause of action. It is sufficient if there is evidence "which appreciably helps the judicial mind to believe one or more of the material statements or facts

---

96   Authorities cited by the court for these principles have been omitted.
97   *Radford v. Macdonald* (1891), 18 O.A.R. 167, at 171 (C.A.); *Sands Estate v. Sonnwald* (1986), 9 C.P.C. (2d) 100, at 110, 22 E.T.R. 282 (H.C.J.).
98   These words are used in ss. 13, 14 and 18(2) of The Ontario *Evidence Act*, R.S.O. 1980, c. 145.
99   *Smallman v. Moore*, [1948] S.C.R. 295, at 301, [1948] 3 D.L.R. 657.

deposed to".[100] This is generally the test in civil cases[101] and incorporates a test of quality or cogency of the proof offered.[102] The corroborative evidence cannot, however, be in respect of irrelevant and immaterial matters; it must be corroborative of the party's evidence in essential matters.[103] Also, some statutory provisions may require corroboration of a particular issue, for example, in support of the promise in an action for breach of promise of marriage,[104] or in support of paternity in affiliation proceedings.[105]

C. *Independence of Corroborative Evidence*

Although the statutory language does not use the term "independent," some courts have interpreted the statutory phrase "some other material evidence" to require the corroborating evidence to derive from a person or source extraneous to the testimony needing corroboration.[106] For instance, in *Little v. Hyslop*,[107] a claim for a debt by the representative of an estate, the defendant relied on a number of separate unconnected payments. It was held that the defendant was

---

100 *Black v. George McKean & Co.* (1921), 62 S.C.R. 290, at 308, 68 D.L.R. 34 (C.A.); *Radford v. Macdonald* (1891), 18 O.A.R. 167, at 173 (Ont. C.A.); *Harvie v. Gibbons* (1980), 12 Alta. L.R. (2d) 72, at 85-87, 109 D.L.R. (3d) 559, 16 R.P.R. 174 (C.A.); *Ken Ertel Ltd. v. Simonian Estate* (1986), 21 E.T.R. 279, at 285, 25 D.L.R. (4th) 233, 53 O.R. (2d) 220, 7 C.P.C. (2d) 106; leave to appeal to C.A. refd. 21 E.T.R. 279n (Ont. C.A.).

101 *R. v. Silverstone* (1934), 61 C.C.C. 258, [1934] 1 D.L.R. 726, [1934] O.R. 94 (C.A.); *Johnson v. Nova Scotia Trust Co.* (1973), 43 D.L.R. (3d) 222, at 236, 6 N.S.R. (2d) 88 (C.A.).

102 *Sands Estate, supra,* note 97, at 293 (E.T.R.).

103 *Bayley v. Trusts & Guarantee Co.* (1930), 66 O.L.R. 254, [1931] 1 D.L.R. 500 (C.A.); *Smallman v. Moore, supra,* note 99, at 303. Recently, Watt J. in *Sands Estate, ibid.,* stated: ". . . the evidence proposed as corroboration should be such as to enhance the probability of truth of the suspect witness' evidence upon a substantive part of the case raised by the pleadings".

104 For example, see the *Saskatchewan Evidence Act,* R.S.S. 1978, c. S-16, s. 43; and see, *Mott v. Trott,* [1943] S.C.R. 256, [1943] 2 D.L.R. 609.

105 Only Northwest Territories maintains a corroboration provision: R.S.N.W.T. 1988, c. C-6, s. 60. Saskatchewan and British Columbia courts had held that a similar provision was unconstitutional, *supra,* note 72. For an earlier case on this provision, see *Luther v. Ryan* (1956), 115 C.C.C. 303, 3 D.L.R. (2d) 693, 39 M.P.R. 122 (Nfld. C.A.).

106 *Sands Estate v. Sonnwald, supra,* note 97, at 293; *Elgin v. Stubbs* (1928), 62 O.L.R. 128 (C.A.).

107 (1912), 23 O.W.N. 247, 4 O.W.N. 285, 7 D.L.R. 478 (S.C.).

required to corroborate his evidence with respect to each distinct payment.[108] The requirement of independence sometimes created difficulty when potentially corroborative documentary evidence could be proved only by the witness whose evidence needed corroboration. In *Walker v. Foster*,[109] a paternity case, the only evidence identifying the disputed handwriting in a letter as that of the putative father was the mother's testimony. The Ontario Court of Appeal refused to accept the writing as corroborative evidence. This interpretation and application of the corroboration rule was not universally followed[110] and it appears inconsistent with the test in *Smallman v. Moore*[111] and the more recent decisions by the Supreme Court of Canada.[112]

D. Corroborative Evidence May be Direct or Circumstantial

Corroboration may be found in direct or circumstantial evidence[113] which renders it probable that the evidence needing corroboration is true upon a material issue.[114] There should not be a more

---

108 However, see *Cook v. Tripp* (1982), 39 O.R. 431, 13 E.T.R. 80, 139 D.L.R. (3d) 136 (Div. Ct.).

109 (1923), 54 O.L.R. 214, [1923] 4 D.L.R. 1204 (C.A.). See also *Thompson v. Thompson* (1902), 4 O.L.R. 442 (C.A.), where it was held that a writing could be admitted and the handwriting compared directly with another document made by the same party which was independently proved.

110 *Jeffery v. Johnson*, [1952] 2 Q.B. 8, [1952] 1 All E.R. 450 (C.A.); *Workun v. Nelson* (1958), 26 W.W.R. 600 (Alta. C.A.); *Myles v. Elliott* (1924), 26 O.W.N. 166, at 168 (S.C.) where the court adopted Phipson's definition of corroboration: "Facts which tend to render more probable the truth of a witness's testimony on any material point are admissible in corroboration thereof, although otherwise irrelevant to the issue, and although happening before the date of the fact to be corroborated", from S.L. Phipson, *The Law of Evidence*, 6th ed. (London: Sweet & Maxwell, 1921), at 487 and cases cited. See now M.N. Howard, P. Crane and D.A. Hochberg, *Phipson on Evidence*, 14th ed. (London: Sweet & Maxwell, 1990), at 321-22.

111 *Supra*, note 99.

112 E.g., *R. v. B. (G.) (No. 1)*, *supra*, note 92.

113 *Walmsley v. Humenick*, [1954] 2 D.L.R. 232, at 237; *Moran v. Richards* (1973), 38 D.L.R. (3d) 171, [1973] 3 O.R. 751; *Paquette v. Chubb* (1988), 65 O.R. (2d) 321, at 334-35, 52 D.L.R. (4th) 1, 29 O.A.C. 243, 31 C.P.C. (2d) 87 (C.A.); *Sands Estate v. Sonnwald*, *supra*, note 97.

114 *Sands Estate*, *supra*, note 97, at 119. But see *Harvie v. Gibbons* (1980), 12 Alta. L.R. 72, at 87, 109 D.L.R. (3d) 559 (C.A.) where inferences or probabilities tending to support the truth of the respondents testimony sufficed.

onerous standard when circumstantial evidence is offered as corroborative evidence.[115] Circumstantial evidence is assessed cumulatively,[116] but if the evidence is equally consistent with the evidence of the party who must supply corroboration and with another view, it is corroborative of neither.[117] But defence evidence that has been rejected by the trier of fact cannot be used to render the evidence equivocal.[118] Corroboration can be found in the evidence of the opposite party,[119] and, indeed, in his or her failure to testify or call available witnesses.[120] In actions by or against the heirs, executors or assigns of a deceased person, the evidence of a claimant may be corroborated by a statement against interest made by the deceased and admitted as an exception under the hearsay rule.[121] Furthermore, the deceased's silence and lack of complaint about nonpayment of a debt, coupled with evidence as to his miserliness, has been held to be corroborative.[122]

E. *Function of Judge and Jury*

It is for the trial judge to determine if the evidence is capable of being corroborative, and it is for the jury to determine if it has this effect.[123] In the absence of corroboration, the party requiring corrob-

---

115 *Sands Estate, ibid.*

116 *Paquette v. Chubb, supra*, note 113, at 330-33, considering *R. v. McNamara (No. 1), supra*, note 95, at 278-79 (propositions 4 and 8), and *R. v. Warkentin*, [1977] 2 S.C.R. 355, 35 C.R.N.S. 21, 30 C.C.C. (2d) 1, 70 D.L.R. (3d) 20, [1976] 5 W.W.R. 1, 9 N.R. 301.

117 *Lahay v. Brown*, [1958] S.C.R. 240, 12 D.L.R. (2d) 785; *MacDonald v. Young*, [1934] 4 D.L.R. 172, 7 M.P.R. 602 (N.S.C.A.); *Thompson v. Coulter* (1903), 34 S.C.R. 261, 3 O.W.R. 82; *Smallman v. Moore, supra*, note 99; *British Columbia (Public Trustee) v. Skoretz* (1973), 32 D.L.R. (3d) 749, [1973] 2 W.W.R. 638.

118 *Paquette v. Chubb, supra*, note 113, at 330.

119 *Goguen v. Bourgeois* (1956), 6 D.L.R. (2d) 19 (N.B.C.A.).

120 *Middleton v. Bryce* (1931), 40 O.W.N. 583 (C.A.); *Moran v. Richards* (1974), 38 D.L.R. (3d) 171, [1973] 3 O.R. 751 (Ont. H.C.J.). But the failure of an accused to testify is not capable of constituting corroboration.

121 *Rigby v. Nova Scotia Trust Co.*, [1938] 2 D.L.R. 583, 13 M.P.R. 70 (N.S.C.A.); *Evans v. Trusts and Guarantee Co.*, [1920] 3 W.W.R. 103 (Alta. S.C.); affd. [1921] 1 W.W.R. 117 (Alta. C.A.).

122 *Green v. McLeod* (1896), 23 O.A.R. 676 (C.A.).

123 *Sands Estate v. Sonnwald* (1986), 9 C.P.C. (2d) 100, at 119-20 (C.P.C.), 22 E.T.R. 282, at 302-03 (point 5) (H.C.J.); and see *R. v. McNamara (No. 1)* (1981), 56 C.C.C. (2d) 193, at 278-79 citing with approval *Manos v. R.*, [1953] 1 S.C.R. 91, 15 C.R. 363, 104 C.C.C. 336.

oration will fail unless the opposing party fails to satisfy a burden of proof cast upon it.[124] If the court is satisfied that the statutory requirement has been met, it then weighs the evidence as if there were no statutory requirement with respect to corroboration.[125] In so weighing the evidence, it is unnecessary to establish the party's credibility before corroborative evidence can be resorted to.[126]

F. Difference Between Civil and Criminal Cases

Although it is difficult to state with a high degree of confidence, a review of the cases decided before *Vetrovec* indicate a more liberal interpretation or a broader definition of the corroboration rule in civil actions than in criminal prosecutions.[127] In *R. v. Silverstone*, Middleton J.A. pointed out this difference:[128]

> ... In civil cases, it is sufficient if the evidence of the party to be corroborated is strengthened by evidence which appreciably helps the judicial mind to believe his evidence in one or more of the facts or statements deposed to. . . . In criminal cases the corroborative evidence need not establish the guilt of the accused throughout but it must show that there was a crime and show the probability of the accused as the criminal; "it must implicate him".

The corroboration test articulated in civil cases corresponds to the common sense approach more recently advocated by the Supreme Court of Canada in the criminal field. For example in *R. v. Warkentin*,[129] Mr. Justice de Grandpré broadly defined

---

124 *Sands Estate, supra,* note 123, at 303.

125 *Buchanan v. Labrash* (1922), 23 O.W.N. 339 (C.A.); *Re Taylor,* [1923] 2 D.L.R. 847, [1923] 2 W.W.R. 180, 19 Alta. L.R. 295 (C.A.); *Teasdale v. Hertel* (1925), 29 O.W.N. 200 (S.C.); *Pieper v. Zinkann* (1927), 60 O.L.R. 443 (C.A.).

126 *Dominion Trust Co. v. Inglis,* [1921] 1 W.W.R. 677, 29 B.C.R. 213 (C.A.).

127 See A. Wakeling, *Corroboration in Canadian Law* (Toronto: Carswell, 1977), at 79.

128 (1934), 61 C.C.C. 258, [1934] 1 D.L.R. 726, [1934] O.R. 94, at 98 (C.A.).

129 *R. v. Warkentin, supra,* note 116. Additionally the *Report of the Federal/Provincial Task Force on Uniform Rules of Evidence* (Toronto: Carswell, 1982), at 364: "It is hard to disagree with the minority view [in the Supreme Court] that the facts in *Warkentin* failed to satisfy either arm of the *Baskerville* test. On the other hand, the majority seemed to realize that technical compliance with the rules did not always work justice and a more flexible approach was desirable."

corroboration:[130]

> Corroboration is not a word of art. It is a matter of common sense. In recent years, this Court has repeatedly refused to give a narrow legalistic reading of that word and to impose upon trial Judges artificial restraints in their instructions to juries or to themselves.

In both *Warkentin* and *R. v. Murphy*,[131] the forerunners of *Vetrovec*, the Supreme Court did not vigorously apply the *Baskerville* test.[132] After the court's decision in *Vetrovec*, writers on evidence[133] and some superior court judges[134] maintained that the technical or *Baskerville* rule applied to the remaining *Criminal Code* corroboration provisions. On the other hand, there was mounting academic[135] and judicial support[136] favouring the application of the new judicially formulated *Vetrovec* test for these statutory rules. The Supreme Court of Canada ended the controversy by adopting the latter interpretation.[137]

In *R. v. B. (G.) (No. 1)*[138] a five year old child was sexually

---

130   *Ibid.*, at 16 (C.C.C.).
131   [1977] 2 S.C.R. 603, 35 C.R.N.S. 44, 29 C.C.C. (2d) 417, [1976] 5 W.W.R. 65, 9 N.R. 329.
132   In *R. v. B. (G.) (No. 1)*, [1990] 2 S.C.R. 3, at 23, 77 C.R. (3d) 327, 56 C.C.C. (3d) 200, 111 N.R. 1, Wilson J. noted that ". . . [T]he judgement [in *Warkentin*] does suggest a weakening of the strict requirement of evidence corroborative of the accused's connection with the offence."
133   See Anthony F. Sheppard, 11 C.E.D. (Ont. 3rd) Title 57 *Evidence*, § 1158, at 584, §§ 1167-72, at 587-89; P.K. McWilliams, *Canadian Criminal Evidence*, 3rd ed. (Aurora: Canada Law Book, 1988), at 26-2–26-16.
134   *R. v. Ookpik*, [1988] N.W.T.R. 67 (C.A.); *R. v. Chayko* (1984), 12 C.C.C. (3d) 157, 31 Alta. L.R. (2d) 113, at 121, 51 A.R. 382 (C.A.) and *R. v. Jackson* (1988), 84 A.R. 278, at 288, 58 Alta. L.R. (2d) 207 (C.A.), per Harradence J. in dissent. *Paquette v. Chubb* (1988), 65 O.R. 321, 52 D.L.R. (4th) 1, 29 O.A.C. 243, 31 C.P.C. (2d) 87 (C.A.) in *obiter*.
135   R. Delisle, *Evidence: Principles and Problems*, 2nd ed. (Toronto: Carswell, 1989), at 313: "This common sense approach to the problem is to be welcomed. It is a pity that the corroboration required by statute cannot be approached in a similar way."
136   *R. v. Chayko, supra*, note 134 (C.A.); *R. v. Jackson, supra*, note 134; *R. v. B. (G.)* (1988), 65 Sask. R. 134 (C.A.); *R. v. Foley* (1988), 67 Sask. R. 247 (C.A.).
137   *R. v. B. (G.) (No. 1), supra*, note 132, at 27 (S.C.R.). See also *R. v. Potvin*, [1989] 1 S.C.R. 525, 47 C.C.C. (3d) 289, 68 C.R. (3d) 193, 93 N.R. 42, 21 Q.A.C. 258.
138   *Ibid.*

assaulted. At trial the child gave unsworn testimony. There was corroboration of the assault, but only the complainant identified the accused as the assailant. The court was required to interpret s. 586 of the *Criminal Code* (now repealed) which provided:[139]

> No person shall be convicted of an offence upon the unsworn evidence of a child unless the evidence of the child is corroborated in a material particular by evidence that implicates the accused.

The court held that corroboration is:[140]

> . . . additional evidence that renders it probable that the complainant's story is true and may be safely acted upon. Provided that the complainant's evidence is corroborated in a material particular, with or without implicating the accused, the veracity of the witness will be strengthened.

Under this approach there is no requirement that there be independent evidence implicating the accused.[141] Thus, corroboration is evidence which shows or tends to show the testimony of the suspect witness is true in relation to a material circumstance[142] or is evidence which tends to support the *allegation* of a criminal act[143] but it need not confirm every element of the offence.[144]

In *R. v. B. (G.) (No. 1)* the court compared the underlying values for the two competing interpretations of the statutory corroboration rule. The court acknowledged that the *Baskerville* interpretation would provide strong protection against false convictions, but nonetheless, it preferred the more liberal approach. The court reasoned that the *Baskerville* interpretation may permit serious offences against children to go unpunished or perhaps continue, and the legislation

---

139 R.S.C. 1970, c. C-34, repealed by *An Act to amend the Criminal Code and the Canada Evidence Act*, S.C. 1987, c. 24, s. 15.

140 *R. v. B. (G.) (No. 1), supra*, note 132, at 28 (S.C.R.).

141 *Ibid.*

142 *R. v. Beliveau* (1986), 30 C.C.C. (3d) 193 (B.C.C.A.).

143 *R. v. Chayko, supra*, note 136, at 116 (Alta. L.R.). See also *R. v. Jackson, supra*, note 136.

144 *R. v. Parish*, [1968] S.C.R. 466, 4 C.C.C. 11, 3 C.R.N.S. 383, 68 D.L.R. (2d) 528, 64 W.W.R. 310; *R. v. B. (G.) (No. 1), supra*, note 132, at 29 (S.C.R.).

should not be interpreted in such a way as to unnecessarily impede prosecution.[145]

The Court noted that the degree of corroboration for unsworn testimony of children was thought to be the same under this provision ("corroborated in a material particular by evidence that implicates the accused") as that set out in the *Canada Evidence Act*[146] ("corroborated by some other material evidence").[147] Provincial legislation which frequently follows the form of the *Canada Evidence Act*, in that it omits the words "that implicates the accused" would, *a fortiori*, receive the broader interpretation which the court gave to s. 586 of the *Criminal Code*.[148]

Historically, the *Baskerville* rule was applied to overturn convictions where there was confirmatory evidence of the main witness and the trier of fact found that the accused committed the offence beyond a reasonable doubt.[149] The Law Reform Commission of Canada[150] and the Task Force[151] recommended that every rule of law that requires corroboration or a corroboration warning be abrogated.[152] The minimal number of statutory corroboration rules in the criminal field reflect a trend against formal legal rules that require confirmatory evidence for potentially unreliable witnesses.[153] In those provincial jurisdictions which do not have a statutory rule in relation to a particular cause of action, the trial courts were nonetheless alive to

---

145 *R. v. B. (G.) (No. 1), ibid.*, at 28-29 (S.C.R.).
146 R.S.C. 1985, c. C-5.
147 *R. v. B. (G.) (No. 1), supra*, note 132, at 14 (S.C.R.); see also *Paige v. R.*, [1948] S.C.R. 349, at 351, 6 C.R. 93, 92 C.C.C. 32; *R. v. Chayko, supra*, note 136, at 119 (Alta. L.R.).
148 E.g., ss. 13 and 14 of the Ontario *Evidence Act*, R.S.O 1980, c. 145.
149 *Hubin v. R.*, [1927] S.C.R. 442, 48 C.C.C. 172, [1927] 4 D.L.R. 760.
150 Law Reform Commission of Canada, *Report on Evidence* (Ottawa: Law Reform Commission of Canada, 1975), s. 88; see also, Criminal Law Revision Committee, *11th Report, Evidence (General)* (London: H.M.S.O., 1972), Cmnd. 4991.
151 The *Report of the Federal/Provincial Task Force on Uniform Rules of Evidence* (Toronto: Carswell, 1982), at 369; however, the task force recommended that the court should continue to warn the jury for the offence of treason.
152 But see the Australian Law Reform Commission, *Evidence*, Report No. 26, Interim, Vol. 1 (Canberra: Australian Government Publishing Service, 1985), at 558 ff; Vol. 2, at 63-64.
153 See *D.P.P. v. Hester*, [1972] 3 All E.R. 1056, [1973] A.C. 296, 57 Cr. App. R. 212 (H.L.); *D.P.P. v. Kilbourne*, [1973] 2 W.L.R. 254, [1973] 1 All E.R. 440, [1973] A.C. 729; *R. v. Spencer*, [1988] 2 All E.R. 928 (H.L.).

potentially untruthful evidence.[154] In a different context, the Supreme Court recently stated:[155]

> The reason we have juries is so that lay persons and not lawyers decide facts. To inject into the process artificial legal rules with respect to the normal human activity of deliberation and decisions would tend to detract from value of the jury system.

A clear warning about the particular grounds of unreliability of the suspect witness' testimony and a caution to search for confirmation of the witness' evidence would be more helpful to the jury in its fact finding task than a *Baskerville* direction. Because an appellate court has jurisdiction to overturn a conviction if a verdict is unreasonable or cannot be supported by the evidence,[156] a remedy is available if a verdict, based on unreliable evidence, is thought to be unsafe.[157]

---

154 *DeCorby v. DeCorby* (1987), 49 Man. R. (2d) 136 (Q.B.); vard (1989), 57 Man. R. (2d) 241 (A.C.). See also *J.M. Lumber King v. Von Transehe-Roseneck Estate* (1988), 31 E.T.R. 243 (B.C.C.A.); *Miller v. Miller Estate* (1987), 14 B.C.L.R. (2d) 42, 26 E.T.R. 243 (B.C.S.C.); *Kong v. Kong* (1979), 5 E.T.R. 67, 14 B.C.L.R. 357, [1979] 6 W.W.R. 673 (B.C.S.C.); *McLeod v. MacLeod* (1980), 22 B.C.L.R. 51 (B.C.S.C.).

155 *R. v. Morin*, [1988] 2 S.C.R. 345, at 362, 66 C.R. (3d) 1, at 19, 44 C.C.C. (3d) 193, 30 O.A.C. 81.

156 In *R. v. Lang* (1987), 46 Man. R. (2d) 135 (C.A.); affd. [1988] 1 S.C.R. 618, 52 Man. R. 80, 83 N.R. 238 the accused was convicted of sexually assaulting an 11 year old girl and the trial court and appeal court agreed that a technical approach to corroboration was not warranted under the former s. 586 of the *Criminal Code* (now R.S.C. 1985, c. C-46, s. 659 [rep. 1985, c. 19 (3rd Supp.), s. 15]). Although the trial judge performed an exhaustive analysis of the credibility of the child's testimony and the surrounding circumstances, the appeal court applied s. 613(1)(a) of the *Criminal Code* [now s. 686] to overturn the conviction because it was unreasonable. See also *R. v. Hayes*, [1989] 1 S.C.R. 44, at 57-58, 48 C.C.C. (3d) 161, 68 C.R. (3d) 245, 89 N.R. 138, 89 N.S.R. (2d) 286 where Sopinka J. held that a failure to warn a jury about the risks of adopting, without more, the evidence of the accomplice may constitute, in some circumstances, a miscarriage of justice.

157 See for example *R. v. Izzard* (1990), 75 C.R. (3d) 342, 54 C.C.C. (3d) 258, 38 O.A.C. 6 (C.A.), an identification case.

V ILLUSTRATIONS OF THE RULE IN CIVIL PROCEEDINGS

We will now examine two of the more prominent provisions requiring corroboration found in the various provincial Evidence Acts.[158] It is beyond the scope of this chapter to examine every corroboration provision set out in various other statutes.[159]

A. Actions by or against Heirs, Executors or Assigns of Deceased Persons or by or against Mentally Incompetent Persons

1. General

This provision concerns actions brought by or against a party who is unable to give evidence either by reason of death or mental disability.[160] At common law, when no interested party was allowed to give evidence, deceased or disabled parties were under no greater incapacity than living litigants. This obstacle, which also applied to a party's spouse, was removed by statute[161] thereby placing a deceased or disabled party at a decided disadvantage. To ameliorate this disadvantage, it became a rule of practice that in actions by or against such persons, an opposite or interested party should not obtain a judgment, decision, or verdict in respect of a matter occurring before the death or disability, unless that party's evidence was corroborated by some other material evidence. This rule of practice was made an absolute requirement by statute and is contained in many provincial Evidence Acts.[162] An illustration is found in s. 11 of the Prince Edward Island

---

158 For an analysis of corroboration requirements for breach of promise to marry and affiliation proceedings see J. Sopinka and S.N. Lederman, *The Law of Evidence in Civil Cases* (Toronto: Butterworths, 1974), at 413-15.

159 For example, s. 69 of the Ontario *Mining Act*, R.S.O. 1980, c. 268; see *Paquette v. Chubb* (1988), 65 O.R. (2d) 321, 52 D.L.R. (4th) 1, 29 O.A.C. 243, 31 C.P.C. (2d) 87 (C.A.) for an interpretation of that section.

160 In *Kirkpatrick v. Lament*, [1965] S.C.R. 538, at 547, [1966] 1 C.C.C. 30, 51 D.L.R. (2d) 699 the court held that corroboration sections governing an action against a deceased and a mental incompetent are *para materia*.

161 Incompetency was first abolished in the U.K. by *The Evidence Act* (1851), 14 & 15 Vict., c. 99.

162 Evidence Acts: Ontario, R.S.O. 1980, c. 145, s. 13 (estates), s. 14 (incompetents); Alberta, R.S.A. 1980, c. A-21, s. 12 (estates), s. 13 (incompetents); British

Evidence Act which states:[163]

In any action or proceeding by or against the heirs, or personal representatives or their assigns of a deceased person, an opposite or interested party to the action shall not obtain a verdict, judgment or decision therein on his own evidence in respect of any matter occurring before the death of the deceased person, unless the evidence is corroborated by some other material evidence.

In Manitoba, where the requirement was not incorporated into a statute, it remains a rule of practice,[164] whereas in Saskatchewan[165] and British Columbia,[166] the courts have held that the evidence must be carefully scrutinized. Since the recent pronouncements by the Supreme Court of Canada as to the meaning of corroboration, differences between a rule of practice, a corroboration rule, and the practice of scrutinizing the evidence may be less important than formerly required. We will now examine the scope of the statutory corroboration provisions for these causes of action.[167]

Columbia, R.S.B.C. 1979, c. 116, s. 9 (incompetents), (the provision re estates, R.S.B.C. 1960, c. 134, s. 11, was repealed S.B.C. 1976, c. 2, s. 20(a)); Newfoundland, R.S.N. 1970, c. 115, s. 14 (estates), s. 15 (incompetents); Nova Scotia, R.S.N.S. 1989, c. 154, s. 45 (estates), (no provision re incompetents); Prince Edward Island, R.S.P.E.I. 1988, c. E-11, s. 11 (estates), s. 12 (incompetents); Yukon, R.S.Y. 1986, c. 57, s. 14 (estates), s. 15 (incompetents); Northwest Territories, R.S.N.W.T. 1988, c. E-8, s. 17 (estates), s. 18 (incompetents).

163 *Ibid.*

164 *Weingarden v. Moss* (1954), 13 W.W.R. 161, [1955] 1 D.L.R. 747, 63 Man. R. 243 (Man. Q.B.); affd. 15 W.W.R. 481, [1955] 4 D.L.R. 63, 63 Man. R., at 253 (Man. C.A.). But see *DeCorby v. DeCorby, supra,* note 154: "[T]he law [in Manitoba] is that the evidence must be examined with scrupulous care, even with suspicion, but if it brings conviction to the court which has to try the case, the court will act on that conviction" per Oliphant J., *ibid.,* at 142 (Man. R.–Q.B.).

165 *Re Riffel Estate* (1987), 28 E.T.R. 1, 64 Sask. R. 190 (Q.B.).

166 *Kong v. Kong, supra,* note 154; *J.M. Lumber King Ltd. v. Von Transehe-Roseneck Estate, supra,* note 154; see also *Re Murray* (1966), 60 D.L.R. (2d) 76 (B.C.S.C.). The British Columbia provision regarding estates (R.S.B.C. 1960, c. 134, s. 11) has been repealed by S.B.C. 1976, c. 2, s. 20(a).

167 In *Ken Ertel Ltd. v. Johnson* (1986), 53 O.R. (2d) 220, 25 D.L.R. (4th) 233, 12 O.A.C. 137, 7 C.P.C. (2d) 106, 21 E.T.R. 279, 283, (*sub nom. Ertel (Ken) Ltd. v. Simonian Estate*) Van Camp J. suggested that the general approach was a strict interpretation as there is a general reluctance by the courts to require corroboration.

2. The Witness Requiring Corroboration: Opposite and Interested Party

An opposite or interested party who is a witness requires corroboration, but a witness called by an interested party who benefits by the judgment does not have to be corroborated.[168] Corroboration is required whether the party is plaintiff or defendant.[169] Neither the spouse,[170] the solicitor,[171] nor the servant of a party[172] are interested parties within the meaning of the statute. In cases in which a corporation is an opposite or interested party, an employee of the corporation is not, and can therefore establish the case for the corporation.[173] Persons financially interested in the corporation, such as shareholders and bondholders, however, are within the statute.[174]

The assignor of a debt is not an opposite or interested party, and in an action by the assignee to recover from the estate of the deceased debtor no corroboration is required of the assignor's evidence.[175] The requirement extends to actions by or against the "assigns of a deceased person", which includes a donee of land from a deceased person.[176]

3. Action by or against Deceased or Mental Incompetent

It is not sufficient to invoke the requirement for corroboration that the estate is merely involved in the action. The judgment, decision or verdict to be obtained must be *by* or *against* the estate. Thus

---

168 *Re Curry* (1900), 32 O.R. 150 (S.C.); *Re Ruby* (1983), 43 O.R. (2d) 277 (Surr. Ct.).
169 S. Schiff, *Evidence in the Litigation Process*, 3rd ed. (Toronto: Carswell: 1988), at 623.
170 *Farrell v. Collerman* (1961), 34 W.W.R. 576 (B.C.S.C.); *Re Critelli* (1960), 24 D.L.R. (2d) 510 (Surr. Ct.). However, Nova Scotia by virtue of the *Evidence Act*, R.S.N.S. 1989, c. 154, s. 45 requires corroboration of the evidence of the spouse of an interested party.
171 *McEwan v. Toronto General Trusts Corp.* (1917), 54 S.C.R. 381, 28 C.C.C. 387, 35 D.L.R. 435.
172 *Re Miller*, [1949] O.W.N. 569 (Surr. Ct.); *Gibbs v. Canada Trust Co.*, [1954] O.W.N. 917 (S.C.).
173 *Kenora (District) Home for the Aged v. Duck Estate* (1987), 62 O.R. (2d) 696, 26 C.P.C. (2d) 70 (Ont. H.C.J.).
174 *Imperial Bank v. Trusts & Guarantee Co.*, [1921] 1 W.W.R. 801, 57 D.L.R. 693, 16 Alta. L.R. 343 (C.A.); *Re Bell*, [1940] O.R. 88, [1940] 1 D.L.R. 133 (C.A.); *Ken Ertel v. Johnson, supra*, note 167.
175 *Watson v. Severn* (1881), 6 O.A.R. 559 (C.A.).
176 *Follis v. Albemarle (Township)*, [1941] O.R. 1, [1941] 1 D.L.R. 178 (C.A.).

in an action by the creditors of the deceased to set aside a conveyance by the deceased to his daughter, it was held that the action was against the grantee of the deceased and corroboration was not required.[177] In actions by an opposite or interested party against a deceased's estate or a mentally disabled party, the onus of proof being generally on the plaintiff, the plaintiff cannot succeed, unless the evidence is corroborated as required by the statute. Once, however, the plaintiff establishes a *prima facie* case and the legal burden of proof is on the estate or disabled person in relation to a defence, the mere allegation of a defence or evidence supporting it does not renew the requirements for corroboration on the part of the plaintiff.

For example, in *Bayley v. Trusts & Guarantee Co.*,[178] an action by a real estate agent to recover a commission against an estate, the evidence of the plaintiff as to the agreement to pay commission was corroborated. Proof by the estate that the agent had received a commission from another person did not cast on the plaintiff the burden of corroborating his reply that the payment of this additional commission was known to the deceased person.

The same view was adopted in *McGregor v. Curry*,[179] in which the plaintiff proved a contract and claimed specific performance. The estate's defence to specific performance was acquiescence, laches and delay. It was held that the plaintiff's uncorroborated testimony could be accepted to negative the defence. Hodgins J.A. said:[180]

> If a plaintiff proved his case on a promissory note against a party deceased, by corroborative evidence, and the defence made was that it was paid, it would be monstrous if the plaintiff could not give effective answer, that the alleged payment was upon another debt, without corroboration.

However, a different view was taken in *Re Jackson*,[181] in which the plaintiff sued on a promissory note. The defendant pleaded the *Statute of Limitations*. To take the case out of the statute, the plaintiff countered by proving that a payment had been made within the six-year

177   *Anderson v. Bradley* (1921), 51 O.R. 94, 64 D.L.R. 707 (C.A.); see also *Brown v. Brown* (1904), 8 O.L.R. 332 (S.C.).
178   (1930), 66 O.L.R. 254, [1931] 1 D.L.R. 500 (C.A.).
179   (1914), 31 O.L.R. 261, 20 D.L.R. 706 (C.A.); affd. (1915), 25 D.L.R. 771 (P.C.).
180   *Ibid.*, at 273 (O.L.R.–C.A.).
181   (1929), 64 O.L.R. 215, [1929] 4 D.L.R. 213 (C.A.).

period by the deceased. It was held that this evidence had to be corroborated. Since the statute merely requires corroboration of the evidence of the opposite or interested party in respect of some material issue, the reasoning in *McGregor v. Curry*[182] and *Bayley v. Trusts & Guarantee Co. Ltd.*[183] is to be preferred.

In an action against the heirs, next-of-kin, executors, administrators or assigns of a deceased person, the statute only requires corroboration in respect of any matter occurring before the death of the deceased person.[184] Claims arising out of the acts of the personal representatives of a deceased person, do not, therefore, have to be corroborated.[185] In actions *by* the representative of a deceased or disabled person, it is only when the representative has made out a *prima facie* case, discharging the representative's evidentiary burden that the statute operates in favour of the plaintiff to prevent judgment being obtained by the opposite party on its own evidence.[186]

4. Multiple Claims and Claimants

In the case of a joint claim where the claimants are both entitled to the fruits of the action, evidence independent of the claimants is required.[187] Similarly, two plaintiffs interested in the same cause of action cannot corroborate each other,[188] nor can two defendants who are sued as joint tortfeasors.[189] This result appears to be justified by the express wording of the statute which requires corroboration "by

---

182 *Supra*, note 179.

183 *Supra*, note 178.

184 This requirement is, of course, absent in actions against mentally incompetent persons, where the concern is not on verification of events occurring before a certain point in time, but on the ability of a party to adequately conduct his or her proceedings. Compare ss. 12 and 13 of the Alberta *Evidence Act*, R.S.A. 1980, c. A-21.

185 *McClenaghan v. Perkins* (1902), 5 O.L.R. 129 (C.A.); *Sproule v. Murray* (1919), 45 O.L.R. 326, 48 D.L.R. 368 (C.A.).

186 *Thompson v. Coulter* (1903), 34 S.C.R. 261, 3 O.W.R. 82; *Groat v. Kinnaird* (1914), 7 W.W.R. 264, 20 D.L.R. 421, 7 Alta. L.R. 390 (Alta. C.A.); *Re Taylor*, [1923] 2 W.W.R. 180, [1923] 2 D.L.R. 847, 19 Alta. L.R. 295 (Alta. C.A.); *Duggan v. Duggan*, [1939] 3 W.W.R. 321 (Alta. S.C.).

187 *Ledingham v. Skinner* (1915), 21 D.L.R. 300, 8 W.W.R. 52, 21 B.C.R. 41 (B.C.C.A.); *Taylor v. Regis* (1895), 26 O.R. 483 (Ch.).

188 *Hallman v. Bricker*, [1943] O.W.N. 311 (S.C.).

189 *Kirkpatrick v. Lament*, [1965] S.C.R. 538, [1966] 1 C.C.C. 30, 51 D.L.R. (2d) 699.

some other material evidence".[190] The other material evidence should, therefore, be some evidence other than that of an interested party. This result can also be supported on the basis of the rule against "mutual corroboration" approved by the Supreme Court of Canada in *Paige v. R.*[191] Mutual corroboration precludes one witness whose evidence requires corroboration from obtaining corroboration from another witness whose evidence also requires corroboration. However, this doctrine has been limited in more recent decisions by the House of Lords[192] and by Canadian appellate courts.[193]

Where several claims are joined in one action, if the claims have underlying connection, and there is corroboration with respect to some of the claims so as to satisfy the court of the truthfulness and correctness of the plaintiff's evidence as to those items and as to his or her general credibility, the statute is satisfied.[194] However, there is authority that if the separate claims could be the subject of an independent cause of action, each claim must be separately corroborated.[195] This later proposition must now be read subject to the less rigid common sense approach which has been adopted in recent criminal cases.[196]

5. Actions for Negligence

The corroboration requirement with respect to actions by or against the representatives of deceased or mentally incompetent persons can arise in negligence actions resulting from motor vehicle collisions. In such cases it is not necessary to have evidence corroborating the evidence of the interested or opposite party as to how the

---

190 The *Evidence Act*, R.S.O. 1980, c. 145, ss. 13 and 14; see also s. 18(2) of *Evidence Act*.

191 [1948] S.C.R. 349, 92 C.C.C. 32, 6 C.R. 93.

192 *D.P.P. v. Hester*, [1972] 3 All E.R. 1056, [1973] A.C. 296, 57 Cr. App. R. 212 (H.L.); *D.P.P. v. Kilbourne*, [1973] 2 W.L.R. 254, [1973] 1 All E.R. 440, [1973] A.C. 729.

193 *R. v. Sigmund*, [1968] 1 C.C.C. 92, 60 W.W.R. 257 (B.C.C.A.); *R. v. Taylor* (1970), 1 C.C.C. (2d) 321, 75 W.W.R. 45 (Man. C.A.). But see *Morris v. New Brunswick (A.G.)* (1975), 63 D.L.R. 337, 12 N.B.R. (2d) 520 (N.B.C.A.).

194 *Voyer v. Lepage* (1914), 7 W.W.R. 933, 19 D.L.R. 52, 8 Alta. L.R. 139 (Alta. S.C.); *Mushol v. Benjamin* (1920), 47 O.L.R. 426, 54 D.L.R. 248 (C.A.); *Thornley v. Royal Trust Co.* (1932), 41 O.W.N. 470 (S.C.).

195 *Re Ross* (1881), 29 Gr. 385 (Ont. S.C.); *Cook v. Grant* (1882), 32 U.C.C.P. 511 (C.A.); *Gerard v. Hudson*, [1928] 1 D.L.R. 839 (Alta. S.C.).

196 See this Chapter, *supra*, II, IV.A. and F.

accident happened, provided that there is corroboration with respect to some material issue.[197] The statute appears to apply to actions under fatal accident legislation whether brought by the personal representative or the dependants.

A case for the contrary point of view would be based on a restrictive meaning being given to the words "by or against the heirs, next-of-kin, executors, administrators or assigns of a deceased person".[198] When an action is brought by an executor, although it is really a derivative action for the benefit of dependents and not the estate, the dependents are usually the heirs or next-of-kin of the deceased. If it is not an action "by the executrix or executor", it will in most cases be an action "by the heirs, next-of-kin". The statutory requirement for corroboration has been held not to apply in an application by a dependent widow for relief against her deceased husband's estate brought pursuant to statute, because the applicant does not seek a judgment "in respect of any matter occurring before the death of the deceased."[199]

B. *Evidence of Children*

There was a common law corroboration rule that a trial judge should warn a jury about the uncorroborated evidence of children.[200] Applying *Vetrovec*,[201] the trial judge now has a discretion to caution a jury about the frailties of the testimony of children.[202] Most provincial Evidence Acts contain a provision for the reception of the unsworn evidence of a child of tender years who is found to be possessed of sufficient intelligence to justify the admission of the evidence, provided that the child understands the duty of speaking the truth.[203] These Acts

---

197 See *Ryan v. Whitton*, [1963] 1 O.R. 97, 36 D.L.R. (2d) 145 (S.C.); *Smythe v. Campbell* (1930), 65 O.L.R. 597, [1930] 4 D.L.R. 376 (C.A.).
198 See s. 13 of the *Evidence Act*, R.S.O. 1980, c. 145.
199 *Re Murray* (1966), 60 D.L.R. (2d) 76 (B.C.S.C.); *Plumb v. Royal Trust Co.*, [1943] 3 W.W.R. 513; affd. [1950] 2 W.W.R. 334 (*sub. nom. Plumb v. Snow*) (C.A.); *Re Blackwell*, [1948] O.R. 522, [1948] 3 D.L.R. 621 (C.A.).
200 *Kendall v. R.*, [1962] S.C.R. 469, 37 C.R. 179, 132 C.C.C. 216.
201 *R. v. Vetrovec*, [1982] 1 S.C.R. 811, 27 C.R. (3d) 304, 67 C.C.C. (2d) 1, 136 D.L.R. (3d) 89.
202 *R. v. B. (G.) (No. 1)*, [1990] 2 S.C.R. 3, 77 C.R. (3d) 327, 56 C.C.C. (3d) 200, 111 N.R. 1; *R. v. K. (V.)* (1991), 4 C.R. (4th) 338 (B.C.C.A.).
203 Evidence Acts: Ontario, R.S.O. 1980, c. 145, s. 18(1); Alberta, R.S.A. 1980, c. A-21, s. 20(1); Manitoba, R.S.M. 1987, c. E150, s. 24(1); Saskatchewan, R.S.S.

however also provide that "no case shall be decided upon such evidence alone and it must be corroborated by some other material evidence".[204] As noted, there is no requirement in British Columbia, New Brunswick or Prince Edward Island for corroboration of children and Parliament has abolished it in criminal cases.[205] There is authority that the unsworn evidence of one child cannot be corroborated by the unsworn evidence of another child[206] but this requirement must be re-examined in light of recent developments on the law of corroboration.[207]

In the competency chapter[208] it was noted that the judicial tests for receiving the sworn and unsworn testimony of a child are extremely similar, and the difference between sworn and unsworn evidence has lost its significance in relation to the child's obligation to testify truthfully. Moreover, it seems anomalous that the uncorroborated evidence of a child is sufficient in order to convict a person for a serious criminal offence, but such testimony is insufficient to support a civil judgement. On these grounds, an argument could be made to do away with corroboration for children's evidence completely.[209] In *R. v. B. (G.) (No. 1)* the Supreme Court commented on Parliament's

---

1978, c. S-16, s. 42(1); Nova Scotia, R.S.N.S. 1989, c. 154, s. 63(1); New Brunswick, R.S.N.B. 1973, c. E-11, s. 24(1); Newfoundland, R.S.N. 1970, c. 115, s. 15A(1) [new S.N. 1972, No. 3, s. 2; 1972, No. 11, s. 2]; Northwest Territories, R.S.N.W.T. 1988, c. E-8, s. 25; Yukon, R.S.Y.T. 1986, c. 57, s. 22. Section 5 of the British Columbia *Evidence Act* has been amended at S.B.C. 1988, c. 46, s. 25, to parallel s. 16 of the Canada *Evidence Act*, R.S.C. 1985, c. C-5 [s. 16 rep. & sub. 1985, c. 19 (3rd Supp.), s. 18].

204   Evidence Acts: Ontario, R.S.O. 1980, c. 145, s. 18(2); Alberta, R.S.A. 1980, c. A-21, s. 20(2); Manitoba, R.S.M. 1987, c. E150, s. 24(2); Saskatchewan, R.S.S. 1978, c. S-16, s. 42(2); Nova Scotia, R.S.N.S. 1989, c. 154, s. 63(2); Newfoundland, R.S.N. 1970, c. 115, s. 15A(2) [new S.N. 1972, No. 3, s. 2; 1972, No. 11, s. 2]; Northwest Territories, R.S.N.W.T. 1988, c. E-8, s. 19; Yukon, R.S.Y. 1986, c. 57, s. 16.

205   R.S.C. 1985, c. 19 (3rd Supp.), s. 15, s. 18. The requirement which did exist in s. 5 of the British Columbia provision has been repealed, *ibid.*; The New Brunswick provision requiring corroboration has been repealed (S.N.B. 1990, c. 17, s. 5).

206   *Paige v. R., supra,* note 191; *R. v. Whistnant* (1912), 20 C.C.C. 322, 5 Alta. L.R. 211, 8 D.L.R. 468, 3 W.W.R. 486 (Alta. C.A.); *R. v. Shorten,* [1918] 3 W.W.R. 5; affd. 57 S.C.R. 118, [1918] W.W.R., at 9, 49 D.L.R. 571.

207   See this Chapter, V.4.

208   Chapter 13, II.D.4.

209   See Government of Canada, *Sexual Offences Against Children: Summary of the Report of the Committee on Sexual Offences Against Children* (Ottawa, 1984).

liberalization of the corroboration requirement for the testimony of children:[210]

> These changes are evidence of the decline in importance of the need for corroboration due to the recognition that the trier of fact is competent to weigh evidence and credibility of all witnesses. It also reflects a desire to overcome technical impediments in the prosecution of offences.

---

210 *R. v. B. (G.) (No. 1)*, *supra*, note 202, at 15 (S.C.R.).

CHAPTER 18

DOCUMENTARY EVIDENCE

I   GENERALLY

A document has been traditionally defined as any written thing capable of being made evidence, no matter on what material it may be inscribed.[1] Some statutes have broadened the meaning of the written word: " 'writing', 'written', or a term of similar import includes words printed, typewritten, painted, engraved, lithographed, photographed or represented or reproduced by any mode of representing or reproducing words in visible form".[2] Statutory provisions, such as s. 30(12) of the *Canada Evidence Act*,[3] broadly define business records to include modern forms of storing information:

> . . . the whole or any part of any book, document, paper, card, tape or other thing on or in which information is written, recorded, stored or reproduced . . . .

Rules of practice, such as the British Columbia Rules of Court,[4] have given an expanded definition of what constitutes a document:[5]

---

1   *R. v. Daye*, [1908] 2 K.B. 333, at 340; also *Fox v. Sleeman* (1897), 17 P.R. 492 (Ont. C.A.).
2   *Interpretation Act*, R.S.B.C. 1979, c. 206, s. 29; see also *Interpretation Act*, R.S.O. 1980, c. 219, s. 30(37); *R. v. Sanghi* (1971), 6 C.C.C. (2d) 123, 3 N.S.R. (2d) 70 (S.C.C.A.).
3   R.S.C. 1985, c. C-5.
4   B.C. Reg. 95/89.
5   *Ibid.*, r. 1(c); see also Ontario Rules of Civil Procedure [Rules of Court], O. Reg. 560/84, r. 30.01(1)(a) define a document as: "a sound recording, videotape, film, photograph, chart, graph, map, plan, survey, book of account and information recorded or stored by means of any device"; Nova Scotia Civil Procedure Rules, r. 1.05(g) (*Judicature Act*, R.S.N.S. 1989, c. 240, s. 47(2): " 'document' includes a sound recording, photograph, film, plan, chart, graph and a record of any kind."

'document' has an extended meaning and includes a photograph, film, recording of sound, any record of a permanent or semi-permanent character and any information recorded or stored by means of any device.

The legislative and judicial trend is to broadly define documents to include modern methods of communicating and storing information.[6] Tape recordings,[7] videotapes,[8] microfiche[9] and computer records[10] have been admitted as documentary evidence in civil and criminal proceedings. In its broadest sense a document could be anything, other than testimony, that can be perceived and presented in a courtroom.

Documents may, for evidential purposes, be roughly classed into three categories. Documents in the first category are public documents, which are normally proven by the introduction of copies. Their content is evidence of the facts stated against strangers as well as parties and privies. Documents in the second category, judicial documents, are proven in the same manner as public documents.[11] In the

---

6   See J.D. Ewart et al., *Documentary Evidence in Canada* (Toronto: Carswell, 1984), at 16-18; *Reichmann v. Toronto Life Publishing Co.* (1988), 66 O.R. (2d) 65, 30 C.P.C. (2d) 280 (H.C.J.); *Tide Shore Logging Ltd. v. Commonwealth Insurance Co.* (1979), 47 C.C.C. (2d) 215, at 216-20, 9 C.R. (3d) 237, 13 B.C.L.R. 316, [1979] 5 W.W.R. 424, 100 D.L.R. (3d) 112 (S.C.); *Grant v. Southwestern and County Properties Ltd.*, [1975] Ch. 185, [1974] 2 All E.R. 465 (Ch. D.).

7   See Ewart, *ibid.*; *Tide Shore Logging v. Commonwealth Insurance Co.*, *ibid.*; *R. v. Swartz* (1977), 37 C.C.C. (2d) 409 (Ont. C.A.), at 410-12; affd., [1979] 2 S.C.R. 256, 45 C.C.C. (2d) 1, at 6-9, 7 C.R. (3d) 185, 93 D.L.R. (3d) 161, 26 N.R. 133 (*sub nom. R. v. Cotroni; Papalia v. R.*).

8   *Kajala v. Noble* (1982), 75 Cr. App. R. 149, at 152 (Div. Ct.).

9   *R. v. Sanghi, supra*, note 2.

10   Ewart, *supra*, note 6; see also *R. v. Vanlerberghe* (1978), 6 C.R. (3d) 222 (B.C.C.A.); *R. v. McMullen* (1978), 42 C.C.C. (2d) 67, 6 C.R. (3d) 218 (Ont. H.C.J.); affd. 47 C.C.C. (2d) 499, 25 O.R. (2d) 301, 100 D.L.R. (3d) 671 (C.A.); *R. v. Bell & Bruce* (1982), 65 C.C.C. (2d) 377, 26 C.R. (3d) 336 (Ont. C.A.); *Tecoglas, Inc. v. Domglas, Inc.* (1985), 51 O.R. (2d) 196, 19 D.L.R. (4th) 738, 3 C.P.C. (2d) 275 (H.C.J.); *Reichmann v. Toronto Life Publishing Co.*, *supra*, note 6; *R. v. Bicknell* (1988), 41 C.C.C. (3d) 545 (B.C.C.A.); *R. v. Cordell* (1982), 39 A.R. 281 (C.A.).

11   Judgments in previous proceedings may be effective to raise a *res judicata* defence or an issue estoppel where they are introduced in subsequent proceedings between parties and their privies, or where the previous judgment is relevant to an issue in a subsequent proceeding between strangers to the judgment or demonstrates an abuse of process. See Chapter 19, III.D. for a discussion of these

third category, private documents are traditionally proven by production of the original document and its evidential value is restricted to parties and privies.[12]

When a document is produced at trial, the primary requirement for its admission is that the document, unless it falls into certain excepted categories to be enumerated below, be "proved". Proof in this context has several aspects or meanings. First, it may mean proof of the document itself.[13] In certain cases mere production of the document or a copy thereof is sufficient for this purpose. For some of these documents, the due execution of the document must also be proved, showing that it was signed or written by the person by whom it purports to be signed or written, and when attestation is necessary, that it was attested. Second, proof means that the document tendered in evidence is a correct copy of the original.[14] For this type of proof it is not necessary that the witness have any knowledge with respect to the preparation of the original. The witness must simply be in a position to say that he or she saw the original and that the copy is in all respects similar. Third, proof means the extent to which the contents of the document are considered to establish the truth of the matters stated therein under the rules of evidence.[15]

II   BEST EVIDENCE RULE

A. *The History of the Rule*

The earliest statement of what became known as the best evidence rule appears to have occurred in the case of *Ford v. Hopkins*,[16] in

---

situations and for examples where a judicial record is admitted although one of the parties is a stranger to it. See also *O'Hara v. Dougherty* (1894), 25 O.R. 347 (C.A.).

12   See M.N. Howard, P. Crane and D.A. Hochberg, *Phipson on Evidence*, 14th ed. (London: Sweet & Maxwell, 1990), at paras. 36-01, 36-27 and 36-69.

13   *R. v. Knittel*, [1983] 3 W.W.R. 42, 22 Sask. R. 101 (C.A.).

14   *R. v. Betterest Vinyl Manufacturing Ltd.* (1989), 52 C.C.C. (3d) 441, 42 B.C.L.R. (2d) 198, [1990] 2 W.W.R. 751 (C.A.).

15   For example, s. 9 of the *Narcotic Control Act*, R.S.C. 1985, c. N-1, provides that a certificate of analysis purported to be signed by an analyst ". . . is admissible in evidence in any prosecution for an offence . . . and, in the absence of evidence to the contrary, is proof of the statements contained in the certificate . . ."; see also *R. v. Yerxa* (1978), 42 C.C.C. (2d) 177, 21 N.B.R. (2d) 569 (C.A.).

16   (1701), 1 Salk. 283, 90 E.R. 964 (K.B.).

which Holt C.J. said, ". . . the best proof that the nature of the thing will afford is only required".[17] The rule rapidly became regarded as the single most important rule in the law of evidence. In *Omychund v. Barker*,[18] the court held that a Gentoo was a competent witness even though his evidence was not given on the Gospel:[19]

> The judges and sages of the law have laid it down that there is but one general rule of evidence, *the best that the nature of the case will admit.* [original emphasis]

The early pronouncements of the rule stressed the inclusionary aspect of the rule as much as its exclusionary effect. Thus, if better evidence was not available the best that was at hand could be received.

During the eighteenth century the rule was of general application excluding hearsay, secondary evidence, and proof of documents by non-attesting witnesses. The rule also excluded circumstantial evidence if direct evidence was available; real evidence unless it was physically produced; opinion evidence of handwriting when the writer of a document could not attend court, and proof of consent by persons other than the consenting party if that party was alive. Where an attesting witness resided abroad, the rule required the issue of a commission to take his or her oral testimony.[20] The exclusionary aspect of the rule had more influence than its inclusionary effect. For example, if hearsay was the best evidence that could be obtained, the rule was not able to overcome the objection to its reception.

After the eighteenth century the rule suffered a progressive decline. In *Garton v. Hunter*,[21] Lord Denning said:[22]

> That old rule has gone by the board long ago. The only remaining instance of it that I know is that if an original document is available in one's hands, one must produce it. One cannot give secondary evidence by producing a copy. Nowadays we do not

---

17   *Ibid.*
18   (1744), 1 Atk. 21, 26 E.R. 15 (Ch.).
19   *Ibid.*, at 33 (E.R.), 49 (Atk.).
20   *Phipson on Evidence, supra*, note 12, at para. 7-14.
21   [1969] 2 Q.B. 37, [1969] 1 All E.R. 451, [1968] 2 W.L.R. 86 (C.A.).
22   *Ibid.*, [1969] 1 All E.R., at 453. His Lordship rejected the well known dictum of Scott L.J. in *Robinson Bros. (Brewers), Ltd. v. Houghton and Chester-le-Street Assessment Committee*, [1937] 2 K.B. 445, [1937] 2 All E.R. 298 (C.A.), at 307.

confine ourselves to the best evidence. We admit all relevant evidence. The goodness or badness of it goes only to weight, and not to admissibility.

Lord Denning's statement as to the scope of the modern rule has been adopted by both Canadian[23] and English[24] appellate courts.

Thus, considerations such as the prevention of fraud and perjury or error in transcription which motivated the early framers of the rule are now thought to affect the weight of the evidence rather than its admissibility.[25] This along with the obvious advantage to a party to adduce the best evidence has contributed to the decline of the rule.

B. *The Application of the Rule*

1. General

The rule is now generally limited to the contents of a document, for example, correspondence. The rule, however, equally applies to modern methods of recording or storing information, such as tape recordings[26] and computer generated evidence.[27] Thus, a party relying on the words used in a document must adduce primary evidence of its contents by producing the original document, but the rule does not apply to a party who tenders a document solely for the purpose of identifying it or proving its existence.[28] There is a common law exception to the rule for public documents which may be proved by copies, and there are numerous provisions in statutes and rules of practice which provide for the admissibility of copies of documents.

---

23 *R. v. Swartz* (1977), 37 C.C.C. (2d) 409 (Ont. C.A.), at 410; affd. (*sub nom. R. v. Cotroni; Papalia v. R.*) (1979), 45 C.C.C. (2d) 1 (S.C.C.), at 9, 26; *R. v. Galarce* (1983), 35 C.R. (3d) 268, at 270, 26 Sask. R. 122 (Q.B.); see also Ewart, *supra*, note 6, at 22.

24 *Kajala v. Noble*, *supra*, note 8; *R. v. Governor of Pentonville Prison, Ex Parte Osman* (1990), 90 Cr. App. R. 281, [1989] 3 All E.R. 701 (Q.B. Div. Ct.).

25 *R. v. Wayte* (1982), 76 Cr. App. R. 110 (C.A.); *Kajala v. Noble, supra*, note 8.

26 *R. v. Swartz*, (1977), 37 C.C.C. (2d) 409 (Ont. C.A.), at 410-12; *R. v. Cotroni; Papalia v. R.* (1979), 45 C.C.C. (2d) 1 (S.C.C.), at 6-9, 26.

27 *R. v. Vanlerberghe, supra*, note 10; *R. v. McMullen, supra*, note 10; *R. v. Bell & Bruce, supra*, note 10; *Tecoglas, Inc. v. Domglas, Inc., supra*, note 10; *Reichmann v. Toronto Life Publishing Co.* (1988), 66 O.R. (2d) 65, 30 C.P.C. (2d) 280 (H.C.J.); *R. v. Bicknell, supra*, note 10; *R. v. Cordell, supra*, note 10.

28 J.D. Ewart et al., *Documentary Evidence in Canada* (Toronto: Carswell, 1984), at 22; *R. v. Elworthy* (1867), 10 Cox C.C. 579, L.R. 1 C.C.R. 103 (C.A.); *Pelrine v. Arron* (1969), 3 D.L.R. (3d) 713 (N.S.C.A.), at 724.

Although the best evidence rule is sometimes used in reference to matters other than the admission of secondary evidence of documents, it is rather by way of a rationale for assigning less weight to the evidence tendered than as a reason for its exclusion.[29]

2. The Distinction Between Primary and Secondary Evidence

The application of the rule requires in the first instance a determination as to what is the primary or best evidence. In *Doe d. Gilbert v. Ross*,[30] Baron Parke enunciated the following test:[31]

> The law does not permit a man to give evidence which from its very nature shows that there is better evidence within his reach, which he does not produce.

And Henry J. stated in *Gunn v. Cox*,[32] "Evidence that carries on its face no indication that better remains behind is not secondary but primary." Accordingly, when parol evidence is tendered of a written instrument it is apparent that there exists or existed better evidence. The same result occurs when a copy of a document is tendered.

If documents are executed in duplicate or in counterparts, each duplicate or counterpart is treated as an original.[33] Although it is often difficult to differentiate between originals and copies for some modern methods of storing information, this has not been a barrier to the admissibility of such evidence.[34]

---

29   *Cohen v. Cohen*, [1971] 1 O.R. 619, 16 D.L.R. (3d) 241, 2 R.F.L. 409 (C.A.); *Crothers v. Northern Taxi Ltd.* (1957), 21 W.W.R. 577, 10 D.L.R. (2d) 87, at 90, 65 Man. R. 146 (C.A.); *Ontario (Attorney-General) v. Bear Island Foundation* (1984), 49 O.R. (2d) 353, at 368, 15 D.L.R. (4th) 321 (H.C.J.); affd. 68 O.R. (2d) 394, 32 O.A.C. 66, 58 D.L.R. (4th) 117, 4 R.P.R. (2d) 252 (C.A.); affd. 4 O.R. (3d) 133*n* (S.C.C.).

30   (1840), 7 M. & W. 102, 151 E.R. 696 (Exch.).

31   *Ibid.*, (1840), 7 M. & W., at 106.

32   (1879), 3 S.C.R. 296, at 304.

33   *R. v. Walsh* (1980), 53 C.C.C. (2d) 568, 6 M.V.R. 125 (Ont. C.A.); but see *R. v. Bergstrom* (1982), 65 C.C.C. (2d) 351, 30 C.R. (3d) 267, [1982] 2 W.W.R. 95, 16 Man. R. (2d) 372, 14 M.V.R. 131 (C.A.). For cases that preclude admissibility until all duplicates are accounted for see: *Hood v. Cronkite* (1869), 29 U.C.Q.B. 98 (Q.B.), at 111; *Cyr v. DeRosier* (1910), 40 N.B.R. 373 (C.A.); see also *Jones v. Burgess* (1914), 43 N.B.R. 126 (C.A.); vard. (March 3, 1916), unreported (S.C.C.); *Kinghorne v. Montreal Telegraph Co.* (1859), 18 U.C.Q.B. 60 (C.A.), at 66.

34   *R. v. Vanlerberghe* (1978) 6 C.R. (3d) 222 (B.C.C.A.); *R. v. McMullen* (1978),

3. Circumstances in Which Secondary Evidence is Admissible

(a) *Loss or Destruction*

Secondary evidence may be admitted when the court is satisfied that the original document existed and it has been lost or destroyed.[35] Proof of its loss or destruction need not be made by direct evidence but may be proved circumstantially by showing that a reasonably diligent search has been made in the places where the document was likely to be found.[36] Whether the inference of loss will be drawn by the court depends upon the sufficiency of the evidence of the search made to find it.[37] The determination of this issue is a question to be decided by the judge.[38] It is, however, a mixed question of law and fact which may be reviewed on appeal.[39] A document, which was alleged to be at the respondent's head office outside of the jurisdiction, could not be presumed to be lost because, due to confusion in moving offices, it could not be found.[40] Similarly, a police officer cannot excuse production of his original notes on the sole ground that he could not find them.[41] In *Saskatchewan Minerals v. Keyes*,[42] the Supreme Court

---

42 C.C.C. (2d) 67, 6 C.R. (3d) 218 (Ont. H.C.J.); affd. 47 C.C.C. (2d) 499, 25 O.R. (2d) 301, 100 D.L.R. (3d) 671 (C.A.); *R. v. Bell & Bruce* (1982), 65 C.C.C. (2d) 377, 26 C.R. (3d) 336 (Ont. C.A.); *Tecoglas, Inc. v. Domglas, Inc.* (1985), 51 O.R. (2d) 196, 19 D.L.R. (4th) 738, 3 C.P.C. (2d) 275 (H.C.J.); *Reichmann v. Toronto Life Publishing Co.* (1988), 66 O.R. (2d) 65, 30 C.P.C. (2d) 280 (H.C.J.); *R. v. Bicknell* (1988), 41 C.C.C. (3d) 545 (B.C.C.A.); *R. v. Cordell* (1982), 39 A.R. 281 (C.A.).

35 *R. v. Swartz* (1977), 37 C.C.C. (2d) 409 (Ont. C.A.), at 410-12; affd., [1979] 2 S.C.R. 256, 45 C.C.C. (2d) 1, at 6-9 and 26, 7 C.R. (3d) 185, 93 D.L.R. (3d) 161, 26 N.R. 133 (*sub nom. R. v. Cotroni; Papalia v. R.*); *R. v. Betterest Vinyl Manufacturing Ltd., supra*, note 14; *Westeel-Rosco Ltd. v. Edmonton Tinsmith Supplies Ltd.*, [1986] 3 W.W.R. 173, 43 Alta. L.R. (2d) 136, 68 A.R. 24 (Q.B.); see also *R. v. Minors* (1988), 89 Cr. App. R. 102 (C.A.).

36 *MacDonald v. Royal Bank of Canada*, [1934] 1 W.W.R. 732 (Sask. C.A.), at 741; *Lilwall v. Stockford*, [1934] 3 W.W.R. 746 (Sask. C.A.), at 749; *Beukenkamp v. Canada (Minister of Consumer and Corporate Affairs)*, [1973] F.C. 1401, 43 D.L.R. (3d) 118 (*sub nom. Beukenkamp and Minister of Consumer and Corporate Affairs, Re*) (T.D.).

37 *Lilwall v. Stockford, ibid.*

38 *Gilbert v. Campbell* (1869), 12 N.B.R. 474 (C.A.).

39 *Brown v. Morrow* (1878), 43 U.C.Q.B. 436 (C.A.).

40 *Newell v. Barker*, [1950] S.C.R. 385, at 394-95, [1950] 2 D.L.R. 289.

41 *Simpson v. Monture* (1966), 56 D.L.R. (2d) 349 (N.S.S.C.).

42 [1972] S.C.R. 703, [1972] 2 W.W.R. 108, 23 D.L.R. (3d) 573.

of Canada refused to admit secondary evidence of the contents of an option tendered by the respondent who testified that he had turned the document over to the solicitor for a third party and had not kept a copy of it. He proceeded to give evidence as to its contents, without first having given any evidence as to any attempt to locate it, or as to his having made an enquiry from the grantor of the option. A party tendering secondary evidence, however, need not negate every possibility of the existence of the best evidence.[43] Loss or destruction need not be proved directly or circumstantively where it is impossible or highly inconvenient to produce the original, for example, where the characters are on something such as a wall, monument or other thing which cannot very well be removed.[44] So far as admissibility is concerned, there are no degrees of secondary evidence, and oral evidence of the contents of a paper from a person who has read it and a copy of the document are put exactly on the same footing.[45] While more weight may be attached to a copy of a document than oral evidence of it, there is no requirement to account for copies before oral evidence can be adduced.[46]

---

43 *Industrial Acceptance Corp. v. Doughan*, [1931] 2 W.W.R. 532 (Sask. K.B.), at 535; revd. on other grounds, [1932] 1 W.W.R. 619 (Sask. C.A.). Leave to appeal to S.C.C. refused, [1932] 2 W.W.R. 279.

44 *Owner v. Bee Hive Spinning Co.*, [1914] 1 K.B. 105; *R. v. Galarce* (1983), 35 C.R. (3d) 268, 26 Sask. R. 122 (Q.B.); *R. v. Donald* (1958), 121 C.C.C. 304, 28 C.R. 206, 41 M.P.R. 127 (N.B.C.A.); *R. v. Wisbey Enterprises Ltd.*, [1969] 3 C.C.C. 109, 1 D.L.R. (3d) 510 (B.C. Co. Ct.).

45 *Doe d. Godsoe v. Jack* (1849), 6 N.B.R. 476 (C.A.), at 483; *Brown v. Woodman* (1834), 6 C. & P. 206, 172 E.R. 1209 (N.P.); *Hansell v. Spink*, [1943] Ch. 396; *Doe d. Gilbert v. Ross* (1840), 7 M. & W. 102, 151 E.R. 696 (Exch.); *R. v. Wayte* (1982), 76 Cr. App. R. 110 (C.A.); but see *Rogers v. Hill* (1972), 29 D.L.R. (3d) 628 (B.C.S.C.); revd. on other grounds, [1973] 4 W.W.R. 606, 37 D.L.R. (3d) 468 (B.C.C.A.).

46 See, however, *Saskatchewan Minerals v. Keyes, supra*, note 42, 23 D.L.R. (3d), at 575, in which Martland J. says: "He [respondent] proceeded to give evidence as to its contents, without first having given any evidence as to any attempt to locate it, or as to his having made any inquiry from the grantor of the option as to the existence of a copy of it." It is doubtful that this statement was intended to mean that the second alternative would have justified reception of oral evidence and thus to overrule a long line of authority to the contrary.

(b) *Documents in Possession of Another Party*

Production of a document in the possession of another party may be compelled by notice to produce.[47] If the other party refuses or neglects to produce the documents in compliance with the notice, the document may be proved by secondary evidence.[48] Possession must, however, be traced to the party to whom the notice to produce is delivered.[49] A document shown to have been delivered to a committee of a municipal corporation is in the possession of the corporation.[50]

There is an exception in the case of notices of dishonour and notices to quit[51] and documents which a party is prohibited by law from producing.[52] In these circumstances secondary evidence is admissible without the necessity of a notice to produce the original.

A party who refuses to produce a document pursuant to a notice to produce cannot contradict the secondary evidence adduced by his or her opponent by proving the original because it then suits his or her purpose.[53] If the opposite party admits that the original document has been destroyed, the service of a notice to produce before secondary evidence may be admitted is unnecessary.[54] Similarly, if the document is by its very nature such that the opposite party knows it will be required, as for example, the agreement sued upon, no notice to produce is required.[55] Also, rules of practice may allow a party to authenticate a document thus providing for the admissibility of a copy of a document at trial.[56]

---

47   See *Reichmann v. Toronto Life Publishing Co., supra*, note 34, where the computer disk was required to be produced.
48   *Cyr v. DeRosier, supra*, note 33; *Hayball v. Shephard* (1866), 25 U.C.Q.B. 536 (C.A.).
49   *Marvin v. Hales* (1857), 6 U.C.C.P. 208 (C.A.).
50   *Riley v. St. John (City)* (1865), 11 N.B.R. 264 (C.A.).
51   *Hood v. Cronkite* (1869), 29 U.C.Q.B. 98 (Q.B.).
52   *R. v. Wisbey Enterprises Ltd., supra*, note 44.
53   *Cyr v. DeRosier, supra*, note 33.
54   *Campbell v. McDonald* (1926), 58 N.S.R. 365 (C.A.).
55   *Gilbert v. Sleeper* (1833), 3 O.S. 135 (C.A.); *R. v. Elworthy* (1867), 10 Cox C.C. 579, L.R. 1 C.C.R. 103 (C.A.).
56   E.g., r. 31(1), Rules of Court, B.C. Reg. 95/89; r. 21.01, Nova Scotia Civil Procedure Rules, *Judicature Act*, R.S.N.S. 1989, c. 240, s. 47(2); Rules of Civil Procedure [Rules of Court], O. Reg. 560/84, r. 51.02; see *Canpotex Ltd. v. Graham* (1985), 5 C.P.C. (2d) 233 (Ont. H.C.J.).

(c) Documents in Possession of a Third Party

Documents in the possession of a third party that are beyond the power of the party seeking to compel production may be proved by secondary evidence. Included in this category are documents in which the third party asserts a lawful privilege.[57]

Ordinarily, a third party within the jurisdiction must be served with a subpoena *duces tecum* and, in the absence of such proceedings to compel production, secondary evidence will be refused.[58] Secondary evidence was admitted, however, when a solicitor refused to answer a subpoena *duces tecum* on the grounds that he had a solicitor's lien for unpaid fees in the document.[59] The fact that a document is outside the jurisdiction is not sufficient justification in itself.[60] At the very least the party tendering the secondary evidence must show reasonable attempts to locate the document and request its production.[61] In a nineteenth century case of *Porter v. Hale*,[62] where it was sought to give secondary evidence of an agreement relied on to create an interest in land, it was suggested that, in addition, the party tendering the evidence must show that production could not be compelled by the issue of a commission to take evidence in the foreign jurisdiction.[63] Proof, however, that the foreign law precluded removal of the document from the jurisdiction would be sufficient to allow secondary proof.[64]

(d) Public and Official Documents

By reason of the great inconvenience and risk which would attend the removal of original documents of a public or official nature, the contents of these documents, whether judicial or non-judicial, were allowed to be proved at common law by secondary evidence and

---

57   *R. v. Connolly* (1894), 1 C.C.C. 468, 25 O.R. 151 (H.C.J.), at 171; *Andrews v. Wirral R.D.C.*, [1916] 1 K.B. 863, at 870; *Dennison v. Gahans*, [1946] 1 D.L.R. 72 (N.B. Ch. D.).
58   *Farley v. Graham* (1852), 9 U.C.Q.B. 438 (C.A.).
59   *Doe d. Gilbert v. Ross* (1840), 7 M. & W. 102, 151 E.R. 696 (Exch.).
60   *Newell v. Barker*, [1950] S.C.R. 385, [1950] 2 D.L.R. 289.
61   *Ibid.*
62   (1894), 23 S.C.R. 265.
63   *Ibid.*, at 272-73.
64   *Doe d. Gilmour v. Witney* (1838), 2 N.B.R. 514 (C.A.).

without notice to produce the originals.[65] The secondary evidence was ordinarily in the form of an exemplification (verified under seal)[66] or examined (verified under oath) or certified copies.[67] Oral evidence was ordinarily admissible only if the records had been destroyed.[68] This common law exception was not limited to public documents[69] but included other official documents whose removal would create inconvenience and which might be required in different places at the same time.[70]

Statutory provisions now provide for the reception of copies authenticated by various means. These provisions extend not only to public and official documents which were provable by secondary evidence at common law, but also to certain private documents which were not within the common law exception relating to public and official documents.[71] For example, ss. 29 and 30 of the *Canada Evidence Act* allow for the admission of copies of books or records of financial institutions and businesses.[72] Indeed, these sections provide that the records may be proven by affidavit.[73]

In cases in which a statute provides for the admission of certified copies, or copies otherwise authenticated, of public or official docu-

---

65 *Paterson v. Todd* (1865), 24 U.C.Q.B. 296 (C.A.), at 302; *O'Hara v. Dougherty* (1894), 25 O.R. 347 (C.A.); *Doe d. William IV v. Roberts* (1844), 13 M. & W. 520, at 530, 153 E.R. 217 (Exch.); *Warren v. Deslippes* (1872), 33 U.C.Q.B. 59 (C.A.); *McLean v. McDonell* (1844), 1 U.C.Q.B. 13 (C.A.); *R. v. Tatomir* (1989), 51 C.C.C. (3d) 322, 69 Alta. L.R. (2d) 305, [1990] 1 W.W.R. 470, 17 M.V.R. (2d) 321. Application for leave to appeal to S.C.C. dismissed February 15, 1990 (C.A.).

66 *Heany v. Parker* (1868), 27 U.C.Q.B. 509 (C.A.); see *R. v. Tatomir, ibid.*, for a discussion of exemplification and a copy of a document.

67 *Warren v. Deslippes, supra*, note 65; *McLean v. McDonell, supra*, note 65.

68 *Heany v. Parker, supra*, note 66.

69 The definition of a public document is a very narrow one; see *Sturla v. Freccia* (1880), 5 App. Cas. 623 (H.L.), at 643-44; *R. v. Kaipiainen* (1953), 107 C.C.C. 377, 17 C.R. 388, [1954] O.R. 43 (C.A.).

70 *McLean v. McDonell, supra*, note 65; *Doe de William IV v. Roberts, supra*, note 65.

71 See this Chapter, III.A.

72 *Canada Evidence Act*, R.S.C. 1985, c. C-5. See: *R. v. McMullen* (1978), 42 C.C.C. (2d) 67, 6 C.R. (3d) 218 (Ont. H.C.J.); affd. 47 C.C.C. (2d) 499, 25 O.R. (2d) 301, 100 D.L.R. (3d) 671 (C.A.); *R. v. Bell & Bruce* (1982), 65 C.C.C. (2d) 377, 26 C.R. (3d) 336 (Ont. C.A.); see also Chapter 6, II.C.2.

73 See ss. 29(2) and (5), s. 30(6); *R. v. Parker* (1984), 16 C.C.C. (3d) 478, 7 O.A.C. 150 (C.A.). *Contra: Re California (State) and Meir & Hazelwood (No. 2)* (1982), 69 C.C.C. (2d) 180 (B.C.S.C.).

ments, the document must be proved in the manner prescribed by the statute, unless the copy has been lost or destroyed and another cannot be reasonably obtained.[74] The effect of the statute is that the certified copies partake of the nature of originals in that the absence of a certified copy must be accounted for before other secondary evidence is admissible. The original document, however, is not excluded unless the statute so provides.[75]

4. Proof by Secondary Evidence

Although secondary evidence of only part of a document can be admitted,[76] the court will refrain from giving effect to it, unless it is convinced that all material terms have been proved.[77] Proof that a copy is a reproduction of the original does not dispense with the necessity of proving execution.[78] In order to prove that a document is a copy of the original, the witness need only have read both.[79] Accordingly, a person who has made a copy of the original, but who has no knowledge of the circumstances of the preparation of the original, nor of the signatures or other handwriting, may yet prove that the document is a copy of the original. To prove execution of a document, however, the witness must have some knowledge of the circumstances under which the document was executed, or of the handwriting of the parties.[80]

Statutory enactments[81] provide a procedure to assist a party in proving the correctness of copies. For example, a party intending to prove the original of a telegram, letter, shipping bill, bill of lading, delivery order, receipt, account or other written instrument used in

---

74   R. v. Troop (1898), 30 N.S.R. 339, 2 C.C.C. 22 (C.A.); Heany v. Parker, supra, note 66; R. v. Purdy (1958), 121 C.C.C. 230 (N.S.S.C.); see also R. v. Pederson (1974), 15 C.C.C. (2d) 323, [1974] 1 W.W.R. 481 (B.C.S.C.); R. v. Tatomir, supra, note 65.
75   Linton v. Wilson (1841), 3 N.B.R. 223 (C.A.).
76   Doe d. Godsoe v. Jack (1849), 6 N.B.R. 476 (C.A.).
77   Ross v. Williamson (1887), 14 O.R. 184 (C.P.); Reichmann v. Toronto Life Publishing Co. (1988), 66 O.R. (2d) 65, 30 C.P.C. (2d) 280 (H.C.J.).
78   Dickson v. McFarlane (1863), 22 U.C.Q.B. 539 (C.A.); Campbell v. Lindsey (1925), 29 O.W.N. 86 (H.C.J.).
79   4 Wigmore, Evidence (Chadbourn rev. 1972), § 1278, at 687.
80   Marcy v. Pierce (No. 2) (1899), 4 Terr L.R. 246 (N.W.T.S.C.).
81   See, for instance, the Ontario Evidence Act, R.S.O. 1980, c. 145, s. 55.

business or other transactions may, by notice to the opposite party, require the latter to admit the correctness or genuineness of the copy, failing which the opposite party may be penalized in costs.[82] The effect of the statutory notice by itself is simply to obtain the admission as to the correctness of the copy and nothing more unless the statute further provides for the genuineness of the signature.[83] In the absence of an admission by the opposite party of the execution or authorship of the document, the party relying on this statutory procedure must still prove execution or authorship of the document.

Parties in civil proceedings may obtain admissions as to the genuineness and authorship of documents at the examination for discovery of the opposite party. Rules of practice may also permit a party to request another party to admit the truth of a fact, for example, authorship of a document as well as that a document is a true copy of the original.[84]

C. *The Modern Rule*

The traditional best evidence rule will continue to have an affect on the admissibility of particular kinds of documents. For example, where the terms of a contract, the authenticity of an affidavit or the validity of a will are disputed, or there is an issue whether a document has been altered or changed, the traditional best evidence rule may be applied to exclude the admission of a copy of the document. However, in the age of photocopies,[85] computer print-outs,[86] facsimile transmissions and video cassettes,[87] it may be a subtle question which docu-

---

82 *Ibid.*
83 *Sharpe v. Lamb* (1840), 11 Ad. & El. 805, 113 E.R. 620 (K.B.).
84 See Rules of Civil Procedure [Rules of Court], O. Reg 560/84, r. 51; *Canpotex Ltd. v. Graham* (1985), 5 C.P.C. (2d) 233 (Ont. H.C.J.). See Chapter 19, I.A.
85 *R. v. Lutz* (1978), 44 C.C.C. (2d) 143, 22 O.R. (2d) 300 (Ont. Prov. Ct.); *Westeel-Rosco Ltd. v. Edmonton Tinsmith Supplies Ltd.*, [1986] 3 W.W.R. 173, 43 Alta. L.R. (2d) 136, 68 A.R. 24 (Q.B.); *R. v. Wayte* (1982), 76 Cr. App. R. 110 (C.A.).
86 *R. v. Bicknell* (1988), 41 C.C.C. (3d) 545 (B.C.C.A.); *R. v. Bell & Bruce* (1982), 65 C.C.C. (2d) 377, 26 C.R. (3d) 336 (Ont. C.A.).
87 *Kajala v. Noble* (1982), 75 Cr. App. R. 149 (Div. Ct.); *R. v. Caughlin* (1987), 40 C.C.C. (3d) 247, 18 B.C.L.R. (2d) 186 (Co. Ct.); Rules of Civil Procedure [Rules of Court], O. Reg. 560/84, r. 34.19.

ment is the original.[88] Also, the rules of evidence should reflect the practices of modern society. In *R. v. Governor of Pentonville Prison, Ex Parte Osman*,[89] Lloyd L.J. said:

> ... this court would be more than happy to say goodbye to the best evidence rule. We accept that it served an important purpose in the days of parchment and quill pens. But since the invention of carbon paper and, still more, the photocopier and the telefacsimile machine, that purpose has largely gone. Where there is an allegation of forgery the Court will obviously attach little, if any, weight to anything other than the original; so also if the copy produced in court is illegible. But to maintain a general exclusionary rule for these limited purposes is, in our view, hardly justifiable.

The modern common law,[90] statutory provisions,[91] rules of practice[92] and modern technology, have rendered the rule obsolete in most cases and the question is one of weight and not admissibility.[93]

---

88   *R. v. Walsh* (1980), 53 C.C.C. (2d) 568, 6 M.V.R. 125 (Ont. C.A.). For an analysis of the use of copies see J.D. Ewart, *Documentary Evidence in Canada* (Toronto: Carswell, 1984), at 25-33.
89   (1990), 90 Cr. App. R. 281 (Q.B. Div. Ct.), at 308-09.
90   See, for example, *Ontario (Attorney-General) v. Bear Island Foundation* (1984), 49 O.R. (2d) 353, at 368, 15 D.L.R. (4th) 321 (H.C.J.); affd. 68 O.R. (2d) 394, 32 O.A.C. 66, 58 D.L.R. (4th) 117, 4 R.P.R. (2d) 252 (C.A.); affd. 4 O.R. (3d) 133*n* (S.C.C.), where the court admitted native oral history on the issue of possession of lands; *R. v. Governor of Pentonville Prison, ibid.*, where the rule was limited to an original document a party refuses to produce; *R. v. Scheel* (1978), 42 C.C.C. (2d) 31, 3 C.R. (3d) 359 (Ont. C.A.); *R. v. Fichter* (1984), 37 Sask. R. 126 (C.A.), where summaries or a complication of documents were admitted; *R. v. Bengert (No. 5)* (1980), 53 C.C.C. (2d) 481, 15 C.R. (3d) 114 (B.C.C.A.), where condensed re-recording of taped conversations were admitted; but see *R. v. Cloutier*, [1979] 2 S.C.R. 709, 48 C.C.C. (2d) 1, 12 C.R. (3d) 10, 28 N.R. 1; *R. v. Pleich* (1980), 55 C.C.C. (2d) 13, at 36-37, 16 C.R. (3d) 194 (Ont. C.A.).
91   See ss. 29 and 30 of the *Canada Evidence Act*, R.S.C. 1985, c. C-5; *R. v. Bell & Bruce, supra*, note 86; *R. v. Cordell* (1982), 39 A.R. 281 (C.A.).
92   See Rules of Civil Procedure [Rules of Court], O. Reg. 560/84.
93   Ewart, *supra*, note 88. Compare *R. v. Lutz, supra*, note 85 and *Rogers v. Hill* (1972), 29 D.L.R. (3d) 628 (B.C.S.C.); revd. on other grounds, [1973] 4 W.W.R. 606, 37 D.L.R. (3d) 468 (B.C.C.A.).

III DOCUMENTS ADMISSIBLE WITHOUT PROOF

A. *Public and Judicial Documents*

A "public document" means ". . . a document that is made for the purpose of the public making use of it, and being able to refer to it".[94] At common law the contents of numerous public documents could be proved by copies of various kinds on account of the inconvenience that would have been occasioned by the production of the originals and the requirement that a public official be present to prove such documents. These documents are admissible without proof on the basis of their inherent reliability because documents made by a public official for the information of the Crown or its subjects, who may require the information they contain, are presumed to be true when they are made. Thus, a "public document" exists for the benefit of the public and the public has the right to see and examine it. Unless the public or a section of the public has the right to see a particular document, the document is not admissible without proof as a "public document".

In *R. v. Kaipiainen*[95] the Ontario Court of Appeal reviewed the leading English authorities[96] on what is a public document. The Court concluded that four conditions must be present for a public document to be admissible without proof: (1) there must be a judicial or semi-judicial inquiry; (2) the inquiry must be with the object that the report be made public; (3) the report must be open to public inspection or an inference to this effect should be drawn from the circumstances; and (4) statements in a public document must relate to matters for which it was the duty of the public officer holding the inquiry to inquire into and report on.[97]

Until all of the above requirements are met, any and all statements in the tendered records (in the instant case, Finnish Army Records) are inadmissible. For example, even though reports of Statistics Canada are made for the use of the public, they gain little or no

---

94   *Sturla v. Freccia* (1880), 5 App. Cas. 623 (H.L.), at 643. For a discussion of public documents as an exception to the hearsay rule, see Chapter 6, II.G.
95   (1953), 107 C.C.C. 377, 17 C.R. 388, [1954] O.R. 43 (C.A.).
96   *Irish Society v. Derry* (1846), 12 Cl. & Fin. 641, 8 E.R. 1561 (H.L.); *Sturla v. Freccia, supra*, note 94; *Lilley v. Pettit*, [1946] K.B. 401, [1946] 1 All E.R. 593 (*sub nom. Pettit v. Lilley*) (D.C.); *Thrasyvoulos Ioannou v. Pappa Christoforos Demetriou*, [1952] A.C. 84, [1952] 1 All E.R. 179 (P.C.).
97   *R. v. Kaipiainen, supra*, note 95, 107 C.C.C., at 382; see also J.D. Ewart, *supra*, note 88, at 149-75.

authority through public scrutiny because the constituent material used to make them up is secret. Accordingly, the reports are inadmissible.[98] This rule governing the admissibility in evidence of writings made in pursuance of a public duty applies equally to a writing made pursuant to a duty under foreign and domestic law.[99]

In *R. v. Bellman*,[100] the New Brunswick Court of Appeal considered the admissibility of admiralty charts and hydrographic charts prepared under government authority and held that such charts were admissible as public documents. In that case the court said that a different standard applied with reference to the admissibility without proof of public documents prepared by officers of the Crown for a public purpose unconnected with the determination of any person's right to do anything represented upon the document. The court reasoned that it was expedient to dispense with the proof of such official publications by public officers as it would be inefficient if they were liable to be called upon to prove the making of all government maps, charts and other official documents. The court presumed that public officers did their duty in the preparation of the documents and relied upon the fact that such documents are open to public inspection resulting in the exposure and correction of any errors. The court stated that there was a substantial guarantee of trustworthiness of such public documents which substituted for cross-examination. In the absence of evidence showing that the chart offered was not an authentic chart, the court took judicial notice that a chart purporting to be an admiralty chart issued by the British Admiralty was a chart issued by the authority of the British Government. Similarly, a Canadian hydrographic chart, purporting to be issued under the authority of the Minister responsible, would be admissible as an authentic government chart without further proof.[101]

---

98 *R. v. Northern Electric Co.* (1955), 111 C.C.C. 241, 21 C.R. 45, [1955] O.R. 431, [1955] 3 D.L.R. 449, 24 C.P.R. 1 (H.C.J.); but see *Competition Act*, R.S.C. 1985, c. C-34, s. 70 (am. R.S.C. 1985, c. 19 (2nd Supp.), s. 41).

99 *Finestone v. R.*, [1953] 2 S.C.R. 107, 17 C.R. 211; *Saari v. Nykanen*, [1944] O.R. 582, [1944] 4 D.L.R. 619 (H.C.J.); *Wyer v. Wyer*, [1947] O.R. 292, [1947] 3 D.L.R. 579 (H.C.J.).

100 (1938), 70 C.C.C. 171, [1938] 3 D.L.R. 548, 13 M.P.R. 37 (N.B.C.A.).

101 *R. v. Ingram* (1978), 9 B.C.L.R. 195 (C.A.).

Domestic judicial records are admissible at common law. The clerk, who has custody of such records, such as an office copy, may certify the copy.[102] Before a copy of a judicial record could be used in another court, or in another cause, it had to be an "examined" copy, that is, a copy examined and sworn to, or an "exemplification", that is, a copy certified under the seal of the court.[103] Foreign judgments could be proved by an exemplification under the seal of the foreign court and upon the proof of that seal,[104] the authenticity of which could be proved by a witness.[105]

Some provincial Evidence Acts provide that foreign judgments, decrees, or other judicial proceedings recovered, made, had or taken, may be proved by an exemplification of the same under the seal of the court without any proof of the authenticity of such seal or other proof.[106] These provisions are limited to judgments, decrees or other judicial proceedings of any court of record in England or Ireland or any of the superior courts of law, equity or bankruptcy in Scotland, or in any court of record in any British colony or possession, or in any court of record in the United States of America, or of any state of the United States of America.[107] The *Canada Evidence Act*[108] and other provincial Evidence Acts[109] are broad enough to include all foreign courts of record and any court in the United Kingdom or Canada, in

---

102 *Denn d. Lucas v. Fulford* (1761), 2 Burr. 1177, at 1179, 97 E.R. 775 (*sub nom. Lucas v. Fulford*) (K.B.), and compare: *R. v. Sawchuk* (1984), 12 W.C.B. 302 (B.C. Co. Ct.); *R. v. Tatomir* (1989), 51 C.C.C. (3d) 322, 69 Alta. L.R. (2d) 305, [1990] 1 W.W.R. 470, 17 M.V.R. (2d) 321. Application for leave to appeal to S.C.C. dismissed February 15, 1990 (C.A.).

103 *Tilton v. McKay* (1874), 24 U.C.C.P. 94 (C.A.); *R. v. Cordes*, [1979] 1 S.C.R. 1062, 47 C.C.C. (2d) 46, 10 C.R. (3d) 186, 16 A.R. 162, 98 D.L.R. (3d) 376, 26 N.R. 612; *R. v. Tatomir, ibid.*; *Industrial Acceptance Corporation v. R.*, [1952] 2 S.C.R. 273, 107 C.C.C. 1, [1953] 4 D.L.R. 369; *R. v. Kobold* (1927), 48 C.C.C. 290, 37 Man. R. 37, [1927] 3 W.W.R. 294 (C.A.); see also Ewart, *supra*, note 88, at 188-95 for a discussion of the statutory provisions governing the admissibility of criminal records.

104 *Warener v. Kingsmill* (1850), 7 U.C.Q.B. 409 (C.A.).

105 *Ibid.*; see also *Junkin v. Davis* (1857), 6 U.C.C.P. 408 (C.A.), at 413.

106 See Evidence Acts: *Alberta Evidence Act*, R.S.A. 1980, c. A-21, s. 45; British Columbia *Evidence Act*, R.S.B.C. 1979, c. 116, s. 29; Ontario *Evidence Act*, R.S.O. 1980, c. 145, s. 38; Nova Scotia *Evidence Act*, R.S.N.S. 1989, c. 154, s. 15.

107 See *Alberta Evidence Act* and Ontario *Evidence Act, ibid.*

108 R.S.C. 1985, c. C-5, s. 23; see Ewart, *supra*, note 88, at 183-95.

109 See British Columbia *Evidence Act* and Nova Scotia *Evidence Act, supra*, note 106.

any British colony or possession, as well as courts of justices of the peace and coroners. In those jurisdictions, which are limited to specific foreign jurisdictions, the authenticity of the seal of the court and any exemplification would still have to be proved. The *Canada Evidence Act (supra)* also provides that where any such court, justice or coroner has no seal, evidence of its proceedings may be given by a copy, purporting to be certified under the signature of a judge or presiding magistrate of such court or of such justice or coroner, without any proof of the authenticity of the signature or other proof whatever.[110] It further provides, however, that reasonable notice of at least seven days be given to the party against whom it is intended to introduce such evidence before such proof may be used.[111] The reasonableness of such notice is determined by the court or other person presiding.[112] The foregoing deals with proof in its first aspect, that is, production of the document or a copy, is sufficient for its admissibility.

The second aspect of proof is the correctness of the copy of the document. In the case of examined copies, they are proved by sworn evidence and in the case of exemplifications and certified copies, judicial notice is generally taken of the seal or certificate of the public official or institution which purports to authenticate the copy.[113] However, a party must comply with the mandatory procedure for authenticating a document if that is required under the governing statute[114] unless the document is alternatively admissible at common law.[115]

The third aspect of proof is the proof of the contents of a document. Public and judicial documents are generally, but not always, admitted as evidence of the truth of their contents, even

---

110 *Supra*, note 108, s. 23(2).

111 *Supra*, note 108, s. 28(1); but see *R. v. Tatomir, supra*, note 102, where the court held that the admissibility of public documents at common law did not require notice.

112 *Supra*, note 108, s. 28(2).

113 M.N. Howard, P. Crane, and D.A. Hochberg, *Phipson on Evidence*, 14th ed. (London: Sweet & Maxwell, 1990), at 38, para. 2-17; *R. v. Cordes, supra*, note 103. See also Chapter 19, II.C.

114 *Re Teen* (1975), 24 C.C.C. (2d) 501 (*sub nom. Re Wong Shue Teen and U.S.A.*), [1975] F.C. 573, 61 D.L.R. (3d) 181, 10 N.R. 271 (*sub nom. U.S.A. v. Teen*) (C.A.), applying the provisions of the *Extradition Act*, R.S.C. 1970, c. E-21 (now R.S.C. 1985, c. E-20); see J.D. Ewart et al., *Documentary Evidence in Canada* (Toronto: Carswell, 1984), at 184-86 for a discussion of this case.

115 *R. v. Tatomir, supra*, note 102.

though statements made therein might otherwise be inadmissible. But, in *Bird v. Keep*,[116] even though the death certificate was admissible, a statement in the death certificate as to the cause of death was ruled inadmissible because this statement was based on information supplied by a coroner. It is difficult to reconcile admission of a public document as an exception to the rule against hearsay with a refusal to accept its contents as proof of facts stated therein.

B. *Documents Admissible Under Statutory Authority*

There are numerous statutory provisions making public documents or other documents, which would not qualify as public documents at common law, admissible on the mere production to the court of the original or a copy, without there being any question of accounting for the original, if a copy is produced, or without proving the accuracy of the copy.[117] Some statutes, which enable the contents of a public document to be proved by means of a copy, also dispense with the necessity of proving that the document has been properly executed;[118] however, in some cases the official character of the person signing the document and the signature of that person may still have to be proven.[119] A statutory provision may dispense with all aspects of proof, that is, genuineness, execution and proof of contents.[120] But the statutory provision does not provide that the admission of the contents of the document, for example, shall be *prima facie* evidence of the

---

116 [1918] 2 K.B. 692, 87 L.J.K.B. 1199 (C.A.); approved in *Chapman v. Amos* (1957), 18 D.L.R. (2d) 140, at 146, 42 M.P.R. 137 (N.B.C.A.); also see Chapter 6, II.G.

117 See *Canada Evidence Act, supra*, note 108, ss. 24, 25, and provisions in provincial Evidence Acts, e.g., Ontario *Evidence Act, supra*, note 106, ss. 29 and 32; *Alberta Evidence Act, supra*, note 106, s. 34.

118 See *Canada Evidence Act, supra*, note 108, s. 24; Ontario *Evidence Act, supra*, note 106, s. 29; British Columbia *Evidence Act, supra*, note 106, s. 31.

119 See, e.g., Ontario *Evidence Act, supra*, note 106, s. 52 [rep. & sub. 1989, c. 68, s. 1], which does not dispense with proof that a medical report, which is made admissible with leave of the court, was signed by a legally qualified medical practitioner licensed to practise in any part of Canada. This fact would, however, generally be admitted by the opposite party.

120 Section 40 of the Ontario *Evidence Act* provides: "A protest of a bill of exchange or promissory note purporting to be under the hand of a notary public wherever made is *prima facie* evidence of the allegations and facts therein stated." See also *Alberta Evidence Act, supra*, note 106, s. 34.

contents thereof, and the document is not a public document within the common law definition, it is doubtful that the contents are proof of the truth thereof, unless they otherwise satisfy the rules of evidence.[121] Thus, a statutory provision may render a document admissible and stipulate that proof of execution is unnecessary but if a party tenders the document to prove the truth of its contents, the provision must specifically so provide.

The following illustrate statutory provisions outside of the *Canada Evidence Act* and provincial Evidence Acts, under which documents of a public nature may be admitted as evidence of the facts stated therein. For example, s. 15 of the Ontario *Registry Act*[122] provides that an abstract furnished by a registrar is *prima facie* evidence of the registration of instruments included in the abstract. Section 184(2) and (3) of the Ontario *Highway Traffic Act*[123] provides that a copy of any writing, paper or document filed with the Ministry of Transportation pursuant to that Act or any statement containing information from the records required to be kept under that Act, purported to be certified by the registrar under the seal of the Ministry, shall be received in evidence in all courts without proof of the seal or signature. Also, a copy is *prima facie* evidence of the facts therein contained and that an engraved, lithographed, printed or otherwise mechanically reproduced facsimile signature of the Registrar is sufficient authentication of any such copy or statement.

Another example of such statutory provisions is found in s. 43(4) of the Ontario *Personal Property Security Act, 1989*,[124] which requires the registrar to provide a certified copy of a registered financing statement filed under the Act. The Act also provides that a certified copy is *prima facie* proof of the contents of the certified document.[125]

---

121 See *Chapman v. Amos, supra*, note 116; *Apsassin v. Canada* (1987), 17 C.P.C. (2d) 187 (F.C.T.D.), at 199.
122 R.S.O. 1980, c. 445.
123 R.S.O. 1980, c. 198, s. 184(2) [am. 1985, c. 13, s. 14(2)); (2) and (2a) rep. & sub. 1989, c. 87, s. 19(2)].
124 S.O. 1989, c. 16.
125 *Ibid.*

The *Canada Evidence Act*[126] and provincial Evidence Acts[127] provide for the proof of the contents of various statutes by the production of copies printed by the Queen's Printer.[128] Proclamations, orders, regulations or appointments to office made or issued by the Governor-General or by the Governor-General in Council, or of various government officials may be proved by the production of a copy of the relevant gazette, by the production of copies of such treaties, proclamations, etc., purported to be printed by the Queen's Printer, or by certified copies.[129]

In some cases the combined effect of more than one statute provides for the admissibility of certain documents without proof. For example, by virtue of the provisions of the Ontario *Registry Act*, the registrar is authorized to give certified copies of a registered "instrument".[130] "Instrument" is broadly defined so as to include not only things which in themselves can be public documents, such as Crown grants and orders-in-council, but also private documents such as deeds, mortgages, and the like, as well as "every [other] instrument whereby . . . land . . . may be transferred, disposed of, charged, encumbered or affected".[131] The Ontario *Evidence Act* provides that a copy of such an instrument, certified under the hand and seal of the registrar to be a true copy, is "*prima facie* evidence of the original"[132] which seems to mean *prima facie* proof of the existence, execution and contents of the original. Before such copy can be used as *prima facie* proof of the execution of the original, the party proposing to use it must give ten days' notice to the opposite party and unless the opposite party gives notice within four days disputing the validity of the original, the certified copy "is sufficient evidence of the instrument . . . and of its validity and contents".[133]

---

126 *Supra*, note 108, ss. 19 and 20.
127 E.g., Nova Scotia *Evidence Act*, R.S.N.S. 1989, c. 154, s. 3; *Saskatchewan Evidence Act*, R.S.S. 1978, c. S-16, s. 4.
128 Ontario *Evidence Act*, R.S.O. 1980, c. 145, s. 26.
129 E.g., *Canada Evidence Act*, R.S.C. 1985, c. C-5, ss. 21 and 22; Ontario *Evidence Act*, R.S.O. 1980, c. 145, s. 26; New Brunswick *Evidence Act*, R.S.N.B. 1973, c. E-11, s. 64.
130 R.S.O. 1980, c. 445, s. 17(1); see also British Columbia *Evidence Act*, R.S.B.C. 1979, c. 116, ss. 44-46.
131 Ontario *Registry Act*, *ibid.*, s. 1(f).
132 Ontario *Evidence Act*, *supra*, note 129, s. 53(2).
133 *Ibid.*, s. 53(3).

Some documents, even though they are not public documents as such, are admissible without proof by the provisions of various provincial Evidence Acts. For example, statutory provisions provide for proof of a will to establish a devise or other testamentary disposition of or affecting real estate.[134] Section 42 of the British Columbia *Evidence Act* states that probate of the will or letters of administration with the will annexed containing such devise or disposition or a certified copy under seal of the court is *prima facie* evidence of the will and of its validity and contents. Section 43 similarly provides for the admissibility of the probate or letters of administration of a person who died in one of Her Majesty's possessions outside of British Columbia to pass real estate within the province provided one month's notice has been given to the opposite party.[135]

Other statutory provisions provide for the admissibility of letters patent or notarized documents. For example, s. 28 of the *Alberta Evidence Act* provides that letters patent under the Great Seal of the United Kingdom or any other of Her Majesty's realms or territories may be proven by the production of an exemplification thereof or of the enrolment under the Great Seal under which such letters patent were issued, and such exemplification has the like force and effect for all purposes as the letters patent thereby exemplified or enrolled against Her Majesty and all other persons whomsoever.[136] Section 40 of the Ontario *Evidence Act* provides that a protest of a bill of exchange or promissory note purporting to be made under the hand of a notary public, wherever made, is *prima facie* evidence of the allegations therein stated. Section 46 of the *Alberta Evidence Act* provides that a copy of a notarial act or instrument in writing made in Quebec before a notary and filed, enrolled or unregistered by such notary and certified by a notary or prothonotary to be a true copy of the original thereby certified to be in her or his possession as such notary or prothonotary, is receivable in evidence in the place and stead of the original, and has the same force and effect as the original would have if produced and proved. However, it is provided that the proof of such certified copy may be rebutted or set aside by proof that there is no

---

134 See Ontario *Evidence Act*, *supra*, note 129, s. 49 [am. 1989, c. 56, s. 13]; British Columbia *Evidence Act*, *supra*, note 130, s. 42.
135 See also Ontario *Evidence Act*, *ibid.*, s. 50.
136 *Alberta Evidence Act*, R.S.A. 1980, c. A-21. See also New Brunswick *Evidence Act*, *supra*, note 129, s. 36.

such original, or that the copy is not a true copy of the original or that the original is not an instrument of such nature, as may, by the law of Quebec, be taken before a notary or be filed, enrolled or unregistered by a notary.[137]

The admission of documents under these statutory provisions is facilitated by general provisions that judicial notice is to be taken of the signatures of judicial officers,[138] and of the handwriting and official position of persons certifying to the truth of any matter or thing to which they are by law authorized or required to certify.[139]

C. *Other Documents Admitted Without Proof*

Of course, documents may be admitted without proof by agreement between the parties whereby one party produces a document at trial and the other waives proof of it and accepts the document's genuineness.[140] An admission made by counsel at trial in a civil action for the purpose of dispensing with proof has been held to preclude any evidence on the point.[141] Admissions in criminal proceedings are governed by s. 655 of the *Criminal Code*.[142] The section eliminates proof of a fact that the Crown is required to prove and the accused is prepared to admit. However, the accused cannot frame the issue to be admitted nor admit a fact until it is alleged by the Crown.[143] The agreed-to factual admission should be unequivocal and if it is unclear whether a fact is admitted the Crown must prove it.[144]

---

137 See also Ontario *Evidence Act, supra*, note 129, s. 39; British Columbia *Evidence Act, supra*, note 130, s. 41.

138 See for instance Ontario *Evidence Act, ibid.*, s. 36; British Columbia *Evidence Act, ibid.*, s. 30; and *Alberta Evidence Act, supra*, note 136, s. 43.

139 This kind of provision is illustrated by the British Columbia Act, *ibid.*, s. 33, the Ontario Act, *ibid.*, s. 37, and the Alberta Act, *ibid.*, s. 44.

140 *General Host Corp. v. Chemalloy Minerals Ltd.*, [1972] 3 O.R. 142, 27 D.L.R. (3d) 561 (H.C.J.).

141 See Chapter 19, I.A.

142 R.S.C. 1985, c. C-46. An accused may admit a fact at a preliminary hearing, *R. v. Ulrich* (1977), 38 C.C.C. (2d) 1, [1978] 1 W.W.R. 422, 10 A.R. 155 (T.D.).

143 *Castellani v. R.*, [1970] S.C.R. 310, [1970] 4 C.C.C. 287, 71 W.W.R. 147, 11 D.L.R. (3d) 92, 9 C.R.N.S. 111; *R. v. Ecker* (1984), 55 A.R. 249, 28 M.V.R. 257 (Q.B.).

144 *R. v. Coburn* (1982), 66 C.C.C. (2d) 463, 27 C.R. (3d) 259 (Ont. C.A.).

Documents may also be admitted in answer to a notice to admit under provincial Evidence Acts[145] or rules of practice.[146] Unless an Evidence Act or the rules of practice specifically provide that failure to answer the notice is deemed to be an admission, the documents listed in the notice will still have to be proved if the opposite party does not admit them pursuant to the notice. If the opposite party admits the authenticity of the document, the admission is subject to all just exceptions relating to the admissibility of such documents. Thus, the party must prove the contents of the document in some other manner or, if there are statements in the document that are inadmissible by reason of an exclusionary rule of evidence, for example hearsay,[147] such statements are not evidence of the facts unless the responding party also admits the truth of a fact specified in the notice.

IV DOCUMENTS ADMISSIBLE ON PROOF OF AUTHORSHIP OR EXECUTION

As stated, before a private document may be admitted in evidence, something more than its mere production is required. The court will require to be satisfied by evidence that it was duly executed, unless it is more than 30 years old and comes from proper custody, in which case there is a presumption of formal validity.[148] In the case of documents not requiring formal execution, proof must be tendered as to the origin and authorship of the document. The due execution or authorship of private documents is proved by showing that in the former case it was signed, and in the latter case prepared or authored by the person by whom it purports to have been written, and, when attestation is necessary, that it was properly attested.[149] Proof of execution is usually required before proof of contents is allowed,[150]

---

145 See British Columbia *Evidence Act*, R.S.B.C. 1979, c. 116, s. 49; Ontario *Evidence Act*, R.S.O. 1980, c. 145, s. 55; *Manitoba Evidence Act*, R.S.M. 1987, c. E150, s. 54.

146 See Rules of Civil Procedure [Rules of Court], O. Reg. 560/84, r. 51 and Form 51A; Court Rules Act, B.C. Reg. 221/90, r. 31 and Form 23; Nova Scotia Civil Procedure Rules, r. 21 and Form 21.02A (*Judicature Act*, R.S.N.S. 1989, c. 240, s. 47(2)).

147 *Canpotex Ltd. v. Graham* (1985), 5 C.P.C. (2d) 233 (Ont. H.C.J.).

148 See this Chapter, V.A. for a full discussion.

149 See this Chapter, VI.A. and VI.B. for illustrative methods by which writings may be proved.

150 *R. v. Culpepper* (1696), Skin. 673, 90 E.R. 301 (K.B.); *Whitfield v. Fausset*

unless it is a case where execution is the only point in dispute.[151] Proof of a private document when it is produced involves two elements, *viz.*, the signature of the person who signed it, and where a document is being proved against a party other than the person signing it, for example, proving that a letter signed by an individual was sent by a company, or proving an assignment of a mortgage executed by the executor of the owner of certain property, the authority of the person signing must also be proved.[152]

Where there are facts from which it may be inferred that a document was executed or authored by a certain party, it is for the trier of fact to say whether such an inference is to be drawn from such facts.[153] An example of the application of this principle is found in the case of *Stevenson v. Dandy*,[154] in which it was held by Beck J. quoting from Wigmore:[155]

When a letter is received by due course of mail, purporting to come in answer from the person to whom a prior letter has been sent, there are furnished thereby over and above mere contents showing knowledge of facts in general, three circumstances evidencing the letter's genuineness: First, the tenor of the letter as a reply to the first indicates a knowledge of the tenor of the first. Secondly, the habitual accuracy of the mails, in delivering a letter to the person addressed and to no other person, indicates that no other person was likely to have received the first letter and to have known its contents. Thirdly, the time of arrival, in due course, lessens the possibility that the letter, having been received by the right person but left unanswered, came subsequently in a different person's hands and was answered by him. To this may be added the empirical argument that in usual

---

(1750), 1 Ves. Sen. 387, 27 E.R. 1097 (L.C.).

151 *Stowe v. Querner* (1870), L.R. 5 Exch. 155, 39 L.J. Ex. 60 (C.A.).

152 *Cochlin v. Massey-Harris Co.* (1915), 8 W.W.R. 286, 23 D.L.R. 397, 8 Alta. L.R. 392 (C.A.); *Doe d. Slason v. Hanson* (1857), 8 N.B.R. 427 (C.A.); *Maynes v. Dolan* (1857), 8 N.B.R. 573 (C.A.); *Doe d. Stevens v. Robinson* (1827), 1 N.B.R. 492 (N.S.S.C.).

153 *Cochlin v. Massey-Harris Co., ibid.; R. v. Armstrong* (1970), 1 C.C.C. (2d) 106, 11 C.R.N.S. 384, 2 N.S.R. (2d) 204 (C.A.); motion for leave to appeal dismissed at 4 N.S.R. (2d) 248 (S.C.C.).

154 [1920] 2 W.W.R. 643 (Alta. C.A.).

155 *Ibid.*, at 661.

experience the answer to a letter is found in fact to come from the person originally addressed. There seems to be here adequate ground for a special rule declaring these facts, namely, the arrival by mail of a reply purporting to be from the addressee of a prior letter duly addressed and mailed, are sufficient evidence of the reply's genuineness to go to the jury. *Such a rule* — varying slightly in the phraseology of different judges — *seems now to be universally accepted.*

Wigmore expands this principle by citing the proposition that if a document lacks a signature, no rule of evidence prevents its execution from being proved in some other way.[156] A rule of substantive law, however, may require a signature, for example, the rule requiring that a will shall signed at the end thereof and not merely bear the name in the midst or in the beginning or on a superscription. Therefore, if there is no signature, and the substantive law makes no requirement as to signature, execution may be established by identifying the handwriting of the contents, or by some oral act of acknowledgement or assent by the opposite party.

In special circumstances, where it can be shown that the contents of a document reveal information or some other peculiar trait referable only to a single person, the contents of the document might be sufficient to prove that the document was authored by a particular person. In *R. v. Armstrong*,[157] evidence that a letter handed to the jailer of the accused and written on paper supplied to the accused by the jailer was held to be evidence for the jury that the writing was that of the accused. It has been held that where a party executes an agreement in several capacities, it is not necessary that she or he sign more than once. Extrinsic evidence is admissible to show the author's intention,[158] but it is desirable that she or he should put into writing all capacities in which she or he signs the document.[159]

It has also been held that an error in receiving a document insufficiently proved may be cured by subsequent evidence in the case,

---

156 7 Wigmore, *Evidence* (Chadbourn rev. 1978), § 2134, at 719.
157 *Supra*, note 153.
158 *Young v. Schuler* (1883), 11 Q.B.D. 651 (C.A.); *Ball v. Dunsterville* (1791), 4 Term. Rep. 313, 100 E.R. 1038 (K.B.).
159 *Prager v. Prager & Goodison* (1913), 29 T.L.R. 556 (Prob., Divorce, and Adm. Div.).

and it is not necessary to again tender the document after the evidence necessary to complete its proof has been disclosed.[160]

Certain statutory provisions have eased the requirement of proof of execution of some documents, provided it can be shown that the document fits into the category envisioned by the statute. The *Canada Evidence Act* and provincial Evidence Acts provide for the admissibility of business records. For example, the *Manitoba Evidence Act* provides:

Any writing or record made of an act, transaction, occurrence or event is admissible as evidence of the act, transaction, occurrence or event if

(a) it is made in the usual and ordinary course of any business; and

(b) it was in the usual and ordinary course of business to make the writing or record at the time of the act, transaction, occurrence or event, or within a reasonable time thereafter.[161]

The statute provides for the giving of seven days' notice of a party's intention to tender such records to all other parties in the action, and also provides that such other parties are entitled to inspect the records set out in the notice after giving five days' notice requiring production of same. Additionally, the statute requires that the circumstances of the making of such writing or records, including the personal knowledge by the maker, may be shown to affect their weight, but such circumstances do not affect their admissibility.[162] The *Canada Evidence Act* business records section provides that if a record made in the usual and ordinary course of business does not contain information in respect of a matter, the occurrence or existence of which might reasonably be expected to be recorded in that record, the court may, upon production of the record, admit the record for the purpose of establishing that fact and may draw the inference that such a matter

---

160   *R. v. Dixon (No. 2)* (1897), 3 C.C.C. 220, 29 N.S.R. 462 (C.A.).
161   R.S.M. 1987, c. E150, s. 49(2); see also British Columbia *Evidence Act*, R.S.B.C. 1979, c. 116, ss. 47 and 48; Ontario *Evidence Act*, R.S.O. 1980, c. 145, s. 35; Nova Scotia *Evidence Act*, R.S.N.S. 1989, c. 154, s. 22; *Saskatchewan Evidence Act*, R.S.S. 1978, c. S-16, s. 31(2).
162   *Ibid.*, *Manitoba Evidence Act*, s. 49(3).

did not occur or exist.[163] Before the record or entry is receivable in evidence, the party tendering it must establish by admissible evidence the statutory conditions for admissibility.[164]

In the case of a document executed by a corporation, the corporate seal may be proved by anyone who knows it without calling a witness who saw it affixed.[165] The corporate seal will be presumed to have been affixed by the proper person, although this may be rebutted by the proof of absence of authority.[166]

Documents required by law to be attested are (subject to the exceptions mentioned below) provable by calling the attesting witnesses.[167] A witness called to prove attested documents is the witness of the court and may be cross-examined by the party calling her or him as to any evidence the witness gives to negate execution.[168] There is, however, no rule that the evidence of an attesting witness is conclusive and others present at the time may be called to contradict her or him.[169] Generally, where there are several attesting witnesses, only one need be called.[170] In a contested will case, however, it has been held that the proponent of the will who has the burden of proof should call and examine all available attesting witnesses.[171] If none of the attesting witnesses are available to testify in person, proof of the signature of one of the attesting witnesses is sufficient.[172] In Ontario for an application of probate or for administration with the will annexed, "the due execution of the will ... shall be proved by affidavit

---

163 *Canada Evidence Act*, R.S.C. 1985, c. C-5, s. 30(2); see also s. 29(4).

164 *Thomas v. Watkins Products Inc.* (1965), 54 D.L.R. (2d) 252, 51 M.P.R. 321 (C.A.). The admissibility of business records is discussed in Chapter 6, II.C.

165 *Doe d. King's College v. Kennedy* (1849), 5 U.C.Q.B. 577 (C.A.).

166 *Clarke v. Imperial Gas Light & Coke Co.* (1832), 4 B. & Ad. 315, 110 E.R. 473 (K.B.).

167 *Crane v. Ayre* (1853), 7 N.B.R. 577 (C.A.); *Nichols & Shepard Co. v. Skedanuk* (1913), 4 W.W.R. 587, 11 D.L.R. 199 (Alta. S.C.); revd. on other grounds, 5 W.W.R. 118, 13 D.L.R. 892, 6 Alta. L.R. 368 (C.A.).

168 *Oakes v. Uzzell*, [1932] P. 19.

169 For a discussion of the history and principle behind the requirement to call attesting witnesses, see M.N. Howard, P. Crane, and D.A. Hochberg, *Phipson on Evidence*, 14th ed. (London: Sweet & Maxwell, 1990), at 944, para. 35-11.

170 *Bell v. Matthewman* (1920), 48 O.L.R. 364, at 370 (H.C.J.).

171 *Madill v. McConnell* (1908), 17 O.L.R. 209 (C.A.), at 213; *Newcombe v. Evans* (1917), 43 O.L.R. 1 (C.A.).

172 *Crane v. Ayre, supra,* note 167; *Nichols & Shepard Co. v. Skedanuk, supra,* note 167; *Doe d. McDonald v. Twigg* (1848), 5 U.C.Q.B. 167 (C.A.), at 170.

of one of the subscribing witnesses . . . but if an affidavit cannot be obtained from either of them, the due execution of the will may be established by other evidence".[173]

Upon proof of authorship and execution, the extent to which the document is admissible to prove the truth of facts stated therein depends on the nature of the statements contained in the document. If the contents are wholly inadmissible, the document cannot be admitted into evidence, even if the preliminary aspect of proof has been satisfied, that is, the document is what it purports to be. Some statements in the document may, however, be admissible while others are not, in which case the document is admitted in evidence, but only the admissible facts are properly before the court.

V DOCUMENTS ADMISSIBLE BY REASON OF CUSTODIAL ORIGIN

A. *Ancient Documents*

Any written document proved or purporting to be not less than 30 years old, which is produced from proper custody, is presumed, in the absence of circumstances of suspicion, to have been duly signed, sealed, attested, delivered, or published according to its purport.[174] Such documents in absence of suspicious circumstances are said to prove themselves. If, however, there is any suspicious appearance on the face of the document by erasure, interlineation or otherwise, the court will require proof of the execution of it in like manner as that of a document of a more recent date.[175] It has also been held that parol evidence will not be admitted of the contents of a document offered on oral evidence alone as being an instrument of 30 years' standing.[176] Whether the rule dispensing with proof of ancient documents should apply to documents sealed by a court or a corporation is open to question, since such seals, being of a permanent type, are not rendered

---

173 Ontario Surrogate Court, R.R.O. 1980, Reg. 925, r. 4.
174 *Doe d. Maclem v. Turnbull* (1848), 5 U.C.Q.B. 129 (C.A.); *Montgomery v. Graham* (1871), 31 U.C.Q.B. 57 (C.A.); *Doe d. Edgett v. Stiles* (1841), 3 N.B.R. 338 (C.A.); *Hayes v. Driscoll* (1973), 36 D.L.R. (3d) 84, 5 N.B.R. (2d) 767 (C.A.); *Tobias v. Nolan* (1985) 71 N.S.R. (2d) 92 (S.C.); affd. 78 N.S.R. (2d) 271 (C.A.), for 20-year period.
175 *Doe d. Edgett v. Stiles, ibid.*
176 *Ibid.*

more difficult to prove through the lapse of time.

Documents are said to be produced from proper custody when they have been in the keeping of some person and in a place where, if authentic, they might reasonably and naturally be expected to be found.[177] The case of *Doe d. Jacobs v. Phillips*[178] has on numerous occasions[179] been approved by Ontario courts as properly setting out the tests as to what constitutes proper custody. That case held that, except in the situation where the party who tenders a particular document is the proper depository of such document, the fact of custody of that document must be properly established by evidence, and that where the fact of proper custody is established, there is no need to inquire what happened to the document between the date of execution and the date of production.[180]

In *Orser v. Vernon*,[181] the court approved the statement of Colleridge J. in *Doe d. Neale v. Samples*, where he stated:[182] "It is sufficient that the custody be one which may be reasonably and naturally explained; though not strictly the proper custody in point of law." One would assume, however, that in the case of documents of which the custody is imposed by statute on a particular person, the rule must perhaps be more strict, and any unusual custody must be properly accounted for.[183]

B. *Documents in the Possession of a Person*

1. Introduction

Documents which are or have been in the possession of a person are generally admissible against that person to show her or his knowledge of their contents.[184] The documents will constitute an admission

---

177 *Thompson v. Bennett* (1872), 22 U.C.C.P. 393 (C.A.), approving the principle stated in *Doe d. Jacobs v. Phillips* (1845), 8 Q.B. 158, 115 E.R. 835; document sworn to have been obtained from the plaintiff's predecessor in title was treated as produced from proper custody in *Hayes v. Driscoll, supra*, note 174.

178 (1845), 8 Q.B. 158, 115 E.R. 835.

179 *Supra*, note 174.

180 In *Tobias v. Nolan, supra*, note 174.

181 (1864), 14 U.C.C.P. 573 (C.A.).

182 (1838), 8 Ad. & El. 154, 112 E.R. 794 (K.B.), at 795 (E.R.).

183 See *Doe d. Arundel (Lord) v. Fowler* (1850), 14 Q.B. 700, 117 E.R. 270.

184 *R. v. Container Materials Ltd.* (1940), 74 C.C.C. 113, [1940] 4 D.L.R. 293 (Ont. H.C.J.); vard. 76 C.C.C. 18, [1941] 3 D.L.R. 145 (Ont. C.A.); affd. [1942]

to prove the truth of their contents if the person has in any way recognized, adopted, or acted on them.[185] For the documents in possession doctrine to apply it must be shown that the person is or had been in possession of the relevant document. In criminal proceedings, a more restrictive definition of constructive possession applies.[186]

A preliminary question is the relevancy of a document tendered in evidence and even if the document is relevant, whether it is inadmissible by reason of an exclusionary rule of evidence. In *R. v. Thompson*,[187] the accused was charged with committing acts of gross indecency and the question arose as to the admissibility of photographs of naked boys. In upholding the ruling at trial of the admission of the photographs, Viscount Reading C.J. stated:[188]

> Of course, evidence would not necessarily be admissible of everything found in the possession of the accused. For instance, if a burglarious implement was found upon him, it could not be given in evidence against him upon a charge of committing acts of gross indecency; it would have no relevance to the issue, and would merely tend to show that he was a person of bad character.

In *R. v. Morris*,[189] the accused was charged with conspiring to import and traffic in heroin orginating from Hong Kong. A clipping of a newspaper article describing the heroin trade in Pakistan was found in the accused's night-table of his bedroom. The majority of the Supreme Court of Canada held that the document was open to the inference that preparatory steps in respect of importing narcotics had

---

S.C.R. 147, 77 C.C.C. 129, [1942] 1 D.L.R. 529; *R. v. Hashem* (1940), 73 C.C.C. 124, [1940] 1 D.L.R. 527, 15 M.P.R. 205 (N.S.C.A.); M.N. Howard, P. Crane, and D.A. Hochberg, *Phipson on Evidence*, 14th ed. (London: Sweet & Maxwell, 1990), at 350, para. 16-10.
185 *Phipson on Evidence, ibid.; R. v. Famous Players* (1932), 58 C.C.C. 50, [1932] O.R. 307, [1932] 3 D.L.R. 791 (S.C.); *Glen Bain (Rural Municipality) v. Haley*, [1928] 2 W.W.R. 184, [1928] 3 D.L.R. 306, 22 Sask. L.R. 559 (C.A.).
186 See J.D. Ewart et al., *Documentary Evidence in Canada* (Carswell: Toronto, 1984), at 234-56.
187 [1917] 2 K.B. 630 (C.C.A.); affd. [1918] A.C. 221, 13 Cr. App. R. 61 (H.L.).
188 *Ibid.*, [1917] 2 K.B., at 634; see also *R. v. Gaich (sub nom. R. v. Gaijic)* (1956), 116 C.C.C. 34, 24 C.R. 196, [1956] O.W.N. 616 (C.A.); *R. v. Hannam*, [1964] 2 C.C.C. 340, 42 C.R. 267, 49 M.P.R. 262 (N.S.C.A.).
189 [1983] 2 S.C.R. 190, 7 C.C.C. (3d) 97, 36 C.R. (3d) 1, [1984] 2 W.W.R. 1, 1 D.L.R. (4th) 385.

been taken or were contemplated. Although the majority were of the view that the probative value of the evidence was low, it was admissible under the *Wray* test. Although Lamer J. acknowledged that the evidence was relevant, he was of the opinion that the clipping was inadmissible. He reasoned that the sole relevancy of the document was to show that the accused had a propensity to commit the type of crime charged in the indictment. If the newspaper clipping had described the laxity of Hong Kong custom officials, however, then Lamer J. was prepared to admit the document as being relevant to the crime. Accordingly, if an accused or a party in a civil action is in possession of a document, privilege or some other exclusionary rule of evidence may render the tendered document inadmissible.

2. Possession by Individuals

The threshold element for the document in possession doctrine is whether the document is or had been in possession of the accused. When an accused is found in actual or constructive possession of a document, an inference may be made that the person had knowledge of its content. But as Mr. Ewart writes:[190]

> ... knowledge of the existence of the document can and must be severed from knowledge of its contents; proof of the former is essential to ground admissibility, and is sufficient to permit the trier of fact to find the party's knowledge of the contents. ...

In criminal cases, s. 3(4) of the *Criminal Code* requires that the Crown adduce evidence from which it may be inferred that the accused had knowledge of the existence of the document in order to establish possession.[191] Once the trier of fact is satisfied that the accused possessed the document, the tribunal may infer that the accused had knowledge of its content. A document found in the personal possession of the accused is sufficient evidence of knowledge of possession in order to trigger the documents in possession doctrine.[192] For

---

190 *Supra*, note 186, at 235.
191 R.S.C. 1970, c. C-34, s. 3(4) [now R.S.C. 1985, s. 4(3)]. See: *R. v. Caccamo*, [1976] 1 S.C.R. 786, 21 C.C.C. (2d) 257, 29 C.R.N.S. 78, 54 D.L.R. (3d) 685, 4 N.R. 133; *R. v. Lovis*, [1975] 2 S.C.R. 294, 17 C.C.C. (2d) 481, [1974] 6 W.W.R. 345 (*sub nom. R. v. Moncini*), 47 D.L.R. (3d) 732, 2 N.R. 551.
192 *R. v. Russell* (1920), 33 C.C.C. 1, [1920] 1 W.W.R. 624, 51 D.L.R. 1 (Man. C.A.).

example, a sheet of paper listing the various prices for illegal drugs that is found on the accused's person upon arrest would be admissible circumstantial evidence from which one or more of the following inferences may be made: the accused's knowledge of the existence of the document, which in turn, permits the inference that the accused had knowledge of its content, the accused's connection with or complicity in a drug crime, or her or his state of mind.[193]

In cases of constructive possession, for example, a document found outside an accused's apartment building or at her or his place of work, the nexus between the accused and the document from which possession may be inferred may be absent.[194] An officer, director, or employee of a corporation will not be found in possession of a document discovered on the premises of the corporation unless there is evidence connecting the individual with the document.[195] No inference may be made that a director of a company, merely because she or he was acting as such, has knowledge of the contents of a company's books, nor that there is a duty upon the director to know their contents.[196] In *R. v. Smart*,[197] the accused were charged with conspiring to defraud customers of a brokerage house, conspiring to fraudulently affect the market price of shares and with gaming in shares, and use thereof by them for their own purposes in the conduct of their business. The court held that books and papers in the custody of the accused constituted *prima facie* evidence against them of the methods, systems and devices of which they availed themselves in their own speculations and in their transactions with their customers and other brokers. The Ontario Court of Appeal stated:[198]

---

193 J.H. Buzzard, R. May, M.N. Howard, *Phipson on Evidence*, 13th ed. (London: Sweet & Maxwell, 1982), at para. 21-09; Ewart, *supra*, note 186, at 232, n. 2.

194 See *R. v. Lal* (1979), 51 C.C.C. (2d) 336, 20 B.C.L.R. 84 (C.A.); *R. v. Caccamo, supra*, note 191; *R. v. Gilson*, [1965] 4 C.C.C. 61, 46 C.R. 368, [1965] 2 O.R. 505, 51 D.L.R. (2d) 289 (C.A.); *R. v. Kozak* (1975), 20 C.C.C. (2d) 175, 30 C.R.N.S. 7 (Ont. C.A.). Because the definition of possession found in s. 3(4) of the *Criminal Code* (R.S.C. 1970, c. C-34 [now R.S.C. 1985, c. C-46, s. 4(3)]) applies, the case law re possession of stolen goods or illegal drugs may assist further analysis.

195 *R. v. Smart* (1931), 55 C.C.C. 310, [1931] O.R. 176, [1931] 2 D.L.R. 207 (C.A.); *Shrewsbury v. Blount* (1841), 2 Man. & G. 475, 133 E.R. 836 (C.P.); Ewart, *supra*, note 186, at 240-42.

196 *Hallmark's Case* (1878), 9 Ch. D. 329 (C.A.).

197 *Supra*, note 195.

198 *R. v. Smart* (1931), 55 C.C.C. 310, [1931] O.R. 176, at 183-84, [1931] 2

Here the books are undoubtedly books kept under the direction of the respective appellants; and, when their meaning and purpose were explained, as they were in each case, by competent testimony, given in more than one instance by employees of the accused, and on the cross-examination of Smart and Young . . . they constituted, in the opinion of the Court, evidence proper to have been admitted by the learned Judge and submitted to the jury for their consideration.

Thus, it is necessary for the Crown to establish a nexus or foundation for a finding that the accused possessed the relevant documents by extrinsic evidence before the document is admissible against an accused person.

In civil proceedings, there is sparse authority that knowledge of the existence of the document is not required in order to establish possession.[199] These authorites deal with ownership of personal property found on premises by persons other than the owner and thus are of questionable relevance in the context of the present subject. The liberal rules governing production of documents and examinations for discoveries give a party an opportunity to establish possession of documents and admissions as to acts referred to therein. Accordingly, the issue of whether a party possesses a document will infrequently arise in civil proceedings.

3. Possession by Corporations

Corporations are capable of possessing documents. Although the case law has arisen mainly in the context of prosecutions for restraint of trade, the issue may arise in both civil and criminal proceedings. Unless governing legislation has specific provisions addressing the issue of the admissibility of documentary evidence, the common law documents in possession doctrine applies.

Documents found on corporate premises are admissible against a corporation if knowledge of their existence can be attributed to a responsible officer or director or an employee acting in the course of

---

D.L.R. 207 (C.A.).

199 *Grafstein v. Holme*, [1957] O.R. 354, 9 D.L.R. (2d) 444 (H.C.J.); affd. [1958] O.R. 296, 12 D.L.R. (2d) 727 (C.A.); *South Staffordshire Water Co. v. Sharman*, [1896] 2 Q.B. 44 (D.C.); *R. v. Caccamo, supra*, note 191, 21 C.C.C. (2d), at 267; Ewart, *supra*, note 186, at 240.

her or his duty.[200] But merely proving that the document was found on the company premises or as part of their corporate records will not be sufficient to establish the corporation's possession of the document.

In the leading case of *R. v. Ash-Temple Co.*,[201] several companies were charged with conspiring to restrain trade. The Crown sought to prove its case almost entirely by documents found on the premises or in the files of the accused companies. No evidence was adduced to show that the acts of the various employees of the company referred to in the documents had been authorized, or even brought to the attention of the board of directors of the company. It was held that there was no evidence that any of the letters found in the possession of any of the accused were written on the authority of the accused, or that anyone having authority to bind the accused knew of the sending or receipt of the letters or of their contents, and that, in the case of an incorporated company it is not sufficient to merely prove that a document was found on the premises of the company or even in the company's files.[202] It was further held that it must be shown that there was corporate possession, and that in order that an incorporated company should be deemed to have knowledge of the contents of a document found among its papers, it must be established by evidence, either that the board of directors had knowledge of it or that it had come to the attention of someone having authority from the company to deal with the matters to which the document relates.[203] The court excluded correspondence where originals of correspondence were found on the premises of one co-conspirator and carbon copies were found on the premises of the sender because there was no evidence anyone was authorized to send the letter or a responsible person of either company had knowledge of the sending, receipt or contents.[204] The same principles would be applicable in civil cases.

The common law rule of documents in possession enunciated by the Ontario Court of Appeal in *Ash-Temple*[205] was abrogated by Parliament for prosecutions under the *Combines Investigation Act*.[206]

---

200   *R. v. Western Grocers Ltd.* (1945), 85 C.C.C. 251, [1945] 3 W.W.R. 451, [1946] 1 D.L.R. 606 (Sask. C.A.).

201   (1949), 93 C.C.C. 267, 8 C.R. 66, [1949] O.R. 315 (C.A.).

202   *Ibid.*, 93 C.C.C., at 280.

203   *Ibid.*

204   *Ibid.*, at 281.

205   *Supra*, note 201.

206   R.S.C. 1927, c. 26 [en. by 1949 (2nd sess.), c. 12, s. 3]. *R. v. McGavin Bakeries*

Section 69(2) of the *Competition Act*[207] provides that a document[208] proved to have been in the possession of or on premises used or occupied by any accused, an unindicted co-conspirator or a party to the offence shall be admitted as *prima facie* proof that the party had knowledge of the record and its contents, that anything recorded as having been done, said or agreed was done, and that where a document appears to be written it was so written by that person. The courts have broadly interpreted the section to render an interoffice memorandum found on the premises of one corporation admissible against another alleged co-conspirator.[209]

4. Possession by Co-conspirators, Agents

Documents that constitute acts or declarations in furtherance of a conspiracy, common design or pre-concert are admissible against an accused or party who, by evidence directly admissible against that person,[210] is shown to be a member of the conspiracy or common design.[211] Thus, documents found in possession of one party which are in furtherance of the common design are admissible under this principle.[212] In civil cases, documents found in possession of a partner in furtherance of the partnership would be admissible against every partner of a firm.

Ltd. (1950), 12 C.R. 343 (Alta. S.C.); *R. v. Anthes Business Forms Ltd.* (1975), 26 C.C.C. (2d) 349, 10 O.R. (2d) 153, 20 C.P.R. (2d) 1 (C.A.); affd., [1978] 1 S.C.R. 970, 32 C.C.C. (2d) 207n, 28 C.P.R. (2d) 33n, 22 N.R. 541.

207 R.S. 1985, c. C-34, s. 69(2) [rep. & sub. R.S.C. 1985, c. 19 (2nd Supp.), s. 40(3)].

208 The term record is broadly defined to include all types of documents, *ibid.*, s. 2(1) [renumbered R.S.C. 1985, c. 19 (2nd Supp.), s. 20(1) as s. 2(1)].

209 *R. v. Howard Smith Paper Mills*, [1957] S.C.R. 403, 118 C.C.C. 321, 26 C.R. 1, 8 D.L.R. (2d) 449, 29 C.P.R. 6.

210 *R. v. Watt*, [1967] 1 C.C.C. 188, 49 C.R. 261, [1966] 2 O.R. 726 (Ont. C.A.).

211 See Chapter 6, II.K.3.(c); *R. v. Russell* (1920), 33 C.C.C. 1, [1920] 1 W.W.R. 624, 51 D.L.R. 1 (Man. C.A.); *R. v. Connolly* (1894), 1 C.C.C. 468, 25 O.R. 151 (H.C.J.); *R. v. Smart, supra*, note 195; *R. v. Kozak, supra*, note 194; *R. v. Parrot* (1979), 51 C.C.C. (2d) 539, 27 O.R. (2d) 333, 106 D.L.R. (3d) 296 (C.A.); leave to appeal to S.C.C. refused 51 C.C.C. (2d) 539n, 27 O.R. (2d) 333n, 106 D.L.R. (3d) 296n (S.C.C.).

212 *Parrot, ibid.*, 51 C.C.C. (2d), at 548.

5. Evidentiary Value of Possession

In a civil case, documents that a party has caused to be made or knowingly used as true in a civil case to prove a particular fact are admissible against him or her in subsequent civil proceedings to prove the same fact, even on behalf of strangers, and documents furnished by persons specifically referred to for information are evidence against the referrer, though a mere general reference will not have this effect.[213]

Failure to answer a letter sent under circumstances which entitle the writer to an answer, or where it is the ordinary practice for people to reply, may imply an admission of its contents. Likewise, in the case of merchants' accounts, an inference of correctness will generally arise unless objection is made within a reasonable time; and objection to one item only may be taken to imply assent to the others.[214]

In criminal proceedings, a document found in actual or constructive possession of an accused constitutes circumstantial evidence of knowledge of the content or connection with the document. The document is inadmissible to prove the truth of their contents unless the possessor has recognized, adopted or acted upon it.[215] In *Patel v. Comptroller of Customs*,[216] the accused was charged with making a false declaration in an import entry form in connection with the importation of seed. On the import entry form, the accused declared that the country of origin was India but the words "Produce of Morocco" were imprinted on the seed bags. The Privy Council held that words on the bags were inadmissible hearsay to prove the truth of the statement, that is, the country of origin. Where documents are found on corporate premises and there is evidence of knowledge of its existence by a director, officer or employee acting in the course of employment, possession is circumstantial evidence imputing knowledge to the company of the content of the document. The documents may also be receivable to prove the truth of the contents, if recognized, adopted

---

213 J.H. Buzzard, R. Amlot, S. Mitchell, *Phipson on Evidence*, 11th ed. (London: Sweet & Maxwell, 1970), at 767, para. 768.
214 *Richard v. Dunn* (1841), 2 Q.B. 218, 114 E.R. 505; *Gaskill v. Skene* (1850), 14 Q.B. 664, 117 E.R. 256; *Wiedemann v. Walpole*, [1891] 2 Q.B. 534 (C.A.).
215 *R. v. Famous Players* (1932), 58 C.C.C. 50, [1932] O.R. 307, at 348, [1932] 3 D.L.R. 791 (S.C.); J.D. Ewart et al., *Documentary Evidence in Canada* (Toronto: Carswell, 1984), at 232-33, 245-59.
216 [1965] A.C. 356, [1965] 3 All E.R. 593 (P.C.).

or acted upon by a person authorized by the corporation.[217]

In criminal conspiracies, the common law evidentiary rule is a three stage process. First, the trier of fact must find that a conspiracy existed. Second, on the basis of evidence admissible against an individual accused, the trier of fact must find that he or she was probably a member of the conspiracy. Third, the trier of fact may consider the acts or declarations of a co-conspirator in furtherance of the conspiracy, such as a bill of lading for goods in which drugs were concealed, to determine if the Crown has proven the guilt of an accused.[218] In proceedings under the *Competition Act*,[219] the common law co-conspirator evidentiary rule has been abrogated.[220] Although this statutory provision makes the document found in possession of one party *prima facie* evidence against the co-conspirator, its evidentiary value may be challenged.[221]

Legislation may provide for both the admissibility and evidentiary value of a document. For example, the Ontario *Business Corporations Act*[222] provides that records required to be kept by that Act are admissible in evidence as *prima facie* proof of all the facts stated therein. Business records of an accused corporation which were made in the ordinary course of business are admissible if the common law or statutory business records exception to the hearsay rule has been satisfied.[223]

---

217 *R. v. Famous Players, supra,* note 215.
218 *R. v. Carter,* [1982] 1 S.C.R. 938, 67 C.C.C. (2d) 568, 31 C.R. (3d) 97, 137 D.L.R. (3d) 387, 47 N.R. 289, 46 N.B.R. (2d) 142.
219 R.S.C. 1985, c. C-34.
220 *R. v. Anthes Business Forms Ltd., supra,* note 206.
221 See *R. v. Rolex Watch Co. of Canada Ltd.* (1980), 53 C.C.C. (2d) 445, 50 C.P.R. (2d) 222 (Ont. C.A.); *R. v. Anthes Business Forms Ltd., supra,* note 206; see also *Sunbeam Corp. (Canada) Ltd. v. R.,* [1969] S.C.R. 221, [1969] 2 C.C.C. 189, 1 D.L.R. (3d) 161, 56 C.P.R. 242; see also Chapter 3, IV.B. in relation to the term *prima facie* proof.
222 R.S.O. 1980, c. 54, s. 149(3).
223 See Chapter 6, II.C.

VI PARTICULAR RULES RELATING TO PROOF OF PRIVATE DOCUMENTS

A. *Handwriting*

Except where judicial notice is taken of official signatures or where an apparent or purported signature is deemed by statute to be the actual signature, the handwriting or signature of unattested documents may be proved by: (1) the writer; (2) a witness who saw the document being written or signed; (3) an admission of the party against whom the document is tendered;[224] (4) a comparison of the disputed document with other documents proved to the satisfaction of the judge to be genuine;[225] (5) a witness who has a general knowledge of the writing of the person whose signature or handwriting is sought to be proved;[226] (6) expert evidence.[227] Prior to the passage of the statutory provisions dealing with "comparison of hands", a witness was allowed to give opinion evidence of disputed writing only if it could be shown that the witness was acquainted with the handwriting or signature of the person alleged to have written or signed the disputed document. The comparison of handwriting by the collation of one paper with another for the purpose of proving that the two documents were written by the same person was regarded as a test so

---

224 *R. v. Attwood* (1891), 20 O.R. 574 (C.A.); *R. v. Armstrong* (1970), 1 C.C.C. (2d) 106, 11 C.R.N.S. 384, 2 N.S.R. (2d) 204 (C.A.); motion for leave to appeal dismissed at 4 N.S.R. (2d) 248 (S.C.C.); *R. v. Voisin*, [1918] 1 K.B. 531, [1918-19] All E.R. Rep. 491 (C.C.A.); *R. v. Gillespie* (1967), 51 Cr. App. R. 172 (C.C.A.); *Stevenson v. Dandy*, [1920] 2 W.W.R. 643 (Alta. C.A.); see M.N. Howard, P. Crane and D.A. Hochberg, *Phipson on Evidence*, 14th ed. (London: Sweet & Maxwell, 1990), at 936, para. 35-03.

225 *Thompson v. Bennett* (1872), 22 U.C.C.P. 393 (C.A.); *Foulds v. Bowler* (1908), 8 W.L.R. 189 (Man. S.C.); *Thompson v. Thompson* (1902), 4 O.L.R. 442 (C.A.). This comparison may be carried out by an expert, the trial judge, the jury (*R. v. Dixon (No.2)* (1897), 3 C.C.C. 220, 29 N.S.R. 462 (C.A.)) or a non-expert: *First National Bank of Boston v. Christy Crops Ltd.* (1981), 47 N.S.R. (2d) 224 (T.D.).

226 *Russell v. Fraser* (1865), 15 U.C.C.P. 375 (C.A.), at 382-83; *Pitre v. R.*, [1933] S.C.R. 69, 59 C.C.C. 148, [1933] 1 D.L.R. 417.

227 See *Canada Evidence Act*, R.S.C. 1985, c. C-5, s. 8; British Columbia *Evidence Act*, R.S.B.C. 1979, c. 116, s. 51; *Alberta Evidence Act*, R.S.A. 1980, c. A-21, s. 59; Ontario *Evidence Act*, R.S.O. 1980, c. 145, s. 57. The Evidence Acts permit a witness to compare a disputed writing with a writing proved to the satisfaction of the court to be genuine and to give evidence as to the genuineness of the disputed writing.

fallacious that it was rejected, and it was not until 1854, that it was by statute made admissible as evidence in England.[228]

It is generally the practice to have the expert witness prepare enlarged photographs, which can be referred to and used by the witness, to show those similarities or differences in the specimen in question upon which the witness relies.[229] It is now common practice for expert witnesses to give opinion evidence as to whether the handwriting on a given document is that of a particular person.[230]

In *R. v. Voisin*,[231] the body of a woman was found in a parcel and a piece of paper with the words "Bladie Beligiam" written upon it was also found in the parcel. While in custody, the accused was asked to write the subject words which he identically misspelled. The writing by the accused was circumstantial evidence of his identity as the killer. At a civil or criminal trial a witness, including the accused, may be required to give a specimen of her or his handwriting for comparison purposes.[232]

B. *Attesting Witnesses*

In *Crane v. Ayre*,[233] Carter C.J. held:[234]

> It cannot be disputed that the rule which has long prevailed, that where there is an attesting witness, he must be called or accounted for, still remains in force. It is equally clear that where the attesting witness is dead, absent in a foreign country, or not amenable to the process of the court, or where he cannot be found after diligent inquiry, proof of his handwriting will be sufficient.

---

228 *Scott v. Crerar* (1887), 14 O.A.R. 152 (Ont. C.A.), at 160; *Gleeson v. Wallace* (1848), 4 U.C.R. 245 (Q.B.).
229 *R. v. Bouffard*, [1964] 3 C.C.C. 14, 43 C.R. 124, [1964] 2 O.R. 111 (C.A.), at 117-18.
230 *R. v. Bouffard*, *ibid*.
231 *Supra*, note 224.
232 *R. v. Whittaker* (1924), 42 C.C.C. 162, [1924] 2 W.W.R. 706, [1924] 3 D.L.R. 63 (Alta. S.C.). This procedure might be challenged under the *Charter*.
233 *Crane v. Ayre* (1853), 7 N.B.R. 577 (C.A.); see also, *Nichols & Shepard Co. v. Skedanuk* (1913), 4 W.W.R. 587, 11 D.L.R. 199 (Alta. S.C.); revd. on other grounds, 5 W.W.R. 118, 13 D.L.R. 892, 6 Alta. L.R. 368 (C.A.); *Doe d. McDonald v. Twigg* (1848), 5 U.C.Q.B. 167 (C.A.); *Tylden v. Bullen* (1846), 3 U.C.Q.B. 10 (C.A.).
234 *Ibid.*, 7 N.B.R., at 578.

It is unnecessary to prove by the attesting witness any instrument which, though attested, does not depend upon attestation for its validity.[235]

C. *Corporate Seal*

In general, a corporation seal may be proved by anyone familiar with it, without calling a witness who saw it affixed.[236]

D. *Typewriting*

It has been held that an expert as to typewriting or even a witness of ordinary capacity and experience, may be able to state whether a particular letter resembles one made by a typewriter produced and operated before the witness, or by a typewriter with whose printing the witness is familiar.[237] Just as a signature or handwriting may be proved to be that of a particular individual by comparing a disputed document with other documents proved to the satisfaction of the judge to be genuine, a particular specimen of typewriting may be shown to come from a particular typewriter upon comparison with another specimen proved to the satisfaction of the judge to have come from the typewriter in question.

E. *Photographs and Videotapes*[238]

It has been held that the admissibility of photographs depends upon: (1) their accuracy in truly representing facts; (2) their fairness and absence of any intention to mislead; (3) their verification on oath by a person capable of doing so.[239] It is not always necessary to have

---

235 *Canada Evidence Act, supra,* note 227, s. 34; *Alberta Evidence Act, supra,* note 227, s. 58; Ontario *Evidence Act, supra,* note 227, s. 56.

236 *Monarch Lumber Co. v. Garrison* (1911), 18 W.L.R. 686, 4 Sask. L.R. 514 (C.A.); *Ontario Salt Co. v. Merchants' Salt Co.* (1871), 18 Gr. 551 (Q.B.); *Doe d. King's College v. Kennedy* (1849), 5 U.C.Q.B. 577 (C.A.).

237 *Scott v. Crerar* (1887), 14 O.A.R. 152 (Ont. C.A.), at 154, 160; *R. v. Petersen* (1983), 45 N.B.R. (2d) 271 (C.A.); leave to appeal to S.C.C. refused 46 N.B.R. (2d) 231, 50 N.R. 80*n* (S.C.C.).

238 See also Chapter 2, I.C. where the reception of such evidence is considered under the topic, Real Evidence.

239 *R. v. Creemer,* [1968] 1 C.C.C. 14, 1 C.R.N.S. 146, 53 M.P.R. 1 (N.S.C.A.); *Hindson v. Ashby,* [1896] 2 Ch. 1 (C.A.); *R. v. Maloney (No. 2)* (1976), 29 C.C.C. (2d) 431 (Ont. Co. Ct.). In this case a number of photographs showing a particular river bank were ordered taken by the court in the presence of agents for both

the sworn evidence of the person who took the photograph. Another witness who is familiar with the objects shown in the photograph may be permitted to identify it.[240] Similarily, a person must be able to authenticate the accuracy of a videotape to represent the matter depicted[241] or the reliability of an unmanned camera to accurately record the event.[242] The surreptious video surveillance of an accused, however, may be subject to exclusion under the *Charter*.[243]

It is an accepted rule that photographs and videotapes, even if relevant to the issue being tried are subject to certain limitations, one of which is that admission will be refused where the inflammatory and prejudicial effect of the photograph or videotape exceeds its potential evidentiary or probative value.[244] In criminal jury trials, the trial judge must be cautious to protect the accused's right to a fair trial if the photographs may inflame the jury especially if they are of low probative value.[245] However, it may be necessary for the trier of fact to observe a photograph if such evidence is necessary to understand other evidence.[246]

F. Plans, Maps and Charts

Plans and maps prepared and filed by public officials in the course of their duty have been held to be admissible without proof

---

parties. *Chippendale v. Winnipeg Electric Co.*, [1928] 1 D.L.R. 920, [1928] 1 W.W.R. 238, 37 Man. R. 207 (C.A.).

240 *R. v. Bannister* (1936), 66 C.C.C. 38, [1936] 2 D.L.R. 795, 10 M.P.R. 391 (N.B.C.A.); *Simpson Timber Co. (Saskatchewan) v. Bonville*, [1986] 5 W.W.R. 180 (Sask. Q.B.).

241 *Kajala v. Noble* (1982), 75 Cr. App. R. 149 (Div. Ct.).

242 *R. v. Caughlin* (1987), 40 C.C.C. (3d) 247, 18 B.C.L.R. (2d) 186 (Co. Ct.); see *R. v. Schaffner* (1988), 44 C.C.C. (3d) 507, 86 N.S.R. (2d) 342 (C.A.); *Taylor v. Chief Constable of Cheshire*, [1987] 1 All E.R. 225 (Q.B.), where the witness testified as to observations of a tape that had been erased.

243 *The Canadian Charter of Rights and Freedoms*, R.S.C. 1985, Appendix II, No. 44. See *R. v. Wong*, [1990] 3 S.C.R. 36, 60 C.C.C. (3d) 460, 1 C.R. (4th) 1, 45 O.A.C. 250, 120 N.R. 34, 2 C.R.R. (2d) 277.

244 *Draper v. Jacklyn*, [1970] S.C.R. 92, 9 D.L.R. (3d) 264; *Quintal v. Datta*, [1988] 6 W.W.R. 481, 68 Sask. R. 104 (C.A.).

245 *Dilabbio v. R.*, [1965] 4 C.C.C. 295, 46 C.R. 131, [1965] 2 O.R. 537 (C.A.); *R. v. Maloney (No. 2)* (1976), 29 C.C.C. (2d) 431 (Ont. Co. Ct.).

246 *R. v. Bannister, supra*, note 240; *R. v. Wildman* (1981), 60 C.C.C. (2d) 289, 5 O.A.C. 268, 55 N.R. 54 (Ont. C.A.); revd. [1984] 2 S.C.R. 311, 14 C.C.C. (3d) 321, 5 O.A.C. 241, 12 D.L.R. (4th) 641, 55 N.R. 27.

other than that they were so prepared in a manner similar to that in which public documents are admissible.[247] Statutory provisions may have the effect of giving some private plans the same status as public documents and of allowing them to be admitted as such.[248] Also, ancient documents, ancient maps and plans are admissible without proof if shown to come from proper custody.[249]

Private maps, plans and surveys are not, in general, admissible in evidence against third parties[250] without being properly proved as is required in the case of any other document, although, as between parties and privies, they may operate as admissions.[251] Thus, if a survey has been accepted and acted upon by the predecessor in title of A, it may be admitted without further proof against A in an action against her or him by B.[252] In addition, such instruments may be admissible for the purpose of establishing public rights.[253]

Presumably, a sketch or a plan is admissible if the person making it, or a witness who can testify as to its accuracy, is called and testifies that it accurately depicts a certain situation or locality, or if the parties consent to its being admitted as correctly showing such situation or locality.[254]

It is quite common in civil actions, particularly negligence actions, for a party to seek to admit a sketch or diagram illustrating the *locus in quo*, to show such a sketch to witnesses being examined,

---

247 *Nicholson v. Page* (1868), 27 U.C.Q.B. 318 (C.A.); *Burford (Bd. of Education) v. Burford (Township)* (1889), 18 O.R. 546 (C.P.); *Haggarty v. Britton* (1870), 30 U.C.Q.B. 321 (C.A.); *R. v. Bellman* (1938), 70 C.C.C. 171, [1938] 3 D.L.R. 548, 13 M.P.R. 37 (N.B.C.A.).

248 See 12 Vict., c. 35, s. 34 (Consolidated Statutes, Cl. C., c. 93, s. 18) as applied in *Van Every v. Drake* (1860), 9 U.C.C.P. 478 (C.A.); *Registry Act*, R.S.O. 1980, c. 445, s. 85.

249 *Burford (Bd. of Education) v. Burford (Township)* (1889), 18 O.R. 546 (C.P.), at 549; *Van Every v. Drake, ibid.; R. v. Wilson* (1835), 2 N.B.R. 3 (C.A.).

250 *Cormier v. LeBlanc*, [1935] 2 D.L.R. 803, 9 M.P.R. 164 (N.B.C.A.); *Mercer v. Denne*, [1904] 2 Ch. 534; affd. [1905] 2 Ch. 538 (C.A.); *VanKoughnet v. Denison* (1885), 11 O.A.R. 699 (C.A.); *R. v. Price Bros. & Co.*, [1926] S.C.R. 28, [1925] 3 D.L.R. 595.

251 *O'Connor v. Dunn* (1876), 39 U.C.Q.B. 597 (Q.B.), at p. 603; revd. on other grounds, 2 O.A.R. 247 (C.A.); *Van Koughnet v. Denison, ibid.*

252 *Van Every v. Drake, supra*, note 248.

253 *VanKoughnet v. Denison, supra*, note 250.

254 See *R. v. Price Bros. & Co.*, [1926] S.C.R. 28, at 44-46, for a critical view of the evidential value of maps.

and to ask them to relate their testimony in such a manner as to point out on such a sketch the specific location of the occurrence in question. Such a sketch may be held inadmissible if it purports to show on its face information bearing on the very point in issue, in such a way that it might have the effect of influencing the testimony of witnesses to whom it is shown.[255]

---

255 *Wattsburg Lumber Co. v. Cooke Lumber Co.* (1912), 2 W.W.R. 248, 17 B.C.R. 410, 4 D.L.R. 8 (C.A.). See especially judgment of MacDonald C.J.A., 2 W.W.R., at 249, approving *Beamon v. Ellice* (1831), 4 C. & P. 585, 172 E.R. 836 (N.P.).

CHAPTER 19

RULES DISPENSING WITH OR FACILITATING PROOF

I   FORMAL ADMISSIONS

A. *In Civil Cases*

A formal admission in civil proceedings is a concession made by a party to the proceeding that a certain fact or issue is not in dispute. Formal admissions[1] made for the purpose of dispensing with proof at trial are conclusive as to the matters admitted. As to these matters other evidence is precluded as being irrelevant,[2] but, if such evidence is adduced the court is bound to act on the admission even if the evidence contradicts it.[3] A formal admission should be distinguished from an informal admission. The latter is admitted into evidence as an exception to the hearsay rule and does not bind the party making it, if it is overcome by other evidence.[4]

A formal admission may be made: (1) by a statement in the pleadings or by failure to deliver pleadings;[5] (2) by an agreed statement

---

1   On occasion they have also been termed "express" or "judicial". In *Doe d. Spence v. Welling* (1866), 11 N.B.R. 470 (C.A.) the terms "solemn admissions" and "admissions in judicio" were employed.
2   *Dominion Act Co. Ltd. v. Murphy* (1923), 54 O.L.R. 332, at 340, 24 O.W.N. 477 (C.A.); *Levesque v. Albert* (1976), 16 N.B.R. (2d) 205, at 208 (C.A.); *Rocca Construction Ltd. v. Gen. Labourer's & Gen. Workers' Union, Local 1079* (1979), 27 N.B.R. (2d) 457 (C.A.).
3   *Copp v. Clancy* (1957), 16 D.L.R. (2d) 415, at 425 (N.B.C.A.); *Urquhart v. Butterfield* (1887), 37 Ch. D. 357, at 369 and 374 (C.A.).
4   See Chapter 6, II.K.
5   See by way of example, the Ontario *Rules of Civil Procedure*, O. Reg. 560/84, as amended, rr. 19.02(1)(a) and 25.07(2).

of facts filed at the trial;[6] (3) by an oral statement made by counsel at trial,[7] or even counsel's silence in the face of statements made to the trial judge by the opposing counsel with the intention that the statements be relied on by the judge;[8] (4) by a letter written by a party's solicitor prior to trial;[9] or (5) by a reply or failure to reply to a request to admit facts.[10] A formal admission of fact, as distinct from an admission of law, cannot be withdrawn except with leave of the court or the consent of the party in whose favour it was made.[11] An admission relating solely to a question of law, on the other hand, may be withdrawn at any time,[12] even in the Court of Appeal.[13] Leave to withdraw an admission should not be granted, however, unless (1) the admission was made clearly without authority,[14] by mistake[15] or under duress; (2) there exists a triable issue concerning the admitted fact, and (3) there will be no prejudice to the party in whose favour it was made. An inadvertent statement of fact by counsel in opening may be withdrawn if retracted before it has been acted upon.[16] The discretion of the court ought to be warily exercised and usually on terms.[17]

---

6   *Patterson v. Scherloski*, [1971] 3 O.R. 753, 21 D.L.R. (3d) 641 (H.C.J.).
7   *Copp v. Clancy, supra*, note 3.
8   *Meunier v. Canadian Northern Ry. Co.* (1911), 17 W.L.R. 539, 3 Alta. L.R. 345 (C.A.).
9   *Ellis v. Allen*, [1914] 1 Ch. 904, [1911-13] All E.R. 906; *Wright v. Pepin*, [1954] 1 W.L.R. 635, 98 Sol. J. 252, [1954] 2 All E.R. 52; *Plainsman Dev. Ltd. v. Builders Contract Mgmt. Ltd.* (1982), 20 Sask. R. 298, at 300 (Q.B.).
10   Requests to admit facts are provided for in the provinces; Alberta, Alta. Reg. 360/68, r. 230; B.C., *Supreme Court Rules*, r. 31; Man., *Queen's Bench Rules*, Man. Reg. 553/88, r. 51, N.B. *Rules of Court*, Reg. 82-73, r. 51; Newfoundland *Rules of the Supreme Court, 1986*, in *Judicature Act, 1986*, S. Nfld. 1986, c. 42, Sched. D, r. 33; Northwest Territories, *Rules of Court*, SOR/79-768, r. 232; Nova Scotia, *Civil Procedure Rules*, r. 21; Ontario, O. Reg. 560/84, r. 51.03; Prince Edward Island, *Supreme Court Rules*, r. 21; Saskatchewan, *Rules of the Court of Queen's Bench*, r. 244.
11   *Patterson v. Scherloski, supra*, note 6.
12   *Highley v. C.P.R.* (1929), 64 O.L.R. 615, 36 C.R.C. 217, [1930] 1 D.L.R. 630 (C.A.), revg. 37 O.W.N. 1, 35 C.R.C. 312; *Henderson v. Tudhope* (1930), 65 O.L.R. 238, 38 O.W.N. 23, [1930] 3 D.L.R. 245 (C.A.).
13   *Re Baty*, [1959] O.R. 13, 16 D.L.R. (2d) 164 (C.A.).
14   *Anderson v. Woods*, [1955] O.W.N. 585 (S.C.).
15   *Hollis v. Burton*, [1892] 3 Ch. 226, 67 L.T. 146 (C.A.); *Gardiner v. M.N.R.* (1963), 17 D.T.C. 1219 (S.C.C.); *Smith v. Smith* (1884), 5 O.R. 690 (Ch.); *Power v. MacFarlane* (1970), 2 N.B.R. (2d) 359 (C.A.).
16   *Jannette v. The Great Western Rly. Co.* (1855), 4 U.C.C.P. 488.
17   *Patterson v. Scherloski, supra*, note 6.

Counsel has the implied authority to make an admission on behalf of a client, which in the honest exercise of his or her judgment he or she thinks is proper, provided it is incidental to the suit. The fact, therefore, that the client has not expressly authorized the admission to be made does not, in itself, entitle a client to subsequently withdraw it.[18]

An admission in a pleading that is struck out cannot be relied on as a formal admission, but it has been suggested that it may still be adduced in evidence as an informal admission.[19]

Formal admissions are only binding for the purposes of the particular case in which they are made.[20] However, there is a conflict of authority as to whether an admission made at the first trial continues to bind when a new trial is ordered.[21] It is submitted that an admission for the purpose of dispensing with evidence is generally intended to apply only to the trial which is in progress or imminent and not in the differing circumstances that may prevail at a new trial. Accordingly, the admission is no longer binding at the new trial in the formal sense, but may be introduced as an informal admission. The party who made the admission may, therefore, lead evidence to explain or contradict the previous statement.[22]

Admissions made in interlocutory proceedings may be binding at the trial, unless they were intended only to facilitate the disposition of the interlocutory proceedings.[23]

---

18 *Dominion Act Co. Ltd. v. Murphy, supra,* note 2.
19 *O'Kelly v. Downie* (1914), 6 W.W.R. 911, 24 Man. R. 210, 17 D.L.R. 395 (C.A.).
20 *Dawson v. Great Central Ry. Co.* (1919), 88 L.J.K.B. 1177, at 1181, 121 L.T. 263 (C.A.); R. Cross and C. Tapper, *Cross on Evidence,* 7th ed. (London: Butterworths, 1990), at 73.
21 Compare *Elton v. Larkins* (1832), 1 Mood. & R. 196, 5 C. & P. 385, 172 E.R. 1020, at 1021; *Dawson v. Great Central Ry., ibid.*
22 *Doe d Wetherell v. Bird* (1835), 7 C. & P. 6, 173 E.R. 3; *McDonald v. Murray* (1884), 5 O.R. 559, at 575 (C.A.); *R. v. Bedere* (1891), 21 O.R. 189 (C.A.); *Domville v. Ferguson* (1877), 17 N.B.R. 40 (C.A.).
23 See *Guy v. Brady* (1885), 24 N.B.R. 563 (C.A.).

B. *In Criminal Proceedings*

1. Guilty Pleas

Formal admissions can also be made in the context of a criminal proceeding. A guilty plea, for example, constitutes an admission of all of the essential elements of the offence charged in the indictment and to be proved by the Crown.[24] A plea which the Crown rejects can still be used as an informal admission in the proceedings.[25] A judge in a criminal trial has a greater role in ensuring that the process is fair to the accused than a judge in a civil proceeding has with respect to any party. Therefore, a judge should make inquiries to ensure that an accused making a guilty plea understands the nature of the charge and the consequences in terms of penalty.[26] The court should not accept the plea if there is any doubt about the accused's understanding.[27] Furthermore, the court should not accept the plea until it appears that the foundational facts disclose the essential ingredients of the offence.[28] Formal proof of those facts is not necessary,[29] but the court should be provided, in open court, with information that demonstrates the facts upon which the guilty plea is based.[30]

---

24 *R. v. Gardiner,* [1982] 2 S.C.R. 368, at 414-15, 30 C.R. (3d) 289, 68 C.C.C. (2d) 477, 140 D.L.R. (3d) 612, 43 N.R. 361; *R. v. Toulejour* (1983), 27 Sask. R. 72 (C.A.); *R. v. Robillard* (1982), 18 Sask. R. 255 (C.A.); *R. v. Milina* (1946), 86 C.C.C. 374, at 378, 2 C.R. 179, [1946] 2 W.W.R. 584 (B.C.C.A.); *R. v. Drysdale* (1932), 59 C.C.C. 83, at 85 (N.S.S.C.); *R. v. Grant* (1924), 42 C.C.C. 344, [1924] 3 D.L.R. 985 (*sub nom. R. v. Roop*), 57 N.B.R. 325; *R. v. MacKenzie* (1935), 65 C.C.C. 104 (N.S.S.C.).

25 R. v. *Dobson* (1985), 19 C.C.C. (3d) 93, 7 O.A.C. 145 (Ont. C.A.); leave to appeal to S.C.C. refd., [1985] 1 S.C.R. viii, 59 N.R. 238*n*, 9 O.A.C. 400*n*.

26 Questions may be asked of the accused and of his or her counsel and the Crown.

27 *Adgey v. R.,* [1975] 2 S.C.R. 426, 13 C.C.C. (2d) 177, 23 C.R.N.S. 298, 39 D.L.R. (3d) 553; *Brosseau v. R.,* [1969] S.C.R. 181, at 188-90, [1969] 3 C.C.C. 129, 5 C.R.N.S. 331, 2 D.L.R. (3d) 139, 65 W.W.R. 751; *R. v. Fraser* (1971), 5 C.C.C. (2d) 439, 17 C.R.N.S. 164, [1972] 2 W.W.R. 248 (B.C.C.A.); *R. v. Bliss* (1936), 67 C.C.C. 1, [1937] 1 D.L.R. 1 (Ont. S.C.); *R. v. Gordon* (1947), 88 C.C.C. 413, 3 C.R. 26, [1947] 1 W.W.R. 468 (B.C.C.A.); see also the *Young Offenders Act,* R.S.C. 1985, c. Y-1, s. 19(1).

28 *R. v. Gordon, ibid.,* at 416; *R. v. Johnson* (1945), 85 C.C.C. 56, [1945] 4 D.L.R. 75, [1945] 3 W.W.R. 201, 62 B.C.R. 199 (C.A.).

29 *R. v. Maynard* (1946), 2 C.R. 81 (Que. C.A.); *R. v. Milina, supra,* note 24.

30 Such as the depositions received by the Crown (*R. v. Bliss, supra,* note 27; *R. v. Clark* (1929), 21 Cr. App. R. 81 (C.A.)), or a confession of the accused (*R. v.*

An accused can withdraw the plea only with leave of the court[31] and, if withdrawn, the plea is of no effect.[32]

2. Specific Facts

An accused either personally or through counsel can admit certain specific facts. Section 655 of the *Criminal Code*[33] provides as follows:

> Where an accused is on trial for an indictable offence, he or his counsel may admit any fact[34] alleged against him for the purpose of dispensing with proof thereof.[35]

This section only applies where the fact has been alleged against the accused by the Crown at the trial[36] on an indictable offence.[37] An agreed statement of facts can be admitted at the trial so long as the facts are clearly agreed upon.[38] However, if the accused's evidence conflicts with the statement the trial judge should require the Crown to call evidence on the point.[39]

There is also scope for the admission of facts at common law. An

---

Vent (1935), 25 Cr. App. R. 55 (C.A.)).

31   *Adgey v. R.*, *supra*, note 27; *Brosseau v. R.*, *supra*, note 27; *Toussaint v. R.* (1984), 40 C.R. (3d) 230, 16 C.C.C. (3d) 544, [1984] C.A. 290 (Que. C.A.); *S. v. Recorder of Manchester*, [1971] A.C. 481 (H.L.); *R. v. Milina*, *supra*, note 24.

32   *Thibodeau v. R.*, [1955] S.C.R. 646, 21 C.R. 265.

33   R.S.C. 1985, c. C-46.

34   This section applies to admissions of fact only, not to admissions of law (such as the voluntariness of a confession: *R. v. Dietrich* (1970), 1 C.C.C. (2d) 49, 11 C.R.N.S. 22, [1970] 3 O.R. 725 (Ont. C.A.) and see *R. v. LeBrun* (1954), 110 C.C.C. 262, 19 C.R. 286, 13 W.W.R. 192 (B.C.S.C.)), or statements of opinion (*R. v. Curry* (1980), 38 N.S.R. (2d) 575 (C.A.)).

35   Overruling the common law with respect to admissions on the trial of a felony: *R. v. Bateman* (1845), 1 Cox. C.C. 186 (Cont. Cr. Ct.).

36   *Castellani v. R.*, [1970] S.C.R. 310, [1970] 4 C.C.C. 287, 9 C.R.N.S. 111, 11 D.L.R. (3d) 92, 71 W.W.R. 147 (S.C.C.); *R. v. Leggo* (1962), 133 C.C.C. 149, 38 C.R. 290, 39 W.W.R. 385 (B.C.C.A.).

37   *R. v. Modeste* (1959), 127 C.C.C. 197, 31 W.W.R. 84 (N.W.T. Terr. Ct.).

38   *R. v. Warkentin*, [1977] 2 S.C.R. 355, 30 C.C.C. (2d) 1, 35 C.R.N.S. 21 (S.C.C.); *R. v. Coburn* (1982), 66 C.C.C. (2d) 463, 27 C.R. (3d) 259 (Ont. C.A.).

39   *R. v. Coburn, ibid.*

accused can admit the voluntariness of a confession and therefore dispense with a *voir dire*.[40] Facts can also be admitted at a preliminary inquiry.[41]

II   JUDICIAL NOTICE

Judicial notice is the acceptance by a court or judicial tribunal, in a civil or criminal proceeding, without the requirement of proof, of the truth of a particular fact or state of affairs. Facts which are (a) so notorious as not to be the subject of dispute among reasonable persons, or (b) capable of immediate and accurate demonstration by resorting to readily accessible sources of indisputable accuracy, may be noticed by the court without proof of them by any party.[42] The practice of taking judicial notice of facts is justified. It expedites the process of the courts, it creates uniformity in decision making and it keeps the courts receptive to societal change. Furthermore, the tacit judicial notice that surely occurs in every hearing is indispensable to the normal reasoning process.

A. *Notorious Facts*

In *Reference re Alberta Statutes*,[43] Duff C.J. said: "It is our duty, as judges, to take judicial notice of facts which are known to intelligent persons generally; ". . . In the simplest terms, the court may and should notice without proof that which "everybody knows".[44] The matter need only be common knowledge in the particular community in

---

40   *R. v. Dietrich, supra,* note 34; *Park v. R.,* [1981] 2 S.C.R. 64, 59 C.C.C. (2d) 385, 21 C.R. (3d) 182, 26 C.R. (3d) 164 (Fr.), 122 D.L.R. (3d) 1, 37 N.R. 501.
41   *R. v. Ulrich* (1977), 38 C.C.C. (2d) 1, [1978] 1 W.W.R. 422 (Alta. T.D.).
42   *R. v. Porter* (1961), 130 C.C.C. 116, at 118 (N.S.S.C.); *R. v. Uvery* (1968), 5 C.R.N.S. 43, 66 W.W.R. 27, 1 D.L.R. (3d) 29, at 34-35 (Sask. Q.B.); *R. v. Potts* (1982), 26 C.R. (3d) 252, 66 C.C.C. (2d) 219, 134 D.L.R. (3d) 227, 36 O.R. (2d) 195 (Ont. C.A.); leave to appeal to S.C.C. refd. [1982] 1 S.C.R. xi, 66 C.C.C. (2d) 219*n*, 134 D.L.R. (3d) 227*n*, 43 N.R. 270*n*; and see G.D. Nokes, "The Limits of Judicial Notice" (1958), 74 L.Q.R 59.
43   [1938] S.C.R. 100, at 128.
44   Per Irving J.A. in *Schnell v. B.C. Electric Rly. Co.* (1910), 14 W.L.R. 586, 15 B.C.R. 378 (B.C.C.A.).

which the judge is sitting.[45] Also, what facts are judicially noticeable may change over time.[46]

Matters that can be judicially noted as notorious facts can be divided into innumerable categories and endless examples can be given.[47] The fact that a certain fact or matter has been noted by a judge of the same court in a previous matter has precedential value and it is, therefore, useful for counsel and the court to examine the case law when attempting to determine whether any particular fact can be noted. However, because the question of what is judicially noticeable is also very dependent on the locality, the time and the particular facts, we intend to do no more than highlight a few of the categories with a limited number of examples.

The character of a certain place or of the community of persons living in a certain locality has been judicially noticed.[48] For example, in *R. v. Potts*[49] the Ottawa trial judge noticed that a certain highway in Ottawa was under the care and control of the National Captial Commission, a fact which was essential to the Crown's case.[50] Geographical facts, such as international, provincial and territorial districts and boundaries, the location of cities,[51] and landmarks, such as lakes and rivers,[52] are often judicially noted. In *R. v. Mallios*[53] the Quebec Supreme Court took notice of the fact that Montreal Harbour was south of the 60th parallel and in Canadian waters. This is perhaps a fact within the common knowledge of most Canadians which could have been recognized within the Quebec courts and the courts of any other province. On the other hand, the fact that Slave Lake is in

---

45   *R. v. Potts, supra,* note 42.

46   See the example in R. Cross and C. Tapper, *Cross on Evidence,* 7th ed. (London: Butterworths, 1990), at 64-65.

47   For a quite detailed listing of such examples, see 11 C.E.D. (Ont. 3rd), Title 57 *Evidence,* at § 597.

48   *R. v. Potts, supra,* note 42; *R. v. Burbridge* (1990), 79 Nfld. & P.E.I.R. 66 (Nfld. Prov. Ct.); *R. v. Kline* (1988), 86 N.S.R. (2d) 443, 218 A.P.R. 443 (N.S.C.A.).

49   *Ibid.*

50   *McCoy v. O'Donnell* (1974), 9 N.B.R. (2d) 609 (N.B.S.C.).

51   *Lick v. Rivers* (1901), 1 O.L.R. 57, 21 C.L.T. 166 (Chambers); *R. v. Cerniuk* (1947), 91 C.C.C. 56, [1948] 1 W.W.R. 653 (B.C.C.A.); *R. v. MacLure* (1979), 21 Nfld. & P.E.I.R. 505 (P.E.I.S.C.); *R. v. Sim* (1934), 62 C.C.C. 268, [1934] 3 W.W.R. 253, at 254 (B.C.S.C.).

52   *R. v. Dubrule* (1978), 14 A.R. 554 (Dist. Ct.).

53   (1978), 42 C.C.C. (2d) 441 (Que. S.C.).

Alberta may be within the common knowledge of most westerners and hence be properly noticed by Alberta judges, but it is not necessarily properly noticed by Ontario judges.[54]

Characteristics of human needs and behaviour ranging from television habits[55] to reactions to alcohol and drugs[56] to the normal period of human gestation[57] have all been the subject of judicial notice.

Another recognized category is that of business and trade practices notorious generally or in the community. In *Sutherland v. Bell*,[58] Beck J. pointed out that:[59]

> It is a matter of common experience . . . We are not to decline to make use of our own knowledge of such ordinary methods of business as are matter of common experience.

For example, notice has recently been taken of the fact that pension benefits generally equal five per cent of employment earnings,[60] of the estate and probate practice in Nova Scotia[61] and of the paraphernalia of the drug trade.[62] Economic trends and political events may also be notorious.[63]

---

54   *R. v. Dubrule, supra*, note 52; see also *R. v. Laurie* (1982), 37 Nfld. & P.E.I.R. 283, 104 A.P.R. 283 (Nfld. T.D.).

55   *Bridlington Relay Ltd. v. Yorkshire Electricity Bd.*, [1965] 1 All E.R. 264, [1965] Ch. 436.

56   *R. v. Penno*, [1990] 2 S.C.R. 865, 59 C.C.C. (3d) 344, 80 C.R. (3d) 97, 115 N.R. 249, 49 C.R.R. 50, 42 O.A.C. 271, per Lamer C.J.C.; *R. v. Litke* (1976), 34 C.R.N.S. 397 (B.C.S.C.); *Legrand v. R.*, [1982] C.S. 767 (Que. S.C.); *R. v. Kays* (1987), 46 M.V.R. 161, 78 N.S.R. (2d) 443 (Co. Ct.); revd. (1987), 3 M.V.R. (2d) 209, 82 N.S.R. (2d) 18, 62 C.R. (3d) 193 (C.A.); leave to appeal to S.C.C. refd. (1988), 64 C.R. (3d) xxx*n*; but see *R. v. Stevenson* (1972), 14 C.C.C. (2d) 412 (B.C.C.A.) for an example of the limitations on the noting of such facts.

57   *Re Chilcott*, 84 D.R.S. 22-514 (Ont. Prov. Ct.); *Fleming v. Pitirri* (1979), 27 O.R. (2d) 115 (Prov. Ct.); *R. v. Luffe* (1807), 8 East. 193, 103 E.R. 316; *Hiuser v. Hiuser*, [1962] O.W.N. 220 (C.A.); but see *Preston-Jones v. Preston-Jones*, [1951] A.C. 391, [1951] 1 All E.R. 124.

58   (1911), 3 Alta. L.R. 497, at 498, 18 W.L.R. 521 (C.A.). See also *Davey v. Harrow Corp.*, [1957] 2 All E.R. 305, [1958] 1 Q.B. 60 (C.A.).

59   *Gollan v. Edmonton Credit Co.*, [1938] 1 W.W.R. 670 (Alta.); *Poole v. Smith's Car Sales (Balham) Ltd.*, [1962] 2 All E.R. 482, at 486, [1962] 1 W.L.R. 744 (C.A.); *R. v. Pinno*, [1925] 1 W.W.R. 737 (Sask.).

60   *Zayac v. Coneco Equipment Ltd.* (1986), 69 A.R. 58, at 59 (Q.B.).

61   *Marchand v. Marchand* (1979), 36 N.S.R. (2d) 264, 64 A.P.R. 264 (T.D.).

62   *R. v. Santangelo* (1981), 9 Man. R. (2d) 370 (Co. Ct.).

63   *Kinnon v. Traynor* (1982), 46 A.R. 75 (Q.B.); *Meyer v. Cronkhite* (1983), 46

Scientific or mechanical facts are sometimes so well known generally that the court can judicially note them without reference to any external sources.[64] The meaning of well known phrases, such as "O.D'd"[65] have been noticed also.[66]

B. Facts Capable of Immediate Accurate Demonstration

There are some facts which, although not immediately within the judge's knowledge, are indisputable and can be ascertained from sources to which it is proper for the judge to refer.[67] These may include texts, dictionaries, almanacs and other reference works, previous case reports, certificates from various officials and statements from witnesses in the case.[68]

1. Official Matters

In *Re Chateau Gai Wines Ltd. v. Canada (A.G.)*,[69] it was material to establish that a trade agreement between Canada and France came into force on a certain date. In order to take judicial notice of this fact a certificate was obtained from the Secretary of State, which was accepted as conclusive.

In the same manner the court may take judicial notice of the

N.B.R. (2d) 439 (Q.B.); *Sperschneider v. Staskiewicz* (1985), 33 Man. R. (2d) 56 (Q.B.); *Reference re Anti-Inflation Act* (Can.), [1976] 2 S.C.R. 373, 68 D.L.R. (3d) 452; *Wallace v. McMaster*, [1931] 1 W.W.R. 79, at 80, [1931] 1 D.L.R. 1016, 25 Sask. L.R. 219; *Re Qualifications for Mayor and Aldermen of Calgary of Persons in Receipt of Relief*, [1933] 3 W.W.R. 385, at 386, [1934] 1 D.L.R. 55 (Alta. C.A.).

64 *Giffin v. R.* (1980), 8 M.V.R. 313 (N.S. Co. Ct.) (function of radar machine) (but see *R. v. Waschuk* (1970), 1 C.C.C. (2d) 463 (Sask. Q.B.)); *R. v. Reeves* (1979), 35 N.S.R. (2d) 369 (Co. Ct.) as to how breathalyzer devices work; *R. v. Orlias* (1983), 42 A.R. 138, [1983] N.W.T.R. 166 (S.C.) as to the process of fermentation and *Fay v. Prentice* (1845), 1 C.B. 828, 135 E.R. 769 (C.P.) as to the fact that rain falls.

65 *R. v. MacAulay* (1975), 11 N.B.R. 44 (N.B.C.A.).

66 But see *Joe v. Director of Family and Childrens Services* (1986), 5 B.C.L.R. (2d) 267 (Y.T.S.C.), as to the meaning of the phrase "fetal alcohol syndrome".

67 *Commonwealth Shipping Representative v. Peninsular & Oriental Branch Service*, [1923] A.C. 191, at 212, [1922] All E.R. Rep. 207 (H.L.).

68 *McQuaker v. Goddard*, [1940] 1 K.B. 687, [1940] 1 All E.R. 471.

69 (1971), 14 D.L.R. (3d) 411, [1970] Ex. C.R. 366, 63 C.P.R. 195, 44 Fox. Pat. C. 167 (Exch. Ct.).

following matters in respect of which the certificate of the appropriate minister of the Crown is conclusive:

(a) a question as to whether a person is a foreign sovereign power,

(b) a question as to what persons must be regarded as constituting the effective Government of a foreign territory,

(c) a question as to whether a particular place must be regarded as being in Canada or as being under the authority of a foreign sovereign authority,

(d) a question as to whether Canada is at peace or at war with a foreign power, or

(e) a question as to whether a person in Canada is entitled to diplomatic privileges as being an ambassador of a foreign power or a member of the entourage of such an ambassador.[70]

Cross on Evidence notes,[71] that such certificates are treated as a source of indisputable accuracy on grounds of public policy; the undesirability of conflict between the executive and the courts.

2. Historical Facts

The court may rely on its own historical knowledge and may examine history texts to enable it to take judicial notice of the facts of ancient[72] and modern history.[73]

---

70 *Re Chateau Gai Wines Ltd. v. Canada (A.G.)*, *ibid.*, at 422 (D.L.R.); *Duff Development Co. Ltd. v. Kelantan Government*, [1924] A.C. 797, [1924] 2 All E.R. 1 (H.L.); *The Fagernes*, [1927] P. 311 (C.A.); *Engelke v. Musmann*, [1928] A.C. 433, [1928] All E.R. 18 (H.L.).
71 R. Cross and C. Tapper, *Cross on Evidence*, 7th ed. (London: Butterworths, 1990), at 65.
72 *Read v. Bishop of Lincoln*, [1892] A.C. 644, at 652-54, 62 L.J.P.C. 1; *Calder v. British Columbia (A.G.)*, [1973] S.C.R. 313, 34 D.L.R. (3d) 145 (S.C.C.), at 169, per Hall J., dissenting.
73 *Monarch SS. Co. Ltd. v. Karlshamns of Oljefabriker*, [1949] A.C. 196, at 234, [1949] 1 All E.R. 1; *R. v. Bartleman* (1984), 13 C.C.C. (3d) 488, at 491-92, 12 D.L.R. (4th) 73, at 77, 55 B.C.L.R. 78, [1984] 3 C.N.L.R. 114 (B.C.C.A.); *R. v. Zundel* (1987), 31 C.C.C. (3d) 97, 56 C.R. (3d) 1, 35 D.L.R. (4th) 338, 58 O.R. (2d) 129, 18 O.A.C. 161, 29 C.R.R. 349; leave to appeal S.C.C. refd. 56 C.R. (3d) xxviii, 23 O.A.C. 317n, 61 O.R. (2d) 588n.

3. Times, Measures and Weights

The courts have examined almanacs to determine the day of the week upon which a particular date fell,[74] but have refused to consult an almanac to ascertain the time of the rising of the sun on a particular day,[75] although they have accepted the information in an almanac as to the time of the rising of the moon on a particular night as *prima facie* evidence.[76]

As far as measurements are concerned the court will take judicial notice of obvious disproportions between weights and measures. For example, the court will note that a pint is less than five gallons,[77] that a metre is longer than a yard, that a foot contains twelve inches and that a pound weighs more than a grain, although it may have to inform itself by the use of texts with respect to some of the more obscure weights or measures.

4. The Course of Nature and Scientific Facts

The cases, however, are in conflict as to the extent to which, if at all, facts of nature and scientific facts, which are capable of accurate demonstration from reliable sources, can be noticed.

In *McQuaker v. Goddard*,[78] the issue was whether a camel was a domesticated or wild animal. In the former case it would have been entitled to the proverbial first bite. The trial judge reached the conclusion that it was domesticated after consulting books about camels and hearing witnesses. This decision was confirmed in the Court of Appeal where Clauson L.J. said that the trial judge was entitled to examine the books and hear witnesses, not as evidence, but for the purpose of ". . . forming his view as to what the ordinary course of nature in this regard in fact is, a matter of which he is supposed to have complete knowledge."[79]

In *Preston-Jones v. Preston-Jones*,[80] however, the House of Lords refused to take judicial notice that a normal child could not be born

---

74 *Page v. Faucet* (1591), Cro. Eliz. 227, 78 E.R. 482 (K.B.); *R. v. Dyer* (1703), 6 Mod. 41, 87 E.R. 803 (K.B.); *Hoyle v. Lord Cornwallis* (1720), 1 Str. 387, 93 E.R. 584 (K.B.).
75 *Collier v. Nokes* (1849), 2 Car. & Ker. 1012, 175 E.R. 426 (N.P.).
76 *R. v. Hillier* (1840), 4 J.P. 155.
77 *Reid v. McWhinnie* (1868), 27 U.C.Q.B. 289 (C.A.)
78 [1940] 1 K.B. 687, [1940] 1 All E.R. 471 (C.A.).
79 *Ibid.*, at 700 (K.B.).
80 [1951] A.C. 391, [1951] 1 All E.R. 124 (H.L.).

360 days after the last intercourse of a man and a woman, even though the court admitted that the contrary was a fantastic suggestion.[81] Undoubtedly, the court could have consulted a medical book which would have put the matter beyond dispute. Indeed, in *M-T v. M-T*,[82] an eminent specialist testified that a lapse of 340 days between coitus and the birth of a normal, healthy baby was impossible and this evidence was accepted by Ormerod J. McGillivray J.A., in *Fletcher v. Kondratiuk*,[83] a Canadian case dealing with the same problem, summed the matter up as follows:[84]

> The Court is not at liberty to speculate upon the course of nature or the wonders of nature or the seemingly curious freaks of nature and is entitled to take judicial notice of the course of nature only in so far as it is a notorious fact that nature follows a certain course.

In *R. v. Savidant*,[85] Campbell C.J. was asked to take judicial notice as to the extent of alcoholic fermentation of a fresh brew. The Chief Justice, declining, to take judicial notice of this fact, said:[86]

> Knowledge so imputed tends to be general, rather than particular, and notorious, rather than obscure or technical. So that, although the scope of judicial notice is constantly enlarging, it lags very far behind the advance of expert scientific knowledge.

The *Preston-Jones* case and the two Canadian cases referred to above can be explained on the ground that the fact under consideration was thought not to be capable of immediate and accurate demonstration by reference to an indisputable source of information. As Chief Justice Campbell points out, judicial certainty about a scientific fact will always lag behind expert scientific knowledge. The court will, therefore, preclude reference to scientific treatises by counsel, except in the examination of expert witnesses,[87] unless it is

---

81   *Ibid.*, at 402 (A.C.), per Lord Simonds.
82   [1949] P. 331, [1949] L.J.R. 378 (H.C.J.).
83   (1939), 60 C.C.C. 119, [1933] 2 W.W.R. 225, [1933] 3 D.L.R. 532 (Alta. C.A.).
84   *Ibid.*, at 235 (W.W.R.), 129-30 (C.C.C.).
85   (1945), 19 M.P.R. 448 (P.E.I.S.C.).
86   *Ibid.*, at 450.
87   *Jackson v. C.P.R.*, [1947] 2 W.W.R. 337 (Alta. Dist. Ct.); *R. v. Anderson* (1914), 5 W.W.R. 1052, 22 C.C.C. 455, 16 D.L.R. 203, 26 W.L.R. 783, 7 Alta.

assured that there will not be a conflict between different treatises on the same subject. Where the scientific facts, although not notorious, can be readily and accurately ascertained from a textbook on the subject, the judge can, and should, take judicial notice of the fact.[88]

C. *Judicial Notice by Statute*

There are innumerable instances in which the court is required by statute to take judicial notice. Thus, courts throughout Canada are bound to take judicial notice of acts, public or private, of the Federal Parliament and of the legislature of the province by which they are passed.[89] The statutory provisions generally extend to ordinances,[90] orders-in-council,[91] proclamations[92] and regulations.[93] In the absence

---

L.R. 102 (C.A.); *Brownell v. Brownell* (1890), 31 N.B.R. 594 (C.A.)

88   *Miller v. Shaffran*, [1951] R.L. 523 (Que. S.C.), at 537; *Shantz v. Hansen* (1956), 20 W.W.R. 196 (Alta. S.C.).

89   Evidence Acts: Can., R.S.C. 1985, c. C-5, s. 17, s. 18; Alta., R.S.A. 1980, c. A-21, s. 33; B.C., R.S.B.C. 1979, c. 116, s. 26(1); Man., R.S.M. 1987, c. E-150, s. 29; Nfld., R.S. Nfld. 1970, c. 115, s. 23 [am. 1976, No. 26, s. 1]; N.B., R.S.N.B. 1973, c. E-11, s. 70(1); N.W.T., R.S.N.W.T. 1988, c. E-8, s. 38; N.S., R.S.N.S. 1989, c. 154, s. 3(3); Sask., R.S.S. 1978, c. S-16, s. 3(2), (3); Yuk., R.S.Y. 1986, c. 57, s. 28; Ontario, *Interpretation Act*, R.S.O. 1980, c. 219, s. 7(1). At common law notice of public and private acts was to be taken, but not of subordinate legislation, see *R. v. "Evgenia Chandris" (The)*, [1977] 2 S.C.R. 97, 27 C.C.C. (2d) 241, 65 D.L.R. (3d) 553, 8 N.R. 338, 12 N.B.R. (2d) 652 per Laskin J., at 106 (S.C.R.); *Royal Bank v. Neher*, [1985] 5 W.W.R. 667, 39 Alta. L.R. (2d) 173, 64 A.R. 22 (Alta. Q.B.).

90   *Ibid.*: see also *Statutory Instruments Act*, R.S.C. 1985, c. S-22, s. 16(1) as to ordinances published in the Canada Gazette (it is not necessary to prove publication); *R. v. Evgenia Chandris, ibid.*).

91   *R. v. Whalen* (1971), 4 C.C.C. (2d) 560, 15 C.R.N.S. 187, 3 N.B.R. (2d) 729 (C.A.).

92   Can., *Interpretation Act*, R.S.C. 1985, c. I-21, s. 18(4); Can., *Statutory Instruments Act*, R.S.C. 1985, c. S-22, s. 16(1); Alta., *Alberta Evidence Act*, R.S.A. 1980, c. A-21, s. 33; B.C., *Interpretation Act*, R.S.B.C. 1979, c. 206, s. 16(3); Man., *Manitoba Evidence Act*, R.S.M. 1987, c. E-150, s. 29; N.B., *Evidence Act*, R.S.N.B. 1973, c. E-11, s. 63(2); N.W.T., *Interpretation Act*, R.S.N.W.T. 1988, c. I-8, s. 7(2); N.S., *Evidence Act*, R.S.N.S. 1989, c. 154, s. 11; Sask., *Saskatchewan Evidence Act*, R.S.S. 1978, s. S-16, s. 10; P.E.I., *Evidence Act*, R.S.P.E.I. 1988, c. E-11, s. 21(4).

93   Can., *Statutory Instruments Act*, R.S.C. 1985, c. S-22, s. 16(1); Alta., *Evidence Act*, R.S.A. 1980, c. A-21, s. 33; B.C., *Regulations Act*, S.B.C. 1979, c. 305, s. 10 and *Evidence Act*, R.S.B.C. 1979, c. 116, s. 26(1); Man., *Manitoba Evidence Act*,

---

of an express statutory provision, a proclamation of the lieutenant-governor of a province bringing an act into force will require proof in the ordinary way.[94] Moreover any subordinate legislation is not judicially noticeable at common law and, therefore, in the absence of an express statutory provision such enactments as municipal by-laws cannot be noticed.[95]

In addition to statutes and regulations, courts are generally required to take judicial notice of all equitable rights and duties, and, subject thereto, to take notice of all legal claims existing by the common law.[96] Although in a provincial court when the law of another province is in issue it must be proved, the Supreme Court of Canada and the Federal Court may take judicial notice of the laws of the various provinces.[97] Various statutory provisions provide that judicial notice shall be taken of the seals and signatures of various persons in official documents, such as court records.[98]

R.S.M. 1987, c. E-150, s. 29, Nfld., *Statutes and Subordinate Legislation Act*, R.S. Nfld. 1977, c. 108, s. 13(2); N.W.T., *Regulation Ordinance Act*, 1974, c. R-4, s. 14(1); N.S., *Regulations Act*, R.S.N.S. 1989, c. 393, s. 9(2); Ont., *Regulations Act*, R.S.O. 1980, c. 446, s. 5(4); P.E.I., *Evidence Act*, R.S.P.E.I. 1988, c. E-11, s. 21(4); Sask., *Regulations Act*, R.S.S. 1978, c. R-16, s. 6; Yuk., *Regulations Act*, R.S.Y. 1986, c. 151, s. 4(1).

94 *R. v. Markin*, [1970] 1 C.C.C. 14, 68 W.W.R. 611, 6 D.L.R. (3d) 497, 7 C.R.N.S. 135 (B.C.C.A.).

95 *R. v. Snelling*, [1952] O.W.N. 214 (H.C.J.); *Danylec v. Kowpak* (1960), 25 D.L.R. (2d) 716 (Man. C.A.), distd in *R. v. Potapchuk*, [1963] 1 O.R. 40 (H.C.J.); *R. v. Ross*, [1966] 4 C.C.C. 175, [1966] 2 O.R. 273 (C.A.); *Garner v. Morin-Heights (Municipalité)*, [1989] R.L. 445 (C.A. Que.); see Ont. *Regulation Act*, R.S.O. 1980, c. 446, s. 5(4); but see B.C. *Offence Act*, R.S.B.C. 1979, c. 305, s. 10 and *R. v. Lum*, [1982] 3 W.W.R. 694 (B.C. Co. Ct.).

96 Alta., *Judicature Act*, R.S.A. 1980, c. J-1, s. 17(4); B.C., *Law and Equity Act*, R.S.B.C. 1979, c. 224, s. 7; Man., *Queen's Bench Act*, R.S.M. 1987, c. 280, s. 63, r. 4;, Nfld., *Judicature Act*, S. Nfld. 1986, c. 42, ss. 89-96 [s. 92 am. 1987, c. 41, s. 9]; N.B., *Judicature Act*, R.S.N.B. 1973, c. J-2, s. 26; N.W.T., *Judicature Ordinance Act*, 1974, c. J-1, s. 18(d); N.S., *Judicature Act*, R.S.N.S. 1989, c. 240, s. 41; Ont., *Courts of Justice Act, 1984*, S.O. 1984, c. 11, s. 109; P.E.I., *Supreme Court Act*, R.S.P.E.I. 1988, c. S-10, s. 29; Sask., *Queen's Bench Act*, R.S.S. 1978, c. Q-1, s. 44(4); Yuk., *Judicature Act*, R.S.Y. 1986, c. 96, s. 12.

97 *Canadian Pacific Rly. Co. v. Parent*, [1917] A.C. 195, 86 L.J.P.C. 123, 116 L.T.R. 165, 33 T.L.R. 180; *John Morrow Screw & Nut Co. v. Hankin* (1918), 58 S.C.R. 74, 45 D.L.R. 685; *Logan v. Lee* (1907), 39 S.C.R. 311, 27 C.L.R. 781; *Zien v. R.* (1986), 26 D.L.R. (4th) 121, 64 N.R. 282 (*sub nom. Zien v. Canada*) (Fed. C.A.).

98 Evidence Acts, *supra*, note 89 for citations: Can., s. 23; Alta., ss. 43, 45; B.C.

D. *Personal Knowledge*

Unless the other criteria for taking judicial notice are present, the judge cannot judicially notice a fact within his personal knowledge even if it has been proved before him in a previous case.[99] There is an exception in the case of a custom which, if proved often enough, may be judicially noticed.[100]

Thorson J.A. of the Ontario Court of Appeal in *R. v. Potts*[101] explained the distinction between reliance on personal knowledge and general knowledge in the following way:[102]

> Where judicial notice of some matter is taken by a trial court, the trier of the facts, (whether judge alone or jury) may or may not share the knowledge that is said to be common knowledge in the community or in a particular class of the community. If it happens that the court does share a personal knowledge of that which is commonly known in the community, well and good. If not, however, the matter may still be judicially noticed, but the court is put on its inquiry as to whether the matter is or is not one which may properly be made part of the case before it without formal proof thereof. Conversely there is the situation where the knowledge that the court has about a particular matter is knowledge of a kind which the court is required to apply repeatedly in the cases that come before it day by day. In *R. v. Miller* (1971), 4 C.C.C. (2d) 70, 15 C.R.N.S. 164, the learned County Court judge, speaking of the procedures that are involved in taking samples of a person's breath for breathalyzer testing, concluded that, on the authorities he had reviewed, 'it is

---

ss. 29, 30; Man., ss. 34-35; Nfld., s. 30; N.B., ss. 75, 77(2); N.W.T., s. 40; N.S., ss. 66(2), 67(2); Ont., ss. 36, 38; P.E.I., s. 22(6); Sask., s. 21; Yuk., s. 39.

99 *R. v. Savidant* (1945), 19 M.P.R. 448, at 449 (P.E.I.S.C.); *R. v. Ostrowski*, [1958] O.R. 708, 122 C.C.C. 196, 29 C.R. 109 (H.C.J.); *Preston-Jones v. Preston-Jones*, [1951] A.C. 391, at 402, [1951] 1 All E.R. 124 (H.L.); *R. v. Potts* (1982), 26 C.R. (3d) 252, 66 C.C.C. (2d) 219, 36 O.R. (2d) 195, 134 D.L.R. (3d) 227, 14 M.V.R. 72 (Ont. C.A.); leave to appeal to S.C.C. refd. [1982] 1 S.C.R. xi, 66 C.C.C. (2d) 219*n*, 134 D.L.R. (3d) 227*n*, 43 N.R. 270*n*.

100 *Barnett v. Brandao* (1846), 12 Cl. & Fin. 787, 8 E.R. 1622 (H.L.); *George v. Davies*, [1911] 2 K.B. 445, at 448.

101 *Supra*, note 99, at 203-04 (O.R.).

102 See also *Joe v. Director of Family and Children's Services* (1986), 5 B.C.L.R. (2d) 267 (Y.T.S.C.).

possible for a Court to take judicial notice of matters that are repeatedly before it' (p. 80, C.C.C.). While in principle this appears to make a good deal of sense, at least where the matters being noticed are not really disputed, it is nevertheless clear that a trial court is not justified in acting on its own personal knowledge of or familiarity with a particular matter, alone and without more.

E. *The Effect of Judicial Notice*

There has been a lively debate among text writers as to whether a fact which is judicially noticed forecloses any evidence on the point.[103]

Some cases support the view that a judicially noted fact raises a factual presumption or is *prima facie* evidence of the fact. On principle, however, it seems that judicial notice is intended to dispense with evidence, assuming the criteria for its application are present.[104] This appears to be the modern view.[105]

In any treatment of this subject it is necessary to carefully distinguish between the conclusiveness of the facts actually noticed, on the one hand, and the inferences drawn on the other. *Commonwealth Shipping Representative v. Peninsular & Oriental Branch Service*[106] provides a helpful illustration. The issue in the case was whether a ship had been sunk while "engaged in a warlike operation". The sinking was caused by a collision with a British ship carrying ambulance wagons and stores from Mudros to Alexandria. In the Court of Appeal two judges took judicial notice that at the time of the collision the British were in the process of evacuating Suvla Bay and Helles in the Gallipoli Peninsula and inferred from this that the British ship was taking part in the evacuation. Viscount Cave in the House of Lords[107]

---

103 J.B. Thayer, *A Preliminary Treatise on Evidence at the Common Law*, reprint of 1898 ed. (New York: Augustus M. Kelley, 1969), at 308-09; 9 Wigmore, *Evidence* (Chadbourn rev. 1981), §§ 2567, 2567a, at 714-19.

104 See, S. Schiff, "The Use of Out-of-Court Information in Fact Determination at Trial" (1963), 41 Can. Bar Rev. 335, at 351-54.

105 See, *R. v. Zundel* (1987), 31 C.C.C. (3d) 97, 56 C.R. (3d) 1, 35 D.L.R. (4th) 338, 58 O.R. (2d) 129, 18 O.A.C. 161, 29 C.R.R. 349; leave to appeal to S.C.C. refd. 56 C.R. (3d) xxviii, 23 O.A.C. 317*n*, 61 O.R. (2d) 588*n*.

106 [1923] A.C. 191, [1922] All E.R. 207 (H.L.).

107 *Ibid.*, at 197 (A.C.).

disapproved of the taking of judicial notice in the Court of Appeal because the opportunity to rebut the inference drawn therefrom was absent. Another more recent Canadian case that explains this distinction is the decision of the Ontario Court of Appeal in *R. v. Zundel*.[108] The Crown asked the trial judge to take judicial notice of the historical fact of the Holocaust. This was an important feature of the Crown's claim that the accused was spreading false news. The Crown contended before the appeal Court that the trial judge had erred in refusing to take judicial notice of this fact. The Court of Appeal noted that admission of the fact would relieve the jury from one factual finding, but would not preclude either of two possible inferences being drawn from that fact:[109]

> The Crown, in order to succeed, was required to prove by circumstantial evidence of inference that the appellant knew the pamphlet was false. If the jury on the evidence concluded that the existence of the Holocaust was so notorious as to be indisputable by reasonable men and women, that would be a circumstance, but only a circumstance, from which the jury might infer that the appellant knew that the pamphlet was false, but the jury would not be required to draw that inference. However, if the trial judge had taken judicial notice of the existence of the Holocaust, he would have been required to so declare to the jury and to direct them to find that the Holocaust existed, which would have been gravely prejudicial to the defence in so far as it would influence the drawing of the inference concerning the appellant's knowledge of the falsity of the pamphlet.

The Court did not say that the fact necessitated the drawing of the inference as to the accused's knowledge; it was simply capable of influencing it to the prejudice of the accused.

While there appears to be formidable authority against the view that a judicially noticed fact is conclusive,[110] it is submitted that no

---

108 *Supra*, note 105.

109 *Ibid.*, at 184 (O.R.), 152 (C.A.).

110 See the approach of Denning L.J. quoted in *Preston-Jones v. Preston-Jones*, [1951] A.C. 391, at 400, [1951] 1 All E.R. 124 (H.L.) and the cases reviewed by S. Schiff, "The Use of Out of Court Information in Fact Determination at Trial" *supra*, note 104, at 351-54.

practical purpose is served by allowing evidence to be led to contradict a judicially noticed fact. If the process is carried out correctly, the judge will already have had the benefit of all available information on the subject and it is unlikely that putting it in the form of evidence will have any greater impact on his or her decision. Furthermore, the fact that a judge has a wide discretion in determining whether to take judicial notice of any fact capable of being noticed[111] will limit the circumstances where the conclusiveness of the fact will prejudice a party or an accused. One advantage, however, to the contrary view is that if the judge was wrong in taking judicial notice, the Court of Appeal can accept the contrary evidence. If no contrary evidence is led, and the fact is a necessary one to determine the appeal, the case would have to be remitted for a new trial.

F. *Judicial Notice in the Court of Appeal*

It has already been pointed out above that a court of appeal is reluctant to take judicial notice of a fact for the first time and to draw inferences therefrom. Subject to this qualification, however, Canadian courts have taken judicial notice of facts for the first time in the appeal courts, and have reversed the findings at trial as a result of facts so noticed.[112] In *R. v. Potts*[113] Thorson J.A. noted that it is not the function of an appellate court to adjudicate upon the correctness of a trial court's decision to take judicial notice of some fact or matter known locally, relying solely upon the appellate court's knowledge of (or, for that matter, its lack of knowledge of) that which was in the court below, unless that knowledge is public knowledge.

III *RES JUDICATA* AND RELATED MATTERS

A. *Statement of the General Principle*

"The principle of *res judicata* in its various manifestations has become far too complicated." So said McEachern C.J.S.C. in *Saska-*

---

111 *R. v. Zundel, supra,* note 105, at 184 (O.R.).
112 *Forrest v. Davidson* (1951), 4 W.W.R. 273 (Sask. C.A.); *Bell v. Hutchings,* [1932] 1 W.W.R. 49, [1932] 1 D.L.R. 468, 40 Man. R. 113 (C.A.); *R. v. Pinno,* [1925] 1 W.W.R. 737 (Sask. Dist. Ct.).
113 *Supra,* note 99, at 204 (O.R.).

toon Credit Union Ltd. v. Central Park Enterprises Ltd.,[114] and there is much truth in this.

The modern rule of estoppel by *res judicata* is grounded upon two broad principles of public policy: first that the state has an interest that there should be an end to litigation (*interest republicae ut sit finis litium*), and secondly that no individual should be sued more than once for the same cause (*nemo debet bis vexari pro una et eadem causa*) or punished more than once for the same offence (*nemo debet bis puniri pro uno et eodem delicto*).[115] The following may be taken as a correct general statement of the common law rule:[116]

> No Court shall try any suit or issue in which the matter directly and substantially in issue has been directly and substantially in issue in a former suit between the same parties, or between parties under whom they or any of them claim, litigating under the same title, in a Court of jurisdiction competent to try such subsequent suit or the suit in which such issue has been subsequently raised, and has been heard and finally decided by such Court.

Although it is sometimes referred to as a rule of substantive law,[117] the better view is that it is a rule of evidence.[118] Essentially, the party

---

114 (1988), 47 D.L.R. (4th) 431, at 435, 22 B.C.L.R. (2d) 89 (B.C.S.C.).

115 *R. v. The Duchess of Kingston* (1776), 20 State Tr. 355, at 537, 1 Leach 146; *Lockyer v. Ferryman* (1877), 2 App. Cas. 519 (H.L.); *Clark v. Phinney* (1896), 25 S.C.R. 633, at 644; *Fenerty v. Halifax (City)* (1920), 50 D.L.R. 435, at 437-38, 53 N.S.R. 457 (N.S.S.C.); *Pickford v. Daley* (1956), 7 D.L.R. (2d) 600 (N.S.T.D.); *Angle v. M.N.R.*, [1975] 2 S.C.R. 248, at 267, 47 D.L.R. (3d) 544, at 550-51. This sentence in the first edition was cited in *Mitchell v. Reiss* (1989), 78 Sask. R. 153 (Q.B.).

116 *Re Ontario Sugar Co.* (1910), 22 O.L.R. 621, at 623 (H.C.J.), at 623; affd. 24 O.L.R. 332 (C.A.); leave to appeal to S.C.C. refd (1911), 44 S.C.R. 659.

117 *Canada and Dominion Sugar Co. Ltd. v. Canadian National (West Indies) Steamships Ltd.*, [1947] A.C. 46, [1946] 3 W.W.R. 759, [1947] 1 D.L.R. 241 (P.C.), at 56 (A.C.), 764 (W.W.R.), 246 (D.L.R.), referring to estoppel by representation.

118 This paragraph in J. Sopinka and S.N. Lederman, *The Law of Evidence in Civil Cases*, Canadian Legal Text Series (Toronto: Butterworths, 1974) was quoted with approval in *Production Equipment Ltd. v. Clayton & Lambert Manufacturing Co.* (1984), 66 N.S.R. (2d) 328, 152 A.P.R. 328 (C.A.). See *Low v. Bouverie*, [1891] 3 Ch. 82 (C.A.), at 105, [1924-34] All E.R. 348; *Humphries v. Humphries*, [1910] 2 K.B. 531 (C.A.), at 536; *Maritime Electric Co. v. General Dairies Ltd.*,

against whom the suit or issue was decided is estopped from proferring evidence to contradict that result. It has been held that the principle of *res judicata* is not inconsistent with ss. 7 or 15 of the *Canadian Charter of Rights and Freedoms*.[119]

Although the underlying theory governing the application of the principle is the same in both civil and criminal cases, the rules are stated somewhat differently and it is, therefore, convenient to deal with them separately.

B. *In Civil Cases*

1. General Rule

The constituent elements of estoppel by *res judicata* were enumerated by Aikens J. in *Re Bullen*:[120]

(i) that the alleged *judicial* decision was what in law is deemed such;

(ii) that the particular judicial decision relied upon was in fact pronounced, as alleged;

(iii) that the judicial tribunal pronouncing the decision had competent jurisdiction in that behalf;

(iv) that the judicial decision was final;

(v) that the judicial decision was, or involved, a determination

---

[1937] A.C. 610, [1937] 1 W.W.R. 591, [1937] 1 All E.R. 748, 46 C.R.C. 1, [1937] 1 D.L.R. 609 (P.C.), at 620 (A.C.); *Morrison Rose & Partners v. Hillman*, [1961] 2 Q.B. 266, [1961] 2 All E.R. 891 (C.A.), at 267 (Q.B.); *Robinson v. McQuaid* (1854), 1 P.E.I. 103 (S.C.).

119 R.S.C. 1985, App. II, No. 44. *Feener v. A.G. (N.S.)* (1987), 78 N.S.R. (2d) 22, 28 C.R.R. 154 (N.S.C.A.); leave to appeal to S.C.C. refd. [1987] 1 S.C.R. viii, 28 C.R.R. 154.

120 (1971), 21 D.L.R. (3d) 628 (B.C.S.C.), at 631, quoting from G. Spencer Bower and A. Turner, *The Doctrine of Res Judicata*, 2nd ed. (London: Butterworths, 1969), at 18-19, para. 19. This passage from Spencer, Bower, and Turner was also quoted with approval in *Duhamel v. R. (No. 2)* (1981), 64 C.C.C. (2d) 538, 25 C.R. (3d) 53, [1982] 1 W.W.R. 127, 17 Alta. L.R. (2d) 127, 33 A.R. 271 (Alta. C.A.), at 542 (C.C.C.); affd. [1984] 2 S.C.R. 555, 15 C.C.C. (3d) 491, 43 C.R. (3d) 1, 14 D.L.R. (4th) 92, 57 N.R. 162, 57 A.R. 204 and in *Re Abacus Cities Ltd.* (1984), 55 A.R. 258 (Q.B.); affd. 45 Alta. L.R. (2d) 113, 70 A.R. 55, [1986] 4 W.W.R. 564 (C.A.); leave to appeal to S.C.C. refd. [1986] 1 S.C.R. v, 69 N.R. 240n (*sub nom. Allan v. Bank of Montreal*).

of the same question as that sought to be controverted in the litigation in which the estoppel is raised;

(vi) that the parties to the judicial decision, or their privies, were the same persons as the parties to the proceeding in which the estoppel is raised, or their privies, or that the decision was conclusive *in rem.* [emphasis added]

The first four of the elements may be grouped under the heading, "A Final Judicial Decision Pronounced by a Court of Competent Jurisdiction". Such a decision is required to constitute a *res judicata.* The other elements are dealt with under the headings, "Identity of Action or Issue" and "Parties and their Privies". Finally, a number of miscellaneous problems encountered in connection with a plea of *res judicata* are discussed under the heading, "Procedural Matters".

2. Final Judicial Decision of a Court of Competent Jurisdiction

(a) *Inferior Courts and Tribunals*

The decision need not be that of a court, but includes the decision of arbitrators[121] or inferior tribunals in respect of matters within their jurisdiction, with respect to later use in proceedings in a higher court.[122] While estoppel by *res judicata* applies to the decisions of administrative tribunals,[123] the tribunal should be one which is

---

121 *Qatar Petroleum Producing Authority v. Shell Internationale Petroleum Maatschapij B.V.*, [1983] 2 Lloyd's Rep. 35 (C.A.); *Northern Regional Health Authority v. Derek Crouch Construction Co.*, [1984] Q.B. 644 (C.A.); *Ayscough v. Sheed, Thompson & Co.* (1924), 93 L.J.K.B. 924, 131 L.T. 610, [1924] All E.R. Ext. 875 (H.L.); *Bell v. Miller* (1862), 9 Gr. 385 (Ch.).

122 *Daniel v. Hess* (1965), 54 W.W.R. 290 (Sask. Dist. Ct.); *Kirk v. Faugh*, [1951] O.W.N. 745 (H.C.J.).

123 *Halam Park Devt. Ltd. v. Hamilton Wentworth, Regional Assessment Commissioner, Region No. 19* (1985), 29 M.P.L.R. 1, 50 O.R. (2d) 437, 17 O.M.B.R. 504 (H.C.J.); affd. (1986), 54 O.R. (2d) 64*n*, 18 O.M.B.R. 351 (Div. Ct.); *Ringrose v. College of Physicians and Surgeons* (1984), 53 A.R. 372 (Alta. C.A.); *Burke v. Arab* (1981), 49 N.S.R. (2d) 181, 96 A.P.R. 181, 130 D.L.R. (3d) 38 (C.A.); leave to appeal to S.C.C. refd. [1983] 1 S.C.R. 55, 141 D.L.R. (3d) 765, 55 N.S.R. (2d) 540; *Macleod v. Campbell* (1918), 57 S.C.R. 517, 44 D.L.R. 210, [1918] 3 W.W.R. 769. See also *Construction Association of Thunder Bay Inc., General Contractors' Div. v. Lumber & Sawmill Workers' Union, Local 2693 of C.J.A.*, [1987] O.L.R.B. Rep. 976, 17 C.L.R.B.R. (N.S.) 317; vard. [1988] O.L.R.B. Rep. 277 for a discussion

required to hold a hearing. Otherwise there is no adjudication.[124]

(b) Foreign Courts

The decision may be that of a foreign court or tribunal,[125] but such a judgment may be impeached on the ground of fraud practised on the foreign court or tribunal. In order to impeach the judgment it is insufficient to show that false evidence was given at the trial; the fraud must be based on something collateral or extraneous and not merely on the evidence given before the foreign tribunal.[126] Judgments of domestic courts can also be impeached on the ground of fraud.[127]

If a domestic action to enforce a foreign judgment fails, that enforcement action will not bar a subsequent domestic action on the merits; but if the first action raises the merits as well as the enforcement issue, then it will constitute a final disposition of the matter and a subsequent domestic action is barred.[128]

(c) Court or Tribunal with Jurisdiction

The requirement that the court or tribunal whose judgment is relied upon must have had jurisdiction to deal with the matter is self evident inasmuch as a judgment made wholly without jurisdiction has

---

of whether a labour relations board can be bound by an earlier *in rem* determination of the same board.

124 *Caffoor (Trustee of Abdul Gaffoor Trust) v. Income Tax Commr. Columbo*, [1961] A.C. 584, [1961] 2 All E.R. 436, [1961] 2 W.L.R. 794 (P.C.); *Shell Co. of Australia Ltd. v. Federal Taxation Commr.*, [1931] A.C. 275, [1930] All E.R. Rep. 671 (P.C.) and see 16 *Halsbury*, 4th ed. (London: Butterworths, 1976), at 1056, 1565, ftn. 1.

125 *Manolopoulos v. Paniffe*, [1930] 2 D.L.R. 169, 1 M.P.R. 366 (N.S.C.A.); *Law v. Hansen* (1895), 25 S.C.R. 69, at 72. *Barwell Food Sales Inc. v. Snyder & Fils Inc.* (1988), 24 C.P.R. (3d) 102, 38 C.P.C. (2d) 192 (Ont. H.C.J.) suggests that the principle may not apply to a foreign judgment granting an injunction. The non-application of *res judicata* was clearly correct inasmuch as there was a pending appeal of the foreign judgment and so it was not final.

126 *Jacobs v. Beaver* (1908), 17 O.L.R. 496 (C.A.), at 508; *Johnston v. Occidental Syndicate Ltd.* (1912), 3 O.W.N. 1384 (*sub nom.* McDougal v. Occidental Syndicate Ltd.), 4 D.L.R. 727, 22 O.W.R. 478 (C.A.); *Manolopoulos v. Paniffe, ibid.*

127 *Sun Alliance Ins. Co. v. Thompson* (1981), 56 N.S.R. (2d) 619, 117 A.P.R. 619 (S.C.T.D.); *Dsane v. Hagan*, [1962] Ch. 193, [1961] 3 All E.R. 380 (Ch. D.); *Rogers v. Porter* (1905), 37 N.B.R. 235 (C.A.); *Johnston v. Barkley* (1905), 10 O.L.R. 724 (C.A.); *Abouloff v. Oppenheimer* (1882), 10 Q.B.D. 295, [1881-5] All E.R. 307 (C.A.), at 303 (Q.B.D.). See Spencer, Bower and Turner, *supra*, note 120.

128 *O'Nory v. Patricia Properties Ltd.* (1983), 144 D.L.R. (3d) 742 (B.C.S.C.).

no effect and can be ignored.[129] In this context, absence of jurisdiction means complete want of authority to enter upon the enquiry or to make the judgment or order, but does not apply to loss of jurisdiction in the course of proceedings by reason of an erroneous decision on the law.[130]

(d) Decision Must be Final

The judgment which raises the estoppel is the final judgment. The judgment is final even if it could have been appealed, but was not.[131] If an appeal is pending, however, the decision is not final.[132] A final decision may be relied upon in subsequent proceedings even if the second proceedings were commenced before the first judgment was given.[133] Although the authorities are in conflict, it would appear that in Canada, a decision in an interlocutory application is binding on the parties with respect to other proceedings in the same action.[134]

---

129 *Rogers v. Wood* (1831), 2 B. & Ad. 245, 109 E.R. 1134 (K.B.); *Toronto Rly. Co. v. Toronto Corp.*, [1904] A.C. 809, [1904-7] All E.R. Ext. 1514 (P.C.); *Duke v. Andler*, [1932] S.C.R. 734, [1932] 4 D.L.R. 529. See also *Manella v. Manella*, [1942] 4 D.L.R. 712, [1942] O.R. 630 (Ont. C.A.).

130 *Tannis Trading Inc. v. Thorne Ernst & Whinney* (1989), 69 O.R. (2d) 120, 60 D.L.R. (4th) 566, 35 C.P.C. (2d) 165 (H.C.J.). See also 16 *Halsbury Laws of England*, 4th ed. (London: Butterworths, 1976), at 1049, § 1554 and at 1058, § 1569; Spencer, Bower and Turner, *supra*, note 120, at 108-10, § 133. In *Gough v. Whyte* (1983), 56 N.S.R. (2d) 68, 117 A.P.R. 68, 32 C.P.C. 232 (T.D.), it was said that a prior decision was not a *res judicata* because the relief sought in the new action was outside the *monetary* jurisdiction of the court in the first claim, but this is questionable; see *Shanks v. J.D. Irving Ltd.* (1985), 7 C.P.C. (2d) 965, 70 N.S.R. (2d) 10, 166 A.P.R. 10 (N.S.T.D.).

131 *Re Flavelle*, [1947] O.R. 229, [1947] 2 D.L.R. 404 (C.A.).

132 *Barwell Food Sales Inc. v. Snyder & Fils Inc.*, *supra*, note 125.

133 *Maynard v. Maynard*, [1951] S.C.R. 346, at 359-60, [1951] 1 D.L.R. 241 relying on *Law v. Hansen, supra*, note 125, at 75, 76; *Bell v. Holmes*, [1956] 1 W.L.R. 1359, [1956] 3 All E.R. 449 (Leeds Assizes).

134 *Stamper v. Finnigan* (1984), 57 N.B.R. (2d) 411, 148 A.P.R. 411, 11 C.P.C. (2d) 175 (Q.B.), citing this sentence in the first edition, but allowing the new application as the issues were different; affd. (*sub nom. Stamper v. C.N.R.*) (1985), 63 N.B.R. (2d) 342, 164 A.P.R. 342 (C.A.), which, however, suggests that *res judicata* applies to interlocutory applications in "special situations"; *Zevest Dev. Corp. v. K Mart Canada Ltd.* (1986), 16 C.P.C. (2d) 301 (Ont. H.C.J.); *Air Canada v. British Columbia* (1985), 67 B.C.L.R. 1, [1986] 1 W.W.R. 342, 21 D.L.R. (4th) 685, at 697 (C.A.), reversed in part on other grounds (*sub nom. Canadian Pacific Airlines Ltd. v. British Columbia*), [1989] 1 S.C.R. 1133, 36 B.C.L.R. (2d) 185, [1989] 4 W.W.R. 137, 59 D.L.R. (4th) 218, vard. on reconsideration [1989] 2

To constitute a *res judicata*, the interlocutory decision must be a judgment on the merits of the application.[135] *Res judicata* will apply in a subsequent application if the applicant relies merely on his or her own failure to present certain material[136] or arguments[137] on the first application because whatever might have been litigated at the first proceeding will be deemed to have been adjudicated on its merits.

(e) *Decision on the Merits*

A judgment which disposes of an action without an adjudication on the merits is not binding on the parties in a subsequent action. Thus a judgment which dismisses an action as premature, because the cause of action has not yet accrued is no bar to a further action once the cause of action has accrued.[138] Similarly, an action dismissed for want of

---

S.C.R. 1067, 63 D.L.R. (4th) 768, 102 N.R. 75; *J.F. Henderson Ltd. v. Athika Enterprises Ltd.* (1974), 5 O.R. (2d) 519 (H.C.J.); *British American Oil Co. v. Born Engineering Co.* (1963), 38 D.L.R. (2d) 523 (Alta. T.C.); *Scotia Construction Co. v. Halifax*, [1935] S.C.R. 124, at 130-31, [1935] 1 D.L.R. 316; *Diamond v. Western Realty Co.*, [1924] S.C.R. 308, at 315-16, [1924] 2 D.L.R. 922; *Desaulniers v. Payette* (1904), 35 S.C.R. 1; *Proulx v. Fraser* (1892), 20 S.C.R. 196; *McKean v. Jones* (1891), 19 S.C.R. 489; *Payne v. Newberry (No. 2)* (1890), 13 P.R. 392 (Ont. Master); *Grand Trunk Ry. Co. v. McMillan* (1889), 16 S.C.R. 543, at 559-60; *contra*: *Talbot v. Pan Ocean Oil Corp.* (1977), 4 C.P.C. 107, 3 Alta. L.R. (2d) 354, 5 A.R. 361 (C.A.); *Lacaille v. Brandl* (1954), 14 W.W.R. 191 (B.C.S.C.); *Kingston (City) v. Salvation Army* (1904), 7 O.L.R. 681 (Div. Ct.).

135 See *Standall v. Standall* (1912), 3 W.W.R. 402, 22 W.L.R. 512, 22 Man. R. 591, 7 D.L.R. 671 (Man. K.B.); *L'Hirondelle v. L'Hirondelle*, [1930] 1 W.W.R. 303, [1930] 2 D.L.R. 134 (Alta. S.C.); *Doty v. Marks* (1925), 57 O.L.R. 623, [1925] 4 D.L.R. 740 (C.A.); *McCowan v. Menasco Manufacturing Co.*, [1941] O.W.N. 133 (H.C.J.); *Lundy v. Patrick Construction Co.* (1952), 6 W.W.R. (N.S.) 564 (Sask. Dist. Ct.).

136 *Scotia Chevrolet Oldsmobile Ltd. v. Whynot* (1970), 1 N.S.R. (2d) 1041, 15 D.L.R. (3d) 438 (C.A.); *Leier v. Shumiatcher* (1962), 37 W.W.R. 605, 32 D.L.R. (2d) 584 (Sask. C.A.); *Lloyd v. Milton (No. 4)*, [1939] 3 W.W.R. 123, [1939] 3 D.L.R. 155 (Sask. C.A.); *Davis v. Ralls*, [1937] 2 W.W.R. 206 (Sask. K.B.); *Covert v. Janzen* (1908), 9 W.L.R. 133, 1 Sask. L.R. 424 (S.C.); *Cyr v. O'Flynn* (1907), 5 W.L.R. 524, 6 Terr. L.R. 299 (N.W.T.S.C.); *R. v. Richardson* (1889), 13 P.R. 303, 17 O.R. 729 (Ont. S.C.); *contra*: *Talbot v. Pan Ocean Oil Corp., supra*, note 134; *Doty v. Marks, ibid.*

137 *McKay v. Chisolm* (1908), 43 N.S.R. 227 (C.A.); *Industrial Acceptance Corp. v. Golisky*, [1967] 1 O.R. 278 (S.C. Master), at 282; *Mulholland v. Toigo*, [1973] 3 W.W.R. 766 (B.C.S.C.); *Winnipegosis Boatworks Ltd. v. Holm* (1983), 21 Man. R. (2d) 282 (Co. Ct.).

138 *Barber v. McQuaig* (1900), 31 O.R. 593 (H.C.J.), at 598.

prosecution is no bar to a subsequent action.[139] But if the action goes to trial and proceeds to judgment, it is a *res judicata* even if the particular claim is abandoned during the trial.[140]

Subject to certain exceptions in cases of fraud or mistake,[141] a judgment by consent raises an estoppel in the same manner as a judgment which has been contested.[142] The exception as to mistake operated to permit a husband, who had consented to an alimony judgment in ignorance of the invalidity of his marriage, to bring an action in which the validity of the marriage was put in question.[143] In *Saskatoon Credit Union Ltd. v. Central Park Enterprises Ltd.*,[144] an order of the trial judge was held to operate as a *res judicata* notwithstanding that an appeal had been allowed, on consent and without reasons, so that a settlement agreement could be implemented.

---

139 *Byrne v. Frere* (1828), 2 Mol. 157 (Ir. Ch.), at 180; *Magnus v. National Bank of Scotland* (1888), 57 L.J. Ch. 902; *Mayzel v. Sturm*, [1957] O.W.N. 240, 10 D.L.R. (2d) 642 (H.C.J.); *Pople v. Evans*, [1969] 2 Ch. 255, [1968] 3 W.L.R. 97, [1968] 2 All E.R. 743 (Ch. D.); *Mills v. Mills* (1971), 5 R.F.L. 286 (N.S. Co. Ct.).
140 *Hennig v. Northern Heights (Sault) Ltd.* (1980), 30 O.R. (2d) 346, 116 D.L.R. (3d) 496, 17 C.P.C. 173; leave to appeal to S.C.C. refd. (1980), 30 O.R. (2d) 346*n* (C.A.).
141 *Re Ontario Sugar Co.* (1911), 24 O.L.R. 332 (C.A.), at 336; leave to appeal to S.C.C. refd. (1911), 44 S.C.R. 659.
142 *Staff Builders International Inc. v. Cohen* (1983), 38 C.P.C. 82 (Ont. H.C.J.); *Kapusta v. Polish Fraternal Aid Society* (1938), 46 Man. R. 161, [1938] 2 W.W.R. 215, [1938] 3 D.L.R. 207, 46 Man. R. 161 (C.A.); leave to appeal to S.C.C. refd. 46 Man. R. 164; *Kinch v. Walcott*, [1929] 3 W.W.R. 13, [1929] A.C. 482, [1929] All E.R. 720 (P.C.); *Re Kline* (1923), 56 N.S.R. 389, [1924] 1 D.L.R. 295 (C.A.); *Hardy Lumber Co. v. Pickerel River Improvement Co.* (1898), 29 S.C.R. 211; but see *Pelrine v. Arron* (1969), 3 D.L.R. (3d) 713 (N.S.C.A.); *Reid v. Reid* (1969), 68 W.W.R. 93 (B.C.S.C.); and *Bonisteel v. Bateman*, [1945] O.W.N. 163 (H.C.J.), in which *Hair v. Meaford (Town)* (1914), 31 O.L.R. 124, 20 D.L.R. 475 (C.A.) was misunderstood as saying, at 128 (O.L.R.) that a consent judgment cannot operate as a *res judicata*, when in fact the case says that such a judgment cannot operate as a judgment *in rem*.
143 *Thompson v. Crawford*, [1932] O.R. 281, [1932] 2 D.L.R. 466 (H.C.J.), at 287 (O.R.); affd. (1932), 41 O.W.N. 231, [1932] 4 D.L.R. 206 (C.A.); leave to appeal to P.C. granted November 18, 1932. See also *Powell v. Cockburn*, [1977] 2 S.C.R. 218, 22 R.F.L. 155, 8 N.R. 215, 68 D.L.R. (3d) 700, which restored the trial judgment setting aside a judgment for alimony based on minutes of settlement. The trial judgment is reported in [1973] 1 O.R. 497 (H.C.J.).
144 (1988), 47 D.L.R. (4th) 431, 22 B.C.L.R. (2d) 89 (B.C.S.C.).

A default judgment, as long as it stands, raises an estoppel by *res judicata* in subsequent proceedings.[145] A default judgment, however, must always be scrutinized with extreme particularity for the purpose of ascertaining the bare essence of what "it must necessarily have decided".[146] A summary judgment clearly constitutes a *res judicata*.[147]

Although a judgment *in rem* is generally binding on everyone, where it is obtained by consent, it is doubtful that it is binding on persons who are not, and do not claim through, the parties to it.[148]

(f) Application to Family Law Judgments

It appears that *res judicata* is applied differently in the area of family law.[149] Perhaps because there is a public law element in the administration of family law,[150] it has been said that *in personam* judgments in this area of the law need not be treated as final. The judge has a discretion whether to allow the matter to be re-litigated.[151] The

---

145 *Kinna v. Reilander* (1978), 85 D.L.R. (3d) 306, 7 C.P.C. 70 (B.C.S.C.); *Re South American and Mexican Co., Ex parte Bank of England*, [1895] 1 Ch. 37, at 45, [1891-4] All E.R. Rep. 680 (C.A.) approved in *Re Ontario Sugar Co., supra*, note 141.

146 *Hill v. Hill* (1966), 57 D.L.R. (2d) 760, 56 W.W.R. 260 (B.C.C.A.), at 767 (D.L.R.); *Kok Hoong v. Leong Cheong Kweng Mines Ltd.*, [1964] A.C. 993, [1964] 1 All E.R. 300, [1964] 2 W.L.R. 150 (P.C.). See D. Kelly, "Issue Estoppel — Judgments Founded on Assumptions — Default Judgments" (1968), 84 L.Q.R. 362.

147 *Bank of Nova Scotia v. Agronin* (1989), 75 C.B.R. (N.S.) 160 (Alta. Q.B.).

148 *Hair v. Meaford, supra*, note 142. See also 16 *Halsbury's Laws of England*, 4th ed. (London: Butterworths, 1976) at 1040, § 1541; G. Spencer Bower and A. Turner, *The Doctrine of Res Judicata*, 2nd ed. (London: Butterworths, 1969), at 214, para. 249; and *Brown v. Bonnycastle*, [1935] 2 W.W.R. 124 (Man. K.B.); affd. [1935] 3 W.W.R. 536, 43 Man. R. 476, 65 C.C.C. 57, [1936] 1 D.L.R. 295 (C.A.).

149 See C. Davies, *Family Law in Canada* (Toronto: Carswell, 1984), at 414-17; H.A. Hubbard, "*Res Judicata* in Matrimonial Causes" in D. Mendes da Costa, ed., *Studies in Canadian Family Law*, Vol. 2 (Toronto: Butterworths, 1972), at 695; and M.N. Howard, P. Crane, and D.A. Hochberg, *Phipson on Evidence*, 14th ed. (London: Sweet & Maxwell, 1990), at 888-92.

150 See *C. v. C.* (1917), 39 O.L.R. 571 (C.A.), at 573: "the relationship of husband and wife is of such great public importance that the doctrine of estoppel cannot here apply." Contrast *Maynard v. Maynard*, [1951] S.C.R. 346, [1951] 1 D.L.R. 241, especially the judgment of Rand J., suggesting that there is no public law element in maintenance disputes and so the principle applies.

151 See *Thoday v. Thoday*, [1964] P. 181, [1964] 1 All E.R. 341; *Thompson v. Thompson*, [1957] P. 19, [1957] 1 All E.R. 161 (C.A.). These decisions are apparently based on a statutory duty of the English court to satisfy itself as to the

scope of this discretion was stated narrowly in *Upper v. Upper*,[152] but much less restrictively in *Mann v. Mann*.[153] It has been doubted whether *res judicata* applies to custody disputes.[154]

3. Identity of Action or Issue

(a) *Two Principles at Play*

There are two principles subsumed under the heading *res judicata*. The first is that any action or issue which has been litigated and upon which a decision has been rendered cannot be retried in a subsequent suit between the same parties or their privies.[155] This principle prevents the *contradiction* of that which was determined in the previous litigation, by prohibiting the relitigation of issues already actually addressed.

The second principle makes it mandatory that a plaintiff asserting a cause of action must claim all possible relief in respect thereto and prevents any second attempt to invoke the aid of the courts in the same cause.[156] It is sometimes called "merger" because the plaintiff's

---

truth of the pleadings. It is argued by Davies, *supra*, note 149, at 415, ftn. 17, that a similar principle should apply in Canadian courts even in the absence of the statutory duty. Of course, all parties and all courts are bound by a decision *in rem*.

152 [1933] O.R. 1 (C.A.); Davies, *supra*, note 149, at 415, ftn. 18, opines that the case is wrong. *Res judicata* was applied in the family context in *Horsfall v. Horsfall* (1988), 14 R.F.L. (3d) 393 (Man. Q.B.), and *Komarniski v. Komarniski* (1982), 29 R.F.L. (2d) 150 (Alta. Q.B.).

153 (1973), 1 O.R. (2d) 416, 40 D.L.R. (3d) 504, 11 R.F.L. 392 (H.C.J.). In *Powell v. Cockburn, supra*, note 143, "husband" succeeded in having the marriage declared void in the Supreme Court of Canada; but the Court ordered that the "wife" be allowed to add a counterclaim for maintenance, and referred the matter back to the trial court. See also *Auld v. Auld*, [1960] O.W.N. 62 (C.A.), where the order of a family court judge was held not to be a bar to a claim for maintenance by the wife in the Supreme Court. The court, however, does not appear to have treated the matter as one involving *res judicata*. The decision was based, rather, on the interpretation of the statute conferring jurisdiction on the family court. See also *Reid v. Reid, supra*, note 142.

154 *Turner v. Turner* (1967), 58 W.W.R. 27, 59 D.L.R. (2d) 277 (B.C.S.C.); *Millett v. Millett* (1974), 9 N.S.R. (2d) 306, 52 D.L.R. (3d) 139, 16 R.F.L. 180 (C.A.); *F. v. F.*, [1968] 2 All E.R. 946 (C.A.).

155 *McIntosh v. Parent* (1924), 55 O.L.R. 552, at 555, 26 O.W.N. 312, [1924] 4 D.L.R. 420 (C.A.).

156 *Clark v. Phinney* (1896), 25 S.C.R. 633; *McIntosh v. Parent, ibid.*; *Gettle Bros. Construction Co. v. Alwinsal Potash of Canada Ltd.* (1973), 34 D.L.R. (3d) 286 (Sask.

cause of action becomes "merged" in the judgment.[157] The judgment actually operates as a comprehensive declaration of the rights of *all* parties in respect of the matters in issue. As a result, the rule applies equally to a defendant who must put forward all defences which will defeat the plaintiff's action, and the defendant who does not will be debarred from raising them subsequently.[158] This principle prevents the *fragmentation* of litigation by prohibiting the litigation of matters that were never actually addressed in the previous litigation, but which properly belonged to it.

In *Henderson v. Henderson*,[159] Wigram V.C. said:[160]

> The plea of *res judicata* applies, except in special cases, not only to points upon which the court was actually required by the parties to form an opinion and pronounce a judgment, but to every point which properly belonged to the subject of litigation, and which the parties, exercising reasonable diligence, might have brought forward at the time.

By reason of the operation of this second principle, estoppel by *res judicata* "also extends to any point whether of assumption or admission

---

C.A.); affd. (1973), 38 D.L.R. (3d) 319n (S.C.C.); *Parna v. G. & S. Properties Ltd.*, [1973] 2 O.R. 765, 35 D.L.R. (3d) 321 (C.A.); *Doering v. Grandview (Town)*, [1976] 2 S.C.R. 621 (*sub nom. Grandview v. Doering*), 61 D.L.R. (3d) 455, [1976] 1 W.W.R. 388, 7 N.R. 299; *Bernier v. Bernier* (1989), 70 O.R. (2d) 372, 35 O.A.C. 367, 62 D.L.R. (4th) 561 (C.A.).

157 *Fidelitas Shipping Co. Ltd. v. V/O Exportchleb*, [1965] 2 All E.R. 4, [1966] 1 Q.B. 630 (C.A.), at 8.

158 *Terroco Industries Ltd. v. Viking Oldfield Supply Ltd.* (1987), 57 Alta. L.R. (2d) 62, [1988] 2 W.W.R. 744, 84 A.R. 274 (C.A.); *Re Abacus Cities Ltd.* (1984), 55 A.R. 258 (Q.B.); affd. 45 Alta. L.R. (2d) 113, 70 A.R. 55 (*sub nom. Abacus Cities Ltd. v. Bank of Montreal*), [1986] 4 W.W.R. 564 (C.A.); leave to appeal to S.C.C. refd. [1986] 1 S.C.R. v (*sub nom. Allan v. Bank of Montreal*); *Malik v. Principal Savings & Trust Co.* (1985), 63 A.R. 109 (Q.B.); *Mire v. Northwestern Mutual Ins. Co. (No. 2)*, [1972] 6 W.W.R. 614, [1973] I.L.R. 1-513, 31 D.L.R. (3d) 746 (Alta. C.A.); *Leutner v. Garbuz*, [1971] 1 W.W.R. 436, 14 D.L.R. (3d) 367 (Alta. T.D.); *Hill v. Hill*, *supra*, note 146; *Daniel v. Hess* (1965), 54 W.W.R. 290 (Sask. Dist. Ct.); *Henderson v. Henderson* (1843), 3 Hare 100, 67 E.R. 313, [1843-60] All E.R. Rep. 378 (Ch.).

159 *Ibid.*, at 115 (Hare) and 381-82 (All E.R. Rep.).

160 Approved in *Maynard v. Maynard*, *supra*, note 150 (S.C.R.) and in *Wahl v. Nugent*, [1924] 2 W.W.R. 1138, at 1143, [1924] 3 D.L.R. 679, 18 Sask. L.R. 592 (C.A.). See also *Ord v. Ord*, [1923] 2 K.B. 432, at 443, 92 L.J.K.B. 859, at 864, [1923] All E.R. 206 (K.B.).

which was in substance the ratio of and fundamental to the decision."[161]

Since there can be estoppel with respect to the whole cause of action or to a single issue therein, the two different aspects of estoppel are often referred to as "cause of action estoppel" and "issue estoppel".[162]

(b) Cause of Action Estoppel

(i) Same Cause of Action

Cause of action estoppel usually results from the application of the second principle above: that parties must not attempt to conduct "law suits by installment".[163] To determine whether there is cause of action estoppel, it is necessary to bear in mind that an adjudication on a particular set of facts does not raise an estoppel with respect to every cause of action which is subsequently based on the same facts, but only those claims which properly belonged to the first proceedings. *Res judicata* concerns itself with the legal consequence of particular facts,[164] although a party may, apparently, be estopped by a specific finding of fact.[165] The point is illustrated by a comparison of some authorities.

In *Hall v. Hall*,[166] the plaintiff's first action was for an accounting of property jointly owned by the plaintiff and her husband. In this action, although the plaintiff tried to trace into the defendant's hands moneys extracted from joint property and invested in a seed business, there was no allegation that the seed business was a partnership of the

---

161 *Hoystead v. Taxation Commr.*, [1926] A.C. 155, [1926] 1 W.W.R. 286, [1925] All E.R. 56 (P.C.).

162 *Angle v. M.N.R.*, [1975] 2 S.C.R. 248, 47 D.L.R. (3d) 544; *Carl Zeiss Stiftung v. Rayner and Keeler Ltd. (No. 2)*, [1967] 1 A.C. 853, [1966] 2 All E.R. 536, at 550, [1966] 3 W.L.R. 125 (H.L.).

163 In the words of Crossley J. in *Melcor Developments Ltd. v. Edmonton (City)* (1982), 20 Alta. L.R. (2d) 179, at 187, 37 A.R. 532, at 540, 136 D.L.R. (3d) 695 (Q.B.).

164 *Fidelitas Shipping Co. Ltd. v. V/O Exportchleb, supra*, note 157, at 9-10; *Aboulof v. Oppenheimer* (1882), 10 Q.B.D. 295 (C.A.); *Foster v. Reaume* (1926), 60 O.L.R. 63, at 70-74, [1927] 1 D.L.R. 1024 *per* Masten J.A. dissenting in part on other grounds.

165 *Maynard v. Maynard, supra*, note 150, at 359 (S.C.R.).

166 (1958), 15 D.L.R. (2d) 638 (Alta. C.A.); approved by the majority in *Doering v. Grandview (Town), supra*, note 156, at 635 (S.C.R.).

parties. In a second action, the plaintiff alleged that she and her husband were partners and claimed an accounting of that partnership. The majority of the Alberta Court of Appeal held that the cause of action raised in the second action concerned a right to property, which was not directly involved in the first case, and, therefore, was a new cause of action to which *res judicata* did not apply.

On the other hand in *Grandview v. Doering (Town)*,[167] the plaintiff sued the defendant municipality in nuisance, alleging that its dam caused the flooding of his land at high water, and claimed damages for losses in 1967 and 1968. He lost. He then started a new action, alleging that the dam caused saturation of his land through a subterranean aquifer, and claiming damages for losses in 1969, 1970, 1971 and 1972. The new theory was based upon the tests and opinions of an expert who was consulted between the dismissal of the first action and the commencement of the second. Ritchie J., for the majority, said that there was no cause of action and so the second action was barred. There was nothing different about the second claim except the expert's view, which presumably could have been obtained before the first action. The court in *Hall's* case addressed itself to the question of the identity of legal issues, whereas *Doering* applied *res judicata* by reason of identity of facts. There is some difficulty in knowing which approach a court will take.[168] The cases can perhaps be rationalized on the basis that in *Hall* a different legal theory of liability was being asserted whereas in *Doering* the same legal theory (that is, nuisance) was re-asserted based on a new theory of the facts. However, in keeping with the general principle that a plaintiff should not conduct litigation of a matter by instalments, the preferrable approach is to

---

167 *Ibid.*
168 See also *Re St. Denis and North Himsworth (Township)* (1985), 50 O.R. (2d) 482, 17 D.L.R. (4th) 289, 8 O.A.C. 307, 17 O.M.B.R. 278 (Div. Ct.), and *McCorriston v. Hayward* (1980), 20 Sask. R. 181 (C.A.), where new actions were allowed for new claims arising out of the same facts. But see *Grant v. Canada (Min. of Indian and Northern Affairs)*, [1990] 2 F.C. 351, 31 F.T.R. 31 (*sub nom. Musqueam Indian Band v. Canada (Min. of Indian and Northern Affairs)*; *Goncalves v. Guerra* (1988), 48 D.L.R. (4th) 134 (B.C.S.C. — in Chambers); and *Morgan Power Apparatus Ltd. v. Flanders Installations Ltd.* (1972), 27 D.L.R. (3d) 249 (B.C.C.A.). In all of these cases *res judicata* (or abuse of process: see this Chapter, III.B.3.(a)) was applied due to the identity of facts, even though a new legal theory was asserted in the second action. See Pinos, "*Res Judicata* Redux" (1988), 26 Osgoode Hall L.J. 713, especially at 727-36.

require all legal theories arising out of the same facts to be put forward in one proceeding.

In *Cahoon v. Franks*,[169] the Supreme Court of Canada held that when a tort causes personal injury and property damage, there is but one cause of action. This principle is generally easy to apply,[170] but the matter may be complicated if an insured party and the insurer bring separate actions for different damages arising out of the same tort. Often a second claim is permitted in such cases.[171]

(ii) New Facts or Circumstances

Even if the same cause of action is being presented, it may be allowed in some circumstances. In *Doering*, Ritchie J. said that the new action was permissible only if there was some new fact which totally changed the aspect of the case, and if that fact was not known before and could not have been known by reasonable diligence.[172] Ritchie J. said:[173]

In my opinion the burden lay upon the respondent to at least allege that the new fact could not have been ascertained by reasonable diligence at the time when the first action was commenced before he could invoke it so as to expose the appellant a second time to litigation arising out of the same conduct.

Hence there must be an important new fact, unascertained and unascertainable at the time of the first trial.[174] There is authority to

---

169   [1967] S.C.R. 455, 60 W.W.R. 684, 63 D.L.R. (2d) 274, declining to follow *Brunsden v. Humphrey* (1884), 14 Q.B.D. 141, [1881-5] All E.R. 357 (C.A.).

170   See *Cox v. Robert Simpson Co.* (1973), 1 O.R. (2d) 333, 40 D.L.R. (3d) 213 (C.A.); *Baker v. Spain*, [1974] 1 W.W.R. 151 (B.C. Co. Ct.); *Fife v. I.C.B.C.* (1978), 9 C.P.C. 106 (B.C. Co. Ct.); *Bashnick v. Mitchell* (1981), 8 Sask. R. 338, 13 M.V.R. 110 (Q.B.); affd. (1988), 69 Sask. R. 311 (C.A.).

171   See *Arrow Transit Lines Ltd. v. Tank Truck Transport Ltd.*, [1968] 1 O.R. 154, 65 D.L.R. (2d) 683 (H.C.J.); *Braithwaite v. Haugh* (1978), 19 O.R. (2d) 288, 84 D.L.R. (3d) 590 (Co. Ct.); *Vaughan v. Scott* (1979), 27 O.R. (2d) 560, 107 D.L.R. (3d) 153, 15 C.P.C. 219 (Co. Ct.); *Gough v. Whyte* (1983), 56 N.S.R. (2d) 68, 117 A.P.R. 68, 32 C.P.C. 232 (T.D.). But if the insured has recovered anything in the action brought for the insurer's benefit, all of the insured's claims will be *res judicatae*: *Fortino v. Randolph* (1983), 32 C.P.C. 315 (Ont. Div. Ct.); leave to appeal to Ont. C.A. refd. 32 C.P.C. 315 (C.A.).

172   Citing *Phosphate Sewage Co. v. Molleson* (1879), 4 App. Cas. 801 (H.L.).

173   *Supra*, note 156, at 638 (S.C.R.).

174   See *Toronto General Trusts Corp. v. Roman*, [1963] 1 O.R. 312, 37 D.L.R.

the effect that a second action will also be allowed if the law has changed since the first decision.[175] There can be no estoppel in the face of an express provision of a statute.[176] Where there is ongoing or continuing damage, a new cause of action accrues each day.[177]

(iii) Tax Assessment

A somewhat anomalous branch of the law of *res judicata* has developed in connection with tax assessments. In *Broken Hill Pty. Co. v. Broken Hill Municipal Council*[178] and *Caffoor (Trustee of Abdul Gaffoor Trust) v. Income Tax Commr. Columbo*,[179] which followed *Broken Hill*, the Privy Council held that a taxpayer cannot set up an estoppel against a taxing authority, based on the decision on the same point, but relating to tax liability in a prior year or period. Briefly stated, the rationale of these decisions is that a tax decision for a particular year merely determines the amount of tax for that year. All other matters which are decided, leading to this determination, are collateral or incidental to it, and will not found issue estoppels. In *Hoystead v. Taxation*,[180] decided about the same time as *Broken Hill*, the Privy

---

(2d) 16 (C.A.); affd. [1963] S.C.R. vi, 41 D.L.R. (2d) 290; *Hennig v. Northern Heights (Sault) Ltd.* (1980), 30 O.R. (2d) 346, 116 D.L.R. (3d) 496, 17 C.P.C. 173 (C.A.); *Lake Manitoba Estates Ltd. v. Communities Economic Development Fund*, [1984] 3 W.W.R. 695, 27 Man. R. (2d) 118 (Q.B.); affd. [1985] 1 W.W.R. 36, 28 Man. R. (2d) 219 (C.A.); and *Smith's Field Manor Development Ltd. v. Halifax (No. 2)* (1988), 87 N.S.R. (2d) 1, 222 A.P.R. 1, 40 M.P.L.R. 45 (S.C.T.D.).

175 *Bouchard v. Wheeler* (1981), 22 R.F.L. (2d) 104 (Ont. Prov. Ct.); *Re Bullen* (1971), 21 D.L.R. (3d) 628 (B.C.S.C.); *Arnold v. National Westminster Bank*, [1990] 1 All E.R. 529, [1990] 2 W.L.R. 304 (C.A.). But see *Reference re Manitoba Language Rights*, [1985] 1 S.C.R. 721, at 757, 19 D.L.R. (4th) 1, [1985] 4 W.W.R. 385, 35 Man. R. (2d) 83, 59 N.R. 321, 3 C.R.R. (3d) 1 (*sub nom. Language Rights Under Manitoba Act, 1870*, special hearing [1985] 2 S.C.R. 347, 26 D.L.R. (4th) 767, [1986] 1 W.W.R. 289 (S.C.C. — Per Curiam): ". . . *res judicata* would preclude the re-opening of cases decided by the courts on the basis of invalid laws."

176 *St. Ann's Island Shooting and Fishing Club Ltd. v. R.*, [1950] S.C.R. 211, at 220, [1950] 2 D.L.R. 225.

177 *McIntosh v. Parent* (1924), 55 O.L.R. 552, [1924] 4 D.L.R. 420 (C.A.); see also *Lake Manitoba Estates Ltd. v. Communities Economic Development Fund, supra*, note 174; but compare *Doering v. Grandview (Town)*, [1976] 2 S.C.R. 621, 61 D.L.R. (3d) 455, [1976] 1 W.W.R. 338, 7 N.R. 299 where the point was not directly addressed.

178 [1926] A.C. 94, [1925] All E.R. 672 (P.C.).

179 [1961] A.C. 584, [1961] 2 All E.R. 436, [1961] 2 W.L.R. 794 (P.C.).

180 *Supra*, note 161.

Council, differently constituted, reached an opposite conclusion. In Canada the continued existence of this anomaly is in jeopardy. In *Angle v. M.N.R.*[181] the majority judgment of the Supreme Court of Canada relied on *Hoystead*, without mentioning *Broken Hill* or *Caffoor*. Laskin J., as he then was, in a dissenting judgment, while acknowledging that the appeal did not involve successive tax assessments, doubted that the anomaly created by the English cases retained any survival value in England and rejected its introduction into Canada. This was followed in *Halam Park Devt. Ltd. v. Hamilton Wentworth Regional Assessment Commr., Region No. 19.*[182]

(c) *Issue Estoppel*

Issue estoppel usually results from the application of the first of the principles described above: that parties cannot call into question issues which have already been decided between them.[183] In dealing with a plea of issue estoppel, the court must determine whether the issue is the same in both proceedings. Thus in *Beeches Working Men's Club and Institute Trustees v. Scott,*[184] an employee under a service agreement was to pay his employer a sum equal to any deficiency of cash or stock "on taking stock". A complaint was made under the statute in question in relation to an alleged misappropriation of property by the employee. A magistrate's court acquitted the employee, whereupon the employer brought an action claiming repayment of the alleged sum in question under the terms of the agreement. Although the county court judge accepted the employee's plea that the matter was identical and, therefore, that the employer was estopped from proceeding, Lord Denning M.R. for a unanimous Court of Appeal held otherwise. Whereas the issue before the magistrate was whether the employee had fraudulently withheld property contrary to statute, the issue before the county court was whether the employee was liable under a contract of service. On the same principle it has been held that a finding of cruelty within the meaning of s. 8(2)(b)(ii) of the *Divorce Act*[185] is not rendered *res judicata* by a decision in an action between the same parties for a judicial separation.

---

181 *Supra*, note 162.
182 (1985), 29 M.P.L.R. 1, 50 O.R. (2d) 437, 17 O.M.B.R. 504 (H.C.J.); affd. (1986), 54 O.R. (2d) 64*n*, 18 O.M.B.R. 351 (Div. Ct.).
183 See this Chapter, III.B.3.(a).
184 [1969] 2 All E.R. 420, [1969] 1 W.L.R. 550 (C.A.).
185 S.C. 1967-68, c. 24 [now R.S.C. 1985, c. 3 (2nd Supp.), s. 8(2)(*b*)(ii)].

The difference in the definition of cruelty in the respective proceedings deprived the issues of the requisite identity.[186]

In *Angle v. M.N.R.*[187] the Supreme Court of Canada held that a previous decision that a taxpayer received a taxable benefit from a corporation did not negative an obligation to pay for the benefit in subsequent proceedings between the Minister of National Revenue and the taxpayer. The majority view was that it was not the same question. Dickson J., as he then was, delivering the majority judgment, said:[188]

> It will not suffice if the question arose collaterally or incidentally in the earlier proceedings or is one which must be inferred by argument from the judgment. . . . The question out of which the estoppel is said to arise must have been "fundamental to the decision arrived at" in the earlier proceedings: *per* Lord Shaw in *Hoystead v. Commissioner of Taxation.*

Laskin J., as he then was, delivering the dissenting judgment, was of the opinion that it was implicit in the first judgment that the taxpayer was not indebted to the corporation.

Issue estoppel applies equally to issues which, although not expressly raised in the previous case, are necessarily assumed in it or negatived by it.[189] In *Hill v. Hill,*[190] an action under a separation agreement, the wife recovered a judgment for arrears of maintenance.

---

186   *Galbraith v. Galbraith* (1969), 5 D.L.R. (3d) 543, 69 W.W.R. 390 (Man. C.A.). See also *Hamilton v. Laurentian Pacific Ins. Co.* (1989), 37 B.C.L.R. (2d) 30, [1989] W.W.R. 467, 58 D.L.R. (4th) 760, 37 C.C.L.I. 190, [1989] I.L.R. 1-2479 (C.A.); *Craig v. Craig* (1989), 65 D.L.R. (4th) 106, 24 R.F.L. (3d) 341, 78 C.B.R. (N.S.) 97, 94 N.S.R. (2d) 196, 247 A.P.R. 196 (C.A.); *Rans Construction (1966) Ltd. v. M.N.R.* (1987), 87 D.T.C. 5415, [1988] 1 F.C. 526, 16 F.T.R. 73 (F.C.T.D.).
187   [1975] 2 S.C.R. 248, 47 D.L.R. (3d) 544.
188   At 255 (S.C.R.) quoting *Hoystead*, [1926] A.C. 155, [1926] 1 W.W.R. 286 (P.C.); Dickson J. also quoted G. Spencer, Bower and A. Turner, *The Doctrine of Res Judicata*, 2nd ed. (London: Butterworths, 1969), at 181-82, para. 211, to the effect that the finding upon which an estoppel is sought to be founded must be "so fundamental to the substantive decision that the latter *cannot stand* without the former." See also *De Champlain v. Maryland Casualty Co.* (1982), 35 O.R. (2d) 428 (Co. Ct.), affd. 40 O.R. (2d) 480n.
189   *Oley v. Fredericton (City)* (1984), 15 D.L.R. (4th) 269, 28 M.P.L.R. 301, 57 N.B.R. (2d) 361, 148 A.P.R. 361 (C.A.).
190   (1966), 57 D.L.R. (2d) 760, 56 W.W.R. 260 (B.C.C.A.).

In a second action, the husband questioned the validity of the separation agreement on the ground that it lacked consideration and that the parties did not intend it to have legal effect. The British Columbia Court of Appeal held that *res judicata* applied to these issues. In the first judgment the wife could not have succeeded unless there was consideration for the separation agreement and it was intended to have legal effect. These matters were, therefore, assumed in the judgment. Put another way, the defendant had failed to raise these matters as defences, and was, therefore, prevented by merger, the second aspect of *res judicata*, from raising them later. In *Mire v. Northwestern Mutual Ins. Co. (No. 2)*,[191] the defendant had pleaded generally a defence, which was not pursued by him, on a successful motion by the plaintiff for summary judgment. In subsequent proceedings, it was alleged that the former judgment was defective. It was held by the appellate division of the Alberta Supreme Court that this defence was negatived by the failure to advance it in the previous proceedings and the matter was, therefore, *res judicata*. Conversely, a previous judgment between the same parties is only conclusive of matters which were essential and necessary to the decision but not on matters which came incidentally into consideration in the course of the reasoning.[192]

(d) *Estoppel as Between Defendants*

One defendant in a previous proceeding may raise an estoppel against another defendant in that proceeding. In order to do so, however, it is necessary to show that there was an issue between the defendants which was finally decided in the previous proceeding.[193]

---

191 [1972] 6 W.W.R. 614, [1973] I.L.R. 1-513, 31 D.L.R. (3d) 746 (Alta. C.A.). *Re Abacus Cities Ltd.* (1984), 55 A.R. 258 (Q.B.); affd. 45 Alta. L.R. (2d) 113, 70 A.R. 55, [1986] 4 W.W.R. 564 (C.A.); leave to appeal to S.C.C. refd. [1986] 1 S.C.R. v (*sub nom. Allan v. Bank of Montreal*) is similar.

192 *I.C.B.C. v. Sherrell* (1988), 23 C.P.R. (3d) 540 (Fed. T.D.); *Penn-Texas Corp. v. Murat Anstaldt (No. 2)*, [1964] 2 Q.B. 647, [1964] 3 W.L.R. 131, [1964] 2 All E.R. 594 (C.A.), at 660 (Q.B.); *Concha v. Concha* (1886), 11 App. Cas. 541, 56 L.J. Ch. 257 (H.L.). Cf. *Komarniski v. Komarniski* (1982), 29 R.F.L. (2d) 150 (Alta. Q.B.).

193 *Kirk v. Faugh*, [1951] O.W.N. 745 (H.C.J.); *Bell v. Holmes*, [1956] 1 W.L.R. 1359, [1956] 3 All E.R. 449 (Leeds Assizes); 16 *Halsbury's Laws of England*, 4th ed. (London: Butterworths, 1976) at 1044-45, § 1547. Contrast *Nesbitt Thomson Deacon Inc. v. Everett* (1989), 37 B.C.L.R. (2d) 341, 60 D.L.R. (4th) 238 (C.A.),

(e) *Parties and Their Privies*

(i) Same Parties

The traditional view is that in order for *res judicata* to operate, the party invoking the estoppel and the party against whom it is invoked must both have been parties to the former proceeding.[194] In the words of Bird J. in *Foggo v. Foggo*:[195] ". . . the doctrine of estoppel . . . cannot be invoked by one who was not a party to a former judgment against another who was a party thereto." In this regard, judgments *in personam* are to be distinguished from judgments *in rem*. The latter are conclusive against all persons whether parties or strangers.[196] Judgments *in rem* are those which affect legal status and include divorce decrees,[197] adjudications of bankruptcy and declarations as to the ownership of land.[198]

(ii) Same Capacity

An estoppel by *res judicata* will not arise if the parties or their privies claim to have brought or defended the previous proceedings in respect of different rights. A plaintiff, who brings an action as a personal representative for damages sustained by relatives of a deceased by reason of his death by accident, is not estopped in a subsequent action for damages caused to the deceased's estate arising out of the same accident.[199] Accordingly an executor, bringing an action in that capacity, is not estopped by reason of a previous

---

where the issues between the defendants were not determined in the first proceedings.

194 This does not mean, however, that all the parties in the former proceeding must be present as parties in the proceeding in which the estoppel is raised. See *Kirk v. Faugh, ibid.*

195 [1952] 2 D.L.R. 701, at 708, 5 W.W.R. (N.S.) 40 (B.C.C.A.).

196 *Law v. Hansen* (1895), 25 S.C.R. 69, at 73; *Cameron v. Rounsefell*, [1933] 3 W.W.R. 121, 47 B.C.R. 401 (S.C.); *Brown v. Bonnycastle*, [1935] 2 W.W.R. 124 (Man. K.B.); affd. 65 C.C.C. 57, [1935] 3 W.W.R. 536, 43 Man. R. 476, [1936] 1 D.L.R. 295 (C.A.).

197 "A decree absolute in a divorce case, therefore, concludes the fact of dissolution of the marriage, but nothing further." *Supra*, note 193, 16 *Halsbury* at 1040, § 1542.

198 *Leutner v. Garbuz*, [1971] 1 W.W.R. 436, 14 D.L.R. (3d) 367 (Alta. S.C.).

199 *Leggott v. Great Northern Rly. Co.* (1876), 1 Q.B.D. 599, [1874-80] All E.R. 625 (Q.B.D.); see also *Marginson v. Blackburn Borough Council*, [1939] 2 K.B. 426, [1939] 1 All E.R. 273 (C.A.), *Kasteel v. Harris* (1970), 75 W.W.R. 572 (Alta. T.D.).

determination in an action in which he or she sued personally, and the same is true if the situation is reversed. In *Canadian Shredded Wheat Co. v. Kellogg Co.*,[200] however, the Supreme Court of Canada held that the appellant was bound by the result in a prior unsuccessful passing off action which it had brought against the respondent. That action failed because it was held that "shredded wheat" had not acquired a secondary meaning, but was merely descriptive of the product. The appellant was now trying to register the mark and the respondent was objecting in the capacity of a member of the public. The court rejected the argument that the matter was not *res judicata* because the respondent appeared in different capacities in the two actions.

(iii) *Application to Those in Privity with Parties*

Res judicata operates not only against the parties, but also against persons in privity with the parties. Privity, it is stated, may arise out of a blood relationship or a coincidence of title or interest.[201] The relationship of ancestor and heir is that of privies in blood.[202] It is suggested that privity of blood is no longer applicable unless privity exists under another head such as title or interest.[203]

Privies in title or estate include vendor and purchaser,[204] and lessor and lessee[205] provided, however, that the privies claim or derive their title from the parties.[206] The suit, of course, must be relevant to that title or interest. For example, if the issue in the first proceeding was whether an easement in favour of the owner of land existed, a subsequent owner could take advantage of this judicial finding.

It is impossible to be categorical about the degree of interest

---

200 [1939] S.C.R. 329, [1939] 3 D.L.R. 641.

201 *Carl Zeiss Stiftung v. Rayner and Keeler Ltd. (No. 2)*, [1967] 1 A.C. 853, [1966] 2 All E.R. 536, at 550, [1966] 3 W.L.R. 125 (H.L.).

202 *Supra*, note 193, 16 *Halsbury* at 1041, § 1543.

203 See *Cassidy v. Ingoldsby* (1875), 36 U.C.Q.B. 339, at 341; *Eccles v. Lowry* (1876), 23 Gr. 167 (C.A.). See also *Bashnick v. Mitchell* (1981), 8 Sask. R. 338, 13 M.V.R. 110 (Q.B.); affd. (1988), 69 Sask. R. 311 (C.A.), in which *res judicata* applied to bar the claim of one plaintiff due to a previous action in his name, but not the claims of his wife and son.

204 *Board v. Board* (1873), L.R. 9 Q.B. 48, 43 L.J.Q.B. 4.

205 E. Coke, *The First Part of the Institutes of the Laws of England; or a Commentary Upon Littleton*, Vol. II (London: J. & W.T. Clarke, 1832), at 352a (hereinafter Co. Litt. 352a.).

206 *Cassidy v. Ingoldsby*, *supra*, note 203.

which will create privity.[207] It has been said that "there must be a sufficient degree of identification between the two to make it just to hold that the decision to which one was party should be binding in proceedings to which the other is party."[208] In *Eccles v. Lowry*[209] it was held that an action against a personal representative of a testator or intestate bound the estate, but not the heirs.

It has been suggested that a party is in privity with another for whose acts it was vicariously responsible,[210] and that a party is bound by a decision in which it *could have* participated.[211] In *Saskatoon Credit Union Ltd. v. Central Park Enterprises Ltd.*,[212] there was an alternative holding that the creditors of a common debtor were in privity, with each other. Also in *Canada (Min. of Trade and Commerce) v. Central Cartage Co.*[213] privity was found between a corporation and its successor. In *Central Trust Co. v. MacDonald*,[214] the plaintiff had been involved in earlier litigation with the employer of the defendant in the current action. Certain issues now raised by the employee had been decided against his employer in the previous proceedings. It was held that in respect of some of these issues, the employee was a privy of his employer and so was estopped from raising them. On other issues there was held to be no privity. In *Altobelli v. Pilot Insurance Co.*,[215] the Ontario District Court found privity between an insured and the insurers. The Ontario Court of Appeal allowed the appeal without addressing the privity issue. The appeal to the Supreme Court of

---

207 This sentence was cited in *Central Trust Co. v. MacDonald* (1987), 80 N.S.R. (2d) 291, 200 A.P.R. 291 (S.C.T.D.), at 296. See, in addition to the cases discussed in the text below, *Cavers v. Laycock* (1963), 40 D.L.R. (2d) 687, [1963] 2 O.R. 639 (Ont. H.C.), where privity was found between a driver and his passenger. In so finding, Landreville J. was clearly responding to the problem of the "wait-and-see" plaintiff, discussed in the text below.

208 *Gleeson v. J. Wippell & Co. Ltd.*, [1977] 1 W.L.R. 510, [1977] 3 All E.R. 54, at 60 (Ch. D.).

209 *Supra*, note 203.

210 *Grewal v. Small* (1985), 69 B.C.L.R. 121 (S.C.).

211 *London Guarantee & Accident Co. v. Davidson*, [1926] 1 W.W.R. 148, 36 B.C.R. 301, [1926] 1 D.L.R. 66 (S.C.); *Saskatoon Credit Union Ltd. v. Central Park Enterprises Ltd.* (1988), 47 D.L.R. (4th) 431, at 438, 22 B.C.L.R. (2d) 89 (S.C.).

212 *Ibid.*

213 (1987), 10 F.T.R. 225; affd. (1990), 109 N.R. 373.

214 (1987), 80 N.S.R. (2d) 291, 200 A.P.R. 291 (T.D.).

215 (1989), 34 C.P.C. (2d) 193 (C.A.), affd. unreported, October 7, 1991 (S.C.C.).

Canada was dismissed on the basis that the identical issue raised in the subsequent action was not previously decided. The prior proceedings involved a factual assessment of damages in a tort action. The subsequent proposed proceedings entailed a legal determination of the plaintiff's disability according to the terms of an insurance contract. The case of *CNA Assurance Co. v. Altobelli*[216] was decided on the same basis. In another case a surety was held to have sufficient interest in the lease, which he guaranteed, to set up a judgment between the lessor and the lessee in bar of the action against him.[217] However, this case seems to have been decided on the basis that the guarantor was relieved once the lessor's liability was gone, and not expressly on the basis that the guarantor was a privy of the lessee. In fact it has been held in an English case that a guarantor is not a privy, but may be bound by a judgment between the creditor and principal debtor, if the language of the guarantee is appropriate.[218]

Though not based on estoppel, but on the theory that there is only one cause of action, a judgment against one or more joint obligors results in a merger of the cause in the judgment, *transit in rem judicatum*.[219] The same principle bars a plaintiff from pursuing a second action when there is an election as to which of two parties will be sued.[220]

If the parties to an action sue or are sued in a representative capacity and the court is satisfied that the representees were fairly represented, the latter are bound by the judgment in subsequent proceedings.[221]

---

216 Unreported, October 7, 1991 (S.C.C.).
217 *Taylor v. Hortop* (1872), 22 U.C.C.P. 542 (C.A.).
218 *Re Kitchin, Ex parte Young* (1881), 17 Ch. D. 668. See also *Gleeson v. J. Wippell & Co. Ltd.*, *supra*, note 208.
219 *Kendall v. Hamilton* (1879), 4 App. Cas. 504, [1874-80] All E.R. 932 (H.L.); *Campbell Flour Mills Co. v. Bowes* (1914), 32 O.L.R. 270 (C.A.), at 277-78.
220 *Modern Air Spray Ltd. v. Homme* (1983), 45 A.R. 95 (Q.B.); *Hawboldt v. Elliott* (1941), 15 M.P.R. 440, [1941] 1 D.L.R. 351 (N.S.C.A.); *M. Brennen & Sons Mfg. Co. v. Thompson* (1915), 33 O.L.R. 465, at 472, 22 D.L.R. 375 (C.A.); *Cooper v. Molson's Bank* (1896), 26 S.C.R. 611; affd. (1899), 26 O.A.R. 571 (P.C.).
221 *Sewers Commrs. of London v. Gellatly* (1876), 3 Ch. D. 610 (M.R.); *Cox v. Dublin City Distillery Co. (No. 3)*, [1917] 1 Ir. R. 203 (Ch. D.); *Cox v. Dublin City Distillery Co. (No. 2)*, [1915] 1 Ir. R. 345 (Ch. D.).

(iv) Requirement of Mutuality

The rule that only parties and their privies can take advantage of a previous decision follows from the maxim that "estoppels must be mutual": a party can take advantage of a judgment only if it would have been bound had the judgment gone the other way. The courts of the U.S. have abandoned mutuality, and will in certain circumstances allow one who was not a party to a previous decision to set it up as an estoppel against the party that previously lost.[222] The use of non-mutual estoppel is subject to some restrictions. For example, if a plaintiff could easily have joined the earlier action, it will not be allowed to use the decision in that action offensively against the unsuccessful defendant.[223] This is to prevent the "wait-and-see" strategy: a plaintiff might stay out of the first action, planning to set it up as an estoppel against the defendant if the defendant loses, but keeping open the possibility of a second attempt to establish liability. Also, it may be unfair to the defendant to allow the previous adverse decision to be used against it, as, for example, where the defendant had no opportunity or incentive to defend the first action.

English courts have insisted that mutuality be retained, and therefore that only the parties to the prior decision or their privies may rely on it.[224] But where the traditional doctrine of *res judicata* is unavailable because the parties are different, resort to the doctrine of abuse of process is sometimes had to prevent duplicative litigation.[225]

---

222 *Blonder-Tongue Laboratories Inc. v. University of Illinois Foundation*, 402 U.S. 313 (1971), allowing the defendant to set up against the plaintiff a prior judgment in which the plaintiff had been unsuccessful against a different defendant ("defensive collateral estoppel"); *Parklane Hosiery Co. v. Shore*, 439 U.S. 322 (1979), allowing the plaintiff to estop the defendant with a previous judgment in which the defendant had been unsuccessful against a different plaintiff ("offensive collateral estoppel").

223 *Parklane Hosiery Co. v. Shore, ibid.*, at 331.

224 *Carl Zeiss Stiftung v. Rayner and Keeler Ltd. (No. 2)*, [1967] 1 A.C. 853, [1966] 3 W.L.R. 125, [1966] 2 All E.R. 536 (H.L.); *Gleeson v. J. Wippell & Co. Ltd., supra*, note 208; *Hunter v. Chief Constable of West Midlands Police*, [1982] A.C. 529, [1981] 3 All E.R. 727 (H.L.).

225 See *Hunter v. Chief Constable of the West Midlands, ibid.* The scope of the doctrine in England is unclear: see *Bragg v. Oceanus Mutual Underwriting Association (Bermuda) Ltd.*, [1982] 2 Lloyd's Rep. 132 (C.A.); *North West Water Authority v. Binnie & Partners* (1990), 140 New L.J. 130 (Q.B.).

In Canada, most courts continue to hold that only the parties to the previous decision and their privies can plead it as an estoppel,[226] but there is some willingness to use the doctrine of abuse of process to derogate from the mutuality requirement.[227] In *Bomac Construction Ltd. v. Stevenson*,[228] the defendant lost a negligence action arising out of an airplane accident. When another passenger sued, it was held that it would be an abuse of process to allow the defendant to dispute that it had been negligent.[229] *Demeter v. British Pacific Life Insurance Co.*[230]

---

226 Following *Angle v. M.N.R.*, [1975] 2 S.C.R. 248, 47 D.L.R. (3d) 544 wherein the Court cited *Carl Zeiss Stiftung v. Rayner and Keeler Ltd. (No. 2)*, *supra*, note 223 on this point. See *Laidlaw Waste Systems Ltd. v. Provincial Sanitation Ltd.* (1989), 100 A.R. 181 (Q.B. Master); *Kibale v. Canada* (1988), 26 F.T.R. 307 (T.D.); revd. (1990) 123 N.R. 153; and the cases cited in the next note and discussed in the text immediately below. But contrast *Nesbitt Thomson Deacon Inc. v. Everett* (1989), 37 B.C.L.R. (2d) 341, 60 D.L.R. (4th) 238 (C.A.), *Romaniuk v. Alberta* (1988), 50 D.L.R. (3d) 480, 44 C.C.L.T. 148, 58 Alta. L.R. (2d) 114 (Q.B.), *LeBar v. Canada* (1987), 8 F.T.R. 250, [1987] 1 F.C. 585, C.W.L.S. 8744 [29]; affd. (1988), 46 C.C.C. (3d) 103, [1989] 1 F.C. 603, 90 N.R. 5 (Fed. C.A.) (where the Trial Court perhaps conflated *res judicata* and *stare decisis*); *Holt v. Ashfield* (1986), 77 N.B.R. (2d) 121, 195 A.P.R. 121 (N.B.Q.B.), *Ralston Purina Canada Inc. v. Canada Packers Inc.* (1985), 55 Nfld. & P.E.I.R. 254, 162 A.P.R. 254 (P.E.I.S.C.) and *Nigro v. Agnew-Surpass Shoe Stores Ltd* (1977), 18 O.R. (2d) 215, 82 D.L.R. (3d) 302, 3 C.P.C. 194 (H.C.J.); affd. (1978), 18 O.R. (2d) 714*n*, 84 D.L.R. (3d) 256*n* (C.A.).
227 For example, *Bank of B.C. v. Singh* (1987), 17 B.C.L.R. (2d) 256 (S.C.), at 265; revd. (1990), 51 B.C.L.R. (2d) 273; *Solomon v. Smith* (1987), 22 C.P.C. (2d) 12, 45 D.L.R. (4th) 266, [1988] 1 W.W.R. 410, 49 Man. R. (2d) 252 (Man. C.A.); *Bank of Montreal v. Crosson* (1979), 23 O.R. (2d) 625, 96 D.L.R. (3d) 765, 11 C.P.C. 30 (Ont. H.C.J.); *Breen v. Saunders* (1986), 69 N.B.R. (2d) 427 (Q.B.); see also *Grant v. Canada (Min. of Indian and Northern Affairs)*, [1990] 2 F.C. 351, 31 F.T.R. 31, (*sub nom. Musqueam Indian Band v. Canada (Min. of Indian and Northern Affairs)* at 368, 380 (F.C.). See M.J. Herman and G.F. Hayden, "Issue Estoppel: Mutuality of Parties Reconsidered" (1986), 64 Can. Bar Rev. 437, and G.D. Watson, "Duplicative Litigation: Issue Estoppel, Abuse of Process and the Death of Mutuality" (1990), 69 Can. Bar Rev. 623.
228 [1986] 5 W.W.R. 21, 48 Sask. R. 62 (C.A.); see also *Saskatoon Credit Union Ltd. v. Central Park Enterprises Ltd.* (1988), 47 D.L.R. (4th) 431, 22 B.C.L.R. (2d) 89.
229 The court did not satisfactorily address the plaintiff's adoption of the "wait-and-see" strategy. See M. Gelowitz, *"Bomac and O'Hara: Abuse and Abdication"* (1989), 53 Sask. L.R. 163. A similar result, and a similar problem, can be seen in *Bjarnarson v. Manitoba* (1987), 21 C.P.C. (2d) 302, 45 D.L.R. (4th) 766, [1988] 1 W.W.R. 422, 50 Man. R. (2d) 178 (Man. C.A.).
230 (1983), 43 O.R. (2d) 33, 150 D.L.R. (3d) 249, 37 C.P.C. 277 (H.C.J.); affd. 48 O.R. (2d) 266, 13 D.L.R. (4th) 318, 7 O.A.C. 143 (C.A.).

was a case in which the plaintiff had been convicted of the murder of his wife. In a civil action, he claimed the proceeds of insurance on her life. The action was dismissed as an abuse of process.[231]

In *Germscheid v. Valois*,[232] the Ontario High Court confronted the problem of a "wait-and-see" plaintiff. The plaintiff and another person had been injured in a fire, and the other person had successfully sued certain defendants. The plaintiff then moved for summary judgment against those defendants who had lost in the first action. Rather than dismiss the motion,[233] which would result in the relitigation of issues addressed in the previous action, the Court allowed it on the ground that it would be an abuse of process for the defendants to dispute their liability. To discourage the "wait-and see" strategy, the plaintiff was ordered to pay the costs of the motion on a solicitor and client basis.

(f) *Procedural Matters*

It is well established that estoppel by *res judicata* must be pleaded.[234] An amendment will, however, be allowed in special circumstances.[235] Although a plea of *res judicata* based on a foreign judgment can be met by an attack on the judgment on the ground of fraud,[236] in the case of domestic judgments rendered by a court of competent jurisdiction, the proper course is to take steps to have the judgment set aside.[237] In order to determine the identity of the actions

---

231 The trial judge and the Court of Appeal both held that *Hollington v. F. Hewthorn & Co.*, [1943] K.B. 587, [1943] 2 All E.R. 35 (C.A.) did not represent the law of Ontario. The Court of Appeal held that a prior criminal conviction was inadmissible in subsequent civil proceedings. See this Chapter, III.D.

232 (1989), 34 C.P.C. (2d) 267, 68 O.R. (2d) 670 (Ont. H.C.J.).

233 As a U.S. court would, following *Parklane Hosiery Co. v. Shore*, *supra*, note 221.

234 *Mann v. Mann* (1973), 1 O.R. (2d) 416, 40 D.L.R. (3d) 504, 11 R.F.L. 392 (H.C.J.), relying on *Cooper v. Molsons Bank*, *supra*, note 219; *Vooght v. Winch*, [1819] 2 B. & Ald. 662, 106 E.R. 507 (K.B.); W.B. Ogders, *Principles of Pleadings and Practice*, 22nd ed. (London: Sweet & Maxwell, 1981), at 190.

235 *Morrison Rose & Partners v. Hillman*, [1961] 2 Q.B. 266, [1937] 1 W.W.R. 591, [1937] 1 All E.R. 748, 46 C.R.C. 1, [1937] 1 D.L.R. 609 (C.A.); *Wytinck v. DeGrouwe*, [1925] 4 D.L.R. 326, at 333, 6 W.W.R. (N.S.) 97, 60 Man. R. 242 (Man. C.A.).

236 *Jacobs v. Beaver* (1908), 17 O.L.R. 496 (C.A.).

237 *McGuire v. Haugh*, [1934] O.R. 9 (C.A.); *Jonesco v. Beard*, [1930] A.C. 298, [1930] All E.R. 483 (H.L.).

or issues, the court should consult the pleadings, judgments, reasons for judgments and other formal documents relating to the previous proceeding. These documents are admissible without formal proof.[238]

C. *Criminal Law*

The same general principles apply in the criminal law.[239] Corresponding to cause of action estoppel, there are the special pleas of *autrefois acquit* (where the accused has already been acquitted of the offence) and *autrefois convict* (where the accused was convicted). Moreover, there is issue estoppel just as in the civil law. But there are additional principles under the rubric of *res judicata*. These include the *Kienapple* rule and s. 11(h) of the *Canadian Charter of Rights and Freedoms*. While all of these rules are aimed at common policy objectives, each must be considered separately.[240] They apparently apply to provincial offences,[241] although it is not clear how they apply when the first proceeding was under the law of one level of government, and the second proceeding is under the law of the other level.[242]

---

238 *Barber v. McQuaig* (1900), 31 O.R. 593, at 596 (H.C.J.); *Kemptville Milling Co. v. Village of Kemptville* (1924), 26 O.W.N. 431, at 432 (H.C.J.); *Wytinck v. DeGrouwe, supra*, note 235.

239 See generally R. E. Salhany, *Canadian Criminal Procedure*, 5th ed. (Aurora: Canada Law Book, 1989), at 223-38; P.G. Barton and N.A. Peel, *Criminal Procedure in Practice*, 2nd ed. (Toronto: Butterworths, 1983), at 128-37; M. L. Friedland, *Double Jeopardy* (Oxford: Clarendon Press, 1969).

240 *R. v. Van Rassel*, [1990] 1 S.C.R. 225, at 233, 53 C.C.C. (3d) 353, 75 C.R. (3d) 150, 27 Q.A.C. 285, 45 C.R.R. 265.

241 *R. v. Browning-Ferris Industries of Winnipeg (1974)*, [1980] 3 W.W.R. 471, 2 Man. R. (2d) 168, 7 M.V.R. 62 (C.A.) applied *Kienapple* to provincial offences; see also *R. v. McKinney* (1979), 46 C.C.C. (2d) 566, 98 D.L.R. (3d) 369, [1979] 2 W.W.R. 545, 2 Man. R. (2d) 403, 31 N.R. 567, [1979] 2 C.N.L.R. 87 (Man. C.A.); revd. in part on other grounds [1980] 1 S.C.R. 401, 50 C.C.C. (2d) 576, 106 D.L.R. (3d) 494*n*, [1981] 1 W.W.R. 448, 31 N.R. 564, 2 Man. R. (2d) 400, [1984] 2 C.N.L.R. 113 where the applicability of the *Kienapple* rule to provincial offences was apparently assumed (although the rule did not apply on the facts). Issue estoppel and the special pleas are also common law rules (see *R. v. Art* (1987), 39 C.C.C. (3d) 563, 7 M.V.R. (2d) 132, 61 C.R. (3d) 204 (B.C.C.A.) on the latter), and so would apply to provincial offences. See *R. v. Wigglesworth*, [1987] 2 S.C.R. 541, 37 C.C.C. (3d) 385, 60 C.R. (3d) 193, [1988] 1 W.W.R. 193, 45 D.L.R. (4th) 235, 24 O.A.C. 321, 61 Sask. R. 105, 28 Admin. L.R. 294, 32 C.R.R. 219 discussed in detail in this Chapter, III.C.4.(b), (c), for s. 11(h) of the *Charter*.

242 See Barton and Peel, *supra*, note 239, at 135.

1. The Special Pleas

The special pleas of *autrefois acquit* and *autrefois convict* are dealt with in ss. 607-610 of the *Criminal Code*.[243] They will be considered individually, and then matters of procedure and of the effect of foreign proceedings will be addressed.

(a) *Autrefois Acquit*

(i) General Principle

The plea of *autrefois acquit* under s. 607 of the *Criminal Code* will estop the Crown from bringing proceedings on a charge upon which the accused has already been in jeopardy and been finally acquitted by a court of competent jurisdiction. This is analogous to the civil cause of action estoppel discussed above: the Crown is estopped because either it is seeking to contradict the earlier judgment in favour of the accused, or it is presenting an argument which properly belonged to the first proceedings.

(ii) Same Charge

For the plea to succeed, the charges must be the same in the required sense. The relevant principles were set out in *R. v. Van Rassel*[244] where McLachlin J., summarizing the effects of ss. 607 and 609 of the *Criminal Code*,[245] said that the accused must show that the following conditions are met:[246]

(1) the matter is the same, in whole or in part; and

(2) the new count must be the same as at the first trial, or be implicitly included in that of the first trial, either in law or on account of the evidence presented if it had been legally possible at that time to make the necessary amendments.

---

243 R.S.C. 1985, c. C-46. There is also the special plea of pardon (s-s. 607(1)) and, on a charge of defamatory libel, the plea of justification (ss. 611-612).
244 *Supra*, note 240.
245 It should be noted that s. 610 is also relevant. Subsection (1) says that a subsequent charge which is merely a more serious version of the former charge is to be treated as the same charge. Although it refers to "an indictment", this includes an information (s. 2). Subsections (2) through (4) provide for an identity of offences among various forms of homicide.
246 *Supra*, note 240, at 234.

She further said:[247]

> ... the substantive point is a simple one: could the accused have been convicted at the first trial of the offence with which he is now charged? If the differences between the charges at the first and second trials are such that it must be concluded that the charges are different in *nature*, the plea of *autrefois acquit* is not appropriate. On the other hand, the plea will apply if, despite the differences between the earlier and the present charges, the offences are the same.

McLachlin J. went on to decide that this was not established in *Van Rassel*. She looked at the elements of the second offence and said that the accused could not have been convicted of that offence at the first trial.

This may be contrasted with *R. v. Plank*.[248] The accused was charged with driving a motor vehicle while his blood alcohol level was greater than 0.08 per cent. The trial judge acquitted the accused because it had not been proved that he had been driving. He refused to allow the information to be amended to read "care and control" instead of "drive", and he did not consider whether it had been proved that the accused had been in care and control of the vehicle. The accused was subsequently charged with being in care and control of a vehicle while his blood alcohol level exceeded 0.08 per cent to which he pleaded *autrefois acquit*. The Court of Appeal held that the driving charge included the offence of being in care or control of a vehicle with a blood alcohol level of greater than 0.08 per cent, and so the first trial judge had been correct in refusing to allow the amendment but had erred in not considering the evidence of care and control. Nonetheless, the accused's acquittal at the first trial was an acquittal of both offences and so *autrefois acquit* succeeded.

(iii) Final Decision

The prior disposition on which it is sought to found the plea must be a final one, and this has given rise to difficulty. If the charge is actually dismissed at the first trial, then the doctrine applies, even if the prosecution presented no evidence. In *R. v. Riddle*,[249] the com-

---

247 *Ibid.*, at 235; emphasis in original.
248 (1986), 28 C.C.C. (3d) 386, 15 O.A.C. 21, 40 M.V.R. 298 (Ont. C.A.).
249 [1980] 1 S.C.R. 380, 48 C.C.C. (2d) 365, 100 D.L.R. (3d) 577, [1980] 1

plainant was not present at the first trial and the Crown sought an adjournment. This was denied, the Crown elected to call no evidence, and the charge was dismissed. The complainant swore a new information and a new charge was laid. It was held that the plea of *autrefois acquit* was available at the new trial. Dickson J., as he then was, said for the Court:[250]

> In my view, a criminal trial commences and an accused is normally in jeopardy from the moment issue is joined before a judge having jurisdiction and the prosecution is called upon to present its case in court. The person accused continues in jeopardy until the final determination of the matter by rendering of the verdict.
>
> . . .
>
> So long as the case has proceeded to a verdict and a dismissal, that should be sufficient.
>
> . . .
>
> There is no basis, in the *Code* or in the common law, for any super-added requirement that there must be a trial "on the merits". That phrase merely serves to emphasize the general requirement that the previous dismissal must have been made by a court of competent jurisdiction, whose proceedings were free from jurisdictional error and which rendered judgment on the charge.

Applying these principles, if a charge has previously been dismissed, even if on procedural grounds and due to an error of law on the part of the judge, then the plea of *autrefois acquit* will bar a subsequent proceeding on the same charge.[251]

But for the prior proceedings to have the requisite finality, there

---

W.W.R. 592. See also *R. v. Ross* (1977), 34 C.C.C. (2d) 483 (B.C.C.A.), and *R. v. Hatherley* (1971), 4 C.C.C. (2d) 242, [1971] 3 O.R. 430 (Ont. C.A.); leave to appeal to S.C.C. refd., [1971] 3 O.R. 431*n*, 4 C.C.C. (2d) 243*n*.

250 *Ibid.*, at 398-99 (S.C.R.).

251 *Petersen v. R.*, [1982] 2 S.C.R. 493, 69 C.C.C. (2d) 385, 140 D.L.R. (3d) 480, 30 C.R. (3d) 165, [1982] 6 W.W.R. 498, 44 N.R. 92, 18 Sask. R. 357. This case and *R. v. Moore*, [1988] 1 S.C.R. 1097, 41 C.C.C. (3d) 289, 65 C.R. (3d) 1, [1988] 5 W.W.R. 1, 29 B.C.L.R. (2d) 1 discussed below, were distinguished in *R. v. Frisbee* (1989), 48 C.C.C. (3d) 386 (B.C.C.A.); leave to appeal to S.C.C. refd. [1989] 2 S.C.R. vii. An indictment had been dismissed in the U.S. so that the accused could be extradited to Canada. It was held (at 406) that the dismissal for this reason was tantamount to a stay and could not found a plea of *autrefois acquit*.

must be "a verdict and a dismissal."[252] In *R. v. Karpinski*,[253] the accused was charged with a hybrid offence. The information was laid more than six months after the offence allegedly occurred, but the Crown chose to proceed summarily. The accused pleaded not guilty and raised the defence that the prosecution was statute barred. The Crown withdrew the charge and then proceeded by indictment on an identical information. The accused pleaded *autrefois acquit* but the plea was not allowed.[254] Fauteux and Abbott JJ. said that *autrefois acquit* did not arise because the information showed on its face that there could be no summary proceedings, and so the judge lacked jurisdiction to receive either a Crown election or a plea. Taschereau J. said that the plea was not available because the withdrawal of the information did not amount to an acquittal, and because the accused was never in jeopardy. Kerwin C.J.C. held that *autrefois acquit* did not apply because there had been no adjudication in the earlier case.[255] Similar reasoning was applied in *R. v. Selhi*.[256] When charges were withdrawn after plea, but before any evidence was led, and then relaid, the plea of *autrefois acquit* did not succeed. There was no question of a lack of jurisdiction in this case, which suggests an agreement with the reasoning of Kerwin C.J.C. and Taschereau J. in *Karpinski*. Again, in *R. v. Tateham*,[257] the Crown stayed proceedings during the first trial and in

---

252 *R. v. Riddle, supra*, note 249, at 398 (S.C.R.), citing a passage from *R. v. Ecker* (1929), 51 C.C.C. 409, [1929] 3 D.L.R. 760, 64 O.L.R. 1 (C.A.) which was adopted by Taschereau J. in *R. v. Welch*, [1950] S.C.R. 412, 97 C.C.C. 177, 10 C.R. 97, [1950] 3 D.L.R. 641.

253 [1957] S.C.R. 343, 117 C.C.C. 241, 25 C.R. 365; applied in *R. v. Belair* (1988), 41 C.C.C. (3d) 329, 64 C.R. (3d) 179, 26 O.A.C. 340 (Ont. C.A.). In *Belair*, the information was not withdrawn but rather was quashed by the Court, but before a plea was entered. Because no plea was entered, the accused was never in jeopardy.

254 Cartwright J. dissenting.

255 In *R. v. Conrad* (1983), 6 C.C.C. (3d) 226, 34 C.R. (3d) 320, 150 D.L.R. (3d) 331, 58 N.S.R. (2d) 150 (C.A.), the Crown withdrew the charge after plea with the permission of the court. The court opined that *R. v. Karpinski, ibid.*, had been narrowed by *R. v. Riddle, supra*, note 249 and *Petersen, supra*, note 251 and held that *autrefois acquit* was available when the same offence was charged. This is questionable in the light of *R. v. Selhi, infra*, note 256 discussed in the text immediately below.

256 (1985), 18 C.C.C. (3d) 131, 38 Sask. R. 90, 32 M.V.R. 299 (Sask. C.A.); affd. [1990] 1 S.C.R. 277, 53 C.C.C. (3d) 576n, 110 N.R. 318, 86 Sask. R. 253.

257 (1982), 70 C.C.C. (2d) 565 (B.C.C.A.). See also *Burrows v. R.* (1983), 6 C.C.C. (3d) 54, 150 D.L.R. (3d) 317, 22 Man. R. (2d) 241 (Man. C.A.); leave to

a subsequent trial on the same charge, the plea was not available.

But a stay entered by the court, rather than by Crown counsel, can be sufficiently final to found a later plea of *autrefois acquit*. In *R. v. Jewitt*,[258] the trial judge ordered a stay after the jury found that the accused had been entrapped (this must now be read in the light of *R. v. Mack*,[259] setting out the correct procedure in respect of entrapment). The issue was whether this stay was an order which the Crown could appeal. Dickson C.J.C., for the Court, said:[260]

> Substance and not form should govern. Whatever the words used, the judge intended to make a final order disposing of the charge against the [accused]. If the order of the Court effectively brings the proceedings to a final conclusion in favour of an accused then I am of opinion that, irrespective of the terminology used, it is tantamount to a judgment or verdict of acquittal and therefore appealable by the Crown.

> We are concerned here with a stay of proceedings because of an abuse of process by the Crown. While a stay of proceedings of this nature will have the same result as an acquittal and will be such a final determination of the issue that it will sustain a plea of *autrefois acquit*, its assimilation to an acquittal should only be for purposes of enabling an appeal by the Crown.

Is the quashing of an indictment or information sufficiently final to support the plea of *autrefois acquit*? In *Lattoni v. R.*,[261] Kerwin C.J.C. said that such a quashing could be appealed and could support the

---

appeal to S.C.C. refd. 6 C.C.C. (3d) 54n, 150 D.L.R. (3d) 317n, 22 Man. R. (2d) 240, 51 N.R. 386n. Apparently *autrefois acquit* was not actually pleaded (see 6 C.C.C. (3d) 65) but the applicability of *Riddle* was considered and rejected when a stay was entered by the Crown during the trial, and then the charge was relaid and a new one added.

258 [1985] 2 S.C.R. 128, 21 C.C.C. (3d) 7, 47 C.R. (3d) 193, 61 N.R. 159, [1985] 6 W.W.R. 127, 20 D.L.R. (4th) 651.

259 [1988] 2 S.C.R. 903, 44 C.C.C. (3d) 513, 67 C.R. (3d) 1, [1989] 1 W.W.R. 577, 90 N.R. 173.

260 *Supra*, note 258, at 147-48 (S.C.R.).

261 [1958] S.C.R. 603, 121 C.C.C. 317. It should be noted that when the Provincial Judge quashed the indictment, he also stated that the accused were acquitted.

plea. This would be so if it were a final decision on a question of law alone, and based not on merely procedural grounds or technical irregularities.[262] But a four to three majority of the Supreme Court of Canada clarified the effects of a quashing and enlarged the boundaries of a "final decision" in *R. v. Moore*.[263] An information was quashed after plea as it failed to set out an essential element of the offence. The majority considered the wide power of a trial judge to amend an indictment,[264] and said that the power must be exercised in preference to quashing the indictment, unless it cannot be exercised without injustice being done. Amendment may be possible even when the indictment fails to set out an essential element.[265] In these circumstances, where the indictment should be quashed only where amendment would lead to injustice, quashing is a final disposition of the case. This leads to two effects. First, quashing is tantamount to an acquittal and will support a plea of *autrefois acquit*. Moreover, the decision to quash is always appealable. The majority explicitly held that quashing where amendment is possible is a reversible error of law.[266] Therefore, the proper course where it is thought that quashing was improper is for the Crown to appeal the quashing order, not to lay a new charge. This is because laying a new charge before another judge would be just like amending the first; but the trial judge in quashing has determined that amendment would lead to injustice, and this decision is deemed to be correct until it is reversed by a Court of Appeal. The majority noted that where the first charge is a nullity, its quashing is for lack of jurisdiction and cannot support *autrefois acquit*.[267]

---

262 As in *R. v. MacDonald* (1952), 104 C.C.C. 184, 30 M.P.R. 71 (N.S.S.C.), where the indictment was quashed as it omitted certain words; when the accused was charged on a new indictment, the plea of *autrefois acquit* was not allowed. This was followed in *R. v. Bury*, [1970] 4 C.C.C. 379, 11 C.R.N.S. 73, 72 W.W.R. 237 (B.C.S.C.), where the information had been quashed.

263 [1988] 1 S.C.R. 1097, 41 C.C.C. (3d) 289, 65 C.R. (3d) 1, [1988] 5 W.W.R. 1, 29 B.C.L.R. (2d) 1, 85 N.R. 195.

264 *Criminal Code*, s. 601. "Indictment" includes an information: s. 2.

265 Section 601(3)(b)(i).

266 *Supra*, note 263, at 1129 (S.C.R.).

267 This is consistent with the reasoning of Fauteux and Abbott JJ. in *R. v. Karpinski, supra*, note 253. In *R. v. Selhi, supra*, note 256, discussed above, the Court indicated that *autrefois acquit* is also unavailable when there has been no adjudication in the case, which was the basis of the decisions of Kerwin C.J.C. and Taschereau J. in *Karpinski. Moore, supra*, note 263 indicates that given the trial judge's wide powers to amend, quashing an indictment amounts to an adjudica-

(iv) Accused Must Have Been in Jeopardy

Even if there was a final determination at the first proceedings, the accused must have been in jeopardy.[268] In *R. v. Belair*,[269] the Crown proceeded by summary conviction outside the six-month limitation period, and the information was quashed by the court prior to plea. It was held that the plea of *autrefois acquit* was not available to bar subsequent proceedings. This may seem inconsistent with *Moore*, but the accused in *Belair* was never in jeopardy because he had not pleaded.[270] Hence, the special plea was unavailable even though the disposition of the first proceedings was apparently final. If the statutory provision upon which the first charge was based is declared invalid, then the accused was never in jeopardy and cannot plead *autrefois acquit* in bar of a subsequent charge.[271] The same is true if the first court lacked jurisdiction,[272] and the burden of proving that there was jurisdiction lies on the accused.[273]

(b) *Autrefois Convict*

(i) General Principle

The Crown, having succeeded previously, is not allowed to make the same claim against the accused. This is another form of cause of action estoppel, based on the rule against splitting one's case. Here, the plea of *autrefois convict* applies.[274]

---

tion of the case.

268   *R. v. Riddle, supra*, note 249; *Petersen v. R., supra*, note 251; *R. v. Moore, supra*, note 263, at 1106, 1128 (S.C.R.)

269   *Supra*, note 253.

270   See *R. v. Riddle*, [1980] 1 S.C.R. 380, at 398, 48 C.C.C. (2d) 365, 100 D.L.R. (3d) 577, [1980] 1 W.W.R. 592: ". . . a criminal trial commences and an accused is normally in jeopardy from the moment *issue is joined* before a judge having jurisdiction and the prosecution is called upon to present its case in court." (emphasis added)

271   *R. v. Logan* (1981), 64 C.C.C. (2d) 238, 25 C.R. (3d) 35, 49 N.S.R. (2d) 59, 131 D.L.R. (3d) 130 (C.A.). Cf. *Reference re Manitoba Language Rights*, [1985] 1 S.C.R. 721, at 757: ". . . *res judicata* would preclude the re-opening of cases decided by the courts on the basis of invalid laws."

272   See *Riddle, supra*, note 270, at 398 (S.C.R.); *R. v. Moore, supra*, note 263, at 1128 (S.C.R.).

273   *R. v. Sanver* (1973), 12 C.C.C. (2d) 105, 28 C.R.N.S. 10, 6 N.B.R. (2d) 192 (C.A.).

274   *Criminal Code*, ss. 607-610. See also G. Spencer, Bower and A. Turner, *The Doctrine of Res Judicata*, 2nd ed. (London: Butterworths & Co., 1962), at 391-96.

(ii) Same Charge

The provisions of the Code which govern whether the two charges are the same apply to both of the special pleas. It can thus be inferred that the statement of the substantive point in *R. v. Van Rassel*,[275] in the context of *autrefois acquit*, also applies to *autrefois convict*. Modified appropriately, it is: was the accused convicted at the previous trial of the offence with which he or she is now charged? A discharge, whether conditional or absolute, will also ground a plea of *autrefois convict*.[276]

In *R. v. Ko*,[277] the two trials were on the same indictment for trafficking and essentially the same evidence was led. In his opening at the first trial, Crown counsel had said that the first trial was to be concerned with the delivery of a sample of narcotics, and that the subsequent trial was to deal with the delivery of a larger amount. Convicted at the first trial, the accused pleaded *autrefois convict* at the second. It was held that these two transactions could constitute separate offences, but only if the Crown alleged the facts in such a way as to isolate the two acts. As the Crown had not done so, the plea was allowed.

Subsection 610(1) of the *Criminal Code* provides that a new proceeding cannot be justified merely by alleging a more serious version of the same offence.[278] This section was relied upon in *R. v. Hemmingway*.[279] The accused was found on a boat in which there were

---

It might be suggested that in Canada, the rule cannot be based on precluding the splitting of the Crown's case, because under the *Kienapple* rule (discussed below) such identical charges cannot even be brought simultaneously. But a prior conviction is a prerequisite of the special plea of *autrefois convict*; and its successful invocation leads to an acquittal. Neither of these statements is true of the *Kienapple* rule.

275 [1990] 1 S.C.R. 225, at 235. Discussed in this Chapter, III.C.1(a).

276 Section 736(3)(c). The provision says that one discharged "may plead *autrefois convict* in respect of any subsequent charge relating to the offence." On its face, this is of little significance, since *any* accused can plead *autrefois convict* in respect of *any* charge; the question is whether the plea will succeed. Presumably that is what this provision stipulates.

277 (1977), 36 C.C.C. (2d) 32, 38 C.R.N.S. 243, [1977] 3 W.W.R. 447 (B.C.C.A.).

278 Although s. 610(1) refers to "an indictment", this includes an information (s. 2). Note also that subs. 610(2) through (4) provide for an identity of offences among various forms of homicide.

279 (1971), 5 C.C.C. (2d) 127 (B.C. Co. Ct.).

narcotics, and he also had narcotics on his person. He pleaded guilty to possession, and no evidence was led regarding the narcotics in the boat. Then he was charged with possession for the purpose of trafficking, and he pleaded *autrefois convict*. It was held that any distinction between the drugs on the boat and those on the accused's person would be an unreal one, and the plea was allowed.

(iii) Final Order of Court with Jurisdiction

As with *autrefois acquit*, there must be a final determination by a court of competent jurisdiction, and again the burden of showing that there was jurisdiction is on the accused.[280]

(c) *Procedural Matters and Foreign Proceedings*

(i) Procedural Matters

The pleas are available in both summary proceedings and proceedings by indictment.[281] If one of these pleas is raised in a jury trial, the judge will deal with it without the jury, and only if the plea fails need the accused plead further.[282] If all special pleas fail, the accused may plead guilty or not guilty.[283]

To make one of these pleas, the accused must state that he or she was acquitted, convicted or discharged of the offence to which the plea is made, and must indicate the date of the previous order.[284] To prove the former proceedings, the accused will likely rely on a certified copy

---

280 *R. v. Taylor* (1914), 22 C.C.C. 234 (Alta. S.C.).

281 This is so even though there is a procedure in s. 808(2) of the Code under which a certificate of the dismissal of a summary proceeding will bar subsequent proceedings. In *R. v. Riddle, supra*, note 270, it was held that the special pleas were available for summary proceedings, despite the certificate of dismissal procedure and even though at that time the special pleas were set out in a part of the Code headed "Procedure by Indictment". Now they are in a Part called "Procedure in Jury Trials and General Provisions". Hence it is no longer the case that the special pleas must be raised in summary conviction matters via a general plea of "not guilty": *R. v. Riddle, supra*, note 270, at 389 (S.C.R.). See also *Petersen v. R.*, [1982] 2 S.C.R. 493, 69 C.C.C. (2d) 385, 30 C.R. (3d) 165, 140 D.L.R. (3d) 480, [1982] 6 W.W.R. 498, 44 N.R. 92, 18 Sask. R. 357 where *autrefois acquit* was allowed where the first proceedings were by summary conviction and the second were by indictment.

282 Section 607(3).

283 Section 607(4).

284 Section 607(5).

of the order of acquittal or conviction,[285] which is sufficient evidence to prove the acquittal or conviction.[286] In deciding whether the charges are the same, the "evidence and adjudication and the notes of the judge and official stenographer" of the former trial are admissible, as is the record for the current charge.[287]

(ii) Foreign Proceedings

It would appear that a foreign acquittal can found the plea of *autrefois acquit*,[288] but the question was left open in *R. v. Van Rassel*.[289] It is less clear whether a foreign conviction will suffice for *autrefois convict*.[290] Under s. 7 of the *Criminal Code*, certain crimes of an international nature committed outside Canada can be deemed to have been committed in Canada.[291] The special pleas are specifically made available to persons alleged to have committed such offences outside Canada, who have been appropriately "tried and dealt with."[292] The plea of *autrefois convict*, however, is specifically taken away from a

---

285   See s. 570 for proceedings by indictment; ss. 806(1), 808(1) for summary proceedings.

286   Section 570(4); see also s. 667, and ss. 23 and 28 of the *Canada Evidence Act*, R.S.C. 1985, c. C-5.

287   Section 608.

288   See 11(1) *Halsbury's Laws of England*, 4th ed. (London: Butterworths, 1976) § 635, at 473; Spencer, Bower and Turner, *supra*, note 274, at 278, para. 328; M.L. Friedland, *Double Jeopardy* (Oxford: Clarendon Press, 1969), at 360-67; *R. v. Frisbee* (1989), 48 C.C.C. (3d) 386, at 407-408 (B.C.C.A.); leave to appeal to S.C.C. refd. [1989] 2 S.C.R. vii; *Libman v. R.*, [1985] 2 S.C.R. 178, at 212, 21 C.C.C. (3d) 206, 21 D.L.R. (4th) 174, 62 N.R. 161, 12 O.A.C. 33; *R. v. Stratton* (1978), 3 C.R. (3d) 289, 42 C.C.C. (2d) 449, 90 D.L.R. (3d) 420, 21 O.R. (2d) 258 (Ont. C.A.). It may be noted that there will be no identity of parties as the prosecuting authority will be different. Issues of sovereignty may also arise: *Van Rassel*, at 232.

289   [1990] 1 S.C.R. 225, at 232-33.

290   Friedland, *supra*, note 288, at 367, states that "[w]hereas little can be said against recognition of foreign acquittals, certain arguments which have a certain degree of force can be made against the automatic recognition of convictions." Nonetheless, he concludes (at 368) that a foreign conviction for an offence committed abroad should bar domestic proceedings.

291   R.S.C. 1985, c. C-46. It should be noted that there are other provisions defining offences of which an essential element may be conduct outside of Canada, and which do not directly address the issue of the availability of the special pleas. See ss. 57, 58, 74, 75, 290(1)(b), 342(1)(c), 354(1), 357, 462.31, and 465(4).

292   Section 7(6).

person accused under s. 7 who was tried and convicted *in absentia* outside Canada and who has not satisfied the sentence imposed by the foreign court.[293]

2. *Issue Estoppel*

In 1976, the House of Lords said that issue estoppel could not be raised in criminal proceedings.[294] This was not followed in Canada. In *R. v. Gushue*,[295] the accused had been acquitted of a murder which had occurred in the course of a robbery. He had testified at that first trial that he did not shoot the deceased. Four years later he confessed that he had tried to rob the deceased and had shot him when he resisted. He was charged with robbery and with perjury in respect of his testimony at the murder trial. He pleaded guilty to both charges and was convicted of robbery, but the perjury charge was dismissed by a Provincial Judge on the ground that the Crown could not relitigate the issue of whether the accused had shot the deceased. Six months later the accused was indicted for perjury and for making contradictory statements in judicial proceedings with intent to mislead, under what is now s. 136 of the *Criminal Code*. At trial the judge directed an acquittal on the perjury indictment, on the ground that a conviction would be inconsistent with the previous jury verdict in the murder trial. Consequently, the accused was convicted on the s. 136 charge. The question before the Supreme Court of Canada was whether the accused could invoke issue estoppel to bar the proceedings on the robbery charge and the s. 136 charge.

Laskin C.J.C., for the Court, said that issue estoppel is part of the criminal law of Canada. As to the s. 136 charge, it was said that the subsequently made statements added a new element to the matter, taking it outside the scope of the murder trial. The gist of the offence was making contradictory statements with intent to mislead, in this case, the court at the murder trial. The accused argued that the Crown was estopped from asserting the intent to mislead because the acquittal at the murder trial must be taken as conclusive proof that the accused

---

293 Section 607(6).
294 *D.P.P. v. Humphrys*, [1977] A.C. 1, [1976] 2 W.L.R. 857, [1976] 2 All E.R. 497 (H.L.).
295 [1980] 1 S.C.R. 798, 50 C.C.C. (2d) 417, 16 C.R. (3d) 39, 106 D.L.R. (3d) 152, 30 N.R. 204.

did not kill the deceased. Laskin C.J.C. said:[296]

> ... what we have to resolve here is a question of policy based on the premise that issue estoppel cannot be founded on false evidence where the falsity is disclosed by subsequent evidence not available at the trial from which issue estoppel is alleged to arise. In my view, unless it can be said that the subsequent prosecution is an attempt by the Crown to re-try the accused — and that is not the case here — the preferable policy is to exclude issue estoppel, especially when the contradictory statements on which the charge under s. 124 [now 136] is founded consist of admissions of the accused himself.

As to the robbery conviction, Laskin C.J.C. said that the accused's plea of guilty on this charge did not necessarily exclude issue estoppel. The accused argued that the evidence at the murder trial showed that the robber and the murderer were the same person. Hence, the acquittal of murder imported a finding that the accused had not committed the robbery. Thus, the Crown was estopped from alleging that he had. Laskin C.J.C. noted that the trial judge at the murder trial had misdirected the jury as to what the Crown needed to prove. He left open whether a misdirection precludes the invocation of issue estoppel, although he quoted a statement of Dixon C.J. in the High Court of Australia to the effect that it does not.[297] Laskin C.J.C. quoted with approval from Friedland on *Double Jeopardy*, to the effect that an issue estoppel arises out of a jury finding only when a certain finding on the relevant issue is "the only rational explanation of the verdict." He said that, because of the way the matter was left to the jury, the murder acquittal did not necessarily import a finding that the accused had not committed robbery. In other words, such a finding was not the only rational explanation for the verdict of not guilty. In the result, issue estoppel was held to be inapplicable in respect of both charges.

This will generally constitute the greatest barrier to the raising of an issue estoppel in criminal law, since the verdict is so often "blank", especially in a jury trial.[298] Often, there is more than one rational

---

296 *Ibid.*, at 805-806 (S.C.R.).
297 *Mraz v. R. (No. 2)* (1956), 96 C.L.R. 62 (H.C. Aust.).
298 See *Feeley v. R.*, [1963] S.C.R. 539, [1963] 3 C.C.C. 201, 40 C.R. 261, 40 D.L.R. (2d) 563; *R. v. Owens*, [1970] 2 C.C.C. 38 (B.C.C.A.); leave to appeal to

explanation for the verdict, and so no individual issue is unequivocally decided. But sometimes an issue estoppel can arise even from a jury verdict.[299] This problem was discussed in *R. v. Greeno*.[300] The accused was acquitted by a judge on a charge of driving with blood alcohol over 0.08 per cent. The judge's reasons made it quite clear that he had a reasonable doubt as to the element of care and control. Subsequently, the accused was convicted by another judge of having care and control of a vehicle while impaired. The Court of Appeal held that the Crown should have been estopped from asserting that the accused had care and control of the vehicle. The accused's appeal was allowed.

The availability of issue estoppel in respect of perjury was clarified in *Grdic v. R.*[301] The accused was acquitted of impaired driving, having given alibi evidence. He was subsequently charged with having perjured himself at the first trial. Lamer J., as he then was, wrote for the majority and said that the only avenue of acquittal at the first trial had been based on identity. Since the accused was acquitted, the only rational explanation for that verdict was a finding that the accused had not been driving the car in question. Lamer J. said[302] that "[f]raud may be set up against an accused so as to deny him the benefit of issue estoppel"; but, the Crown must present new evidence, since otherwise the new case is but an attempt to relitigate the matter. Moreover, to be fair to the accused, the new evidence must have been unavailable to the Crown at the first trial by the exercise of reasonable diligence.

S.C.C. refd. [1971] S.C.R. x.

299 See *R. v. Carlson*, [1970] 5 C.C.C. 147, [1970] 3 O.R. 213 (Ont. H.C.J.); *R. v. Quinn* (1905), 11 O.L.R. 242, 10 C.C.C. 412 (C.A.). In *R. v. Sweetman*, [1939] O.R. 131, [1931] 2 D.L.R. 70, 71 C.C.C. 171 (C.A.), the court said that if the Crown presented "substantially the same evidence" at the second trial, an acquittal should be directed. *Quaere* whether this gives effect to the rule against splitting a case; compare *Gill v. R.*, [1962] Que. Q.B. 368, 38 C.R. 122 (C.A.), where the Crown was estopped even though it wanted to lead further evidence at the second trial. In all of these cases, the first trial was by jury. See also *R. v. Dooley* (1978), 43 C.C.C. (2d) 288, [1978] 6 W.W.R. 79 (Sask. C.A.) (judge alone).

300 (1983), 6 C.C.C. (3d) 325, 58 N.S.R. (2d) 261 (C.A.). Macdonald J.A., for the court, stated that *R. v. Riddle*, [1980] 1 S.C.R. 380, 48 C.C.C. (2d) 365, 100 D.L.R. (3d) 577, [1980] 1 W.W.R. 592, 29 N.R. 91, made issue estoppel applicable to summary conviction matters.

301 [1985] 1 S.C.R. 810, 19 C.C.C. (3d) 289, 46 C.R. (3d) 1, 19 D.L.R. (4th) 385, [1985] 4 W.W.R. 437, 59 N.R. 61; applied in *R. v. Skanes* (1988), 44 C.C.C. (3d) 273, 71 Nfld. & P.E.I.R. 248 (C.A.).

302 *Ibid.*, at 827 (S.C.R.).

Here there was new evidence presented, but it was available at the first trial and so the accused's invocation of issue estoppel succeeded. Wilson J. wrote for the dissenting four judges. She said that a finding that the accused was not driving the car was not necessarily inherent in the original verdict, and so issue estoppel was unavailable. She said that the invocation of issue estoppel requires affirmative findings of fact at the first trial, and could not depend on inferences. She agreed that fraud precluded the raising of issue estoppel, and that new evidence must be presented in such a case, but she said that the Crown could introduce evidence that was available at the first trial, which might have been of marginal relevance to the issues at that trial. Both judgments in *Grdic* implicitly held that whether an issue estoppel has arisen, and on which issues the Crown is estopped, are questions for the trial judge and not the jury.[303]

In *Duhamel v. R.*,[304] the accused was charged on two counts of robbery and each charge was tried separately. At the first trial, certain statements of the accused were declared inadmissible following a *voir dire* and the accused was acquitted. The issue was whether the Crown was estopped from relitigating the admissibility of the statements at the second trial. It was held that since there is no autonomous appeal from the findings of a *voir dire*, no issue estoppel can arise from one.[305] Lamer J., as he then was, for the Court, noted that mutuality does not form part of the criminal law of issue estoppel, because in each case the Crown must prove all of the elements of the offence charged. In other words, the previous decision can operate as an estoppel against the Crown, but it can never operate against the accused to alleviate the burden on the Crown of proving every element in each trial.[306]

R. v. Van Rassel[307] left open whether a foreign proceeding can found an issue estoppel in a Canadian trial. As with the special pleas,

---

303 See Hon. R. E. Salhany, *Canadian Criminal Procedure*, 5th ed. (Aurora: Canada Law Book, 1988), at 232-33.
304 [1984] 2 S.C.R. 555, 15 C.C.C. (3d) 491, 43 C.R. (3d) 1, [1985] 2 W.W.R. 251, 35 Alta. L.R. (2d) 1, 57 A.R. 204, 57 N.R. 162, 14 D.L.R. (4th) 92; applied in *R. v. Van Den Meerssche* (1989), 53 C.C.C. (3d) 449, 74 C.R. (3d) 161 (B.C.C.A.).
305 Compare *Desaulniers v. Payette* (1904), 35 S.C.R. 1. Taschereau C.J.C. said (at 4): "As we have often said, an interlocutory judgment that cannot be appealed from is *res judicata*." But he was referring to the preclusive effect that such a judgment has on relitigation within the same proceedings.
306 See *ibid.*, at 23-26 for a discussion of mutuality in the civil law context.
307 [1990] 1 S.C.R. 225.

one problem in such a case is that the current "plaintiff" or Crown is not the party against whom an adverse finding was made in the earlier proceeding.[308] Similarly, it has been said that an accused cannot found an issue estoppel on matters established at another's trial.[309]

There is no special plea to raise an issue estoppel; the accused must plead not guilty.[310]

3. Kienapple v. R.[311]

(a) *General Principle*

In essence, this case states that a person should not be convicted of more than one offence arising out of the same matter. Laskin J., writing for the majority, stated[312] that "the term *res judicata* best expresses the theory of precluding multiple convictions for the same delict, although the matter is the basis of two separate offences." Later, he said:[313]

> The relevant inquiry so far as *res judicata* is concerned is whether the same cause or matter (rather than the same offence) is comprehended by two or more offences. Moreover, it cannot be the case that if an accused is tried on several counts charging different offences, he is liable to be convicted and sentenced on each count, and yet if he was tried and convicted on one only he would be entitled to set up the defence of *res judicata* as a defence to other charges arising out of the same cause or matter.
>
> . . .
>
> If there is a verdict of guilty on the first count and the same or substantially the same elements make up the offence charged in the second count, the situation invites application of a rule against multiple convictions. . . .

---

308 See Friedland, *supra*, note 288, at 366, for the view that *res judicata* nonetheless applies.

309 *R. v. Speid* (1985), 20 C.C.C. (3d) 534, 46 C.R. (3d) 22, 9 O.A.C. 237 (Ont. C.A.), at 556.

310 Section 613. See *R. v. Fitzpatrick* (1975), 28 C.C.C. (2d) 483 (Ont. Prov. Ct.), and *R. v. Sweetman* (1939), 71 C.C.C. 171, [1939] O.R. 131, [1939] 2 D.L.R. 70 (C.A.).

311 [1975] 1 S.C.R. 729, 15 C.C.C. (2d) 524, 26 C.R.N.S. 1, 44 D.L.R. (3d) 351, 1 N.R. 322.

312 *Ibid.*, at 748 (S.C.R.).

313 *Ibid.*, at 750-51 (S.C.R.).

In *McGuigan v. R.*,[314] Parliament was held to have departed from the *Kienapple* rule by the enactment of provisions which clearly envisaged multiple convictions arising out of the same matter. The offences were attempted robbery while armed with an offensive weapon and use of a firearm while attempting to commit a robbery. In *R. v. Krug*,[315] similar offences were said to be outside the *Kienapple* rule because the elements of the offences were different. *Kienapple* was, however, held to apply to preclude a conviction for pointing a firearm, given a conviction for using a firearm while attempting to commit an indictable offence. Moreover, the Court approved the decision of the trial judge that the same conviction precluded a conviction for the unlawful possession of a weapon.[316]

(b) *Sufficient Proximity between Facts and Charges*

In *R. v. Prince*,[317] the Supreme Court of Canada refined and narrowed *Kienapple*. Dickson C.J.C., for the Court, held that the rule against multiple convictions applies when there is sufficient proximity

---

314 [1982] 1 S.C.R. 284, 66 C.C.C. (2d) 97, 26 C.R. (3d) 289, 134 D.L.R. (3d) 625, 40 N.R. 499.

315 [1985] 2 S.C.R. 255, 21 C.C.C. (3d) 193, 48 C.R. (3d) 97, 62 N.R. 263, 21 D.L.R. (4th) 161, 11 O.A.C. 187. *Krug* is discussed in more detail in this Chapter, III.C.4. See *R. v. Switzer* (1987), 32 C.C.C. (3d) 303, 56 C.R. (3d) 107, 75 A.R. 167 (Alta. C.A.), where the same result was reached.

316 *Krug, ibid.*, at 263 (S.C.R.).

317 [1986] 2 S.C.R. 480, 30 C.C.C. (3d) 35, 54 C.R. (3d) 97, 33 D.L.R. (4th) 724, [1987] 1 W.W.R. 1, 45 Man. R. (2d) 93. Before *Prince*, the *Kienapple* rule was held to be inapplicable in *Sheppe v. R.*, [1980] 2 S.C.R. 22, 51 C.C.C. (2d) 481, 15 C.R. (3d) 381, [1980] 5 W.W.R. 598 (where the offences were trafficking and conspiracy to traffic) and in *R. v. McKinney* (1979), 46 C.C.C. (2d) 566, 98 D.L.R. (3d) 369, [1979] 2 W.W.R. 545, 2 Man. R. (2d) 403 (Man. C.A.); affd. [1980] 1 S.C.R. 401, 50 C.C.C. (2d) 576, 106 D.L.R. (3d) 494*n*, [1981] 1 W.W.R. 448, 31 N.R. 564 (where the offences were hunting out of season and hunting at night with lights). In *Doré v. Canada (A.G.)*, [1975] 1 S.C.R. 756, 15 C.C.C. (2d) 542, 27 C.R.N.S. 237, 44 D.L.R. (3d) 370; application for rehearing granted at 15 C.C.C. (2d) 542*n*, [1975] 1 S.C.R. 756, at 760 and *Doré v. Canada (A.G.) (No. 2)*, [1975] 1 S.C.R. 756, at 784, 17 C.C.C. (2d) 359, 27 C.R.N.S. 237, at 258, and the *Kienapple* rule prevented convictions for accepting bribes from standing with convictions for criminal breach of trust. The result might be different after *Prince*. In *Hagenlocher v. R.* (1981), 65 C.C.C. (2d) 101, [1982] 1 W.W.R. 410; affd. [1982] 2 S.C.R. 531, 70 C.C.C. (2d) 41, [1982] 6 W.W.R. 480, 18 Man. R. (2d) 361, the offences were arson and manslaughter, and *Kienapple* was held to be applicable; this result clearly could not survive *Prince*.

between the facts grounding the charges, and between the charges laid. The factual nexus is usually found if the same act of the accused grounds both charges. Subject to a clearly expressed legislative intention to the contrary, the sufficient nexus between the offences can be found if there is no additional and distinguishing element that goes to guilt contained in the offence for which a conviction is sought to be precluded by the rule against multiple convictions. Where the offences are of unequal gravity, the rule may bar a conviction on the less grave charge, notwithstanding that there are additional elements in the graver charge, if there are no additional elements in the lesser offence. Elements are not distinct (subject to a contrary legislative intention) where an element in one offence is a particularization of an element in another offence;[318] nor where they are simply alternative ways to prove the same delict;[319] nor where one is really the deemed proof of the other.[320]

In *Prince*, the accused stabbed a pregnant woman. The child was born alive but then died, allegedly due to the stabbing. The accused was charged with the attempted murder of the mother, and later with manslaughter in respect of the child. On the first charge, she was convicted of causing bodily harm; then, she was committed to stand trial on the other charge. She moved for a stay of proceedings based on *Kienapple*. Applying the tests above, Dickson C.J.C. said that the factual nexus was present, but not the legal one. An essential element of the first charge was harm to the mother. An essential element of the manslaughter charge was the death of the child. The offences had

---

318 An example was discussed in *R. v. Krug, supra*, note 314, at 268 (S.C.R.). "Pointing" a firearm is just a particularization of "using" it. See ss. 85(1)(a) and 86 of the *Criminal Code*, R.S.C. 1985, c. C-46.

319 An example is *R. v. Gushue* (1976), 32 C.C.C. (2d) 189, 35 C.R.N.S. 304, 74 D.L.R. (3d) 473, 14 O.R. (2d) 620 (Ont. C.A.), at 207; affd. on other grounds [1980] 1 S.C.R. 798, 50 C.C.C. (2d) 417, 16 C.R. (3d) 39, 106 D.L.R. (3d) 152, 30 N.R. 204. The giving of contradictory evidence (s. 136) is an offence which makes it easier to prove the delict of perjury (s. 131), because the s. 136 charge does not require that any statement be proved false.

320 An example of this would be the charges of impaired driving and driving with over 0.08 per cent blood alcohol: see *Terlecki v. R.*, [1985] 2 S.C.R. 483, 22 C.C.C. (3d) 224, 64 N.R. 233, 65 A.R. 401; affg. (1983), 4 C.C.C. (3d) 522 (Alta. C.A.). There is also *Kienapple* itself, in which the charges were rape and unlawful intercourse with a female under fourteen years. The tender years of the victim serve as a substitute for the element of non-consent. The rule was applied to these offences in *R. v. T. (F.M.)* (1988), 39 C.C.C. (3d) 491 (Alta. C.A.).

different victims and so could not be the same.

The legal nexus required by *Prince* was not satisfied in *R. v. Iuculano*,[321] where the offences were accepting bribes and conspiring to import narcotics. Nor was it satisfied in *Wigman v. R.*,[322] where the offences were attempted murder and "breaking and entering and committing robbery". Again, the test was not met in *R. v. Van Rassel*,[323] where the offences were violations of U.S. and Canadian anti-corruption laws. As in *Prince*, the offences had different victims. Similarly, there was no legal nexus in *R. v. Berryman*,[324] where the charges were forging a passport and making a written statement on a passport application known to be false. The factual nexus will of course be absent where, following a conviction and an order, the order is disobeyed and the same offence committed a second time; in such a case, there is not a single "delict".[325]

The *Kienapple* rule was applied in *R. v. Imperial Oil*[326] in which the Ontario Court of Appeal affirmed[327] the trial judge's decision that a single spill of gasoline could not ground convictions under both the *Environmental Protection Act*[328] and the *Ontario Water Resources Act*.[329] It was also applied in *R. v. B. (J.E.)*[330] where the offences were gross indecency and sexual assault, and in *R. v. T. (F.M.)*,[331] where the charges were sexual assault and having sexual intercourse with a female under fourteen years. In *R. v. Voutsis*,[332] the rule applied to prevent two convictions for trafficking two types of narcotics to the same person at the same time. In *R. v. Sullivan*,[333] *Kienapple* was applied, with no

---

321 [1988] 1 S.C.R. 667, 41 C.C.C. (3d) 288, 84 N.R. 234; revg. (1986), 29 C.C.C. (3d) 498, 53 C.R. (3d) 236, 3 Q.A.C. 152 (Que. C.A.).
322 [1987] 1 S.C.R. 246, 33 C.C.C. (3d) 97, 38 D.L.R. (4th) 530, [1987] 4 W.W.R. 1.
323 [1990] 1 S.C.R. 225.
324 (1990), 57 C.C.C. (3d) 375, 78 C.R. (3d) 376, 48 B.C.L.R. (2d) 105 (B.C.C.A.).
325 *Re United Nurses of Alberta v. Alberta (A.G.)* (1990), 54 C.C.C. (3d) 1, 66 D.L.R. (4th) 385, 73 Alta. L.R. (2d) 152, 90 CLLC 14,022; leave to appeal to S.C.C. granted November 15, 1990 (C.A.).
326 (1990), 59 C.C.C. (3d) 201, 75 O.R. (2d) 28, 40 O.A.C. 333 (Ont. C.A.).
327 *Ibid.*, at 211 (C.C.C.).
328 R.S.O. 1980, c. 141.
329 R.S.O. 1980, c. 361.
330 (1989), 52 C.C.C. (3d) 224, 94 N.S.R. (2d) 312 (C.A.).
331 *Supra*, note 320.
332 (1989), 47 C.C.C. (3d) 451, 73 Sask. R. 287 (Sask. C.A.).
333 (1987), 37 C.C.C. (3d) 143, 20 O.A.C. 323 (Ont. C.A.).

discussion of *Prince*, to quash a conviction for unlawful confinement where there was a conviction for sexual assault arising out of the same facts. But *Prince* was applied in *R. v. Harris*[334] and *Kienapple* was held inapplicable where the charges were making obscene video tapes, and possessing these tapes for the purpose of distribution.

(c) *Procedural Issues*

The correct procedure for trial judges was set out in *R. v. P. (D.W.)*[335] The *Kienapple* question does not arise until after the trier of fact has determined whether or not all of the elements of the offence have been proved. When culpability is found but a conviction is precluded by reason of another conviction and the application of the rule in *Kienapple*, a conditional stay should be entered rather than an acquittal. When the accused's appeal routes on the conviction are exhausted, the stay on the other charge becomes absolute. In accordance with *R. v. Jewitt*,[336] this absolute stay is tantamount to an acquittal for the purpose of the plea of *autrefois acquit*; but it is not a true acquittal, because all elements of the offence have been found against the accused. If the accused's appeal is successful, the Court of Appeal can remit to the trial judge the count or counts conditionally stayed, and the trial judge can enter a conviction pursuant to the findings made earlier. This preserves the accused's right to appeal a second time.

R. v. Loyer[337] had suggested that an acquittal should be entered on the other offence, and to this extent it is superseded by *R. v. P. (D.W.)*. *Loyer* also stipulated that if the accused is charged with two offences arising out of the same matter and pleads guilty to the less serious one, that plea should be held in abeyance pending the resolution of the more serious charge. This procedure can survive *R. v. P. (D.W.)*. The result is that if the accused is acquitted on the more serious charge, the guilty plea on the other is accepted, but if there is a conviction on the more serious charge, a stay on the lesser one is

---

334 (1987), 35 C.C.C. (3d) 1, 57 C.R. (3d) 356, 20 O.A.C. 26 (C.A.); leave to appeal to S.C.C. refd. 25 O.A.C. 240.
335 [1989] 2 S.C.R. 3, 49 C.C.C. (3d) 417, 70 C.R. (3d) 315, 97 N.R. 209 (*sub nom. R. v. Provo*), [1989] 5 W.W.R. 97, 59 Man. R. (2d) 1.
336 [1985] 2 S.C.R. 128, 21 C.C.C. (3d) 7, 47 C.R. (3d) 193, 20 D.L.R. (4th) 651, [1985] 6 W.W.R. 127, 61 N.R. 159.
337 [1978] 2 S.C.R. 631, 40 C.C.C. (2d) 291, 3 C.R. (3d) 105, 85 D.L.R. (3d) 101, 21 N.R. 181.

substituted for the guilty plea.

Although a Court of Appeal normally has no jurisdiction to disturb an acquittal when there has been no Crown appeal,[338] the situation is different if such an acquittal was granted only due to the rule in *Kienapple*. If that is the case, a Court of Appeal which allows an accused's appeal from conviction on the other charge has wider powers because even in the absence of a Crown appeal from an acquittal, the Court of Appeal may remit the matter to the trial judge, either for a new trial or to enter a conviction.[339] *A fortiori* the Court of Appeal may do the same where the trial judge has found all elements of the offence against the accused and entered a conditional stay following *R. v. P. (D.W.)*? In *R. v. Sullivan*,[340] the Supreme Court of Canada declined to widen this power of the Courts of Appeal. In the latter case, it was held that the powers of the Court of Appeal embodied in s. 686(8) of the *Criminal Code* can only apply to a count which is properly before the Court. A count which has not been appealed from the court below is not properly before the Court of Appeal when it does not fall within the exception relating to the *Kienapple* rule.

4. Section 11(d) of the Charter

(a) *General Principle*

11. Any person charged with an offence has the right

. . .

(h) if finally acquitted of the offence, not to be tried for it again and, if finally found guilty and punished for the offence, not to be tried or punished for it again. . . .

In *R. v. Krug*[341] this provision was raised in respect of the offences of using a firearm while attempting to commit an offence, and

---

338 *R. v. Rickard*, [1970] S.C.R. 1022, 12 C.R.N.S. 172, 1 C.C.C. (2d) 153, 13 D.L.R. (3d) 591, 12 Cr. L.Q. 437; *R. v. Guillemette*, [1986] 1 S.C.R. 356, 26 C.C.C. (3d) 1, 51 C.R. (3d) 273, 27 D.L.R. (4th) 682, 66 N.R. 19.

339 Pursuant to s. 686(8) of the *Criminal Code, Terlecki v. R.*, [1985] 2 S.C.R. 483, 22 C.C.C. (3d) 224, 64 N.R. 233, 65 A.R. 401; affg. (1983), 4 C.C.C. (3d) 522 (Alta. C.A.), and *R. v. P. (D.W.), supra*, note 335.

340 (1991), 63 C.C.C. (3d) 97, 3 C.R. (4th) 277, 55 B.C.L.R. (2d) 1, 122 N.R. 166.

341 [1985] 2 S.C.R. 255, 21 C.C.C. (3d) 193, 48 C.R. (3d) 97, 21 D.L.R. (4th) 161, 62 N.R. 263.

attempting to steal while armed. These were similar to the offences in *McGuigan v. R.*,[342] where the *Kienapple* principle was held to be inapplicable. The accused argued that *McGuigan* rested on a finding that *Kienapple* was inapplicable because the legislation evidenced an intention of Parliament to exclude it; but, ss. 7 and 11(h) of the *Charter* now made it impossible for Parliament to do so. La Forest J., for the Court, held that it was inherent in *McGuigan* that Parliament had achieved its intended purpose by creating offences with different elements. This difference itself makes *Kienapple* inapplicable. Accordingly, the *Kienapple* rule was not applicable in *Krug* either. This made consideration of s. 11(h) unnecessary, presumably because it had no application in view of the difference in the two offences.

(b) *"Charged with an Offence"*

It was held in *R. v. Schmidt*[343] that s. 11(h) does not apply to an extradition proceeding because it is not a proceeding in which a person is charged with an offence. Section 11 was also examined in *R. v. Wigglesworth*,[344] and guidance was provided on the words "charged with an offence". It was held that s. 11 applies only to proceedings which are criminal by nature, or which may lead to true penal consequences. "Criminal by nature" includes matters of a public nature, intended to promote public order and welfare.[345] This brings within the section all criminal offences and quasi-criminal offences under provincial legislation. Other matters are within the section if they involve "true penal consequences". This includes any term of imprisonment, and any fine imposed to redress a public wrong.[346] Still, s. 11(h) is not violated unless the two proceedings are for the same offence, and in this case they were not, even though the two offences were based on the same act of the accused.[347] One offence was an internal disciplinary matter, which required an accounting to the

---

342   [1982] 1 S.C.R. 284, 66 C.C.C. (2d) 97, 26 C.R. (3d) 289, 134 D.L.R. (3d) 625, 40 N.R. 499. See this Chapter, III.C.3.

343   [1987] 1 S.C.R. 500 (*sub nom. Canada v. Schmidt*), 33 C.C.C. (3d) 193, 58 C.R. (3d) 1, 39 D.L.R. (4th) 18, 61 O.R. (2d) 530*n*, 20 O.A.C. 161, 76 N.R. 12, 28 C.R.R. 280.

344   [1987] 2 S.C.R. 541, 37 C.C.C. (3d) 385, 60 C.R. (3d) 193, 45 D.L.R. (4th) 235, 24 O.A.C. 321, 61 Sask. R. 105, 28 Admin. L.R. 294, 32 C.R.R. 219.

345   *Ibid.*, at 560 (S.C.R.).

346   *Ibid.*, at 561 (S.C.R.).

347   Estey J. dissented on this point.

accused's profession. The other was a crime, requiring an accounting to society. Therefore, even though the accused had been punished for the former offence, s. 11(h) did not bar the criminal proceedings. A similar conclusion was reached in *R. v. Van Rassel*.[348] Section 11(h) did not bar proceedings for a criminal breach of trust in Canada following an acquittal in the United States under an anti-corruption provision. The Canadian provision required an accounting to the Canadian public, and so it was not the same as the United States offence.

In *R. v. Shubley*,[349] the majority held that s. 11(h) did not bar criminal proceedings following disciplinary proceedings against a prison inmate. Applying *Wigglesworth*, it was held that the disciplinary offence was not criminal in nature, nor did it involve the imposition of true penal consequences. Hence, it was not an "offence" within s. 11.

(c) *Same Offence*

It appears that the test for identity of offences under s. 11(h) is similar to that under the *Kienapple* rule. In *Wigglesworth*, Wilson J. quoted from *R. v. Prince*[350] when considering whether the new proceeding was for the same offence. In *Krug*, having concluded that the offences were not the same within *Kienapple*, La Forest J. said, for the Court:[351]

> In view of my conclusion on the question of multiple convictions, it becomes unnecessary to discuss s. 11(h) of the *Charter*.

It has been held that the section is inapplicable, for want of identity of offences, to the situation where a single act leads to conviction for a

---

348 [1990] 1 S.C.R. 225.
349 (1988), 39 C.C.C. (3d) 481, 63 O.R. (2d) 161, 25 O.A.C. 66 (C.A.); affd. [1990] 1 S.C.R. 3, 52 C.C.C. (3d) 481, 74 C.R. (3d) 1, 65 D.L.R. (4th) 193, 71 O.R. (2d) 63*n*, 37 O.A.C. 63, 104 N.R. 81, 42 Admin. L.R. 118.
350 [1986] 2 S.C.R. 480, 30 C.C.C. (3d) 35, 54 C.R. (3d) 97, 33 D.L.R. (4th) 724, [1987] 1 W.W.R. 1, 45 Man. R. (2d) 93.
351 [1985] 2 S.C.R. 255, 21 C.C.C. (3d) 193, 48 C.R. (3d) 97, 21 D.L.R. (4th) 161, at 268 (S.C.R.). For other cases touching on the requirement of identity of offences, see *D'Ettore v. R.* (1984), 11 W.C.B. 318 (Ont. H.C.J.) and *Dacey v. R.* (1983), 61 N.S.R. (2d) 255, 24 M.V.R. 74 (C.A.) (no identity); contrast *R. v. Caseley* (1989), 7 W.C.B. (2d) 351 (P.E.I. Prov. Ct.) (identity between different provisions of the *Income Tax Act*).

substantive criminal offence, and subsequently to conviction for breach of a pre-existing parole order.[352]

The section requires that the accused be "finally" acquitted or found guilty and punished. It does not apply where proceedings are stayed during the trial and a new information is laid with an additional charge.[353] Nor does it apply when the first proceedings are terminated for jurisdictional reasons.[354] It has been suggested that being discharged at a preliminary inquiry does not attract the protection of the section.[355]

(d) Final Acquittal or Conviction

The section can be invoked where the subject has been "found guilty and punished" to prevent the subject's being "tried or punished again". In *R. v. Art*,[356] the accused was stopped while driving and given a 24-hour driving suspension. Later he was charged with impaired driving. It was held that the criminal proceedings were not barred, as he had never before been "charged with an offence". Nor, indeed, had he been found guilty or punished. It has been said that some dispositions following a result adverse to the subject may not amount to "punishment" as required by the section. This may include certain results which flow from being adjudged a juvenile delinquent;[357] the

---

352 *R. v. Daniels* (1985), 38 Sask. R. 68, 44 C.R. (3d) 184, 15 C.R.R. 85 (Q.B.); *R. v. Savary* (unreported, 27 May 1985, Alta. Prov. Ct., Marshall P.C.J.). Contrast *R. v. Cardinal* (1982), 40 A.R. 342 (Q.B.), where the section was held applicable in such a situation and the accused was given an absolute discharge. But if the section applied, the accused had the right "not to be tried or punished". On this, see *R. v. Genaille* (1983), 22 Man. R. (2d) 186, 6 C.C.C. (3d) 440, 1 D.L.R. (4th) 207 (Q.B.).
353 *Burrows v. R.* (1983), 6 C.C.C. (3d) 54, 150 D.L.R. (3d) 317, 22 Man. R. (2d) 241 (C.A.); leave to appeal to S.C.C. refd. (1983), 6 C.C.C. (3d) 54n, 150 D.L.R. (3d) 317n, 22 Man. R. (2d) 240, 51 N.R. 386n.
354 *R. v. Timmons* (1985), 69 N.S.R. (2d) 133 (T.D.).
355 *Re Lamberti* (1983), 26 Sask. R. 213 (Q.B.).
356 (1987), 39 C.C.C. (3d) 563, 61 C.R. (3d) 204, 7 M.V.R. (2d) 132 (B.C.C.A.).
357 *R. v. R. (T.)* (1983), 28 Alta. L.R. (2d) 383 (Q.B.); *R. v. R. (T.) (No. 2)* (1984), 11 C.C.C. (3d) 49, 7 D.L.R. (4th) 263, 30 Alta. L.R. (2d) 241, 51 A.R. 63 (Q.B.). See also *R. v. M.(D.)* (1982), 2 C.C.C. (3d) 296, (*sub nom. R. v. M.*) 30 C.R. (3d) 210 (Ont. Fam. Ct.) approved in *R. v. W.* (1983), 41 O.R. (2d) 576, 4 C.C.C. (3d) 575, 34 C.C.C. (3d) 575n, 147 D.L.R. (3d) 575 (H.C.), and *R. v. C. (D.A.)* (1982), 9 W.C.B. 201 (Man. Prov. Ct.); affd. (1983), 6 C.C.C. (3d) 246, 150 D.L.R. (3d) 151, 22 Man. R. (2d) 92 (Q.B.).

loss of driving privileges following a conviction for impaired driving;[358] deportation;[359] the denial of citizenship;[360] and certain other administrative orders.[361] Similarly, s. 738(4) of the *Criminal Code*[362] provides that where a convicted person receives a suspended sentence and is put on probation, and then commits another offence, a sentence may be imposed in respect of the initial offence. It has been held that the initial suspended sentence and probation order are not "punishment" within s. 11(h), at least where the probation order was made to rehabilitate.[363] Statutory provisions which allow past convictions to be relevant in sentencing decisions apparently do not violate s. 11(h).[364]

---

358 *Johnston v. British Columbia (Superintendent of Motor Vehicles)* (1987), 46 M.V.R. 59, 27 C.R.R. 206 (B.C.S.C.); *Perry v. P.E.I.* (1987), 70 Nfld. & P.E.I.R. 32, 7 M.V.R. (2d) 16 (P.E.I.S.C.); *Workman v. R.* (1987), 37 C.C.C. (3d) 187 (*sub nom. Breshears v. R.*) (Y.T.S.C.); *R. v. Vanderlinden* (1987), 3 W.C.B. (2d) 160 (Ont. Prov. Ct.).
359 *Hurd v. Canada (Minister of Employment & Immigration)*, [1989] 2 F.C. 594, 90 N.R. 31 (*sub nom. Hurd v. Minister of Employment & Immigration*) (C.A.).
360 *Re Noailles*, [1985] 1 F.C. 852 (T.D.).
361 *Eagle Disposal Systems Ltd. v. Ontario (Minister of the Environment)* (1983), 9 C.C.C. (3d) 500, 44 O.R. (2d) 518, 5 D.L.R. (4th) 70, 13 C.E.L.R. 13 (H.C.J.); affd. (1984), 13 C.C.C. (3d) 351, 47 O.R. (2d) 332, 12 D.L.R. (4th) 639 (C.A.) (clean-up order under the *Environmental Protection Act*, R.S.O. 1980, c. 141); *R. v. Yes Holdings Ltd.* (1987), 40 C.C.C. (3d) 30, 83 A.R. 81, 48 D.L.R. (4th) 642, 52 Alta. L.R. (2d) 227 (C.A.); leave to appeal to S.C.C. refd. [1988] 1 S.C.R. xv, 58 Alta. L.R. (2d) xlivn, *R. v. Georges Contracting Ltd.* (1987), 15 B.C.L.R. (2d) 240, 36 C.C.C. (3d) 411, 30 C.R.R. 69 (S.C.) and *R. v. Ferraro* (1983), 10 W.C.B. 204 (Ont. Prov. Ct.) (penalty assessed for unpaid taxes); *Hardy v. Man. Public Insurance Corp.* (1984), 29 Man. R. (2d) 279, 28 M.V.R. 101 (Co. Ct.) (increased insurance premiums following conviction on a driving offence).
362 R.S.C. 1985, c. C-46.
363 *R. v. Linklater* (1983), 9 C.C.C. (3d) 217, 7 C.R.R. 299 (Y.T.C.A.). Taggart J.A., with whom Seaton J.A. concurred, said that the situation might be different if the original probation order was of a punitive character. He also said that if he were wrong, then for the rehabilitative type of order in issue, s. 1 of the *Charter* could cure any violation of s. 11(h). Hutcheon J.A. agreed as to s. 1.
364 *R. v. Bourne* (1983), 21 M.V.R. 216 (B.C.S.C.); *R. v. Latham* (1987), 47 Man. R. (2d) 81 (Q.B.). *A fortiori*, a provision which regulates sentencing based only on the facts of the offence in issue is consistent with s. 11(h): *R. v. Parlee* (1988), 92 N.B.R. (2d) 390 (Q.B.); *R. v. Sewid* (1986), 1 W.C.B. (2d) 319 (B.C. Co. Ct.) (but contrast *R. v. Youngman* (1987), 22 B.C.L.R. (2d) 14, [1988] 3 C.N.L.R. 135 (Co. Ct.); *R. v. Green* (1983), 41 O.R. (2d) 557, 5 C.C.C. (3d) 95, 148 D.L.R. (3d) 767, 9 C.R.R. 78 (H.C.J.); *R. v. Porter* (1989), 26 F.T.R. 69, 48 C.C.C. (3d) 252, 40

(e) *Precludes Appeals by Way of Trial de Novo*

Section 11(h) does not preclude a Crown right of appeal on a question of law.[365] But in *Corporation professionnelle des médecins (Qué.) v. Thibault*,[366] it was held that the provision does preclude a prosecutorial appeal as of right by way of a trial *de novo*. Lamer J., for the Court, said:[367]

> The proceeding in the case at bar is not a true appeal, but actually a new trial disguised as an appeal. As I mentioned, an appeal by trial *de novo* can raise questions of fact as well as questions of law; the appeal is as of right, and the prosecutor does not have to allege errors committed by the justice of the peace. There can thus be a second trial even if the trial judgment was rendered in accordance with all the rules of law. In fact, it is just as if once the accused was acquitted the prosecutor filed a new information alleging the same offence based on the same facts. This is precisely the type of abuse that s. 11(h) seeks to prevent. Section 11(h) guarantees the accused the right to plead *autrefois acquit* if the prosecution attempts to have him tried again for an offence of which he has been acquitted.

5. Conclusion

The criminal manifestations of *res judicata* can be seen to be broadly similar to the civil law rules. *Autrefois acquit* and issue estoppel preclude the Crown from contradicting a previous judgment. *Autrefois convict* precludes the Crown from splitting its case, by making allegations against the accused upon which it has previously relied in obtaining a conviction.

The *Kienapple* rule has the effect of preventing the Crown from obtaining multiple convictions by bringing charges simultaneously, where one of the special pleas would be available if the charges were

---

C.R.R. 263. Again, the use of a past conviction as evidence in a proceeding for citizenship is permissible as there is no new trial or punishment for the past offence: *Canada (Secretary of State) v. Delezos* (1988), 22 F.T.R. 135, 6 Imm. L.R. (2d) 12 (F.C.T.D.).
365 *R. v. Morgentaler*, [1988] 1 S.C.R. 30, 37 C.C.C. (3d) 449, 62 C.R. (3d) 1, 44 D.L.R. (4th) 385, 63 O.R. (2d) 281*n*, 82 N.R. 1, 26 O.A.C. 1, 31 C.R.R. 1.
366 [1988] 1 S.C.R. 1033, 42 C.C.C. (3d) 1, 84 N.R. 247, 14 Q.A.C. 173.
367 *Ibid.*, at 1044-45.

brought successively. It will be recalled that in *Kienapple*,[368] Laskin C.J.C. said:

> . . . it cannot be the case that if an accused is tried on several counts charging different offences, he is liable to be convicted and sentenced on each count, and yet if he was tried and convicted on one only he would be entitled to set up the defence of *res judicata* as a defence to other charges arising out of the same cause or matter.

But it must be noted that a successful invocation by the accused of *Kienapple* leads only to a stay, while a successful invocation of one of the special pleas leads to an acquittal. Where a special plea succeeds, the accused was previously either acquitted of the charge, in which case the Crown is estopped from contradicting the previous judgment; or, the accused was convicted, in which case the accused is entitled to an acquittal because the Crown is not allowed to split its case and litigate by instalments. If the Crown brings the charges in the same proceeding, neither of these complaints can be made, but for policy reasons, only one conviction will be entered, and proceedings for the other charge will be stayed.

It is clear that the *Kienapple* principle has been narrowed since it was first pronounced. In *Kienapple*,[369] Laskin C.J.C. said:

> The relevant inquiry so far as *res judicata* is concerned is whether the same cause or matter (rather than the same offence) is comprehended by two or more offences.

This led to cases such as *R. v. Hagenlocher*,[370] where *Kienapple* was held to be applicable to the offences of arson and manslaughter. But this result cannot stand with subsequent developments, particularly *R. v. Prince*.[371] As explained above,[372] that case requires that the offences be substantially identical.

The current formulation of the *Kienapple* rule, and the require-

---

368 [1975] 1 S.C.R. 729, 15 C.C.C. (2d) 524, 26 C.R.N.S. 1, 44 D.L.R. (3d) 351, at 750 (S.C.R.).
369 *Ibid.*
370 (1981), 65 C.C.C. (2d) 101, [1982] 1 W.W.R. 410; affd. [1982] 2 S.C.R. 531, 70 C.C.C. (2d) 41, [1982] 6 W.W.R. 480, 18 Man. R. (2d) 361.
371 [1986] 2 S.C.R. 480, 30 C.C.C. (3d) 35, 54 C.R. (3d) 97, 33 D.L.R. (4th) 724, [1987] 1 W.W.R. 1, 45 Man. R. (2d) 93.
372 See this Chapter, III.C.3.(b).

ment of identity of offences for the special pleas, can be seen to be consistent with the view taken above[373] in relation to civil *res judicata*. That is, *res judicata* does not apply where a new legal theory is presented, even if the underlying facts are the same.

The role of s. 11(h) of the *Charter* is to guarantee the continued existence of the special pleas in the criminal law. While criminal issue estoppel and the *Kienapple* rule could, perhaps, be amended or eliminated by Parliament, the continued existence of the special pleas is guaranteed by virtue of s. 11(h).

D. *Evidentiary Effect of Prior Judicial Determinations*

1. General

A prior judicial decision will have conclusive effect in cases where the party to the proceedings makes out a case of *res judicata* or issue estoppel. However, as the above discussion shows, the application of these principles is limited by various factors, most important of which is that the issue must have arisen as between the parties and their privies.[374] In addition to these principles, a judicial decision is conclusive against the world with respect to the matters which it actually effects.[375] Therefore, if the issue is whether the defendant has ever been convicted of a criminal offence, evidence of the conviction by a court will be relevant and admissible. In a defamation action for example where the defamatory words impute the commission of a crime to the plaintiff, the fact of the plaintiff's previous conviction for that crime may be conclusive proof on the issue of justification (perhaps even if the words suggest commission and not just conviction).[376]

However, the determination of the facts upon which a conviction or other judgment is rendered is not conclusive as against all the

---

373 See this Chapter, III.B.3.

374 *La Foncière Cie d'assurance v. Perras*, [1943] S.C.R. 165, [1943] 2 D.L.R. 129, 10 I.L.R. 45 illustrates the requirement in criminal cases. However, see this Chapter, III.B.3.(e)(iv) for a discussion about the relaxing of the requirement of mutuality.

375 The plea of guilty in a previous criminal proceeding is admissible as an admission of a party: see *Re Charlton*, [1969] 1 O.R. 706, 3 D.L.R. (3d) 623 (C.A.).

376 *Jorgensen v. News Media (Auckland) Ltd.*, [1969] N.Z.L.R. 961 (C.A.).

world.[377] The issue explored in this section is whether it has any evidentiary effect in a proceeding between parties where they or their privies were not both parties to the previous proceeding in which the judgment was given. So, for example, is evidence of the previous conviction for careless driving admissible as evidence of negligence against the defendant in a civil negligence suit brought by the victim? The answer to this question in Canada involves a review of both common law and statutory principles.

The leading English common law case, applying to the admissibility of prior judicial determinations in both civil and criminal cases, is *Hollington v. Hewthorn & Co. Ltd.*[378] The English Court of Appeal held that proof of a previous conviction was not admissible in a civil case as evidence of the underlying facts upon which the judgment was based. Goddard L.J. advanced a number of reasons for the rule:[379] (1) a conviction is the inadmissible opinion evidence of the criminal court,[380] (2) a conviction is hearsay since it would be the equivalent of a statement of negligence by a person who is not a witness,[381] (3) a conviction lacks evidentiary value on the underlying issues,[382] (4) a conviction is between other parties and therefore it would be unfair to use it against a party in another proceeding,[383] (5) the civil court would have to review the evidence before the criminal court in order to weigh the conviction,[384] and (6) the acceptance of the conviction would mean that an acquittal could be admitted in defence.[385] *Cross on Evidence*[386] describes the points with respect to the hearsay rule and the opinion rule as "indefensible technicalities".

---

377 R. Cross and C. Tapper, *Cross on Evidence*, 7th ed. (London: Butterworths, 1990), at 100.
378 [1943] K.B. 587, [1943] 2 All E.R. 35 (C.A.).
379 See *Report of the Federal/Provincial Task Force on Uniform Rules of Evidence* (Toronto: Carswell, 1982), at 212.
380 *Ibid.*, at 595 (K.B.).
381 *Ibid.*
382 *Ibid.*, at 594-95 (K.B.).
383 *Ibid.*, at 596 (K.B.). This is referred to as the *res inter alios acta* principle.
384 *Ibid.*
385 *Ibid.*, at 601 (K.B.).
386 *Supra*, note 377, at 101.

2. Application of the Rule in Canada

(a) *In Civil Cases*

(i) Previous Criminal Convictions: Common Law

The injustice of the rule in *Hollington v. Hewthorn & Co. Ltd.*,[387] particularly to the extent to which it allows a convicted criminal from benefitting from his or her wrongdoing by denying the act in a subsequent criminal proceeding, has been noted by many law reform bodies, judges and academics.[388] It is unclear, however, whether the rule ever formed part of the common law in Canada.[389] In *Demeter v. Pacific Life Insurance Co.*[390] it was held by both the trial judge and the Ontario Court of Appeal that the rule in *Hollington v. Hewthorn* was never part of the law of Ontario. *Demeter* decided that a criminal conviction is admissible as *prima facie* proof that the party against whom the conviction was rendered committed the offence. That party can rebut this finding, but only so long as it would not be an abuse of process for it to do so.[391]

The conviction is not, however, admissible as *prima facie* proof of every factual finding made in the previous criminal proceeding, only those necessary for the court's determination of the charge.[392]

---

387 *Supra*, note 378.

388 See the Task Force Report, *supra*, note 379 and studies cited at 213, note 8; 15th Report of the Law Reform Committee (London: H.M.S.O., 1967), Cmnd. 3391, para. 3. The rule was overruled in England so far as it governs proof of convictions and findings of adultery and paternity in civil proceedings by the *Civil Evidence Act, 1968*, c. 60, ss. 11 and 13 and so far as it governs proof of convictions in criminal proceedings by the *Police and Criminal Evidence Act 1984*, c. 60, s. 74. See also C.A. Wright, "Case and comment" (1943), 21 Can. Bar Rev. 653, at 658, a case comment on *Hollington v. Hewthorn*.

389 See the review of the case law by Osler J. in *Demeter v. British Pacific Life Insurance Co.* (1983), 43 O.R. (2d) 33, 150 D.L.R. (3d) 249, 2 C.C.L.I. 246, 37 C.P.C. 277, [1983] I.L.R. 1-1689 (H.C.J.); affd. 48 O.R. (2d) 266, 13 D.L.R. (4th) 318, 8 C.C.L.I. 286, [1985] I.L.R. 1-1862 (C.A.).

390 *Ibid.*

391 Abuse of process is considered in this Chapter, III.B.3.(e)(iv). In fact, subsequent cases seem to ignore *Hollington v. Hewthorn* and skip right to the issue of abuse of process: see for example, *Van Rooy v. M.N.R.*, 88 D.T.C. 6323, [1989] 1 F.C. 489, 87 N.R. 13 (F.C.A.).

392 *Taylor v. Baribeau* (1985), 51 O.R. (2d) 541, 21 D.L.R. (4th) 140, 35 M.V.R. 79, 12 O.A.C. 344, 4 C.P.C. (2d) 52 (Ont. Div. Ct.). Although, to relitigate a particular factual issue may be an abuse of process.

The criminal conviction must, of course, be relevant to the civil proceedings, but the lack of an exact identity of issues between the criminal and civil proceedings goes to weight only, a matter for the trier of fact.[393] Any factor mitigating the effect of or explaining the conviction will be relevant. If the party defended the criminal proceeding on the merits and took every avenue of appeal these will be factors giving the conviction greater weight. Where the prejudicial effect of the previous conviction outweighs its probative force, the judge may exercise his or her discretion to exclude it.[394] This principle applies to convictions under federal, provincial or municipal legislation.[395] The conviction is admissible not only as evidence against the party convicted, but also against any other party to the proceeding,[396] whether or not the person convicted is a party in the subsequent proceedings.

(ii) Previous Criminal Convictions: Statutory Reform

Alberta and British Columbia have ensured that the rule in *Hollington v. Hewthorn & Co. Ltd.*[397] does not form a part of their law by enacting provisions in their Evidence Acts permitting the introduction into evidence of previous convictions.[398] These statutes specifically provide that where a person has been convicted or found guilty of an offence anywhere in Canada and the commission of that offence is relevant to an issue in an action, then, whether or not that person is a party to the action, proof of the conviction or the finding of guilt is admissible in evidence for the purpose of proving that the person

---

393   *Demeter v. Pacific Life Insurance Co., supra,* note 387; *Del Core v. College of Pharmacists (Ontario)* (1985), 51 O.R. (2d) 1, 19 D.L.R. (4th) 68, 10 O.A.C. 57, 15 Admin. L.R. 227 (Ont. C.A.) per Houlden J.A., at 247, and Blair J.A., at 251; *Jorgensen v. News Media (Auckland) Ltd.,* [1969] N.Z.L.R. 961 (C.A.); *Q. v. Minto Management Ltd.* (1984), 46 O.R. (2d) 756, 44 C.P.C. 6 (H.C.J.); leave to appeal to S.C.C. refd. (1984), 44 C.P.C. 13 (Ont. H.C.J.).

394   See for example, *Catty v. James* (1985), 10 C.P.C. (2d) 313 (Ont. Dist. Ct.), where the judge excluded the previous conviction for speeding on this basis. See also, Chapter 2, II.C. for a general discussion of the judge's discretion to exclude relevant evidence.

395   *Catty, ibid.* — provincial offence of careless driving.

396   *Q. v. Minto Management Ltd., supra,* note 393.

397   *Supra,* note 378.

398   *Alberta Evidence Act,* R.S.A. 1980, c. A-21, s. 27; British Columbia *Evidence Act,* R.S.B.C. 1979, c. 116, ss. 80, 81 [am. 1983, c. 10, Sched. 2].

committed the offence.[399] The contents of the information, complaint or indictment relating to the offence are also admissible.[400] Both statutes provide that the weight to be given to the conviction or finding of guilt is to be determined by the trier of fact.[401]

These statutes also put the question of the effect of a criminal conviction in a defamation action beyond question.[402] They provide that when proof of the conviction or finding of guilt is tendered in evidence in an action for defamation, the conviction of that person or the finding of guilt against that person is *conclusive* proof that he or she committed the offence.[403] The Task Force described the reason for such a rule as follows:[404]

> The reason for admitting a previous conviction as conclusive evidence and estopping the opposing party from attacking its weight, is to prevent a convicted person from recovering damages for libel from a newspaper because it described him as "guilty" of a crime (instead of "convicted") and cannot make proof of his guilt in the defamation action to establish the defense of justification.

In Saskatchewan a special statutory rule allows the introduction of evidence of certain criminal offences in matrimonial proceedings.[405] In an action for dissolution of marriage, alimony or judicial separation proof of a conviction for any offence against the *Criminal Code* for which proof of sexual intercourse is required is admissible as *prima facie* proof of adultery.[406]

---

399 Alberta, *ibid.*, s. 27(2); B.C., *ibid.*, s. 80(2).

400 Alberta, *ibid.*, s. 27(5); B.C., *ibid.*, s. 80(5).

401 Alberta, *ibid.*, s. 27(6), B.C., s. 81. In *Tally v. Klatt* (1979), 106 D.L.R. (3d) 33, 17 A.R. 237, 10 Alta. L.R. (2d) 336 (Alta. C.A.) the trial judge's failure to point out to the jury that it was to determine the weight constituted a misdirection. See also *Latta v. London Life Insurance Co.* (1977), 4 A.R. 359, 76 D.L.R. (3d) 265, [1977] I.L.R. 1-895; affd. (1977), 1 C.R. (3d) 92, 83 D.L.R. (3d) 204, [1978] 1 W.W.R. 434, 5 C.P.C. 157, [1978] I.L.R. 1-972, 8 A.R. 219.

402 As noted above, III.D.1., at common law the criminal conviction was probably admissible as proof of the commission of the offence.

403 Alberta, *supra*, note 398, s. 27(4); B.C., s. 80(4). The *Report of the Federal/Provincial Task Force on Uniform Rules of Evidence* (Toronto: Carswell, 1982), also recommended the adoption of such a provision.

404 *Ibid.*, at 219.

405 *Saskatchewan Evidence Act*, R.S.S. 1978, c. S-16, s. 27 [rep. & sub. S.S. 1984-85-86, c. 38, s. 35].

406 Presumably the referred to sexual intercourse would have to be with someone other than the spouse.

(iii) Previous Acquittal

An acquittal in a criminal trial is not admissible in a subsequent civil trial as proof that the party did not commit the offence. Because of the burden of proof that is placed on the Crown in a criminal trial the fact that an accused is acquitted is no evidence that the accused did not commit the offence. The previous acquittal is not admissible simply because it is irrelevant.[407]

(iv) Previous Civil Judgment

Where the rule in *Hollington v. Hewthorn* does not apply, a judgment in a criminal case finding an accused guilty of a particular crime will often be very strong evidence of a party's negligence or the fact that an assault took place, as the case may be, because of the fact that the prosecution had to prove its case beyond a reasonable doubt. A judgment of a civil court, however, need only be based on proof to a balance of probabilities. A civil judgment is, therefore, worthy of less respect in a subsequent proceeding and should not as a general rule be admissible as *prima facie* proof of the commission of the relevant acts or the existence of negligent conduct.[408] It cannot logically raise such a presumption of fact or law. It is not, however, logically irrelevant; it just has less weight. If the rule in *Hollington v. Hewthorn* is not to be recognized so far as it relates to a previous criminal conviction, then logically it also should not apply so far as it relates to a previous civil judgment. The fact that it is a civil judgment only would be significant in terms of weight. The party against whom the judgment was rendered would have a greater opportunity to explain it or suggest mitigating circumstances. So, for example, if an auditor is found to owe a duty of care to a shareholder of a company arising out of her or his negligent preparation of financial statements, that judicial finding would have some evidential value in a subsequent proceeding brought by another shareholder. The weight to be given to it may, however, be quite low if the auditor were to show that she or he did not vigorously

---

407 *Fishman v. R.*, [1970] Ex. C.R. 784, at 826; *Hollington v. Hewthorn & Co. Ltd.*, [1943] K.B. 587, at 601, [1943] 2 All E.R. 35 (C.A.).
408 Subject to the principle of abuse of process, see this Chapter, III.B.3.(e)(iv). The issue of admissibility of a previous judgment must be distinguished from the issue of *res judicata*. When the latter principle applies, the judgment is not only admissible but it is binding.

defend the first proceeding because the damages in issue were minimal or that it was a consent judgment to implement a settlement. In other circumstances it may be an abuse of process for the auditor to dispute the previous judicial decision. For example, there may have been a lengthy trial, with many expert witnesses and several appeals.[409]

The Task Force on the Uniform Rules of Evidence recommended that the law as to the non-applicability of the rule in *Hollington v. Hewthorn* be clarified for findings of adultery and paternity, but made no comment with respect to the effect of civil judgments in general.[410] In Ontario, it was held, prior to *Demeter*, that notwithstanding the rule in *Hollington v. Hewthorn* a decree of divorce obtained on the grounds of adultery is admissible in a subsequent proceeding in which adultery is in issue.[411] Cases in other jurisdictions have held otherwise.[412]

(b) *Criminal Proceedings*

The previous conviction of a person other than an accused could be relevant in a criminal proceeding to prove that the person committed the offence charged. For example, where the charge is being an accessory to a crime the conviction of the principal is very relevant in proof of one of the elements of the crime. In fact, the Supreme Court of Canada has held that the principal can testify as to his or her guilty plea, conviction and sentence in a previous criminal proceeding as evidence of his or her guilt in a proceeding against the accessory.[413] It should be no more offensive to allow documentary evidence of the conviction.[414]

---

409 See for example, *Saskatoon Credit Union Ltd. v. Central Park Enterprises Ltd.* (1988), 47 D.L.R. (4th) 431, 22 B.C.L.R. (2d) 89 (B.C.S.C.) where the court held that it was an abuse of process for the defendants to deny that a certain transfer was fraudulent where that issue had been determined against them after a full and fair trial in a previous proceeding between different parties.

410 *Supra*, note 403, at 216-18.

411 *McGregor v. McGregor* (1977), 20 O.R. (2d) 680, 88 D.L.R. (2d) 419 (H.C.J.).

412 *Meshwa v. Meshwa* (1970), 75 W.W.R. 459, 13 D.L.R. (3d) 502, 2 R.F.L. 234 (B.C.S.C.); *Stevenson v. Stevenson* (1956), 19 W.W.R. 90 (Sask. Q.B.).

413 *R. v. Vinette*, [1975] 2 S.C.R. 222, 19 C.C.C. (2d) 1, 50 D.L.R. (3d) 697, 4 N.R. 181.

414 The Task Force, *supra*, note 403 recommended that a conviction of a person for theft in connection with property or mail should be admitted on a charge of receiving stolen property.

Generally, the rule with respect to the introduction of evidence of bad character will prevent evidence of the accused's or his or her associates' previous convictions being admitted.[415]

---

415 See Chapters 10 and 11 for a review of the circumstances when they can be admitted.

Index

A

ACCOMPLICE. See CORROBO-
RATION
ACCUSED. See SIMILAR FACT

ADMISSIBILITY
burden of proof relationship, 94, 95
character. See CHARACTER
circumstantial evidence. See CIR-
CUMSTANTIAL EVIDENCE
classification for, 9
conditional, 43
conditions
factors involved, 21
relevance. See RELEVANCE
confessions. See CONFESSIONS
curative, 44, 45
demonstrative evidence. See real
evidence, *infra*
direct evidence. See DIRECT
EVIDENCE
documents. See DOCUMENTS
electronic surveillance, 425-426
experiments, 19, 20
expert. See OPINION
illegally obtained evidence. See
ILLEGALLY OBTAINED
EVIDENCE
judicial discretion, 28-37
judicial notice, 976-988
limited, 43, 44
procedure

appeal
grounds
objection at trial
advisability, 47
criminal cases, 48-51
prejudice factor, 49
remedy, relevance to, 50
waiver, 48
tendering, 45, 46
real evidence
appearance, personal, 19
definition, 14, 15
demeanour, personal, 19
effectiveness, 15
problems of, 15
things
audiotape, 17, 18
general, 14, 15
identification, 15
photographs, 16
videotape, 16, 17
types, 14, 15
view, 18
self-serving evidence. See SELF-
SERVING EVIDENCE
similar fact evidence. See SIMILAR
FACT
sworn statements
affidavits, 14
commission
civil cases, 10-12
criminal cases, 12, 13
discovery, 13, 14

general, 9
testimonial evidence. See sworn
    statements, *supra*; unsworn state-
    ments, *infra*
unsworn statements, 14
ADMISSIONS
  by a party. See HEARSAY
  civil cases
    authority of counsel, 973
    matters constituting, 971, 972
  criminal cases
    guilty plea, 974
    specific facts, 975, 976
  co-conspirators and agents, 293,
    295-299
  effect, 281-283, 299, 300
  exceptions. See HEARSAY
  vicarious, 289-293
ADULTEROUS CONDUCT,
    privilege. See PRIVILEGE, self-
    incrimination
ADVANCEMENT, presumption,
    117-119
AFFIRMATION. See COMPE-
    TENCE
APPEARANCE, personal, admis-
    sibility, 19
ARREST, statements on, admis-
    sibility, 319
AUDIOTAPE, admissibility, 17, 18
AUTHENTIFICATION. See
    DOCUMENTS
AUTREFOIS ACQUIT. See *RES
    JUDICATA* special pleas
AUTREFOIS CONVICT. See *RES
    JUDICATA*, special pleas

B

BEST EVIDENCE RULE. See
    DOCUMENTS
BODILY SAMPLES, 428-430
BOLSTERING. See WITNESSES
BURDEN OF PROOF

allocation
  admissibility issues, 94, 95
  causation issues, 93, 94
  civil cases, 93
  conditional, 75
  exceptions, exemptions, 84-90
  factual determination basis
    civil, 75, 76
    criminal, 76, 77
  fairness, 91, 92
  formulae, 83, 84
  historical approach, 80
  party's own knowledge, 89, 90
  policy factors, 91
  probability, 91, 92
  public welfare offenses, 92
  res ipsa loquitur, 81, 82
  statutory, 82, 83
  tactical factors, 77
concepts, 53-55
evidential. See EVIDENTIAL
    BURDEN
facts within knowledge of accused,
    89, 90
legal. See LEGAL BURDEN
meaning, 53
presumption, as, 80
rules applicable, general, 53
shifting
  distribution distinguished, 74
  tactical, 77-79
  terminology problem, 74
standard. See STANDARD OF
    PROOF
types
  distinction, 54, 55
  terminology, 53, 54
BUSINESS RECORDS. See HEAR-
    SAY

C

CHARACTER
  definition, 431

fact in issue, as
civil cases
animals, 439
breach of promise to marry, 438, 439
defamation
bad character of plaintiff
defence, supporting, 434
mitigation of damages, 435-437
rumours, 437
good character of plaintiff, 433, 434
scope admissible, 437, 438
places, 439
things, 439
criminal cases, 440
fact in issue, proving
civil cases, 440-443
criminal cases
accused
bad character
co-accused, 456
cross-examination of accused, 458-460
cross-examination of witness, 457
general rule, 454, 455
previous convictions, 462-465
putting in issue, 456, 457
raised by accused, 455, 456
reform proposals, 465, 466
reply by Crown, 460-462
good character
expert opinion, 450-453
methods, 443
reputation, 444-447
specific acts, 447-450
use of evidence, 453, 454
previous convictions
Canada Evidence Act, 463-465
Criminal Code, 462
complainants

general, 467, 468
sexual offences, 468-474
general rule, 443
third parties, 467
witnesses
general, 474, 475
previous convictions, 475, 476
historical role, 432, 433
significance, 431
CHARTER OF RIGHTS AND FREEDOMS
compellability, 604-607
confessions. See CONFESSIONS
freedom of press, 710-712
illegally obtained evidence. See ILLEGALLY OBTAINED EVIDENCE
presumptions. See PRESUMPTIONS
res judicata. See RES JUDICATA
self-incrimination. See PRIVILEGE; CONFESSIONS
similar fact evidence, 482, 483
CHILDREN. See COMPETENCE; HEARSAY, sexual abuse
CIRCUMSTANTIAL EVIDENCE
definition, 38, 39
similar fact. See SIMILAR FACT
direct evidence distinguished, 37-40
treatment
civil cases, 40
criminal cases
general, 40
Hodge's Case, 40
warning
form, 41
rejection of rule, 42, 43
requirement, 40, 41
COLLATERAL FACT RULE. See WITNESSES, reply evidence
COMPELLABILITY
civil proceedings
Crown, foreign, 621

diplomats, foreign, 621
foreign statutory illegality, 621,
    622
judges, 619-621
parties, 618
privilege, 622
spouses, 619
criminal proceedings
    accused
        general rule, 600
        co-accused, 601-603
        collateral proceedings
            post-Charter, 607-610
            pre-Charter, 604-607
        parallel civil proceedings, 611
        provincial offences, 603, 604
    spouse of accused
        common law, 611-615
        statutory provisions
            exceptions, 616, 617
            general, 615, 616
    definition, 599, 600
    general rule, 577
COMPETENCE
    burden of proof, 598, 599
    disqualifications
        children, 583, 584
        communicative deficiencies, 585,
            586
        judges, 597
        jurors, 597
        lawyers, 598
        mental impairment, 580-583
    general rule, 577, 578
    historical restrictions
        criminal record, 578-580
        interest in proceedings, 578-580
        statutory abolition, 578-580
    oath
        affirmation, 590
        children
            sworn evidence, 591, 592
            unsworn evidence
                intellectual understanding,
                    594, 595

statutory provisions, 592,
    593, 595-597
    truth obligations, under-
        standing, 593, 594
    form, 586-589
    necessity, 586
CONDITIONAL ADMIS-
    SIBILITY, 43
CONFESSIONS
    admissibility
        Charter effect
            right to counsel, 369-373
            right to silence, 376, 377
            self-incrimination, 373-376
        future prospects, 377, 378
        onus of proof, 358
        role of judge, 356-358
        standard of proof, 358-360
    cross-examination use, 363-366
    evidential value
        entire statement rule, 361
        joint accused, 363
        lack of personal knowledge, 362,
            363
        res gestae statements, 362
    inadmissible
        evidence obtained from, 367-369
    jury, review by, 357
    role of judge, 356-358
    rule
        applicability, 326, 327
        operating mind requirement
            factors involved, 335-338
            origin, 334
        operating mind requirement,
            rationale, 334-338
        person in authority
            meaning, 350
            objective test, 352
            subjective test, 351
        rationale
            operating mind requirement,
                334-338
        voluntariness
            development, 330-334

general, 327, 328
historical position, 328, 329
scope, 326, 327
voluntariness
objective test, 330
oppression
circumstances constituting, 345-347
English position, 342, 343
relevance, 344
other factors, relationship, 332, 333
police questioning
accuracy of record, 348, 349
electronic recording, 349
factors involved, 347, 348
relevance, 347
rationale. See rationale, *supra*
reliability, 330-332
test, general, 338
threats or inducements
effect, 338-342
intent, 339
morality, 342
relationship to offence, 340
spiritual, 341
time lapse, 341
statements constituting
exculpatory, 324, 325
inculpatory, 323
spontaneous, 326
voir dire
procedure, 354-356
requirement, 353, 354
CONFIDENTIAL COMMUNI-
CATIONS. See PRIVILEGE
CORROBORATION
civil case examples
child, unsworn evidence
discretion, 923
statutory provisions, 923, 924
deceased or disabled parties
by or against estate, 919-921
multiple claims, 921, 922
negligence actions, 922, 923

scope of provisions, 917, 918
witness requiring corro-
boration, 919
common law
discretion, 894-896
rigid rule, rejection, 893, 894
nature of
circumstantial evidence, 911
civil cases, 912
criminal cases, 912-916
definition, 905-908
degree required, 908, 909
direct evidence, 910
independence, 909, 910
judicial function, 911, 912
jury function, 911
rules
mandatory requirement, 892
warning requirement, 891, 892
statutory provisions
civil law
affiliation, 902
breach of promise to marry, 901
categories, 901
child, unsworn evidence, 904
estate actions, 903
mental incompetents, actions
against, 903
rules of practice, 904, 905
criminal law
express requirement, 899, 900
repeals
child, unsworn evidence, 898
effect, 898, 899
sexual offences, 896, 897
CREDIBILITY. See CORRO-
BORATION; WITNESSES,
impeachment
CROSS-EXAMINATION. See
WITNESSES, impeachment;
OPINION, cross-examination
CROWN PRIVILEGE. See PUB-
LIC INTEREST IMMUNITY
CURATIVE ADMISSIBILITY, 44, 45

D

DEATH, presumption
  occurrence, 114-116
  order, 116, 117
DECLARATIONS AGAINST
  INTEREST. See HEARSAY,
  exceptions
DECLARATIONS AS TO PEDI-
  GREE. See HEARSAY, exceptions
DECLARATIONS BY CHIL-
  DREN. See HEARSAY, exceptions
DECLARATIONS INDICATING
  PHYSICAL, MENTAL OR
  EMOTIONAL STATE. See *RES
  GESTAE*
DECLARATIONS MADE IN
  COURSE OF BUSINESS
  DUTY. See HEARSAY, exceptions
DEMEANOUR, personal, admissi-
  bility, 19
DIRECT EVIDENCE
  circumstantial evidence distin-
    guished, 37-40
  definition, 37, 38
  superiority, 38
DIRECTED VERDICT, 135
DISCOVERY, admissibility, 13, 14
DISCREDITING WITNESS. See
  WITNESSES
DISCRETION. See JUDICIAL
  DISCRETION
DOCTOR-PATIENT. See PRIVI-
  LEGE
DOCUMENTS
  admissibility
    custodial origin
      ancient documents, 955, 956
      possession of person, admissi-
        bility against
        agents, 962
        co-conspirators, 962
        corporations, 960-962
        evidentiary value, 963, 964
        individuals, 958-960

rationale, 956-958
general, 20, 21
proof of authorship or execution
  contents, 955
  corporations, 954
  inference, 951
  procedure, 950
  statutory provisions, 953
  unsigned documents, 952
admissibility without proof
  agreement, 949
  judicial documents, 943, 944
  notice to admit, 950
  public documents, 941, 942, 944
  statutory authority
    Evidence Act, 945, 946
    general, 946-948
    letters patent, 948
    notarized documents, 948
best evidence rule
  applicability, 931
  history, 929-931
  modern rule, scope, 939, 940
  secondary evidence
    admissibility
      destruction, 933, 934
      loss, 933, 934
      official documents, 936-938
      possession of another party,
        935
      possession of third party, 936
      public documents,
        936-938
    primary distinguished, 932
    proof by, procedure, 938, 939
business records. See HEARSAY,
  exceptions
categories, 928
definition, 927
private, proof
  attesting witnesses, 966
  corporate seal, 967
  handwriting, 965, 966
  maps, 968, 969
  photographs, 967, 968

plans, 968, 969
sketches, 969, 970
typewriting, 967
videotapes, 968
proof
best evidence rule. See best evidence rule, *supra*
meanings, 929
public. See HEARSAY, exceptions
DYING DECLARATIONS. See HEARSAY, exceptions

E

EVIDENCE
confessions. See CONFESSIONS
documentary. See DOCUMENTS
illegally obtained. See ILLEGALLY OBTAINED EVIDENCE
rules. See RULES OF EVIDENCE
self-serving. See SELF-SERVING EVIDENCE
EVIDENTIAL BURDEN
allocation
exceptions, exemptions, 84-89
multiple issues, 60
policy, 91-99
statutory, 63, 64
discharge, effect
compelling fact determination, 66, 67
permitting decision on issue, 65, 66
prima facie proof, 69-73
types of burden, 67
effect, general 57
jury system, relationship, 61
legal burden
coexistence, 62, 63
concurrence, 64, 65
legal burden distinguished, general, 56-58
meaning, general, 56
non-discharge, effect, 68, 69

prima facie, 69-73
presumption. See PRESUMPTIONS
role
civil cases, 61, 62
criminal cases, 61
shifting burdens, 74-79
significance, 58, 60
standard of proof. See STANDARD OF PROOF
terminology problems, 69-73
EXAMINATION OF WITNESSES. See WITNESSES
EXCLUSIONARY RULES
hearsay. See HEARSAY
nature of, 24, 25
relevance distinguished, 24-26
EXPERIMENTS, admissibility, 19, 20
EXPERT EVIDENCE, opinion. See OPINION

G

GUILTY PLEA. See ADMISSIONS

H

HANDWRITING. See DOCUMENTS, private; OPINION
HEARSAY
conduct constituting, 160
expert opinion. See OPINION
purpose for which tendered
general, 160-162
implied assertions
acts constituting, 170-172
danger analysis, 166-168
discretionary approach, 172, 173
intent, 165, 166
perception problems, 169, 170
policy factors, 168
reliability, 168

non-hearsay use of words,
162-165
rule
exceptions
admissions
effect against others, 299, 300
effect, 281-283
matters constituting
conduct, 284-286
silence, 286-289
statements, 284
rationale, 279-283
representatives, by
co-conspirators and com-
mon purpose, 295-299
identity of interest, 293,
294
vicarious admissions,
289-293
ancient documents, interest in
land, 228-230
business duty declarations
common law
Ares v. Venner
aftermath, 195-198
decision, 192
effect, 195
scope, 192-194
conditions, early, 188-192
nature, 187
rationale, 188
statute
computer systems, 214
contemporaneous record,
203, 204
duty of declarant, 204-208
factual record, 208-210
general, 198, 199
investigation, records
made in course, 212
motive to misrepresent,
absence, 210-212
negative inferences, 213
notice requirement, 215
other rules applicable, 213

personal knowledge,
204-208
reform proposals, 215, 216
usual and ordinary course
of business, 200-203
declarations against interest
pecuniary, 176, 177
penal
conditions, 178, 179
criteria, application,
185-187
exculpation test, 184, 185
mixed statements, 181-183
origin, 177, 178
safeguards, 180
unavailability, 183, 184
proprietary, 176, 177
declarations indicating physical,
mental or emotional state. See
RES GESTAE
development process, 173-176
dying declarations
rationale, 267, 268
requirements
expectation of death, 268
homicide charge, 269
injuries of declarant subject of charge, 269, 270
scope, 267, 268
former proceedings testimony
conditions
cross-examination oppor-
tunity, 273
issues substantially same,
272
parties same, 272, 273
criminal proceedings,
274-277
discovery transcript, 273, 274
led by party against whom
tendered, 278
other rules relationship, 277,
278
rationale, 270-272
pedigree declarations

ante litem motam rule, 223, 224
  conditions, 223-228
  conduct, 227, 228
  genealogical question test, 228
  independent evidence, 225-227
  origin, 222
  rationale, 223
  significance, 222, 223
public documents
  conditions, 231, 232
  definition, 232, 233
  knowledge, sufficiency, 234
  rationale, 231
  statute, 235
reputation declarations
  general, 216, 217
  history, 222
  marriage, 220-222
  public rights, 217-220
res gestae. See *Res gestae*
sexual abuse, child victims
  criteria, 301
  necessity, 303
  origin of exception, 301
  rationale, 300
  reform proposal, 303
  reliability, 301, 302
  scope of rule, 302
  sodium amytol testing, 304
non-applicability
  administrative proceedings, 305
  sentencing, 306
origin, 156
rationale
  general, 157-159
  veracity, 157
statement, 156
status of, 155
HUSBAND AND WIFE COMMU-NICATIONS. See PRIVILEGE
HYPOTHETICAL QUESTION. See OPINION

I

IDENTIFICATION
handwriting. See OPINION; DOC-UMENTS
persons and places. See OPINION
prior eye witness. See SELF-SERVING EVIDENCE
ILLEGALLY OBTAINED EVI-DENCE
admissibility
  Charter effect
    administration of justice, dis-repute
      burden of proof, 396, 397
      factors relevant, 400, 401
      mandatory exclusion, 399, 400
      probability, degree, 397, 398
      significance, 396
      standard for disrepute, 398, 399
    exclusion, effect on reputation of justice, 423, 424
    historical development, 387, 388
    section 24 remedy
      causation, 392-396
      court of competent juris-diction, 390
      exclusion power, 391, 392
      scope, general, 388-390
      standing, 392
    seriousness of violation
      availability of alternatives, 420, 421
      factors affecting, 422, 423
      general, 410-412
      good faith, 412-418
      necessity, 418-420
      urgency, 418-420
    trial fairness
      effect, 410
      factors overriding, 407-410
      general factors, 403-405

real evidence, 405-407
self-incrimination, 401-403
common law
civil cases, 384-387
criminal cases, 380-384
rationale, 380
Criminal Code
bodily samples
Charter issues, 429
consent, 428
general, 428
statutory conditions, 429, 430
general, 425
wiretap
admissibility, 427
prohibition, 425, 426
general rule, 379
confession, inadmissible, from,
367-369
right to counsel, 369-373
right against self-incrimination,
373-376
right to remain silent, 376-377
IMMUNITY
public interest. See PUBLIC
INTEREST IMMUNITY
IMPEACHMENT. See
WITNESSES
INFORMERS. See PUBLIC
INTEREST IMMUNITY
INTEREST, declarations against.
See HEARSAY
ISSUE ESTOPPEL. See *RES JUDI-
CATA*

J

JOURNALISTS' PRIVILEGE. See
PRIVILEGE
JUDICIAL DECISION
evidentiary effect
civil cases
prior acquittal, 1045
prior civil judgment, 1045, 1046

prior criminal convictions
common law, 1042, 1043
statutory provisions, 1043,
1044
criminal cases, 1046, 1047
general rules, 1040, 1041
res judicata. See *RES JUDICATA*
JUDICIAL DISCRETION
civil cases
general, 33
real evidence
factors involved, 33, 34
prejudice test, 34-37
criminal cases
accused, in favour of
inflammatory real evidence, 33
scope, 30-32
statutory, 32
trial fairness rule, 28-30
Crown, in favour of, 33
third persons, in favour of, 33
role, 28
JUDICIAL NOTICE
appeal court, 988
definition, 976
demonstrable facts
categories, 979
historical, 980
measures, 981
nature, course of, 981-983
official matters, 979, 980
scientific facts, 981-983
times, 981
weights, 981
effects, 986-988
notorious facts, 976-979
personal knowledge, 985, 986
statutory, 983, 984

K

KIENAPPLE RULE. See *RES
JUDICATA*

L

LANGUAGE
proceedings
official, 831, 832
translation, 828
witnesses. See WITNESSES
LAWYER-CLIENT. See PRIVI-
LEGE
LEADING QUESTIONS. See
WITNESSES, examination
LEGAL BURDEN
allocation
civil cases, 59, 60
criminal cases, 59
confessions, 358-360
effect, 58
evidence, 94-95
evidential burden distinguished
general, 56-58
illegally obtained evidence, 396-397
meaning, 57
multiple issues, 59
significance, 58
standard of proof. See STANDARD
OF PROOF
substantive rules applicable, 58, 59
LEGITIMACY, presumption, 112,
113
LIFE, presumption, 113, 114
LIMITED ADMISSIBILITY, 43, 44

N

NON-SUIT, 130

O

OPINION
experts
court appointments, 573, 574
hearsay issues
authoritative literature, 560-563
cross-examination, 563-565

knowledge component, 546,
547
opinion component
basis for admissibility,
551-553
development, 547, 548
factual foundation, 553-556
rationale, 548-551
public opinion polls, 558-560
surveys, 556-558
new scientific evidence
categories, 567, 568
general acceptance test, 565,
566
multiple standards, 567
polygraph, 568, 569
probability statistics, 569-571
problems, 569
reliability factors, 566, 567
United States test, 565
notice requirement, 572, 573
number limits, 571, 572
principles
development of exception,
533-536
hypothetical question,
537-540
qualifying, 536, 537
ultimate issue
admissibility, 540-543
inadmissibility
judicial function
credibility, 543, 544
interpretation, 543
legal question, 545
superfluity, 546
jury function relationship, 540
lay persons
admissibility
identification
handwriting, 530-532
persons, 528, 529
places, 529, 530
mental capacity, 532
state of mind, 532

rationale
  development, 524, 525
  exclusion, 523
  fact and inference distinction,
    524, 525
  helpfulness concept, 526-528

P

PARTIES, exclusion
power, 827
PHOTOGRAPHS, admissibility, 16.
  See also DOCUMENTS
POSSESSION
  explanatory statements on, admissi-
    bility, 320, 321
PRESUMPTIONS
  basic facts, with, nature of, 97
  basic facts, without
    constitutional rights, 99
    nature of, 98, 99
  categories, 97
  Charter effect
    presumption of innocence
      components, 123
      interpretation, 123
      justifiable limits, 124-127
      nature, 121
      reverse onus, 122
  conflicting, 120, 121
  evidential burden, distinguished
    from, 80
  fact, of
    effect, 100
    inference drawn, 101-103
    law distinguished, 103, 104
    maxims, 101
    nature of, 99
    scope, 100, 101
    terminology problem, 103, 104
  law, of
    conclusive
      effect, 104
      nature of, 104-107

statutory, 104-106
rebuttable
  definition, 107, 108
  effect
    civil cases
      advancement, 117-119
      death, occurrence, 114-116
      death, order, 116, 117
      general, 112
      legitimacy, 112, 113
      life, 113, 114
      regularity, 119, 120
      resulting trust, 117-119
    criminal cases, 109-111
  terminology problems, 97
PREVIOUS CONSISTENT
  STATEMENT. See SELF-
  SERVING EVIDENCE
PRIMA FACIE EVIDENCE, 69-73
PRIOR CONVICTIONS. See
  WITNESSES
PRIOR INCONSISTENT STATE-
  MENT. See WITNESSES
PRIVILEGE
  anticipation of litigation, 653
  confidentiality
    conditions for protection
      Wigmore test
        applicability, 627-635
        solicitor-client communica-
          tions. See solicitor-client,
          infra
      doctor and patient. See doctor
        and patient, infra
      husband and wife. See husband
        and wife, infra
      journalist. See journalists, infra
      settlements. See settlement com-
        munications, infra
      significance, 626
      spiritual advisers. See spiritual
        advisers, infra
  doctor and patient
    court ordered psychiatric assess-
      ments, 718

discretion, Wigmore criteria, 717, 718
general, 712, 713
psychiatric consultations, 713-717
foundation
confidentiality. See confidentiality, *supra*
policy balance, 623
relationships protected, 624-626
social values, 623
husband and wife
abolition proposal, 690-692
intercepted communications, 684-686
marital status, 681-684
origin, 678
persons entitled, 687, 688
rationale, 677-679, 690
sexual intercourse, as to, 692-694
subject matter, 679-681
waiver, 688-690
informant identity. See PUBLIC INTEREST IMMUNITY
journalists
news sources identity, 700-702
newspaper rule, 702-706
qualified privilege
Charter, freedom of press, 710-712
judicial discretion, 706-708
Wigmore criteria, 708-710
public interest. See PUBLIC INTEREST IMMUNITY
self-incrimination
adulterous conduct
origins, 768
proceedings in consequence, 769-771
scope, 768, 769
waiver, 771, 772
Charter provision
any other proceeding, 749-752
automatic protection, 739, 740

evidence subject to, 741, 742
fundamental justice
derivative use immunity
factors relevant, 756, 757
theories, 753-756
right of silence
investigations included, 759, 760
rationale, 757-759
incriminating use
Crown
case in chief, 744
cross-examination, 744-749
forfeitures, 744
penalties, 744
time for assessment, 743, 744
persons entitled to protection, 752, 753
proceedings included, 742, 743
text, 739
common law
scope, 735, 736
statutory modification, 736, 737
protection
failure to give explanation
comments, prohibition, 765-767
relevance, 767, 768
failure to testify
adverse inference, 763-765
comments
charge to jury, prohibition, 761-763
prohibition, 760
rationale, 734, 735
statutory provisions
enactment, 736-739
settlement communications
applicability
subsequent proceedings, different parties, 725-728
conditions for recognition
litigious dispute in existence, 722

non-disclosure intention,
722-724
purpose of communication,
724, 725
scope, 722
exceptions
concluded agreement in issue,
730
costs, 731
limitation periods, 731
prejudice to recipient, 729
rationale, 728
unlawful communications, 728,
729
mediators, effect, 732-734
rationale
alternative theories, 720, 721
public policy, 719
scope, 721, 722
solicitor-client
advisers included, 648-650
agents, 650
anticipation of litigation, materials
inclusion in privilege
conditions, 655, 656
dominant purpose test, 656
policy, 653-655
rationale, 653
third party communications,
657
assertion, 645-648
confidential nature
general, 637
joint interests, 638, 639
subject matter, 639
third party disclosure, 637, 638
corporate clients
corporate counsel, 651
identification of individuals,
651, 652
duration
death of client
general, 660
wills cases, 660-663
other proceedings, 658-660

evidentiary rule, 628-635
loss of, waiver, 663-671
rationale, 635, 636
scope
communications
confidential. See confidentiality, supra
purpose
legal advice, seeking, 642,
643
unlawful conduct, 644, 645
restriction to, 641
professional relationship,
within, 640, 641
time for assertion, 645-648
waiver ·
implied
disclosure to third person,
669-671
fairness test, 666-668
inadvertent disclosure,
672-677
persons entitled, 663, 664
statutory, 672
voluntary, 664-666
spiritual advisers
common law approach
historic, 694
nature of relationship, 697
policy factors, 695-697
Wigmore criteria, 697-700
statutory approach, 695
PROOF
burden. See BURDEN OF
PROOF; EVIDENTIAL BUR-
DEN; LEGAL BURDEN
dispensing with. See ADMIS-
SIONS; CONFESSIONS; JUDI-
CIAL NOTICE; RES JUDICATA
standard. See STANDARD OF
PROOF
PUBLIC INTEREST IMMUNITY
assertion
general, 774
judicial role, 774, 775

balancing interests, 773
criteria for grant
  balancing factors, 790, 791
  claim
    categories, 791
    class, rationale
      candour, 792-794
      harassment of cabinet, 794,
        795
    contents, 791, 792
    level of government, 795, 796
    outside source of information,
      796-802
    police reports, 802-805
    statements to police, 802-805
  Crown as party
    basis, 776-778
    statutory provisions, 777, 778
  determination
    affidavit, government, of, 789
    government opinion
      conclusiveness, statutory,
        779-781
      evaluation, 778, 779
    judicial power
      certificate of minister
        consideration, 782
        contents, 789
        common law, 782, 783
        inspection, 781
        scope, 784-789
      oral evidence, 789
  informant identity
    general rule
      exception, full answer and
        defence
        general, 809-813
        search warrant information,
          813-815
        wiretap information, 815-819
    nature of, 806-808
    policy, 806
    relationship included, 809
    scope, 805
  privilege distinguished, 773

significance, 819
terminology, 773

R

REAL EVIDENCE
  admissibility. See ADMISSIBILITY
REASONABLE DOUBT. See
    STANDARD OF PROOF
RECEIVABILITY. See ADMISSI-
    BILITY
RECENT COMPLAINT. See
    SELF-SERVING EVIDENCE
RECENT FABRICATION. See
    SELF-SERVING EVIDENCE
RE-EXAMINATION. See
    WITNESSES
REFRESHING MEMORY. See
    WITNESSES, refreshing memory
REGULARITY, presumption, 119,
    120
RELEVANCE
  conditional, 28
  definition, 22
  exclusionary rules distinguished, 24-
    26
  fact in issue
    determination, 23
    relationship to
      direct, 23
      indirect, 24
  judicial discretion. See JUDICIAL
    DISCRETION
  materiality distinguished, 27
  significance, general, 21
  weight distinguished, 26, 27
REPLY EVIDENCE. See
    WITNESSES
REPUTATION. See CHARACTER
RES GESTAE
  doctrine
    declarations included
      accompanying relevant acts,
        253-256

bodily feelings and condition,
238-242
confessions, 362
mental condition, 242-245
rights created by assertion,
236-238
spontaneous exclamations
contemporaneity test, 258,
259, 261, 262
rationale, 257
relationship to event, 264-267
reliability, 259-264
statement of intention
general, 245-251
testators, 251-253
general, 235
situations justifying, 235, 236
self-serving evidence, 318, 319
RES IPSA LOQUITUR, effect, 81,
82
RES JUDICATA
civil cases
final judicial decision
family law judgments, 996
finality, 993, 994
foreign courts, 992
inferior courts, 991
jurisdiction, 992, 993
merits, decision on, 994-996
tribunals, 991
general rule, 990, 991
identity of issue
cause of action estoppel
new facts, 1001, 1002
same cause, 999-1001
tax assessment, 1002, 1003
defendants, between, 1005
issue estoppel, 1003-1005
parties
mutuality, 1010-1012
privity with, 1007-1009
same capacity, 1006, 1007
same, 1006
principles involved, 997-999
procedure, 1012, 1013

criminal cases
Charter provision
appeal by trial *de novo*, 1038
charged with offence, 1034,
1035
finality, 1036, 1037
Kienapple rule distinguished,
1033, 1034
same offence, 1035, 1036
text, 1033
effects, 1038-1040
general rule, 1013
issue estoppel
applicability, 1024, 1025
perjury, 1026, 1027
problems of, 1025, 1026
procedure, 1028
voir dire findings, 1027
Kienapple rule
effects, 1039, 1040
general principle, 1028
procedure, 1032, 1033
proximity, 1029-1032
scope, 1028, 1029
special pleas
autrefois acquit
finality, 1015-1019
general rule, 1014
jeopardy test, 1020
same charge, 1014, 1015
autrefois convict
finality, 1022
general principle, 1020
same charge, 1021, 1022
foreign proceedings, 1023,
1024
procedure, 1022, 1023
evidentiary effect, 1040
general principles, 988-990
RESULTING TRUST,
presumption, 117-119
RULES OF EVIDENCE
goals
trial process
efficiency, 2, 3

fairness, 3, 4
interests outside, 4
truth, ascertainment, 1, 2
logically relevant facts
definition, 1
significance, 1
nature
dynamic reform, 5-7
static, 5
role of, 1

S

SCIENTIFIC EVIDENCE. See
OPINION
SELF-INCRIMINATION
Charter
right to counsel, 369-373
right to silence, 376-377
self-incrimination, 373-376
trial fairness, 401-403
privilege. See PRIVILEGE
SELF-SERVING EVIDENCE
admissibility
arrest, statements on, 319
bases for, 308, 309
possession, explanatory statements, 320, 321
prior eye-witness identification,
313, 314
rebutting recent fabrication
allegation
form, 311, 312
raising, 310, 311
scope, 309, 310
recent complaint
historical development, 315
procedure, 317, 318
rationale, problems of, 316
sexual offences included, 315,
316
statutory amendment, 317
res gestae, 318, 319
exclusionary rule

exceptions. See admissibility, *supra*
rationale, 307, 308
scope, 307
SETTLEMENT COMMUNICA-
TIONS. See PRIVILEGE
SIMILAR FACT
admissibility
principles
civil cases
agency, 521
condition of premises or
objects, 519-521
disposition alone, 514, 515
general, 512-514
market value, 521
ownership, 521
purpose, explaining, 518, 519
rebutting evidence, 521, 522
standard practice, 521
system, fact in issue, 515-518
title, 521
criminal cases
probative value against
prejudicial effect, 512
relevance, 510, 511
rule. See rule, *infra*
rule
Australian cases, 506-510
Canadian cases
credibility
exclusion, 501
disposition
circumstantial evidentiary
connection, 499-501
expert evidence, 503, 504
non-criminal acts, 502, 503
prejudice test, 505, 506
striking similarity, 504, 505
propensity
linking factor requirement,
499
special circumstances,
496-499
character evidence rules relationship, 477

English development
origin, 485
rule in Makin case
application, 486-489
balancing probative value
and prejudice, 490-496
categories, expansion, 489,
490
scope, 485, 486
future development, 522
nature of, 477, 478
rationale
Charter rights
presumption of innocence,
483
trial only on indictment
charges, 482
dangers, 482
law enforcement system,
adverse effect, 484
relevance, 481
scope, 479-481
terminology, 478
SOLICITOR-CLIENT COMMU-
NICATIONS. See PRIVILEGE
SPIRITUAL ADVISERS, communications with. See PRIVILEGE
SPONTANEOUS EXCLAMA-
TIONS. See HEARSAY, exceptions; *RES GESTAE*
STANDARD OF PROOF
evidential burden
defendant, of, 137-140
directed verdict
multiple defendants, 137
non-suit relationship, 136
test, 135
non-suit
election of defendant, 133
judge's role, 130, 131
jury verdict, taking, 133, 134
multiple defendants, 132
procedure, 131, 132
question of law, 131
risks to defendant, 134

factors involved, 129
legal burden
categories, 141, 142
civil cases
definition, 142
degrees, 144-146
determination, 143
policy aspect, 141
special scrutiny, 146-148
criminal cases
charge to jury
circumstantial evidence, 149
general, 148, 150-152
definition, 148
policy issues, 129
STATEMENTS. See CON-
FESSIONS; SELF-SERVING
EVIDENCE; WITNESSES

T

TESTIMONY IN FORMER PRO-
CEEDINGS. See HEARSAY,
exceptions, 270

V

VICTIM. See CHARACTER, com-
plainants
VIDEOTAPE, admissibility, 16, 17
VIEW, admissibility, 18
VOIR DIRE. See CONFESSIONS

W

WITNESS
accused. See COMPELLABILITY
adverse, hostile. See one's own witness, *infra*
child. See COMPETENCE
compellability. See COMPELLA-
BILITY
competence. See COMPETENCE
expert. See OPINION

judges, jurors, lawyers. See COM-
PETENCE
oath. See COMPETENCE
spouse. See COMPELLABILITY
WITNESSES
calling, general rule, 821
character. See CHARACTER
corroboration. See CORROBORA-
TION
cross-examination
  documents, 864-866
  multiple parties
    civil cases, 862, 863
    criminal cases, 863
  persons not subject to, 861, 862
  purposes, 857
  right of parties, 822
  scope
    discretion of court, 860, 861
    relationship to evidence in
      chief, 859
    suggestions, 857-859
  tendering for, 875
examination
  chief
    function, 832, 833
    leading question
      form, 833, 834
      rule
        exception, 834-838
        rationale, 833
    judge, right of
      limits, 824, 825
      recall, 825, 826
      scope, 824
exclusion
  discretion
    breach of order, 827, 828
    rationale, 826, 827
impeachment
  notice of intention, 876-879
  prior convictions, 873-875
  prior inconsistent statements
    collateral fact rule, 870, 871
    denial, effect, 871

discovery transcript, 869
exhibiting, 872
inconsistent, definition, 870
statutory provisions, 868, 869
testimonial capabilities, 866-868
interpreter
  choice, 830, 831
  entitlement, 828-830
one's own witness
  bolstering, 838
  contradicting by prior inconsis-
    tent statements
    common law, 838
    evidential value of prior incon-
      sistent statements, 847-849
  Canada Evidence Act
    development, 842
    procedure, 843-845
    provincial Acts distinguished,
      845, 846
  provincial Evidence Acts
    adverse witness
      definition, 840
      hostile, relationship, 841,
        842
    federal Act distinguished,
      845, 846
  statutory provisions
    enactment, 839
    text, 839, 840
re-examination
  purpose, 879
  scope, 879, 880
refreshing memory
  contemporaneity of record, 850,
    851
  general rule, 849, 850
  independent recollection, absence
    of, 851-854
  procedure, 856, 857
  records permissible, 854-856
reply evidence
  restrictions
    collateral fact rule
      applicability, 883, 884

exceptions
    bias, 885
    categories, 884
    mental condition for
        untruthfulness, 886
    partiality, 885
    physical condition for
        untruthfulness, 886
    prior convictions, 885
    prior inconsistent state-
        ments, 885, 886
    reputation for untruthful-
        ness, 887-890
general rule, 880-883
scope, 880
significance, 821
    open court, 823
    presence of parties, 822